GLENCOE
LITERATURE

The Reader's Choice

Program Consultants

Beverly Ann Chin

Denny Wolfe

Jeffrey Copeland

Mary Ann Dudzinski

William Ray

Jacqueline Jones Royster

Jeffrey Wilhelm

American
Literature

Glencoe McGraw-Hill

New York, New York　　Columbus, Ohio　　Woodland Hills, California　　Peoria, Illinois

Acknowledgments

Grateful acknowledgment is given authors, publishers, photographers, museums, and agents for permission to reprint the following copyrighted material. Every effort has been made to determine copyright owners. In case of any omissions, the Publisher will be pleased to make suitable acknowledgments in future editions.

Acknowledgments continued on page R132.

The Standardized Test Practice pages in this book were written by The Princeton Review, the nation's leader in test preparation. Through its association with McGraw-Hill, The Princeton Review offers the best way to help students excel on standardized assessments.

The Princeton Review is not affiliated with Princeton University or Educational Testing Service.

Glencoe/McGraw-Hill

A Division of The McGraw-Hill Companies

Printed in the United States of America

Send all inquiries to:
Glencoe/McGraw-Hill
8787 Orion Place
Columbus, OH 43240-4027

ISBN 0-02-635423-3
(Student Edition)

ISBN 0-02-635424-1
(Teacher's Wraparound Edition)

5 6 7 8 9 10   071/043   04 03 02 01

Senior Program Consultants

Beverly Ann Chin is Professor of English, Co-Director of the English Teaching Program, former Director of the Montana Writing Project, and former Director of Composition at the University of Montana in Missoula. In 1995–1996, Dr. Chin served as President of the National Council of Teachers of English. She currently serves as a Member of the Board of Directors of the National Board for Professional Teaching Standards. Dr. Chin is a nationally recognized leader in English language arts standards, curriculum, and assessment. Formerly a high school English teacher and adult education reading teacher, Dr. Chin has taught in English language arts education at several universities and has received awards for her teaching and service.

Denny Wolfe, a former high school English teacher and department chair, is Professor of English Education, Director of the Tidewater Virginia Writing Project, and Director of the Center for Urban Education at Old Dominion University in Norfolk, Virginia. For the National Council of Teachers of English, he has served as Chairperson of the Standing Committee on Teacher Preparation, President of the International Assembly, member of the Executive Committee of the Council on English Education, and editor of the SLATE Newsletter. Author of more than seventy-five articles and books on teaching English, Dr. Wolfe is a frequent consultant to schools and colleges on the teaching of English language arts.

Program Consultants

Jeffrey S. Copeland is Professor and Head of the Department of English Language and Literature at the University of Northern Iowa, where he teaches children's and young adult literature courses and a variety of courses in English education. A former public school teacher, he has published many articles in the professional journals in the language arts. The twelve books he has written or edited include *Speaking of Poets: Interviews with Poets Who Write for Children and Young Adults* and *Young Adult Literature: A Contemporary Reader.*

Mary Ann Dudzinski is a former high school English teacher and recipient of the Ross Perot Award for Teaching Excellence. She also has served as a member of the core faculty for the National Endowment for the Humanities Summer Institute for Teachers of Secondary School English and History at the University of North Texas. After fifteen years of classroom experience in grades 9–12, she currently is a language arts consultant.

William Ray has taught English in the Boston Public Schools; at Lowell University; University of Wroclaw, Poland; and, for the last fourteen years, at Lincoln-Sudbury Regional High School in Sudbury, Massachusetts. He specializes in world literature. He has worked on a variety of educational texts, as editor, consultant, and contributing writer.

Jacqueline Jones Royster is Associate Professor of English at The Ohio State University. She is also on the faculty of the Bread Loaf School of English at Middlebury College in Middlebury, Vermont. In addition to the teaching of writing, Dr. Royster's professional interests include the rhetorical history of African American women and the social and cultural implications of literate practices.

Jeffrey Wilhelm, a former English and reading teacher, is currently an assistant professor at the University of Maine where he teaches courses in middle and secondary level literacy. Author of several books and articles on the teaching of reading and the use of technology, he also works with local schools as part of the fledgling Adolescent Literacy Project and is the director of two annual summer institutes: the Maine Writing Project and Technology as a Learning Tool.

Teacher Reviewers

Rahn Anderson
Arapahoe High School
Littleton Public Schools
Littleton, Colorado

Linda Antonowich
West Chester Area School District
West Chester, Pennsylvania

Mike Bancroft
Rock Bridge High School
Columbia, Missouri

Luella Barber
Hays High School
Hays, Kansas

Lori Beard
Cypress Creek High School
Houston, Texas

Hugh Beattie
Bergenfield Public School District
Bergenfield, New Jersey

Patricia Blatt
Centerville High School
Centerville, Ohio

Edward Blotzer III
Wilkinsburg High School
Pittsburgh, Pennsylvania

Ruby Bowker
Mt. View High School
Mt. View, Wyoming

Darolyn Brown
Osborn High School
Detroit, Michigan

Rob Bruno
Atholton High School
Columbia, Maryland

Mary Beth Crotty
Bridgetown Junior High
Cincinnati, Ohio

Susan Dawson
Sam Barlow High School
Portland, Oregon

Thomas A. Della Salla
Schenectady City School District
Schenectady, New York

Sandra Denton
East High School
Columbus, Ohio

Charles Eisele
St. John Vianney High School
St. Louis, Missouri

Mel Farberman
Benjamin Cardozo High School
Bayside, New York

Caroline Ferdinandsen
San Joaquin Memorial High School
Fresno, California

Tye Ferdinandsen
San Joaquin Memorial High School
Fresno, California

Randle Frink
East Rowan High School
Salisbury, North Carolina

Pamela Fuller
Capital High School
Charleston, West Virginia

Tara Gallagher
River Hill High School
Columbia, Maryland

June Gatewood
Rio Americano
Sacramento, California

Ellen Geisler
Mentor High School
Mentor, Ohio

Leslie Gershon
Annapolis Senior High
Mitchellville, Maryland

Kim Hartman
Franklin Heights High School
Columbus, Ohio

Charlotte Heidel
Gaylord High School
Gaylord, Michigan

Keith Henricksen
Sutton Public Schools
Sutton, Nebraska

Patricia Herigan
Central Dauphin High School
Harrisburg, Pennsylvania

Azalie Hightower
Paul Junior High School
Washington, D.C.

Bobbi Ciriza Houtchens
San Bernardino High School
San Bernardino, California

Cheri Jefferson
Atholton High School
Columbia, Maryland

Marsha Jones
Seymour High School
Seymour, Indiana

Cheryl Keast
Glendale High School
Glendale, California

Glenda Kissell
Littleton High School
Littleton, Colorado

Jan Klein
Cypress Lake High School
Fort Myers, Florida

Beth Koehler
Nathan Hale High School
West Allis, Wisconsin

Sister Mary Kay Lampert
Central Catholic High School
Portland, Oregon

Elaine Loughlin
Palo Duro High
Amarillo, Texas

Tom Mann
Franklin Heights High School
Columbus, Ohio

Carolyn Sue Mash
Westerville North High School
Westerville, Ohio

Eileen Mattingly
McDonough High School
Pomfret, Maryland

Wanda McConnell
Statesville High School
Statesville, North Carolina

Victoria McCormick
John Jay High School
San Antonio, Texas

Sandra Sue McPherson
McKeesport Area High School
McKeesport, Pennsylvania

Jill Miller
Odessa High School
Odessa, Texas

Karmen Miller
Cypress Falls High School
Houston, Texas

Catherine Morse
Shelby High School
Shelby, Ohio

Tom Omli
Rogers High School
Puyallup, Washington

John O'Toole
Solon High School
Solon, Ohio

Helen Pappas
Bridgewater-Raritan High School
Bridgewater, New Jersey

Jill Railsback
Seymour High School
Seymour, Indiana

Doug Reed
Franklin Heights High School
Columbus, Ohio

Mary Jane Reed
Solon High School
Solon, Ohio

Dorlea Rikard
Bradshaw High School
Florence, Alabama

Diane Ritzdorf
Arapahoe High School
Littleton, Colorado

Leonor Rodriguez
Breckenridge High School
San Antonio, Texas

Susanne Rubenstein
Wachusett Regional High School
Holden, Massachusetts

Steve Slagle
San Gabriel High School
San Gabriel, California

Tammy Smiley
Littleton High School
Littleton, Colorado

Carol Smith
Moses Lake School District
Moses Lake, Washington

Helen Spaith
Franklin Heights High School
Columbus, Ohio

Marsha Spampinato
High School of Enterprise,
Business, and Technology
Smithtown, New York

Nora Stephens
Huntsville High School
Huntsville, Alabama

David Stocking
Wachusett Regional High School
Holden, Massachusetts

Mark Tavernier
Norfolk Public Schools
Norfolk, Virginia

Martin Tierney
Bishop Dwenger High School
Fort Wayne, Indiana

Elysa Toler-Robinson
Detroit Public Schools
Detroit, Michigan

Megan Trow
Sprague High School
Salem, Oregon

Joseph Velten Jr.
Archbishop Wood High School
Warminster, Pennsylvania

Margaret Wildermann
McDonough High School
Pomfret, Maryland

Kathy Young
Walnut Ridge High School
Columbus, Ohio

Mary Young
Greenville High School
Greenville, Illinois

Book Overview

Contents

Guide to Active Reading

UNIT ❧ ONE

From the Earliest Days 36

indicates world literature

CONTENTS

CONTENTS

Theme 3   Gaining Insight 201

CONTENTS

CONTENTS

UNIT ❦ FOUR

Regionalism and Realism . . .448

Theme 6   The Energy of the Everyday 459

CONTENTS

CONTENTS

UNIT ❧ 6

Midcentury Voices

Theme 9 Personal Discoveries

CONTENTS

Theme 10   Acting on an Idea 907

UNIT ❦ 7

Toward the Twenty-First Century 1018

CONTENTS

CONTENTS

Reference Section

Selections by Genre

Poetry

SELECTIONS BY GENRE

Features

COMPARING selections

Literature FOCUS

Active Reading Strategies

✒ Writing Workshop

Interdisciplinary Connection

Skills

Grammar Link

Listening, Speaking, and Viewing

Reading & Thinking Skills

Technology Skills

Vocabulary Skills

Writing Skills

Literary Map of

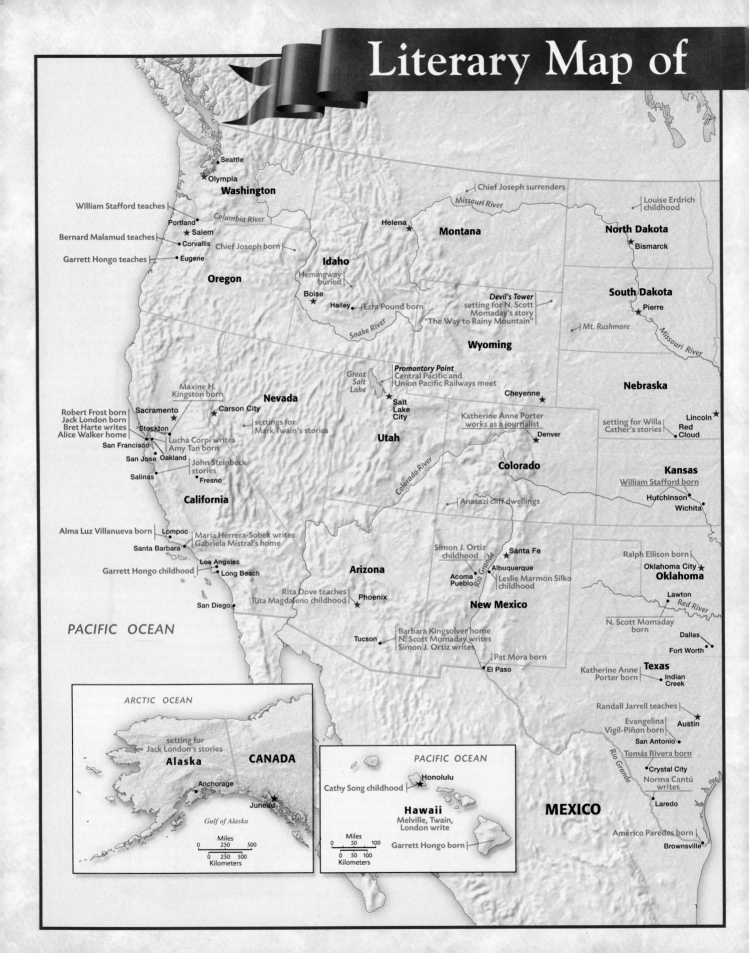

Seattle
★ Olympia
Washington

William Stafford teaches
Portland
Columbia River
Bernard Malamud teaches
★ Salem
• Corvallis
Garrett Hongo teaches
• Eugene
Chief Joseph born

Oregon

Chief Joseph surrenders
Missouri River

Helena
★
Montana

Louise Erdrich
childhood

North Dakota
★ Bismarck

Idaho
Hemingway
buried
Boise
★
Hailey • Ezra Pound born

Snake River

Devil's Tower
setting for N. Scott
Momaday's story
"The Way to Rainy Mountain"

South Dakota
• Pierre

Mt. Rushmore
Missouri River

Wyoming

Maxine H.
Kingston born

Promontory Point
Central Pacific and
Union Pacific Railways meet

Great
Salt
Lake

Salt
Lake
City
★

Cheyenne
★

Nebraska

Robert Frost born
Jack London born
Bret Harte writes
Alice Walker home

Sacramento
★
Carson City
Nevada

settings for
Mark Twain's stories

Katherine Anne Porter
works as a journalist

Denver
•

Lincoln ★
setting for Willa
Cather's stories
Red
Cloud •

Stockton •
Lucha Corpi writes
Amy Tan born
San Francisco •
San Jose • Oakland
Salinas •
John Steinbeck
stories
• Fresno

Utah

Colorado

Kansas
William Stafford born
Hutchinson •
Wichita •

California

Alma Luz Villanueva born
Lompoc •
María Herrera-Sobek writes
Gabriela Mistral's home
Santa Barbara •

Colorado River

Anasazi cliff dwellings

Garrett Hongo childhood
Los Angeles •
• Long Beach

Arizona

Simon J. Ortiz
childhood
Acoma
Pueblo
Santa Fe •
Albuquerque •
Leslie Marmon Silko
childhood

Rio Grande

Ralph Ellison born
Oklahoma City ★
Oklahoma

Lawton •
Red River

San Diego •

Rita Dove teaches
Rita Magdaleno childhood
Phoenix
★

New Mexico

N. Scott Momaday
born

Dallas •
Fort Worth •

PACIFIC OCEAN

Tucson •

Barbara Kingsolver home
N. Scott Momaday writes
Simon J. Ortiz writes

El Paso •

Pat Mora born

Katherine Anne
Porter born

Texas
Indian
Creek •

Randall Jarrell teaches
Evangelina
Vigil-Piñon born
San Antonio •
Tomás Rivera born

Austin
★

Rio Grande

• Crystal City
Norma Cantú
writes

Laredo •

MEXICO

Américo Paredes born •
• Brownsville

ARCTIC OCEAN

setting for
Jack London's stories
Alaska
CANADA

Anchorage •

Juneau ★

Gulf of Alaska

Miles
0   250   500

0   250 500
Kilometers

PACIFIC OCEAN

Cathy Song childhood
Honolulu
★

Hawaii
Melville, Twain,
London write

Garrett Hongo born

Miles
0   50   100

0   50 100
Kilometers

the United States

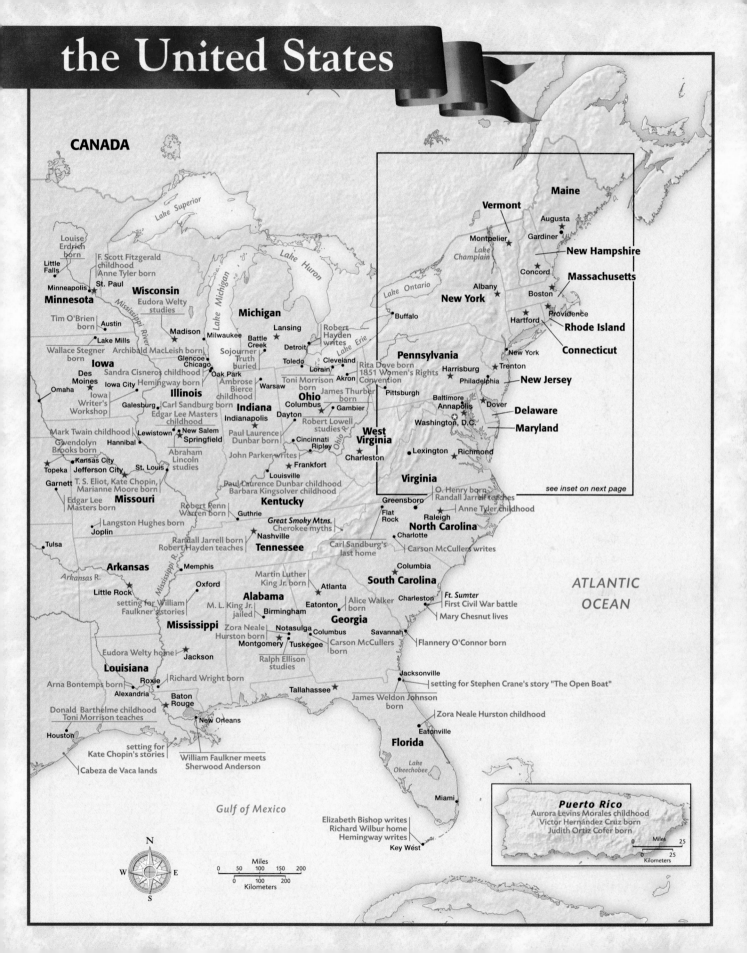

CANADA

Lake Superior

Louise Erdrich born
Little Falls
Minneapolis
St. Paul
F. Scott Fitzgerald childhood
Anne Tyler born
Minnesota
Wisconsin
Eudora Welty studies
Mississippi River

Tim O'Brien born
Austin
Lake Mills
Wallace Stegner born
Archibald MacLeish born
Iowa
Des Moines
Iowa City
Hemingway born
Iowa Writer's Workshop
Omaha
Glencoe
Chicago
Oak Park
Ambrose Bierce childhood
Sandra Cisneros childhood
Galesburg
Carl Sandburg born
Illinois
Edgar Lee Masters childhood
Indianapolis
New Salem
Springfield
Abraham Lincoln studies

Michigan
Lake Michigan
Lake Huron
Lansing
Madison
Milwaukee
Battle Creek
Sojourner Truth buried
Detroit
Toledo
Robert Hayden writes
Lake Erie
Cleveland
Lorain
Akron
Warsaw
Toni Morrison born
James Thurber born
Ohio
Columbus
Gambier
Dayton
Rita Dove born
1851 Women's Rights Convention
Pittsburgh
Pennsylvania
Harrisburg
Philadelphia

Mark Twain childhood
Gwendolyn Brooks born
Hannibal
Lewistown
Indiana
Paul Laurence Dunbar born
Cincinnati
Ripley
John Parker writes
Frankfort
Louisville
Robert Lowell studies
Ohio R.
West Virginia
Charleston

Kansas City
Topeka
Jefferson City
St. Louis
T. S. Eliot, Kate Chopin, Marianne Moore born
Garnett
Edgar Lee Masters born
Missouri
Paul Laurence Dunbar childhood
Barbara Kingsolver childhood
Kentucky
Robert Penn Warren born
Guthrie
Lexington
Richmond
Virginia

Langston Hughes born
Joplin
Tulsa
Arkansas R.
Arkansas
Little Rock
Memphis
Oxford
setting for William Faulkner's stories
Randall Jarrell born
Robert Hayden teaches
Nashville
Tennessee
Great Smoky Mtns.
Cherokee myths
Carl Sandburg's last home
Flat Rock
Greensboro
O. Henry born
Randall Jarrell teaches
Anne Tyler childhood
Raleigh
North Carolina
Charlotte
Carson McCullers writes

Columbia
South Carolina
Charleston
Ft. Sumter
First Civil War battle
Mary Chesnut lives

Mississippi R.
Alabama
M. L. King Jr. jailed
Birmingham
Eatonton
Alice Walker born
Georgia
Columbus
Carson McCullers born
Savannah
Flannery O'Connor born

Martin Luther King Jr. born
Atlanta
Mississippi
Zora Neale Hurston born
Notasulga
Montgomery
Tuskegee
Ralph Ellison studies
Eudora Welty home
Jackson
Louisiana
Arna Bontemps born
Roxie
Richard Wright born
Alexandria
Baton Rouge
New Orleans
Tallahassee
Jacksonville
setting for Stephen Crane's story "The Open Boat"
James Weldon Johnson born
Zora Neale Hurston childhood
Eatonville

Donald Barthelme childhood
Toni Morrison teaches
Houston
setting for Kate Chopin's stories
Cabeza de Vaca lands
William Faulkner meets Sherwood Anderson
Florida
Lake Okeechobee
Miami

Gulf of Mexico

Elizabeth Bishop writes
Richard Wilbur home
Hemingway writes
Key West

Inset (top right)

Maine
Vermont
Augusta
Gardiner
Montpelier
Lake Champlain
New Hampshire
Concord
Massachusetts
Albany
Boston
New York
Hartford
Providence
Rhode Island
Buffalo
New York
Connecticut
Trenton
New Jersey
Lake Ontario
Baltimore
Annapolis
Dover
Delaware
Washington, D.C.
Maryland
see inset on next page

ATLANTIC OCEAN

Puerto Rico (inset)

Puerto Rico
Aurora Levins Morales childhood
Victor Hernández Cruz born
Judith Ortiz Cofer born

Miles
0   25
Kilometers
0   25

Compass / Scale

N W E S

Miles
0   50   100   150   200

0   100   200
Kilometers

Map of Eastern U.S.

CANADA

MAINE

North Brooklyn — E. B. White writes

Augusta ★

Gardiner — Edwin A. Robinson childhood

Montpelier ★

VERMONT

N.H.

Margaret Atwood studies
E. E. Cummings born
H. W. Longfellow writes
Harvard University

Concord ★

Robert Frost's farm

Nathaniel Hawthorne born
Witch trials

Phillis Wheatley writes
R. W. Emerson born
Sylvia Plath born
Robert Lowell born
Oliver Wendell Holmes born
Anne Sexton writes
Helene Johnson born

Walden Pond
H. D. Thoreau writes

Salem

Mary Rowlandson writes

Emily Dickinson home

Albany ★

Cambridge
Boston

Lancaster

Richard Wilbur home

Amherst

Elizabeth Bishop born

Cummington

MASS.

Worcester

Plymouth

Great Barrington

Mayflower lands
Massachusetts Bay Colony
William Bradford writes
Anne Bradstreet writes
Jonathan Edwards writes

NEW YORK

William C. Bryant writes

Hartford ★

Providence

CONN.

RHODE ISLAND

Lake Ontario

Sojourner Truth born

Wallace Stevens home

E. B. White born

Amistad trial

William Carlos Williams home

Thomas Paine home

Rutherford
Newark

New Rochelle

Stephen Crane born

Mt. Vernon

New York

Herman Melville born
Washington Irving born
Arthur Miller born
James Baldwin childhood
Edna St. Vincent Millay writes
Dorothy Parker writes
Jean Toomer writes
Ralph Ellison writes
Claude McKay writes
Edwidge Danticat writes
Julia Alvarez writes
Victor Cruz writes
Diana Chang writes
Sandra M. Esteves writes
Bernard Malamud born

PENNSYLVANIA

Trenton ★

NEW JERSEY

Marianne Moore late childhood/
early adulthood

Benjamin Franklin writes
Donald Barthelme born

Harrisburg ★

Reading

Philadelphia

Carlisle

Camden

Shillington

Walt Whitman home

Lincoln's
Gettysburg Address

John Updike born

Wallace Stevens born

Pittsburgh

Frederick Douglass childhood

Henry Louis Gates Jr. childhood

Barbara Kingsolver born

Baltimore

Dover

DEL.

Piedmont

Annapolis ★

Jean Toomer born
Frederick Douglass born
Abigail Adams writes
from White House
Archibald MacLeish writes

☆ Washington, D.C.

WEST VIRGINIA

MARYLAND

Fredericksburg

ATLANTIC OCEAN

Walt Whitman at Civil War battlefront

Monticello

Richmond ★

Hillsboro

Lexington

Thomas Jefferson home

Robert E. Lee home

Patrick Henry's "liberty or death" speech
Edgar Allan Poe boyhood

Norfolk

Pearl S. Buck born

VIRGINIA

Huron Myths
Iroquois Nation
Dekanawida creates
Iroquois Constitution

Miles
0 — 50 — 100

Kilometers
0 — 50 — 100

Guide to
Active Reading

FICTION

POETRY

NONFICTION

Active Reading Strategies

Fiction

Think of an experience—a sports event, a movie, or maybe a special concert—during which you completely forgot your surroundings or the passage of time. Your involvement was what drew you in. You can experience a short story or a novel in exactly the same way. Don't be passive! Interact with the fiction. Talk it over in your head. The strategies described below can make your reading a richer experience.

● For more about related reading strategies, see **Reading Handbook,** pp. R86–R93.

PREDICT

Predicting helps you anticipate events and appreciate less obvious parts of a story. Combine clues the author provides with your own understanding of people. Make educated guesses about what will happen to the characters.

> **Say to yourself . . .**
> ● The title indicates that the story might be about . . .
> ● This character will probably . . .
> ● This story is different from my original prediction. Now I think . . .

CONNECT

Draw parallels to connect the people, events, and settings in the story with those in your life and in other fiction you have enjoyed.

> **Ask yourself . . .**
> ● How might I act in this character's situation?
> ● When have I felt the same way as this character?
> ● What historical or current events does this bring to mind?
> ● What other stories does this remind me of?

QUESTION

Ask yourself questions to clarify the story.

> **Ask yourself . . .**
> ● Do I understand what I've just read?
> ● Why did he or she say that?
> ● How does this action fit into the overall conflict?

VISUALIZE

In your imagination, form pictures of the setting, the characters, and the action. Pay close attention to sensory details and descriptions and your responses to them.

Ask yourself . . .
- Can I see the characters and setting in my mind?
- Where are the characters in relation to one another and to their surroundings?
- How do the descriptions of a character's expressions, body stance, and tone of voice help to develop the scene?

EVALUATE

As you read, form opinions and make judgments about the characters and their actions. Review and, if necessary, revise opinions and judgments.

Ask yourself . . .
- Does this turn of events make sense for these characters?
- Is this character acting or responding in a realistic way?
- What is particularly effective about this writer's style?

REVIEW

As you read, summarize related events and paraphrase difficult language.

Say to yourself . . .
- These events have happened so far . . .
- That event caused this event to happen . . .
- In other words, this character means . . .

RESPOND

Respond to the story *while* you are reading it. React spontaneously to the story.

Say to yourself . . .
- That character's actions were so . . . !
- I'd like to ask the author why . . .
- I wish I could see this place because . . .

Applying the Strategies

1. Read the following story, "The Life You Save May Be Your Own," by Flannery O'Connor. Use the Active Reading Model notes in the margins to help you.

2. Read another short story using appropriate Active Reading Strategies. Write your comments and questions on a sheet of paper. When you finish, evaluate your use of the strategies.

Before You Read

The Life You Save May Be Your Own

Meet Flannery O'Connor

Award-winning author Flannery O'Connor often delighted in telling friends and interviewers that the highlight of her life occurred when, as a five-year-old, she taught a chicken to walk backwards. It was on such odd yet mundane experiences that O'Connor was later to base her work. "The first and most obvious characteristic of fiction," she said, "is that it deals with reality through what can be seen, heard, smelt, tasted, and touched."

Mary Flannery O'Connor grew up in Georgia. After graduating from college in 1945, she attended the prestigious Iowa Writers' Workshop at the University of Iowa. In 1952 O'Connor was stricken with a near fatal attack of lupus, the disease from which her father had died, and was forced to move back to her mother's farm. Her writing reflects the vivid details of these rural surroundings and describes seemingly simple yet extremely complex characters. Her themes are often the harsh and unsettling realities of hard luck, hypocrisy, and failed expectations.

O'Connor died at the age of thirty-nine, but her great talent had earned her recognition as a major literary voice of the American South. A review appearing in *Time* magazine hailed O'Connor as "highly unladylike [with] a brutal irony, a slam-bang humor, and a style of writing as balefully direct as a death sentence."

"Fiction is . . . the most modest and the most human of the arts."

—*O'Connor*

Flannery O'Connor was born in 1925 and died in 1964.

FOCUS ACTIVITY

What do you look for when you meet someone for the first time? Are your first impressions usually correct?

JOURNAL Briefly describe an experience you have had as you sized up a new acquaintance and then got to know the person better.

SETTING A PURPOSE Read to discover the first impressions two characters have about each other and whether those impressions prove to be correct.

BACKGROUND

The Time and Place

Widespread unemployment during the Depression of the 1930s brought hard times to many. Unemployed men, and occasionally women, often became wanderers, referred to as "tramps" or "hoboes." They went from city to city and house to house, particularly in rural areas, seeking odd jobs in return for food, clothes, or shelter. When World War II began, many regularly employed workers joined the armed forces. As a result, the previously unemployed and men wounded and sent home from the war frequently filled in at temporary jobs.

VOCABULARY PREVIEW

gaunt (gônt) *adj.* thin, bony, and hollow-eyed, as from hunger or illness; p. 8
list (list) *v.* to tilt or lean to one side; p. 8
ravenous (rav′ ə nəs) *adj.* extremely hungry; p. 11
stately (stāt′ lē) *adj.* noble; dignified; majestic; p. 12
morose (mə rōs′) *adj.* bad-tempered, gloomy, and withdrawn; p. 14
rue (rōō) *v.* to regret; to be sorry for; p. 16

The Life You Save May Be Your Own

Flannery O'Connor ∿

Active
Reading Model

THE OLD WOMAN AND HER DAUGHTER WERE SITTING ON their porch when Mr. Shiftlet came up their road for the first time. The old woman slid to the edge of her chair and leaned forward, shading her eyes from the piercing sunset with her hand. The daughter could not see far in front of her and continued to play with her fingers. Although the old woman lived in this desolate[1] spot with only her daughter and she had never seen Mr. Shiftlet before, she could tell, even from a distance, that he was a tramp and no one to be afraid of.

---

1. A *desolate* spot is miserable, lonely, and cheerless.

The Life You Save May Be Your Own

His left coat sleeve was folded up to show there was only half an arm in it and his gaunt figure listed slightly to the side as if the breeze were pushing him. He had on a black town suit and a brown felt hat that was turned up in the front and down in the back and he carried a tin tool box by a handle. He came on, at an amble, up her road, his face turned toward the sun which appeared to be balancing itself on the peak of a small mountain.

The old woman didn't change her position until he was almost into her yard; then she rose with one hand fisted on her hip. The daughter, a large girl in a short blue organdy dress, saw him all at once and jumped up and began to stamp and point and make excited speechless sounds.

Mr. Shiftlet stopped just inside the yard and set his box on the ground and tipped his hat at her as if she were not in the least afflicted; then he turned toward the old woman and swung the hat all the way off. He had long black slick hair that hung flat from a part in the middle to beyond the tips of his ears on either side. His face descended in forehead for more than half its length and ended suddenly with his features just balanced over a jutting steel-trap jaw. He seemed to be a young man but he had a look of composed dissatisfaction as if he understood life thoroughly.

"Good evening," the old woman said. She was about the size of a cedar fence post and she had a man's gray hat pulled down low over her head.

The tramp stood looking at her and didn't answer. He turned his back and faced the sunset. He swung both his whole and his short arm up slowly so that they indicated an expanse of sky and his figure formed a crooked cross. The old woman watched him with her arms folded across her chest as if she were the owner of the sun, and the daughter watched, her head thrust forward and her fat helpless hands hanging at the wrists. She had long pink-gold hair and eyes as blue as a peacock's neck.

He held the pose for almost fifty seconds and then he picked up his box and came on to the porch and dropped down on the bottom step. "Lady," he said in a firm nasal voice, "I'd give a fortune to live where I could see me a sun do that every evening."

"Does it every evening," the old woman said and sat back down. The daughter sat down too and watched him with a cautious sly look as if he were a bird that had come up very close. He leaned to one side, rooting in his pants pocket, and in a second he brought out a package of chewing gum and offered her a piece. She took it and unpeeled it and began to chew without taking her eyes off him. He offered the old woman a piece but she only raised her upper lip to indicate she had no teeth.

Mr. Shiftlet's pale sharp glance had already passed over everything in the yard—the pump near the corner of the house and the big fig tree that three or four chickens were preparing to roost in—and had moved to a shed where he saw the square rusted back of an automobile. "You ladies drive?" he asked.

PREDICT

Given the story title and this description of Mr. Shiftlet, what do you think the story will be about?

VISUALIZE

Form a detailed picture of both the mother and daughter in your mind.

Vocabulary
gaunt (gônt) *adj.* thin, bony, and hollow-eyed, as from hunger or illness
list (list) *v.* to tilt or lean to one side

Active Reading Model

"That car ain't run in fifteen year," the old woman said. "The day my husband died, it quit running."

"Nothing is like it used to be, lady," he said. "The world is almost rotten."

"That's right," the old woman said. "You from around here?"

"Name Tom T. Shiftlet," he murmured, looking at the tires.

"I'm pleased to meet you," the old woman said. "Name Lucynell Crater and daughter Lucynell Crater. What you doing around here, Mr. Shiftlet?"

He judged the car to be about a 1928 or '29 Ford. "Lady," he said, and turned and gave her his full attention, "lemme tell you something. There's one of these doctors in Atlanta that's taken a knife and cut the human heart—the human heart," he repeated, leaning forward, "out of a man's chest and held it in his hand," and he held his hand out, palm up, as if it were slightly weighted with the human heart, "and studied it like it was a day-old chicken, and lady," he said, allowing a long significant pause in which his head slid forward and his clay-colored eyes brightened, "he don't know no more about it than you or me."

"That's right," the old woman said.

"Why, if he was to take that knife and cut into every corner of it, he still wouldn't know no more than you or me. What you want to bet?"

"Nothing," the old woman said wisely. "Where you come from, Mr. Shiftlet?"

He didn't answer. He reached into his pocket and brought out a sack of tobacco and a package of cigarette papers and rolled himself a cigarette, expertly with one hand, and attached it in a hanging position to his upper lip. Then he took a box of wooden matches from his pocket and struck one on his shoe. He held the burning match as if he were studying the mystery of flame while it traveled dangerously toward his skin. The daughter began to make loud noises and to point to his hand and shake her finger at him, but when the flame was just before touching him, he leaned down with his hand cupped over it as if he were going to set fire to his nose and lit the cigarette.

He flipped away the dead match and blew a stream of gray into the evening. A sly look came over his face. "Lady," he said, "nowadays, people'll do anything anyways. I can tell you my name is Tom T. Shiftlet and I came from Tarwater, Tennessee, but you never have seen me before: how you know I ain't lying? How you know my name ain't Aaron Sparks, lady, and I come from Singleberry, Georgia, or how you know it's not George Speeds and I come from Lucy, Alabama, or how you know I ain't Thompson Bright from Toolafalls, Mississippi?"

PREDICT

Why might Mr. Shiftlet be so interested in the car?

EVALUATE

What do you think of Mr. Shiftlet and his values? Do you trust him?

Red Barn with Junkyard, 1986. John Salt. Watercolor on paper, 19 x 28 in. O.K. Harris Works of Art, New York.

Viewing the painting: What items in the painting might you also expect to see around the Crater farm? Explain.

The Life You Save May Be Your Own

"I don't know nothing about you," the old woman muttered, irked.[2]

"Lady," he said, "people don't care how they lie. Maybe the best I can tell you is, I'm a man; but listen lady," he said and paused and made his tone more ominous[3] still, "what is a man?"

The old woman began to gum a seed. "What you carry in that tin box, Mr. Shiftlet?" she asked.

"Tools," he said, put back. "I'm a carpenter."

"Well, if you come out here to work, I'll be able to feed you and give you a place to sleep but I can't pay. I'll tell you that before you begin," she said.

QUESTION

What work arrangement does Mrs. Crater offer Mr. Shiftlet?

There was no answer at once and no particular expression on his face. He leaned back against the two-by-four that helped support the porch roof. "Lady," he said slowly, "there's some men that some things mean more to them than money." The old woman rocked without comment and the daughter watched the trigger that moved up and down in his neck. He told the old woman then that all most people were interested in was money, but he asked what a man was made for. He asked her if a man was made for money, or what. He asked her what she thought she was made for but she didn't answer, she only sat rocking and wondered if a one-armed man could put a new roof on her garden house. He asked a lot of questions that she didn't answer. He told her that he was twenty-eight years old and had lived a varied life. He had been a gospel singer, a foreman on the railroad, an assistant in an undertaking parlor, and he had come over the radio for three months with Uncle Roy and his Red Creek Wranglers. He said he had fought and bled in the Arm Service of his country and visited every foreign land and that everywhere he had seen people that didn't care if they did a thing one way or another. He said he hadn't been raised thataway.

A fat yellow moon appeared in the branches of the fig tree as if it were going to roost there with the chickens. He said that a man had to escape to the country to see the world whole and that he wished he lived in a desolate place like this where he could see the sun go down every evening like God made it to do.

REVIEW

Summarize what you know about Mr. Shiftlet's background.

"Are you married or are you single?" the old woman asked.

There was a long silence. "Lady," he asked finally, "where would you find you an innocent woman today? I wouldn't have any of this trash I could just pick up."

The daughter was leaning very far down, hanging her head almost between her knees, watching him through a triangular door she had made in her overturned hair; and she suddenly fell in a heap on the floor and began to whimper. Mr. Shiftlet straightened her out and helped her get back in the chair.

"Is she your baby girl?" he asked.

"My only," the old woman said, "and she's the sweetest girl in the world. I wouldn't give her up for nothing on earth. She's smart too. She can sweep the floor, cook, wash, feed the chickens, and hoe. I wouldn't give her up for a casket of jewels."

---

2. To be *irked* is to be annoyed or bothered.
3. Something *ominous* is, or seems to be, threatening.

"No," he said kindly, "don't ever let any man take her away from you."

"Any man come after her," the old woman said, " 'll have to stay around the place."

Mr. Shiftlet's eye in the darkness was focused on a part of the automobile bumper that glittered in the distance. "Lady," he said, jerking his short arm up as if he could point with it to her house and yard and pump, "there ain't a broken thing on this plantation that I couldn't fix for you, one-arm jackleg[4] or not. I'm a man," he said with a sullen dignity, "even if I ain't a whole one. I got," he said, tapping his knuckles on the floor to emphasize the immensity of what he was going to say, "a moral intelligence!" and his face pierced out of the darkness into a shaft of doorlight and he stared at her as if he were astonished himself at this impossible truth.

The old woman was not impressed with the phrase. "I told you you could hang around and work for food," she said, "if you don't mind sleeping in that car yonder."

"Why listen, Lady," he said with a grin of delight, "the monks of old slept in their coffins!"

"They wasn't as advanced as we are," the old woman said.

The next morning he began on the roof of the garden house while Lucynell, the daughter, sat on a rock and watched him work. He had not been around a week before the change he had made in the place was apparent. He had patched the front and back steps, built a new hog pen, restored a fence, and taught Lucynell, who was completely deaf and had never said a word in her life, to say the word "bird." The big rosy-faced girl followed him everywhere, saying "Burrttddt ddbirrrttdt," and clapping her hands. The old woman watched from a distance, secretly pleased. She was ravenous for a son-in-law.

Mr. Shiftlet slept on the hard narrow back seat of the car with his feet out the side window. He had his razor and a can of water on a crate that served him as a bedside table and he put up a piece of mirror against the back glass and kept his coat neatly on a hanger that he hung over one of the windows.

In the evenings he sat on the steps and talked while the old woman and Lucynell rocked violently in their chairs on either side of him. The old woman's three mountains were black against the dark blue sky and were visited off and on by various planets and by the moon after it had left the chickens. Mr. Shiftlet pointed out that the reason he had improved this plantation was because he had taken a personal interest in it. He said he was even going to make the automobile run.

He had raised the hood and studied the mechanism and he said he could tell that the car had been built in the days when cars were really built. You

---

4. A *jackleg,* like a jack-of-all-trades, can do many different kinds of work for which he or she has not been trained.

Vocabulary
ravenous (rav′ ə nəs) *adj.* extremely hungry

The Life You Save May Be Your Own

RESPOND

What do you think about Mr. Shiftlet's theory on how cars should be made?

take now, he said, one man puts in one bolt and another man puts in another bolt and another man puts in another bolt so that it's a man for a bolt. That's why you have to pay so much for a car: you're paying all those men. Now if you didn't have to pay but one man, you could get you a cheaper car and one that had had a personal interest taken in it, and it would be a better car. The old woman agreed with him that this was so.

Mr. Shiftlet said that the trouble with the world was that nobody cared, or stopped and took any trouble. He said he never would have been able to teach Lucynell to say a word if he hadn't cared and stopped long enough.

"Teach her to say something else," the old woman said.

"What you want her to say next?" Mr. Shiftlet asked.

The old woman's smile was broad and toothless and suggestive. "Teach her to say 'sugarpie,'" she said.

Mr. Shiftlet already knew what was on her mind.

The next day he began to tinker with the automobile and that evening he told her that if she would buy a fan belt, he would be able to make the car run.

The old woman said she would give him the money. "You see that girl yonder?" she asked, pointing to Lucynell who was sitting on the floor a foot away, watching him, her eyes blue even in the dark. "If it was ever a man wanted to take her away, I would say, 'No man on earth is going to take that sweet girl of mine away from me!' but if he was to say, 'Lady, I don't want to take her away, I want her right here,' I would say, 'Mister, I don't blame you none. I wouldn't pass up a chance to live in a permanent place and get the sweetest girl in the world myself. You ain't no fool,' I would say."

"How old is she?" Mr. Shiftlet asked casually.

EVALUATE

Do you think Mrs. Crater's tender feelings for her daughter are genuine?

"Fifteen, sixteen," the old woman said. The girl was nearly thirty but because of her innocence it was impossible to guess.

"It would be a good idea to paint it too," Mr. Shiftlet remarked. "You don't want it to rust out."

"We'll see about that later," the old woman said.

The next day he walked into town and returned with the parts he needed and a can of gasoline. Late in the afternoon, terrible noises issued from the shed and the old woman rushed out of the house, thinking Lucynell was somewhere having a fit. Lucynell was sitting on a chicken crate, stamping her feet and screaming, "Burrddttt! bddurrddtttt!" but her fuss was drowned out by the car. With a volley of blasts it emerged from the shed, moving in a fierce and stately way. Mr. Shiftlet was in the driver's seat, sitting very erect. He had an expression of serious modesty on his face as if he had just raised the dead.

That night, rocking on the porch, the old woman began her business at once. "You want you an innocent woman, don't you?" she asked sympathetically. "You don't want none of this trash."

Vocabulary

stately (stāt′ lē) *adj.* noble; dignified; majestic

"No'm, I don't," Mr. Shiftlet said.

"One that can't talk," she continued, "can't sass you back or use foul language. That's the kind for you to have. Right there," and she pointed to Lucynell sitting cross-legged in her chair, holding both feet in her hands.

"That's right," he admitted. "She wouldn't give me any trouble."

"Saturday," the old woman said, "you and her and me can drive into town and get married."

Mr. Shiftlet eased his position on the steps.

"I can't get married right now," he said. "Everything you want to do takes money and I ain't got any."

"What you need with money?" she asked.

"It takes money," he said. "Some people'll do anything anyhow these days, but the way I think, I wouldn't marry no woman that I couldn't take on a trip like she was somebody. I mean take her to a hotel and treat her. I wouldn't marry the Duchesser Windsor,"[5] he said firmly, "unless I could take her to a hotel and give her something good to eat.

"I was raised thataway and there ain't a thing I can do about it. My old mother taught me how to do."

"Lucynell don't even know what a hotel is," the old woman muttered. "Listen here, Mr. Shiftlet," she said, sliding forward in her chair, "you'd be getting a permanent house and a deep well and the most innocent girl in the world. You don't need no money. Lemme tell you something: there ain't any place in the world for a poor disabled friendless drifting man."

The ugly words settled in Mr. Shiftlet's head like a group of buzzards in the top of a tree. He didn't answer at once. He rolled himself a cigarette and lit it and then he said in an even voice, "Lady, a man is divided into two parts, body and spirit."

The old woman clamped her gums together.

"A body and a spirit," he repeated. "The body, lady, is like a house: it don't go anywhere; but the spirit, lady, is like a automobile: always on the move, always . . ."

"Listen, Mr. Shiftlet," she said, "my well never goes dry and my house is always warm in the winter and there's no mortgage on a thing about this place. You can go to the courthouse and see for yourself. And yonder under that shed is a fine automobile." She laid the bait carefully. "You can have it painted by Saturday. I'll pay for the paint."

In the darkness, Mr. Shiftlet's smile stretched like a weary snake waking up by a fire. After a second he recalled himself and said, "I'm only saying a man's spirit means more to him than anything else. I would have to take my wife off for the weekend without no regards at all for cost. I got to follow where my spirit say to go."

EVALUATE
Does Mr. Shiftlet's reason for needing money seem reasonable? Why or why not?

QUESTION
Why, do you think, does Mr. Shiftlet smile in the darkness?

5. Shiftlet is referring to the American woman for whom Britain's King Edward VIII gave up the throne in 1936. The new king gave them the titles Duke and Duchess of *Windsor*.

The Life You Save May Be Your Own

"I'll give you fifteen dollars for a weekend trip," the old woman said in a crabbed voice. "That's the best I can do."

"That wouldn't hardly pay for more than the gas and the hotel," he said. "It wouldn't feed her."

"Seventeen-fifty," the old woman said. "That's all I got so it isn't any use you trying to milk me. You can take a lunch."

Mr. Shiftlet was deeply hurt by the word "milk." He didn't doubt that she had more money sewed up in her mattress but he had already told her he was not interested in her money. "I'll make that do," he said and rose and walked off without treating[6] with her further.

On Saturday the three of them drove into town in the car that the paint had barely dried on and Mr. Shiftlet and Lucynell were married in the Ordinary's[7] office while the old woman witnessed. As they came out of the courthouse, Mr. Shiftlet began twisting his neck in his collar. He looked morose and bitter as if he had been insulted while someone held him. "That didn't satisfy me none," he said. "That was just something a woman in an office did, nothing but paper work and blood tests. What do they know about my blood? If they was to take my heart and cut it out," he said, "they wouldn't know a thing about me. It didn't satisfy me at all."

"It satisfied the law," the old woman said sharply.

"The law," Mr. Shiftlet said and spit. "It's the law that don't satisfy me."

He had painted the car dark green with a yellow band around it just under the windows. The three of them climbed in the front seat and the old woman said, "Don't Lucynell look pretty? Looks like a baby doll." Lucynell was dressed up in a white dress that her mother had uprooted from a trunk and there was a Panama hat on her head with a bunch of red wooden cherries on the brim. Every now and then her placid[8] expression was changed by a sly isolated little thought like a shoot of green in the desert. "You got a prize!" the old woman said.

Mr. Shiftlet didn't even look at her.

They drove back to the house to let the old woman off and pick up the lunch. When they were ready to leave, she stood staring in the window of the car, with her fingers clenched around the glass. Tears began to seep sideways out of her eyes and run along the dirty creases in her face. "I ain't ever been parted with her for two days before," she said.

Mr. Shiftlet started the motor.

"And I wouldn't let no man have her but you because I seen you would do right. Good-bye, Sugarbaby," she said, clutching at the sleeve of the

---

6. Here, *treating* means "negotiating or discussing terms."
7. An *Ordinary* is a local judge who, in many states, is called the "justice of the peace."
8. *Placid* means "calm" or "peaceful."

Vocabulary

morose (mə rōs′) *adj.* bad-tempered, gloomy, and withdrawn

white dress. Lucynell looked straight at her and didn't seem to see her there at all. Mr. Shiftlet eased the car forward so that she had to move her hands.

The early afternoon was clear and open and surrounded by pale blue sky. Although the car would go only thirty miles an hour, Mr. Shiftlet imagined a terrific climb and dip and swerve that went entirely to his head so that he forgot his morning bitterness. He had always wanted an automobile but he had never been able to afford one before. He drove very fast because he wanted to make Mobile[9] by nightfall.

Occasionally he stopped his thoughts long enough to look at Lucynell in the seat beside him. She had eaten the lunch as soon as they were out of the yard and now she was pulling the cherries off the hat one by one and throwing them out the window. He became depressed in spite of the car. He had driven about a hundred miles when he decided that she must be hungry again and at the next small town they came to, he stopped in front of an aluminum-painted eating place called The Hot Spot and took her in and ordered her a plate of ham and grits. The ride had made her sleepy and as soon as she got up on the stool, she rested her head on the counter and shut her eyes. There was no one in The Hot Spot but Mr. Shiftlet and the boy behind the counter, a pale youth with a greasy rag hung over his shoulder. Before he could dish up the food, she was snoring gently.

_____

9. *Mobile* (mō′ bēl) is a port city in southwestern Alabama.

VISUALIZE
Picture Lucynell's appearance and actions on her wedding day. What might her actions suggest about her feelings?

Blue Diner with Figures, 1981. Ralph Goings. Oil on canvas, 48 x 62½ in. O.K. Harris Works of Art, New York.

Viewing the painting: How does this scene compare with your vision of the lunch counter where Mr. Shiftlet takes Lucynell? Explain.

The Life You Save May Be Your Own

Active Reading Model

QUESTION

Why does Mr. Shiftlet lie to the boy behind the counter?

"Give it to her when she wakes up," Mr. Shiftlet said. "I'll pay for it now."

The boy bent over her and stared at the long pink-gold hair and the half-shut sleeping eyes. Then he looked up and stared at Mr. Shiftlet. "She looks like an angel of Gawd," he murmured.

"Hitchhiker," Mr. Shiftlet explained. "I can't wait. I got to make Tuscaloosa."[10]

The boy bent over again and very carefully touched his finger to a strand of the golden hair and Mr. Shiftlet left.

He was more depressed than ever as he drove on by himself. The late afternoon had grown hot and sultry and the country had flattened out. Deep in the sky a storm was preparing very slowly and without thunder as if it meant to drain every drop of air from the earth before it broke. There were times when Mr. Shiftlet preferred not to be alone. He felt too that a man with a car had a responsibility to others and he kept his eye out for a hitchhiker. Occasionally he saw a sign that warned: "Drive carefully. The life you save may be your own."

The narrow road dropped off on either side into dry fields and here and there a shack or a filling station stood in a clearing. The sun began to set directly in front of the automobile. It was a reddening ball that through his windshield was slightly flat on the bottom and top. He saw a boy in overalls and a gray hat standing on the edge of the road and he slowed the car down and stopped in front of him. The boy didn't have his hand raised to thumb the ride, he was only standing there, but he had a small cardboard suitcase and his hat was set on his head in a way to indicate that he had left somewhere for good. "Son," Mr. Shiftlet said, "I see you want a ride."

The boy didn't say he did or he didn't but he opened the door of the car and got in, and Mr. Shiftlet started driving again. The child held the suitcase on his lap and folded his arms on top of it. He turned his head and looked out the window away from Mr. Shiftlet. Mr. Shiftlet felt oppressed.[11] "Son," he said after a minute, "I got the best old mother in the world so I reckon you only got the second best."

The boy gave him a quick dark glance and then turned his face back out the window.

"It's nothing so sweet," Mr. Shiftlet continued, "as a boy's mother. She taught him his first prayers at her knee, she give him love when no other would, she told him what was right and what wasn't, and she seen that he done the right thing. Son," he said, "I never rued a day in my life like the one I rued when I left that old mother of mine."

The boy shifted in his seat but he didn't look at Mr. Shiftlet. He unfolded his arms and put one hand on the door handle.

---

10. *Tuscaloosa,* in west central Alabama, is nearly 200 miles north of Mobile.
11. Here, *oppressed* means "distressed" or "burdened."

Vocabulary
rue (rōō) *v.* to regret; to be sorry for

I'll Take the High Road, 1944. Emil J. Kosa Jr. Oil on Masonite, 24 x 30 in. Private collection. Permission courtesy of Mrs. Emil J. Kosa, Jr.

Viewing the painting: What are the key images in this painting? How do they affect your response to Mr. Shiftlet's action?

"My mother was an angel of Gawd," Mr. Shiftlet said in a very strained voice. "He took her from heaven and giver to me and I left her." His eyes were instantly clouded over with a mist of tears. The car was barely moving.

The boy turned angrily in the seat. "You go to the devil!" he cried. "My old woman is a flea bag and yours is a stinking pole cat!" and with that he flung the door open and jumped out with his suitcase into the ditch.

Mr. Shiftlet was so shocked that for about a hundred feet he drove along slowly with the door still open. A cloud, the exact color of the boy's hat and shaped like a turnip, had descended over the sun, and another, worse looking, crouched behind the car. Mr. Shiftlet felt that the rottenness of the world was about to engulf him. He raised his arm and let it fall again to his breast. "Oh Lord!" he prayed. "Break forth and wash the slime from this earth!"

The turnip continued slowly to descend. After a few minutes there was a guffawing peal of thunder from behind and fantastic raindrops, like tin-can tops, crashed over the rear of Mr. Shiftlet's car. Very quickly he stepped on the gas and with his stump sticking out the window he raced the galloping shower into Mobile.

EVALUATE

Is Mr. Shiftlet's treatment of the young hitchhiker true to his character?

RESPOND

What is your opinion of Mr. Shiftlet at the end of the story?

Responding to Literature

Personal Response

Were you surprised by the outcome of the story? Explain.

Active Reading Response

Which one of the Active Reading Strategies described on pages 4–5 did you use most often? What did this strategy add to your appreciation of the story?

——— ANALYZING LITERATURE ———

RECALL

1. How does Mr. Shiftlet present himself to Mrs. Crater?
2. What does Mr. Shiftlet accomplish during his week on the Crater farm?
3. What is Lucynell's disability, and how does it affect her?
4. What two agreements do Mr. Shiftlet and Mrs. Crater make?
5. What happens to each of the characters at the end of the story?

INTERPRET

6. Why does Mrs. Crater assume that Mr. Shiftlet is no one to fear? What clues to his true character does she fail to notice?
7. What does Mr. Shiftlet want from Mrs. Crater? How do you know?
8. Why does Mrs. Crater think that Mr. Shiftlet is a good match for her daughter? Support your answer with examples from the story.
9. What factors might motivate Mr. Shiftlet to make each agreement? Do you think he intended to honor the second one? Why or why not?
10. Whose life, if anyone's, do you think may have been saved at the end of the story? Explain your choice.

EVALUATE AND CONNECT

11. How might this story be different if it were set in a modern-day city instead of on a country farm in the 1940s? Explain your answer.
12. How is your response to the Focus Activity on page 6 like Mrs. Crater's initial response to Shiftlet? How is it different?
13. The planting of clues about what may happen later in a story is **foreshadowing.** Which parts of the story foreshadow the end?
14. **Situational irony** occurs when the outcome of a situation is different from the expectations of a character or of a reader. Explain the situational irony in this story.
15. A hypocrite is someone who claims to have certain beliefs, but whose actions prove otherwise. Do you think Mr. Shiftlet is a hypocrite? Why or why not? Is Mrs. Crater a hypocrite? Explain.

Literary ELEMENTS

Description

A **description** is a detailed portrayal of a person, place, or thing. When authors write descriptions, they include vivid and precise adjectives, nouns, and verbs. Authors may use details to describe tangible things, such as the appearance of a character, place, or object. Or they may use details to describe intangible things, such as a character's personality traits. Authors often use **sensory details** to help readers understand what characters see, hear, touch, smell, or taste.

1. Identify details in the story that describe the Crater farm.
2. Which character in this story do you think is described most vividly? Cite details from the story to support your choice.

● See **Literary Terms Handbook,** p. R4.

LITERATURE AND WRITING

Writing About Literature

Evaluating the Title   Why might O'Connor have chosen the slogan from a highway safety sign as the title of her story? Write a brief evaluation of the title's effectiveness. Explain why it is effective, or suggest an alternate title and provide support for your suggestion.

Creative Writing

Lucynell's Story   What might happen to Lucynell after she wakes up? Will she be able to communicate her problem? Will she get home? Is it likely that anyone will befriend her? Write a one- or two-page sequel to the story, showing Lucynell's fate.

EXTENDING YOUR RESPONSE

Literature Groups

O'Connor's Characters   Flannery O'Connor was known for having a flair for the absurd and for depicting characters who felt alone or isolated. With your group, discuss the appearance, thoughts, dialogue, manners, and actions of the characters in "The Life You Save May Be Your Own." In what ways are the characters loners? What exaggerated qualities do they have? How do these qualities affect the story? Share your conclusions with the class.

Learning for Life

Police Report   Write up a police report on Shiftlet's theft and his abandonment of Lucynell. State the crime and note all the facts of the case, including descriptions of Shiftlet and the stolen car. Summarize his background, and record witnesses' statements.

Interdisciplinary Activity

Theater: Play Proposal   Imagine that you are to stage a production of "The Life You Save May Be Your Own." With a partner, write a proposal stating your plans for sets, props, and costumes. If you wish, create a portfolio of detailed illustrations of how the scenes from the story should look.

📖 **Save your work for your portfolio.**

Skill Minilesson

VOCABULARY · Analogies

An **analogy** is a type of comparison that is based on the relationships between things or ideas. Some analogies are based on what may be called "degree of intensity."

     happy : ecstatic :: angry : furious

One who is extremely *happy* is *ecstatic,* just as one who is extremely *angry* is *furious.* In both cases, the second word conveys something similar to, but more intense than, the first.

● For more on analogies, see **Communications Skills Handbook,** pp. R83–R84.

PRACTICE   Choose the word pair that best completes each analogy.

1. slender : gaunt ::
   a. true : accurate   d. moral : ethical
   b. courageous : fearful   e. expensive : impractical
   c. good : excellent

2. hungry : ravenous ::
   a. cold : frigid   d. sad : lonely
   b. tall : heavy   e. wise : educated
   c. lucky : fortunate

Active Reading Strategies

Poetry

"Poetry has always seemed the most natural way of saying what I feel," poet Elizabeth Bishop once said. How can poetry help us say what we feel? It can capture intense experiences or creative perceptions of the world with musical language. If prose is like talking, poetry is like singing. Also, poems can express deep thoughts or paint vivid images in just a few lines, or they can present extended comparisons and descriptive passages about a single idea. To get the most from a poem, try the following strategies.

● For more about related reading strategies, see **Reading Handbook,** pp. R86–R93.

LISTEN

Read a poem aloud, concentrating on the way it sounds. As you read, pay attention to punctuation marks and the form of **stanzas,** or groups of lines. These items are signals for natural pauses.

Ask yourself . . .

● What type of rhythm do I hear in this poem? Is it rapid or slow?

● What rhyme scheme or pattern, if any, does each stanza have?

● Can I detect alliteration (the repetition of consonant sounds at the beginnings of words)?

● Do I hear assonance (the repetition of vowel sounds)?

● Does the poem have consonance (the repetition of consonant sounds within words or at the ends of words)?

● Is there onomatopoeia (the use of a word or phrase that imitates the sound it names)?

● How do these devices affect the musical quality of the poem?

IMAGINE

Re-create in your mind the sights, sounds, smells, tastes, and feel of objects mentioned in the poem.

Ask yourself . . .

● Which specific details appeal to my senses?

● What comparisons does the poet make?

● What human attributes, if any, do the inanimate objects have?

● What types of visual images does the poet include?

● What figures of speech help me "see" objects in the poem?

THE **LANGSTON** **HUGHES** READER

T. S. ELIOT   SELECTED POEMS   HARCOURT BRACE

HOMECOMING   JULIA ALVAREZ

SANDBURG THE PEOPLE, YES   HARCOURT BRACE

FROST The Road Not Taken

Collected Poems Edna St. Vincent Millay

ACROSS SPOON RIVER Master

CLARIFY

Work to unlock the meaning of each line or sentence.

Ask yourself . . .
- What does this image (or line or phrase) mean? Why might the poet have chosen to include it?
- How does this image relate to other thoughts and ideas in the poem?

INTERPRET

Reread the poem several times, focusing on its meaning.

Ask yourself . . .
- What clues about the poem's message does the title provide?
- What words or phrases do the rhyme and rhythm help to emphasize?
- How do the images and symbols work together to support this message, or theme?
- How would I state the theme of this poem?

RESPOND

Think about how the poem affects you. React spontaneously. Consider the ideas about your own life that come to mind as you read the poem.

Say to yourself . . .
- This poem reminds me of . . .
- This poem makes me feel . . .
- I'd like to read or write a poem about . . .
- This image is so . . .

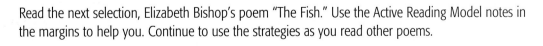

Applying the Strategies

Read the next selection, Elizabeth Bishop's poem "The Fish." Use the Active Reading Model notes in the margins to help you. Continue to use the strategies as you read other poems.

Meet Elizabeth Bishop

The poet Elizabeth Bishop once told her writing class at Harvard University, "Use the dictionary. It's better than the critics." Bishop's wit and devotion to careful, precise language came through in her own writing, which earned her nearly every major poetry prize in the United States.

For Bishop, writing poetry was an act of "self-forgetfulness," in which she focused on shaping and sharing her impressions of the physical world rather than on giving the details of her personal life. Her childhood in Worcester, Massachusetts, was difficult. When she was very young, her father died and her mother was permanently hospitalized, so Bishop was raised by her grandparents in Canada. After graduating from Vassar College in 1934, Bishop traveled frequently and lived in many places, including Florida, New York, and Europe. For sixteen years, she made her home in Brazil, writing, editing, and translating. She kept in touch with people she met in her travels through thousands of letters, some of which were collected and published in her book *One Art*. Over her fifty-year writing career, Bishop published five slim volumes of poetry with a total of just 101 poems. However, she also wrote nonfiction, including several travel books. Besides writing, Bishop taught writing at Harvard for seven years and served as a poetry consultant to the Library of Congress.

"I never intended to 'be' a poet, as I think people set out to do today. . . . [It is] far more important to just keep writing poetry than to think of yourself as a poet whose job is to write poetry all the time."

—*Bishop*

Elizabeth Bishop was born in 1911 and died in 1979.

FOCUS ACTIVITY

Imagine yourself fishing from a small boat. What might the fish you catch look like?

LIST IT! Make a list of words and phrases to describe the fish you "caught." Choose words that suggest your reaction to the fish.

SETTING A PURPOSE Read to discover one speaker's impressions of a fish she catches.

BACKGROUND

Literary Influences

Bishop was a college student when she met the poet Marianne Moore, who was to become her mentor and lifelong friend.

A lover of animals and the physical world, Bishop wrote careful descriptions of scenes she witnessed or experienced outdoors. The following passage from a letter Bishop wrote to Moore may have developed into her poem "The Fish."

> The other day I caught a parrot fish, almost by accident. They are ravishing fish—all iridescent, with a silver edge to each scale, and a real bull-like mouth just like turquoise; the eye is very big and wild, and the eyeball is turquoise too—they are very humorous-looking fish. A man on the dock immediately scraped off three scales, then threw him back; he was sure it wouldn't hurt him. I'm enclosing one [scale], if I can find it.

The Fish

Elizabeth Bishop

I caught a tremendous fish
and held him beside the boat
half out of water, with my hook
fast in a corner of his mouth.
5   He didn't fight.
He hadn't fought at all.
He hung a grunting weight,
battered and venerable°
and homely. Here and there
10 his brown skin hung in strips
like ancient wall-paper,
and its pattern of darker brown
was like wall-paper:
shapes like full-blown roses
15 stained and lost through age.
He was speckled with barnacles,
fine rosettes of lime,
and infested
with tiny white sea-lice,
20 and underneath two or three
rags of green weed hung down.
While his gills were breathing in
the terrible oxygen
—the frightening gills,
25 fresh and crisp with blood,
that can cut so badly—
I thought of the coarse white flesh
packed in like feathers,
the big bones and the little bones,
30 the dramatic reds and blacks
of his shiny entrails,°
and the pink swim-bladder°
like a big peony.
I looked into his eyes
35 which were far larger than mine

---

8   *Venerable* means "deserving respect because of age."
31 *Entrails* are internal organs.
32 A *swim-bladder,* or air bladder, is an air sac that enables some fish to maintain buoyancy and equilibrium.

but shallower, and yellowed,
the irises backed and packed
with tarnished tinfoil
seen through the lenses
40   of old scratched isinglass.°
They shifted a little, but not
to return my stare.
—It was more like the tipping
of an object toward the light.
45   I admired his sullen face,
the mechanism of his jaw,
and then I saw
that from his lower lip
—if you could call it a lip—
50   grim, wet, and weapon-like,
hung five old pieces of fish-line,
or four and a wire leader
with the swivel still attached,
with all their five big hooks
55   grown firmly in his mouth.
A green line, frayed at the end
where he broke it, two heavier lines,
and a fine black thread
still crimped from the strain and snap
60   when it broke and he got away.
Like medals with their ribbons
frayed and wavering,
a five-haired beard of wisdom
trailing from his aching jaw.
65   I stared and stared
and victory filled up
the little rented boat,
from the pool of bilge°
where oil had spread a rainbow
70   around the rusted engine
to the bailer rusted orange,
the sun-cracked thwarts,°
the oarlocks on their strings,
the gunnels°—until everything
75   was rainbow, rainbow, rainbow!
And I let the fish go.

Trout Leap, 1993. Paul Riley.
Monoprint. Private collection.

INTERPRET

Why hasn't the fish
fought for his survival
this time?

CLARIFY

Whose victory fills up
the boat?

RESPOND

What effect does the
ending have on you?

40 *Isinglass* (ī′ zin glas′) was used in windows before glass panes
    became common.
68 *Bilge* (bilj) is stagnant water in the bottom of a boat.
72 *Thwarts* (thwôrts) are seats going across a small boat.
74 *Gunnels* (gun′ əlz) are the upper edges of the sides of a boat.

Responding to Literature

Personal Response

Would you have thrown the fish back, as the speaker does? Why?

Active Reading Response

Which Active Reading Strategy was most helpful to you as you read the poem? Explain.

—————— **ANALYZING LITERATURE** ——————

RECALL AND INTERPRET

1. What details about the fish are provided in lines 1–21? How would you characterize the fish based on these details? Cite words and phrases from the poem to support your conclusion.
2. What thoughts does the speaker have while the fish's gills are breathing in "the terrible oxygen"? What do these thoughts suggest about her perception of the fish?
3. To what does the speaker compare the fish-lines hanging from the fish's mouth? What does this comparison tell you about how the speaker sees the fish? What might the fish symbolize?
4. In line 66, what does the speaker say fills the boat? What does everything become, according to line 75? What, in your opinion, motivates the speaker to let the fish go?

EVALUATE AND CONNECT

5. Have you ever experienced a sense of wonder or awe when confronted with some aspect of nature? What happened?
6. Do you think this poem is mostly about the fish or the speaker? Why?
7. How do the **sensory details** (see page R14) Bishop uses compare with the words you listed for the Focus Activity on page 22? Explain.
8. How is Bishop's description of the fish like that of a scientist or a naturalist? How is her description different? Which approach interests you more, and why?

Literary ELEMENTS

Simile

A **simile** states a comparison of two things by using a word or phrase that clearly indicates the comparison, such as *like* or *as.* Writers use similes to make an experience more vivid for the reader or to explain something unfamiliar by comparing it to something familiar. In this poem, Bishop uses similes to help the reader visualize the fish and to communicate her feelings about it.

1. To what does Bishop compare the fish's brown skin in line 11? What does this comparison reveal about Bishop's attitude toward the fish?
2. To what does the speaker compare the fish's white flesh? Why might she make this comparison?

● See **Literary Terms Handbook**, p. R14.

—————— **EXTENDING YOUR RESPONSE** ——————

Literature Groups

Discuss the Question   One critic wrote that Bishop focused less on an event than on what she "saw and felt and shared with others." In your group, discuss the ways "The Fish" supports or contradicts this statement. Then present your conclusions to the class.

Creative Writing

Describing the Ordinary   Write ten or fifteen lines in which you describe an ordinary object, using **figurative language** (see page R6) as Bishop does in "The Fish."

💼 **Save your work for your portfolio.**

Active Reading Strategies

Nonfiction

How can you get the most out of the essays, biographies, articles, and other types of nonfiction that you read? Active readers use many of the same strategies they use when reading fiction. However, as an active reader you'll need to adjust the strategies to the particular type of nonfiction you are reading.

● For more about related reading strategies, see **Reading Handbook,** pp. R86–R93.

PREDICT Make educated guesses about what you are reading. Preview the topic and the type of nonfiction. You can do this by making inferences from the title and skimming the text. Then try to figure out the author's main idea by looking for a thesis statement in the introductory paragraph. Also, think about the facts, reasons, and details the author may use to support the main idea.

> ### Ask yourself . . .
> ● What will this selection be about?
> ● What main idea will the writer have about the topic?
> ● What evidence might the writer use to back up his or her ideas?

CONNECT Consider what you already know about the topic. Compare people and events with those in your own life. Reflect on any experiences you have had that relate to the topic. Read with the purpose of getting information or a new point of view on the topic.

> ### Ask yourself . . .
> ● What have I heard or read about this topic?
> ● Whom or what does this selection remind me of?
> ● When have I been in a situation like the one described here?

QUESTION As you read, pause occasionally to question anything you do not understand. Reread any section that seems unclear to you. Read on to find answers to your questions. Discuss lingering questions with other readers.

> ### Ask yourself . . .
> ● What is the writer's point here?
> ● Why is the writer giving me these facts?
> ● What does this point have to do with the writer's main idea?

VISUALIZE

Note details the writer provides, and use them to form mental images. Think about the physical appearance of people, places, and objects. In your mind, picture events, the steps in a process, or the way something works.

Ask yourself . . .
- What does this person or scene look like?
- What happens after this step, and what came just before?
- How does this part fit in with the rest of the selection?

EVALUATE

Make judgments about the material. Don't accept a statement if it isn't supported with plenty of evidence.

Ask yourself . . .
- Is this a fact or an opinion? Do I agree with it?
- Do these facts and examples really support the author's point?
- Are the author's cause-and-effect relationships logical and realistic?

REVIEW

As you read, pause occasionally to check your understanding of the material.

Say to yourself . . .
- The thesis statement is . . .
- The evidence that supports the thesis is . . .
- The steps in this process are . . .
- This effect was caused by . . .
- The author's purpose for writing is . . .

RESPOND

As you read, think about your reactions to the facts and ideas you are reading. Note the spontaneous thoughts and feelings that you have about what the author is saying.

Say to yourself . . .
- I'd like to ask the writer why . . .
- I'd like to know more about . . .

Applying the Strategies

The next selection is an essay, "Thoughts on the African-American Novel," by Toni Morrison. As you read it, use the Active Reading Model notes in the margins. Then practice the strategies as you read another work of nonfiction.

Before You Read

Thoughts on the African-American Novel

Meet
Toni Morrison

"Black people had some choices. They could say life is limited for you, make the best of it. . . . Or they said all things are possible and don't let anybody tell you that you can't do something. I came from a family that said the latter."

—Morrison

Highly acclaimed as a novelist, essayist, and literary critic, Toni Morrison won the Nobel Prize for Literature in 1993. Upon receiving it, Morrison responded, "I am outrageously happy. But what is most wonderful for me, personally, is to know that the prize at last has been awarded to an African American. Winning as an American is very special—but winning as a black American is a knockout."

Born Chloe Anthony Wofford, Morrison grew up in northern Ohio, a setting that figures prominently in many of her novels. She graduated from Howard University and received an M.A. degree from Cornell University. Throughout her career, Morrison has also held prestigious teaching positions at various colleges and universities.

When she was thirty-eight, she published *The Bluest Eye*, her first of seven novels. Her novel *Beloved* won the 1988 Pulitzer Prize for Fiction.

Morrison has always emphasized both her African American heritage and her experiences as a woman as influences that have shaped her storytelling talents. When asked whether she considered herself a black writer or a female writer, Morrison responded, "I've just insisted—insisted!—upon being called a black woman novelist."

Toni Morrison was born in 1931.

FOCUS ACTIVITY

In your opinion, why do people read novels?

FREEWRITE Spend a few minutes freewriting to explore this question.

SETTING A PURPOSE Read to explore one writer's ideas about why a society needs novels.

BACKGROUND

Literary Influences

The music, legends, and oral traditions of her African heritage influence Morrison's poetic and precise language. Much like some jazz music defies traditional structure, many of Morrison's own novels float back and forth through time.

VOCABULARY PREVIEW

aristocracy (ar' is tok' rə sē) *n.* people with high social status due to birth or title; p. 30
didactic (dī dak' tik) *adj.* intended to instruct, especially with regard to morals; p. 30
exclusively (iks' klōō' siv lē) *adv.* without the inclusion or involvement of any others; p. 30
enlighten (en līt' ən) *v.* to give knowledge or wisdom to; p. 31
meandering (mē an' dər ing) *adj.* following a winding course; p. 33
unorthodox (un ôr' thə doks') *adj.* not customary or traditional; unusual; p. 33
paradigm (par' ə dīm') *n.* an example that acts as a model; a pattern; p. 33

Thoughts on the African-American Novel

Toni Morrison ~

Slow Down Freight Train, 1946–1947. Rose Piper. Oil on canvas, 29½ x 23⅛ in. Ackland Art Museum, University of North Carolina at Chapel Hill. Ackland Fund.

The label "novel" is useful in technical terms because I write prose that is longer than a short story. My sense of the novel is that it has always functioned for the class or the group that wrote it. The history of the novel as a form began when there was a new class, a middle class, to read it; it was an art form that they needed. The lower classes didn't need novels at that time because they had an art form already: they had songs, and dances, and ceremony, and gossip, and celebrations. The aristocracy didn't need it because they had the art that they had patronized,[1] they had their own pictures painted, their own houses built, and they made sure their art separated them from the rest of the world. But when the industrial revolution[2] began, there emerged a new class of people who were neither peasants nor aristocrats. In large measure they had no art form to tell them how to behave in this new situation. So they produced an art form: we call it the novel of manners, an art form designed to tell people something they didn't know. That is, how to behave in this new world, how to distinguish between the good guys and the bad guys. How to get married. What a good living was. What would happen if you strayed from the fold. So that early works such as *Pamela,* by Samuel Richardson, and the Jane Austen material provided social rules and explained behavior, identified outlaws, identified the people, habits, and customs that one should approve of. They were didactic in that sense. That, I think, is probably why the novel was not missed among the so-called peasant cultures. They didn't need it, because they were clear about what their responsibilities were and who and where was evil, and where was good.

But when the peasant class, or lower class, or what have you, confronts the middle class, the city, or the upper classes, they are thrown a little bit into disarray. For a long time, the art form that was healing for Black people was music. That music is no longer *exclusively* ours, we don't have exclusive rights to it. Other people sing it and play it; it is the mode[3] of contemporary music everywhere. So another form has to take that place, and it seems to me that the novel is needed by African Americans now in a way that it was not needed before—and it is following along the lines of the function of novels everywhere. We don't live in places where we can hear those stories anymore; parents don't sit around and tell their children those classical, mythological archetypal stories[4] that we heard years ago. But new information has got to get out, and there are

PREDICT

What do you think Morrison might say about the necessity of novels for the middle class?

QUESTION

Why does Morrison say that the early "lower classes" didn't need novels?

CONNECT

Can you think of novels you have read that explained how to behave in your own world?

---

1. Here, *patronize* (pā′ trə nīz′) means "to give financial support or encouragement to."
2. The *industrial revolution* helped develop a middle class of workers who began to gain some control over where, for whom, and for what wages they would work.
3. Here, *mode* means "a manner of expression." The type of music once considered an art form belonging to African Americans is now the preferred form of contemporary music for many modern listeners.
4. *Archetypal* (är′ kə tī′ pəl) *stories* come from ideas inherited through the ages by members of a race.

Vocabulary

aristocracy (ar′ is tok′ rə sē) *n.* people with high social status due to birth or title
didactic (dī dak′ tik) *adj.* intended to instruct, especially with regard to morals
exclusively (iks′ kl oo′ siv lē) *adv.* without the inclusion or involvement of any others

Church Picnic, 1988. Faith Ringgold. Painted canvas, pieced, dyed, printed fabrics, 74½ x 75½ in. Collection, High Museum at Georgia-Pacific Center, Atlanta, GA.

Viewing the quilt: In "Thoughts on the African-American Novel," Morrison says "one should be able to hear" a novel. What do you "hear" when you look at this quilt?

several ways to do it. One is in the novel. I regard it as a way to accomplish certain very strong functions—one being the one I just described.

It should be beautiful, and powerful, but it should also *work*. It should have something in it that enlightens; something in it that opens the door and points the way. Something in it that suggests what the conflicts are, what the problems are. But it need not solve those problems because it is not a case study, it is not a recipe. There are things that I try to incorporate into my fiction that are directly and deliberately related to what I regard as the major characteristics of Black art, wherever it is. One of which is the ability to be both print and oral literature: to combine those two aspects so that the stories can be read in silence, of course, but one should be able to hear them as well. It should try deliberately to make you stand up and make you feel something profoundly in the same way that a Black preacher requires his congregation to speak, to join him in the sermon, to behave in a certain way, to stand up and to weep and to cry and to accede or to change and to modify—to expand on the sermon that is being delivered. In the same way that a musician's music is enhanced when there is a response from the audience. Now in a book, which closes, after all— it's of some importance to me to try to make that connection—to try to make that happen also. And, having at my disposal only the letters of the alphabet and some punctuation, I have to provide the places and spaces so that the reader can participate. Because it is the affective and participatory relationship[5] between the artist or the speaker and the audience that is of primary importance, as it is in these other art forms that I have described.

REVIEW

Paraphrase what Morrison means when she says that a novel must "work."

EVALUATE

Do you think a novel can succeed if it doesn't invite the reader to get involved?

5. An *affective and participatory relationship* influences one's emotions and encourages one to take an active part in the relationship.

Vocabulary
enlighten (en līt′ ən) *v.* to give knowledge or wisdom to

Autobiography: Water/Ancestors/Middle Passage/Family Ghosts, 1988. Howardena Pindell. Acrylic, tempera, cattle markers, oil stick, paper, polymer-photo transfer, and vinyl tape on sewn canvas, 299.7 x 180.3 cm. Wadsworth Atheneum, Hartford, CT. The Ella Galup Sumner and Mary Catlin Sumner Collection Fund. Courtesy the artist.

Viewing the art: How does your response to this image help you understand Morrison's point about the relationship between an artist and the audience?

Toni Morrison

To make the story appear oral, <u>meandering</u>, effortless, spoken—to have the reader *feel* the narrator without *identifying* that narrator, or hearing him or her knock about, and to have the reader work *with* the author in the construction of the book—is what's important. What is left out is as important as what is there. To describe sexual scenes in such a way that they are not clinical, not even explicit—so that the reader brings his own sexuality to the scene and thereby participates in it in a very personal way. And owns it. To construct the dialogue so that it is heard. So that there are no adverbs attached to them: "loudly," "softly," "he said menacingly." The menace should be in the sentence. To use, even formally, a chorus. The real presence of a chorus. Meaning the community or the reader at large, commenting on the action as it goes ahead.

In the books that I have written, the chorus has changed but there has always been a choral note, whether it is the "I" narrator of *Bluest Eye,* or the town functioning as a character in *Sula,* or the neighborhood and the community that responds in the two parts of town in *Solomon.* Or, as extreme as I've gotten, all of nature thinking and feeling and watching and responding to the action going on in *Tar Baby,* so that they are in the story: the trees hurt, fish are afraid, clouds report, and the bees are alarmed. Those are the ways in which I try to incorporate, into that traditional genre the novel, <u>unorthodox</u> novelistic characteristics—so that it is, in my view, Black, because it uses the characteristics of Black art. I am not suggesting that some of these devices have not been used before and elsewhere—only the reason why I do. I employ them as well as I can. And those are just some; I wish there were ways in which such things could be talked about in the criticism. My general disappointment in some of the criticism that my work has received has nothing to do with approval. It has something to do with the vocabulary used in order to describe these things. I don't like to find my books condemned as bad or praised as good, when that condemnation or that praise is based on criteria from other <u>paradigms</u>. I would much prefer that they were dismissed or embraced based on the success of their accomplishment within the culture out of which I write.

I don't regard Black literature as simply books written *by* Black people, or simply as literature written *about* Black people, or simply as literature that uses a certain mode of language in which you just sort of drop *g*'s. There is something very special and very identifiable about it and it is my struggle to *find* that elusive but identifiable style in the books. My joy is when I think that I have approached it; my misery is when I think I can't get there.

REVIEW

What are some of the devices the author uses to inject aspects of black culture into her writing?

RESPOND

How does Morrison make you feel about writing?

Vocabulary

meandering (mē an′ dər ing) *adj.* following a winding course
unorthodox (un ôr′ thə doks′) *adj.* not customary or traditional; unusual
paradigm (par′ ə dīm′) *n.* an example that acts as a model; a pattern

Responding to Literature

Personal Response

Which of Morrison's ideas about novels did you find most surprising?

Active Reading Response

Which one of the Active Reading Strategies on pages 26–27 best helped you understand Morrison's essay? Why?

——— ANALYZING LITERATURE ———

RECALL

1. According to Morrison, what event and what class of people caused the birth of the novel as a literary form?
2. In Morrison's view, what lessons did the novel of manners teach?
3. What reasons does Morrison give for explaining how African American culture developed a need for the novel?
4. What specific qualities does Morrison say an African American novel should contain?
5. What does Morrison find disappointing in criticism of her work?

INTERPRET

6. If the upper classes "made sure their art separated them from the rest of the world," why might the novel have been of little use to them?
7. What factors may have caused the lower classes to understand their responsibilities and to distinguish between good and evil?
8. Why might music have been a "healing" form of art to African Americans of an earlier time?
9. Explain Morrison's comparison between a novel and an African American preacher.
10. What do you think Morrison means by the final comment in her essay: "my misery is when I think I can't get there"?

EVALUATE AND CONNECT

11. Look at your response to the Focus Activity on page 28. How does your response compare with Morrison's ideas about the novel?
12. In your opinion, have novels the power to help readers distinguish between "the good guys and the bad guys"? Explain.
13. Morrison says that a novel should present problems but needn't solve them. Do you agree or disagree? Why?
14. Morrison strives for an African American style (see page R15) in her writing. What qualities do you strive to include in your work?
15. Does this essay make you want to read Morrison's novels? Explain.

Literary ELEMENTS

Informal Essay

An essay is a type of nonfiction that presents opinions and ideas on a specific topic. Essays may be formal or informal. An informal essay has a lighter tone and a more fluid structure than a formal essay, which features a carefully structured progression of opinions and supporting information. A formal essay may sound like a dignified speech, but an informal essay often sounds like a conversation. "Thoughts on the African-American Novel" is an informal essay.

1. An informal essay may contain sentence fragments and informal language. Find examples of each of these features in Morrison's essay.
2. How do these examples contribute to the overall tone of the essay?
3. An informal essay might include humor. Find one or more examples in Morrison's essay and explain what the humor adds to your reading of the piece.

• See Literary Terms Handbook, p. R5.

LITERATURE AND WRITING

Writing About Literature

Dialogue   Several critics have praised Morrison for her use of realistic dialogue in novels. Reread her comments about dialogue on page 33. Write a passage of dialogue that you think Morrison would not like. Then write a passage of dialogue that you believe she would like. Explain the differences between the two passages.

Personal Writing

Exploring New Insights   If you've ever been to a concert, you may agree with Morrison that "a musician's music is enhanced when there is a response from the audience." Write a journal entry about a time when you had a strong response to something you read. Describe your response and explain how your reaction contributed to the experience of reading that piece.

EXTENDING YOUR RESPONSE

Literature Groups

Critic's Corner   Toni Morrison's work is often the subject of critical reviews. With your group, begin a critical discussion about her essay. Which ideas did you particularly like or agree with? What did you dislike or disagree with? Why? Be sure to support your opinions with facts, examples, and sound reasoning. Summarize the group's views, and share them with the class.

Learning for Life

New Lessons for Novels   The "novel of manners" emerged to tell people how to behave in the world after the Industrial Revolution. With a partner, brainstorm a list of lessons that novels should teach young readers today. Be prepared to explain the reasoning behind each choice when you share your list with the class.

Interdisciplinary Activity

Music: A Healing Source   Research the roots of African American music, including spirituals, blues, and jazz. Select one African American musician and prepare a brief report about the person's contribution to African American culture.

Save your work for your portfolio.

Skill Minilesson

VOCABULARY • Etymology

The **etymology** of a word is its history—a sort of family tree that helps explain the meanings carried by the word in a variety of times and by many writers. The word *novel,* for example, once meant "new." While it has that meaning today, it also refers to a literary genre, *the novel,* which is not new to modern readers.

PRACTICE   Use the following words to complete the sentences.

unorthodox	enlighten	aristocracy
paradigm	meandering	didactic

1. In Greek, *krátos* means "strength" and *áristos* is "best." People who fit this description were the

   _____ .

2. The Büyük Menderes River winds through Turkey. Its name is related to a Greek word we use to describe anything or anyone that wanders:

   _____ .

3. The Greek word *orthós* means "correct," and *dóxa* means "opinion." Ideas not generally accepted as correct may be called _____ .

4. *Didaskein,* in Greek, means "to teach." Something that is designed to provide instruction is _____ .

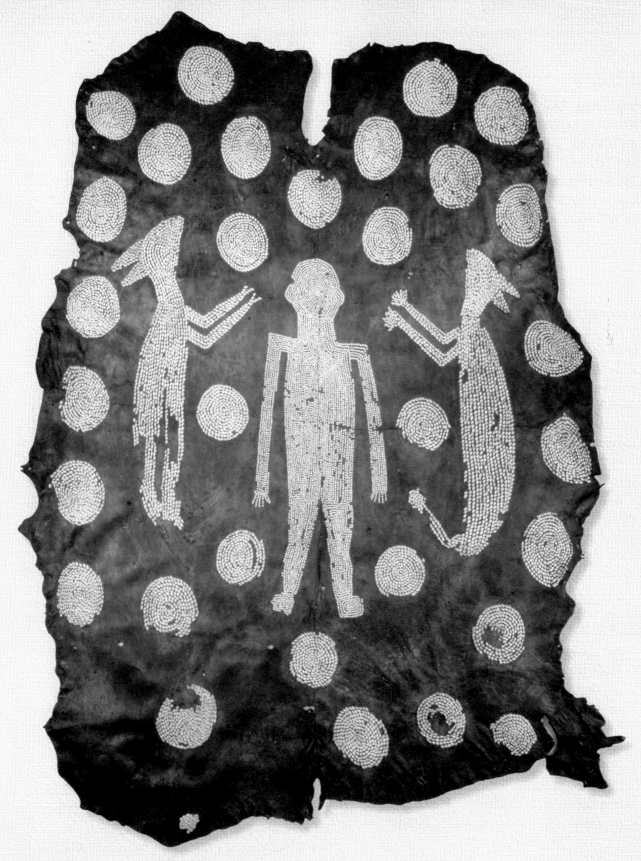

Powhatan's Mantle. Late 16th–early 17th century, Native North American, Virginia. Deerskin with shell patterns. The Ashmolean Museum, Oxford, UK.

36

UNIT ❧ ONE

From the Earliest Days

Prehistory to 1750

"*Come with me now through time and mind,*
for the past beckons to be known.
And the future,
crouched like a panther on the bough of a tree,
waits to see if we . . .
if we
have truly
grown
while it growls
impatiently."

—*White Deer of Autumn*

Theme 1
Beginnings and Change
pages 45–113

Setting the Scene

According to a story generations of Delaware Indians have passed down, Indians fishing off the Atlantic coast in the fall of 1609 saw "something remarkably large floating on the water." Some thought it was "an uncommonly large fish or animal, while others were of [the] opinion it must be a very big house floating on the sea." As the object approached the shore, the curious observers concluded that it was "positively a house full of human beings, of quite a different color from that of the Indians, and dressed quite differently from them."

The unusual looking visitors came ashore on the land that would one day be the state of New York. They held a brief, pleasant meeting with Indian leaders, explaining that they would return the following year. Then they sailed away. These visitors, probably Dutch sailors under the command of Henry Hudson, were among the first Europeans to visit the land that is now the United States. The Delaware, like other Native Americans throughout North America, would have many more encounters with white visitors, though not all would be so friendly.

The Landing of Henry Hudson, c. 1838. Robert W. Weir. Oil on canvas, 68 x 108 in. David David Gallery, Philadelphia.

North America

c. 35,000 B.C.
People begin moving across land bridge from Asia to North America

Leif Eriksson visits North America

1492
Christopher Columbus lands in America

1565
Spain founds St. Augustine, Florida, the first permanent European settlement in what is now the United States

40,000 B.C.   **1000**   1275   **1500**   1517   **1575**

World

1275
Venetian traveler Marco Polo visits China

1517
In Germany, Martin Luther ignites the Protestant Reformation

1546
The Songhay defeat the Mali in West Africa

History of the Time

Native Americans

The Delaware Indians who greeted Hudson's sailors descended from migrants to America who probably arrived roughly 35,000 years earlier. Archeological evidence indicates that the first Americans came from Asia. They traveled across a land bridge that once linked Alaska and Russia across the Bering Strait. As groups of people migrated south and east throughout the Americas, they developed into hundreds of thriving societies. Though diverse, these Native Americans shared basic outlooks that in many ways differed dramatically from those of Europeans. Some central traditions of Native Americans were:

- The land is sacred—a living entity that benefits all life and that must be treated with great respect. No one can own the land.

- Lives are organized around cycles of nature, not around concepts of past, future, and progress.

- Traditions pass verbally from generation to generation through folktales, fables, and sacred stories.

- Speechmaking and storytelling are important parts of life.

Age of Exploration

Between 1000 and 1492, the year Christopher Columbus sailed across the Atlantic, a cultural revival known as the Renaissance increased Europeans' curiosity about the world. Trade with Arabs taught Europeans about the great wealth of Asia, as well as about improved techniques for building and navigating ships. These changes stimulated a period of European expansion in the 1400s that is often called the Age of Exploration. Led at first by the Portuguese and the Spanish, Europeans brought all parts of the world into meaningful contact with one another for the first time in history.

English Settlements

The first successful English settlement in North America began when a group of 105 colonists landed in Jamestown, Virginia, in 1607. Within seven months, all but thirty-two were dead. Still, the colony survived and began to prosper by the mid-1600s. About 550 miles north of Virginia, in Plymouth, Massachusetts, English immigrants started another colony in 1620. Many of the original settlers were Pilgrims, members of a reform movement known as Puritanism.

The English colonies also attracted many Dutch, German, and Scots-Irish immigrants. In addition, many Africans were captured and taken to America by force. By 1750, enslaved Africans accounted for about one-fifth of the population in the English colonies. By the late 1700s, the English colonies in North America were already a home for diverse cultures.

1620
Pilgrims land at Plymouth, Massachusetts

1624
First Dutch settlers arrive in the North American lands they name New Netherlands

1669
La Salle begins to explore the Great Lakes

1732
The English found their last North American colony, Georgia

1600

1603
Powerful Tokugawa shogunate begins to rule in Japan

1624
The Dutch begin thirty years of control over Brazil

1675

1744–1748
The French and British battle over control of India

1750

Life of the Time

People are talking about

Slavery Wanting laborers to work their land, colonists, particularly in Virginia, begin buying enslaved Africans. By 1700, ships crowded with enslaved men and women arrive regularly. Some colonists disapprove. In 1688, Quakers in Germantown, Pennsylvania, issue the first antislavery protest. Slave revolts become a constant fear among slaveholders. ▶

◀ **Religion** In the Massachusetts Bay Colony, Puritans exile Roger Williams in 1636 for his religious beliefs. He founds Rhode Island, which tolerates religious diversity. In 1660, Mary Dyer is publicly hanged on the Boston Common for her Quaker beliefs. Most Native Americans and enslaved Africans continue to practice their own beliefs.

New Fauna and Flora Everywhere in America, Europeans come upon exotic animals and vegetation unlike anything they have ever imagined—the opossum, for example.

"An animal which has a head like a sucking pig . . . hair like a badger . . . the tail like a rat, the paws like a monkey, which has a purse beneath its belly, where it produces its young and nourishes them." —*Le Moyne d'Iberville, 1699* ▶

Firsts

- Spanish explorers bring horses to the Americas. (1500s)
- John Rolfe harvests first tobacco crop in Virginia. (1612)
- Mail service in the colonies begins temporarily between Boston and New York. (1673)
- The first theater in the colonies opens in Williamsburg, Virginia. (1716)

Virginian Opossum, 1827–1836. John James Audubon. Color lithograph. Private collection.

North America

40,000 B.C. | **1600**

1619 — Twenty enslaved Africans brought to Virginia

1636 — Roger Williams founds Rhode Island

1640 — The English colonies include about 26,000 Europeans and 600 Africans

1621 — Potatoes first planted in Germany

1630

1632 — Italian scientist Galileo publishes *Two Chief Systems of the World*

1644 — China's Ming Dynasty collapses

1653 — Taj Mahal completed in India

1660

1664–1665 — Plague kills nearly 70,000 in London

World

Food & Fashion

- Native foods—corn, squash, beans, fish—are abundant, but cattle and pigs are brought from Europe. Some settlers adopt the Native American habit of chewing the resin of some trees.

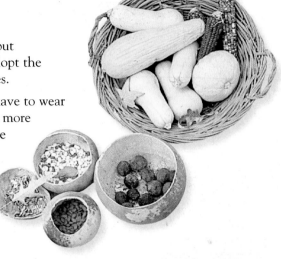

- Puritans favor plain, dark clothing, though women still have to wear layers of petticoats and underskirts. Other colonists dress more lavishly, especially wealthy southern planter families. One Englishman writes from Virginia in 1759:

"I assure you . . . the common Planter's Daughters here go every Day in finer Cloath than I have seen content you for a Summer's Sunday. . . . I'm nothing amongst the Lace and Lac'd fellows . . . here."

Arts & Entertainment

Native American cultures create objects both useful and beautiful—decorated clothing, baskets, pottery, and blankets. ▶

◀ Among European settlers, especially in the South, girls learn to sew and embroider. Samplers displaying a variety of stitches hang in many homes.

Amusements

- Native American recreations include sleight-of-hand games, dice games, and athletic games such as lacrosse and hoop-and-spear, in which a hoop rolling along the ground is speared with a wooden pole.

- Early colonists make their own entertainment. Many play musical instruments. Southern plantation owners give grand dance parties.

- Puritans outlaw dice, cards, and nine-pin bowling; some colonists invent a new game—ten-pin bowling.

1692
Witchcraft trials begin in Salem, Massachusetts

1700
English colonies include about 220,000 Europeans and 27,000 Africans

1730s and 1740s
Religious revivals, known as the Great Awakening, spread through colonies

1670s
Ice cream becomes a popular treat in Paris

1669
Dutch painter Rembrandt dies

1690

1687
English scientist Isaac Newton publishes his *Principia Mathematica*

1720

German composer Johann Sebastian Bach completes his *Brandenburg Concertos*

1750

Literature of the Time

PEOPLE ARE READING . . .

Fliers and Pamphlets   In England, people are enticed by fliers that promote the delights of a "new life" across the sea but that often overlook the hardships and hazards that come with it.

"Poor people (both Men and Women) of all kinds, can here get three times the Wages for their Labour they can in *England* or *Wales*. . . . Here are no Beggars to be seen." —Gabriel Thomas, *Historical and Geographical Account of Pensilvania* (1698) ▷

◁ **Religious Books**   After its publication in 1611, the English translation of the Bible ordered by King James I of England becomes the most widely read book in English. To enable more people to read the Bible, in 1647, Massachusetts Bay Colony passes the first colonial law requiring communities to support public schools. Another colonial best-seller is the hymnbook known as the *Bay Psalm Book*.

Newspapers   English settlers hungry for news get their first colonial newspaper in 1704, the *Boston News-Letter*. In 1734 officers arrest John Peter Zenger for allowing his *New York Weekly Journal* to criticize the governor. After ten months in prison, Zenger wins acquittal from a jury—an important victory for freedom of the press.

People Are Writing

Journals and Diaries   Puritans often keep diaries and include comments on their religious experiences. This allows people to reflect upon and examine their own spiritual development. Sarah Kemble Knight records her Boston-to-New York trip by horseback in 1704. The idea of a female traveling so far alone shocks many, including one woman who insists that she has never seen "a woman on the road so dreadful late in all the days of my versal [whole] life."

Letters   Educated colonists stay in touch with Europe and with one another through letters. Southern gentlemen and ladies who live far apart correspond often to share details of their daily lives.

North America			**1640** One of first books published in America, *Bay Psalm Book*	**1643** Roger Williams writes a key to the language of the Narragansett Indians
		William Bradford begins *Of Plymouth Plantation*		**1650** Anne Dudley Bradstreet, *The Tenth Muse Lately Sprung Up in America*

40,000 B.C.　　**1600**　　　　**1630**　　　　**1660**

World	**1601** Bento Teixeira Pinto publishes the Brazilian epic *Prosopopéa*	**1605–1606** First performances of Shakespeare's *King Lear* and *Macbeth* **1605** Spanish writer Miguel de Cervantes publishes first part of *Don Quixote*	**1670** First performance of French playwright Molière's *The Bourgeois Gentleman*

Literary Trends: Plain Style

"[John Billington was] found guilty of willful murder, by plain and notorious evidence. And was for the same accordingly executed. This, as it was the first execution among them [the Pilgrims], so was it a matter of great sadness unto them. . . . His fact was that he waylaid a young man, one John Newcomen, about a former quarrel and shot him with a gun, whereof he died." —*William Bradford*

The Puritans strive for simplicity in writing, just as they do in clothing, food, architecture, household furnishings, and religious practices. For example, Pilgrim leader William Bradford records the dramatic story of the settlement in "a plain style, with singular regard unto the simple truth in all things." Plain style focuses on communicating ideas as clearly as possible. This marks a change from ornate style, the complicated and decorative style used by writers in Europe at that time. Colonial writers such as Bradford think of writing as a practical tool for spiritual self-examination and religious instruction, not as an opportunity to demonstrate cleverness.

FOCUS ON . . .

The Power of Nature

The environment of North America astonishes newcomers to the continent. Some, like William Bradford, view it as a frightening place, a "hideous and desolate wilderness, full of wild beasts and wild men." However, others see in America an enormous garden, a vast, untouched earthly paradise:

"But the territorie and soil of the Chesepeans [Native Americans living on Chesapeake Bay] (being distant fifteene miles from the shoare) was for pleasantnes of seate, for temperature of climate, for fertilitie of soyle and for the commodity of the sea, besides multitude of beares (being an excellent good victuall [food]) with great woods of sassafras, and wallnut trees, . . . not to be excelled by any other whatsoever." —*Ralph Lane, 1585*

Hooker and Company Journeying Through the Wilderness from Plymouth to Hartford, in 1636, 1846. Frederic Edwin Church. Oil on canvas, 40¼ x 60⅜ in. Wadsworth Atheneum, Hartford, CT.

This view of a land filled with earthly blessings and of unlimited possibilities helps shape an emerging American spirit and literature.

1735
The Zenger trial in New York helps establish free press

1682
A Narrative of the Captivity and Restoration of Mrs. Mary Rowlandson is published

1704
First English colonial newspaper, *Boston News-Letter*

1741
Jonathan Edwards delivers sermon "Sinners in the Hands of an Angry God"

1679
Japanese poet Bashō writes poetry that breaks with the traditional haiku form

1690

1720

1726
Irish-born writer Jonathan Swift publishes *Gulliver's Travels*

1750

Language of the Time

How People Speak

More Than One English Language   In the early 1600s, each region of England has its own distinctive dialect. For example, Shakespeare uses rhymes based on the pronunciations common to his native town of Stratford-upon-Avon. English colonists carry their regional speech patterns with them to North America. Traces of these regional differences continue to distinguish American dialects today.

- Because most Virginia settlers come from western England while most settlers in Massachusetts come from eastern England, they speak differently. Certain distinguishing features of the two dialects will carry into modern speech—not pronouncing the *r* after vowels in New England, for instance.

- Scots-Irish people settle mostly in the middle colonies. Here, the *r* is still pronounced in words such as *lord* and *here*.

- The following language features of the 1600s and 1700s fade in England but persist in America:
    - "flat" *a* in *fast, path* (rather than "broad" *a* of *father*)
    - first vowel sound in *either* pronounced *ee*
    - *mad* for "angry"
    - *gotten* instead of *got*
    - *fall* for "autumn"

Thee, Thou, Thy   *Thee, thou,* and *thy* are old-fashioned words for "you" and "your" that some people use to address children, close friends, and God. Quakers and Puritans use them to address everyone.

How People Write

Spelling   More and more people are reading and writing in sixteenth-century England, and they cry out for spelling rules. The spelling system that settlers bring with them is similar to modern spelling. Exceptions include occasional final *e*: *kinde*; *ll* and *sse* at the end of words: *gratefull, kindnesse*; and *ick* for *ic*: *logick, magick*.

New Words and Expressions

From Other Languages   In America, English speakers encounter new languages and new items that need names. Below are some of the useful words from Native American and African languages that enter English in colonial times.

Native American Languages		African Languages	
Original Word	**English Word**	**Original Word**	**English Word**
xocolatl (Aztec)	chocolate	mbanza (Kimbundu)	banjo
arathkone (Algonquian)	raccoon	banäna (Mande)	banana

Theme 1 — Beginnings and Change

How do you feel at the beginning of the school year? Excited? Nervous? How about other beginnings, such as the first days in a new neighborhood or the beginning of a friendship? After all these beginnings, things eventually change. How well do you adapt to change? Many of the writers in this theme tell of beginnings, from the beginnings of the world to the start of a life in a new land. And many of them faced great change, such as a change of government, a change in plans, or a change in their way of life.

THEME PROJECTS

Interdisciplinary Activity

Art   Choose two selections from this theme that tell of different kinds of beginnings. Create an illustration for each one.

1. Think about a critical moment in the selection that involves a beginning. What people or objects were present at that moment? What colors best describe that beginning?

2. Make a drawing or painting to represent each beginning. Include details that show how the two beginnings are alike and different.

3. Show your work to the class. Invite classmates to identify the beginnings you have illustrated and discuss their similarities and differences.

Performing

Theater   With a small group, choose a selection from this theme that shows a person or a group facing an important change. Rewrite the selection as a play, turning as much narrative as you can into dialogue and adding simple stage directions. Edit and revise your script. Assign roles to members of your group and put on an informal presentation of the play.

Sunrise–A Gift No Gem Could Equal, 1970. Charles F. Lovato. Oil on Masonite, 30½ x 21⅞ in. The Philbrook Museum of Art, Tulsa, OK.

Literature FOCUS

Native American Mythology

Centuries before the first Europeans arrived on the shores of North America, Native Americans had established hundreds of thriving nations, each with a unique culture and heritage. Each nation had its own tradition of **oral literature**—stories that were passed down from one generation to the next as they were told and retold in the privacy of households and in tribal ceremonies.

An important part of the oral tradition of each culture was its myths. A **myth** is an anonymous, traditional story that relies on the supernatural to explain a natural phenomenon, an aspect of human behavior, or a mystery of the universe. Myths try to explain why the world is the way it is. They provide imaginative ways to help people feel at home in the world and make sense of it. **Creation myths** tell how the world and human life came to exist. Some myths, called **origin myths,** explain how natural phenomena such as the stars, moon, and mountains came to be or why a society has certain beliefs and customs. Often, the qualities of creation myths and origin myths appear in one story. A Taos Pueblo story explains:

"When Earth was still young and giants still roamed the land, a great sickness came upon them. All of them died except for a small boy. One day while he was playing, a snake bit him. The boy cried and cried. The blood came out, and finally he died. With his tears our lakes became. With his blood the red clay became. With his body our mountains became, and that was how Earth became."

Many Native American myths emphasize a strong spiritual bond between the Creator, humanity, and the entire natural world. They emphasize that it is the duty of humanity to maintain a balance within their natural world.

In many cultures, each family group, or clan, believed it descended from a particular animal or other natural object, called the **totem.** Members of the bear clan, for example, honored the bear. The bear in turn served as the group's guardian spirit, helping and protecting its members. The bear clan was responsible for preserving the myths of the bear.

Another common feature of Native American mythology is the **trickster.** These animal characters have two sides to their personalities. Tricksters are rebels who defy authority and sometimes create trouble and chaos. However, they are also curious, clever, and creative figures who can unexpectedly reveal wisdom. In many myths, the trickster is a coyote, a raven, or a mink. In one Native American myth, the coyote brings death into the world when he realizes the earth will become too crowded if people live forever.

Myths and rituals continue to play a central role in traditional Native American cultures. They are used to give people a sense of order and identity, to heal the sick, to ensure a plentiful supply of food, to initiate young people into adulthood, and to teach moral lessons.

Before You Read

How the World Was Made and *The Sky Tree*

The Oral Tradition

Both of these stories come from an **oral tradition.** Storytellers passed along such tales by word of mouth. No one really knows where the stories originated. Native Americans have written down these stories only in the past hundred years. Long before that, however, the storytellers helped groups understand and record their daily lives and their history.

Native American storytellers often tell tales of nature. The two pieces you are about to read are **origin myths.** They tell how the world or some part of it came to be.

These two stories have been passed down for many hundreds of years. They come from different cultures, yet both stories show a great reverence for the natural world. "How the World

Was Made" comes from the Cherokee people, who lived in the forests of the Great Smoky Mountains. "The Sky Tree" comes from the Huron people of the Great Lakes region.

FOCUS ACTIVITY

In what ways does nature, or the natural world, affect your life? For example, are you more cheerful on a sunny day?

SHARE IDEAS In a group, share experiences of the natural world and your reactions to them—anything from the sense of awe at seeing a mountain to the frustration of being caught in a downpour.

SETTING A PURPOSE Read to learn the attitudes these tales reflect about nature and the place of humans in the natural world.

BACKGROUND

Recording the Oral Tradition

The Cherokee passed down the myth "How the World Was Made" from generation to generation. Then, around 1890, James Mooney, an anthropologist for the Smithsonian Institution in Washington, D.C., listened to the tale and wrote it down. He first published the story in 1891.

The Huron myth "The Sky Tree" is retold by Joseph Bruchac, a member of the Abenaki Native American group in northern New York State. Bruchac published this myth in 1991.

VOCABULARY PREVIEW

vault (vôlt) *n.* an arched structure forming a roof or ceiling; p. 48

alight (ə līt′) *v.* to descend and come to rest; p. 48

conjurer (kon′ jər ər) *n.* one who performs magic; sorcerer; p. 49

How the World

(Cherokee—Great Smoky Mountains)

Retold by James Mooney :~

THE EARTH IS A GREAT ISLAND FLOATING IN A SEA OF WATER,

and suspended at each of the four cardinal points[1] by a cord hanging down from the sky vault, which is of solid rock. When the world grows old and worn out, the people will die and the cords will break and let the earth sink down into the ocean, and all will be water again. The Indians are afraid of this.

When all was water, the animals were above in Gălûñ′lătĭ (go lun(g) lot′ i), beyond the arch; but it was very much crowded, and they were wanting more room. They wondered what was below the water, and at last Dâyuni′sĭ (dô yun ē′ si), "Beaver's Grandchild," the little Water-beetle, offered to go and see if it could learn. It darted in every direction over the surface of the water, but could find no firm place to rest. Then it dived to the bottom and came up with some soft mud, which began to grow and spread on every side until it became the island which we call the earth. It was afterward fastened to the sky with four cords, but no one remembers who did this.

At first the earth was flat and very soft and wet. The animals were anxious to get down, and sent out different birds to see if it was yet dry, but they found no place to alight and came back again to Gălûñ′lătĭ. At last it seemed to be time, and they sent out the Buzzard and told him to go and make ready for them. This was the Great Buzzard, the father of all the buzzards we see now. He flew all over the earth, low down near the ground, and it was still soft. When he reached the Cherokee country, he was very tired, and his wings began to flap and strike the ground, and wherever they struck the earth there was a valley, and where they turned up again there was a mountain. When the animals above saw this, they were afraid that the whole world would be mountains, so they called him back, but the Cherokee country remains full of mountains to this day.

When the earth was dry and the animals came down, it was still dark, so they got the sun and set it in a track to go every day across the island from east to west, just overhead. It was too hot this way, and Tsiska′gĭlĭ′ (chēs kä′ gi li′), the Red Crawfish, had his shell scorched a bright red, so that his meat was

---

1. The *four cardinal points* are the four main directions on a compass (north, south, east, and west).

Vocabulary

vault (vôlt) *n.* an arched structure forming a roof or ceiling
alight (ə līt′) *v.* to descend and come to rest

Was Made

spoiled; and the Cherokee do not eat it. The conjurers put the sun another hand-breadth[2] higher in the air, but it was still too hot. They raised it another time, and another, until it was seven handbreadths high and just under the sky arch. Then it was right, and they left it so. This is why the conjurers call the highest place Gûlkwâ′gine Di′gălûñ′lătiyûñ′ (gul kwô′ gē nā dē′ gol un(g) lot ē yun(g′)), "the seventh height," because it is seven hand-breadths above the earth. Every day the sun goes along under this arch, and returns at night on the upper side to the starting place.

There is another world under this, and it is like ours in everything—animals, plants, and people—save that the seasons are different. The streams that come down from the mountains are the trails by which we reach this underworld, and the springs at their heads are the doorways by which we enter it, but to do this one must fast and go to water and have one of the underground people for a guide. We know that the seasons in the underworld are different from ours, because the water in the springs is always warmer in winter and cooler in summer than the outer air.

When the animals and plants were first made—we do not know by whom—they were told to watch and keep awake for seven nights, just as young men now fast and keep awake when they pray to their medicine.[3] They tried to do this, and nearly all were awake through the first night, but the next night several dropped off to sleep, and the third night others were asleep, and then others, until, on the seventh night, of all the animals only the owl, the panther, and one or two more were still awake. To these were given the power to see and to go about in the dark, and to make prey of the birds and animals which must sleep at night. Of the trees only the cedar, the pine, the spruce, the holly, and the laurel were awake to the end, and to them it was given to be always green and to be greatest for medicine, but to the others it was said: "Because you have not endured to the end you shall lose your hair every winter."

Men came after the animals and plants. At first there were only a brother and sister until he struck her with a fish and told her to multiply, and so it was. In seven days a child was born to her, and thereafter every seven days another, and they increased very fast until there was danger that the world could not keep them. Then it was made that a woman should have only one child in a year, and it has been so ever since.

---

2. A *hand-breadth* is a unit of measurement based on the width of a hand. It varies from 2½ to 4 inches.

3. Many Native American cultures believe that each plant, animal, and human has its own natural spirit that gives it power. *Medicine,* in this instance, refers to this spirit.

Vocabulary

conjurer (kon′ jər ər) *n.* one who performs magic; sorcerer

Sky Woman, 1936. Ernest Smith. Oil on canvas, 24¼ x 18⅛ in. Rochester Museum & Science Center, Rochester, NY.

The Sky Tree

(Huron—Eastern Woodland)

Retold by Joseph Bruchac

IN THE BEGINNING, EARTH WAS COVERED with water. In Sky Land, there were people living as they do now on Earth. In the middle of that land was the great Sky Tree. All of the food which the people in that Sky Land ate came from the great tree. The old chief of that land lived with his wife, whose name was Aataentsic, meaning "Ancient Woman," in their longhouse near the great tree. It came to be that the old chief became sick and nothing could cure him. He grew weaker and weaker until it seemed he would die. Then a dream came to him and he called Aataentsic to him.

Did You Know?
A *longhouse* was a bark-covered communal home that could have space for as many as ten families as well as rooms for meetings and religious ceremonies.

"I have dreamed," he said, "and in my dream I saw how I can be healed. I must be given the fruit which grows at the very top of Sky Tree. You must cut it down and bring that fruit to me."

Aataentsic took her husband's stone ax and went to the great tree. As soon as she struck it, it split in half and toppled over. As it fell a hole opened in Sky Land and the tree fell through the hole. Aataentsic returned to the place where the old chief waited.

"My husband," she said, "when I cut the tree it split in half and then fell through a great hole. Without the tree, there can be no life. I must follow it."

Then, leaving her husband she went back to the hole in Sky Land and threw herself after the great tree.

As Aataentsic fell, Turtle looked up and saw her. Immediately Turtle called together all the water animals and told them what she had seen.

"What should be done?" Turtle said.

Beaver answered her. "You are the one who saw this happen. Tell us what to do."

"All of you must dive down," Turtle said. "Bring up soil from the bottom, and place it on my back."

Immediately all of the water animals began to dive down and bring up soil. Beaver, Mink, Muskrat, and Otter each brought up pawfuls of wet soil and placed the soil on the Turtle's back until they had made an island of great size. When they were through, Aataentsic settled down gently on the new Earth and the pieces of the great tree fell beside her and took root.

Responding to Literature

Personal Response

What passages from the myths are the most memorable to you? Why?

ANALYZING LITERATURE

How The World Was Made

RECALL AND INTERPRET

1. What is Water-beetle's role in the creation of Earth? What does this tell you about Cherokee reverence for all creatures?
2. What do the "conjurers" do? Who do you think the "conjurers" are? Explain.
3. Name three natural phenomena explained in this myth. Why might people create stories about how such things came to be?

EVALUATE AND CONNECT

4. For the Cherokee people, are humans more important than plants and animals, or are humans equal to them? Give examples from the myth to support your view.
5. At some points, the narrator says "No one remembers" or "We do not know." How do you think these phrases enhance the myth? Explain.

The Sky Tree

RECALL AND INTERPRET

6. Why was the Sky Tree important to the inhabitants of Sky Land?
7. Why does the old woman try to cut down the Sky Tree? What does this tell you?
8. According to the myth, how was the Earth formed? What **imagery** (see page R8) is used to describe Earth in the myth?

EVALUATE AND CONNECT

9. Theme Connections   Would this great beginning have occurred without the old chief's dream? Do you think his dream comes true?
10. Consider Turtle's role in this myth. If you saw a turtle in a Huron work of art, what might be its meaning within the work?

EXTENDING YOUR RESPONSE

Writing About Literature

Comparison of the Myths   Both selections tell how life on Earth came to be. Write a paragraph that compares and contrasts one of the following aspects of the myths: what life was like before Earth was created; how the sky and Earth are described; significant roles played by plants, animals, or humans.

Creative Writing

Your Own Myth   Using these two myths as a model, write an origin myth of your own about some element of nature. Tell what the world was like before this element existed. Tell how it came to be and how it made the world different. For ideas, think about the reactions to nature you shared in the Focus Activity on page 47.

💼 **Save your work for your portfolio.**

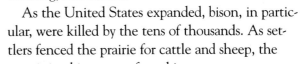

Living in Harmony with Nature

The story of the Sky Tree reflects Native American understanding of and appreciation for the interdependence of all parts of nature. **Ecology** is the study of the relationship among plants, animals, and people and their environments.

In nature, a community of living things and its environment is called an **ecosystem.** A pond, for example, is an ecosystem. The microscopic life-forms, plants, insects, fish, birds, and animals that live in or near the pond or that visit the pond are all part of that ecosystem.

The living things in an ecosystem all pass through cycles of birth, reproduction, consumption, and death. Under normal circumstances, these cycles maintain a balance, but external influences can throw the cycles out of balance.

The North American prairie, for example, once consisted of millions of acres of grassland; it was the home of free-grazing bison and antelope. Natural predators such as wolves controlled the bison and antelope populations. Native Americans also helped by killing what they needed for food, clothing, and shelter.

As the United States expanded, bison, in particular, were killed by the tens of thousands. As settlers fenced the prairie for cattle and sheep, the remaining bison were forced into smaller areas. Starvation and disease devastated the bison herds.

Meanwhile, herds of cattle and sheep grazed countless acres of prairie grasses down to the bare ground. In other areas, farmers plowed up the prairie in order to plant crops. Without the deep-rooted grasses to anchor it, wind and rain eroded the rich topsoil. The once-fertile prairie was transformed into the "Dust Bowl" when a drought in the early 1930s attacked the already struggling ecosystem. Thousands of families lost their farms after watching their soil— and their life's work—blow away.

Decades later, ecologists are still learning how to maintain an ecological balance on the prairie. The North American prairie will never be what it once was. Perhaps through careful use, however, the plants, animals, and people that depend on one another for survival can find a balance.

Activity

List the ways in which humans have affected the ecosystem of the North American prairie. Then work with a small group to do the following.

- Discuss what people might have done to maintain rather than destroy the prairie ecosystem.
- Find out how farmers and ranchers are maintaining the balance of the prairie's ecosystem today.

Before You Read

from *The Iroquois Constitution*

Meet Dekanawida

"The Word that I bring is that all peoples shall love one another and live together in peace."

—*Dekanawida*

Dekanawida (dək uhn′ ä wē′ dä), whose name means "Two River Currents Flowing Together," joined together not two, but five warring Iroquois tribes. Traditional accounts of his life vary. Some identify the great leader as a Huron, and others say he was born an Onondaga and later was adopted by the Mohawks. There is no doubt, however, that Dekanawida believed he was predestined to unite the Iroquois nation.

Dekanawida began to fulfill his destiny when he was a teenager. "It is my business to stop the shedding of blood among human beings," he said. Hiawatha, a Mohawk, forged a strong friendship with Dekanawida, and together the two men established an alliance among the Seneca, Cayuga, Oneida, Onondaga, and Mohawk nations. Because Dekanawida was not a gifted speaker, the eloquent Hiawatha presented their plan to the tribes. Once the Iroquois Confederacy was established and his task was completed, Dekanawida mysteriously vanished.

Dekanawida was born around 1550 and vanished around 1600.

FOCUS ACTIVITY

Read the following quotation, imagining that you are listening to Hiawatha speak these words:

"We must unite ourselves into one common band of brothers. We must have but one voice. . . . We must have one fire, one pipe, and one war. This will give us strength."

—*Hiawatha*

QUICKWRITE In your journal, describe your reaction to Hiawatha's call to unite.

SETTING A PURPOSE Read to learn Dekanawida's ideas about unity.

BACKGROUND

The Time and Place

In the 1400s, the Mohawk, Oneida, Onondaga, Cayuga, and Seneca tribes of the Iroquois nation occupied what is now New York State. These tribes continually fought with one another, which made them vulnerable to attack by other warring tribes. Then, around 1570, Dekanawida led them to form the Iroquois Confederacy, also known as the League of Five Nations. Two centuries after its formation, the confederacy came to an end as the remaining members withdrew to Canada or reluctantly settled on U.S. reservation lands.

VOCABULARY PREVIEW

disposition (dis′ pə zish′ ən) *n.* one's general way of thinking or feeling; p. 55

convene (kən vēn′) *v.* to come together; assemble; p. 56

posterity (pos ter′ ə tē) *n.* generations of the future; all of one's descendants; p. 56

progenitor (prō jen′ ə tər) *n.* direct ancestor; originator of an ancestral line; p. 57

mentor (men′ tər) *n.* wise and trusted adviser; p. 57

temper (tem′ pər) *v.* to modify or moderate; soften; p. 57

deliberation (di lib′ ə rā′ shən) *n.* careful consideration; p. 57

from
The Iroquois Constitution

Dekanawida ∿

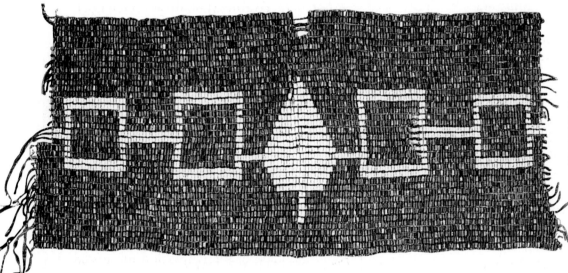

Hiawatha Wampum Belt. Iroquois. Wover beads, 21½ x 10½ in. New York State Museum, Albany.

The Tree of the Great Peace

I am Dekanawida and with the Five Nations' Confederate Lords I plant the Tree of the Great Peace. I plant it in your territory, Adodarho, and the Onondaga Nation, in the territory of you who are Firekeepers.

I name the tree the Tree of the Great Long Leaves. Under the shade of this Tree of the Great Peace we spread the soft white feathery down of the globe thistle[1] as seats for you, Adodarho, and your cousin Lords.

We place you upon those seats, spread soft with the feathery down of the globe thistle, there beneath the shade of the spreading branches of the Tree of Peace. There shall you sit and watch the Council Fire of the Confederacy of the Five Nations, and all the affairs of the Five Nations shall be transacted at this place.

Roots have spread out from the Tree of the Great Peace, one to the north, one to the east, one to the south, and one to the west. The name of these roots is the Great White Roots and their nature is Peace and Strength.

If any man or any nation outside the Five Nations shall obey the laws of the Great Peace and make known their disposition to the Lords of the Confederacy, they may trace the Roots to the Tree and if their minds are clean and they are obedient and promise to obey the wishes of the Confederate Council, they shall be welcomed to take shelter beneath the Tree of the Long Leaves.

---

1. *Globe thistle* is a plant that has prickly leaves and blue flowers. Like a dandelion, the flower becomes a mass of white, silky fuzz, or down, when it goes to seed.

Vocabulary
disposition (dis′ pə zish′ ən) *n.* one's general way of thinking or feeling

from The Iroquois Constitution

We place at the top of the Tree of the Long Leaves an Eagle who is able to see afar. If he sees in the distance any evil approaching or any danger threatening, he will at once warn the people of the Confederacy.

The Care of the Fire

The Smoke of the Confederate Council Fire shall ever ascend and pierce the sky so that other nations who may be allies may see the Council Fire of the Great Peace.

You, Adodarho, and your thirteen cousin Lords shall faithfully keep the space about the Council Fire clean and you shall allow neither dust nor dirt to accumulate. I lay a Long Wing before you as a broom. As a weapon against a crawling creature I lay a staff with you so that you may thrust it away from the Council Fire.

The Laws of the Council

Whenever the Confederate Lords shall assemble for the purpose of holding a council, the Onondaga Lords shall open it by expressing their gratitude to their cousin Lords and greeting them, and they shall make an address and offer thanks to the earth where men dwell, to the streams of water, the pools, the springs and the lakes, to the maize[2] and the fruits, to the medicinal herbs and trees, to the forest trees for their usefulness, to the animals that serve as food and give their pelts for clothing, to the great winds and the lesser winds, to the Thunderers, to the Sun, the mighty warrior, to the moon, to the messengers of the Creator who reveal his wishes and to the Great Creator who dwells in the heavens above, who gives all the things useful to men, and who is the source and the ruler of health and life.

All the business of the Five Nations' Confederate Council shall be conducted by the two combined bodies of Confederate Lords. First the question shall be passed upon by the Mohawk and Seneca Lords; then it shall be discussed and passed by the Oneida and Cayuga Lords. Their decisions shall then be referred to the Onondaga Lords (Firekeepers) for final judgment.

When the Council of the Five Nation Lords shall <u>convene</u>, they shall appoint a speaker for the day. He shall be a Lord of either the Mohawk, Onondaga, or Seneca Nation.

No individual or foreign nation interested in a case, question, or proposition shall have any voice in the Confederate Council except to answer a question put to him or them by the speaker for the Lords.

If the conditions which shall arise at any future time call for an addition to or change of this law, the case shall be carefully considered, and if a new beam seems necessary or beneficial, the proposed change shall be voted upon and, if adopted, it shall be called, "Added to the Rafters."[3]

The Clans

Among the Five Nations and their <u>posterity</u> there shall be the following original clans: Great Name Bearer, Ancient Name Bearer,

---

2. *Maize* is corn.

3. The Iroquois leaders thought of their confederacy of five nations as a longhouse, a communal Iroquois dwelling with an east door, a west door, and a central fire. The terms *beam* and *Added to the Rafters* continue this comparison.

Vocabulary
convene (kən vēn′) *v.* to come together; assemble
posterity (pos ter′ ə tē) *n.* generations of the future; all of one's descendants

Great Bear, Ancient Bear, Turtle, Painted Turtle, Standing Rock, Large Plover, Little Plover, Deer, Pigeon Hawk, Eel, Ball, Opposite-Side-of-the-Hand, and Wild Potatoes. These clans, distributed through their respective Nations, shall be the sole owners and holders of the soil of the country, and in them is it vested as a birthright.

People of the Five Nations [who are] members of a certain clan shall recognize every other member of that clan, irrespective of the Nation, as relatives.

The lineal descent of the people of the Five Nations shall run in the female line. Women shall be considered the <u>progenitors</u> of the Nation. They shall own the land and the soil. Men and women shall follow the status of the mother.

The Leaders

The Lords of the Confederacy of the Five Nations shall be <u>mentors</u> of the people for all time. The thickness of their skin shall be seven spans—which is to say that they shall be proof against anger, offensive actions, and criticism. Their hearts shall be full of peace and good will and their minds filled with a yearning for the welfare of the people of the Confederacy. With endless patience they shall carry out their duty, and their firmness shall be <u>tempered</u> with a tenderness for their people. Neither anger nor fury shall find lodgment in their minds, and all their words and actions shall be marked by calm <u>deliberation</u>.

The Festivals

The rites and festivals of each Nation shall remain undisturbed and shall continue as before because they were given by the people of old times as useful and necessary for the good of men.

The recognized festivals of Thanksgiving shall be the Midwinter Thanksgiving, the Maple or Sugar Making Thanksgiving, the Raspberry Thanksgiving, the Strawberry Thanksgiving, the Corn Planting Thanksgiving, the Corn Hoeing Thanksgiving, the Little Festival of Green Corn, the Great Festival of Ripe Corn, and the complete Thanksgiving for the Harvest.

The Symbols

A large bunch of shell strings, in the making of which the Five Nations' Confederate Lords have equally contributed, shall symbolize the completeness of the union and certify the pledge of the Nations represented by the Confederate Lords of the Mohawk, the Oneida, the Onondaga, the Cayuga, and the Seneca, that all are united and formed into one body or union called the Union of the Great Law, which they have established.

Five arrows shall be bound together very strong, and each arrow shall represent one nation. As the five arrows are strongly bound, this shall symbolize the complete union of the nations. Thus are the Five Nations united completely and enfolded together, united into one head, one body, and one mind. Therefore they shall labor, legislate, and council together for the interest of future generations.

Vocabulary

progenitor (prō jen′ ə tər) *n.* direct ancestor; originator of an ancestral line
mentor (men′ tər) *n.* wise and trusted adviser
temper (tem′ pər) *v.* to modify or moderate; soften
deliberation (di lib′ ə rā′ shən) *n.* careful consideration

Responding to Literature

Personal Response

What is your reaction to Dekanawida's words? Compare your reaction with the notes you made for the Focus Activity on page 54.

——— ANALYZING LITERATURE ———

RECALL AND INTERPRET

1. What happens at the Tree of the Great Peace? Why is the tree an appropriate **symbol** for peace? (See page R16.)
2. What purpose does the Council Fire serve? Based on details in "The Laws of the Council," what position do the firekeepers hold?
3. Why do you think Dekanawida compares laws to beams and rafters?
4. What is the role of women in the Iroquois Confederacy? What does this information tell you about women in Iroquois society?
5. Theme Connections   Summarize the final two paragraphs. What do they tell you about Dekanawida's dream for a new beginning?

EVALUATE AND CONNECT

6. Why might an Iroquois chief have been reluctant to join the confederacy? In your opinion, were there more advantages to belonging to the confederacy or to remaining independent? Explain.
7. What qualities do you think made Dekanawida a powerful leader?
8. Use what you know about U.S. democracy to identify some similarities between it and the Iroquois Constitution.
9. What kinds of laws do you think are important for people to live peacefully in society today? List three examples.
10. How is the **symbolism** of the American flag similar to the symbolism of the five arrows that represent the Iroquois Confederacy?

Literary ELEMENTS

Repetition

Repetition in literature occurs when the same sound, word, phrase, line, or grammatical structure appears more than once in a piece of writing. Writers of both prose and poetry use repetition to link related ideas and to emphasize key points. Repetition was used in the Iroquois Constitution as a memorization aid because the constitution originally was communicated by word of mouth; it was part of the Iroquois **oral tradition.**

1. What examples of repetition in the Iroquois Constitution serve to emphasize or link ideas?
2. Find one example of repetition in the constitution that may have been used to help speakers memorize the text.

● See **Literary Terms Handbook,** p. R13.

——— EXTENDING YOUR RESPONSE ———

Writing About Literature

Analyze Iroquois Laws   Review "The Laws of the Council" to discover the values the Iroquois held sacred. What was important to these people? In two paragraphs, explain what the laws and procedures reveal about the convictions of the founders of the Iroquois Confederacy.

Interdisciplinary Activity

Geography: What's in a Name?   Various places in New York State are named for Iroquois clans and tribes. Research several of these cities, towns, rivers, and lakes. Then prepare a travel brochure and map for visitors to what was once the land of the Iroquois.

📖 **Save your work for your portfolio.**

Vo·cab·u·lar·y Skills

Understanding Analogies

An **analogy** is a way of showing that two relationships are the same.

eagle : sky :: worm : ground

This analogy would be read "eagle is to sky as worm is to ground." In other words, **an eagle moves across the sky; a worm moves across the ground.** Most analogy test questions ask you to identify the pair of words that best represents the relationship expressed by the first pair of words. For example, a test item might look like this:

Tree : ax ::
a. knife : blade   b. clippers : hedge   c. flower : stem   d. paper : scissors

To complete the analogy, follow these steps:

1. Describe the relationship of the first pair of words. (In the sample, that would be "A tree can be cut by an ax.")

2. Try that relationship with each answer choice. The one that makes sense is the right answer. ("Paper can be cut by scissors.")

3. The words in the second pair should be the same parts of speech as those in the first pair.

4. If none of the choices makes sense, your description may have been too vague or too specific. Look for another relationship for the first pair of words and try again.

Analogies can be based on a variety of relationships. Here are some examples.

Association or Usage	A *carpenter* is associated with or uses a *hammer.*
Part/Whole	A *core* is part of an *apple.*
Example/Class	A *cannoli* is a type of *pastry.*
Synonym or Antonym	*Selfish* is the opposite of *generous.*
Object/Characteristic	An *antique* is an *old* item.

● For more about analogies, see **Communications Skills Handbook,** pp. R83–R84.

EXERCISE

Choose the pair that best completes each analogy.

1. brother : family ::

   a. sibling : sister   b. soprano : choir   c. army : country

2. thankfulness : ingratitude ::

   a. regret : sorrow   b. active : still   c. bravery : cowardice

MEDIA Connection

Newspaper Article

How might you begin again and change your life if you survived a near-death experience? Three Mexican fishermen recall their dramatic rescue at sea and comment on their plans for the future.

Shipwreck Survivors Recall Ordeal in Shark-filled Waters

by Patrick J. McDonnell—*Los Angeles Times*, July 21, 1997

[Jorge] Bello and his two colleagues [Pedro Fontan and José Luís Diego] lived to tell the tale Saturday of the shipwreck of their 25-foot wooden fishing boat in stormy seas last Sunday 40 miles west of Acapulco. After 55 hours adrift on floating debris, the trio was literally saved by *Magic*—a Dutch freighter ferrying bananas from Panama to Long Beach that spotted the Mexican fishermen and plucked them from the sea. All three men have scratches, burns, and bumps, but no serious injuries.

The fishermen, who were the only ones aboard the sinking vessel, are due to return Monday, to their home in Acapulco, where grieving relatives had initially assumed they were dead, the latest area fishermen to perish in a high-risk occupation. Search parties had concluded they were lost after finding sandals and other personal effects at sea.

Indeed, the three were not far from the end when the crew of the *Magic* spotted them waving frantically.

They had had no fresh water or food for more than two days, suffered from a scorching sun and chilly nights, and hung desperately to a floating gasoline tank, and, later, a filled plastic garbage bag that miraculously appeared and provided a kind of life raft.

And then there were the ominous sharks, whose dorsal fins proved an unnerving sight as the three clung to life amid an unexpected, pounding storm that lashed them with 12-foot waves. Ironically, the three are shark fishermen—and, indeed, were heading back to Acapulco with more than 600 pounds of cooling shark when the storm swamped their modest fishing vessel. It was the foul smell of the gasoline from the floating tank that kept the sharks at bay, the three suspect.

Despite their ordeal, the three say they will go back to

the sea. They have lived off its bounty all their lives, making an implicit pact with its inherent risks. Six fellow fishermen died last year, they said, presumably shipwrecked and finished off by sharks. No trace of them was ever found.

"We have mouths to feed, children to send to school," said Fontan with a smile. "The sea is our way of life. What else can we do?"

Respond

1. Do you agree that the men should return to fishing? Why or why not?

2. Even though the fishermen will continue to go to sea, in what other ways might their lives change?

Before You Read

from *La Relación*

Meet Álvar Núñez Cabeza de Vaca

"... we were entering a land for which we had no description, without knowing what kind of place it was, nor by what people it was inhabited, nor in which part of it we were."

—*Cabeza de Vaca*

The Spanish explorer Álvar Núñez Cabeza de Vaca (äl′ vär nōō′ nyez kä bä′ zä dā bä′ kä) wrote these words in *La Relación* (*The Account*), a description of a hazardous eight-year odyssey in the New World. Of a group originally numbering six hundred men, only four survived, and Cabeza de Vaca was the only one to return to Spain, embarking from Mexico in 1537. In 1540, Cabeza de Vaca was appointed governor of several Spanish posts in what is now Paraguay, but was later arrested for reasons not clear to historians. Cabeza de Vaca was returned to Spain in chains. Eventually, however, the Spanish government freed him. He is believed to have died in poverty.

Álvar Núñez Cabeza de Vaca was born around 1490 and died sometime around 1556.

FOCUS ACTIVITY

Imagine that you are planning an expedition to an unknown or little-known place—a distant planet or Antarctica, perhaps. What problems might you encounter? How might you best prepare?

CHART IT! Create a two-column chart to prepare for your expedition. In one column, list concerns or problems that you might face along the way. In the second column, describe ways to solve or prevent these problems. Share your ideas with the class.

Problems	Solutions
1.	1.

SETTING A PURPOSE Read to learn how one group of explorers responded to great difficulties.

BACKGROUND

The Time and Place

Cabeza de Vaca's expedition set sail from Spain in June, 1527, with five ships and about six hundred men, and arrived in Florida on April 14, 1528. Facing harsh conditions, all but sixty of the party died. The others set sail for the coast of present-day Texas. Many more died, but the survivors encountered a group of Native Americans, as described in this selection. Eventually, only Cabeza de Vaca and three others survived, wandering the land for eight years until they met Spanish soldiers in Mexico.

VOCABULARY PREVIEW

ration (rash′ ən) *n.* fixed portion or share; p. 62

rouse (rouz) *v.* to awaken from sleep; p. 62

revive (ri vīv′) *v.* to give new strength and vitality, or to bring back to consciousness; p. 62

embark (em bärk′) *v.* to set out on a venture; p. 64

from La Relación

Álvar Núñez Cabeza de Vaca

Translated by Martin A. Favata and José B. Fernández

We sailed in this manner together for four days, eating a daily ration of half a handful of raw corn. After four days a storm came up and caused the other boat to be lost. We did not sink because of God's great mercy. The weather was rough, very cold, and wintery. We had been suffering from hunger for many days and had been pounded so much by the sea that the following day many men began to faint. By nightfall all the men in my boat had passed out, one on top of another, so near death that few of them were conscious and fewer than five were still upright. During the night only the sailing master and I were left to sail the boat. Two hours after nightfall he told me I should take over because he was in such a condition that he thought he would die that very night; so I took the tiller. In the middle of the night, I went to see if the sailing master had died, but he told me that he was better and that he would steer until daybreak. At that time I certainly would have rather died than see so many people before me in that condition. After the sailing master took over the boat, I tried to rest some but could not, and sleep was the furthest thing from my mind.

Near dawn I thought I heard the roar of the breakers[1] near shore, which was very loud because the coast was low. Surprised by this, I roused the sailing master, who said he thought we were near land. We took a sounding and found that the water was seven fathoms[2] deep. He thought that we should stay out until dawn. So I took an oar and rowed along the coast, which was a league[3] distant. Then we set our stern[4] to sea.

Near land a great wave took us and cast the boat out of the water as far as a horseshoe can be tossed. The boat ran aground with such force that it revived the men on it who were almost dead. When they saw they were near land they pushed themselves overboard and crawled on their hands and knees. When they got to the beach, we lit a fire by some rocks and toasted some of the corn we had and found rain water. With the warmth of the fire, the men revived and began to regain some of their strength. We arrived at this place on the sixth of November.

Once our people had eaten, I sent Lope de Oviedo, who was stronger and fitter than the

tiller

Did You Know?
A *tiller* is a lever attached to the rudder of a boat. It is used to steer the boat.

---

1. *Breakers* are waves that foam as they break on rocks or a shoreline.
2. A *fathom* is a linear measure equal to six feet, used mainly in measuring the depth of water.
3. A *league* is a measure of distance equal to three miles.
4. The *stern* is the rear part of a boat or ship.

Vocabulary
ration (rash′ ən, rā′ shən) *n.* fixed portion or share
rouse (rouz) *v.* to awaken from sleep
revive (ri vīv′) *v.* to give new strength and vitality, or bring back to consciousness

Cabeza de Vaca in the Desert, 1906. Frederic Remington. Oil on canvas. Courtesy Frederic Remington Art Museum, Ogdensburg, NY.

Viewing the painting: How would you describe Cabeza de Vaca's (center) expression? What might account for this expression?

rest of us, to climb one of the trees nearby to sight the land and find out something about it. He did this and saw that we were on an island, and that the land appeared to have been trampled by livestock. He thought for this reason that it must be a country of Christians, and told us so. I told him to look again very carefully to see if there were any paths that could be followed, but not to go too far because of possible danger. He found a path and followed it for half a league and found some unoccupied Indian huts, for the Indians had gone into the fields. He took a pot from one of them, a small dog and some mullet[5] and started back.

We thought he was taking a long time to return, so I sent two other Christians to look for him and find out what had happened to him. They found him near there, pursued by three Indians with bows and arrows. They were calling out to him and he was trying to speak to them through sign language. He got to where we were and the Indians stayed back a bit seated on the same shore. Half an hour later another one hundred Indian bowmen appeared. We were so scared that they seemed to us to be giants, whether they were or not. They stopped near us, where the first three were. We could not even think of defending ourselves, since there were scarcely six men who could even get up from the ground. The Inspector and I went towards them and called them, and they approached us. As best we could we tried to reassure them and ourselves, and gave them beads and little bells. Each of them gave me an arrow, which is a sign of friendship. In sign language they told us that they would return in the morning and bring us food, since they did not have any at the time.

The following day at sunrise, at the time the Indians had indicated, they came to us as promised, bringing us much fish, some roots which they eat, the size of walnuts, some larger or smaller. Most of these are pulled with great difficulty from under the water. In the evening they returned to bring us more fish and the same kind of roots. They had their women and children come to see us and they considered themselves rich with little bells and beads that we gave them. The following days they returned to visit with the same things as before.

Seeing that we were provisioned with fish, roots, water, and the other things we requested, we agreed to <u>embark</u> on our voyage once again. We dug up the boat from the sand. We had to strip naked and struggle mightily to launch it, because we were so weak that lesser tasks would have been enough to exhaust us. Once we were out from the shore the distance of two crossbow shots, a wave struck us quite a blow and got us all wet. Since we were naked and it was very cold, we let go of the oars. Another strong wave caused the boat to capsize. The Inspector and two other men held on to it to survive, but quite the opposite occurred because the boat pulled them under and they drowned. Since the surf was very rough, the sea wrapped all the men in its waves, except the three that had been pulled under by the boat, and cast them on the shore of the same island. Those of us who survived were as naked as the day we were born and had lost everything we had. Although the few things we had were of little value, they meant a lot to us.

It was November then and the weather was very cold. We were in such a state that our bones could easily be counted and we looked like the picture of death. I can say for myself that I had not eaten anything but parched corn since the previous May, and sometimes I had to eat it raw. Although the horses were

---

5. A *mullet* is a type of fish.

Vocabulary
embark (em bärk´) *v.* to set out on a venture

slaughtered while we were building the boats, I was never able to eat them, and I had eaten fish fewer than ten times. This is but a brief comment, since anyone can imagine what shape we were in. On top of all this, the north wind began to blow, and so we were closer to death than to life. It pleased our Lord to let us find some embers among the coals of the fire we had made, and we made large fires. In this way we asked our Lord's mercy and the forgiveness of our sins, shedding many tears, with each man pitying not only himself but all the others who were in the same condition.

At sunset the Indians, thinking that we had not gone, looked for us again and brought us food. When they saw us in such a different state of attire and looking so strange, they were so frightened that they drew back. I went out to them and called them and they returned very frightened. I let them know through sign language that one of our boats had sunk and that three of our men had drowned. And there before their very eyes they saw two of the dead men, and those of us who were alive seemed as if we would soon join them.

The Indians, seeing the disaster that had come upon us and brought so much misfortune and misery, sat down with us. They felt such great pain and pity at seeing us in such a state that they all began to cry so loudly and sincerely that they could be heard from afar. This went on for more than half an hour. In fact, seeing that these crude and untutored people, who were like brutes, grieved so much for us, caused me and the others in my company to suffer more and think more about our misfortune. When their crying ceased, I told the Christians that, if they agreed, I would ask those Indians to take us to their lodges. And

> **The Indians, seeing the disaster that had come upon us and brought so much misfortune and misery, sat down with us.**

some who had been in New Spain[6] responded that we should not even think about it, because if they took us to their lodges they would sacrifice us to their idols.[7] But seeing that we had no other recourse and that any other action would certainly bring us closer to death, I did not pay attention to what they were saying and I asked the Indians to take us to their lodges. They indicated that they would be very pleased to do this. They asked us to wait a bit and then they would do what we wanted. Then thirty of them loaded themselves with firewood and went to their lodges, which were far from there. We stayed with the others until nearly nightfall, when they held on to us and took us hastily to their lodges. Since it was so cold and they feared that someone might faint or die on the way, they had provided for four or five large fires to be placed at intervals, and they warmed us at each one. Once they saw that we had gained some strength and gotten warmer, they took us to the next one so rapidly that our feet scarcely touched the ground. In this way we went to their lodges and found that they had one ready for us with many fires lighted in it. Within an hour of our arrival they began to dance and have a great celebration that lasted all night. For us there was no pleasure nor celebration nor sleep because we were waiting to see when they would sacrifice us. In the morning they again gave us fish and roots and treated us so well that we were a little reassured and lost some of our fear of being sacrificed.

---

6. *New Spain* was a part of the Spanish Empire in the 1500s. It included Venezuela, Florida, Mexico, Central America, and other territory. Mexico City was its capital.

7. *Idols* are images of gods used as objects of worship.

Responding to Literature

Personal Response

What questions would you like to ask Cabeza de Vaca?

─────── **ANALYZING LITERATURE** ───────

RECALL AND INTERPRET

1. How do Cabeza de Vaca and his men reach the island? Why might their landing on the island seem like a miracle to them?
2. Why do the native people chase Lope de Oviedo? How does the behavior of Oviedo and his pursuers reveal each group's assumptions about the other?
3. How do the native people help Cabeza de Vaca and his men? What do you think prompts natives to act as they do?
4. What do the Spanish fear in the narrative at the end of the selection? In your opinion, is their fear well-founded? Explain your position.

EVALUATE AND CONNECT

5. What might have motivated Cabeza de Vaca to continue his journey in spite of overwhelming difficulties?
6. In your opinion, were the explorers sufficiently prepared for their journey? What might you have done differently? Refer to your responses for the Focus Activity on page 61.
7. *La Relación* is still valued as a first-person account of the early history and culture of North America. To whom might this narrative be important? What questions might it answer?
8. What situations in contemporary life might require skills and courage similar to that displayed by Cabeza de Vaca? Explain your response.

Literary ELEMENTS

Narrator

The **narrator** tells what happens in a story. When the work is nonfiction and the narrator is also a character in the story, a reader must be aware of a certain degree of **bias**. Keep in mind that a narrator recalls what he or she considers important and relates it in a way that suits the writer's purpose.

1. In *La Relación,* the narrator gives accounts of people, places, and events. How might this story have been different if one of Cabeza de Vaca's men had told it? How might it have been different if told by one of the Native Americans?
2. Cabeza de Vaca as portrayed in this selection is a strong, resourceful character. What details create this positive image?

● See **Literary Terms Handbook,** p. R10.

─────── **EXTENDING YOUR RESPONSE** ───────

Writing About Literature

Description   Description helps writers bring events to life. Choose a passage in *La Relación,* and examine Cabeza de Vaca's choice of descriptive words. Evaluate the effectiveness of his descriptions and the ways in which they add to the value of the work for readers hundreds of years later. Organize your comments in a one-page paper.

Literature Groups

Justice for All?   In your group, read aloud passages in which Cabeza de Vaca interacts with the native people and evaluate the attitudes he displays. Discuss whether later European explorers and settlers in the Americas would agree or disagree with his attitudes. Have one person in your group summarize the discussion for the class.

📖 **Save your work for your portfolio.**

Reading & Thinking Skills

Recognizing Bias

Cabeza de Vaca's account of his travels was written for the king of Spain. The explorer hoped to give the king useful information about his discoveries and experiences. His report, however, is not totally objective; it contains bias. **Bias** is "a mental inclination toward some opinion or position." A writer might have many reasons to be biased. Cabeza de Vaca, for example, probably wanted to present the best possible picture of himself as a loyal, courageous, and long-suffering servant of the Spanish king.

Good readers always look for an author's bias. To detect possible author bias, try these methods:

- Identify emotionally charged words. For example, Cabeza de Vaca uses words such as "picture of death," "misery," and "pity" to describe himself and his crew.
- Consider whether the author has a special interest in the issue. Cabeza de Vaca, for example, depended upon the generosity and support of the king for his livelihood. As a result, he wanted the king to think highly of him.
- Analyze the writer's reasoning. Does the writer give reliable evidence for certain claims? Consider Cabeza de Vaca's description of the Indians as "crude and untutored" in spite of the fact that they had homes, food, and a comfortable life.
- Look for oversimplification or exaggeration. Cabeza de Vaca describes the Indians as "giants."

Many pieces of writing, especially nonfiction, contain bias. Recognizing bias reminds you that there are differing viewpoints on many issues. Knowing that, you can decide to read further on an issue to gain a broader perspective.

- For more about related modes of reasoning, see **Reading Handbook,** pp. R86–R93.

EXERCISE

Identifying Bias   Identify any of the following statements that you think are biased. Write the word clues that led you to make that decision, and the strategy that helped you recognize the bias.

1. I, Cabeza de Vaca, am willing to perform without question any service for my king.

2. Because the Spaniards were the first Europeans to visit the island, the place and its people rightfully belonged to Spain.

3. Arrogant and careless of his crew's suffering, the captain insisted on setting sail despite the heavy waves and approaching storm.

4. Cabeza de Vaca was the greatest and bravest explorer to visit the Americas.

5. When Lope de Oviedo saw that livestock lived on the island, he knew it was a land occupied by Christians.

Before You Read

from *Of Plymouth Plantation*

Meet William Bradford

"All great and honorable actions are accompanied with great difficulties, and must be both enterprised and overcome with answerable courage."
—*Bradford*

Violent storms tossed the creaking ship and blew it far off course. It was 1620 and the passengers aboard the *Mayflower* were traveling to the Americas. Among the passengers was thirty-year-old William Bradford.

Bradford was orphaned while still an infant and was raised by relatives. As a youth, he studied the Bible, and at about the age of seventeen he became a Separatist. Separatists were Puritans who wanted to break from the Church of England. Bradford and other Separatists decided to establish their own colony in the Americas.

Aboard the *Mayflower* Brad-ford helped write the Mayflower Compact (the colony's rules of government). In 1621 this group, known today as the Pilgrims, elected Bradford their leader. Although nearly half the colonists died of scurvy, fever, or starvation that first brutal winter, the colony grew into a thriving community under Bradford's leadership.

William Bradford was born in 1590 and died in 1657.

FOCUS ACTIVITY

Think of someone you have read about who has endured very harsh weather or other hardships. What were the main difficulties they faced?

MAP IT! What qualities do you think would help a person endure great hardship? List your ideas in a word web like the one shown.

Facing hardship

SETTING A PURPOSE Read to learn how the Pilgrims faced their hardships.

BACKGROUND

The Time and Place

Ocean travel in seventeenth-century England was hazardous. Ships were made of wood and were easily damaged if they hit shoals (sandbars or shallow spots in the water). Sometimes strong waves caused ships to "seele," or lurch suddenly from side to side. In fierce winds, sails were lowered by heavy ropes called "halyards," and ships would have to "hull" or drift at sea. Storms and wind shifts sometimes made it necessary for the *Mayflower* to change directions ("tack about") and to head for (or "stand for") a different course. Destined for Virginia, the *Mayflower* eventually landed on the coast of what is now Massachusetts.

VOCABULARY PREVIEW

resolve (ri zolv´) *v.* to decide; determine; p. 70
providence (prov´ ə dəns) *n.* divine care or guidance; foresight; p. 70
succor (suk´ ər) *n.* assistance in time of need; relief; p. 71

procure (prə kyo͞or´) *v.* to obtain by care or effort; p. 72
commodity (kə mod´ə tē) *n.* a product or economic good; p. 72
feigned (fānd) *adj.* fictitious; not genuine; p. 72

The Landing of the Pilgrims at Plymouth, Mass. Dec. 22nd 1620, 1876. Currier & Ives.
Color lithograph. Museum of the City of New York.

from
Of Plymouth
Plantation

William Bradford

from Chapter 9
Of Their Voyage, and How They Passed the Sea; and of Their Safe Arrival at Cape Cod

IN SUNDRY[1] OF THESE STORMS the winds were so fierce and the seas so high, as they could not bear a knot of sail, but were forced to hull for divers[2] days together. And in one of them, as they thus lay at hull in a mighty storm, a lusty[3] young man called John Howland, coming upon some occasion above the gratings was, with a seele of the ship, thrown into sea; but it pleased God that he caught hold of the topsail halyards which hung overboard and ran out at length. Yet he held his hold (though he was sundry fathoms under water) till he was hauled up by the same rope to the brim of the water, and then with a boat hook and other means got into the ship again and his life saved. And though he was something ill with it, yet he lived many years after and became a profitable member both in church and commonwealth. In all this voyage there died but one of the passengers, which was William Butten, a youth, servant to Samuel Fuller, when they drew near the coast.

But to omit other things (that I may be brief) after long beating at sea they fell with that land which is called Cape Cod; the which being made and certainly known to be it, they were not a little joyful. After some deliberation had amongst themselves and with the master of the ship, they tacked about and resolved to stand for the southward (the wind and weather being fair) to find some place about Hudson's River for their habitation. But after they had sailed that course about half the day, they fell amongst dangerous shoals and roaring breakers, and they were so far entangled therewith as they conceived themselves in great danger; and the wind shrinking upon them withal,[4] they resolved to bear up again for the Cape and thought themselves happy to get out of those dangers before night overtook them, as by God's good providence they did. And the next day they got into the Cape Harbor where they rid[5] in safety. . . .

Being thus arrived in a good harbor, and brought safe to land, they fell upon their knees and blessed the God of Heaven who had brought them over the vast and furious ocean, and delivered them from all the perils and miseries thereof, again to set their feet on the firm and stable earth, their proper element. And no marvel if they were thus joyful, seeing wise Seneca[6] was so affected with sailing a few miles on the coast of his own Italy, as he affirmed, that he had rather remain twenty years on his way by land than pass by sea to any place in a short time, so tedious and dreadful was the same unto him.

But here I cannot but stay and make a pause, and stand half amazed at this poor people's present condition; and so I think will the

Did You Know?
Cape Cod is a point of land on the east coast of Massachusetts.

---

1. *Sundry* refers to an indefinite number.
2. *Divers* means "several."
3. *Lusty* here means "strong."
4. *Also* is another word for *withal.*
5. *Rid* means "rode."
6. *Seneca* was a Roman philosopher and writer.

Vocabulary
resolve (ri zolv′) *v.* to decide; determine
providence (prov′ ə dəns) *n.* divine care or guidance; foresight

reader, too, when he well considers the same. Being thus passed the vast ocean, and a sea of troubles before in their preparation (as may be remembered by that which went before), they had now no friends to welcome them nor inns to entertain or refresh their weatherbeaten bodies; no houses or much less towns to repair to, to seek for succor. It is recorded in Scripture[7] as a mercy to the Apostle and his shipwrecked company, that the barbarians showed them no small kindness in refreshing them, but these savage barbarians, when they met with them (as after will appear) were readier to fill their sides full of arrows than otherwise. And for the season it was winter, and they that know the winters of that country know them to be sharp and violent, and subject to cruel and fierce storms, dangerous to travel to known places, much more to search an unknown coast.

from Chapter 11
The Starving Time

But that which was most sad and lamentable was, that in two or three months' time half of their company died, especially in January and February, being the depth of winter, and wanting houses and other comforts; being infected with the scurvy[8] and other diseases which this long voyage and their inaccommodate condition had brought upon them. So as there died some times two or three of a day in the foresaid time, that of 100 and odd persons, scarce fifty remained. And of these, in the time of most distress, there was but six or seven sound persons who to their great commendations, be it spoken, spared no pains

night nor day, but with abundance of toil and hazard of their own health, fetched them wood, made them fires, dressed them meat, made their beds, washed their loathsome clothes, clothed and unclothed them. In a word, did all the homely[9] and necessary offices for them which dainty and queasy stomachs cannot endure to hear named; and all this willingly and cheerfully, without any grudging in the least, showing herein their true love unto their friends and brethren; a rare example and worthy to be remembered. Two of these seven were Mr. William Brewster, their reverend Elder, and Myles Standish, their Captain and military commander, unto whom myself and many others were much beholden in our low and sick condition. And yet the Lord so upheld these persons as in this general calamity they were not at all infected either with sickness or lameness. . . .

Indian Relations

All this while the Indians came skulking about them, and would sometimes show themselves aloof off, but when any approached near them, they would run away; and once they [the Indians] stole away their [the colonists'] tools where they had been at work and were gone to dinner. But about the 16th of March, a certain Indian came boldly amongst them and spoke to them in broken English, which they could well understand but marveled at it. At length they understood by discourse with him, that he was not of these parts, but belonged to the eastern parts where some English ships came to fish, with whom he was acquainted and could name sundry of them by their names, amongst whom he had got his language. He became profitable to them in acquainting them with many things

7. The reference here to *Scripture,* or the Bible, is Acts of the Apostles 28, which tells of the kindness shown to St. Paul and his companions by the natives of Malta after they were shipwrecked on that island.
8. A severe lack of vitamin C causes a disease called *scurvy.*

9. *Homely* here means "domestic."

Vocabulary
succor (suk′ ər) *n.* assistance in time of need; relief

concerning the state of the country in the east parts where he lived, which was afterwards profitable unto them; as also of the people here, of their names, number and strength, of their situation and distance from this place, and who was chief amongst them. His name was Samoset. He told them also of another Indian whose name was Squanto, a native of this place, who had been in England and could speak better English than himself.

Being, after some time of entertainment and gifts dismissed, a while after he came again, and five more with him, and they brought again all the tools that were stolen away before, and made way for the coming of their great Sachem, called Massasoit. Who, about four or five days after, came with the chief of his friends and other attendance, with the aforesaid Squanto. With whom, after friendly entertainment and some gifts given him, they made a peace with him (which hath now continued this 24 years) in these terms:

1. That neither he nor any of his should injure or do hurt to any of their people.

2. That if any of his did hurt to any of theirs, he should send the offender, that they might punish him.

3. That if anything were taken away from any of theirs, he should cause it to be restored; and they should do the like to his.

4. If any did unjustly war against him, they would aid him; if any did war against them, he should aid them.

5. He should send to his neighbors confederates to certify them of this, that they might not wrong them, but might be likewise comprised in the conditions of peace.

6. That when their men came to them, they should leave their bows and arrows behind them.

After these things he returned to his place called Sowams, some 40 miles from this place, but Squanto continued with them and was their interpreter and was a special instrument sent of God for their good beyond their expectation. He directed them how to set their corn, where to take fish, and to procure other commodities, and was also their pilot to bring them to unknown places for their profit, and never left them till he died.

from Chapter 12
First Thanksgiving

They began now to gather in the small harvest they had, and to fit up their houses and dwellings against winter, being all well recovered in health and strength and had all things in good plenty. For as some were thus employed in affairs abroad, others were exercised in fishing, about cod and bass and other fish, of which they took good store, of which every family had their portion. All the summer there was no want; and now began to come in store of fowl, as winter approached, of which this place did abound when they came first (but afterward decreased by degrees). And besides waterfowl there was great store of wild turkeys, of which they took many, besides venison, etc. Besides they had about a peck of meal a week to a person, or now since harvest, Indian corn to that proportion. Which made many afterwards write so largely of their plenty here to their friends in England, which were not feigned but true reports.

Vocabulary

procure (prə kyoor′) *v.* to obtain by care or effort
commodity (kə mod′ə tē) *n.* a product or economic good; an article of trade
feigned (fānd) *adj.* fictitious; not genuine

Responding to Literature

Personal Response

What was your reaction to Bradford's experiences?

——— ANALYZING LITERATURE ———

RECALL AND INTERPRET

1. Theme Connections   What hardships did the Pilgrims face aboard the *Mayflower* and in Plymouth? Do you think the Pilgrims were skilled at adapting to unexpected changes? Explain.
2. Explain how the Pilgrims survived during "the Starving Time." What do Bradford's comments reveal about the Pilgrims?
3. What did Samoset and Squanto accomplish? Explain the effects of their actions on the Pilgrims. Give examples to support your response.
4. Compare the time of plenty in "the First Thanksgiving" to the Pilgrims' situation in "the Starving Time." What do you think might have happened to the Pilgrims without Squanto's help?

EVALUATE AND CONNECT

5. Think about your response to the Focus Activity on page 68. In your opinion, were the Pilgrims' qualities of endurance similar to those you listed? Use evidence from the selection to support your views.
6. Which episode from Bradford's account did you find the most interesting? Why?
7. In what ways might Bradford's narrative have meaning for people today? Explain your response.
8. Do you think that the celebration of Thanksgiving today has a strong connection to the experiences of the Pilgrims on the First Thanksgiving? Explain.

Literary ELEMENTS

Diction

Diction is the choice of words used by a writer. Bradford's diction reflects the language that was used in the seventeenth century. Many of the words and expressions he chose are rarely used in present-day writing. Also, compared with most writers today, Bradford uses long, complicated sentences.

1. Explain what you think the following sentence means: ". . . after long beating at sea they *fell with* that land. . . ."
2. Choose one of Bradford's long, complicated sentences with archaic words and reword it in language used today.

● See **Literary Terms Handbook,** p. R5.

——— EXTENDING YOUR RESPONSE ———

Creative Writing

Another Viewpoint   Imagine that you are one of the Native Americans who first encountered William Bradford and the other Pilgrims. What might be your impression of their arrival? How might you react to the newcomers' clothing and language? Record your observations and descriptions as a journal entry.

Performing

You Are There   Choose an event from Bradford's narrative and retell it to the class in the form of a dramatic monologue. Speak as if you were Bradford, but use modern language. If you would like, you may present your monologue to the class as a poem or rap.

📔 **Save your work for your portfolio.**

Technology Skills

Using a Video Camera

Video cameras, or camcorders, are often used to record major life events—births, graduations, weddings, and holiday celebrations. A video camera also allows you the chance to respond to your reading in a way that stretches your imagination as you help create a work of art.

Choosing the Literature

Think over the literature selections you've read in class this year. Work with a group to choose a selection that provides material for an impressive video. Use the literature as a basis for the video, but don't feel you have to follow the writer's work exactly.

Using a Video Camera

TRY THIS TECHNIQUE	COMMENTS
Use a tripod	If you've ever gotten seasick watching a video of a family picnic, then you know the importance of a steady camera.
Lean against something	When a tripod is unavailable, try balancing yourself against something steady, like a wall or a piece of heavy furniture.
Experiment with the camera before you start filming	The time to push buttons is before you have actors on the set. Simulate filming conditions before shooting begins. The great thing about videotape is that you can try something over and over again on the same tape until you get it right.
Keep each scene short	Long, drawn-out scenes can be boring. Actors should stop at least every five minutes so you can move the camera to other angles, change to close-ups, or otherwise vary the shot.
Keep actors' faces visible	Unless the scene calls for the back of someone's head, keep the actors turned toward the camera.
Make sure your viewfinder image makes sense	When you zoom in or move the camera close to the actors, make sure the audience can see who is talking. Don't worry about keeping all the actors visible all the time.
Use cut-aways or cut-ins	When you just turn the camera off at the end of filming a scene, the next scene pops up in the video as if by magic. To avoid this, try panning to an inanimate object before turning the camera off, or focus on an inanimate object before filming the next action.
Don't "overzoom"	Constant zooming in and out disorients the viewer.
Experiment with composition	Practice various angles to achieve different effects. If you stand on a chair and shoot a scene from above, viewers feel they are listening in. If the camera is tilted away from horizontal, viewers will feel uneasy. Also, try to vary the position of the main subject within the frame.

TECHNOLOGY TIP

The closer the camera gets to a specific actor, the closer the relationship he or she develops with the audience. Such camera work can help point out the main character.

Making the Movie

Step 1: Planning

The most important (and longest) stage is planning. Time spent getting ready reduces the need for retakes and makes editing easier. Planning is best handled by several groups:

- **Script**   A script-writing team needs good writers, students who can envision each scene and the finished product, and a leader who can motivate others to stay on task and meet deadlines.
- **Storyboard**   This series of sketches translates the script into images and sounds. Each crucial shot has a sketch with the accompanying audio written beside it. The storyboarders work to maintain a consistent flow from scene to scene.
- **Equipment**   The equipment team locates, acquires, uses, maintains, and returns all necessary equipment. The group prepares for every need, from batteries and extension cords to extra recording tape and props. The group also develops a contingency plan in case something breaks. Each equipment team member should learn how to operate each piece of equipment.

Step 2: Rehearsal and Videotaping

The filming phase is often enjoyable, but it can have its pitfalls. Filming requires that all elements focused upon in the planning stage come together smoothly.

- **Actors**   All actors must memorize their lines from the script. They must also know the storyboard well enough to move through each scene. Actors need to rehearse until they can work smoothly with one another and with the crew.
- **Crew**   The crew includes a camera operator, several people to set up and monitor lighting and sound, and an equipment manager. You may also require people to work on makeup, costumes, and props.
- **Direction**   The direction team oversees all aspects of filming—the performance of the actors, the positioning of the camera, the length of scenes. It's best to have only one person as director. That person should make decisions based on input from several assistants.

Step 3: Editing and Final Production

The final product is created in the editing stage. Unnecessary takes are removed, and titles, credits, and music are added. Because editing equipment varies, the editing team should book training time with an A/V professional during the planning stage.

ACTIVITIES

1. Show your completed video to another class and get their response.

2. Produce a video illustrating literature concepts for younger viewers.

3. Volunteer to film activities at a local community center or a facility for the elderly.

Before You Read

Upon the Burning of Our House and
To My Dear and Loving Husband

Meet
Anne Bradstreet

"[Anne Bradstreet wrote] . . . the first good poems in America, while rearing eight children, lying frequently sick, keeping house at the edge of the wilderness, [and] managed a poet's range and extension within confines as severe as any American poet has confronted."

—Adrienne Rich

Anne Bradstreet wrote poems whenever she could—while caring for teething infants or mending clothes by the fire at night. She is remarkable not only because she was essentially the first American poet, but also because she composed her poems during a time when writing was considered an unsuitable occupation for a woman.

Bradstreet grew up in England, where she was educated by her father, Thomas Dudley. When she was eighteen, she traveled to the Massachusetts Bay Colony with her husband Simon and her parents to join the Puritan community there. Without her knowledge, her brother-in-law collected her poems and had them published in England under the title of *The Tenth Muse Lately Sprung Up in America*. Her best works explore her love for her husband, her sadness at the death of her parents and other family members, and her struggle to accept as God's will the losses she suffered.

Anne Bradstreet was born in 1612 and died in 1672.

FOCUS ACTIVITY

Think about something you own that you treasure. How would you feel if you lost that cherished object?

JOURNAL In your journal, write a short paragraph describing the object and your possible reaction to its loss.

SETTING A PURPOSE Read to find out the speaker's reactions to losing something she cherishes and her comments about someone she treasures.

BACKGROUND

The Time and Place

In seventeenth-century New England, poetry was acceptable reading for Puritans only if it was religious. However, as a Puritan, Anne Bradstreet viewed all events within the context of God's divine plan. She found similarities between the domestic details of daily life and the spiritual details of her religious life. Unlike traditional verse of her day, Bradstreet's poems speak of everyday occurrences and personal emotions. With directness and sincerity, Anne Bradstreet recorded both her earthly concerns and the Puritan faith that sustained her.

Literary Technique

Like many early poets, Bradstreet used **inversion**; that is, she changed the usual order of words. For example, in her poem "Upon the Burning of Our House" she wrote, "For sorrow near I did not look" instead of "I did not look nearby for sorrow." These inversions are designed to maintain the rhyme scheme and the rhythm of the poem.

Upon the Burning of Our House

July 10th, 1666

Anne Bradstreet

In silent night when rest I took
For sorrow near I did not look
I wakened was with thund'ring noise
And piteous shrieks of dreadful voice.
5 That fearful sound of "Fire!" and "Fire!"
Let no man know is my desire.
I, starting up, the light did spy,
And to my God my heart did cry
To strengthen me in my distress
10 And not to leave me succorless.°
Then, coming out, beheld a space
The flame consume my dwelling place.
And when I could no longer look,
I blest His name that gave and took,°
15 That laid my goods now in the dust.
Yea, so it was, and so 'twas just.
It was His own, it was not mine,
Far be it that I should repine;°
He might of all justly bereft°
20 But yet sufficient for us left.
When by the ruins oft I past
My sorrowing eyes aside did cast,
And here and there the places spy
Where oft I sat and long did lie:
25 Here stood that trunk, and there that
     chest,
There lay that store I counted best.
My pleasant things in ashes lie,
And them behold no more shall I.

Under thy roof no guest shall sit,
30 Nor at thy table eat a bit.
No pleasant tale shall e'er be told,
Nor things recounted done of old.
No candle e'er shall shine in thee,
Nor bridegroom's voice e'er heard
     shall be.
35 In silence ever shall thou lie,
Adieu, Adieu,° all's vanity.°
Then straight I 'gin my heart to chide,°
And did thy wealth on earth abide?
Didst fix thy hope on mold'ring dust?
40 The arm of flesh didst make thy trust?
Raise up thy thoughts above the sky
That dunghill mists away may fly.
Thou hast an house on high erect,
Framed by that mighty Architect,
45 With glory richly furnished,
Stands permanent though this be fled.
It's purchased and paid for too
By Him who hath enough to do.
A price so vast as is unknown
50 Yet by His gift is made thine own;
There's wealth enough, I need no more,
Farewell, my pelf,° farewell my store.
The world no longer let me love,
My hope and treasure lies above.

---

10 *Succorless* means "without assistance" or "helpless."
14 This is a biblical reference to Job 1:21, ". . . the Lord gave, and the Lord hath taken away; blessed be the name of the Lord."
18 *Repine* means "to express unhappiness" or "to complain."
19 *Bereft* means "deprived of the possession or use of something."

---

36 *Adieu* (ə dōō′) is French for "good-bye." *All's vanity* is a biblical reference to Ecclesiastes 1:2 and 12:8, "Vanity of vanities: all is vanity."
37 To *chide* is to find fault with or to blame.
52 *Pelf* is a term for money or wealth, often used disapprovingly.

To My Dear and Loving Husband

Anne Bradstreet

If ever two were one, then surely we.
If ever man were loved by wife, then thee;
If ever wife was happy in a man,
Compare with me, ye women, if you can.
5   I prize thy love more than whole mines of gold
Or all the riches that the East doth hold.
My love is such that rivers cannot quench,
Nor ought° but love from thee, give recompense.°
Thy love is such I can no way repay,
10   The heavens reward thee manifold,° I pray.
Then while we live, in love let's so persevere
That when we live no more, we may live ever.

---

8 *Ought* means "anything." *Recompense* is "something given in return
for something else" or "compensation."
10 Here, *manifold* means "in many different ways."

Responding to Literature

Personal Response

What lines from the poems do you find the most memorable? Share your ideas with the class.

ANALYZING LITERATURE

Upon the Burning of Our House

RECALL AND INTERPRET

1. At first, how does the speaker feel about the loss of her house in the fire? What different emotions does the speaker express? Point out specific lines to support your answer.
2. How did the speaker view her possessions before the fire, and how did she later change her views? Explain what she wanted to dispel.
3. In your opinion, what does the last sentence of the poem mean?

EVALUATE AND CONNECT

4. How is Bradstreet's reaction to losing the things she values similar to or different from your response to the Focus Activity on page 76?
5. How do people today accept or deal emotionally with losing their homes in a natural disaster? Do you think modern reactions are similar to or different from Bradstreet's reaction? Explain your response.

To My Dear and Loving Husband

RECALL AND INTERPRET

6. What does the speaker prize "more than whole mines of gold"? Why do you think she compares the way she feels to mines of gold?
7. What does the speaker say would compensate her for loving her husband, and how does she hope he will be rewarded for his love? In your opinion, how do the ideas in these lines relate to the ideas in the first four lines?
8. What is the seeming contradiction in the last line? What do you think this contradiction means?

EVALUATE AND CONNECT

9. If this poem were written today, how might the style and content be different? Explain your answer.
10. Describe a couple you know from real life, a movie, or a book who, in your opinion, feel for each other the way the speaker and her husband do.

Literary ELEMENTS

Extended Metaphor

A **metaphor** is a figure of speech that compares two things by saying that one thing is another. For example, in the sentence "the desert became a sweltering oven," the desert is said to be an oven—a fitting comparison because they are both hot. Occasionally, a writer will use an **extended metaphor,** developing a metaphor beyond a single line. This is what Bradstreet does,

beginning with line 43 of "Upon the Burning of Our House." Reread lines 43–50.

1. In your own words, summarize what you think the speaker is describing in the extended metaphor.
2. How do you think this extended metaphor relates to the speaker's description in lines 21–30?

🔵 See **Literary Terms Handbook,** p. R6.

LITERATURE AND WRITING

Writing About Literature

Poetry Review   Write a review of either "Upon the Burning of Our House" or "To My Dear and Loving Husband." Discuss what you liked or disliked about either of the two poems or whether you agreed with the speaker's views. You might also want to explain the effect of such devices as rhyme, rhythm, and metaphor. Use lines from the poems to support your opinions.

Creative Writing

Upon the Loss of . . .   Using the paragraph you wrote for the Focus Activity on page 76, write your own poem about what it feels like to lose something that is important to you. If you wish, you might try using **rhyme, repetition** (see page R13), or **paradox** (see page R11) as Bradstreet does in her poems.

EXTENDING YOUR RESPONSE

Literature Groups

Confusing Couplets   Both "To My Dear and Loving Husband" and "Upon the Burning of Our House" are written in **couplets,** or pairs of lines whose final syllables rhyme. To maintain the rhyme scheme, Bradstreet occasionally inverted word order or used unusual words, such as *succorless.* With your group, identify couplets that you find difficult to understand, and interpret their meaning. Then collaborate in rewording the sentences to make the meanings more clear.

Interdisciplinary Activity

Family and Consumer Sciences: Quilting Bee   With a partner, design squares for a quilt that Anne Bradstreet might have made. Use images from "To My Dear and Loving Husband" and "Upon the Burning of Our House" to illustrate your squares. Design individual squares and

then tape or glue them together and present your finished paper quilt to the class. If you have access to a computer graphics program, you could use it to design some or all of your squares. Print each square in color and assemble your quilt.

Performing

Oral Interpretation   With a small group of classmates, plan and perform an oral reading of "Upon the Burning of Our House." Decide which parts of the poem will be read by one person or several people. Agree on appropriate words to emphasize, gestures to make, and when to vary the tone and volume of speakers voices. Explain to the class how your reading helps to reveal the meaning of the poem.

🛍 **Save your work for your portfolio.**

Song

What is romantic love? Is it only a beginning, or does it last through many changes?

By Peter Gabriel

In Your Eyes

love I get so lost, sometimes
days pass and this emptiness fills my heart
when I want to run away
I drive off in my car
but whichever way I go
I come back to the place you are

all my instincts, they return
and the grand façade, so soon will burn
without a noise, without my pride
I reach out from the inside

in your eyes
the light the heat
in your eyes
I am complete
in your eyes
I see the doorway to a thousand churches
in your eyes
the resolution of all the fruitless searches
in your eyes
I see the light and the heat
in your eyes
oh, I want to be that complete
I want to touch the light
the heat I see in your eyes

love, I don't like to see so much pain
so much wasted and this moment keeps slipping away
I get so tired of working so hard for our survival
I look to the time with you to keep me awake and alive

and all my instincts, they return
and the grand façade, so soon will burn
without a noise, without my pride
I reach out from the inside

in your eyes
the light the heat
in your eyes
I am complete
in your eyes
I see the doorway to a thousand churches
in your eyes
the resolution of all the fruitless searches
in your eyes
I see the light and the heat
in your eyes
oh, I want to be that complete
I want to touch the light,
the heat I see in your eyes
in your eyes in your eyes
in your eyes in your eyes
in your eyes in your eyes

Respond

1. What does the writer seem to be saying about love?

2. Do you agree with the portrayal of love in this song?

Writing Skills

Using Specific, Vivid Words

Consider these words from Anne Bradstreet's poem "Upon the Burning of Our House."

> **"I wakened was with thund'ring noise**
> **And piteous shrieks of dreadful voice."**

Notice the powerful way Bradstreet conveys her image of a *thund'ring noise, piteous shrieks,* and a *dreadful voice.*

Writers use various strategies to make scenes come alive. First, they choose specific rather than general words. For instance, how might the example be different if Bradstreet had used the word *calls* instead of *shrieks?* A call is a loud yell. A shriek is also a loud yell, but it is more specifically one that is frantic and high-pitched.

In selecting a specific word, writers consider the word's **connotation.** A word's connotation is made up of the feelings and values that readers associate with that word. In the example above, Bradstreet uses the term *dreadful.* She might have chosen words such as *horrible* or *terrifying.* The word *dreadful,* however, conveys an ominous feeling, fear of something that is about to happen. This connotation is different from the connotations of the other words.

Good writers also strive to use vivid, original words rather than overused ones. In the example, Bradstreet uses the word *thund'ring* to describe the noise she heard. *Great* and *loud* have similar meanings, but are more commonly used and no longer convey the vividness of the sound. For help in finding more precise, vivid, and fresh words, check a thesaurus.

EXERCISE

Replacing Overused Words   Rewrite the following sentences. Replace inexact or overused words with more specific, vivid ones. Use a thesaurus for help.

1. The moon shone over the lonely town.

2. The visitors were quite surprised by the tall buildings in our city.

3. Fed by a strong wind, the noisy fire burned one home after another.

4. The angry crowd moved closer and closer to the speaker.

5. Slowly, the tired stranger came out of the ugly old house.

Before You Read

from *The Captivity of Mrs. Mary Rowlandson*

Meet
Mary Rowlandson

❝I can remember the time, when I used to sleep quietly without workings in my thoughts, whole nights together, but now it is other ways with me.❞

Mary White Rowlandson wrote these words after being held prisoner for eleven weeks and five days. She had experienced the terror of war and kidnapping.

Born in England, Mary White moved to Lancaster, Massachusetts. Around 1656 she married Joseph Rowlandson, a minister in Lancaster.

When Lancaster was attacked at dawn on February 10, 1676, Rowlandson, her six-year-old daughter, and her two older children were among those captured by a party of Wampanoag warriors.

Looking back on her captivity, she wrote, "I have been in the midst of those roaring lions, and savage bears, that feared neither God, nor man, nor the devil." Yet her captors were neither "lions" nor "bears." Instead they were starving people displaced from their own land, and they wanted ransom money to buy food and other supplies. Indeed, they never hurt Rowlandson.

Eventually, Rowlandson's husband paid twenty pounds for her ransom, and Rowlandson was released. This narrative recounts parts of her ordeal.

Mary Rowlandson was born in approximately 1636 and died in 1710 or 1711.

FOCUS ACTIVITY

How do you feel when you find yourself in a group of strangers? What does the word *stranger* mean to you? What is the literal meaning of *stranger*?

SHARE IDEAS Talk with classmates about situations in which people who live near each other remain strangers. Share your ideas about the negative effects of such situations and how you might relieve them.

SETTING A PURPOSE Read this narrative to notice Mary Rowlandson's attitude toward Native Americans and to see whether it changes.

BACKGROUND

As a child, the Wampanoag chief Metacomet had watched his father, Massasoit, help the Pilgrims who arrived on the *Mayflower.* By 1665, there were about 25,000 Puritans in Massachusetts Bay Colony. With each passing year, more arrived; with each passing year, the Native Americans had less and less land, and some even had to work for the English to earn a living. Foreseeing the destruction of his own way of life and that of all the native people, Metacomet began forming alliances with other tribes against the settlers. In 1675, after three Wampanoag were executed by the Puritans, a swift, desperate war broke out.

VOCABULARY PREVIEW

doleful (dōl′ fəl) *adj.* full of grief or sorrow; sad; p. 85

desolation (des′ ə lā′ shən) *n.* devastation; misery; sadness; p. 85

daunt (dônt) *v.* to overcome with fear; intimidate; p. 86

compassion (kəm pash′ ən) *n.* deep awareness of another's suffering with a desire to help; p. 86

discern (di surn′) *v.* to recognize as different and distinct; distinguish; p. 88

lament (lə ment′) *v.* to express deep sorrow or grief; p. 89

savory (sā′ vər ē) *adj.* agreeable to the taste or smell; appetizing; p. 89

from
A Narrative of the Captivity and Restoration of Mrs. Mary Rowlandson

Mary Rowlandson ⁓

O the <u>doleful</u> sight that now was to behold at this house! *Come, behold the works of the Lord, what <u>desolation</u> he has made in the earth.*[1] Of thirty seven persons who were in this one house, none escaped either present death or a bitter captivity, save only one, who might say as he, *Job*[2] i. 15, *And I only am escaped alone to tell the news.* There were twelve killed, some shot, some stabbed with their spears, some knocked down with their hatchets. When we are in prosperity, oh, the little that we think of such dreadful sights; and to see our dear friends and relations lie bleeding out their heart-blood upon the ground! . . .

---

1. The author is quoting Psalms 46:8.
2. In the Bible, *Job* is a good man. His faith in God is tested by many afflictions. Messengers bring word of catastrophes affecting his possessions and family members. Each messenger tells Job that he alone has escaped to tell the news.

Vocabulary
doleful (dōl′ fəl) *adj.* full of grief or sorrow; sad
desolation (des′ ə lā′ shən) *n.* devastation, misery, sadness

from *The Captivity of Mrs. Mary Rowlandson*

I had often before this said, that if the Indians should come, I should choose rather to be killed by them than taken alive; but when it came to the trial my mind changed; their glittering weapons so <u>daunted</u> my spirit, that I chose rather to go . . . than that moment to end my days. And that I may the better declare what happened to me during that grievous captivity, I shall particularly speak of the several removes[3] we had up and down the wilderness.

There remained nothing to me but one poor wounded babe, and it seemed at present worse than death that it was in such a pitiful condition, bespeaking <u>compassion</u>, and I had no refreshing for it, nor suitable things to revive it. . . .

The second remove.—But now (the next morning) I must turn my back upon the town, and travel with them into the vast and desolate wilderness, I know not whither.[4] It is not my tongue or pen can express the sorrows of my heart and bitterness of my spirit that I had at this departure: but God was with me in a wonderful manner, carrying me along, and bearing up my spirit, that it did not quite fail. One of the Indians carried my poor wounded babe upon a horse: it went moaning all along, I shall die, I shall die! I went on foot after it, with sorrow that cannot be expressed. At length I took it off the horse, and carried it in my arms, till my strength failed, and I fell down with it. Then they set me upon a horse, with my wounded child in my lap. . . .

Thus nine days I sat upon my knees, with my babe in my lap, till my flesh was raw again. My child, being even ready to depart this sorrowful world, they bad me carry it out to another wigwam; (I suppose because they would not be troubled with such spectacles;) whither I went with a very heavy heart, and down I sat with the picture of death in my lap. About two hours in the night, my sweet babe, like a lamb, departed this life, on Feb. 18, 1675 [1676] it being about six years and five months old. It was nine days (from the first wounding) in this miserable condition, without any refreshing of one nature or other, except a little cold water. I cannot but take notice how, at another time, I could not bear to be in the room where any dead person was; but now the case is changed; I must and could lie down by my dead babe, side by side, all the night after. I have thought since of the wonderful goodness of God to me, in preserving me so in the use of my reason and senses in that distressed time, that I did not use wicked and violent means to end my own miserable life. In the morning, when they understood that my child was dead, they sent for me home to my master's wigwam; (by my master, in this writing, must be understood Quannopin, who was a Saggamore,[5] and married King Philip's wife's sister; not that he first took me, but I was sold to him by another Narrhaganset Indian, who took me when first I came out of the garrison).[6] I went to take up my dead

---

3. Here, *removes* means "changes of residence"; we would say *moves* today.
4. *Whither* means "to what place."
5. A *saggamore* was a subordinate chief in the hierarchy of various Native American peoples.
6. A *garrison* is a military post.

Vocabulary

daunt (dônt) *v.* to overcome with fear; to intimidate
compassion (kəm pash′ ən) *n.* deep awareness of another's suffering with a desire to help

child in my arms to carry it with me, but they bid me let it alone; there was no resisting, but go I must and leave it. When I had been a while at my master's wigwam, I took the first opportunity I could get to go look after my dead child. When I came, I asked them what they had done with it. They told me it was upon the hill; then they went and shewed me where it was, where I saw the ground was newly dug, and there they told me they had buried it; there I left that child in the wilderness, and must commit it, and myself also, in this wilderness condition, to Him who is above all.

Hearing that my son was come to this place, I went to see him, and found him lying flat upon the ground. . . .

. . . During my abode in this place Philip spake to me to make a shirt for his boy, which I did; for which he gave me a shilling;[7] I offered the money to my master, but he bade me keep it; and with it I bought a piece of horse flesh. Afterwards I made a cap for his boy, for which he invited me to dinner; I went, and he gave me a pancake about as big as two fingers; it was made of parched wheat, beaten and fried in bear's grease, but I thought I never tasted pleasanter meat in my life. There was a squaw who spake to me to make a shirt for her sannup; for which she gave me a piece of bear. Another asked me to knit a pair of stockings, for which she gave me a quart of peas. I boiled my peas and bear together, and invited my master and mistress to dinner; but the proud gossip, because I served them both in one dish, would eat nothing, except one bit that he gave her upon the point of his knife. Hearing that my son was come to this place, I went to see him, and found him lying flat upon the ground; I asked him how he could sleep so? he answered me, that he was not asleep, but at prayer; and lay so, that they might not observe what he was doing. I pray God he may remember these things, now he is returned in safety. At this place (the sun now getting higher) what with the beams and heat of the sun, and the smoke of the wigwams, I thought I should have been blind; I could scarce discern one wigwam from another. There was here one Mary Thurston of Medfield, who, seeing how it was with me, lent me a hat to wear; but as soon as I was gone, the squaw (who owned that Mary Thurston) came running after me, and got it away again. Here there was a squaw who gave me one spoonful of meal;[8] I put it in my pocket to keep it safe; yet, notwithstanding, somebody stole it, but put five Indian corns in the room of it; which corns were the greatest provision I had in my travel for one day.

The Indians returning from Northampton, brought with them some horses and sheep, and other things which they had taken;

---

7. A *shilling* was an English or early American coin, whose value was 20 pence (pennies) or ¹⁄₂₀ pound.

8. *Meal* is coarsely ground grain.

Vocabulary
discern (di surn′) *v.* to recognize as different and distinct; distinguish

I desired them that they would carry me to Albany upon one of those horses, and sell me for powder; for so they had sometimes discoursed.[9] I was utterly hopeless of getting home on foot the way that I came. I could hardly bear to think of the many weary steps I had taken to come to this place.

. . . My son being now about a mile from me, I asked liberty to go and see him; they bade me go, and away I went; but quickly lost myself, travelling over hills and through swamps, and could not find the way to him. And I cannot but admire at the wonderful power and goodness of God to me, in that though I was gone from home, and met with all sorts of Indians, and those I had no knowledge of, and there being no Christian soul near me; yet not one of them offered the least imaginable miscarriage to me. I turned homeward again, and met with my master; he showed me the way to my son: when I came to him I found him not well; and withal he had a boil on his side, which much troubled him; we bemoaned one another a while, as the Lord helped us, and then I returned again. When I was returned, I found myself as unsatisfied as I was before. I went up and down moaning and lamenting; and my spirit was ready to sink with the thoughts of my poor children; my son was ill, and I could not but think of his mournful looks; and no Christian friend was near him to do any office of love for him, either for soul or body. And my poor girl, I knew not where she was, nor whether she was sick or well, or alive or dead. I repaired under these thoughts to my Bible (my great comforter in that time) and that scripture came to my hand, *Cast thy burden upon the Lord, and he shall sustain thee.* Psal. lv. 22.

But I was fain[10] to go and look after something to satisfy my hunger; and going among the wigwams, I went into one, and there found a squaw who showed herself very kind to me, and gave me a piece of bear. I put it into my pocket, and came home; but could not find an opportunity to broil it, for fear they would get it from me, and there it lay all that day and night in my stinking pocket. In the morning I went again to the same squaw, who had a kettle of ground nuts boiling; I asked her to let me boil my piece of bear in her kettle, which she did, and gave me some ground nuts to eat with it, and I cannot but think how pleasant it was to me. I have seen bear baked very handsomely amongst the English, and some liked it, but the thoughts that it was bear made me tremble: but now that was savory to me that one would think was enough to turn the stomach of a brute creature.

One bitter cold day I could find no room to sit down before the fire; I went out, and could not tell what to do, but I went into another wigwam where they were also sitting round the fire; but the squaw laid a skin for me, and bid me sit down; and gave me some ground nuts, and bade me come again; and told me they would buy me if they were able; and yet these were strangers to me that I never knew before.

. . . *The fourteenth remove.*—Now must we pack up and be gone from this thicket, bending

---

9. *Discoursed* means "discussed."

10. In this instance, *fain* means "obliged."

Vocabulary
lament (lə ment′) *v.* to express deep sorrow or grief
savory (sā′vər ē) *adj.* agreeable to the taste or smell; appetizing

our course towards the bay-towns. I having nothing to eat by the way this day, but a few crumbs of cake, that an Indian gave my girl the same day we were taken. She gave it me, and I put it into my pocket; there it lay till it was so moldy (for want of good baking) that one could not tell what it was made of; it fell all to crumbs, and grew so dry and hard, that it was like little flints;[11] and this refreshed me many times when I was ready to faint. It was in my thoughts when I put it into my mouth; that if ever I returned, I would tell the world what a blessing the Lord gave to such mean food. As we went along, they killed a deer, with a young one in her; they gave me a piece of the fawn, and it was so young and tender, that one might eat the bones as well as the flesh, and yet I thought it very good. When night came on we sat down; it rained, but they quickly got up a bark wigwam, where I lay dry that night. I looked out in the morning, and many of them had lain in the rain all night. I saw by their reeking.[12] Thus the Lord dealt mercifully with me many times; and I fared better than many of them.

. . . O the wonderful power of God that I have seen, and the experiences that I have had! I have been in the midst of those roaring lions and savage bears, that feared neither God nor man, nor the devil, by night and day, alone and in company, sleeping all sorts together; and yet not one of them ever offered the least abuse or unchastity to me in word or action. Though some are ready to say I speak it for my own credit; but I speak it in the presence of God, and to His glory.

. . . If trouble from smaller matters begins to arise in me, I have something at hand to check myself with, and say when I am troubled, it was but the other day, that if I had had the world, I would have given it for my freedom. . . . I have learned to look beyond present and smaller troubles, and to be quieted under them, as *Moses* said, *Exod.* xiv. 13, *Stand still, and see the salvation of the Lord.*

FINIS[13]

> *. . . O the wonderful power of God that I have seen, and the experiences that I have had!*

---

11. *Flints* refers to pieces of flint, a very hard type of quartz.
12. *Reeking* here means "steaming"; that is, water was evaporating from their hair and clothing.

---

13. *Finis* means "The End."

Responding to Literature

Personal Response

What incident or observation surprised you most in the Rowlandson account? Why was it surprising?

ANALYZING LITERATURE

RECALL AND INTERPRET

1. What is the "doleful sight" of which Mary Rowlandson speaks? How does she cope with it? In your opinion, does she make the right decision in her manner of surviving?
2. How does Rowlandson help her captors? How do they help her? Do you think Rowlandson continues to see her captors as strangers? Review your description of a stranger in the Focus Activity on page 84.
3. What happens to other members of Rowlandson's family who are taken captive? What supports her each day during her captivity?
4. How does Rowlandson view her captors? Use examples from the narrative to support your answer.

EVALUATE AND CONNECT

5. Do you think Rowlandson portrays her captors fairly? Explain, using details from the selection.
6. What qualities or behaviors help Rowlandson through her ordeal?
7. What details would you remove from this narrative, and what facts would you add to make it a more balanced account of both the Native Americans' and colonists' sides of the story?
8. This narrative and others about colonists in captivity were very popular in their time. What effect do you think this type of literature might have had on attitudes toward and policy regarding Native Americans?

Literary ELEMENTS

Analogy

An **analogy** is a comparison made between two things to show the similarities between them. Writers use analogies in order to make experiences more vivid for the reader or to explain things unfamiliar by comparing them to things familiar. In her account, Rowlandson draws an analogy between her experiences and those of figures from the Bible to make her suffering vivid to the reader.

1. To whom does Rowlandson indirectly compare herself in the first paragraph of the account? Why might she have chosen to compare herself to this person?
2. In your opinion, why did Rowlandson choose to compare herself to biblical figures instead of figures from her own time?

● See **Literary Terms Handbook**, p. R1.

EXTENDING YOUR RESPONSE

Literature Groups

And the Verdict Is . . .   Rowlandson's home was burned to the ground; one of her children and many of her neighbors died. The Puritans retaliated: among other things, they killed Metacomet and sold his wife and son into slavery in the West Indies. Conduct two trials. In one, try Metacomet for his actions. In the other, try the Puritans for theirs.

Creative Writing

Future Perfect or Future Tense?   Imagine that in the early twenty-first century, a descendant of Mary Rowlandson meets a descendant of Metacomet in a restaurant in Lancaster. As they eat together, they discuss the past and the present. What do they say to each other? Write the dialogue for this meeting.

👜 **Save your work for your portfolio.**

Before You Read

from *Stay Alive, My Son*

Meet
Pin Yathay

"It is said that history is a mirror of the future. I pray that this is not necessarily so."

—*Pin Yathay*

Pin Yathay (pin yä' tī) was born in the village of Oudong, just north of Phnom Penh, Cambodia's largest city and capital. As a high school student, he won the Cambodian national prize for mathematics and earned a government scholarship to study abroad in Montreal. There he learned French and studied engineering. After completing his studies, Pin Yathay returned to his homeland and started a family.

When the Khmer Rouge, a communist political organization, seized power in Cambodia in 1975, Pin Yathay knew he was in danger because of his position as an employee of the state. As the situation worsened, he and his family joined the refugees who clogged the roads, seeking safety away from the cities. Eventually, all of Pin Yathay's family died of malnutrition, disease, or murder. Pin Yathay outlived his nightmare and now tells audiences around the world about his experience.

Pin Yathay was born in 1944.

FOCUS ACTIVITY

Do you want the freedom to choose how you live your life? Freedom of choice seems an obvious basic human right, one that we exercise every day of our lives.

JOURNAL In your journal, list some of the types of choices you make every day. Which would be the most difficult to surrender? Then, list choices you think it would be impossible to live without.

SETTING A PURPOSE Read to learn how one family makes a difficult choice.

BACKGROUND

The Time and Place

The years before the Khmer Rouge's rise to power were very turbulent ones in Cambodia. In 1970, the prime minister and army chief, Lon Nol, overthrew Prince Sihanouk, the king since World War II. The Khmer Rouge, led by Communist Party member Pol Pot, then rose to power by presenting itself as a party of patriots in search of peace and freedom. It seized control of the Cambodian government on April 17, 1975, and controlled it until 1979. Over three years, the Khmer Rouge executed an estimated one to three million citizens—anyone it felt was a threat. Pol Pot's regime also drove the 200,000 residents of Phnom Penh—including 20,000 hospital patients—out of the city because it believed that cities were evil and that people should live off the land. As a result, thousands of people died from disease and starvation.

VOCABULARY PREVIEW

enormity (i nôr' mə tē) *n.* outrageousness; state of being monstrous; p. 93

inevitable (i nev' ə tə bəl) *adj.* incapable of being avoided or evaded; p. 96

irrevocable (i rev' ə kə bəl) *adj.* not possible to undo; p. 96

ensure (en shoor') *v.* to make certain; guarantee; p. 96

from
Stay Alive, My Son

Pin Yathay
with John Man

My first reaction was to give way to despair, to give up, to surrender to my fate. Everything was lost, I was going to die anyway, I knew that. There was no escape. We swelled up[1] and died. It was the law of nature, unalterable. We all died one after another. There was nothing to be done. What did it matter? I would die, and the sooner the better, there in the house with my wife and son.

Then the true enormity of my situation struck me. There would be no such choice. Even that tiny freedom would be taken from me. There would be no gentle, natural passing with my family beside me. They were going to slaughter me, like an animal, away in the forest.

At that thought, I felt another sensation, a surge of raw energy that drove out all other feelings. The instinct for self-preservation took over, and I suddenly, desperately, wanted to stay alive. I told myself: "Pull yourself together! Sharpen up! Get out of this! You've always succeeded before! This is your last chance! Do something!"

I began to think. What was to be done? Leave alone? But there was Nawath across the hut, lying prostrate,[2] his limbs swollen. I could hardly bear the thought of leaving him and Any. But neither could I imagine escaping with them. Better they should have a chance to live here than die with me. Better that I should get away, and give myself a chance to live, or at least die on my own terms.

It was all very simple. My mind was made up. I had to tell Any of my decision, that very evening.

---

1. Their bodies *swelled up,* or became bloated, from malnutrition and vitamin deficiencies.
2. *Prostrate* means "flat on the ground," in this case from exhaustion.

Vocabulary
enormity (i nôr′ mə tē) *n.* outrageousness; state of being monstrous

Untitled. Sompear Hong Sot. Mixed media.

Viewing the painting: Explain how this painting might express the way Pin Yathay feels in the midst of his great dilemma.

Pin Yathay ~

After we had eaten, as we sat on the floor opposite each other, with Nawath sleeping behind his cloth partition across the hut, I prepared myself to speak. I was certain of my course, but that did not make me any less nervous. It was a terrible thing to do to us as a family, a terrible thing to impose on Any. But as I glanced up at her, and saw her sweet and wasted features lit dimly by the flickering flames of the cooking fire, I knew there was no other course. It was purposeless to stay on there merely to face death. They would be alone all too soon, anyway.

"Any, my dearest," I said, "I have something to tell you." She looked up, without surprise, and I realized she had been expecting a decision of some kind. She too must have known that I could not stay. Speaking softly in order not to wake Nawath—I could see his little bloated face round the edge of the partition—I began to explain. I was doomed, I said. All the former high officials had disappeared. I was trained in the West. I was irredeemable[3] in the eyes of the Khmer Rouge. They would come for me in a week, and that would be that. "But you're a woman, Any, if you were alone with Nawath I don't think they would harm you."

She said nothing, but I saw her gaze turn to one of horror.

"You can live on here with Nawath," I went on. "It's the only answer. I'll take my chances in the forest. If I succeed, we'll meet again. But I have to go soon. In one week, it'll be too late."

"You'll leave?" she said. "Leave me here with Nawath?" And suddenly she began to sob as if she were being torn apart.

3. *Irredeemable* here refers to being unable to be changed or reformed to accept the new government.

"Yes, my dearest. It's the only way," I said, desperately. For the first time, I began to realize that she had not come to the same conclusion as me. "What did you think?"

"Not that. Not that."

I said nothing, for there was only one other course open, the one that was impossible to contemplate. She would see that in a few minutes, I thought, and accept my decision.

But no. With hesitations and bitter sobs, she went on, "It's impossible, my dearest Thay . . . I don't want to be separated from you . . . I prefer to die with you rather than to stay here . . ." As I listened to her in silence, unable to say anything to stem the slow, whispered outpouring of words and sobs and tears, I couldn't believe that she understood what she was saying. Soon, soon, she would see, and know why I had to go alone. "I cannot live without you!" she sobbed. "I prefer to die quickly and cleanly, with you."

She paused, wracked by sobs. I waited for her to say: But if you think it is for the best, of course that is how it must be.

Silence.

To my astonishment, I began to realize she meant what she said. For the first time in our lives, she was refusing to accept my judgment of what was best.

The silence dragged on, broken only by her gasps. She was looking at me. I could see the highlights cast by the fire on her cheeks and in her eyes. Still she said nothing further. I knew then she had understood all along what she was saying.

I felt the strength of her, as well. Once, she had asked my opinion even before buying a dress. Now she had been hardened by experience. She knew what she was doing, knew that in any event she and Nawath would die, knew that we were in the process not of choosing life over death, but of choosing different ways of dying.

And she knew that, having chosen, there was one more fearful choice still to make. There seemed nothing I could do or say to help her through it. It was too awful for me to put into words. If I spoke the words, it would turn something that was merely a nightmarish fear into dreadful reality. I could not say them.

"But," she said at last. "But what shall we do with Nawath?"

Yes: those were the words I had refused to utter.

"Tell me, Thay dearest. What shall we do with Nawath?" She broke down again as she struggled to express the thought. "He can't come with us. We can't carry him, and he can't walk far. They would catch us and kill us before . . ." She paused, her face working to control her emotion. "We . . . we have to leave him behind. But . . . what are we going to do with him if we leave him?" She broke off again, overcome by sobs.

Could she really contemplate leaving Nawath? It seemed an extraordinary thing for a mother to do. I realize now that she had made a mother's supreme sacrifice. People say that for a mother the supreme sacrifice is to die with her child. No—if death is <u>inevitable</u>, the mother's supreme sacrifice is to abandon her child, if thereby she can prolong her own life.

I did not understand all that right then and there. But I felt her resolve, and knew there was nothing I could say to make her change her mind. After what we had been through,

after being made one body with her by what we had endured together, it never even occurred to me to argue her out of her decision. I don't think I could have done so. I simply had to accept that things were different now.

Any was still sobbing. "What do we do with Nawath?" she asked again, and fell silent. I knew from her tone of voice, and the silence, that she already knew the answer, for there was only one. Knowing it, again neither of us could bring ourselves to express it. Again, expressing it would make it <u>irrevocable</u>.

I glanced at Nawath, still asleep. I felt I wanted to go to him, stroke his head, provide some comfort for him, or myself. But I did not move. I couldn't risk waking him. I glanced back at Any. Her eyes were lowered, as if waiting for me to pronounce sentence.

After another eternal minute, the burden of silence became intolerable. I felt it as an accusation against me for evading responsibility.

"You know there is only one thing to do," I whispered. "We must take him to the hospital."

The hospital, where people went only to die.

I looked into the shadows of her eyes. "We must," I said.

She knew that this time I was right. Nawath's chances were better in that morgue of a place than in the forest, while ours were better in the forest than there in the village. We would all die anyway; but to <u>ensure</u> we all lived as long as possible we had to leave him. While we would at least die together, he would die alone, abandoned by the only ones who cared for him.

Vocabulary
inevitable (i nev′ ə tə bəl) *adj.* incapable of being avoided or evaded
irrevocable (i rev′ ə kə bəl) *adj.* not possible to undo
ensure (en shoor′) *v.* to make certain; guarantee

Responding to Literature

Personal Response
What went through your mind as you finished reading?

——— ANALYZING LITERATURE ———

RECALL AND INTERPRET

1. What is Pin Yathay's first reaction to the knowledge that he will be killed? How does his attitude change? Why does it change?
2. What decision does Pin Yathay privately make? How does Any react to his decision? What does this episode reveal about the couple?
3. At what point does Pin Yathay realize how Any has changed? What, in your opinion, has brought about the change?
4. What decision must the couple make regarding their son? What makes the decision especially difficult?

EVALUATE AND CONNECT

5. Describe the **tone** of *Stay Alive, My Son*. (See page R16.) Is it effective in carrying out the writer's purpose? Explain.
6. Pin Yathay writes of the difficulty in making his final decision. Does he effectively describe why the issue was so complex? Explain your answer.
7. Are you persuaded by Pin Yathay's statement in the last paragraph that he made the only reasonable choice? Explain why or why not. To help you consider other choices, use a chart like the one below.
8. How do you think you might act in a similar situation?

Possible Choice	Advantages	Disadvantages

Literary ELEMENTS

Rhetorical Question
A **rhetorical question** is a question to which no answer is expected. It is used to emphasize the obvious answer to what is asked. The result is a point well made. For example, in the first paragraph of *Stay Alive, My Son*, Pin Yathay writes, "What did it matter?" showing his resignation to his coming death.

1. Any asks her husband, "What shall we do with Nawath? . . . what are we going to do with him if we leave him?" Are these rhetorical questions? Explain.
2. Why does Pin Yathay ask, "Could she really contemplate leaving Nawath?" Does he know the answer? Explain.

● See **Literary Terms Handbook**, p. R13.

——— EXTENDING YOUR RESPONSE ———

Creative Writing
What Now?   Review your notes from the Focus Activity on page 92. Imagine you must give up the one choice that you said you could not do without. Write several paragraphs about what happens next. What decisions will you be forced to make? Will anyone's destiny besides your own be affected? Will you be able to remain objective in making your decisions?

Literature Groups
Values and Ideals   With your group, debate whether Pin Yathay and Any acted according to their values and ideals or whether they were simply trying to save themselves. After your discussion, tally the number of students in the group who have modified their original opinion about the speaker's decision. Summarize the discussion for the class.

📔 **Save your work for your portfolio.**

COMPARING *selections*

from *The Captivity of Mrs. Mary Rowlandson* **and** from **Stay Alive, My Son**

COMPARE **EXPERIENCES**

With a small group, discuss similarities and differences in the experiences of Rowlandson and Pin Yathay. Use a Venn diagram like the one here to record your ideas.

1. Discuss the different attitudes Rowlandson and Pin Yathay take toward their situations.

2. Think about the circumstances in which Rowlandson and Pin Yathay find themselves and the attitudes of both people. How might these factors influence the different ways they cope with their situations?

COMPARE **GOALS**

Mary Rowlandson and Pin Yathay both desire the same thing, but they achieve their goals in different ways. Write a few paragraphs to answer these questions.

- What do they both want for themselves and their families?
- How do the paths they take to their goals differ?
- To what similar destination do their different paths take Rowlandson and Pin Yathay?

COMPARE **MOTIVATIONS**

Acts of political aggression or oppression often have similar results—loss of freedom, captivity, death. However, the motivation for such acts can be quite different. People may act aggressively if they are desperate for food, or they may be aggressive if they want to expand an empire. Use sources from the library, the Internet, or CD-ROM research materials to research both Rowlandson's situation and that of Cambodia in 1975. In a brief report, explain the differences between the motivation of Rowlandson's captors and that of Cambodia's Khmer Rouge.

Untitled. Sompear Hong Sot.

LISTENING, SPEAKING, and VIEWING

Conducting an Interview

In *Stay Alive, My Son,* Pin Yathay tells a horrifying story of war and the loss of a loved one. Stories like Pin Yathay's expose us to a variety of experiences and valuable lessons.

Another way to gather information about people's experiences is through an interview. In an interview, one person questions another person to obtain specific information. The interviewer then shares his or her findings—perhaps in a news article, a television broadcast, or a book.

In any career, however, you might conduct an interview. An employer might interview a potential employee, or a software developer might interview potential customers. For any interview, remember these guidelines.

Before the Interview
- Focus on the purpose of the interview. What do you want to learn?
- Find out as much as you can about the person and the topic.
- Plan a logical list of questions that ask *who, what, when, where, why,* and *how.*

During the Interview
- Be courteous.
- Do not argue or disagree. Focus on the ideas of the person being interviewed.
- Keep your questions brief and to the point.
- Listen carefully so you can ask appropriate and thoughtful follow-up questions.
- Take notes or, better yet, record the interview. (Be sure to ask permission.)

After the Interview
- Write a detailed account of the interview as soon as possible.
- If necessary, contact the person you interviewed or other sources to verify facts.
- Organize the material. Eliminate any information that is unrelated to your topic.
- Write an introduction for your interview that provides background and sets the scene.

ACTIVITIES

1. Interview a person who was a teenager a few decades ago. Focus on how that person's life as a teenager was similar to and different than yours. Discuss what you learn with your classmates.

2. Find a person who is an "expert" on football, TV trivia, gardening, or just about anything. Conduct a brief interview with that person to learn about his or her expertise. Report your findings to the class.

Before You Read

from *Sinners in the Hands of an Angry God*

Meet
Jonathan Edwards

"I think it is a reasonable thing to fright persons away from hell. . . . Is it not a reasonable thing to fright a person out of a house on fire?"

—*Edwards*

The son and grandson of Puritan ministers, Jonathan Edwards was ordained a minister at the age of twenty-three. He soon became known for his "preaching of terror," which grew out of his belief that God was all powerful and human beings had no free will. Edwards preached that God had predestined people to go to heaven or hell. By 1750 some members of his congregation in Northampton, a village in the Massachusetts Bay Colony, were no longer comfortable with his extreme teachings and dismissed Edwards. He moved his family to a frontier village and worked as a missionary with Native Americans. During this time he wrote important theological works, including *Freedom of Will*.

Jonathan Edwards was born in 1703 and died in 1758.

FOCUS ACTIVITY

Think about a time you tried to change someone's mind. Did you use a gentle approach, scare tactics, or something in between?

QUICKWRITE In your journal, write about a time when you tried to persuade someone to accept your point of view. How did you do it? How successful were you?

SETTING A PURPOSE Read to discover how Edwards tries to persuade others.

BACKGROUND

The Time and Place

In 1740 the well-known British evangelist George Whitefield joined with Jonathan Edwards to spark a religious revival that swept New England. The Great Awakening, as it was called, was a backlash against what many believed was a church that had grown far too lenient. Edwards preached a return to strict Calvinism, religious teachings popular in the 1720s that had begun to fade. Calvinist ideas are reflected in his most famous sermon, "Sinners in the Hands of an Angry God."

Calvinism stressed predestination, the belief that only a select few chosen by God would be saved. No individual could earn grace by doing good deeds, so everyone was equally powerless to control their own fates.

VOCABULARY PREVIEW

wrath (rath) *n.* extreme anger; vengeful punishment; p. 102

appease (ə pēz′) *v.* to bring to a state of peace or quiet; soothe; p. 102

abate (ə bāt′) *v.* to lessen or reduce in force or intensity; p. 102

incensed (in senst′) *adj.* made very angry; p. 102

prudence (prōōd′ əns) *n.* exercise of good and cautious judgment; p. 102

abhor (ab hôr′) *v.* to regard with disgust; p. 103

abominable (ə bom′ə nə bəl) *adj.* disgusting; detestable; p. 103

Jonathan Edwards

John Foster Headstone, 1681. Attributed to The Charlestown Stonecutter. Slate, carved area 23⅜ x 18¼ in., depth 2³⁄₁₆ in. Boston Parks and Recreation Commission, on loan to Museum of Fine Arts, Boston.

from
SINNERS IN THE HANDS OF AN ANGRY GOD

*S*o that thus it is, that natural men[1] are held in the hand of God over the pit of hell; they have deserved the fiery pit, and are already sentenced to it; and God is dreadfully provoked, his anger is as great towards them as to those that are actually suffering the executions of the fierceness of his <u>wrath</u> in hell, and they have done nothing in the least, to <u>appease</u> or <u>abate</u> that anger, neither is God in the least bound by any promise to hold them up one moment; the devil is waiting for them, hell is gaping for them, the flames gather and flash about them, and would fain[2] lay hold on them and swallow them up; the fire pent up in their own hearts is struggling to break out; and they have no interest in any Mediator, there are no means within reach that can be any security to them. In short, they have no refuge, nothing to take hold of; all that preserves them every moment is the mere arbitrary will, and uncovenanted, unobliged forbearance of an <u>incensed</u> God.

Application

The use may be of awakening to unconverted persons in this congregation. This that you have heard is the case of every one of you that are out of Christ.[3] That world of misery, that lake of burning brimstone, is extended abroad under you. There is the dreadful pit of the glowing flames of the wrath of God; there is hell's wide gaping mouth open; and you have nothing to stand upon, nor any thing to take hold of. There is nothing between you and hell but the air; it is only the power and mere pleasure of God that holds you up.

You probably are not sensible of this; you find you are kept out of hell, but do not see the hand of God in it; but look at other things, as the good state of your bodily constitution, your care of your own life, and the means you use for your own preservation. But indeed these things are nothing; if God should withdraw his hand, they would avail no more to keep you from falling, than the thin air to hold up a person that is suspended in it.

Your wickedness makes you as it were heavy as lead, and to tend downwards with great weight and pressure towards hell; and if God should let you go, you would immediately sink and swiftly descend and plunge into the bottomless gulf, and your healthy constitution, and your own care and <u>prudence</u>, and best contrivance,[4] and all your righteousness, would have no more influence to uphold you and keep you out of hell, than a spider's web would have to stop a falling rock.

1. *Natural men* are those who have not been "born again" or received God's grace.
2. Here, *fain* means "willingly" or "gladly."
3. Those who are *out of Christ* are not in God's grace.
4. A *contrivance* is a clever scheme or plan.

Vocabulary
wrath (rath) *n.* extreme anger; vengeful punishment
appease (ə pēz′) *v.* to bring to a state of peace or quiet; soothe
abate (ə bāt′) *v.* to lessen or reduce in force or intensity
incensed (in senst′) *adj.* made very angry
prudence (prōōd′ əns) *n.* exercise of good and cautious judgment

The bow of God's wrath is bent, and the arrow made ready on the string, and justice bends the arrow at your heart, and strains the bow, and it is nothing but the mere pleasure of God, and that of an angry God, without any promise or obligation at all, that keeps the arrow one moment from being made drunk with your blood.

Thus are all you that never passed under a great change of heart, by the mighty power of the Spirit of God upon your souls; all that were never born again, and made new creatures, and raised from being dead in sin, to a state of new, and before altogether unexperienced light and life, (however you may have reformed your life in many things, and may have had religious affections, and may keep up a form of religion in your families and closets,[5] and in the houses of God, and may be strict in it) you are thus in the hands of an angry God; it is nothing but his mere pleasure that keeps you from being this moment swallowed up in everlasting destruction.

The God that holds you over the pit of hell, much as one holds a spider, or some loathsome insect, over the fire, abhors you, and is dreadfully provoked; his wrath towards you burns like fire; he looks upon you as worthy of nothing else, but to be cast into the fire; he is of purer eyes than to bear to have you in his sight; you are ten thousand times so abominable in his eyes, as the most hateful and venomous serpent is in ours.

George Whitefield, c. 1742. John Wollaston. Oil on canvas, 32⅝ x 26 in. National Portrait Gallery, London.

Viewing the painting: Does the painting capture the tone of Jonathan Edwards's sermon? Support your opinion.

O sinner! consider the fearful danger you are in: it is a great furnace of wrath, a wide and bottomless pit, full of the fire of wrath, that you are held over in the hand of that God, whose wrath is provoked and incensed as much against you, as against many of the damned in hell: you hang by a slender thread, with the flames of divine wrath flashing about it, and ready every moment to singe it, and burn it asunder;[6] and you have no interest in any Mediator, and nothing to lay

---

5. Here, *closets* refers to small rooms used especially for prayer and meditation.

6. *Asunder* means "into separate pieces."

Vocabulary
abhor (ab hôr′) *v.* to regard with disgust
abominable (ə bom′ ə nə bəl) *adj.* disgusting; detestable

hold of to save yourself, nothing to keep off the flames of wrath, nothing of your own, nothing that you ever have done, nothing that you can do, to induce God to spare you one moment.

There is reason to think, that there are many in this congregation now hearing this discourse, that will actually be the subjects of this very misery to all eternity. We know not who they are, or in what seats they sit, or what thoughts they now have. It may be they are now at ease, and hear all these things without much disturbance, and are now flattering themselves that they are not the persons; promising themselves that they shall escape. If we knew that there was one person, and but one, in the whole congregation, that was to be the subject of this misery, what an awful thing it would be to think of! If we knew who it was, what an awful sight would it be to see such a person! How might all the rest of the congregation lift up a lamentable and bitter cry over him! But alas! Instead of one, how many is it likely will remember this discourse in hell! And it would be a wonder, if some that are now present should not be in hell in a very short time, before this year is out. And it would be no wonder if some persons, that now sit here in some seats of this meeting-house in health, and quiet and secure, should be there before to-morrow morning.

Those of you that finally continue in a natural condition, that shall keep out of Hell longest, will be there in a little time! Your damnation does not slumber; it will come swiftly, and in all probability very suddenly upon many of you. You have reason to wonder that you are not already in Hell. 'Tis doubtless the case of some that heretofore you have seen and known, that never deserved Hell more than you, and that heretofore appeared as likely to have been now alive as you: Their case is past all hope. They are crying in extreme misery and perfect despair. But here you are in the land of the living, and in the house of God, and have an opportunity to obtain salvation. What would not those poor damned, helpless souls give for one day's such opportunity as you now enjoy!

And now you have an extraordinary opportunity, a day wherein Christ has flung the door of mercy wide open, and stands in the door calling and crying with a loud voice to poor sinners; a day, wherein many are flocking to him, and pressing into the kingdom of God. Many are daily coming from the east, west, north and south; many that were very lately in the same miserable condition that you are in, are in now a happy state, with their hearts filled with love to Him that has loved them and washed them from their sins in His own blood, and rejoicing in hope of the Glory of God.[7] How awful is it to be left behind at such a day! To see so many others feasting, while you are pining and perishing! To see so many rejoicing and singing for joy of heart, while you have cause to mourn for sorrow of heart and howl for vexation of spirit! How can you rest one moment in such a condition? . . .

Therefore let everyone that is out of Christ now awake and fly from the wrath to come. The wrath of Almighty God is now undoubtedly hanging over a great part of this congregation: Let everyone fly out of Sodom![8] *Haste and escape for your lives, look not behind you, escape to the mountain, lest you be consumed.*

---

7. The author is referring to the many people who were part of the Great Awakening, a movement that urged people to experience religion on a personal, emotional level.
8. In Genesis 19:15–17, angels warn Lot, the only virtuous inhabitant of the sinful city of Sodom, to flee the city before it is destroyed.

Responding to Literature

Personal Response

Imagine that you are in the congregation, listening to Edwards's sermon. How might you respond?

——— ANALYZING LITERATURE ———

RECALL AND INTERPRET

1. In the first paragraph, what generalization does Edwards make about all people? Why do you think Edwards makes this statement?
2. A **metaphor** is a comparison made without using the words *like* or *as*. What metaphors does Edwards use to explain God's mercy? How do these metaphors reflect Edwards's view of the relationship between God and humanity?
3. What does the minister say to command the attention of those who think they will not fall victim to God's wrath?
4. Near the end of the sermon, what does Edwards say Christ has done? What might have been the minister's purpose in closing with this image?

EVALUATE AND CONNECT

5. **Repetition** is the frequent use of a word or phrase for emphasis. Evaluate the effect of repeating *you* throughout the sermon.
6. Edwards used fear to rekindle his congregation's interest. Compare his style with that of a more recent religious leader, such as Martin Luther King Jr. How are their appeals and goals similar and different?
7. Edwards wanted his sermon to frighten people into a "change of heart." In what other ways might a person have reacted to the sermon? Explain.
8. Reread what you wrote for the Focus Activity on page 100. Have your thoughts on persuasion changed at all since reading the sermon? Explain.

Literary ELEMENTS

Imagery

Imagery is the collection of mental pictures, or images, in a literary work. Visual imagery is most common but a writer can also use other **sensory details** that appeal to the reader's sense of sound, taste, smell, or touch.

Edwards's sermon is filled with images meant to frighten listeners into seeking God and avoiding hell.

1. What frightening images occur in the first two paragraphs? To what senses do they appeal?
2. What sensory details does Edwards include in the fourth paragraph? What effect does the imagery have on the reader?
3. List five additional images in the sermon, each of which appeals to a different sense.

● See **Literary Terms Handbook**, p. R8.

——— EXTENDING YOUR RESPONSE ———

Personal Writing

Emotional Appeals   Edwards preached with a "fiery rhetoric," a speaking style intended to elicit a highly emotional response. In your opinion, when can emotional appeals be effective? In what situations are they inappropriate? Write a brief set of guidelines for the appropriate use of emotional appeals.

Interdisciplinary Activity

Art: Illustrating Images   Choose a passage from Edwards's sermon that contains vivid imagery, such as his comparison of sinners to "the most hateful and venomous serpent." Sketch the passage, or use a computer graphics program to illustrate the scene. Then, with other students, organize your images to create a visual presentation of the sermon.

 Save your work for your portfolio.

Grammar Link

Avoiding Sentence Fragments

A fragment is something that is incomplete. It might be a fragment of a conversation, a fragment of a song, or a fragment of a sentence. A **sentence fragment** is a word or group of words that makes up only part of a sentence.

Problem 1 Some sentence fragments lack a subject, a verb, or both.
> *Succeeded his grandfather as a minister in Northampton, Massachusetts.* [lacks a subject]
> *Many people in Edwards's church that Sunday.* [lacks a verb]

Solution Add the missing subject and/or verb.
> *Edwards succeeded his grandfather as a minister in Northampton, Massachusetts.*
> *Many people sat in Edwards's church that Sunday.*

Problem 2 Some sentence fragments are subordinate clauses that have been mistaken for a complete sentence. A subordinate clause has a subject and verb, but it does not express a complete thought and cannot stand alone as a sentence.
> *Because some Northampton Puritans disagreed with Edwards.*

Solution A Join the subordinate clause to a main clause.
> *Because some Northampton Puritans disagreed with Edwards, he moved to the village of Stockbridge.*

Solution B Remove the subordinating conjunction at the beginning of the clause.
> *Some Northampton Puritans disagreed with Edwards.*

Writers sometimes deliberately use sentence fragments. Edwards uses the phrase "But alas!" in "Sinners in the Hands of an Angry God." It is an exclamation and its meaning is clear. Later, he uses the fragment "To see so many others feasting, while you are pining and perishing!" Here the meaning is less clear but can be understood within the context of the selection. Although you will find similar examples in other writing, beware of using fragments in your own writing because readers can often become confused.

● For more about sentence fragments, see **Language Handbook,** pp. R18–R19.

EXERCISES

1. **Proofreading** Use the strategies above to correct the sentence fragments in this paragraph.

   Jonathan Edwards was a Puritan minister and one of the foremost early American writers. Who was born in 1703. "Sinners in the Hands of an Angry God" may be his best known sermon. Written in 1741. In this sermon, preaches about the dangers of sin. Edwards's theme, however, is not the anger of God. But God's grace.

2. Revise a piece of your own writing using these strategies to eliminate sentence fragments.

Before You Read

Offer of Help

Meet Canassatego

❝We are a powerful Confederacy; and by your observing the same methods our wise forefathers have taken, you will acquire such strength and power. Therefore whatever befalls you, never fall out with one another.❞

—*Canassatego*

Canassatego was a leader of the Onondaga people and a powerful *tadadaho,* or orator. A British colonial official, after hearing him speak, described Canassatego as "a tall, well-made man," with "a very full chest and brawny limbs. . . . He was about sixty years of age, very active, strong, and had a surprising liveliness in his speech."

The Onondaga were, in fact, allies of the British. Between 1689 and 1763, France and England battled over land in North America. To strengthen their forces, each nation developed alliances with Native American groups.

One powerful alliance forged by the British was with the Six Nations of the Iroquois—the Onondaga, Mohawk, Seneca, Oneida, Cayuga, and Tuscarora peoples. (The Tuscarora had joined the Iroquois in 1722.)

As leader of the Onondaga, Canassatego served as a representative of the united Iroquois at several meetings with British colonists. At one meeting in 1744, Canassatego urged the British colonies to unite, like the Iroquois, to form a strong, centralized government.

The unity of the colonies, based on the model of Canassatego's united Iroquois, ultimately came into being shortly before the American Revolution; inspired by Canassatego's original advice, "Never fall out with one another," the American patriots' rallying cry became, "United we stand, divided we fall."

Canassatego was born around 1690 and died in 1750.

FOCUS ACTIVITY

In your opinion, what skills should young people learn in school in order to prepare themselves most effectively for "real life"?

LIST IDEAS In your journal, create a list entitled "The Top Ten Skills a Person Needs for a Successful, Fulfilling Life."

SETTING A PURPOSE Read to see what one man valued as the best skills for his people.

BACKGROUND

The Time and Place

European settlers rarely respected the cultural traditions and territorial rights of Native Americans. A statement by Boston church leader Cotton Mather (1663–1728) illustrates the attitudes of many settlers: "We, God's chosen people, must conquer the earth. . . ." Ironically, such feelings of superiority occasionally led settlers to make gestures of "generosity." For example, representatives from Virginia gave an "offer of help" to Canassatego. They invited him to send a group of young Native Americans to Virginia to attend college, free of charge. The message you are about to read is Canassatego's response to this offer.

VOCABULARY PREVIEW

esteem (es tēm′) *v.* to regard favorably; value highly; p. 108
proposal (prə pō′zəl) *n.* something put forward for consideration as a plan of action; p. 108

conception (kən sep′shən) *n.* mental image or idea; thought or notion; p. 108

Offer of Help

Canassatego

We know you highly <u>esteem</u> the kind of learning taught in these colleges, and the maintenance of our young men, while with you, would be very expensive to you. We are convinced, therefore, that you mean to do us good by your <u>proposal</u>; and we thank you heartily. But you who are so wise must know that different nations have different <u>conceptions</u> of things; and you will not therefore take it amiss,[1] if our ideas of this kind of education happens not to be the same with yours. We have had some experience of it. Several of our young people were formerly brought up in the colleges of the northern provinces; they were instructed in all your sciences; but, when they came back to us, they were bad runners, ignorant of every means of living in the woods, unable to bear either cold or hunger, knew neither how to build a cabin, take a deer, or kill an enemy, spoke our language imperfectly, were therefore neither fit for hunters, warriors, nor counsellors, they were totally good for nothing. We are however not the less obliged for your kind offer, tho' we decline accepting it; and to show our grateful sense of it, if the gentlemen of Virginia shall send us a dozen of their sons, we will take great care of their education, instruct them in all we know, and make men of them.

---

1. To *take amiss* is "to take offense at."

Vocabulary
esteem (es tēm′) *v.* to regard favorably; value highly
proposal (prə pō′zəl) *n.* something put forward for consideration as a plan of action
conception (kən sep′shən) *n.* mental image or idea; thought or notion

Responding to Literature

Personal Response

What questions would you like to ask Canassatego? Why?

—————— ANALYZING LITERATURE ——————

RECALL AND INTERPRET

1. Canassatego begins by thanking the colonists for their offer. What reasons does he give for saying that he knows they mean well? How might this beginning affect the colonists?
2. According to Canassatego, what skills did Iroquois men need? Why might these skills have been particularly important to them? Explain.
3. What does Canassatego say about the Native Americans who had gone to college in the northern provinces? How do you think the colonists might have responded to his comments? Why?
4. What counteroffer does Canassatego make? What reason does he give for making this offer? What might be his real reason? Explain.

EVALUATE AND CONNECT

5. In your own words, state what Canassatego wants the men from Virginia to understand. Do you think he makes his point effectively?
6. Theme Connections   In your opinion, why are the colonists interested in changing Canassatego's people? Explain.
7. Canassatego states, "Different nations have different conceptions of things." In your own life, would you say that different groups have different ideas about things? Support your response with details.
8. Being a diplomat requires tact and sensitivity, especially when dealing with people of different cultural backgrounds. Based on "Offer of Help," do you think Canassatego had effective skills as a diplomat? Explain.

Literary ELEMENTS

Tone

Tone is the attitude that a writer expresses toward his or her subject matter. When we speak, we choose a tone of voice to give clues to such underlying attitudes as humor, formality, anger, or sadness. Similarly, when we write, we carefully choose our words and structure our sentences in order to set the tone.

1. How would you describe the tone of Canassatego's speech? Cite examples of words or sentences that you feel indicate the tone.
2. In your opinion, why did Canassatego choose this particular tone?

● See **Literary Terms Handbook,** p. R16.

—————— EXTENDING YOUR RESPONSE ——————

Literature Groups

An Effective Education   In your group, discuss this question: *What practical skills should schools teach in order to prepare students for "real life"*? Refer to the list you created for the Focus Activity on page 107, adding any new ideas that you may have gained by reading Canassatego's thoughts. Present and explain the group's ideas to the class.

Creative Writing

R.S.V.P.   Write a letter that the representatives from Virginia might have written to respond to Canassatego. Choose your words carefully to express your reaction clearly. Be sure that your letter conveys respect for Canassatego and appreciation for his offer.

📖 **Save your work for your portfolio.**

～: Writing Workshop :～

Narrative Writing: Historical Narrative

Does reading about the past make you wonder what it would have been like to have lived during another time in history? If so, writing about a historical period is the next best thing to being there. **In this workshop, you will write a historical narrative in the first person.** In other words, you will use your imagination to enter into the time and place of one of the selections from this unit, then you'll write about the past from the point of view of someone who was there.

● As you write your narrative, refer to the **Writing Handbook,** pp. R62–R77.

The Writing Process

PREWRITING

PREWRITING TIP
If you find it difficult to imagine living in a different time period, think first about the similarities between people who lived then and people who live now. Then take it from there.

Explore ideas

Obviously, you weren't alive hundreds of years ago, so the personal experiences you describe in your narrative will be fictional. However, the sites and situations you write about should be real. To help you choose which literary setting to "visit," try some of these strategies.

● As you scan the selections, jot down "What if" questions, such as, "What if a group of colonists bumped into Mary Rowlandson and her captors?"
● Complete some sentence starters, such as, "When Aataentsic threw herself after the big tree, I went _____ ."
● Quiz yourself about your own strengths and limitations by asking such questions as, "How would I have survived the first winter at Plymouth?"

Choose an audience

To some extent, the content and style of your narrative will depend on your audience. For example, if you write for children, you might want to include a great deal of dialogue and action to keep them interested. If you write for your peers, you might have your narrator be a teenager.

Consider your purpose

No matter who your audience is, the main purpose of your narrative will probably be to help readers understand what it would have been like to live during a particular time in history.

Make a plan

The first step in developing a plan for your historical narrative is to decide on the time and place—the **setting**—of your narrative. Then, think about the other main elements of a story. You might want to jot down your thoughts on a chart like the one below:

STUDENT MODEL

Setting	Where and when does the action occur? What does the place look like? What details will bring the setting to life?	The settlement of Plymouth, on the Atlantic coast, in 1620. I'll try to get pictures and a map of the reconstruction.
Point of view	Who's telling your story? Since this is a first-person narrative, the narrator of your tale will use words like *I* and *me.* However, that narrator doesn't have to be you. He or she can be a fictional character or a historical figure.	When I visited the modern reconstruction of Plymouth Plantation, I wondered about the people who used to live there. I think the narrator will be one of the colonists—a fictional one.
Characters	Who are they? Are they real people or fictional characters? How can you make them come alive in your narrative?	The other characters will be Captain Standish and the settlers that were really there. I'll re-read *Of Plymouth Plantation* and look in other sources to find out more about what they were like.
Plot	What is the problem or conflict? What relationship does your plot have to the actual historical events?	Problem = survival during the first winter. Captain Standish, one of the few healthy men, is struggling to keep the others alive. The climax will come when some of the sick people get well enough to bury the ones who didn't make it.

Note any factual information you will need to fill out background details. Is the information easily available from the library or other sources? If not, you may want to rethink your plans.

~: Writing \ Workshop :~

DRAFTING

DRAFTING TIP
To help imagine yourself in the role of the narrator, keep asking yourself such questions as, "What is the narrator feeling now?"

Write your draft
Before you start writing, you might want to close your eyes for a few minutes and imagine yourself in the role of your narrator. Notice what you see, hear, smell, and feel. Then open your eyes and start writing about all those things. Don't concern yourself with what is important and what's not. You'll have time to filter and refine your details later.

Set the scene
In order for your historical narrative to take readers somewhere they've never been before, you have to create a strong sense of time and place. Bring your readers into the narrative by using distinctive details and specific, vivid words that appeal to the readers' sense of smell, touch, or hearing as well as their sense of sight.

STUDENT MODEL

> Wherever I looked, I saw gray—the murky gray sky, the restless gray sea, the bare and shivering gray trees. The smoke from the houses was gray, and it scratched at my throat painfully. It was as if a gray blanket of illness lay over everything and was seeping through our skin.

REVISING

REVISING TIP
Be selective. Ask yourself whether each detail really adds to the flow and impact of the narrative. If it doesn't, throw it out.

TECHNOLOGY TIP

When revising on the computer, don't delete anything. Instead, cut unwanted sentences and paste them at the end of the file. Later, review this material for ideas or details to add.

Be your own critic
Do not review your narrative right away. Wait a few hours or a few days, then approach the story as if you were reading it for the first time. Put a check mark beside passages that are unclear, unnecessary, flat, or underdeveloped. When you're done reading, go back and try to improve those passages.

Ask another critic
Ask another student to review your narrative. Using the **Questions for Revising** as a guide, he or she should write questions and comments in the margins of your story. When you get your narrative back, consider which suggestions you want to follow.

QUESTIONS FOR REVISING
- ☑ Is the sense of time and place clear? How could it be strengthened?
- ☑ Where could details be added to make events or characters more vivid? Which details should be left out?
- ☑ How can the central conflict be strengthened?
- ☑ Which lines of dialogue sound realistic and which do not? How could the unrealistic ones be improved?
- ☑ Do the characters' thoughts and motivations seem real?
- ☑ Is the opening attention-getting? Is the ending satisfying?

STUDENT MODEL

> I wondered where the deadly illness had come from. Had it come from the ^crowded, reeking^ ship? Was it waiting for us on ^this new^ shore? (we had come so far to find)

EDITING/PROOFREADING

When you think your narrative reads smoothly, proofread it. Go over the story carefully several times, referring to the **Proofreading Checklist** on the inside back cover of this book to make sure you check for the most common types of errors.

Grammar Hint

Be sure each verb agrees with its subject, even when other words come between the subject and verb.

*The strong **arms** of Captain Standish gently **raise** the shivering woman's head so that she can sip the hot soup.*

● For more on subject-verb agreement, see **Language Handbook,** p. R21.

STUDENT MODEL

The days of last week was bitter cold. This week, any warmth, even during our mid-day chores, are hard to find.

[handwritten edits: "were" inserted above "was"; "is" inserted after "are"]

PUBLISHING/PRESENTING

How will your narrative reach its proper audience? If you've written for children, you may want to turn your story into an illustrated mini-book for a grade-school library. If you've written for your peers, think about collaborating with them. You could form a historical fiction collection by binding your narrative with others that take place in the same setting.

PRESENTING TIP
Did you come across any maps of your story's setting? Consider making a copy to illustrate your narrative.

Reflecting

Think over your writing experience in this workshop. In your journal, comment on how writing about another time and place affected your process. Is your historical narrative something you would like to include in your portfolio? Why or why not?

Set goals for your next piece of writing. Consider what you hope to accomplish and what you plan to do differently.

📖 **Save your work for your portfolio.**

Unit Wrap-Up

PERSONAL RESPONSE

1. Rank the selections in this unit from most to least interesting. Give a reason for each ranking.
2. What did your work in this unit teach you about:
   - differences and similarities between oral and written literature?
   - literary genres, such as myth, poetry, or narrative?
   - how to use literature to learn about history?
   - how to gain insight into different cultures from their literature?

ANALYZING LITERATURE

Comparing Attitudes Compare and contrast the attitudes that Native Americans and Europeans displayed toward one another in the years covered by this unit. Use Cabeza de Vaca's *La Relación,* Canassatego's "Offer of Help," and Rowlandson's narrative of her captivity for evidence. Write a few paragraphs to explain your conclusions. Use specific facts and statements from the selections to support your ideas.

EVALUATE AND SET GOALS

Evaluate

1. Make a list of three things you contributed to the class as you studied this unit. Check the best one.
2. What aspect of this unit was the most challenging for you?
   - How did you approach the challenge?
   - What was the result?
3. If you had another week to work on this unit, what would you hope to learn; what skills would you hope to strengthen?
4. How would you assess your work in this unit using the following scale? Give at least two reasons for your assessment.
   4 = outstanding   **3** = good   **2** = fair   **1** = weak

Set Goals

1. Set a goal for your work in the next unit. Try to focus on improving a skill area, such as speaking or critical thinking.
2. Discuss your goal with your teacher.
3. Plan specific steps to achieve the goal.
4. Plan two or more points at which to stop and judge your work.
5. Think of a method to evaluate finished work.

 # BUILD YOUR PORTFOLIO

Select From the writing you did in this unit, choose two pieces to put into your portfolio. Use the following questions as guides when choosing:
- Which taught you the most?
- Which are you likely to share?
- Which was the most difficult to complete?

Reflect Include some explanatory notes with the portfolio pieces you chose. Use these questions to guide you:
- What are the piece's strengths and weaknesses?
- What did working on the piece teach you about writing (or about other skills the piece displays)?
- How would you revise the piece today to make it stronger?

Reading on Your Own

If you have enjoyed the literature in this unit, you might also be interested in the following books.

The Autobiography of Benjamin Franklin

by Benjamin Franklin While Franklin did not live to complete this autobiography, the great American leader tells of his life from an impoverished childhood in Boston to his successful careers as a printer, inventor, and writer.

The Account: Álvar Núñez Cabeza de Vaca's *Relación*

translated by Martin A. Favata and José B. Fernández This dramatic narrative, published in Spain in 1542, chronicles one of the first Spanish explorations of America. The story of the extreme hardships of the expedition is intertwined with vivid descriptions of the lush landscape and the cultures of native peoples.

The Works of Anne Bradstreet

edited by Jeannine Hensley This book provides an opportunity to read more of the works of this skilled poet.

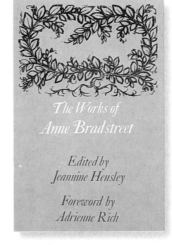

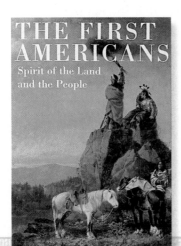

The First Americans

by Josepha Sherman An excellent, intelligent, and richly illustrated overview of Native American cultures, this book includes information about customs, beliefs, living conditions, and contacts with white settlers.

Standardized Test Practice

> <u>Directions:</u> The following sentences test correctness and effectiveness of expression. In choosing answers, follow the requirements of standard written English; that is, pay attention to grammar, choice of words, sentence construction, and punctuation.
>
> In each of the following sentences, part of the sentence or the entire sentence is underlined. Beneath each sentence you will find five ways of phrasing the underlined part. Choice A repeats the original; the other four are different.
>
> Choose the answer that best expresses the meaning of the original sentence. If you think the original is better than any of the alternatives, choose it; otherwise choose one of the others. Your choice should produce the most effective sentence—clear and precise, without awkwardness or ambiguity. Write the corresponding letter on your paper.

1. Many times reporters are privy to more information than they include in a piece, <u>this restraint helps create an especially compelling story.</u>
   - (A) this restraint helps create an especially compelling story
   - (B) with this restraint helping create an especially compelling story
   - (C) and an especially compelling story being the creation of their restraint
   - (D) and this restraint helps create an especially compelling story
   - (E) an especially compelling story created from this restraint.

2. Climbing without supplemental oxygen at high altitudes is hard on the body, but it enables some climbers to explore remote areas <u>and they can ascend</u> without stopping.
   - (A) and they can ascend
   - (B) as well as ascending
   - (C) so they can ascend
   - (D) and an ascension
   - (E) and to ascend

3. With all its high-powered winds, <u>the Statue of Liberty was caused to sway no more than five inches by the hurricane.</u>
   - (A) the Statue of Liberty was caused to sway no more than five inches by the hurricane.
   - (B) the hurricane caused the Statue of Liberty to sway no more than five inches
   - (C) no more than five inches was how far the Statue of Liberty was swayed by the hurricane
   - (D) the Statue of Liberty's movement was kept to no more than five inches by the hurricane
   - (E) the hurricane swayed no more than five inches to the Statue of Liberty

4. The lecturer argued that though the program has excelled at training future scholars, <u>the failure is in its not educating</u> vocational students in the value of scholarly interests.
   - (A) the failure is in its not educating
   - (B) the failure it has is in its not educating
   - (C) it failed not to educate
   - (D) it has failed to educate
   - (E) failing in its education of

116 ❧ UNIT 1

Directions: The following sentences test your knowledge of grammar, usage, diction (choice of words), and idiom.

Some sentences are correct.
No sentence contains more than one error.

You will find that the error, if there is one, is underlined and lettered. Elements of the sentence that are not underlined will not be changed. In choosing answers, follow the requirements of standard written English.

If there is an error, select the one underlined part that must be changed to make the sentence correct. Write the corresponding letter on your paper.

If there is no error, select answer E.

1. Only after the curtains had <u>rose</u> ten feet
   A
   <u>was</u> the crowd able <u>to see</u> the <u>layout of the</u>
   B   C   D
   stage. <u>No error</u>
         E

2. The new minor-league players <u>attracted a</u>
                      A
   crowd of fans, <u>for</u> <u>it</u> had <u>never been seen</u>
          B   C   D
   in public before. <u>No error</u>
               E

3. The building of a float for homecoming
   <u>was first proposed</u> in the spring,
         A
   <u>but not until</u> school opened in the fall did
       B
   <u>such a project</u> become <u>a reality.</u> <u>No error</u>
       C   D   E

4. If one <u>is interested</u> <u>in learning</u> <u>even more</u>
           A   B   C
   about aeronautics, <u>you should</u> take a flying
                  D
   lesson. <u>No error</u>
          E

5. Meteorologists have discovered that public
   concern is heightened <u>considerably</u>
                     A
   <u>whenever</u> television stations <u>forecasted</u>
      B   C
   weather advisories early <u>in the day.</u>
                  D
   <u>No error</u>
     E

6. An organized team sport allows students
   <u>to undertake</u> challenges that <u>encourages</u>
      A   B
   each of <u>them</u> to be <u>both</u> competitive
       C   D
   and cooperative. <u>No error</u>
             E

Kindred Spirits, 1849. Asher Brown Durand. Oil on canvas, 46 x 36 in. The New York Public Library, New York.

UNIT ❧ TWO

A New Nation

1750–1850

*"Liberty, when it begins
to take root, is a plant
of rapid growth."*
—George Washington

Theme 2
Breaking Free
Pages 129–200

Theme 3
Gaining Insight
Pages 201–311

Setting the Scene

On December 16, 1773, three British ships filled with chests of dried tea leaves lay in Boston harbor. A group of colonists, furious at the faraway king for taxing and restricting the sale of tea, refused to let the ships unload their cargo. That night about two hundred colonists decided to take more direct action. Disguised as Mohawk Indians, with red paint on their faces and blankets tied around their waists, the men marched to the waterfront. They used the ship's cranes to hoist 342 chests of tea out of the ship's hold and toss the chests into the harbor. The Boston Tea Party, as it came to be known, infuriated the British king and became a symbol of colonial resistance. Less than two years later, shots fired in Lexington, Massachusetts—what American author Ralph Waldo Emerson called "the shot heard 'round the world"—signaled the start of the American Revolution.

U.S.A.

1754
French and Indian War begins (French and British fight over control of North America)

1775
Revolutionary War begins

1765
Parliament imposes Stamp Act on colonies

1776
Declaration of Independence is signed

1783
United States wins its independence

1791
Bill of Rights is ratified

1750   **1770**   1789   **1790** 1791

The French Revolution begins

1787
Sierra Leone is founded as a settlement for freed slaves

1791
Toussaint l'Ouverture leads African slaves in Haiti in a revolt against French rulers

World

History of the Time

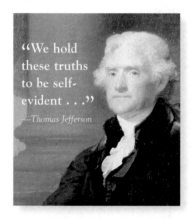

"We hold these truths to be self-evident . . ."
—Thomas Jefferson

The Revolution

The American colonists were angry. They had hoped America would be a land of freedom and opportunity and had labored hard, endured severe weather, and risked disease and starvation in order to build towns and farms. They had fought alongside British soldiers to defeat France in the French and Indian War. However, that war had put Britain in debt, and to raise money, the British government looked to the colonies.

The British Parliament passed a series of unpopular laws, forcing the colonists to house British soldiers and taxing everyday items such as newspapers, almanacs, and legal documents. Some colonial political leaders refused to comply, and Britain "dissolved" their power. Then, in 1770, British troops fired on a disorderly mob in Boston. The event came to be known as the Boston Massacre.

After Parliament had levied new taxes on imports such as paint and tea, further violence broke out. In December 1773, the colonists dumped 342 chests of tea from British ships into Boston Harbor. King George III was furious and responded by passing the Intolerable Acts of 1774, a series of laws meant to punish the colonies for their disobedience.

The Acts so outraged the colonists that even the moderate George Washington declared, "the crisis is arrived when we must assert our rights." When the British troops fired at the colonial militia, on April 19, 1775, the colonists responded with force. The war had begun.

Independence

American leaders justified their revolt against British authority in the remarkable Declaration of Independence, approved by the Second Continental Congress on July 4, 1776. The United States went on to wage a war in which the ragtag colonial volunteers ultimately managed to defeat the splendidly outfitted and trained British soldiers.

Winning a war, however, does not create a nation. In 1781 the Second Continental Congress met to establish a government for the new nation. At first, they created a set of laws called the Articles of Confederation, which provided for a weak central government. Realizing the need for a more powerful national government, leaders of all the states met in Philadelphia in 1787. There they crafted the Constitution of the United States. Two years later, in 1789, George Washington was inaugurated as the first president of the United States.

The area and population of the new nation grew rapidly because of the acquisition of the Louisiana Territory and an influx of immigrants. This growth, as well as technological advances and other developments, helped create a flourishing and unique nation.

1803
United States negotiates Louisiana Purchase

1812
War of 1812 against Britain begins

1836
Texas declares independence from Mexico

1848
Mexican American War ends, adding territory to United States

1808–1826
Most Latin American countries succeed in gaining independence

1810

1815
Napoleon I is defeated at Waterloo and later exiled

1830

1842
China opens five ports to trade with Western nations

1850

Life of the Time

People are talking about

◀ **The First "People's President"**   Americans inaugurate Andrew Jackson as their seventh president in 1829. Lacking the upper-class background and manners of previous presidents, Jackson is popular among the common people. Thousands attend Jackson's inauguration. As the new president arrives at the White House on horseback, a great crowd follows him.

"Thronging the East Room, the crowd fell on the refreshments, breaking china and smashing furniture."

—*William V. Shannon*

"We, the People"   Democracy is a hot topic in political circles, though its practice does not apply to all Americans. In 1848, Elizabeth Cady Stanton and Lucretia Mott hold the first women's rights convention at Seneca Falls, New York. They present a statement modeled on the Declaration of Independence. They call their resolutions the "Declaration of Sentiments" and profess "that all men and women are created equal."

Travel   Roads are still primitive. As late as 1842, visiting British novelist Charles Dickens reports riding on a road that was ". . . at the best but a track through the wild forest, and among the swamps, bogs, and morasses of the withered bush." Americans develop trails, turnpikes, canals, bridges, steamboats, and railroads. ▶

Firsts

- America's first streetlights are used in Philadelphia. (1757)
- Chocolate is first manufactured in the United States. (1765)
- Elizabeth Blackwell is the first American woman to receive a medical degree. (1849)

U.S.A.

1752 Franklin experiments with electricity using kite and key

1769 Dartmouth College is founded

1772 Charles Wilson Peale, portrait of George Washington

1780 American Academy of Arts and Sciences is established in Boston

1789 Thanksgiving is first celebrated as national holiday

1794 Eli Whitney patents cotton gin

1750

1770

1790

1700s Introduction of power-driven machinery heralds the Industrial Revolution in England

1782 King Rama I of Siam (now Thailand) makes Bangkok his capital

1786 Wolfgang Amadeus Mozart's comic opera *Le nozze de Figaro* premieres in Vienna

World

Food & Fashion

Most Americans are wearing comfortable, sturdy woolen clothing they make by hand.

- Most pioneer women wear smock-like dresses and petticoats over their skirts. Woolen or cotton bonnets protect their faces. ▶
- Frontiersmen wear loose-fitting, thigh-length hunting shirts—made from deerskin or homemade cloth—without buttons and belted or tied at the waist. Deerskin trousers are also worn. ▶

◀ Wealthy Americans are influenced by styles from England and France.

Diets vary, as do clothes.

- On the frontier and farms, a meal usually consists of corn grown in the family's fields and meat provided by the family's cattle, hogs, sheep, and chickens or from wild game.

- On southern plantations, wealthy owners may begin their dinner at three o'clock and continue into the evening. Most of what they eat is produced on their own property. Their meal may start with a rich soup, followed by a choice of mutton, ham, beef, turkey, duck, greens, vegetables, potatoes, beets, and hominy, and end with pudding, tarts, and ice cream.

Portrait of the Children of William Rankin Sr., 1838. Oliver Tarbell Eddy. Oil on canvas, 71 x 60 in. Collection of The Newark Museum, Newark, NJ.

Arts & Entertainment

- American artists such as John Singleton Copley, Charles Wilson Peale, and Gilbert Charles Stuart paint portraits of notable Americans.
- In 1787 Royall Tyler's *The Contrast* is the first American comedy performed by professional actors. The play compares the English and American people.
- In 1815 the Handel and Haydn Society of Boston is founded to perform choral music, and the Philharmonic Society of New York is established in 1842.
- Something close to modern baseball evolves in the 1840s when the British game "rounders" is modified by the use of a hard ball and the tagging of runners.
- In rural areas, at corn-gathering time, as many as forty or fifty people may gather to dance, hold contests, eat, and tell jokes.

Paul Revere, 1768. John Singleton Copley. Oil on canvas, 35 x 28½ in. Museum of Fine Arts, Boston. Gift of Joseph W. Revere, William B. Revere, and Edward H. R. Revere.

1800
Library of Congress founded

1803
Ludwig van Beethoven completes his longest, grandest symphony, the *Third Symphony,* "Eroica"

1810

1814
Francis Scott Key, "Star Spangled Banner"

1825
First successful steam railroad is built in England

1825
Erie Canal opens

1826
First overland route to California opens

1830

1839
First successful photographic process, French physicist Louis Jacques Daguerre

1840
Samuel Morse patents telegraph

1849
Harriet Tubman escapes from slavery and joins the Underground Railroad

1850

Literature of the Time

PEOPLE ARE READING . . .

Magazines   Sarah Josepha Hale, American writer and editor, becomes well-known for being a forceful editor at *Ladies' Magazine* in Boston from 1828 to 1837 and at the *Godey's Lady's Book* in Philadelphia from 1837 to 1877. In addition to other works, in 1830 she writes *Poems for Our Children*, which contains the popular rhyme "Mary Had a Little Lamb."

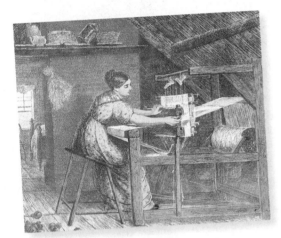

Newspapers   As of 1765, America has more than thirty newspapers, and by 1830 it has about a thousand. In 1833 Benjamin H. Day develops the "penny paper," which he says is designed "to lay before the public, at a price within the means of every one, all the news of the day."

◀ *The Frugal Housewife*
This bestseller by Lydia Maria Child is published in 1829. It is full of tips for cooking, house-keeping, and home remedies.

People Are Writing

About America   Americans and Europeans, ordinary and famous (including Charles Dickens), jot down their impressions of this new country. Some are published, such as Crévecoeur's *Letters of an American Farmer*, which describes the American as "a new man, who acts upon new principles."

About Politics   Americans like to express themselves on the issues of the day. Broadsides—sheets of papers containing various kinds of writing—are tacked up everywhere. The writing, though not sophisticated, is earnest and has popular appeal.

U.S.A.

1773 — Phillis Wheatley, *Poems on Various Subjects, Religious and Moral*

1783 — Noah Webster, *American Spelling Book*, the first attempt to standardize spelling of American English

1796 — Amelia Simmons, *American Cookery*

1750

1770

— China: Wu Ching-tzu, *The Scholars*

1790

1792 — England: Mary Wollstonecraft, *A Vindication of the Rights of Woman*

World

Literary Trends: From Reason to Romanticism

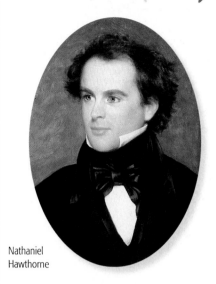

Nathaniel
Hawthorne

In the new century, as democracy is spreading, so is the importance of the common person. Romanticism, which focuses on individualism and the concerns of the heart, rather than the mind, emerges as a movement. Personal experience, emotions, intuition, the splendors of nature, and love of one's country find their way into poetry and prose. The new literature, still being shaped by European writing, begins to feature Americans dealing with American problems.

For the most part, as in the writings of Ralph Waldo Emerson, Romanticism is in tune with the optimism of the growing nation. However, the movement also has a dark side, expressed by such writers as Edgar Allan Poe and Nathaniel Hawthorne. Emerson finds Hawthorne's tales gloomy, while Hawthorne thinks Emerson is "a mystic, stretching his hand out of cloudland, in vain search for something real." Optimism and pessimism, individualism and nationalism, a love of nature and a fascination with the supernatural—all are part of the American consciousness.

Edgar Allan Poe

FOCUS ON . . .

The Transcendentalists

Transcendentalists such as Emerson believe that basic truths can be reached only by "going beyond," or transcending, reason and reflecting on the world of the spirit. Real knowledge, they argue, comes from a person's deep and free intuition and is available to everyone. They believe that the individual can transform the world—and that is what they aim to do, not only through their writings but through antislavery activity and other social action.

Ralph Waldo
Emerson

Nathaniel Hawthorne,
The Scarlet Letter

1817
William Cullen Bryant,
"Thanatopsis"

1828
Noah Webster, *American Dictionary of the English Language*

1841
Ralph Waldo Emerson,
"Self-Reliance" and
Essays

1849
Frances Parkman,
The Oregon Trail

1798
England: Samuel Taylor Coleridge and William Wordsworth, *Lyrical Ballads*

1810

1812–1815
Germany: *Grimm's Fairy Tales*

1833
Russia: Aleksandr Pushkin, *Eugene Onegin*

1830

1847
England: Charlotte Brontë (under pseudonym Currer Bell), *Jane Eyre*

1850

Novels of the Time

Stirred by the spirit of a young nation and its untarnished beauty, American writers during the second half of the eighteenth century hope to produce a truly American literature. At the same time, however, they remain strongly influenced by established European traditions. The first novels written by Americans use British models to explore American themes. Charles Brockden Brown's 1798 novel, Wieland, for example, follows the Gothic style—characterized by the grotesque and mysterious. By the 1820s, however, the first truly American novels emerge. By then, Romanticism is beginning to take hold in Europe—a movement stressing individualism, freedom from old forms, and a love of nature. American writers embrace the movement and make it their own.

The Last of the Mohicans
by James Fenimore Cooper (1826)

Cooper's popular five-part series *The Leather-Stocking Tales*, about a nature guide called Natty Bumppo, contains the first novels to depict realistic American frontier scenes and characters. *The Last of the Mohicans*, the second installment in the series, is set during the French and Indian War and portrays a group of Native Americans whose way of life is fast disappearing. The novel presents a thrilling chase, punctuated by captures, escapes, unexpected attacks, and heroic rescues. The novel contrasts two ways of life: the Native American's freedom and reverence of nature, and the settlers' drive to build farms and towns.

Two Years Before the Mast
by Richard Henry Dana (1840)

Dana's novel is based on his own experience on the crew of a ship for two years. Americans were fascinated by the day-to-day duties of a Yankee captain and crew. Dana's vivid descriptions of the captain's cruelty toward the crew lead to public outcry and legal action against such treatment aboard ship. The novel's factual details influence Herman Melville, whose novel *Moby-Dick* becomes the standard for all sea adventures.

U.S.A.			
		1789 — William Hill Brown, *The Power of Sympathy*	1792–1815 H. H. Brackenridge, *Modern Chivalry*
1750	1759–1767 England: Laurence Sterne, *Tristram Shandy* **1770**	1787 — Germany: Johann Wolfgang von Goethe, *The Sorrows of Young Werther*	**1790**
World			

Critics Corner

The Scarlet Letter Praised by a Peer

"[*The Scarlet Letter*] is so terrible in its pictures of diseased human nature as to produce most questionable delight. The reader's interest never flags for a moment. There is nothing of episode or digression. The author is always telling his one story with a concentration of energy which, as we can understand, must have made it impossible for him to deviate. The reader will certainly go on with it to the end very quickly, entranced, excited, shuddering, and at times almost wretched. His consolation will be that he too has been able to see into these black deeps of the human heart."

—Anthony Trollope, *The North American Review*,
September 1879

The Scarlet Letter
by Nathaniel Hawthorne (1850)

Rooted in American Puritanism, this tragic tale of colonial New England examines three complex characters—a woman who follows her heart rather than Puritan standards of behavior, a minister torn by guilt, and a husband consumed by hatred and revenge. Hawthorne, who calls this a novel of "frailty and human sorrow," peers deeply into the mind and heart of each character to reveal torturous moral dilemmas.

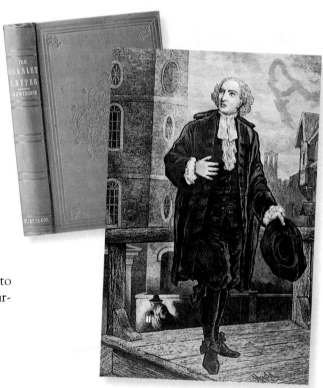

1798
Charles Brockden Brown, *Wieland*

1822
Washington Irving, *Bracebridge Hall*

1835
William Kilgore Simms, *The Yemansee*

1846
Herman Melville, *Typee*

1810

1825
England: Sir Walter Scott discloses his identity as the author of the popular *Waverly Novels,* a series of romantic tales

1830

France: Marie-Henri Beyle, also known as Stendhal, *The Red and the Black*

1840
Russia: Mikhail Lermontov, *A Hero of Our Time*

1850

Language of the Time

How People Speak

Americanisms   The term *Americanism* is used as early as 1781 to mean "a way of speaking peculiar to this country [America]." British visitors begin to notice Americanisms such as these:

Americanism	British Counterpart
clever	worthy, obliging
smart	clever
I guess	I suppose
elegant	excellent
I reckon	I think

Noah Webster

How People Write

An American Dictionary   Noah Webster proposes that the nation "have a system of our own, in language as well as government." In 1828 he publishes *An American Dictionary of the English Language*, with seventy thousand entries. It is fiercely attacked in Britain for its Americanized spelling and usage.

More Dictionaries   Between 1806 and 1860, thirty general dictionaries appear as people race to keep up with the flood of new terms and concepts pouring in from industry, science, and medicine. Finally, American writers have guides, though sometimes conflicting ones, to the spellings of both new and old words.

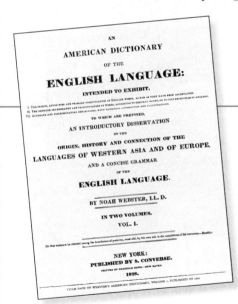

New Words and Expressions

"Native" Words   In the 1800s, expressions that are supposedly Native American enter American English. Actually these expressions have been made up by writers who imagine how Native Americans speak.

- Great White Father
- paleface
- warpath
- war paint
- How!

Dining Out   The French word *restaurant*, meaning an eating establishment, is used in America in 1827, even before it is used in England. Soon after that, diners are looking at *menu cards* or *menus*.

Theme 2

Breaking Free

From the time that we are old enough to do things for ourselves we crave independence. We want to have the freedom to try new things and to do them our own way. In what ways do you desire to be independent? Would you like to break free from any particular traditions or habits? The selections in this theme deal with the efforts of individuals and groups to break free.

THEME PROJECTS

Listening and Speaking

The individuals portrayed in these selections have vivid life experiences. Some of these experiences are the result of the individual's efforts to break free or begin anew. Other experiences inspire the desire for independence.

1. With a small group, choose three pieces of literature in this theme that you think best express the idea of breaking free.

2. Choose important parts of each selection to develop into a series of dramatic monologues and choral readings that express the theme. Try to arrange the monologues and readings in an order that brings out the theme powerfully.

3. Rehearse your series of readings and present it to the class.

Learning for Life

Create a Booklet   In their struggles to break free, the characters in these selections undergo strenuous times and difficulties in many settings.

1. Choose several characters presented in the selections. Then create a ten-page booklet of images that show how the characters represent the theme of breaking free.

2. Use a series of hand-drawn illustrations or collages to depict particular moments or change.

3. Write a brief caption or paragraph to help explain each visual.

4. Share your booklet with classmates.

Before You Read

from *The Autobiography of Benjamin Franklin* and
from *Poor Richard's Almanack*

Meet Benjamin Franklin

"The next thing most like living one's life over again seems to be a recollection of that life, and to make that recollection as durable as possible by putting it down in writing."

—*Franklin*

Even though he was born the tenth of seventeen children in an impoverished Boston family, Benjamin Franklin achieved success and fame as a printer, inventor, statesman, and writer. When Franklin was thirteen, he began working in his brother's print shop. Ten years later, he had his own thriving printing business and newspaper.

Franklin's many inventions include the lightning rod, bifocal eyeglasses, and the Franklin stove. He also first proposed daylight savings time. His experiments with lightning and electricity give him a permanent place in the history of science.

Franklin is best known for his diplomacy and his championship of liberty. He helped edit the Declaration of Independence, procured French aid for the colonies, and signed the Treaty of Paris.

In addition to speeches, letters, essays, and his annual almanac, Franklin wrote his autobiography.

Benjamin Franklin was born in 1706 and died in 1790.

FOCUS ACTIVITY

What are some familiar sayings or words to live by that you know or have heard?

DISCUSS Choose a favorite saying and share it with a group of classmates. Then put it in your own words and explain why it is effective.

SETTING A PURPOSE Read to learn some of Benjamin Franklin's sayings.

BACKGROUND

The Time and Place
The passage from Franklin's autobiography begins with his arrival in Philadelphia in the 1720s, when the city was a bustling metropolis of five thousand people.

Colonial Almanacs
Almanacs were one of the earliest types of publication and were the forerunners of today's magazines. Colonial almanacs provided a wide variety of content, including puzzles, articles, humor, and the common sense **aphorisms,** or witty sayings, of the type that made Franklin famous. Franklin published *Poor Richard's Almanack* every year for twenty-five years (1733–1758).

VOCABULARY PREVIEW

indentured (in den' chərd) *adj.* bound by contract to serve another person for a period of time; p. 131

ambulatory (am' byə lə tôr´ē) *adj.* moving from place to place; p. 131

ingenious (in jēn' yəs) *adj.* exhibiting creative ability; inventive; p. 131

infidel (in' fə del´) *n.* an unbeliever; p. 131

mortification (môr´ tə fi kā´ shən) *n.* feeling of shame, humiliation, or embarrassment; p. 132

from

The Autobiography of Benjamin Franklin

Benjamin Franklin ⌒

In the evening I found myself very feverish and went to bed; but having read some where that cold water drunk plentifully was good for fever, I followed the prescription and sweat plentifully most of the night. My fever left me, and in the morning, crossing the ferry, I proceeded on my journey on foot, having fifty miles to go to Burlington,[1] where I was told I should find boats that would carry me the rest of the way to Philadelphia.

It rained very hard all the day; I was thoroughly soaked, and by noon a good deal tired; so I stopped at a poor inn, where I stayed all night, beginning now to wish I had never left home. I made so miserable a figure, too, that I found, by the questions asked me, I was suspected to be some runaway indentured servant and in danger of being taken up on that suspicion. However, I proceeded next day and got in the evening to an inn within eight or ten miles of Burlington,

kept by one Dr. Brown. He entered into conversation with me while I took some refreshment, and finding I had read a little, became very obliging and friendly. Our acquaintance continued all the rest of his life. He had been, I imagine, an ambulatory quack doctor, for there was no town in England nor any country in Europe of which he could not give a very particular account. He had some letters,[2] and was ingenious, but he was an infidel, and wickedly undertook, some years after, to turn the Bible into doggerel[3] verse, as Cotton had formerly done with Virgil. By this means he set many facts in a ridiculous light, and might have done mischief with weak minds if his work had been published; but it never was.

At his house I lay that night, and arrived the next morning at Burlington, but had the

---

1. *Burlington,* New Jersey, is not far from Philadelphia, on the opposite side of the Delaware River.

2. Here, *letters* means "education or knowledge, especially of literature."

3. English poet Charles Cotton (1630–1687) wrote a *doggerel* version, or parody, of Virgil's epic poem the *Aeneid.*

Vocabulary

indentured (in den′ chərd) *adj.* bound by contract to serve another person for a period of time
ambulatory (am′ byə lə tôr′ ē) *adj.* moving from place to place
ingenious (in jēn′ yəs) *adj.* exhibiting creative ability; inventive
infidel (in′ fə del′) *n.* an unbeliever

Benjamin Franklin, Printer, c. 1928. John Ward Dunsmore. Oil on canvas, 28 x 36 in. The New York Historical Society, New York.

Viewing the painting: What might Benjamin Franklin have been discussing with the other people in this scene?

mortification to find that the regular boats were gone a little before, and no other expected to go before Tuesday, this being Saturday. Wherefore I returned to an old woman in the town, of whom I had bought some gingerbread to eat on the water, and asked her advice. She proposed to lodge me till a passage by some other boat occurred. I accepted her offer, being much fatigued by traveling on foot. Understanding I was a printer, she would have had me remain in that town and follow my business, being ignorant what stock was necessary to begin with. She was very hospitable, gave me a dinner of oxcheek with great good-will, accepting only of a pot of ale in return; and I thought myself fixed till Tuesday should come. However, walking in the evening by the side of the river, a boat came by, which I found was going toward Philadelphia with several people in her. They took me in, and as there was no wind we rowed all the way; and about midnight, not having yet seen the city, some of the company were confident we must have passed it and would row no further;

Vocabulary

mortification (môrʹ tə fi kāʹ shən) *n.* feeling of shame, humiliation, or embarrassment

the others knew not where we were, so we put toward the shore, got into a creek, landed near an old fence, with the rails of which we made a fire, the night being cold, in October, and there we remained till daylight. Then one of the company knew the place to be Cooper's Creek, a little above Philadelphia, which we saw as soon as we got out of the creek, and arrived there about eight or nine o'clock on the Sunday morning and landed at Market Street wharf.

I have been the more particular in this description of my journey, and shall be so of my first entry into that city, that you may in your mind compare such unlikely beginnings with the figure I have since made there. I was in my working dress, my best clothes coming round by sea. I was dirty, from my being so long in the boat. My pockets were stuffed out with shirts and stockings, and I knew no one nor where to look for lodging. Fatigued with walking, rowing, and the want of sleep, I was very hungry; and my whole stock of cash consisted in a single dollar, and about a shilling[4] in copper coin, which I gave to the boatmen for my passage. At first they refused it, on account of my having rowed; but I insisted on their taking it. Man is sometimes more generous when he has little money than when he has plenty; perhaps to prevent his being thought to have but little.

I walked toward the top of the street, gazing about till near Market Street, when I met a boy with bread. I had often made a meal of dry bread, and inquiring where he had bought it, I went immediately to the baker's he directed me to. I asked for biscuits, meaning such as we had at Boston; that sort, it seems, was not made at Philadelphia. I then asked for a threepenny loaf and was told they had none. Not knowing the different prices nor the names of the different sorts of bread, I told him to give me threepenny worth of any sort. He gave me accordingly three great puffy rolls. I was surprised at the quantity, but took it, and having no room in my pockets, walked off with a roll under each arm and eating the other. Thus I went up Market Street as far as Fourth Street, passing by the door of Mr. Read, my future wife's father; when she, standing at the door, saw me, and thought I made, as I certainly did, a most awkward, ridiculous appearance. Then I turned and went down Chestnut Street and part of Walnut Street, eating my roll all the way; and coming round found myself again at Market Street wharf, near the boat I came in, to which I went for a draught[5] of the river water; and being filled with one of my rolls, gave the other two to a woman and her child that came down the river in the boat with us and were waiting to go further.

Thus refreshed I walked again up the street, which by this time had many clean-dressed people in it, who were all walking the same way. I joined them, and thereby was led into the great meeting-house of the Quakers,[6] near the market. I sat down among them, and after looking round a while and hearing nothing said,[7] being very drowsy through labor and want of rest the preceding night, I fell fast asleep and continued so till the meeting broke up, when some one was kind enough to rouse me. This, therefore, was the first house I was in, or slept in, in Philadelphia.

---

4. A *shilling* is a British coin equal to one-twentieth of a pound.

5. Here, *draught* means "a gulp" or "a swallow."
6. *Quakers* are members of the Society of Friends, a Christian religious group founded in the seventeenth century.
7. Quaker religious meetings often include long periods of silence.

from POOR RICHARD'S ALMANACK

Benjamin Franklin

Who judges best of a man, his enemies or himself?

If you would keep your secret from an enemy,
   tell it not to a friend.

The worst wheel of the cart makes the most noise.

He that cannot obey, cannot command.

No gains without pains.

'Tis easier to prevent bad habits than to break them.

A rolling stone gathers no moss.

Today is yesterday's pupil.

Most fools think they are only ignorant.[1]

An empty bag cannot stand upright.

---

1. *Ignorant* means "uneducated" or "uninformed."

Experience keeps a dear[2] school, yet fools will learn
    in no other.

What signifies[3] your patience, if you can't find it
    when you want it.

He that lies down with dogs, shall rise up with fleas.

Well done is better than well said.

What you would seem to be, be really.

Honesty is the best policy.

Dost thou love life? Then do not squander time;
    for that's the stuff life is made of.

Keep thy shop, and thy shop will keep thee.

Beware of little expenses,
    a small leak will sink a great ship.

A penny saved is a penny earned.

Don't count your chickens before they are hatched.

Buy what thou hast no need of;
    and e'er long thou shalt sell thy necessaries.

Not to oversee workmen, is to leave them your purse open.

Fish and visitors smell in three days.

Quarrels never could last long,
    if on one side only lay the wrong.

Love thy neighbor; yet don't pull down your hedge.

---

2. Here, *dear* means "expensive."
3. *Signifies* means "has importance or meaning."

Responding to Literature

Personal Response

Do you think you would have felt as young Franklin did arriving in a new city, with little money, no place to live, and no job? Explain.

ANALYZING LITERATURE

from
The Autobiography of Benjamin Franklin

RECALL AND INTERPRET

1. Whom does Franklin meet before he takes the boat to Philadelphia? What do you learn about him from these encounters?
2. Why do the boatmen at first refuse to accept money from Franklin? Why do you think he offers to pay?
3. What does Franklin do during the Quakers' meeting? What do you think the last sentence of this selection reveals about Franklin?

EVALUATE AND CONNECT

4. How important is self-reliance in the world today? Do you think people are more or less self-reliant today than they were in Franklin's time? Explain.

from
POOR RICHARD'S ALMANACK

RECALL AND INTERPRET

5. According to Franklin, how can a secret be kept from an enemy? Describe in your own words the advice given in the second saying.
6. What does Franklin say will sink a great ship? What do you think he means by this?
7. In the final aphorism, what does Franklin say about "thy neighbor"? What might he mean by "don't pull down your hedge"?

EVALUATE AND CONNECT

8. In your opinion, which aphorism gives the best advice? Explain.

Literary ELEMENTS

Aphorisms

Aphorisms are short, memorable statements that convey a general truth or an observation about life. The aphorisms that Franklin wrote in *Poor Richard's Almanack* reflect his clever use of language. For example, when Franklin says, "An empty bag cannot stand upright," he presents a humorous **metaphor** for a spineless person who can't stand up for his or her beliefs.

1. Choose one aphorism. Explain how Franklin's word choices help make it easy to remember.
2. Using language of today and references to contemporary life, reword one of Franklin's aphorisms.

● See **Literary Terms Handbook,** p. R1.

LITERATURE AND WRITING

Writing About Literature
Personality Profile   What do you know about Franklin from the two selections that you have read? What personal characteristics does Franklin reveal? Use the personal details and experiences that Franklin presents to create a personality profile of Franklin as a young man. Use vivid language and quotes from the selections to enliven Franklin's profile.

Creative Writing
Advice by Aphorism   The colonists found advice in the aphorisms of the *Almanack,* while today we read advice columns in the newspaper. Select a letter written to a newspaper advice columnist and compose an aphorism that sums up your advice to the letter writer. Refer to your response to the Focus Activity on page 130 and review the elements that made your favorite saying effective. Then use those elements to help you write your own aphorism.

EXTENDING YOUR RESPONSE

Literature Groups
Getting the Point   The meanings of some of Franklin's aphorisms, such as "Honesty is the best policy," are clear and straightforward. With others, however, the meaning must be inferred, or figured out. Take turns in your group choosing the aphorisms you find most thought-provoking, or perhaps hardest to understand, and discuss their meanings with your group.

Listening and Speaking
On My Own   Ask one or more family members or older friends to recall a time in their life when they went out on their own, had to make a new start, or, like Franklin, arrived in a city as a stranger. Invite them to discuss the thoughts and feelings they had at the time. Take notes or tape record their memories and then share the oral histories with your classmates.

Internet Connection
Franklin on the Web   You can find the entire text of Benjamin Franklin's *Autobiography* on-line, made available by Project Gutenberg. For further information about Franklin, including a visit to the Benjamin Franklin National Memorial, type "Benjamin Franklin" into a search engine and surf the Web sites listed.

Save your work for your portfolio.

Skill Minilesson

VOCABULARY   • The Latin Root *gen*

The word *ingenious* contains the Latin root *gen,* which means "to give birth to" or "to produce." To *generate* is to bring into existence.

Recognizing the root *gen* in an unfamiliar word can help you get a sense of the word's meaning.

PRACTICE   Use your knowledge of the root *gen* and these clues to match each word to its meaning.

Clues: *con-* means "with"; *de-* means "away from"; *pro-* means "forth"; *primo-* means "first"; *-alogy* means "the study of"

1. congenital
2. degenerate
3. progeny
4. primogenitor
5. genealogy

a. offspring
b. oldest ancestor
c. acquired at birth
d. recorded history of one's ancestry
e. to fall away from a former condition

Before You Read

Dichos

Meet Américo Paredes

❝The proverb presents conventional wisdom in a neat package . . .❞

—*Paredes*

To many people it might not sound like work at all: visiting restaurants and other public gathering places and listening to people tell jokes. Yet, some of Américo Paredes's most serious writings are his analyses of such informal humor. Paredes is a folklorist—a scholar who collects and records the oral traditions, including the sayings, beliefs, tales, and practices of a particular people. His focus is the folklore of Mexican Americans. Having grown up in a Mexican American family that has called the Rio Grande region of Texas home since the 1700s, Paredes brings an insider's insight to his work. He was a professor at the University of Texas at Austin for more than forty years, teaching anthropology and English. Paredes is also a prolific poet, has published a novel, and has been a professional singer, guitarist, and composer, performing throughout the Texas-Mexico border region. His essay "Dichos" appeared in the book *Mexican-American Authors* in 1972.

❝. . . For I was born beside your waters,
And since very young I knew
That my soul had hidden currents,
That my soul resembled you, . . .❞

—*Paredes*

Américo Paredes was born in 1915 in Brownsville, Texas, and died in 1999.

FOCUS ACTIVITY

Think of an occasion when you made what you would classify as a perfect comment—or when you later thought of what would have been a perfect comment.

DISCUSS In a small group, share your "perfect" sayings and describe the situations in which they occurred. Discuss possible improvements on the sayings.

SETTING A PURPOSE Read to learn what *dichos* are and how they are helpful to speakers and writers.

BACKGROUND

Literary Influences

A rich oral tradition has always been an important part of Mexican American culture. This culture includes people who have lived in Texas, New Mexico, and California since Europeans first came to North America. It also embraces the urban lifestyles of the Mexican American neighborhoods of most major cities in the United States. Paredes sheds light on this varied culture with his collection of sayings in common usage among Mexican Americans.

VOCABULARY PREVIEW

distinctive (dis ting′ tiv) *adj.* different in quality or kind; separate; p. 139

absolute (ab′ sə lo͞ot′) *adj.* complete; certain; final; p. 140

sluggard (slug′ ərd) *n.* one who is usually lazy or idle; p. 141

conspire (kən spīr′) *v.* to join or act together, especially to carry out some secret or evil deed or for a hidden or illegal purpose; p. 141

Peasants, 1947.
Diego Rivera.
Oil on canvas.
Museu de Arte,
São Paulo, Brazil.

Américo Paredes :~

Proverbs have been called "the wisdom of many and the wit of one." They are "the wit of one" because it was some one person, at some particular time and place, who put the thought of each proverb into just the right words. To put something into "just the right words" is to create poetry, and the unknown persons who created proverbs were poets in their own right. Proverbs are "the wisdom of many" because they express the feelings and attitudes of whole groups of people rather than just the feelings of an individual. They are part of the literature of <u>distinctive</u> groups of people that we refer to as "folk." That is, proverbs are one of the basic forms of folk poetry, and a very ancient kind. Proverbs are found in the Old Testament, for example.

The formal word for "proverb" in Spanish is *refrán* but most Mexicans and Mexican-Americans call them *dichos,*[1] "sayings." They are a special way of saying things, of making a point, and they are used in ordinary conversation everywhere that Mexican-Americans speak to each other in Spanish, whether

---

1. *refrán* (rä frän′), *dichos* (dē′ chōs)

Vocabulary
distinctive (dis ting′ tiv) *adj.* different in quality or kind; separate

Dichos

on a farm in South Texas or at a steel mill in Gary, Indiana. To those unfamiliar with the culture, the effect of *dichos* is to make the language "colorful." To the sayer of *dichos*, they are a time-honored way of expressing himself, of putting over a point in just the right way.

Dichos do not contain absolute truths; that is, they are not a set of rules telling one exactly how to behave at all times. They are a storehouse of good advice to be used according to specific situations. That is why two *dichos* may give opposite advice. This is also true of proverbs in English; for example, "Look before you leap" and "He who hesitates is lost."

There are two kinds of *dichos* most commonly used. One is called by folklorists[2] the "true proverb." It is always a complete statement, a sentence. It is also a complete little poem, using the same kinds of effects that are found in other poetry. One of the simplest poetic effects, and perhaps the oldest, is balanced structure—the balancing of the two parts of the *dicho* on either side of a center, like two weights on an old-fashioned type of scales. For example: *Arrieros somos / y en el camino andamos.*[3] This is the same type of structure used in the Old Testament, in the Psalms: "The Lord is my shepherd; / I shall not want."

Contrast may be added to balanced structure, and the effect is even more pleasing. In the following *dichos* the two underlined words are contrasted with each other: *Mucho ruido / y pocas nueces; A buena hambre / no hay mal pan.*[4] Another effect is made by adding rhyme, as in much poetry we are familiar with: *Cada oveja / con su pareja; A Dios rogando / y con el mazo dando.*[5] Other *dichos* may use alliteration, the repetition of the first sounds of words, rather than the final sounds as in rhyme—"rough and ready." Alliteration is not common in Spanish poetry, but assonance is used very frequently. In assonance, only the vowel sounds are matched (*olas* and *hoja*, for example), instead of vowel and consonant sounds, as we do to make rhymes (*olas* and *solas*). The following *dicho* uses both assonance and alliteration: *Quien da pan a perro ajeno / pierde el pan y pierde el perro.*[6]

The other kind of *dicho* is known as a "comparison." It is not a complete sentence, but a phrase beginning with the word *como*, "like." Most *dichos* of this kind have stories behind them, stories that everybody knows, so that when somebody says, "I was left there like the man who whistled on the hill," everybody knows just how the speaker was left—holding the bag.

(*These* dichos *were collected and translated by* Américo Paredes.)

True Proverbs

A buena hambre no hay mal pan.
> No food is bad when you're good and hungry.

A Dios rogando y con el mazo dando.
> Pray to God, but keep hammering away (at your problem).

¿A dónde ha de ir el buey, que no ha de seguir arando?
> Where can the ox go that he will not have to plow? (Where can a poor man go, that he

---

2. **Folklorists** study the tales, beliefs, customs, and traditions of a people as handed down from generation to generation orally.

3. *arrieros somos / y en el camino andamos* (ar′ rē er′ ōs sō′ mōs ē en el kə mē′ nō än dä′ mōs) This proverb and the next two are fully translated later in the selection.

4. *Mucho ruido / y pocas nueces; A buena hambre / no hay mal pan* (mōō′ chō rōō ē′ dō ē pō′ käs nwä′ säs ä bwe′ nä äm′ brä nō ī mäl pän) The underlined words mean, in order, "much," "few," "good," and "bad."

5. *Cada oveja / con su pareja; A Dios rogando / y con el mazo dando* (kä′ dä ō vä′ hä′ kôn sōō pä rä′ hä′ ä dyōs rō gän′ dō ē kôn el mä′ zō dän′ dō)

6. *Quien da pan a perro ajeno / pierde el pan y pierde el perro* (kēen dä pän ä per′ rō ä hä′ nō pē er′ dä el pän ē pē er′ dä el per′ rō)

Vocabulary
absolute (ab′ sə lōōt′) *adj.* complete; certain; final

will not be given the hardest kind of job for the lowest pay?)

Ahora es cuando, yerbabuena, le has de dar sabor al caldo.
Now is the time, peppermint, when you must flavor the soup. (Now is the time to do or die; now or never; put up or shut up.)

Al pan, pan y al vino, vino.
Let us call bread, bread and wine, wine. (Be realistic.)

Arrieros somos y en el camino andamos.
We are all drovers,[7] traveling down the same road. (We are all the same, living in the same hard world; we are all in it together; the world is not so wide that we will not meet again.)

Cada oveja con su pareja.
Each ewe to its ram. (To each his own.)

Cada quien en su casa, y Dios en la de todos.
Each man in his house, and God in all houses. (Let each man mind his own business, and God will smile on all of us.)

Caras vemos, corazones no sabemos.
We see their faces, but we do not know their hearts.

Como quiera nace el maíz, estando la tierra en punto.
Nothing will keep the corn from growing, as long as the land is ready. (Nothing will stop us, if we have planned well.)

Cuando se pelean las comadres, salen las verdades.
When gossips fight, then truths will out.

Da y ten, y harás bien.
Give (some of your goods) and keep (a part), and you will do well.

El flojo y el mezquino andan dos veces el camino.
The sluggard and the miser[8] travel the same road twice. (Lazy and stingy people do not give their all to what they do, so they often have to do it again.)

El pan ajeno hace al hijo bueno.
Another man's food will make your son good. (Going out into the world and earning his own keep makes a son more considerate of his parents.)

Él que carga su costal sabe lo que lleva dentro.
He who shoulders the bag knows what he carries in it. (No one really knows your troubles except yourself.)

Él que con lobos anda, a aullar se enseña.
He who runs with wolves will learn to howl. (If you run around with unsavory[9] characters, you will pick up their ways.)

Él que nace pa' tamal, del cielo le caen las hojas.
If you're born to be a *tamal*, heaven will send you the cornshucks. (Tamales are made wrapped in cornshucks, so they go together like hamburgers and buns. You will be what you're going to be, and circumstances will conspire to keep you from being anything else.)

---

7. A group of animals moving or being driven along together is called a *drove,* and *drovers* are the people who keep the group moving.

8. A *miser* is someone who is reluctant to give or spend money.
9. Characters who are *unsavory* have criminal, evil, or morally offensive qualities.

Vocabulary
sluggard (slug′ərd) *n.* one who is usually lazy or idle
conspire (kən spīr′) *v.* to join or act together, especially to carry out some secret or evil deed or for a hidden or illegal purpose

Dichos

Él que no habla, Dios no lo oye.
> If you don't speak up, God will not hear you. (You have to speak up for your rights, or you won't get them.)

Entre menos burros, más olotes.
> The fewer donkeys, the more corncobs. (The fewer to share, the more to go around.)

Es poco el amor, ¡y gastándolo en celos!
> So little love—why waste it in jealous quarrels? (Let us not waste the little we have.)

Haz bien, y no mires a quien.
> Do good, without caring to whom.

Las cuentas claras y el chocolate espeso.
> I like my accounts clear and my chocolate thick.

Lo pescaron en las tunas, con las manos coloradas.
> They caught him in the prickly-pear patch, with his hands all red.

Los golpes hacen al buen vaquero.
> Hard knocks make a good horseman.

Manso como un cordero, mientras hago lo que quiero.
> I'm as gentle as a lamb, as long as I'm doing what I want to do.

Más vale pobre que solo.
> It's better to be poor than to live alone.

Mucho ruido y pocas nueces.
> Much noise and few nuts (harvested or shelled). (Much ado about nothing.)

No creas que la luna es queso, nomás porque la ves redonda.
> Don't think the moon is made of cheese, just because you see it's round.

Comparisons

Como agua pa' chocolate.
> Like water for making chocolate. (Very hot, that is. When someone is very angry, he is "like water for making chocolate.")

Como atole de enfermo.
> Like a sick man's gruel.[10] (This is all a sick man is fed, so it stands for something that is very boring, that you just can't stand any more.)

Como el burro del aguador (or del zacatero).
> Like the water seller's (or the hay seller's) burro. (The poor burro carries water or hay on his back all day, for sale, but he never gets any of it. When you are close to something you want very much but cannot have it, you say you are like the water seller's burro.)

Como él que chifló en la loma.
> Like the man who whistled on the hill. (There is a story about several thieves or smugglers who posted one man on a hill as a lookout. The lookout was supposed to whistle, to warn them if police were coming. But the others saw the police officers before the lookout did, and they ran away. When the lookout saw the officers, he began to whistle as loudly as he could; but nobody answered him. So he kept whistling and whistling until he was caught.)

---

10. *Gruel* is a thin porridge.

Responding to Literature

Personal Response

Which three *dichos* are your favorites? Why do you like each *dicho* you selected?

——— ANALYZING LITERATURE ———

RECALL AND INTERPRET

1. Why does Paredes call proverbs "the wisdom of many and the wit of one"? How is Paredes's wit expressed in the proverbs *(dichos)* he chooses for this selection? Explain your answer.
2. According to Paredes, what are the effects of a *dicho* on the language? On the speaker of the *dicho?* Do you agree? Explain.
3. How do comparisons differ from true proverbs? Which type of *dichos,* in your opinion, would be more easily understood by non-Mexican American listeners? Why?
4. Name two poetic devices that Paredes mentions. What do you think might be the effect of these devices on the person hearing a *dicho?*

EVALUATE AND CONNECT

5. Theme Connections   In terms of **imagery** and meaning, which *dicho* might add to a conversation on the concept of "breaking free"? Explain.
6. The *dichos* in this selection are all translated from Spanish. Which do not seem to translate well into English? Explain why you think these particular *dichos* do not translate as well as others.
7. Do any of these *dichos* seem similar in meaning to any English sayings or proverbs that you know? Discuss the similarities.
8. Are any of these *dichos* similar to the "perfect response" you discussed for the Focus Activity on page 138? If so, explain the similarities. If not, try to turn your "perfect response" into a *dicho.*

Literary ELEMENTS

Exposition

Exposition, along with description, narration, and persuasion, is a type of prose writing. Expository writing informs and explains, using a variety of techniques including definition, illustration, analysis, and classification. In "Dichos," Américo Paredes defines the term *dichos,* illustrates the definition with examples, analyzes the poetic qualities of *dichos,* and classifies them according to type.

1. In "Dichos," find examples of the four methods of exposition.
2. What information from Paredes's essay did you find most helpful in understanding the *dichos?*

● See **Literary Terms Handbook,** p. R6.

——— EXTENDING YOUR RESPONSE ———

Literature and Writing

Guide to Often-Used Proverbs   Write a brief essay on proverbs in the English language. Use Paredes's essay as a model. To begin, list proverbs you already know. Ask friends and family to add to your list. Look through books of proverbs. Try finding proverbs on the Internet. Then choose your favorites, and use them as examples.

Learning for Life

Creating a Storyboard   Choose one of your favorite *dichos* and create a storyboard for an animated cartoon to illustrate it. Use the *dicho* as the title of the cartoon or include it as dialogue.

📖 **Save your work for your portfolio.**

COMPARING
selections

COMPARE **TECHNIQUES**

Paredes's essay discusses the different poetic effects used in the *dichos*—
balanced structure, contrast, rhyme, alliteration, and assonance.

● What similarities and differences do you see in the techniques that Franklin and
Paredes used?

● Try to write some of the *dichos* in Franklin's style and some of Franklin's sayings
more in the style of a *dicho*.

COMPARE **ADVICE**

Franklin's aphorisms and Paredes's *dichos* both give advice.

● In your opinion, which of the aphorisms and *dichos* give
the best advice? Which give the worst advice? Discuss
and provide real-life examples.

● With a partner, write a skit of someone asking advice
of either Franklin or Paredes. For your script, describe
modern-day problems that might be solved by the
advice of one or more of the sayings or *dichos*.

Peasants, 1947.

COMPARE **CULTURES**

Franklin and Paredes come from very different times and cultures. Investigate whether
the advice they give reflects any differences in values, imagery, or humor.

1. Identify three or more categories to classify some of the aphorisms and the *dichos*.
   For example, both kinds give advice about spending money. On a large chart, list
   sayings and *dichos* that fall into each category. Is the advice similar?

2. Look for additional sayings from different cultures. You can use books of proverbs,
   quotations, or folklore, and do research on the Internet. Add these to your chart.

3. With the class, discuss similarities or differences in values you note by comparing
   sayings from different cultures or time periods.

LISTENING, SPEAKING, and VIEWING

Analyzing Advertising Slogans

As Américo Paredes explains, people remember *dichos* because the sayings use just the right words. Advertising slogans are somewhat similar to *dichos* in that they are meant to be memorable—to stay in our minds and influence our buying decisions. Like *dichos* they might have two balanced parts or use contrasting words within a statement. Other times, they use alliteration (repeated first sounds of words) or assonance (repeated vowel sounds). Some might compare one thing to another. Following are some advertising slogans that use these techniques:

Balanced parts: "The quality of platinum. The strength of steel."
Balanced parts with contrast: "Tough on stains. Easy on your hands."
Alliteration or assonance: "Discover the difference."
                              "Care for what you wear."
Comparison: "Like the tools your grandfather cherished."

When you see or hear such slogans, certain images usually come to mind. These mental images connect you with the slogan's message and help you to remember it. Also, because of a slogan's rhythm, rhyme, or perhaps its association with a catchy tune or melody, you often "hear" a slogan over and over in your mind, which in turn helps you remember it. Viewing slogans on billboards or on television fixes the words visually in your mind, and when you see or hear the slogan again, you are more easily persuaded because you are familiar with the message. Being aware of advertising techniques can help you understand how slogans persuade you to buy a product or service.

ACTIVITY

As you watch a television program or listen to the radio, jot down any ads you hear that use the techniques mentioned. Analyze the words and/or the visuals of the ads to determine what makes the ads effective. Then use similar techniques to create and present an advertising slogan for a product you use every day. Use visuals and/or music to help you present your slogan in a memorable and persuasive way.

Before You Read

Speech to the Second Virginia Convention

Meet Patrick Henry

"**Give me liberty, or give me death.**"

—*Henry*

On March 23, 1775, Patrick Henry stood before fellow delegates at the Second Virginia Convention and thundered his famous challenge. Thomas Marshall, a delegate to the convention, recalled that the speech was "one of the most bold, vehement, and animated pieces of eloquence that had ever been delivered."

As a young lawyer, Henry developed his gift for public speaking. That talent served him well when he became a member of the Virginia House of Burgesses at the age of twenty-nine.

Supporting the colonists' right to make their own laws, Henry defiantly exclaimed, "If this be treason, make the most of it." For the next decade, he continued to argue boldly for colonial rights.

A man of action as well as a compelling speaker, Henry played a prominent role in the Revolution that soon followed his famous speech. In 1776, as the battles of the Revolution raged around them, the citizens of Virginia elected Henry to be the first governor of the commonwealth under its new constitution. He served three terms as governor.

Patrick Henry was born in 1736 and died in 1799.

FOCUS ACTIVITY

What does the phrase "Give me liberty, or give me death" mean to you?

LIST IDEAS In your journal, explore some of the liberties you enjoy. Would you risk your life to preserve any one of these freedoms? Why or why not?

SETTING A PURPOSE Read to find out what Patrick Henry says about liberty.

BACKGROUND

The Time and Place
The speech you are about to read was delivered in 1775 to the Second Virginia Convention meeting in Richmond, Virginia.

Colonists' Protests
The Seven Years War with France in the mid-eighteenth century strained Britain's treasury. Consequently, the British Parliament passed a series of taxes on its colonies designed to replenish Britain's treasury. American colonists protested these taxes, and thousands of British troops were sent to Boston to keep the peace.

VOCABULARY PREVIEW

arduous (är′jōō əs) *adj.* requiring great exertion or endurance; difficult; p. 148
insidious (in sid′ē əs) *adj.* slyly treacherous and deceitful; deceptive; p. 148
subjugation (sub′jə gā′ shən) *n.* act of bringing under control; domination; p. 148
remonstrate (ri mon′strāt) *v.* to object; to protest; p. 148
spurn (spurn) *v.* to reject with disdain; p. 149

Patrick Henry Arguing the Parson's Cause. Artist unknown. Oil on canvas. Virginia Historical Society, Richmond.

Speech to the Second Virginia Convention

Patrick Henry ~

MR. PRESIDENT:[1] No man thinks more highly than I do of the patriotism, as well as abilities, of the very worthy gentlemen who have just addressed the house. But different men often see the same subject in different lights; and, therefore, I hope it will not be thought disrespectful to those gentlemen, if, entertaining,[2] as I do, opinions of a character very opposite to theirs, I shall speak forth my sentiments freely and without reserve. This is no time for ceremony.

---

1. *Mr. President* refers to Peyton Randolph, president of the Virginia Convention.
2. In this case, *entertaining* means "having in mind."

The question before the house is one of awful moment[3] to this country. For my own part, I consider it as nothing less than a question of freedom or slavery. And in proportion to the magnitude of the subject ought to be the freedom of the debate. It is only in this way that we can hope to arrive at truth, and fulfill the great responsibility which we hold to God and our country. Should I keep back my opinions at such a time, through fear of giving offense, I should consider myself as guilty of treason toward my country, and of an act of disloyalty toward the Majesty of Heaven, which I revere above all earthly kings.

Mr. President, it is natural for man to indulge in the illusions of hope. We are apt to shut our eyes against a painful truth, and listen to the song of that siren, till she transforms us into beasts. Is this the part of wise men, engaged in a great and arduous struggle for liberty? Are we disposed to be of the number of those who, having eyes, see not, and having ears, hear not, the things which so nearly concern their temporal[4] salvation? For my part, whatever anguish of spirit it may cost, I am willing to know the whole truth; to know the worst and to provide for it.

I have but one lamp by which my feet are guided; and that is the lamp of experience. I know of no way of judging of the future but by the past. And judging by the past, I wish to know what there has been in the conduct of the British ministry for the last ten years to justify those hopes with which gentlemen have been pleased to solace themselves and the House? Is it that insidious smile with which our petition

Give me liberty,

has been lately received? Trust it not, sir; it will prove a snare to your feet. Suffer not yourselves to be betrayed with a kiss. Ask yourselves how this gracious reception of our petition comports with these warlike preparations which cover our waters and darken our land. Are fleets and armies necessary to a work of love and reconciliation? Have we shown ourselves so unwilling to be reconciled, that force must be called in to win back our love? Let us not deceive ourselves, sir. These are the implements of war and subjugation; the last arguments to which kings resort. I ask gentlemen, sir, what means this martial array,[5] if its purpose be not to force us to submission? Can gentlemen assign any other possible motives for it? Has Great Britain any enemy, in this quarter of the world, to call for all this accumulation of navies and armies? No, sir, she has none. They are meant for us; they can be meant for no other. They are sent over to bind and rivet upon us those chains which the British ministry have been so long forging. And what have we to oppose to them? Shall we try argument? Sir, we have been trying that for the last ten years. Have we anything new to offer on the subject? Nothing. We have held the subject up in every light of which it is capable; but it has been all in vain. Shall we resort to entreaty[6] and humble supplication?[7] What terms shall we find which have not been already exhausted? Let us not, I beseech you, sir, deceive ourselves longer. Sir, we have done everything that could be done to avert the storm which is now coming on. We have petitioned; we have remonstrated; we have

---

3. The phrase *of awful moment* means "of great consequence."
4. The word *temporal* means "in time; relating to life on earth."

5. A *martial array* is a military display.
6. An *entreaty* is a plea or request.
7. Here, *supplication* means "begging."

Vocabulary

arduous (är′jŏŏ əs) *adj.* requiring great exertion or endurance; difficult
insidious (in sid′ ē əs) *adj.* slyly treacherous and deceitful; deceptive
subjugation (sub′ jə gā′ shən) *n.* act of bringing under control; domination
remonstrate (ri mon′ strāt) *v.* to object; to protest

supplicated; we have prostrated[8] ourselves before the tyrannical hands of the ministry and parliament. Our petitions have been slighted; our remonstrances have produced additional violence and insult; our supplications have been disregarded; and we have been <u>spurned</u>, with contempt, from the foot of the throne. In vain, after these things, may we indulge the fond[9] hope of peace and reconciliation. There is no longer any room for hope. If we wish to be free—if we mean to preserve inviolate[10] those inestimable privileges for which we have been so long contending—if we mean not basely[11] to abandon the noble struggle in which we have been so long engaged, and which we have pledged ourselves never to abandon until the glorious

or give me death!

object of our contest shall be obtained, we must fight! I repeat it, sir, we must fight! An appeal to arms and to the God of Hosts is all that is left us!

They tell us, sir, that we are weak; unable to cope with so formidable an adversary. But when shall we be stronger? Will it be the next week, or the next year? Will it be when we are totally disarmed, and when a British guard shall be stationed in every house? Shall we gather strength by irresolution and inaction? Shall we acquire the means of effectual resistance by lying supinely on our backs, and hugging the delusive phantom of hope, until our enemies shall have bound us hand and foot? Sir, we are not weak, if we make a proper use of the means which the God of nature hath placed in our power. Three millions of people, armed in the holy cause of liberty, and in such a country as that which we possess, are invincible by any force which our enemy can send against us. Besides, sir, we shall not fight our battles alone. There is a just God who presides over the destinies of nations; and who will raise friends to fight our battles for us. The battle, sir, is not to the strong alone; it is to the vigilant, the active, the brave. Besides, sir, we have no election.[12] If we were base enough to desire it, it is now too late to retire from the contest. There is no retreat but in submission and slavery! Our chains are forged! Their clanking may be heard on the plains of Boston! The war is inevitable—and let it come! I repeat it, sir, let it come!

It is in vain, sir, to extenuate[13] the matter. Gentlemen may cry peace, peace—but there is no peace. The war is actually begun! The next gale that sweeps from the North will bring to our ears the clash of resounding arms![14] Our brethren are already in the field! Why stand we here idle? What is it that gentlemen wish? What would they have? Is life so dear, or peace so sweet, as to be purchased at the price of chains and slavery? Forbid it, Almighty God! I know not what course others may take; but as for me, give me liberty, or give me death!

---

8. *Prostrated* means "bowed down."
9. Here, *fond* means "foolish."
10. The word *inviolate* means "unharmed and intact."
11. Here, *basely* means "dishonorably."

12. In this instance, *election* means "choice."
13. To *extenuate* means "to make a situation seem less serious by offering excuses."
14. *[The next gale . . . arms!]* Colonists in Massachusetts were already engaged in open opposition to the British.

Vocabulary
spurn (spurn) *v.* to reject with disdain

Responding to Literature

Personal Response

On a scale of 1–5, how convincing is Patrick Henry's speech? Explain.

unconvincing • —— • —— • —— • —— • convincing
1   2   3   4   5

———— ANALYZING LITERATURE ————

RECALL AND INTERPRET

1. To what two choices facing the colonists does Patrick Henry refer in his opening lines? How does he defend his need to speak about them?
2. Why does Henry feel that he must speak freely? Why, do you think, does he give so many reasons to support his need to speak out?
3. What does Henry say to the argument that the colonists are no match for the British military? What does he imply in the statement, "There is a just God who presides over the destinies of nations. . . ."?
4. What are the choices Henry recognizes for himself as he concludes his speech? How might these words summarize his position?

EVALUATE AND CONNECT

5. Which emotions come through in the speech? In your opinion, does Henry's passion add to his effectiveness? Explain.
6. What choices for the colonists does Henry outline? In your opinion, does he include all of the possible choices in his fiery speech? Explain.
7. To what situation does Henry compare the injustices suffered by the colonists? In your opinion, is this comparison justified? Explain.
8. Consider the freedoms you listed for the Focus Activity on page 146 in light of Patrick Henry's passion for liberty. Select an item from your list, and explain to what extent you would defend it.

Literary ELEMENTS

Author's Purpose

Political decisions are not made without passion and dissension, and these elements are reflected in political speeches. A committed speaker such as Patrick Henry must make every word count by supporting arguments and appealing to the hearts and minds of the audience.

1. What, in your opinion, is the purpose of Henry's speech? What is he trying to accomplish?
2. Henry uses two techniques extensively—**rhetorical questions** and **literary allusions.** Choose one example of each technique and explain how it furthers the speaker's purpose.

● See **Literary Terms Handbook,** p. R13.

———— EXTENDING YOUR RESPONSE ————

Performing

Freedom's Firebrand   Eyewitnesses report that Patrick Henry's speech rose to a dramatic climax. The orator, with wrists held together as if in chains and head bowed, sank to one knee, then rose up and yanked apart the imaginary chains. At the words ". . . or give me death!" he plunged an imaginary dagger into his heart. Plan and present a dramatic reading of Henry's speech.

Creative Writing

Reporting the News   Place yourself in pre-Revolutionary America. Write a news report on Patrick Henry's speech to the Second Virginia Convention. Summarize the speech, and provide your readers with background material by reporting on the events leading up to his speech.

📖 **Save your work for your portfolio.**

Magazine Article

Are today's political speakers as exciting as Patrick Henry? Could they persuade anyone to break free? Modern-day writer Wen Smith gives his opinion.

Give Me Rhetoric!
What if Patrick Henry had said things a little differently?

by Wen Smith—*Saturday Evening Post*, September/October, 1996

My wife touched my shoulder. "Wake up! You've snored through the last ten minutes of the convention."

"I wasn't snoring," I said. "I was helping Patrick Henry write a speech."

"Sure you were."

"Really," I said. "He was writing on a pad. Wads of yellow paper were strewn around him. He was complaining about how hard it is to get the wording just right."

"Go back to sleep," she said, and turned back to the TV. I slipped again into my reverie with Patrick Henry.

"I know what I want to say," he said, "but I'm not saying it right. This rhetoric business is tough going."

"What are you trying to say?" I asked him.

"It's all about freedom," he said. "You know how precious that is."

"Sure," I said. "If you're not free, you're dead."

"That's it!" he said. "Now I just have to get that into

the right words and put 'em in the right order."

I thought I had done that for him, but he ignored my version. He scratched on the pad again, ripped off the sheet, and threw it to the floor.

"When we orators get up to speak," he said, "we don't want to depend too much on a prepared script. We want to be at liberty to . . ."

"*Liberty!*" I exclaimed. "Maybe that's the word."

"Eureka!" he said.

"This will work!" he said, scratching again at his yellow pad. He stood up and raised his right hand in a gesture.

"Give me liberty, or give me death!"

"Bingo!" I shouted.

My own voice woke me. The candidates were still talking on the TV. I turned to my wife. "The rhetoric's not very exciting."

"Orators these days aren't what they used to be," my wife said.

"I know," I said. "They used to work at it."

Respond

1. What does Wen Smith seem to be saying about the process of writing?

2. What, do you think, are Smith and his wife saying about today's "orators," or political speakers?

Literature **F O C U S**

Analyzing Essays

An essay is any fairly short, nonfiction work that explores the author's opinions and ideas on a topic. French writer Michel de Montaigne is credited with writing the first essays. In 1580, he published several short works in which he attempted to answer such questions as: Are we responsible for each other? How can we gain self-knowledge? He called these works *essais*, the French word meaning "attempts," and translated into English as "essays."

During colonial times in America, essays helped stir the American spirit. For example, *Common Sense*, written by Thomas Paine, helped spark the American Revolution and the founding of our nation.

Essays can be divided into two main categories, formal and informal. A **formal essay** presents a carefully structured argument and has a serious, scholarly tone. By contrast, the **informal**, or **personal, essay** has a lighter tone, is less structured (almost conversational), and typically includes personal details and references as well as humor.

A writer might compose an essay for one or more purposes. A **narrative essay** relates true events, usually in chronological order. A **descriptive essay** describes actual people, places, or things. An **expository essay** simply presents information and explains ideas. A **persuasive essay,** such as Thomas Paine's *The Crisis*, tries to persuade the reader that a certain point of view is correct.

The Structure of an Essay

Most essays you read will be made up of three parts—**introduction, body,** and **conclusion.** Each part has a specific function

and contributes to the essay's overall purpose. In the introduction, the writer usually begins with the "big picture," the essay's main idea, or **thesis.** The thesis will appear in a sentence or statement called the **thesis statement.** Next, in the body of the essay, the writer presents the information supporting the thesis, piece by piece in an orderly and logical sequence. Finally, in the conclusion, the writer might restate the thesis statement and explain how it has been supported.

Part of Essay	Function
Introduction	Captures the reader's interest Introduces the thesis Sets the tone of the essay
Body	Develops and supports the thesis with appropriate information arranged in a logical and orderly form
Conclusion	Ends with a strong impression Effectively brings the writing to a close

Organizing the Details

The writer of an essay tries to present the supporting information in the most effective way possible. Information and details in an essay can be organized in several ways, depending on the writer's purpose and topic. The chart on page 153 shows several ways to organize an essay.

Organizing Supporting Details	
Compare/ Contrast	Shows similarities and differences between objects, people, incidents, or ideas
Pro/Con	Explains reasons to do or believe something and reasons not to
Order of Importance	Presents details in increasing (or decreasing) order of importance
Chronological Order	Describes events in the order they occurred
Problem/ Solution	Presents a problem and offers a solution(s)
Cause/Effect	Explains how one event causes another event to happen

Tone and Style

Two other important elements of an essay are its **tone** and its **style.** Tone is the writer's attitude toward the subject.

The tone may be angry, whimsical, or urgent, for example. Through an essay's tone, some of the writer's personality becomes evident. A good writer chooses a tone to fit the topic and purpose.

Tone is just one part of a writer's style, or the way that writer uses language. What words does the writer choose? How complex or simple is the language? How long are the sentences? These are some factors that make up a writer's style.

As you read *The Crisis, No.1* by Thomas Paine, notice how his tone and style fit his topic and purpose.

Understanding an Essay

The following questions may be helpful in analyzing essays you read.

Guidelines for Analyzing an Essay

- What is the writer's overall purpose?
- What is the writer's thesis?
- How does the writer first gain the reader's attention and interest?
- What form of organization does the writer use? Is this type of organization helpful?
- What supporting details does the writer provide to develop the thesis?
- How effectively do these details support the writer's thesis?
- Does the conclusion effectively restate the thesis?
- Is the essay formal or informal? What tells you which it is?
- What is the tone of the essay? Does this tone add to the effectiveness of the essay?
- How would you describe the style of the essay? Does the style add to the essay's effectiveness?
- Does the essay accomplish its overall purpose? For example, if it is a persuasive essay, were you persuaded? Why or why not?

ACTIVITY

With a small group, locate an essay that is meant to entertain, such as one of Dave Barry's newspaper columns. Read the essay and analyze it by applying the questions above.

Before You Read

from *The Crisis, No. 1*

Meet Thomas Paine

"My country is the world and my religion is to do good."

—*Paine*

Corset maker, cobbler, teacher, tax-collector—Thomas Paine failed miserably at every line of work he attempted in his native England. Finally, at age thirty-seven, Paine set sail for the colonies to start a new life. It was 1774, and colonists were weighing the pros and cons of a break with England. Always a friend of the "little guy," Paine sympathized with the revolutionary forces. In January 1776, he published the pamphlet *Common Sense*, the first cry for complete independence from Britain. The pamphlet quickly sold half a million copies, and Paine followed it with a series of essays called *The Crisis*.

After the war, Paine returned to Europe—and to trouble. Banned in England as a traitor, he moved to France, where he was imprisoned during the French Revolution for being an Englishman! In 1794, Paine returned to the United States, but he got no hero's welcome. Many Americans had misunderstood his later writings and harassed him because they thought he was an atheist, or someone who does not believe in God. When Paine's life ended, he was poor, alone, and swollen with dropsy, a disease of the body's connective tissue. Even after his death, the insults continued. His remains were dug up, shipped to Britain, and then lost.

Thomas Paine was born in 1737 and died in 1809.

FOCUS ACTIVITY

A *crisis* is a moment when a crucial change is about to occur. Whom do you know that has been through a life-changing crisis?

JOURNAL Write a journal entry about a crisis that someone you know has faced. (Choose a crisis that you can share with other students, not something private.) How did the person handle the crisis? Was this tactic effective? Discuss your response with the class.

SETTING A PURPOSE Read to learn of the crisis Thomas Paine describes.

BACKGROUND

The Time and Place

Written by the light of an army campfire, *The Crisis, No. 1,* is the first of sixteen pamphlets Paine issued beginning in December 1776. At that time, the morale of General Washington's army was low. Soldiers were limping through the snow without boots or supplies. Washington had Paine's stirring words read to his troops just before crossing the icy Delaware River to defeat the British in Trenton, New Jersey.

VOCABULARY PREVIEW

tyranny (tir′ ə nē) *n.* cruel use of authority; oppressive power; p. 155

ravage (rav′ ij) *n.* a destructive or ruinous action or its result; p. 156

resolution (rez′ ə loo′ shən) *n.* firmness of purpose; p. 156

relinquish (ri ling′ kwish) *v.* to give up control of; to surrender; p. 156

petrified (pet′ rə fīd) *adj.* paralyzed with fear; stiff or like stone; p. 156

exploit (eks′ ploit) *n.* notable, heroic deed; feat; p. 156

hypocrisy (hi pok′ rə sē) *n.* an expression of feelings or beliefs not actually possessed or held; p. 156

ardor (är′ dər) *n.* intensity of emotion; passion; enthusiasm; p. 157

from The Crisis, No. 1

Thomas Paine

These are the times that try men's souls.

The summer soldier and the sunshine patriot will, in this crisis, shrink from the service of his country; but he that stands it now, deserves the love and thanks of man and woman. Tyranny, like hell, is not easily conquered; yet we have this consolation with us, that the harder the conflict, the more glorious the triumph. What we obtain too cheap, we esteem[1] too lightly: it is dearness only that gives everything its value. Heaven knows how to put a proper price upon its goods; and it would be strange indeed if so celestial an article as FREEDOM should not be highly rated. Britain, with an army to enforce her tyranny, has declared that she has a right (not only to TAX) but "to BIND us in ALL CASES WHATSOEVER";[2] and if being bound in that manner is not slavery, then is there not such a thing as slavery upon earth. Even the expression is impious;[3] for so unlimited a power can belong only to God.

---

1. *Esteem* means "to value" or "to appreciate."
2. In March 1766 the British Parliament repealed the Stamp Act but also passed the Declaratory Act, which extended their right to impose taxes on the colonies and *"to bind [the colonies] in all cases whatsoever."*
3. *Impious* (im′ pē əs) means "lacking in reverence for God."

Vocabulary

tyranny (tir′ ə nē) *n.* cruel use of authority; oppressive power

Whether the independence of the continent was declared too soon, or delayed too long, I will not now enter into as an argument; my own simple opinion is, that had it been eight months earlier it would have been much better. We did not make a proper use of last winter; neither could we, while we were in a dependent state. However, the fault, if it were one, was all our own; we have none to blame but ourselves. But no great deal is lost yet. All that Howe[4] has been doing for this month past is rather a <u>ravage</u> than a conquest, which the spirit of the Jerseys[5] a year ago would have quickly repulsed, and which time and a little <u>resolution</u> will soon recover.

I have as little superstition in me as any man living; but my secret opinion has ever been, and still is, that God Almighty will not give up a people to military destruction, or leave them unsupportedly to perish, who have so earnestly and so repeatedly sought to avoid the calamities of war, by every decent method which wisdom could invent. Neither have I so much of the infidel[6] in me as to suppose that He has <u>relinquished</u> the government of the world, and given us up to the care of devils; and as I do not, I cannot see on what grounds the king of Britain can look up to heaven for help against us: a common murderer, a highwayman,[7] or a housebreaker, has as good a pretense as he.

It is surprising to see how rapidly a panic will sometimes run through a country. All nations and ages have been subject to them: Britain has trembled like an ague[8] at the report of a French fleet of flat-bottomed boats; and in the fourteenth century the whole English army, after ravaging the kingdom of France, was driven back like men <u>petrified</u> with fear; and this brave <u>exploit</u> was performed by a few broken forces collected and headed by a woman, Joan of Arc. Would that heaven might inspire some Jersey maid to spirit up her countrymen, and save her fair fellow sufferers from ravage and ravishment! Yet panics, in some cases, have their uses; they produce as much good as hurt. Their duration is always short; the mind soon grows through them, and acquires a firmer habit than before.

Did You Know?
Joan of Arc (1412?–1431) was a French peasant who became a military leader and led French troops in victories against the English, saving her country from British domination. She was declared a saint after her death.

But their peculiar advantage is, that they are the touchstones[9] of sincerity and <u>hypocrisy</u>, and bring things and men to light, which might otherwise have lain forever undiscovered. In fact, they have the same effect on secret traitors which an imaginary apparition[10] would have

---

4. Major General Sir William *Howe* was commander in chief of the British forces in America during part of the Revolutionary War.
5. At one time New Jersey was divided into two sections, East Jersey and West Jersey. The two parts were reunited as a royal colony in 1702.
6. Here, *infidel* means "someone who does not believe in God."
7. A thief who stole from travelers on a public road was a *highwayman.*

---

8. An *ague* is a fit of shivering.
9. A *touchstone* is anything that tests the quality or genuineness of something.
10. An *apparition* is a ghost.

Vocabulary

ravage (rav′ ij) *n.* a destructive or ruinous action or its result
resolution (rez′ ə loo′ shən) *n.* firmness of purpose
relinquish (ri ling′ kwish) *v.* to give up control of; to surrender
petrified (pet′ rə fīd) *adj.* paralyzed with fear; stiff or like stone
exploit (eks′ ploit) *n.* notable, heroic deed; feat
hypocrisy (hi pok′ rə sē) *n.* an expression of feelings or beliefs not actually possessed or held

upon a private murderer. They sift out the hidden thoughts of man, and hold them up in public to the world. Many a disguised tory has lately shown his head, that shall penitentially solemnize[11] with curses the day on which Howe arrived upon the Delaware.

. . . Quitting this class of men, I turn with the warm ardor of a friend to those who have nobly stood, and are yet determined to stand the matter out: I call not upon a few, but upon all: not on *this* State or *that* State, but on *every* State: up and help us; lay your shoulders to the wheel; better have too much force than too little, when so great an object is at stake. Let it be told to the future world that in the depth of winter, when nothing but hope and virtue could survive, that the city and the country, alarmed at one common danger, came forth to meet and to repulse it. Say not that thousands are gone—turn out your tens of thousands; throw not the burden of the day upon Providence, but *"show your faith by your works,"*[12] that God may bless you. It matters not where you live, or what rank of life you hold, the evil or the blessing will reach you all. The far and the near, the home counties

> *. . . he whose heart is firm, and whose conscience approves his conduct, will pursue his principles unto death.*

and the back, the rich and poor, will suffer or rejoice alike. The heart that feels not now is dead; the blood of his children will curse his cowardice who shrinks back at a time when a little might have saved the whole, and made *them* happy. I love the man that can smile in trouble, that can gather strength from distress and grow brave by reflection. It is the business of little minds to shrink; but he whose heart is firm, and whose conscience approves his conduct, will pursue his principles unto death. My own line of reasoning is to myself as straight and clear as a ray of light. Not all the treasures of the world, so far as I believe, could have induced[13] me to support an offensive war, for I think it murder; but if a thief breaks into my house, burns and destroys my property, and kills or threatens to kill me or those that are in it, and to *"bind me in all cases whatsoever"* to his absolute will, am I to suffer[14] it? What signifies[15] it to me, whether he who does it is a king or a common man; my countryman or not my countryman; whether it be done by an individual villain, or an army of them? If we reason to the root of things we shall find no difference; neither can any just cause be assigned why we should punish in the one case and pardon in the other. . . .

11. A colonist who supported British rule was a *tory*. *Penitentially solemnize* means "to celebrate formally with sorrow and regret."
12. Here, *Providence* means "God." *["show . . . your works"]* This phrase is a reference to the Book of James in the Bible.

13. *Induced* means "persuaded."
14. Here, *suffer* means "to put up with."
15. Here, *signifies* means "to make important."

Vocabulary
ardor (är′ dər) *n.* intensity of emotion; passion; enthusiasm

Responding to Literature

Personal Response

Suppose you were going to choose a sentence or two from Thomas Paine's essay to post on your bulletin board as a memorable quotation. Which sentence would you choose, and why?

——— ANALYZING LITERATURE ———

RECALL

1. Which Americans does Paine criticize? Which does he praise?
2. To whom does Paine compare the English king in the third paragraph?
3. What lessons does Paine draw from the panics in European history that he mentions?
4. In the last paragraph, what does Paine want everyone to do?
5. What **analogy,** or comparison, does Paine make at the end of the essay to argue that this is not an "offensive" war?

INTERPRET

6. What, do you think, are Paine's opinions of the people he criticizes in the first paragraph?
7. What emotions does Paine appeal to when describing the king?
8. What connection do you think Paine sees between the panics in European history and the experience America now faces?
9. What feelings do you think Paine wants to inspire in his audience with the biblical **allusion** "show your faith by your works"? (See page R1.)
10. Why do you think Paine might have chosen the analogy he used in his final argument? List some reasons for your answer.

EVALUATE AND CONNECT

11. Thomas Paine said that his goal as a writer was to use plain language. Cite some sentences from *The Crisis* that you think achieve this goal.
12. In your opinion, how might a British sympathizer have answered Paine's main arguments? Use a chart like the one on the right to help organize your answer.
13. What lessons does this essay teach you about persuasive writing? Explain with examples from the text.
14. How effectively, do you think, does Paine use religion as part of his argument? Explain your answer with examples.
15. Many aspects of *The Crisis* made it successful in Paine's time. What aspect of it means the most to you? Its directness? Its emotion? Or something else? Explain.

Hyperbole

Persuasive writers often use **hyperbole,** or exaggeration, to rouse the emotions of their audiences. By calling King George "a common murderer, a highwayman, or a housebreaker," for example, Paine emphasizes the king's faults by exaggerating them. In addition, by claiming that *all* nations experience panics, Paine is downplaying the low morale felt by the Revolutionary forces.

1. Find at least two more examples of hyperbole in Paine's speech and explain how Paine is exaggerating in each.
2. For each hyperbole you have identified, evaluate its effectiveness as part of Paine's argument.
- See **Literary Terms Handbook,** p. R8.

Paine's argument	Possible response of British sympathizer

LITERATURE AND WRITING

Writing About Literature

Emotional Appeals   Thomas Paine uses vivid images to appeal to his readers' feelings of loyalty and service in the fight against British rule. Reread the essay and find several images that might have appealed to a reader's sense of loyalty to the Revolution. For each example, write a few sentences describing why the words would have had an emotional effect on readers.

Personal Writing

Persuasive Letter   Look over the crises that you and your classmates listed for the Focus Activity on page 154. Choose one crisis that you feel strongly about. Then write a persuasive letter that would motivate a person to solve the crisis by following your advice. Be sure to use some of the persuasive techniques that you found in Paine's essay, such as vivid language and hyperbole.

EXTENDING YOUR RESPONSE

Literature Groups

What Does It Mean?   Have each group member identify one passage in *The Crisis* that he or she found difficult to understand. Discuss the meaning of the passage or passages. Have a group note taker write down the group's explanation (or differing explanations) of each passage chosen. Then present the passages and the group's interpretations to the entire class to get other possible opinions.

Interdisciplinary Activity

History: General Washington Wants You   Thomas Paine calls upon all colonists to support the war effort. Create an enlistment poster to encourage young patriots to join the Continental Army. Use a memorable quote from Paine's essay as part of the text of your poster.

Performing

Soul-Trying Times   Imagine that General Washington has asked you to read *The Crisis* aloud to the troops as they prepare to cross the Delaware and attack the British at Trenton. How would you read the paragraphs for maximum dramatic impact? Practice reading the text, varying your speed, tone, and volume. When you think you are ready, read the essay aloud to the class.

Reading Further

To learn more about the Continental Army between 1776 and 1778, read the following books:

The Winter Soldiers, by Richard M. Ketchum, offers a military history.

Winter Quarters, by Noel F. Busch, portrays Washington and his troops at Valley Forge.

Save your work for your portfolio.

Skill Minilesson

VOCABULARY • **Words with Multiple Meanings**

Many English words have more than one meaning. The vocabulary word *resolution,* for example, means "firmness of purpose" in this selection, but it can also mean "a formal statement of a decision." Similarly, the vocabulary word *petrified* is used to mean "paralyzed with fear," but it can also mean "turned into stone."

PRACTICE   For each word below, give the meaning used in *The Crisis* and one other meaning. Then write a sentence using the word according to the second meaning.

try	article	state	spirit	common
report	mind	shrinks	reflection	case

Before You Read

from *The Histories*

Meet Herodotus

"**These are the researches of Herodotus of Halicarnassus, which he publishes, in the hope of thereby preserving from decay the remembrance of what men have done. . . .**"

—*Herodotus of Greece*

So begins one of the first histories of Western civilization. Between 430 and 424 B.C., Herodotus (hə rod′ ə təs) published *The Histories*, a lively account of the Persian Wars interspersed with wide-ranging analyses.

Modern historian K. H. Waters comments, "The Persian Empire was by far the greatest foreign . . . power encountered by the Greeks, and their [eventual] escape from subjugation to it dominated their patriotic thinking for generations." The events of the Persian Wars inspired Herodotus and others to attempt an overthrow of the pro-Persian tyrant in power. For his role in this plot, Herodotus was forced into exile.

Herodotus was born in 484 B.C. The date of his death is unknown. It may have been as early as 430 B.C. or after 408 B.C.

FOCUS ACTIVITY

Have you ever watched an unevenly matched contest—a competition in which one contestant is stronger than the other? Perhaps you have seen sports events, listened to verbal exchanges, or read about battles between unevenly matched contestants.

SHARE IDEAS Make a list of unevenly matched contests you have watched, read about, or taken part in. Pick the one that seems most interesting, and discuss it with a partner. Who were the contestants? What happened during each contest? How did the contest end? How did it make you feel?

SETTING A PURPOSE As you read, note the important developments in the battle.

BACKGROUND

The Time and Place

In the fifth century B.C., the Persian Empire ruled the Middle East. Persia was a strong, wealthy empire with an overwhelming army. Greece was made up of small, independent city-states, each with its own government and army.

In 499 B.C., the Greek city-states encouraged the Ionian cities of Asia Minor to rebel against their Persian rulers. When King Darius I of Persia tried to punish the Greeks for their actions, the Greeks fought back. Xerxes, the son of Darius, succeeded his father and carried on the conflict, which became known as the Persian Wars. In 480 B.C., Xerxes invaded Greece. The Persian and Greek armies first met in battle at Thermopylae, a narrow pass where the mountains meet the sea.

In his account of the battle, Herodotus mentions Peloponnesians, Phocians, Locrians, Spartans, and other groups from different Greek city-states.

VOCABULARY PREVIEW

indignation (in′ dig nā′ shən) *n.* restrained, dignified anger in response to meanness, injustice, or ingratitude; p. 161

feint (fānt) *n.* a deceptive movement intended to draw an opponent's attention from the real attack; deception; p. 162

onslaught (ôn′ slôt′) *n.* a vigorous or destructive attack; p. 163

disperse (dis purs′) *v.* to go off in different directions; to scatter; p. 163

remorselessly (ri môrs′ lis lē) *adv.* mercilessly; p. 165

signal (sig′ nəl) *adj.* remarkable; striking; notable; p. 165

from THE HISTORIES

Herodotus
Translated by Aubrey de Sélincourt

THERMOPYLAE

The Persian army was now close to the pass, and the Greeks, suddenly doubting their power to resist, held a conference to consider the advisability of retreat. It was proposed by the Peloponnesians generally that the army should fall back upon the Peloponnese and hold the Isthmus; but when the Phocians and Locrians expressed their indignation at this suggestion, Leonidas[1] gave his voice for staying where they were and sending, at the same time, an appeal for reinforcements to the various states of the confederacy, as their numbers were inadequate to cope with the Persians.

During the conference Xerxes sent a man on horseback to ascertain[2] the strength of the Greek force and to observe what the troops were doing. He had heard before he left Thessaly that a small force was concentrated here, led by the Lacedaemonians under Leonidas of the house of Heracles. The Persian rider approached the camp and took a thorough survey of all he could see—which was not, however, the whole Greek army; for the men on the further side of the wall which, after its reconstruction, was now guarded, were out of sight. He did, nonetheless, carefully observe the troops who were stationed on the outside of the wall. At that moment these happened to be the Spartans, and some of them

---

1. *Leonidas* was the leader of the Lacedaemonians and commanded the battle at Thermopylae.
2. To *ascertain* is to find with certainty; to determine.

Vocabulary
indignation (in′ dig nā′ shən) *n.* restrained, dignified anger in response to meanness, injustice, or ingratitude

were stripped for exercise, while others were combing their hair. The Persian spy watched them in astonishment; nevertheless he made sure of their numbers, and of everything else he needed to know, as accurately as he could, and then rode quietly off. No one attempted to catch him, or took the least notice of him.

Back in his own camp he told Xerxes what he had seen. Xerxes was bewildered; the truth, namely that the Spartans were preparing themselves to kill and to be killed according to their strength, was beyond his comprehension, and what they were doing seemed to him merely absurd. Accordingly he sent for Demaratus, the son of Ariston, who had come with the army, and questioned him about the spy's report, in the hope of finding out what the unaccountable behavior of the Spartans might mean. "Once before," Demaratus said, "when we began our march against Greece, you heard me speak of these men. I told you then how I saw this enterprise would turn out, and you laughed at me. I strive for nothing, my lord, more earnestly than to observe the truth in your presence; so hear me once more. These men have come to fight us for possession of the pass, and for that struggle they are preparing. It is the common practice of the Spartans to pay careful attention to their hair when they are about to risk their lives. But I assure you that if you can defeat these men and the rest of the Spartans who are still at home, there is no other people in the world who will dare to stand firm or lift a hand against you. You have now to deal with the finest kingdom in Greece, and with the bravest men."

Xerxes, unable to believe what Demaratus said, asked further how it was possible that so small a force could fight with his army. "My lord," Demaratus replied, "treat me as a liar, if what I have foretold does not take place." But still Xerxes was unconvinced.

For four days Xerxes waited, in constant expectation that the Greeks would make good their escape; then, on the fifth, when still they had made no move and their continued presence seemed mere impudent[3] and reckless folly, he was seized with rage and sent forward the Medes and Cissians[4] with orders to take them alive and bring them into his presence. The Medes charged, and in the struggle which ensued[5] many fell; but others took their places, and in spite of terrible losses refused to be beaten off. They made it plain enough to anyone, and not least to the king himself, that he had in his army many men, indeed, but few soldiers. All day the battle continued; the Medes, after their rough handling, were at length withdrawn and their place was taken by Hydarnes and his picked Persian troops—the King's Immortals[6]—who advanced to the attack in full confidence of bringing the business to a quick and easy end. But, once engaged, they were no more successful than the Medes had been; all went as before, the two armies fighting in a confined space, the Persians using shorter spears than the Greeks and having no advantage from their numbers.

On the Spartan side it was a memorable fight; they were men who understood war pitted against an inexperienced enemy, and amongst the feints they employed was to turn their backs in a body and pretend to be retreating in confusion, whereupon the enemy would come on with a great clatter and roar, supposing the battle won; but the Spartans, just as the Persians were

---

3. *Impudent* means "offensively bold; arrogant."
4. The *Medes* and *Cissians* were two of many armies that made up the Persian force.
5. What *ensued* was what occurred as a consequence.
6. Strictly speaking, an *immortal* is one who has eternal life, such as a god in Greek mythology. Here, however, the name *King's Immortals* suggests that these are the king's finest soldiers and that they will be celebrated for all eternity.

Vocabulary
feint (fānt) *n.* a deceptive movement intended to draw an opponent's attention from the real attack; deception

on them, would wheel and face them and inflict in the new struggle innumerable casualties. The Spartans had their losses too, but not many. At last the Persians, finding that their assaults upon the pass, whether by divisions or by any other way they could think of, were all useless, broke off the engagement and withdrew. Xerxes was watching the battle from where he sat; and it is said that in the course of the attacks three times, in terror for his army, he leapt to his feet.

Next day the fighting began again, but with no better success for the Persians, who renewed their <u>onslaught</u> in the hope that the Greeks, being so few in number, might be badly enough disabled by wounds to prevent further resistance. But the Greeks never slackened; their troops were ordered in divisions corresponding to the states from which they came, and each division took its turn in the line except the Phocian, which had been posted to guard the track over the mountains. So when the Persians found that things were no better for them than on the previous day, they once more withdrew.

How to deal with the situation Xerxes had no idea; but while he was still wondering what his next move should be, a man from Malis got himself admitted to his presence. This was Ephialtes, the son of Eurydemus, and he had come, in hope of a rich reward, to tell the king about the track which led over the hills to Thermopylae—and the information he gave was to prove the death of the Greeks who held the pass. . . .

The Greeks at Thermopylae had their first warning of the death that was coming with the dawn from the seer Megistias, who read their doom in the victims of sacrifice; deserters, too,

Statue of Leonidas, at Thermopylae.

had begun to come in during the night with news of the Persian movement to take them in the rear, and, just as day was breaking, the look-out men had come running from the hills. At once a conference was held, and opinions were divided, some urging that they must on no account abandon their post, others taking the opposite view. The result was that the army split: some <u>dispersed</u>, the men returning to their various homes, and others made ready to stand by Leonidas.

There is another account which says that Leonidas himself dismissed a part of his force, to spare their lives, but thought it unbecoming for the Spartans under his command to desert the post which they had originally come to guard. I myself am inclined to think that he dismissed them when he realized that they had

---

Vocabulary
onslaught (ôn′ slôt′) *n.* a vigorous or destructive attack
disperse (dis purs′) *v.* to go off in different directions; to scatter

no heart for the fight and were unwilling to take their share of the danger; at the same time honor forbade that he himself should go. And indeed by remaining at his post he left a great name behind him, and Sparta did not lose her prosperity, as might otherwise have happened; for right at the outset of the war the Spartans had been told by the oracle,[7] when they asked for advice, that either their city must be laid waste by the foreigner or one of their kings be killed. The prophecy was in hexameter verse[8] and ran as follows:

Hear your fate, O dwellers in Sparta of the
  wide spaces;
Either your famed, great town must be sacked
  by Perseus' sons,
Or, if that be not, the whole land of
  Lacedaemon
Shall mourn the death of a king of the house
  of Heracles,
For not the strength of lions or of bulls shall
  hold him,
Strength against strength; for he has the power
  of Zeus,
And will not be checked till one of these two
  he has consumed.

I believe it was the thought of this oracle, combined with his wish to lay up for the Spartans a treasure of fame in which no other city should share, that made Leonidas dismiss those troops; I do not think that they deserted, or went off without orders, because of a difference of opinion. Moreover, I am strongly supported in this view by the case of Megistias, the seer from Acarnania who foretold the coming doom by his inspection of the sacrificial victims: this man—he was said to be descended from Melampus—was with the army, and quite plainly received orders from Leonidas to quit Thermopylae, to save him from sharing the army's fate. But he refused to go, sending away instead an only son of his, who was serving with the forces.

Thus it was that the confederate troops, by Leonidas' orders, abandoned their posts and left the pass, all except the Thespians and the Thebans who remained with the Spartans. The Thebans were detained by Leonidas as hostages very much against their will—unlike the loyal Thespians, who refused to desert Leonidas and his men, but stayed, and died with them. They were under the command of Demophilus the son of Diadromes.

In the morning Xerxes poured a libation[9] to the rising sun, and then waited till about the time of the filling of the marketplace, when he began to move forward. This was according to Ephialtes' instructions, for the way down from the ridge is much shorter and more direct than the long and circuitous ascent. As the Persian army advanced to the assault, the Greeks under Leonidas, knowing that the fight would be their last, pressed forward into the wider part of the pass much further than they had done before; in the previous days' fighting they had been holding the wall and making sorties[10] from behind it into the narrow neck, but now they left the

---

7. In ancient Greece, an *oracle* was a priest through whom the gods sometimes answered the questions of worshipers.
8. Each line of *hexameter verse* has six feet–that is, six sets of accented and unaccented syllables.
9. *Libation* is the ritual of pouring out wine as an offering to a god. (Today, the word is often used to refer to any drink, especially an alcoholic beverage.)
10. *Sorties* are sudden attacks by troops in a besieged position upon their besiegers. (The word comes from the French, and the singular form is *sortie*.)

confined space and battle was joined on more open ground. Many of the invaders fell; behind them the company commanders plied their whips, driving the men remorselessly on. Many fell into the sea and were drowned, and still more were trampled to death by their friends. No one could count the number of the dead. The Greeks, who knew that the enemy were on their way round by the mountain track and that death was inevitable,[11] fought with reckless desperation, exerting every ounce of strength that was in them against the invader. By this time most of their spears were broken, and they were killing Persians with their swords.

In the course of that fight Leonidas fell, having fought like a man indeed. Many distinguished Spartans were killed at his side—their names, like the names of all the three hundred, I have made myself acquainted with, because they deserve to be remembered. Amongst the Persian dead, too, were many men of high distinction—for instance, two brothers of Xerxes, Habrocomes and Hyperanthes, both of them sons of Darius by Artanes' daughter Phratagune.

There was a bitter struggle over the body of Leonidas; four times the Greeks drove the enemy off, and at last by their valor[12] succeeded in dragging it away. So it went on, until the fresh troops with Ephialtes were close at hand; and then, when the Greeks knew that they had come, the character of the fighting changed. They withdrew again into the narrow neck of the pass, behind the walls, and took up a position in a single compact body—all except the Thebans—on the little hill at the entrance to the pass, where the stone lion in memory of Leonidas stands today. Here they resisted to the last, with their swords, if they had them, and, if not, with their hands and teeth, until the Persians, coming on from the front over the ruins of the wall and closing in from behind, finally overwhelmed them.

Of all the Spartans and Thespians who fought so valiantly on that day, the most signal proof of courage was given by the Spartan Dieneces. It is said that before the battle he was told by a native of Trachis that, when the Persians shot their arrows, there were so many of them that they hid the sun. Dieneces, however, quite unmoved by the thought of the terrible strength of the Persian army, merely remarked: "This is pleasant news that the stranger from Trachis brings us: for if the Persians hide the sun, we shall have our battle in the shade." He is said to have left on record other sayings, too, of a similar kind, by which he will be remembered. After Dieneces the greatest distinction was won by the two Spartan brothers, Alpheus and Maron, the sons of Orsiphantus; and of the Thespians the man to gain the highest glory was a certain Dithyrambus, the son of Harmatides.

The dead were buried where they fell, and with them the men who had been killed before those dismissed by Leonidas left the pass. Over them is this inscription, in honor of the whole force:

*Four thousand here from Pelops' land
Against three million once did stand.*

---

11. Something that is *inevitable* cannot be avoided or prevented.
12. *Valor* is outstanding courage, especially in battle.

Vocabulary
remorselessly (ri môrs′ lis lē) *adv.* mercilessly
signal (sig′ nəl) *adj.* remarkable; striking; notable

Responding to Literature

Personal Response

What was your strongest reaction as you finished reading this selection?

ANALYZING LITERATURE

RECALL AND INTERPRET

1. What does Xerxes decide to do after he speaks with Demaratus? What do his actions tell you about his attitude toward battle?
2. What is the outcome of the first three days of battle? How do the strategies of the Greeks and Persians differ?
3. How do the Persians gain their ultimate advantage? What does the Greek reaction to inevitable defeat tell you about them?
4. What is the outcome of the battle? What do you think Herodotus wants readers to understand from reading his account? Explain.

EVALUATE AND CONNECT

5. How did this uneven contest compare to other contests you discussed for the Focus Activity on page 160? Did the selection reinforce or change your thoughts about unevenly matched contests? Explain.
6. In your opinion, how would the account of the battle at Thermopylae have differed if a Persian historian had told it?
7. Theme Connections   The Greeks eventually won the Persian Wars. From what you learned in reading this selection, what advantages do you think the Greeks had over the Persians? What motivation did the Greeks have that the Persions did not? Explain
8. What evidence from the selection indicates that Herodotus intended to give a factual account of the battle at Thermopylae?

Literary ELEMENTS

Historical Narrative

Herodotus's *Histories* is a **historical narrative,** a work of nonfiction that tells the story, in chronological order, of important historical events or developments.

The Histories was the first attempt by the Greeks to record their history in a factual manner. *The Histories* remains as Herodotus wrote it more than two thousand years ago.

1. Do you see any evidence of **bias,** favoring one side or another, in Herodotus's account? Explain with examples from the selecton.
2. Review the conversation between Xerxes and Demaratus. How does this conversation affect your opinion of the factual nature of the selection? Explain.

• See **Literary Terms Handbook,** p. R8.

EXTENDING YOUR RESPONSE

Literature Groups

Views on War   In the introduction to his work, *The Histories,* Herodotus says that his purpose for writing is to preserve the "great and wonderful actions of the Greeks." Do you agree that the Persian Wars and other hard-fought wars should be remembered? Should war be glorified? What are some ways nations might avoid war? Discuss these questions with your group. Then share your group's views with the class.

Literature and Writing

A Battle in Verse   Write a poem about Thermopylae and what happened there. For inspiration, you might read part of the epic poem the *Iliad* or other poems about war. "Charge of the Light Brigade" by Alfred Tennyson, "40" by E. E. Cummings, and "War" by Joseph Langland are a few examples. Read your poem to the class.

📖 **Save your work for your portfolio.**

COMPARING selections

from The Crisis, No. 1 **and** *from* **THE HISTORIES**

COMPARE **SITUATIONS**

Both Paine and Herodotus describe nations at war. On a separate piece of paper, write a few paragraphs answering the following questions:

1. How is the war between the Persians and the Greeks similar to the war between the British and the colonists?

2. In what ways are the two wars different? You might use encyclopedias or other reference books to learn more about ancient Greece and Persia.

3. In your opinion, what could the British and the colonists have learned from reading Herodotus's account of the Persian Wars?

COMPARE **IDEAS OF BRAVERY**

Both Herodotus and Paine give their views on true bravery against an invading enemy. With a small group, discuss the following:

1. Which statements from each selection show the writer's idea of bravery?

2. What idea does Herodotus have of true bravery? What idea does Paine have?

3. Compare and contrast the ideas of bravery expressed by Herodotus and Paine.

COMPARE **SOLDIERS**

More than two thousand years separate the battle at Thermopylae from the battle at Trenton. Despite this time gap, many aspects of soldiering remained unchanged.

- With a small group of classmates, research the Persian, Greek, British, or the Patriot (colonial) soldiers. Learn about their weapons, battle preparations, and fighting tactics.

- On a piece of poster board, make a large drawing representing a soldier from the group you selected. Label the various parts of the uniform and fighting gear. Add margin notes to provide additional details about the soldier.

- Display your poster with those of classmates. Then discuss your work with the class. Make a class chart of the similarities and differences among the soldiers.

Before You Read

Declaration of Independence

Meet Thomas Jefferson

"...to place before mankind the common sense of the subject, in terms so plain and firm as to command their assent, and to justify ourselves in the independent stand we are compelled to take."

—*Jefferson*

With his purpose defined, Thomas Jefferson crafted what many believe is the most powerful argument for freedom ever written. When the Continental Congress debated breaking away from Britain in 1776, the members turned to Jefferson to put their ideas about liberty and freedom into writing. Jefferson did indeed express those ideas in the writing of the Declaration of Independence.

This skilled writer was also a man of many other talents and interests. James Parton, a Jefferson biographer, describes him as "a gentleman of thirty-two who could calculate an eclipse, tie an artery, plan an edifice, try a case, break a horse, dance a minuet, and play the violin."

Jefferson was a native Virginian. He graduated from the College of William and Mary, studied law, and became a member of the Virginia House of Burgesses. He served as governor of Virginia, minister to France, secretary of state, vice-president, and president of the United States.

Jefferson died on July 4, 1826, the fiftieth anniversary of the signing of the Declaration of Independence.

Thomas Jefferson was born in 1743 and died in 1826.

FOCUS ACTIVITY

Just how much freedom should an individual or a country have? What, if anything, should limit freedom?

WORD WEB Create a word web with the word "freedom" at the center. Then complete the word web with your ideas on personal and national freedom.

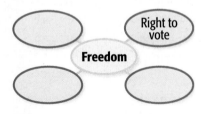

Right to vote

Freedom

SETTING A PURPOSE Read to learn more about Jefferson's views of freedom.

BACKGROUND

The Time and Place

In 1776 the Second Continental Congress created a committee to draft a statement declaring independence from Britain. Jefferson did most of the writing.

The Idea of Natural Law

Some of Jefferson's ideas about independence were not new. He studied John Locke's theory of "natural law." According to Locke, people are "by nature free, equal and independent . . ." Following his lead, Jefferson stressed that the American Revolution was a struggle for the basic rights of all.

VOCABULARY PREVIEW

usurpation (ū′ sər pā′ shən) *n.* act of seizing power without legal right or authority; p. 169

endeavor (en dev′ ər) *v.* to make an effort to; to try; p. 171

tenure (ten′ yər) *n.* conditions or terms under which something is held; p. 171

acquiesce (ak′ wē es′) *v.* to consent or agree silently, without objections; to comply passively; p. 172

rectitude (rek′ tə tood′) *n.* uprightness of moral character; honesty; p. 172

Declaration of Independence

In Congress, July 4, 1776

Thomas Jefferson ~

WHEN, IN THE COURSE OF HUMAN EVENTS, it becomes necessary for one people to dissolve the political bands which have connected them with another, and to assume, among the powers of the earth, the separate and equal station to which the laws of nature and nature's God entitle them, a decent respect to the opinions of mankind requires that they should declare the causes which impel them to the separation.

We hold these truths to be self-evident: that all men are created equal, that they are endowed by their Creator with certain unalienable rights;[1] that among these are life, liberty, and the pursuit of happiness; that to secure these rights, governments are instituted among men, deriving their just powers from the consent of the governed; that whenever any form of government becomes destructive of these ends, it is the right of the people to alter or to abolish it, and to institute new government, laying its foundation on such principles, and organizing its powers in such form, as to them shall seem most likely to effect their safety and happiness. Prudence,[2] indeed, will dictate that governments long established should not be changed for light and transient causes; and accordingly all experience hath shown that mankind are more disposed to suffer, while evils are sufferable, than to right themselves by abolishing the forms to which they are accustomed. But when a long train of abuses and usurpations, pursuing invariably the same object, evinces[3] a design to reduce

---

1. *Unalienable rights* cannot be taken away.

2. The exercise of good judgment is called *prudence*.
3. *Evinces* means "makes clear or evident."

Vocabulary

usurpation (u´ sər pā´ shən) *n.* act of seizing power without legal right or authority

them under absolute despotism,[4] it is their right, it is their duty, to throw off such government, and to provide new guards for their future security.

Such has been the patient sufferance of these colonies; and such is now the necessity which constrains[5] them to alter their former systems of government. The history of the present King of Great Britain is a history of repeated injuries and usurpations, all having in direct object the establishment of an absolute tyranny[6] over these states. To prove this, let facts be submitted to a candid world.

He has refused his assent[7] to laws, the most wholesome and necessary for the public good.

He has forbidden his governors to pass laws of immediate and pressing importance, unless suspended in their operation till his assent should be obtained; and when so suspended, he has utterly neglected to attend to them.

He has refused to pass other laws for the accommodation of large districts of people,

---

4. *Despotism* is government by a ruler who has absolute authority.
5. *Constrains* means "forces."

---

6. The arbitrary or oppressive exercise of power is *tyranny*.
7. *Assent* is agreement.

Declaration of Independence, 1824. John Trumbull. Oil on canvas, 21⅛ x 31⅛ in. Yale University Art Gallery, New Haven, CT.

Viewing the painting: Do you think the artist accurately captured the spirit of the moment? Explain why or why not.

unless those people would relinquish the right of representation in the legislature, a right inestimable to them, and formidable to tyrants only.

He has called together legislative bodies at places unusual, uncomfortable, and distant from the depository of their public records, for the sole purpose of fatiguing them into compliance with his measures.

He has dissolved representative houses repeatedly, for opposing, with manly firmness, his invasions on the rights of the people.

He has refused, for a long time after such dissolutions, to cause others to be elected; whereby the legislative powers, incapable of annihilation, have returned to the people at large for their exercise; the state remaining, in the meantime, exposed to all the dangers of invasion from without and convulsions within.

He has endeavored to prevent the population of these states; for that purpose obstructing the laws for naturalization[8] of foreigners, refusing to pass others to encourage their migrations hither, and raising the conditions of new appropriations of lands.

He has obstructed the administration of justice, by refusing his assent to laws for establishing judiciary powers.

He has made judges dependent on his will alone for the tenure of their offices, and the amount of payment of their salaries.

He has erected a multitude of new offices, and sent hither swarms of officers to harass our people and eat out their substance.

He has kept among us, in times of peace, standing armies, without the consent of our legislatures.

He has affected to render the military independent of, and superior to, the civil power.

He has combined with others to subject us to a jurisdiction foreign to our constitution and unacknowledged by our laws, giving his assent to their acts of pretended legislation:

For quartering[9] large bodies of armed troops among us;

For protecting them, by a mock trial, from punishment for any murders which they should commit on the inhabitants of these states;

For cutting off our trade with all parts of the world;

For imposing taxes on us without our consent;

For depriving us, in many cases, of the benefits of trial by jury;

For transporting us beyond seas, to be tried for pretended offenses;

For abolishing the free system of English laws in a neighboring province,[10] establishing therein an arbitrary government, and enlarging its boundaries, so as to render it at once an example and fit instrument for introducing the same absolute rule into these colonies;

For taking away our charters, abolishing our most valuable laws, and altering fundamentally the forms of our governments;

For suspending our own legislatures, and declaring themselves invested with power to legislate for us in all cases whatsoever.

He has abdicated government here, by declaring us out of his protection and waging war against us.

He has plundered our seas, ravaged our coasts, burned our towns, and destroyed the lives of our people.

He is at this time transporting large armies of foreign mercenaries[11] to complete the works

---

8. *Naturalization* is the process by which foreigners become citizens of another country.

9. Here, *quartering* means "providing with living accommodations; lodging."

10. The *neighboring province* is Quebec, Canada.

11. Soldiers who serve in a foreign army for pay are *mercenaries.*

Vocabulary
endeavor (en dev′ ər) *v.* to make an effort to; to try
tenure (ten′ yər) *n.* conditions or terms under which something is held

of death, desolation, and tyranny already begun with circumstances of cruelty and perfidy[12] scarcely paralleled in the most barbarous ages, and totally unworthy the head of a civilized nation.

He has constrained our fellow-citizens, taken captive on the high seas, to bear arms against their country, to become the executioners of their friends and brethren, or to fall themselves by their hands.

He has excited domestic insurrections among us, and has endeavored to bring on the inhabitants of our frontiers, the merciless Indian savages, whose known rule of warfare is an undistinguished destruction of all ages, sexes, and conditions.

In every stage of these oppressions we have petitioned for redress[13] in the most humble terms; our repeated petitions have been answered only by repeated injury. A prince whose character is thus marked by every act which may define a tyrant is unfit to be ruler of a free people.

Nor have we been wanting in our attentions to our British brethren. We have warned them, from time to time, of attempts by their legislature to extend an unwarrantable jurisdiction over us. We have reminded them of the circumstances of our emigration and settlement here. We have appealed to their native justice and magnanimity;[14] and we have conjured[15] them, by the ties of our common kindred, to disavow these usurpations, which would inevitably interrupt our connections and correspondence. They, too, have been deaf to the voice of justice and consanguinity.[16] We must, therefore, acquiesce in the necessity which denounces[17] our separation, and hold them, as we hold the rest of mankind, enemies in war, in peace, friends.

We, therefore, the representatives of the United States of America, in General Congress assembled, appealing to the Supreme Judge of the world for the rectitude of our intentions, do, in the name and by the authority of the good people of these colonies, solemnly publish and declare that these United Colonies are, and of right ought to be, free and independent states; that they are absolved from all allegiance to the British crown, and that all political connection between them and the state of Great Britain is, and ought to be, totally dissolved; and that, as free and independent states, they have full power to levy war, conclude peace, contract alliances, establish commerce, and do all other acts and things which independent states may of right do. And for the support of this declaration, with a firm reliance on the protection of Divine Providence, we mutually pledge to each other our lives, our fortunes, and our sacred honor.

---

12. *Perfidy* means "a deliberate betrayal of trust."
13. A compensation for a wrong done is a *redress*.
14. *Magnanimity* means "nobility of mind and heart."
15. Here, *conjured* means "solemnly appealed to."

16. *Consanguinity* is a relationship based on having ancestors in common; a blood relationship.
17. Here, *denounces* means "announces" or "proclaims."

Vocabulary
acquiesce (ak′ wē es′) *v.* to consent or agree silently, without objections; to comply passively
rectitude (rek′ tə tōōd′) *n.* uprightness of moral character; honesty

Responding to Literature

Personal Response

How has your reading of the Declaration of Independence affected your ideas about freedom?

——— ANALYZING LITERATURE ———

RECALL AND INTERPRET

1. What is the purpose of the document? To which "opinions of mankind" might Jefferson be referring?
2. According to Jefferson, which human rights are unalienable? How do you interpret the phrase "pursuit of happiness"?
3. What accusations does Jefferson make against the British king? In a statement, summarize the complaints against the king.
4. How have the colonists met with "these oppressions"? Why might the King have ignored the colonists' petitions for redress?
5. What do the signers pledge in the final paragraph? What does the pledge in the final paragraph reveal about the signers' commitment?

EVALUATE AND CONNECT

6. In listing the grievances, Jefferson uses the technique of **repetition** (see page R13), beginning each item with the phrase *He has.* How does this technique help make the document clear?
7. Identify and explain what you consider to be Jefferson's strongest argument for freedom.
8. Think back to the ideas you expressed for the Focus Activity on page 168. Do you think the basic ideas expressed in the Declaration of Independence reflect your beliefs? Use details from the document to support your opinion.

Literary
ELEMENTS

Connotation
Beyond their literal meaning, words carry with them suggestions or associations of feeling. Such suggestions or associations are called the word's **connotations.** In the Declaration of Independence, Jefferson uses words having strongly negative connotations: He speaks of the king's "abuses," "usurpations," and "despotism."

Identify words having negative connotations in the following passage: "He has plundered our seas, ravaged our Coasts, burned our towns, and destroyed the lives of our people." Explain the connotation of each.

● See **Literary Terms Handbook,** p. R4.

——— EXTENDING YOUR RESPONSE ———

Writing About Literature

Effective Presentation of Ideas   Jefferson's presentation of the rights of all people proved so effective that the Declaration of Independence is universally admired. Identify at least three elements in the Declaration that, in your opinion, give it strength. Explain how each contributes to the power of the whole.

Literature Groups

Freedom for All   "When in the course of human events it becomes necessary for one people to dissolve the political bands which have connected them with another . . ." With your group, discuss what conditions or situations in today's world might justify such a declaration of independence.

 Save your work for your portfolio.

Technology Skills

E-mail: Business Writing

E-mail has made exercising your right of free speech easier than ever. Many newspapers, magazines, television shows, and radio broadcasts list their E-mail addresses so you can voice your opinion with a few minutes at the keyboard and the click of a mouse button. But if you decide to comment via E-mail, you'll need to remember several points about business writing.

The E-mail Business Letter

Server space on office computers is valuable. Mail that is too memory-intensive has been known to bring more than one network crashing down. Consequently, a business letter via E-mail should not be as lengthy or as elaborate as those destined for the post office. Look at the sample below:

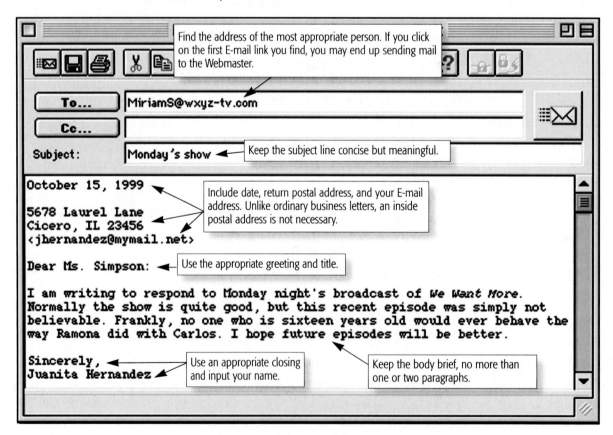

As with any letter, business E-mails should be checked for grammar and spelling *before* they are sent. Though most E-mail programs offer an "unsend" feature, you shouldn't make a habit of relying upon it too heavily.

TIPS FOR EFFECTIVE BUSINESS E-MAIL COMMUNICATIONS
• **Be certain.** If you respond immediately to something you view or read, you may react with emotion, which can get in the way of what you want to express. If you're writing an E-mail to voice an extreme response, you might want to wait a day or two before clicking Send.
• **Be cordial.** Even if you are writing to express displeasure, don't neglect common courtesy. You don't need to be overly gracious in your letter, but don't flame the reader.
• **Be brief.** Dispense with any unnecessary formalities, and say what you want to say.
• **Be clear.** Because we know what we mean, sometimes we mistakenly think others will, too. Ask a friend to read through your E-mail before you send it if you think there might be confusing elements.
• **Avoid E-mail acronyms and emoticons.** Acronyms (such as BTW for By the Way) and emoticons (like smiley faces) are useful for saving valuable server space, but save them for your friendly letters.
• **Remember your audience.** Adapt your correspondence to the needs of the person to whom you are writing. A business E-mail should be formal, but not stilted.
• **Include your addresses.** Make sure you include your E-mail address as well as your postal address.

E-mail is an excellent way of sharing your opinions quickly and easily, but you might consider following up your electronic correspondence with a letter mailed through the post office. E-mail is often viewed as remote, whereas traditional forms of business communication add a personal touch.

ACTIVITIES

1. Surf the Web to find sites of major newspapers and television programs. Search within the site to locate the E-mail address of a public relations official or customer service representative. (Note: the E-mail address at the bottom of the Web site is usually that of the Webmaster. Only comments about the site itself should be sent to her or him.) Practice writing E-mail letters that provide feedback to the newspaper or television show. Ask an older friend or relative to critique your letters and offer suggestions on how they might be improved.

2. Working with a partner, role-play a consumer and a television executive engaged in an E-mail correspondence. Some possible situations include: a letter of praise, a comment or suggestion, a criticism, a request for information.

Before You Read

To His Excellency, General Washington

Meet Phillis Wheatley

❝We whose Names are under-written, do assure the World, that the Poems . . . were (as we verily believe) written by Phillis, a young Negro Girl, who . . . [is] under the Disadvantage of serving as a Slave. . . .❞

In 1773 most readers would have doubted that an enslaved woman had written a book of poetry. The above statement was taken from the introduction to Phillis Wheatley's book of poetry, *Poems on Various Subjects, Religious and Moral,* published when Wheatley was only nineteen or twenty years old. Signed by eighteen of "the most respectable charac-ters in Boston," including John Hancock and the royal governor, the letter was testimony to the authenticity of the poems. Wheatley was the first African American to publish a book of poetry.

Wheatley was kidnapped from her home in the Senegal/Gambia region on the west coast of Africa and brought to New England on the slave ship *Phillis* when she was just seven or eight. In 1761 John Wheatley, a wealthy Bostonian, purchased her to be a personal attendant for his wife, Susanna. Recognizing the child's intelligence, the Wheatley family took great interest in educating her.

Given the family name Wheatley and the first name Phillis (the name of the ship she arrived on), the young woman gained free use of the home library and was supported and encouraged in her studies and writing. She quickly mastered English and Latin. She stud-ied the Bible and read many of the ancient Greek and Latin classics.

In May of 1773, the Wheatleys sent Phillis to London. A doctor had recommended a sea voyage for Phillis's health, and the Wheatley's son Nathaniel was bound for London on business. It was there that Wheatley was finally able to publish her only volume of poetry, *Poems on Various Subjects, Religious and Moral.* On her return from England, the family freed her from enslavement. The poet remained in the Wheatley household until the death of John Wheatley in 1778.

In April of that same year, Phillis Wheatley married John Peters, a freed African American. Poverty and the death of two infants marked their difficult marriage. In 1784 Wheatley wrote her last poem, her husband died in debtor's prison, and on December 5, she died of malnu-trition. A brief announcement in Boston's *Independent Chronicle* read, "Last Lord's Day, died Mrs. Phillis Peters (formerly Phillis Wheatley), aged thirty-one, known to the world by her celebrated miscellaneous poems."

❝You were . . . a sickly little Black girl, snatched from your home and country and made a slave; a woman who still struggled to sing the song that was your gift . . . It is not so much what you sang, as that you kept alive, in so many of our ancestors, the notion of song.❞

—*Alice Walker*

Phillis Wheatley was born around 1753 and died in 1784.

Reading Further

If you would like to read more by Phillis Wheatley, you might read:

The Collected Works of Phillis Wheatley, edited by John C. Shields.

———— FOCUS ACTIVITY ————

What would you write in a letter to the President or another leader? Would you ask the leader to support new laws? Would you propose solutions to problems?

FREEWRITE List messages you might send to the President or to another leader. Consider local or national problems that need to be solved. Think about accomplishments you might thank the leader for.

SETTING A PURPOSE Read to learn Phillis Wheatley's message to George Washington.

———— BACKGROUND ————

The Time and Place

When General George Washington traveled to Boston in 1775 to assume leadership of the Continental Army and to rid the city of occupying British soldiers, Phillis Wheatley wrote to him. Her letter and poem to the General were sent to his headquarters in nearby Cambridge. Washington responded by expressing his appreciation for the poem and invited her to visit him. The two met at his Cambridge headquarters.

Liberty vs. Slavery

The "Columbia" Wheatley speaks of in her poem is America, personified as a goddess of liberty. Wheatley herself, however, had not yet attained her own freedom in the New England colonies. Critics have ridiculed Wheatley for glorifying our nation's freedom yet never speaking out against slavery. Others, however, see Wheatley as a woman who was painfully aware of the need to ingratiate herself with her supporters and patrons.

Literary Influences

Wheatley's poetry is written in the neoclassical style, characterized by formal elegance, simplicity, dignity, order, and proportion. The content of her poetry reflects her strong Christian values.

George Washington. Artist unknown, after Charles Willson Peale. Oil on canvas. Chateau de Versailles, France.

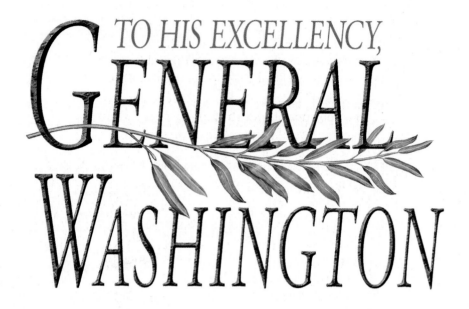

TO HIS EXCELLENCY, GENERAL WASHINGTON

Phillis Wheatley

Sir.

I Have taken the freedom to address your Excellency in the enclosed poem, and entreat your acceptance, though I am not insensible of its inaccuracies. Your being appointed by the Grand Continental Congress to be Generalissimo of the armies of North America, together with the fame of your virtues, excite sensations not easy to suppress. Your generosity, therefore, I presume, will pardon the attempt. Wishing your Excellency all possible success in the great cause you are so generously engaged in. I am,

   Your Excellency's most obedient humble servant,
    Phillis Wheatley.

Providence, Oct. 26, 1775.
His Excellency Gen. Washington.

> Celestial choir! enthron'd in realms of light,
> Columbia's scenes of glorious toils I write.
> While freedom's cause her anxious breast alarms,
> She flashes dreadful in refulgent° arms.
> 5 See mother earth her offspring's fate bemoan,
> And nations gaze at scenes before unknown!
> See the bright beams of heaven's revolving light
> Involved in sorrows and the veil of night!

---

4 *Refulgent* means "radiant."

The goddess comes, she moves divinely fair,
10   Olive and laurel binds her golden hair:
  Wherever shines this native of the skies,
  Unnumber'd charms and recent graces rise.
     Muse!° bow propitious° while my pen relates
  How pour her armies through a thousand gates,
15   As when Eolus° heaven's fair face deforms,
  Enwrapp'd in tempest and a night of storms;
  Astonish'd ocean feels the wild uproar,
  The refluent° surges beat the sounding shore;
  Or thick as leaves in Autumn's golden reign,
20   Such, and so many, moves the warrior's train.
  In bright array they seek the work of war,
  Where high unfurl'd the ensign° waves in air.
  Shall I to Washington their praise recite?
  Enough thou know'st them in the fields of fight.
25   Thee, first in peace and honours,—we demand
  The grace and glory of thy martial band.
  Fam'd for thy valour, for thy virtues more,
  Hear every tongue thy guardian aid implore!
    One century scarce perform'd its destined round,
30   When Gallic° powers Columbia's fury found;
  And so may you, whoever dares disgrace
  The land of freedom's heaven-defended race!
  Fix'd are the eyes of nations on the scales,
  For in their hopes Columbia's arm prevails.
35   Anon° Britannia° droops the pensive head,
  While round increase the rising hills of dead.
  Ah! cruel blindness to Columbia's state!
  Lament thy thirst of boundless power too late.
    Proceed, great chief, with virtue on thy side,
40   Thy ev'ry action let the goddess guide.
  A crown, a mansion, and a throne that shine,
  With gold unfading, WASHINGTON! be thine.

---

13 The poet asks for aid from a *Muse*. In Greek mythology, the Muses
    (goddesses) preside over arts and sciences. Here, *propitious* means "favorably."
15 In Greek mythology, *Eolus* is the god of the winds.
18 *Refluent* means "back-flowing."
22 The *ensign* here is a flag.
30 *Gallic* means "French." Washington had fought the French during the French
    and Indian War (1754–1763).
35 *Anon* means "soon." *Britannia* is Great Britain, personified as a goddess.

Responding to Literature

Personal Response

What is your impression of Wheatley from reading this letter and poem?

ANALYZING LITERATURE

RECALL AND INTERPRET

1. In your own words, restate the message in Wheatley's letter to General Washington. What seems to have been her opinion of Washington?
2. In lines 1–8, describe what the speaker asks the Celestial Choir to see.
3. What image of Columbia is described in lines 9–12? What does the **imagery** convey about the speaker's view of America?
4. In lines 13–22, to what three things does the speaker compare the colonial army? In your opinion, why did she choose these images?
5. To whom are lines 29–38 addressed? How does this section of the poem differ from the rest?

EVALUATE AND CONNECT

6. Did reading the letter help you understand the poem? Why or why not?
7. Which lines from the poem did you have the most trouble understanding? Why do you think they were especially troublesome?
8. How does Wheatley's portrait of Washington compare with other interpretations of him, based on your reading and on television or film portrayals?
9. How might most readers today view Wheatley's poem if it appeared in a newspaper or magazine? Give examples.
10. **Theme Connections**   What is your reaction to Wheatley's attitude toward the colonial cause of freedom? Explain your response.

Literary ELEMENTS

The Heroic Couplet
A **couplet** is two consecutive lines of poetry that rhyme. A **heroic couplet** has a specific rhythm, or meter, called **iambic pentameter**. In this meter, each line consists of five units, or feet, and each foot consists of two syllables, an unstressed one followed by a stressed one. This form of couplet became known as "heroic" because it was commonly used in epics that told of heroes and heroic deeds.

1. Read aloud three heroic couplets from the poem. In your opinion, does the heroic couplet form add to or detract from the meaning and tone of the poem? Explain your position.
2. Why do you think Wheatley might have chosen to write this poem in heroic couplets?

● See **Literary Terms Handbook,** p. R7.

EXTENDING YOUR RESPONSE

Creative Writing

Letter to a Leader   Review your freewrite from the Focus Activity on page 177. Choose one message you would like to send to the President or any other leader. Then write a short poem that captures the essence of your message. Write your poem in couplets; if you want a greater challenge, try writing it in heroic couplets. Read your work to the class.

Interdisciplinary Activity

Art: Create an Image   Choose one of the images from Wheatley's poem to illustrate. Then, in a drawing or a painting, create your own visual image to convey the image in the poem. If possible, you might use a computer to create your image. Display your art for the class.

📖 **Save your work for your portfolio.**

Writing Skills

Effective Conclusions

Phillis Wheatley wrote a cover letter to accompany her poem to President Washington. In her cover letter she presents the reasons for writing her poem and concludes with a sincere wish for Washington's success. Being able to write an effective cover letter is an essential skill. For example, you may need to write a letter to accompany a college or job application. In a cover letter, you should state your purpose for writing at the beginning of the letter. However, in the conclusion you have the opportunity to make your final, strongest point.

Your conclusion should:

- Restate your main ideas and create a sense of closure.
- State what you want to happen as a result of your letter.
- Ask for a specific action or response.

For example, in concluding your cover letter accompanying a college application, you might summarize your key activities or the interests that make you unique. Or, you might emphasize your reasons for wanting to attend the particular school to which you are applying and stress the areas in which you excel. Another way to conclude is to make a general statement that demonstrates the overall importance of any specific qualities or accomplishments you have mentioned.

> **"I have outlined my accomplishments and strong interest in both art and computer science. I believe that these factors, in addition to my excellent grades, make me a prime candidate for Holden College of Art and Design. I sincerely hope you will give strong consideration to my application for admission. I await your response. Thank you."**

Make sure that your conclusion does not introduce new or unexplained information that will confuse your reader. Also, do not let your conclusion be too lengthy or too informal.

EXERCISES

1. Explain what is wrong with the following conclusion and rewrite it to make it more effective: "Well, I have mentioned most of the reasons why I would like to go to your school. Let me know if I am accepted."

2. Imagine that you are writing a letter responding to an ad for a job. Write an effective conclusion that will ensure a response.

Before You Read

Letter to Her Daughter from the New and Unfinished White House

Meet Abigail Adams

"Do not put such unlimited power into the hands of husbands. Remember all men would be tyrants if they could."

—*Adams*

She was the wife of a president and the mother of another, but Abigail Adams was a remarkable woman in her own right. She grew up in one of the most prestigious families in Massachusetts at a time when women did not pursue an education. Intelligent and curious, Adams educated herself by reading everything she could. She was a strong believer in a woman's right to own property and to receive a formal education. Women should move "beyond the limits of drawing room and kitchen," she once wrote. As the nation's first lady from 1797 to 1801, Adams often advised the president on national affairs. She also ran their farm in Massachusetts, managed the family finances, and raised four children, including John Quincy Adams, the sixth president of the United States (1825–1829).

Abigail Adams was born in 1744 and died in 1818.

FOCUS ACTIVITY

Think of a time when you had difficulty adjusting to a new situation, or when a place or situation did not live up to your expectations. How did you feel?

DISCUSS Share with the class examples of expectations dashed by reality or exceeded by reality. List techniques for coping.

SETTING A PURPOSE Read to discover how writing might be a way to cope with a challenging situation.

BACKGROUND

The Time and Place

In 1790 the United States government formed the District of Columbia as the new nation's capital. Irish architect James Hoban was chosen to design the presidential house. President John Adams and First Lady Abigail Adams moved into the still unfinished residence on November 1, 1800. The building was not officially known as the White House until 1902.

VOCABULARY PREVIEW

extricate (eks′ trə kāt′) *v.* to set free from; to remove; p. 183

accommodate (ə kom′ ə dāt′) *v.* to provide room or facilities for; p. 184

render (ren′ dər) *v.* to cause to be; to make; p. 184

recourse (rē′ kôrs′) *n.* resorting to a person or thing for help; p. 185

Letter to Her Daughter

from the New and Unfinished White House

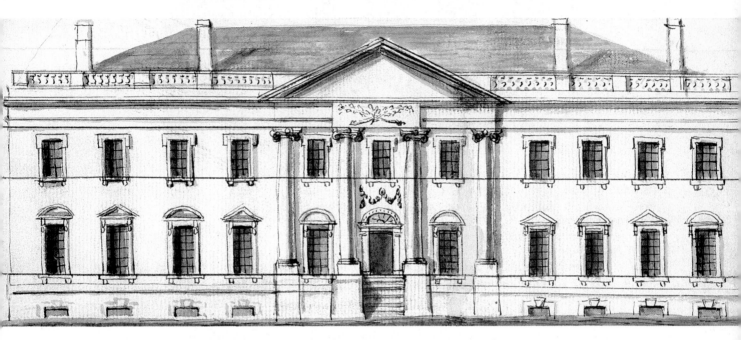

The President's House, Sketch of the North Front, c. 1800. Samuel Blodget. Pen and ink drawing. The White House Collection, © White House Historical Association.

Abigail Adams

Washington, 21 November, 1800.

My Dear Child,

I arrived here on Sunday last, and without meeting with any accident worth noticing, except losing ourselves when we left Baltimore, and going eight or nine miles on the Frederick road, by which means we were obliged to go the other eight through woods, where we wandered two hours without finding a guide, or the path. Fortunately, a straggling black came up with us, and we engaged him as a guide, to <u>extricate</u> us out of our difficulty; but woods are all you see, from Baltimore until you reach *the city*, which is only so in name. Here and there is a small cot,[1] without a glass window, interspersed amongst the forests, through which you travel miles without seeing any human being.

1. A *cot* is a small house.

Vocabulary
extricate (eks′ trə kāt′) *v.* to set free from; to remove

Abigail Adams Hanging Laundry in the East Wing of the Unfinished White House. Gordon Phillips. Oil on canvas. Collection of White House Historical Association.

Viewing the painting: What further insight into the character of Abigail Adams does this painting give you? Explain your reasoning.

In the city there are buildings enough, if they were compact and finished, to accommodate Congress and those attached to it; but as they are, and scattered as they are, I see no great comfort for them. The river, which runs up to Alexandria, is in full view of my window, and I see the vessels as they pass and repass. The house is upon a grand and superb scale, requiring about thirty servants to attend and keep the apartments in proper order, and perform the ordinary business of the house and stables; an establishment very well proportioned to the President's salary. The lighting of the apartments, from the kitchen to parlors and chambers, is a tax indeed; and the fires we are obliged to keep to secure us from daily agues is another very cheering comfort. To assist us in this great castle, and render less attendance necessary, bells are wholly wanting, not one single one being hung through the whole house, and promises are all you can obtain. This is so great an inconvenience, that I know not what to do, or how to do. The ladies from Georgetown and in the city have many of them visited me. Yesterday I returned fifteen visits,—but such a place as Georgetown appears,—why, our Milton is beautiful. But no comparisons;—if they will put me up some bells, and let me have wood enough to keep fires, I design to be pleased. I could content myself almost anywhere three months; but, surrounded with forests, can you believe that wood is not to be had, because people cannot be found to cut and cart it! Briesler entered into a contract with a man to supply him with wood. A small part, a few cords[2]

2. A *cord* is a quantity of wood equal to 128 cubic feet. The sawed wood is usually arranged in a pile 4 feet wide, 4 feet high, and 8 feet long.

Vocabulary
accommodate (ə kom′ ə dāt′) *v.* to provide room or facilities for
render (ren′ dər) *v.* to cause to be; to make

only, has he been able to get. Most of that was expended to dry the walls of the house before we came in, and yesterday the man told him it was impossible for him to procure it to be cut and carted. He has had <u>recourse</u> to coals; but we cannot get grates made and set. We have, indeed, come into a *new country*.

You must keep all this to yourself, and, when asked how I like it, say that I write you the situation is beautiful, which is true. The house is made habitable, but there is not a single apartment finished, and all withinside, except the plastering, has been done since Briesler came. We have not the least fence, yard, or other convenience, without, and the great unfinished audience-room I make a drying-room of, to hang up the clothes in. The principal stairs are not up, and will not be this winter. Six chambers are made comfortable; two are occupied by the President and Mr. Shaw; two lower rooms, one for a common parlor, and one for a levee-room.[3] Upstairs there is the oval room, which is designed for the drawing-room, and has the crimson furniture in it. It is a very handsome room now; but, when completed, it will be beautiful. If the twelve years, in which this place has been considered as the future seat of government, had been improved, as they would have been if in New England, very many of the present inconveniences would have been removed. It is a beautiful spot, capable of every improvement, and, the more I view it, the more I am delighted with it.

Since I sat down to write, I have been called down to a servant from Mount Vernon,[4] with a billet[5] from Major Custis, and a haunch of venison, and a kind, congratulatory letter from Mrs. Lewis, upon my arrival in the city, with Mrs. Washington's love, inviting me to Mount Vernon, where, health permitting, I will go, before I leave this place. . . .

Thomas comes in and says a House[6] is made; so to-morrow, though Saturday, the President will meet them. Adieu, my dear. Give my love to your brother, and tell him he is ever present upon my mind.

Affectionately your mother,
A. Adams

---

3. A *levee-room* is a room for holding formal receptions.
4. *Mount Vernon,* located near Washington, D.C., was the home of the first U.S. president, George Washington, and his wife, Martha.
5. Here, *billet* means "a short letter."
6. A sufficient number of members of the *House* of Representatives had arrived in the new capital to enable a session of Congress to take place.

Vocabulary
recourse (rē′ kôrs′) *n.* resorting to a person or thing for help

Responding to Literature

Personal Response

Would you like to have known Abigail Adams? Why or why not?

——— ANALYZING LITERATURE ———

RECALL AND INTERPRET

1. What situations complicated Abigail Adams's journey to Washington, D.C.? How do you think she felt about these complications?
2. Does she think that the members of Congress will find their own residences comfortable? Explain.
3. Which inconveniences appear to be most important to Abigail Adams? Why, in your opinion, is this so?
4. In the middle of the letter, what instructions does Adams give her daughter? Why do you think Adams makes this request?

EVALUATE AND CONNECT

5. **Tone** (see page R16) is the attitude a writer takes toward his or her subject. Describe Adams's tone in this letter.
6. What character traits would you attribute to Abigail Adams based solely on this letter? Support your response with details from the letter.
7. What kinds of information do you think can be learned from publishing the private letters of famous people from the past?
8. Personal writings are sources of information about daily life in earlier times. What kinds of modern-day communications might people in the future study to learn about life in your generation?

Literary ELEMENTS

Description

Description is the use of details in a piece of writing to give the reader a picture of a person, place, or thing. These details appeal to the five senses—sight, sound, taste, smell, and touch. Good descriptive writing includes details that contribute to the overall purpose of the writing and avoids irrelevant details.

1. What impression of Abigail Adams's new home do you get from her letter? Which details contribute to that impression?
2. Which description in her letter is most surprising to you? most memorable? Why?

● See **Literary Terms Handbook**, p. R4.

——— EXTENDING YOUR RESPONSE ———

Learning for Life

Running the White House   In a small group, research the inner workings of the White House. Focus your research on one of the topics listed below.

● How many people are employed at the White House, and what are some of their specific jobs?
● Describe a typical day at the White House.
● About how much does it cost to maintain the White House each year, and how is the money spent?

Pull together your group's findings into a brief presentation that includes pie charts or other visuals.

Personal Writing

Something New   Look back at your response to the Focus Activity on page 182. Write a letter to someone who is moving to the area where you live. Try to present a picture of your region that will create realistic expectations. Describe the pros and cons of living in your area.

💾 **Save your work for your portfolio.**

MEDIA *Connection*

Web Site

Throughout history, people have made heroic efforts to break free. Participants in the project Amistad America™ hope to remind us of one group of enslaved Africans who did break free.

Amistad America™ The Amistad Incident

Address: ▼   http://www.amistadamerica.org

AMISTAD *America* ™

The *Amistad* incident began off the coast of Cuba in 1839 with a shipboard rebellion by 53 Africans who had been illegally enslaved. Wandering up the Atlantic coast, the ship was seized by a United States revenue cutter off the coast of Long Island and towed into New London harbor, where the Africans were initially imprisoned. They were tried for murder in Connecticut, and eventually won their freedom after John Quincy Adams argued their case in the United States Supreme Court. The ship that was transporting them into slavery and then to freedom was named *Amistad,* which means "friendship" in Spanish.

Now, more than 150 years later, the *Amistad* will sail again. When complete the freedom schooner *Amistad* will ply the nation's waterways as an educational ambassador, teaching lessons of history, cooperation, and leadership to Americans of all ages, interests, and cultural backgrounds.

Take a look at this picture perfect project:

While Steven Spielberg puts the *Amistad* saga on the big screen, Amistad America™ will take the story on the open sea aboard freedom schooner *Amistad.* . . .

Mystic Seaport's *Amistad* project coordinator Quentin Snediker will lead the charge in transforming wood, metal, and fabric into the $2.8 million, 77-foot, hand-hewn freedom schooner *Amistad.*

Amistad will set sail . . . with Captain Bill Pinkney at the helm. The vessel will ply the nation's waterways as an educational ambassador. . . .

Respond

1. What do you think motivates people to participate in a project like Amistad America™?

2. Do you think the project will be successful? Explain your answer.

Before You Read

from *The Life of Olaudah Equiano*

Meet Olaudah Equiano

"... I might say my sufferings were great; but when I compare my lot with that of most of my countrymen, I regard myself as a particular favorite of heaven...."

—*Equiano*

Olaudah Equiano (ō lau′ dä e kwē ä′ nō), the son of a chieftain of the Igbo group, was born in 1745 in the African village of Essaka (now northeastern Nigeria). When he was only eleven years old, he was kidnapped by slave traders and shipped to the island of Barbados in the Caribbean Sea.

In Barbados, Equiano traded the "cheerfulness and affability . . . the leading characteristics of our nation" for the "shrieks of the women and the groans of the dying [that made] a scene of horror almost inconceivable."

Equiano had been in Barbados for nearly a year when an officer of the British Royal Navy bought him and renamed him Gustavus Vassa. By the age of twelve Equiano learned to read and write. At age twenty-one he was finally able to buy his freedom. He settled in England and devoted himself to the antislavery movement. His autobiography, *The Interesting Narrative of the Life of Olaudah Equiano, or Gustavus Vassa, the African*, was first published in 1789. It would forever change the European and American view of slavery.

Olaudah Equiano was born in 1745 and died in 1797.

FOCUS ACTIVITY

"No man has received from nature the right to give orders to others. Freedom is a gift from heaven, and every individual of the same species has the right to enjoy it as soon as he is in enjoyment of his reason."

—*Denis Diderot*

SHARE IT! Discuss with a classmate this statement by French philosopher Diderot. Try to summarize the statement in just a few words. Consider how you might feel if someone took away your freedom.

SETTING A PURPOSE Read to discover Equiano's attitude toward his loss of freedom.

BACKGROUND

The Time and Place

From the 1500s to the 1800s, about twelve million Africans suffered unspeakable horrors on the forced journey from their homes to enslavement in the Western Hemisphere. The longest and most arduous portion of the journey, known as the Middle Passage, was a two-month voyage from West Africa to the West Indies. Almost two million Africans died from malnutrition, disease, suffocation, beatings, and despair.

VOCABULARY PREVIEW

countenance (koun′ tə nens) *n.* face; facial features; p. 190
apprehension (ap′ ri hen′ shən) *n.* fear of what may happen in the future; anxiety; p. 191
copious (kō′ pē əs) *adj.* large in quantity; plentiful; p. 192

gratify (grat′ ə fī′) *v.* to satisfy or indulge; p. 193
clamor (klam′ ər) *n.* confused, insistent shouting; p. 194
scruple (skroo′ pəl) *n.* moral principle that restrains action; p. 194

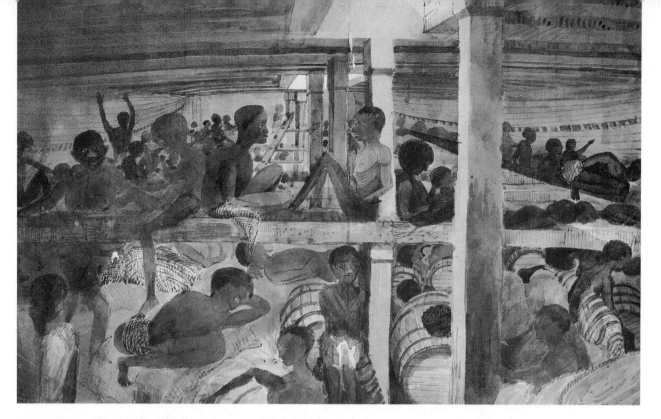

The Slavedeck of the Albaroz, *Prize to the H.M.S.* Albatros, 1846. Daniel Henry Meynell. Watercolor. National Maritime Museum, London, UK.

from The Life of Olaudah Equiano

Olaudah Equiano ~

THE FIRST OBJECT WHICH SALUTED[1] MY EYES WHEN I arrived on the coast, was the sea, and a slave ship, which was then riding at anchor, and waiting for its cargo. These filled me with astonishment, which was soon converted into terror, when I was carried on board. I was immediately handled, and tossed up to see if I were sound, by some of the crew; and I was now persuaded that I had gotten into a world of bad spirits, and that they were going to kill me.

1. Here, *saluted* means "became noticeable to" or "struck."

from The Life of Olaudah Equiano

Their complexions, too, differing so much from ours, their long hair, and the language they spoke, (which was very different from any I had ever heard) united to confirm me in this belief. Indeed, such were the horrors of my views and fears at the moment, that, if ten thousand worlds had been my own, I would have freely parted with them all to have exchanged my condition with that of the meanest[2] slave in my own country. When I looked round the ship too, and saw a large furnace of copper boiling, and a multitude of black people of every description chained together, every one of their countenances expressing dejection and sorrow, I no longer doubted of my fate; and, quite overpowered with horror and anguish, I fell motionless on the deck and fainted. When I recovered a little, I found some black people about me, who I believed were some of those who had brought me on board, and had been receiving their pay; they talked to me in order to cheer me, but all in vain.[3] I asked them if we were not to be eaten by those white men with horrible looks, red faces, and long hair. They told me I was not: and one of the crew brought me a small portion of spirituous liquor in a wine glass, but, being afraid of him, I would not take it out of his hand. One of the blacks, therefore, took it from him and gave it to me, and I took a little down my palate,[4] which, instead of reviving me, as they thought it would, threw me into the greatest consternation[5] at the strange feeling it produced, having never tasted any such liquor before. Soon after this, the blacks who brought me on board went off, and left me abandoned to despair.

I now saw myself deprived of all chance of returning to my native country, or even the least glimpse of hope of gaining the shore, which I now considered as friendly; and I even wished for my former slavery in preference to my present situation, which was filled with horrors of every kind, still heightened by my ignorance of what I was to undergo. I was not long suffered[6] to indulge my grief; I was soon put down under the decks, and there I received such a salutation in my nostrils as I had never experienced in my life: so that, with the loathsomeness of the stench, and crying together, I became so sick and low that I was not able to eat, nor had I the least desire to taste any thing. I now wished for the last friend, death, to relieve me; but soon, to my grief, two of the white men offered me eatables; and, on my refusing to eat, one of them held me fast by the hands, and laid me across, I think the windlass,[7] and tied my feet, while the other flogged me severely. I had never experienced any thing of this kind before, and although not being used to the water, I naturally feared that element the first time I saw it, yet, nevertheless, could I have got over the nettings,[8] I would have jumped over the side, but I could not; and besides, the crew used to watch us very closely who were not chained down to the decks, lest we should leap into the water; and I have seen some of these poor African prisoners most severely cut, for attempting to do so, and hourly whipped for not eating. This indeed was often the case with myself. In a little time after, amongst the poor chained men, I found some of my own nation, which in a small degree gave ease to my mind. I inquired of these what was to be done with us? They gave

---

2. Here, *meanest* means "of the lowest social position or rank."
3. Something done *in vain* is done without effect or success.
4. The *palate,* here, is the mouth and throat.
5. *Consternation* is paralyzing dismay or fear.
6. Here, *suffered* means "allowed."
7. A *windlass* is a type of crank with a handle. It is used to raise or lower a heavy object such as an anchor.
8. *Nettings* were networks of small ropes on the sides of a ship. On slavers, nettings were used to prevent captives from jumping overboard.

Vocabulary
countenance (koun′ tə nəns) *n.* face; facial features

me to understand, we were to be carried to these white people's country to work for them. I then was a little revived, and thought, if it were no worse than working, my situation was not so desperate; but still I feared I should be put to death, the white people looked and acted, as I thought, in so savage a manner; for I had never seen among any people such instances of brutal cruelty; and this not only shown towards us blacks, but also to some of the whites themselves. One white man in particular I saw, when we were permitted to be on deck, flogged so unmercifully with a large rope near the foremast, that he died in consequence of it;

Did You Know?
The *foremast* is the mast (pole that supports the sails and rigging) nearest the bow, or front area, of a sailing ship.

and they tossed him over the side as they would have done a brute. This made me fear these people the more; and I expected nothing less than to be treated in the same manner. I could not help expressing my fears and <u>apprehensions</u> to some of my countrymen; I asked them if these people had no country, but lived in this hollow place? (the ship) they told me they did not, but came from a distant one. "Then," said I, "how comes it in all our country we never heard of them?" They told me because they lived so very far off. I then asked where were their women? had they any like themselves? I was told they had. "And why," said I, "do we not see them?" They answered, because they were left behind. I asked how the vessel could go? they told me they could not tell; but that there was cloth put upon the masts by the help of the ropes I saw, and then the vessel went on; and the white men had some spell or magic they put in the water when they liked, in order to stop the vessel. I was exceedingly amazed at this account, and really thought they were spirits. I therefore wished much to be from amongst them, for I expected they would sacrifice me; but my wishes were vain—for we were so quartered that it was impossible for any of us to make our escape.

While we stayed on the coast I was mostly on deck; and one day, to my great astonishment, I saw one of these vessels coming in with the sails up. As soon as the whites saw it, they gave a great shout, at which we were amazed; and the more so, as the vessel appeared larger by approaching nearer. At last, she came to an anchor in my sight, and when the anchor was let go, I and my countrymen who saw it, were lost in astonishment to observe the vessel stop—and were now convinced it was done by magic. Soon after this the other ship got her boats out, and they came on board of us, and the people of both ships seemed very glad to see each other. Several of the strangers also shook hands with us black people, and made motions with their hands, signifying I suppose, we were to go to their country, but we did not understand them.

At last, when the ship we were in, had got in all her cargo, they made ready with many fearful noises, and we were all put under deck, so that we could not see how they managed the vessel. But this disappointment was the least of my sorrow. The stench of the hold while we were on the coast was so intolerably loathsome, that it was dangerous to remain there for any time, and some of us had been permitted to stay on the deck for the fresh air; but now that the whole ship's

Vocabulary
apprehension (ap′ ri hen′ shən) *n.* fear of what may happen in the future; anxiety

Viewing the art: In what ways does this image express the horrors of slavery? Use details from the art to explain your answer.

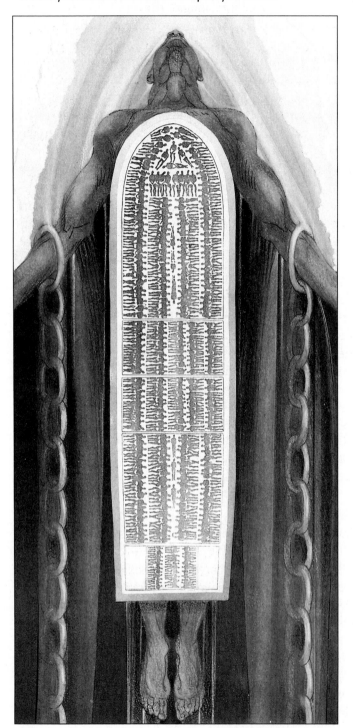

cargo were confined together, it became absolutely pestilential.[9] The closeness of the place, and the heat of the climate, added to the number in the ship, which was so crowded that each had scarcely room to turn himself, almost suffocated us. This produced copious perspirations, so that the air soon became unfit for respiration, from a variety of loathsome smells, and brought on a sickness among the slaves, of which many died—thus falling victims to the improvident[10] avarice,[11] as I may call it, of their purchasers. This wretched situation was again aggravated by the galling[12] of the chains, now became insupportable; and the filth of the necessary tubs,[13] into which the children often fell, and were almost suffocated. The shrieks of the women, and the groans of the dying, rendered[14] the whole a scene of horror almost inconceivable. Happily perhaps, for myself, I was soon reduced so low here that it was thought necessary to keep me almost always on deck; and from my extreme youth I was not put in fetters.[15] In this situation I expected every hour to share the fate of my companions, some of whom were almost daily brought upon deck at the point of death, which I began to hope would soon put an end to my miseries. Often did I think many of the inhabitants of the deep much more happy than myself. I envied them the freedom they enjoyed, and as often

---

9. *Pestilential* means "poisonous" or "likely to cause disease or death."
10. *Improvident* means "lacking foresight" or "not providing for the future."
11. *Avarice* is greed.
12. *Galling* is the chafing or rubbing that causes irritation of the skin.
13. *Necessary tubs* are containers for bodily waste.
14. *Render* means "to cause to be" or "to make."
15. *Fetters* are leg irons.

Vocabulary
copious (kō′ pē əs) *adj.* large in quantity; plentiful

wished I could change my condition for theirs. Every circumstance I met with, served only to render my state more painful, and heightened my apprehensions, and my opinion of the cruelty of the whites.

One day they had taken a number of fishes; and when they had killed and satisfied themselves with as many as they thought fit, to our astonishment who were on deck, rather than give any of them to us to eat, as we expected, they tossed the remaining fish into the sea again, although we begged and prayed for some as well as we could, but in vain; and some of my countrymen, being pressed by hunger, took an opportunity, when they thought no one saw them, of trying to get a little privately; but they were discovered, and the attempt procured them some very severe floggings. One day, when we had a smooth sea and moderate wind, two of my wearied countrymen who were chained together, (I was near them at the time,) preferring death to such a life of misery, somehow made through the nettings and jumped into the sea: immediately, another quite dejected fellow, who, on account of his illness, was suffered to be out of irons, also followed their example; and I believe many more would very soon have done the same, if they had not been prevented by the ship's crew, who were instantly alarmed. Those of us that were the most active, were in a moment put down under the deck, and there was such a noise and confusion amongst the people of the ship as I never heard before, to stop her, and get the boat out to go after the slaves. However, two of the wretches were drowned, but they got the other, and afterwards flogged him unmercifully, for thus attempting to prefer death to slavery. In this manner we continued to undergo more hardships than I can now relate, hardships which are inseparable from this accursed trade. Many a time we were near suffocation from the want of fresh air, which we were often without for whole days together.

This, and the stench of the necessary tubs, carried off many.

During our passage, I first saw flying fishes, which surprised me very much; they used frequently to fly across the ship, and many of them fell on the deck. I also now first saw the use of the quadrant; I had often with astonishment seen the mariners make observations with it, and I could not think what it meant. They at last took notice of my surprise; and one of them, willing to increase it, as well as to <u>gratify</u> my curiosity, made me one day look through it. The clouds appeared to me to be land, which disappeared as they passed along. This heightened my wonder; and I was now more persuaded than ever, that I was in another world, and that every thing about me was magic. At last, we came in sight of the island of Barbadoes, at which the whites on board gave a great shout, and made many signs of joy to us. We did not know what to think of this; but as the vessel drew nearer, we plainly saw the harbor, and other ships of different kinds and sizes, and we soon anchored amongst them, off Bridgetown.[16] Many merchants and planters now came on board, though it was in the evening. They put us in separate parcels,[17] and examined us attentively. They also made us jump, and pointed to the land, signifying we were to go there. We thought by this, we should be eaten by these ugly men, as they appeared to us; and, when soon after we were all put down under the

Did You Know?
A *quadrant* is an instrument with a scale of 90° used in navigating a ship.

---

16. *Bridgetown* is the capital of Barbados.
17. Here, *parcels* means "groups."

Vocabulary
gratify (grat′ ə fī′) *v.* to satisfy or indulge

deck again, there was much dread and trembling among us, and nothing but bitter cries to be heard all the night from these apprehensions, insomuch, that at last the white people got some old slaves from the land to pacify us. They told us we were not to be eaten, but to work, and were soon to go on land, where we should see many of our country people. This report eased us much. And sure enough, soon after we were landed, there came to us Africans of all languages.

We were conducted immediately to the merchant's yard, where we were all pent up together, like so many sheep in a fold, without regard to sex or age. As every object was new to me, every thing I saw filled me with surprise. What struck me first, was, that the houses were built with bricks and stories, and in every other respect different from those I had seen in Africa; but I was still more astonished on seeing people on horseback. I did not know what this could mean; and, indeed, I thought these people were full of nothing but magical arts. While I was in this astonishment, one of my fellow-prisoners spoke to a countryman of his, about the horses, who said they were the same kind they had in their country. I understood them, though they were from a distant part of Africa; and I thought it odd I had not seen any horses there; but afterwards, when I came to converse with different Africans, I found they had many horses amongst them, and much larger than those I then saw.

We were not many days in the merchant's custody, before we were sold after their usual manner, which is this:—On a signal given, (as the beat of a drum,) the buyers rush at once into the yard where the slaves are confined, and make choice of that parcel they like best.

The noise and clamor with which this is attended, and the eagerness visible in the countenances of the buyers, serve not a little to increase the apprehension of terrified Africans, who may well be supposed to consider them as the ministers of that destruction to which they think themselves devoted. In this manner, without scruple, are relations and friends separated, most of them never to see each other again. I remember, in the vessel in which I was brought over, in the men's apartment, there were several brothers, who, in the sale, were sold in different lots; and it was very moving on this occasion, to see and hear their cries at parting. O, ye nominal[18] Christians! might not an African ask you—Learned you this from your God, who says unto you, Do unto all men as you would men should do unto you?[19] Is it not enough that we are torn from our country and friends, to toil for your luxury and lust of gain? Must every tender feeling be likewise sacrificed to your avarice? Are the dearest friends and relations, now rendered more dear by their separation from their kindred, still to be parted from each other, and thus prevented from cheering the gloom of slavery, with the small comfort of being together, and mingling their sufferings and sorrows? Why are parents to lose their children, brothers their sisters, or husbands their wives? Surely, this is a new refinement in cruelty, which, while it has no advantage to atone[20] for it, thus aggravates distress, and adds fresh horrors even to the wretchedness of slavery.

---

18. *Nominal* means "in name only."
19. "Therefore all things whatsoever ye would that men should do to you, do ye even so to them." (Matthew 7:12)
20. *Atone* means "to make amends" or "to compensate for."

Vocabulary
clamor (klam′ ər) *n.* confused, insistent shouting
scruple (skrōō′ pəl) *n.* moral principle that restrains action

Responding to Literature

Personal Response

What images or details from this narrative linger in your mind?

——— ANALYZING LITERATURE ———

RECALL AND INTERPRET

1. What does Equiano fear will happen to him when he is taken aboard the ship? Why might he be so afraid?
2. How does Equiano react to the fatal flogging of a white crew member? Why do you think the incident has such a strong impact on Equiano?
3. Although terrified, Equiano also displays great curiosity. Relate an incident that reveals his curiosity. What does it reveal about his character?
4. In the last paragraph, what does Equiano describe as perhaps the greatest tragedy of slavery? What do you think he means when he says it "adds fresh horrors even to the wretchedness of slavery"?

EVALUATE AND CONNECT

5. **Theme Connections**   In this part of his story, does Equiano give any indication that he might soon break free of his enslavement? Explain.
6. Describe the **tone** (see page R16) of this work. At what point does the tone shift? Evaluate the effectiveness of this change in tone.
7. Think back to your discussion for the Focus Activity on page 188. How would you describe Equiano's attitude toward his loss of freedom? How might you react to such an extreme loss of freedom?
8. What insights have you gained from reading this work? For example, has it affected your attitudes about personal freedom, human nature, or our nation's history of enslavement of Africans?

Literary ELEMENTS

Slave Narrative
A **slave narrative** is an autobiographical account of a former enslaved person's life. By personally documenting their own experiences, African Americans helped to expose the cruelty and inhumanity of slavery. Briton Hammon wrote the first slave narrative in 1760. After Equiano's account was published in 1789, many other formerly enslaved people published their autobiographies during the 1800s.

1. To whom do you think Equiano wrote this account?
2. How might this audience have shaped Equiano's tone?
3. Equiano wrote this account to expose the horrors of slavery. In your opinion, how well does he fulfill his purpose?

● See **Literary Terms Handbook,** p. R14.

——— EXTENDING YOUR RESPONSE ———

Internet Connection

First-Hand Accounts   Log on to the Library of Congress's on-line African American History and Culture page. There you can find photographs of original texts, letters, and posters related to the topic of slavery. You can also find art by and about enslaved African Americans. Download and print a story or photograph you find interesting and share it with your class.

Writing About Literature

Two Thumbs Up   Imagine that you have just produced a feature film based on the life of Olaudah Equiano. Write a press release that summarizes the story and encourages viewers to attend a screening of the film.

📖 **Save your work for your portfolio.**

~: Writing ✒ Workshop :~

Personal Writing: Reflective Essay

What does "breaking free" mean to you? What are your thoughts about oppression and independence? Your mind is deep, and when you take the trouble to explore it, you can find surprising wisdom. The selections you have read so far express ideas about oppression, freedom, and crucial choices. One way to explore such ideas is to write a reflective essay, a piece of writing that examines in-depth your own thoughts on a particular subject. **In this workshop, you will write a reflective essay.** You will examine, develop, and write about your own insights on one of the ideas in this theme.

● As you write your reflective essay, refer to **Writing Handbook,** pp. R62–R77.

The Writing Process

PREWRITING

PREWRITING TIP

To start your exploration, ask a friend to interview you about freedom, oppression, or choices in this theme and in today's world. Jot down your answers to the interview questions.

Explore ideas

Many selections in this theme are more than two hundred years old, yet they speak to people today. Look back through the theme for selections or passages that have special meaning for you. Ask yourself questions like these:

● How do these selections make me feel? Proud? Angry? Hopeful? Confused? Sad? Curious? Why do I feel this way?
● With which of Benjamin Franklin's proverbs do I agree or disagree? Why?
● What are Patrick Henry's ideas about freedom? What are my ideas about freedom?
● What parts of Thomas Paine's *The Crisis, No. 1* do I still remember from my first reading? Why?
● What aspects of Abigail Adams's personality do I like or dislike?
● What current events or issues came to mind when I read the Declaration of Independence?
● If Phillis Wheatley saw the world today, what would she think?
● How can I understand or relate to Olaudah Equiano's experience?
● Of the selections I have read, which ones might apply to my life or to the lives of people I know? How do they apply?

Connect your thoughts

To explore an idea further, try using a word web. In the center circle of your web, identify a striking passage. In the connecting circles, write your initial reactions. Add circles to raise questions, respond to them, or give examples. Show how one thought leads to another.

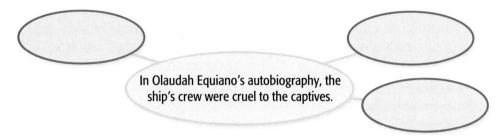

In Olaudah Equiano's autobiography, the ship's crew were cruel to the captives.

Choose an audience

You might want to express your thoughts by writing a column for your school newspaper, a letter to the editor of a local publication, or simply a journal entry. Decide on your audience before you begin to write.

Consider your purpose

Your main purpose will be to express your reflections on a subject in an essay.

Make a plan

Look over your notes. In a statement to yourself, sum up what you want to say. Then select points to elaborate on your thesis. Use a chart like the one shown here to arrange your points in an order that makes sense.

Thesis: Olaudah Equiano's autobiography shows one group of people treating another inhumanely; such cruelty has terrible costs.	
Point	**Examples/Details**
Cruelty recurs through history	Concentration camps Trail of Tears Political prisoners tortured today
Cruelty undermines civilizations	Lack of physical safety and trust = Lack of freedom Radio interview of woman whose parents survived Nazi concentration camps
Cruelty harms perpetrators as well as victims	How must perpetrator view victims? Loss of compassion = Loss of humanness Victims may take revenge if they have the opportunity
Conclusion	**Action Needed**
Can such cruelty be prevented?	Deal with violence in media Look at my personal behavior

∴ Writing ❧ Workshop ∾

DRAFTING

DRAFTING TIP

A reflective essay is like a one-way conversation. Imagine you are talking with someone as you draft.

Begin your draft

Jump in and begin drafting, using your prewriting plan as a guide. Write as yourself, using the pronouns *I* and *me*. Put your thoughts, feelings, insights, and observations down on paper. Take the time to stop occasionally and reflect on your unfinished draft. If your writing is leading you in an unexpected direction, follow it. You may gain new insights about your topic—and yourself. Don't get bogged down trying to find the perfect word or make your ideas flow smoothly at this point. You can polish your essay later.

Flesh out main points

Your opinions and observations about your topic will be more believable if you back them up with details, facts, and examples. Look over the main points in your draft and find two or more pieces of information to support each point. If you need more information, do some research or reread the selection for new ideas. Include them, and add transitions where necessary to guide readers from one main point or supporting detail to the next.

STUDENT MODEL

Equiano is one of millions of people who have been treated in ways that I find shocking and unbearable. For example, between 1492 and 1870, about 11 million Africans were snatched from their homes, crammed aboard ships, and sold into slavery in the New World. Meanwhile, American colonists hungry for land were pushing native peoples out of their homes. ~~The "Trail of Tears" is one example of this cruelty toward Native Americans.~~ In 1838, American soldiers forced 16,000 Cherokee people to leave their homeland in the southeastern United States and resettle in Oklahoma. During this journey, known as the "Trail of Tears," thousands of Cherokee died from disease, starvation, or exposure to the cold.

REVISING

Evaluate your work

Take a break from your essay, then come back to it after several hours or a day. Reread your draft and mark parts that seem weak or confusing. Use the **Questions for Revising** as a guide.

Ask for comments

Read your work aloud to a classmate. Ask questions and discuss possible changes. Then make changes that seem right to you.

TECHNOLOGY TIP
On a word processor, work with two screens at once. Make changes on one screen and then compare it with the original. Be sure your changes are really improvements.

QUESTIONS FOR REVISING

- ☑ How well does my writing reflect my thoughts on the topic?
- ☑ How might I state my main idea more clearly?
- ☑ How might I make the order of my ideas more logical or effective? Where might appropriate transitions help?

- ☑ Which (if any) parts wander off the point?
- ☑ Which parts might be clarified by adding details or discussion?
- ☑ How can I make my conclusion more effective?
- ☑ How does the format and writing style fit my purpose and audience?

STUDENT MODEL

According to some people, watching violence in films and on television makes people less sensitive to cruelty. ~~My parents refuse to watch some programs.~~ There were no movies or television during Olaudah Equiano's lifetime, but There was plenty of violence. How could the ship's crew treat Equiano and the other captives so cruelly? I think that the crew became hardened to the violence after seeing so much of it. Today, violence is a big part of television programming. I think we are all somewhat hardened to violence and cruelty, even if it doesn't touch us directly.

EDITING/PROOFREADING

When you are satisfied with your essay, proofread for errors in grammar, usage, mechanics, and spelling. Use the **Proofreading Checklist** on the inside back cover of this book.

Grammar Hint

Add an apostrophe and *s* to form the possessive of a singular noun, even a noun that ends in *s*. Do the same for a plural noun that does not end in *s*.

Charles's *kindness impressed me.*

What could explain ***people's*** *cruelty?*

Simply add an apostrophe to form the possessive of a plural noun that ends in *s*.

The ***captives'*** *experience was truly horrible.*

STUDENT MODEL

In those men's minds, the captives were not people.

PUBLISHING/PRESENTING

PRESENTING TIP

If you decide to read your essay aloud to an audience, rehearse. You want your thoughts to be worth listening to, so practice expressing them with confidence.

If you plan to send your essay to a newspaper or a television station, attach a cover letter. In it, briefly explain who you are, why you wrote your essay, and why you are sending it. You might also mention why you think the letter should be published or read on the air. Be sure your essay is neatly typed or printed.

Reflecting

Look back on the experience of writing this essay. What did you learn about your own attitudes and ideas? How did the process of writing help you strengthen your ideas about the topic? For another reflective essay, what would you do differently? Discuss these questions with a classmate.

Save your work for your portfolio.

Theme 3  Gaining Insight

Think of a time when you had a flash of understanding and saw the deeper, hidden meaning of something. Maybe you suddenly saw the logic behind a geometry proof, or discovered the perfect new ingredient to add to your chili recipe. In either case you would have gained an insight, *an understanding that goes deeper than the surface of things. In this theme you will read selections that reflect the writers' insights—about themselves, about nature, and about humankind.*

THEME PROJECTS

Internet Connection

Design a Web Site   With a partner, design a Web site for one of the authors in this theme.

1. Together, choose an author and plan what to include about his or her life, works, and thoughts.

2. Search the Internet to find other sites related to the author and add "links" to those sites on your own Web site.

3. Design your Web site to be visually appealing and to reflect the nature of the author's insights.

4. If possible, design an actual Web site. Otherwise, create your site on paper as it would look on a monitor screen. Share your Web site with the class.

Interdisciplinary Project

Art: Collage Gallery   Choose three speakers or authors from this theme and create a collage for each one that conveys that person's ideas.

1. Use paper, newspaper and magazine clippings, fabric, photographs, objects from nature, and any other media you can think of to express your view of the subject. However, do not use your subject's name in the collage.

2. Display your collages for the class. Ask classmates to try to name the person each collage represents and to give reasons for their guesses.

Shield of Memory, Robin Holder.
Stencil monotype, 19¾ x 30 in.
Collection of the artist.

Before You Read

The Devil and Tom Walker

Meet Washington Irving

The youngest of eleven children, Washington Irving trained to be a lawyer, but his real love was writing.

Irving's first book, *A History of New York,* was a humorous, tongue-in-cheek combination of history, folklore, and opinion. Published under the pseudonym Diedrich Knickerbocker when Irving was twenty-six, it extended his reputation worldwide and established him as the first American writer to achieve international fame. A few years later Irving traveled to Europe, where he stayed for almost two decades.

While in London, he published *The Sketch Book of Geoffrey Crayon, Gent.* An immediate success, this book contained two of Irving's most famous stories, "The Legend of Sleepy Hollow" and "Rip Van Winkle."

In his sixties, Irving returned to New York to stay. When asked which of his works was his favorite, he said:

"I scarcely look with full satisfaction on any. . . . I often wish that I could have twenty years more, to take them down from the shelf one by one, and write them over."

Washington Irving was born in 1783 and died in 1859.

FOCUS ACTIVITY

Have you ever made a decision or commitment that you later regretted?

JOURNAL Write for a few minutes in your journal about the results of your decision and how you might have acted differently.

SETTING A PURPOSE Read to find out the results of the main character's decision.

BACKGROUND

The Time and Place

"The Devil and Tom Walker" takes place in New England in the 1720s—when Puritanism was fading and the urge to acquire wealth was growing.

Literary Influences

Both Irving and his readers would have been familiar with two references that appear in this tale. The first reference is to Captain William Kidd (c. 1645–1701), a real pirate who became the subject of many legends. The second is to Faust, who makes a deal with the devil. A version of this story had been published by Johann Wolfgang von Goethe.

VOCABULARY PREVIEW

prevalent (prev′ ə lent) *adj.* widespread; p. 204

discord (dis′ kôrd) *n.* lack of agreement or harmony; conflict; p. 204

impregnable (im preg′ nə bəl) *adj.* incapable of being taken by force; able to resist attack; p. 205

melancholy (mel′ ən kol′ ē) *adj.* depressing; dismal; gloomy; p. 205

surmise (sər mīz′) *v.* to infer from little evidence; to guess; p. 207

obliterate (ə blit′ ə rāt) *v.* to remove all traces of; to erase; p. 207

speculate (spek′ yə lāt′) *v.* to engage in risky business ventures, hoping to make quick profits; p. 210

parsimony (pär′ sə mō nē) *n.* excessive frugality; stinginess, p. 211

The Devil and Tom Walker, 1856. John Quidor. Oil on canvas, 27 x 34 in.
The Cleveland Museum of Art, Cleveland, OH.

The Devil and Tom Walker

Washington Irving ~

A FEW MILES FROM BOSTON, in Massachusetts, there is a deep inlet,
winding several miles into the interior of the country from Charles Bay,
and terminating in a thickly wooded swamp or morass. On one side of this
inlet is a beautiful dark grove; on the opposite side the land rises abruptly
from the water's edge into a high ridge, on which grow a few scattered oaks
of great age and immense size.

The Devil and Tom Walker

Under one of these gigantic trees, according to old stories, there was a great amount of treasure buried by Kidd the pirate. The inlet allowed a facility to bring the money in a boat, secretly and at night, to the very foot of the hill; the elevation of the place permitted a good lookout to be kept that no one was at hand; while the remarkable trees formed good landmarks by which the place might easily be found again. The old stories add, moreover, that the devil presided at the hiding of the money, and took it under his guardianship; but this, it is well known, he always does with buried treasure, particularly when it has been ill gotten. Be that as it may, Kidd never returned to recover his wealth, being shortly after seized at Boston, sent out to England, and there hanged for a pirate.

About the year 1727, just at the time that earthquakes were <u>prevalent</u> in New England and shook many tall sinners down upon their knees, there lived near this place a meager, miserly fellow, of the name of Tom Walker. He had a wife as miserly as himself; they were so miserly that they even conspired to cheat each other. Whatever the woman could lay hands on she hid away; a hen could not cackle but she was on the alert to secure the new laid egg. Her husband was continually prying about to detect her secret hoards, and many and fierce were the conflicts that took place about what ought to have been common property. They lived in a forlorn-looking house that stood alone and had an air of starvation. A few straggling savin trees, emblems of sterility, grew near it; no smoke ever curled from its chimney, no traveler stopped at its door. A miserable horse, whose ribs were as articulate as the bars of a gridiron, stalked about a field where a thin carpet of moss, scarcely covering the ragged beds of pudding stone,[1] tantalized and balked his hunger; and sometimes he would lean his head over the fence, look piteously at the passer-by, and seem to petition deliverance from this land of famine.

The house and its inmates had altogether a bad name. Tom's wife was a tall termagant,[2] fierce of temper, loud of tongue, and strong of arm. Her voice was often heard in wordy warfare with her husband, and his face sometimes showed signs that their conflicts were not confined to words. No one ventured, however, to interfere between them. The lonely wayfarer shrunk within himself at the horrid clamor and clapperclawing,[3] eyed the den of <u>discord</u> askance, and hurried on his way, rejoicing, if a bachelor, in his celibacy.

One day that Tom Walker had been to a distant part of the neighborhood, he took what he considered a short cut homeward, through the swamp. Like most short cuts it was an ill-chosen route. The swamp was thickly grown with great gloomy pines and hemlocks, some of them ninety feet high, which made it dark at noonday, and a retreat for all the owls of the neighborhood. It was full of pits and quagmires, partly covered with weeds and mosses, where the green surface often betrayed the traveler into a gulf of black, smothering mud; there were also dark and stagnant pools, the abodes of the

Did You Know?
Savin trees are a type of juniper. Dark green in summer, their scalelike leaves turn a dingy green in winter.

---

1. *Pudding stone* is a rock consisting of pebbles and gravel embedded in cement, like plums in a pudding.
2. A *termagant* is a quarrelsome, scolding woman.
3. *Clapperclawing* is scratching or clawing with the fingernails.

Vocabulary
prevalent (prev′ ə lent) *adj.* widespread
discord (dis′ kôrd) *n.* lack of agreement or harmony; conflict

tadpole, the bullfrog, and the water snake, where the trunks of pines and hemlocks lay half drowned, half rotting, looking like alligators sleeping in the mire.

Tom had long been picking his way cautiously through this treacherous forest, stepping from tuft to tuft of rushes and roots, which afforded precarious footholds among deep sloughs, or pacing carefully, like a cat, along the prostrate[4] trunks of trees, startled now and then by the sudden screaming of the bittern or the quacking of a wild

Did You Know?
A *bittern* is a marsh-dwelling wading bird with mottled brownish plumage and a deep, booming cry.

duck rising on the wing from some solitary pool. At length he arrived at a firm piece of ground, which ran out like a peninsula into the deep bosom of the swamp. It had been one of the strongholds of the Indians during their wars with the first colonists. Here they had thrown up a kind of fort, which they had looked upon as almost impregnable, and had used as a place of refuge for their squaws and children. Nothing remained of the old Indian fort but a few embankments, gradually sinking to the level of the surrounding earth, and already overgrown in part by oaks and other forest trees, the foliage of which formed a contrast to the dark pines and hemlocks of the swamp.

It was late in the dusk of evening when Tom Walker reached the old fort, and he paused there awhile to rest himself. Any one

but he would have felt unwilling to linger in this lonely, melancholy place, for the common people had a bad opinion of it, from the stories handed down from the time of the Indian wars, when it was asserted that the savages held incantations[5] here, and made sacrifices to the evil spirit.

Tom Walker, however, was not a man to be troubled with any fears of the kind. He reposed himself for some time on the trunk of a fallen hemlock, listening to the boding cry of the tree toad, and delving with his walking staff into a mound of black mold at his feet. As he turned up the soil unconsciously, his staff struck against something hard. He raked it out of the vegetable mold, and lo! a cloven[6] skull, with an Indian tomahawk buried deep in it, lay before him. The rust on the

Did You Know?
A male *tree toad,* or tree frog, calls to attract females. When certain types of these frogs call, their throat expands to look like a bubble.

weapon showed the time that had elapsed since this death blow had been given. It was a dreary memento of the fierce struggle that had taken place in this last foothold of the Indian warriors.

"Humph!" said Tom Walker, as he gave it a kick to shake the dirt from it.

"Let that skull alone!" said a gruff voice. Tom lifted up his eyes, and beheld a great black man seated directly opposite him on the stump of a tree. He was exceedingly surprised, having neither heard nor seen any

---

4. *Prostrate* means "lying down."

5. *Incantations* are the recitations of verbal charms or spells to produce a magical effect.
6. *Cloven* means "split" or "divided."

Vocabulary
impregnable (im preg′ nə bəl) *adj.* incapable of being taken by force; able to resist attack
melancholy (mel′ ən kol′ ē) *adj.* depressing; dismal; gloomy

The Devil and Tom Walker

one approach, and he was still more perplexed on observing, as well as the gathering gloom would permit, that the stranger was neither negro nor Indian. It is true he was dressed in a rude, half Indian garb,[7] and had a red belt or sash swathed round his body, but his face was neither black nor copper color, but swarthy and dingy, and begrimed with soot, as if he had been accustomed to toil among fires and forges. He had a shock of coarse black hair, that stood out from his head in all directions, and bore an ax on his shoulder.

He scowled for a moment at Tom with a pair of great red eyes.

"What are you doing on my grounds?" said the black man, with a hoarse, growling voice.

"Your grounds!" said Tom with a sneer, "no more your grounds than mine; they belong to Deacon Peabody."

"Deacon Peabody be d——d," said the stranger, "as I flatter myself he will be if he does not look more to his own sins and less to those of his neighbors. Look yonder, and see how Deacon Peabody is faring."

Tom looked in the direction that the stranger pointed, and beheld one of the great trees, fair and flourishing without, but rotten at the core, and saw that it had been nearly hewn through, so that the first high wind was likely to blow it down. On the bark of the tree was scored the name of Deacon Peabody, an eminent man who had waxed[8] wealthy by driving shrewd bargains with the Indians. He now looked around, and found most of the tall trees marked with the name of some great man of the colony, and all more or less scored by the ax. The one on which he had been seated, and which had evidently just been hewn down, bore the name of Crowninshield, and he recollected a mighty rich man of that name, who made a vulgar display of wealth which it was whispered he had acquired by buccaneering.[9]

"He's just ready for burning!" said the black man, with a growl of triumph. "You see I am likely to have a good stock of firewood for winter."

"But what right have you," said Tom, "to cut down Deacon Peabody's timber?"

"The right of a prior claim," said the other. "This woodland belonged to me long before one of your white-faced race put foot upon the soil."

"And pray, who are you, if I may be so bold?" said Tom.

"Oh, I go by various names. I am the wild 'huntsman' in some countries, the 'black miner' in others. In this neighborhood I am known by the name of the 'black woodsman.' I am he to whom the red men consecrated this spot, and in honor of whom they now and then roasted a white man, by way of sweet-smelling sacrifice. Since the red men have been exterminated by you white savages, I amuse myself by presiding at the persecutions of Quakers and Anabaptists;[10] I am the great patron and prompter of slave dealers, and the grand master of the Salem witches."

"The upshot of all which is that, if I mistake not," said Tom sturdily, "you are he commonly called 'Old Scratch.'"[11]

"The same, at your service!" replied the black man, with a half civil nod.

Such was the opening of this interview, according to the old story, though it has almost too familiar an air to be credited. One would think that to meet with such a singular personage, in this wild, lonely place, would have shaken any man's nerves; but Tom was a hard-minded fellow, not easily

---

7. *Garb* means "clothing" or "attire."
8. Here, *waxed* means "grown" or "become."
9. *Buccaneering* is robbing ships at sea (piracy).
10. The *Quakers* and the *Anabaptists* were two religious groups in Massachusetts that were persecuted for their beliefs.
11. *Old Scratch* is a nickname for the devil.

daunted, and he had lived so long with a ter-magant wife that he did not even fear the devil.

It is said that after this commencement they had a long and earnest conversation together, as Tom returned homeward. The black man told him of great sums of money buried by Kidd the pirate under the oak trees on the high ridge, not far from the morass. All these were under his command, and pro-tected by his power, so that none could find them but such as propitiated[12] his favor. These he offered to place within Tom Walker's reach, having conceived an especial kindness for him; but they were to be had only on certain conditions. What these con-ditions were may be easily surmised, though Tom never disclosed them publicly. They must have been very hard, for he required time to think of them, and he was not a man to stick at trifles when money was in view. When they had reached the edge of the swamp the stranger paused. "What proof have I that all you have been telling me is true?" said Tom. "There's my signature," said the black man, pressing his finger on Tom's forehead. So saying, he turned off among the thickets of the swamp, and seemed, as Tom said, to go down, down, down into the earth, until nothing but his head and shoulders could be seen, and so on, until he totally disappeared.

When Tom reached home he found the black print of a finger burned, as it were, into his forehead, which nothing could obliterate.

The first news his wife had to tell him was the sudden death of Absalom Crowninshield, the rich buccaneer. It was announced in the papers with the usual

flourish, that a great man had fallen in Israel.[13]

Tom recollected the tree which his black friend had just hewn down, and which was ready for burning. "Let the freebooter[14] roast," said Tom; "who cares!" He now felt convinced that all he had heard and seen was no illusion.

He was not prone to let his wife into his confidence, but as this was an uneasy secret he willingly shared it with her. All her avarice was awakened at the mention of hid-den gold, and she urged her husband to com-ply with the black man's terms, and secure what would make them wealthy for life. However Tom might have felt disposed to sell himself to the devil, he was determined not to do so to oblige his wife, so he flatly refused, out of the mere spirit of contradic-tion. Many and bitter were the quarrels they had on the subject, but the more she talked the more resolute was Tom not to be damned to please her.

At length she determined to drive the bargain on her own account, and, if she suc-ceeded, to keep all the gain to herself. Being of the same fearless temper as her husband, she set off for the old Indian fort towards the close of a summer's day. She was many hours absent. When she came back she was reserved and sullen in her replies. She spoke something of a black man whom she had met about twilight hewing at the root of a tall tree. He was sulky, however, and would not come to terms; she was to go again with a

12. *Propitiated* means "won over" or "gained by pleasing acts."

13. Here, *Israel* is a biblical reference to 2 Samuel 3:38: "Know ye not that there is a prince and a great man fallen this day in Israel?" The Puritans referred to New England as "Israel," their Promised Land.

14. A *freebooter* is a pirate.

Vocabulary
surmise (sər mīz′) *v.* to infer from little evidence; to guess
obliterate (ə blit′ ə rāt) *v.* to remove all traces of; to erase

The Devil and Tom Walker

propitiatory offering, but what it was she forbore to say.

The next evening she set off again for the swamp, with her apron heavily laden. Tom waited and waited for her, but in vain; midnight came, but she did not make her appearance; morning, noon, night returned, but still she did not come. Tom now grew uneasy for her safety, especially as he found she had carried off in her apron the silver teapot and spoons and every portable article of value. Another night elapsed, another morning came, but no wife. In a word, she was never heard of more.

What was her real fate nobody knows, in consequence of so many pretending to know. It is one of those facts which have become confounded by a variety of historians. Some asserted that she lost her way among the tangled mazes of the swamp, and sank into some pit or slough; others, more uncharitable, hinted that she had eloped with the household booty,[15] and made off to some other province; while others surmised that the tempter had decoyed her into a dismal quagmire, on the top of which her hat was found lying. In confirmation of this it was said a great black man, with an ax on his shoulder, was seen late that very evening coming out of the swamp, carrying a bundle tied in a check apron, with an air of surly triumph.

---

15. *Booty* is stolen goods.

Swamp Sunset. Harold Rudolph (c. 1850–1884). Oil on canvas, 12 x 18 in. The Ogden Museum of Southern Art, University of New Orleans.

Viewing the painting: What mood does this painting evoke? How would the mood change if the scene had been depicted in broad daylight? How is the swamp scene in the painting similar to or different from the one where Tom Walker first met the Devil?

The most current and probable story, however, observes that Tom Walker grew so anxious about the fate of his wife and his property that he set out at length to seek them both at the Indian fort. During a long summer's afternoon he searched about the gloomy place, but no wife was to be seen. He called her name repeatedly, but she was nowhere to be heard. The bittern alone responded to his voice, as he flew screaming by, or the bullfrog croaked dolefully from a neighboring pool. At length, it is said, just in the brown hour of twilight, when the owls began to hoot and the bats to flit about, his attention was attracted by the clamor of carrion crows[16] hovering about a cypress tree. He looked up, and beheld a bundle tied in a check apron and hanging in the branches of the tree, with a great vulture perched hard by, as if keeping watch upon it. He leaped with joy, for he recognized his wife's apron and supposed it to contain the household valuables.

"Let us get hold of the property," said he consolingly to himself, "and we will endeavor to do without the woman."

As he scrambled up the tree the vulture spread its wide wings and sailed off, screaming, into the deep shadows of the forest. Tom seized the check apron, but, woeful sight! found nothing but a heart and liver tied up in it!

Such, according to this most authentic old story, was all that was to be found of Tom's wife. She had probably attempted to deal with the black man as she had been accustomed to deal with her husband; but though a female scold is generally considered a match for the devil, yet in this instance she appears to have had the worst of it. She must have died game, however, for it is said Tom noticed many prints of cloven feet deeply stamped about the tree, and found handfuls of hair that looked as if they had been plucked from the coarse black shock of the woodman. Tom knew his wife's prowess by experience. He shrugged his shoulders as he looked at the signs of a fierce clapperclawing. "Egad," said he to himself, "Old Scratch must have had a tough time of it!"

Tom consoled himself for the loss of his property with the loss of his wife, for he was a man of fortitude. He even felt something like gratitude towards the black woodman, who, he considered, had done him a kindness. He sought, therefore, to cultivate a further acquaintance with him, but for some time without success; the old blacklegs played shy, for whatever people may think, he is not always to be had for calling for; he knows how to play his cards when pretty sure of his game.

At length, it is said, when delay had whetted Tom's eagerness to the quick, and prepared him to agree to anything rather than not gain the promised treasure, he met the black man one evening in his usual woodman's dress, with his ax on his shoulder, sauntering along the swamp, and humming a tune. He affected to receive Tom's advances with great indifference, made brief replies, and went on humming his tune.

By degrees, however, Tom brought him to business, and they began to haggle about the terms on which the former was to have the pirate's treasure. There was one condition which need not be mentioned, being generally understood in all cases where the devils grants favors; but there were others about which, though of less importance, he was inflexibly obstinate. He insisted that the money found through his means should be employed in his service. He proposed, therefore, that Tom should employ it in the black traffic,—that is to say, that he should fit out a slave ship. This, however, Tom resolutely refused; he was bad enough, in all conscience, but the devil himself could not tempt him to turn slave trader.

---

16. *Carrion crows* are crows that feed on dead or decaying flesh.

The Devil and Tom Walker

Finding Tom so squeamish on this point, he did not insist upon it, but proposed, instead, that he should turn usurer,[17] the devil being extremely anxious for the increase of usurers, looking upon them as his peculiar[18] people.

To this no objections were made, for it was just to Tom's taste.

"You shall open a broker's shop in Boston next month," said the black man.

"I'll do it tomorrow, if you wish," said Tom Walker.

"You shall lend money at two percent a month."

"Egad, I'll charge four!" replied Tom Walker.

"You shall extort[19] bonds, foreclose mortgages, drive the merchants to bankruptcy"—

"I'll drive them to the d—l!" cried Tom Walker.

"You are the usurer for my money!" said blacklegs with delight. "When will you want the rhino?"[20]

"This very night."

"Done!" said the devil.

"Done!" said Tom Walker. So they shook hands and struck a bargain.

A few days' time saw Tom Walker seated behind his desk in a countinghouse in Boston.

His reputation for a ready-moneyed man, who would lend money out for a good consideration, soon spread abroad. Everybody remembers the time of Governor Belcher,[21] when money was particularly scarce. It was a time of paper credit. The country had been deluged with government bills; the famous Land Bank[22] had been established; there had been a rage for speculating; the people had run mad with schemes for new settlements, for building cities in the wilderness; land jobbers[23] went about with maps of grants and townships and Eldorados,[24] lying nobody knew where, but which everybody was ready to purchase. In a word, the great speculating fever which breaks out every now and then in the country had raged to an alarming degree, and everybody was dreaming of making sudden fortunes from nothing. As usual the fever had subsided, the dream had gone off, and the imaginary fortunes with it; the patients were left in doleful plight, and the whole country resounded with the consequent cry of "hard times."

At this propitious time of public distress did Tom Walker set up as usurer in Boston. His door was soon thronged by customers. The needy and adventurous, the gambling speculator, the dreaming land jobber, the thriftless tradesman, the merchant with cracked credit,— in short, everyone driven to raise money by desperate means and desperate sacrifices hurried to Tom Walker.

Thus Tom was the universal friend of the needy, and acted like a "friend in need"; that is to say, he always exacted good pay and good security. In proportion to the distress of

---

17. A *usurer* is a person who lends money, especially at an excessive or unlawfully high rate of interest.
18. Here, *peculiar* means "special."
19. *Extort* means "to obtain by threats, force, or other types of oppression."
20. *Rhino* is a slang term for money.
21. Jonathan *Belcher* was governor of Massachusetts and New Hampshire from 1730 to 1741.
22. Boston merchants organized the *Land Bank* in 1739. Landowners could borrow money in the form of mortgages on their property and then repay the loans with cash or manufactured goods. When the bank was outlawed in 1741, many colonists lost money.
23. *Land jobbers* are people who buy and sell land for profit.
24. *Eldorados* are places of great wealth or opportunity. The term comes from the name El Dorado, a legendary region of South America sought by Spanish explorers for its gold and jewels.

Vocabulary
speculate (spek′ yə lāt′) *v.* to engage in risky business ventures, hoping to make quick profits

the applicant was the hardness of his terms. He accumulated bonds and mortgages, gradually squeezed his customers closer and closer, and sent them at length, dry as a sponge, from his door.

In this way he made money hand over hand, became a rich and mighty man, and exalted his cocked hat upon 'Change.[25] He built himself, as usual, a vast house, out of ostentation,[26] but left the greater part of it unfinished and unfurnished, out of parsimony. He even set up a carriage in the fullness of his vainglory,[27] though he nearly starved the horses which drew it; and as the ungreased wheels groaned and screeched on the axletrees you would have thought you heard the souls of the poor debtors he was squeezing.

As Tom waxed old, however, he grew thoughtful. Having secured the good things of this world, he began to feel anxious about those of the next. He thought with regret on the bargain he had made with his black friend, and set his wits to work to cheat him out of the conditions. He became, therefore, all of a sudden, a violent churchgoer. He prayed loudly and strenuously, as if heaven were to be taken by force of lungs. Indeed, one might always tell when he had sinned most during the week by the clamor of his Sunday devotion. The quiet Christians who had been modestly and steadfastly traveling Zionward,[28] were struck with self-reproach at seeing themselves so suddenly outstripped in their career by this new-made convert. Tom was as rigid in religious, as in money, matters; he was a stern supervisor and

censurer of his neighbors, and seemed to think every sin entered up to their account became a credit on his own side of the page. He even talked of the expediency of reviving the persecution of Quakers and Anabaptists. In a word, Tom's zeal became as notorious as his riches.

Still, in spite of all this strenuous attention to forms, Tom had a lurking dread that the devil, after all, would have his due. That he might not be taken unawares, therefore, it is said he always carried a small Bible in his coat pocket. He had also a great folio Bible on his countinghouse desk, and would frequently be found reading it when people called on business. On such occasions he would lay his green spectacles in the book, to mark the place, while he turned round to drive some usurious bargain.

Some say that Tom grew a little crack-brained in his old days, and that, fancying his end approaching, he had his horse new shod, saddled, and bridled, and buried with his feet uppermost, because he supposed that at the last day the world would be turned upside down, in which case he should find his horse standing ready for mounting, and he was determined at the worst to give his old friend a run for it. This, however, is probably a mere old wives' fable. If he really did take such a precaution it was totally superfluous; at least, so says the authentic old legend, which closes his story in the following manner.

One hot summer afternoon in the dog days,[29] just as a terrible, black thunder gust was coming up, Tom sat in his counting-house, in his white linen cap and India silk morning gown. He was on the point of foreclosing a mortgage, by which he would complete the ruin of an

25. The 'Change, or Exchange, was a financial center where merchants, bankers, and brokers met to do business.
26. Ostentation means "a display meant to impress others."
27. Vainglory is boastful, undeserved pride in one's accomplishments or qualities.
28. Zionward means "toward heaven."
29. Dog days are the hot, sultry days of summer.

Vocabulary
parsimony (pär′ sə mō nē) n. excessive frugality; stinginess

The Devil and Tom Walker

unlucky land speculator for whom he had professed the greatest friendship. The poor land jobber begged him to grant a few months' indulgence. Tom had grown testy and irritated, and refused another day.

"My family will be ruined and brought upon the parish," said the land jobber.

"Charity begins at home," replied Tom; "I must take care of myself in these hard times."

"You have made so much money out of me," said the speculator.

Tom lost his patience and his piety. "The devil take me," said he, "if I have made a farthing."[30]

Just then there were three loud knocks at the street door. He stepped out to see who was there. A black man was holding a black horse, which neighed and stamped with impatience.

"Tom, you're come for," said the black fellow gruffly. Tom shrank back, but too late. He

---

30. A *farthing* was a British coin worth one-fourth of a penny.

Tom Walker's Flight, c. 1856. John Quidor. Oil on canvas, 26¾ x 33¾ in. The Fine Arts Museums of San Francisco.
Viewing the painting: In what ways does this painting reflect the fantastic nature of the story?

had left his little Bible at the bottom of his coat pocket, and his big Bible on the desk buried under the mortgage he was about to foreclose; never was sinner taken more unawares. The black man whisked him like a child into the saddle, gave the horse a lash, and away he galloped, with Tom on his back, in the midst of the thunderstorm. The clerks stuck their pens behind their ears, and stared after him from the windows. Away went Tom Walker, dashing down the streets, his white cap bobbing up and down, his morning gown fluttering in the wind, and his steed striking fire out of the pavement at every bound. When the clerks turned to look for the black man he had disappeared.

Tom Walker never returned to foreclose the mortgage. A countryman, who lived on the border of the swamp, reported that in the height of the thunder gust he had heard a great clattering of hoofs and a howling along the road, and running to the window caught sight of a figure such as I have described, on a horse that galloped like mad across the fields, over the hills, and down into the black hemlock swamp towards the old Indian fort, and that shortly after, a thunderbolt falling in that direction seemed to set the whole forest in a blaze.

The good people of Boston shook their heads and shrugged their shoulders, but had been so much accustomed to witches and goblins, and tricks of the devil, in all kinds of shapes, from the first settlement of the colony, that they were not so much horror-struck as might have been expected. Trustees were appointed to take charge of Tom's effects. There was nothing, however, to administer upon. On searching his coffers,[31] all his bonds and mortgages were found reduced to cinders. In place of gold and silver his iron chest was filled with chips and shavings; two skeletons lay in his stable instead of his half starved horses; and the very next day his great house took fire and was burned to the ground.

Such was the end of Tom Walker and his ill-gotten wealth. Let all griping money brokers lay this story to heart. The truth of it is not to be doubted. The very hole under the oak trees, whence he dug Kidd's money, is to be seen to this day, and the neighboring swamp and old Indian fort are often haunted in stormy nights by a figure on horseback, in morning gown and white cap, which is doubtless the troubled spirit of the usurer. In fact, the story has resolved itself into a proverb, and is the origin of that popular saying, so prevalent throughout New England, of "the devil and Tom Walker."

---

31. *Coffers* are strongboxes used to hold money or other valuables.

Responding to Literature

Personal Response

How did you react to Tom and his wife? Share your responses.

─── ANALYZING LITERATURE ───

RECALL

1. What kind of people are Tom Walker and his wife? Describe what you know about them.
2. How does Tom react to the devil and his offer?
3. What happens to Tom's wife?
4. What business does Tom go into? What makes this possible, and what makes this a good time to go into such a business?
5. What finally happens to Tom Walker?

INTERPRET

6. How are Tom and his wife alike? In your opinion, does Tom's wife contribute to Tom's cooperation with the devil? Explain.
7. What does Tom's agreement with the devil tell you about Tom?
8. The narrator offers different versions of what might have happened to Tom's wife. What might the narrator want us to believe? Explain.
9. What can you infer about the narrator's attitude toward money and the people who care about it? What evidence supports your inference?
10. The narrator tells us what happens to Tom's possessions. What do you understand from this?

EVALUATE AND CONNECT

11. What do you think is the purpose of this story? How does this story differ from the histories, religious tracts, and political papers that most American writers of the time were producing?
12. **Satire** is a form of writing that uses humor, not as an end in itself, but as a weapon against someone or something—a person, a group, or a habit. In what ways is this story a satire? What is made fun of?
13. Think about your response to the Focus Activity on page 202. Compare the decision you regretted with Tom Walker's decision and its consequences.
14. The narrator often issues disclaimers by saying "people said" or "it is said." How did you respond to these disclaimers? How do you think other readers might respond? Explain.
15. Theme Connections   What are some of the insights that this story conveys? In your opinion what is the most powerful message? Explain.

Tall Tale

"The Devil and Tom Walker" is a **tall tale,** a type of folklore associated with the American frontier. Tall tales are humorous stories that contain exaggerations and invention. Typically, their heroes are bold but foolish characters who may have superhuman abilities or who may act as if they do. Tall tales are not intended to be believable; their exaggerations are used for comic effect. When Irving writes that Tom "had lived so long with a termagant wife that he did not even fear the devil," he stretched the truth to gain a laugh.

1. When Tom's wife disappears, what does Tom do and say? What makes this comic instead of sad?
2. Tom's greed is exaggerated. How does Irving show this?
3. What other comic exaggerations can you find?

● See **Literary Terms Handbook,** p. R16.

LITERATURE AND WRITING

Writing About Literature

Character Sketch Irving describes Tom Walker's appearance, his actions, his words, and the reactions of other characters to him. Write a brief character sketch of Tom using details from the story to support your description.

Creative Writing

Story in Song Many folk songs tell the story of events and characters from history and legends. Using the tune of a song that you like, write a few verses that tell what happened to Tom Walker.

EXTENDING YOUR RESPONSE

Literature Groups

Test of Time Do you think "The Devil and Tom Walker" has lasting appeal, or is it interesting mainly as a historical piece? Give your opinion, using evidence from the story to support your answer. Then, as a group, summarize the opinions expressed and report to the class.

Performing

The Devil to Pay Imagine that you are one of the minor characters from this story and you are giving an interview years later. In a monologue, tell what happened to the Walker family. Include your reactions, opinions, and any gossip of the time. Present your monologue to the class.

Learning for Life

The Cost of Borrowing What kind of living would Tom Walker earn today as a moneylender? Work with a group to investigate how much interest would be charged on a loan of $1,000. Examine several sources, such as a cash advance from a credit card company, a long-term mortgage, and a loan from a commercial lender. Present your findings in a brief report.

Reading Further

To read more by Washington Irving, look for these books:

Short Story: *The Legend of Sleepy Hollow: Found Among the Papers of the Late Diedrich Knickerbocker,* an illustrated edition of the story about a schoolmaster and a headless horseman.

Collection: *The Sketch Book,* contains short stories, travel sketches, and essays.

📖 **Save your work for your portfolio.**

Skill Minilesson

VOCABULARY • Analogies

Analogies are comparisons based on relationships between ideas. The word pairs in some analogies are antonym variants. For example,

> weak : strong :: dark : light

Weak is the opposite of *strong; dark* is the opposite of *light.*

To finish an analogy, decide on the relationship represented by the first pair of words. Then apply that relationship to the second set of words.

● For more about analogies, see **Communications Skills Handbook,** pp. R83–R85.

PRACTICE Choose the word that best completes each analogy.

1. discord : harmony :: conflict :
   a. agreement   b. fight   c. tension
2. calm : nervous :: melancholy :
   a. gloomy   b. cheerful   c. sad
3. generosity : parsimony :: wealth :
   a. greed   b. riches   c. poverty
4. prevalent : uncommon :: often :
   a. frequent   b. common   c. seldom

MEDIA Connection

In this *Simpsons* episode, Bart jokingly sells his "soul" ("Bart Simpson's Soul" written on a piece of paper) to his friend, Milhouse, for five dollars. Later, Bart has a dream about his soul.

Bart Sells His Soul

EXTERIOR: SPRINGFIELD CENTRAL PARK

[*As Bart approaches the park, he hears sounds of kids having fun. As he gets closer, he sees that each child is playing with his or her own soul (milky-white ghostly versions of themselves). He sees kids and their souls pushing each other on swings, riding bicycles built for two, and having chicken fights.*]

*　　*　　*

[*Martin and his soul, in matching sailor outfits, run down to the shore of a lake and stand by a bunch of rowboats. They hop into a rowboat, each grabbing an oar, and row off. Other kids and their souls follow and head off toward a glowing Emerald City on the other side of the lake. Milhouse runs by, hand-in-hand with his own soul and Bart's soul. The souls get on the bench and do all the rowing as Milhouse relaxes in the back of the boat. Bart tries to follow, but without a soul to grab the other oar, he can only row around and around in a circle.*]

BART
Wait! Wait for me!

[*Sherri, Terri, and their souls row by.*]

SHERRI, TERRI, & THEIR SOULS
Bart, it's time to end this dream / And don't forget the standard scream.

BACK TO REALITY

[*Bart sits upright in bed.*] [*Scream.*]

*　　*　　*

EXTERIOR: SPRINGFIELD STREET— MORNING

[*As Bart walks home, it starts to rain.*]

INTERIOR: BART'S ROOM—A LITTLE LATER

[*Bart walks into his room, kneels by his bed, and prays.*]

BART
Are you there, God? It's me, Bart Simpson. I know I never paid too much attention in church, but I could really use some of that good stuff now. . . . I'm afraid some weirdo's got my soul and I don't know what they're doing to it. I just want it back. Please. [*Starts to cry.*] I hope you can hear this . . .

[*The soul flutters down onto the bed, ragged and . . . crumpled. Bart looks up to see Lisa.*]

BART
Lisa? You bought this?

LISA
With the change in my piggy bank.

BART
There's no change in your piggy bank.

LISA
Not in any of the ones *you* know about.

BART
Oh, Lisa, thank you.

[*Bart is so happy he kisses her.*]

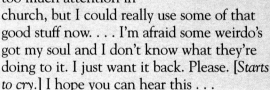

The Simpsons™ © and ™ Twentieth Century Fox Corp. All Rights Reserved.

Respond

1. How does Bart's "joke" backfire on him?

2. Do you think Lisa does the right thing by helping Bart? Explain.

Vo·cab·u·lar·y Skills

Using Roots to
Understand New Words

When you read, you are likely to come across unfamiliar words. There are several techniques that can help you understand these words. One good way to begin is to identify the word's **root**—the element that expresses the basic meaning of the word. Although English borrows words from many languages, a great number of root words trace their origins to Greek or Latin words. Knowing some common Greek and Latin roots can boost your understanding of what you read.

In "The Devil and Tom Walker," Washington Irving uses the word *recognize.* The word's root comes from the Latin *cogn,* meaning "to know." In the story, Tom Walker *recognizes* his wife's apron as he searches for her. In other words, he sees something he has previously *known.* The following words contain the same root as *recognize:*

cognitive   cognizant   cognition   incognito

Since a number of words may come from the same root, a knowledge of common roots can help you recognize the meaning of many words. Here are a few useful roots to know.

Root	Meaning	Example
facilis	easy	facilitate
cult	to care for	agriculture
vivi	live	vivacious
verb	word	verbal

Words change over time, of course, and you may not know what a word means even if you recognize its root. Still, looking at the root of an unfamiliar word is one good place to begin as you try to figure out that word's meaning.

EXERCISES

1. The words below appear in "The Devil and Tom Walker." The root of each word is listed above. Find the word in the story and define it as it is used there.

   a. facility (page 204)
   b. cultivate (page 209)
   c. reviving (page 211)
   d. proverb (page 213)

2. The root of each word below is underlined. For each word, write another word with the same root.

   a. determine
   b. versatile
   c. objection
   d. unfinished
   e. report

Before You Read

To a Waterfowl and *Thanatopsis*

Meet
William Cullen Bryant

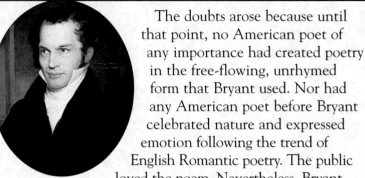

"The remarkable thing about 'Thanatopsis' was not that Bryant entertained the thoughts it contains . . . but that he expressed them in verses that were so beautiful and so different from anything ever written before in America."

—*Percy H. Boynton*

As a boy, William Cullen Bryant spent much time exploring the mysteries of the forests and hills in the isolated countryside of Cummington, Massachusetts. Encouraged by his father, who loved poetry, Bryant also enjoyed literary pursuits. While still in his teens, Bryant wrote "Thanatopsis," which his father sent to the *North American Review*, a major literary magazine. The editors found the poem so impressive that some doubted its true origins. "No one on this side of the Atlantic is capable of writing such verse," said one editor.

The doubts arose because until that point, no American poet of any importance had created poetry in the free-flowing, unrhymed form that Bryant used. Nor had any American poet before Bryant celebrated nature and expressed emotion following the trend of English Romantic poetry. The public loved the poem. Nevertheless, Bryant continued to revise it over the next ten years.

Bryant first worked as a lawyer, but at thirty-one, he gave up the profession and moved to New York City. There he became the editor of the *Evening Post* newspaper, a position he held for half a century. As an editor, Bryant became an outspoken advocate of freedom and human rights. He supported women's rights, the abolition of slavery, and freedom of speech. Bryant continued to express his ideas through poetry and speeches into his eighties.

William Cullen Bryant was born in 1794 and died in 1878.

FOCUS ACTIVITY

"Let nature be your teacher," advised the English Romantic poet William Wordsworth. What lessons have you learned from nature?

LIST IDEAS List some personal insights you have gained from natural events and scenes.

SETTING A PURPOSE Read to discover the insights that one poet gained from observing and contemplating nature.

BACKGROUND

Literary Influences
Romanticism began in Europe during the late eighteenth century and has affected art, music, and literature ever since. A reaction against earlier, rational schools of thought, Romanticism celebrated the individual and emotional, imaginative, and spiritual experiences. Bryant was influenced by the English Romantics, including William Wordsworth and Samuel Taylor Coleridge.

Blank Verse
The poem "Thanatopsis" is written in **blank verse** (see page R2), a poetic form not used by American poets before Bryant. Blank verse is unrhymed poetry that is written in a rhythmic pattern called **iambic pentameter.** In iambic pentameter, each line has five feet, or beats; each foot contains one unstressed syllable followed by a stressed syllable. Pauses do not always come at the ends of lines but wherever they make sense. Bryant introduced this poetic form into mainstream American poetry.

To a Waterfowl

William Cullen Bryant

Whither, midst falling dew,
While glow the heavens with the last steps of day
Far, through their rosy depths, dost thou persue
    Thy solitary way?

5   Vainly the fowler's° eye
Might mark thy distant flight to do thee wrong,
As, darkly seen against the crimson sky,
    Thy figure floats along.

      Seek'st thou the plashy° brink
10   Of weedy lake, or marge° of river wide,
Or where the rocking billows rise and sink
    On the chafed ocean side?

      There is a Power whose care
Teaches thy way along that pathless coast,—
15   The desert and illimitable air,—
    Lone wandering, but not lost.

      All day thy wings have fanned,
At that far height, the cold, thin atmosphere,
Yet stoop not, weary, to the welcome land,
20   Though the dark night is near.

      And soon that toil shall end;
Soon shalt thou find a summer home, and rest,
And scream among thy fellows; reeds shall bend,
    Soon, o'er thy sheltered nest.

25   Thou'rt gone, the abyss° of heaven
Hath swallowed up thy form; yet, on my heart
Deeply hath sunk the lesson thou hast given,
    And shall not soon depart.

      He who, from zone to zone,
30   Guides through the boundless sky thy certain flight,
In the long way that I must tread alone,
    Will lead my steps aright.

Canada Goose, 1834. Robert Havell. Hand-colored engraving with aquatint after a painting by John James Audubon. National Gallery of Art, Washington, DC.

---

5 A *fowler* is a hunter of wild birds.
9 *Plashy* means "swampy" or "marshy."
10 *Marge* means "margin" or "edge."
25 Here, *abyss* (ə bis′) refers to "an immeasurably large space."

Thanatopsis

William Cullen Bryant

To him who in the love of Nature holds
Communion with her visible forms, she speaks
A various language; for his gayer hours
She has a voice of gladness, and a smile
5 And eloquence of beauty, and she glides
Into his darker musings, with a mild
And healing sympathy, that steals away
Their sharpness, ere° he is aware. When thoughts
Of the last bitter hour come like a blight
10 Over thy spirit, and sad images
Of the stern agony, and shroud,° and pall,°
And breathless darkness, and the narrow house,
Make thee to shudder, and grow sick at heart;—
Go forth, under the open sky, and list°
15 To Nature's teachings, while from all around—
Earth and her waters, and the depths of air—
Comes a still voice.°—Yet a few days, and thee
The all-beholding sun shall see no more
In all his course; nor yet in the cold ground,
20 Where thy pale form was laid, with many tears,
Nor in the embrace of ocean, shall exist
Thy image. Earth, that nourished thee, shall claim
Thy growth, to be resolved to earth again,
And, lost each human trace, surrendering up
25 Thine individual being, shalt thou go
To mix for ever with the elements,
To be a brother to the insensible rock
And to the sluggish clod, which the rude swain°
Turns with his share,° and treads upon. The oak
30 Shall send his roots abroad, and pierce thy mould.

---

8 *Ere* means "before."
11 A *shroud* is a cloth used to wrap a dead body. A *pall* refers to both a
 coffin cover and the coffin itself.
14 Here, *list* means "listen."
17 The voice of Nature begins here.
28 A *rude swain* is an uneducated country boy.
29 A *share*, or plowshare, is the cutting blade of a plow.

Yet not to thine eternal resting-place
Shalt thou retire alone, nor couldst thou wish
Couch° more magnificent. Thou shalt lie down
With patriarchs of the infant world—with kings,
35 The powerful of the earth—the wise, the good,
Fair forms, and hoary seers° of ages past,
All in one mighty sepulchre.° The hills
Rock-ribbed and ancient as the sun,—the vales
Stretching in pensive quietness between;
40 The venerable woods—rivers that move
In majesty, and the complaining brooks
That make the meadows green; and, poured round all,
Old Ocean's gray and melancholy waste,—
Are but the solemn decorations all
45 Of the great tomb of man. The golden sun,
The planets, all the infinite host of heaven,
Are shining on the sad abodes of death,
Through the still lapse of ages. All that tread

---

33 Here, *couch* means "bed."
36 *Hoary seers* are white-haired prophets.
37 A *sepulchre* is a burial place, in particular, a vault or tomb.

Landscape, Scene from "Thanatopsis," 1850. Asher Brown Durand. Oil on canvas, 39½ x 61 in. The Metropolitan Museum of Art, New York.

Thanatopsis

The globe are but a handful to the tribes
50   That slumber in its bosom.—Take the wings
Of morning,° pierce the Barcan wilderness,°
Or lose thyself in the continuous woods
Where rolls the Oregon,° and hears no sound,
Save his own dashings—yet the dead are there:
55   And millions in those solitudes, since first
The flight of years began, have laid them down
In their last sleep—the dead reign there alone.
So shalt thou rest, and what if thou withdraw
In silence from the living, and no friend
60   Take note of thy departure? All that breathe
Will share thy destiny. The gay will laugh
When thou art gone, the solemn brood of care
Plod on, and each one as before will chase
His favorite phantom; yet all these shall leave
65   Their mirth and their employments, and shall come
And make their bed with thee. As the long train
Of ages glides away, the sons of men,
The youth in life's green spring, and he who goes
In the full strength of years, matron and maid,
70   The speechless babe, and the gray-headed man—
Shall one by one be gathered to thy side
By those, who in their turn shall follow them.

     °So live, that when thy summons comes to join
The innumerable caravan, which moves
75   To that mysterious realm, where each shall take
His chamber in the silent halls of death,
Thou go not, like the quarry-slave at night,
Scourged to his dungeon, but, sustained and soothed
By an unfaltering trust, approach thy grave,
80   Like one who wraps the drapery of his couch
About him, and lies down to pleasant dreams.

50–51 This is a biblical reference to Psalm 139:9, "If I take the wings of the
      morning . . ."
  51 *Barcan wilderness* refers to Barca, a desert in Libya, a nation in northern
      Africa.
  53 *Oregon* is an early name for the Columbia River, which flows between Oregon
      and Washington.
  73 The speaker's voice resumes here.

Responding to Literature

Personal Response

What do these poems make you wonder about? Jot down questions and ideas in your journal.

ANALYZING LITERATURE

To a Waterfowl

RECALL AND INTERPRET
1. What questions does the speaker ask in the first three stanzas? Rephrase the questions.
2. What guides the bird? How do you think the speaker feels about the bird's situation?
3. What comparison does the speaker make between the bird's flight and his own life? What "lesson" does the speaker receive, and why might the lesson "not soon depart"? Explain.

EVALUATE AND CONNECT
4. This poem has a regular **rhyme scheme** and form (see page R13). What impact does this regular pattern have on your reading of the poem? Explain.
5. Seeing the waterfowl makes the speaker reflect upon his own life. Reread your response to the Focus Activity on page 218. What situations in nature might affect you?

Thanatopsis

RECALL AND INTERPRET
6. According to the speaker, what does Nature do during happy times?
7. In lines 17–30, what does Nature say will happen to the reader? Why will the reader not be alone? In your own words, how would you describe what Nature says in lines 31–72?
8. What suggestion does the speaker make at the end of the poem? What conclusions do you draw about the speaker's views of life and death?

EVALUATE AND CONNECT
9. *Thanatopsis* means "view of death." How is the view of death expressed in this poem the same or different from others that you know about?
10. Do you think the poem's message is still valid today? Explain.

EXTENDING YOUR RESPONSE

Writing About Literature

Compare Themes   A **theme** is a main idea in a story or poem, a message that can be expressed as a general statement about life. What are the themes of "To a Waterfowl" and "Thanatopsis"? Write a paragraph or two comparing the themes, using details from the poems to support your ideas.

Internet Connection

Birds of a Feather   Use the Internet to research waterfowl. What species of bird might Bryant's poem be describing? Is this species, or species like it, alive today? Create a short booklet about waterfowl from information you gather on the Internet. Include maps and pictures if possible. Share your booklet with the class.

📖 **Save your work for your portfolio.**

Before You Read

Old Ironsides and The Chambered Nautilus

Meet Oliver Wendell Holmes

Henry James: "Holmes, you are intellectually the most alive man I ever knew." Holmes: "I am, I am. From the crown of my head to the sole of my foot, I'm alive, I'm alive!"

—Reported by *Henry James*

There were hardly enough hours in the day for Oliver Wendell Holmes. Working as a doctor and as a poet, he also took a strong interest in boxing, photography, rowing, rattlesnakes, and much more. As a college student, he was a leader of Harvard College's Hasty Pudding Club, a group of students who wrote and performed humorous skits about college life. He earned his medical degree from Harvard in 1836 and published his first book of poetry that same year.

For forty years, Holmes was an enthusiastic member of the Saturday Club, a group of Cambridge, Massachusetts, writers and philosophers who met over dinner to share conversation and their writings. For more than thirty years, beginning at the age of thirty-eight, Holmes was a popular professor of anatomy at Harvard. One student recalled that Holmes was greeted with "a mighty shout and stamp of applause" when he entered the classroom.

When friend and fellow poet James Russell Lowell started the *Atlantic Monthly* magazine, Holmes contributed humorous essays that ran under the title "The Autocrat of the Breakfast Table." Holmes also published many poems, including "The Chambered Nautilus," in the *Atlantic*.

Oliver Wendell Holmes was born in 1809 and died in 1894.

FOCUS ACTIVITY

As you mature, you often put aside the toys and other reminders of childhood. How do you decide which items are worth saving and which are not?

SHARE IDEAS Jot down some ideas about this question. Then discuss your notes with a partner.

SETTING A PURPOSE Read to learn how the speaker in each poem feels about reminders of the past.

BACKGROUND

The Time and Place

Oliver Wendell Holmes was a Harvard student in 1830 when he learned that the frigate *Constitution* was going to be scrapped. This ship had won important battles in the War of 1812. Although it was actually made of oak, it had earned the nickname "Old Ironsides" by withstanding the repeated assaults of British warships. The news about the ship's fate so upset Holmes that in an "outburst of feeling" he wrote the poem "Old Ironsides." When published in the *Boston Daily Advertiser* two days later, it triggered such a protest that the ship was saved.

The Chambered Nautilus

The chambered nautilus is a remarkable sea creature. As a nautilus grows, it builds a beautiful spiral shell, chamber by chamber. At each stage, the living animal moves out of its old, small chamber into a new, larger chamber. A nautilus shell can grow to be more than ten inches across.

Old Ironsides

Oliver Wendell Holmes

Ay, tear her tattered ensign° down!
   Long has it waved on high,
And many an eye has danced to see
   That banner in the sky;
5 Beneath it rung the battle shout,
   And burst the cannon's roar;—
The meteor of the ocean air
   Shall sweep the clouds no more.

Her deck, once red with heroes' blood,
10   Where knelt the vanquished° foe,
When winds were hurrying o'er the flood,
   And waves were white below,
No more shall feel the victor's tread,
   Or know the conquered knee;—
15 The harpies° of the shore shall pluck
   The eagle of the sea!

Oh, better that her shattered hulk
   Should sink beneath the wave;
Her thunders shook the mighty deep,
20   And there should be her grave;
Nail to the mast her holy flag,
   Set every threadbare sail,
And give her to the god of storms,
   The lightning and the gale!

Old Ironsides, 1863. James Hamilton. Oil on canvas, 60 x 48 in.
The Pennsylvania Academy of the Fine Arts, Philadelphia.

---

1 Here, *ensign* means "flag."
10 *Vanquished* means "defeated."
15 In Greek mythology, the *harpies* are ugly monsters having
   the head and body of a woman and the tail, wings, and claws
   of a bird. The name literally means "robbers" or "snatchers."
   Here, the word refers to those who prey on others.

Sea Change, 1937. John Hollis Kaufmann. Oil on canvas, 30 x 40 in. Private collection.

The Chambered Nautilus

Oliver Wendell Holmes ᔰ

This is the ship of pearl, which, poets feign,°
    Sails the unshadowed main,°—
    The venturous bark° that flings
On the sweet summer wind its purpled wings
5   In gulfs enchanted, where the Siren° sings,
      And coral reefs lie bare,
Where the cold sea-maids° rise to sun their streaming hair.

---

1 Here, *feign* means "imagine."
2 Here, *main* means "the boundless ocean."
3 A *bark* is a sailing ship.
5 In Greek mythology, a *Siren* is a sea nymph whose enchanting songs lure sailors to their death on the rocks.
7 *Sea-maids* are mermaids or sea nymphs.

Its webs of living gauze no more unfurl;
    Wrecked is the ship of pearl!
10   And every chambered cell,
Where its dim dreaming life was wont to dwell,
As the frail tenant shaped his growing shell,
    Before thee lies revealed,—
Its irised° ceiling rent,° its sunless crypt unsealed!

15   Year after year beheld the silent toil
      That spread his lustrous coil;
      Still, as the spiral grew,
He left the past year's dwelling for the new,
Stole with soft step its shining archway through,
20   Built up its idle door,
Stretched in his last-found home, and knew the old no more.

Thanks for the heavenly message brought by thee,
    Child of the wandering sea,
    Cast from her lap, forlorn!
25   From thy dead lips a clearer note is born
Than ever Triton° blew from wreathèd° horn!
    While on mine ear it rings,
Through the deep caves of thought I hear a voice that sings:—

Build thee more stately mansions, O my soul,
30   As the swift seasons roll!
      Leave thy low-vaulted past!
Let each new temple, nobler than the last,
Shut thee from heaven with a dome more vast,
    Till thou at length art free,
35   Leaving thine outgrown shell by life's unresting sea!

---

14 *Irised* means "like a rainbow" or "rainbow-colored." In Greek mythology, Iris is
the goddess of the rainbow. Here, *rent* means "torn apart."

26 In Greek mythology, *Triton* is a sea god who resembles a fish from the waist
down. He is commonly pictured blowing a conch-shell horn. *Wreathèd* means
"spiral-shaped" or "coiled."

Responding to Literature

Personal Response

What do you think is the most powerful image from each poem? Write your ideas in your journal.

ANALYZING LITERATURE

Old Ironsides

RECALL AND INTERPRET

1. According to the speaker, what kinds of events have taken place on the ship? What does his description of these events suggest about his attitude toward "Old Ironsides"?
2. What images do lines 15 and 16 contain? What do you think they represent?
3. What end does the speaker finally suggest for the ship? Why might he prefer this end to the one described in lines 15 and 16?

EVALUATE AND CONNECT

4. Refer to your answer to the Focus Activity on page 224. Holmes wrote this poem to preserve a part of our nation's history. Why might it also be important to preserve reminders of your own personal history?

The Chambered Nautilus

RECALL AND INTERPRET

5. According to lines 1–14, what has happened to the chambered nautilus? What does the speaker's attitude toward the nautilus seem to be? Explain.
6. What does the speaker describe in lines 15–21? What do these lines add to your understanding of the speaker's attitude toward the nautilus? Explain.
7. For what is the speaker thanking the chambered nautilus in lines 22–28? What has the speaker learned from the chambered nautilus, as revealed in lines 29–35?

EVALUATE AND CONNECT

8. List some of the **imagery** (see page R8) used in this poem. In your opinion, how effective is it in supporting the poet's purpose? Explain.

Literary ELEMENTS

Verbal Irony

If someone threatens to destroy an object that you treasure, you might say, "Sure. Go ahead. Break my heart!" Your statement would be an example of **verbal irony,** the use of words that say one thing but really mean something quite different.

Find an example of verbal irony in "Old Ironsides." Do you think the example you have found is effective? Explain.

● See **Literary Terms Handbook,** p. R8.

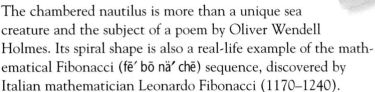

Math Under the Sea?

The chambered nautilus is more than a unique sea creature and the subject of a poem by Oliver Wendell Holmes. Its spiral shape is also a real-life example of the mathematical Fibonacci (fē′ bō nä′ chē) sequence, discovered by Italian mathematician Leonardo Fibonacci (1170–1240).

In the Fibonacci sequence, each number is the sum of the two numbers that come before it in the series: 1, 1, 2, 3, 5, 8, 13, 21, and so on.

It works this way:

$$1 + 1 = \underline{2}, 1 + 2 = \underline{3}, 2 + 3 = \underline{5}, 3 + 5 = \underline{8}, 5 + 8 = \underline{13}, \text{ and so on}$$

The Fibonacci Spiral and the Nautilus

How can a chambered nautilus have anything to do with a mathematical sequence? Take a look at the diagrams below to find out.

Start with two small squares, side by side (Figure 1). The sides of the squares can be any length, as long as they're small—an inch, a half-inch, a centimeter. Call that length "one unit." Above the first two squares, place a third square with sides of 2 units (1 + 1) (Figure 2).

▢▢ **Figure 1**   ▢ **Figure 2**

Then continue adding squares in a clockwise direction. For example, the next square should be to the right of the first three. Each new square should have a side equal to the sum of a side of each of the previous two squares. The length of the sides follows the Fibonacci sequence of 1, 1, 2, 3, 5, 8, 13.

Finally, draw a spiral through the diagram, crossing each square from one corner to its opposite, as shown (Figure 3). The curve will form a spiral pattern that is very close to the shape of Holmes's chambered nautilus.

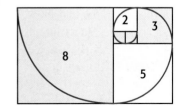

Figure 3

The Fibonacci sequence appears surprisingly often in nature. The petals of some flowers, the seeds in flower heads and pine cones, and the leaves of many trees have shapes that follow the Fibonacci sequence.

Activity

On a large sheet of paper, create a set of Fibonacci squares with the largest square having sides of 13 inches. Use a ruler to be sure your measurements are accurate. Once you have completed this set of Fibonacci squares, draw a curved line across each to create the chambered nautilus shape.

Before You Read

The First Snow-Fall

Meet James Russell Lowell

"[Reading] enables us to see with the keenest eyes, hear with the finest ears, and listen to the sweetest voices of all time."

—*Lowell*

Born in Cambridge, Massachusetts, James Russell Lowell had a happy childhood. At age fifteen, he entered Harvard College. Lowell wrote many letters to friends in those Harvard days, and from evidence in these letters has been described as "a scatterbrain, eagerly enthusiastic, devoted to his friends, . . . [opposed] to hard work." Still, he graduated from Harvard and then from Harvard Law School four years later. At twenty-five Lowell married Maria White, a poet and abolitionist. Maria White provided a stabilizing influence on Lowell's often unfocused life. In fact, he published his first book of poetry the year after they were engaged to be married.

Then, at the height of his literary fame, three of his four children died. These losses were followed by the death of Maria in 1853. For a time, it seemed that Lowell had buried with Maria his enthusiasm for poetry. He turned his energy toward interests other than writing. Lowell married Frances Dunlap in 1857 but continued to grieve over the death of Maria.

In 1855 he became a professor of modern languages at Harvard. He helped found the *Atlantic Monthly*, a literary magazine that is still published today, and he served as its first editor. By the 1860s, Lowell began writing extensively again. His poetry and essays during this period helped him regain his literary fame, yet Lowell took on new challenges.

In 1877, he served as ambassador to Spain, and then in 1880 he became ambassador to Great Britain. In 1885 Lowell returned home from England and lived until his death at Elmwood, the house of his birth.

James Russell Lowell was born in 1819 and died in 1891.

FOCUS ACTIVITY

Sometimes our moods seem to match the weather. What kind of weather do you associate with joy? with sorrow?

CHART IT! Make a chart that matches different moods to the weather you would associate with each. For example, what weather do you associate with anger?

SETTING A PURPOSE Read to see how a snowfall brings out a strong emotion in the speaker.

BACKGROUND

The Time and Place
The time is the mid-1800s. Lowell is at home with his daughter Mabel in Cambridge, Massachusetts.

Lowell's Tragedy
Lowell's experience of the death of a child was not uncommon in the 1800s. About one-third of the children who lived in urban areas died before they reached the age of twenty-one. Most were victims of diseases that are now controlled by vaccines and medication. Measles, diphtheria, and smallpox—all contagious—took the lives of many children. The death of women from childbirth, or from complications following birth, was also common.

The First Snow-Fall

James Russell Lowell

The snow had begun in the gloaming,°
   And busily all the night
Had been heaping field and highway
   With a silence deep and white.

5 Every pine and fir and hemlock
   Wore ermine° too dear° for an earl,
And the poorest twig on the elm-tree
   Was ridged inch deep with pearl.

From sheds new-roofed with Carrara°
10   Came Chanticleer's° muffled crow,
The stiff rails softened to swan's-down,
   And still fluttered down the snow.

I stood and watched by the window
   The noiseless work of the sky,
15 And the sudden flurries of snow-birds,
   Like brown leaves whirling by.

1 *Gloaming* means "twilight" or "dusk."
6 The fur of an *ermine,* a weasel of northern regions, turns white in winter. Here, *dear* means "expensive."

9 *Carrara* is a type of white marble from Italy.
10 A *chanticleer* is a rooster.

The First Snow-Fall

I thought of a mound in sweet Auburn°
    Where a little headstone stood;
How the flakes were folding it gently,
20   As did robins the babes in the wood.

Up spoke our own little Mabel,
    Saying, "Father, who makes it snow?"
And I told of the good All-father
    Who cares for us here below.

25 Again I looked at the snow-fall,
    And thought of the leaden sky
That arched o'er our first great sorrow,
    When that mound was heaped so high.

30 I remembered the gradual patience
    That fell from that cloud like snow,
Flake by flake, healing and hiding
    The scar that renewed our woe.

And again to the child I whispered,
    "The snow that husheth all,
35 Darling, the merciful Father
    Alone can make it fall!"

Then, with eyes that saw not, I
    kissed her;
And she, kissing back, could
    not know
That *my* kiss was given to her sister,
40   Folded close under deepening snow.

---

17 *Auburn* is Mt. Auburn Cemetery in Cambridge, Massachusetts.

Last Touch of Sun. John Henry Twachtman (1853–1902). Oil on canvas, 24¾ x 30 in. Private collection.

Viewing the painting: Which images from "The First Snow-Fall" are reflected in this painting?

Responding to Literature

Personal Response

Which lines from the poem did you find most powerful or surprising? Copy these lines into your journal.

Literary **ELEMENTS**

--- **ANALYZING LITERATURE** ---

RECALL AND INTERPRET

1. What has the snowfall done to the specific places and things mentioned in lines 1–14? What general atmosphere has the snowfall created? Use specific words from those lines to support your answer.
2. What does the speaker remember in lines 17–20? How would you characterize the tone of his remembrance in this stanza?
3. What answer does the speaker give Mabel when she asks where the snow comes from? What does his response tell you about his beliefs?
4. As the speaker again looks out at the snow, he is reminded of an event in the family's life. What is that event? How do you know?
5. What has the family experienced since the event described in lines 27–28? How is this experience similar to the snowfall?

EVALUATE AND CONNECT

6. How did the last stanza affect your understanding of the poem?
7. What might the speaker say to a family who had recently lost a child?
8. Does the **tone** change through this poem (see Literary Terms Handbook, page R16)? Use specific words and images to support your answer.
9. Think about your own writing experiences, including journals. How can writing about personal loss help people work through their sorrow?
10. Do you think this poem would comfort someone who had suffered a loss but did not share Lowell's religious beliefs? Why or why not?

Theme

The **theme** of a work of literature is the main idea, or point, that it conveys to the reader. In some works, the theme is stated directly. In other works, events, dialogue, or imagery suggest the theme indirectly. Short stories, drama, and poetry often contain a suggested theme. One must read carefully to infer the theme from the details in the work.

1. State the theme of "The First Snow-Fall" in your own words.
2. Is the theme of the poem stated or implied? How do you know?
3. List details that point to or support the theme of this poem.

● See **Literary Terms Handbook,** p. R16.

--- **EXTENDING YOUR RESPONSE** ---

Personal Writing

Weather and Emotion   Consider your response to the Focus Activity on page 230. Think of an intense feeling you have had. What kind of weather do you associate with that feeling? Connect the weather to the feeling or experience in a poem or short narrative. For help, you might use Lowell's poem as a model. Share your work with classmates.

Interdisciplinary Activity

Art: Expressive Images   Images created by artists catch the eye and then the heart. Those created by poets capture the mind's eye and then the heart. Use paint, clay, a computer program, or other medium to create a work of art that expresses a particular emotion. Share your work with the class.

 Save your work for your portfolio.

Grammar Link

Making Pronouns and Their Antecedents Agree

Using **pronouns** in place of nouns allows you to avoid repetition in your writing. However, be careful to make pronouns agree with their antecedents—the nouns they replace. Pronouns and their antecedents must agree in gender (masculine, feminine, or neuter), number (singular or plural), and person (first, second, or third). Here are two common problems you might encounter in pronoun-antecedent agreement.

Problem 1 A masculine pronoun used with an antecedent that can be masculine or feminine
A poet must make careful word choices in his work.

Solution A   Reword the sentence to include both a masculine and feminine pronoun.
A poet must make careful word choices in his or her work.

Solution B   Make the pronoun and its antecedent plural.
Poets must make careful word choices in their work.

Solution C   Reword the sentence to eliminate the pronoun.
A poet must make careful word choices.

Problem 2 The second-person pronoun *you* used to refer to a third-person antecedent
After some people read "The First Snow-Fall," you feel sad but peaceful.

Solution A   Use the appropriate third-person pronoun.
After some people read "The First Snow-Fall," they feel sad but peaceful.

Solution B   Use an appropriate noun rather than the pronoun.
After some people read "The First Snow-Fall," those readers feel sad but peaceful.

● To learn more about pronoun-antecedent agreement, see **Language Handbook,** pp. R23–R24.

EXERCISES

1. Rewrite the sentences below, correcting errors in pronoun-antecedent agreement.

   a. A reader might be surprised if he discovered that James Russell Lowell was once a student of law.

   b. Many students have studied poetry because it allows you to be more creative.

   c. A writer might have been amused or horrified to find himself portrayed in one of Lowell's articles.

2. Review an essay or story you have written recently. Check it to make sure that all pronouns agree with their antecedents.

Before You Read

The Tide Rises, the Tide Falls

Meet Henry Wadsworth Longfellow

"We can make our lives
      sublime,
   And, departing, leave
      behind us
   Footprints on the sands of time."

— *Longfellow*

Henry Wadsworth Longfellow was a poet for the people—a man who always seemed to please his readers. Longfellow's poems often focused on noble sentiments that caught the spirit of his time. This sense of nobility, along with his enthusiastic optimism, won him a huge and devoted audience.

Longfellow had great success in making poetry popular in America. His works often brought to life stories from the past. They include *Evangeline*, *The Courtship of Miles Standish*, and "Paul Revere's Ride."

A professor of European languages and literature at Bowdoin College and then at Harvard College, Longfellow was also a popular figure on campus. He was known as a stylish dresser—a good-looking man with a sense of humor, well liked by his students.

Personal sorrow cast a shadow over Longfellow's extraordinary public success, however. His first wife died four years after their marriage. His second wife was killed in a fire, and Longfellow was badly burned when he tried to save her. Late in life, Longfellow took refuge from his grief by translating *The Divine Comedy*, an epic poem by the fourteenth-century Italian poet Dante.

When Longfellow turned seventy-five, people in the United States celebrated the popular poet's birthday as if it were a national holiday. When he died, statues were dedicated in his honor across the country.

Henry Wadsworth Longfellow was born in 1807 and died in 1882.

FOCUS ACTIVITY

Imagine you are having a hectic day. Suddenly you have the chance to sit by the sea, by a mountain, or in a forest for an hour. How do you think that would make you feel?

DISCUSS With a group of classmates, discuss how sitting in a natural setting like the seashore might make you feel on such a day.

SETTING A PURPOSE Read to notice the role of the sea in the poem.

BACKGROUND

The Time and Place

Cambridge, Massachusetts, was a country town when Henry Wadsworth Longfellow and his friends Oliver Wendell Holmes and James Russell Lowell lived there as young men in the 1830s. The three young men gathered informally with other writers to exchange ideas and conversation, encouraging one another and fostering a great flowering of ideas and literature.

The Ebb and Flow of Fame

As a poet, Longfellow encouraged positive values. He reached out to readers of all ages and backgrounds with easy, satisfying rhythms and rich yet simple imagery. However, by the twentieth century, Longfellow's poetry had fallen out of favor. Many readers complained that his work was too sentimental, moralizing, or unrealistic. Nevertheless, Longfellow's best poems still have the power to stir the feelings and imaginations of their readers.

Time and Tide, c. 1873. Alfred Thompson Bricher. Oil on canvas, 20¼ x 50 in. Dallas Museum of Art.

The Tide Rises, the Tide Falls

The tide rises, the tide falls,
The twilight darkens, the curlew° calls;
Along the sea-sands damp and brown
The traveler hastens toward the town,
5   And the tide rises, the tide falls.

Darkness settles on roofs and walls,
But the sea, the sea in the darkness calls;
The little waves, with their soft, white hands,
Efface° the footprints in the sands,
10   And the tide rises, the tide falls.

The morning breaks; the steeds in their stalls
Stamp and neigh, as the hostler° calls;
The day returns, but nevermore
Returns the traveler to the shore,
15   And the tide rises, the tide falls.

Henry Wadsworth
Longfellow

---

2 A *curlew* is a small, long-legged shore bird.
9 *Efface* means "wipe out" or "erase."
12 A *hostler* is a person who cares for horses, especially at an inn.

Responding to Literature

Personal Response

Write three words that describe the reactions that this poem inspires in you. In your journal, explain why you have chosen each word.

Literary
ELEMENTS

ANALYZING LITERATURE

RECALL AND INTERPRET

1. What events occur in the first stanza? Which one of them stands out from the rest? In what ways is it different?
2. Refer to lines 8–10. What evidence does the traveler leave behind? What happens to the evidence? What comment do you think the speaker is making by describing what happens to that evidence?
3. Summarize lines 13–15. What do these lines suggest to you about an individual's place in nature?

EVALUATE AND CONNECT

4. Do you think the poet's use of **consonance** (see page R4) is effective in helping him convey the mood, or feeling, of the poem? Explain.
5. Think about your response to the Focus Activity on page 235. Compare your response to the feelings evoked by the sea and the tide in this poem.
6. In what ways would you like to leave footprints in "the sands of time," or make your mark on the world? How might you kindle the spirit of humanity?

Rhythm

Rhythm is the arrangement of stressed and unstressed syllables in a poem. Many poems have a regular rhythm. In other words, patterns of stressed syllables repeat line after line. The rhythm of "The Tide Rises, the Tide Falls" is not regular. It varies. Read the first two lines aloud to a partner. How would you describe the rhythm of these lines?

> The tide rises, the tide falls,
> The twilight darkens, the curlew calls.

Read the next two lines aloud with your partner. What contrast do you see between the rhythm and content of the first two lines and the rhythm and content of the second two lines?

● See **Literary Terms Handbook**, p. R13.

EXTENDING YOUR RESPONSE

Performing

Rhythms of the World If you look around, you'll notice many rhythms in the world. The tides rise and fall. City traffic stops and goes. With a group, choose some rhythms from life and express them through movement. You might create original dance movements, mime, or styles of walking to match the rhythms you choose. Begin with a rhythmic exploration of the tides. Then go on to other rhythms. Perform for a group of younger children.

Writing About Literature

Interview Longfellow Imagine that you are interviewing Henry Wadsworth Longfellow for your school newspaper. Prepare a series of questions about the meaning and elements of "The Tide Rises, the Tide Falls." Then, using your own knowledge of the poet and the poem, write answers to the questions from Longfellow's point of view.

📖 **Save your work for your portfolio.**

Before You Read

Concord Hymn, from *Nature,* from *Self-Reliance*

Meet Ralph Waldo Emerson

"It was a high counsel that I once heard given to a young person, 'Always do what you are afraid to do.'"

—*Emerson*

Philosopher, poet, essayist, and public speaker, Ralph Waldo Emerson is one of the most quoted men of his time. He urged people to think for themselves rather than follow rules that had been handed down for generations. "Nothing is at last sacred," said Emerson, "but the integrity of your own mind."

Emerson was born in 1803 in Boston, where his father was a Unitarian minister. His father died when the boy was eight, leaving the family with financial problems. When Emerson was fourteen, he received a scholarship to attend Harvard College, and in 1825 he entered Harvard Divinity School. By 1829 Emerson had become a successful Boston minister. He also had married.

Two years later, however, Emerson's life took a new path. His wife died, and he grieved for her tremendously. Also, he had long been developing his own beliefs. He maintained that each person contained a spark of divinity and that people should search for truths in nature and within themselves. Emerson realized that his personal beliefs conflicted with those of his church, so he decided to leave the ministry.

Emerson then sailed for Europe, where he met and was influenced by the English writers William Wordsworth, Samuel Taylor Coleridge, and Thomas Carlyle. When he returned to the United States in 1833, he settled in Concord, Massachusetts, and began a life as a writer and lecturer. Two years later, he remarried.

In Concord Emerson helped found the Transcendental Club, a group devoted to discussions of literature, philosophy, and religion. At thirty-three, he published "Nature," a long essay that set forth the major ideas of transcendentalism. This work attracted little notice at the time. A year later, however, Emerson gave two lectures that made him famous: "The American Scholar" and "The Divinity School Address." These works, like "Nature," urged Americans to think for themselves and to resist the bonds of conformity. During the next decades, Emerson lectured extensively and published many works.

In his last years, Emerson's memory failed. His inquisitive mind noted even that change:

> It is time to be old,
> To take in sail:
> The god of bounds,
> Who sets to seas a shore,
> Came to me in his fatal rounds,
> And said: "No more! . . ."

"The end of the human race will be that it will eventually die of civilization."

—*Emerson*

Ralph Waldo Emerson was born in 1803 and died in 1882.

FOCUS ACTIVITY

What can you learn from history—the history of your own life, of your community, and of your country? How does history help you deal with the present and the future?

FREEWRITE Take a few minutes to freewrite about the benefits of remembering the details of important events both in your own history and in the nation's history.

SETTING A PURPOSE Read to learn how one writer helps others remember an historic event of great importance.

BACKGROUND

The Time and Place

On July 4, 1837, a monument was unveiled in Concord, Massachusetts. There, in 1775, the American Minutemen had fought against the British in one of the first battles of the Revolutionary War. At the request of the Monument Committee, Emerson wrote the words to "Concord Hymn," which was sung at the memorial ceremony.

Literary Influences

Emerson was involved in the nineteenth-century philosophical and literary movement known as Transcendentalism, which stemmed from the Romantic movement in art, literature, and music. Transcendentalists believed in the unity of all creation and that human nature contained something that transcended, or went beyond, ordinary experience. They thought that every person was divine, and so to trust or rely on the self was to trust God who spoke within us. Transcendentalists maintained that through intuition we transcend the limits of our senses and reason and come to know higher truths.

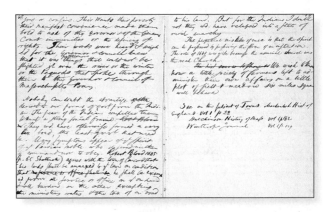

Emerson's journal.

VOCABULARY PREVIEW

perpetual (pər pech′ ōō əl) *adj.* lasting forever; eternal; p. 242

integrate (in′ tə grāt) *v.* to bring all parts together into a whole; p. 242

decorum (di kôr′ əm) *n.* conformity to the approved standards of good taste; p. 243

perennial (pə ren′ ē əl) *adj.* continuing year after year; enduring; p. 243

blithe (blīth) *adj.* lighthearted and carefree; cheerful; p. 243

occult (ə kult′) *adj.* beyond human understanding; mysterious; p. 243

admonition (ad′ mə nish′ ən) *n.* a warning; cautionary advice; p. 245

latent (lā′ tənt) *adj.* present but not evident; hidden; p. 245

sage (sāj) *n.* a person of profound wisdom and judgment; p. 245

manifest (man′ ə fest′) *adj.* apparent to the eye or the mind; evident; obvious; p. 246

benefactor (ben′ ə fak′ tər) *n.* one who gives help or financial aid; p. 246

integrity (in teg′ rə tē) *n.* moral uprightness; honesty; p. 247

Concord Hymn

Ralph Waldo Emerson

*Sung at the completion of Concord Monument,
July 4, 1837.*

By the rude bridge that arched the flood,
Their flag to April's breeze unfurled,
Here once the embattled farmers stood,
And fired the shot heard round the world,

5   The foe long since in silence slept,
Alike the Conqueror silent sleeps,
And Time the ruined bridge has swept
Down the dark stream which seaward creeps.

On this green bank, by this soft stream,
10 We set to-day a votive stone,
That memory may their deed redeem,
When like our sires our sons are gone.

Spirit! who made those freemen dare
To die, or leave their children free,
15 Bid time and nature gently spare
The shaft we raise to them and Thee.

Minute Man, 1874. Daniel Chester French. Bronze, approximately 7 x 4 x 4 ft. Minuteman National Park, Old North Bridge, Concord, MA.

Responding to Literature

Personal Response

What were your reactions to this poem? Note them in your journal.

ANALYZING LITERATURE

RECALL AND INTERPRET

1. What did the farmers do at the bridge in Concord? What does the speaker imply about the impact of their activities?
2. Where are the battle's participants now? What has happened to the bridge?
3. What are people doing on the day the poem is sung? According to the speaker, what purpose will be served by what they are doing?
4. What does the speaker ask in the last stanza? In your opinion, why does he ask this?
5. A hymn is a song of praise or thanksgiving. What do you think Emerson is praising or being thankful for in this poem? Cite details from the poem to support your response.

EVALUATE AND CONNECT

6. Look at the words Emerson used, the way he arranged them, and the poem's rhythm pattern. Based on these factors, how would you describe the **mood** (see page R10) created in the poem? In your opinion, does the mood fit the message of the poem? Why or why not?
7. Consider your response to the Focus Activity on page 239. What do you think are the advantages of memorializing an important person or historic event in a song or poem? What contemporary songs do you know that pay tribute to people or significant events?
8. Emerson wrote about an important event in U.S. history. What historic event would you choose to commemorate? Explain your choice.

Literary ELEMENTS

Metonymy

Emerson often uses a type of figurative language called **metonymy** (mi ton′ ə mē). Metonymy is the use of one word to stand for a related term. When Emerson writes that the sun shines into a child's heart, he uses *heart* to stand for deep emotions. In "Concord Hymn," he uses metonymy when he refers to "the shot heard round the world." He is actually referring to the entire battle, not just one bullet.

1. In "Concord Hymn," when Emerson writes that "like our sires our sons are gone," what does he mean? How else could he have said this?
2. What does Emerson mean by the word "children" in the last stanza? Do you think the meaning would change if a freeman had no children? Why or why not?

● See **Literary Terms Handbook**, p. R10.

EXTENDING YOUR RESPONSE

Literature Groups

Why a Poem?   Should Emerson have written a speech instead of a poem? Which form do you think would be more effective? In your group, discuss these questions and use evidence from the poem to support your ideas. Summarize your ideas and share them with the class.

Creative Writing

Modern Song   Work with a partner to write a new version of the "Concord Hymn." Put Emerson's ideas into new words and perhaps a new form. Then add music from a favorite melody or a contemporary song. Record your song or perform it for the class.

from Nature

Ralph Waldo Emerson

TO GO INTO SOLITUDE, a man needs to retire as much from his chamber as from society. I am not solitary whilst I read and write, though nobody is with me. But if a man would be alone, let him look at the stars. The rays that come from those heavenly worlds will separate between him and what he touches. One might think the atmosphere was made transparent with this design, to give man, in the heavenly bodies, the perpetual presence of the sublime. Seen in the streets of cities, how great they are! If the stars should appear one night in a thousand years, how would men believe and adore; and preserve for many generations the remembrance of the city of God which had been shown! But every night come out these envoys[1] of beauty, and light the universe with their admonishing[2] smile.

The stars awaken a certain reverence, because though always present, they are inaccessible; but all natural objects make a kindred impression, when the mind is open to their influence. Nature never wears a mean[3] appearance. Neither does the wisest man extort her secret, and lose his curiosity by finding out all her perfection. Nature never became a toy to a wise spirit. The flowers, the animals, the mountains, reflected the wisdom of his best hour, as much as they had delighted the simplicity of his childhood.

When we speak of nature in this manner, we have a distinct but most poetical sense in the mind. We mean the integrity of impression made by manifold[4] natural objects. It is this which distinguishes the stick of timber of the wood-cutter from the tree of the poet. The charming landscape which I saw this morning is indubitably[5] made up of some twenty or thirty farms. Miller owns this field, Locke that, and Manning the woodland beyond. But none of them owns the landscape. There is a property in the horizon which no man has but he whose eye can integrate all the parts, that is, the poet. This is the best part of these men's farms, yet to this their warranty-deeds[6] give no title.

To speak truly, few adult persons can see nature. Most persons do not see the sun. At least they have a very superficial seeing. The sun illuminates only the eye of the man, but shines into the eye and the heart of the child. The lover of nature is he whose inward and outward senses are still truly adjusted to each other; who has retained the spirit of infancy even into the era of manhood. His intercourse with heaven and earth becomes part of his daily food. In the presence of nature a wild delight runs through the man, in spite of real sorrows. Nature says,—he is my creature, and maugre[7] all his impertinent[8]

---

1. *Envoys* are those sent as representatives of another.
2. *Admonishing* means "gently warning" or "scolding."
3. Here, *mean* means "poor," "inferior," or "shabby."
4. *Manifold* means "many kinds or varieties."
5. *Indubitably* means "without a doubt" or "certainly."
6. *Warranty-deeds* are legal documents that state ownership of property.
7. *Maugre* means "in spite of."
8. *Impertinent* means "irrelevant."

Vocabulary

perpetual (pər pech′ oo əl) *adj.* lasting forever; eternal
integrate (in′ tə grāt) *v.* to bring all parts together into a whole

griefs, he shall be glad with me. Not the sun or the summer alone, but every hour and season yields its tribute of delight; for every hour and change corresponds to and authorizes a different state of the mind, from breathless noon to grimmest midnight. Nature is a setting that fits equally well a comic or a mourning piece. In good health, the air is a cordial[9] of incredible virtue. Crossing a bare common,[10] in snow puddles, at twilight, under a clouded sky, without having in my thoughts any occurrence of special good fortune, I have enjoyed a perfect exhilaration. I am glad to the brink of fear. In the woods, too, a man casts off his years, as the snake his slough, and at what period soever of life is always a child. In the woods is perpetual youth. Within these plantations of God, a decorum and sanctity reign, a perennial festival is dressed, and the guest sees not how he should tire of them in a thousand years. In the woods, we return to reason and faith. There I feel that nothing can befall me in life,—no disgrace, no calamity (leaving me my eyes), which nature cannot repair. Standing on the bare ground,—my head bathed by the blithe air and uplifted into infinite space,—all mean egotism vanishes. I become a transparent eyeball; I am nothing; I see all; the currents of the Universal Being circulate through me; I am part or parcel of God. The name of the nearest friend sounds then foreign and accidental: to be brothers, to be acquaintances, master or servant, is then a trifle and a disturbance. I am the lover of uncontained and immortal beauty. In the wilderness, I find something more dear and connate[11] than in streets or villages. In the tranquil landscape, and especially in the distant line of the horizon, man beholds somewhat as beautiful as his own nature.

The greatest delight which the fields and woods minister is the suggestion of an occult relation between man and the vegetable. I am not alone and unacknowledged. They nod to me, and I to them. The waving of the boughs in the storm is new to me and old. It takes me by surprise, and yet is not unknown. Its effect is like that of a higher thought or a better emotion coming over me, when I deemed I was thinking justly or doing right.

Yet it is certain that the power to produce this delight does not reside in nature, but in man, or in a harmony of both. It is necessary to use these pleasures with great temperance. For nature is not always tricked[12] in holiday attire, but the same scene which yesterday breathed perfume and glittered as for the frolic of the nymphs is overspread with melancholy today. Nature always wears the colors of the spirit. To a man laboring under calamity, the heat of his own fire hath sadness in it. Then there is a kind of contempt of the landscape felt by him who has just lost by death a dear friend. The sky is less grand as it shuts down over less worth in the population.

---

9. A *cordial* is a stimulant, such as a drink or medicine.
10. A *common* is community property, such as a park, owned or used by the public.

---

11. *Connate* means "being in harmony or sympathy."
12. Here, *tricked* means "dressed."

Vocabulary

decorum (di kôr′ əm) *n.* conformity to the approved standards of good taste
perennial (pə ren′ ē əl) *adj.* continuing year after year; enduring
blithe (blīth) *adj.* lighthearted and carefree; cheerful
occult (ə kult′) *adj.* beyond human understanding; mysterious

Responding to Literature

Personal Response

Which of Emerson's ideas most impressed you? Explain.

ANALYZING LITERATURE

RECALL AND INTERPRET

1. According to Emerson, why should people look at the stars if they wish to be alone? How would people respond if the stars appeared only once in a thousand years? What does this suggest about Emerson's view of human nature?

2. In Emerson's view, how do adults and children differ in the way they view nature? What does Emerson suggest accounts for this difference?

3. How do changing seasons affect lovers of nature? Why might Emerson have felt exhilarated by crossing a park on a snowy evening?

4. What scenes in nature does Emerson describe? What effect does being in nature have on Emerson? What conclusions does he draw from this?

5. In your opinion, what does Emerson mean when he states, "Nature always wears the colors of the spirit"? Do you agree with him? Explain.

EVALUATE AND CONNECT

6. Do you consider yourself to be one of the people who can truly see nature as Emerson describes? Explain your response.

7. What, do you think, is the difference between the meaning Emerson finds in nature and the meaning a scientist finds?

8. How do you think people today can connect with nature in a meaningful way, even if they live in a city? What benefits might they receive?

EXTENDING YOUR RESPONSE

Literature Groups

Theme Connections: Spread the Word   How would you summarize Emerson's main points about nature in order to share his insights with others? Work with your group to outline the main ideas of this selection. Then add necessary supporting details. Share your outline with the class.

Personal Writing

I Should Have Said   What would you say to Emerson if you could meet him? Would you agree with him or argue? Would you ask him how you might become in touch with nature? Imagine yourself free to speak your mind to him. In your journal, write what you would say.

📖 **Save your work for your portfolio.**

from Self-Reliance

Ralph Waldo Emerson

I READ THE OTHER DAY SOME VERSES written by an eminent[1] painter which were original and not conventional. Always the soul hears an admonition in such lines, let the subject be what it may. The sentiment they instill is of more value than any thought they may contain. To believe your own thought, to believe that what is true for you in your private heart, is true for all men,—that is genius. Speak your latent conviction and it shall be the universal sense; for always the inmost becomes the outmost,—and our first thought is rendered back to us by the trumpets of the Last Judgment. Familiar as the voice of the mind is to each, the highest merit we ascribe to Moses, Plato, and Milton is that they set at naught books and traditions, and spoke not what men, but what they thought. A man should learn to detect and watch that gleam of light which flashes across his mind from within, more than the lustre of the firmament of bards[2] and sages. Yet he dismisses without notice his thought, because it is his. In every work of genius we recognize our own rejected thoughts: they come back to us with a certain alienated majesty. Great works of art have no more affecting lesson for us than this.

---

1. *Eminent* means "distinguished" or "prominent."
2. *Bards* are poets.

Vocabulary

admonition (ad′ mə nish′ ən) *n.* a warning; cautionary advice
latent (lā′ tənt) *adj.* present but not evident; hidden
sage (sāj) *n.* a person of profound wisdom and judgment

from Self-Reliance

They teach us to abide by our spontaneous impression with good humored inflexibility then most when the whole cry of voices is on the other side. Else, tomorrow a stranger will say with masterly good sense precisely what we have thought and felt all the time, and we shall be forced to take with shame our own opinion from another.

There is a time in every man's education when he arrives at the conviction that envy is ignorance; that imitation is suicide; that he must take himself for better, for worse, as his portion; that though the wide universe is full of good, no kernel of nourishing corn can come to him but through his toil bestowed on that plot of ground which is given to him to till. The power which resides in him is new in nature, and none but he knows what that is which he can do, nor does he know

John Milton, c. 1629. Artist unknown. Oil on canvas, 23½ x 19 in. National Portrait Gallery, London.

until he has tried. Not for nothing one face, one character, one fact makes much impression on him, and another none. It is not without preëstablished harmony, this sculpture in the memory. The eye was placed where one ray should fall, that it might testify of that particular ray. Bravely let him speak the utmost syllable of his confession. We but half express ourselves, and are ashamed of that divine idea which each of us represents. It may be safely trusted as proportionate and of good issues, so it be faithfully imparted, but God will not have his work made <u>manifest</u> by cowards. It needs a divine man to exhibit any thing divine. A man is relieved and gay when he has put his heart into his work and done his best; but what he has said or done otherwise, shall give him no peace. It is a deliverance which does not deliver. In the attempt his genius deserts him; no muse[3] befriends; no invention, no hope.

Trust thyself: every heart vibrates to that iron string. Accept the place the divine Providence[4] has found for you; the society of your contemporaries, the connection of events. Great men have always done so and confided themselves childlike to the genius[5] of their age, betraying their perception that the Eternal was stirring at their heart, working through their hands, predominating[6] in all their being. And we are now men, and must accept in the highest mind the same transcendent[7] destiny; and not pinched in a corner, not cowards fleeing before a revolution, but redeemers and <u>benefactors</u>, pious aspirants[8] to be noble clay plastic under the Almighty effort, let us advance and advance on Chaos and the Dark. . . .

---

3. In Greek mythology, the Muses were goddesses who presided over the arts and sciences. Here, *muse* is used to mean "a source of genius or inspiration."
4. The *divine Providence* is God.
5. Here, *genius* means "the distinctive character" or "predominant spirit."
6. *Predominating* means "having controlling power or influence."
7. *Transcendent* means "concerned with a spiritual reality that is beyond the limits of experience and knowable only through intuition."
8. *Aspirants* are those who seek, or aspire to, advancement or honors.

Vocabulary
manifest (man′ ə fest′) *adj.* apparent to the eye or the mind; evident; obvious
benefactor (ben′ ə fak′ tər) *n.* one who gives help or financial aid

Society everywhere is in conspiracy against the manhood of every one of its members. Society is a joint-stock company in which the members agree for the better securing of his bread to each shareholder, to surrender the liberty and culture of the eater. The virtue in most request is conformity. Self-reliance is its aversion. It loves not realities and creators, but names and customs.

Whoso would be a man must be a nonconformist. He who would gather immortal palms[9] must not be hindered by the name of goodness, but must explore if it be goodness. Nothing is at last sacred but the integrity of your own mind. . . .

What I must do, is all that concerns me, not what the people think. This rule, equally arduous[10] in actual and in intellectual life, may serve for the whole distinction between greatness and meanness.[11] It is the harder, because you will always find those who think they know what is your duty better than you know it. It is easy in the world to live after the world's opinion; it is easy in solitude to live after our own; but the great man is he who in the midst of the crowd keeps with perfect sweetness the independence of solitude.

Viewing the sculpture:
In what ways does this sculpture of Moses capture the spirit of self-reliance?

---

9. *Palm* leaves are a traditional symbol of victory or success.
10. *Arduous* means "difficult."
11. Here, *meanness* means "the state of having little importance, worth, or consequence."

Vocabulary
integrity (in teg′ rə tē) *n.* moral uprightness; honesty

Responding to Literature

Personal Response

Do you agree with Emerson's views about the value of nonconformity? Share your opinions with your class.

——— ANALYZING LITERATURE ———

RECALL

1. According to Emerson, what is genius?
2. What is the lesson Emerson would have people learn from great works of art?
3. In what way, according to Emerson, should a person approach his or her work?
4. How does Emerson describe society? What approach to society does Emerson say a person must strive for?
5. What does Emerson say is his main concern? According to Emerson, who is a great man?

INTERPRET

6. In Emerson's view, what are the benefits of genius?
7. What do you think Emerson's references to art say about his values and his view of human thought?
8. What kind of "work" do you think Emerson is describing? Explain.
9. How does society affect what people value?
10. How do you think a person can become "great" according to Emerson's view? Give examples.

EVALUATE AND CONNECT

11. Theme Connections In your opinion, how might people react if Emerson's essay were published today? What insights might they gain from reading the essay?
12. Under what circumstances might conformity be wise? When might it be foolish?
13. Describe how people today might show self-reliance. What roles might self-reliant people play in society today?
14. What parts of Emerson's essay did you find most persuasive? What techniques did Emerson use to make these parts effective?
15. Do you think it's possible for people to live in society the way Emerson recommends? Why or why not?

Literary ELEMENTS

Figurative Language

Figurative language is language that conveys ideas beyond what the words literally mean. For example, Emerson says that a person "should learn to detect and watch that gleam of light which flashes across his mind from within." The gleam of light that Emerson writes about refers to a person's ideas. Emerson uses figurative language to help us understand an abstract thought. Figurative language can also make commonplace ideas fresh and vivid.

1. When Emerson writes, "no kernel of nourishing corn can come to him but through his toil bestowed on that plot of ground which is given to him to till," what do you think he means?

2. Find at least three other examples of figurative language in "Self-Reliance." Tell how each image helps explain an idea or makes it concrete.

● See **Literary Terms Handbook,** p. R6.

LITERATURE AND WRITING

Writing About Literature

Understanding Emerson's Message   What value does Emerson place on human ideas? How does he view the connection between nature and people? Write a brief analysis of Emerson's ideas about human nature using details from "Nature" and "Self-Reliance."

Personal Writing

Take Yourself Seriously   Emerson thought deeply about matters that interested him. Try following his example. Review your freewriting for the Focus Activity on page 239. Choose one key point you made about remembering past events. Write a journal entry in which you more fully explain the advantages and the effect on your life.

EXTENDING YOUR RESPONSE

Literature Groups

Being Courageous   In what ways would it take courage for students today to "trust" themselves and live according to their own convictions? Discuss this question in your group. How might their behavior change? What might they risk, if anything? What might they gain? Share your ideas with the class.

Internet Connection

Scavenger Hunt   Have an informal scavenger hunt and try to find the following information about Emerson on the Internet: Emerson home pages; excerpts from his journal; his opinion of Nathaniel Hawthorne's novel *The House of the Seven Gables;* quotations by Emerson; the text of some of his speeches. Print out an interesting Web page to post on a bulletin board in your classroom.

Performing

Press Conference   Imagine that Emerson has appeared today, having recently published "Concord Hymn" and the essays "Nature" and "Self-Reliance." With a group, create a press conference in which Emerson answers reporters' questions about his work. Decide what questions the reporters might ask and how Emerson might respond. Then perform your press conference for the class.

Reading Further

If you would like to read more by or about Emerson, you might enjoy these works:

Collections: *The Topical Notebooks of Ralph Waldo Emerson,* edited by Ronald A. Bosco, includes Emerson's notebooks as well as annotations by the editor.

History: *Emerson Among the Eccentrics: A Group Portrait,* by Carlos Baker, a glimpse into the daily life of Emerson and his circle of friends.

📖 **Save your work for your portfolio.**

Skill Minilesson

VOCABULARY • The Prefix *com-*

A **prefix** is a word part that is added at the beginning of a base word or a word root. One common Latin prefix, *com-* (also *col-, con-,* or *cor-*) means "together," "with," or "jointly." Notice how this prefix contributes to the meaning of this word:

concord—being in agreement; harmony

PRACTICE   Write a definition for each word below. Include the meaning of the prefix *com-* in each definition. Feel free to use a dictionary.

1. collaborate
2. committee
3. colleague
4. corresponds

Before You Read

from *Walden* and from *Civil Disobedience*

Meet Henry David Thoreau

"If a man does not keep pace with his companions, perhaps it is because he hears a different drummer."

—*Thoreau*

When Henry David Thoreau (thə rō′) died at age forty-four, few people outside Concord, Massachusetts, had ever heard of him. It was not until the twentieth century that Thoreau became famous around the world as a thinker and environmentalist.

After graduating from Harvard College, Thoreau took a job as a schoolteacher. He enjoyed teaching, but when he was ordered to discipline his students by whipping them, he resigned.

Except for brief periods, Thoreau made the Concord area his home. There he devoted his time to nature study, reading, and writing, and he supported himself with odd jobs. When his brother John died suddenly of tetanus, Thoreau was deeply affected. About three years after John's death, Thoreau decided to pay tribute to his brother by writing an account of the camping and canoeing trip that he and John had taken a few years before.

Thoreau needed a quiet place to write, so he persuaded his friend Ralph Waldo Emerson to allow him to build a cabin on Emerson's land at Walden Pond. Thoreau was a keen observer of nature and had kept detailed notes in his journals about what he saw on his trip. He used these notes as the basis for his first book, *A Week on the Concord and Merrimack Rivers*. Thoreau continued his extensive nature writing during the two years that he lived alone at Walden Pond. His masterpiece, *Walden*, was based on his observations there.

Thoreau was a dedicated abolitionist and helped slaves escape to the North through the Underground Railroad. He also wrote an impassioned defense of abolitionist John Brown, who had been sentenced to be hanged for attempting to incite a slave rebellion. Thoreau scheduled a public meeting to present the defense of Brown, but local officials refused to announce the meeting. Thoreau rang the Town Hall bell himself to announce the meeting. Once he presented his defense of Brown, he won over many to his viewpoint.

Although very few copies of Thoreau's first book sold during his lifetime, *Walden* was well received. Published in 1854, the first edition sold out in five years.

Thoreau and his friend Emerson, who outlived him by two decades, are buried near each other in Concord.

"Time never passes so quickly and unaccountably as when I am engaged in composition, i.e. in writing down my thoughts. Clocks seem to have been put forward."

—*Thoreau*

"He declined to give up his large ambition of knowledge and action for any narrow craft or profession, aiming at a much more comprehensive calling, the art of living well."

—*Ralph Waldo Emerson*

Henry David Thoreau was born in 1817 and died in 1862.

FOCUS ACTIVITY

What do you think are the most essential things that people do in everyday life?

CHART IT! Thoreau believed "Our life is frittered away by detail." What are the unimportant details in your life? What is really important? Record your responses in a chart like the one shown.

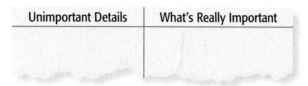

Unimportant Details	What's Really Important

SETTING A PURPOSE Read to learn one writer's thoughts about what is really important in life.

BACKGROUND

Did You Know?
Thoreau lived at Walden Pond for two years, two months, and two days in a cabin that measured ten feet by fifteen feet. He built the cabin himself. It was simple and sturdy, with plastered walls and a shingled roof. His equipment consisted of an ax, two knives and a fork, three plates, one cup, one spoon, a jug for oil, a jug for molasses, and one lamp. He made his own furniture, including a bed, table, desk, and three chairs. At Walden, Thoreau devoted himself to observing the seasons, the animals, the plants, and to writing his journals; but he was not a hermit. Since the pond was only a mile from Concord, Thoreau was able to visit his relatives and friends nearly every day.

Thoreau in Jail
When he was twenty-nine years old, Thoreau refused to pay a small tax that supported the Mexican-American War and the continuation of slavery. His action was an example of his philosophy of "passive resistance," a means of nonviolent protest. The jailer offered to pay the tax for Thoreau, but Thoreau refused, on principle. He spent one night in jail before his aunt paid the tax. To explain his actions, Thoreau wrote the essay "Resistance to Civil Government," now known as "Civil Disobedience."

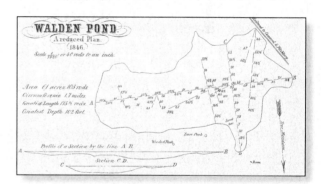

VOCABULARY PREVIEW

deliberately (di lib′ ər it lē) *adv.* in a careful, thoughtful way; p. 253

resignation (rez′ ig nā′ shən) *n.* unresisting acceptance; submission; p. 253

sublime (sə̄b līm′) *adj.* of great spiritual or intellectual value; noble; p. 253

rudiment (ro͞o′ də mənt) *n.* an imperfect or undeveloped part; p. 254

myriad (mir′ ē əd) *adj.* countless; innumerable; p. 255

expedient (iks pē′ dē ənt) *n.* something employed to bring about a desired result; a means to an end; p. 258

din (din) *n.* loud, continuous noise; p. 258

alacrity (ə lak′ rə tē) *n.* speed; swiftness; p. 258

inherent (in hēr′ ənt) *adj.* existing as a basic quality; belonging to by nature; p. 258

sanction (sangk′ shən) *n.* approval or support; p. 261

from

WALDEN

Henry David Thoreau

from Where I Lived and What I Lived For

I WENT TO THE WOODS because I wished to live <u>deliberately</u>, to front only the essential facts of life, and see if I could not learn what it had to teach, and not, when I came to die, discover that I had not lived. I did not wish to live what was not life, living is so dear; nor did I wish to practice <u>resignation</u>, unless it was quite necessary. I wanted to live deep and suck out all the marrow[1] of life, to live so sturdily and Spartanlike[2] as to put to rout all that was not life, to cut a broad swath and shave close,[3] to drive life into a corner, and reduce it to its lowest terms, and, if it proved to be mean,[4] why then to get the whole and genuine meanness of it, and publish its meanness to the world; or if it were <u>sublime</u>, to know it by experience, and be able to give a true account of it in my next excursion. For most men, it appears to me, are in a strange uncertainty about it, whether it is of the devil or of God, and have *somewhat hastily* concluded that it is the chief end of man here to "glorify God and enjoy him forever."

Still we live meanly, like ants; though the fable tells us that we were long ago changed into men;[5] like pygmies we fight with cranes;[6] it is error upon error, and clout upon clout, and our best virtue has for its occasion a superfluous and evitable[7] wretchedness. Our life is frittered away by detail. An honest man has hardly need to count more than his ten fingers, or in extreme cases he may add his ten toes, and lump the rest. Simplicity, simplicity, simplicity! I say, let your affairs be as two or three, and not a hundred or a thousand; instead of a million count half a dozen, and keep your accounts on your thumb nail. In the midst of this chopping sea of civilized life, such are the clouds and storms and quicksands and thousand-and-one items to be allowed for, that a man has to live, if he would not founder[8] and go to the bottom and not make his port at all, by dead reckoning,[9] and he must be a great calculator indeed who succeeds. Simplify, simplify. Instead of three meals a day, if it be necessary eat but one; instead of a hundred dishes, five; and reduce other things in proportion. . . .

Why should we live with such hurry and waste of life? We are determined to be starved before we are hungry. Men say that a stitch in time saves nine, and so they take a

---

1. *Marrow* is the soft tissue inside bones. It also means "the best or most essential part."
2. Spartans were inhabitants of the ancient Greek city-state of Sparta. *Spartanlike* means simple, economical, and disciplined.
3. *[to cut . . . close]* means "to gather as much of the essence of life as possible."
4. Here, *mean* means "of little importance, worth, or consequence" or "ignoble."
5. The *fable* referred to is a Greek myth in which Zeus changes *ants* into *men.*
6. In Homer's *Iliad,* the Trojans are compared to *cranes* battling *pygmies.*
7. *Evitable* means "avoidable."

8. *Founder* means "to sink, as a boat."
9. *Dead reckoning* is a method of navigation used by sailors when the stars cannot be seen.

Vocabulary
deliberately (di lib′ ər it lē) *adj.* in a careful, thoughtful way
resignation (rez′ ig nā′ shən) *n.* unresisting acceptance; submission
sublime (səb līm′) *adj.* of great spiritual or intellectual value; noble

thousand stitches today to save nine tomorrow. As for *work*, we haven't any of any consequence. We have the Saint Vitus' dance,[10] and cannot possibly keep our heads still. If I should only give a few pulls at the parish bell-rope, as for a fire, that is, without setting the bell, there is hardly

A Cabin on Greenwood Lake, 1879. Jasper Francis Cropsey. Oil on canvas, 23.3 x 41.4 cm. Private collection.
Viewing the painting: How might your own life be simpler if you lived in a cabin like this one?

a man on his farm in the outskirts of Concord, notwithstanding that press of engagements which was his excuse so many times this morning, nor a boy, nor a woman, I might almost say, but would forsake all and follow that sound, not mainly to save property from the flames, but, if we will confess the truth, much more to see it burn, since burn it must, and we, be it known, did not set it on fire,—or to see it put out, and have a hand in it, if that is done as handsomely; yes, even if it were the parish church itself. Hardly a man takes a half hour's nap after dinner, but when he wakes he holds up his head and asks, "What's the news?" as if the rest of mankind had stood his sentinels. Some give directions to be waked every half hour, doubtless for no other purpose; and then, to pay for it, they tell what they have dreamed. After a night's sleep the news is as indispensable as the breakfast. "Pray tell me any thing new that has happened to a man any where on this globe,"—and he reads it over his

coffee and rolls, that a man has had his eyes gouged out this morning on the Wachito River;[11] never dreaming the while that he lives in the dark unfathomed mammoth cave of this world, and has but the rudiment of an eye himself.

For my part, I could easily do without the post-office. I think that there are very few important communications made through it. To speak critically, I never received more than one or two letters in my life—I wrote this some years ago—that were worth the postage. The penny-post is, commonly, an institution through which you seriously offer a man that penny for his thoughts which is so often safely offered in jest. And I am sure that I never read any memorable news in a newspaper. If we read of one man robbed, or murdered, or killed by accident, or one house burned, or one vessel wrecked, or one steam-boat blown up, or one cow run over on the Western Railroad, or one mad dog killed, or

---

10. *Saint Vitus' dance* is a nervous disorder characterized by involuntary twitching of the muscles in the face, arms, and legs.

11. The *Wachito River* (now called the Ouachita) flows from southern Arkansas into northern Louisiana. People in Thoreau's time thought that criminals went to that region to escape from the law.

Vocabulary
rudiment (rōō′ də mənt) *n.* an imperfect or undeveloped part

one lot of grasshoppers in the winter,—we never need read of another. One is enough. If you are acquainted with the principle, what do you care for a <u>myriad</u> instances and applications? . . .

Time is but the stream I go a-fishing in. I drink at it; but while I drink I see the sandy bottom and detect how shallow it is. Its thin current slides away, but eternity remains. I would drink deeper; fish in the sky, whose bottom is pebbly with stars. I cannot count one. I know not the first letter of the alphabet. I have always been regretting that I was not as wise as the day I was born. The intellect is a cleaver; it discerns and rifts its way into the secret of things. I do not wish to be any more busy with my hands than is necessary. My head is hands and feet. I feel all my best faculties concentrated in it. My instinct tells me that my head is an organ for burrowing, as some creatures use their snout and fore-paws, and with it I would mine and burrow my way through these hills. I think that the richest vein is somewhere hereabouts; so by the divining rod[12] and thin rising vapors I judge; and here I will begin to mine.

from Conclusion

. . . I left the woods for as good a reason as I went there. Perhaps it seemed to me that I had several more lives to live, and could not spare any more time for that one. It is remarkable how easily and insensibly we fall into a particular route, and make a beaten track for ourselves. I had not lived there a week before my feet wore a path from my door to the pond-side; and though it is five or six years since I trod it, it is still quite distinct. It is true, I fear that others may have fallen into it, and so helped to keep it open. The surface of the earth is soft and impressible by the feet of men; and so with the paths which the mind travels. How worn and dusty, then, must be the highways of the world, how deep the ruts of tradition and conformity! I did not wish to take a cabin passage,[13] but rather to go before the mast and on the deck of the world, for there I could best see the moonlight amid the mountains. I do not wish to go below now.

I learned this, at least, by my experiment; that if one advances confidently in the direction of his dreams, and endeavors to live the life which he has imagined, he will meet with a success unexpected in common hours. He will put some things behind, will pass an invisible boundary; new, universal, and more liberal laws will begin to establish themselves around and within him; or the old laws be expanded, and interpreted in his favor in a more liberal sense, and he will live with the license of a higher order of beings. In proportion as he simplifies his life, the laws of the universe will appear less complex, and solitude will not be solitude, nor poverty poverty, nor weakness weakness. If you have built castles in the air, your work need not be lost; that is where they should be. Now put the foundations under them. . . .

---

12. A *divining rod* is a forked stick believed to indicate the presence of underground minerals or water.

13. A person who took a *cabin passage* on a sailing ship would travel in a private compartment, sheltered from the weather.

Vocabulary
myriad (mir′ ē əd) *adj.* countless; innumerable

Responding to Literature

Personal Response

Which of Thoreau's ideas do you strongly agree or disagree with? Note them in your journal.

ANALYZING LITERATURE

RECALL AND INTERPRET

1. What did Thoreau hope to do at Walden? How might being there have helped him achieve his goal?
2. What are Thoreau's views of the news and the mail? Why do you think he held these views? What does his discussion tell you about what he values?
3. Why did Thoreau leave Walden? What might this suggest about him?
4. What did Thoreau learn at Walden? In your opinion, did he see his time there as well spent or wasted? Give reasons for your response.

EVALUATE AND CONNECT

5. Look back at the list of "What's Really Important" that you created in response to the Focus Activity on page 251. Which of those items do you think Thoreau might have considered unessential? Explain.
6. How do you think your life might change if you took Thoreau's advice to "Simplify, simplify"? To help answer this question, use a cause-and-effect diagram.
7. Theme Connections   In your opinion, what insights did Thoreau gain by his "experiment" in the woods?
8. Thoreau urges us to "live deep and suck out all the marrow of life." How could you apply this to your own life? Explain and give examples.

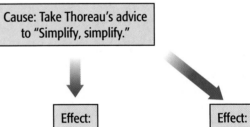

Cause: Take Thoreau's advice to "Simplify, simplify."

Effect: Effect: Effect:

EXTENDING YOUR RESPONSE

Literature Groups

No Ambition?   Ralph Waldo Emerson once said of Thoreau, "I cannot help counting it a fault in him that he had no ambition." In your group, discuss whether or not you agree with Emerson. First, define *ambition*. Debate the statement with your group and use evidence to support your opinions. Summarize the group's ideas for the class.

Listening and Speaking

Guest Speaker   Thoreau earned money and spread his ideas by giving lectures to local groups. Write and deliver a lecture that Thoreau might have given to high school students in which he explains his ideas about nature, materialism, and progress. Include examples from *Walden*.

 Save your work for your portfolio.

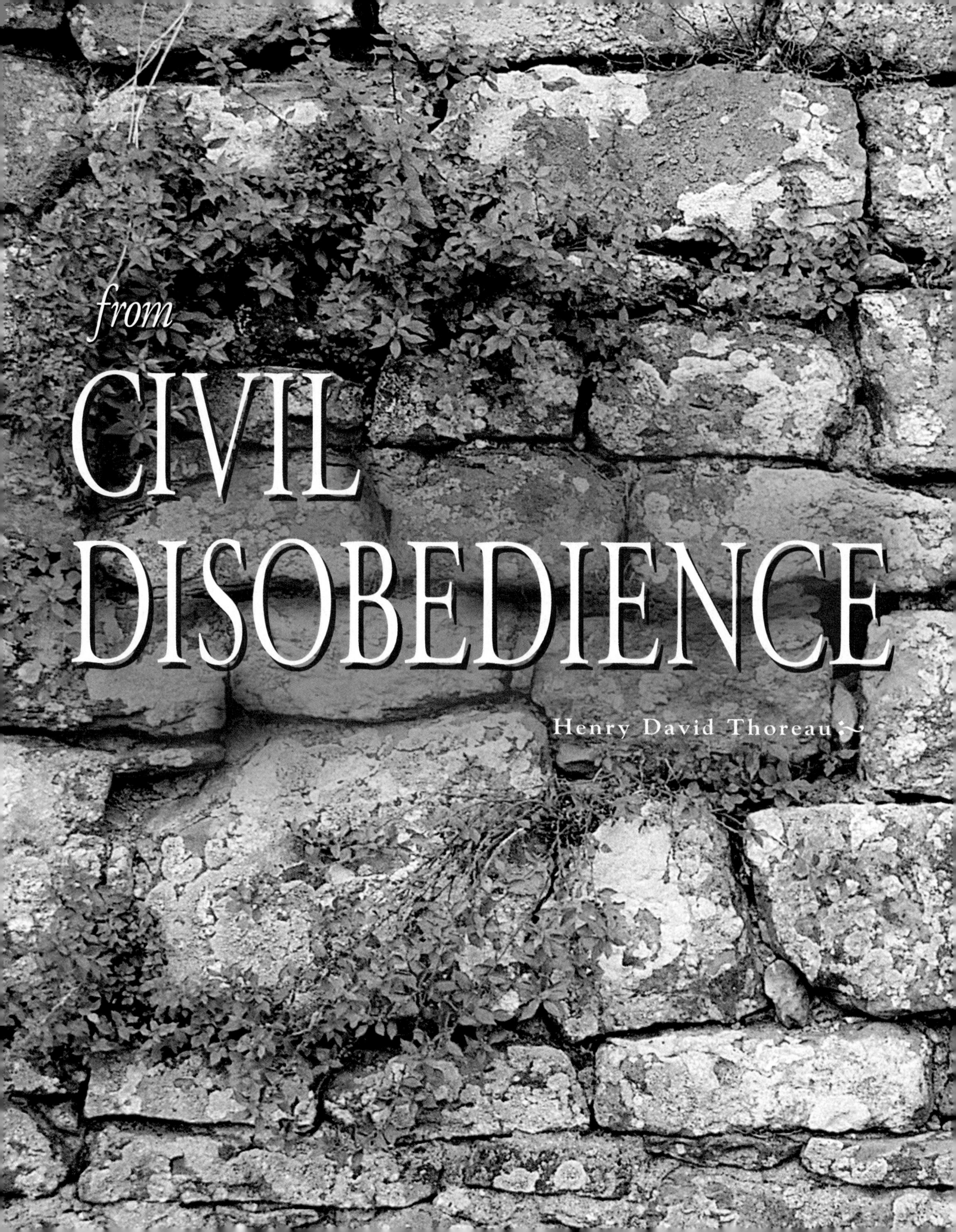

from

CIVIL DISOBEDIENCE

Henry David Thoreau

I heartily accept the motto, "That government is best which governs least"; and I should like to see it acted up to more rapidly and systematically. Carried out, it finally amounts to this, which also I believe—"That government is best which governs not at all"; and when men are prepared for it, that will be the kind of government which they will have. Government is at best but an expedient; but most governments are usually, and all governments are sometimes, inexpedient. The objections which have been brought against a standing army, and they are many and weighty, and deserve to prevail, may also at last be brought against a standing government. The standing army is only an arm of the standing government. The government itself, which is only the mode which the people have chosen to execute their will, is equally liable to be abused and perverted before the people can act through it. Witness the present Mexican war, the work of comparatively a few individuals using the standing government as their tool; for, in the outset, the people would not have consented to this measure.

This American government—what is it but a tradition, though a recent one, endeavoring to transmit itself unimpaired to posterity,[1] but each instant losing some of its integrity? It has not the vitality and force of a single living man; for a single man can bend it to his will. It is a sort of wooden gun to the people themselves. But it is not the less necessary for this; for the people must have some complicated machinery or other, and hear its din, to satisfy that idea of government which they have. Governments show thus how successfully men can be imposed on, even impose on themselves, for their own advantage. It is excellent, we must all allow. Yet this government never of itself furthered any enterprise, but by the alacrity with which it got out of its way. *It* does not keep the country free. *It* does not settle the West. *It* does not educate. The character inherent in the American people has done all that has been accomplished; and it would have done somewhat more, if the government had not sometimes got in its way. For government is an expedient by which men would fain[2] succeed in letting one another alone; and, as has been said, when it is most expedient, the governed are most let alone by it. Trade and commerce, if they were not made of india-rubber, would never manage to bounce over the obstacles which legislators are continually putting in their way; and, if one were to judge these men wholly by the effects of their actions and not partly by their intentions, they would deserve to be classed and punished with those mischievous persons who put obstructions on the railroads.

But, to speak practically and as a citizen, unlike those who call themselves no-government men, I ask for, not at once no government, but *at once* a better government. Let every man make known what kind of government would command his respect, and that will be one step toward obtaining it.

After all, the practical reason why, when the power is once in the hands of the people, a majority are permitted, and for a long period continue, to rule is not because they are most likely to be in the right, nor because this seems fairest to the minority, but because they are physically the strongest. But a government in which the majority rule in all cases cannot be based on justice, even as far as men understand it. Can there not be a government in which majorities do not virtually decide right and wrong, but conscience?—in which majorities

---

1. *Posterity* means "future generations."

2. *Fain* means "gladly" or "willingly."

Vocabulary

expedient (iks pē′ dē ənt) *n.* something employed to bring about a desired result; a means to an end

din (din) *n.* loud, continuous noise

alacrity (ə lak′ rə tē) *n.* speed; swiftness

inherent (in hēr′ ənt) *adj.* existing as a basic quality; belonging to by nature

decide only those questions to which the rule of expediency is applicable? Must the citizen ever for a moment, or in the least degree, resign his conscience to the legislator? Why has every man a conscience, then? I think that we should be men first, and subjects afterward. It is not desirable to cultivate a respect for the law, so much as for the right. The only obligation which I have a right to assume is to do at any time what I think right. It is truly enough said that a corporation has no conscience; but a corporation of conscientious men is a corporation *with* a conscience. Law never made men a whit[3] more just; and, by means of their respect for it, even the well-disposed are daily made the agents of injustice. . . .

Some years ago, the State met me in behalf of the Church, and commanded me to pay a certain sum toward the support of a clergyman whose preaching my father attended, but never I myself. "Pay," it said, "or be locked up in the jail." I declined to pay. But, unfortunately, another man saw fit to pay it. I did not see why the schoolmaster should be taxed to support the priest, and not the priest the schoolmaster; for I was not the State's schoolmaster, but I supported myself by voluntary subscription. I did not see why the lyceum[4] should not present its tax-bill, and have the State to back its demand, as well as the Church. However, at the request of the selectmen,[5] I condescended to make some such statement as this in writing:—"Know all men by these presents, that I, Henry Thoreau, do not wish to be regarded as a member of any incorporated society which I have not joined." This I gave to the town clerk; and he has it. The State, having thus learned that I did not wish to be regarded as a member of that church, has never made a like demand on me since; though it said that it must adhere to its original presumption

The only obligation which I have a right to assume is to do at any time what I think right.

that time. If I had known how to name them, I should then have signed off in detail from all the societies which I never signed on to; but I did not know where to find a complete list.

I have paid no poll-tax[6] for six years. I was put into a jail once on this account, for one night; and, as I stood considering the walls of solid stone, two or three feet thick, the door of wood and iron, a foot thick, and the iron grating which strained the light, I could not help being struck with the foolishness of that institution which treated me as if I were mere flesh and blood and bones, to be locked up. I wondered that it should have concluded at length that this was the best use it could put me to, and had never thought to avail itself of my services in some way. I saw that, if there was a wall of stone between me and my townsmen, there was a still more difficult one to climb or break through before they could get to be as free as I was. I did not for a moment feel confined, and the walls seemed a great waste of stone and mortar. I felt as if I alone of all my townsmen had paid my tax. They plainly did not know how to treat me, but behaved like persons who are underbred. In every threat and in every compliment there was a blunder; for they thought that my chief desire was to stand the other side of that stone wall. I could not but smile to see how industriously they locked the door on my meditations, which followed them out again without let[7] or hindrance, and *they* were really all that was dangerous. As they could not reach me, they had resolved to punish my body; just as boys, if they cannot come at some person against whom they have a spite, will abuse his dog. I saw that the State was half-witted, that it was timid as a lone woman with her silver spoons, and that it did not know its friends from its foes, and I lost all my remaining respect for it, and pitied it.

---

3. *Whit* means "a tiny amount" or "a bit."
4. A *lyceum* is an organization that sponsors educational programs, such as concerts and lectures.
5. *Selectmen* refers to a group of elected local officials.

6. A *poll-tax,* now illegal, was a tax on people (not property). Payment was often required in order to vote.
7. Here, *let* means "an obstruction" or "an obstacle."

from CIVIL DISOBEDIENCE

Thus the State never intentionally confronts a man's sense, intellectual or moral, but only his body, his senses. It is not armed with superior wit or honesty, but with superior physical strength. I was not born to be forced. I will breathe after my own fashion. Let us see who is the strongest. What force has a multitude? They only can force me who obey a higher law than I. They force me to become like themselves. I do not hear of *men* being *forced* to live this way or that by masses of men. What sort of life were that to live? When I meet a government which says to me, "Your money or your life," why should I be in haste to give it my money? It may be in a great strait, and not know what to do: I cannot help that. It must help itself; do as I do. It is not worth the while to snivel about it. I am not responsible for the successful working of the machinery of society. I am not the son of the engineer. I perceive that, when an acorn and a chestnut fall side by side, the one does not remain inert to make way for the other, but both obey their own laws, and spring and grow and flourish as best they can, till one, perchance, overshadows and destroys the other. If a plant cannot live according to its nature, it dies; and so a man.

The night in prison was novel and interesting enough. The prisoners in their shirt-sleeves were enjoying a chat and the evening air in the doorway, when I entered. But the jailer said, "Come, boys, it is time to lock up"; and so they dispersed, and I heard the sound of their steps returning into the hollow apartments. My roommate was introduced to me by the jailer as "a first-rate fellow and a clever man." When the door was locked, he showed me where to hang my hat, and how he managed matters there. The rooms were whitewashed once a month; and this one, at least, was the whitest, most simply furnished, and probably the neatest apartment in the town. He naturally wanted to know where I came from, and what brought me there; and, when I had told him, I asked him in my turn how he came there, presuming him to be an honest man, of course; and, as the world goes, I believe he was. "Why," said he, "they accuse me of burning a barn; but I never did it." As near as I could discover, he had probably gone to bed in a barn when drunk, and smoked his pipe there; and so a barn was burnt. He had the reputation of being a clever man, had been there some three months waiting for his trial to come on, and would have to wait as much longer; but he was quite domesticated and contented, since he got his board for nothing, and thought that he was well treated.

He occupied one window, and I the other; and I saw that if one stayed there long, his principal business would be to look out the window. I had soon read all the tracts[8] that were left there, and examined where former prisoners had broken out, and where a grate had been sawed off, and heard the history of the various occupants of that room; for I found that even here there was a history and a gossip which never circulated beyond the walls of the jail. Probably this is the only house in the town where verses are composed, which are afterward printed in a circular form, but not published. I was shown quite a long list of verses which were composed by some young men who had been detected in an attempt to escape, who avenged themselves by singing them.

I pumped my fellow-prisoner as dry as I could, for fear I should never see him again; but at length he showed me which was my bed, and left me to blow out the lamp.

It was like traveling into a far country, such as I had never expected to behold, to lie there for one night. It seemed to me that I never had heard the town clock strike before, nor the evening sounds of the village; for we slept with the windows open, which were inside the grating. It was to see my native village in the light of the Middle Ages, and our Concord was turned into a Rhine[9] stream, and visions of knights and

---

8. *Tracts* are leaflets or pamphlets, especially those on religious or political topics.
9. *Concord* refers to the Concord River. The *Rhine* River flows through Germany and the Netherlands.

castles passed before me. They were the voices of old burghers[10] that I heard in the streets. I was an involuntary spectator and auditor[11] of whatever was done and said in the kitchen of the adjacent village inn—a wholly new and rare experience to me. It was a closer view of my native town. I was fairly inside of it. I never had seen its institutions before. This is one of its peculiar institutions; for it is a shire town.[12] I began to comprehend what its inhabitants were about.

In the morning, our breakfasts were put through the hole in the door, in small oblong-square tin pans, made to fit, and holding a pint of chocolate, with brown bread, and an iron spoon. When they called for the vessels again, I was green enough to return what bread I had left; but my comrade seized it, and said that I should lay that up for lunch or dinner. Soon after he was let out to work at haying in a neighboring field, whither he went every day, and would not be back till noon; so he bade me good-day, saying that he doubted if he should see me again.

When I came out of prison—for some one interfered, and paid that tax—I did not perceive that great changes had taken place on the common, such as he observed who went in a youth and emerged a tottering and gray-headed man; and yet a change had to my eyes come over the scene—the town, and State, and country—greater than any that mere time could effect. I saw yet more distinctly the State in which I lived. . . .

> *Is a democracy, such as we know it, the last improvement possible in government?*

The authority of government, even such as I am willing to submit to—for I will cheerfully obey those who know and can do better than I, and in many things even those who neither know nor can do so well—is still an impure one: to be strictly just, it must have the sanction and consent of the governed. It can have no pure right over my person and property but what I concede to it. The progress from an absolute to a limited monarchy, from a limited monarchy to a democracy, is a progress toward a true respect for the individual. Even the Chinese philosopher[13] was wise enough to regard the individual as the basis of the empire. Is a democracy, such as we know it, the last improvement possible in government? Is it not possible to take a step further towards recognizing and organizing the rights of man? There will never be a really free and enlightened State until the State comes to recognize the individual as a higher and independent power, from which all its own power and authority are derived, and treats him accordingly. I please myself with imagining a State at least which can afford to be just to all men, and to treat the individual with respect as a neighbor; which even would not think it inconsistent with its own repose if a few were to live aloof from it, not meddling with it, nor embraced by it, who fulfilled all the duties of neighbors and fellow-men. A State which bore this kind of fruit, and suffered it to drop off as fast as it ripened, would prepare the way for a still more perfect and glorious State, which also I have imagined, but not yet anywhere seen.

---

10. *Burghers* is a term for inhabitants of a city.
11. Here, *auditor* means "someone who hears" or "a listener."
12. A *shire town,* or county town, is similar to a county seat.

13. The *Chinese philosopher* referred to is Confucius (c. 551–479 B.C.).

Vocabulary
sanction (sangk′ shən) *n.* approval or support

Responding to Literature

Personal Response

Did Thoreau persuade you to share his views of government? Why or why not?

—— ANALYZING LITERATURE ——

RECALL

1. What kind of government does Thoreau say is best?
2. What is the one thing Thoreau feels obligated to follow?
3. What action did Thoreau take after refusing to pay the tax to support a clergyman? What was the outcome of this action?
4. Why was he put in jail? How did he feel about being there? Explain.
5. In Thoreau's opinion, what is needed for a government to be just?

INTERPRET

6. According to Thoreau, what problems might arise from government?
7. What does Thoreau mean when he says "we should be men first, and subjects afterward"? Cite specific details from the essay to support your response.
8. How do Thoreau's actions reflect his thoughts about himself as part of society?
9. What does Thoreau conclude about freedom while he is in jail?
10. What does Thoreau suggest should be the relationship between government and the individual?

EVALUATE AND CONNECT

11. Based on the ideas in "Civil Disobedience," how might Thoreau suggest that people today become involved in their government?
12. Thoreau mentions the Mexican-American War as an example of a government acting against the people's will. What other examples of unpopular government actions can you think of? Explain.
13. An **anecdote** is a short account of an interesting event in a person's life. What does Thoreau's anecdote about his night in jail contribute to his essay?
14. In general, what is Thoreau trying to persuade readers to believe? Why might this essay have been persuasive in a country that was relatively newly independent?
15. Do you think this essay is optimistic or pessimistic? In what ways? Explain.

Literary ELEMENTS

Argument

In "Civil Disobedience," Thoreau presents an **argument,** a piece of writing in which reason is used to influence someone else's ideas or actions. An argument is a form of persuasive writing. Some persuasive writing depends mainly on emotion for its power. An argument uses logic, reasons, and evidence. For instance, Thoreau writes that government does not further any enterprise. He supports this by giving examples: "*It* does not keep the country free. *It* does not settle the West. *It* does not educate."

1. List the reasons that Thoreau presents for not paying a tax to support a clergyman.
2. Identify another of Thoreau's topics and give examples of the supporting logic, reasons, and evidence he uses.

● See **Literary Terms Handbook,** p. R2.

LITERATURE AND WRITING

Writing About Literature

A Different Drummer?   Look again at the first quote on page 250. Do you think Thoreau followed his own advice? In a few paragraphs explain whether Thoreau's actions or writings followed the idea he expressed in the quote. Use evidence from these selections to support your ideas.

Creative Writing

Report on the Prisoner   When Thoreau refused to pay the poll tax, Samuel Staples, the local tax collector, constable, and jailer, had to arrest him. Write the arrest report that Staples might have submitted to his boss about taking Thoreau into custody and putting him in jail.

EXTENDING YOUR RESPONSE

Literature Groups

Debate   Hold a debate on one of the issues that Thoreau writes about. In your group, form two teams—one to defend Thoreau's point of view, and the other to defend an opposing view. Each team should work together to provide evidence to support their arguments. Summarize the key points and arguments presented by each team, and share your summary with the class.

Performing

A One-Act Play   Use the jail scene in "Civil Disobedience" as the basis for a one-act play or a short skit. Experiment with using minimal props to create the physical place and the atmosphere. Use some of the quotes Thoreau provides as starting points for dialogue. You may also want to have a narrator explain the historical setting or provide other information. Rehearse your play and present it to the class.

Listening and Speaking

"I Have a Dream"   "Civil Disobedience" influenced many world leaders, including Dr. Martin Luther King Jr. Locate a copy of Dr. King's speech "I Have a Dream." Select a passage that you think relates to Thoreau's essay. Deliver that passage to the class and explain how Dr. King's speech shows the influence of "Civil Disobedience."

Reading Further

If you'd like to read more by and about Henry David Thoreau, look for these books:

Memoirs: *Journal 1837–1844: The Writings of Henry D. Thoreau,* a personal glimpse into the writer's life.

Walking, a celebration of the joys of "sauntering."

Biography: *The Cambridge Companion to Henry David Thoreau,* edited by Joel Myerson, essays about Thoreau.

📖 **Save your work for your portfolio.**

Skill Minilesson

VOCABULARY • Analogies

Analogies are comparisons based on relationships between ideas. Some analogies are based on a relationship of *definition.*

   teacher : instructs :: carpenter : builds

A *teacher* by definition *instructs;* a *carpenter builds.*

   To finish an analogy, decide on the relationship of the first pair of words. Apply that relationship to the second set of words.

PRACTICE   Choose the word that best completes each analogy.

1. hindrance : obstructs :: sanction :
   a. assists   b. shelters   c. approves

2. sentinels : guard :: chaperones :
   a. flourish   b. watch   c. founder

● For more about analogies, see **Communications Skills Handbook,** pp. R83–R85.

Before You Read

Meet Nathaniel Hawthorne

"I don't want to be a doctor, and live by men's diseases; nor a minister to live by their sins; nor a lawyer to live by their quarrels. So I don't see there's anything left for me but to be an author."

—*Hawthorne*

Thus, some may say, Nathaniel Hawthorne became one of the United States' great writers by default.

Hawthorne was born in the port town of Salem, Massachusetts. When Hawthorne was only four, his father, a sea captain, died of yellow fever in South America. Raised by his eccentric, reclusive mother, young Hawthorne became an avid reader of poetry and exotic adventure stories.

At age seventeen Hawthorne began his four years at Bowdoin College in Maine. His friends there included a future president and a future poet: Franklin Pierce and Henry Wadsworth Longfellow.

After graduating from Bowdoin, Hawthorne sought seclusion in Salem, where he spent twelve years studying Puritan history and developing his writing skills. Out of those twelve years came two books, a novel called *Fanshawe* and a collection of short stories called *Twice-Told Tales*. *Fanshawe* was never popular—Hawthorne himself destroyed all the copies he could find—but reviewers praised *Twice-Told Tales*, and the book enjoyed a modest success with the public.

In his writing, Hawthorne explored issues of moral and social responsibility in Puritan New England. He hated intolerance, hypocrisy, and any other sentiment that separated one from the rest of humanity. Hawthorne explored these issues in tales he called "allegories of the heart"—stories that teach a moral principle.

At the age of thirty-eight, Hawthorne married Sophia Peabody and moved to the Old Manse, the house in Concord, Massachusetts, where writer Ralph Waldo Emerson had lived. However, unable to support his family as a writer, Hawthorne returned to Salem. There he served as Surveyor of the Port but lost the job when the political administration changed. Hawthorne then began writing *The Scarlet Letter*. This novel, published when Hawthorne was forty-six, was a sensation. He followed up the success with another novel, *The House of the Seven Gables*.

In 1853, when his friend Franklin Pierce became president of the United States, Hawthorne was awarded the position of U.S. consul to the city of Liverpool, England. He held that position for four years. Then he toured Italy and returned to England to write his last complete novel, *The Marble Faun*. By 1860, he returned to the United States—in ill health, struggling to continue writing, and despondent. Four years later, while traveling with Franklin Pierce, Hawthorne died in his sleep.

"Mr. Hawthorne's distinctive trait is invention, creation, imagination."

—*Edgar Allan Poe*

Nathaniel Hawthorne was born in 1804 and died in 1864.

FOCUS ACTIVITY

How do you behave when you feel guilty about something?

CREATE A WEB Make a word web like the one below. Write the word *guilt* in the center oval. Take five minutes to complete the web with ways people might behave when they feel guilty.

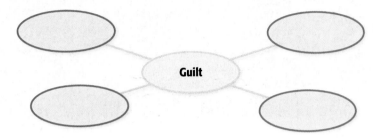

SETTING A PURPOSE Read to notice how guilt affects the people in the story.

BACKGROUND

The Time and Place

Seventeenth-century Puritan New England, the setting of "The Minister's Black Veil," was steeped as much in superstition as in religion. Hawthorne's story balances on the line that separated the two.

The Puritans

Puritanism was a movement that began in the Church of England in the 1500s. Puritans wanted to "purify" the church of practices they said had no basis in the Bible. In the 1600s, Puritans came to New England and founded a community based on biblical laws. They believed that God was all-powerful and all-knowing. They also held that people were sinful by nature and deserved eternal punishment but that God had "elected" some to be saved. No one could be sure of salvation, but Puritans strove to lead

a moral life as a sign that they had been saved. This involved keeping a constant watch over oneself and others to fight the "natural" tendency to sin.

Parables

The subtitle of "The Minister's Black Veil" is "A Parable." A parable is a story that illustrates a moral lesson. In this way, parables resemble fables. Fables, however, usually have animal characters, whereas parables have human characters. Many famous parables appear in the Bible. The parable of the prodigal son, for example, teaches that one who turns away from evil should be forgiven. Hawthorne included the subtitle "A Parable" to alert his readers that he intended "The Minister's Black Veil" to convey a moral lesson.

VOCABULARY PREVIEW

perturbation (pur´ tər bā´ shən) *n.* agitation; anxiety; uneasiness; p. 268

venerable (ven´ ər ə bəl) *adj.* deserving respect because of age, character, or position; p. 268

iniquity (in ik´ wə tē) *n.* sin; p. 268

sagacious (sə gā´ shəs) *adj.* having or showing wisdom and keen perception; p. 269

irreproachable (ir´ i prō´ chə bəl) *adj.* free from blame; faultless; p. 274

zealous (zel´ əs) *adj.* filled with enthusiastic devotion; passionate; p. 274

torpor (tôr´ pər) *n.* a state of being unable to move or feel; p. 274

The Minister's Black Veil

A Parable

Nathaniel Hawthorne

THE SEXTON STOOD IN THE PORCH of Milford meeting-house, pulling busily at the bell-rope. The old people of the village came stooping along the street. Children, with bright faces, tripped merrily beside their parents, or mimicked a graver gait, in the conscious dignity of their Sunday clothes. Spruce[1] bachelors looked sidelong at the pretty maidens, and fancied that the Sabbath sunshine made them prettier than on week days. When the throng had mostly streamed into the porch, the sexton[2] began to toll the bell, keeping his eye on the Reverend Mr. Hooper's door. The first glimpse of the clergyman's figure was the signal for the bell to cease its summons.

"But what has good Parson Hooper got upon his face?" cried the sexton in astonishment.

All within hearing immediately turned about, and beheld the semblance of Mr. Hooper, pacing slowly his meditative way towards the meeting-house. With one accord[3] they started,[4] expressing more wonder than if some strange minister were coming to dust the cushions of Mr. Hooper's pulpit.[5]

"Are you sure it is our parson?" inquired Goodman[6] Gray of the sexton.

"Of a certainty it is good Mr. Hooper," replied the sexton. "He was to have exchanged pulpits with Parson Shute, of Westbury; but Parson Shute sent to excuse himself yesterday, being to preach a funeral sermon."

The cause of so much amazement may appear sufficiently slight. Mr. Hooper, a gentlemanly person, of about thirty, though still a bachelor, was dressed with due clerical neatness, as if a careful wife had starched his band, and brushed the weekly dust from his Sunday's garb. There was but one thing remarkable in his appearance. Swathed[7] about his forehead, and hanging down over his face, so low as to be

---

1. *Spruce* means "neat and trim in appearance" or "dapper."
2. A *sexton* is a church employee who cares for church property and who may also ring the bells and dig graves.
3. *With one accord* means "with complete agreement" or "with unity."
4. Here, *started* means "made a sudden involuntary movement, as from fear or surprise."
5. A *pulpit* is a raised structure from which a minister delivers a sermon or conducts a worship service.
6. *Goodman* is a title of polite address similar to "Mister."
7. *Swathed* means "wrapped."

shaken by his breath, Mr. Hooper had on a black veil. On a nearer view it seemed to consist of two folds of crepe,[8] which entirely concealed his features, except the mouth and chin, but probably did not intercept his sight, further than to give a darkened aspect to all living and inanimate things. With this gloomy shade before him, good Mr. Hooper walked onward, at a slow and quiet pace, stooping somewhat, and looking on the ground, as is customary with abstracted[9] men, yet nodding kindly to those of his parishioners who still waited on the meeting-house steps. But so wonder-struck were they that his greeting hardly met with a return.

"I can't really feel as if good Mr. Hooper's face was behind that piece of crepe," said the sexton.

---

8. *Crepe* is a light, soft fabric with a crinkled surface.
9. Here, *abstracted* means "lost in thought" or "preoccupied."

"I don't like it," muttered an old woman, as she hobbled into the meeting-house. "He has changed himself into something awful, only by hiding his face."

"Our parson has gone mad!" cried Goodman Gray, following him across the threshold.

A rumor of some unaccountable phenomenon had preceded Mr. Hooper into the meeting-house, and set all the congregation astir. Few could refrain from twisting their heads towards the door; many stood upright, and turned directly about; while several little boys clambered upon the seats, and came down again with a terrible racket. There was a general bustle, a rustling of the women's gowns and shuffling of the men's feet, greatly at variance with that hushed repose which should attend the entrance of the minister. But Mr. Hooper appeared not to notice the

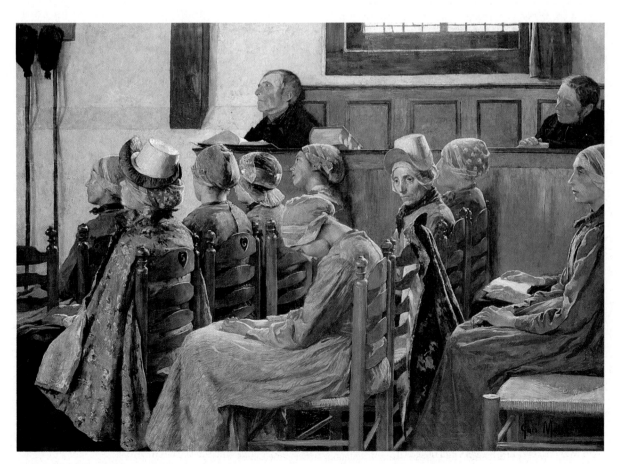

The Sermon, 1886. Julius Gari Melchers. Oil on canvas, 62⅝ x 86½ in. National Museum of American Art, Smithsonian Institution, Washington, D.C.

Viewing the painting: In what ways do the attitudes of the people in the painting reflect those of Mr. Hooper's congregation?

Viewing the sketch: How might the pulpit's placement in this sketch reflect Mr. Hooper's position in Milford?

perturbation of his people. He entered with an almost noiseless step, bent his head mildly to the pews on each side, and bowed as he passed his oldest parishioner, a white-haired great-grandsire, who occupied an arm-chair in the center of the aisle. It was strange to observe how slowly this venerable man became conscious of something singular in the appearance of his pastor. He seemed not fully to partake of the prevailing wonder, till Mr. Hooper had ascended the stairs, and showed himself in the pulpit, face to face with his congregation, except for the black veil. That mysterious emblem was never once withdrawn. It shook with his measured breath, as he gave out the psalm; it threw its obscurity between him and the holy page, as he read the Scriptures; and while he prayed, the veil lay heavily on his uplifted countenance.[10] Did he

seek to hide it from the dread Being whom he was addressing?

Such was the effect of this simple piece of crepe, that more than one woman of delicate nerves was forced to leave the meeting-house. Yet perhaps the pale-faced congregation was almost as fearful a sight to the minister, as his black veil to them.

Mr. Hooper had the reputation of a good preacher, but not an energetic one: he strove to win his people heavenward by mild, persuasive influences, rather than to drive them thither by the thunders of the Word. The sermon which he now delivered was marked by the same characteristics of style and manner as the general series of his pulpit oratory. But there was something, either in the sentiment of the discourse itself, or in the imagination of the auditors,[11] which made it greatly the most powerful effort that they had ever heard from their pastor's lips. It was tinged, rather more darkly than usual, with the gentle gloom of Mr. Hooper's temperament. The subject had reference to secret sin, and those sad mysteries which we hide from our nearest and dearest, and would fain[12] conceal from our own consciousness, even forgetting that the Omniscient[13] can detect them. A subtle power was breathed into his words. Each member of the congregation, the most innocent girl, and the man of hardened breast, felt as if the preacher had crept upon them, behind his awful veil, and discovered their hoarded iniquity of deed or thought. Many spread their clasped hands on their bosoms. There was nothing terrible in what Mr. Hooper said, at least, no violence; and yet, with every tremor of his melancholy voice, the hearers quaked. An

---

10. *Countenance* means "face."

11. *Auditors* are "those who hear" or "listeners."
12. *Fain* means "gladly" or "willingly."
13. *The Omniscient* is "the all knowing," or God.

Vocabulary

perturbation (pur′ tər bā′ shən) *n.* agitation; anxiety; uneasiness
venerable (ven′ ər ə bəl) *adj.* deserving respect because of age, character, or position
iniquity (in ik′ wə tē) *n.* sin

unsought pathos[14] came hand in hand with awe. So sensible were the audience of some unwonted[15] attribute in their minister, that they longed for a breath of wind to blow aside the veil, almost believing that a stranger's visage[16] would be discovered, though the form, gesture, and voice were those of Mr. Hooper.

At the close of the services, the people hurried out with indecorous confusion, eager to communicate their pent-up amazement, and conscious of lighter spirits the moment they lost sight of the black veil. Some gathered in little circles, huddled closely together, with their mouths all whispering in the center; some went homeward alone, wrapped in silent meditation; some talked loudly, and profaned the Sabbath day with ostentatious laughter. A few shook their sagacious heads, intimating that they could penetrate the mystery; while one or two affirmed that there was no mystery at all, but only that Mr. Hooper's eyes were so weakened by the midnight lamp, as to require a shade. After a brief interval, forth came good Mr. Hooper also, in the rear of his flock. Turning his veiled face from one group to another, he paid due reverence to the hoary heads,[17] saluted the middle aged with kind dignity as their friend and spiritual guide, greeted the young with mingled authority and love, and laid his hands on the little children's heads to bless them. Such was always his custom on the Sabbath day. Strange and bewildered looks repaid him for his courtesy. None, as on former occasions, aspired to the honor of walking by their pastor's side. Old Squire Saunders, doubtless by an accidental lapse of memory, neglected to invite Mr. Hooper to his table, where the good clergyman had been wont[18] to

bless the food, almost every Sunday since his settlement. He returned, therefore, to the parsonage, and, at the moment of closing the door, was observed to look back upon the people, all of whom had their eyes fixed upon the minister. A sad smile gleamed faintly from beneath the black veil, and flickered about his mouth, glimmering as he disappeared.

"How strange," said a lady, "that a simple black veil, such as any woman might wear on her bonnet should become such a terrible thing on Mr. Hooper's face!"

"Something must surely be amiss with Mr. Hooper's intellects," observed her husband, the physician of the village. "But the strangest part of the affair is the effect of this vagary,[19] even on a sober-minded man like myself. The black veil, though it covers only our pastor's face, throws its influence over his whole person, and makes him ghostlike from head to foot. Do you not feel it so?"

"Truly do I," replied the lady; "and I would not be alone with him for the world. I wonder he is not afraid to be alone with himself!"

"Men sometimes are so," said her husband.

The afternoon service was attended with similar circumstances. At its conclusion, the bell tolled for the funeral of a young lady. The relatives and friends were assembled in the house, and the more distant acquaintances stood about the door, speaking of the good qualities of the deceased, when their talk was interrupted by the appearance of Mr. Hooper, still covered with his black veil. It was now an appropriate emblem. The clergyman stepped into the room where the corpse was laid, and bent over the coffin, to take a last farewell of his deceased parishioner. As he stooped, the veil hung straight down from his forehead, so that, if her eyelids had not been closed forever,

14. *Pathos* is a feeling of pity, compassion, or sorrow.
15. *Unwonted* means "not customary" or "unusual."
16. *Visage* means "face."
17. *Hoary heads* are white-haired heads.
18. *Wont* means "accustomed."

19. A *vagary* is an odd or erratic action or idea.

Vocabulary
sagacious (sə gā′ shəs) *adj.* having or showing wisdom and keen perception

The Minister's Black Veil

the dead maiden might have seen his face. Could Mr. Hooper be fearful of her glance, that he so hastily caught back the black veil? A person who watched the interview between the dead and living, scrupled[20] not to affirm, that, at the instant when the clergyman's features were disclosed, the corpse had slightly shuddered, rustling the shroud[21] and muslin cap, though the countenance retained the composure of death. A superstitious old woman was the only witness of this prodigy.[22] From the coffin Mr. Hooper passed into the chamber of the mourners, and thence to the head of the staircase, to make the funeral prayer. It was a tender and heart-dissolving prayer, full of sorrow, yet so imbued with celestial hopes, that the music of a heavenly harp, swept by the fingers of the dead, seemed faintly to be heard among the saddest accents of the minister. The people trembled, though they but darkly understood him when he prayed that they, and himself, and all of mortal race, might be ready, as he trusted this young maiden had been, for the dreadful hour that should snatch the veil from their faces. The bearers went heavily forth, and the mourners followed, saddening all the street, with the dead before them, and Mr. Hooper in his black veil behind.

"Why do you look back?" said one in the procession to his partner.

"I had a fancy," replied she, "that the minister and the maiden's spirit were walking hand in hand."

"And so had I, at the same moment," said the other.

That night, the handsomest couple in Milford village were to be joined in wedlock. Though reckoned a melancholy man, Mr. Hooper had a placid cheerfulness for such occasions, which often excited a sympathetic smile where livelier merriment would have been thrown away. There was no quality of his disposition which made him more beloved than this. The company at the wedding awaited his arrival with impatience, trusting that the strange awe, which had gathered over him throughout the day, would now be dispelled. But such was not the result. When Mr. Hooper came, the first thing that their eyes rested on was the same horrible black veil, which had added deeper gloom to the funeral, and could portend[23] nothing but evil to the wedding. Such was its immediate effect on the guests that a cloud seemed to have rolled duskily from beneath the black crepe, and dimmed the light of the candles. The bridal pair stood up before the minister. But the bride's cold fingers quivered in the tremulous hand[24] of the bridegroom, and her deathlike paleness caused a whisper that the maiden who had been buried a few hours before was come from her grave to be married. If ever another wedding were so dismal, it was that famous one where they tolled the wedding knell.[25] After performing the ceremony, Mr. Hooper raised a glass of wine to his lips, wishing happiness to the new-married couple in a strain of mild pleasantry that ought to have brightened the features of the guests, like a cheerful gleam from the hearth. At that instant, catching a glimpse of his figure in the looking-glass, the black veil involved his own spirit in the horror with which it overwhelmed all others. His frame shuddered, his lips grew white, he spilt the untasted wine upon the carpet, and rushed forth into the darkness. For the Earth, too, had on her Black Veil.

The next day, the whole village of Milford talked of little else than Parson Hooper's black veil. That, and the mystery concealed behind it, supplied a topic for discussion between acquaintances meeting in the street, and good

---

20. *Scrupled* means "hesitated."
21. A *shroud* is a cloth used to wrap a dead body for burial.
22. Here, *prodigy* means "an extraordinary event that causes amazement."

23. *Portend* means "to be a warning or an indication of."
24. A *tremulous hand* is one that is trembling or shaking.
25. Hawthorne is referring to his own short story "The Wedding Knell." A *knell* is the solemn sound of a bell ringing, as at a funeral.

women gossiping at their open windows. It was the first item of news that the tavern-keeper told to his guests. The children babbled of it on their way to school. One imitative little imp covered his face with an old black handkerchief, thereby so affrighting his playmates that the panic seized himself, and he well-nigh lost his wits by his own waggery.[26]

It was remarkable that of all the busybodies and impertinent people in the parish, not one ventured to put the plain question to Mr. Hooper, wherefore he did this thing. Hitherto, whenever there appeared the slightest call for such interference, he had never lacked advisers, nor shown himself averse to be guided by their judgment. If he erred at all, it was by so painful a degree of self-distrust, that even the mildest censure would lead him to consider an indifferent action as a crime. Yet, though so well acquainted with this amiable weakness, no individual among his parishioners chose to make the black veil a subject of friendly remonstrance. There was a feeling of dread, neither plainly confessed nor carefully concealed, which caused each to shift the responsibility upon another, till at length it was found expedient to send a deputation[27] of the church, in order to deal with Mr. Hooper about the mystery, before it should grow into a scandal. Never did an embassy so ill discharge its duties. The minister received them with friendly courtesy, but became silent, after they were seated, leaving to his visitors the whole burden of introducing their important business. The topic, it might be supposed, was obvious enough. There was the black veil swathed round Mr. Hooper's forehead, and concealing every feature above his placid mouth, on which, at times, they could perceive the glimmering of a melancholy smile. But that piece of crepe, to their imagination, seemed to hang down before his heart, the symbol of a fearful secret between him and

them. Were the veil but cast aside, they might speak freely of it, but not till then. Thus they sat a considerable time, speechless, confused, and shrinking uneasily from Mr. Hooper's eye, which they felt to be fixed upon them with an invisible glance. Finally, the deputies returned abashed[28] to their constituents, pronouncing the matter too weighty to be handled, except by a council of the churches, if, indeed, it might not require a general synod.[29]

But there was one person in the village unappalled by the awe with which the black veil had impressed all beside herself. When the deputies returned without an explanation, or even venturing to demand one, she, with the calm energy of her character, determined to chase away the strange cloud that appeared to be settling round Mr. Hooper, every moment more darkly than before. As his plighted wife,[30] it should be her privilege to know what the black veil concealed. At the minister's first visit, therefore, she entered upon the subject with a direct simplicity, which made the task easier both for him and her. After he had seated himself, she fixed her eyes steadfastly upon the veil, but could discern nothing of the dreadful gloom that had so overawed the multitude: it was but a double fold of crepe, hanging down from his forehead to his mouth, and slightly stirring with his breath.

"No," said she aloud, and smiling, "there is nothing terrible in this piece of crepe, except that it hides a face which I am always glad to look upon. Come, good sir, let the sun shine from behind the cloud. First lay aside your black veil: then tell me why you put it on."

Mr. Hooper's smile glimmered faintly.

"There is an hour to come," said he, "when all of us shall cast aside our veils. Take it not amiss, beloved friend, if I wear this piece of crepe till then."

---

26. *Waggery* is mischievous or joking behavior.
27. A *deputation* is a delegation.
28. *Abashed* means "ashamed" or "embarrassed."
29. A *synod* is a council of church officials or a governing body of all the churches.
30. *Plighted wife* means "intended wife" or "fiancée."

The Minister's Black Veil

"Your words are a mystery, too," returned the young lady. "Take away the veil from them, at least."

"Elizabeth, I will," said he, "so far as my vow may suffer me. Know, then, this veil is a type and a symbol, and I am bound to wear it ever, both in light and darkness, in solitude and before the gaze of multitudes, and as with strangers, so with my familiar friends. No mortal eye will see it withdrawn. This dismal shade must separate me from the world: even you, Elizabeth, can never come behind it!"

"What grievous affliction hath befallen you," she earnestly inquired, "that you should thus darken your eyes forever?"

"If it be a sign of mourning," replied Mr. Hooper, "I, perhaps, like most other mortals, have sorrows dark enough to be typified by a black veil."

"But what if the world will not believe that it is the type of an innocent sorrow?" urged Elizabeth. "Beloved and respected as you are, there may be whispers that you hide your face under the consciousness of secret sin. For the sake of your holy office, do away this scandal!"

The color rose into her cheeks as she intimated the nature of the rumors that were already abroad in the village. But Mr. Hooper's mildness did not forsake him. He even smiled again—that same sad smile, which always appeared like a faint glimmering of light, proceeding from the obscurity beneath the veil.

"If I hide my face for sorrow, there is cause enough," he merely replied; "and if I cover it for secret sin, what mortal might not do the same?"

And with this gentle, but unconquerable obstinacy did he resist all her entreaties.[31] At length Elizabeth sat silent. For a few moments she appeared lost in thought, considering, probably, what new methods might be tried to withdraw her lover from so dark a fantasy, which, if it had no other meaning, was perhaps a symptom of mental disease. Though of a firmer character than his own, the tears rolled down her cheeks. But, in an instant, as it were, a new feeling took the place of sorrow: her eyes were fixed insensibly on the black veil, when, like a sudden twilight in the air, its terrors fell around her. She arose, and stood trembling before him.

"And do you feel it then, at last?" said he mournfully.

She made no reply, but covered her eyes with her hand, and turned to leave the room. He rushed forward and caught her arm.

"Have patience with me, Elizabeth!" cried he, passionately. "Do not desert me, though this veil must be between us here on earth. Be mine, and hereafter there shall be no veil over my face, no darkness between our souls! It is but a mortal veil—it is not for eternity! O! you know not how lonely I am, and how frightened, to be alone behind my black veil. Do not leave me in this miserable obscurity forever!"

"Lift the veil but once, and look me in the face," said she.

"Never! It cannot be!" replied Mr. Hooper.

"Then farewell!" said Elizabeth.

She withdrew her arm from his grasp, and slowly departed, pausing at the door, to give one long shuddering gaze, that seemed almost to penetrate the mystery of the black veil. But, even amid his grief, Mr. Hooper smiled to think that only a material emblem had separated him from happiness, though the horrors, which it shadowed forth, must be drawn darkly between the fondest of lovers.

From that time no attempts were made to remove Mr. Hooper's black veil, or, by a direct appeal, to discover the secret which it was supposed to hide. By persons who claimed a superiority to popular prejudice, it was reckoned merely an eccentric whim, such as often mingles with the sober actions of men otherwise rational, and tinges them all with its own semblance of insanity. But with the multitude, good Mr. Hooper was irreparably a bugbear.[32] He

---

31. *Entreaties* are pleas.

32. A *bugbear* is a real or imaginary object of fear.

could not walk the street with any peace of mind, so conscious was he that the gentle and timid would turn aside to avoid him, and that others would make it a point of hardihood[33] to throw themselves in his way. The impertinence of the latter class compelled him to give up his customary walk at sunset to the burial ground; for when he leaned pensively over the gate, there would always be faces behind the gravestones, peeping at his black veil. A fable went the rounds that the stare of the dead people drove him thence. It grieved him, to the very depth of his kind heart, to observe how the children fled from his approach, breaking up their merriest sports, while his melancholy figure was yet afar off. Their instinctive dread caused him to feel more strongly than aught else, that a preternatural[34] horror was interwoven with the threads of the black crepe. In truth, his own antipathy[35] to the veil was known to be so great, that he never willingly passed before a mirror, nor stooped to drink at a still fountain, lest, in its peaceful bosom, he should be affrighted by himself. This was what gave plausibility to the whispers, that Mr. Hooper's conscience tortured him for some great crime too horrible to be entirely concealed, or otherwise than so obscurely intimated. Thus, from beneath the black veil, there rolled a cloud into the sunshine, an ambiguity of sin or sorrow, which enveloped the poor minister, so that love or sympathy could never reach him. It was said that ghost and fiend consorted with him there. With self-shudderings and outward terrors, he walked continually in its shadow, groping darkly within his own soul, or gazing through a medium that saddened the whole world. Even the lawless wind, it was believed, respected his dreadful secret, and never blew aside the veil. But still good Mr. Hooper sadly smiled at the pale visages of the worldly throng as he passed by.

Viewing the sketch: How do you picture the meeting-house in Milford? How is the building in the sketch similar or different?

Among all its bad influences, the black veil had the one desirable effect, of making its wearer a very efficient clergyman. By the aid of his mysterious emblem—for there was no other apparent cause—he became a man of awful power over souls that were in agony for sin. His converts always regarded him with a dread peculiar to themselves, affirming, though but figuratively, that, before he brought them to celestial light, they had been with him behind the black veil. Its gloom, indeed, enabled him to sympathize with all dark affections. Dying sinners cried aloud for Mr. Hooper, and would not yield their breath till he appeared; though ever, as he stooped to whisper consolation, they shuddered at the veiled face so near their own. Such were the terrors of the black veil, even when Death had bared his visage! Strangers came long distances to attend service at his church, with the mere idle purpose of gazing at his figure, because it was forbidden them to behold his face. But many were made to quake ere they departed! Once, during Governor Belcher's[36]

---

33. *Hardihood* is offensive boldness or daring.
34. *Preternatural* means "supernatural."
35. *Antipathy* is a feeling of intense dislike.

36. Jonathan *Belcher* was governor of Massachusetts and New Hampshire from 1730 to 1741.

The Minister's Black Veil

administration, Mr. Hooper was appointed to preach the election sermon.[37] Covered with his black veil, he stood before the chief magistrate, the council, and the representatives, and wrought[38] so deep an impression, that the legislative measures of that year were characterized by all the gloom and piety of our earliest ancestral sway.[39]

In this manner Mr. Hooper spent a long life, irreproachable in outward act, yet shrouded in dismal suspicions; kind and loving, though unloved, and dimly feared; a man apart from men, shunned in their health and joy, but ever summoned to their aid in mortal anguish. As years wore on, shedding their snows above his sable veil,[40] he acquired a name throughout the New England churches, and they called him Father Hooper. Nearly all his parishioners, who were of mature age when he was settled, had been borne away by many a funeral: he had one congregation in the church, and a more crowded one in the churchyard; and having wrought[41] so late into the evening, and done his work so well, it was now good Father Hooper's turn to rest.

Several persons were visible by the shaded candlelight, in the death chamber of the old clergyman. Natural connections[42] he had none. But there was the decorously grave, though unmoved physician, seeking only to mitigate[43] the last pangs of the patient whom he could not save. There were the deacons, and other eminently pious members of his church. There, also, was the Reverend Mr. Clark, of Westbury, a young and zealous divine, who had ridden in haste to pray by the bedside of the expiring minister. There was the nurse, no hired handmaiden of death, but one whose calm affection had endured thus long in secrecy, in solitude, amid the chill of age, and would not perish, even at the dying hour. Who, but Elizabeth! And there lay the hoary head of good Father Hooper upon the death pillow, with the black veil still swathed about his brow, and reaching down over his face, so that each more difficult gasp of his faint breath caused it to stir. All through life that piece of crepe had hung between him and the world: it had separated him from cheerful brotherhood and woman's love, and kept him in that saddest of all prisons, his own heart; and still it lay upon his face, as if to deepen the gloom of his darksome chamber, and shade him from the sunshine of eternity.

For some time previous, his mind had been confused, wavering doubtfully between the past and the present, and hovering forward, as it were, at intervals, into the indistinctness of the world to come. There had been feverish turns, which tossed him from side to side, and wore away what little strength he had. But in his most convulsive struggles, and in the wildest vagaries of his intellect, when no other thought retained its sober influence, he still showed an awful solicitude[44] lest the black veil should slip aside. Even if his bewildered soul could have forgotten, there was a faithful woman at his pillow, who, with averted eyes, would have covered that aged face, which she had last beheld in the comeliness of manhood. At length the death-stricken old man lay quietly in the torpor

---

37. Mr. Hooper was given the honor of preaching at the governor's inaugural ceremony.
38. Here, *wrought* means "made."
39. Here, *sway* means "influence."
40. *[As years . . . veil]* This phrase refers to the fact that his hair was turning white with time.
41. Here, *wrought* means "worked."
42. *Natural connections* are relatives.
43. *Mitigate* means "to make less intense, severe, or painful."

44. *Solicitude* means "concern" or "anxiety."

Vocabulary

irreproachable (ir´ i prō´ chə bəl) *adj.* free from blame; faultless
zealous (zel´ əs) *adj.* filled with enthusiastic devotion; passionate
torpor (tôr´ pər) *n.* a state of being unable to move or feel

of mental and bodily exhaustion, with an imperceptible pulse, and breath that grew fainter and fainter, except when a long, deep, and irregular inspiration seemed to prelude the flight of his spirit.

The minister of Westbury approached the bedside.

"Venerable Father Hooper," said he, "the moment of your release is at hand. Are you ready for the lifting of the veil that shuts in time from eternity?"

Father Hooper at first replied merely by a feeble motion of his head; then, apprehensive, perhaps, that his meaning might be doubtful, he exerted himself to speak.

"Yea," said he, in faint accents, "my soul hath a patient weariness until that veil be lifted."

"And is it fitting," resumed the Reverend Mr. Clark, "that a man so given to prayer, of such a blameless example, holy in deed and thought, so far as mortal judgment may pronounce; is it fitting that a father in the church should leave a shadow on his memory, that may seem to blacken a life so pure? I pray you, my venerable brother, let not this thing be! Suffer us to be gladdened by your triumphant aspect as you go to your reward. Before the veil of eternity be lifted, let me cast aside this black veil from your face!"

And thus speaking, the Reverend Mr. Clark bent forward to reveal the mystery of so many years. But, exerting a sudden energy, that made all the beholders stand aghast, Father Hooper snatched both his hands from beneath the bedclothes, and pressed them strongly on the black veil, resolute to struggle, if the minister of Westbury would contend with a dying man.

"Never!" cried the veiled clergyman. "On earth, never!"

"Dark old man!" exclaimed the affrighted minister, "with what horrible crime upon your soul are you now passing to the judgment?"

Father Hooper's breath heaved; it rattled in his throat; but, with a mighty effort, grasping forward with his hands, he caught hold of life, and held it back till he should speak. He even raised himself in bed; and there he sat, shivering with the arms of death around him, while the black veil hung down, awful, at that last moment, in the gathered terrors of a lifetime. And yet the faint, sad smile, so often there, now seemed to glimmer from its obscurity, and linger on Father Hooper's lips.

"Why do you tremble at me alone?" cried he, turning his veiled face round the circle of pale spectators. "Tremble also at each other! Have men avoided me, and women shown no pity, and children screamed and fled, only for my black veil? What, but the mystery which it obscurely typifies, has made this piece of crepe so awful? When the friend shows his inmost heart to his friend; the lover to his best beloved; when man does not vainly shrink from the eye of his Creator, loathsomely treasuring up the secret of his sin; then deem me a monster, for the symbol beneath which I have lived, and die! I look around me, and, lo! on every visage a Black Veil!"

While his auditors shrank from one another, in mutual affright, Father Hooper fell back upon his pillow, a veiled corpse, with a faint smile lingering on the lips. Still veiled, they laid him in his coffin, and a veiled corpse they bore him to the grave. The grass of many years has sprung up and withered on that grave, the burial stone is moss-grown, and good Mr. Hooper's face is dust; but awful is still the thought that it moldered[45] beneath the Black Veil!

---

45. *Moldered* means "turned to dust" or "crumbled."

Responding to Literature

Personal Response

What was your first reaction to the minister's black veil? Did your reaction change as the story developed?

--- ANALYZING LITERATURE ---

RECALL

1. How do the people react when they see Mr. Hooper wearing the veil?
2. What is the subject of Mr. Hooper's sermon on the first day he wears the black veil?
3. What reasons does Mr. Hooper give for refusing to remove the veil for his fiancée, Elizabeth? How does she react?
4. How does Mr. Hooper's life change as he continues to wear the veil?
5. What does Mr. Hooper say on his deathbed about veils?

INTERPRET

6. Why might the veil affect the parishioners as it does?
7. What do you think is the connection between the veil and the congregation's interpretation of Mr. Hooper's sermon? Explain.
8. Why might Elizabeth react as she does when Mr. Hooper refuses to remove the veil for her? How does this show her feelings for him?
9. Why do you think Mr. Hooper refuses to remove his veil over the course of his life? What does this tell you about his character?
10. What might Mr. Hooper's black veil represent for him? Explain.

EVALUATE AND CONNECT

11. Why do you think Hawthorne chose not to explain why Mr. Hooper wears the veil? How does this secret contribute to the story?
12. Compare Mr. Hooper's parishioners to people in your community today. How might people in your community respond to the veil?
13. The story is told from the **third-person point of view** (see page R12). How does the point of view affect the drama of the story? How might the story have been different if told from another point of view?
14. Something that **foreshadows** an event gives a clue to that event before it happens. What foreshadows Mr. Hooper's deathbed scene?
15. If you had been Mr. Hooper, would you have given your reason for wearing the black veil? Explain. Refer to the web you created for the Focus Activity on page 265. Is Mr. Hooper's reaction to guilt similar to the reactions you listed?

Literary ELEMENTS

Short Story

Hawthorne is one writer responsible for creating the American short story, a popular literary genre today. The **short story,** a brief prose narrative that usually can be read in one sitting, generally includes the following elements:

- **Setting:** the time and place in which the events occur.
- **Characters:** the participants in the author's story. The main character is the **protagonist.** There may also be an **antagonist,** or character in conflict with the protagonist.
- **Point of view:** the perspective of the storyteller, or narrator.
- **Theme:** the central message of the story that readers can apply to life. A theme may be stated clearly or inferred.
- **Plot:** the sequence of related events in a story. Most plots deal with a problem and develop around a conflict, a struggle between opposing forces.

1. List the main events of this short story. What is the conflict?
2. What is the setting of "The Minister's Black Veil"? Explain how the setting is important to the story.

⬤ See **Literary Terms Handbook,** p. R14.

— LITERATURE AND WRITING —

Writing About Literature

Analyzing a Parable "The Minister's Black Veil" is a parable, a story that illustrates a moral lesson. In three paragraphs, discuss the development of the parable. First, explain the lesson this parable conveys. Then explain how the story illustrates the lesson. Finally, state your opinion of Hawthorne's success in communicating this lesson.

Creative Writing

Interview the Parson Imagine you have the opportunity to interview Parson Hooper on his deathbed. You must agree to one condition, however: you cannot ask him directly why he has worn the black veil. What questions would you ask? How might he answer? Write a dialogue of the interview as you imagine it might develop.

— EXTENDING YOUR RESPONSE —

Literature Groups

Picture This Hawthorne gives a detailed description of his main character, Parson Hooper; yet the minister is elusive. Have each member of your group draw a portrait of Mr. Hooper based on their impressions of him. Discuss what each portrait reveals about Mr. Hooper.

Listening and Speaking

The Sermon The story describes Mr. Hooper's first sermon after he begins to wear the veil. Reread the description and try to imagine what he might have said. Write a few lines that might have been included. Deliver them to the class the way you think Mr. Hooper might have said them.

Performing

Behind the Veil Imagine that Mr. Hooper decides to reveal his secret to Elizabeth. Create a dramatic scene in which the minister explains to Elizabeth why he wears the veil and why she is the only person who will ever know.

Reading Further

If you would like to read more by or about Nathaniel Hawthorne, you might enjoy these works:

Novel: *The House of the Seven Gables,* a story about a family who lives for generations under a curse.

Short Story Collection: *Twice-Told Tales,* stories that show Hawthorne's fascination with people's inner lives.

📖 Save your work for your portfolio.

Skill Minilesson

VOCABULARY • Etymology

How the etymology, or history, of a word connects to the word's modern meaning may be straightforward, or it may require a bit of thought. For example, *perturbation* comes from the Latin prefix *per-,* meaning "thoroughly," and *turbare,* meaning "to disturb." That connection is quite clear. However, *eccentric* comes from the Greek prefix *ec-,* meaning "out of," and *kentros,* meaning "center." What, then, is an *eccentric* person?

PRACTICE Use the etymologies given to answer the questions.

venerable: from the Latin *venerari,* "to worship"

torpor: from the Latin *torpere,* "to be numb"

1. Who would you be most likely to describe as *venerable*—your hero, your boss, or your friend?

2. Would a person most likely be in a state of *torpor* because of laziness or wanting to be unnoticed?

Before You Read

The Three-Piece Suit

Meet Ali Deb

Ali Deb, known mostly for his poetry, is from the northern African nation of Tunisia. In addition to his poems, Deb has published short stories, studies, and plays. Many of his works have been broadcast on Tunisian radio. Currently, Deb teaches in a secondary school and is on the board of directors of the Tunisian Writers' Union.

Ali Deb was born in 1941.

BACKGROUND

The Time and Place

The story takes place in present-day Tunisia, the smallest country in North Africa. Tunisia was ruled by France from 1881 until 1956 when it became an independent nation. Today, Tunisia is an Arab republic, and Arabic is the official language. However, French is still taught in schools and is commonly used in government and in publications. Islam is the state religion.

In Tunisian cities, many people wear clothing similar to that worn in the United States. However, Tunisian men in rural areas most often wear traditional attire, including a turban or skullcap and long, loose robes or gowns.

FOCUS ACTIVITY

How does what you wear affect the way you feel and act?

QUICKWRITE Jot down notes about how the way you dress affects you. How do you feel and act when you are dressed up? How do you feel and act when you are wearing casual clothing?

SETTING A PURPOSE Read to note how some people respond to articles of clothing.

VOCABULARY PREVIEW

affability (a fə′ bi′ lə tē) *n.* the quality of being easy to approach and talk to; pleasantness; p. 280

repertoire (rep′ ər twär′) *n.* the skills that a person has and is prepared to demonstrate; p. 280

discreet (dis krēt′) *adj.* cautious; prudent; p. 280

accost (ə kôst′) *v.* to approach and speak to, especially in an aggressive manner; p. 280

supplication (sup′ lə kā′ shən) *n.* an earnest and humble request; p. 280

Souks in Tunis, 1931. Leon Gaspard. Oil on canvas laid down on board, 12⅛ x 13⅜ in. Private collection.

The Three-Piece Suit

Ali Deb

Translated by Alice Copple-Tošić

Café a Tunis, 1934. Raoul Dufy. Watercolor, 49 x 65 cm. Private collection.

THIS MONTH, FOR THE FIRST TIME, the household budget has been met and . . . even left me a little supplement . . . I don't know why, I went against my habits and bought myself an elegant three-piece suit, tailored in a magnificent English fabric of lovely sky-blue—the color of sunlit days— in which the tailor's skill was displayed so well that one would say we were born together, one for the other . . .

The Three-Piece Suit

The buttons sparkling in the sun were like stars on the shoulder of a sailor swollen with courage. The spinning sensation that its price aroused did not last long, and I said to myself as I straightened my head and shoulders, "Tell me how you dress, and I'll say who you are."

I made my way without hesitation toward the largest café on the main street. As expected, my friends made a fuss over me, touching, feeling and dusting me with their fingers. I strutted, proud as a peacock, then I took out a package of paper handkerchiefs and cigarettes and offered them to eager hands. "Usually I don't smoke, but they are truly fine, what a pleasure!" exclaimed one of them.

I murmured: "Ordinary cigarettes are infested with tar and nicotine."

Naturally I paid for the drinks and left a fat tip for the waiter who gave me his best compliments. There was glib talk of the rise in prices and the high cost of living.

At this point one of them murmured into my ear, "What kind of shirt and tie are these?" Then he led me to a shop that was celebrated for the high quality of its merchandise and for its voraciousness.[1] His good taste and affability were such that my pockets were emptied and it was only with great difficulty that I managed to pay the ticket home.

For one whole week, I concentrated on straightening out my accounts and forced myself to exactitude[2] and strict austerity.[3] I was thus obliged to forgo[4] luxury and excess such as eggs and butter. I also reduced by half my consumption of meat and cigarettes and pretended to lack the time for entertainment with my friends. . . . I managed somehow or other to put my accounts back in order, while still not forgetting to trim my mustache, smooth my face with a close shave and spray myself with aftershave.

There I was, strolling about, puffed up with pride, on the main street, taking care to pass by the women since their tastes are more refined and assured and their eyes are sharper . . . I heard as though a murmur in my ear, "The flaw is in your shoes"? I turned and noticed a light blush on the face of a young girl. I counted the age of my shoes on my fingers. Goodness, how quickly the months had flown by. "Only a pair of shoes stands between me and perfection!" I chose a pair on Liberty Avenue, then returned to my friends. They directed their entire repertoire of flattering expressions my way and I was literally overcome by a delicious peace that was only troubled by the price of a cup of coffee. I almost proposed another spot in which to drink it but gave up, this café was better suited to my attire.[5] My only recourse[6] was a long but discreet sigh.

On the way home, the weather took a sudden turn and fine little drops fell on my oh-so-proud nose. "Abominable[7] sky," and I bought an umbrella that saved me, in spite of its poor quality.

On Barcelona Square, I was accosted by young beggars. Their sullen faces, extended hands and supplications surrounded me to the

---

1. *Voraciousness* is being greedy or overeager in eating or some other activity. It appears that the shop's voraciousness has to do with its high prices.
2. Here, *exactitude* means "complete accuracy."
3. *Austerity* is the practice of living simply and plainly.
4. *Forgo* means "do without."
5. *Attire* means "clothing."
6. Here, *recourse* means "choice" or "alternative."
7. Here, *abominable* means "very unpleasant, disagreeable."

Vocabulary

affability (a fə′ bi′ lə tē) *n.* the quality of being easy to approach and talk to; pleasantness
repertoire (rep′ ər twär′) *n.* the skills that a person has and is prepared to demonstrate
discreet (dis krēt′) *adj.* cautious; prudent
accost (ə kôst′) *v.* to approach and speak to, especially in an aggressive manner
supplication (sup′ lə kā′ shən) *n.* an earnest and humble request

point of suffocation. There were three of them, I handed fifty millimes[8] to each one and, rid of their harassment, I gave a sigh of relief, but their leader came after me, repeating, "You're worth much more," showing the coin to all the passers-by. I bought his silence for double the amount . . .

I walked prudently,[9] taking the sidewalk, avoiding the dust on cars and jostling[10] pedestrians. I fled the crowd and buses and never forgot to polish my shoes and iron my shirts carefully, often using the fire to dry them faster. The January cold suddenly came to mind and I anticipated the need to buy a coat and change my suit when winter had passed. Should I hold out my hand for a loan or draw directly from the company's cash box? Finally, I got on the train. I breathed in the fetid[11] breath of the passengers. I leaned on the armrest of a seat; a lady grumbled and said to her neighbor, "They're even contesting our second-class seats."

---

8. The *millime* (mə lēm′) is a Tunisian unit of money of very low value.
9. To walk *prudently* is to do so cautiously, in a way that shows good judgment.
10. *Jostling* pedestrians are bumping, pushing, or shoving each other in a crowd.
11. *Fetid* (fet′ id) breath is offensive-smelling.

So I slipped into the first class where a seat and a supplementary fee of some consequence awaited me. I went into the local supermarket. It had been quite some time since I had taken care of my shopping. Upon seeing me, a neighbor literally shrieked for joy, shook my hand and then, raising his flat voice, asked me for a loan that I would have naturally refused him if I had not been wearing my suit.

I bought several items and held them in my arms against my chest. The salesgirl greeted me and unhooked a suitable basket. I had no other alternative but to deposit my purchases inside, and since the proper sort of people, my sort, buy without consideration for the price, I did not even bother to look at the cash register total. When I had returned home, my blood pressure was at its peak, my head was literally boiling, my tongue twisted and my chest heaving. I no longer saw where I walked or where I threw my jacket, vest, and trousers. I clenched my teeth and gritted them as I cursed the traps of this century and the folly of fools. I finally went back to being my old self and since that day no one has troubled me anymore.

Responding to Literature

Personal Response

Did the story's ending surprise you, or not? Explain.

——— ANALYZING LITERATURE ———

RECALL AND INTERPRET

1. What enables the narrator to buy the new suit? How does he feel about the suit? What conclusions can you draw from this about his usual financial status and way of dressing?

2. What comment does a friend in the café make about the narrator's clothing? What is the friend implying? What does this comment cause the narrator to do?

3. What does the narrator do when someone calls attention to his shoes? How does he feel when his friends compliment him? Why do you think he feels this way?

4. **Theme Connections**   What decision does the narrator make at the end of the story? What insights do you think he has gained into his own identity–about who he really is–from this experience?

EVALUATE AND CONNECT

5. Did you find this story humorous, serious, or both? Explain.

6. This story is told from the **first-person point of view** (see page R12). What does this point of view add to the story? Explain.

7. How do you feel when a friend wears something new and very appealing? Are you at all like any of the characters in the story? Support your response using details from the selection.

8. Review what you wrote for the Focus Activity on page 278. How do you act when you are dressed up or wearing new clothes? How does your response compare to the narrator's behavior?

Literary ELEMENTS

Rising Action

The **rising action** in a plot is the action that leads up to the climax of the story. In this part of the story, the complications and plot twists help develop the conflict. For example, in "The Three-Piece Suit" the rising action consists of a series of problems for the narrator. Each time he attempts to solve a problem, a new one arises.

1. What is the first problem that the narrator encounters? How does it set the stage for the next problem?

2. What additional problems does the narrator face? How does each one prepare the reader for what will follow?

⬤ See **Literary Terms Handbook,** p. R13.

——— EXTENDING YOUR RESPONSE ———

Literature Groups

Discuss the Issue   Was the narrator responsible for his own problems in this story, or was he the victim of other people's reactions? Let each member of your group give an opinion on this question. Use evidence from the story to support your position. Summarize the group's responses and share the results with the class.

Personal Writing

The Real You   Imagine that you have just won a contest and your prize is the opportunity to choose a completely new wardrobe. Price is no object. In one paragraph, describe in detail the clothing you would choose. Tell what pieces really shout, "This is who I am!" and explain why.

📖 **Save your work for your portfolio.**

COMPARING selections

The Minister's Black Veil **and** *The Three-Piece Suit*

COMPARE **SYMBOLS**

In both selections, an article of clothing becomes a symbol—an object that represents something else. Write a brief essay that answers the following questions about these symbols.

1. What is the symbol in each story and what might it represent? How are the symbols alike? How are they different?
2. In which story does the symbol more accurately represent the character who wears it? Explain.
3. With which symbol or character do you identify? Why?

COMPARE **MOTIVATION**

Which character has the greater motivation to change his appearance the way he does—Mr. Hooper or the narrator of "The Three-Piece Suit"? With a small group of classmates, discuss the reasons each character has for changing his appearance. Support your opinions with details from the stories. Discuss points such as these:

- What statement was each character trying to make with the change in appearance?
- What might be the effects of these statements?
- How important might these effects be to the characters and to others around them?

COMPARE **CULTURES**

With a partner, research modes of dress in seventeenth-century Puritan New England and in modern-day Tunisia or another Islamic nation. What importance does each culture place on attire? What symbolic meaning do various articles of clothing carry? On poster board, create a visual presentation of the clothing of each culture.

Reading & Thinking Skills

Scanning

Let's say you have just read a fascinating news story. It might be about a discovery on Mars or under Egypt's desert sands. It might be about a student summer work program in national parks. You'd like to learn more.

You might begin by checking the listings in your library or by using a search engine on the Internet. You might find a vast amount of information but not have time to read it all. Once you have chosen an appropriate source, how can you quickly find the specific information you need?

Many readers use a technique called scanning. **Scanning** is one process of searching through writing for a particular fact or piece of information. When you scan, your eyes sweep across a page, looking for key words that may lead you to information you want. Whether you're looking through library listings, a textbook, or the want ads, scanning can make your information searches more efficient.

You can also use scanning to find specific information in material that you've already read. For example, when it's time to answer the questions following "The Three-Piece Suit" or another selection, scanning can help you locate relevant sections to review.

Use the following guidelines to make scanning work for you.

- Choose from two to four key words or phrases that relate to your topic and the information you want to locate. For example, to learn more about summer work programs in national parks, you might look for *work program* and *national parks.*
- Move your eyes quickly over the material. Stay focused. Look only for the key words you have chosen; don't try to read every word.
- Pay special attention to titles, headings and subheadings, and boldfaced words.
- When you find a key word, read the material around it.

● For more about related reading strategies, see **Reading Handbook,** pp. R86–R93.

ACTIVITIES

1. Scan "The Three-Piece Suit" to find answers to the following questions. List the key words you used in your search. Write your answers.

   a. In addition to the suit, what other articles of clothing did the narrator buy?

   b. What other financial burdens did the narrator accept in his effort to appear rich?

2. Read a brief magazine article and write a question about it. Then write three key words or phrases that will lead to the answer. Exchange articles and questions with a partner. Scan the article to answer your partner's question. Did you find the information quickly? Discuss what other approaches you might have taken to find the information.

Before You Read

To Helen, The Raven, and The Pit and the Pendulum

Meet
Edgar Allan Poe

Known primarily as a master of horror and suspense tales, Edgar Allan Poe is also credited with inventing the detective story and contributing to the development of science fiction. Despite his talent, however, Poe led a troubled life.

Poe attended the University of Virginia and the United States Military Academy at West Point, but he encountered personal problems and left each school before graduating. In between schools, Poe lived in Boston, where he published his first collection of poetry,

Tamerlane, and Other Poems, before he turned twenty. Poe spent much of his adult life struggling—moving from city to city, from job to job.

At twenty-six, Poe married Virginia Clemm. For a time he was happy, but Virginia died of tuberculosis after twelve years of marriage, and Poe never fully recovered from the loss. At the age of forty, Poe died in Baltimore—alone.

"I was never *really* insane, except on occasions where my heart was touched."
—*Poe*

Edgar Allan Poe was born in 1809 and died in 1849.

FOCUS ACTIVITY

Have you ever enjoyed a song, movie, or story that dealt with extremes of emotion? Perhaps it was a sad song about lost love, a suspenseful film of high adventure, or an eerie, terrifying tale with unexplained events.

BRAINSTORM With a partner, spend five minutes brainstorming reasons that stories involving extremes of emotion are popular.

SETTING A PURPOSE Read to experience one author's expressions of extreme emotion.

BACKGROUND

The Spanish Inquisition

The Spanish Inquisition began in the late 1400s and lasted more than three hundred years. Throughout Europe at this time, the Roman Catholic Church appointed judges, called inquisitors, to prosecute those who might have religious beliefs that disagreed with those of the Church. In Spain inquisitors persecuted, tortured, and murdered thousands of people.

Who Is Helen?

In "To Helen" the speaker addresses a woman of great beauty. Some scholars believe Poe was alluding to Helen of Troy, who, according to legend, was the most beautiful woman in Greece.

VOCABULARY PREVIEW

deduce (di dōōs′) *v.* to draw a conclusion from something known or assumed; p. 294

impede (im pēd′) *v.* to slow or block progress or action; to obstruct; p. 295

lethargy (leth′ ər jē) *n.* sluggish inactivity or drowsiness; p. 298

cognizance (kog′ nə zəns) *n.* knowledge; awareness; p. 299

proximity (prok sim′ ə tē) *n.* closeness in space, time, sequence, or degree; nearness; p. 302

diffuse (di fūz′) *v.* to spread widely; to scatter in all directions; p. 303

TO HELEN

Edgar Allan Poe

The Pink Rose. Lilla Cabot Perry (1848–1933). Oil on canvas, 40 x 30 in. David David Gallery, Philadelphia.

Helen, thy beauty is to me
    Like those Nicéan barks of yore,°
That gently, o'er a perfumed sea,
    The weary, way-worn wanderer bore
5   To his own native shore.

On desperate seas long wont° to roam,
    Thy hyacinth° hair, thy classic face,
Thy Naiad° airs have brought me home
    To the glory that was Greece,
10   And the grandeur that was Rome.

Lo! in yon brilliant window niche°
    How statue-like I see thee stand,
    The agate lamp° within thy hand!
Ah, Psyche,° from the regions which
15   Are Holy Land!

---

2 *Barks of yore* means "boats of long ago." Poe may be referring to boats from the ancient Greek city of Nicaea in Asia Minor.

6 *Wont* means "accustomed."

7 Here, *hyacinth* means "wavy and perfumed."

8 In Greek mythology, a *naiad* (nī' ad) is a water nymph.

11 A *niche* is a recessed area in a wall, sometimes used for displaying a statue.

13 *Agate* is a type of quartz. An *agate lamp* is a symbol of immortality.

14 In classical mythology, *Psyche* (sī' kē) is the goddess of the soul.

THE RAVEN

Edgar Allan Poe

Once upon a midnight dreary, while I pondered, weak and weary,
Over many a quaint and curious volume of forgotten lore—
While I nodded, nearly napping, suddenly there came a tapping,
As of someone gently rapping, rapping at my chamber° door.
5   "'Tis some visitor," I muttered, "tapping at my chamber door—
     Only this and nothing more."

Ah, distinctly I remember it was in the bleak December;
And each separate dying ember wrought its ghost upon the floor.
Eagerly I wished the morrow;—vainly I had sought to borrow
10   From my books surcease° of sorrow—sorrow for the lost Lenore—
For the rare and radiant maiden whom the angels name Lenore—
     Nameless *here* for evermore.

And the silken, sad, uncertain rustling of each purple curtain
Thrilled me—filled me with fantastic terrors never felt before;
15   So that now, to still the beating of my heart, I stood repeating
"'Tis some visitor entreating entrance at my chamber door—
Some late visitor entreating entrance at my chamber door;—
     This it is and nothing more."

---

4 A *chamber* is a room, especially a bedroom.
10 *Surcease* means "an end."

THE RAVEN

Presently my soul grew stronger; hesitating then no longer,
20   "Sir," said I, "or Madam, truly your forgiveness I implore;
But the fact is I was napping, and so gently you came rapping,
And so faintly you came tapping, tapping at my chamber door,
That I scarce was sure I heard you"—here I opened wide the door;—
     Darkness there and nothing more.

25   Deep into that darkness peering, long I stood there wondering, fearing,
Doubting, dreaming dreams no mortal ever dared to dream before;
But the silence was unbroken, and the stillness gave no token,
And the only word there spoken was the whispered word, "Lenore!"
This I whispered, and an echo murmured back the word, "Lenore!"
30   Merely this and nothing more.

Back into the chamber turning, all my soul within me burning,
Soon again I heard a tapping somewhat louder than before.
"Surely," said I, "surely that is something at my window lattice;°
Let me see, then, what thereat is, and this mystery explore—
35   Let my heart be still a moment and this mystery explore;—
     'Tis the wind and nothing more!"

Open here I flung the shutter, when, with many a flirt and flutter
In there stepped a stately Raven of the saintly days of yore.°
Not the least obeisance° made he; not a minute stopped or stayed he;
40   But, with mien of lord or lady, perched above my chamber door—
Perched upon a bust° of Pallas° just above my chamber door—
     Perched, and sat, and nothing more.

Then this ebony bird beguiling° my sad fancy into smiling,
By the grave and stern decorum of the countenance° it wore,
45   "Though thy crest be shorn and shaven, thou," I said, "art sure no craven,
Ghastly grim and ancient Raven wandering from the Nightly shore—
Tell me what thy lordly name is on the Night's Plutonian° shore!"
     Quoth the Raven "Nevermore."

---

33 A *lattice* is a structure of crisscrossed strips, commonly wood or metal, that forms a pattern of openings.
38 *Days of yore* means "days of long ago." Here Poe is referring to a Bible story
  (1 Kings 17:1–7) in which ravens feed the Hebrew prophet Elijah during a sojourn in the wilderness.
39 *Obeisance* means "a movement or gesture, such as a bow, that expresses respect."
41 A *bust* is a statue of someone's head and shoulders. *Pallas* refers to Pallas Athena, the Greek goddess
  of wisdom.
43 *Beguiling* means "influencing by deceit" or "tricking."
44 Here, *countenance* means "facial expression."
47 *Plutonian* refers to Pluto, the Roman god of the dead and ruler of the underworld.

Much I marveled this ungainly fowl to hear discourse so plainly,
50   Though its answer little meaning—little relevancy bore;
For we cannot help agreeing that no living human being
Ever yet was blessed with seeing bird above his chamber door—
Bird or beast upon the sculptured bust above his chamber door,
        With such name as "Nevermore."

55   But the Raven, sitting lonely on the placid° bust, spoke only
That one word, as if his soul in that one word he did outpour.
Nothing farther then he uttered—not a feather then he fluttered—
Till I scarcely more than muttered "Other friends have flown before—
On the morrow *he* will leave me, as my Hopes have flown before."
60   Then the bird said "Nevermore."

Startled at the stillness broken by reply so aptly spoken,
"Doubtless," said I, "what it utters is its only stock and store
Caught from some unhappy master whom unmerciful Disaster
Followed fast and followed faster till his songs one burden bore—
65   Till the dirges° of his Hope that melancholy burden bore
        Of 'Never—nevermore.'"

But the Raven still beguiling all my fancy into smiling,
Straight I wheeled a cushioned seat in front of bird, and bust and door;
Then, upon the velvet sinking, I betook myself to linking
70   Fancy unto fancy, thinking what this ominous bird of yore—
What this grim, ungainly, ghastly, gaunt, and ominous bird of yore
        Meant in croaking "Nevermore."

This I sat engaged in guessing, but no syllable expressing
To the fowl whose fiery eyes now burned into my bosom's core;
75   This and more I sat divining,° with my head at ease reclining
On the cushion's velvet lining that the lamplight gloated o'er,
But whose velvet violet lining with the lamplight gloating o'er,
        She shall press, ah, nevermore!

---

55 *Placid* means "calm," "peaceful," or "undisturbed."
65 *Dirges* are slow, mournful pieces of music, such as funeral hymns.
75 *Divining* means "knowing through insight or intuition" or "guessing."

THE RAVEN

Then, methought, the air grew denser, perfumed from an unseen censer°
80 Swung by Seraphim° whose foot-falls tinkled on the tufted floor.
"Wretch," I cried, "thy God hath lent thee—by these angels he hath sent thee
Respite°—respite and nepenthe° from thy memories of Lenore;
Quaff,° oh quaff this kind nepenthe and forget this lost Lenore!"
        Quoth the Raven "Nevermore."

85 "Prophet!" said I, "thing of evil!—prophet still, if bird or devil!—
Whether Tempter° sent, or whether tempest° tossed thee here ashore,
Desolate yet all undaunted, on this desert land enchanted—
On this home by Horror haunted—tell me truly, I implore—
Is there—*is* there balm° in Gilead?°—tell me—tell me, I implore!"
90   Quoth the Raven "Nevermore."

"Prophet!" said I, "thing of evil!—prophet still, if bird or devil!
By that Heaven that bends above us—by that God we both adore—
Tell this soul with sorrow laden if, within the distant Aidenn,°
It shall clasp a sainted maiden whom the angels name Lenore—
95 Clasp a rare and radiant maiden whom the angels name Lenore."
        Quoth the Raven "Nevermore."

"Be that word our sign of parting, bird or fiend!" I shrieked, upstarting—
"Get thee back into the tempest and the Night's Plutonian shore!
Leave no black plume as a token of that lie thy soul hath spoken!
100 Leave my loneliness unbroken!—quit the bust above my door!
Take thy beak from out my heart, and take thy form from off my door!"
        Quoth the Raven "Nevermore."

And the Raven, never flitting, still is sitting, *still* is sitting
On the pallid° bust of Pallas just above my chamber door;
105 And his eyes have all the seeming of a demon's that is dreaming,
And the lamp-light o'er him streaming throws his shadow on the floor;
And my soul from out that shadow that lies floating on the floor
        Shall be lifted—nevermore!

---

79 A *censer* is a container in which incense is burned. During a religious service, it may be swung from
   connecting chains.
80 *Seraphim* are angels of the highest rank.
82 A *respite* is a period of rest or relief, as from work or sorrow. The ancient Greeks believed the drug
   nepenthe (ni pen' thē) would ease pain and grief by causing forgetfulness.
83 *Quaff* means "to drink heartily and deeply."
86 *Tempter* refers to the devil. A *tempest* is a violent storm.
89 *Balm* is something that heals or soothes, as an ointment. *Gilead* was a region in ancient Palestine. Here
   Poe uses a phrase from the Bible (Jeremiah 8:22): "Is there no balm in Gilead?" By this he means, "Is
   there no relief from my suffering?"
93 Aidenn means "Eden" or "Heaven."
104 *Pallid* means "lacking in color" or "pale."

Responding to Literature

Personal Response

In your opinion, what is the most haunting image from either of these poems?

ANALYZING LITERATURE

TO HELEN

RECALL AND INTERPRET

1. In the first stanza, to what does the speaker compare Helen's beauty? What might the speaker be saying about the way Helen's beauty makes him feel?
2. What does the **imagery** (see page R8) in lines 7–8 suggest to you about the speaker's feelings for Helen?
3. In lines 11–12, where is Helen when the speaker sees her? What does that detail and his description of her in the following lines suggest about his relationship with her?

EVALUATE AND CONNECT

4. The speaker in this poem describes his response to a beautiful woman. What, in your mind, is perfect beauty? Explain.

THE RAVEN

RECALL AND INTERPRET

5. Why is the speaker reading at the beginning of the poem? How would you describe his emotional state in the first six stanzas?
6. How does the speaker's mood change after the raven enters his room? What conclusion does the speaker express in lines 81–83 about the raven's presence?
7. Summarize the speaker's questions to the raven in lines 85–95. How does he react to the raven's response? Describe the speaker's emotional response by the end of the poem.

EVALUATE AND CONNECT

8. Reread the poem, paying particular attention to the repetition of sounds Poe uses. How does this repetition influence the effect of the poem?

EXTENDING YOUR RESPONSE

Writing About Literature

Character Description   Based on the statements and actions of the speaker in "The Raven," write a description of his character. Be sure to mention events that seem to have had a strong influence on his mental and emotional state. Comment on whether you think the raven's visit helped or harmed the speaker's condition.

Creative Writing

My Advice to You   Imagine that the speaker in "To Helen" has written to you for advice on how to pursue a relationship with his love. Write a letter of advice in reply. Be sure to consider what you know about Helen, the speaker's feelings for her, and the nature of their relationship.

📖 **Save your work for your portfolio.**

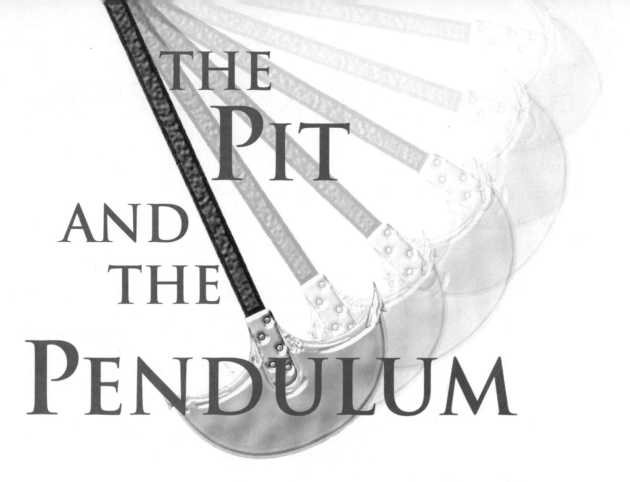

THE PIT AND THE PENDULUM

Edgar Allan Poe ~

I WAS SICK—sick unto death with that long agony; and when they at length unbound me, and I was permitted to sit, I felt that my senses were leaving me. The sentence—the dread sentence of death—was the last of distinct accentuation which reached my ears.

After that, the sound of the inquisitorial voices seemed merged in one dreamy indeterminate hum. It conveyed to my soul the idea of *revolution*—perhaps from its association in fancy with the burr of a millwheel. This only for a brief period; for presently I heard no more. Yet, for a while, I saw; but with how terrible an exaggeration! I saw the lips of the black-robed judges. They appeared to me white—whiter than the sheet upon which I trace these words—and thin even to grotesqueness;[1] thin with the intensity of their expression of firmness—of immovable resolution—of stern contempt of human torture. I saw that the decrees of what to me was Fate, were still issuing from those lips. I saw them writhe with a deadly locution.[2] I saw them fashion the syllables of my name; and I shuddered because no sound succeeded. I saw, too, for a few moments of delirious horror, the soft and nearly imperceptible waving of the sable draperies which enwrapped the walls of the apartment. And then my vision fell upon the seven tall candles upon the table. At first they wore the aspect of charity, and seemed white slender angels who would save me; but then, all

---

1. *Grotesqueness* is the state of being distorted or unnatural in shape or appearance.

2. *Locution* is a form or style of verbal expression.

at once, there came a most deadly nausea over my spirit, and I felt every fiber in my frame thrill as if I had touched the wire of a galvanic battery,[3] while the angel forms became meaningless specters,[4] with heads of flame, and I saw that from them there would be no help. And then there stole into my fancy, like a rich musical note, the thought of what sweet rest there must be in the grave. The thought came gently and stealthily, and it seemed long before it attained full appreciation; but just as my spirit came at length properly to feel and entertain it, the figures of the judges vanished, as if magically, from before me; the tall candles sank into nothingness; their flames went out utterly; the blackness of darkness supervened; all sensations appeared swallowed up in a mad rushing descent as of the soul into Hades.[5] Then silence, and stillness, and night were the universe.

I had swooned; but still will not say that all of consciousness was lost. What of it there remained I will not attempt to define, or even to describe; yet all was not lost. In the deepest slumber—no! In delirium—no! In a swoon—no! In death—no! even in the grave all *is not* lost. Else there is no immortality[6] for man. Arousing from the most profound[7] of slumbers, we break the gossamer web of *some* dream. Yet in a second afterward, (so frail may that web have been) we remember not that we have dreamed. In the return to life from the swoon there are two stages; first, that of the sense of mental or spiritual; secondly, that of the sense of physical, existence. It seems probable that if, upon reaching the second stage, we could recall the impressions of the first, we should find these impressions eloquent in memories of the gulf beyond. And that gulf is—what? How at least shall we distinguish its shadows from those of the tomb? But if the impressions of what I have termed the first stage, are not, at will, recalled, yet, after long interval, do they not come unbidden, while we marvel whence they come? He who has never swooned, is not he who finds strange palaces and wildly familiar faces in coals that glow; is not he who beholds floating in midair the sad visions that the many may not view; is not he who ponders over the perfume of some novel[8] flower—is not

---

8. A *novel* flower is new and unusual.

Seven Tall Candles. Barry Moser. Watercolor, 6½ x 3⅞ in. Private collection.

Viewing the painting: The narrator describes the candles first as "white slender angels," then as "specters, with heads of flame." How would you describe the candles in the painting?

---

3. In a *galvanic battery*, direct electric current is produced by means of chemical action.
4. *Specters* are ghosts or ghostly visions.
5. In Greek myth, *Hades* is the underground place of the dead.
6. Here, *immortality* means "eternal life."
7. Here, *profound* means "complete" or "deep."

THE PIT AND THE PENDULUM

he whose brain grows bewildered with the meaning of some musical cadence which has never before arrested his attention.

Amid frequent and thoughtful endeavors to remember; amid earnest struggles to regather some token of the state of seeming nothingness into which my soul had lapsed, there have been moments when I have dreamed of success; there have been brief, very brief periods when I have conjured up remembrances which the lucid reason of a later epoch assures me could have had reference only to that condition of seeming unconsciousness. These shadows of memory tell, indistinctly, of tall figures that lifted and bore me in silence down—down—still down—till a hideous dizziness oppressed me at the mere idea of the interminableness[9] of the descent. They tell also of a vague horror at my heart, on account of that heart's unnatural stillness. Then comes a sense of sudden motionlessness throughout all things; as if those who bore me (a ghastly train!) had outrun, in their descent, the limits of the limitless, and paused from the wearisomeness of their toil. After this I call to mind flatness and dampness; and that all is *madness*—the madness of a memory which busies itself among forbidden things.

Very suddenly there came back to my soul motion and sound—the tumultuous motion of the heart, and, in my ears, the sound of its beating. Then a pause in which all is blank. Then again sound, and motion, and touch—a tingling sensation pervading my frame. Then the mere consciousness of existence, without thought—a condition which lasted long. Then, very suddenly, *thought*, and shuddering terror, and earnest endeavor to comprehend my true state. Then a strong desire to lapse into insensibility.[10] Then a rushing revival of soul and a successful effort to move. And now a full memory of the trial, of the judges, of the sable draperies, of the sentence, of the sickness, of the swoon. Then entire forgetfulness of all that followed; of all that a later day and much earnestness of endeavor have enabled me vaguely to recall.

So far, I had not opened my eyes. I felt that I lay upon my back, unbound. I reached out my hand, and it fell heavily upon something damp and hard. There I suffered[11] it to remain for many minutes, while I strove to imagine where and *what* I could be. I longed, yet dared not to employ my vision. I dreaded the first glance at objects around me. It was not that I feared to look upon things horrible, but that I grew aghast lest there should be *nothing* to see. At length, with a wild desperation at heart, I quickly unclosed my eyes. My worst thoughts, then, were confirmed. The blackness of eternal night encompassed me. I struggled for breath. The intensity of the darkness seemed to oppress and stifle me. The atmosphere was intolerably close. I still lay quietly, and made effort to exercise my reason. I brought to mind the inquisitorial proceedings,[12] and attempted from that point to deduce my real condition. The sentence had passed; and it appeared to me that a very long interval of time had since elapsed. Yet not for a moment did I suppose myself actually dead. Such a supposition, notwithstanding what we read in fiction, is altogether inconsistent with real existence;—but where and in what state was I? The condemned to death, I knew, perished usually at the *autos-da-fé*,[13] and one of these had

---

9. *Interminableness* means "endlessness."
10. The narrator is describing his wish to return to unconsciousness *(insensibility)*.
11. Here, *suffered* means "allowed."
12. During the Inquisition, a person's refusal to confess was taken as evidence of guilt.
13. Often, the sentence was to be burned alive in public ceremonies called *autos-da-fé* (ô′ tōz də fā′). The phrase is Portuguese for "acts of faith," referring to the Inquisitors' faith that the condemned persons were guilty as charged.

Vocabulary
deduce (di dōōs′) *v.* to draw a conclusion from something known or assumed

Brücke, 1987. Christa Näher. Oil on canvas, 90 x 50 cm. Private collection.

Viewing the painting: How might you feel if you were isolated, as the narrator was, in a place like the one depicted in the painting? Explain.

been held on the very night of the day of my trial. Had I been remanded to my dungeon, to await the next sacrifice which would not take place for many months? This I at once saw could not be. Victims had been in immediate demand. Moreover, my dungeon, as well as all the condemned cells at Toledo,[14] had stone floors, and light was not altogether excluded.

A fearful idea now suddenly drove the blood in torrents upon my heart, and for a brief period, I once more relapsed into insensibility. Upon recovering, I at once started to my feet, trembling convulsively in every fiber. I thrust my arms wildly above and around me in all directions. I felt nothing; yet dreaded to move a step, lest I should be <u>impeded</u> by the walls of the *tomb*. Perspiration burst from every pore and stood in cold big beads on my forehead. The agony of suspense grew at length intolerable, and I cautiously moved forward, with my arms extended, and my eyes straining from their sockets, in the hope of catching some faint ray of light. I proceeded for many paces; but still all was blackness and vacancy. I breathed more freely. It seemed evident that mine was not, at least, the most hideous of fates.

And now, as I still continued to step cautiously onward, there came thronging upon my recollection a thousand vague rumors of the horrors of Toledo. Of the dungeons there

---

14. The Spanish city of *Toledo* was important during the Inquisition.

Vocabulary

impede (im pēd′) *v.* to slow or block progress or action; obstruct

had been strange things narrated—fables I had always deemed them—but yet strange, and too ghastly to repeat, save in a whisper. Was I left to perish of starvation in the subterranean[15] world of darkness; or what fate, perhaps even more fearful, awaited me? That the result would be death, and a death of more than customary bitterness, I knew too well the character of my judges to doubt. The mode and the hour were all that occupied or distracted me.

My outstretched hands at length encountered some solid obstruction. It was a wall, seemingly of stone masonry—very smooth, slimy, and cold. I followed it up; stepping with all the careful distrust with which certain antique narratives had inspired me. This process, however, afforded me no means of ascertaining the dimensions of my dungeon; as I might make its circuit, and return to the point whence I set out, without being aware of the fact; so perfectly uniform seemed the wall. I therefore sought the knife which had been in my pocket, when led into the inquisitorial chamber; but it was gone; my clothes had been exchanged for a wrapper of coarse serge. I had thought of forcing the blade in some minute crevice of the masonry, so as to identify my point of departure. The difficulty, nevertheless, was but trivial; although, in the disorder of my fancy, it seemed at first insuperable.[16] I tore a part of the hem from the robe and placed the fragment at full length, and at right angles to the wall. In groping my way around the prison I could not fail to encounter this rag upon completing the circuit. So, at least I thought: but I had not counted upon the extent of the dungeon, or upon my own weakness. The ground was moist and slippery. I staggered onward for some time, when I stumbled and fell. My excessive fatigue induced me to remain prostrate; and sleep soon overtook me as I lay.

Upon awakening, and stretching forth an arm, I found beside me a loaf and a pitcher with water. I was too much exhausted to reflect upon this circumstance, but ate and drank with avidity.[17] Shortly afterward, I resumed my tour around the prison, and with much toil, came at last upon the fragment of the serge. Up to the period when I fell I had counted fifty-two paces, and upon resuming my walk, I counted forty-eight more;—when I arrived at the rag. There were in all, then, a hundred paces; and admitting two paces to the yard, I presumed the dungeon to be fifty yards in circuit. I had met, however, with many angles in the wall, and thus I could form no guess at the shape of the vault; for vault I could not help supposing it to be.

I had little object—certainly no hope—in these researches; but a vague curiosity prompted me to continue them. Quitting the wall, I resolved to cross the area of the enclosure. At first I proceeded with extreme caution, for the floor, although seemingly of solid material, was treacherous with slime. At length, however, I took courage, and did not hesitate to step firmly; endeavoring to cross in as direct a line as possible. I had advanced some ten or twelve paces in this manner, when the remnant of the torn hem of my robe became entangled between my legs. I stepped on it, and fell violently on my face.

In the confusion attending my fall, I did not immediately apprehend a somewhat startling circumstance, which yet, in a few seconds afterward, and while I still lay prostrate, arrested my attention. It was this—my chin rested upon the floor of the prison, but my lips and the upper portion of my head, although seemingly at a less elevation than the chin, touched nothing. At the same time my forehead seemed bathed in a clammy vapor, and the peculiar smell of decayed fungus arose to

---

15. Most commonly, *subterranean* describes things that exist or occur below the earth's surface, but it can also mean "out of sight" or "secret."

16. Something that's *insuperable* cannot be overcome.

17. *Avidity* is eagerness and enthusiasm.

my nostrils. I put forward my arm, and shuddered to find that I had fallen at the very brink of a circular pit, whose extent, of course, I had no means of ascertaining at the moment. Groping about the masonry just below the margin, I succeeded in dislodging a small fragment, and let it fall into the abyss.[18] For many seconds I hearkened to its reverberations as it dashed against the sides of the chasm in its descent; at length there was a sullen plunge into water, succeeded by loud echoes. At the same moment there came a sound resembling the quick opening, and a rapid closing of a door overhead, while a faint gleam of light flashed suddenly through the gloom, and as suddenly faded away.

I saw clearly the doom which had been prepared for me, and congratulated myself upon the timely accident by which I had escaped. Another step before my fall, and the world had seen me no more. And the death just avoided, was of that very character which I had regarded as fabulous and frivolous[19] in the tales respecting the Inquisition. To the victims of its tyranny, there was the choice of death with its direst physical agonies, or death with its most hideous moral horrors. I had been reserved for the latter. By long suffering my nerves had been unstrung, until I trembled at the sound of my own voice, and had become in every respect a fitting subject for the species of torture which awaited me.

Shaking in every limb, I groped my way back to the wall; resolving there to perish rather than risk the terrors of the wells, of which my imagination now pictured many in various positions about the dungeon. In other conditions of mind I might have had courage to end my misery at once by a plunge into one of these abysses; but now I was the veriest of cowards. Neither could I forget what I had read of these pits—that the *sudden* extinction of life formed no part of their most horrible plan.

Agitation of spirit kept me awake for many long hours; but at length I again slumbered. Upon arousing, I found by my side as before, a loaf and a pitcher of water. A burning thirst consumed me, and I emptied the vessel at a draught. It must have been drugged; for scarcely had I drunk, before I became irresistibly drowsy. A deep sleep fell upon me—a sleep like that of death. How long it lasted of course, I know not; but when, once again, I unclosed my eyes, the objects around me were visible. By a wild sulphurous luster, the origin of which I could not at first determine, I was enabled to see the extent and aspect of the prison.

In its size I had been greatly mistaken. The whole circuit of its walls did not exceed twenty-five yards. For some minutes this fact occasioned me a world of vain trouble; vain indeed! for what could be of less importance, under the terrible circumstances which environed[20] me, than the mere dimensions of my dungeon? But my soul took a wild interest in trifles, and I busied myself in endeavors to account for the error I had committed in my measurement. The truth at length flashed upon me. In my first attempt at exploration I had counted fifty-two paces, up to the period when I fell; I must then have been within a pace or two of the fragments of serge; in fact, I had nearly performed the circuit of the vault. I then slept, and upon awaking, I must have returned upon my steps—thus supposing the circuit nearly double what it actually was. My confusion of mind prevented me from observing that I began my tour with the wall to the left, and ended it with the wall to the right.

I had been deceived, too, in respect to the shape of the enclosure. In feeling my way around I had found many angles, and thus deduced an idea of great irregularity; so potent

---

18. Here, *abyss* (ə bis′) refers to "an extremely deep hole."
19. Here, *fabulous* means "fictional," and *frivolous* means "silly" or "unimportant."

---

20. To *environ* is to encircle or surround.

is the effect of total darkness upon one arousing from lethargy or sleep! The angles were simply those of a few slight depressions, or niches, at odd intervals. The general shape of the prison was square. What I had taken for masonry seemed now to be iron, or some other metal, in huge plates, whose sutures or joints occasioned the depression. The entire surface of this metallic enclosure was rudely daubed in all the hideous and repulsive devices[21] to which the charnel[22] superstitions of the monks has given rise. The figures of fiends in aspects of menace, with skeleton forms, and other more really fearful images, overspread and disfigured the walls. I observed that the outlines of these monstrosities were sufficiently distinct, but that the colors seemed faded and blurred, as if from the effects of a damp atmosphere. I now noticed the floor, too, which was of stone. In the center yawned the circular pit from whose jaws I had escaped; but it was the only one in the dungeon.

All this I saw distinctly and by much effort: for my personal condition had been greatly changed during slumber. I now lay upon my back, and at full length, on a species of low framework of wood. To this I was securely bound by a long strap resembling a surcingle.[23] It passed in many convolutions about my limbs and body, leaving at liberty only my head, and my left arm to such extent that I could, by dint of much exertion, supply myself with food from an earthen dish which lay by my side on the floor. I saw, to my horror, that the pitcher had been removed. I say to my horror; for I was consumed with intolerable thirst. This thirst it appeared to be the design of my persecutors to stimulate: for the food in the dish was meat pungently seasoned.

Looking upward I surveyed the ceiling of my prison. It was some thirty or forty feet overhead, and constructed much as the side walls. In one of its panels a very singular figure riveted my whole attention. It was the painted figure of Time as he is commonly represented, save that, in lieu of[24] a scythe, he held what, at a casual glance, I supposed to be the pictured image of a huge pendulum such as we see on antique clocks. There was something, however, in the appearance of this machine which caused me to regard it more attentively. While I gazed directly upward at it (for its position was immediately over my own) I fancied that I saw it in motion. In an instant afterward the fancy was confirmed. Its sweep was brief, and of course slow. I watched it for some minutes, somewhat in fear, but more in wonder. Wearied at length with observing its dull movement, I turned my eyes upon the other subjects in the cell.

A slight noise attracted my notice, and, looking to the floor, I saw several enormous rats traversing it. They had issued from the well, which lay just within view to my right. Even then, while I gazed, they came up in troops, hurriedly, with ravenous eyes, allured by the scent of the meat. From this it required much effort and attention to scare them away.

It might have been half an hour, perhaps even an hour, (for I could take but imperfect note of time) before I again cast my eyes upward. What I then saw confounded and amazed me. The sweep of the pendulum had increased in extent by nearly a yard. As a natural consequence, its velocity was also much greater. But what mainly disturbed me was the idea that it had perceptibly *descended*. I now observed—with what horror it is needless to say—that its

---

21. Here, the *devices* are ornamental designs.
22. Here, *charnel* means "gruesome" or "deathlike." As a noun, it refers to a cemetery or vault where the bones or bodies of the dead are placed.
23. A *surcingle* is a belt or band used to hold a saddle or pack on a horse or pack animal.

24. The expression *in lieu* (in lōō) *of* means "in place of" or "instead of."

Vocabulary
lethargy (leth′ ər jē) *n.* sluggish inactivity or drowsiness

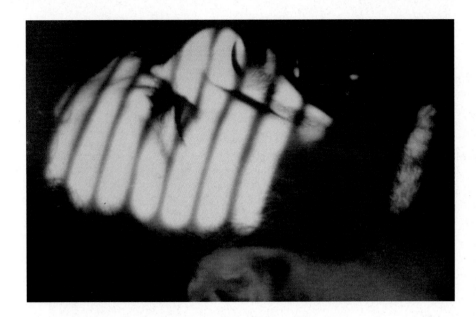

Viewing the photograph: How might this photograph reflect the torment of the narrator?

nether extremity[25] was formed of a crescent of glittering steel, about a foot in length from horn to horn; the horns upward, and the under edge evidently as keen as that of a razor. Like a razor also, it seemed massy and heavy, tapering from the edge into a solid and broad structure above. It was appended to a weighty rod of brass, and the whole *hissed* as it swung through the air.

I could no longer doubt the doom prepared for me by monkish ingenuity[26] in torture. My cognizance of the pit had become known to the inquisitorial agents—*the pit* whose horrors had been destined for so bold a recusant[27] as myself—*the pit,* typical of hell, and regarded by rumor as the Ultima Thule[28] of all their punishments. The plunge into this pit I had avoided by the merest of accidents, and I knew that surprise, or entrapment into torment, formed an important portion of all the grotesquerie of these dungeon deaths. Having

failed to fall, it was no part of the demon plan to hurl me into the abyss; and thus (there being no alternative) a different and a milder destruction awaited me. Milder! I half smiled in my agony as I thought of such application of such a term.

What boots it[29] to tell of the long, long hours of horror more than mortal, during which I counted the rushing vibrations of the steel! Inch by inch—line by line—with a descent only appreciable at intervals that seemed ages—down and still down it came! Days passed—it might have been that many days passed—ere it swept so closely over me as to fan me with its acrid breath. The odor of the sharp steel forced itself into my nostrils. I prayed—I wearied heaven with my prayer for its more speedy descent. I grew frantically mad, and struggled to force myself upward against the sweep of the fearful scimitar.[30] And then I fell suddenly calm, and lay smiling at the glittering death, as a child at some rare bauble.[31]

---

25. The pendulum's *nether extremity* is its lower end.
26. *Ingenuity* (in′ jə nōō′ ə tē)—the noun form of *ingenious*—is creative ability or inventiveness.
27. A *recusant* (re′ kyə zənt) is one who refuses to accept or obey established authorities.
28. Here, *Ultima Thule* (ul′ tə mə   thōō lē) means "extreme limit" or "greatest degree." In ancient times, this was the name of the northernmost part of the known world.

29. *What boots it?* is an expression meaning "What good is it?"
30. A *scimitar* is a curved, single-edged sword of Asian origin.
31. A *bauble* is any showy but worthless trinket.

Vocabulary
cognizance (kog′ nə zəns) *n.* knowledge; awareness

A Prison Scene, 1793–94. Francisco José de Goya y Lucientes. Oil on canvas, 42.9 x 31.7 cm. Bowes Museum, County Durham, England.

Viewing the painting: In what ways does the mood of the painting evoke the narrator's experience?

There was another interval of utter insensibility; it was brief; for, upon again lapsing into life there had been no perceptible descent in the pendulum. But it might have been long; for I knew there were demons who took note of my swoon, and who could have arrested the vibration at pleasure. Upon my recovery, too, I felt very—oh, inexpressibly sick and weak, as if through long inanition.[32] Even amid the agonies of that period, the human nature craved food. With painful effort I outstretched my left arm as far as my bonds permitted, and took possession of the small remnant which had been spared me by the rats. As I put a portion of it within my lips, there rushed to my mind a half formed thought of joy—of hope? Yet what business had I with hope? It was, as I say, a half formed thought—man has many such which are never completed. I felt that it was of joy—of hope; but I felt also that it had perished in its formation. In vain I struggled to perfect—to regain it. Long suffering had nearly annihilated all my ordinary powers of mind. I was an imbecile—an idiot.

The vibration of the pendulum was at right angles to my length. I saw that the crescent was designed to cross the region of the heart. It would fray the serge of my robe—it would return and repeat its operations—again—and again. Notwithstanding its terrifically wide sweep (some thirty feet or more) and the hissing vigor of its descent, sufficient to sunder these very walls of iron, still the fraying of my robe would be all that, for several minutes, it would accomplish. And at this thought I paused. I dared not go farther than this reflection. I dwelt upon it with a pertinacity[33] of attention—as if, in so dwelling, I could arrest *here* the descent of the steel. I forced myself to ponder upon the sound of the crescent as it should pass across the garment—upon the peculiar thrilling sensation which the friction of cloth produces on the nerves. I pondered upon all this frivolity until my teeth were on edge.

Down—steadily down it crept. I took a frenzied pleasure in contrasting its downward with its lateral velocity. To the right—to the left—far and wide—with the shriek of a damned spirit; to my heart with the stealthy pace of the tiger! I alternately laughed and howled as the one or the other idea grew prominent.

Down—certainly, relentlessly down! It vibrated within three inches of my bosom! I struggled violently, furiously, to free my left arm. This was free only from the elbow to the hand. I could reach the latter, from the platter beside me, to my mouth, with great effort, but no farther. Could I have broken the fastenings above the elbow, I would have seized and attempted to arrest the pendulum. I might as well have attempted to arrest an avalanche!

Down—still unceasingly—still inevitably down! I gasped and struggled at each vibration. I shrunk convulsively at its every sweep. My eyes followed its outward or upward whirls with the eagerness of the most unmeaning despair; they closed themselves spasmodically at the descent, although death would have been a relief, oh! how unspeakable! Still I quivered in every nerve to think how slight a sinking of the machinery would precipitate that keen, glistening axe upon my bosom. It was *hope* that prompted the nerve to quiver—the frame to shrink. It was *hope*—the hope that triumphs on the rack[34]—that whispers to the death-condemned even in the dungeons of the Inquisition.

I saw that some ten or twelve vibrations would bring the steel in actual contact with my robe, and with this observation there suddenly came over my spirit all the keen, collected calmness of despair. For the first time during many hours—or perhaps days—I *thought*. It now occurred to me that the bandage, or

---

32. The exhaustion caused by a lack of food or water is called *inanition*.
33. *Pertinacity* is stubborn persistence.

34. The *rack* was an instrument of torture used to stretch or pull a victim's body in different directions.

surcingle, which enveloped me, was *unique*. I was tied by no separate cord. The first stroke of the razor-like crescent athwart any portion of the band, would so detach it that it might be unwound from my person by means of my left hand. But how fearful, in that case, the proximity of the steel! The result of the slightest struggle how deadly! Was it likely, moreover, that the minions of the torturer had not foreseen and provided for this possibility! Was it probable that the bandage crossed my bosom in the track of the pendulum? Dreading to find my faint, and, as it seemed, my last hope frustrated, I so far elevated my head as to obtain a distinct view of my breast. The surcingle enveloped my limbs and body close in all directions—*save in the path of the destroying crescent*.

Scarcely had I dropped my head back into its original position, when there flashed upon my mind what I cannot better describe than as the unformed half of that idea of deliverance to which I have previously alluded, and of which a moiety[35] only floated indeterminately through my brain when I raised food to my burning lips. The whole thought was now present—feeble, scarcely sane, scarcely definite,—but still entire. I proceeded at once, with the nervous energy of despair, to attempt its execution.

For many hours the immediate vicinity of the low framework upon which I lay, had been literally swarming with rats. They were wild, bold, ravenous; their red eyes glaring upon me as if they waited but for motionlessness on my part to make me their prey. "To what food," I thought, "have they been accustomed in the well?"

They had devoured, in spite of all my efforts to prevent them, all but a small remnant of the contents of the dish. I had fallen into an habitual seesaw, or wave of the hand about the platter: and, at length, the unconscious uniformity of the movement deprived it of effect. In their voracity the vermin[36] frequently fastened their sharp fangs into my fingers. With the particles of the oily and spicy viand which now remained, I thoroughly rubbed the bandage wherever I could reach it; then, raising my hand from the floor, I lay breathlessly still.

At first the ravenous animals were startled and terrified at the change—at the cessation of movement. They shrank alarmedly back; many sought the well. But this was only for a moment. I had not counted in vain upon their voracity. Observing that I remained without motion, one or two of the boldest leaped upon the frame-work, and smelt at the surcingle. This seemed the signal for a general rush. Forth from the well they hurried in fresh troops. They clung to the wood—they overran it, and leaped in hundreds upon my person. The measured movement of the pendulum disturbed them not at all. Avoiding its strokes they busied themselves with the anointed bandage. They pressed—they swarmed upon me in ever accumulating heaps. They writhed upon my throat; their cold lips sought my own; I was half stifled by their thronging pressure; disgust, for which the world has no name, swelled my bosom, and chilled, with a heavy clamminess, my heart. Yet one minute, and I felt that the struggle would be over. Plainly I perceived the loosening of the bandage. I knew that in more than one place it must be already severed. With a more than human resolution I lay *still*.

---

35. A *moiety* of something is a portion of it.

36. *Voracity* is another form of the noun *voraciousness*. This kind of greedy hunger is one of the traits often associated with *vermin*—animals that are destructive or troublesome.

Vocabulary
proximity (prok sim′ ə tē) *n.* closeness in space, time, sequence, or degree; nearness

Nor had I erred in my calculations—nor had I endured in vain. I at length felt that I was *free*. The surcingle hung in ribands from my body. But the stroke of the pendulum already pressed upon my bosom. It had divided the serge of the robe. It had cut through the linen beneath. Twice again it swung, and a sharp sense of pain shot through every nerve. But the moment of escape had arrived. At a wave of my hand my deliverers hurried tumultuously away. With a steady movement—cautious, sidelong, shrinking, and slow—I slid from the embrace of the bandage and beyond the reach of the scimitar. For the moment, at least, *I was free.*

Free!—and in the grasp of the Inquisition! I had scarcely stepped from my wooden bed of horror upon the stone floor of the prison, when the motion of the hellish machine ceased and I beheld it drawn up, by some invisible force through the ceiling. This was a lesson which I took desperately to heart. My every motion was undoubtedly watched. Free!—I had but escaped death in one form of agony, to be delivered unto worse than death in some other. With that thought I rolled my eyes nervously around the barriers of iron that hemmed me in. Something unusual— some change which at first I could not appreciate distinctly—it was obvious, had taken place in the apartment. For many minutes in a dreamy and trembling abstraction,[37] I busied myself in vain, unconnected conjecture.[38] During this period, I became aware, for the first time, of the origin of the sulphurous light which illuminated the cell. It proceeded from a fissure, about half an inch in width, extending entirely around the prison at the base of the walls, which thus appeared, and were completely separated from the floor. I endeavored, but of course in vain, to look through the aperture.

As I arose from the attempt, the mystery of the alteration in the chamber broke at once upon my understanding. I have observed that, although the outlines of the figures upon the walls were sufficiently distinct, yet the colors seemed blurred and indefinite. These colors had now assumed, and were momentarily assuming, a startling and most intense brilliancy, that gave to the spectral and fiendish portraitures an aspect that might have thrilled even firmer nerves than my own. Demon eyes, of a wild and ghastly vivacity, glared upon me in a thousand directions, where none had been visible before, and gleamed with the lurid luster[39] of a fire that I could not force my imagination to regard as unreal.

Unreal!—Even while I breathed there came to my nostrils the breath of the vapour of heated iron! A suffocating odor pervaded the prison! A deeper glow settled each moment in the eyes that glared at my agonies! A richer tint of crimson diffused itself over the pictured horrors of blood. I panted! I gasped for breath! There could be no doubt of the design of my tormentors—oh! most unrelenting! oh! most demoniac of men! I shrank from the glowing metal to the center of the cell. Amid the thought of the fiery destruction that impended, the idea of the coolness of the well came over my soul like balm.[40] I rushed to its deadly brink. I threw my straining vision below. The glare from the enkindled roof illumined its inmost recesses.

---

37. *Abstraction* is the state of being lost in thought.
38. *Conjecture* is the forming of an opinion without definite or sufficient evidence.

39. The eyes are full of life *(vivacity),* with a fiery, reddish glare, (a *lurid* luster).
40. Although destruction was about to occur *(impended),* the idea of coolness seemed to be something calming or soothing (a *balm*).

Vocabulary
diffuse (di fūz′) *v.* to spread widely; to scatter in all directions

Yet, for a wild moment, did my spirit refuse to comprehend the meaning of what I saw. At length it forced—it wrestled its way into my soul—it burned itself in upon my shuddering reason.—Oh! for a voice to speak! oh! horror!—oh! any horror but this! With a shriek, I rushed from the margin, and buried my face in my hands—weeping bitterly.

The heat rapidly increased, and once again I looked up, shuddering as with a fit of the ague.[41] There had been a second change in the cell—and now the change was obviously in the *form*. As before, it was in vain that I, at first, endeavoured to appreciate or understand what was taking place. But not long was I left in doubt. The Inquisitorial vengeance had been hurried by my two-fold escape, and there was to be no more dallying[42] with the King of Terrors.[43] The room had been square. I saw that two of its iron angles were now acute—two, consequently, obtuse. The fearful difference quickly increased with a low rumbling or moaning sound. In an instant the apartment had shifted its form into that of a lozenge.[44] But the alteration stopped not here—I neither hoped nor desired it to stop. I could have clasped the red walls to my bosom as a garment of eternal peace. "Death," I said, "any death but that of the pit!" Fool! might I have not known that *into the pit* it was the object of the burning iron to urge me? Could I resist its glow? or, if even that, could I withstand its pressure? And now, flatter and flatter grew the lozenge, with a rapidity that left me no time for contemplation. Its center, and of course, its greatest width, came just over the yawning gulf. I shrank back—but the closing walls pressed me resistlessly onward. At length for my seared and writhing body there was no longer an inch of foothold on the firm floor of the prison. I struggled no more, but the agony of my soul found vent in one loud, long, and final scream of despair. I felt that I tottered upon the brink—I averted my eyes—

There was a discordant hum of human voices! There was a loud blast of many trumpets! There was a harsh grating as of a thousand thunders! The fiery walls rushed back! An outstretched arm caught my own as I fell, fainting, into the abyss. It was that of General Lasalle.[45] The French army had entered Toledo. The Inquisition was in the hands of its enemies.

---

41. *Ague* (ā′ gū) is a fever accompanied by chills and shivering.
42. To *dally* is to "linger," "delay," or "waste time."
43. The *King of Terrors* could be either the "Inquisitorial vengeance" or death.
44. Here, the *lozenge* is a diamond shape.

---

45. *Lasalle* was an officer of the French emperor Napoleon Bonaparte, whose army invaded Spain in 1808.

Responding to Literature

Personal Response

What emotions did you experience while reading this story? Were you surprised by the ending? Why or why not?

--- ANALYZING LITERATURE ---

RECALL

1. To what fate has the narrator been sentenced? How does he react to his sentence?
2. How does the narrator determine the size of his prison? What error does he make?
3. Describe the narrator's first encounter with the pit.
4. In what new horror does the narrator find himself after he first encounters the pit? How does he react to this new torture?
5. What is the third method of torture the captors use on the narrator? What finally happens?

INTERPRET

6. What do you learn about the narrator from the way he describes his reaction to the sentence?
7. Why might the narrator feel that he must find out about his surroundings?
8. What kind of death does he associate with the pit? Why might the pit put him in such a state of terror?
9. Why do you think the narrator makes the efforts he does in response to the second horror?
10. How do you account for what finally happens to the narrator?

EVALUATE AND CONNECT

11. What do the narrator's struggles and thoughts throughout his ordeal tell you about Poe's views of human nature?
12. How did you react to the character of the narrator? Do you think his actions are realistic for his situation? Explain.
13. What words would you use to describe the overall **mood** (see page R10) of this story? How does Poe achieve this mood? Choose one of the situations the narrator faces, and give details to support your answer.
14. How effectively does Poe convey the state of mind of the narrator? How would you describe that state of mind? Explain.
15. Compare and contrast the actions and ideas expressed in this story with those of a modern adventure story or film you know.

Suspense

Suspense is the increasing feeling of interest and excitement—even a sense of impending disaster—that readers experience as the plot of a work of literature builds to a climax. In "The Pit and the Pendulum," Edgar Allan Poe, widely recognized as a master of suspense, uses tension and uncertainty to maintain and build readers' interest. The reader becomes more and more involved in the story and concerned about what will happen to the narrator as he faces one horror after another.

1. The narrator undergoes moments of both physical and psychological torment. Give two examples of each. Describe the event, the narrator's emotional reaction, and how each event adds to the story's suspense.
2. In your opinion, what is the most suspenseful moment in the story? Explain your choice.

● See **Literary Terms Handbook**, p. R16.

LITERATURE AND WRITING

Writing About Literature
Abstract and Concrete Language   Concrete words describe things that can be identified by the senses, such as rats and fire. Abstract words express ideas or qualities, such as hope and despair. Using details from the selection, analyze how Poe's use of concrete and abstract words affects your overall impression of "The Pit and the Pendulum."

Creative Writing
A Bird's-Eye View   Rewrite "The Raven" from the raven's point of view. Try to mimic the style and rhythm Poe used in his poem. Share your finished work with the class.

EXTENDING YOUR RESPONSE

Literature Groups
Reality or a Dream?   Does Poe expect readers to believe that the events in "The Pit and the Pendulum" really happened? Or are readers supposed to view what happened as a dream or hallucination the narrator experienced? Discuss this question in your group, using evidence from the story to support your position. Share your conclusions with the rest of the class.

Learning for Life
A Marketing Plan   With a partner, create a plan to market one of the selections here as a film or a music video. Develop a rough idea of what your final product would be. Then, based on the brainstorming you did for the

Focus Activity on page 285, decide which specific aspects of the selection would be especially appealing to today's audiences. Use posters, magazine ads, or radio or television commercials to present your campaign to the class.

Internet Connection
Poe On-line   Would you like to take a cyber-tour of the Poe museum in Richmond, Virginia? Do you want to learn more about Poe's life? Would you like to hear "The Raven" read aloud? You can do all this and more on-line. Use any major search engine to begin your investigation, entering key words and phrases such as *Edgar Allan Poe* and *"The Raven,"* or other titles of Poe's works.

💼 **Save your work for your portfolio.**

Skill Minilesson

VOCABULARY • **Pronunciation**

Pronunciation guides in dictionaries and textbooks help readers properly say words that they have read but have never heard pronounced.

   Dictionaries show the pronunciations of words in "respellings" that use letters and symbols. For example, a vowel without a symbol has a "short" sound, as in *pat, pet, pit, pot,* and *putt.* A vowel with a straight line over it has a "long" sound as in *a, e, i, o,* and *u.* There are several other symbols for vowel pronunciation, such as ä for the "ah" sound, as in *father.*

PRACTICE   Use the pronunciation guides below to answer the questions.

1. bleak (blēk)   Does *bleak* rhyme with *peek, peck,* or *pack?*

2. entreat (en trēt′)   Does *entreat* rhyme with *sweat* or *sweet?*

3. beguile (bi gīl′)   Does the second syllable in *beguile* rhyme with *you'll, while,* or *pull?*

4. quaff (kwäf)   Does the *a* in *quaff* sound like the *a* in *ha, lawn,* or *day?*

MEDIA Connection

What appeal might the dark, macabre works of Edgar Allan Poe have for rock singers, actors, and CD producers today? To one CD producer, Poe's chilling words seem perfect for a project highlighting major stars.

Dead Singer Buckley's Voice Haunts Poe Disc

by Steve James—Reuters news service, January 14, 1998

Rock musician Jeff Buckley's death by drowning in the Mississippi River last year had a quality of Edgar Allan [Poe] about it.

All the more uncanny then that Buckley's ghostly voice can be heard on a new album of poems and short stories by the 19th-century master of the macabre. Even weirder is the fact that "beat" poet Allen Ginsberg, who visited Buckley to help coach him on reading the Poe verse, died less than a month after the recording.

"Allen died way too prematurely. Jeff's (death) was tragic," said Hal Willner, who produced the album, "Closed on Account of Rabies."

A Beautiful Memory

"In Jeff's performance you hear he had discovered how to read poetry," Willner told Reuters in an interview. Buckley's reading, with guitars in the background, was one of his last recordings.

"With Allen in the session, Jeff's discovery comes

through and leaves a beautiful memory in my head," Willner said.

The two-CD spoken-word collection on Mouth Almighty Records features actors Christopher Walken and Gabriel Byrne and singers Marianne Faithfull, Deborah Harry, Dr. John and Iggy Pop, along with Buckley, performing Poe's work.

Such well-known works as "The Tell-Tale Heart," "The Raven," "The Black Cat," and "The Masque of the Red Death" are given spine-tingling renditions that marry Poe's trademark mix of horror, madness, and decay with Willner's unique vision of music production. The title of the album is a reference to the disease that is believed to have killed the poet nearly 150 years ago at the age of 40 in Baltimore. "Now Edgar Allan Poe, by all contemporary accounts a loser, who died broke and unappreciated, gets a ghostly last laugh over his 19th-century critics with an unusual tribute

offered by such 20th-century hipsters," *People* magazine said of the CD.

More Romantic Approach

Willner said that, when he was growing up, he always associated Poe's words with such horror movie actors as Vincent Price, Peter Lorre, Basil Rathbone and Boris Karloff. For the "Rabies" project, "I wanted to try different people with a more romantic approach."

Respond

1. Do you agree with the writer that Jeff Buckley's death had a Poe-like quality about it? Explain.

2. Would you be interested in hearing this CD? Why or why not?

∿: Writing ✒ Workshop :∿

Descriptive Writing: Travel Article

Travel is certainly one way to gain insight. You might even enjoy visiting the setting of a favorite literature selection. Many of the writers in this theme wrote about real places around the United States and the world. Now you will describe a real place. **Follow the process on these** **pages to write your own travel article.** Your challenge is to create a verbal snapshot of a location that will make your readers want to go there.

● As you write your travel article, refer to the **Writing Handbook,** pp. R77–R85.

The Writing Process

PREWRITING

PREWRITING TIP
Reread some of the selections in this theme. Jot down descriptive words and phrases that grab your attention or help you picture the setting.

Explore locations
List places you might write about. Ideas can come from your experiences, magazines, encyclopedias, or any source that is helpful. You might choose and research a place from one of the selections, such as Walden Pond in Concord, Massachusetts, where Thoreau wrote *Walden.* Next to each location, write some of its highlights.

STUDENT MODEL

Guadalupe Mountains, Tex. Camping trip last year. No cars allowed. Entered park on foot. Very rugged, huge area—lots of wildlife, plant life. Had wheelchair trails for my sister. Climbed to Guadalupe peak for incredible view. Land changes from desert to forest. El Paso and Mexico nearby.

Outer Banks, NC. Untamed beauty. Lots of history. Not much development. Good for nature and beach lovers. Fishing. Boating. Watching wild ponies. Reading on beach. Sea grass and sand dollars everywhere. Great family cottages.

Choose one place
Choose the place on your list you would most like to explore. What attracts you to this place? Put your thoughts on paper. To get more information, interview someone who has been there recently and study photographs. Note facts and details that make the place remarkable.

Consider your audience and purpose

Who will read your travel article? You might send it to a company that publishes travel guides or magazines. You might post it on an Internet chat site for travel and vacations. You might even create a travel brochure to send to the chamber of commerce closest to your destination, or you might just share your work with other students. Whoever your audience is, remember that your purpose is to make readers want to visit the place. Choose specific words and a writing style that will persuade your readers and bring the travel location to life.

Organize your ideas

Review your notes. Use a highlighter or colored pen to mark main features that will appeal to your audience. Circle the best supporting details for each feature. Then organize your information by using one of the models below.

Three Ways of Organizing Details	
Order of impression	Present details in order they are noticed Creates a "you are there" feeling
Order of importance	Start or end with most important detail Helps writer emphasize what is important
Spatial order	Arrange according to location Helps reader travel through setting

DRAFTING

Get ready to write

Build your draft around your model for organizing ideas. As you begin to write, think of yourself as a camera with a zoom lens. Zoom in on one striking object or feature. Pull back slowly, letting your lens range over a wider and wider area until you take in the whole picture.

Draft tour description

Let your ideas and words flow. Stick to the overall impression, but remain open to any vivid details that will engage your audience. End with a strong image. Leave readers eager to see the place for themselves.

DRAFTING TIP

Ask, "What does it remind me of?" to help you create similes and metaphors. A **simile** compares or identifies one thing with another using the words *like* or *as*. (The leaves are like orange and yellow flames.) A **metaphor** is a comparison that doesn't use *like* or *as*. (The leaves were flames against the sky.)

REVISING

REVISING TIP

Too many sensory details can overwhelm your reader. Let the strongest details carry the description.

Take a fresh look

Take a break from your description, then pick it up again and imagine you are reading it for the first time. Do you *show* readers what the place is like, or do you just *tell* about it? Every detail should appeal to one of the five senses or help create an image in your reader's mind. Add transitions to help your writing flow smoothly. Then review your work, using the **Questions for Revising**.

Let a friend read your description

Invite a friend to read your description. Have your friend answer the **Questions for Revising**, and discuss with your friend ideas for improving and presenting your work. For example, you could add a sidebar—a short article that accompanies a major story—that tells readers how to get to the place.

QUESTIONS FOR REVISING

- ☑ Is the opening attention-getting?
- ☑ How might the order of supporting details be more effective?
- ☑ Are there enough vivid details to bring the location to life for the reader?
- ☑ Which details could be more lively?
- ☑ Where could you use more precise words?
- ☑ How well does the writing express your own enthusiasm for the location?
- ☑ Does the ending make readers want to visit the place?

STUDENT MODEL

Visit the Guadalupe Mountains in the fall, and the leaves take center stage. A ~~colorful~~ *brilliant* display of maple, walnut, and oak leaves ~~spreads out~~ *shimmers* across McKittrick Canyon. Walking up the canyon, *toward the woods,* you see traces of autumn yellow. You notice fallen leaves *crackling* beneath your feet. You notice also the ~~smell~~ *woody scent* of dried leaves. Soon a variety of colors surrounds you—the *fiery* ~~brilliant~~ reds, yellows, and oranges of the maples.

EDITING/PROOFREADING

When your description is as vivid as you can make it, proofread for errors in grammar, usage, mechanics, and spelling. Use the **Proofreading Checklist** on the inside back cover of this book.

EDITING TIP

Make sure that all words in your description—especially the names of people and places—are spelled correctly.

Grammar Hint

In a series of three or more words or terms with a single conjunction, use a comma after each word or term except the last.

More than eighty miles of trails weave through the deserts,
steep-walled canyons, and rugged highlands of the Guadalupe
Mountains.

● For more about using commas, see **Language Handbook**, p. R53.

STUDENT MODEL

Tarantulas, black bears, jackrabbits, elk, and bobcats
are among the creatures that inhabit these
mountains of southwestern Texas.

PUBLISHING/PRESENTING

The format of your description depends on your intended audience. If you write an article for the travel section of a newspaper, send a computer printout along with your own illustrations, photographs, maps, or sidebars. If you create a brochure for an office of tourism, you might design a layout with space for headings, text, and images. If you read your description to a group, consider adding poster-size images, appropriate music, a diorama, or even a T-shirt.

PRESENTING TIP

If you send your description to a publisher, include a cover letter. Introduce yourself, explain your interest in the topic, and ask them to consider publishing your writing.

Reflecting

Think about your experience in writing a description. Answer questions like the following in your journal. Which part of the writing project was the most challenging? the most fun?

Set goals for your next piece of writing. Given what you have learned about drafting and revising a description, how will you approach your next assignment differently?

📖 **Save your work for your portfolio.**

Unit Wrap-Up

PERSONAL RESPONSE

1. Which selections in this unit had the greatest impact on you? the least impact? Give reasons.
2. As a result of the work you did in this unit, what new ideas about the following topics do you have?
   - the use of literature to learn about U.S. history
   - the power of literature to influence history
   - how writers can show different aspects of the human spirit and imagination
   - your own reaction to different genres—nonfiction, short stories, and poetry

ANALYZING LITERATURE

What issues stood out for you as you read the selections? Choose one issue, such as:
- freedom
- individuality
- nature
- good vs. evil

Identify three or four selections that treat the issue you have chosen. Using specific examples from the selections, write a few paragraphs discussing the ideas those selections express about the issue. Conclude with a statement about how the selections are similar or different.

EVALUATE AND SET GOALS

Evaluate
1. Make a list of three things you contributed to the class as you studied this unit.
2. What aspect of this unit was the most challenging?
   - What made it so challenging?
   - How did you approach the challenge?
   - What was the result?
3. How would you assess your work in this unit using the following scale? Give at least two reasons for your assessment.
   4 = outstanding   **3** = good   **2** = fair   **1** = weak
4. If you had another week to work on this unit, what would you hope to learn; what would you hope to make or create; what skills would you hope to strengthen?

Set Goals
1. Set a goal for your work in the next unit. Try to focus on improving a skill such as speaking or critical thinking.
2. Discuss your goal with your teacher.
3. Plan specific steps to achieve the goal.
4. Plan checkpoints at which you can judge your work.
5. Think of a method to evaluate your finished work.

💼 BUILD YOUR PORTFOLIO_____

Select   From the writing you have done for this unit, choose two pieces to put into your portfolio. Use the following questions as guides when choosing:
- Which taught you the most?
- Which are you likely to share?
- Which was the most fun to do?

Reflect   Include some explanatory notes with the portfolio pieces you have chosen. Use these questions to guide you:
- What are the piece's strengths and weaknesses?
- What did working on the piece teach you about writing (or about other skills the piece displays)?
- How would you revise the piece to make it stronger?

Reading on Your Own

If you have enjoyed the literature in this unit, you might also be interested in the following books.

The Scarlet Letter
by Nathaniel Hawthorne
In this tragic masterpiece of American literature, Hawthorne tells a story rooted in the Puritanism of colonial New England. Hester Prynne is a young woman who has violated Puritan standards of behavior. Hawthorne delves deeply into the mind and heart of Hester and of the two other main characters—Roger Chillingworth, Hester's obsessive and vengeful husband, and Arthur Dimmesdale, the town's guilt-ridden minister.

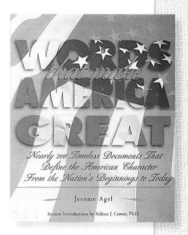

Words That Make America Great
edited by Jerome Agel This book presents 200 documents that have helped define America's character and ideals from its earliest days to the present. Included are many documents of the years 1750–1850, from the Declaration of Independence to the earliest rules of baseball.

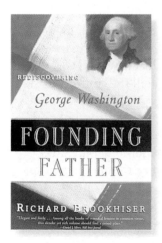

Rediscovering George Washington: Founding Father
by Richard Brookhiser Some current historians see much of the story of George Washington as folk legend. Brookhiser disagrees, though, as he traces Washington's accomplishments as a statesman, soldier, and founder of our nation.

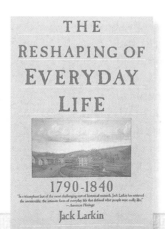

The Reshaping of Everyday Life: 1790–1840
by Jack Larkin Larkin investigates the daily concerns and activities of everyday Americans in a time of great social and economic change. The author is chief historian at Old Sturbridge Village, an outdoor history museum in Massachusetts.

Standardized Test Practice

The passage below is followed by seven questions based on its content. Select the best answer and write the corresponding letter on your paper.

This excerpt is from "Walking," an essay written by Henry David Thoreau in 1862.

I have met with but one or two persons in the course of my life who understood the art of Walking, that is, of taking walks—
Line who had a genius, so to speak, for SAUN-
(5) TERING, which word is beautifully derived "from idle people who roved about the country, in the Middle Ages, and asked charity, under pretense of going *a la Sainte Terre*," to the Holy Land, till the children
(10) exclaimed, "There goes a *Sainte-Terrer*," a Saunterer, a Holy-Lander. They who never go to the Holy Land in their walks, as they pretend, are indeed mere idlers and vagabonds; but they who do go there are
(15) saunterers in the good sense, such as I mean. Some, however, would derive the word from sans terre without land or a home, which, therefore, in the good sense, will mean, having no particular home, but
(20) equally at home everywhere. For this is the secret of successful sauntering. He who sits still in a house all the time may be the greatest vagrant of all; but the saunterer, in the good sense, is no more vagrant than the
(25) meandering river, which is all the while sedulously seeking the shortest course to the sea. But I prefer the first, which, indeed, is the most probable derivation. For every walk is a sort of crusade, preached by some
(30) Peter the Hermit in us, to go forth and reconquer this Holy Land from the hands of the Infidels.

It is true, we are but faint-hearted crusaders, even the walkers, nowadays, who
(35) undertake no persevering, never-ending enterprises. Our expeditions are but tours, and come round again at evening to the old hearth-side from which we set out. Half the walk is but retracing our steps. We should
(40) go forth on the shortest walk, perchance, in the spirit of undying adventure, never to return—prepared to send back our embalmed hearts only as relics to our desolate kingdoms. If you are ready to leave
(45) father and mother, and brother and sister, and wife and child and friends, and never see them again—if you have paid your debts, and made your will, and settled all your affairs, and are a free man—then you
(50) are ready for a walk.

To come down to my own experience, my companion and I, for I sometimes have a companion, take pleasure in fancying ourselves knights of a new, or rather an old,
(55) order—not Equestrians or Chevaliers, not Riders, but Walkers, a still more ancient and honorable class, I trust. The Chivalric and heroic spirit which once belonged to the Rider seems now to reside in, or per-
(60) chance to have subsided into, the Walker—not the Knight, but Walker, Errant. He is a sort of fourth estate, outside of Church and State and People. We have felt that we almost alone hereabouts practiced this
(65) noble art; though, to tell the truth, at least if their own assertions are to be received, most of my townsmen would fain walk sometimes, as I do, but they cannot. No wealth can buy the requisite leisure, free-
(70) dom, and independence which are the capital in this profession. It comes only by the grace of God. It requires a direct dispensation from Heaven to become a walker. You must be born into the family of the
(75) Walkers. *Ambulator nascitur, non fit.* Some of my townsmen, it is true, can remember and have described to me some walks which they took ten years ago, in which they were so blessed as to lose themselves

(80) for half an hour in the woods; but I know very well that they have confined themselves to the highway ever since, whatever pretensions they may make to belong to this select class. No doubt they were ele-

(85) vated for a moment as by the reminiscence of a previous state of existence, when even they were foresters and outlaws.

1 In line 26, the word "sedulously" most nearly means

(A) steadily
(B) unevenly
(C) thoughtfully
(D) quickly
(E) rebelliously

2 In lines 19–21, Thoreau suggests that the "secret of successful sauntering" is

(A) to rove about aimlessly
(B) to find the shortest distance to the sea
(C) to not feel tied to any one particular place
(D) to go forth and conquer
(E) to not be constrained by time

3 In line 53, "fancying" most nearly means

(A) appearing
(B) lavishing
(C) becoming
(D) imagining
(E) occurring

4 Thoreau's comments about his townsmen (lines 66–71) indicate that he regards them as

(A) admirable and brave
(B) too materialistic to enjoy nature
(C) lazy and cheap
(D) optimistic and blithe
(E) forgetful of the past

5 Thoreau claims to "prefer the first" (line 27) definition of sauntering because

(A) the first definition denotes a sense of purpose.
(B) the first definition involves acting on impulse.
(C) the second definition involves acting like a vagrant.
(D) the second definition is more about the destination than the travel itself.
(E) the first definition is more historically accurate.

6 With which of the following statements would Thoreau most likely agree?

(A) It is only possible to enjoy a walk in solitude.
(B) One must be prepared to give up everything to truly experience a walk.
(C) It is enough to walk along a well-trod path.
(D) Walking can be an excellent form of exercise.
(E) Once you have been lost in the woods, you'll never want to walk again.

7 Thoreau uses the phrase "to lose themselves" (line 79) to describe people who

(A) have abandoned all hope
(B) are cut off from their families and friends
(C) fulfill all their obligations
(D) reject all offers of help
(E) are free to fully enjoy an activity

STOP

> **"Our National Sin has found us out. . . .**
> **We have sown the wind, only to reap the whirlwind."**
>
> —Frederick Douglass, 1861,
> speaking of slavery and the Civil War

C.S.S. Manassas Pushing a Fire Barge into the U.S.S. Hartford in New Orleans Harbor.
Xanthus R. Smith (1839–1929). Oil on paper, 5¼ x 9¼ in. Private collection.

The
Civil War
and
Its Aftermath
1845–1880

Setting the Scene

Mary Boykin Chesnut went to bed on April 11, 1861, but could not sleep. Like many others in Charleston, South Carolina, that night, she knew that federal troops under Major Robert Anderson were holed up in Fort Sumter on a rocky island in the city's harbor. South Carolina, which had seceded from the Union four months earlier, had issued these troops an ultimatum. "If Anderson will not surrender," Chesnut noted in her private journal, "tonight the bombardment begins." At 4:30 A.M. on April 12, she heard the sound she had dreaded: "the booming of the cannon." Racing to her rooftop, she witnessed the beginning of the thirty-four-hour shelling of Fort Sumter— the event that began the American Civil War.

Flag of Fort Sumter, October 20, 1863, 1864. Conrad Wise Chapman. Oil on board, 10 x 14 in. The Museum of the Confederacy, Richmond, VA.

U.S.A.

1846
War begins between the United States and Mexico

1848
First women's rights convention held in Seneca Falls, New York

1850
Compromise of 1850 strengthens the Fugitive Slave Act

1859
John Brown leads antislavery raid

1860
Abraham Lincoln elected president

1861
Confederate forces win First Battle of Bull Run

1845   **1855**

World

1847
In West Africa, formerly enslaved African Americans declare Liberia an independent nation

1850
Taiping Rebellion erupts in China

1858
Benito Juárez becomes president of Mexico

1861
Nationalists proclaim a united Italy; Russian serfs freed

History of the Time

The Path to War

Regional economic differences helped bring about the outbreak of the Civil War in 1861. In the South, enslaved African Americans provided the labor needed for an agricultural economy based on raising and selling cotton. In the North, free people, both white and black, worked for wages in the mines, factories, and trading companies of a growing industrial economy.

As the nation expanded westward, many Southerners wanted slavery to expand with it, but most Northerners did not. In November 1860, Abraham Lincoln, who opposed the expansion of slavery, won the presidential election. In response, South Carolina and other Southern states—together known as the Confederacy—began to secede from the United States. Lincoln vowed to preserve the Union. When Confederate cannons fired at Fort Sumter, the Civil War began.

The War

The long tradition of military service in the South gave the eleven states that seceded an edge during the first year of fighting. By the end of 1862, however, the North's naval blockades and larger armies began to bring it victories. Then, on January 1, 1863, events took a dramatic turn. Lincoln issued the Emancipation Proclamation, which declared that all enslaved people in the rebellious states were free. The North's fight to save the Union immediately became a war to end slavery. In the spring of 1865, after more than 600,000 deaths, the war ended in a victory for the North. The slave economy was destroyed.

The Aftermath

The eleven-year period after the Civil War, referred to as Reconstruction, was marked by economic growth. Northern industry had prospered during the Civil War and continued to expand. The South, devastated by the war, began to rebuild. In both regions, however, groups fought against long-existing oppression:

- African Americans, though no longer enslaved, still battled discrimination and racism. One victory was the ratification of the Fourteenth Amendment in 1868, which required states to provide "equal protection of the laws" to all persons.

- Women fought for equality and the right to vote. One leader, Susan B. Anthony, was arrested in 1872 for attempting to vote in a New York election.

- Sioux, Cheyenne, Arapaho, and other Native Americans continued the struggle to protect their land from the spread of white settlements.

The efforts of African Americans, women, and Native Americans to achieve justice would help shape American history after the Civil War.

Civil War ends; Lincoln is assassinated; Thirteenth Amendment bans slavery

1867
United States buys Alaska from Russia

1870
Hiram Revels becomes the first African American in the U.S. Senate

1876
Sioux forces defeat General George Custer at the Battle of Little Bighorn

1865

1868
Meiji Restoration reforms Japan's government

1870
Franco-Prussian War begins in Europe

1875

1879
Zulu War starts in South Africa

1880

Life of the Time

People are talking about

The Underground Railroad   Harriet Tubman escapes slavery and then secretly returns to the South nineteen times to help others escape. She becomes the most famous guide on the Underground Railroad—a secret network of hideouts for people fleeing slavery.

"I had reasoned this out in my mind: There was two things I had a right to, liberty and death. If I could not have one, I would have the other, for no man should take me alive." —*Harriet Tubman*

Harriet Tubman

Portrait of John Brown, c. 1859. Ole Peter Hansen Balling. Oil on canvas, 30 x 25 in. The National Portrait Gallery, Washington, DC.

◀ **John Brown's Raid**   Brown and his followers kill five proslavery men in Kansas in 1856. Three years later, he and about twenty followers seize weapons and ammunitions from a federal arsenal at Harpers Ferry, Virginia. Brown hopes his actions will ignite an uprising to free enslaved African Americans "on a larger scale." He is captured, tried, and executed.

Otis's Elevators   In 1852, Elisha Otis announces his invention of the first elevator with an automatic safety device to prevent it from falling if the cable breaks. Otis personally demonstrates his new elevator by having the cable cut after he has ascended. The device works. ▶

Firsts

- The first transatlantic telegraph cable is laid. (1858)
- Christopher Sholes and associates produce the first practical typewriter. (1867)
- Alexander Graham Bell demonstrates the first telephone. (1876)

U.S.A.

1846 Elias Howe patents the sewing machine

1848 Discovery of gold ignites the California Gold Rush; Stephen Foster publishes "Oh! Susannah"

1850 Printmakers Currier and Ives begin working together

1863 James Whistler exhibits *Arrangement in Grey and Black No 1: The Artist's Mother*

1862 Richard J. Gatling demonstrates an improved machine gun

1845

1855

1856 British inventor Henry Bessemer develops an efficient steel making process

Potato blight causes the Great Famine in Ireland

British explorer David Livingstone names Victoria Falls in Africa

World

Food & Fashion

- Whiskey, long a staple drink in the United States, comes under increasing attack. Between 1846 and 1857, thirteen states pass laws prohibiting consumption of alcohol.

- Machine production transforms what people wear. Invention of the sewing machine makes possible production of inexpensive, ready-to-wear clothing.

- In the 1870s, a clothing maker in San Francisco begins making rugged pants out of blue denim reinforced with copper rivets. Levi's blue jeans will eventually become widely popular.

- Fashionable women wear skirts that are held out from their bodies with wire frameworks. ▶

Arts & Entertainment

◀ Winslow Homer draws and paints scenes of army camp life. His work often makes the cover of *Harper's Weekly* magazine. Critics will later praise Homer as one of the greatest American painters.

More than one thousand photographers record the Civil War. The best known is Mathew Brady, who will produce 3,500 photographs of the war. ▶

Home, Sweet Home, c. 1863. Winslow Homer. Oil on canvas, 21½ x 16½ in. The National Gallery of Art, Washington, DC.

Amusements

- Baseball is a popular pastime. In 1869, the Cincinnati Red Stockings become the first team of all professional players.

- In 1850 Swedish singer Jenny Lind tours the United States, creating a sensation wherever she goes.

1865

1867
Swedish industrialist Alfred Nobel receives a British patent on dynamite; diamond rush begins in South Africa

1871
Chicago Fire destroys much of the city, killing 250 people

1869
The Suez Canal opens in Egypt

1873
French painter Claude Monet completes *Impression: Sunrise*

1875
Thomas Eakins paints *The Gross Clinic*

1879
Thomas Edison demonstrates the first practical electrical lightbulb

1876
The first full production of German composer Richard Wagner's opera *The Ring of Nibelung* is staged

1880

Literature of the Time

PEOPLE ARE READING . . .

Antislavery Writings *The Liberator*, a newspaper founded by William Lloyd Garrison in 1831, is dedicated to the abolition of slavery. Harriet Beecher Stowe's anti-slavery novel, *Uncle Tom's Cabin*, appears first as a newspaper serial and then in book form in 1852. It sells 300,000 copies in its first year.

William Lloyd Garrison

William Gilmore Simms A proud native of South Carolina, Simms writes a popular series of romantic tales about his state's frontier past. He emerges as a defender of slavery and a critic of excessive federal government power.

Harper's Weekly Readers look forward to the political cartoons of Thomas Nast, a Union supporter. Nast popularizes the Democratic Party's donkey symbol and creates the Republican elephant. ▶

"A LIVE JACKASS KICKING A DEAD LION."
And such a Lion! and such a Jackass!

People Are Writing

Letters and Diaries During the war many people record their daily lives in letters and diaries. In 1873 they begin using postcards to correspond.

Memoirs Soldiers and civilians publish their memoirs after the war. These accounts provide day-to-day details of the major campaigns of the war.

U.S.A.

Frederick Douglass publishes his autobiography

1847 Henry Wadsworth Longfellow, *Evangeline*

1854 Sara Josepha Hale, *Woman's Record* (encyclopedia)

Walt Whitman, *Leaves of Grass*

1863 Abraham Lincoln, "The Gettysburg Address"

1845

1855

World

1850 England: Elizabeth Barrett Browning, *Sonnets from the Portuguese*

1854 England: Alfred Tennyson, "The Charge of the Light Brigade"

1858 Kenya: Mwana Kupona binti Msham, "Poem of Mwana Kupona"

Literary Trends: From Romanticism to Realism

"The new age [after the Civil War] began with the putting away of the outworn dress of eighteenth-century romantic liberalism. In the hurrying new days there was no time for abstract theories. . . . [There] emerged eventually a spirit of realistic criticism, seeking to evaluate the worth of this new America, and discover if possible other philosophies to take the place of those which had gone down in the fierce battles of the Civil War." —*Vernon L. Parrington*

Before the Civil War, most fiction and poetry depicts people and situations that are highly imaginative, like Poe's and Irving's, or romanticized and idealized, like Hawthorne's. All of that changes. People who have entertained romantic notions of war are shocked into reality by war's brutality.

The Ambrose Bierce story in this unit, "An Occurrence at Owl Creek Bridge," represents the new wave in fiction: Realism. Writers such as Bierce portray real human experience with all of its imperfections and find truth in everyday people and experiences.

FOCUS ON . . .

Two Unique Geniuses

Walt Whitman and Emily Dickinson redefine American poetry, but it would be hard to find two more different people. Whitman, outgoing and outspoken, publishes nine editions of *Leaves of Grass,* creating both enemies and admirers. Dickinson, reserved and reclusive, publishes only seven poems in her lifetime. Both writers, however, are innovators who set the stage for twentieth-century poetry.

Mark Twain, "The Celebrated Jumping Frog of Calaveras County"

1868
Bret Harte, "The Luck of Roaring Camp"

1873
Henry Timrod, "The Cotton Boll"

Mary Baker Eddy, *Science and Health*

1879
George W. Cable, *Old Creole Days*

1865

1872
Argentina: José Hernández, *The Gaucho Martin Fierro*

1875

1879
Norway: Henrik Ibsen, *A Doll's House*

1880

England: Lewis Carroll, *Alice's Adventures in Wonderland*

Novels of the Time

Responding to the brutality of the Civil War, American novelists turn more and more toward realism. Writers of this time try to observe society closely and to show life as it really is. Many important books of this period analyze economic conditions of the day and conflicts between people from different social classes.

Moby-Dick: or, The Whale
by Herman Melville (1851)

Although Melville's previous novels of sea adventure are quite successful, this story of a whaling voyage is dismissed as absurd, wild, or mad by most readers of his time. In years to come, however, *Moby-Dick* becomes recognized as one of the greatest American novels, the first to struggle with such profound issues as the place of humanity in the universe. The tragic figure of Captain Ahab and his obsessive, doomed search for a great white whale dominate the story.

The Red Badge of Courage
by Stephen Crane (1895)

Although written thirty years after the Civil War ends, this short novel realistically depicts the psychological terror experienced by soldiers. It portrays young Henry Fleming's intense fear in his first battle and his response to that fear. Crane uses what is most likely the Battle of Chancellorsville as the model for the fighting portrayed in the book.

Herman Melville

U.S.A.			
	1852 Harriet Beecher Stowe, *Uncle Tom's Cabin*		**1860** Ann Sophia Stephens, *Malaeska: The Indian Wife of the White Hunter*
1850 Nathaniel Hawthorne, *The Scarlet Letter*	**1853** William Wells Brown, *Clotelle*	**1857** Herman Melville, *The Confidence-Man*	

1845	**1847** England: Emily Brontë, *Wuthering Heights*	**1849** England: Charles Dickens, *David Copperfield*	**1855**	**1857** France: Gustave Flaubert, *Madame Bovary*	**1864** Germany: Wilhelm Raabe, *The Hunger-pastor*
World					

Critics Corner

Little Women's Enduring Appeal

"The natural progress of events which is involved in the growing up of four lively girls and the boy who lives next door would make plot enough, but the course of the story follows a more distinctive pattern which should not be overlooked. . . . Sitting on the grass the girls and Laurie fall to talking of the future and each one voices his or her ambition, telling of the thing that is at the back of every growing young person's mind, 'What would I like to be?'"

—*Cornelia Meigs, 1968*

"Her [Alcott's] girls were jealous, mean, silly and lazy; and for 100 years jealous, mean, silly and lazy girls have been ardently grateful for the chance to read about themselves."

—*Elizabeth Janeway, 1968*

Louisa May Alcott

Little Women, or, Meg, Jo, Beth, and Amy
by Louisa May Alcott (1868–1869)

This tale of four sisters growing up in Concord, Massachusetts, during the Civil War era has become one of the best-loved American novels about the transition from adolescence to adulthood. Alcott gives each sister in the March family a distinctive personality. Meg, the oldest, is the most refined. Jo, fiery and independent, wants to be a writer. Beth is shy and musical. Amy, the youngest and most pragmatic, is the most beautiful. Alcott modeled the sisters, their levelheaded mother, and their idealistic father on her own family.

Mary Mapes Dodge, *Hans Brinker and His Silver Skates*

1873 William Dean Howells, *A Chance Acquaintance*

1876 Mark Twain, *Tom Sawyer*

1878 Henry James, *Daisy Miller* and *The Europeans*

1865

1867 Colombia: Jorge Isaacs, *María*

Bengal: Bankim Chandra Chatterjee, *Daughter of the Lord of the Fort*

1871 England: George Eliot, *Middlemarch*

1875

1874 Spain: Pedro Antonio de Alarcón, *The Three-Cornered Hat*

1880

Language of the Time

How People Speak

Cajun and Gullah   Beginning in the 1740s, the British government forces into exile many of the French-speaking colonists in the Acadia region of eastern Canada. Many settle in Louisiana, where they become known as Cajuns. They bring their own variety of French, adding to it words from several languages spoken in Louisiana, such as *bootleg* (English), *gris-gris* (West African), and *bayou* (Choctaw).

Meanwhile, in the Sea Islands of Georgia and South Carolina, enslaved people speak Gullah, a mixture of English and West African languages. Gullah words include *nyam* (eat), *cooter* (turtle), *pinder* (peanut), and *ki,* an exclamation used to express wonder.

Dialects   Everyone speaks a dialect—a variety of a language common to a region or group. In the 1800s, writers such as James Russell Lowell and Mark Twain write in dialects. For example, in Twain's *The Adventures of Tom Sawyer,* Huckleberry Finn tells Tom how sharing a treasure with Tom is ruining his life: "Tom, I wouldn't ever got into all this trouble if it hadn't 'a' been for that money . . . becuz I don't give a dern for a thing 'thout it's tollable hard to git."

How People Write

Simple, Clear Language   William Cullen Bryant, a journalist and poet, demands simple, clear language in his newspaper, the *New York Evening Post.* For example, he insists on *begin* instead of *commence, dinner* instead of *banquet,* and *artist* instead of *artiste.*

William Cullen Bryant

New Words and Expressions

From Science   Tremendous progress in some of the sciences brings an out-pouring of new terms in the middle 1800s. Here are just a few: *chloroform, sucrose, ohm, ampere, pasteurization, hemophilia, diphtheria, aphasia, claustrophobia.*

Because of the War   The Civil War makes food canning so popular that people are using the expressions *to can, canning, canned food,* and *can opener.* Also, people are sending more cards and letters. As a result, these improvements appear along with the terms to describe them: *first-, second-,* and *third-class mail; postcard; branch post office; mailbox.*

Theme 4 — The Union Is Tested

Have you ever felt you were facing a test, or a great challenge? The United States was put to a great test during the mid-1800s. Deeply felt differences of opinion threatened to destroy the nation. Writers in this theme tell of the conflicts that drew the United States into a bloody civil war. They also tell of the heroism and the horrors of that war.

Fort Federal Hill at Sunset–Baltimore, c. 1862. Sanford Robinson Gifford. Oil on canvas, 18 x 32 in. The Seventh Regiment Fund, Inc. Photograph courtesy of the Metropolitan Museum of Art, New York.

THEME PROJECTS

Interdisciplinary Project

Geography: Mapping   With a group, create a large map of the United States at the time of the Civil War. Then, as you come across an important location in a selection, do the following.

1. Draw a dot on your map to show the location. Label the place with its name and write a brief description of what happened there.

2. At the end of this theme look at your labeled map and discuss what story it might tell beyond any of the individual selections.

Creative Writing

Epigraphs   An epigraph is a quotation that summarizes the theme, or meaning, of a piece of writing.

1. Choose a quote from each selection that reflects its theme.

2. Create a title page for each piece with the title, the author's name, and the quote you chose. Share your epigraphs with classmates and discuss your choices for each selection.

Before You Read

from *My Bondage and My Freedom*

Meet Frederick Douglass

"Where justice is denied, where poverty is enforced, where ignorance prevails, and where any one class is made to feel that society is in an organized conspiracy to oppress, rob, and degrade them, neither persons nor property will be safe."

—*Douglass*

How did Frederick Douglass journey from enslavement on Southern plantations to Washington, D.C., where he delivered these words in 1886? The road was long and treacherous.

Born on a Maryland plantation as Frederick Bailey, Douglass never knew his white father and was separated from his enslaved mother soon after birth. At the age of eight, he was sent to the Auld family of Baltimore, where Mrs. Auld introduced him to the magic of reading. Realizing that education was the path to freedom, Frederick taught himself to read and write. The more he learned, the more restless he became about his enslavement. To make him more obedient, Mr. Auld hired Bailey out to Edward Covey, a "slave breaker" who beat him for the slightest offense. Rather than breaking the young man's spirit, the experience made Bailey even more determined to gain freedom.

At the age of twenty, Frederick Bailey finally escaped to freedom, settling in Massachusetts. There, he changed his name to Douglass to avoid capture and a forced return to his master.

Douglass's life changed dramatically again in 1841 when he was asked to speak at an antislavery meeting. He later wrote, "It was a severe cross, and I took it up reluctantly. The truth was, I felt myself a slave, and the idea of speaking to white people weighed me down." But Douglass gave a moving speech, inspiring abolitionist leaders to ask him to work for the Massachusetts Anti-Slavery Society. Touring tirelessly for the group, Douglass developed a reputation as a great orator.

However, many doubted that such an educated man could really have been enslaved. Urged to authenticate his experience, Douglass wrote *Narrative of the Life of Frederick Douglass* in 1845. Because the autobiography included information that might have led to his capture, Douglass fled to England where abolitionist groups welcomed him. Douglass wrote, "The entire absence of anything that looked like prejudice against me, on the account of the color of my skin—contrasted so strongly with my long and bitter experience in the United States, that I look with wonder and amazement at the transition."

In 1847 English friends raised money to purchase Douglass's freedom, and he returned to the United States where he began publishing an antislavery newspaper. He also expanded and republished his autobiography as *My Bondage and My Freedom* (1855) and *Life and Times of Frederick Douglass* (1881).

"He stood there like an African prince, conscious of his dignity and power, grand in his proportions, majestic in his wrath; as with keen wit, satire, and indignation he portrayed the bitterness of slavery."

—*Elizabeth Cady Stanton*

Frederick Douglass was born around 1818 and died in 1895.

Do you agree with the saying "knowledge is power"? Does knowledge give you greater control over your life?

QUICKWRITE Spend three or four minutes writing to explore your response to this question. Include specific examples.

SETTING A PURPOSE Read to see what kind of power knowledge gives to one young man.

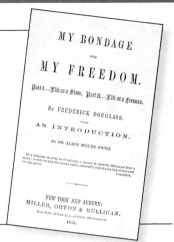

────────── **BACKGROUND** ──────────

The Time and Place

When Douglass first arrived in Baltimore in 1825, the city was already a busy seaport on Chesapeake Bay. Shipbuilding thrived, and the docks along the Patapsco River were crowded with goods headed for inland cities. Unlike other parts of Maryland, free blacks formed a majority of the black population in Baltimore. The seaport thus seemed a haven for African Americans living in the state.

Life as a Free Man

Once Douglass no longer had to worry about being captured and sent back to slavery, he funneled all of his energy into the promotion of justice. Not only did he speak against slavery, he championed the rights of African Americans and women. He participated in the first women's rights convention in Seneca Falls, New York, in 1848. He also became involved in politics. In 1872 he ran for vice-president on the Equal Rights Party ticket headed by feminist Victoria Woodhull. During the Civil War, Douglass supported the recruitment of free and enslaved African Americans into the Union Army, and near the end of his life, he served as United States minister to Haiti.

Baltimore, 1857.

────────── **VOCABULARY PREVIEW** ──────────

benevolent (bə nev′ə lent) *adj.* doing or desiring to do good; kind; p. 330

depravity (di prav′ə tē) *n.* the state of being morally bad or corrupt; p. 330

induce (in do͞os′) *v.* to lead by persuasion or influence; p. 330

upbraiding (up brā′ding) *adj.* criticizing or harshly scolding; p. 333

vanquish (vang′ kwish) *v.* to defeat; p. 333

avarice (av′ ər is) *n.* excessive desire for wealth; greed; p. 333

censure (sen′shər) *v.* to express disapproval of; to find fault with; to blame; p. 334

from MY BONDAGE AND MY FREEDOM

Frederick Douglass

I LIVED IN THE FAMILY OF MASTER Hugh, at Baltimore, seven years, during which time—as the almanac[1] makers say of the weather—my condition was variable. The most interesting feature of my history here, was my learning to read and write, under somewhat marked disadvantages. In attaining this knowledge, I was compelled to resort to indirections by no means congenial to my nature, and which were really humiliating to me. My mistress—who, as the reader has already seen, had begun to teach me—was suddenly checked in her benevolent design, by the strong advice of her husband. In faithful compliance with this advice, the good lady had not only ceased to instruct me, herself, but had set her face as a flint against my learning to read by any means. It is due, however, to my mistress to say, that she did not adopt this course in all its stringency at the first. She either thought it unnecessary, or she lacked the depravity indispensable to shutting me up in mental darkness. It was, at least, necessary for her to have some training, and some hardening, in the exercise of the slaveholder's prerogative, to make her equal to forgetting my human nature and character, and to treating me as a thing destitute of a moral or an intellectual nature. Mrs. Auld—my mistress—was, as I have said, a most kind and tender-hearted woman; and, in the humanity of her heart, and the simplicity of her mind, she set out, when I first went to live with her, to treat me as she supposed one human being ought to treat another.

It is easy to see, that, in entering upon the duties of a slaveholder, some little experience is needed. Nature has done almost nothing to prepare men and women to be either slaves or slaveholders. Nothing but rigid training, long persisted in, can perfect the character of the one or the other. One cannot easily forget to love freedom; and it is as hard to cease to respect that natural love in our fellow creatures. On entering upon the career of a slaveholding mistress, Mrs. Auld was singularly deficient; nature, which fits nobody for such an office, had done less for her than any lady I had known. It was no easy matter to induce her to think and to feel that the curly-headed boy, who stood by her side, and even leaned on her lap; who was loved by little Tommy, and who loved little Tommy in turn; sustained to her only the relation of a chattel.[2] I was *more* than that, and she felt me to be more than that. I could talk and sing; I could laugh and weep; I could reason and remember; I could

---

1. An *almanac* is a reference book that is published yearly. It includes calendars with weather forecasts and astronomical information.

2. An article of movable, personal property, such as furniture or livestock, is *chattel*. Enslaved people were sometimes referred to as *chattel*.

Vocabulary

benevolent (bə nev′ə lent) *adj.* doing or desiring to do good; kind
depravity (di prav′ə tē) *n.* the state of being morally bad or corrupt
induce (in do͞os′) *v.* to lead by persuasion or influence

Frederick Douglass Series No. 8, 1938–39. Jacob Lawrence.
Casein tempera on gessoed hardboard, 17⅞ x 12 in.
Hampton University Museum, Hampton, VA.

love and hate. I was human, and she, dear lady, knew and felt me to be so. How could she, then, treat me as a brute, without a mighty struggle with all the noble powers of her own soul. That struggle came, and the will and power of the husband was victorious. Her noble soul was overthrown; but, he that overthrew it did not, himself, escape the consequences. He, not less than the other parties, was injured in his domestic peace by the fall.

When I went into their family, it was the abode of happiness and contentment. The mistress of the house was a model of affection and tenderness. Her fervent piety and watchful uprightness made it impossible to see her without thinking and feeling—*"that woman is a Christian."* There was no sorrow nor suffering for which she had not a tear, and there was no innocent joy for which she had not a smile. She had bread for the hungry, clothes for the naked, and comfort for every mourner that came within her reach. Slavery soon proved its ability to divest her of these excellent qualities, and her home of its early happiness. Conscience cannot stand much violence. Once thoroughly broken down, *who* is he that can repair the damage? It may be broken toward the slave, on Sunday, and toward the master on Monday. It cannot endure such shocks. It must stand entire, or it does not stand at all. If my condition waxed bad, that of the family waxed not better. The first step, in the wrong direction, was the violence done to nature and to conscience, in arresting the benevolence that would have enlightened my young mind. In ceasing to instruct me, she must begin to justify herself *to* herself; and, once consenting to take sides in such a debate, she was riveted to her position. One needs very little knowledge of moral philosophy, to see *where* my mistress now landed. She finally became even more violent in her opposition to my learning to read, than was her husband himself. She was not satisfied with simply doing as *well* as her husband had commanded her, but seemed resolved to better his instruction. Nothing appeared to make my poor mistress—after her turning toward the downward path—more angry, than seeing me, seated in some nook or corner, quietly reading a book or a newspaper. I have had her rush at me, with the utmost fury, and snatch from my hand such newspaper or book, with something of the wrath and consternation which a traitor might be supposed to feel on being discovered in a plot by some dangerous spy.

Mrs. Auld was an apt woman, and the advice of her husband, and her own experience, soon demonstrated, to her entire satisfaction, that education and slavery are incompatible with each other. When this conviction was thoroughly established, I was most narrowly watched in all my movements. If I remained in a separate room from the family for any considerable length of time, I was sure to be suspected of having a book, and was at once called upon to give an account of myself. All this, however, was entirely *too late*. The first, and never to be retraced, step had been taken. In teaching me the alphabet, in the days of her simplicity and kindness, my mistress had given me the *"inch,"* and now, no ordinary precaution could prevent me from taking the *"ell."*[3]

Seized with a determination to learn to read, at any cost, I hit upon many expedients to accomplish the desired end. The plea which I mainly adopted, and the one by which I was most successful, was that of using my young white playmates, with whom I met in the street, as teachers. I used to carry, almost constantly, a copy of Webster's spelling book in my pocket; and, when sent of errands, or when play time was allowed me, I would step, with my young friends, aside, and take a lesson in spelling. I generally paid my *tuition fee* to the boys, with bread, which I also carried in my pocket. For a single biscuit, any of my hungry little comrades would give me a lesson more valuable to me than bread. Not every one, however, demanded this consideration, for there were those who took pleasure in

teaching me, whenever I had a chance to be taught by them. I am strongly tempted to give the names of two or three of those little boys, as a slight testimonial of the gratitude and affection I bear them, but prudence forbids; not that it would injure me, but it might, possibly, embarrass them; for it is almost an unpardonable offense to do any thing, directly or indirectly, to promote a slave's freedom, in a slave state. It is enough to say, of my warm-hearted little play fellows, that they lived on Philpot street, very near Durgin & Bailey's shipyard.

Although slavery was a delicate subject, and very cautiously talked about among grown up people in Maryland, I frequently talked about it—and that very freely—with the white boys. I would, sometimes, say to them, while seated on a curb stone or a cellar door, "I wish I could be free, as you will be when you get to be men." "You will be free, you know, as soon as you are twenty-one, and can go where you like, but I am a slave for life. Have I not as good a right to be free as you have?" Words like these, I observed, always troubled them; and I had no small satisfaction in wringing from the boys, occasionally, that fresh and bitter condemnation of slavery, that springs from nature, unseared and unperverted. Of all consciences, let me have those to deal with which have not been bewildered by the cares of life. I do not remember ever to have met with a *boy*, while I was in slavery, who defended the slave system; but I have often had boys to console me, with the hope that something would yet occur, by which I might be made free. Over and over again, they have told me, that "they believed *I* had as good a right to be free as *they* had"; and that "they did not believe God ever made any one to be a slave." The reader will easily see, that such little conversations with my play fellows, had no tendency to weaken my love of liberty, nor to render me contented with my condition as a slave.

When I was about thirteen years old, and had succeeded in learning to read, every increase of knowledge, especially respecting

---

3. An *ell* is an old English measure of length used mainly for cloth. It is equal to forty-five inches. Douglass is referring to the adage "Give him an inch and he'll take an ell."

the FREE STATES, added something to the almost intolerable burden of the thought—"I AM A SLAVE FOR LIFE." To my bondage I saw no end. It was a terrible reality, and I shall never be able to tell how sadly that thought chafed my young spirit. Fortunately, or unfortunately, about this time in my life, I had made enough money to buy what was then a very popular school book, viz:[4] the "Columbian Orator." I bought this addition to my library, of Mr. Knight, on Thames street, Fell's Point, Baltimore, and paid him fifty cents for it. I was first led to buy this book, by hearing some little boys say that they were going to learn some little pieces out of it for the Exhibition. This volume was, indeed, a rich treasure, and every opportunity afforded me, for a time, was spent in diligently perusing it. Among much other interesting matter, that which I had perused and reperused with unflagging satisfaction, was a short dialogue between a master and his slave. The slave is represented as having been recaptured, in a second attempt to run away; and the master opens the dialogue with an upbraiding speech, charging the slave with ingratitude, and demanding to know what he has to say in his own defense. Thus upbraided, and thus called upon to reply, the slave rejoins, that he knows how little anything that he can say will avail, seeing that he is completely in the hands of his owner; and with noble resolution, calmly says, "I submit to my fate." Touched by the slave's answer, the master insists upon his further speaking, and recapitulates the many acts of kindness which he has performed toward the slave, and tells him he is permitted to speak for himself. Thus invited to the debate, the quondam[5] slave made a spirited defense of himself, and thereafter the whole argument, for and against slavery, was brought out. The master was vanquished at every turn in the argument; and seeing himself to be thus vanquished, he generously and meekly emancipates the slave, with his best wishes for his prosperity. It is scarcely necessary to say, that a dialogue, with such an origin, and such an ending—read when the fact of my being a slave was a constant burden of grief—powerfully affected me; and I could not help feeling that the day might come, when the well-directed answers made by the slave to the master, in this instance, would find their counterpart in myself. . . .

I had now penetrated the secret of all slavery and oppression, and had ascertained their true foundation to be in the pride, the power and the avarice of man. The dialogue and the speeches were all redolent of the principles of liberty, and poured floods of light on the nature and character of slavery. . . . Nevertheless, the increase of knowledge was attended with bitter, as well as sweet results. The more I read, the more I was led to abhor and detest slavery, and my enslavers. "Slaveholders," thought I, "are only a band of successful robbers, who left their homes and went into Africa for the purpose of stealing and reducing my people to slavery." I loathed them as the meanest and the most wicked of men. As I read, behold! the very discontent so graphically predicted by Master Hugh, had already come upon me. I was no longer the light-hearted, gleesome boy, full of mirth and play, as when I landed first at Baltimore. Knowledge had come; light had penetrated the moral dungeon where I dwelt; and, behold! there lay the bloody whip, for my back, and here was the iron chain; and my good,

---

4. *Viz* is an abbreviation for the Latin word *videlicet,* meaning "namely" or "that is."

5. *Quondam* means "that once was" or "former."

Vocabulary
upbraiding (up brā′ ding) *adj.* criticizing or harshly scolding
vanquish (vang′kwish) *v.* to defeat
avarice (av′ər is) *n.* excessive desire for wealth; greed

kind master, he was the author of my situation. The revelation haunted me, stung me, and made me gloomy and miserable. As I writhed under the sting and torment of this knowledge, I almost envied my fellow slaves their stupid contentment. This knowledge opened my eyes to the horrible pit, and revealed the teeth of the frightful dragon that was ready to pounce upon me, but it opened no way for my escape. I have often wished myself a beast, or a bird—anything, rather than a slave. I was wretched and gloomy, beyond my ability to describe. I was too thoughtful to be happy. It was this everlasting thinking which distressed and tormented me; and yet there was no getting rid of the subject of my thoughts. All nature was redolent of it. Once awakened by the silver trump[6] of knowledge, my spirit was roused to eternal wakefulness. Liberty! the inestimable birthright of every man, had, for me, converted every object into an asserter of this great right. It was heard in every sound, and beheld in every object. It was ever present, to torment me with a sense of my wretched condition. The more beautiful and charming were the smiles of nature, the more horrible and desolate was my condition. I saw nothing without seeing it, and I heard nothing without hearing it. I do not exaggerate, when I say, that it looked from every star, smiled in every calm, breathed in every wind, and moved in every storm.

I have no doubt that my state of mind had something to do with the change in the treatment adopted, by my once kind mistress toward me. I can easily believe, that my leaden, downcast, and discontented look, was very offensive to her. Poor lady! She did not know my trouble, and I dared not tell her. Could I have freely made her acquainted with the real state of my mind, and given her the reasons therefor, it might have been well for both of us. Her abuse of me fell upon me like the blows of the false prophet upon his ass; she did not know that an *angel* stood in the way;[7] and—such is the relation of master and slave—I could not tell her. Nature had made us *friends*; slavery made us *enemies*. My interests were in a direction opposite to hers, and we both had our private thoughts and plans. She aimed to keep me ignorant; and I resolved to know, although knowledge only increased my discontent. My feelings were not the result of any marked cruelty in the treatment I received; they sprung from the consideration of my being a slave at all. It was *slavery*—not its mere *incidents*—that I hated. I had been cheated. I saw through the attempt to keep me in ignorance; I saw that slaveholders would have gladly made me believe that they were merely acting under the authority of God, in making a slave of me, and in making slaves of others; and I treated them as robbers and deceivers. The feeding and clothing me well, could not atone for taking my liberty from me. The smiles of my mistress could not remove the deep sorrow that dwelt in my young bosom. Indeed, these, in time, came only to deepen my sorrow. She had changed; and the reader will see that I had changed, too. We were both victims to the same overshadowing evil—*she,* as mistress, *I,* as slave. I will not censure her harshly; she cannot censure me, for she knows I speak but the truth, and have acted in my opposition to slavery, just as she herself would have acted, in a reverse of circumstances.

---

6. *Trump* is a trumpet.

7. Douglass is referring to a biblical tale (Numbers 22:21–35) in which an ass (donkey), despite being beaten by its master, Balaam, cannot obey and move on because its way is blocked by an angel whom Balaam cannot see.

Vocabulary
censure (sen′shər) *v.* to express disapproval of; to find fault with; to blame

Responding to Literature

Personal Response

How did this narrative affect your attitude toward your own personal freedom?

——— ANALYZING LITERATURE ———

RECALL AND INTERPRET

1. How does Mrs. Auld treat Douglass when he first arrives? How does Mrs. Auld's "inexperience" with slavery help Douglass?
2. How and why does Mrs. Auld's behavior toward Douglass change? In your opinion, who is hurt more by the change, Douglass or the Auld family? Support your answer with details from the selection.
3. Who finally agrees to teach Douglass to read and why? Compare these teachers' attitudes toward slavery with Mrs. Auld's attitudes.
4. To whom is Douglass referring and what do you think he means when he says, "Nature had made us *friends;* slavery made us *enemies*"?

EVALUATE AND CONNECT

5. Evaluate the effectiveness of Douglass's use of the **first-person point of view** in conveying his message. (See Literary Terms Handbook, page R12.)
6. How did knowledge help Douglass gain control over his life? Refer to your notes from the Focus Activity on page 329. Do you think that Douglass might agree with the ideas you expressed there? Explain.
7. Douglass blames the system of slavery more than he blames the Aulds for his situation. Do you agree or disagree? Explain, using a chart like the one on this page.
8. Douglass was physically held captive in slavery; yet, his mind and spirit were free. In what ways might a person held in captivity keep his or her mind free? Explain your response.

Literary ELEMENTS

Autobiography

An **autobiography** is the story a person writes about his or her own life. Douglass's autobiography recounts his experiences both during his enslavement and as a free man, but it has another purpose—to provide a persuasive argument against slavery.

1. What do you think is Douglass's main idea or purpose in this particular portion of his autobiography?
2. Do you think that Douglass presents himself as he really was, or might he be presenting a **biased,** or one-sided, view? Support your response.

● See **Literary Terms Handbook,** p. R2.

Blame for Douglass's situation	
the institution of slavery	the Aulds

——— EXTENDING YOUR RESPONSE ———

Creative Writing

Mrs. Auld's Journal   Take Mrs. Auld's point of view. Write three journal entries that show how you feel about teaching young Frederick to read. Write the first entry from a time soon after Douglass's arrival in your household; the second, from the day of the confrontation with your husband; the third, from one year later.

Performing

Role-Play   Picture Frederick Douglass meeting Mrs. Auld again later in life, when he is famous and free. In a group, discuss what they might talk about. Then write a dialogue between these two characters and have two group members act out the dialogue for the class.

▪ **Save your work for your portfolio.**

Before You Read

Three Spirituals

Who Wrote These Spirituals?

The spirituals featured here came out of the oral tradition of African Americans enslaved in the South before the outbreak of the Civil War. These "sorrow songs," as they were called, were created by anonymous artists and transmitted by word of mouth. As a result, several versions of a spiritual may exist.

African American spirituals combined the tunes and texts of Christian hymns with the rhythms, finger-snapping, clapping, and stamping of traditional African music. Many followed a call-and-response pattern in which a leader sang the verses and was answered by a group of singers.

Enslaved African Americans sang spirituals both in worship and while laboring in the field. Many of the songs have a dual meaning, expressing both religious faith and a hunger for freedom from slavery.

Some spirituals served as encoded messages through which enslaved field workers, forbidden to speak to each other, could communicate practical information about escape. Some typical "code" words included *Egypt*, referring to the South or the state of bondage, and the *Promised Land* or *Heaven*, referring to the North or freedom. The spiritual "Follow the Drinking Gourd," for example, tells people escaping enslavement how to follow the Underground Railroad, a secret network of free blacks and white sympathizers who accompanied and sheltered thousands on the dangerous journey north to freedom.

FOCUS ACTIVITY

Think of a song you find particularly inspiring, such as a patriotic song, a school fight song, or even a popular song from the radio.

DISCUSS Talk with a partner about what makes your song inspirational. Is it the music, the lyrics, an association with a particular time or place, or is it a combination of these elements?

SETTING A PURPOSE Read to enjoy songs that have inspired millions of people.

BACKGROUND

The Biblical Connection

Some enslaved African Americans likened their situation to that of the Jews in Egypt in biblical times. According to the Bible, the Jews were forced into slavery by a pharaoh, or ruler of Egypt. Moses, a leader of the Jews, asked the pharaoh to free his people. Moses explained that if his people were not freed, God would send ten plagues upon the Egyptians. The plagues indeed came and the pharaoh released the Jews. Moses led his people out of Egypt, but the pharaoh changed his mind and sent soldiers after them. The soldiers chased the Jews to the shores of the Red Sea. Then Moses called upon God to part the waters so his people could cross. The sea rolled back for the Jews to pass, but closed in on the Egyptian soldiers. Thus, when the Jews "reached the other shore," they were free people once again.

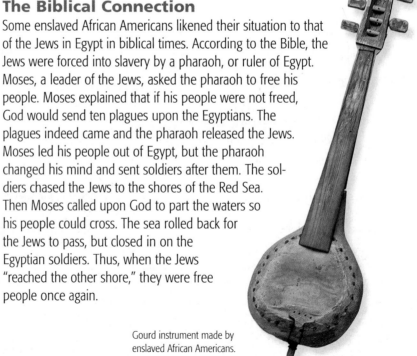

Gourd instrument made by enslaved African Americans.

Swing Low, Sweet Chariot

Swing low, sweet chariot,
Coming for to carry me home,
Swing low, sweet chariot,
Coming for to carry me home.

5   I looked over Jordan° and what did I see,
Coming for to carry me home?
A band of angels coming after me,
Coming for to carry me home.

If you get there before I do,
10   Coming for to carry me home,
Tell all my friends I'm coming too;
Coming for to carry me home.

I'm sometimes up, I'm sometimes down,
Coming for to carry me home,
15   But still my soul feels heavenly bound;
Coming for to carry me home.

Swing low, sweet chariot,
Coming for to carry me home,
Swing low, sweet chariot,
20   Coming for to carry me home.

---

5 *Jordan* refers to the Jordan River. In the Book of Exodus in the Bible, when the Jews were fleeing from slavery in Egypt, they had to cross the Jordan to reach their Promised Land.

Swing Low, Sweet Chariot, c. 1939. William H. Johnson. Oil on board, 28½ x 26½ in. National Museum of American Art, Smithsonian Institution, Washington, DC. Do you think this painting effectively conveys the mood of the song? Which details seem to relate specifically to lines in the song?

Go Down, Moses

Go down, Moses,
'Way down in Egypt's land;
Tell ole Pharaoh
Let my people go.

5   When Israel was in Egypt's land,
Let my people go;
Oppressed so hard they could not stand,
Let my people go.

Thus saith the Lord, bold Moses said,
10 Let my people go;
Let them come out with Egypt's spoil,
Let my people go.

The Lord told Moses what to do,
Let my people go;
15 To lead the children of Israel thro',
Let my people go.

When they had reached the other shore,
Let my people go;
They sang a song of triumph o'er.
20 Let my people go.

Go down, Moses,
'Way down in Egypt's land;
Tell ole Pharaoh
Let my people go.

Harriet Tubman Series No. 11, 1939–40. Jacob Lawrence. Casein tempera on gessoed hardboard, 12 x 17⅞ in. Hampton University Museum, Hampton, VA.

Follow the Drinking Gourd

Harriet Tubman Series No. 10, 1939–40. Jacob Lawrence. Casein tempera on gessoed hardboard, 17⅞ x 12 in. Hampton University Museum, Hampton, VA.

When the sun comes back and the first
    quail calls,
    Follow the drinking gourd,°
For the old man is a-waiting for to carry
    you to freedom
    If you follow the drinking gourd.

5   Follow the drinking gourd,
    Follow the drinking gourd,
For the old man is a-waiting for to carry
    you to freedom
    If you follow the drinking gourd.

The river bank will make a very good
    road,
10   The dead trees show you the way,

Left foot,° peg foot° traveling on
    Follow the drinking gourd.

The river ends between two hills
    Follow the drinking gourd.
15   There's another river on the other side,
    Follow the drinking gourd.

Where the little river meets the great
    big river,°
    Follow the drinking gourd.
The old man is a-waiting for to carry
    you to freedom,
20   If you follow the drinking gourd.

---

2 The *drinking gourd* was the Big Dipper, which points directly to Polaris, the North Star, and the direction of freedom for African Americans escaping from enslavement.

11 One "conductor," or guide, on the Underground Railroad was a man named Peg Leg Joe. This one-legged sailor taught slaves this song and made marks—a *left foot* and a *peg foot*—for them to follow on their journey north.

13–17 The first river is the Tombigbee River in Alabama; the second is the Tennessee River; and the third is the Ohio River.

Responding to Literature

Personal Response

Which phrases or lines from these spirituals do you find most memorable? Share your reactions with a partner.

ANALYZING LITERATURE

Swing Low, Sweet Chariot

RECALL AND INTERPRET

1. To what vehicle does the speaker refer? What might this vehicle represent? Whom or what might the "band of angels" in line 7 represent?
2. Where does the speaker want to go? In your opinion, where or what is this place? Explain.
3. How does the speaker feel in lines 13–16? Why do you think the speaker's "soul feels heavenly bound"?

EVALUATE AND CONNECT

4. In what ways does this spiritual reflect the history of enslaved African Americans? Might the spiritual in any way point to their future? Explain.
5. Think about your discussion for the Focus Activity on page 336. Then explain how the song you picked compares with "Swing Low, Sweet Chariot" both in terms of its words and its effect on you.

Go Down, Moses

RECALL AND INTERPRET

6. In lines 1–8, what is the speaker asking Moses to do? What hidden message might these words have given to enslaved African Americans?
7. According to the song, who is telling Moses what to do? What might these lines say about the hopes and beliefs of many enslaved African Americans?

EVALUATE AND CONNECT

8. Describe the **mood,** or overall feeling or emotion, created by this song. Use specific examples from the song to support your response.
9. Who might have reason to sing this song or another like it today? Why?

Follow the Drinking Gourd

RECALL AND INTERPRET

10. According to the song, what reward would come to a person who followed the drinking gourd? What might the drinking gourd be a **symbol** for (see page R16)?
11. What other landmarks does the song mention? How might these landmarks have been helpful to people escaping enslavement?

EVALUATE AND CONNECT

12. Imagine that you are an enslaved person. Might this song have helped you to build up courage and trust in the Underground Railroad? Explain your answer.

Literary ELEMENTS

Refrain

A repeated line or lines in a song is called a **refrain.** For example, the line "Follow the drinking gourd" is repeated in every stanza of the spiritual of that name. Spirituals usually contain at least one refrain that emphasizes the central idea, or **theme,** and helps establish the **mood.** The refrain also helps create **rhythm.** In a spiritual, the refrain is often sung by a chorus, or group of singers, with the other words sung by a leader.

1. What mood is created by the refrain in the spiritual "Swing Low, Sweet Chariot"?
2. The words "Let my people go" are repeated in every stanza of "Go Down, Moses." What impact does the repetition create?
3. What idea is emphasized by the refrain in "Follow the Drinking Gourd"?

◉ See **Literary Terms Handbook,** p. R13.

LITERATURE AND WRITING

Writing About Literature

Keeping the Spirit These three spirituals remain popular even though people no longer need the encoded messages the songs contain. Consider why these songs are still so popular. What role might they play today? What might people enjoy about these songs? Where might people be likely to sing these spirituals? Write two or three paragraphs explaining your answer.

Creative Writing

Code Writers The spiritual "Follow the Drinking Gourd" includes specific, encoded directions to help fugitives from slavery escape. Imagine a situation in which a friend or family member is in danger. Then consider what important message you might need to send that person. Encode the message in a poem or song and ask a friend to try to decipher the message.

EXTENDING YOUR RESPONSE

Literature Groups

Entitled to a New Title? You have probably noticed that the title of each spiritual is also a phrase that is repeated in the song. Discuss with your group possible new titles for each spiritual. Be sure each title encompasses the song's **theme,** or message. Then compare your titles with those of other groups, as well as with the existing title. Vote for the best title for each spiritual.

Interdisciplinary Activity

Music: "Ain't Nothin' Like the Real Thing" Choose one of these spirituals and, working with a group, prepare a performance of the piece. Feel free to improvise by adding, for example, hand clapping or foot stamping or new words or phrases. Perform your spiritual for the class.

Listening and Speaking

Follow the Drinking Gourd Prepare a brief how-to talk on navigating by the North Star. Create at least one visual that shows the Big Dipper, the Little Dipper, and the North Star. Explain how to use this star as a natural compass.

Reading Further

If you enjoyed learning about these spirituals, you might want to listen to or view these productions:

Listening: *Trav'ling Home,* a compact disc of American spirituals composed between 1770 and 1870, performed by the Boston Camerata.

Viewing: *Sing Spirituals,* a 91-minute videocassette on which opera great Kathleen Battle performs spirituals, including "Swing Low, Sweet Chariot."

📖 **Save your work for your portfolio.**

INTERDISCIPLINARY CONNECTION

From Spirituals to Rock and Roll

What is your favorite kind of music? "Swing Low, Sweet Chariot" and other spirituals, or "sorrow songs," are the ancestors of much of the music of today, from country to rock and roll. Spirituals of the 1700s and 1800s told stories of suffering and salvation. Many, like the three you have just read, reflected the experiences of enslavement. These spirituals often combined phrases from English hymns with the harmonies and complex rhythms found in African music. They also used blue, or slightly flatted, notes, which created a sad, mournful sound.

Jelly Roll Morton

Since the late 1800s and early 1900s, performers have modified traditional spirituals, creating new styles of music. For example:

- In the late 1800s, musicians such as W. C. Handy began dropping the religious elements of these songs. However, they continued to use the blue, or flatted, notes, and this style became known as the blues.

- In the late 1800s, some musicians began writing down spirituals, adding more precise melodies and more complex harmonies. Thomas Dorsey and Mahalia Jackson helped make this music, called gospel, famous in the 1930s.

- In the early 1900s, Jelly Roll Morton and others added faster rhythms and variations in form to blues tunes, creating the style known as jazz.

- In the 1940s, performers such as Hank Williams combined the traditional music of the American Southwest and Southeast with blues and gospel to develop what is now called country music.

- In the 1950s and 1960s, Little Richard, Elvis Presley, the Beatles, and others drew upon gospel, country, blues, and jazz traditions to develop rock and roll. Others such as Aretha Franklin and Sam Cooke used these same traditions to develop rhythm and blues and soul music.

Activity

In a small group, share your favorite popular songs. Then discuss how these songs are similar to or different than the spirituals you have studied. For example: Does your favorite song tell of someone's suffering? Can the song be accompanied by foot tapping or dancing? Does it have a sad, mournful sound? See if you can find the "spiritual" roots of some of today's popular music.

MEDIA *Connection*

Magazine Article

The article below tells of a robot exploring Mars in 1997. Yet it's also about an African American woman who lived during the 1800s. How are the two connected? Read on to find out.

Mars Robot 'Sojourner' Named by Black Girl to Honor Abolitionist Sojourner Truth

Jet, July 29, 1997

Black history heroine Sojourner Truth is being remembered in a special, grand way.

NASA (National Aeronautics and Space Administration) selected the name "Sojourner" for its new robot recently used to kick off a historic exploration of the planet Mars. The *Sojourner* is the first mobile vehicle to roam and explore another planet.

Valerie Ambroise of Bridgeport, CT, was 12 years old when she came up with the name "Sojourner" in a worldwide essay contest. She won the contest a year later at age 13 and is now 15.

The *Sojourner* is a tribute to Sojourner Truth, an abolitionist and champion of women's rights who lived during the Civil War era. She was born a slave in 1797 or thereabouts in upstate New York and died in 1883.

Truth's legal name was Isabella Van Wagener, but she changed it to Sojourner Truth.

She said, "The Lord named me Sojourner because I am to travel up and down the land showing the people their sins and being a sign unto them," according to noted historian and EBONY Magazine Executive Editor Lerone Bennett Jr. in his book, *Pioneers in Protest.*

Students were invited to select a heroine and submit an essay about her historical accomplishments. Most of the students in the contest were between 5 and 18.

The students were asked to address in their essays how a robot rover named for their heroine would translate these accomplishments to the Mars environment.

NASA agreed that the name of the Mars robot should be "Sojourner" because the name means "traveler."

In her essay, Ambroise wrote:

"I chose Sojourner because she was a heroine to Blacks, slaves, and women. She acted on her strong feelings about life and the way it should be. Her greatest companions were God and her beliefs."

Respond

1. Do you think "Sojourner" is a fitting name for the Mars robot explorer? Explain.

2. In what ways might the robot be tested as Sojourner Truth was?

Before You Read

And Ain't I a Woman?

Meet Sojourner Truth

"She had taken us up in her strong arms and carried us safely over the slough of difficulty, turning the whole tide in our favor."

—*Francis Gage*

Armed with her common sense and sharp wit, Sojourner Truth went to battle against slavery and in support of the rights of women. Nearly six feet tall, Truth had a deep, smooth voice that quieted rowdy crowds and won devoted supporters.

Sojourner Truth was born into slavery and endured cruel slave owners, backbreaking work, and harsh beatings. At age twenty-nine she finally escaped from slavery. Given refuge by Isaac and Maria Van Wagener, she took the name Isabella Van Wagener.

For many years, Isabella believed she heard messages from God. At age forty-six, she took the name Sojourner Truth—meaning that she would become a traveler preaching the truth of God. Truth preached throughout the northeastern United States. Before long, she began to weave antislavery messages into her preaching.

Truth also adopted the cause of women's rights, especially the right to vote. She delivered her famous "And Ain't I a Woman?" speech at the Akron, Ohio, Women's Rights Convention in 1851.

Later in the 1850s, Truth settled in Battle Creek, Michigan, where she continued her preaching and her work for equal rights. During the Civil War, Truth helped gather supplies and money for the black volunteer regiments. Toward the end of the war, Truth moved to Washington, D.C., where she accepted a job with the National Freedmen's Relief Association, counseling former slaves.

At age seventy-eight, Truth returned to Battle Creek. She remained there until her death, which is said to have occasioned the largest funeral ever held in that city.

Sojourner Truth was born in 1797 and died in 1883.

FOCUS ACTIVITY

Think of a time in your life when you felt you were treated unfairly. What was the situation?

JOURNAL Write about the time you were treated most unfairly. Explain how it made you feel and how you responded.

SETTING A PURPOSE Read to find out how one woman spoke out against unfair treatment.

BACKGROUND

The Time and Place

On the second day of the 1851 Women's Rights Convention in Akron, Ohio, a number of male ministers spoke, insisting that women were too weak and intellectually inferior to vote. One man gave religious reasons against woman suffrage, or right to vote. Sojourner Truth's speech is her answer to these critics.

The Real Words?

Truth's speech was not written, and many versions have survived—some in what might be interpreted as the dialect of an enslaved person from the South. In reality, Truth spoke Standard English. So, whose exact words are these? We may never know, but the spirit is certainly that of Sojourner Truth.

And Ain't I a Woman?

Address to the Ohio Women's Rights Convention, 1851

Sojourner Truth ❧

In Sojourner Truth I Fought for the Rights of Women as Well as Blacks, 1947. Elizabeth Catlett. Linocut. 22.5 x 15 cm. Hampton University Museum, Hampton, VA/©Elizabeth Catlett/Licensed by VAGA, New York..

And Ain't I a Woman?

WELL, CHILDREN, WHERE THERE IS SO MUCH RACKET
there must be something out of kilter.[1] I think that 'twixt[2] the Negroes
of the South and the women at the North, all talking about rights, the
white men will be in a fix pretty soon. But what's all this here talking
about? That man over there says that women need to be helped into carriages, and lifted over ditches, and to have the best place everywhere.
Nobody ever helps me into carriages, or over mud-puddles, or gives me
any best place! And ain't I a woman? Look at me! Look at my arm. I have
ploughed and planted, and gathered into barns, and no man could head[3]
me! And ain't I a woman? I could work as much and eat as much as a
man—when I could get it—and bear the lash as well! And ain't I a
woman? I have borne thirteen children, and seen them most all sold off to
slavery, and when I cried out with my mother's grief, none but Jesus heard
me! And ain't I a woman?

Then they talk about this thing in the head; what's this they call it?
[Intellect, someone whispers.] That's it, honey. What's that got to do with
women's rights or Negroes rights? If my cup won't hold but a pint, and
yours holds a quart, wouldn't you be mean not to let me have my little
half-measure full?

Then that little man in black there, he says women can't have as
much rights as men, 'cause Christ wasn't a woman! Where did your Christ
come from? Where did your Christ come from? From God and a woman!
Man had nothing to do with Him.

If the first woman God ever made was strong enough to turn the
world upside down all alone, these women together ought to be able to
turn it back, and get it right side up again! And now they is asking to do
it, the men better let them.

Obliged to you for hearing me, and now old Sojourner ain't got
nothing more to say.

---

1. The phrase *out of kilter* means "out of order" or "mixed up."
2. *'Twixt,* the shortened form of *betwixt,* is an Old English word meaning "between."
3. Here, Truth uses *head* to mean "to do better than" or "to get ahead of."

Responding to Literature

Personal Response

What visual image did you have in your mind as you finished reading this speech? Explain.

ANALYZING LITERATURE

RECALL AND INTERPRET

1. According to Truth, what evidence is there that something is "out of kilter"? What does the first paragraph suggest about Truth's opinion on the issue of inequality?
2. How does she contradict the first two reasons given against woman suffrage? What do her arguments tell you about her character?
3. How does Truth refute the "religious" arguments against woman suffrage? What does this indicate about the importance of religion to Truth? Explain, using details from the selection.
4. How does Truth end her speech? What impression of the speaker does this ending leave you with?

EVALUATE AND CONNECT

5. What **repetition** (see page R13) does Truth use in her first argument? What effect does the repetition have on the effectiveness of the speech?
6. An **allusion** is a reference to a literary work or character. What allusion to the Bible does Truth make in the final paragraph before her closing statement? Evaluate the impact of that allusion on her message.
7. How does Truth introduce the antislavery message into her speech? Do you think this message adds to or detracts from her argument? Explain.
8. Identify the qualities that you think make this speech effective. In your opinion, would those qualities appeal to contemporary audiences? Use details from the speech to support your answer.

Persuasion

In **persuasion,** the writer or speaker attempts to influence other people to think or act in a particular way. Thus, the writer or speaker must have a clear purpose.

A persuasive argument also should take into account the audience and the occasion. To be effective, a persuasive argument also needs clear and logical supporting evidence. One common form of evidence can be the personal experience of the writer. Sojourner Truth uses this technique.

1. Who is Truth trying to persuade? In what way does she want them to change their thinking?
2. Identify examples from personal experience that Truth uses in her persuasive argument.

● See **Literary Terms Handbook,** p. R11.

EXTENDING YOUR RESPONSE

Literature Groups

After the Speech   With your group, discuss a conversation Truth might have had after the speech. Some men in the audience had spoken out against women's rights. Imagine them speaking to Truth after the speech. Discuss what they might have said and how Truth might have responded.

Personal Writing

And Ain't I a . . . ?   Look back at your response to the Focus Activity on page 344. Follow Truth's pattern as you write an argument against the way that you were treated unfairly. Then write your argument in a brief essay. Be sure to add an effective introduction and conclusion.

📖 **Save your work for your portfolio.**

LISTENING, SPEAKING, and VIEWING

Making a Persuasive Speech

As "And Ain't I a Woman?" demonstrates, Sojourner Truth was a persuasive, convincing speaker. Persuasive speaking skills are survival skills. Like Sojourner Truth, you can use persuasive skills when you want someone to think as you do. You might use these skills at school to gain support for a policy or in the community to encourage neighbors to recycle.

How do you become a strong persuasive speaker? Here are some guidelines.

Guidelines for Persuasive Speaking

- Choose a topic about which you feel strongly.
- Gather and present strong reasons and persuasive evidence to support your argument.
- Write out the introduction and conclusion ahead of time. Decide whether the rest of the speech needs to be written or only outlined.
- Practice your speech to be sure it will fit into the time allotted. Also practice gestures and different points of emphasis.
- Know your audience—who they are and what their mood and opinions might be.
- Stay focused as you speak, and your point will be remembered. Avoid using so many anecdotes that your audience loses track of your message.
- Take your time. Do not rush; your audience may miss your point.
- Use techniques to draw your audience to your message. Make eye contact with individuals in the audience. Use gestures for emphasis, but keep them natural.
- Vary your volume, pitch, and rhythm as needed to support your message.
- Believe in yourself and in your message. If you, like Sojourner Truth, are passionate about your message, the rest will fall into place.

ACTIVITY

Plan and deliver a three- to five-minute persuasive speech. For the greatest success, choose a topic that is important to you. Before you give your speech, practice it in front of family or friends. Ask for their honest input. Use suggestions from your test audience to make adjustments to your speech. When you feel confident, present your speech to the class.

Before You Read

from *His Promised Land*

Meet
John P. Parker

"He gloried in danger. . . . He would go boldly over into the enemy's camp and filch the fugitives to freedom."

—*Cincinnati Commercial Tribune*

Born into slavery, John P. Parker was just eight years old when he was chained to an elderly enslaved man who was whipped to death. The experience ignited a rage in Parker that fueled his desire for freedom and later gave him the courage to help other victims of slavery.

Soon after this horrific experience, Parker was chained to a gang of four hundred enslaved persons and marched across the Southeast from Richmond, Virginia, to Mobile, Alabama. There he was sold to a doctor.

"I was trudging along a trail called a road through the mountains of Virginia. It was June. Every flower was in bloom. . . . Everything seemed to be gay except myself. Picking up a stick, I struck each flowering shrub, taking delight in smashing down particularly those in bloom."

Parker would soon strike out against slavery with the same intensity. At fourteen he was sold to a widow who allowed him to work in an iron foundry to earn money to buy his freedom. After four years of labor, Parker paid her $1800 and went north as a free man.

In 1850, Parker and his wife settled in Ripley, Ohio, a town with an active abolitionist community. There he worked in his own foundry during the day, and at night helped people who were escaping from enslavement. During the next fifteen years, he helped hundreds escape to freedom.

John P. Parker was born in 1827 and died in 1900.

FOCUS ACTIVITY

To what lengths would you go to preserve your freedom?

QUICKWRITE Take a few minutes to list some situations that might threaten your freedom. Next to each item write what you might do to overcome that threat.

SETTING A PURPOSE Read to discover how one woman faced great danger to win her freedom.

BACKGROUND

The Time and Place

In 1850 Ripley, Ohio, on the northern bank of the Ohio River, had a solid community of abolitionists, which included Southerners who had moved there because they opposed slavery. Because the Ohio River formed the border between free states and slave states, many fugitives from slavery arrived in Ripley and other towns along the river.

In 1850 Congress passed the Fugitive Slave Act. This act permitted slaveholders to go into free states to capture runaways. Anyone caught aiding a fugitive paid a fine, served six months in prison, and forfeited all property.

VOCABULARY PREVIEW

agitated (aj′ ə tā′ təd) *adj.* disturbed; upset; p. 351
venture (ven′chər) *n.* an undertaking, often involving risk or danger; p. 351
refugee (ref′ū jē′) *n.* a person who flees to safety, especially one who leaves home or a homeland because of persecution, war, or danger; p. 352

from

His Promised Land

John P. Parker

W hile I am on the subject of John Brown,[1] I am reminded of the most important incident that ever took place at Ripley, during all the years of the activities of the abolition group. Strange as it may seem, no one placed any importance to the episode when it occurred, because we did not know what was in the mind of Harriet Beecher Stowe. It was she who took the incident and wove it into the pages of *Uncle Tom's Cabin*, making it one of the most appealing and forceful attacks of this epoch-making book.

I am referring to that incident of Eliza with her babe in arms crossing on the ice, chased by dogs to the water's edge. This all really happened, and it took place at Ripley. I was not involved in this adventure, so I have to depend upon my friends who were and what I actually heard, though I did not know at the time what the trouble was.

I have the story directly from Rev. John Rankin, to whom Eliza told her story within an hour after she had made the crossing, as she sat by his fireside in his hilltop home. Eliza was a young mulatto woman who lived back in Kentucky. She was not married but her baby was ascribed to[2] the overseer of the planta-tion. The day before her flight, a slave dealer had been in close conference with

---

1. *John Brown* was an ardent abolitionist who led a revolt at Harpers Ferry, Virginia, in an attempt to liberate enslaved persons. He was tried and hanged in 1859.
2. *Ascribed to* means "attributed to" or "belonged to."

her master, which meant some of the slaves were being sold down the river, as Kentucky was a slave-breeding and not to any extent a slave-using state. This alarmed her to the point she decided she would run away with her baby, rather than be sent to the cotton fields, which had a bad reputation for treatment of slaves.

Making her plans for escape, she left home early in the morning in midwinter, without any preparations for the journey or knowing how she would get across the river or to whom she was to apply for aid. In other words, she up and left, trusting to the future taking care of itself. How she stood the journey carrying her baby is still a mystery to me.

But she did it with a mother's determination and courage, arriving on the banks of the Ohio after dark, exhausted and driven to desperation by the cold. Seeing a light in a cabin, she took her chances, opened the door, and walked right into the arms of a white man. She was badly scared, but so utterly miserable she did not care what happened to her. Fortunately, the man was a gentleman living alone, and was not a slave owner. Her condition so aroused the sympathy of the man he immediately made a place for her by his fire.

While she was thawing out [he] prepared food for her. While she ate, he accused her of being a runaway, which she freely confessed. Then he told her how helpless her case was; though the river was still frozen over, it had been thawing for several days and the ice was so rotten that no one dared go on, let alone attempt to cross on it.

He further advised her to give herself up and go back home. She admitted she had about made up her mind to follow the . . . [gentleman's] advice when she heard the baying of the dogs, which she knew were on her trail. This made her so afraid she determined to go ahead and take her chances.

When the white man heard the dogs he became greatly agitated, again and again advising . . . Eliza to abandon her plans, which meant sure death. Seeing that she was determined to make the venture, the old fellow gave her a woolen shawl to put around her baby. He then led the way out of his cabin towards the river. On the way he took a long wooden rail off the top of his fence, advising her that when she broke through the ice, the rail would catch on both sides of her, preventing her from being drowned. He then went back to his cabin, leaving her alone.

She had gotten down to the river's edge, stepped on soft ice, and went through. This made her stop and hesitate. As she was standing there trying to make up her mind [what] to do, the men and the dogs came down the bank at her, with such a rush she was forced to hurry on or be captured.

As she ran out on the ice the dogs were at her heels, but refused to go further. Strange as it may seem, the ice held until she disappeared in[to] the darkness. When the men came down the bank they yelled for her to come back and then began firing their pistols over her head. The sound of the bullets drove her on faster and faster until, coming to a weak spot, she went through the soft ice into the river. Throwing her baby from her, she clung fast to the rail, thus was prevented from sinking to the bottom of the river.

Scrambling out as best she could, she felt around in the darkness for her baby. She did not know what way she had thrown [it] in her desperate effort to save herself, [so] it was some

> How she stood the journey carrying her baby is still a mystery to me.

Vocabulary

agitated (aj′ ə tā′ təd) *adj.* disturbed; upset

venture (ven′ chər) *n.* an undertaking, often involving risk or danger

from His Promised Land

time before she found it. All the while the dogs on the bank kept up a fearful noise, while the men were yelling and firing in her direction.

These unnerving things set her more determinedly on her way, until again she broke through the ice, and again she threw the baby from her, while she held on to the rail. Now cold, wet, and weary, she struggled out to find her baby and wearily continued her journey. A third time she broke through and a third time she had to go through the same efforts to secure her baby. This time she was so weak and exhausted, her clothes frozen to her body, she did not have the strength to even pull the rail along with her, so simply left to trust that the ice would hold, or else it would swallow her and her baby up.

The ice did hold until she reached the firm land. As she stepped off the shore ice onto the land, weary and disheartened, a caring hand came from some unknown source out of the dark and grabbed her. She told Rev. Rankin this was the last straw. She sank down on the ground and began to cry, feeling she was lost. Then the baby began to cry and a voice out of the darkness said, "Any woman who crossed that river, carrying her baby, has won her freedom."

It was Chance Shaw, one of the Ohio patrol. Shaw now helped her to her feet [and], threw the wet shawl away, which the old gentleman had given her to protect the baby. Carrying the baby in his arms, he helped Eliza up the bank, guiding her through the streets of the town until he came in sight of the Rankin beacon light, which shone every night in the window. Pointing to the light, he told her if she would follow it she would find friends.

The first any of the Rankin household knew of the presence of Eliza was when Rev. John heard someone poking the fire in the sitting room. The door being always open to <u>refugees</u>, she made her way into the house and was poking the fire to warm her cold body and restore comfort to the baby. Later Rankin supplied dry clothes for mother and baby. While she sat by the fire, she told the story of the escape and crossing to Rev. Rankin . . .

On the subject of Eliza, she [Harriet Beecher Stowe] had this to say: "Last spring while the author was in New York, a Presbyterian clergyman of Ohio came to me and said: 'I understand they dispute that fact about the woman's crossing the river. Now I know all about that; for I got the story from the very man that helped her up the bank. I know it is true, for she is now living in Canada.'"

The Presbyterian minister we now know was Rev. John Rankin, as he was of that denomination. Furthermore, he was the only one that could know that Eliza had traveled to Canada over the Underground Railroad, of which he was an active conductor at that time. Rev. John Rankin did not dare confess his knowledge of Eliza openly; nor could Mrs. Harriet Beecher Stowe associate him with the crossing. If she had, he and his sons would have been sent to jail, their property confiscated. So there was every reason why neither the minister [n]or Mrs. Stowe should openly declare his connection with the affair, nor specify Ripley as the point where the episode took place.

Vocabulary
refugee (ref′ū jē′) *n.* a person who flees to safety, especially one who leaves home or a
homeland because of persecution, war, or danger

Responding to Literature

Personal Response

Which character in this passage did you identify with most strongly? Why?

——— ANALYZING LITERATURE ———

RECALL AND INTERPRET

1. Why does Eliza flee her home? What conclusions can you draw about Eliza from the manner in which she left?
2. Who first helps Eliza? What can you infer about his views on slavery? Use specific examples to support your response.
3. Identify the obstacles that Eliza faces on her journey. In your opinion, if she had known the danger she was about to face, would she have left her home? Explain.
4. According to the narrator, what could have happened to Reverend Rankin if he had confessed to helping Eliza? What does Rankin's silence and the behavior of Eliza's first helper suggest about the risks involved in helping fugitives escape?

EVALUATE AND CONNECT

5. Do you detect any **bias**—a mental inclination toward some opinion or position—in this story? Cite specific lines in this account that point to bias, or explain why you think there might be no bias.
6. In *Uncle Tom's Cabin,* Harriet Beecher Stowe gives a melodramatic, or highly emotional, account of Eliza's flight. Describe the **tone** Parker uses to tell the same story. (See Literary Terms Handbook, page R16.)
7. Refer to your list from the Focus Activity on page 349. Would you ever take risks comparable to those taken by Eliza? Explain.
8. In this account, several persons take risks to attain freedom for a stranger and her baby. What degree of risk might you take to protect a family member, a friend, or a stranger? Explain.

● See **Literary Terms Handbook,** p. R7.

Literary ELEMENTS

Foreshadowing

Foreshadowing is a method of increasing suspense by presenting events or characters in such a way as to hint at what is going to happen. Writers often foreshadow what will occur in a story by giving hints or clues. Sometimes these clues are subtle. Sometimes they are ominous and are used to create an aura of **suspense**. For example, when the dogs refuse to follow Eliza onto the ice, you realize that they sense danger. This detail foreshadows Eliza's first fall through the ice, and prompts the reader to continue reading to learn the outcome of the story.

1. What other examples of foreshadowing can you find in the narrative about Eliza?
2. How does foreshadowing build suspense in the story?

——— EXTENDING YOUR RESPONSE ———

Interdisciplinary Activity

American History: Routes to Freedom With a partner, create a map that shows major routes on the Underground Railroad from the South to the North and into Canada. Indicate the place on the Ohio River where Eliza crossed. Share your work with the class.

Creative Writing

My Name Is Eliza Write this story from Eliza's perspective. Tell about your harrowing river crossing and what kept you going. Explain why you risked your life and that of your baby.

📔 **Save your work for your portfolio.**

Technology Skills

Internet: Writing Resources on the Web

Unless you have a photographic memory, you might find it difficult to recall the countless rules of grammar and mechanics. As you compose, you may ask yourself:

- Do I use commas or semicolons to separate items in a list?
- Is it really wrong to end a sentence with a preposition?
- When do I use a colon?
- How can I tell if this is a sentence fragment?
- Is this a run-on sentence?

The answers to these questions and more are available on the World Wide Web.

Find Your Problems

Look back at papers you have written that were marked and returned to you. Based on your teacher's comments, record the major grammar, usage, and mechanics items that gave you trouble. To supplement your list, or, in the unlikely event that you don't have a single item of your own to list, refer to the following items:

Do you get confused between the words in these pairs?		
accept / except	complement / compliment	it's / its
affect / effect	confident / confidante	lay / lie
allusion / illusion	counsel / council	personal / personnel
a lot / allot	desert / dessert	principal / principle
already / all ready	every day / everyday	stationary / stationery
altogether / all together	farther / further	their / there / they're
beside / besides	fewer / less	whose / who's
capital / capitol	immigrate / emigrate	your / you're
Can you explain the difference between each of the following pairs?		
• an adjective and an adverb		
• a relative pronoun and a demonstrative pronoun		
• a transitive verb and an intransitive verb		
• a compound sentence and a complex sentence		
• a direct object and an indirect object		
Do you always know when and how to use each kind of punctuation?				
period	comma	colon	semicolon	quotation marks
apostrophe	hyphen	dash	italics	parentheses

From the list you compiled, and including at least one item from each group in the boxed lists, write ten questions or problems about grammar, usage, and mechanics you'd like answered. You will then find the answers to your questions.

1. Use a search engine to locate the resources listed below. Write their URLs in your notebook for future reference. A good place to begin your search is at the National Writing Centers Association site: http://departments.colgate.edu/diw/NWCA.html.
   - an on-line writing lab (OWL)
   - a grammar hotline
   - Modern Language Association (MLA) guidelines for citing electronic sources
   - an on-line dictionary
   - an on-line thesaurus

2. On a sheet of paper, or on your word processor, write your ten questions, their answers, and the URLs of the Web sites where you found the information.

ACTIVITIES

1. With a partner or a small group, create a reference handbook of Web sites that offer assistance to writers. Describe the features of each site and rate it using a star system.
   - ★★★★ Super Site
   - ★★★ Good Site
   - ★★ Fair Site
   - ★ Don't Bother

2. Volunteer to help students in a nearby middle school use the Internet to improve their writing skills.

Before You Read

from *Mary Chesnut's Civil War*

Meet
Mary Chesnut

"If the only true history concerns itself not so much with what statesmen and generals *did* at a given time as with what men and women *were*, then this diary is a masterpiece of history in the highest and fullest sense."

—Ben Ames Williams

Mary Boykin Chesnut's life was one of opposites. Before the Civil War, she experienced the kind of luxury that accompanied growing up on a large South Carolina plantation. After the war, she struggled to make ends meet. While she abhorred slavery, her family owned hundreds of enslaved people and her father was a proslavery senator and governor.

At seventeen she married James Chesnut Jr., a lawyer from a large, neighboring plantation. When James was elected to the Senate in 1858, the Chesnuts moved to Washington, where they entertained politicians who would become the leading figures of the Confederacy. When not charming friends with her sharp wit and keen intellect, Chesnut immersed herself in reading, enjoying English and French novels and history books above all.

When the war broke out, Chesnut remained loyal to the South despite her opposition to slavery. She visited hospitals, rejoiced with her friends at Confederate victories, and cried with them over Confederate defeats. Through it all, she lamented the cruelties and evils of war in detailed journals that recorded what people of the time believed, felt, and said. Hers is an insider's view of the real war as it ripped through the South.

Mary Chesnut was born in 1823 and died in 1886.

FOCUS ACTIVITY

Picture yourself and your friends at a time of crisis—perhaps during a flood, an ice storm, a hurricane, an earthquake, or a war.

JOURNAL Choose one of the crisis situations listed above. Visualize yourself in the middle of it. What part might you play? How might other people behave? What might you talk about? Write your ideas in your journal.

SETTING A PURPOSE Read to find out Mary Chesnut's thoughts and observations during a crisis.

BACKGROUND

The Time and Place

By early 1861, South Carolina had seceded from the Union and claimed ownership of all federal property within the state. Only Fort Sumter remained under federal control. Confederate authorities demanded the removal of U.S. troops from Fort Sumter. President Lincoln refused their request, and on April 12, 1861, Confederate forces opened fire on the fort.

VOCABULARY PREVIEW

allusion (ə loo′ zhən) *n.* an indirect or casual reference; an incidental mention; p. 358

capitulate (kə pich′ ə lāt′) *v.* to surrender or yield; to give up; p. 358

audaciously (ô dā′ shəs lē) *adv.* boldly; arrogantly; p. 358

prostrate (pros′ strāt) *adj.* bowing or kneeling down in humility, adoration, or submission; p. 359

delusion (di loo′ zhen) *n.* a false impression or belief; p. 359

pervade (pər vād′) *v.* to spread through every part; p. 360

from
MARY CHESNUT'S
CIVIL WAR

Mary Chesnut

APRIL 7, 1861. . . . Today things seem to have settled down a little. One can but hope still. Lincoln or Seward[1] have made such silly advances and then far sillier drawings back. There may be a chance for peace, after all.

Things are happening so fast.

My husband has been made an aide-de-camp[2] of General Beauregard.[3] Three hours ago we were quietly packing to go home. The convention has adjourned.

Now he tells me the attack upon Fort Sumter may begin tonight. Depends upon Anderson and the fleet outside. The *Herald* says that this show of war outside of the bar[4] is intended for Texas.[5]

John Manning came in with his sword and red sash. Pleased as a boy to be on Beauregard's staff while the row goes on. He has gone with Wigfall to Captain Hartstene with instructions.

1. William Henry *Seward* was U.S. Secretary of State from 1861 to 1869.
2. An officer who serves as an assistant to a superior officer is an *aide-de-camp.*
3. *General Beauregard* commanded the Confederate forces surrounding Fort Sumter.

4. *Bar* refers to a sand bar.
5. *Texas,* a pro-slavery state, had recently voted to secede from the Union.

from MARY CHESNUT'S CIVIL WAR

Mr. Chesnut[6] is finishing a report he had to make to the convention.

Mrs. Hayne called. She had, she said, "but one feeling, pity for those who are not here."

Jack Preston, Willie Alston—"the take-life-easys," as they are called—with John Green, "the big brave," have gone down to the island—volunteered as privates.

Seven hundred men were sent over. Ammunition wagons rumbling along the streets all night. Anderson burning blue lights—signs and signals for the fleet outside, I suppose.

Today at dinner there was no allusion to things as they stand in Charleston Harbor. There was an undercurrent of intense excitement. There could not have been a more brilliant circle. In addition to our usual quartet (Judge Withers, Langdon Cheves, and Trescot) our two governors dined with us, Means and Manning.

These men all talked so delightfully. For once in my life I listened.

That over, business began. In earnest, Governor Means rummaged a sword and red sash from somewhere and brought it for Colonel Chesnut, who has gone to demand the surrender of Fort Sumter.

— ★ —

And now, patience—we must wait.

— ★ —

Why did that green goose Anderson go into Fort Sumter? Then everything began to go wrong.

Now they have intercepted a letter from him, urging them to let him surrender. He paints the horrors likely to ensue if they will not.

He ought to have thought of all that before he put his head in the hole.

APRIL 12, 1861.   Anderson will not capitulate.

— ★ —

Yesterday was the merriest, maddest dinner we have had yet. Men were more audaciously wise and witty. We had an unspoken foreboding it was to be our last pleasant meeting. Mr. Miles dined with us today. Mrs. Henry King rushed in: "The news, I come for the latest news—all of the men of the King family are on the island"—of which fact she seemed proud.

While she was here, our peace negotiator—or envoy—came in. That is, Mr. Chesnut returned—his interview with Colonel Anderson had been deeply interesting—but was not inclined to be communicative, wanted his dinner. Felt for Anderson. Had telegraphed to President Davis for instructions.

What answer to give Anderson, &c&c.[7] He has gone back to Fort Sumter, with additional instructions.

When they were about to leave the wharf, A. H. Boykin sprang into the boat, in great excitement; thought himself ill-used. A likelihood of fighting—and he to be left behind!

— ★ —

I do not pretend to go to sleep. How can I? If Anderson does not accept terms—at four—the orders are—he shall be fired upon.

---

6. *Mr. Chesnut* (also called Colonel Chesnut) refers to Mary's husband James, who served as the liaison between Confederate President Jefferson Davis and Colonel Anderson.

7. *&c&c* means "et cetera" or "and others."

Vocabulary
allusion (ə lōō′zhən) *n.* an indirect or casual reference; an incidental mention
capitulate (kə pich′ə lāt′) *v.* to surrender or yield; to give up
audaciously (ô dā′shəs lē) *adv.* boldly; arrogantly

I count four—St. Michael chimes. I begin to hope. At half-past four, the heavy booming of a cannon.

I sprang out of bed. And on my knees—prostrate—I prayed as I never prayed before.

There was a sound of stir all over the house—pattering of feet in the corridor—all seemed hurrying one way. I put on my double gown and a shawl and went, too. It was to the housetop.

The shells were bursting. In the dark I heard a man say "waste of ammunition."

I knew my husband was rowing about in a boat somewhere in that dark bay. And that the shells were roofing it over—bursting toward the fort. If Anderson was obstinate—he was to order the forts on our side to open fire. Certainly fire had begun. The regular roar of the cannon—there it was. And who could tell what each volley accomplished of death and destruction.

The women were wild, there on the housetop. Prayers from the women and imprecations[8] from the men, and then a shell would light up the scene. Tonight, they say, the forces are to attempt to land.

The *Harriet Lane*[9] had her wheelhouse smashed and put back to sea.

Did You Know?
The *wheelhouse* is the enclosed area on the deck of a ship that shelters the steering equipment and the pilot.

We watched up there—everybody wondered. Fort Sumter did not fire a shot.

Today Miles and Manning, colonels now—aides to Beauregard—dined with us. The latter hoped I would keep the peace. I give him only good words, for he was to be under fire all day and night, in the bay carrying orders, &c.

Last night—or this morning truly—up on the housetop I was so weak and weary I sat down on something that looked like a black stool.

"Get up, you foolish woman—your dress is on fire," cried a man. And he put me out. It was a chimney, and the sparks caught my clothes. Susan Preston and Mr. Venable then came up. But my fire had been extinguished before it broke out into a regular blaze.

Do you know, after all that noise and our tears and prayers, nobody has been hurt. Sound and fury, signifying nothing.[10] A delusion and a snare. . . .

Somebody came in just now and reported Colonel Chesnut asleep on the sofa in General Beauregard's room. After two such nights he must be so tired as to be able to sleep anywhere. . . .

APRIL 13, 1861. Nobody hurt, after all. How gay we were last night.

Reaction after the dread of all the slaughter we thought those dreadful cannons were making such a noise in doing.

Not even a battery[11] the worse for wear.

---

8. *Imprecations* are curses.
9. The *Harriet Lane* was a federal ship that brought provisions to the troops at Fort Sumter.
10. *"Sound and fury, signifying nothing"* is taken from *Macbeth* (act 5, scene 5, lines 27–28), a play by William Shakespeare. Macbeth questions the meaning of life after learning that his wife has died.
11. A *battery* is an artillery unit.

Vocabulary
prostrate (pros′trāt) *adj.* bowing or kneeling down in humility, adoration, or submission
delusion (di lōō′zhen) *n.* a false impression or belief

Fort Sumter has been on fire. He has not yet silenced any of our guns. So the aides—still with swords and red sashes by way of uniform—tell us.

But the sound of those guns makes regular meals impossible. None of us go to table. But tea trays <u>pervade</u> the corridors, going everywhere.

Some of the anxious hearts lie on their beds and moan in solitary misery. Mrs. Wigfall and I solace ourselves with tea in my room.

These women have all a satisfying faith. . . .

APRIL 15, 1861.   I did not know that one could live such days of excitement.

They called, "Come out—there is a crowd coming."

A mob indeed, but it was headed by Colonels Chesnut and Manning.

The crowd was shouting and showing these two as messengers of good news. They were escorted to Beauregard's headquarters. Fort Sumter had surrendered.

Those up on the housetop shouted to us, "The fort is on fire." That had been the story once or twice before.

— ★ —

When we had calmed down, Colonel Chesnut, who had taken it all quietly enough—if anything, more unruffled than usual in his serenity—told us how the surrender came about.

Wigfall was with them on Morris Island when he saw the fire in the fort, jumped in a little boat and, with his handkerchief as a white flag, rowed over to Fort Sumter. Wigfall went in through a porthole.

When Colonel Chesnut arrived shortly after and was received by the regular entrance, Colonel Anderson told him he had need to pick his way warily, for it was all mined.

As far as I can make out, the fort surrendered to Wigfall.

But it is all confusion. Our flag is flying there. Fire engines have been sent to put out the fire.

Everybody tells you half of something and then rushes off to tell something else or to hear the last news. . . .

Equipment 61. William Ludwell Sheppard (1833–1912). Watercolor on paper, 11 x 8 in. The Museum of the Confederacy, Richmond, VA.

Viewing the painting: What attitude does the soldier in this painting seem to have about preparing for war? How might his attitude compare with those of the soldiers Mary Chesnut describes?

Vocabulary
pervade (pər vād′) *v.* to spread through every part

Responding to Literature

Personal Response

What insights about the Civil War did these journal entries give you?

─────── **ANALYZING LITERATURE** ───────

RECALL AND INTERPRET

1. What activities in Chesnut's entry for April 7 suggest that war is about to begin? In your opinion, what attitude does Chesnut express toward these activities?
2. What momentous event occurs on April 12? What hopes and fears does Chesnut convey in the entry for that date?
3. What bit of good news does Chesnut report in her entry for April 13? What does the entry reveal about Chesnut's attitude toward war?
4. What historical event occurred on April 15? What does the entry for this date convey about being caught up in war?

EVALUATE AND CONNECT

5. Describe the **tone,** the writer's feelings about her topic and characters, in the first journal entry. Is it what you might expect under the circumstances described? Why or why not?
6. Look back at the journal entry you wrote for the Focus Activity on page 356. How do Chesnut's reactions on April 7 compare with the imagined thoughts and reactions you wrote in your journal?
7. Is Mary Chesnut someone you would like to know? Explain.
8. Theme Connections   Chesnut writes, "There may be a chance for peace, after all." Based on your reading here, do you think the events that took place at Fort Sumter could have been avoided? Explain.

Literary ELEMENTS

Journal

A **journal** is a day-to-day account that a person writes of his or her life. The journal writer includes whatever he or she chooses, such as thoughts, observations, and personal feelings. Most writers don't plan to publish their journals, though some write with an audience in mind. The special quality of a journal like Mary Chesnut's is that it transports the reader into the daily life of the writer's time. Chesnut captures the flavor of Southern society and the impact of the war on Southerners.

1. How is Chesnut's journal different from a history or memoir that a politician or general of the time might have written? Explain.
2. What do you think is unique about Chesnut's style of writing? Consider line length, tone, and description.

● See **Literary Terms Handbook,** p. R9.

─────── **EXTENDING YOUR RESPONSE** ───────

Literature Groups

Understanding the Past   What can Chesnut's journal entries teach you about the past? What are their strengths and limitations? Discuss these questions in your group, using details from the selection to support your opinions. Then, as a group, summarize the opinions expressed and report to the class.

Creative Writing

Fort Sumter Drama   Write a one-act play based on Mary Chesnut's journals. Determine which characters you will include and write their **dialogue.** Remember to include **stage directions** (see pages R4 and R15) and a description or sketch of the set for this particular scene.

💼 **Save your work for your portfolio.**

Before You Read

Letters to His Family

Meet Robert E. Lee

❝There was not a man in the Confederacy whose influence with the whole people was as great as his.❞

—*Ulysses S. Grant*

Robert E. Lee was born into the famous Lee family of Virginia, who, according to President John Adams, had "more men of merit in it than any other family." Lee's ancestors included two signers of the Declaration of Independence. His father was both a Revolutionary War hero and a governor of Virginia.

Despite his prestigious background, Lee experienced much hardship. His father squandered the family fortune and died when Lee was young, leaving him to help support the household. Many believe that these early difficulties motivated Lee to excel at whatever he did.

As a student at the United States Military Academy at West Point, Lee received many honors, including a commission to the elite Army Corps of Engineers. During the Mexican War (1846–1848), Lee rose to the rank of captain and was described by a general as "the very best soldier I ever saw in the field."

In 1861 Lee faced an agonizing decision. President Lincoln asked him to head the Union forces in the Civil War. Opposed to secession but unwilling to fight against his family and state, Lee declined and resigned his position in the United States Army. He then accepted the command of Virginia's armed forces as commander in chief. Mary Custis Lee wrote to a friend, "My husband has wept tears of blood over this terrible war, but as a man of honor and a Virginian, he must follow the destiny of his state."

Robert E. Lee was born in 1807 and died in 1870.

FOCUS ACTIVITY

Think of a time when you felt torn by conflicting loyalties–perhaps to two friends, to a friend and a family member, or to school and a job.

JOURNAL In your journal, describe your feelings about being caught in the middle. How did you resolve the situation?

SETTING A PURPOSE Read to find out Lee's reaction to having to choose between conflicting loyalties.

BACKGROUND

The Time and Place
Robert E. Lee wrote a number of letters to his family as the Southern states were seceding from the Union. Lee's home state of Virginia, however, did not secede until several months after the following excerpts were written–when the Civil War broke out in April of 1861.

VOCABULARY PREVIEW

perusal (pə rōo′ zəl) *n.* the process of examining carefully; p. 363
virtuous (vur′ chōo əs) *adj.* righteous; good; p. 363
anarchy (an′ ər kē) *n.* the absence of government; p. 363
array (ə rā′) *v.* to place in proper or methodical order; p. 364

redress (rē′ dres′) *n.* compensation, as for wrong done; p. 364
contend (kən tend′) *v.* to argue; to dispute; p. 364
prosperity (pros per′ə tē) *n.* success; wealth; good fortune; p. 364

Letters to His Family

Robert E. Lee ～

Confederate volunteers from the First Virginia Militia, 1861.

I received Everett's[1] *Life of Washington* which you sent me, and enjoyed its perusal. How his spirit would be grieved could he see the wreck of his mighty labors! I will not, however, permit myself to believe, until all ground of hope is gone, that the fruit of his noble deeds will be destroyed, and that his precious advice and virtuous example will so soon be forgotten by his countrymen. As far as I can judge by the papers, we are between a state of anarchy and civil war. May God avert[2] both of these evils from us! I fear that mankind will not for years be sufficiently Christianized to bear the absence of restraint and force. I see that four states[3] have declared themselves out of the Union; four more will apparently follow their example.

---

1. Edward *Everett* was a noted American politician and orator.
2. Here, *avert* means "to ward off."
3. The first *four states* to secede from the Union were South Carolina, Mississippi, Florida, and Alabama. With Georgia, Louisiana, Texas, Virginia, Arkansas, Tennessee, and North Carolina, these states would make up the Confederate States of America.

Vocabulary
perusal (pə rōō′ zəl) *n.* the process of examining carefully
virtuous (vur′ chōō əs) *adj.* righteous; good
anarchy (an′ ər kē) *n.* the absence of government

Letters to His Family

Then, if the border states are brought into the gulf of revolution, one half of the country will be <u>arrayed</u> against the other. I must try and be patient and await the end, for I can do nothing to hasten or retard it.

The South, in my opinion, has been aggrieved by the acts of the North, as you say. I feel the aggression and am willing to take every proper step for <u>redress</u>. It is the principle I <u>contend</u> for, not individual or private benefit. As an American citizen, I take great pride in my country, her <u>prosperity</u> and institutions, and would defend any state if her rights were invaded. But I can anticipate no greater calamity for the country than a dissolution of the Union. It would be an accumulation of all the evils we complain of, and I am willing to sacrifice everything but honor for its preservation. I hope, therefore, that all constitutional means will be exhausted before there is a resort to force. Secession is nothing but revolution. The framers of our Constitution never exhausted so much labor, wisdom, and forbearance in its formation, and surrounded it with so many guards and securities, if it was intended to be broken by every member of the Confederacy at will. It was intended for "perpetual union," so expressed in the preamble, and for the establishment of a government, not a compact, which can only be dissolved by revolution or the consent of all the people in convention assembled. It is idle to talk of secession. Anarchy would have been established, and not a government, by Washington, Hamilton, Jefferson, Madison, and the other patriots of the Revolution. . . . Still, a Union that can only be maintained by swords and bayonets,[4] and in which strife and civil war are to take the place of brotherly love and kindness, has no charm for me. I shall mourn for my country and for the welfare and progress of mankind. If the Union is dissolved, and the government disrupted, I shall return to my native state and share the miseries of my people; and, save in defense, will draw my sword on none.

State Seal of Virginia, Civil War era.

---

4. A *bayonet* is a large knife or dagger that can be attached to the muzzle of a rifle.

Vocabulary

array (ə rā′) *v.* to place in proper or methodical order
redress (rē′ dres′) *n.* compensation, as for wrong done
contend (kən tend′) *v.* to argue; to dispute
prosperity (pros per′ə tē) *n.* success; wealth; good fortune

Responding to Literature

Personal Response

What questions would you like to ask Robert E. Lee?

——— ANALYZING LITERATURE ———

RECALL AND INTERPRET

1. How does Lee describe George Washington? What do you learn about Lee's character from his description of Washington?

2. What two calamities does Lee say the country is between? What do you think Lee means when he says, "I fear that mankind will not for years be sufficiently Christianized to bear the absence of restraint and force"?

3. What opinions about secession does Lee express? How does he support these opinions? What can you infer from this about Lee's attitude toward his country?

4. What decision does Lee announce at the end of the selection? What does this final sentence reveal about Lee's character?

EVALUATE AND CONNECT

5. What is the **thesis** of Lee's letter? Do you think he supports it well? Explain, using details from the selection. (See page R16.)

6. If you were related to Lee, how might you react to receiving one of these letters?

7. Theme Connections   Summarize Lee's message about how the Union was being tested. In your opinion, how is the United States being tested today? Give specific examples.

8. What is your opinion of Lee? Based on what you know of his character, how do you think Lee might react to events taking place today? Explain.

Literary ELEMENTS

Diction

Diction is a writer's choice of words. It involves the use of exactly the right word or words to convey the desired **tone** and meaning. The diction of nineteenth-century writers may seem formal to us. For example, Lee wrote, "But I can anticipate no greater calamity for the country than a dissolution of the Union." His diction appears stilted, especially because it is excerpted from personal letters.

   As you read, keep in mind that diction changes with time.

1. Rewrite the last sentence in the letter as it might be written today.

2. Choose one other sentence, and "translate" it into contemporary informal diction.

● See **Literary Terms Handbook**, p. R5.

——— EXTENDING YOUR RESPONSE ———

Personal Writing

Taking Sides   Use your journal notes from the Focus Activity on page 362 to write a letter to a friend explaining how you resolved the conflict you wrote about. Did you have a discussion or an argument with the people involved? Were you forced to choose one person over another?

Performing

I, Robert E. Lee . . .   Based on what you have learned about Lee, enact a **dramatic monologue** (see page R5) in which you, as Robert E. Lee, volunteer to serve the Confederate Army. Include the reasons for your offer.

💼 **Save your work for your portfolio.**

Grammar Link

Making Subjects and Verbs Agree

In both speaking and writing, a verb must match its subject in number. Always use a singular verb with a singular noun and a plural verb with a plural noun.

Problem 1 A subject that is separated from the verb by a prepositional phrase (A subject is never the object of a preposition.)
Lee's letters to his family <u>shows</u> his great respect for the Union.

> Solution   Make the verb agree with the subject.
> *Lee's letters to his family <u>show</u> his great respect for the Union.*

Problem 2 A predicate nominative that differs in number from the subject (A **predicate nominative** is a noun or pronoun that follows a linking verb and points back to the subject to identify it further.)
Aggressive acts <u>was</u> the issue with Lee.

> Solution   Ignore the predicate nominative. Make the verb agree with the subject.
> *Aggressive acts <u>were</u> the issue with Lee.*

Problem 3 In an inverted sentence, a subject that follows the verb
With these acts <u>fall</u> the last hope for the survival of the Union.

> Solution   Look for the subject *after* the verb. Then make sure the verb agrees with the subject.
> *With these acts <u>falls</u> the last hope for the survival of the Union.*

Problem 4 A collective noun as the subject
The assembly <u>rise</u> and <u>cheer</u> the speaker.
The committee <u>signs</u> their names to the report.

> Solution A   If the collective noun refers to a group as a whole, use a singular verb.
> *The assembly <u>rises</u> and <u>cheers</u> the speaker.*

> Solution B   If the collective noun refers to each member of a group individually, use a plural verb.
> *The committee <u>sign</u> their names to the report.*

● For more on subject-verb agreement, see **Language Handbook,** p. R21.

EXERCISES

1. Rewrite these sentences, correcting any errors in subject-verb agreement.
   a. There exists several reasons for his reluctance to go to war.
   b. The threats of secession bothers him greatly.
   c. The Confederacy need a leader of Lee's abilities.
   d. Lee feared that secession were a calamity and an accumulation of evils.
2. Reread a recent journal entry. Correct errors in subject-verb agreement.

Before You Read

An Occurrence at Owl Creek Bridge

Meet Ambrose Bierce

> "Insurrection, An unsuccessful revolution. Disaffection's failure to substitute misrule for bad government."
>
> —*Bierce*

In 1913, writer Ambrose Bierce traveled to Mexico to report on the revolution there. On December 26, he sent a letter to his daughter. Soon after sending that letter, he disappeared. The mysterious circumstances of his disappearance could have been a story from his own writings.

The tenth of thirteen children, Bierce had a difficult childhood on an Indiana farm. Extreme poverty robbed him of a formal education and led him to work as a printer's apprentice, a waiter, a clerk, and a farmhand. When the Civil War broke out, Bierce was among the first to enlist in the Union Army. He fought valiantly and eventually was promoted to the rank of first lieutenant.

After the war, Bierce launched a successful career as a journalist in San Francisco. He wrote scathing articles attacking politicians, writers, and others he suspected of wrongdoing or bad taste. These pieces earned him many enemies and the nickname "Bitter Bierce."

Bierce also became famous for his short stories about the Civil War and the supernatural. Often compared to Edgar Allan Poe, Bierce wrote with dark humor and psychological insight about bizarre characters and events.

Ambrose Bierce was born in 1842 and disappeared in 1914.

FOCUS ACTIVITY

Imagine facing a life-or-death situation involving, for example, an automobile accident or a natural disaster. What thoughts might flash through your mind?

FREEWRITE Spend a few minutes freewriting to explore your response to this question.

SETTING A PURPOSE Read to learn one character's response to a life-or-death situation.

BACKGROUND

The Time and Place

Bierce served with distinction in battles at Chickamauga, Georgia, and at Shiloh and Kennesaw Mountain in Tennessee, where he suffered a serious head wound. Profoundly influenced by these experiences, Bierce explored the theme of war in his writings up until his disappearance. "An Occurrence at Owl Creek Bridge" is a fictionalized account of an event that took place in 1862 at the Battle of Shiloh.

VOCABULARY PREVIEW

protrude (prō trōōd') v. to stick out; to project; p. 369

adorn (ə dôrn') v. to make beautiful; to decorate; p. 369

deference (def'ər əns) n. courteous respect or regard; p. 369

ardently (ärd'ent lē) adv. passionately; enthusiastically; p. 371

imperious (im pēr' ē əs) adj. imperative; urgent; p. 371

assent (ə sent') v. to express agreement; p. 371

poignant (poin' yənt) adj. sharp; severe; causing emotional or physical anguish; p. 372

efface (i fās') v. to destroy; to erase; p. 373

The Red Bridge, 1896. Julian Alden Weir. Oil on canvas, 24¼ x 33¾ in. The Metropolitan Museum of Art, New York.

An Occurrence at Owl Creek Bridge

Ambrose Bierce

I

A man stood upon a railroad bridge in northern Alabama, looking down into the swift water twenty feet below. The man's hands were behind his back, the wrists bound with a cord. A rope closely encircled his neck. It was attached to a stout cross-timber above his head

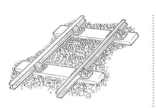

Did You Know?
Sleepers are the horizontal ties that support railroad rails.

and the slack fell to the level of his knees. Some loose boards laid upon the sleepers supporting the metals of the railway supplied a footing for him and his executioners— two private soldiers of the Federal army, directed by a sergeant who in civil life may have been a deputy sheriff. At a short remove upon the same temporary platform was an officer in the uniform of his rank, armed. He was a captain. A sentinel[1] at each end of the bridge stood with his rifle in the position known as "support," that is to say, vertical in front of the left shoulder, the hammer[2] resting on the forearm thrown straight across the chest—a formal and unnatural position, enforcing an erect carriage of the body. It did not appear to be the duty of these two men to know what was occurring at the center of the bridge; they merely blockaded the two ends of the foot planking that traversed it.

Beyond one of the sentinels nobody was in sight; the railroad ran straight away into a forest for a hundred yards, then, curving, was lost to view. Doubtless there was an outpost farther along. The other bank of the stream was open ground—a gentle acclivity[3] topped with a stockade of vertical tree trunks, loop-holed for rifles, with a single embrasure through which protruded the muzzle of a brass cannon commanding the bridge. Midway of the slope between bridge and fort were the

Did You Know?
An *embrasure* (em brā′ zhər) is an opening in a wall or parapet through which a gun can be fired.

spectators—a single company of infantry in line, at "parade rest," the butts of the rifles on the ground, the barrels inclining slightly backward against the right shoulder, the hands crossed upon the stock. A lieutenant stood at the right of the line, the point of his sword upon the ground, his left hand resting upon his right. Excepting the group of four at the center of the bridge, not a man moved. The company faced the bridge, staring stonily, motionless. The sentinels, facing the banks of the stream, might have been statues to adorn the bridge. The captain stood with folded arms, silent, observing the work of his subordinates, but making no sign. Death is a dignitary who when he comes announced is to be received with formal manifestations of respect, even by those most familiar with him. In the code of military etiquette silence and fixity[4] are forms of deference.

---

1. A *sentinel* is a soldier who guards a point of passage.
2. A *hammer* is the part of a gun that helps to ignite the cartridge.

---

3. An *acclivity* is an upward slope.
4. *Fixity* refers to a steady and unmoving stance.

Vocabulary
protrude (prō trōōd′) *v.* to stick out; to project
adorn (ə dôrn′) *v.* to make beautiful; to decorate
deference (def′ ər əns) *n.* courteous respect or regard

An Occurrence at Owl Creek Bridge

The man who was engaged in being hanged was apparently about thirty-five years of age. He was a civilian, if one might judge from his habit,[5] which was that of a planter. His features were good— a straight nose, firm mouth, broad forehead, from which his long, dark hair was combed straight back, falling behind his ears to the collar of his well-fitting frock-coat. He wore a mustache and pointed beard, but no whiskers; his eyes were large and dark gray, and had a kindly expression which one would hardly have expected in one whose neck was in the hemp. Evidently this was no vulgar assassin. The liberal military code makes provision for hanging many kinds of persons, and gentlemen are not excluded.

Did You Know?
A *frock-coat* is a man's coat that reaches to the knees. Popular in the nineteenth century, it is usually double-breasted and fitted at the waist.

The preparations being complete, the two private soldiers stepped aside and each drew away the plank upon which he had been standing. The sergeant turned to the captain, saluted and placed himself immediately behind that officer, who in turn moved apart one pace. These movements left the condemned man and the sergeant standing on the two ends of the same plank, which spanned three of the cross-ties[6] of the bridge. The end upon which the civilian stood almost, but not quite, reached a fourth. This plank had been held in place by the weight of the captain; it was now held by that of the sergeant. At a signal from the former the latter would step aside, the plank would tilt and the condemned man go down between two ties. The arrangement commended itself to his judgment as simple and effective. His face had not been covered nor his eyes bandaged. He looked a moment at his "unsteadfast footing," then let his gaze wander to the swirling water of the stream racing madly beneath his feet. A piece of dancing driftwood caught his attention and his eyes followed it down the current. How slowly it appeared to move! What a sluggish stream!

He closed his eyes in order to fix his last thoughts upon his wife and children. The water, touched to gold by the early sun, the brooding mists under the banks at some distance down the stream, the fort, the soldiers, the piece of drift—all had distracted him. And now he became conscious of a new disturbance. Striking through the thought of his dear ones was a sound which he could neither ignore nor understand, a sharp, distinct, metallic percussion like the stroke of a blacksmith's hammer upon the anvil; it had the same ringing quality. He wondered what it was, and whether immeasurably distant or near by—it seemed both. Its recurrence was regular, but as slow as the tolling of a death knell.[7] He awaited each stroke with impatience and—he knew not why—apprehension. The intervals of silence grew progressively longer; the delays became maddening. With their greater infrequency the sounds increased in strength and sharpness. They hurt his ear like the thrust of a knife; he feared he would shriek. What he heard was the ticking of his watch.

He unclosed his eyes and saw again the water below him. "If I could free my hands," he thought, "I might throw off the noose and spring into the stream. By diving I could evade the bullets and, swimming vigorously, reach the bank, take to the woods and get away

---

5. *Habit* refers to a distinctive manner of dressing or type of clothing.
6. *Cross-ties* are the wooden pieces to which railroad rails are secured.

7. A *knell* is the solemn sound of a bell ringing.

home. My home, thank God, is as yet outside their lines; my wife and little ones are still beyond the invader's farthest advance."

As these thoughts, which have here to be set down in words, were flashed into the doomed man's brain rather than evolved from it the captain nodded to the sergeant. The sergeant stepped aside.

II

Peyton Farquhar was a well-to-do planter, of an old and highly respected Alabama family. Being a slave owner and like other slave owners a politician he was naturally an original secessionist[8] and <u>ardently</u> devoted to the Southern cause. Circumstances of an <u>imperious</u> nature, which it is unnecessary to relate here, had prevented him from taking service with the gallant army that had fought the disastrous campaigns ending with the fall of Corinth, and he chafed[9] under the inglorious restraint, longing for the release of his energies, the larger life of the soldier, the opportunity for distinction. That opportunity, he felt, would come, as it comes to all in war time. Meanwhile he did what he could. No service was too humble for him to perform in aid of the South, no adventure too perilous for him to undertake if consistent with the character of a civilian who was at heart a soldier, and who in good faith and without too much qualification <u>assented</u> to at least a part of the frankly villainous dictum[10] that all is fair in love and war.

One evening while Farquhar and his wife were sitting on a rustic bench near the entrance to his grounds, a gray-clad[11] soldier rode up to the gate and asked for a drink of water. Mrs. Farquhar was only too happy to serve him with her own white hands.[12] While she was fetching the water her husband approached the dusty horseman and inquired eagerly for news from the front.

"The Yanks are repairing the railroads," said the man, "and are getting ready for another advance. They have reached the Owl Creek bridge, put it in order and built a stockade[13] on the north bank. The commandant has issued an order, which is posted everywhere, declaring that any civilian caught interfering with the railroad, its bridges, tunnels or trains will be summarily[14] hanged. I saw the order."

"How far is it to the Owl Creek bridge?" Farquhar asked.

"About thirty miles."

"Is there no force on this side the creek?"

"Only a picket post[15] half a mile out, on the railroad, and a single sentinel at this end of the bridge."

"Suppose a man—a civilian and student of hanging—should elude the picket post and perhaps get the better of the sentinel," said Farquhar, smiling, "what could he accomplish?"

The soldier reflected. "I was there a month ago," he replied. "I observed that the flood of last winter had lodged a great quantity of driftwood against the wooden pier at

---

8. A *secessionist* was one in favor of breaking away from the Union.
9. *Chafe* means "to fret; to feel irritation."
10. A *dictum* is a formal, authoritative pronouncement.

11. Confederate soldiers wore *gray* uniforms.
12. [*Mrs. Farquhar . . . hands*] Ordinarily, a servant or slave would have served the guest. In this case, Mrs. Farquhar brought the soldier a drink of water.
13. A *stockade* is an enclosure made of posts in which prisoners may be kept.
14. *Summarily* means "without delay; arbitrarily."
15. A *picket post* is a group of soldiers sent ahead to watch for and to warn of a surprise attack.

Vocabulary
ardently (ärd' ent lē) *adv.* passionately; enthusiastically
imperious (im pēr' ē əs) *adj.* imperative; urgent
assent (ə sent') *v.* to express agreement

An Occurrence at Owl Creek Bridge

this end of the bridge. It is now dry and would burn like tow."[16]

The lady had now brought the water, which the soldier drank. He thanked her ceremoniously, bowed to her husband and rode away. An hour later, after nightfall, he repassed the plantation, going northward in the direction from which he had come. He was a Federal scout.[17]

---

16. *Tow* (tō) is the coarse fibers of flax or hemp used to make yarn and twine.
17. Here, a *Federal scout* is a Union spy.

III

As Peyton Farquhar fell straight downward through the bridge he lost consciousness and was as one already dead. From this state he was awakened—ages later, it seemed to him—by the pain of a sharp pressure upon his throat, followed by a sense of suffocation. Keen, <u>poignant</u> agonies seemed to shoot from his neck downward through every fiber of his body and limbs. These pains appeared to flash along well-defined lines of ramification[18] and to beat

---

18. Here, *ramification* means "the act of branching out."

Vocabulary
poignant (poin′ yənt) *adj.* sharp; severe; causing emotional or physical anguish

Sugar Bridge Over Coulee, 1973. George Rodrigue. Oil on canvas, 48 x 75 in. Private collection.

Viewing the painting: Does this painting look as if it could depict a scene from "An Occurrence at Owl Creek Bridge"? Explain.

with an inconceivably rapid periodicity.[19] They seemed like streams of pulsating fire heating him to an intolerable temperature. As to his head, he was conscious of nothing but a feeling of fullness—of congestion. These sensations were unaccompanied by thought. The intellectual part of his nature was already effaced; he had power only to feel, and feeling was torment. He was conscious of motion. Encompassed in a luminous cloud, of which he was now merely the fiery heart, without material substance, he swung through unthinkable arcs of oscillation,[20] like a vast pendulum. Then all at once, with terrible suddenness, the light about him shot upward with the noise of a loud plash;[21] a frightful roaring was in his ears, and all was cold and dark. The power of thought was restored; he knew that the rope had broken and he had fallen into the stream. There was no additional strangulation; the noose about his neck was already suffocating him and kept the water from his lungs. To die of hanging at the bottom of a river!—the idea seemed to him ludicrous. He opened his eyes in the darkness and saw above him a gleam of light, but how distant, how inaccessible! He was still sinking, for the light became fainter and fainter until it was a mere glimmer. Then it began to grow and brighten, and he knew that he was rising toward the surface—knew it with reluctance, for he was now very comfortable. "To be hanged and drowned," he thought, "that is not so bad; but I do not wish to be shot. No; I will not be shot; that is not fair."

He was not conscious of an effort, but a sharp pain in his wrist apprised him that he was trying to free his hands. He gave the struggle his attention, as an idler[22] might observe the feat of a juggler, without interest in the outcome. What splendid effort!—what magnificent, what superhuman strength! Ah, that was a fine endeavor! Bravo! The cord fell away; his arms parted and floated upward, the hands dimly seen on each side in the growing light. He watched them with a new interest as first one and then the other pounced upon the noose at his neck. They tore it away and thrust it fiercely aside, its undulations[23] resembling those of a water-snake. "Put it back, put it back!" He thought he shouted these words to his hands, for the undoing of the noose had been succeeded by the direst pang that he had yet experienced. His neck ached horribly; his brain was on fire; his heart, which had been fluttering faintly, gave a great leap, trying to force itself out at his mouth. His whole body was racked and wrenched with an insupportable anguish! But his disobedient hands gave no heed to the command. They beat the water vigorously with quick, downward strokes, forcing him to the surface. He felt his head emerge; his eyes were blinded by the sunlight; his chest expanded convulsively, and with a supreme and crowning agony his lungs engulfed a great draft of air, which instantly he expelled in a shriek!

He was now in full possession of his physical senses. They were, indeed, preternaturally[24] keen and alert. Something in the awful disturbance of his organic system had so exalted and refined them that they made record of things never before perceived. He felt the ripples upon his face and heard their separate sounds as they struck. He looked at the forest on the bank of the stream, saw the individual trees, the leaves and the veining of each leaf—saw the very insects upon them: the locusts, the

---

19. *Periodicity* means "recurrence at regular intervals."
20. *Oscillation* is swinging back and forth with regular rhythm.
21. *Plash* is a splash or the sound of a splash.
22. An *idler* is a person who is lazy or not employed.
23. *Undulations* are regular movements that come in waves.
24. *Preternaturally* (prē′ tər nach′ ər əl ē) means "going beyond what is normal" or "extraordinarily."

Vocabulary
efface (i fās′) *v.* to destroy; to erase

brilliant-bodied flies, the gray spiders stretching their webs from twig to twig. He noted the prismatic colors in all the dewdrops upon a million blades of grass. The humming of the gnats that danced above the eddies[25] of the stream, the beating of the dragon-flies' wings, the strokes of the water-spiders' legs, like oars which had lifted their boat—all these made audible music. A fish slid along beneath his eyes and he heard the rush of its body parting the water.

He had come to the surface facing down the stream; in a moment the visible world seemed to wheel slowly round, himself the pivotal point, and he saw the bridge, the fort, the soldiers upon the bridge, the captain, the sergeant, the two privates, his executioners. They were in silhouette against the blue sky. They shouted and gesticulated, pointing at him. The captain had drawn his pistol, but did not fire; the others were unarmed. Their movements were grotesque and horrible, their forms gigantic.

Suddenly he heard a sharp report[26] and something struck the water smartly within a few inches of his head, spattering his face with spray. He heard a second report, and saw one of the sentinels with his rifle at his shoulder, a light cloud of blue smoke rising from the muzzle. The man in the water saw the eye of the man on the bridge gazing into his own through the sights of the rifle. He observed that it was a gray eye and remembered having read that gray eyes were keenest, and that all famous marksmen had them. Nevertheless, this one had missed.

A counter-swirl had caught Farquhar and turned him half round; he was again looking into the forest on the bank opposite the fort. The sound of a clear, high voice in a monotonous singsong now rang out behind him and came across the water with a distinctness that pierced and subdued all other sounds, even the beating of the ripples in his ears. Although no soldier, he had frequented camps enough to know the dread significance of that deliberate, drawling, aspirated[27] chant; the lieutenant on shore was taking a part in the morning's work. How coldly and pitilessly—with what an even, calm intonation, presaging,[28] and enforcing tranquillity in the men—with what accurately measured intervals fell those cruel words:

"Attention, company! . . . Shoulder arms! . . . Ready! . . . Aim! . . . Fire!"

Farquhar dived—dived as deeply as he could. The water roared in his ears like the voice of Niagara, yet he heard the dulled thunder of the volley[29] and, rising again toward the surface, met shining bits of metal, singularly flattened, oscillating slowly downward. Some of them touched him on the face and hands, then fell away, continuing their descent. One lodged between his collar and neck; it was uncomfortably warm and he snatched it out.

As he rose to the surface, gasping for breath, he saw that he had been a long time under water; he was perceptibly farther down stream—nearer to safety. The soldiers had almost finished reloading; the metal ramrods[30] flashed all at once in the sunshine as they were drawn from the barrels, turned in the air, and thrust into their sockets. The two sentinels fired again, independently and ineffectually.

The hunted man saw all this over his shoulder; he was now swimming vigorously with the current. His brain was as energetic as his arms and legs; he thought with the rapidity of lightning.

"The officer," he reasoned, "will not make that martinet's[31] error a second time. It is as easy to dodge a volley as a single shot. He

---

25. *Eddies* are currents that move contrary to the main current in a river or stream, usually in a circular motion.
26. Here, a *report* is an explosive sound or noise, especially from a rifle or a pistol when fired.
27. Here, *aspirated* refers to a breathy sort of speech.
28. *Presaging* means "acting as a sign or a warning of."
29. Here, a *volley* is a discharge of bullets in rapid succession.
30. *Ramrods* are rods used for stuffing the charge down the barrel of a rifle that is loaded from the muzzle.
31. A *martinet* is one who stresses strict attention to forms and rules.

has probably already given the command to fire at will. God help me, I cannot dodge them all!"

An appalling plash within two yards of him was followed by a loud, rushing sound *diminuendo*,[32] which seemed to travel back through the air to the fort and died in an explosion which stirred the very river to its deeps! A rising sheet of water curved over him, fell down upon him, blinded him, strangled him! The cannon had taken a hand in the game. As he shook his head free from the commotion of the smitten[33] water he heard the deflected shot humming through the air ahead, and in an instant it was cracking and smashing the branches in the forest beyond.

"They will not do that again," he thought; "the next time they will use a charge of grape.[34] I must keep my eye upon the gun; the smoke will apprise me—the report arrives too late; it lags behind the missile. That is a good gun."

Suddenly he felt himself whirled round and round—spinning like a top. The water, the banks, the forests, the now distant bridge, fort and men—all were commingled and blurred. Objects were represented by their colors only; circular horizontal streaks of color—that was all he saw. He had been caught in a vortex[35] and was being whirled on with a velocity of advance and gyration that made him giddy and sick. In a few moments he was flung upon the gravel at the foot of the left bank of the stream—the southern bank—and behind a projecting point which concealed him from his enemies. The sudden arrest of his motion, the abrasion of one of his

hands on the gravel, restored him, and he wept with delight. He dug his fingers into the sand, threw it over himself in handfuls and audibly blessed it. It looked like diamonds, rubies, emeralds; he could think of nothing beautiful which it did not resemble. The trees upon the bank were giant garden plants; he noted a definite order in their arrangement, inhaled the fragrance of their blooms. A strange, roseate[36] light shone through the spaces among their trunks and the wind made in their branches the music of æolian harps.[37] He had no wish to perfect his escape—was content to remain in that enchanting spot until retaken.

A whiz and rattle of grapeshot among the branches high above his head roused him from his dream. The baffled cannoneer had fired him a random farewell. He sprang to his feet, rushed up the sloping bank, and plunged into the forest.

All that day he traveled, laying his course by the rounding sun. The forest seemed interminable; nowhere did he discover a break in it, not even a woodman's road. He had not known that he lived in so wild a region. There was something uncanny[38] in the revelation.

By nightfall he was fatigued, footsore, famishing. The thought of his wife and children urged him on. At last he found a road which led him in what he knew to be the right direction. It was as wide and straight as a city street, yet it seemed untraveled. No fields bordered it, no dwelling anywhere. Not so much as the barking of a dog suggested human habitation. The black bodies of the trees formed a straight wall on both sides, terminating on the horizon in a point, like a diagram in a lesson in perspective. Overhead, as he looked up through this rift in the wood, shone great golden stars looking unfamiliar

---

32. *Diminuendo* (di min′ ū en′ dō) is a musical term that describes a gradual decrease in volume.

33. Here, *smitten* means that the water has been bombarded with ammunition from the cannon.

34. *Grape* refers to grapeshot, a cluster of small iron balls that disperse when shot from a cannon.

35. Here, a *vortex* is a whirling mass of water that pulls everything to its center.

36. *Roseate* means "rose-colored."

37. *Æolian harps* produce musical sounds when air passes through the strings.

38. *Uncanny* means "eerie" or "weird."

and grouped in strange constellations. He was sure they were arranged in some order which had a secret and malign[39] significance. The wood on either side was full of singular noises, among which—once, twice, and again—he distinctly heard whispers in an unknown tongue.

His neck was in pain and lifting his hand to it he found it horribly swollen. He knew that it had a circle of black where the rope had bruised it. His eyes felt congested; he could no longer close them. His tongue was swollen with thirst; he relieved its fever by thrusting it forward from between his teeth into the cold air. How softly the turf had carpeted the untraveled avenue—he could no longer feel the roadway beneath his feet!

Doubtless, despite his suffering, he had fallen asleep while walking, for now he sees another scene—perhaps he has merely recovered from a delirium. He stands at the gate of his own home. All is as he left it, and all bright and beautiful in the morning sunshine. He must have traveled the entire night. As he pushes open the gate and passes up the wide white walk, he sees a flutter of female garments; his wife, looking fresh and cool and sweet, steps down from the veranda to meet him. At the bottom of the steps she stands waiting, with a smile of ineffable[40] joy, an attitude of matchless

Sanford Robinson Gifford, c. 1868. George Peter Alexander Healy. Oil on canvas, 35.6 x 30.5 cm. The Detroit Institute of Art, Founders Society Purchase, Merrill Fund.

Viewing the painting: What qualities does the man in this painting seem to have in common with Peyton Farquhar? Explain.

grace and dignity. Ah, how beautiful she is! He springs forward with extended arms. As he is about to clasp her he feels a stunning blow upon the back of the neck; a blinding white light blazes all about him with a sound like the shock of a cannon—then all is darkness and silence!

Peyton Farquhar was dead; his body, with a broken neck, swung gently from side to side beneath the timbers of the Owl Creek bridge.

---

39. *Malign* (mə līn′) means "evil or harmful in nature or effect."
40. *Ineffable* means "indescribable" or "unspeakable."

Responding to Literature

Personal Response

What was your immediate reaction to the end of this story?

ANALYZING LITERATURE

RECALL

1. Summarize the scene presented in the first two paragraphs. What reactions does the narrator describe?
2. What does Farquhar try to think about as he waits to be hanged? What sound disturbs his thoughts? What plan occurs to him?
3. In sections 1 and 2, what do you learn about Farquhar's appearance, personality, and background? Who recently visited his home?
4. Summarize the action in section 3. Describe some of the physical sensations Farquhar experiences.
5. What happens at the end of the story?

INTERPRET

6. In your opinion, why do those witnessing the event respond to it in the way they do?
7. Why do you think Farquhar experiences time in the way he does in section 1? Explain your answer using details from the selection.
8. What can you infer about the narrator's attitude toward Farquhar from the descriptions of the character's appearance and his life? What crime do you think Farquhar has committed?
9. What changes do you see in Farquhar's thoughts and sensations from the beginning to the end of section 3? What do these changes suggest?
10. What accounts for Farquhar's thoughts in the next to last paragraph?

EVALUATE AND CONNECT

11. In section 1, Bierce uses a series of **similes** to describe the ticking of the watch. In your opinion, what effect do the similes have on the **mood** of the story? (See Literary Terms Handbook, pages R14 and R10.)
12. Based on what you wrote for the Focus Activity on page 367, do you think the description of Farquhar's final thoughts is realistic? Explain.
13. What view of war do you think Bierce expresses in this selection? Do you think he supports one side or the other in the story? Explain.
14. Theme Connections   In your opinion, in what ways does this selection show the Union being tested?
15. Farquhar stands on the plank waiting to be hanged. What role might hope play in such a desperate situation?

Literary ELEMENTS

Point of View

Point of view is the vantage point from which a story is told. A story with a **third-person point of view** is told from the perspective of a narrator outside the story. The narrator uses the pronouns *she, he,* and *they* to refer to characters. A third-person narrator may be either **omniscient** or **limited**. An omniscient third-person narrator knows and sees everything, including the thoughts of all the characters. A narrator with a limited third-person point of view knows only the thoughts and feelings of one character. Most of this story is told from the limited third-person point of view.

1. What parts of the story are told from the omniscient point of view?
2. In your opinion, how does the limited third-person point of view affect the level of **suspense** in the story?

● See **Literary Terms Handbook,** p. R12.

— LITERATURE AND WRITING —

Writing About Literature

Back to the Past A **flashback** is a scene that interrupts the flow of the narrative to describe events that occurred earlier. Do you think the flashback in section 2 helps build **suspense** (see page R16)? Write several paragraphs responding to the question. Use details from the story to support your conclusions.

Creative Writing

Your Own "Occurrence" Look again at your freewriting for the Focus Activity on page 367. Use what you wrote as a starting point for a brief story about a life-or-death situation. Use some of Bierce's techniques in your story such as distorted perception, **foreshadowing** (see page R7), and a surprise ending. Share your story with a partner.

— EXTENDING YOUR RESPONSE —

Literature Groups

Surprise Debate In your group, debate the following question: Did Bierce expect the reader to be completely surprised by the story's ending, or did he provide hints along the way? Support opinions with details from the story. Then summarize the results of the debate and present them to the class.

Interdisciplinary Activity

History: Behind Enemy Lines Research spying, or espionage, during the Civil War. Were spies common on the Union side? on the Confederate side? What did they do?

Performing

Theme Music Imagine that you are staging a production of "An Occurrence at Owl Creek Bridge." Choose background music to evoke the **mood** of each section. Record the pieces you select and then play them for the class. Ask the class to identify which parts of the story go with each piece of music.

📖 **Save your work for your portfolio.**

Skill Minilesson

VOCABULARY • **Synonyms**

Words that have the same or nearly the same meaning are called **synonyms.** The words *evade* and *elude,* for example, are synonyms. They both convey the idea of avoiding or escaping. Other synonyms for these words are *circumvent* and *skirt.* Note that synonyms are always the same part of speech.

PRACTICE Find five pairs of synonyms in the lists below. Use a dictionary if you need help.

assented	effaced	audaciously
destroyed	ardently	adorn
confiscated	upbraided	protruded
projected	agreed	prostrate
obstinate	decorate	enthusiastically

Television Script and Commentary

TV viewers of the 1950s and 1960s waited anxiously each Friday night for the eerie stories of *The Twilight Zone*. One Friday, *The Twilight Zone* presented "An Occurrence at Owl Creek Bridge."

"An Occurrence at Owl Creek Bridge" (2/28/64)

from *The Twilight Zone Companion* by Marc Scott Zicree

[Words in italics are those of *The Twilight Zone* host Rod Serling.]

"Tonight a presentation so special and unique that, for the first time in the five years we've been presenting The Twilight Zone, we're offering a film shot in France by others [than the Twilight Zone staff]. *Winner of the Cannes Film Festival of 1962, as well as other international awards, here is a haunting study of the incredible, from the past master of the incredible, Ambrose Bierce. Here is the French production of 'An Occurrence at Owl Creek Bridge.'"*

[The article presents a plot summary of the story, followed by Serling's closing comments (in italics).]

"An occurrence at Owl Creek Bridge—in two forms, as it was dreamed, and as it was lived and died. This is the stuff of fantasy, the thread of imagination . . . the ingredients of the Twilight Zone."

Commentary

Some time previously, [*Twilight Zone* producer William Froug] had seen *An Occurrence at Owl Creek Bridge*, a French film that had won first prize for short subjects at the 1962 Cannes Film Festival. Based on the story by Ambrose Bierce, it told the story of a condemned Confederate spy who, during the instant that he's falling before the rope breaks his neck, imagines an involved and successful escape.

The film was shortened by several minutes and an introduction by Serling was added. "An Occurrence at Owl Creek Bridge" was aired February 28, 1964, and repeated September 11, 1964. A coup for the show, it was well received. *Variety*'s [an entertainment newspaper] reaction was typical: "This French short film, which has been nominated for an Oscar, undoubtedly received more exposure than any such candidate in Oscar history when aired on Rod Serling's *Twilight Zone* Friday. A fascinating and eerie Ambrose Bierce tale . . . it fits perfectly into the *Zone* format."

Subsequently, the film won its Oscar—another first for *Twilight Zone*.

Respond

1. Review the descriptive words and phrases used above to describe the film *An Occurrence at Owl Creek Bridge*. Would you apply those same words to the story you read? Explain.

2. Do you think the film of *An Occurrence at Owl Creek Bridge* would be popular with people today? Explain.

Reading & Thinking Skills

Sequencing: Order of Events

In narrative writing, or writing that tells a story, the author usually relates events in **chronological order**—the order in which the events occurred. Transition words and phrases that show time, such as *after, before, finally, later,* or *the next day,* can help the reader keep track of the chronology. Sometimes, however, a writer disrupts this order. For example, a writer may begin a story with an important event and then interrupt the chronological order with a **flashback,** a scene that occurred before the narrative's plot began. Again, the reader should pay special attention to transitional words in order to follow the time sequence.

In "An Occurrence at Owl Creek Bridge," Ambrose Bierce relates events out of chronological order, but he doesn't use transition words to signal this. Instead, he divides his story into three numbered sections. The reader must figure out the sequence in which the sections occur by using the clues provided in each. For example, in the first section the reader learns that a man who looks like a wealthy planter is being hanged from a bridge in Alabama. In the second section, Bierce states that "Peyton Farquhar was a well-to-do planter" from an Alabama family. Farquhar longs "for the release of his energies, the larger life of the soldier, the opportunity for distinction." Already the reader can guess that the character in the first section is now being described at an earlier moment in time, since he was about to be hanged when the author introduced him. Further in the story, that guess is confirmed; a federal scout gives Farquhar the idea of destroying Owl Creek Bridge and states that the punishment for that offense is hanging.

In the third section, Farquhar, with the noose around his neck, falls through the bridge, suffers from the pressure around his throat, but loosens the noose. He has seemingly just escaped being hanged, so this section probably occurs after the other two. By disrupting the chronological order, Bierce captures the reader's interest and adds suspense to the story.

Narrative fiction is not the only type of writing that may be written out of chronological order. Newspaper articles often tell the outcome of an event in the opening paragraph or even in the headline. Then they go back and relate the actions that led up to it. Transitions and other clues can help the reader figure out the sequence of this type of writing also.

● For more about the order of events, see **Reading Handbook,** pp. R86–R93.

ACTIVITIES

1. Review "An Occurrence at Owl Creek Bridge." On a piece of paper, list each important event in the sequence that Bierce presents it. Then list the events in the order they really happened.

2. Find a newspaper article that describes an event out of time sequence. Rewrite it, reconstructing the events in chronological order. Discuss your work with a partner. What clues did you use in putting events in chronological order?

Before You Read

Shiloh

Meet Herman Melville

"A whale ship was my Yale College and my Harvard."

—*Melville*

Herman Melville was a writer ahead of his time—and he knew it. During his lifetime, Melville's readers and critics never appreciated his greatest and most serious works. Years later, however, a new generation of readers recognized Melville as one of America's finest writers—a writer who had spoken for them before their time.

Melville's youthful experiences probably contributed to the dark vision of humankind reflected in his writings. Though Melville was born into a prominent New York family, his father went bankrupt, suffered a nervous breakdown, and died when Melville was twelve. Melville had to discontinue much of his schooling to help support his family.

Melville's real adventures began when, at the age of twenty-one, he sailed on a whaling ship bound for the South Pacific. He abandoned ship in the Marquesas Islands and lived for a month with the supposedly cannibalistic Typee people, who, in fact, turned out to be gentle and gracious.

After numerous voyages, Melville returned to New York, where he wrote adventure novels inspired by his seagoing experiences. He quickly became one of the country's most celebrated writers. Melville then began to write his greatest work, *Moby-Dick* (1851), a complex story of the hunt for a fierce white whale.

Ironically, the same critics who had loved Melville's adventure tales panned his serious work; worse yet, the public ignored it. A few years later, Melville abandoned novel writing for poetry and, for financial reasons, took a job as a customs inspector. He composed "Shiloh" and the other poems contained in the book *Battle-Pieces and Aspects of the War* (1866) in response to the horrific sights he encountered visiting a cousin in the Union army.

Herman Melville was born in 1819 and died in 1891.

FOCUS ACTIVITY

Think about a time when you visited or saw pictures of a cemetery, a former battlefield, or a monument. What emotions did you experience?

QUICKWRITE Jot down some reactions you had when visiting or viewing a place that honors the dead.

SETTING A PURPOSE Read to discover one speaker's reactions to visiting a Civil War battlefield.

BACKGROUND

The Time and Place

The Battle of Shiloh, named after a church on the battlefield, was fought in Pittsburg Landing, Tennessee, on April 6 and 7, 1862. The Union Army suffered 13,000 casualties (dead, wounded, missing, or captured), and the smaller Confederate contingent had 10,700 casualties.

A Poetic Tribute

Melville subtitled this poem a **requiem.** In the Roman Catholic Church, a requiem is a mass, or ceremony, held for a deceased person in which people pray for the person's soul. Many composers, including Wolfgang Mozart and Giuseppe Verdi, have written compositions for requiem masses. Writers, too, have used the concept in poetic tributes to the dead.

Shiloh

Herman Melville

Shiloh National Battlefield, Tennessee.

A Requiem
(April 1862)

Skimming lightly, wheeling° still,
  The swallows fly low
Over the field in clouded days,
  The forest-field of Shiloh—
5 Over the field where April rain
  Solaced° the parched° ones stretched
    in pain
Through the pause of night
That followed the Sunday fight
  Around the church of Shiloh—

10 The church so lone, the log-built one,
That echoed to many a parting groan
  And natural prayer
  Of dying foemen° mingled there—
Foemen at morn, but friends at eve—
15   Fame or country least their care:
(What like a bullet can undeceive!)
  But now they lie low,
While over them the swallows skim,
  And all is hushed at Shiloh.

---

1 *Wheeling* means "moving in a circle."
6 *Solaced* means "comforted" or "soothed." *Parched* means
  "dried" or "thirsty."

---

13 *Foemen* are opponents, or enemies, in a war.

Responding to Literature

Personal Response

Describe your emotions after you finished reading the poem. Were they similar to those you described for the Focus Activity on page 381?

ANALYZING LITERATURE

RECALL AND INTERPRET

1. Describe the movements of the swallows in lines 1–4. What does this sight suggest to you about the speaker's reaction to the battlefield?
2. What does the rain do for the wounded soldier? What might this suggest about the speaker's view of the natural world and human pain?
3. According to lines 13–16, what happens between Union and Confederate soldiers following the battle? What accounts for the change between them? What attitude toward war do you think the speaker expresses in this poem?
4. What might the speaker mean by "What like a bullet can undeceive!"?

EVALUATE AND CONNECT

5. List the pairs of words Melville uses to create **end rhyme** (see page R13) with *Shiloh.* What **mood** do these rhymes create?
6. Why do you think Melville focuses on the church at Shiloh? What might the church symbolize? Explain.
7. If you had been a family member or friend of a soldier killed at Shiloh, how might you have responded to this poem? Explain your answer.
8. Theme Connections   If those responsible for the Civil War had experienced the insight offered by Melville in "Shiloh," do you think the war would have been fought? Explain.

Literary ELEMENTS

Alliteration

Poets take advantage of words' sounds as well their meanings. One device poets use is **alliteration,** or the repetition of similar consonant sounds at the beginning of words. Alliteration helps to create a musical effect and a **mood** that evokes an emotional response. For example, in "Shiloh," the repetition of the *s* sound creates a mood of quiet, peace, and sadness. Alliteration can also help the poet reinforce meaning and create unity.

1. In lines 3–5, notice the repetition of the *f* sound. In your opinion, what effect does this have?

2. In your opinion, what effect is created by the repetition of the *p* sound in lines 6 and 7?

● See **Literary Terms Handbook,** p. R1.

EXTENDING YOUR RESPONSE

Creative Writing

Capture the Feeling   Melville wrote "Shiloh" after visiting the scene of a bloody battle. Choose a place that is often crowded with people, such as a football stadium or a school auditorium. Then write either a paragraph or a poem describing the way it looks on the day after a major event. Try to convey your feelings about what happened and to capture echoes or memories of the event. Share your work with the class.

Listening and Speaking

The Sounds of Shiloh   How would you present the poem "Shiloh" on the radio? Would you emphasize the poem's **rhyme** and **alliteration?** Would you add sound effects? How and where would you vary the volume and pitch of your voice? Plan, practice, and audiotape a dramatic reading of "Shiloh" and then play the tape for the class.

■ **Save your work for your portfolio.**

Before You Read

The Gettysburg Address

Meet
Abraham Lincoln

❝With malice toward none, with charity for all . . . let us strive on to finish the work we are in, to bind up the nation's wounds, to care for him who shall have borne the battle, and for his widow and his orphan, to do all which may achieve and cherish a just and lasting peace among ourselves, and with all nations.❞

—*Lincoln*

One of the United States' greatest presidents, Abraham Lincoln led the country through the Civil War, helping to preserve the Union and to end slavery. Lincoln and the United States showed the world that democracy can be a durable form of government.

For many, Lincoln's journey from a Kentucky log cabin to the White House symbolizes American opportunity. Born in Hardin County, Kentucky, Lincoln grew up mainly on frontier farms in Indiana, where he received little formal education. He read every book he could find, and, following a move to New Salem, Illinois, studied the law. At twenty-five, Lincoln was elected to the Illinois state legislature, marking the beginning of an astounding political career that led to his election as president in 1860.

A man who had once described military glory as "that attractive rainbow that rises in showers of blood—that serpent's eye that charms to destroy" became a great war leader only because it was necessary to preserve the Union. Lincoln believed that a Confederate victory would most likely have resulted in at least two separate nations. That, he felt, would have marked the failure of democracy.

Abraham Lincoln was born in 1809 and died from an assassin's bullet in 1865.

FOCUS ACTIVITY

What do you know about President Abraham Lincoln? What kind of person was he? What were his accomplishments as president?

JOURNAL Write for a few minutes in your journal to explore your own impression of Lincoln.

SETTING A PURPOSE Read to find out Lincoln's thoughts when he visits the site of a major Civil War battle.

BACKGROUND

The Time and Place

On November 19, 1863, a solemn group of people gathered on the battlefield at Gettysburg, Pennsylvania, to dedicate a cemetery to the soldiers killed there. Edward Everett, a highly respected orator and politician, spoke before Lincoln—for two hours. Lincoln then spoke for just two minutes. Afterward, the press all but ignored Lincoln's speech. Even Lincoln regarded it as a "flat failure." Everett, however, said, "I should be glad if I could flatter myself that I came as near to the central idea of the occasion, in two hours as you did in two minutes."

VOCABULARY PREVIEW

score (skôr) *n.* a group of twenty items; p. 385

consecrate (kon′sə krāt′) *v.* to set apart as sacred; to make or declare holy; p. 385

hallow (hal′ō) *v.* to make or select as holy; to regard or honor as sacred; p. 385

perish (per′ish) *v.* to pass from existence; to disappear; p. 385

Gettysburg National Military Park, Pennsylvania.

The Gettysburg Address

Abraham Lincoln ⋟

FOUR <u>SCORE</u> AND SEVEN YEARS AGO OUR FATHERS BROUGHT forth on this continent, a new nation, conceived in liberty, and dedicated to the proposition that all men are created equal. Now we are engaged in a great civil war, testing whether that nation or any nation so conceived and so dedicated, can long endure. We are met on a great battle-field of that war. We have come to dedicate a portion of that field, as a final resting place for those who here gave their lives that that nation might live. It is altogether fitting and proper that we should do this.

But, in a larger sense, we can not dedicate—we can not <u>consecrate</u>—we can not <u>hallow</u>—this ground. The brave men, living and dead, who struggled here, have consecrated it, far above our poor power to add or detract. The world will little note, nor long remember what we say here, but it can never forget what they did here. It is for us the living, rather, to be dedicated here to the unfinished work which they who fought here have thus far so nobly advanced. It is rather for us to be here dedicated to the great task remaining before us—that from these honored dead we take increased devotion to that cause for which they gave the last full measure of devotion—that we here highly resolve that these dead shall not have died in vain—that this nation, under God, shall have a new birth of freedom—and that government of the people, by the people, for the people, shall not <u>perish</u> from the earth.

Vocabulary

score (skôr) *n.* a group of twenty items
consecrate (kon′sə krāt′) *v.* to set apart as sacred; to make or declare holy
hallow (hal′ ō) *v.* to make or select as holy; to regard or honor as sacred
perish (per′ish) *v.* to pass from existence; to disappear

Responding to Literature

Personal Response

Which part of this speech made the greatest impression on you? Why?

—— ANALYZING LITERATURE ——

RECALL

1. What words does Lincoln use to describe the United States in the opening sentence?
2. For what reason, according to Lincoln, are he and those in the audience gathered together?
3. According to Lincoln, who has already consecrated the battlefield?
4. In Lincoln's opinion, to what should "the living" dedicate themselves?
5. How does Lincoln describe the government of the United States?

INTERPRET

6. From the opening sentence, what can you infer about Lincoln's ideas about government? What might he address in the rest of the speech?
7. Theme Connections   How, in your opinion, does Lincoln believe the nation is being tested? Explain, using details from the speech.
8. In your opinion, in what ways does Lincoln believe that the battlefield has already been consecrated?
9. What, in your opinion, are the "unfinished work" and the "great task remaining before us" to which Lincoln refers? Support your answer with details from the speech.
10. Reread Lincoln's final words in which he describes the government of the United States. What do you think this description means?

EVALUATE AND CONNECT

11. What, in your opinion, was Lincoln's **purpose** (or what were his purposes) in presenting the Gettysburg Address? Cite details from the speech to support your answer.
12. Describe Lincoln's **tone** (see page R16) in his speech. How does his tone support his message?
13. Refer to your response to the Focus Activity on page 384. How does Lincoln's speech affect your impressions of Lincoln? What have you learned about Lincoln? Explain, using details from the speech.
14. Lincoln made his Gettysburg Address well over one hundred years ago. Do you think the speech is relevant to Americans now? Explain.
15. This speech is often quoted. What, in your opinion, makes it so memorable and inspiring? Support your opinion with examples.

Literary ELEMENTS

Parallelism

Parallelism is the use of a series of words, phrases, or sentences that have similar grammatical form. The Gettysburg Address contains one of the most famous examples of parallelism in American history: "of the people, by the people, for the people." The grammatical structure that is repeated here is the prepositional phrase.

Parallelism affects a piece of writing in many ways. It helps words flow together; it calls attention to important ideas; and it unifies different ideas in a composition. When used appropriately, parallelism can be a very effective writing tool.

1. Identify another example of parallelism in this speech. Explain how it affects you as a reader.
2. Using the example you identified above or another example, explain how parallelism ties together ideas in this speech.

● See **Literary Terms Handbook,** p. R11.

LITERATURE AND WRITING

Writing About Literature

Opposite Ideas   Writers sometimes position opposite ideas next to each other to emphasize a point. This technique is called antithesis. In a short paper, identify at least two uses of antithesis in Lincoln's speech, and describe their roles in conveying Lincoln's message.

Creative Writing

A Letter from Gettysburg   Imagine that you were in the audience listening to the Gettysburg Address. Write a letter to a friend describing the speech and the effects it had on you. Reread the information on page 384 to help you set the scene.

EXTENDING YOUR RESPONSE

Literature Groups

What He Didn't Say   Lincoln could have said a great deal more in the Gettysburg Address. Why do you think his speech was so brief? There was certainly plenty Lincoln could have said about the Civil War and about ending slavery. In your group, discuss why Lincoln might have avoided talking about these subjects. How might the effect of the speech have been different if Lincoln had spoken for a longer time and focused on the war and slavery? Share your opinions with the class.

Performing

In Rehearsal   Prepare to present the Gettysburg Address. Practice reading the speech aloud, using changes in emphasis, speed, and volume, as well as appropriate pauses and gestures, to create a dramatic effect. When you are ready, perform the speech for the class.

Learning for Life

Gettysburg Goes Interactive   Imagine that a museum or park has hired you to create an interactive display to commemorate the Gettysburg Address. Assume you will have a space no larger than a typical classroom in which to work. With a partner or a small group, create a floor plan and write a brief description of your exhibit. Share your completed project with the class.

📕 Save your work for your portfolio.

Skill Minilesson

VOCABULARY • **Analogies**

Analogies are comparisons based on relationships between words and ideas. Some analogies express the relationship of *degree.*

    mad : furious :: sad : miserable

Mad is a similar but less intense feeling than *furious; sad* is a similar but less intense feeling than *miserable.*

    To finish an analogy, determine the relationship between the first two words. Then apply that relationship to the second set of words.

● For more about analogies, see **Communications Skills Handbook,** pp. R83–R84.

PRACTICE   Choose the word that best completes each analogy.

1. deep : bottomless :: tall :
   a. high   b. low   c. towering
2. impenetrable : dense :: eternal :
   a. lasting   b. momentary   c. seldom
3. survive : flourish :: eat :
   a. taste   b. gorge   c. starve
4. despise : dislike :: hallow :
   a. perish   b. consecrate   c. honor

Before You Read

The Gift in Wartime

Meet Tran Mong Tu

"War is a terrible thing," says Tran Mong Tu (trän mông tōō), who has firsthand experience. Tran Mong Tu was born in Hai Dong, North Vietnam. She and her family were forced to relocate to South Vietnam in 1954, she says, "due to the French-Indochina war," in which communist forces battled and eventually drove out the French. Yet South Vietnam did not remain safe for long; a civil war soon raged between communist and non-communist sympathizers.

By the time the United States became heavily involved in the Vietnam War in the 1960s, Tran worked for the Associated Press (a large U.S. news service) in Saigon, the capital of South Vietnam. When the United States pulled its troops out of Vietnam in 1975, the Associated Press evacuated its Vietnamese employees because it feared communist reprisal against those working for American companies. Tran's immediate family and thousands of other Vietnamese also fled to the United States at that time.

Although Tran had wanted to be a writer since elementary school, her poetry was not published until she reached the United States. Today, Tran frequently contributes poems and short stories to Vietnamese literary publications in the United States and overseas.

Tran Mong Tu was born in 1943.

FOCUS ACTIVITY

Have you experienced the death of someone close to you? If not, think about a famous person who has died in recent years.

CHART IT! Use a cause-and-effect chart like the one on this page to describe the immediate effects that person's death had on you and others.

SETTING A PURPOSE As you read this poem, notice how the speaker responds to the death of a loved one.

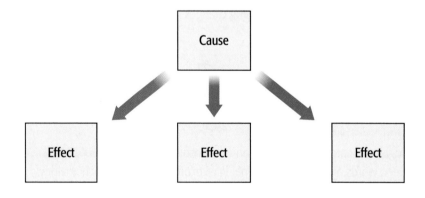

BACKGROUND

The Vietnam War

When asked what she wanted people to know about the Vietnam War, Tran Mong Tu replied, "The Vietnam War is a shameful experience, for both Vietnamese and Americans." Indeed, many people in both countries felt the terrible tragedy of the war. During the war, student protests were common in the United States; protests were also frequent in South Vietnam, especially among Buddhists and other religious groups. Losses in the war were heavy; more than two million Vietnamese and 57,000 Americans died.

The Gift in Wartime

Tran Mong Tu
Translated by Vann Phan

I offer you roses
Buried in your new grave
I offer you my wedding gown
To cover your tomb still green with grass

5   You give me medals
Together with silver stars
And the yellow pips° on your badge
Unused and still shining

I offer you my youth
10   The days we were still in love
My youth died away
When they told me the bad news

You give me the smell of blood
From your war dress
15   Your blood and your enemy's
So that I may be moved

I offer you clouds
That linger on my eyes on summer days
I offer you cold winters
20   Amid my springtime of life

You give me your lips with no smile
You give me your arms without tenderness
You give me your eyes with no sight
And your motionless body

25   Seriously, I apologize to you
I promise to meet you in our next life
I will hold this shrapnel° as a token
By which we will recognize each other

---

7 *Pips* are military badges of rank worn on the shoulder.
27 *Shrapnel* are fragments scattered from an exploding shell or bomb.

Photographs found on the body of a dead
North Vietnamese soldier.

Responding to Literature

Personal Response

What was your immediate reaction to this poem? Share your response with a classmate.

─────── **ANALYZING LITERATURE** ───────

RECALL AND INTERPRET

1. What does the speaker "offer" in this poem? Based on what she offers, what can you infer about the speaker's feelings for the person addressed as "you"?
2. What does the person addressed as "you" give in return? In your opinion, how do these gifts differ from those of the speaker? What does this difference suggest about the speaker's attitude toward war?
3. Where is the person that the speaker addresses? In what ways do you think this person's fate has affected the speaker? Explain with details from the selection.
4. What does the speaker do at the end of the poem? Why do you think the speaker does this?

EVALUATE AND CONNECT

5. Find at least one example of **repetition** (see page R13) in the poem. Why do you think the writer uses the technique? What impact does it have?
6. Think about your response to the Focus Activity on page 388. Compare the speaker's response to death to your own response. How are they similar or different?
7. One way to work through grief is to write or talk about it. In your opinion, how might the speaker in this poem have benefited from saying what she did? Explain.
8. What **imagery** from the poem made the greatest impression on you? Why? (See Literary Terms Handbook, page R8.)

Literary
ELEMENTS

Apostrophe

Apostrophe is a figure of speech in which a writer addresses an absent person, an inanimate object, or an idea as if it were present and capable of understanding. In "The Gift in Wartime," Tran Mong Tu addresses an absent person. For example, as she says, "I offer you roses," the person to whom she is speaking is not there and cannot hear or understand what she is saying.

1. In "The Gift in Wartime," who is the speaker addressing and why can that person not hear or understand what she is saying?
2. In your opinion, how does the use of apostrophe contribute to the impact of the poem?

● See **Literary Terms Handbook,** p. R1.

─────── **EXTENDING YOUR RESPONSE** ───────

Writing About Literature

Analyze the Images   In two or three paragraphs, discuss the use of contrasting images in this poem and whether the images can be classified in any way. Comment on the overall impact of the contrasting images you choose to highlight.

Interdisciplinary Activity

Art: Design and Illustrate a Page   Use a word processor or hand-lettering to reproduce this poem on a sheet of paper. Then sketch in drawings you think appropriate for the poem. Once you are satisfied with the design, complete the drawings and show the final page to the class.

📖 **Save your work for your portfolio.**

COMPARING *selections*

The Gettysburg Address **and** *The Gift in Wartime*

COMPARE **AUDIENCE AND PURPOSE**

Lincoln addressed a crowd at a public event; Tran Mong Tu wrote her thoughts in a poem. With a small group of students, discuss these questions:

1. Who is the audience for each selection?

2. How is each writer's purpose different? How is it the same?

3. How does the word choice in each selection reflect a different sense of audience and purpose? For example, think about the use of the first, second, and third person in each selection.

COMPARE **CULTURES**

Often a written work reveals much about the writer's culture—the ways of life of that time and place. Write a journal entry in which you consider these questions:

● Which selection tells more about the writer's culture? Support your answer with details from the selection. (Culture can include many things, such as ways of speaking and writing, ideas about government, and ways of dressing.)

● In your opinion, which of these two selections seems like it could have been written by someone in the United States today? Explain your answer.

Statue in Gettysburg National Military Park, Pennsylvania.

COMPARE **IDEAS ABOUT WAR**

With a partner, create a visual display that represents the ideas about war expressed in the Gettysburg Address and another to represent the ideas about war expressed in "The Gift in Wartime." You might do a painting, a collage, a poster, or a multimedia presentation, for example. Brainstorm with your partner to develop ideas for your displays. When you have completed your displays, set them out for the class to view. Invite comments from the class. Do they agree with your depiction of each writer's ideas about war?

~∴ Writing ⟍ Workshop ∴~

Persuasive Writing: Essay

What is a situation that needs to be improved upon? What is a policy or practice you believe is unfair? The writers in this theme all believed passionately in something and worked, wrote, or lectured to persuade others to share their vision. **Your goal in this workshop is to write** **an essay persuading others to act on an issue about which you feel strongly.** This is your chance to talk about what is on your mind. How persuasive can you be?

● As you write your persuasive essay, refer to the **Writing Handbook,** pp. R62–R67.

The Writing Process

PREWRITING

PREWRITING TIP

The best persuasive essays take sides in a debate. Are there opposing views on your topic? If not, your topic may be weak.

Explore ideas

Choose a topic that you feel strongly about. The following questions may help you get some ideas:

● What issues would Frederick Douglass be fighting for if he were alive today?
● What would Sojourner Truth be fighting for today?
● What makes you angry or frustrated? How could the situation be changed for the better?
● What news items capture your attention? How do they relate to your community?

Consider your purpose

What problem or situation do you want your readers to understand? Your goal is to persuade them to take action that will help solve the problem or improve the situation.

Identify an audience

Your audience should include those who have the power to carry out the action that you suggest. Will you write for local officials? for voters? for classmates who will then persuade their parents? The audience you choose will determine the kinds of arguments you present.

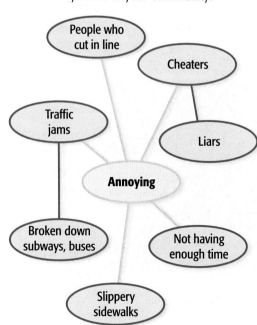

Make a plan

Get your ideas flowing by jotting down notes in response to the following questions:

- How can I state my goal clearly and suggest a specific action?
- What reasons and examples can I give to support my position?
- How can I appeal to the audience in a way that they will respond to? What **tone** will appeal to them? what facts?

STUDENT MODEL

> I want to persuade town officials to vote against a proposed law that sets a curfew for teenagers. Curfews should be set by parents, not the government. We'll need to hire more police to enforce the curfew, and hiring police costs money this town doesn't have. Officials will respond to that.

In your introduction, describe the problem and present a solution—your thesis. In the body of your paper, give information that supports your position. The organizers below show two ways of organizing this information.

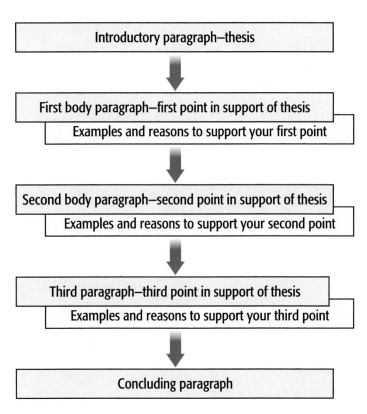

Order of Increasing Importance to Your Audience

Thesis: Town officials should vote against a proposed law setting a curfew for teenagers.

- Parents should set curfew, not government.
- Problem-causing teens won't obey curfew.
- ✓Hiring more police to enforce curfew costs money.

Order of Decreasing Importance to Your Audience

Thesis: Town officials should vote against a proposed law setting a curfew for teenagers.

- ✓Hiring more police to enforce the law costs money.
- Problem-causing teens won't obey curfew.
- Parents should set curfew, not government.

Introductory paragraph—thesis

↓

First body paragraph—first point in support of thesis

Examples and reasons to support your first point

↓

Second body paragraph—second point in support of thesis

Examples and reasons to support your second point

↓

Third paragraph—third point in support of thesis

Examples and reasons to support your third point

↓

Concluding paragraph

DRAFTING

Write your draft
Refer back to your plan, but don't be afraid to change the order of your points if you think that will make your essay more persuasive. Try to end your essay with a call to action.

Support your opinions
Include specific details, facts, expert opinions, and direct quotations that support your thesis. This support will persuade your readers that you are well informed about your subject, and it will strengthen your argument.

Acknowledge objections
Don't ignore viewpoints that oppose yours. Instead, acknowledge the opposition in your writing and show why your ideas are better. This tactic will strengthen your argument and assure your readers that you are both fair and knowledgeable.

STUDENT MODEL

Supporters of the curfew law say that since most teen crimes are committed after 10:00 P.M., the juvenile crime rate will go down if teens aren't allowed out past that time. I think this reasoning is faulty. Not all teens commit crimes, but the few who do are not going to hesitate to break the curfew law. A curfew will restrict law-abiding teens while doing nothing to stop those who don't respect the law.

Jeanne Washington, the mother of a sixteen-year-old, agrees. "My daughter and her friend study together until 10:00 or 10:30 every night. Sometimes they like to go get ice cream after that. These are hardworking girls who have never done anything wrong. Why shouldn't they be allowed that freedom?" Under the proposed curfew law, Jeanne Washington would lose the authority to give her daughter permission to go out and get a late night snack. Is that fair?

REVISING

Evaluate your work

Let your draft sit for a while. Then reread it, imagining that you are one of the people you are trying to persuade. What questions might your argument raise? Think about how you can address those questions in your revision. Using the **Questions for Revising** as a guide, look for other flaws or weak points in your argument. Then highlight your best and strongest sentences. How can you make your other sentences more like them?

Talk it over

Have a partner play the role of a listener who disagrees with your position. Read your essay aloud and ask your partner to react. Have your partner answer the **Questions for Revising.** Take notes on your partner's comments and consider them carefully. Keep in mind, however, you are the author and have the final say.

REVISING TIP
Notice how effective persuasive writers begin their essays, and use some of their strategies to improve your own opening.

TECHNOLOGY TIP
If you are revising on a word processor, don't delete sentences or paragraphs right away. Instead, cut the material you don't want and paste it at the end of your document. Then you can retrieve it if you change your mind later.

QUESTIONS FOR REVISING

Opening
- ☑ Does the opening grab the reader's attention?
- ☑ Does the opening describe a problem and suggest an action?
- ☑ Does the opening address the intended audience?

Body
- ☑ Are good reasons given to support the action?
- ☑ Are the reasons presented in logical order?
- ☑ Have the opposing arguments been addressed?

Conclusion
- ☑ Does the conclusion sum up the argument?
- ☑ Does the conclusion end on a memorable note and call for specific action?

In General
- ☑ Is the language clear?
- ☑ Does the content and language fit the audience?
- ☑ Are there strong verbs and specific nouns?

STUDENT MODEL

As you can see, the ~~proposed~~ curfew law ~~is one that~~ won't ~~be able to~~ lower teen crime or restrain teenagers who can't be controlled by their parents. What it will do is reduce families' authority *increase taxes* and limit teenagers' freedom. If the community is serious about reducing juvenile crime, attention *citizens and police should pay* ~~should be paid~~ to the real criminals.

EDITING/PROOFREADING

PROOFREADING TIP
Use the **Proofreading Checklist** on the inside back cover of this book to help you identify errors.

When you are satisfied with the content of your essay, proofread it carefully for errors in grammar, usage, mechanics, and spelling.

Grammar Hint

Avoid the indefinite use of the pronoun they. Substitute a noun for the pronoun.

In some parts of the country, they arrest jaywalkers.

In some parts of the country, police arrest jaywalkers.

● For more about using pronouns, see **Language Handbook,** pp. R23–R26.

STUDENT MODEL

In a small southwestern town, ~~they~~ finally conceded that a curfew was unworkable.

city officials ᵈ

PUBLISHING/PRESENTING

PRESENTING TIP
Include visual aids if they will help you make a more convincing argument.

How you present your essay depends on who you are trying to persuade. You may want to send it as a letter to the editor of the local paper. If so, follow the guidelines the newspaper provides. If you want to send it to your town council, follow a business-letter format. Make the essay as neat and attractive as you can. Remember to check one final time for mistakes.

Reflecting

In your journal, describe how you will decide whether or not your essay is successful. Think about your experience writing this essay. What have you learned about yourself and about persuasive writing? Are you happy with the finished product? How will you know if your essay is successful? Set goals for your next piece of writing. What might you do differently?

📕 **Save your work for your portfolio.**

Theme 5

Two New American Voices

What does the word voice mean to you? Is it simply the way you sound to others, or is it more than that? Is it the most essential ideas you would like to express? Is it the unique way you express your ideas? In this theme, two writers express their unique voices through poetry. One tells of the people and places around him—of war, suffering, and hard work. The other looks inward, expressing deeply personal thoughts and feelings.

THEME PROJECTS

Listening and Speaking

A Voice Like Your Own As you read the poems in this theme, try to decide which writer's poems express ideas that are closest to your own.

1. Choose three poems from this theme that most closely express your own views. Then choose three poems that express ideas most unlike your own.

2. Read each poem to a small group of class-mates. Read expressively. Explain why you feel the poems express ideas similar to or unlike your own. Invite group members to give their opinions.

Investigate and Report

You Be the Poet Choose one of the two poets in this theme to role-play in a one-person show.

1. Do further research and write an outline of the poet's life.

2. From your outline, list three major parts of the poet's life. For each item on your list, choose a poem that was clearly influenced by an event from the poet's life.

3. Put on a one-person show in which you play the poet. Use props, costumes, and makeup to help create the image of the poet. As the poet, tell about each event you chose and explain how the event might have influenced the writing of that poem.

Blockade on Broadway,
c. 1880s. Taylor and Meeker.
Hand-colored woodcut.

Literature F O C U S

Poetry

Poetry is a type of literature that shares intense experiences or unique insights through the imaginative use of language. Poets rely on the **form** of their writing to convey meaning, using **lines** and **stanzas** rather than sentences and paragraphs as the basic units of composition. Understanding these and other basic elements of poetry will help you analyze the poems you read.

ELEMENTS OF POETRY

MODELS

Speaker

Every poem has a **speaker,** or voice, that talks to the reader. Like a narrator in prose, the speaker is not necessarily the author. The speaker can be a fictional person, an animal, or even a thing.

> The speaker in "The Raven" is a man who has just lost his beloved Lenore.

Rhythm

Rhythm is the pattern of sound created by the arrangement of stressed and unstressed syllables in a line. Rhythm can be regular or irregular. **Meter** is a regular pattern of stressed and unstressed syllables that sets the overall rhythm of certain poems. The basic unit of meter is the **foot,** which typically is made up of at least one stressed and one unstressed syllable. Stressed syllables are marked with (´) and unstressed syllables with (˘).

> For the rare and radiant maiden whom the
> angels name Lenore—
> *from "The Raven" by Edgar Allan Poe*

Rhyme

Rhyme is the repetition of similar sounds in words that appear close to each other in a poem.

- **Internal rhyme** occurs within a line of poetry.
- **End rhyme** occurs at the ends of lines.
- **Slant rhyme** refers to words that almost rhyme, but not quite.
- **Rhyme scheme,** the pattern of rhyme formed by end rhyme, is identified by assigning a different letter of the alphabet to each new rhyme.

> Judge Tenderly—of Me   ⎤ internal
> *from "This is my letter to the World"*   ⎦ rhyme
> *by Emily Dickinson*

> How statue-like I see thee stand,   ⎤ end
> The agate lamp within thy hand!   ⎦ rhyme
> *from "To Helen" by Edgar Allan Poe*

> Who took the Flag today   ⎤
> Can tell the definition   ⎥ slant
> So clear of Victory   ⎦ rhyme
> *from "Success is counted sweetest" by Emily Dickinson*

Other Sound Devices

Sound devices contribute to the musical nature of a poem and help emphasize certain words.

- **Alliteration** is the repetition of sounds, most often consonant sounds, at the beginning of words.
- **Assonance** is the repetition of vowel sounds.
- **Consonance** is the repetition of consonant sounds within words or at the ends of words.
- **Onomatopoeia** is the use of a word or phrase that imitates or suggests the sound it describes.

While I nodded, nearly napping ⎤— alliteration

And the Raven, never flitting, still is sitting, *still* is sitting ⎤— assonance

Some late visitor entreating entrance at my chamber door. ⎤— consonance

tapping, rapping ⎤— onomatopoeia
from "The Raven"

Imagery

Imagery is descriptive language that evokes an emotional response and appeals to the senses—sight, sound, touch, taste, or smell. Some images appeal to more than one sense at the same time.

And the silken, sad, uncertain rustling of each purple curtain ⎤— (appeals to the senses of touch, sound, and sight)
from "The Raven"

Figurative Language

Figurative language is language that is used for descriptive effect and is not meant to be read literally. Usually, figurative language expresses meaning beyond the literal level.

- A **simile** is a figure of speech that uses words such as *like* or *as* to compare seemingly unlike things.
- A **metaphor** compares or equates seemingly unlike things by stating that one thing *is* another. Metaphors do not use *like* or *as.*
- A **symbol** is a person, place, or object that has meaning in itself and also stands for something other than itself. Poets often use symbols to suggest something without actually stating it.
- **Personification** is a figure of speech in which an animal, an object, or an idea is given human characteristics.

Helen, thy beauty is to me
Like those Nicean barks of yore ⎤— simile
from "To Helen"

[the grass] is the handkerchief of the Lord, ⎤— metaphor
from Song of Myself by Walt Whitman

The agate lamp in "To Helen" is a classic symbol of immortality

Quoth the Raven "Nevermore." ⎤— personification
from "The Raven"

Newspaper Article

Walt Whitman was truly a new American voice during the 1800s. He remained a significant figure throughout the 1900s, as shown by this story of thievery and an FBI investigation.

Stolen Whitman Papers Surface After 50 Years

by David Streitfeld and Elizabeth Kastor—*Washington Post*, February 18, 1995

Four long-lost notebooks by Walt Whitman, stolen from the Library of Congress a half-century ago, have been recovered, Sotheby's auction house said yesterday. Found by a man among his late father's papers, the notebooks will be returned to the library.

"This is definitely the most important literary material we could have hoped to recover of anything known in American literature," said David Wigdor, assistant chief of the library's manuscript division.

Six Whitman notebooks are still missing. The 10 stolen volumes were part of a total of 24 donated to the library in 1920 by Thomas B. Harned.

The man who brought the notebooks to Sotheby's in New York has chosen to remain anonymous. He told the auction house that his father had received the material as a gift about 30 years ago. The FBI, which investigated the case in the '40s, is once again pursuing it, according to the Library of Congress.

If the notebooks were not stolen material, they would have brought a presale estimate of $350,000 to $500,000, said Selby Kiffer, a vice president in Sotheby's books and manuscripts department.

The man who approached Sotheby's with the documents was "stunned" when he was told what he had, Kiffer said. "When he realized that he wouldn't be selling them he was stunned and I think slightly depressed, as I think anyone would be. On the other hand, he was incredibly cooperative. . . . He feels he has done his part, and his role is ended." No money is changing hands in the return of the papers.

The rediscovered notebooks include essays on perception and the human senses, names and addresses of friends, and drafts of Civil War poems. Whitman also kept notes about some of the wounded soldiers he tended in Washington [D.C.] in 1862. "bed 15—wants an orange . . . bed 59 wants some liquorice . . . 27 wants some figs and a book," he wrote. Next to some of these jottings were crosses, suggesting the nameless subjects had died.

Respond

1. Why, in your opinion, would the notebooks of a nineteenth-century poet be so valuable?

2. What more would you like to know about this story? Why?

Before You Read

Whitman's Poetry

Meet Walt Whitman

As a young man, Walt Whitman loved to wander through the streets of Manhattan. As he walked, he recorded in a notebook his impressions of the city's sights, sounds, and intriguing cast of characters. Using these notes, Whitman created a revolutionary kind of poetry that celebrated the democratic spirit of his native land.

Whitman lived almost his entire life in Long Island, Manhattan, and Brooklyn, New York. A great believer in gathering a wide range of experiences, he worked as a schoolteacher, office boy, journalist, editor, printer, house builder, and nurse. He also traveled down the Mississippi River, soaking up the voices and sights of America.

In 1854, when Whitman was in his midthirties, he began to devote more of his energy to writing poetry. By this time he had moved back in with his parents in Brooklyn. "Walt," his mother later said, "had no business [during this period] but going out and coming in to eat, drink, write, and sleep." Little did she know that her son was at that time composing what would be one of the greatest books in American literature—*Leaves of Grass*.

In long, unmetered lines called free verse, Whitman celebrated the diversity, energy, and turbulence of nineteenth-century American life. No subject was too commonplace for his attention: not the mechanic or the prisoner, or the lowly blade of grass. Many people were shocked by the poems' unconventional style and by their content. One poet, John Greenleaf Whittier, was even said to have thrown his copy into the fire. Ralph Waldo Emerson, on the other hand, wrote to Whitman: "I greet you at the beginning of a great career."

Through the years, Whitman revised, rearranged, and added new poems to *Leaves of Grass*, publishing a total of nine editions. He imagined the work as one long poem that expressed his all-embracing view of the world. Despite the acclaim from Emerson and others, Whitman had to publish the first five editions of the work at his own expense and lived all his life close to poverty. Today, the 383 poems included in the final edition of *Leaves of Grass* (1892) are read and celebrated throughout the world for capturing the colorful speech and brash, optimistic spirit of a vital young nation.

"You cannot really understand America without Walt Whitman, without *Leaves of Grass*."

—Mary Smith Whitall Costelloe

"I think of art as something to serve the people—the mass: when it fails to do that it's false to its promises."

"The United States themselves are essentially the greatest poem."

—Whitman

Walt Whitman was born in 1819 and died in 1892.

What kind of spirit do you see in the people you know? For example, do you think they feel mostly optimistic or pessimistic? Why?

THINK-PAIR-SHARE Think about these questions on your own for a few minutes. Then discuss your responses with a partner. Finally, share your responses with your classmates and briefly discuss whether people in the United States seem generally optimistic or pessimistic.

SETTING A PURPOSE Read to find out how Whitman views the spirit of his country and its citizens.

──────── **BACKGROUND** ────────

Whitman and the War

In 1862 Whitman's brother was wounded in the first battle of Fredericksburg, and Whitman traveled to the battlefront in Virginia to care for him. Deeply moved by the suffering he encountered and finding his brother's condition stable, Whitman went on to Washington, D.C., to work as a volunteer nurse in army hospitals. There he comforted and cared for both Union and Confederate soldiers, dressing their wounds, writing letters for them, and bringing them items they needed, such as apples, oranges, and books. Writing about this experience, Whitman noted, "I supply often to some of these dear suffering boys . . . that which doctors nor medicines nor skill nor any routine assistance can give."

The Time and Place

Following the Civil War, the United States experienced tremendous economic growth and social change. Railroad construction and a series of new technological advances, such as the telephone, the typewriter, and the automobile, led to a burst of industrial activity. Great social and political change accompanied this growth. For example, many people moved from farms to cities, the number of immigrants increased dramatically, and the country expanded westward. While some individuals profited greatly from these changes, many others suffered. Deplorable working and living conditions in the cities led to labor disputes and eventually to the

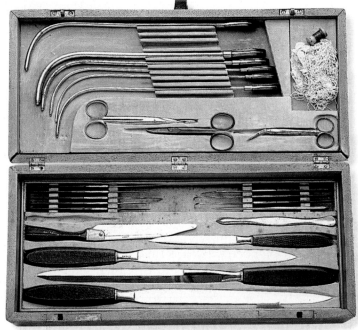

Civil War surgeon's kit

creation of labor unions and political organizations serving workers' needs.

In this growth and turmoil, Whitman saw common people coming alive and asserting their freedom as individuals. He imagined Americans breaking free from conventional ways of life and following their own visions. Recalling this time, Whitman said, "My Book and I—what a period we have presumed to span! those thirty years from 1850 to '80—and America in them!"

I Hear America Singing

Walt Whitman ∼

I hear America singing, the varied carols I hear,
Those of mechanics, each one singing his as it should be blithe° and strong,
The carpenter singing his as he measures his plank or beam,
The mason singing his as he makes ready for work, or leaves off work,
5   The boatman singing what belongs to him in his boat,
       the deckhand singing on the steamboat deck,
The shoemaker singing as he sits on his bench, the hatter singing as he stands,
The wood-cutter's song, the ploughboy's on his way in the morning,
       or at noon intermission or at sundown,
The delicious singing of the mother, or of the young wife at work,
       or of the girl sewing or washing,
Each singing what belongs to him or her and to none else,
10   The day what belongs to the day—at night the party of young fellows,
       robust, friendly,
Singing with open mouths their strong melodious songs.

---

2 *Blithe* means "lighthearted" or "cheerful."

Cradling Wheat, 1938. Thomas Hart Benton. Tempera and oil on board, 31 x 38 in. ©T.H. Benton and R.P. Benton Testamentary Trusts/Licensed by VAGA, New York/The St. Louis Art Museum, St. Louis, MO. Look closely at the people in this painting. What words might Whitman have used to describe them in "I Hear America Singing"? Explain.

Twilight #4, 1997. Peter Sickles. Oil on canvas, 18 x 24 in. Private collection.

When I Heard the Learn'd Astronomer

Walt Whitman ∾

When I heard the learn'd astronomer,
When the proofs, the figures, were ranged in columns before me,
When I was shown the charts and diagrams, to add, divide, and measure them,
When I sitting heard the astronomer where he lectured with much applause
　　in the lecture-room,
How soon unaccountable I became tired and sick,
Till rising and gliding out I wander'd off by myself,
In the mystical moist night-air, and from time to time,
Look'd up in perfect silence at the stars.

Responding to Literature

Personal Response

Which poem did you prefer? Why?

ANALYZING LITERATURE

I Hear America Singing

RECALL AND INTERPRET

1. What occupations does the speaker say represent America? What do these occupations tell you about Whitman's view of his country?
2. According to line 9, what does each laborer sing about? What do the laborers' "songs" suggest about the work they do?
3. What happens at night? Why do you think the poem ends the way it does?

EVALUATE AND CONNECT

4. What **catalog,** or list of images and details, is included in this poem? What effect does the catalog have on your reading of the poem?
5. Look back at your responses to the Focus Activity on page 402. Based on this poem, do you think Whitman would agree or disagree with your ideas? Explain.

*W*hen I Heard the Learn'd Astronomer

RECALL AND INTERPRET

6. What techniques does the astronomer use to present information? What does this suggest to you about the astronomer's approach to his subject?
7. What does the speaker do in lines 6–8? What conclusions can you draw about the speaker based on these actions?
8. How does the speaker's method for "studying" the stars differ from the astronomer's method? What does this difference imply about the speaker's values?

EVALUATE AND CONNECT

9. How does the use of **parallelism** (see page R11) reinforce the message of the poem?
10. What might be some advantages of viewing the stars as the astronomer does? as the speaker does? Which way of viewing do you prefer?

EXTENDING YOUR RESPONSE

Creative Writing

Interview   What would you like to ask Whitman about the themes and distinctive features of "I Hear America Singing" and "When I Heard the Learn'd Astronomer"? With a partner, write questions for Whitman and answers from his point of view.

Interdisciplinary Activity

Astronomy: Your View   In "When I Heard the Learn'd Astronomer," Whitman expresses one opinion about astronomy. Form your own opinion by researching the field. Report your findings to the class.

📖 **Save your work for your portfolio.**

A Sight in Camp in the Daybreak Gray and Dim

Walt Whitman

A sight in camp in the daybreak gray and dim,
As from my tent I emerge so early sleepless,
As slow I walk in the cool fresh air the path near by the hospital tent,
Three forms I see on stretchers lying, brought out there untended lying,
5   Over each the blanket spread, ample brownish woolen blanket,
Gray and heavy blanket, folding, covering all.

Curious I halt and silent stand,
Then with light fingers I from the face of the nearest the first just lift the blanket;
Who are you elderly man so gaunt and grim, with well-gray'd hair, and flesh all sunken
     about the eyes?
10   Who are you my dear comrade?

Then to the second I step—and who are you my child and darling?
Who are you sweet boy with cheeks yet blooming?

Then to the third—a face nor child nor old, very calm, as of beautiful yellow-white ivory;
Young man I think I know you—I think this face is the face of the Christ himself,
15   Dead and divine and brother of all, and here again he lies.

Civil War soldiers awaiting medical treatment, 1864.

Beat! Beat! Drums!

Walt Whitman

The Wounded Drummer Boy, 1871.
Eastman Johnson. Oil on canvas,
40 x 36 in. The Brooklyn Museum,
New York.

Beat! beat! drums!—blow! bugles! blow!
Through the windows—through doors—burst like a ruthless force,
Into the solemn church, and scatter the congregation,
Into the school where the scholar is studying;
5   Leave not the bridegroom quiet—no happiness must he have now with his bride,
Nor the peaceful farmer any peace, ploughing his field or gathering his grain,
So fierce you whirr and pound you drums—so shrill you bugles blow.

Beat! beat! drums!—blow! bugles! blow!
Over the traffic of cities—over the rumble of wheels in the streets;
10   Are beds prepared for sleepers at night in the houses? no sleepers must sleep in those beds,
No bargainers' bargains by day—no brokers or speculators°—would they continue?
Would the talkers be talking? would the singer attempt to sing?
Would the lawyer rise in the court to state his case before the judge?
Then rattle quicker, heavier drums—you bugles wilder blow.

15   Beat! beat! drums!—blow! bugles! blow!
Make no parley°—stop for no expostulation,°
Mind not the timid—mind not the weeper or prayer,
Mind not the old man beseeching the young man,
Let not the child's voice be heard, nor the mother's entreaties,
20   Make even the trestles° to shake the dead where they lie awaiting the hearses,
So strong you thump O terrible drums—so loud you bugles blow.

---

11 *Speculators* are people who engage in risky business ventures hoping to make quick or large profits.
16 A *parley* is a conference between enemies to discuss terms of a truce or an agreement. *Expostulation* is the act of reasoning
    with a person to correct or dissuade him or her.
20 *Trestles* are structures in which a beam is supported by four diverging legs.

Responding to Literature

Personal Response

Which image or idea from these two poems stands out in your mind? Why?

ANALYZING LITERATURE

A Sight in Camp in the Daybreak Gray and Dim

RECALL AND INTERPRET

1. According to the first stanza, what does the speaker see at daybreak? What item does the speaker describe in lines 5–6? Why might the speaker have focused on this item?
2. Describe the first two soldiers. What do the speaker's questions imply about his feelings toward the soldiers?
3. To whom does the speaker compare the third soldier? What does this tell you about the speaker's emotional reaction to what he sees?

EVALUATE AND CONNECT

4. What does each soldier add to your understanding of the poem's message?
5. How do you think you might have reacted to the situation described in the poem?

Beat! Beat! Drums!

RECALL AND INTERPRET

6. What instruments are mentioned in this poem? What might they represent?
7. What kinds of activities do the instruments interrupt? What does the variety of activities suggest to you about the speaker's message?
8. According to the third stanza, what should the instruments ignore? What message does this stanza convey? Explain your answer.

EVALUATE AND CONNECT

9. To whom is the poem addressed? How does this add to its impact?
10. What attitude toward war does this poem express? Support your answer.

EXTENDING YOUR RESPONSE

Creative Writing

A Story Gray and Dim   Write a short story based on "A Sight in Camp in the Daybreak Gray and Dim." Think of this brief event as the beginning of the story. Begin by writing an outline of your story. Then complete the story and present it to a group of classmates.

Interdisciplinary Activity

Music History: The Sounds of Drums and Bugles Research Civil War drums and bugles. What did they look like? What did they sound like? What roles did these instruments play on the battlefront? Report your findings to the class.

📖 **Save your work for your portfolio.**

Before You Read

from *Song of Myself*

Have you ever felt "connected" to nature or to all of humankind? What would it take for you to have such feelings?

DISCUSS As a class, have a brief discussion of what it might mean to feel "connected" to nature or to all of humankind and about what might make someone feel that way.

SETTING A PURPOSE Read to learn of the speaker's feelings of connection to the natural world and to all of humankind.

BACKGROUND

Literary Influences

When Whitman was young, he read Homer's classic epic poem the *Iliad* while "in a shelter'd hollow of rocks and sand, with the sea on each side." He felt that only the "presence of Nature" prevented him from being completely overwhelmed by the experience of reading this poem and other great works of world literature. Several years later Whitman would create his own epic poem—*Song of Myself.* As in the *Iliad,* this poem describes the journey of a hero. The hero in this poem, however, is the poet himself, not a fictional or historic character, and his journey is in part a spiritual one. As the poem progresses, the poet attempts to connect with the spirit of the reader, of the American landscape, of the American people, and, finally, of the universe itself.

Song of Myself encourages each reader to share the poet's journey and to celebrate his or her own heroic spirit. In writing this work, Whitman tried to show that his fellow citizens were as heroic as the "godlike or lordly born characters" written of in ancient Greece.

Authors Among Ourselves

In the 1840s and 1850s, the most popular novelists among readers in the United States were the Scottish writer Sir Walter Scott and the English novelist Charles Dickens. Although Whitman admired these two authors, he deplored what he described as the "tinsel sentimentality" of much of European writing at that time. He asked in one of his essays, "Shall [Nathaniel] Hawthorne get a paltry *seventy-five dollars* for a two-volume work—shall real American genius shiver with neglect—while the public run after this foreign trash?" He urged his fellow citizens to cast aside the "unwholesome reading from abroad" and look for authors among "ourselves."

Eaton's Neck, Long Island, 1872. John Frederick Kensett. Oil on canvas, 18 x 36 in. The Metropolitan Museum of Art, New York.

from Song of Myself

Walt Whitman

1

I celebrate myself, and sing myself,
And what I assume you shall assume,
For every atom belonging to me as good belongs to you.

I loafe and invite my soul,
5   I lean and loafe at my ease observing a spear of summer grass.

My tongue, every atom of my blood, form'd from this soil, this air,
Born here of parents born here from parents the same, and their parents the same,
I, now thirty-seven years old in perfect health begin,
Hoping to cease not till death.

10 Creeds and schools in abeyance,°
Retiring back a while sufficed at what they are, but never forgotten,
I harbor for good or bad, I permit to speak at every hazard,
Nature without check with original energy.

6

A child said *What is the grass?* fetching it to me with full hands;
15 How could I answer the child? I do not know what it is any more than he.

I guess it must be the flag of my disposition, out of hopeful green stuff woven.

Or I guess it is the handkerchief of the Lord,
A scented gift and remembrancer° designedly dropt,
Bearing the owner's name someway in the corners, that we may see and remark,
    and say *Whose?*

20 What do you think has become of the young and old men?
And what do you think has become of the women and children?

---

10 *In abeyance* means "suspended" or "in a state of being undetermined."
18 A *remembrancer* is a reminder.

Haymaking, 1864. Winslow Homer. Oil on canvas, 16 x 11 in. The Columbus Museum of Art, Columbus, OH.

Viewing the painting: In what ways does this painting capture the mood of the poem? Explain, using details from both the painting and the poem.

They are alive and well somewhere,
The smallest sprout shows there is really no death,
And if ever there was it led forward life, and does not wait at the end to arrest it,
25 And ceas'd the moment life appear'd.

All goes onward and outward, nothing collapses,
And to die is different from what any one supposed, and luckier.

16

I am of old and young, of the foolish as much as the wise,
Regardless of others, ever regardful of others,
30 Maternal as well as paternal, a child as well as a man,
Stuff'd with the stuff that is coarse and stuff'd with the stuff that is fine,
One of the Nation of many nations, the smallest the same and the largest the same,
A Southerner soon as a Northerner, a planter nonchalant° and hospitable down by the
    Oconee° I live,
A Yankee bound my own way ready for trade, my joints the limberest joints on earth and
    the sternest joints on earth,
35 A Kentuckian walking the vale of the Elkhorn in my deer-skin leggings, a Louisianian
    or Georgian,
A boatman over lakes or bays or along coasts, a Hoosier,° Badger,° Buckeye;°
At home on Kanadian snow-shoes or up in the bush, or with fishermen off Newfoundland,
At home in the fleet of ice-boats, sailing with the rest and tacking,
At home on the hills of Vermont or in the woods of Maine, or the Texan ranch,
40 Comrade of Californians, comrade of free North-Westerners, (loving their big proportions,)
Comrade of raftsmen and coalmen, comrade of all who shake hands and welcome
    to drink and meat,
A learner with the simplest, a teacher of the thoughtfullest,
A novice beginning yet experient of myriads of seasons,
Of every hue and caste am I, of every rank and religion,
45 A farmer, mechanic, artist, gentleman, sailor, quaker,
Prisoner, fancy-man, rowdy,° lawyer, physician, priest.

I resist any thing better than my own diversity,
Breathe the air but leave plenty after me,
And am not stuck up, and am in my place.

50 (The moth and the fish-eggs are in their place,
The bright suns I see and the dark suns I cannot see are in their place,

The palpable° is in its place and the impalpable is in its place.)

---

33 *Nonchalant* means "showing a lack of interest or enthusiasm." The *Oconee* is a river in Georgia.
36 *Hoosier, Badger,* and *Buckeye* are nicknames for natives or residents of Indiana, Wisconsin, and Ohio, respectively.
46 A *rowdy* is a rough, disorderly person.
52 *Palpable* means "able to be touched or felt."

17

These are really the thoughts of all men in all ages and lands, they
　　are not original with me,
If they are not yours as much as mine they are nothing, or next to nothing,
55　If they are not the riddle and the untying of the riddle they are nothing,
If they are not just as close as they are distant they are nothing.

This is the grass that grows wherever the land is and the water is,
This is the common air that bathes the globe.

46

I know I have the best of time and space, and was never measured and
　　never will be measured.

60　I tramp a perpetual journey, (come listen all!)
My signs are a rain-proof coat, good shoes, and a staff cut from the woods,
No friend of mine takes his ease in my chair,
I have no chair, no church, no philosophy,
I lead no man to a dinner-table, library, exchange,
65　But each man and each woman of you I lead upon a knoll,°
My left hand hooking you round the waist,
My right hand pointing to landscapes of continents and the public road.

Not I, not any one else can travel that road for you,
You must travel it for yourself.

70　It is not far, it is within reach,
Perhaps you have been on it since you were born and did not know,
Perhaps it is everywhere on water and on land.

Shoulder your duds° dear son, and I will mine, and let us hasten forth,
Wonderful cities and free nations we shall fetch as we go.

75　If you tire, give me both burdens, and rest the chuff of your hand° on my hip,

And in due time you shall repay the same service to me,
For after we start we never lie by again.

This day before dawn I ascended a hill and look'd at the crowded heaven,
And I said to my spirit *When we become the enfolders of those orbs, and the pleasure and*
　　knowledge of every thing in them, shall we be fill'd and satisfied then?
80　And my spirit said *No, we but level that lift to pass and continue beyond.*

---

65 A *knoll* is a small, rounded hill.
73 *Duds* are personal belongings.
75 *Chuff of your hand* refers to the fat part of the palm.

You are also asking me questions and I hear you,
I answer that I cannot answer, you must find out for yourself.

Sit a while dear son,
Here are biscuits to eat and here is milk to drink,
85   But as soon as you sleep and renew yourself in sweet clothes, I kiss you with a good-by kiss
         and open the gate for your egress hence.°

Long enough have you dream'd contemptible dreams,
Now I wash the gum from your eyes,
You must habit yourself to the dazzle of the light and of every moment of your life.

Long have you timidly waded holding a plank by the shore,
90   Now I will you to be a bold swimmer,
      To jump off in the midst of the sea, rise again, nod to me, shout, and laughingly dash with
         your hair.

---

85 *Egress hence* means "departure from this place."

The Sand Team, 1917. George Bellows. Oil on canvas, 30½ x 44¼ in. The Brooklyn Museum, New York.

Viewing the painting: In your opinion, what spirit of America does this painting convey? How is it similar to or different from Whitman's view of the American spirit?

The past and present wilt—I have fill'd them, emptied them,
And proceed to fill my next fold of the future.

Listener up there! what have you to confide to me?
95 Look in my face while I snuff the sidle of evening,°
(Talk honestly, no one else hears you, and I stay only a minute longer.)

Do I contradict myself?
Very well then I contradict myself,
(I am large, I contain multitudes.)

100 I concentrate toward them that are nigh,° I wait on the door-slab.

Who has done his day's work? who will soonest be through with his supper?
Who wishes to walk with me?

Will you speak before I am gone? will you prove already too late?

52

The spotted hawk swoops by and accuses me, he complains of my gab and my loitering.

105 I too am not a bit tamed, I too am untranslatable,
I sound my barbaric yawp° over the roofs of the world.

The last scud° of day holds back for me,
It flings my likeness after the rest and true as any on the shadow'd wilds,
It coaxes me to the vapor and the dusk.

110 I depart as air, I shake my white locks at the runaway sun,
I effuse° my flesh in eddies, and drift it in lacy jags.

I bequeath myself to the dirt to grow from the grass I love,
If you want me again look for me under your boot-soles.

You will hardly know who I am or what I mean,
115 But I shall be good health to you nevertheless,
And filter and fibre your blood.

Failing to fetch me at first keep encouraged,
Missing me one place search another,
I stop somewhere waiting for you.

---

95 *Snuff the sidle of evening* means "to put out the last light of the day, which is moving sideways across the sky."
100 *Nigh* means "near."
106 A *yawp* is a loud, sharp cry.
107 *Scud* refers to wind-driven clouds or rain.
111 *Effuse* means "to pour out or forth."

Responding to Literature

Personal Response

How did you react to the speaker in the poem? Explain your answer.

—— ANALYZING LITERATURE ——

RECALL

1. What is the main topic of section 1? What is the speaker saying in lines 10–13 about his past learning and his future?
2. What does the speaker say about death in lines 20–27?
3. A **paradox** is a statement that seems to contradict itself, but may actually be true. What paradoxes does Whitman list in section 16?
4. Summarize the speaker's advice to his "son" in lines 73–91.
5. Briefly state what the speaker is saying in sections 51 and 52.

INTERPRET

6. How does the speaker seem to view himself in relation to nature and to the rest of the world?
7. What do lines 20–27 suggest about the speaker's ideas of life and death?
8. What, in your opinion, do the paradoxes in section 16 reveal about the speaker's feelings toward humankind? What do these lines suggest about Whitman's attitude toward himself?
9. In your opinion, what is the deeper meaning of the advice the speaker gives? Explain your answer using details from the poem.
10. What do sections 51 and 52 suggest to you about the speaker's attitude toward the relationship between his physical body and his spirit? between humankind and nature?

EVALUATE AND CONNECT

11. How does Whitman's use of **catalogs** in this selection help get across his message? (See Literary Terms Handbook, page R3.)
12. Which of Whitman's ideas about nature, death, or people do you find most interesting? Explain, using details from the poem.
13. An **epic poem** recounts the adventures of a hero. In your opinion, is the speaker of *Song of Myself* a hero? Explain your answer with details from the poem.
14. Think back to the ideas you discussed for the Focus Activity on page 409. Then use a chart like the one shown to compare Whitman's ideas about being connected to nature and humankind with yours.
15. What would you like to say to the speaker after reading this poem?

Free Verse

Whitman is famous for using **free verse**—a type of poetry that has no set **meter**, line length, stanza arrangement, or rhyme. Though free verse lacks a regular pattern of stressed and unstressed syllables, it does not lack rhythm. Whitman used free verse because it echoes the rising and falling cadences of everyday speech.

1. With a partner, read one of Whitman's poems aloud, paying close attention to its rhythm. Do you find the rhythm of the poem similar to everyday speech? Explain.
2. In what ways might *Song of Myself* have a different effect if it were written in a regular rhythm pattern?

● See **Literary Terms Handbook**, p. R7.

Connection to nature, humankind	
Whitman's ideas	My ideas

LITERATURE AND WRITING

Writing About Literature

Details, Details In *Song of Myself* and other poems, Whitman uses specific details to enrich his poetry. Choose one of Whitman's poems and list the details in that poem that you find most powerful. Then write a few paragraphs explaining the effect those details have on the poem. For example: Do they bring out the meaning more clearly? Do they make the images more memorable? Be specific in supporting your explanations.

Creative Writing

Celebrate! Write a short poem celebrating your America. Use free verse and other devices Whitman used to create rhythm in his work, such as **repetition** and **parallelism** (see pages R11 and R13). Begin the poem with one of the following lines:

> "I celebrate myself, and sing myself."
> "I hear America singing."

EXTENDING YOUR RESPONSE

Literature Groups

Nature, Death, and Spirit Debate whether or not Whitman succeeds in reaching today's reader. Consider, for example, whether his ideas about nature, death, the spirit of America, and the human spirit are still relevant, and whether his style remains fresh. Summarize the group's responses and share the results with the class.

Internet Connection

Where's Walt? Search the Internet for sites devoted to Whitman. Determine your favorite site and present a short review of it to your classmates. Include the address, the options at the site, and any interesting facts you discovered.

Performing

Sing "a Song" With a group of classmates, perform a choral reading of a section of *Song of Myself*. Decide beforehand who will read each line or stanza: an individual, a pair of students, or the entire group. Also decide when a line should be read loudly or softly, fast or slowly. Try to speak as naturally as possible.

📖 **Save your work for your portfolio.**

Skill Minilesson

VOCABULARY • The Latin Root *pos*

Latin roots form the basis of many English words. The root is usually combined with a prefix, a suffix, or both. The meaning of the English word is usually related to the meaning of the root it contains. For example, the words *disposition* (line 16) and *supposed* (line 27), from *Song of Myself,* contain the Latin root *pos,* meaning "to put" or "to place." *Disposition* can be interpreted as "the way a person's temperament or mood is arranged or placed"; *suppose* can mean "to place under belief."

PRACTICE Define each word below, using a dictionary if necessary. Then discuss with a partner how the meaning of the Latin root *pos* contributes to the meaning of each word.

1. deposit
2. oppose
3. transpose
4. position
5. expose

Before You Read

The Useless and The Butterfly Dream

Meet
Chuang Tzu

"I know about letting the world alone, not interfering. I do not know about running things. Letting things alone so that men will not blow their nature out of shape! Not interfering, so that men will not be changed into something they are not!"

—*Chuang Tzu*

Chuang Tzu (zhwäng dzoo) was born more than two thousand years ago into a world of war and chaos. From the 900s to about 220 B.C., China was embroiled in civil war, as warlords fought for power and land. In search of peace and stability, Chuang Tzu and other philosophers tried to show China's rulers a better way to govern. Great thinkers sought to create a society in harmony with nature.

Little is known of Chuang Tzu's life. According to one Chinese historian, Chuang may have been born in the town of Meng, somewhere in the present-day province of Anhui or Henan. His given name was Chuang Chou. The title *Tzu*, meaning "Master," was added to honor his role as a founder of the way of thinking that became known as Taoism (dou′ iz′ əm).

Philosophers Chuang Tzu, Lao Tzu, and Lieh Tzu are considered the founders of Taoism—a philosophy based on the principle that happiness and tranquility can be achieved by understanding one's own true nature and living in harmony with it.

"Tao" is the name given to the powerful, invisible reality believed by Taoists to be the source of everything in the universe. Followers believe that if they live by Taoist principles they will eventually become good and enlightened beings. Chuang Tzu believed that an individual gains freedom by living a life of purity and simplicity. In his writings, he described politics, fame, and fortune as threats to health, freedom, and integrity.

Chuang Tzu was born c. 369 B.C. and died c. 286 B.C.

FOCUS ACTIVITY

Think of a time when something made you look at your life from an entirely different perspective. Maybe the new view was spurred by a dream, an event, or advice.

CHART IT! Use a flow chart like the one on this page to describe the chain of events that led you to a new and unusual perspective on life.

SETTING A PURPOSE Read to discover the new perspectives Chuang Tzu offers.

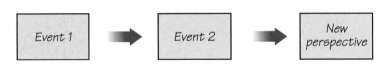

Event 1 → Event 2 → New perspective

BACKGROUND

Ancient Words

The book that shares its author's name—*Chuang Tzu*—is considered a masterpiece of Chinese literature and philosophy. Only the first seven chapters, or "Inner Chapters," are attributed to Chuang Tzu. The other writings have been added or edited over the centuries and contain a wide variety of stories, essays, and legends that deal with Taoist philosophy. Many legends about the life of Chuang Tzu appear throughout the book, although historians do not consider them to be reliable.

The Useless

Chuang Tzu
Translated by Martin Palmer

Hui Tzu said to Chuang Tzu:
"All your teaching is centered on what has no use."

Chuang replied:
"If you have no appreciation for what has no use
You cannot begin to talk about what can be used.
The earth, for example, is broad and vast
But of all this expanse a man uses only a few inches
Upon which he happens to be standing.
Now suppose you suddenly take away
All that he is not actually using
So that, all around his feet a gulf
Yawns, and he stands in the Void,
With nowhere solid except right under each foot:
How long will he be able to use what he is using?"

Hui Tzu said: "It would cease to serve any purpose."

Chuang Tzu concluded:
　　"This shows
　　The absolute necessity
　　Of what has 'no use.'"

Magical Butterfly. Wang Wu (1632–1690) and Da Chongguang (1623–1692). Ink and color on paper. Private collection.

The Butterfly Dream

Chuang Tzu
Translated by Martin Palmer

ONCE UPON A TIME, I, Chuang Tzu, dreamt that I was a butterfly, flitting around and enjoying myself. I had no idea I was Chuang Tzu. Then suddenly I woke up and was Chuang Tzu again. But I could not tell, had I been Chuang Tzu dreaming I was a butterfly, or a butterfly dreaming I was now Chuang Tzu?

Responding to Literature

Personal Response

What do "The Useless" and "The Butterfly Dream" leave you thinking about?

ANALYZING LITERATURE

RECALL AND INTERPRET

1. What statement does Hui Tzu first make to Chuang Tzu? What do you think the statement means?
2. How does Chuang reply to Hui? What example does Chuang use to support his reply? Is the example, in your opinion, an appropriate response to Hui's statement? Explain.
3. What is Chuang's final conclusion? Restate this conclusion in your own words and explain what Chuang seems to be saying.

EVALUATE AND CONNECT

4. Did Chuang's argument convince you? Why or why not?
5. A **paradox** is a statement that seems to contradict itself but may actually be true. What effect does paradox have on your reading of the selection?

RECALL AND INTERPRET

6. What does Chuang Tzu say he once dreamt? Why do you think he would want to relate the story of such a dream?
7. During the dream, what does he have "no idea" of? Why might he have added this statement to the story of his dream?
8. What does Chuang Tzu wonder when he wakes from the dream? What does this tell you about his way of thinking?

EVALUATE AND CONNECT

9. What do you think the butterfly might symbolize? Do you think it is an effective **symbol** (see page R16)? Explain your answer with details from the selection.
10. What lesson, or **moral**, do you gain from this story? Explain your conclusion.

EXTENDING YOUR RESPONSE

Personal Writing

Your Own Dream   In your journal, write about an interesting and unique dream you have had. Tell what lesson you might learn from that dream. You might try to write your dream in the style of Chuang Tzu. Also look for symbols in your dream–like the butterfly in Chuang's dream.

Literature Groups

New Views   With your group, discuss the question: Do "The Butterfly Dream" and "The Useless" cause you to look at life in a different way? If so, how? Review your answers to the Focus Activity on page 418 to help you. Share your ideas with other groups.

💼 **Save your work for your portfolio.**

COMPARING selections

from **Song of Myself** and The Useless and The Butterfly Dream

COMPARE IDEAS

Imagine Walt Whitman and Chuang Tzu in conversation. In a group, discuss questions such as the following. Support your discussion with details from the selections.

1. What questions might each want to ask the other? What answers might they get?
2. What else might they talk about?
3. About what might they agree? About what might they disagree?

Have two group members improvise a discussion between the writers for the class.

COMPARE IMPRESSIONS

Create illustrations that convey your impressions of *Song of Myself,* "The Butterfly Dream," and "The Useless." Sketch two illustrations, one for *Song of Myself* and another for one or both pieces by Chuang Tzu. Then share your work with a partner and discuss similarities and differences in your impressions.

Magical Butterfly. Wang Wu (1632–1690) and Da Chongguang (1623–1692).

COMPARE CULTURES

Whitman was influenced by an American movement known as Transcendentalism. Chuang Tzu was a founder of an Asian way of thought called Taoism.

- Use an encyclopedia to research Transcendentalism and Taoism.
- In your own words, write five to ten sentences that tell the basic ideas of Transcendentalism. Do the same for Taoism.
- Then write an answer to each of these questions: If Whitman had lived in China in the time of Chuang Tzu, might he have been a Taoist? If Chuang Tzu had lived in the United States when Whitman did, might he have accepted the ideas of Transcendentalism? Explain, using details from your research and from the selections.

Vo·cab·u·lar·y Skills

Understanding Prefixes and Suffixes

One way to determine the meaning of an unfamiliar word is to analyze its parts. If you recognize the root, or base of a word, you are well on your way to understanding the new word's meaning. By learning the meanings of **prefixes** (word parts attached to the beginning of a word) and **suffixes** (word parts attached to the end of a word) you can decipher new words. For example, here is how you might analyze the word *expostulation* from Walt Whitman's "Beat! Beat! Drums!"

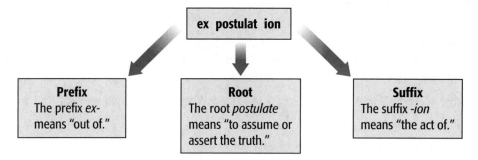

The word *expostulation* means "the act of reasoning with someone to correct or dissuade"—that is, the act of trying to talk someone out of an idea. Although a word's parts usually add up to its meaning, it is a good idea to confirm your interpretation with a dictionary.

Here are some frequently used prefixes and suffixes and their meanings:

	Meaning	Examples
Prefixes		
il-, im-, in-, ir-	without, not	illegal, incomplete
trans-	across	translate, transport
Suffixes		
-able, -ible	capable of	laughable, visible
-ical	related to	symmetrical, geological

EXERCISE

Use prefixes and suffixes from the lists to help you complete the following sentences.

1. A transcontinental airline flight would fly

   a. across a continent.

   b. between more than two continents.

   c. from one continent to another.

2. A hierarchy can be a classification of people based on their status. So, in a hierarchical society, people would

   a. all have the same status.

   b. all be related to one another.

   c. be divided by their status.

Before You Read

Dickinson's Poetry

Meet Emily Dickinson

"Forgive me if I am frightened; I never see strangers and hardly know what I say," Emily Dickinson said to Thomas Wentworth Higginson the first time she met him in her home in Amherst, Massachusetts. Higginson was a well-known critic, with whom she had been corresponding for eight years but had never met. Indeed, Dickinson didn't see strangers often: she rarely went out into the world or received visitors.

Dickinson lived almost her entire life in her family's home, watching the life of Amherst from her second-story bedroom window and writing poetry. She composed approximately eighteen hundred poems, though only seven were published during her lifetime. After Dickinson died, her younger sister Lavinia discovered a number of Dickinson's poems in a dresser drawer and became the principal agent of their publication. Dickinson enjoyed a close relationship with Lavinia and with her older brother Austin, but felt distant from her mother and intimidated by her stern, but loving, father, who was one of Amherst's most distinguished citizens.

As she neared the end of her life, Dickinson hardly ever ventured downstairs, instead sending little notes to visitors who waited below. Dickinson's quiet exterior, however, disguised a passionate inner life. She was a poet far ahead of her time, a poet of keen awareness and startling originality. She created her own distinctive style, experimenting with grammar, capitalization, punctuation, rhyme, and meter—and heartily confusing the few critics of her day who actually saw her poems. Many years would pass before most readers came to fully understand the genius that spoke from her poems.

No matter how common or ordinary the occurrence, Dickinson could find meaning in it. A slant of light during the afternoon, a bird coming down a walk, a long shadow on the lawn; in just eight, twelve, or sixteen lines, she could turn the everyday into the miraculous, and the apparently meaningless into the deeply meaningful. After reading Dickinson's poems, critic Allen Tate rejected Dickinson's description of herself as "frightened" and the world's assessment of her life as quiet or barren. He said, "All pity for Miss Dickinson's 'starved life' is misdirected. Her life was one of the richest and deepest ever lived on this continent." So it is that the "facts" of Dickinson's outer life seem to tell one story, but the proof of Dickinson's inner life, her poetry, tells an entirely different story.

> **"To live is so startling, it leaves but little room for other occupations."**
>
> **"I had no monarch in my life, and cannot rule myself; and when I try to organize, my little force explodes and leaves me bare and charred."**
>
> —Dickinson

Emily Dickinson was born in 1830 and died in 1886.

FOCUS ACTIVITY

How important are your friends to you? What are your views of death? What is success? What is wisdom?

FREEWRITE Spend three or four minutes freewriting to explore your response to one of the questions above.

SETTING A PURPOSE Read to learn one poet's views of relationships, death, success, and other topics.

BACKGROUND

Dickinson's Dashes and Capitalization

Much of Dickinson's poetry features her characteristic use of dashes. The dashes serve as interrupters. They signal pauses, but more than that, they call attention to the words they enclose. They may break off a line or thought suddenly; they may call attention to a shift in meaning or action; they may interrupt the rhythm; or they may draw attention to the moment of silence they create in an oral reading of the poems. To understand these poems, you need to think about not only the words but also the dashes. Each one is carefully placed, and each one affects the reading of the poem.

Dickinson was also innovative in her use of capitalization. Like most poets of her day, she capitalized the first letter of each line of a poem and all proper nouns. Additionally, however, she capitalized many common nouns, thereby calling attention to them and emphasizing their importance.

Literary Influences

Books, Dickinson once said, were her "enthralling friends." She particularly enjoyed reading William Shakespeare, Ralph Waldo Emerson, and women writers of her day, including George Eliot, Charlotte and Emily Brontë, and Elizabeth Barrett Browning. Dickinson's interest in the complexity and turmoil of the human soul and in humankind's relationship to nature drew her to these writers. Dickinson also steeped herself in the Bible, particularly the Book of Revelation. Her poems refer to various religious concepts, such as heaven, hell, sin, and immortality.

Technically, Dickinson's poems owe much to the hymns she heard in childhood, whose rhythms she adapted to her poetry. Many of her poems consist of alternating six- and eight-syllable lines. This is the most popular form of rhythm in old Protestant hymns.

Dickinson Homestead, Amherst, Massachusetts.

If you were coming in the Fall

Emily Dickinson

If you were coming in the Fall,
I'd brush the Summer by
With half a smile, and half a spurn,
As Housewives do, a Fly.

5   If I could see you in a year,
I'd wind the months in balls—
And put them each in separate Drawers,
For fear the numbers fuse—

If only Centuries, delayed,
10 I'd count them on my Hand,
Subtracting, till my fingers dropped
Into Van Dieman's Land.°

If certain, when this life was out—
That yours and mine, should be
15 I'd toss it yonder, like a Rind,
And take Eternity—

But, now, uncertain of the length
Of this, that is between,
It goads me, like the Goblin Bee—
20 That will not state—its sting.

12 *Van Dieman's Land* is the former name for Tasmania, an
island that is part of Australia.

Waiting, 1885. Clement Rollins Grant. Oil on canvas, 20 x 30 in. Private collection.

My life closed twice before its close

Emily Dickinson

My life closed twice before its close—
It yet remains to see
If Immortality unveil
A third event to me

So huge, so hopeless to conceive
As these that twice befell.
Parting is all we know of heaven,
And all we need of hell.

The Soul selects her own Society

Emily Dickinson

The Soul selects her own Society—
Then—shuts the Door—
To her divine Majority—
Present no more—

5   Unmoved—she notes the Chariots—pausing—
At her low Gate—
Unmoved—an Emperor be kneeling
Upon her Mat—

I've known her—from an ample nation—
10 Choose One—
Then—close the Valves of her attention—
Like Stone—

Responding to Literature

Personal Response

What questions would you like to ask the speakers of these poems?

────────── ANALYZING LITERATURE ──────────

If you were coming in the Fall

RECALL AND INTERPRET

1. What periods of time does the speaker suggest in each of the first four stanzas? What action does the speaker take in the first four stanzas? Why, in your opinion, do the periods of time change from stanza to stanza?
2. According to the fifth stanza, what is the speaker uncertain about? Why might she compare this uncertainty to a bee's sting?

EVALUATE AND CONNECT

3. Would you call this a love poem? Why or why not?
4. What might Dickinson be saying about the nature of waiting? Do you agree? Explain.

My life closed twice before its close

RECALL AND INTERPRET

5. What has already happened twice to the speaker? To what kind of event might the speaker be referring?
6. What does the speaker say about parting? How, in your opinion, do partings affect the speaker?

EVALUATE AND CONNECT

7. Have you ever seen a life close before its close? What form did that closing take?
8. Only one dash is used in this poem, and only one word is capitalized that isn't at the beginning of a line. What effect, in your opinion, do the dash and capitalized word have on the meaning of the poem? Explain your answer.

The Soul selects her own Society

RECALL AND INTERPRET

9. What does the soul select? From among how many does the soul choose just one? What does this suggest about the soul?
10. According to the second stanza, what things fail to "move" the soul? In your opinion, why are the examples of what the soul is "unmoved" by significant?
11. What words does the speaker use to refer to the soul? From these words, what can you infer about the speaker's relationship to the soul?

EVALUATE AND CONNECT

12. What image do you see in your mind's eye when you imagine the soul closing "the Valves of her attention"? How does the use of this **metaphor** affect your understanding of the poem? (See Literary Terms Handbook, page R9.)

A Day Dream, 1877. Eastman Johnson. Oil on paperboard, 24 x 12 in. Fine Arts Museums of San Francisco. Gift of Mr. and Mrs. John D. Rockefeller III.

Much Madness is divinest Sense

Emily Dickinson ∿

Much Madness is divinest Sense—
To a discerning Eye—
Much Sense—the starkest Madness—
'Tis the Majority
In this, as All, prevail—
Assent—and you are sane—
Demur°—you're straightway dangerous—
And handled with a Chain—

---

7 *Demur* means "to hesitate" or "to protest."

Success is counted sweetest

Emily Dickinson ∿

Success is counted sweetest
By those who ne'er succeed.
To comprehend a nectar°
Requires sorest need.

5　Not one of all the purple Host°
Who took the Flag today
Can tell the definition
So clear of Victory

As he defeated—dying—
10　On whose forbidden ear
The distant strains of triumph
Burst agonized and clear!

_____

3　*Nectar* is a sweet liquid secreted by plants and used by bees in the making of honey. In Greek mythology, nectar is the drink of the gods that makes all who drink it immortal.
5　*Purple Host* means "winning army."

Taps, c. 1907–1909. William Gilbert Gaul. Oil on canvas, 32¾ x 43 in. The Birmingham Museum of Art, Birmingham, AL.
How does this painting enhance your understanding of Dickinson's message in this poem?

Responding to Literature

Personal Response

What new insights or ideas did the poems give you? Share your thoughts with classmates.

ANALYZING LITERATURE

Much Madness is divinest Sense

RECALL AND INTERPRET

1. According to the speaker, in lines 1–3, what is sense often confused with? Who does the speaker say knows the difference?
2. What or who determines what "Sense" of the third line is? What might the difference be between the "Sense" in line 1 and the "Sense" in line 3?
3. According to the poem, what does a person have to do to be considered "sane"? How would you describe the poet's attitude toward this concept of sanity?
4. How is a person regarded who disagrees with accepted ideas? What does the last word of the poem, *chain,* suggest about what happens to such a person?

EVALUATE AND CONNECT

5. This poem is filled with dashes. What effect, in your opinion, do they have on the poem? What words and ideas do they seem to emphasize?

Success is counted sweetest

RECALL AND INTERPRET

6. According to the first stanza, who most values success? Why?
7. What example of success is given in the second stanza? How well do those who succeed in this manner understand success?
8. According to the speaker, who understands success better than the "purple Host"? How does this person react to hearing the "strains of triumph"?

EVALUATE AND CONNECT

9. In your own words, state Dickinson's viewpoint on success as expressed in this poem. Do you agree or disagree with this view? Explain your reasons.
10. Why, in your opinion, did Dickinson choose war **imagery** (see page R8)? If you were writing a poem about success, what images might you include?

EXTENDING YOUR RESPONSE

Listening and Speaking

Subject to Interpretation With a partner, take turns reading aloud this pair of poems. Vary the **rhythm** (see page R13) by emphasizing different words or pauses. Discuss how hearing the poems read in different rhythms might affect your interpretations of them.

Writing About Literature

Compare and Contrast Find one similarity in these two poems and one difference between them. Then write a paragraph describing the similarity and one describing the difference.

📖 **Save your work for your portfolio.**

I heard a Fly buzz when I died

Emily Dickinson ～

I heard a Fly buzz—when I died—
The Stillness in the Room
Was like the Stillness in the Air—
Between the Heaves of Storm—

5 The Eyes around—had wrung them dry—
And Breaths were gathering firm
For that last Onset—when the King
Be witnessed—in the Room—

I willed my Keepsakes—Signed away
10 What portion of me be
Assignable—and then it was
There interposed a Fly—

With Blue—uncertain stumbling Buzz—
Between the light—and me—
15 And then the Windows failed—and then
I could not see to see—

The Bustle in a House

Emily Dickinson ～

The Bustle in a House
The Morning after Death
Is solemnest of industries
Enacted upon Earth—

The Sweeping up the Heart
And putting Love away
We shall not want to use again
Until Eternity.

Because I could not stop for Death

Emily Dickinson

Because I could not stop for Death—
He kindly stopped for me—
The Carriage held but just Ourselves—
And Immortality.

5 We slowly drove—He knew no haste
And I had put away
My labor and my leisure too,
For His Civility°—

We passed the School, where Children strove
10 At Recess—in the Ring—
We passed the Fields of Gazing Grain—
We passed the Setting Sun—

Or rather—He passed Us—
The Dews drew quivering and chill—
15 For only Gossamer,° my Gown—
My Tippet°—only Tulle°—

We paused before a House that seemed
A Swelling of the Ground—
The Roof was scarcely visible—
20 The Cornice°—in the Ground—

Since then—'tis Centuries—and yet
Feels shorter than the Day
I first surmised the Horses' Heads
Were toward Eternity—

---

8 An old meaning of *civility* is "a community of citizens." Among the more modern meanings is "courtesy." Dickinson could have had either or both meanings in mind.

15 *Gossamer* is a light gauzelike fabric.
16 A *tippet* is a scarf for the neck and shoulders with loose ends that hang down in front. *Tulle* is fine netting used in making scarves and veils.
20 A *cornice* is the projecting, decorative molding along the top of a building.

Responding to Literature

Personal Response

Which images from these poems did you find the most surprising and memorable? Why?

ANALYZING LITERATURE

I heard a Fly buzz when I died

RECALL AND INTERPRET

1. According to the first stanza, what is the atmosphere in the room like? What effect does the buzzing fly seem to have on the speaker?
2. In lines 5 and 6, what are the "eyes" and "breaths" doing? What do the "eyes" and "breaths" await? Explain your answer.
3. According to stanzas three and four, what does the fly come between? What happens next? In your opinion, what point about dying does the speaker make in this poem?

EVALUATE AND CONNECT

4. How does Dickinson's account of someone dying compare with other representations you have read or seen?

The Bustle in a House

RECALL AND INTERPRET

5. What words does the speaker use that suggest everyday household chores? In your opinion, is the poem really referring to everyday household chores? Explain.
6. According to the second stanza, when will we again "use" the love we put aside on the morning after death? What does this suggest about Dickinson's religious faith?

EVALUATE AND CONNECT

7. In your opinion, is bustle helpful or burdensome in times of grief? Explain.
8. An **analogy** is a comparison between two things to show their similarities. What analogy does the speaker make in this poem? In your opinion, is this an effective comparison?

Because I could not stop for Death

RECALL AND INTERPRET

9. According to the first stanza, why does "Death" stop? How is "Death" portrayed?
10. What places and things does the speaker pass while taking the ride with "Death"? What might these places and things represent?
11. What revelation does the speaker make in the last stanza? Why? What can you infer from this about the speaker's attitude toward death?

EVALUATE AND CONNECT

12. If you wrote a poem with this title, what places and things would the speaker pass in your poem? How would the speaker be dressed? Where would the speaker end up?

Writing Skills

Elaborating on an Idea

Elaboration is the filling in of details that flesh out an idea. In "Because I could not stop for Death," Emily Dickinson elaborates on the carriage journey with specific details. For example, when the speaker mentions passing a school, she describes the children at recess. Elaboration not only enriches poetry, it also adds depth and clarity to prose. Besides details, elaboration can also include the following:

- facts and statistics
- anecdotes
- reasons
- expert opinions
- quotations
- examples

The kind of writing you do determines how you will elaborate. To prove a point, you might elaborate by using facts and quotations. For example, in a letter to protest the loss of a neighborhood park you might include

- the results of a poll showing that 150 preschool children use the playground equipment several times a week.
- a quote from the former mayor: "The citizens of Midville need travel no more than a few blocks to picnic or play ball in one of the many small parks that make our community the envy of its neighbors."

To describe someone or something, you might use an anecdote.

> Jonathan Marks finished the last bit of oatmeal in his bowl, got to his feet, and ambled to the sink to wash his dishes. He walked to the door, checked the empty mailbox, and brought in the morning newspaper.
> "Max," he said to the old mixed-breed hound devotedly following him, "wait until I reread this letter my niece wrote last week. Then we'll go for our morning walk."

ACTIVITIES

1. Use facts and expert opinions to elaborate for your parents on the reasons you should receive a laptop computer (or any other gift).

2. Use examples and an anecdote to describe one friend to another.

There's a certain Slant of light

Emily Dickinson

There's a certain Slant of light,
Winter Afternoons—
That oppresses, like the Heft°
Of Cathedral Tunes—

5   Heavenly Hurt, it gives us—
We can find no scar,
But internal difference,
Where the Meanings, are—

None may teach it—Any—
10   'Tis the Seal° Despair—
An imperial affliction
Sent us of the Air—

When it comes, the Landscape listens—
Shadows—hold their breath—
15   When it goes, 'tis like the Distance
On the look of Death—

---

3 Here, *heft* means "heaviness."
10 Here, *seal* means "emblem."

This is my letter to the World

Emily Dickinson

At the Window, 1870. Karl Harald Alfred Broge. Oil on canvas, 21 x 17¼ in. Private collection.

This is my letter to the World
That never wrote to Me—
The simple News that Nature told—
With tender Majesty

Her Message is committed°
To Hands I cannot see—
For love of Her—Sweet—countrymen—
Judge tenderly—of Me

---

5 *Committed* means "entrusted."

Responding to Literature

Personal Response

What reactions did you have while reading these poems?

ANALYZING LITERATURE

There's a certain Slant of light

RECALL AND INTERPRET

1. When does the speaker observe the "certain Slant of light"? What effect does the light have on the speaker?
2. In the third stanza, what words or phrases does the speaker use to name the slant of light? What can you infer about the speaker's feelings toward the light?
3. What happens when the light comes, and what happens when it goes? What might the light **symbolize**, or represent?

EVALUATE AND CONNECT

4. Have you ever experienced the kind of winter afternoon light the speaker describes? What might be different about the light or a person's mood on a winter afternoon than at other times of year or day?
5. What feelings does Dickinson evoke as she describes that "certain Slant of light"? Does she bring out these feelings effectively? Use details from the poem to explain your answer.
6. **Personification** is the giving of human qualities or characteristics to an object, an idea, or an animal. Identify two or more examples of personification in this poem. Explain how they affect the poem's meaning.

This is my letter to the World

RECALL AND INTERPRET

7. To whom is the speaker's letter addressed? To what do you think the speaker is referring with the words "my letter"?
8. What "News" does the letter contain? What, in your opinion, is the speaker's relationship to nature?
9. What plea does the speaker make in the second stanza? Why do you think the speaker makes this plea?

EVALUATE AND CONNECT

10. Do you think this poem would make a suitable introduction to a collection of Dickinson's work? Explain your answer.
11. What new impressions of Dickinson did this poem give you?
12. If you could send a letter to the world, what would it say?

Literary ELEMENTS

Slant Rhyme

Slant rhyme, also called imperfect rhyme or eye rhyme, refers to the words at the ends of lines of poetry that almost—but don't quite—rhyme. Dickinson makes constant use of slant rhyme in her poems. For example, in "I heard a Fly buzz when I died," the words *room* and *storm,* which appear at the ends of lines 2 and 4, almost rhyme. Similarly, the words *be* and *fly,* at the ends of lines 10 and 12, are slant rhymes. In this case, the words do not almost rhyme; instead, they end with letters that sometimes rhyme or may look as if they rhyme.

1. Identify one other use of slant rhyme in "I heard a Fly buzz when I died."
2. Identify the two examples of slant rhyme in "The Bustle in a House."
3. Identify two other uses of slant rhyme in other poems by Dickinson. Give at least one reason why Dickinson may have chosen to use slant rhyme in each case.

● See **Literary Terms Handbook,** p. R13.

— LITERATURE AND WRITING —

Writing About Literature

Identify Themes   Based on the poems you have read, what would you identify as the **themes,** or central messages, of Dickinson's poetry? Begin by jotting down notes about the theme of each poem in this lesson. Then write two or three paragraphs in which you identify Dickinson's primary themes and give examples of how she states them. Finally, compare Dickinson's themes with the ideas you expressed in the Focus Activity on page 424.

Creative Writing

Remodeling Job   Take one of the topics expressed in Dickinson's poems, such as "Death" picking up a rider and taking the rider to the cemetery, and present the topic in a different form. For example, you might choose to create a cartoon, comic strip, diary entry, monologue, script, or itinerary. Title your work with a relevant quote from Dickinson's poetry.

— EXTENDING YOUR RESPONSE —

Literature Groups

Finding the Meaning   With your group, go back over two or three poems and identify words, phrases, and lines that you found difficult to understand. Discuss these passages with one another and offer ideas on how to interpret them. Build an interpretation of each poem based on everyone's combined input. Be ready to share your interpretations with the class.

Internet Connection

Visit Emily Dickinson On-line   The life of this very private poet has become very public on the Internet. Conduct a search to find Web sites devoted to Dickinson's life and poetry. Visit one site and present a short review of it to your classmates. Include the address, the options at the site, and aspects of the site that make visiting it a worthwhile or time-wasting experience.

Performing

Play Charades   Working as a group, choose an image or scene from one of the poems to act out for another group. See how quickly others can identify the poem. When you are done, watch the charades of other groups and identify the poems they correspond to.

📔 **Save your work for your portfolio.**

Web Page

Imitation, people say, is the highest form of flattery. Does that statement include humorous imitation, or **parody?** The poems below placed first and second in an on-line Emily Dickinson Parody Poetry Contest.

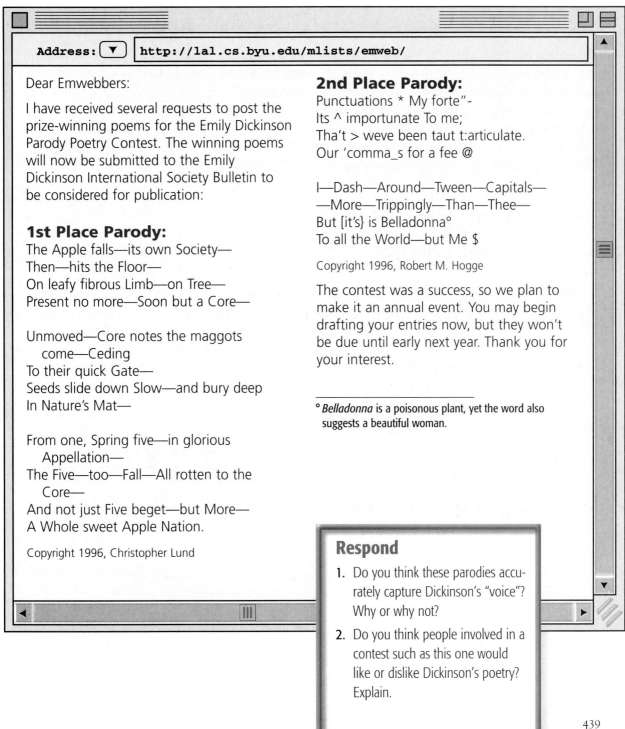

Address: ▼ `http://lal.cs.byu.edu/mlists/emweb/`

Dear Emwebbers:

I have received several requests to post the prize-winning poems for the Emily Dickinson Parody Poetry Contest. The winning poems will now be submitted to the Emily Dickinson International Society Bulletin to be considered for publication:

1st Place Parody:
The Apple falls—its own Society—
Then—hits the Floor—
On leafy fibrous Limb—on Tree—
Present no more—Soon but a Core—

Unmoved—Core notes the maggots
    come—Ceding
To their quick Gate—
Seeds slide down Slow—and bury deep
In Nature's Mat—

From one, Spring five—in glorious
    Appellation—
The Five—too—Fall—All rotten to the
    Core—
And not just Five beget—but More—
A Whole sweet Apple Nation.

Copyright 1996, Christopher Lund

2nd Place Parody:
Punctuations * My forte"-
Its ^ importunate To me;
Tha't > weve been taut t:articulate.
Our 'comma_s for a fee @

I—Dash—Around—Tween—Capitals—
—More—Trippingly—Than—Thee—
But [it's} is Belladonna°
To all the World—but Me $

Copyright 1996, Robert M. Hogge

The contest was a success, so we plan to make it an annual event. You may begin drafting your entries now, but they won't be due until early next year. Thank you for your interest.

_____

° *Belladonna* is a poisonous plant, yet the word also suggests a beautiful woman.

Respond
1. Do you think these parodies accurately capture Dickinson's "voice"? Why or why not?

2. Do you think people involved in a contest such as this one would like or dislike Dickinson's poetry? Explain.

~: Writing · Workshop :~

Expository Writing: Analyzing a Poem

Using relatively few words, poets can communicate vast meanings and evoke deep emotions. How do they do it? They use rhythm, sound, form, figurative language, and numerous other methods to get the most out of their words. As a reader, you try to understand the poem, and one of the best ways to understand a poem is to write an analysis of it. **In this workshop, you will analyze a poem by identifying its meaning and then writing an essay that explains how various techniques help create that meaning.** You may choose a poem from this theme or any other poem that appeals to you.

● As you write your analysis, refer to the **Writing Handbook,** pp. R62–R77.

The Writing Process

PREWRITING

PREWRITING TIP
Keep a dictionary beside you as you read the poem. You will need to understand the meaning of each word.

Explore ideas

Choose a poem from this unit or any poem that has made a strong impression on you. For example, you might want to write about a poem that gave you a surprising view of death, as in Dickinson's "I heard a Fly buzz when I died." Or you might choose a poem that expresses your own feelings about nature, as in Whitman's *Song of Myself.* Then use the following steps to help you get inside the poem.

● Read the poem once all the way through, noting how it makes you feel and any new insights it provides.
● Read the poem again, highlighting sections you might not understand.
● Read it a third and fourth time, jotting down questions, thoughts, feelings—anything you think of.
● Discuss the poem with a partner. Remember, though, that you don't have to agree on everything.

Choose an audience

You can write your poetry analysis for other high school students. Perhaps your class can even put together a literary magazine with articles on favorite poems.

Consider your purpose

No matter who your audience is, you must explain your interpretation of the poem and show how the poet conveys that meaning. To do this, you will have to identify the techniques the poet uses and give examples from the poem.

Make a plan

In the introduction to your essay, state your interpretation of the poem's meaning. You will also want to summarize the techniques that the poet uses to convey the meaning. Then, in the body of your essay, you will devote a separate paragraph to each technique. The chart below will help you plan the content of your essay.

STUDENT MODEL

Meaning	Does the poem focus on an idea? Does it focus on a feeling? What message is the poet trying to convey?	"I heard a Fly buzz" focuses on the moment of death. It makes me imagine what it must be like to die.
Form	Do the poem's form and content seem related? Has the poet done anything unusual with punctuation or capitalization? If so, how does that help communicate the poet's message?	The poem's form does not really relate to its content. Certain words are capitalized, though, and that's probably important.
Meter	Does the poem have regular meter, or is it written in free verse? Why might the poet have chosen one pattern instead of another?	The poem is in free verse, but it has a distinct rhythm. The poet uses dashes to break up the rhythm and hold our attention.
Language	What images does the poet create? To what senses do the images appeal? Does the poet use figurative language, such as metaphors or similes? Does the poem contain any symbols? Do the imagery and figurative language help you see new connections between ideas? How do the imagery and figurative language help bring out the poem's meaning?	Room's stillness is compared to the stillness between a storm's heaves. Other figurative language: Eyes had wrung dry, breaths gathering, failing windows.
Speaker	Is there a definite speaker? If so, does the speaker's identity affect the poem's meaning?	The speaker is someone who has just died. The poet is imagining what it must be like to die.

Remember you don't need to discuss all the techniques mentioned in the chart. Focus on the ones that contribute to the meaning of the poem you are writing about and discuss them in order of importance.

~: Writing ✒ Workshop :~

DRAFTING

DRAFTING TIP

Keep your plan in mind, but don't be afraid to change it if you discover new ideas about the poem as you draft.

Draft openings

When drafting, you can experiment with different openings until you find the best way to get your readers' attention. One approach is to begin your essay with a provocative question.

Write your draft

Elaborate on each point you make by giving examples from the poem. For more help with elaboration, refer to Writing Skills page 434.

STUDENT MODEL

FIRST OPENING

In the poem "I heard a Fly buzz when I died," Emily Dickinson sets out to describe the moment of death. This essay will examine three techniques Dickinson uses to convey her vision of death.

SECOND OPENING

The moment of death— what is it like? In the poem "I heard a Fly buzz when I died," Emily Dickinson thinks about death and imagines what the experience must be like. This essay will discuss her use of three techniques in an unromantic portrayal of death.

REVISING

REVISING TIP

Make sure the lines you cite from the poem are stated correctly.

TECHNOLOGY TIP

Use the cut-and-paste function on your computer to be sure your sentences and paragraphs are concise. Cut out all words, phrases, and sentences that are redundant or unnecessary.

Evaluate your work

Let your draft sit for at least a few hours before you begin revising it. Then look for places where you could have expressed your ideas more clearly. Using the **Questions for Revising** as a guide, make revisions to your draft.

Talk it over

Read your essay aloud to a partner. Take notes on your partner's comments and questions, and consider his or her responses as you revise.

STUDENT MODEL

By focusing
~~Because~~ Dickinson looks at ~~on~~ the
moment of death, the poem makes
what that moment might be like.
me think about ~~death.~~

QUESTIONS FOR REVISING

☑ Does the opening generate interest?

☑ Is your thesis, or central idea, clearly stated in the opening paragraph?

☑ Do the points you make support your thesis?

☑ Is there evidence from the poem to support each point?

☑ Does the concluding paragraph sum up your major points?

EDITING/PROOFREADING

PROOFREADING TIP
Use the **Proofreading Checklist** on the inside back cover of this book to help catch mistakes.

When you are satisfied with the content and flow of your essay, proofread it carefully for errors in grammar, usage, mechanics, and spelling.

Grammar Hint

Nonessential appositives should be preceded and followed by commas.

To see if an appositive is nonessential, ask yourself, "Does the sentence still make sense without the appositive?"

Giselle Gonzales, last year's winner of the poetry contest, will present the award.

● For more on using commas, see **Language Handbook**, p. R53.

The appositive phrase, *last year's winner of the poetry contest,* is not essential to the meaning of the sentence and therefore is set off by commas.

STUDENT MODEL

Emily Dickinson, my favorite poet, remained a recluse all for her life, and had a stark, and often uncompromising view of the universe.

PUBLISHING/PRESENTING

PRESENTING TIP
Giving your essay an intriguing title will help focus your readers' attention on what you want to say.

If you are planning to put together a class literary magazine, agree on ways to make the essays look similar. For example, you might decide to use the same lettering and the same size headings. If you are presenting your essay to teachers or classmates, make the copy as attractive as you can. Remember to check it one final time for mistakes.

Reflecting

Think about the writing experience you have just had. In your journal, reflect on other ways you might use the analyzing skills you developed while writing this essay. What would you do differently in your next analysis of a literary work?

📖 **Save your work for your portfolio.**

Unit Wrap-Up

PERSONAL RESPONSE

1. Which selection in Unit 3 made the strongest impression on you? What created this impression—the events of a story, the language and imagery of a poem, the facts you learned, or some other element?
2. Which selection or selections taught you the most about our nation's history?
3. What new ideas do you have about understanding history through different kinds of literature?
4. How did the poems in Unit 3 affect your feelings and ideas about poetry?

ANALYZING LITERATURE

Compare and Contrast   A number of the selections in Unit 3 focus on the topics of slavery and the Civil War. Choose one of those topics and then select two pieces of literature from Unit 3 on that topic. (Count Whitman's two Civil War poems as one selection.) Explain the ways the two pieces are alike and different. For example, do they provide similar or different viewpoints? Do they convey impressions and lessons that are similar or different? Which piece taught you more about the topic you chose?

EVALUATE AND SET GOALS

Evaluate
1. What was the most significant thing you contributed to the class as you studied this unit?
2. Which aspect of this unit was the most interesting to you?
   - What made it so interesting?
   - In what ways could you pursue this interest further?
3. How would you assess your work in this unit using the following scale? Give at least two reasons for your assessment.
   4 = outstanding   **3** = good   **2** = fair   **1** = weak
4. If you had another week to work on this unit, what would you hope to learn? What would you hope to make or create? What skills would you hope to strengthen?

Set Goals
1. Set a goal for your work in the next unit. Try to focus on improving a skill such as writing or listening.
2. Discuss your goal with your teacher.
3. Plan specific steps to achieve the goal.
4. Plan checkpoints at which you can judge your work.
5. Think of a method to evaluate your finished work.

BUILD YOUR PORTFOLIO

Select   From the writing you have done for this unit, choose two pieces to put in your portfolio. Use the following questions as guides when choosing:
- Which taught you the most?
- Which are you likely to share?
- Which was the most fun to do?
- Which was the most difficult to complete?

Reflect   Include some explanatory notes with the portfolio pieces you have chosen. Use these questions to guide you:
- What are the piece's strengths and weaknesses?
- What did working on the piece teach you about writing (or about other skills the piece displays)?
- How would you revise the piece today to make it stronger?

Reading on Your Own

If you have enjoyed the literature in this unit, you might also be interested in the following books.

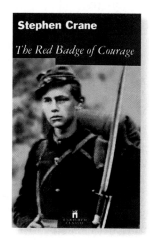

The Red Badge of Courage
by Stephen Crane A Civil War soldier's grand notions of glory abandon him as he faces the slaughter of battle. Crane had no experience of warfare when he wrote this novel, yet he successfully depicts the experiences, the terror, and the bravery of an ordinary soldier.

America Goes to War: The Civil War and Its Meaning in American Culture
by Bruce Catton Catton offers many interesting and useful facts and insights into the Civil War. The author also relates the Civil War to more current events in American and world history.

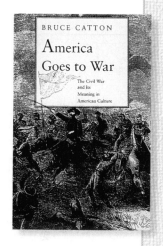

The Negro's Civil War: How American Blacks Felt and Acted During the War for the Union
by James M. McPherson This book reads like a well-written diary with the addition of historical explanations. Numerous quotations reveal the ideas and feelings of African American Union soldiers in their own words. Photographs, songs, tables, and charts offer a variety of additional source materials.

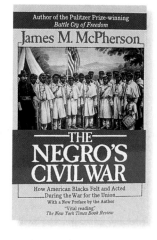

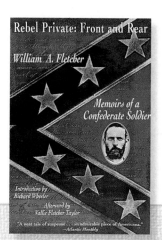

Rebel Private: Front and Rear
by William A. Fletcher In this memoir, a former Confederate soldier tells of the harsh realities of the Civil War. Fletcher describes many important battles, including the Battle of Gettysburg. The book provides an interesting perspective—that of an ordinary citizen and Confederate soldier.

Standardized Test Practice

Directions: The following sentences test your knowledge of grammar, usage, diction (choice of words), and idiom.

Some sentences are correct.
No sentence contains more than one error.

You will find that the error, if there is one, is underlined and lettered. Elements of the sentence that are not underlined will not be changed. In choosing answers, follow the requirements of standard written English.

If there is an error, select the one underlined part that must be changed to make the sentence correct. Write the corresponding letter on your paper.

If there is no error, select answer E.

1. Despite the community's urgent appeal,
   A
   the city government decided to build a
                         B
   new highway through the park and close
                     C
   the park for an indecisive period. No error
                     D   E

2. No matter how cautious mountain bikes
   A   B
   are ridden, they are capable of damaging
                     C   D
   · the land over which they travel. No error
                                      E

3. People are sometimes employed to complete
                                 A
   a small part of one process in one section

   of one company, and so having no sense
                            B
   of the process in its entirety. No error
   C   D   E

4. The doctor omitted from his article any
                  A
   mention of subjects who had experienced
                            B
   adverse reactions to the medication
                     C
   prescribed for them. No error
                  D   E

5. An administrator at the state university

   announced that an extraordinarily high
                A   B
   percentage of their fund-raising results
                  C
   directly from money donated to it by
           D
   generous alumni. No error
                    E

6. Many scholars have written about the
                     A
   Renaissance, but never before has the
                     B   C
   contributions of the painters been

   so completely recorded. No error
   D   E

Directions: The following sentences test correctness and effectiveness of expression. In choosing answers, follow the requirements of standard written English; that is, pay attention to grammar, choice of words, sentence construction, and punctuation.

In each of the following sentences, part of the sentence or the entire sentence is underlined. Beneath each sentence you will find five ways of phrasing the underlined part. Choice A repeats the original; the other four are different.

Choose the answer that best expresses the meaning of the original sentence and write the corresponding letter on your paper. If you think the original is better than any of the alternatives, choose it; otherwise choose one of the others. Your choice should produce the most effective sentence—clear and precise, without awkwardness or ambiguity.

1. Jean Louis David's art depicts classical figures and they were both historically and stylistically accurate for the neo-classical period.

   (A) figures and they were
   (B) figures that were
   (C) figures, being that they were
   (D) figures, and making them
   (E) figures, they

2. The community center, once about to close due to lack of funds, is now a busy, fun place to visit.

   (A) The community center, once about to close due to lack of funds, is
   (B) The community center was once about to close due to lack of funds, it is
   (C) The community center that once having been about to close due to lack of funds is
   (D) The community center, because it was once about to close due to lack of funds, is
   (E) The community center was once about to close due to lack of funds, and it is

3. For many a talented writer, being free to create is more important than being highly paid.

   (A) being free to create is more important
   (B) having freedom to create is more important
   (C) there is more importance in the freedom to create
   (D) freedom to create has more importance
   (E) to have the freedom to create is more important

4. In most offices, employees keep copies of all documents, a focus on detail that is important.

   (A) a focus on detail that is important
   (B) inasmuch as they show a focus on detail, it is important
   (C) this makes it important in showing their focus on detail
   (D) an idea that is important in showing their focus on detail
   (E) which is important and it shows a focus on detail

Breezing Up (A Fair Wind), 1873–1876. Winslow Homer. Oil on canvas, 24⅛ x 38⅛ in. National Gallery of Art, Washington, DC. Gift of the W. L. and May T. Mellon Foundation.

UNIT ✲ FOUR

Regionalism and Realism

1865–1910

❝The history of every country begins in the heart of a man or a woman.❞

—Willa Cather

Theme 6
The Energy of the Everyday
pages 459–581

Setting the Scene

On May 10, 1869, at Promontory Point, Utah, Grenville M. Dodge, chief engineer of the Union Pacific Railway, witnessed "the driving of the last spike." This famous spike marked the completion of the long, arduous work of connecting two railway lines across North America. Workers had extended the Central Pacific line eastward from California and the Union Pacific line westward from Iowa. Dodge recorded what he saw:

"The two trains pulled up facing each other, each crowded with workmen. . . . The officers and invited guests formed on each side of the track. . . . a number of spikes were driven in the two adjoining rails, each one of the prominent persons present taking a hand, but very few hitting the spikes, to the great amusement of the crowd. . . . thus the two roads were wedded into one great trunk line from the Atlantic to the Pacific."

The Last Spike, 1877–1881 (detail). Thomas Hill. Oil on canvas, 96½ x 240½ in. California State Railroad Museum, Sacramento.

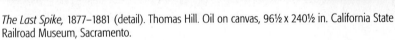

U.S.A.

1869
Elizabeth Cady Stanton and Susan B. Anthony organize the National Woman Suffrage Association

1870
John D. Rockefeller forms the Standard Oil Company

1877
Pursued by the U.S. Army, Chief Joseph and the Nez Percé surrender in Montana

1886
Labor leaders organize the American Federation of Labor; the Statue of Liberty is dedicated in New York

1865

1875

1885

1870
General Tomás Guardia begins his twelve-year dictatorship in Costa Rica

1871
German regions unite to form the German Empire

The Indian National Congress is formed to give the people of India more power in that British-ruled nation

World

History of the Time

An Age of Growth

The railroads—their mighty engines hauling raw materials, hopeful migrants, and wealthy business owners across the country—symbolized the United States in the late 1800s. Like the nation itself, the railroads were powerful, noisy money-makers and always on the move.

Part of this movement was from rural to urban areas. The rapid growth of cities and industry undermined Thomas Jefferson's vision of a nation of small towns and family farms. Between 1870 and 1910, the nation's largest city, New York, tripled in size. In Chicago, the city that poet Carl Sandburg labeled "the nation's freight handler," the population multiplied an astounding seven times. Each major industry created a handful of incredibly wealthy men. Among the richest were Andrew Carnegie in steel, John D. Rockefeller in oil, J. P. Morgan in finance, and Cornelius Vanderbilt in railroads.

Reconstruction in the South

From 1865 to 1877 the South went through a period known as Reconstruction. As the former Confederate states reentered the Union, the U.S. Congress supported the establishment of new state governments. These governments were led by African Americans, Northerners who came to the South, and "scalawags," Southern whites who cooperated with the new governments. There was significant resistance, however, to these new governments and the policies of Reconstruction, and by 1877 the Democratic Party—then the party of conservative white Southerners—had regained control of state governments in the South.

The shifting of economic power and Reconstruction were two of the many developments occurring in the nation.

- The last great land rush took place when the government opened Cherokee territory in Oklahoma for settlement by non-Indians. At noon on April 22, 1889, fifty thousand frantic settlers rode wagons, ran, pushed, and stumbled to claim plots of land.

- Immigrants poured into the country—more than 15 million between 1885 and 1910, mostly from southern or eastern Europe. In 1882 the Chinese Exclusion Act prohibited Chinese workers from immigrating to the United States.

- Laborers, including many children, suffered low wages, long hours, and hazardous conditions. Despite sometimes violent opposition from factory owners, workers formed unions and used strikes to demand fair treatment on the job.

- A burst of inventiveness led to dazzling changes in the daily lives of Americans. Cameras, lightbulbs, telephones, typewriters, automobiles, phonographs, bicycles, moving pictures, skyscrapers, airplanes—new or improved products came in a flurry.

1896
The Supreme Court upholds laws supporting racial segregation; the Klondike gold rush begins in Canada and Alaska

1901
Theodore Roosevelt becomes president after the assassination of William McKinley

1906
An earthquake kills 500 people in San Francisco

1890
Congress creates Yosemite National Park in California

1893
New Zealand adopts woman suffrage

1894
War begins between China and Japan

1895

1899
The South African (Boer) War between British and Dutch settlers begins

1905
Strikes and mass protests bring reform in Russia

1910

Life of the Time

People are talking about

A Continuing Struggle   Although African Americans have gained freedom and citizenship, they still must struggle for equality and opportunity. The U.S. Freedmen's Bureau provides food and medical assistance and builds hospitals and more than 1,000 schools. However, President Andrew Johnson returns abandoned lands to pardoned Southerners, thus forcing many freed African Americans into oppressive sharecropping arrangements.

◀ **Grand Expositions**   At the 1876 Centennial Exposition in Philadelphia, people are amazed by typewriters, telephones, and a gigantic steam engine. In 1893 a highlight for many of the 21 million visitors to the World's Columbian Exposition in Chicago is the gigantic Ferris wheel. Each car on the 264-foot-high Ferris wheel holds up to sixty people.

Going Places   In addition to moving around the country on railroads, people travel about cities on trolleys. The first subways in the country open in Boston in 1897 and in New York in 1904. Then, in 1908, Henry Ford presents his Model T automobile, the car that will enable Americans to take to the road.

A Welcome for Immigrants   Beginning in 1886, the Statue of Liberty, a gift from France, welcomes immigrants to New York Harbor. In 1892 a receiving facility for immigrants opens on New York's Ellis Island that will be an entry point for about 17 million immigrants over the next fifty years. ▶

Firsts

- Scientists create the first plastics—celluloid (1869) and Bakelite in (1909).
- Orville and Wilbur Wright make the first airplane flight (1903).

Immigrants at Ellis Island, 1905.

U.S.A.

1866
More than eighty African Americans are killed in Memphis and New Orleans race riots

1871
P. T. Barnum's circus, the "Greatest Show on Earth," opens in Brooklyn

1879
F. W. Woolworth opens his first five-and-ten-cent store

1880
George Eastman patents roll film for cameras

1883
Buffalo Bill Cody opens his first Wild West show

1865

1869
Russian chemist Dmitry Mendeleyev devises the periodic table of the elements

1875

1876
China's first railway opens

1883
On an island between Java and Sumatra, the volcano Krakatoa explodes, killing 36,000

1885

World

Food & Fashion

In the new department stores, ready-made clothes are available. In women's fashion, the bustle of the 1870s gives way in the 1890s to the shirtwaist, a tailored blouse first popular among women in clerical jobs. ▶

- Beauty salons appear throughout American cities. By 1910 "the mania for make-up has spread from the theatrical profession up and down the line, from the aristocratic lady . . . to the saleswoman and the factory girl," according to Elizabeth Reid, a beauty writer of the time.

- At the 1876 Centennial Exposition, Americans enjoy ice cream sodas. In 1904 David Strickler, a pharmacy apprentice in Pennsylvania, creates the first banana split.

◀ Prepared food is packaged in cans, jars, and boxes. Heavily advertised products include Kellogg and Post cereals, Heinz and Campbell canned goods, and Swift and Armour meats.

Arts & Entertainment

- Art, like everything else, becomes available for mass consumption. Even department stores feature art galleries.

- Architects design lavish mansions, grand railroad stations, and, beginning in Chicago in 1885, towering skyscrapers. ▶

Amusements

- George Eastman's handheld Kodak camera, patented in 1888, and his cheap and simple Brownie camera, first sold in 1900, turn photography into one of the nation's most popular hobbies.

- Americans become spectators, enjoying baseball, football, boxing, vaudeville shows, and moving-picture nickelodeons.

Chicago, around 1900.

1889 — The Eiffel Tower is completed in Paris

1891 James A. Naismith invents the game of basketball

1893 — Russian composer Peter Tchaikovsky completes his *Pathétique* symphony

1895

1896 The first modern Olympic games are held in Greece; famine that will kill 2 million people begins in India

1900 — Hawaii becomes a territory of the United States

1904 — Construction of the Panama Canal begins

1898 In France Marie Sklodowska Curie and Pierre Curie discover radium

1905

1908 — The Ford Motor Company introduces the Model T

1908 — Oil production begins in the Middle East

1910

Literature of the Time

PEOPLE ARE READING . . .

◄ **Newspapers and Magazines**   Newspapers with screaming headlines become part of everyday life, delivering news, sensational stories, features, and advertisements. Magazines flood homes and newsstands. *Ladies' Home Journal* reaches out to women. *McClure's Magazine* features journalists such as Ida Tarbell and Lincoln Steffens and fiction writers, including Jack London and Willa Cather.

Mail-Order Catalogs   In the late 1800s, Montgomery Ward and Sears, Roebuck begin mailing out catalogs. These huge "wish books" become standard in homes across the nation, and people shop by mail for everything from the latest fashions to tractors.

Books for Young People   L. Frank Baum writes fourteen books set in the magical land of Oz. Edward Stratemeyer writes several series, including the Rover Boys and the Bobbsey Twins. Horatio Alger sells 20 million copies of his books about boys who work hard to escape poverty for wealth and fame.   ►

Ida Tarbell

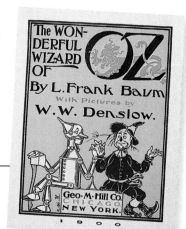

People Are Writing

Letters and Postcards   Americans on the move write postcards and letters—to ask about immigrant relatives, to keep in touch with parents back home, to order goods, to declare their love. In the late 1800s, Americans write twice as many letters per person as do Europeans.

Memoirs and Life Stories   Newspapers feature first-person accounts of the daily lives of workers and immigrants. Many immigrants write autobiographies about coming to the United States. Among the best-known is *The Promised Land* (1912), by Mary Antin, a Jewish immigrant from Russian-controlled Poland.

U.S.A.

1866
John Greenleaf Whittier, *Snow-Bound*

1877
Sidney Lanier, *Song of the Chattahoochee*

Mary Baker Eddy, *Science and Health*

1881
Helen Hunt Jackson, *A Century of Dishonor*

1865

1870
Japan: Scholar Nishi Amane begins writing a series of lectures, *Chain of a Hundred Studies*

1875

1876
France: Stéphane Mallarmé, *The Afternoon of a Faun*

1885

1886
Germany: Friedrich Nietzsche, *Beyond Good and Evil*

World

Literary Trends: Local Color and Naturalism

"Consciously, I was always, as I still am, trying to fashion a piece of literature out of the life next at hand." —*William Dean Howells*

Illustration from a story by Sarah Orne Jewett.

After the Civil War ends in 1865, writers begin crafting realistic, detailed studies of everyday life. Some find inspiration for colorful portrayals of their own local region. In doing so, they feed Americans' curiosity about distinctive language, landforms, and customs in other parts of the country. Mark Twain and Bret Harte convey to the nation the rough excitement of the West. Kate Chopin depicts Louisiana's unique mix of cultures. Sarah Orne Jewett writes about life in rural New England.

Other writers, influenced by the achievements of natural scientists such as Charles Darwin, attempt to write objectively about people and their lives. These writers, called naturalists, focus on the powerful economic, social, and environmental forces that shape the lives of individuals. One of the best naturalist works is Frank Norris's *The Octopus*, which shows how the power of railroads can control and destroy the lives of individual ranchers.

FOCUS ON . . .

The Natural World

In Stephen Crane's "The Open Boat," four shipwrecked men face the relentless sea. Like other naturalists, Crane writes about how individuals face a challenge to survive in an environment that they do not understand and cannot control.

Unlike the religious Puritans, the rationalists of Revolutionary times, and the optimistic Transcendentalists, naturalist writers view this battle with nature—or with the economic system—through everyday experiences of typical people. They look hard at the world, and do not soften the depiction of the struggle they see.

Gulf Stream, 1899. Winslow Homer. Oil on canvas, 28⅛ x 49½ in. The Metropolitan Museum of Art, New York.

1893
Paul Laurence Dunbar, *Oak and Ivy*

1894
Kate Chopin, *Bayou Folk*

1902
Helen Keller, *The Story of My Life*

1903
W. E. B. Du Bois, *The Souls of Black Folk*

Edith Wharton, *The House of Mirth*

1889
Ireland: William Butler Yeats, "The Wanderings of Oisin"

1895

1897
Russia: Anton Chekhov, *Uncle Vanya*

1898
France: Émile Zola, *I Accuse*

1900
Uruguay: José Enrique Rodó, *Ariel*

1902
Brazil: Euclides da Cunha, *Rebellion in the Backlands*

1905

1910

Novels of the Time

Novelists portraying the world in the late 1800s and early 1900s find inspiration in different directions. Some turn inward. Using insights from psychology, they focus on the thoughts and perceptions of their characters. Others turn outward. Struck by the turmoil of rapid industrialization, they portray the vast, impersonal economic forces that overwhelm individuals.

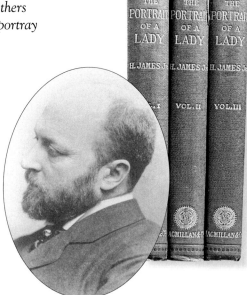

Henry James

The Portrait of a Lady
by Henry James (1881)

Isabel Archer, a vibrant, talented young woman with a powerful sense of independence, leaves Albany, New York, to live with her aunt in London. Marriage to a man who wants to control her every action makes Archer sadder but wiser. James's masterful portrayal of Archer's inner thoughts makes this portrait one of the most captivating sagas in American literature.

Frank Norris

The Octopus
by Frank Norris (1901)

In this epic battle between the grasping, powerful railroads and California wheat farmers, Norris exposes the dangers of concentrated economic power. The railroads have become a multi-tentacled monster, dominating every aspect of life, from the state legislature to the land on which farmers work. Farmers fight back, only to learn that the railroads have become the masters of those they were intended to serve.

U.S.A.

1871 Edward Eggleston, *The Hoosier Schoolmaster*	**1884** Helen Hunt Jackson, *Ramona*
	1877 Sarah Orne Jewett, *Deephaven*

1865 — **1866** Russia: Fyodor Dostoyevsky, *Crime and Punishment*

1874 Spain: Juan Valera, *Pepita Jiménez*

1875

1878 England: Thomas Hardy, *The Return of the Native*

1883 Cape Colony (South Africa): Olive Schreiner, *The Story of an African Farm*

1885
1887–89 Japan: Futabatei Shimei, *The Drifting Clouds*

World

Critics Corner

Huckleberry Finn Barred Out

The Concord, Mass. Public Library committee has decided to exclude Mark Twain's latest book from the library. One member of the committee says that, while he does not wish to call it immoral, he thinks [it] contains but little humor, and that of a very coarse type. He regards it as the veriest trash. The librarian and the other members of the committee entertain similar views, characterizing it as rough, coarse and inelegant, dealing with a series of experiences not elevating, the whole book being more suited to the slums than to intelligent, respectable people.

—*The Boston Transcript*, March 17, 1885

"All modern American literature comes from one book by Mark Twain called *Huckleberry Finn*."

—*Ernest Hemingway*

The Adventures of Huckleberry Finn
by Mark Twain (1885)

Huckleberry Finn first appears as a character in Mark Twain's popular book *The Adventures of Tom Sawyer*, about a boy growing up in Missouri. *The Adventures of Huckleberry Finn* tells of the travels of the runaway orphan Huck, and of Jim, who is escaping enslavement. Huck's reflections on various aspects of life in the prewar South are delivered in a slangy, colloquial voice that will be influential for later writers. The story moves between funny episodes of satire or slapstick and touching portrayals of the relationship between Huck and Jim.

Mark Twain

1888
Edward Bellamy,
*Looking Backward,
2000–1887*

1899
Charles Waddell
Chesnutt, *The
Conjure Woman*

1900
L. Frank Baum, *The Wonderful
Wizard of Oz*; Theodore Dreiser,
Sister Carrie

1901
Frank Norris, *The Octopus*

1906
Upton Sinclair, *The
Jungle*

1888
Nicaragua:
Rubén
Darío, *Azul*

1890
Bengal:
Rabindranath
Tagore, *Mānāsi*

1892
Germany: Gerhart
Hauptmann, *The Weavers*

1895

1902
England: Beatrix Potter,
The Tale of Peter Rabbit

1904–07
China: Liu E, *The
Travels of Lao Ts'an*

1905

1907
Basutoland (Lesotho):
Thomas Mofolo, *The
Traveller of the East*

1910

Language of the Time

How People Speak

◄ **On the Phone**   By 1887 there are more than 150,000 telephones in the United States. The need for something to say when one picks up a ringing phone makes the word "Hello" popular. Compared with letters, phone conversations tend to be brisk and informal.

Recorded Voices   Thomas Edison's phonograph, patented in 1877, preserves the sound of voices for the first time. Florence Nightingale's voice is among those preserved on a recording kept at London's Science Museum. ►

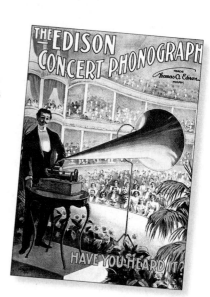

How People Write

On Postcards   Postcards become a craze after their introduction in the United States in 1873 as a promotional device. As the telephone does with the spoken language, postcards encourage a clipped, conversational style of writing.

As They Speak   Regional writers try to capture the flavor of local dialects, including the increasing use of Americanisms. In 1886 one of the nation's leading literary figures, William Dean Howells, writes, "I would have them [our novelists] use 'Americanisms' whenever these serve their turn; and when their characters speak, I should like to hear them speak true American, with all the varying Tennesseean, Philadelphian, Bostonian, and New York accents."

New Words and Expressions

Phone Language   New telephone-related expressions are heard:

Give me a ring.	exchange	long distance
I'll give you a buzz.	trunk line	phone book
Number, please.	central	telephone booth
operator	telephone number	yellow pages
switchboard	party line	

The Melting Pot   The title of a 1908 play by British writer Israel Zangwill, the term *melting pot* becomes part of American English, meaning "a location in which a blending of peoples and cultures takes place." Immigrants contribute numerous words to the language, including *delicatessen, kindergarten, kosher, spaghetti,* and *tutti-frutti.*

Theme 6

The Energy of the Everyday

Would people find your everyday life interesting, maybe even fascinating? You might be surprised. A skilled writer can turn everyday events into great stories. Many of the authors in this theme provide realistic studies of everyday life—the experiences of people in various regions, each region with its own landscapes and customs. As you read, notice how a simple event can become an unforgettable tale.

THEME PROJECTS

Learning for Life

News Broadcasts   Imagine you are a news broadcaster and that the selections in this theme are news items that reporters have passed on to you. You have to present a ten-minute newscast about four of these stories.

1. Choose the four stories that seem the most "newsworthy."

2. Take notes on the most important points of each story. Remember, a newscast must tell *who, what, when, where, why,* and *how,* but it must also be brief and clear.

3. Practice your broadcast. To get ideas about presentation, watch or listen to a local news broadcast.

4. Present your ten-minute newscast to the class.

Interdisciplinary Project

Science: A Multimedia Science Display
Science is important to several selections in this theme. With a small group, choose a selection that sparks your scientific curiosity. Plan, research, and present a display that "tells the story" of the scientific fact or idea in the selection. Be sure to connect your research to the selection that sparked the idea.

May Day, Central Park, c. 1905. William Glackens. Oil on canvas, 25⅛ x 30¼ in. The Fine Arts Museums of San Francisco.

Meet
Mark Twain

Called the "Lincoln of our literature" by one critic, Mark Twain captured the experiences and everyday speech of ordinary people in works that sparkle with humor. Born Samuel Langhorne Clemens, Twain grew up in Hannibal, Missouri, on the west bank of the Mississippi River. There he became enchanted with the sights and sounds of river life and its colorful inhabitants. The death of Twain's father when the boy was just eleven forced Twain to curtail his boyhood escapades and his schooling in order to work as a printer's apprentice.

At twenty-one, Twain fulfilled his lifelong dream of becoming a pilot on a Mississippi riverboat. In writing about this profession, Twain declared that he loved it better than any other because "a pilot was the only unfettered and entirely independent being that lived on the earth." Piloting so captivated him that he used as his pen name a pilot's term for water that is two fathoms deep, or just barely deep enough for safe passage: *mark twain.*

When the Civil War broke out, the Mississippi closed to commercial traffic, and Twain ventured west to seek his fortune. He prospected unsuccessfully for silver and gold in Nevada and California, then settled in San Francisco, where he took up journalism and enthralled lecture audiences with his wit and humor. While there, Twain wrote the story that brought him his first taste of fame: "The Celebrated Jumping Frog of Calaveras County." Twain then wrote *The Innocents Abroad,* a book that poked fun at American tourists and cemented his reputation as a popular writer.

Flush with success, Twain married a wealthy easterner named Olivia Langdon and built a palatial home in Hartford, Connecticut. It was there that he wrote *The Adventures of Tom Sawyer,* the book that for many represents American boyhood, and his masterpiece *The Adventures of Huckleberry Finn.* In the latter, Twain used the characters of a runaway slave and a white youth to critique the injustices of a slaveholding society. Both books include poetic descriptions of life along the Mississippi River that were inspired by Twain's childhood memories.

During his later years, financial and professional setbacks and personal tragedy caused Twain to become increasingly bitter. Though he dwelled in his final books on the depravity of human nature, Twain is chiefly remembered today for capturing the brash, optimistic spirit and youthful vitality of his fellow Americans.

"Everyone is a moon, and has a dark side which he never shows to anybody."

"My books are water; those of the great geniuses are wine. Everybody drinks water."

—*Twain*

Mark Twain was born in 1835 and died in 1910.

FOCUS ACTIVITY

Have you ever heard someone use a humorous exaggeration, such as "I'm so hungry, I could eat a horse"?

LIST IDEAS Jot down two or more examples of humorous exaggerations that you have heard and explain why you think each one is funny.

SETTING A PURPOSE Read to enjoy a story that is filled with humorous exaggerations.

BACKGROUND

The Time and Place

This story takes place in the early 1860s in a small mining town called Angel's Camp, which still exists in Calaveras County, California. In 1848 James W. Marshall discovered

Sutter's Mill, California

rich deposits of gold at Sutter's mill, near the Calaveras County town of Coloma. This discovery led to the California Gold Rush, during which many adventurous people thronged to California to prospect for gold, hoping to "strike it rich." At Angel's Camp, Twain first heard someone tell the story that he later developed into "The Celebrated Jumping Frog of Calaveras County."

Did You Know?

In the remote mining camps and frontier towns of the 1800s, life was hard and entertainment was scarce. To create some fun and laughter, people invented tall tales—stories containing such quirky, larger-than-life characters as Pecos Bill and Paul Bunyan. Many stories celebrated characters with incredible physical skills, while others related the follies of people who had been tricked by clever villains. Such tales were often first passed by word of mouth, with each person adding a few details. Later these tales frequently appeared in newspapers. As a miner and a journalist, Mark Twain probably heard and read dozens of tall tales.

VOCABULARY PREVIEW

garrulous (gar′ ə ləs) *adj.* talkative; p. 462

conjecture (kən jek′ chər) *v.* to form an opinion without definite evidence; to guess; p. 462

reminiscence (rem′ ə nis′ əns) *n.* an account of a past experience or event; p. 462

dilapidated (di lap′ ə dā′ tid) *adj.* fallen into ruin or decay; shabby; p. 462

interminable (in tur′ mi nə bəl) *adj.* seemingly endless; p. 463

enterprising (en′ tər prī′ zing) *adj.* showing energy and initiative, especially in beginning new projects; p. 468

vagabond (vag′ ə bond′) *n.* someone who wanders from place to place, having no visible means of support; p. 468

The Celebrated Jumping

In compliance with the request of a friend of mine, who wrote me from the East, I called on good-natured, <u>garrulous</u> old Simon Wheeler, and inquired after my friend's friend, *Leonidas W.* Smiley, as requested to do, and I hereunto append[1] the result. I have a lurking suspicion that *Leonidas W.* Smiley is a myth; that my friend never knew such a personage; and that he only <u>conjectured</u> that, if I asked old Wheeler about him, it would remind him of his infamous *Jim* Smiley, and he would go to work and bore me nearly to death with some infernal[2] <u>reminiscence</u> of him as long and tedious as it should be useless to me. If that was the design, it certainly succeeded.

I found Simon Wheeler dozing comfortably by the bar-room stove of the old <u>dilapidated</u> tavern in the ancient mining camp of Angel's,[3] and I noticed that he was fat and bald-headed, and had an expression of winning gentleness and simplicity upon his tranquil countenance.[4] He roused up and gave me good-day. I told him a friend of mine had commissioned me to make some inquiries about a cherished companion of his boyhood named *Leonidas W.* Smiley—*Rev. Leonidas W.* Smiley—a young minister of the Gospel, who he had heard was at one time a resident of Angel's Camp. I added that, if Mr. Wheeler could tell me any thing about this Rev. Leonidas W. Smiley, I would feel under many obligations to him.

---

1. *Append* means "to add as a supplement" or "to attach."
2. *Infernal* means "awful" or "thoroughly unpleasant."
3. *Angel's* refers to Angel's Camp.
4. A *tranquil countenance* is a calm face.

Vocabulary

garrulous (gar′ ə ləs) *adj.* talkative
conjecture (kən jek′ chər) *v.* to form an opinion without definite evidence; to guess
reminiscence (rem′ ə nis′ əns) *n.* an account of a past experience or event
dilapidated (di lap′ ə dā′ tid) *adj.* fallen into ruin or decay; shabby

Frog of Calaveras County

Mark Twain

The Country Store, 1872. Winslow Homer. Oil on wood, 11⅞ x 18⅛ in. Hirshhorn Museum and Sculpture Garden, Smithsonian Institution, Washington, D.C. Gift of Joseph H. Hirshhorn, 1966.

Viewing the painting: What do the attitudes of the men in this painting suggest to you about the ways stories such as the one about Jim Smiley might have spread in the mid-1800s?

Simon Wheeler backed me into a corner and blockaded me there with his chair, and then sat me down and reeled off the monotonous narrative which follows this paragraph. He never smiled, he never frowned, he never changed his voice from the gentle-flowing key to which he tuned the initial sentence, he never betrayed the slightest suspicion of enthusiasm; but all through the interminable

Vocabulary
interminable (in tur′ mi nə bəl) *adj.* seemingly endless

narrative there ran a vein of impressive earnestness and sincerity, which showed me plainly that, so far from his imagining that there was any thing ridiculous or funny about his story, he regarded it as a really important matter, and admired its two heroes as men of transcendent[5] genius in finesse.[6]

To me, the spectacle of a man drifting serenely along through such a queer yarn without ever smiling, was exquisitely absurd. As I said before, I asked him to tell me what he knew of Rev. Leonidas W. Smiley, and he replied as follows. I let him go on in his own way, and never interrupted him once:

There was a feller here once by the name of *Jim Smiley*, in the winter of '49—or may be it was the spring of '50—I don't recollect exactly, somehow, though what makes me think it was one or the other is because I remember the big flume wasn't finished when he first came to the camp; but any way, he was the curiosest man about always betting on any thing that turned up you ever see, if he could get any body to bet on the other side; and if he couldn't he'd change sides. Any way that suited the other man would suit him—any way just so's he got a bet, *he* was satisfied. But still he was lucky, uncommon lucky; he most always come out winner. He was always ready and laying for a chance; there couldn't be no solitry thing mentioned but that feller'd offer to bet on it, and take any side you please, as I was just telling you. If there was a horse race, you'd find him flush,[7] or you'd find

Did You Know?
A *flume* is a trough or chute, often inclined, that carries water.

him busted at the end of it; if there was a dog-fight, he'd bet on it; if there was a cat-fight, he'd bet on it; if there was a chicken-fight, he'd bet on it; why, if there was two birds setting on a fence, he would bet you which one would fly first; or if there was a camp-meeting,[8] he would be there reg'lar, to bet on Parson Walker, which he judged to be the best exhorter[9] about here, and so he was, too, and a good man. If he even seen a straddle-bug[10] start to go anywheres, he would bet you how long it would take him to get wherever he was going to, and if you took him up, he would foller that straddle-bug to Mexico but what he would find out where he was bound for and how long he was on the road. Lots of the boys here has seen that Smiley, and can tell you about him. Why, it never made no difference to *him*—he would bet on *any* thing—the dangdest feller. Parson Walker's wife laid very sick once, for a good while, and it seemed as if they warn't going to save her; but one morning he come in, and Smiley asked how she was, and he said she was considerable better—thank the Lord for his inf'nit mercy—and coming on so smart that, with the blessing of Prov'dence,[11] she'd get well yet; and Smiley, before he thought, says, "Well, I'll risk two-and-a-half[12] that she don't, any way."

Thish-yer[13] Smiley had a mare—the boys called her the fifteen-minute nag, but that was only in fun, you know, because, of course, she was faster than that—and he used to win money on that horse, for all she was so slow and always had the asthma, or the distemper, or the consumption,[14] or something of that kind. They

---

5. *Transcendent* means "surpassing others" or "superior."
6. *Finesse* is the smooth or artful handling of a situation.
7. Here, *flush* means "having a large amount of money" or "rich."
8. A *camp-meeting* is an outdoor religious gathering, sometimes held in a tent.
9. An *exhorter* is someone who urges by giving strong advice or warnings; here, a preacher.
10. A *straddle-bug* is a long-legged beetle.
11. *Prov'dence* (Providence) is God.
12. *Risk two-and-a-half* means "risk, or bet, $2.50."
13. *Thish-yer* is dialect for "this here."
14. *Consumption* is another name for tuberculosis.

used to give her two or three hundred yards start, and then pass her under way; but always at the fag-end[15] of the race she'd get excited and desperate-like, and come cavorting[16] and straddling up, and scattering her legs around limber, sometimes in the air, and sometimes out to one side amongst the fences, and kicking up m-o-r-e dust, and raising m-o-r-e racket with her coughing and sneezing and blowing her nose—and always fetch up at the stand[17] just about a neck ahead, as near as you could cipher it down.[18]

And he had a little small bull pup, that to look at him you'd think he wan't worth a cent, but to set around and look ornery, and lay for a chance to steal something. But as soon as money was up on him, he was a different dog; his under-jaw'd begin to stick out like the fo'castle of a steamboat, and his teeth would uncover, and

Did You Know?
The *fo'castle*, or forecastle (fōk′ səl), of a steamboat is a raised deck at the front of the boat.

shine savage like the furnaces. And a dog might tackle him, and bully-rag[19] him, and bite him, and throw him over his shoulder two or three times, and Andrew Jackson—which was the name of the pup—Andrew Jackson would never let on but what *he* was satisfied, and hadn't expected nothing else—and the bets being doubled and doubled on the other side all the time, till the money was all up; and then all of a sudden he would grab that other dog jest by the j'int of his hind leg and freeze to it—not chaw, you understand, but only jest grip and hang on till they throwed up the sponge,[20] if it was a year. Smiley always come out winner on that pup, till he harnessed[21] a dog once that didn't have no hind legs, because they'd been sawed off by a circular saw, and when the thing had gone along far enough, and the money was all up, and he come to make a snatch for his pet holt,[22] he saw in a minute how he'd been imposed on, and how the other dog had him in the door,[23] so to speak, and he 'peared surprised, and then he looked sorter discouraged-like, and didn't try no more to win the fight, and so he got shucked out[24] bad. He give Smiley a look, as much as to say his heart was broke, and it was *his* fault, for putting up a dog that hadn't no hind legs for him to take holt of, which was his main dependence in a fight, and then he limped off a piece and laid down and died. It was a good pup, was that Andrew Jackson, and would have made a name for hisself if he'd lived, for the stuff was in him, and he had genius—I know it, because he hadn't had no opportunities to speak of, and it don't stand to reason that a dog could make such a fight as he could under them circumstances, if he hadn't no talent. It always makes me feel sorry when I think of that last fight of his'n, and the way it turned out.

Well, thish-yer Smiley had rat-tarriers,[25] and chicken cocks,[26] and tom-cats, and all them kind of things, till you couldn't rest, and you couldn't fetch nothing for him to bet on but he'd match you. He ketched a frog one day, and took him home, and said he cal'klated[27] to edercate him; and so he never done nothing

---

15. The *fag-end* is the last part.
16. *Cavorting* means "running and jumping around playfully."
17. *Fetch up at the stand* means "arrive at the grandstand," which was placed at the finish line.
18. *Cipher it down* means "calculate it."
19. *Bully-rag* means "to intimidate" or "to abuse."

20. *Throwed up the sponge* means "gave up the contest."
21. Here, *harnessed* means "set up a fight with."
22. A *pet holt* is a favorite hold.
23. *Had him in the door* means "had him at a disadvantage or in a tight place."
24. *Shucked out* means "beaten" or "defeated."
25. *Rat-tarriers* are dogs (terriers) once used for catching rats.
26. *Chicken cocks* are adult male chickens (roosters) that are trained to fight.
27. *Cal'klated* is dialect for calculated, meaning "planned."

Yellow Frog. Christian Pierre (b. 1962). Oil on canvas, 18 x 25 in. Private collection.

Viewing the painting: Do you think the frog depicted in this painting is a "jumping frog" like Dan'l Webster? Why or why not?

for three months but set in his back yard and learn[28] that frog to jump. And you bet you he *did* learn him, too. He'd give him a little punch behind, and the next minute you'd see that frog whirling in the air like a doughnut—see him turn one summerset, or may be a couple, if he got a good start, and come down flat-footed and all right, like a cat. He got him up so in the matter of catching flies, and kept him in practice so constant, that he'd nail a fly every time as far as he could see him. Smiley said all a frog wanted was education, and he could do most any thing—and I believe him. Why, I've seen him set Dan'l Webster[29] down here on this floor—Dan'l Webster was the name of the frog—and sing out, "Flies, Dan'l, flies!" and quicker'n you could wink, he'd spring straight up, and snake a fly off'n the counter there, and flop down on the floor again as solid as a gob of mud, and fall to scratching the side of his head with his hind foot as indifferent as if he hadn't no idea he'd been doin' any more'n any frog might do. You never see a frog so modest and straightfor'ard as he was, for all he was so gifted. And when it come to fair and square jumping on a dead level, he could get over more ground at one straddle[30] than any animal of his breed you ever see. Jumping on a dead level was his strong suit, you understand; and when it come to that, Smiley would ante up[31] money on him as long as he had a red.[32] Smiley was monstrous proud of his frog, and well he might be, for fellers that had traveled and been everywheres, all said he laid over any frog that ever *they* see.

Well, Smiley kept the beast in a little lattice box, and he used to fetch him down town sometimes and lay for a bet. One day a feller—

a stranger in the camp, he was—come across him with his box, and says:

"What might it be that you've got in the box?"

And Smiley says, sorter indifferent like, "It might be a parrot, or it might be a canary, may be, but it an't—it's only just a frog."

And the feller took it, and looked at it careful, and turned it round this way and that, and says, "H'm—so 'tis. Well, what's *he* good for?"

"Well," Smiley says, easy and careless, "He's good enough for *one* thing, I should judge—he can outjump any frog in Calaveras county."

The feller took the box again, and took another long, particular look, and give it back to Smiley, and says, very deliberate, "Well, I don't see no p'ints[33] about that frog that's any better'n any other frog."

"May be you don't," Smiley says, "May be you understand frogs, and may be you don't understand 'em; may be you've had experience, and may be you an't only a amature, as it were. Anyways, I've got *my* opinion, and I'll risk forty dollars that he can outjump any frog in Calaveras county."

And the feller studied a minute, and then says, kinder sad like, "Well, I'm only a stranger here, and I an't got no frog; but if I had a frog, I'd bet you."

And then Smiley says, "That's all right—that's all right—if you'll hold my box a minute, I'll go and get you a frog." And so the feller took the box, and put up his forty dollars along with Smiley's, and set down to wait.

So he set there a good while thinking and thinking to hisself, and then he got the frog out and prized his mouth open and took a teaspoon and filled him full of quail shot[34]—filled him pretty near up to his chin—and set him on the floor. Smiley he went to the

---

28. Here, *learn* means "teach."
29. *Dan'l Webster* refers to Daniel Webster (1782–1852), a famous orator who served as a U.S. senator and a U.S. secretary of state.
30. Here, *straddle* means "to jump."
31. *Ante up* means "to put into the pool" or "to bet."
32. *A red* refers to a red cent, meaning "any money at all."

33. *P'ints* is dialect for points, meaning "qualities" or "characteristics."
34. *Quail shot* is ammunition made up of small lead pellets.

swamp and slopped around in the mud for a long time, and finally he ketched a frog, and fetched him in, and give him to this feller, and says:

"Now, if you're ready, set him alongside of Dan'l, with his fore-paws just even with Dan'l, and I'll give the word." Then he says, "One—two—three—jump!" and him and the feller touched up the frogs from behind, and the new frog hopped off, but Dan'l give a heave, and hysted up his shoulders—so—like a Frenchman, but it wan't no use—he couldn't budge; he was planted as solid as an anvil, and he couldn't no more stir than if he was anchored out. Smiley was a good deal surprised, and he was disgusted too, but he didn't have no idea what the matter was, of course.

The feller took the money and started away; and when he was going out at the door, he sorter jerked his thumb over his shoulders—this way—at Dan'l, and says again, very deliberate, "Well, *I* don't see no p'ints about that frog that's any better'n any other frog."

Smiley he stood scratching his head and looking down at Dan'l a long time, and at last he says, "I do wonder what in the nation that frog throw'd off for—I wonder if there an't something the matter with him—he 'pears to look mighty baggy, somehow." And he ketched

> "Well, thish-yer Smiley had a yaller one-eyed cow that didn't have no tail . . ."

Dan'l by the nap of the neck, and lifted him up and says, "Why, blame my cats, if he don't weigh five pound!" and turned him upside down, and he belched out a double handful of shot. And then he see how it was, and he was the maddest man—he set the frog down and took out after that feller, but he never ketched him. And—

[Here Simon Wheeler heard his name called from the front yard, and got up to see what was wanted.] And turning to me as he moved away, he said: "Just set where you are, stranger, and rest easy—I an't going to be gone a second."

But, by your leave, I did not think that a continuation of the history of the enterprising vagabond *Jim* Smiley would be likely to afford[35] me much information concerning the Rev. *Leonidas W.* Smiley, and so I started away.

At the door I met the sociable Wheeler returning, and he buttonholed[36] me and recommenced:

"Well, thish-yer Smiley had a yaller one-eyed cow that didn't have no tail, only jest a short stump like a bannanner, and——"

"Oh! hang Smiley and his afflicted cow!" I muttered, good-naturedly, and bidding the old gentleman good-day, I departed.

---

35. *Afford* means "to give" or "to provide."
36. *Buttonholed* means "detained in conversation."

Vocabulary

enterprising (en′ tər prī′ zing) *adj.* showing energy and initiative, especially in beginning new projects

vagabond (vag′ ə bond′) *n.* someone who wanders from place to place, having no visible means of support

Responding to Literature

Personal Response

What questions would you like to ask Simon Wheeler?

ANALYZING LITERATURE

RECALL

1. How does the narrator come to meet Simon Wheeler and to hear his story? How does the narrator describe Wheeler's storytelling style?
2. For what reason does Wheeler call Smiley "the curiosest man"? What evidence does Wheeler use to support his statement?
3. Summarize the methods that Smiley's mare and bull pup use to win. What eventually becomes of Smiley's dog?
4. What amazing things can Smiley's frog do? What personality traits does Wheeler attribute to the frog?
5. Summarize what happens after Smiley meets the stranger.

INTERPRET

6. What can you infer about the narrator's attitude toward Wheeler? Support your answer using details from the story.
7. What conclusions can you draw about Smiley's character, based on the tale Wheeler tells? Use details from the story to support your ideas.
8. Why do you think Wheeler tells about the mare and bull pup first, before focusing on the frog?
9. What aspects of Wheeler's description of Smiley's frog do you find particularly absurd?
10. What event or events determine the outcome of the encounter with the stranger? Explain your answer.

EVALUATE AND CONNECT

11. Refer to your response to the Focus Activity on page 461. Compare the exaggerations you listed with your favorite exaggerations from this story. Which ones are funnier? Why?
12. How do Wheeler's personality and manner of speaking add to the story's humor? Use specific examples to support your ideas.
13. Would you have stayed to hear Wheeler's story about Smiley's "yaller one-eyed cow that didn't have no tail"? Why or why not?
14. Think of a performer who uses exaggeration for comic effect. How does this person's use of exaggeration compare with Wheeler's?
15. In this selection, one story serves as a **frame** for another story. Why might Mark Twain have chosen this structure? What role does the narrator play? (See Literary Terms Handbook, page R7.)

Literary ELEMENTS

Colloquial Language

Colloquial language refers to the informal speech that people use in everyday conversation. Often, the vocabulary and expressions people use, as well as their manner of speaking, are specific to a particular geographical region. To represent colloquial language accurately, writers often break the standard rules of punctuation, spelling, and grammar. In "The Celebrated Jumping Frog of Calaveras County," Twain uses colloquial language to evoke the region and the people he is writing about, as in this example: "He *ketched* a frog one day, and took him home, and said he *cal'klated* to *edercate* him . . ."

1. Identify at least two other examples of colloquial language in the story. Explain which rules of grammar, spelling, or punctuation are ignored in the characters' speech.
2. Why might colloquial language be inappropriate in a formal essay or an article that explains how to do something?

● See **Literary Terms Handbook,** p. R3.

LITERATURE AND WRITING

Writing About Literature

Analyze the Effect of Setting   In three paragraphs, describe the **setting** in which Simon Wheeler tells his story, and explore the following questions: Why might Twain have selected this setting? How might the story have been different if the narrator had met Wheeler in a city? Support your opinions with details from the selection.

Creative Writing

Smiley's Yaller Cow   Tell your version of the story of Smiley's "yaller one-eyed cow," using Simon Wheeler as the narrator. In your story, bend the standard rules of grammar, punctuation, and spelling in order to accurately represent Wheeler's manner of speaking. Try to include as many humorous exaggerations as you can.

EXTENDING YOUR RESPONSE

Literature Groups

Believe It or Not   A **tall tale** is narrated in a sober manner in order to convince the listener that the story is true, no matter how fantastic the events or characters may be. In your group, compare and contrast Smiley's three tales—the mare, the dog, and the frog—and discuss which story was the most convincing. Use specific details from the selection to support your ideas. Share your conclusions with the class.

Performing

An Interview with Simon Wheeler   Work with another student to write an interview with Simon Wheeler. Compose answers that you think would be consistent with

his character. Present your interview to the class, with one student playing the role of interviewer and the other the role of Wheeler.

Learning for Life

An Advertisement   Create a newspaper advertisement for a performance by Jim Smiley's amazing frog. For ideas, look at real newspaper advertisements for plays, circuses, and other live performances. Use language and graphics to capture readers' attention and to persuade them that they won't want to miss this performance by a truly amazing amphibian.

📖 Save your work for your portfolio.

Skill Minilesson

VOCABULARY • The Latin Root *ject*

The word *conjecture* comes from the Latin prefix *con-*, meaning "together," and the root *ject*, meaning "to throw." When you *conjecture*, you don't have enough evidence to draw a logical conclusion, so you throw thoughts together; you guess.

Since the prefix *e-* means "out," an ejected player is one who is thrown out of a game. A rejected suitor or fish or idea is thrown back.

PRACTICE   Use your knowledge of the root *ject* and familiar prefixes to answer the following questions.

1. Does a person with *dejected* spirits feel hopeful, sad, or outraged?

2. What might a person giving a speech do to *inject* some humor?

3. Which is used as a *projectile*—a cannonball, a life raft, or a rocking chair?

4. In the following sentence, which word is an *interjection?* "No, I did not tell him what I thought; but—oh!—how I wanted to!"

Photography/ Science Book

The frogs many of us know from everyday life are green and they jump. The red-eyed tree frog (below), however, usually just strolls around the rain forest. Read to learn more frog facts.

Frogs

from *Frogs*, by David Badger, photographs by John Netherton

"Well, I don't see no p'ints about that frog that's any better'n any other frog."

That sentiment, voiced by a compulsive gambler in Mark Twain's acclaimed short story, "The Celebrated Jumping Frog of Calaveras County," first appeared in a New York literary journal in 1865. Of course, that was before color photography was invented—and before nature photographers like John Netherton began to distill the beauty of the natural world through their artistic images.

Frog-jumping contests such as the annual event in Calaveras County, California, have conditioned many people to think of frogs primarily as "leapers," but these adroit animals move by other means as well. Toads, for example, hop. Arboreal tree frogs climb. Flying frogs glide (or freefall) with webbed feet serving as makeshift parachutes. Senegal running frogs walk or run. Walking frogs stride slowly. Burrowing toads shuffle and dig. Northern cricket frogs skitter. And all manner of aquatic and terrestrial species swim.

Still, it is the leapers and the climbers, endowed with long hind legs, that amaze observers. When a leopard frog launches itself into the air, or a jittery bullfrog jumps into the water, the powerful extensor muscles in its rear legs perform a remarkable feat [allowing it to leap incredibly long distances].

The size of a frog sometimes fools observers into assuming that the bigger the frog, the longer the leap. Yet the goliath frog of Africa, which exceeds 15 inches (375 mm) from snout to rump, is actually a rather poor jumper, and entrants in the Calaveras County frog-jumping contest have proved embarrassing duds.

Well-hyped bullfrogs can excite audiences with their proven ability to leap nine times the length of their body, but smaller frogs can jump even farther relative to their size. The leopard frog, for example, can leap fifteen times its body length, and the southern cricket frog can jump an astonishing thirty-six times its body length.

Respond

1. Which fact about frogs surprised you the most? Explain.

2. Why do you think frogs have developed so many ways of getting around?

Literature F O C U S

Short Story

A **short story** is a brief piece of fiction, usually focusing on a single major event and on a few characters. In a review of Nathaniel Hawthorne's *Twice-Told Tales*, Edgar Allan Poe wrote that the short story belonged "to the loftiest region of art." Learning the language of literary analysis can help you understand and discuss how short stories are created and what makes them effective.

SHORT STORY ELEMENTS

MODEL: "The Celebrated Jumping Frog of Calaveras County"

Setting

Setting is the time and location of a story's events; it may also include the ideas, beliefs, and values of the characters or of the particular society.

> Since the story is a tale within a tale, it has two settings. It opens in the mining community of Angel's Camp, California, some years after a particular frog-jumping contest.

Characters

Characters are the actors in a story. Most characters are people, but they can also be animals, elements of nature, or other forces.

- The **protagonist** is the main character.
- The **antagonist** is the person or thing that opposes the main character. Not all stories have antagonists.

> The **protagonist** of the inner story is Jim Smiley, and the **antagonist** is the stranger who bets against Smiley's frog.

Point of View

Point of view is the perspective from which the narrator tells a story.

- In **first-person** point of view, the narrator is a character in the story and uses "I" or "me" in telling it.
- In **third-person** point of view, the narrator is not a character, but describes the action and the characters from outside the story. In **third-person omniscient** point of view, the narrator is all-knowing. In **third-person limited,** the narrator describes only what one character could know.

> The narrator describes his visit with Simon Wheeler from a **first-person point of view.**

Theme

Theme is the central message of a story—an insight about life that readers can apply to their own lives. Most short stories have one major theme.

- **Stated themes** are directly presented in a story.
- **Implied themes** must be inferred by considering all the elements of a story.

> The main theme is **implied** by the stories that are told: even those who should know better can be outsmarted.

Plot

Plot is the series of related events through which characters explore a problem and solve it. The plot grows out of a **conflict,** a struggle that may involve people, ideas, or other forces.

- **External conflicts** are struggles between a character and a force outside the character.
- **Internal conflicts** are struggles between forces within a character.

> The events that make up the **plot** of the inner tale are shown in the diagram below.
>
> The **conflict** is external—Smiley versus the stranger, betting on whether Smiley's frog can jump farther than any other frog in the county.

Most plots develop in five stages.

- In the **exposition,** the author introduces the characters and the setting to prepare for the conflict that follows.
- The conflict develops during the **rising action** stage.
- The **climax** is the high point of the story.
- During the **falling action** stage, the author explains the results of the climax. Stories that end immediately after the climax may not have this stage.
- The **resolution** shows how the conflict is finally resolved.

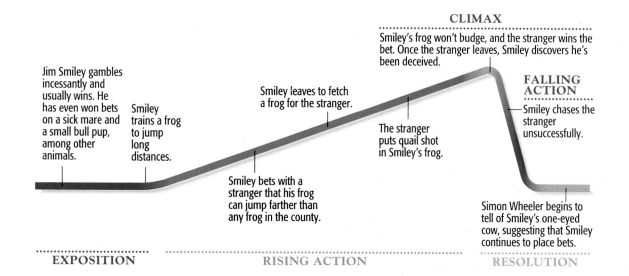

CLIMAX
Smiley's frog won't budge, and the stranger wins the bet. Once the stranger leaves, Smiley discovers he's been deceived.

FALLING ACTION
Smiley chases the stranger unsuccessfully.

Jim Smiley gambles incessantly and usually wins. He has even won bets on a sick mare and a small bull pup, among other animals.

Smiley trains a frog to jump long distances.

Smiley leaves to fetch a frog for the stranger.

The stranger puts quail shot in Smiley's frog.

Smiley bets with a stranger that his frog can jump farther than any frog in the county.

Simon Wheeler begins to tell of Smiley's one-eyed cow, suggesting that Smiley continues to place bets.

EXPOSITION   **RISING ACTION**   **RESOLUTION**

Meet
Bret Harte

If American newspapers of the early 1870s had featured best-seller lists, one name would have appeared regularly at the top: Bret Harte. Not only was he one of the most widely read writers in the United States at the time, but he was also the best paid. Harte wrote colorful, romantic stories about America's West. In many of his stories, he conjured up the flavor and characters of the California gold rush long after it had ended.

Harte was born in Albany, New York, and he ventured west when he was only eighteen years old. In the 1850s, California was a booming frontier, rough and colorful. Harte briefly tried prospecting, worked as a drugstore clerk and a Wells Fargo guard, and then found work in journalism.

By 1860 Harte was thriving as an editor of a newpaper, the *Northern Californian*. However, when he wrote an editorial condemning the massacre of sixty Indians by local white men, he so outraged readers that he had to quit the paper and leave town.

Harte went on to co-found the weekly *Californian* and hired Mark Twain, who was then relatively unknown, to write articles. "Harte," Twain later wrote, "trimmed, trained, and schooled me patiently, until he changed me from an awkward utterer of coarse grotesqueries to a writer of paragraphs and chapters." Later in his career, Twain would become a harsh critic of Harte and his work.

While serving as editor of the *Overland Monthly*, a literary magazine, Harte wrote the story that made him famous: "The Luck of Roaring Camp." He followed that success with "The Outcasts of Poker Flat." Readers in the United States and England were eager for descriptions of California and the Wild West, and Harte gave them the stories they wanted. However, when the prestigious Boston literary magazine *Atlantic Monthly* offered Harte a contract, the writer accepted the offer and left California for the East. He never looked back.

Harte's future looked bright, but personal and family problems prevented him from maintaining his early success. He spent the last twenty-four years of his life in Germany, Scotland, and England. In England Harte found an enthusiastic audience for his work long after Americans had grown tired of his literary formula.

Many popular films and television programs about the West owe a debt to Harte's fiction. In his early works, screenwriters and producers found the prototypes for characters now considered standard in media Westerns. The stereotypical seedy prospector, the dance-hall girl with a heart of gold, and the cynical gambler all originated in Harte's stories. Because these characters have become part of American culture, Harte's portrait of the West has endured.

"Give me a man that is capable of a devotion to anything, rather than a cool, calculating average of all the virtues!"

—Harte

"Bret Harte was one of the pleasantest men I have ever known. He was also one of the unpleasantest men I have ever known."

—Mark Twain

Bret Harte was born in 1836 and died in 1902.

FOCUS ACTIVITY

Have you ever seen reruns of popular television Westerns such as *Bonanza* or *Gunsmoke*? What are your favorite films about the Old West?

DISCUSS In a small group, discuss some of the standard, or stereotypical, characters that appear in films or television series about the Old West. What makes these characters interesting or appealing?

SETTING A PURPOSE Read to encounter a colorful cast of characters from the Old West.

BACKGROUND

The Time and Place

After James Marshall discovered gold in California in 1848, the transformation of the West was immediate and spectacular. Mining towns sprang up almost overnight and small towns rapidly grew into cities. By the end of 1849, nearly one hundred thousand people had entered California to seek their fortune. They were called "forty-niners." Their common destination was a region known as the Mother Lode, a belt more than a hundred miles long that ran from Mariposa, near Yosemite, to Georgetown.

During this period, farmers, businesspeople, criminals, journalists—people from virtually all walks of life—mixed in rough, lawless,

"Jack of the Tules," by Bret Harte in *Harper's Weekly*, July 10, 1886.

and sometimes violent circumstances. As fortunes were made and lost, a new way of life was established. The colorful incidents of western life and the vivid anecdotes of old-timers fired the imagination of Bret Harte, who used this material for his stories.

A Closer Look at Language

Bret Harte was the first writer of the **local color** trend in American literature—a trend that was popular until the turn of the century. One technique Harte used to convey the local color of the West was to incorporate the vernacular, or local speech, into his dialogue. This technique creates vivid, realistic dialogue that typifies the time and place of the story.

VOCABULARY PREVIEW

impropriety (im′ prə prī′ ə tē) *n.* the quality of being improper; improper behavior; p. 477

expatriated (eks pā′ trē āt′ əd) *adj.* banished; exiled; p. 477

malevolence (mə lev′ ə ləns) *n.* a disposition to wish harm to others; ill will; p. 478

equanimity (ek′ wə nim′ ə tē) *n.* evenness of temper; calmness; p. 479

jocular (jok′ yə lər) *adj.* humorous; p. 480

hypothesis (hī poth′ ə sis) *n.* an unproved explanation or assumption; p. 480

seclusion (si klōō′ zhən) *n.* separation from others; isolation; p. 481

querulous (kwer′ ə ləs) *adj.* complaining; whining; p. 483

The OUTCASTS of Poker Flat

Bret Harte

AS MR. JOHN OAKHURST, gambler, stepped into the main street of Poker Flat on the morning of the 23d of November, 1850, he was conscious of a change in its moral atmosphere since the preceding night. Two or three men, conversing earnestly together, ceased as he approached, and exchanged significant glances. There was a Sabbath lull in the air, which, in a settlement unused to Sabbath influences, looked ominous.

Mr. Oakhurst's calm, handsome face betrayed small concern in these indications. Whether he was conscious of any predisposing cause was another question. "I reckon they're after somebody," he reflected; "likely it's me." He returned to his pocket the handkerchief with which he had been whipping away the red dust of Poker Flat from his neat boots, and quietly discharged his mind of any further conjecture.

In point of fact, Poker Flat was "after somebody." It had lately suffered the loss of several thousand dollars, two valuable horses, and a prominent citizen. It was experiencing a spasm of virtuous reaction, quite as lawless and ungovernable as any of the acts that had provoked it. A secret committee had determined to rid the town of all improper persons. This was done permanently in regard of two men who were then hanging from the boughs of a sycamore in the gulch,[1] and temporarily in the banishment of certain other objectionable characters. I regret to say that some of these were ladies. It is but due to the sex, however, to state that their impropriety was professional, and it was only in such easily established standards of evil that Poker Flat ventured to sit in judgment.

Mr. Oakhurst was right in supposing that he was included in this category. A few of the committee had urged hanging him as a possible example and a sure method of reimbursing themselves from his pockets of the sums he had won from them. "It's agin[2] justice," said Jim Wheeler, "to let this yer young man from Roaring Camp—an entire stranger—carry away our money." But a crude sentiment of equity residing in the breasts of those who had been fortunate enough to win from Mr. Oakhurst overruled this narrower local prejudice.

Mr. Oakhurst received his sentence with philosophic calmness, none the less coolly that he was aware of the hesitation of his judges. He was too much of a gambler not to accept fate. With him life was at best an uncertain game, and he recognized the usual percentage in favor of the dealer.

A body of armed men accompanied the deported wickedness of Poker Flat to the outskirts of the settlement. Besides Mr. Oakhurst, who was known to be a coolly desperate man, and for whose intimidation the armed escort was intended, the expatriated party consisted of a young woman familiarly known as "The Duchess;" another who had won the title of "Mother Shipton;"[3] and "Uncle Billy," a suspected sluice-robber[4] and confirmed drunkard. The cavalcade[5] provoked no comments from the spectators, nor was any word uttered by the escort. Only

---

1. A *gulch* is a small, narrow valley, especially one eroded by running water.

2. *Agin* is dialect for *against.*
3. The original *Mother Shipton* (1488–1560) was an English woman accused of witchcraft.
4. A *sluice-robber* is someone who steals gold from sluices, long water troughs used by miners to separate gold ore from other materials.
5. A *cavalcade* (kav′ əl kād′) is a procession, especially of people on horseback.

Vocabulary
impropriety (im′ prə prī′ ə tē) *n.* the quality of being improper; improper behavior
expatriated (eks pā′ trē āt′ əd) *adj.* banished; exiled

when the gulch which marked the uttermost limit of Poker Flat was reached, the leader spoke briefly and to the point. The exiles were forbidden to return at the peril of their lives.

As the escort disappeared, their pent-up feelings found vent in a few hysterical tears from the Duchess, some bad language from Mother Shipton, and a Parthian[6] volley of expletives from Uncle Billy. The philosophic Oakhurst alone remained silent. He listened calmly to Mother Shipton's desire to cut somebody's heart out, to the repeated statements of the Duchess that she would die in the road, and to the alarming oaths that seemed to be bumped out of Uncle Billy as he rode forward. With the easy good humor characteristic of his class, he insisted upon exchanging his own riding-horse, "Five-Spot," for the sorry mule which the Duchess rode. But even this act did not draw the party into any closer sympathy. The young woman readjusted her somewhat draggled plumes with a feeble, faded coquetry;[7] Mother Shipton eyed the possessor of "Five-Spot" with <u>malevolence</u>, and Uncle Billy included the whole party in one sweeping anathema.[8]

The road to Sandy Bar—a camp that, not having as yet experienced the regenerating influences of Poker Flat, consequently seemed to offer some invitation to the emigrants—lay over a steep mountain range. It was distant a day's severe travel. In that advanced season the party soon passed out of the moist, temperate regions of the foothills into the dry,

cold bracing air of the Sierras. The trail was narrow and difficult. At noon the Duchess, rolling out of her saddle upon the ground, declared her intention of going no farther, and the party halted.

Did You Know?
Sierras refers to the Sierra Nevada, a mountain range in eastern California.

The spot was singularly wild and impressive. A wooded amphitheatre, surrounded on three sides by precipitous cliffs of naked granite, sloped gently toward the crest of another precipice that overlooked the valley. It was, undoubtedly, the most suitable spot for a camp, had camping been advisable. But Mr. Oakhurst knew that scarcely half the journey to Sandy Bar was accomplished, and the party were not equipped or provisioned for delay. This fact he pointed out to his companions curtly, with a philosophic commentary on the folly of "throwing up their hand before the game was played out." But they were furnished with liquor, which in this emergency stood them in place of food, fuel, rest, and prescience.[9] In spite of his remonstrances, it was not long before they were more or less under its influence. Uncle Billy passed rapidly from a bellicose[10] state into one of stupor, the Duchess became maudlin,[11] and Mother Shipton snored. Mr. Oakhurst alone remained erect, leaning against a rock, calmly surveying them.

Mr. Oakhurst did not drink. It interfered with a profession which required coolness, impassiveness, and presence of mind, and, in

---

6. Here, *Parthian* means "delivered when parting or retreating." The cavalry of the ancient country of Parthia (now part of Iran) was known for shooting arrows while retreating or pretending to retreat.
7. *Coquetry* (kō′ kə trē) means "flirtation."
8. An *anathema* (a nath′ ə mə) is a strong denunciation or a curse.

9. *Prescience* (prē′ shē əns) is foresight.
10. *Bellicose* (bel′ ə kōs) means "showing an eagerness to fight" or "quarrelsome."
11. *Maudlin* (môd′ lin) means "excessively sentimental."

Vocabulary
malevolence (mə lev′ ə ləns) *n.* a disposition to wish harm to others; ill will

his own language, he "couldn't afford it." As he gazed at his recumbent[12] fellow exiles, the loneliness begotten of his pariah trade,[13] his habits of life, his very vices, for the first time seriously oppressed him. He bestirred himself in dusting his black clothes, washing his hands and face, and other acts characteristic of his studiously neat habits, and for a moment forgot his annoyance. The thought of deserting his weaker and more pitiable companions never perhaps occurred to him. Yet he could not help feeling the want of that excitement which, singularly enough, was most conducive to that calm equanimity for which he was notorious. He looked at the gloomy walls that rose a thousand feet sheer above the circling pines around him, at the sky ominously clouded, at the valley below, already deepening into shadow; and, doing so, suddenly he heard his own name called.

A horseman slowly ascended the trail. In the fresh, open face of the newcomer Mr. Oakhurst recognized Tom Simson, otherwise known as "The Innocent," of Sandy Bar. He had met him some months before over a "little game," and had, with perfect equanimity, won the entire fortune—amounting to some forty dollars—of that guileless youth. After the game was finished, Mr. Oakhurst drew the youthful speculator behind the door and thus addressed him: "Tommy, you're a good little man, but you can't gamble worth a cent. Don't try it over again." He then handed him his money back, pushed him gently from the room, and so made a devoted slave of Tom Simson.

There was a remembrance of this in his boyish and enthusiastic greeting of Mr. Oakhurst. He had started, he said, to go to Poker Flat to seek his fortune. "Alone?" No, not exactly alone; in fact (a giggle), he had run away with Piney Woods. Didn't Mr. Oakhurst remember Piney? She that used to wait on the table at the Temperance House? They had been engaged a long time, but old Jake Woods had objected, and so they had run away, and were going to Poker Flat to be married, and here they were. And they were tired out, and how lucky it was they had found a place to camp, and company. All this the Innocent delivered rapidly, while Piney, a stout, comely damsel of fifteen, emerged from behind the pine-tree, where she had been blushing unseen, and rode to the side of her lover.

Mr. Oakhurst seldom troubled himself with sentiment, still less with propriety; but he had a vague idea that the situation was not fortunate. He retained, however, his presence of mind sufficiently to kick Uncle Billy, who was about to say something, and Uncle Billy was sober enough to recognize in Mr. Oakhurst's kick a superior power that would not bear trifling.[14] He then endeavored to dissuade Tom Simson from delaying further, but in vain. He even pointed out the fact that there was no provision, nor means of making a camp. But, unluckily, the Innocent met this objection by assuring the party that he was provided with an extra mule loaded with provisions, and by the discovery of a rude attempt at a log house near the trail. "Piney can stay with Mrs. Oakhurst," said the Innocent, pointing to the Duchess, "and I can shift for myself."

Nothing but Mr. Oakhurst's admonishing foot saved Uncle Billy from bursting into a roar of laughter. As it was, he felt compelled to retire up the cañon[15] until he could recover his gravity. There he confided the joke to the tall pine-trees, with many slaps of his leg,

---

12. *Recumbent* (ri kum′ bənt) means "lying down" or "resting."
13. A *pariah* (pə rī′ ə) is an outcast, someone who is despised by others. A *pariah trade* is an occupation that is socially unacceptable.
14. Here, *trifling* means "joking" or "mocking."
15. *Cañon* (kä nyōn′) is Spanish for *canyon*.

Vocabulary
equanimity (ek′ wə nim′ ə tē) *n.* evenness of temper; calmness

contortions of his face, and the usual profanity. But when he returned to the party, he found them seated by a fire—for the air had grown strangely chill and the sky overcast—in apparently amicable conversation. Piney was actually talking in an impulsive girlish fashion to the Duchess, who was listening with an interest and animation she had not shown for many days. The Innocent was holding forth, apparently with equal effect, to Mr. Oakhurst and Mother Shipton, who was actually relaxing into amiability. "Is this yer a d—d picnic?" said Uncle Billy, with inward scorn, as he surveyed the sylvan[16] group, the glancing firelight, and the tethered animals in the foreground. Suddenly an idea mingled with the alcoholic fumes that disturbed his brain. It was apparently of a jocular nature, for he felt impelled to slap his leg again and cram his fist into his mouth.

As the shadows crept slowly up the mountain, a slight breeze rocked the tops of the pine-trees and moaned through their long and gloomy aisles. The ruined cabin, patched and covered with pine boughs, was set apart for the ladies. As the lovers parted, they unaffectedly exchanged a kiss, so honest and sincere that it might have been heard above the swaying pines. The frail Duchess and the malevolent Mother Shipton were probably too stunned to remark upon this last evidence of simplicity, and so turned without a word to the hut. The fire was replenished, the men lay down before the door, and in a few minutes were asleep.

Mr. Oakhurst was a light sleeper. Toward morning he awoke benumbed and cold. As he stirred the dying fire, the wind, which was now blowing strongly, brought to his cheek that which caused the blood to leave it,—snow!

He started to his feet with the intention of awakening the sleepers, for there was no time to lose. But turning to where Uncle Billy had been lying, he found him gone. A suspicion leaped to his brain, and a curse to his lips. He ran to the spot where the mules had been tethered—they were no longer there. The tracks were already rapidly disappearing in the snow.

The momentary excitement brought Mr. Oakhurst back to the fire with his usual calm. He did not waken the sleepers. The Innocent slumbered peacefully, with a smile on his good-humored, freckled face; the virgin Piney slept beside her frailer sisters as sweetly as though attended by celestial guardians; and Mr. Oakhurst, drawing his blanket over his shoulders, stroked his mustaches and waited for the dawn. It came slowly in a whirling mist of snowflakes that dazzled and confused the eye. What could be seen of the landscape appeared magically changed. He looked over the valley, and summed up the present and future in two words, "Snowed in!"

A careful inventory of the provisions, which, fortunately for the party, had been stored within the hut, and so escaped the felonious[17] fingers of Uncle Billy, disclosed the fact that with care and prudence they might last ten days longer. "That is," said Mr. Oakhurst sotto voce[18] to the Innocent, "if you're willing to board us. If you ain't—and perhaps you'd better not—you can wait till Uncle Billy gets back with provisions." For some occult[19] reason, Mr. Oakhurst could not bring himself to disclose Uncle Billy's rascality, and so offered the hypothesis that he had wandered from the camp and had accidentally stampeded the animals. He dropped a warning to the Duchess and Mother Shipton,

16. *Sylvan* means "situated in the woods."

17. *Felonious* means "evil" or "villainous."
18. *Sotto voce* (sot' ō vō' chē) means "in a low tone of voice." The Italian words literally mean "under the voice."
19. *Occult* means "mysterious."

Vocabulary
jocular (jok' yə lər) *adj*. humorous
hypothesis (hī poth' ə sis) *n*. an unproved explanation or assumption

who of course knew the facts of their associate's defection. "They'll find out the truth about us *all* when they find out anything," he added significantly, "and there's no good frightening them now."

Tom Simson not only put all his worldly store at the disposal of Mr. Oakhurst, but seemed to enjoy the prospect of their enforced seclusion. "We'll have a good camp for a week, and then the snow'll melt, and we'll all go back together." The cheerful gayety of the young man and Mr. Oakhurst's calm infected the others. The Innocent, with the aid of pine boughs, extemporized[20] a thatch for the roofless cabin, and the Duchess directed Piney in the rearrangement of the interior with a taste and tact that opened the blue eyes of that provincial maiden to their fullest extent. "I reckon now you're used to fine things at Poker Flat," said Piney. The Duchess turned away sharply to conceal something that reddened her cheeks through their professional tint, and Mother Shipton requested Piney not to "chatter." But when Mr. Oakhurst returned from a weary search for the trail, he heard the sound of happy laughter echoed from the rocks. He stopped in some alarm, and his thoughts first naturally reverted to the whiskey, which he had prudently cachéd.[21] "And yet it don't somehow sound like whiskey," said the gambler. It was not until he caught sight of the blazing fire through the still blinding storm, and the group around it, that he settled to the conviction that it was "square fun."

Whether Mr. Oakhurst had cachéd his cards with the whiskey as something debarred the free access of the community, I cannot say. It was certain that, in Mother Shipton's

words, he "didn't say 'cards' once" during that evening. Haply the time was beguiled by an accordion, produced somewhat ostentatiously by Tom Simson from his pack. Notwithstanding some difficulties attending the manipulation of this instrument, Piney Woods managed to pluck several reluctant melodies from its keys, to an accompaniment by the Innocent on a pair of bone castanets. But the crowning festivity of the evening was reached in a rude[22]

Did You Know?
Castanets are pairs of concave shells, often made of ivory or wood. The shells are held in the hand and played by clicking them together.

camp-meeting[23] hymn, which the lovers, joining hands, sang with great earnestness and vociferation. I fear that a certain defiant tone and Covenanter's swing[24] to its chorus, rather than any devotional quality, caused it speedily to infect the others, who at last joined in the refrain:—

"I'm proud to live in the service of the Lord,
    And I'm bound to die in His army."

The pines rocked, the storm eddied and whirled above the miserable group, and the flames of their altar leaped heavenward, as if in token of the vow.

At midnight the storm abated, the rolling clouds parted, and the stars glittered keenly above the sleeping camp. Mr. Oakhurst, whose

---

20. *Extemporized* means "made without preparation" or "improvised."
21. *Cachéd* (kasht) means "hidden."

22. Here, *rude* means "vigorous" or "robust."
23. A *camp-meeting* is an outdoor religious gathering.
24. *Covenanter's swing* implies a lively rhythm. The Covenanters were Scottish Presbyterians who made covenants, or agreements, to resist rule by the Church of England.

Vocabulary
seclusion (si klōō′ zhən) *n.* separation from others; isolation

professional habits had enabled him to live on the smallest possible amount of sleep, in dividing the watch with Tom Simson somehow managed to take upon himself the greater part of that duty. He excused himself to the Innocent by saying that he had "often been a week without sleep." "Doing what?" asked Tom. "Poker!" replied Oakhurst sententiously.[25] "When a man gets a streak of luck, he don't get tired. The luck gives in first. Luck," continued the gambler reflectively, "is a mighty queer thing. All you know about it for certain is that it's bound to change. And it's finding out when it's going to change that makes you. We've had a streak of bad luck since we left Poker Flat,—you came along, and slap you get into it, too. If you can hold your cards right along you're all right. For," added the gambler, with cheerful irrelevance—

"'I'm proud to live in the service of the Lord,
    And I'm bound to die in His army.'"

The third day came, and the sun, looking through the white-curtained valley, saw the outcasts divide their slowly decreasing store of provisions for the morning meal. It was one of the peculiarities of that mountain climate that its rays diffused a kindly warmth over the wintry landscape, as if in regretful commiseration of the past. But it revealed drift on drift of snow piled high around the hut,—a hopeless, uncharted, trackless sea of white lying below the rocky shores to which the castaways still clung. Through the marvelously clear air the smoke of the pastoral[26] village of Poker Flat rose miles away. Mother Shipton saw it, and from a remote pinnacle of her rocky fastness hurled in that direction a final malediction.[27] It was her last vituperative[28]

attempt, and perhaps for that reason was invested with a certain degree of sublimity. It did her good, she privately informed the Duchess. "Just you go out there and cuss, and see." She then set herself to the task of amusing "the child," as she and the Duchess were pleased to call Piney. Piney was no chicken, but it was a soothing and original theory of the pair thus to account for the fact that she didn't swear and wasn't improper.

When night crept up again through the gorges, the reedy notes of the accordion rose and fell in fitful spasms and long-drawn gasps by the flickering campfire. But music failed to fill entirely the aching void left by insufficient food, and a new diversion was proposed by Piney,—story-telling. Neither Mr. Oakhurst nor his female companions caring to relate their personal experiences, this plan would have failed too, but for the Innocent. Some months before he had chanced upon a stray copy of Mr. Pope's[29] ingenious translation of the Iliad.[30] He now proposed to narrate the principal incidents of that poem—having thoroughly mastered the argument and fairly forgotten the words—in the current vernacular of Sandy Bar. And so for the rest of that night the Homeric demi-gods again walked the earth. Trojan bully and wily Greek wrestled in the winds, and the great pines in the cañon seemed to bow to the wrath of the son of Peleus.[31] Mr. Oakhurst listened with quiet satisfaction. Most especially was he interested in the fate of "Ashheels," as the Innocent persisted in denominating the "swift-footed Achilles."

So, with small food and much of Homer and the accordion, a week passed over the heads of the outcasts. The sun again forsook them, and

---

25. *Sententiously* (sen ten′ shəs lē) means "in a concise, energetic manner."
26. *Pastoral* means "of, or relating to, rural life."
27. A *malediction* (mal′ ə dik′ shən) is a curse.
28. *Vituperative* (vī tōō′ pə rā′ tiv) means "characterized by abusive language and harsh criticism."

29. *Mr. Pope's* refers to the English poet Alexander Pope (1688–1744).
30. Homer's Greek epic poem the *Iliad* (i′ lē əd) describes the war between the Trojans, natives of ancient Troy, and the Greeks.
31. The *son of Peleus* (pēl′ yüs′) is Achilles, Greek warrior and a hero in the *Iliad*.

Study of a Head (Portrait of Algernon Graves), c. 1881–1885. James A. McNeill Whistler. Oil on canvas, 22⅝ x 14½ in. The Columbus Museum of Art, OH. Bequest of Frederick W. Schumacher.

Viewing the painting: What characteristics does this man appear to have that Mr. Oakhurst might also have?

again from leaden skies the snowflakes were sifted over the land. Day by day closer around them drew the snowy circle, until at last they looked from their prison over drifted walls of dazzling white, that towered twenty feet above their heads. It became more and more difficult to replenish their fires, even from the fallen trees beside them, now half hidden in the drifts. And yet no one complained. The lovers turned from the dreary prospect and looked into each other's eyes, and were happy. Mr. Oakhurst settled himself coolly to the losing game before him. The Duchess, more cheerful than she had been, assumed the care of Piney. Only Mother

Shipton—once the strongest of the party—seemed to sicken and fade. At midnight on the tenth day she called Oakhurst to her side. "I'm going," she said, in a voice of querulous weakness, "but don't say anything about it. Don't waken the kids. Take the bundle from under my head, and open it." Mr. Oakhurst did so. It contained Mother Shipton's rations for the last week, untouched. "Give 'em to the child," she said, pointing to the sleeping Piney. "You've starved yourself," said the gambler. "That's what they call it," said the woman querulously, as she lay down again, and turning her face to the wall, passed quietly away.

The accordion and the bones were put aside that day, and Homer was forgotten. When the body of Mother Shipton had been committed to the snow, Mr. Oakhurst took the Innocent aside, and showed him a pair of snowshoes, which he had fashioned from the old pack-saddle. "There's one chance in a hundred to save her yet," he said, pointing to Piney; "but it's there," he added, pointing toward Poker Flat. "If you can reach there in two days she's safe." "And you?" asked Tom Simson. "I'll stay here," was the curt reply.

The lovers parted with a long embrace. "You are not going, too?" said the Duchess, as she saw Mr. Oakhurst apparently waiting to accompany him. "As far as the cañon," he replied. He turned suddenly and kissed the Duchess, leaving her pallid[32] face aflame, and her trembling limbs rigid with amazement.

Night came, but not Mr. Oakhurst. It brought the storm again and the whirling snow. Then the Duchess, feeding the fire, found that some one had quietly piled beside the hut enough fuel to last a few days longer. The tears rose to her eyes, but she hid them from Piney.

---

32. *Pallid* means "pale."

Vocabulary
querulous (kwer′ ə ləs) *adj.* complaining; whining

The women slept but little. In the morning, looking into each other's faces, they read their fate. Neither spoke, but Piney, accepting the position of the stronger, drew near and placed her arm around the Duchess's waist. They kept this attitude for the rest of the day. That night the storm reached its greatest fury, and, rendering asunder the protecting vines, invaded the very hut.

Toward morning they found themselves unable to feed the fire, which gradually died away. As the embers slowly blackened, the Duchess crept closer to Piney, and broke the silence of many hours: "Piney, can you pray?" "No, dear," said Piney simply. The Duchess, without knowing exactly why, felt relieved, and, putting her head upon Piney's shoulder, spoke no more. And so reclining, the younger and purer pillowing the head of her soiled sister upon her virgin breast, they fell asleep.

The wind lulled as if it feared to waken them. Feathery drifts of snow, shaken from the long pine boughs, flew like white winged birds, and settled about them as they slept. The moon through the rifted clouds looked down upon what had been the camp. But all human stain, all trace of earthly travail, was hidden beneath the spotless mantle mercifully flung from above.

They slept all that day and the next, nor did they waken when voices and footsteps broke the silence of the camp. And when

> *Toward morning they found themselves unable to feed the fire, which gradually died away.*

pitying fingers brushed the snow from their wan faces, you could scarcely have told from the equal peace that dwelt upon them which was she that had sinned. Even the law of Poker Flat recognized this, and turned away, leaving them still locked in each other's arms.

But at the head of the gulch, on one of the largest pine-trees, they found the deuce of clubs[33] pinned to the bark with a bowie-knife. It bore the following, written in pencil in a firm hand:

✝

BENEATH THIS TREE
LIES THE BODY
OF
JOHN OAKHURST,
WHO STRUCK A STREAK OF BAD LUCK
ON THE 23RD OF NOVEMBER 1850,
AND
HANDED IN HIS CHECKS
ON THE 7TH DECEMBER, 1850.

✝

And pulseless and cold, with a derringer by his side and a bullet in his heart, though still calm as in life, beneath the snow lay he who was at once the strongest and yet the weakest of the outcasts of Poker Flat.

---

33. The *deuce of clubs* is the two of clubs. In a deck of cards, it has the lowest value.

Responding to Literature

Personal Response

Did the ending of the story surprise you? Why or why not?

——— ANALYZING LITERATURE ———

RECALL

1. What has the secret committee of Poker Flat decided to do? Why? How is this decision carried out?
2. Summarize what happens on the outcasts' first day together.
3. What happens on the second day in camp?
4. What happens to Mother Shipton? Why? What actions does Mr. Oakhurst take in the last part of the story?
5. When the people from Poker Flat arrive at the camp, what do they find?

INTERPRET

6. What is the narrator's **tone,** or attitude, toward Poker Flat's secret committee and its "improper persons"? What words convey that tone?
7. What can you infer about Mr. Oakhurst's character, based on the way he treats Tom and Piney?
8. What do you learn about the characters, based on the way each one behaves on the second day in camp?
9. What do you think the narrator means when he says that Oakhurst is "at once the strongest and yet the weakest of the outcasts"?
10. In your opinion, what message, or lesson, does this story convey? Support your ideas, using details from the selection.

EVALUATE AND CONNECT

11. Which story character or characters do you admire the most? the least? Give reasons for your answers.
12. How does the author use **foreshadowing** (see page R7) to help prepare the reader for future events? Give specific examples.
13. Do you think the secret committee of Poker Flat is justified in acting as it does? Why or why not?
14. Recall the ideas you discussed in response to the Focus Activity on page 475. Which story characters resemble the stereotypical characters you've seen in films or television series about the Old West? Explain.
15. Do you believe that people are sometimes capable of acting in a completely unselfish way—even sacrificing themselves for the good of others? Explain.

Literary ELEMENTS

Character

A **character** is a person in a literary work. Some characters are **flat**–that is, they reveal or represent a single personality trait. Stereotypes, or stock characters, such as the noble hero or the innocent young lover, are usually flat characters. A **round character,** on the other hand, shows varied and sometimes contradictory traits–just as real people do. A **static character** remains mostly the same throughout a story; a **dynamic character** grows and changes. In "The Outcasts of Poker Flat," Harte creates both flat and round characters; some characters are static, while others are dynamic.

1. What flat characters does Harte create in this story? What personality trait does each character reveal or represent?
2. Who are the round characters in this story? What varied and contradictory traits does each one exhibit?
3. Who are the static characters? Who are the dynamic characters? Explain your choices.

● See **Literary Terms Handbook,** p. R3.

LITERATURE AND WRITING

Writing About Literature

Analyzing Local Color   When writers evoke a particular region by recreating the language, customs, and geography of the area, they use a technique called **local color** (see page R9). In a few paragraphs, analyze how Harte uses local color in "The Outcasts of Poker Flat." Explain how local color adds to your understanding of the story.

Creative Writing

Happily Ever After   Write a happy ending for this story—if not for all the characters, at least for the ones you like the best. Share and compare your new ending with those created by your classmates.

EXTENDING YOUR RESPONSE

Literature Groups

Frontier Justice   In your group, discuss the type of "justice" that is meted out to the characters in this story. Consider questions like these: What gives the secret committee of Poker Flat the authority to force the outcasts to leave town? Shouldn't the outcasts be given a chance to defend themselves? Should the members of the secret committee be held responsible for what happens to the outcasts? Why or why not? Use specific details from the selection to support your opinions. Share your opinions with the class.

Learning for Life

Incident Report   Imagine that Poker Flat has a sheriff's office and you work for it. Tom Simson, looking half-frozen and utterly exhausted, stumbles into your office on a December afternoon in 1850. Write an incident report based on the information Tom gives you.

Listening and Speaking

Discussing a Film   View the 1952 film *The Outcasts of Poker Flat,* directed by Joseph M. Newman and starring Anne Baxter. Note similarities and differences between the film and Harte's original story. Then hold a roundtable discussion in which you compare the story and the film. Which did you prefer? Why?

📖 **Save your work for your portfolio.**

VOCABULARY • Etymology

A word's etymology is its history or an explanation of its origin. Often a word can be traced back through several languages, as is the case with the word *querulous.*

> *querulous:* Middle English *querulose,* from Old French *querelos,* from Late Latin *querulosus,* from Latin *querulus,* from *queri,* meaning "to complain."

Dictionaries usually list etymologies in brackets.

PRACTICE   Use a dictionary to find the etymology of each of the following words from "The Outcasts of Poker Flat."

1. gulch
2. bellicose
3. castanet
4. pastoral
5. pariah
6. impropriety
7. malevolent
8. equanimity
9. jocular
10. hypothesis

Before You Read

Chief Sekoto Holds Court

Meet Bessie Head

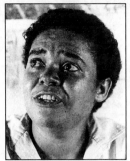

❝I write best if I can hear the thunder behind my ears.❞

—*Head*

One of Africa's best-known writers, Bessie Head began her life in a South African mental hospital. Because of racist attitudes in South Africa, Head's Scottish mother was judged insane and committed to an asylum when she became pregnant by a black man. Taken from her mother at birth, Head was brought up in a foster home until she was thirteen; then she was sent to a mission school.

After training to be a teacher and teaching a few years, Head launched a new career as a journalist. She had difficulty achieving recognition for her work, however, because of prejudice and discrimination toward her gender and racial heritage. The white minority that ruled South Africa at that time practiced apartheid, an official policy of racial segregation and discrimination against nonwhites. This policy made it difficult for people like Head to advance in their careers.

In 1964 Head abandoned journalism and moved to Botswana. There, in a small rural village, she wrote the novels that brought her international acclaim: *When Rain Clouds Gather* (1969), *Maru* (1971), and *A Question of Power* (1973). In these works, Head drew upon her own experiences to explore the themes of racial and sexual discrimination and poverty. While Head's writings often tell of brutality, they also express faith in the power of love and the belief that justice ultimately triumphs.

Bessie Head was born in 1937 and died in 1986.

FOCUS ACTIVITY

How might you respond if your friends and neighbors unjustly accused you of committing a horrible crime? To whom might you turn for help?

FREEWRITE Spend three minutes exploring your response to these questions.

SETTING A PURPOSE Read to find out what happens when a woman is accused of committing a terrible crime.

BACKGROUND

The Time and Place

This story takes place in Botswana, a small nation in southern Africa, some time between the 1960s and the early 1980s. During that period, ninety-four percent of the population lived in small rural villages ruled by tribal chiefs. In addition to their village duties, these chiefs also served as regional law enforcement officers, judges, and representatives at tribal conferences. A House of Chiefs, representing the eight major tribes of the Botswanan people, advised the national government on various tribal matters.

VOCABULARY PREVIEW

concede (kən sēd′) *v.* to acknowledge as true; to admit; p. 489
dally (dal′ ē) *v.* to linger; to delay; to waste time; p. 489
ashen (ash′ ən) *adj.* pale; p. 490

grievously (grē′ vəs lē) *adv.* very seriously; gravely; p. 490
derangement (di rānj′ ment) *n.* disturbance of normal functioning; disorder; p. 491

Chief Sekoto Holds Court

Bessie Head

Even those who did not like chiefs had to <u>concede</u> that Paramount Chief Sekoto was a very charming man. His charm lay not so much in his outer appearance as in his very cheerful outlook on life. In fact, so fond was he of the sunny side of life that he was inclined to regard any gloomy, pessimistic person as insane and make every effort to avoid his company. It was his belief that a witty answer turneth away wrath and that the oil of reason should always be poured on troubled waters.[1]

Every weekday morning, Chief Sekoto listened to cases brought before his court, while the afternoons were spent at leisure unless there were people who had made appointments to interview him. This particular Monday morning a lively and rowdy case was in session when, out of the corner of his eye, Chief Sekoto saw his brother Matenge drive up and park his car opposite the open clearing where court was held. Nothing upset Chief Sekoto more than a visit from his brother, whom he had long classified as belonging to the insane part of mankind. He determined to <u>dally</u> over the proceedings for as long as possible in the hope that his brother would become bored and leave. Therefore he turned his full attention on the case at hand.

The case had been brought in from one of the outlying villages, called Bodibeng, and the cause of its rowdiness was that the whole village of Bodibeng had turned up to witness the trial. A certain old woman of the village, named Mma-Baloi, was charged with allegedly[2] practising witchcraft, and so certain were the villagers of her guilt that they frequently forgot themselves and burst out into loud chatter and had to be brought to order by the president of the court with threats of fines.

---

1. The Chief's first belief is a variation of Proverbs 15:1, which says, "A soft answer turneth away wrath." The second belief refers to the fact that oil floats on, rather than mixing with, water; thus, metaphorically, the *oil of reason* would have a calming effect on the *troubled waters* of a dispute.
2. Here, *allegedly* (ə lej′id lē) means "presumedly" or "supposedly."

Vocabulary
concede (kən sēd′) *v.* to acknowledge as true; to admit
dally (dal′ ē) *v.* to linger; to delay; to waste time

Chief Sekoto Holds Court

Evidence was that Mma-Baloi had always lived a secret and mysterious life apart from the other villagers. She was also in the habit of receiving strangers from far-off places into her home who would not state what dealings they had with Mma-Baloi. Now, over a certain period, a number of the children of the village had died sudden deaths, and each time a mother stood up to describe these sudden deaths, the crowd roared in fury because the deaths of the children and the evil practices of Mma-Baloi were one and the same thing in their minds. The accused, Mma-Baloi, sat a little apart from the villagers in a quaking, ashen, crumpled heap and each time the villagers roared, she seemed about to sink into the earth. Noting this, Chief Sekoto's kindly heart was struck with pity.

Further evidence was that about a week ago a strange young woman had turned up in the village of Bodibeng and made straight for the hut of Mma-Baloi, where she had died a sudden death. This had made Mma-Baloi run screaming from her hut, and it was only the intervention[3] of the police that had saved Mma-Baloi from being torn to pieces by the villagers.

Chief Sekoto was silent for some time. The insanity of mankind never ceased to amaze him. At last he turned to the accused and said gently, "Well, mother, what do you have to say in defense of yourself?"

"Sir, I am no witch," said the quavering old voice. "Even though I am called the mother of the witches, I am no witch. Long ago I was taught by the people who live in the bush how to cure ailments with herbs and that is my business."

She pointed a shaking finger at a bag placed near her.

"I would like to see the contents of the bag," Chief Sekoto said with a great show of interest. The bag was brought to him and its contents tipped out on the ground. They were a various assortment of dried leaves, roots, and berries. He examined them leisurely, picking up a few items for closer inspection. This very deliberate gesture was meant to puncture a hole in the confidence of the crowd, who annoyed him. While he fiddled about he was aware of how silent and intent they had become, following his every movement with their eyes. Thus holding the stage, he turned to the old woman and said:

"Proceed with your defense, mother."

"About the deaths of the children of which I am accused, I know nothing, sir," she said. "About the young woman who died in my home last Saturday, I am also innocent. This young woman came to me on recommendation, being grievously ill. We were discussing the ailment when she fell dead at my feet. Never has such a thing occurred before, and this caused me to lose my mind and run out of the house."

"That is quite understandable, mother," Chief Sekoto said sympathetically. "Even I should have been grieved if some stranger was struck with death in my home."

He swept the crowd with a stern glance. "Who issues the certificates of death in Bodibeng?" he asked.

There was a short, bewildered silence. Then a car and a messenger had to be found to fetch the doctor of the Bodibeng hospital. There was a delay of two hours as the doctor was engaged in an operation. Throughout this long wait the court remained in session. At one stage Chief Sekoto received an impatient

---

3. Here, *intervention* means "the act of coming between opposing parties."

Vocabulary
ashen (ash′ ən) *adj.* pale
grievously (grē′ vəs lē) *adv.* very seriously; gravely

note: "Dear Brother," it said. "Please spare a few moments to discuss an urgent matter."

Chief Sekoto replied: "Is it life or death? I am at the moment faced with the life or death of an old woman. I cannot move."

It was near noon when the doctor arrived. His evidence was brief and to the point. Yes, it was true, he said. There had been a surprising number of child deaths in the village of Bodibeng, and death in each case had been due to pneumonia; and yes, he said, he had performed a postmortem[4] on the body of a young woman last Saturday afternoon. The young woman had died of a septic womb. . . .[5] He would say that the septic condition of the womb had been of three months' duration.

All that was left now was for Chief Sekoto to pass judgement on the case. This he did sternly, drawing himself up to his full height.

"People of Bodibeng," he said. "It seems to me you are all suffering from derangement of the brain."

He paused long enough to allow the villagers to look at each other uneasily.

"Your children die of pneumonia," he thundered, "and to shield yourselves from blame you accuse a poor old woman of having bewitched them into death. Not only that.

---

4. A *postmortem,* or autopsy, is the examination of a corpse that a physician performs to discover the cause of death.
5. In this case, the doctor's discovery of a *septic womb* indicated the absorption of certain poisonous bacteria into the bloodstream from an infection in the womb.

You falsely accuse her of a most serious crime which carries the death sentence. How long have you planned the death of a poor old woman, deranged people of Bodibeng? How long have you caused her to live in utter misery, suspicion, and fear? I say: Can dogs bark forever? Oh no, people of Bodibeng, today you will make payment for the legs of the old mother who has fled before your barking. I say: The fault is all with you, and because of this I fine each household of Bodibeng one beast. From the money that arises out of the sale of these beasts, each household is to purchase warm clothing for the children so that they may no longer die of pneumonia."

He turned and looked at the old woman, changing his expression to one of kindness.

"As for you, mother," he said. "I cannot allow you to go and live once more among the people of Bodibeng. It is only hatred that the people of Bodibeng feel for you, and this has driven them out of their minds. As hatred never dies, who knows what evil they will not plot against you. I have a large house, and you are welcome to the protection it offers. Besides, I suffer from an ailment for which I am always given penicillin injections at the hospital. Now I am tired of the penicillin injections and perhaps your good herbs may serve to cure me of my troubles."

He stood up, signifying the end of the case. The people of Bodibeng fled in confusion from the courtyard, but the old woman sat for a long time on the ground, silent tears of gratitude dripping down into her lap.

Vocabulary
derangement (di rānj´ ment) *n.* disturbance of normal functioning; disorder

Responding to Literature

Personal Response

What was your reaction to the end of the story?

ANALYZING LITERATURE

RECALL AND INTERPRET

1. Describe Chief Sekoto's personality. What can you infer about the narrator's attitude toward him? Support your ideas by using details from the story.
2. What charge is brought against Mma-Baloi? What evidence do her accusers use to support this charge? Why do you think Chief Sekoto doubts the sanity of the woman's accusers?
3. Summarize what Mma-Baloi says in her own defense. How does Chief Sekoto respond to the woman's testimony? What do his words and actions seem to suggest about his character?
4. What evidence does the doctor present? Compare this evidence with that presented by the villagers and by Mma-Baloi.
5. Summarize Chief Sekoto's verdict in this case. What punishment does he impose? What effect might this punishment have on the villagers?

EVALUATE AND CONNECT

6. Refer to your response in the Focus Activity on page 487. Compare your imagined response with Mma-Baloi's actual response to being accused of a horrible crime.
7. In your opinion, what lesson, or **moral**, does this story teach? Explain your answer.
8. Have you ever witnessed or heard a story about a person being accused of wrongdoing based on flimsy evidence? Explain the situation and its outcome.

Literary ELEMENTS

Climax and Resolution

Most stories contain a central conflict, or struggle between two opposing forces. In the story you have just read, the central conflict involves the decision that Chief Sekoto must make regarding Mma-Baloi's guilt or innocence. The point at which the central conflict reaches its highest emotional pitch is called the **climax**. The **resolution** is the point in the story when the outcome of the central conflict is revealed.

1. Identify the climax of "Chief Sekoto Holds Court." What gives this event such emotional impact?
2. Describe the resolution of the central conflict.
3. How might the ending of the story differ if Chief Sekoto had reached a different verdict? Explain.

● See **Literary Terms Handbook,** pp. R3 and R13.

EXTENDING YOUR RESPONSE

Literature Groups

Judge the Judge   In your group, discuss and evaluate Chief Sekoto's ruling in the case of *The People of Bodibeng* v. *Mma-Baloi.* Do you agree or disagree with his ruling? Do you think the fine he imposes is fair? Support your opinions with facts and reasons. Share your conclusions with the class.

Personal Writing

Mob Mentality?   How did you respond to the way Mma-Baloi was treated by the villagers? Why, do you think, didn't a single villager speak out in her defense? Record your responses to these questions in your journal.

📖 **Save your work for your portfolio.**

Comparing selections

The OUTCASTS of Poker Flat and Chief Sekoto Holds Court

COMPARE CONFLICTS AND RESOLUTIONS

Each selection contains a central conflict involving one or more characters labeled as outcasts. On a separate sheet of paper, write a few paragraphs answering the following questions:

1. In each story, who are the outcasts? What reasons do others have for labeling these characters as outcasts?

2. What punishment does each group intend for its outcasts? In each story, compare the intended punishment with what actually happens to the outcasts.

3. Evaluate the resolution of the central conflict in each story. Do you think the characters deserve their fates? Why or why not?

COMPARE CULTURES

Each story demonstrates the power of the accepted rules or customs of a particular culture or subculture, such as its ideas of justice. In a small group, discuss how the following cultural factors affected the characters in each story. Have one member record your group's ideas and opinions.

- accepted ideas about law and justice
- accepted rules of social behavior
- time and place in which events occur

COMPARE PROTAGONISTS

In "The Outcasts of Poker Flat," John Oakhurst is the **protagonist,** or central character; Chief Sekoto is the protagonist in "Chief Sekoto Holds Court." Think about the major traits of each character. Then create a diagram like the one at the right to compare and contrast the two protagonists. Identify traits they share as well as traits that set them apart from each other. Share your diagram with a small group of classmates.

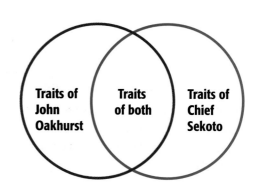

Traits of John Oakhurst | Traits of both | Traits of Chief Sekoto

LISTENING, SPEAKING, and VIEWING

Storytelling

Through stories, people pass traditions, customs, and values from generation to generation. In "Chief Sekoto Holds Court," for example, listeners learn that they should not condemn an innocent person just because she is different from them.

Good storytellers don't just tell a story; they perform it, with dramatic pauses, lively gestures, and sound effects. You can use these techniques to become an effective storyteller yourself.

Before Your Performance

- Read your story several times to remember the key events in the order they appear. Don't try to memorize the words; you might panic if you forget exactly what comes next. However, don't bore your listeners by simply reading the story aloud.
- Experiment with gestures, facial expressions, and posture to show excitement, confusion, and other emotions. Practice in front of a mirror, varying your voice to help listeners distinguish among the characters in the story.
- Consider playing background music to set the mood for your story. Alternatively, add sound effects using your voice, hands, simple instruments, or other tools.
- Ask a friend to watch and listen for ways you can tell your story more effectively, or videotape your performance and critique it.

During Your Performance

- Begin by telling your audience where and when the story takes place, but don't give away the plot. You might pose a question such as, "Do you ever wonder what your cat is thinking? The boy in this story was even more curious than his cat."
- Relax and enjoy yourself. If you're tense, your audience will sense it. If you forget an important detail, add it later, saying something like, "Oops! There's something else you need to know."

ACTIVITIES

1. Watch a storyteller in a taped performance or in person. Notice how he or she uses a variety of voices, gestures, and expressions to create interesting characters and an intriguing plot. Present a brief analysis of the performance to the class.

2. Choose a myth, folktale, or other story to tell. Practice it; then tell the story to an appropriate audience. Young children will let you know if you need to add more drama or perhaps shorten your presentation for your next performance.

Web Site

Some people, in their everyday lives, face powerful natural forces such as bitterly cold weather. For anyone in such a frigid setting, this Web site could be quite important.

Feeling Chilly? Check Out These Hypothermia Tips

Address: ▼ http://www.alaska-movie.com

Hypothermia occurs when a person gets too cold. It is very dangerous and can even kill. People can get hypothermia gradually (which is called exposure) through cool temperatures, sweating, wet clothes, or clothes that aren't warm enough. They can also get acute hypothermia if they fall into cold water or are outside without shelter during a blizzard or other extremely cold weather.

Gradual hypothermia is especially dangerous because it can occur even when the temperature is mild, and because people often don't realize it is even happening.

The Warning Signs of Hypothermia

These are some of the symptoms of hypothermia. A person who is suffering from exposure (or extreme low temperatures) may demonstrate some or all of these symptoms:

1. Shivering, which means the body is trying to warm itself.

2. Increased heart rate and faster breathing.

3. Cold and [pallid] hands and feet, which means that the body is diverting blood from the person's extremities to try to keep the internal organs warm.

4. Irritable, irrational, and/or confused behavior.

5. Blue-colored lips or skin (an indication the hypothermia is getting severe).

6. Eventual unconsciousness.

How to Help People with Hypothermia

Mild cases of hypothermia are easier to treat than severe ones. For [people] with a mild case, you can encourage them to stay active, which will help them to warm up. Try to get them to a warm, dry shelter, and make sure that their clothes are dry and their heads are covered. If possible, it is good to apply warm objects (like a hot water bottle). They should drink something warm, but not if it has caffeine or alcohol in it.

[When] suffering from extreme acute hypothermia, [people] may become drowsy or nearly unconscious. It is important to get them to a hospital as soon as possible. In the meantime, [locate] a warm dry place, and handle them very gently (jostling them around or rubbing their skin can actually cause them to have a heart attack!).

Make sure they are gently warmed, but not by placing anything hot on them, because that can cause a heart attack as well.

Respond

1. What are the different types of hypothermia and how do they differ?

2. Describe some things you should do or not do to help someone suffering from hypothermia.

Meet Jack London

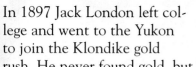

"It was in the Klondike I found myself. There nobody talks. Everybody thinks. You get your true perspective. I got mine."

—*London*

In 1897 Jack London left college and went to the Yukon to join the Klondike gold rush. He never found gold, but he did find something that proved more precious to him: a wealth of raw material for the stories that eventually made him famous.

Born in San Francisco to an unstable mother and a father who refused to claim him, London was raised mainly by a family friend and a stepsister. From the age of eleven, the boy worked to earn money for his family. London loved the sea, so he hung around the harbor, doing odd jobs and learning to be an expert sailor. While still in his teens, he signed on to a schooner sailing to Siberia. From that adventure came his first published story.

At eighteen, London set off to ride the rails, living the life of a hobo as he traveled across the country on freight trains. This journey became a turning point in his life as he saw up close the raw, painful lives of men who did not seem to belong. London vowed to educate himself so he could survive by his mental powers rather than his physical strength.

After completing high school in one year, London attended college for a semester before rushing off to the Klondike. He failed to strike it rich, so he came home and turned to writing for his livelihood. In 1903 London published *The Call of the Wild*, the novel that firmly established his reputation. In time, he became the country's best-paid author—a stunning reversal of fortune for the once-impoverished writer.

Throughout his life, London worked under pressure to support not only himself but also family members and friends. He set himself the task of writing at least a thousand publishable words every day, and he rarely deviated from that schedule. But despite publishing more than fifty books and becoming the country's first millionaire author, London habitually spent more than he earned, and he often wrote stories in order to pay urgent debts.

In the last years of his life, London bought a ranch in northern California and began to build his dream house on it. In 1913, shortly before he was to move into the house, it burned down. The fire devastated London both emotionally and financially. He continued to live on the ranch but never rebuilt the house. Three years later, plagued by health problems and financial difficulties, London died. He was forty years old.

"The proper function of [a person] is to live, not to exist. I shall not waste my days in trying to prolong them. I shall use my time."

—*London*

Jack London was born in 1876 and died in 1916.

FOCUS ACTIVITY

Think of a time when you experienced extreme weather.

CHART IT! Complete a chart like the one shown, naming the kind of weather you experienced and listing the physical and mental effects the weather had on you.

Extreme Weather Experienced:	
Physical Effects	Mental Effects

SETTING A PURPOSE Read to discover how one man copes with extreme weather.

BACKGROUND

The Time and Place

On July 17, 1897, sixty-eight miners arrived in Seattle on the steamship *Portland* carrying boxes, suitcases, and gunnysacks filled with a total of more than two tons of gold. Thousands of prospectors soon poured into the Klondike region of Canada, where gold had been discovered in the sands of Bonanza Creek, a tributary of the Klondike River. Many of the prospectors were unprepared for the brutal conditions in the north, where temperatures could sink below minus fifty degrees Fahrenheit and overland transportation was by foot or dogsled.

The Yukon River

The remarkable Yukon River, which begins in the streams of Chilkoot Pass in British Columbia, Canada, is about 1,875 miles long. Its drainage basin includes 330,000 square miles in the Yukon Territory in Canada and the eastern and central parts of Alaska. The Yukon and its tributaries flow across Alaska's interior plateau, which comprises millions of acres of subarctic forest. The Klondike River is one of the Yukon's tributaries.

Klondike goldminers, 1908.

VOCABULARY PREVIEW

intangible (in tan′ jə bəl) *adj.* not easily defined or evaluated by the mind; p. 498

pall (pôl) *n.* that which covers with an atmosphere of darkness and gloom; p. 498

immortality (im′ ôr tal′ ə tē) *n.* the condition of having eternal life; p. 499

compel (kəm pel′) *v.* to force; p. 501

intervene (in′ tər vēn′) *v.* to come or lie between; p. 502

conflagration (kon′ flə grā′ shən) *n.* a large, destructive fire; p. 504

acute (ə kūt′) *adj.* intense; severe; p. 506

apathetically (ap′ ə the′ ti klē) *adv.* in a manner showing little interest or concern; p. 507

TO BUILD A FIRE

Jack London ❧

Day had broken cold and gray, exceedingly cold and gray, when the man turned aside from the main Yukon[1] trail and climbed the high earthbank, where a dim and little-traveled trail led eastward through the fat spruce timberland. It was a steep bank, and he paused for breath at the top, excusing the act to himself by looking at his watch. It was nine o'clock. There was no sun nor hint of sun, though there was not a cloud in the sky. It was a clear day, and yet there seemed an <u>intangible</u> <u>pall</u> over the face of things, a subtle gloom that made the day dark, and that was due to the absence of sun.

---

1. Here, *Yukon* refers to the Yukon River. The river was a major route to the Klondike gold fields.

Vocabulary
intangible (in tan′ jə bəl) *adj.* not easily defined or evaluated by the mind
pall (pôl) *n.* that which covers with an atmosphere of darkness and gloom

A Very Gallant Gentleman, late 19th century (detail). John Charles Dollman. Oil on canvas. The Cavalry Club, England.

⬅

This fact did not worry the man. He was used to the lack of sun. It had been days since he had seen the sun, and he knew that a few more days must pass before that cheerful orb, due south, would just peep above the skyline and dip immediately from view.

The man flung a look back along the way he had come. The Yukon lay a mile wide and hidden under three feet of ice. On top of this ice were as many feet of snow. It was all pure white, rolling in gentle undulations[2] where the ice jams of the freeze up had formed. North and south, as far as his eye could see, it was unbroken white save for a dark hairline that curved and twisted from around the spruce-covered island to the south, and that curved and twisted away into the north, where it disappeared behind another spruce-covered island. This dark hairline was the trail—the main trail—that led south five hundred miles to the Chilkoot Pass, Dyea, and saltwater; and that led north seventy miles to Dawson, and still on to the north a thousand miles to Nulato,[3] and finally to St. Michael on Bering Sea, a thousand miles and half a thousand more.

But all this—the mysterious, far-reaching hairline trail, the absence of sun from the sky, the tremendous cold, and the strangeness and weirdness of it all—made no impression on the man. It was not because he was long used to it. He was a newcomer in the land, a *chechaquo*,[4] and this was his first winter. The trouble with him was that he was without imagination. He was quick and alert in the things of life, but only in the things, and not in the significances. Fifty

degrees below zero meant eighty-odd degrees of frost. Such fact impressed him as being cold and uncomfortable, and that was all. It did not lead him to meditate upon his frailty in general, able only to live within certain narrow limits of heat and cold; and from there on it did not lead him to the conjectural[5] field of <u>immortality</u> and man's place in the universe. Fifty degrees below zero stood for a bite of frost that hurt and that must be guarded against by the use of mittens, earflaps, warm moccasins, and thick socks. Fifty degrees below zero was to him just precisely fifty degrees below zero. That there should be anything more to it than that was a thought that never entered his head.

As he turned to go on, he spat speculatively. There was a sharp, explosive crackle that startled him. He spat again. And again, in the air, before it could fall to the snow, the spittle crackled. He knew that at fifty below spittle crackled on the snow, but this spittle had crackled in the air. Undoubtedly it was colder than fifty below—how much colder he did not know. But the temperature did not matter. He was bound for the old claim[6] on the left fork of Henderson Creek, where the boys were already. They had come over across the divide[7] from the Indian Creek country, while he had come the roundabout way to take a look at the possibilities of getting out logs in the spring from the islands in the Yukon. He would be in to camp by six o'clock; a bit after dark, it was true, but the boys would be there, a fire would be going, and a hot supper would be ready. As for lunch, he pressed his hand against the protruding bundle under his jacket. It was also under his shirt, wrapped up in a handkerchief and lying against the naked

---

2. *Undulations* are rippling or wavelike forms or outlines.
3. *Dyea* (dī ā) was a mining village in Alaska at the beginning of the route to the gold fields. The trail led through the *Chilkoot Pass* and to northern gold-mining centers in the Yukon such as *Dawson* and *Nulato* (nōō lä′ tō).
4. In the language of the Chinook, Native Americans of the Pacific Northwest, a *chechaquo* (chē chä′ kō) is a "newcomer" or a "tenderfoot."

5. *Conjectural* means "based on guesswork or indefinite evidence."
6. A *claim* is a piece of land registered for mining rights.
7. A *divide* is a ridge of land that separates two river drainage systems.

Vocabulary

immortality (im′ ôr tal′ ə tē) *n.* the condition of having eternal life

skin. It was the only way to keep the biscuits from freezing. He smiled agreeably to himself as he thought of those biscuits, each cut open and sopped in bacon grease, and each enclosing a generous slice of fried bacon.

He plunged in among the big spruce trees. The trail was faint. A foot of snow had fallen since the last sled had passed over, and he was glad he was without sled, traveling light. In fact, he carried nothing but the lunch wrapped in the handkerchief. He was surprised, however, at the cold. It certainly was cold, he concluded, as he rubbed his numb nose and cheekbones with his mittened hand. He was a warm-whiskered man, but the hair on his face did not protect the high cheekbones and the eager nose that thrust itself aggressively into the frosty air.

At the man's heel trotted a dog, a big native husky, the proper wolf dog, gray-coated and without any visible or temperamental difference from its brother, the wild wolf. The animal was depressed by the tremendous cold. It knew that it was no time for traveling. Its instinct told a truer tale than was told to the man by the man's judgment. In reality, it was not merely colder than fifty below zero; it was colder than sixty below, than seventy below. It was seventy-five below zero. Since the freezing point is thirty-two above zero, it meant that one hundred and seven degrees of frost obtained. The dog did not know anything about thermometers. Possibly in its brain there was no sharp consciousness of a condition of very cold such as was in the man's brain. But the brute had its instinct. It experienced a vague but menacing apprehension that subdued it and made it slink along at the man's heels, and that made it question eagerly every unwonted[8] movement of the man as if expecting him to go into camp or to seek shelter somewhere and build a fire. The dog had learned fire, and it wanted fire, or else to burrow under the snow and cuddle its warmth away from the air.

The frozen moisture of its breathing had settled on its fur in a fine powder of frost, and especially were its jowls, muzzle, and eyelashes whitened by its crystalled breath. The man's red beard and mustache were likewise frosted, but more solidly, the deposit taking the form of ice and increasing with every warm, moist breath he exhaled. Also, the man was chewing tobacco, and the muzzle of ice held his lips so rigidly that he was unable to clear his chin when he expelled the juice. The result was that a crystal beard of the color and solidity of amber was increasing

Did You Know?
Amber is a hard, translucent fossil resin that is yellowish-orange or yellowish-brown.

its length on his chin. If he fell down it would shatter itself, like glass, into brittle fragments. But he did not mind the appendage.[9] It was the penalty all tobacco-chewers paid in that country, and he had been out before in two cold snaps. They had not been so cold as this, he knew, but by the spirit thermometer[10] at Sixty Mile he knew they had been registered at fifty below and at fifty-five.

He held on through the level stretch of woods for several miles and dropped down a bank to the frozen bed of a small stream. This was Henderson Creek, and he knew he was ten miles from the forks. He looked at his watch. It was ten o'clock. He was making four miles an hour, and he calculated that he would arrive at the forks at half-past twelve. He decided to celebrate that event by eating his lunch there.

The dog dropped in again at his heels, with a tail drooping discouragement, as the man swung along the creek bed. The furrow[11] of the old sled

---

8. *Unwonted* means "unusual."

9. An *appendage* is something that is added on or attached.
10. A *spirit thermometer* is an alcohol thermometer. It is used in areas of extreme cold, where the more common mercury thermometer would freeze.
11. A *furrow* is a long, narrow groove or depression.

trail was plainly visible, but a dozen inches of snow covered the marks of the last runners. In a month no man had come up or down that silent creek. The man held steadily on. He was not much given to thinking, and just then particularly he had nothing to think about save that he would eat lunch at the forks and that at six o'clock he would be in camp with the boys. There was nobody to talk to; and, had there been, speech would have been impossible because of the ice muzzle on his mouth. So he continued monotonously to chew tobacco and to increase the length of his amber beard.

Once in a while the thought reiterated[12] itself that it was very cold and that he had never experienced such cold. As he walked along he rubbed his cheekbones and nose with the back of his mittened hand. He did this automatically, now and again changing hands. But rub as he would, the instant he stopped his cheekbones went numb, and the following instant the end of his nose went numb. He was sure to frost his cheeks; he knew that, and experienced a pang of regret that he had not devised a nose strap of the sort Bud wore in cold snaps. Such a strap passed across the cheeks, as well, and saved them. But it didn't matter much, after all. What were frosted cheeks? A bit painful, that was all; they were never serious.

Empty as the man's mind was of thoughts, he was keenly observant, and he noticed the changes in the creek, the curves and bends and timber jams, and always he sharply noted where he placed his feet. Once, coming around the bend, he shied[13] abruptly, like a startled horse, curved away from the place where he had been walking, and retreated several paces back along the trail. The creek he knew was frozen clear to the bottom—no creek could contain water in

that arctic winter—but he knew also that there were springs that bubbled out from the hillsides and ran along under the snow and on top the ice of the creek. He knew that the coldest snaps never froze these springs, and he knew likewise their danger. They were traps. They hid pools of water under the snow that might be three inches deep, or three feet. Sometimes a skin of ice half an inch thick covered them, and in turn was covered by the snow. Sometimes they were alternate layers of water and ice skin, so that when one broke through he kept on breaking through for a while, sometimes wetting himself to the waist.

That was why he had shied in such panic. He had felt the give under his feet and heard the crackle of a snow-hidden ice skin. And to get his feet wet in such a temperature meant trouble and danger. At the very least it meant delay, for he would be forced to stop and build a fire, and under its protection to bare his feet while he dried his socks and moccasins. He stood and studied the creek bed and its banks, and decided that the flow of water came from the right. He reflected awhile, rubbing his nose and cheeks, then skirted to the left, stepping gingerly and testing the footing for each step. Once clear of the danger, he took a fresh chew of tobacco and swung along at his four-mile gait.

In the course of the next two hours he came upon similar traps. Usually the snow above the hidden pools had a sunken, candied appearance that advertised the danger. Once again, however, he had a close call; and once, suspecting danger, he compelled the dog to go on in front. The dog did not want to go. It hung back until the man shoved it forward, and then it went quickly across the white, unbroken surface. Suddenly it broke through, floundered to one side, and got away to firmer footing. It had wet its forefeet and legs, and almost immediately the water that clung to it turned to ice. It made

---

12. *Reiterated* means "repeated."
13. *Shied* means "moved suddenly, as in fear."

Vocabulary
compel (kəm pel′) v. to force

quick efforts to lick the ice off its legs, then dropped down in the snow and began to bite out the ice that had formed between the toes. This was a matter of instinct. To permit the ice to remain would mean sore feet. It did not know this. It merely obeyed the mysterious prompting that arose from the deep crypts[14] of its being. But the man knew, having achieved a judgment on the subject, and he removed the mitten from his right hand and helped tear out the ice particles. He did not expose his fingers more than a minute, and was astonished at the swift numbness that smote[15] them. It certainly was cold. He pulled on the mitten hastily, and beat the hand savagely across his chest.

At twelve o'clock the day was at its brightest. Yet the sun was too far south on its winter journey to clear the horizon. The bulge of the earth intervened between it and Henderson Creek, where the man walked under a clear sky at noon and cast no shadow. At half-past twelve, to the minute, he arrived at the forks of the creek. He was pleased at the speed he had made. If he kept it up, he would certainly be with the boys by six. He unbuttoned his jacket and shirt and drew forth his lunch. The action consumed no more than a quarter of a minute, yet in that brief moment the numbness laid hold of the exposed fingers. He did not put the mitten on, but, instead, struck the fingers a dozen sharp smashes against his leg. Then he sat down on a snow-covered log to eat. The sting that followed upon the striking of his fingers against his leg ceased so quickly that he was startled. He had had no chance to take a bite of biscuit. He struck the fingers repeatedly and returned them to the mitten, baring the other hand for the purpose of eating. He tried to take a mouthful, but the ice muzzle prevented. He had forgotten to build a fire and thaw out. He chuckled at his foolishness, and as he chuckled he noted the numbness creeping into his exposed fingers. Also, he noted that the stinging which had first come to his toes when he sat down was already passing away. He wondered whether the toes were warm or numb. He moved them inside the moccasins and decided that they were numb.

He pulled the mitten on hurriedly and stood up. He was a bit frightened. He stamped up and down until the sting returned into the feet. It certainly was cold, was his thought. That man from Sulphur Creek had spoken the truth when telling how cold it sometimes got in the country. And he had laughed at him at the time! That showed one must not be too sure of things. There was no mistake about it, it *was* cold. He strode up and down, stamping his feet and threshing his arms, until reassured by the returning warmth. Then he got out matches and proceeded to make a fire. From the undergrowth, where high water of the previous spring had lodged a supply of seasoned twigs, he got his firewood. Working carefully from a small beginning, he soon had a roaring fire, over which he thawed the ice from his face and in the protection of which he ate his biscuits. For the moment the cold of space was outwitted. The dog took satisfaction in the fire, stretching out close enough for warmth and far enough away to escape being singed.

When the man had finished, he filled his pipe and took his comfortable time over a smoke. Then he pulled on his mittens, settled the earflaps of his cap firmly about his ears, and took the creek trail up the left fork. The dog was disappointed and yearned back toward the fire. This man did not know cold. Possibly all the generations of his ancestry had been ignorant of cold, of real cold, of cold one hundred and seven degrees below freezing point. But the dog knew; all its ancestry knew, and it had

---

14. Here, *crypts* means "hidden recesses."
15. *Smote* (past tense of *smite*) means "afflicted" or "attacked."

Vocabulary
intervene (in´ tər vēn´) *v.* to come or lie between

inherited the knowledge. And it knew that it was not good to walk abroad in such fearful cold. It was the time to lie snug in a hole in the snow and wait for a curtain of cloud to be drawn across the face of outer space whence this cold came. On the other hand, there was no keen intimacy between the dog and the man. The one was the toil slave of the other, and the only caresses it had ever received were the caresses of the whiplash and of harsh and menacing throat sounds that threatened the whiplash. So the dog made no effort to communicate its apprehension to the man. It was not concerned in the welfare of the man; it was for its own sake that it yearned back toward the fire. But the man whistled, and spoke to it with the sound of whiplashes, and the dog swung in at the man's heels and followed after.

The man took a chew of tobacco and proceeded to start a new amber beard. Also, his moist breath quickly powdered with white his mustache, eyebrows, and lashes. There did not seem to be so many springs on the left fork of the Henderson, and for half an hour the man saw no signs of any. And then it happened. At a place where there were no signs, where the soft, unbroken snow seemed to advertise solidity beneath, the man broke through. It was not deep. He wet himself to the knees before he floundered out to the firm crust.

He was angry, and cursed his luck aloud. He had hoped to get into camp with the boys at six o'clock, and this would delay him an hour, for he would have to build a fire and dry out his foot gear. This was imperative[16] at that low temperature—he knew that much; and he turned aside to the bank, which he climbed. On top, tangled in the underbrush about the trunks of several small spruce trees, was a high-water deposit of dry firewood—sticks and twigs, principally, but also larger portions of seasoned branches and fine, dry, last-year's grasses. He threw down several large pieces on

top of the snow. This served for a foundation and prevented the young flame from drowning itself in the snow it otherwise would melt. The flame he got by touching a match to a small shred of birch bark that he took from his pocket. This burned even more readily than paper. Placing it on the foundation, he fed the young flame with wisps of dry grass and with the tiniest dry twigs.

He worked slowly and carefully, keenly aware of his danger. Gradually, as the flame grew stronger, he increased the size of the twigs with which he fed it. He squatted in the snow, pulling the twigs out from their entanglement in the brush and feeding directly to the flame. He knew there must be no failure. When it is seventy-five below zero, a man must not fail in his first attempt to build a fire—that is, if his feet are wet. If his feet are dry, and he fails, he can run along the trail for half a mile and restore his circulation. But the circulation of wet and freezing feet cannot be restored by running when it is seventy-five below. No matter how fast he runs, the wet feet will freeze the harder.

All this the man knew. The old-timer on Sulphur Creek had told him about it the previous fall, and now he was appreciating the advice. Already all sensation had gone out of his feet. To build the fire he had been forced to remove his mittens, and the fingers had quickly gone numb. His pace of four miles an hour had kept his heart pumping blood to the surface of his body and to all the extremities. But the instant he stopped, the action of the pump eased down. The cold of space smote the unprotected tip of the planet, and he, being on that unprotected tip, received

---

16. *Imperative* means "absolutely necessary."

the full force of the blow. The blood of his body recoiled before it. The blood was alive, like the dog, and like the dog it wanted to hide away and cover itself up from the fearful cold. So long as he walked four miles an hour, he pumped that blood, willy-nilly,[17] to the surface; but now it ebbed[18] away and sank down into the recesses of his body. The extremities were the first to feel its absence. His wet feet froze the faster, and his exposed fingers numbed the faster, though they had not yet begun to freeze. Nose and cheeks were already freezing, while the skin of all his body chilled as it lost its blood.

But he was safe. Toes and nose and cheeks would be only touched by the frost, for the fire was beginning to burn with strength. He was feeding it with twigs the size of his finger. In another minute he would be able to feed it with branches the size of his wrist, and then he could remove his wet foot gear, and, while it dried, he could keep his naked feet warm by the fire, rubbing them at first, of course, with snow. The fire was a success. He was safe. He remembered the advice of the old-timer on Sulphur Creek, and smiled. The old-timer had been very serious in laying down the law that no man must travel alone in the Klondike after fifty below. Well, here he was; he had had the accident; he was alone; and he had saved himself. Those old-timers were rather womanish, some of them, he thought. All a man had to do was to keep his head, and he was all right. Any man who was a man could travel alone. But it was surprising, the rapidity with which his cheeks and nose

> **All a man had to do was to keep his head, and he was all right.**

were freezing. And he had not thought his fingers could go lifeless in so short a time. Lifeless they were, for he could scarcely make them move together to grip a twig, and they seemed remote from his body and from him. When he touched a twig, he had to look and see whether or not he had hold of it. The wires were pretty well down between him and his finger-ends.

All of which counted for little. There was the fire, snapping and crackling and promising life with every dancing flame. He started to untie his moccasins. They were coated with ice; the thick German socks were like sheaths of iron halfway to the knees; and the moccasin strings were like rods of steel all twisted and knotted as by some conflagration. For a moment he tugged with his numb fingers, then, realizing the folly of it, he drew his sheath-knife.

But before he could cut the strings, it happened. It was his own fault or, rather, his mistake. He should not have built the fire under the spruce tree. He should have built it in the open. But it had been easier to pull twigs from the brush and drop them directly on the fire. Now the tree under which he had done this carried a weight of snow on its boughs. No wind had blown for weeks, and each bough was fully freighted. Each time he had pulled a twig he had communicated a slight agitation to the tree—an imperceptible agitation, so far as he was concerned, but an agitation sufficient to bring about the disaster. High up in the tree one bough capsized its load of snow. This fell on the boughs beneath, capsizing them. This process continued, spreading out and involving the whole tree. It grew like an avalanche, and it descended without warning upon the man and

---

17. *Willy-nilly* means "without choice."
18. *Ebbed* means "flowed back" or "receded."

Vocabulary
conflagration (kon′ flə grā′ shən) *n.* a large, destructive fire

the fire, and the fire was blotted out! Where it had burned was a mantle of fresh and disordered snow.

The man was shocked. It was as though he had just heard his own sentence of death. For a moment he sat and stared at the spot where the fire had been. Then he grew very calm. Perhaps the old-timer on Sulphur Creek was right. If he had only had a trail mate he would have been in no danger now. The trail mate could have built the fire. Well, it was up to him to build the fire over again, and this second time there must be no failure. Even if he succeeded, he would most likely lose some toes. His feet must be badly frozen by now, and there would be some time before the second fire was ready.

Such were his thoughts, but he did not sit and think them. He was busy all the time they were passing through his mind. He made a new foundation for a fire, this time in the open, where no treacherous tree could blot it out. Next, he gathered dry grasses and tiny twigs from the high-water flotsam.[19] He could not bring his fingers together to pull them out, but he was able to gather them by the handful. In this way he got many rotten twigs and bits of green moss that were undesirable, but it was the best he could do. He worked methodically, even collecting an armful of the larger branches to be used later when the fire gathered strength. And all the while the dog sat and watched him, a certain yearning wistfulness[20] in its eyes, for it looked upon him as the fire provider, and the fire was slow in coming.

When all was ready, the man reached in his pocket for a second piece of birch bark. He knew the bark was there, and, though he

could not feel it with his fingers, he could hear its crisp rustling as he fumbled for it. Try as he would, he could not clutch hold of it. And all the time, in his consciousness, was the knowledge that each instant his feet were freezing. This thought tended to put him in a panic, but he fought against it and kept calm. He pulled on his mittens with his teeth, and threshed his arms back and forth, beating his hands with all his might against his sides. He did this sitting down, and he stood up to do it; and all the while the dog sat in the snow, its wolf brush of a tail curled around warmly over its forefeet, its sharp wolf ears pricked forward intently as it watched the man. And the man, as he beat and threshed with his arms and hands, felt a great surge of envy as he regarded the creature that was warm and secure in its natural covering.

After a time he was aware of the first far-away signals of sensation in his beaten fingers. The faint tingling grew stronger till it evolved into a stinging ache that was excruciating, but which the man hailed with satisfaction. He stripped the mitten from his right hand and fetched forth the birch bark. The

---

19. *Flotsam* (flot´ səm) is floating debris, here left behind by a river or stream in the spring when the water rises with the runoff from melting snow and ice.
20. *Wistfulness* means "thoughtful sadness."

exposed fingers were quickly going numb again. Next he brought out his bunch of sulphur matches. But the tremendous cold had already driven the life out of his fingers. In his effort to separate one match from the others, the whole bunch fell in the snow. He tried to pick it out of the snow, but failed. The dead fingers could neither touch nor clutch. He was very careful. He drove the thought of his freezing feet, and nose, and cheeks, out of his mind, devoting his whole soul to the matches. He watched, using the sense of vision in place of that of touch, and when he saw his fingers on each side of the bunch, he closed them— that is, he willed to close them, for the wires were down, and the fingers did not obey. He pulled the mitten on the right hand, and beat it fiercely against his knee. Then, with both mittened hands, he scooped the bunch of matches, along with much snow, into his lap. Yet he was no better off.

After some manipulation he managed to get the bunch between the heels of his mittened hands. In this fashion he carried it to his mouth. The ice crackled and snapped when by a violent effort he opened his mouth. He drew the lower jaw in, curled the upper lip out of the way, and scraped the bunch with his upper teeth in order to separate a match. He succeeded in getting one, which he dropped on his lap. He was no better off. He could not pick it up. Then he devised a way. He picked it up in his teeth and scratched it on his leg. Twenty times he scratched before he succeeded in lighting it. As it flamed he held it with his teeth to the birch bark. But the burning brimstone[21] went up his nostrils and into his lungs, causing him to cough spasmodically.[22] The match fell into the snow and went out.

The old-timer on Sulphur Creek was right, he thought in the moment of controlled despair that ensued;[23] after fifty below, a man should travel with a partner. He beat his hands, but failed in exciting any sensation. Suddenly he bared both hands, removing his mittens with his teeth. He caught the whole bunch between the heels of his hands. His arm muscles not being frozen enabled him to press the hand heels tightly against the matches. Then he scratched the bunch along his leg. It flared into flame, seventy sulphur matches at once! There was no wind to blow them out. He kept his head to one side to escape the strangling fumes, and held the blazing bunch to the birch bark. As he so held it, he became aware of sensation in his hand. His flesh was burning. He could smell it. Deep down below the surface he could feel it. The sensation developed into pain that grew <u>acute</u>. And still he endured it, holding the flame of the matches clumsily to the bark that would not light readily because his own burning hands were in the way, absorbing most of the flame.

At last, when he could endure no more, he jerked his hands apart. The blazing matches fell sizzling into the snow, but the birch bark was alight. He began laying dry grasses and the tiniest twigs on the flame. He could not pick and choose, for he had to lift the fuel between the heels of his hands. Small pieces of rotten wood and green moss clung to the twigs, and he bit them off as well as he could with his teeth. He cherished the flame carefully and awkwardly. It meant life, and it must not perish. The withdrawal of blood from the surface of his body now made him begin to shiver, and he grew more awkward. A large piece of green moss fell squarely on the little fire. He tried to poke it out with his fingers, but his shivering frame made him poke too far, and he disrupted the nucleus of

---

21. *Brimstone* is sulfur.
22. *Spasmodically* means "in a sudden, violent manner" or "convulsively."

---

23. *Ensued* means "happened afterward" or "followed."

Vocabulary
acute (ə kūt′) *adj.* intense; severe

the little fire, the burning grasses and tiny twigs separating and scattering. He tried to poke them together again, but in spite of the tenseness of the effort, his shivering got away with him, and the twigs were hopelessly scattered. Each twig gushed a puff of smoke and went out. The fire provider had failed. As he looked <u>apathetically</u> about him, his eyes chanced on the dog, sitting across the ruins of the fire from him, in the snow, making restless, hunching movements, slightly lifting one forefoot and then the other, shifting its weight back and forth on them with wistful eagerness.

Viewing the photograph: As you look at this photograph, jot down the first five words that come to mind. Which of these words best describes the tone of "To Build a Fire"? Explain.

The sight of the dog put a wild idea into his head. He remembered the tale of the man, caught in a blizzard, who killed a steer and crawled inside the carcass, and so was saved. He would kill the dog and bury his hands in the warm body until the numbness went out of them. Then he could build another fire. He spoke to the dog, calling it to him; but in his voice was a strange note of fear that frightened the animal, who had never known the man to speak in such way before. Something was the matter, and its suspicious nature sensed danger—it knew not what danger, but somewhere, somehow, in its brain arose an apprehension of the man. It flattened its ears down at the sound of the man's voice, and its restless, hunching movements and the liftings and shiftings of its forefeet became more pronounced; but it would not come to the man. He got on his hands and knees and crawled toward the dog. This unusual posture again excited suspicion, and the animal sidled mincingly[24] away.

The man sat up in the snow for a moment and struggled for calmness. Then he pulled on his mittens, by means of his teeth, and got upon his feet. He glanced down at first in order to assure himself that he was really standing up, for the absence of sensation in his feet left him unrelated to the earth. His erect position in itself started to drive the webs of suspicion from the dog's mind; and when he spoke peremptorily,[25] with the sound of whiplashes in his voice, the dog rendered its customary allegiance and came to him. As it came within reaching distance, the man lost his control. His arms flashed out to the dog, and he experienced genuine surprise when he discovered that his hands could not clutch, that there was neither bend nor feeling in the fingers. He had forgotten for the moment that they were frozen and that they were freezing more and more. All this happened quickly, and before the animal could get away, he encircled its body with his arms. He sat down in the snow, and in this fashion held the dog, while it snarled and whined and struggled.

---

24. *Sidled mincingly* means "moved sideways in a careful manner."

25. *Peremptorily* (pe remp′ tə rə lē) means "authoritatively" or "dictatorially."

Vocabulary
apathetically (ap′ ə the′ ti klē) *adv.* in a manner showing little interest or concern

But it was all he could do, hold its body encircled in his arms and sit there. He realized that he could not kill the dog. There was no way to do it. With his helpless hands he could neither draw nor hold his sheath knife nor throttle the animal. He released it, and it plunged wildly away, with tail between its legs, and still snarling. It halted forty feet away and surveyed him cautiously, with ears sharply pricked forward. The man looked down at his hands in order to locate them, and found them hanging on the ends of his arms. It struck him as curious that one should have to use his eyes in order to find out where his hands were. He began threshing his arms back and forth, beating the mittened hands against his sides. He did this for five minutes, violently, and his heart pumped enough blood up to the surface to put a stop to his shivering. But no sensation was aroused in the hands. He had an impression that they hung like weights on the ends of his arms, but when he tried to run the impression down, he could not find it.

A certain fear of death, dull and oppressive, came to him. This fear quickly became poignant[26] as he realized that it was no longer a mere matter of freezing his fingers and toes, or of losing his hands and feet, but that it was a matter of life and death with the chances against him. This threw him into a panic, and he turned and ran up the creek bed along the old, dim trail. The dog joined in behind and kept up with him. He ran blindly, without intention, in fear such as he had never known in his life. Slowly, as he ploughed and floundered through the snow, he began to see things again—the banks of the creek, the old timber jams, the leafless aspens, and the sky. The running made him feel better. He did not shiver. Maybe, if he ran on, his feet would thaw out; and, anyway, if he ran far enough, he would reach camp and the boys. Without doubt he would lose some fingers and

toes and some of his face; but the boys would take care of him, and save the rest of him when he got there. And at the same time there was another thought in his mind that said he would never get to the camp and the boys; that it was too many miles away, that the freezing had too great a start on him, and that he would soon be stiff and dead. This thought he kept in the background and refused to consider. Sometimes it pushed itself forward and demanded to be heard, but he thrust it back and strove to think of other things.

It struck him as curious that he could run at all on feet so frozen that he could not feel them when they struck the earth and took the weight of his body. He seemed to himself to skim along above the surface, and to have no connection with the earth. Somewhere he had once seen a winged Mercury, and he wondered if Mercury felt as he felt when skimming over the earth.

Did You Know?
In Roman mythology, *Mercury* is the messenger of the gods. He is portrayed wearing a winged hat and winged sandals.

His theory of running until he reached camp and the boys had one flaw in it: he lacked the endurance. Several times he stumbled, and finally he tottered, crumpled up, and fell. When he tried to rise, he failed. He must sit and rest, he decided, and next time he would merely walk and keep on going. As he sat and regained his breath, he noted that he was feeling quite warm and comfortable. He was not shivering, and it even seemed that a warm glow had come to his chest and trunk. And yet, when he touched his nose or cheeks, there was no sensation. Running would not thaw them out. Nor would it thaw out his hands and feet. Then the thought came to him that the frozen portions of his

---

26. *Poignant* (poin′ yənt) means "sharply felt" or "intensely distressing."

body must be extending. He tried to keep this thought down, to forget it, to think of something else; he was aware of the panicky feeling that it caused, and he was afraid of the panic. But the thought asserted itself, and persisted, until it produced a vision of his body totally frozen. This was too much, and he made another wild run along the trail. Once he slowed down to a walk, but the thought of the freezing extending itself made him run again.

And all the time the dog ran with him, at his heels. When he fell down a second time, it curled its tail over its forefeet and sat in front of him, facing him, curiously eager and intent. The warmth and security of the animal angered him, and he cursed it till it flattened down its ears appeasingly. This time the shivering came more quickly upon the man. He was losing in his battle with the frost. It was creeping into his body from all sides. The thought of it drove him on, but he ran no more than a hundred feet, when he staggered and pitched headlong. It was his last panic. When he had recovered his breath and control, he sat up and entertained in his mind the conception of meeting death with dignity. However, the conception did not come to him in such terms. His idea of it was that he had been making a fool of himself, running around like a chicken with its head cut off— such was the simile that occurred to him. Well, he was bound to freeze anyway, and he might as well take it decently. With this new-found peace of mind came the first glimmerings of drowsiness. A good idea, he thought, to sleep off to death. It was like taking an anæsthetic.[27] Freezing was not so bad as people thought. There were lots worse ways to die.

He pictured the boys finding his body next day. Suddenly he found himself with them, coming along the trail and looking for himself. And, still with them, he came around a turn in the trail and found himself lying in the snow. He did not belong with himself any more, for even then he was out of himself, standing with the boys and looking at himself in the snow. It certainly was cold, was his thought. When he got back to the States he could tell the folks what real cold was. He drifted on from this to a vision of the old-timer on Sulphur Creek. He could see him quite clearly, warm and comfortable, and smoking a pipe.

"You were right, old hoss; you were right," the man mumbled to the old-timer on Sulphur Creek.

Then the man drowsed off into what seemed to him the most comfortable and satisfying sleep he had ever known. The dog sat facing him and waiting. The brief day drew to a close in a long, slow twilight. There were no signs of a fire to be made, and, besides, never in the dog's experience had it known a man to sit like that in the snow and make no fire. As the twilight drew on, its eager yearning for the fire mastered it, and with a great lifting and shifting of its forefeet, it whined softly, then flattened its ears down in anticipation of being chidden[28] by the man. But the man remained silent. Later, the dog whined loudly. And still later it crept close to the man and caught the scent of death. This made the animal bristle and back away. A little longer it delayed, howling under the stars that leaped and danced and shone brightly in the cold sky. Then it turned and trotted up the trail in the direction of the camp it knew, where were the other food providers and fire providers.

27. An *anaesthetic* is something that produces a loss of sensation.

28. *Chidden* (past participle of *chide*) means "scolded."

Responding to Literature

Personal Response

Which images from the story are the most vivid and memorable?

——— ANALYZING LITERATURE ———

RECALL

1. Where is the man going? What is his attitude toward his journey and the conditions he faces?
2. Describe how the man's dog behaves. What reasons does the narrator give for this behavior?
3. What mishap occurs shortly after the man eats lunch and resumes his journey? Summarize his attempts to recover from this mishap.
4. Describe what the man does after releasing the dog. How do his feelings of panic affect his behavior?
5. What happens to the man and the dog at the end of the story?

INTERPRET

6. What can you infer about the man's personality and character, based on the information in the first five paragraphs?
7. What events does the dog's behavior **foreshadow** (see page R7)?
8. What external and internal forces must the man struggle against?
9. At what point do you think the man knows his fate? Explain.
10. What lesson or lessons might be learned from reading this story? Support your ideas by using details from the selection.

EVALUATE AND CONNECT

11. Explain how the **mood,** or atmosphere, changes as the story develops. How are the events of the story reflected in the change of mood?
12. Complete a chart like the one you made for the Focus Activity on page 497 for the man in this story. Compare your chart with this new one and explain any differences.
13. Find at least three examples of **sensory details** (see page R14) in the selection and evaluate how well each one helps you see, hear, feel, smell, or taste what is being described.
14. Is the dog merely a **foil,** a character used to contrast with another character, or is it an important character in its own right? Explain.
15. Think of a time when you faced a dangerous or potentially dangerous situation alone. How did you handle it? Would you do anything differently in a similar situation today? Explain.

Literary ELEMENTS

Setting

The **setting** is the time and place in which the events of a literary work occur. "To Build a Fire" is set in a specific historical time and place. The setting of London's story is well defined and essential; without the setting, this particular story could not have been written. The setting establishes the story's central **conflict,** or struggle between opposing forces, and is vital to the development of the plot, or sequence of events that make up the story's action. The setting also allows London to develop the character of the man through his interactions with the physical environment.

1. In what historical time and place is this story set? What details and references in the story help establish the setting?
2. How does the setting of the story establish the central conflict? How does it influence the resolution, or final outcome, of this conflict?
3. How does London reveal the man's character through his interactions with the physical environment? Give specific examples.

● See **Literary Terms Handbook,** p. R14.

LITERATURE AND WRITING

Writing About Literature

Explain a Literary Technique   London names specific places in the story but does not give names to any of the characters. In a paragraph, explain why you think the places are named but the people are not. How does London's choice help you better understand the story's **theme,** or message? Support your ideas with evidence.

Creative Writing

I'm So Sorry to Inform You   Imagine that you are one of the main character's camp mates and that you are writing to the man's family to inform them of his death. Write a tactful letter in which you gently break the news without dwelling on all the gory details. Focus on the fact that the man died while pursuing an adventurous dream.

EXTENDING YOUR RESPONSE

Literature Groups

Consider the Possibilities   In your opinion, how might the man have altered his fate? What decisions might he have made if he had not been a person "without imagination"? In your group, brainstorm different actions the man might have taken at each turn of events in the story. Share your ideas with the class.

Interdisciplinary Activity

Biology: The Effects of Extreme Cold   Investigate how different parts of the human body are affected by severe cold. Find out what actually happens when a person freezes to death. Use diagrams, charts, or other visual aids to present your findings to the class.

Learning for Life

News Story   Imagine that you are a journalist covering the Klondike gold rush in 1897. Write a news story in which you report the death of the man in this selection. In your story's lead, or opening paragraph, be sure to cover the five Ws: *who, what, where, when,* and *why.* Give additional details in the body of your news story.

Reading Further

You might enjoy reading these novels by Jack London: *The Call of the Wild, White Fang,* and *The Sea Wolf* are based on London's adventures in the Yukon and at sea.

📖 **Save your work for your portfolio.**

Skill Minilesson

VOCABULARY • Analogies

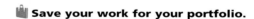

Analogies are comparisons based on relationships between words and ideas. Sometimes the relationship between the words in a pair is that of *synonym variants.* Such words have similar meanings, but they are not exact synonyms. The words in each pair may or may not be the same part of speech.

surprised : astonishment :: joyful : happiness

Someone who is *surprised* is astonished; he or she exhibits *astonishment.* Someone who is *joyful* is happy; he or she exhibits *happiness.*

● For more about analogies, see **Communications Skills Handbook,** p. R83.

PRACTICE   Choose the pair that best completes each analogy.

1. funny : humor ::
   a. angry : gloom
   b. cold : ice
   c. strong : muscles
   d. brave : courage
   e. dishonest : integrity
2. acute : severity ::
   a. strong : weakness
   b. lively : energy
   c. friendly : hostility
   d. careful : accident
   e. white : blizzard

Vo·cab·u·lar·y Skills

Using Context Clues

In "To Build a Fire," Jack London uses some words that you might not recognize, but **context clues** can help you figure out their meanings. There are two main types of context clues.

Clues on the Page

- An unfamiliar word may be used as a **synonym** for another term. Jack London writes, "It had been days since he had seen the sun; . . . a few more days must pass before that cheerful *orb* . . . would just peep above the skyline." By reading carefully, you can determine that *orb,* in this context, is another word for *sun.*
- Sometimes writers **define** unusual words. For instance, London says the nearly frozen man "*threshed* his arms back and forth, beating his hands with all his might." So here, *threshed* means "beat."
- **Other words in the sentence** may also provide clues, as when London describes snow as "rolling in gentle *undulations.*" The words *rolling* and *gentle* can help you see that *undulation* means "a rising and falling in waves."

Clues from Your Own Knowledge

When faced with an unfamiliar word, think of other words that would make sense in the sentence. For example, London writes, ". . . the thought *reiterated* itself that it was very cold." The thought must have "presented" itself. You know the prefix *re-* means that something is repeated, so *reiterate* means "to present again" or "to repeat something."

When you come upon an unfamiliar word in your reading, don't skip over it. Use context clues to figure out what it means.

- For more about using context clues, see **Reading Handbook,** pp. R86–R93.

EXERCISES

1. Use context clues from the sentences to define the words in italics.

   a. The *furrow* of the old sled-trail was plainly visible, but snow covered the marks of the last runners.

   b. The dog stretched out close enough to the fire for warmth and far enough away to escape being *singed.*

   c. His heart kept pumping blood to the surface of his body and to all the *extremities.*

2. For each sentence, think of a word or phrase that would make sense in place of the italicized word. Then use a dictionary to find out whether your word or phrase is similar in meaning to the italicized word.

   a. He worked *methodically,* even collecting an armful of the larger branches to be used later.

   b. He could barely move his fingers together, and they seemed *remote* from his body and from him.

   c. The dog flattened its ears in anticipation of being *chidden* by the man.

Before You Read

I Will Fight No More Forever

Meet Chief Joseph

"**Whenever the white man treats the Indian as they treat each other, then they shall have no more wars.**"

—*Chief Joseph*

Joseph—whose given name was Hinmaton Yalaktit (hin mə tō′ yä läkh′ tet) or "Thunder Rolling Down the Mountain"—was born in the Wallowa Valley in what is now northeastern Oregon. When his father died in 1871, Joseph was elected to succeed him as a chief of the Nez Percé (nez purs).

Although this tribe had maintained peace with the whites for seventy years, Chief Joseph inherited a volatile situation. Eight years earlier, following a gold rush into Nez Percé territory, the U.S. government had reclaimed nearly all the land it had ceded to the tribe in an 1855 treaty. Chief Joseph successfully resisted efforts to remove his band from the Wallowa Valley until 1877, when the government threatened removal by force.

To avoid bloodshed, Chief Joseph decided to cooperate, but as he led his band toward a reservation, some of his men killed a group of white settlers. To protect his people from retaliation by the U.S. Army, he led them on a long, grueling march for the Canadian border. Within forty miles of their destination, however, they were forced to surrender.

Chief Joseph's people were then removed to what is now Oklahoma, where many became sick and died. In 1885 the tribe was returned to the Pacific Northwest, but about half, including Chief Joseph, were taken to a non–Nez Percé reservation in Washington. There Chief Joseph died, according to his doctor, "of a broken heart."

"**I have asked some of the great white chiefs where they get their authority to say to the Indian that he shall stay in one place, while he sees white men going where they please. They can not tell me.**"

—*Chief Joseph*

Chief Joseph was born around 1840 and died in 1904.

FOCUS ACTIVITY

Have you ever been forced to defend yourself, either physically or verbally?

JOURNAL Write about a time when you had to defend yourself. How did you handle the situation?

SETTING A PURPOSE Read to understand a man's defense of his decisions.

BACKGROUND

The Long Trek to Canada

Chief Joseph tried to take his people to Canada because he felt he had no choice. For more than three months, from June 17 to September 30, 1877, he led some two hundred warriors and their families on a journey that covered more than a thousand miles. The warriors fought off pursuing federal troops again and again, despite being outnumbered at least ten to one. Because of his constant attention to the needs of the women, children, and aged among his people, because of his humane treatment of prisoners, and because of his honorable behavior in victory and defeat, Chief Joseph won many admirers and supporters among Native Americans and whites.

Chief Joseph Rides to Surrender, 1979. Howard Terpning. Oil on canvas. ©1979 Howard Terpning. ©1979 The Greenwich Workshop® Inc. Courtesy of The Greenwich Workshop Inc., Shelton, CT.

I Will Fight No More Forever

Chief Joseph ∾

"Tell General Howard[1] I know his heart. What he told me before, I have in my heart. I am tired of fighting. Our chiefs are killed. Looking Glass[2] is dead. Too Hul Hul Suit[3] is dead. The old men are all dead. It is the young men who say yes and no. He who led on the young men is dead.[4] It is cold and we have no blankets. The little children are freezing to death. My people, some of them, have run away to the hills and have no blankets, no food; no one knows where they are—perhaps freezing to death. I want to have time to look for my children and see how many I can find. Maybe I shall find them among the dead. Hear me, my chiefs. I am tired; my heart is sick and sad. From where the sun now stands I will fight no more forever."

---

1. *General* (Oliver Otis) *Howard* (1830–1909) had been a Union general in the Civil War. He sent troops to fight the Nez Percé in the Battle of White Bird Canyon.
2. *Looking Glass* was a respected leader of the Nez Percé. He took part in the 1877 retreat.
3. *Too Hul Hul Suit,* or Tu Ku Lxu C'uut (tœ kœl' hu sœt'), leader of the White Bird tribe, was a member of the negotiating team that met with General Howard. He favored fighting for the Nez Percé land rather than moving to a reservation.
4. *[He who led . . . dead.]* refers to Chief Joseph's younger brother, Ollikut (ōl okh' ut).

Responding to Literature

Personal Response

If you could speak to Chief Joseph, what would you say to him?

ANALYZING LITERATURE

RECALL AND INTERPRET

1. What has happened to the chiefs and the old men of the tribe? Who is left to carry on the fight? In your opinion, how might these developments have affected Chief Joseph's decision?
2. What other reasons does Chief Joseph give for his decision? What can you infer about his values and his character, based on these reasons?
3. What words does Chief Joseph use to describe his heart? How do the feelings he describes help you better understand the decision he has made?
4. In your words, restate the last sentence of Chief Joseph's speech.

EVALUATE AND CONNECT

5. What words and phrases does Chief Joseph repeat? What is the effect of this **repetition?** (See Literary Terms Handbook, page R13.)
6. In this short speech, Chief Joseph explains a decision that will have an enormous impact on the lives of his people. Do you think a longer, more detailed speech would have been more effective or more convincing? Why or why not?
7. Chief Joseph was a brave, proud warrior. In your opinion, what inner qualities did he summon in order to accept defeat with dignity? Explain.
8. Read the journal entry you made for the Focus Activity on page 513. After reading Chief Joseph's speech, can you imagine a different solution to the situation you wrote about? Explain.

Literary ELEMENTS

Tone

Tone is the writer's attitude toward the subject of a work. The tone of a piece of writing conveys one or more emotions. In "I Will Fight No More Forever," the tone conveys feelings of weariness, resignation, sadness, and dignity. Writers create the tone of a work primarily through word choice, but sentence structure and length can also be important. For example, Chief Joseph's use of brief sentences and simple, direct language emphasizes the overwhelming sense of loss.

1. What words and phrases help create a tone that is weary, resigned, and sad, yet dignified?
2. Find examples of simple, direct language and brief sentences. How do they affect the tone of the speech?

● See **Literary Terms Handbook,** p. R16.

EXTENDING YOUR RESPONSE

Personal Writing

In Defense   In "I Will Fight No More Forever," Chief Joseph eloquently defends his decision to surrender. Using the selection as a model, write a speech defending your response to the situation you described for the Focus Activity on page 513.

Internet Connection

Wounded Knee   In 1890 federal troops killed more than 150 unarmed Sioux men, women, and children at Wounded Knee, South Dakota. Use the Internet to research the massacre. In a presentation to the class, compare this situation with that of Chief Joseph and his people.

📋 **Save your work for your portfolio.**

Technology Skills

Multimedia: American Literature Through American History

Multimedia presentations involve the sharing of information using more than one medium. Strictly speaking, a speech accompanied by background music would be a multimedia presentation. Today, however, the word *multimedia* suggests the use of computer software that enables users to combine text, graphic images, and sound.

Multimedia Presentations

Following are three options for putting together a multimedia presentation.

Method	Hardware/Software Needed	Description of Presentation
Low-tech (non-computer presentation)	Camera, slide projector or overhead projector and screen, tape recorder	Use 35mm slides or overhead transparencies for your visuals (text and images). Use a tape recorder for narration, music, or other sounds.
Hypertext presentation	Computer and Hypercard, HyperStudio, or other hypertext software *Also useful:* microphone, digital camera	Use a hypertext program to combine text, graphic images, and sound on a series of "cards" that make up a stack that can be shown in sequence on a computer monitor.
Slide-show presentation	Computer and PowerPoint, Persuasion, or other presentation software *Also useful:* microphone, digital camera	Use presentation software to create a group of "slides" that make up a computer-based slide show combining text, graphic images, and sound.

TECHNOLOGY TIP

Most presentation software will include templates for different slide designs, textures and colors for slide backgrounds, clip art, and other features that can help you create your presentation. The program may also include a tutorial that will help you learn how to use it.

Hypertext cards are generally meant to be seen by a single viewer on a personal computer or via the Internet. Slide-show presentations are meant to be viewed on a big screen by a large audience. Slide-show programs automatically encourage brief text and large type; hypertext programs do not. It's a good idea to use large typefaces for any presentation meant to be seen by more than one person.

Create a Presentation

Working with a small group, create a simple multimedia presentation.

1. From the literature you've studied so far, choose a selection from a historical period. Using a search engine, look on the Web for information about that historical period. Search also for sites that relate to the work of literature you chose and its author.

2. Think about how the author may have been influenced by the time in which he or she worked. Take notes, print relevant information, or save important text to a disk. Pay particular attention to:

   a. sociological aspects of the time, such as class structures, the roles of women and children, and the positions of minorities

   b. political events, such as conflicts over the economy, foreign affairs, and domestic policy

   c. if and how the literary work reflects the time in which it was written

3. Look for a pattern in your research—something that will connect your chosen work of literature, its author, and the historical period in which the work was written. Organize your notes in a logical order. Then summarize the information in concise statements.

4. Think about what illustrations or sounds could augment your text. Create an outline or storyboard that shows the text, images, and sounds of each segment. (These instructions will refer to each segment as a slide, although it may be a slide, a card, or a transparency, depending on which method of presentation you use.) Remember to save your work often!

5. Keep text information succinct. Rather than long paragraphs, use a few numbered or bulleted lists.

6. Begin with a title slide that names your presentation and its creators. Add at least eight additional slides with text or visuals. Add sounds when appropriate.

7. Go through your completed presentation several times, looking for ways you can improve it. Then show your presentation to your class.

Walt Whitman's Civil War

A Multimedia Presentation by Amy Tsai

Main Idea

- **Supporting detail**

- **Supporting detail**

- **Supporting detail**

ACTIVITIES

1. Prepare a multimedia presentation about a historical character you admire.

2. Volunteer to create a multimedia presentation for a local community group.

Before You Read

Let Us Examine the Facts

Meet the Cherokee of Corn Tassel's Era

"Remember that the whites are near us. . . . [U]nless you can speak their language, read and write as they do, they will be able to cheat you and trample on your rights."

—Cherokee elder

Until the middle of the 1700s, the Cherokee were a powerful nation of more than 20,000 people who occupied 40,000 square miles of land in the central and southeastern regions of what became the United States. They lived in villages and made their living by hunting, farming, fishing, and trading. Their prosperity diminished during the 1760s and 1770s, when white settlers began to move into Cherokee territory and claim ownership of the land.

During the American Revolution, some Cherokee sided with the British, who supplied them with food and other goods. Unwilling to distinguish between neutral and hostile Cherokee, revolutionary militias destroyed nearly forty Cherokee towns. In 1777 they forced the Cherokee to sign a binding "peace" treaty. Like many Native American peoples, the Cherokee soon learned that white officials designed such treaties primarily to deprive them of their lands.

In the selection you are about to read, Corn Tassel, a head chief of the Cherokee, responds to a peace treaty proposed by U.S. officials. Though suspicious of the treaty, the Cherokee signed it on November 28, 1785. Three years later Corn Tassel was killed by a young white man in retribution for a crime the chief did not commit.

The date of Corn Tassel's birth is unknown; he died in 1788.

FOCUS ACTIVITY

Imagine that someone comes to your home and demands that you and your family agree to move out so that he or she can move in. How would you react? What would you say and do?

FREEWRITE Spend three minutes writing a response to these questions.

SETTING A PURPOSE Find out how a head chief of the Cherokee responds to the demands of a treaty.

BACKGROUND

Did You Know?

In 1821 a Cherokee named Sequoyah presented to tribal elders the alphabet he had invented to represent the sounds and syllables in the Cherokee language. The elders immediately adopted this alphabet. Because the Cherokee had no written language before 1821, this selection, dated 1785, probably does not contain Corn Tassel's actual words. The ideas communicated in the selection, however, do most likely reflect those that Corn Tassel expressed.

VOCABULARY PREVIEW

exorbitant (ig zôr′ bə tənt) *adj.* exceeding what is reasonable; excessive; p. 519

pretension (pri ten′ shən) *n.* a claim; an assertion; p. 519

vigilance (vij′ ə ləns) *n.* the state of being alert or watchful; p. 520

mishap (mis′ hap′) *n.* an unfortunate accident or mistake; a misfortune; p. 520

propriety (prə prī′ ə tē) *n.* the quality of being proper; appropriateness; p. 520

doctrine (dok′ trin) *n.* a principle that is taught and advocated; a tenet; p. 520

sustenance (sus′ tə nəns) *n.* that which sustains life, especially food; p. 520

Let Us Examine the Facts

Corn Tassel ≈

It is a little surprising that when we entered into treaties with our brothers, the whites, their whole cry is *more land!* Indeed, formerly it seemed to be a matter of formality with them to demand what they knew we durst[1] not refuse. But on the principles of fairness, of which we have received assurances during the conducting of the present treaty, and in the name of free will and equality, I must reject your demand. Suppose, in considering the nature of your claim (and in justice to my nation I shall and will do it freely), I were to ask one of you, my brother warriors, under what kind of authority, by what law, or on what pretense he makes this exorbitant demand of nearly all the lands we hold between your settlements and our towns, as the cement and consideration of our peace.

Would he tell me that it is by right of conquest? No! If he did, I should retort on him that *we* had last marched over his territory; even up to this very place which he has *fortified* so far within his former limits; nay, that some of our young warriors (whom we have not yet had an opportunity to recall or give

Our People Lived Here, c. 1967. Paul Pahsetopah (Four Hills or Humps on the Buffalo). Watercolor on board, 24½ x 31¹⁵⁄₁₆ in. The Philbrook Museum of Art, Tulsa, OK.

notice to, of the general treaty) are still in the woods, and continue to keep his people in fear, and that it was but till lately that these identical walls were your strongholds, out of which you durst scarcely advance.

If, therefore, a bare march, or reconnoitering[2] a country is sufficient reason to ground a claim to it, we shall insist upon transposing the demand, and your relinquishing your settlements on the western waters and removing one hundred miles back towards the east, whither some of our warriors advanced against you in the course of last year's campaign.

Let us examine the facts of your present eruption into our country, and we shall discover your pretensions on that ground. What

---

1. *Durst* means "dared."

2. *Reconnoitering* (rē kə noi′ tər ing) is inspecting or surveying an area in order to obtain information.

Vocabulary
exorbitant (ig zôr′ bə tənt) *adj.* exceeding what is reasonable; excessive
pretension (pri ten′ shən) *n.* a claim; an assertion

did you do? You marched into our territories with a superior force; our <u>vigilance</u> gave us no timely notice of your maneuvers; your numbers far exceeded us, and we fled to the stronghold of our extensive woods, there to secure our women and children.

Thus, you marched into our towns; they were left to your mercy; you killed a few scattered and defenseless individuals, spread fire and desolation wherever you pleased, and returned again to your own habitations. If you meant this, indeed, as a conquest you omitted the most essential point; you should have fortified the junction of the Holstin and Tennessee rivers, and have thereby conquered all the waters above you. But, as all are fair advantages during the existence of a state of war, it is now too late for us to suffer for your <u>mishap</u> of generalship!

Again, were we to inquire by what law or authority you set up a claim, I answer, *none!* Your laws extend not into our country, nor ever did. You talk of the law of nature and the law of nations, and they are both against you.

Indeed, much has been advanced on the want of what you term civilization among the Indians; and many proposals have been made to us to adopt your laws, your religion, your manners, and your customs. But, we confess that we do not yet see the <u>propriety</u>, or practicability of such a reformation, and should be better pleased with beholding the good effect of these <u>doctrines</u> in your own practices than with hearing you talk about them, or reading your papers to us upon such subjects.

You say: Why do not the Indians till the ground and live as we do? May we not, with equal propriety, ask, Why the white people do not hunt and live as we do? You profess[3] to think it no injustice to warn us not to kill our deer and other game from the mere love of waste; but it is very criminal in our young men if they chance to kill a cow or a hog for their <u>sustenance</u> when they happen to be in your lands. We wish, however, to be at peace with you, and to do as we would be done by. We do not quarrel with you for killing an occasional buffalo, bear or deer on our lands when you need one to eat; but you go much farther; your people hunt to gain a livelihood by it; they kill all our game; our young men resent the injury, and it is followed by bloodshed and war.

This is not a mere affected[4] injury; it is a grievance which we equitably[5] complain of, and it demands a permanent redress.[6]

The great God of Nature has placed us in different situations. It is true that he has endowed you with many superior advantages; but he has not created us to be your slaves. *We are a separate people!* He has given each their lands, under distinct considerations and circumstances; he has stocked yours with cows, ours with buffalo; yours with hog, ours with bear; yours with sheep, ours with deer. He has, indeed, given you an advantage in this, that your cattle are tame and domestic while ours are wild and demand not only a larger space for range, but art[7] to hunt and kill them; they are, nevertheless, as much our property as other animals are yours, and ought not to be taken away without our consent, or for something equivalent.

---

3. *Profess* means "claim."
4. *Affected* means "assumed for show to make an impression."
5. *Equitably* means "fairly" or "justly."
6. *Redress* means "compensation."
7. Here, *art* means "skill."

Vocabulary

vigilance (vij′ ə ləns) *n.* the state of being alert or watchful

mishap (mis′ hap′) *n.* an unfortunate accident or mistake; a misfortune

propriety (prə prī′ ə tē) *n.* the quality of being proper; appropriateness

doctrine (dok′ trin) *n.* a principle that is taught and advocated; a tenet

sustenance (sus′ tə nəns) *n.* that which sustains life, especially food

Responding to Literature

Personal Response

Were you convinced by Corn Tassel's arguments? Explain why or why not.

ANALYZING LITERATURE

RECALL AND INTERPRET

1. How much land are the white officials demanding from the Cherokee? What are they promising in return?

2. According to Corn Tassel, what is the basis of the white officials' claim to Cherokee lands? What is Corn Tassel's opinion of that claim? Use details from the selection to support your answer.

3. What specific grievance do the Cherokee have against the white people? In your opinion, how does this grievance reflect the cultural clash between the two groups?

4. Summarize the ideas that Corn Tassel expresses in the last paragraph. What can you infer about his view of the rights held by the Cherokee and the white people?

EVALUATE AND CONNECT

5. Compare your response to the Focus Activity on page 518 with Corn Tassel's response to the proposed peace treaty.

6. Describe Corn Tassel's **tone,** or attitude toward his subject. Do you think his tone suits the subject? Why or why not?

7. If you could interview Corn Tassel, what questions would you ask him? What advice might you give to him?

8. Theme Connections   Corn Tassel points out how the everyday lives of the Cherokee and the white people differ. Do you think one group of people ever has the right to force another group to change or give up its way of life? Explain.

Literary ELEMENTS

Argument

Argument is the use of reason to influence ideas or actions. In "Let Us Examine the Facts," Corn Tassel argues that the white officials are wrong to think that Cherokee lands belong to them. To support his argument, he presents facts and reasons, such as the failure of the whites to occupy the Cherokee towns that they entered and destroyed.

1. What facts and reasons does Corn Tassel give to support his statement that both "the law of nature and the law of nations" are against the claim of the white officials?

2. Would you have been influenced by Corn Tassel's argument? Explain, using details from the selection as support.

● See **Literary Terms Handbook,** p. R2.

EXTENDING YOUR RESPONSE

Literature Groups

Mediating Conflict   People involved in conflict sometimes call in a mediator to help them work toward a compromise. Imagine that Corn Tassel has asked your group to mediate the conflict between the Cherokee and the white officials. As a group, use specific details from Corn Tassel's speech and suggest compromises to resolve the problems. Share your ideas with the class.

Creative Writing

The Pain of Loss   Corn Tassel, like many Native American leaders of the 1700s and 1800s, had learned from experience that "peace" treaties often led to the loss of tribal lands. In a poem, a song, or an essay, try to capture how Corn Tassel might have felt about that loss.

💾 **Save your work for your portfolio.**

Writing Skills

Using Transitions Effectively

When you read a story or an article, do you ever think, "This is too choppy and hard to understand"? The selection might be missing transitions, words and phrases that help show the relationships between ideas in a piece of writing. Transitions lead readers smoothly from sentence to sentence and from paragraph to paragraph.

Contrast

One group of transitional words and phrases, including *but, yet, on the other hand, however,* and *nevertheless,* indicates that two ideas contradict or contrast with each other. Notice how transitions are used to show contradictions between ideas in these sentences from "Let Us Examine the Facts."

- *It is true that he has endowed you with many superior advantages; but he has not created us to be your slaves.*
- *Your cattle are tame . . . while ours are wild . . . ; they are, nevertheless, as much our property as other animals are yours.*

Other Transitions

Transitional words such as *because* or *as a result* also indicate relationships, showing that one event caused another. Phrases such as *for instance* and *that is* alert readers to expect an example. Transitions also indicate time *(first, next, now),* position *(above, in the middle, outside),* and importance *(especially, above all, in fact).*

EXERCISES

---

1. Copy the following summary of "Let Us Examine the Facts," underlining the transitional words and phrases you find. Indicate the relationship each transition shows.

> Corn Tassel, the author, explained why his people would continue to resist white domination. First, the whites had no legal claim to his people's land. The whites could not, for example, claim the land just because they marched over it. Second, the whites wanted the Indians to adopt their religion, but the whites did not themselves live according to the values they professed to hold dear. Most importantly, the whites and the Indians were separate peoples.

2. Write a paragraph responding to "Let Us Examine the Facts" or to another selection, using transitions to make your ideas flow more smoothly. Underline the transitions that you include.

Before You Read

The Story of an Hour

Meet Kate Chopin

Kate Chopin (shō′ pan) was the first female writer in the United States to portray frankly the passions and discontents of women confined to traditional roles as wives and mothers. For this she was roundly condemned in her time and is widely praised today.

She was born Katherine O'Flaherty in St. Louis to an Irish-born merchant and a mother of French descent. When Kate was five, her father died in a railroad accident. She left school, and for the next two years, she studied at home with her mother, grandmother, and great-grandmother, who became her tutor. Growing up in a household of strong, independent women did much to shape Kate as a person and a writer.

At age twenty, Kate married Oscar Chopin, a cotton broker, and moved with him to New Orleans. The cosmopolitan city suited her, and she was unhappy when business problems forced them to move to Oscar's rural hometown of Cloutierville, Louisiana. At first the small town held little attraction for Kate, but the area would later inspire many of her stories.

When her husband died in 1882, Chopin was left with children to raise and support. She ran her husband's businesses for a year. Then she moved her household back to St. Louis to be near her family there. When her mother died a year later, Chopin was overwhelmed with grief. At her doctor's advice, she turned to writing and published her first work in 1889.

Chopin earned praise for stories that captured the local color of Louisiana, but drew criticism for those that questioned the role of women in contemporary society. Her novel *The Awakening*, published in 1899, was acknowledged for its technique and harshly criticized for its content. Possibly as a result of that criticism, the publication of Chopin's last story collection, which included "The Story of an Hour," was canceled.

"When the theme of a story occurs to her, she writes it out immediately, often at one sitting, then, after a little, copies it out carefully, seldom making corrections. She never retouches after that."

—*William Schuyler*

"There are stories that seem to write themselves, and others which positively refuse to be written—which no amount of coaxing can bring to anything."

"Story-writing—at least with me—is the spontaneous expression of impressions gathered from goodness knows where."

"The artist must possess the courageous soul that dares and defies."

—*Chopin*

Kate Chopin was born in 1851 and died in 1904.

Have you ever experienced a feeling of great relief—a moment when you suddenly felt very free and unburdened?

QUICKWRITE Take five minutes to write about a time when you felt as though the weight of the world had just been lifted from your shoulders. What caused you to feel this way? How long did the feeling last?

SETTING A PURPOSE Read to discover how quickly one woman's emotions change.

BACKGROUND

The Time and Place

The 1890s were a period of social tension. Organizations were pushing hard for woman suffrage. Women were also meeting for social, intellectual, and philanthropic purposes. Some women began attending college and entering professions previously open only to men.

Women marching for the right to vote, early 1900s.

At the same time, however, many women, especially in the South, were being raised with a special sense of "a woman's place" in the home. Although their roles as wives and mothers were glorified, women had few legal rights. For example, when Chopin's husband died, she had to petition the court to be appointed the legal guardian of her own children.

Chopin was critical of cultural expectations for women. In much of her fiction, she criticized the institution of marriage and wrote about women who struggled against social convention to be individuals.

Literary Influences

Perhaps the strongest influence on Chopin's writing style was the French writer Guy de Maupassant. Here she talks about his ability to craft a story:

"I read his stories and marveled at them. Here was life, not fiction. . . . Here was a man who had escaped from tradition and authority, who had entered into himself and looked out upon life through his own being and with his own eyes; and who, in a direct and simple way, told us what he saw."

VOCABULARY PREVIEW

repression (ri presh′ ən) *n.* the state of being held back or kept under control; p. 526

elusive (i loo′ siv) *adj.* difficult to explain or grasp; p. 526

tumultuously (too mul′ choo əs lē) *adv.* in an agitated manner; violently; p. 526

exalted (ig zôl′ təd) *adj.* elevated; p. 527

perception (pər sep′ shən) *n.* an awareness; an insight; p. 527

persistence (pər sis′ təns) *n.* stubborn or determined continuance; p. 527

impose (im pōz′) *v.* to inflict, as by authority; to dictate; p. 527

illumination (i loo′ mə nā′ shən) *n.* intellectual enlightenment; p. 527

The Lady Anne, 1899. Edwin Austin Abbey. Oil on canvas, 48 x 24 in.
The Butler Institute of American Art, Youngstown, OH.

THE STORY OF AN HOUR

Kate Chopin

Knowing that Mrs. Mallard was afflicted with a heart trouble, great care was taken to break to her as gently as possible the news of her husband's death. It was her sister Josephine who told her, in broken sentences; veiled[1] hints that revealed in half concealing. Her husband's friend Richards was there, too, near her. It was he who had been in the newspaper office when intelligence of the railroad disaster was received, with Brently Mallard's name leading the list of "killed." He had only taken the time to assure himself of its truth by a second telegram, and had hastened to forestall[2] any less careful, less tender friend in bearing the sad message.

She did not hear the story as many women have heard the same, with a paralyzed inability to accept its significance. She wept at once, with sudden, wild abandonment, in her sister's arms. When the storm of grief had spent[3] itself she went to her room alone. She would have no one follow her.

There stood, facing the open window, a comfortable, roomy armchair. Into this she sank, pressed down by a physical exhaustion that haunted her body and seemed to reach into her soul.

She could see in the open square before her house the tops of trees that were all aquiver with the new spring life. The delicious breath of rain was in the air. In the street below a peddler was crying his wares. The notes of a distant song which some one was singing reached her faintly, and countless sparrows were twittering in the eaves.

There were patches of blue sky showing here and there through the clouds that had met and piled one above the other in the west facing her window.

She sat with her head thrown back upon the cushion of the chair, quite motionless, except when a sob came up into her throat and shook her, as a child who has cried itself to sleep continues to sob in its dreams.

She was young, with a fair, calm face, whose lines bespoke repression and even a certain strength. But now there was a dull stare in her eyes, whose gaze was fixed away off yonder on one of those patches of blue sky. It was not a glance of reflection, but rather indicated a suspension of intelligent thought.

There was something coming to her and she was waiting for it, fearfully. What was it? She did not know; it was too subtle and elusive to name. But she felt it, creeping out of the sky, reaching toward her through the sounds, the scents, the color that filled the air.

Now her bosom rose and fell tumultuously. She was beginning to recognize this thing that was approaching to possess her, and she was striving to beat it back with her will— as powerless as her two white slender hands would have been.

When she abandoned herself a little whispered word escaped her slightly parted lips. She said it over and over under her breath: "free, free, free!" The vacant stare and the look of terror that had followed it went from her eyes. They stayed keen and bright. Her pulses beat fast, and the coursing[4] blood warmed and relaxed every inch of her body.

She did not stop to ask if it were or were not a monstrous joy that held her. A clear and

---

1. *Veiled* means "disguised" or "obscure."
2. *Forestall* means "to hinder or prevent by action taken in advance."
3. Here, *spent* means "exhausted."

---

4. *Coursing* means "swiftly moving."

Vocabulary

repression (ri presh′ ən) *n.* the state of being held back or kept under control
elusive (i lōō′ siv) *adj.* difficult to explain or grasp
tumultuously (tōō mul′ chōō əs lē) *adv.* in an agitated manner; violently

exalted <u>perception</u> enabled her to dismiss the suggestion as trivial.

She knew that she would weep again when she saw the kind, tender hands folded in death; the face that had never looked save[5] with love upon her, fixed and gray and dead. But she saw beyond that bitter moment a long procession of years to come that would belong to her absolutely. And she opened and spread her arms out to them in welcome.

There would be no one to live for her during those coming years; she would live for herself. There would be no powerful will bending hers in that blind <u>persistence</u> with which men and women believe they have a right to <u>impose</u> a private will upon a fellow-creature. A kind intention or a cruel intention made the act seem no less a crime as she looked upon it in that brief moment of <u>illumination</u>.

And yet she had loved him—sometimes. Often she had not. What did it matter! What could love, the unsolved mystery, count for in face of this possession of self-assertion which she suddenly recognized as the strongest impulse of her being!

"Free! Body and soul free!" she kept whispering.

Josephine was kneeling before the closed door with her lips to the keyhole, imploring for admission. "Louise, open the door! I beg; open the door—you will make yourself ill.

What are you doing, Louise? For heaven's sake open the door."

"Go away. I am not making myself ill." No; she was drinking in a very elixir of life[6] through that open window.

Her fancy was running riot along those days ahead of her. Spring days, and summer days, and all sorts of days that would be her own. She breathed a quick prayer that life might be long. It was only yesterday she had thought with a shudder that life might be long.

She arose at length and opened the door to her sister's importunities.[7] There was a feverish triumph in her eyes, and she carried herself unwittingly like a goddess of Victory. She clasped her sister's waist, and together they descended the stairs. Richards stood waiting for them at the bottom.

Some one was opening the front door with a latchkey. It was Brently Mallard who entered, a little travel-stained, composedly carrying his grip-sack[8] and umbrella. He had been far from the scene of accident, and did not even know there had been one. He stood amazed at Josephine's piercing cry; at Richards' quick motion to screen him from the view of his wife.

But Richards was too late.

When the doctors came they said she had died of heart disease—of joy that kills.

---

5. Here, *save* means "except."

6. An *elixir* (i lik′ sər) *of life* is a substance thought to prolong life indefinitely.

7. *Importunities* are persistent requests or demands.

8. A *grip-sack* is a small traveling bag.

Vocabulary

exalted (ig zôl′ təd) *adj.* elevated

perception (pər sep′ shən) *n.* an awareness; an insight

persistence (pər sis′ təns) *n.* stubborn or determined continuance

impose (im pōz′) *v.* to inflict, as by authority; to dictate

illumination (i l ̅oo′ mə nā′ shən) *n.* intellectual enlightenment

Responding to Literature

Personal Response

What emotions did you experience as you read this story? How did the ending affect you?

ANALYZING LITERATURE

RECALL AND INTERPRET

1. How does Mrs. Mallard first react to the news her sister tells her? What does her reaction seem to indicate about her feelings toward her husband?
2. Summarize what happens while Mrs. Mallard is in her room. How do her feelings change? Why, do you think, does she fear this change at first but later welcomes it?
3. What words does the narrator use to describe Mrs. Mallard's appearance and behavior as she leaves her room? Based on this description, what might you infer about her attitude and outlook?
4. What happens to Mrs. Mallard at the end of the story? Do you agree with the explanation the doctors give? Why or why not?

EVALUATE AND CONNECT

5. What is your opinion of Mrs. Mallard's character? Support your evaluation by using details from the story.
6. **Dramatic irony** occurs when the reader knows something that characters in a literary work do not. How does the dramatic irony in the last paragraph add to your understanding and appreciation of the story?
7. Review your response to the Focus Activity on page 524. Compare and contrast Mrs. Mallard's experience with your own.
8. This story takes place more than a century ago, at a time when most American women lived very restricted lives. Do you think this story would be believable if it were set in the present? Why or why not?

Literary ELEMENTS

Plot

The **plot** is the sequence of events in a story. The events of a story develop its central **conflict,** or struggle between opposing forces. When a character struggles against an outside force, the conflict is external; when a character experiences a struggle inside his or her own mind, the conflict is internal. The conflict builds until the story reaches its **climax**—the point of greatest emotional intensity. The story concludes with the **resolution,** or final outcome of the conflict.

1. What is the central conflict of "The Story of an Hour"? Is this conflict external, internal, or both? Explain.
2. Identify the climax. Do you think this story might have two climaxes?
3. How does the resolution of the story help you better understand its **theme,** or message?

● See **Literary Terms Handbook,** p. R12.

EXTENDING YOUR RESPONSE

Writing About Literature

Evaluate the Title   The original title of "The Story of an Hour" was "The Dream of an Hour." Why might the title have been changed? How are the titles similar? different? Which title do you think is more appropriate? Why? Write a paragraph or two in which you answer these questions.

Interdisciplinary Activity

History: Women's Roles   Reread the Time and Place section on page 524. Then research the social, political, and legal issues that concerned Kate Chopin and other women of her time. Share your findings with the class.

📖 **Save your work for your portfolio.**

Mysteries of the Mind

Psychologists study the mysteries of human behavior. Many of the characters in Theme 6 would be interesting subjects for a psychologist. While the characters exhibit types of behavior you might recognize, they often show them to an exaggerated degree.

What Is Psychology?

A psychologist's work is to understand why people think and act as they do—ways people learn, how they form and express emotions, and how they develop their personalities and relationships. Psychologists also may counsel individuals, advise parents on raising children, help an employer organize a productive workplace, or explain why a TV commercial influences buying choices.

Some Ideas About the Mind

- Austrian psychologist Sigmund Freud (1856–1939) is considered by many to be the father of modern psychology. Freud developed a number of methods for discovering people's hidden thoughts and conflicts. One method was **free association,** in which he encouraged the patient to express random thoughts.
- U.S. psychologist John B. Watson (1878–1958) developed a method of psychology known as **behaviorism.** Behaviorism focuses on people's actions—their behavior—rather than on their thoughts.

This chart shows different theories about how people learn.

Theory	Example
People respond to rewards or punishments for specific behaviors.	A basketball coach demonstrates skills, provides incentives for practicing, and rewards successful performance.
People develop knowledge and skills when they reach the proper mental, emotional, or physical stage. Different people learn at different rates.	The coach takes extra time to help each player improve.
People learn by processing new information and relating it to what they already know.	The coach explains how the position of a player's hands on the ball can affect shooting success.

Activity

1. Which character from this theme's selections do you find most interesting from a psychological point of view? Explain.
2. How do you learn most effectively? Explain.

Before You Read

A Wagner Matinée

Meet Willa Cather

When she was only nine years old, Willa Cather's life changed drastically. That year, her family left the forests and hills of Virginia for the wide-open prairie of frontier Nebraska. For Cather, the change was both difficult and exhilarating:

❝I was little and homesick and lonely and my mother was homesick and nobody paid any attention to us. So the country and I had it out together and by the end of the first autumn, that shaggy grass country had gripped me with a passion I have never been able to shake.❞

Cather's family first lived on a homesteading ranch and then moved into the village of Red Cloud, which, though a frontier town, offered Cather intellectual nourishment. There she learned French, German, Latin, and Greek from her European neighbors, took part in plays, and enjoyed performances by traveling companies in the local opera house.

In 1891 Cather left home to study at the University of Nebraska, where she supported herself by writing reviews for school and local newspapers. Cather's articles earned her statewide recognition and eventually a job as a magazine editor in Pittsburgh. While there, she began to pursue writing seriously, publishing her first collection of poetry and the collection of stories that includes "A Wagner Matinée." Entitled *The Troll Garden*, this book so impressed the head of *McClure's Magazine* in New York City that he offered Cather a job. She soon became the magazine's managing editor. In 1911, at the urging of her friend Sarah Orne Jewett, Cather left journalism in order to devote all her energy to writing fiction.

Cather remained in New York for the rest of her life, but her childhood memories of the prairie and its people inspired many of her greatest works. Her earlier stories often focused on the desolation of pioneers' lives—lives that were often devoid of art, music, and other pleasures of civilization. In her later works, however, Cather began to celebrate the freedom and simplicity of pioneer life and the haunting beauty of the prairie landscape.

Between 1912 and 1923, Cather wrote five novels that drew upon her memories of frontier Nebraska: *O Pioneers!*, *The Song of the Lark*, *My Ántonia*, *One of Ours*, and *A Lost Lady*. Today, Cather is celebrated for her carefully crafted writing style as well as her evocative portraits of artists in conflict and immigrant pioneers struggling to fashion lives for themselves on the harsh Nebraska prairie.

❝That love of great spaces, of rolling open country like the sea,—it's the grand passion of my life. I tried for years to get over it. I've stopped trying. It's incurable.❞

—*Cather*

❝[Cather's] strongest and most bitter criticism of the prairie culture was that it could not understand or abide the artistic soul.❞

—*Frederick Hoffman*

Willa Cather was born in 1873 and died in 1947.

FOCUS ACTIVITY

Have you ever moved from one neighborhood, city, or town to another? If not, have you ever imagined what it would be like to move?

JOURNAL Write about a time when you moved to a new home. What did you miss most about your former home? If you've never had to move, write about what you might miss if you did move.

SETTING A PURPOSE Read to find out how a character's life is changed by a move to another part of the country.

BACKGROUND

The Time and Place

Willa Cather based "A Wagner Matinée" on her Uncle George and Aunt Franc's experience of moving to Nebraska after the passage of the Homestead Act in 1862. According to this law, U.S. citizens (or those about to become citizens) who were at least twenty-one years old could obtain a quarter section, or 160 acres, of land just by living on it for five years. Together with the coming of the railroad, the Homestead Act encouraged thousands of hopeful pioneers to move west.

About the Story's Title

The Wagner (väg′ nər) in the title of "A Wagner Matinée" is the German composer Wilhelm Richard Wagner (1813–1883). A brilliant composer, Wagner revolutionized opera by creating works with uninterrupted musical scores and passionate, crashing sounds. His highly dramatic spectacles of sight and sound were often based on Germanic legends. The opera *Tannhäuser* (tän′ hoi′ zər), for example, was inspired by the adventures of a German poet of that name.

Other works by Wagner mentioned in the story include the operas *The Flying Dutchman, Tristan and Isolde* (tris′ tən and i zōl′ də), and *The Ring of the Nibelung* (nē′ bə loong′) (actually a cycle of four operas), as well as "Prize Song," an aria from the opera *Die Meistersinger von Nürnberg* (dē mīs′ tər zing′ ər fon noorn′ berk′).

Opera star Hildegarde Behrens performing Wagner.

VOCABULARY PREVIEW

legacy (leg′ ə sē) *n.* an inheritance; p. 533
kindle (kind′ əl) *v.* to stir up; to excite; p. 533
reproach (ri prōch′) *n.* an expression of disapproval; a reprimand; p. 533
doggedly (dô′ gid lē) *adv.* in a stubbornly persistent manner; obstinately; p. 535
inert (i nurt′) *adj.* inactive; sluggish; p. 536
trepidation (trep′ ə dā′ shən) *n.* nervous anticipation; anxiety; p. 536

turmoil (tur′ moil) *n.* a state of confused agitation; commotion; p. 537
obliquely (ə blēk′ lē) *adv.* in a slanting or sloping direction; p. 537
prevail (pri vāl′) *v.* to use persuasion successfully; p. 539
deluge (del′ ūj) *n.* anything that overwhelms or rushes like a flood; p. 539

A Wagner Matinée

Willa Cather

In the Loge, 1879. Mary Cassatt. Oil on canvas, 32 x 26 in. The Hayden Collection. Museum of Fine Arts, Boston.

I received one morning a letter, written in pale ink on glassy, blue-lined note-paper, and bearing the postmark of a little Nebraska village. This communication, worn and rubbed, looking as if it has been carried for some days in a coat pocket that was none too clean, was from my uncle Howard, and informed me that his wife had been left a small <u>legacy</u> by a bachelor relative, and that it would be necessary for her to go to Boston to attend to the settling of the estate. He requested me to meet her at the station and render[1] her whatever services might be necessary. On examining the date indicated as that of her arrival, I found it to be no later than tomorrow. He had characteristically delayed writing until, had I been away from home for a day, I must have missed my aunt altogether.

The name of my Aunt Georgiana opened before me a gulf of recollection so wide and deep that, as the letter dropped from my hand, I felt suddenly a stranger to all the present conditions of my existence, wholly ill at ease and out of place amid the familiar surroundings of my study. I became, in short, the gangling farmer-boy my aunt had known, scourged[2] with chilblains[3] and bashfulness, my hands cracked and sore from the corn husking. I sat again before her parlour organ, fumbling the scales with my stiff, red fingers, while she, beside me, made canvas mittens for the huskers.

The next morning, after preparing my landlady for a visitor, I set out for the station. When the train arrived I had some difficulty in finding my aunt. She was the last of the passengers to alight, and it was not until I got her into the carriage that she seemed really to recognize me. She had come all the way in a day coach; her linen duster[4] had become black with soot and her black bonnet grey with dust during the journey. When we arrived at my boarding-house the landlady put her to bed at once and I did not see her again until the next morning.

Whatever shock Mrs. Springer experienced at my aunt's appearance, she considerately concealed. As for myself, I saw my aunt's battered figure with that feeling of awe and respect with which we behold explorers who have left their ears and fingers north of Franz-Joseph-Land,[5] or their health somewhere along the Upper Congo.[6] My Aunt Georgiana had been a music teacher at the Boston Conservatory, somewhere back in the latter sixties. One summer, while visiting in the little village among the Green Mountains[7] where her ancestors had dwelt for generations, she had <u>kindled</u> the callow[8] fancy of my uncle, Howard Carpenter, then an idle, shiftless boy of twenty-one. When she returned to her duties in Boston, Howard followed her, and the upshot of this infatuation was that she eloped with him, eluding the <u>reproaches</u> of her family and the criticism of her friends by going

---

1. *Render* means "to make available" or "to provide."
2. *Scourged* means "afflicted."
3. *Chilblains* are red, swollen sores on the skin caused by exposure to the cold.

4. A *duster* is a long, lightweight coat worn to protect one's clothing from dust.
5. *Franz-Joseph-Land* is a group of islands in the Arctic Ocean.
6. The *Congo* River in central Africa is also called the Zaire River.
7. The *Green Mountains* extend from western Massachusetts through Vermont and into Canada.
8. *Callow* means "inexperienced" or "immature."

Vocabulary

legacy (leg′ ə sē) *n.* an inheritance
kindle (kind′ əl) *v.* to stir up; to excite
reproach (ri prōch′) *n.* an expression of disapproval; a reprimand

Boston Commons, 1901. Childe Hassam. Oil on canvas, 16 x 20 in. David David Gallery, Philadelphia.

Viewing the painting: Look closely at the painting. Suppose Aunt Georgiana saw this scene as soon as she arrived in Boston. How might she have reacted? Explain.

with him to the Nebraska frontier. Carpenter, who, of course, had no money, took up a homestead in Red Willow County, fifty miles from the railroad. There they had measured off their land themselves, driving across the prairie in a wagon, to the wheel of which they had tied a red cotton handkerchief, and counting its revolutions. They built a dug-out in the red hillside, one of those cave dwellings whose inmates so often reverted to primitive conditions. Their water they got from the lagoons where the buffalo drank, and their slender stock of provisions was always at the mercy of bands of roving Indians. For thirty years my aunt had not been farther than fifty miles from the homestead.

Did You Know?
Early settlers on the prairie often lived in a *dug-out*, a home dug into the side of a hill or ravine, until they were able to build an above-ground home.

I owed to this woman most of the good that ever came my way in my boyhood, and had a reverential[9] affection for her. During the years when I was riding herd for my uncle, my aunt, after cooking the three meals—the first of which was ready at six o'clock in the morning—and putting the six children to bed, would often stand until midnight at her ironing-board, with me at the kitchen table beside her, hearing me recite Latin declensions and conjugations,[10] gently shaking me when my drowsy head sank down over a page of irregular verbs. It was to her, at her ironing

or mending, that I read my first Shakspere, and her old text-book on mythology was the first that ever came into my empty hands. She taught me my scales and exercises on the little parlor organ which her husband had bought her after fifteen years, during which she had not so much as seen a musical instrument. She would sit beside me by the hour, darning and counting, while I struggled with the "Joyous Farmer."[11] She seldom talked to me about music, and I understood why. Once when I had been <u>doggedly</u> beating out some easy passages from an old score of *Euryanthe*[12] I had found among her music books, she came up to me and, putting her hands over my eyes, gently drew my head back upon her shoulder, saying tremulously,[13] "Don't love it so well, Clark, or it may be taken from you."

When my aunt appeared on the morning after her arrival in Boston, she was still in a semi-somnambulant[14] state. She seemed not to realize that she was in the city where she had spent her youth, the place longed for hungrily half a lifetime. She had been so wretchedly train-sick throughout the journey that she had no recollection of anything but her discomfort, and, to all intents and purposes, there were but a few hours of nightmare between the farm in Red Willow County and my study on Newbury Street. I had planned a little pleasure for her that afternoon, to repay her for some of the glorious moments she had given me when we used to milk together in the straw-thatched cowshed and she, because I was more than usually tired, or because her husband had spoken

---

9. *Reverential* means "with a feeling of deep respect and awe."
10. *Declensions* are different forms of nouns, pronouns, and adjectives. *Conjugations* are different forms of verbs. Students often memorize these forms when learning a new language.
11. *Joyous Farmer* is one of a series of compositions for children by Robert Shumann (1810–1856).
12. *Euryanthe* (ā ûr i än tā) is an opera by the German composer Carl Maria von Weber (1786–1826).
13. *Tremulously* means "in a trembling or shaking manner."
14. *Semi-somnambulant* (sem′ ē   som nam′ byə lənt) means "bewildered or dazed, as if sleepwalking."

Vocabulary
doggedly (dô′ gid lē) *adv.* in a stubbornly persistent manner; obstinately

sharply to me, would tell me of the splendid performance of the *Huguenots*[15] she had seen in Paris, in her youth.

At two o'clock the Symphony Orchestra was to give a Wagner program, and I intended to take my aunt; though, as I conversed with her, I grew doubtful about her enjoyment of it. I suggested our visiting the Conservatory and the Common[16] before lunch, but she seemed altogether too timid to wish to venture out. She questioned me absently about various changes in the city, but she was chiefly concerned that she had forgotten to leave instructions about feeding half-skimmed milk to a certain weakling calf, "old Maggie's calf, you know, Clark," she explained, evidently having forgotten how long I had been away. She was further troubled because she had neglected to tell her daughter about the freshly-opened kit of mackerel in the cellar, which would spoil if it were not used directly.

I asked her whether she had ever heard any of the Wagnerian operas, and found that she had not, though she was perfectly familiar with their respective situations, and had once possessed the piano score of *The Flying Dutchman*. I began to think it would be best to get her back to Red Willow County without waking her, and regretted having suggested the concert.

From the time we entered the concert hall, however, she was a trifle less passive and inert, and for the first time seemed to perceive her surroundings. I had felt some trepidation lest she might become aware of her queer, country clothes, or might experience some painful embarrassment at stepping suddenly into the world to which she had been dead for a quarter of a century. But, again, I found how superficially I had judged her. She sat looking about her with eyes as impersonal, almost as stony, as those with which the granite Rameses[17] in a museum watches the froth and fret that ebbs and flows[18] about his pedestal. I have seen this same aloofness in old miners who drift into the Brown hotel at Denver, their pockets full of bullion,[19] their linen soiled, their haggard faces unshaven; standing in the thronged corridors as solitary as though they were still in a frozen camp on the Yukon.[20]

The matinée audience was made up chiefly of women. One lost the contour of faces and figures, indeed any effect of line whatever, and there was only the color of bodices past counting, the shimmer of fabrics soft and firm, silky and sheer; red, mauve, pink, blue, lilac, purple, écru,[21] rose, yellow, cream, and white, all the colors that an impressionist[22] finds in a sunlit landscape, with here and there the dead shadow of a frock coat. My Aunt Georgiana regarded them as though they had been so many daubs of tube-paint on a palette.

When the musicians came out and took their places, she gave a little stir of anticipation, and looked with quickening interest down over the rail at that invariable grouping, perhaps the first wholly familiar thing that had greeted her eye since she had left old Maggie and her weakling calf. I could feel how all those details sank into her soul, for I had not forgotten how they had sunk into mine when I came fresh from

---

15. *Huguenots* (hū′ gə nots′) is a French opera by the German composer Giacomo Meyerbeer (1791–1864).
16. *Common* refers to Boston Common, a public park.
17. *Rameses* (ram′ ə sēz) is the name shared by several kings of ancient Egypt.
18. *[froth and fret . . . flows]* This phrase refers to the general busy activity that would come and go past a museum statue.
19. Here, *bullion* (bool′ yən) is gold.
20. *Yukon* refers to the Yukon River, a major route to the Klondike gold fields in Canada.
21. *Écru* (ā′ krōō) is beige.
22. An *impressionist* is a member of a movement in French painting that emphasized the play of light and color.

Vocabulary
inert (i nurt′) *adj.* inactive; sluggish
trepidation (trep′ ə dā′ shən) *n.* nervous anticipation; anxiety

ploughing forever and forever between green aisles of corn, where, as in a treadmill, one might walk from daybreak to dusk without perceiving a shadow of change. The clean profiles of the musicians, the gloss of their linen, the dull black of their coats, the beloved shapes of the instruments, the patches of yellow light on the smooth, varnished bellies of the 'cellos and the bass viols in the rear, the restless, wind-tossed forest of fiddle necks and bows—I recalled how, in the first orchestra I ever heard, those long bow-strokes seemed to draw the heart out of me, as a conjurer's stick reels out yards of paper ribbon from a hat.

Did You Know?
The *cello* (short for violon-cello) and the *bass viol* (also called the double bass) are stringed instruments played with a bow. Cellos are usually located on one side of an orchestra, with bass viols on the same side in the back.

The first number was the *Tannhauser* overture. When the horns drew out the first strain of the Pilgrim's chorus, Aunt Georgiana clutched my coat sleeve. Then it was I first realized that for her this broke a silence of thirty years. I saw again the tall, naked house on the prairie, black and grim as a wooden fortress; the black pond where I had learned to swim, its margin pitted with sun-dried cattle tracks; the rain gullied clay banks about the naked house, the four dwarf ash seedlings where the dish-cloths were always hung to dry before the kitchen door. The world there was the flat world of the ancients;[23] to the east, a cornfield that stretched to daybreak; to the west, a corral that reached to sunset; between, the conquests of peace, dearer-bought than those of war.

The overture closed, my aunt released my coat sleeve, but she said nothing. She sat staring dully at the orchestra. What, I wondered, did she get from it? She had been a good pianist in her day, I knew, and her musical education had been broader than that of most music teachers of a quarter of a century ago. She had often told me of Mozart's operas and Meyerbeer's, and I could remember hearing her sing, years ago, certain melodies of Verdi.[24] When I had fallen ill with a fever in her house she used to sit by my cot in the evening—when the cool, night wind blew in through the faded mosquito netting tacked over the window and I lay watching a certain bright star that burned red above the cornfield—and sing "Home to our mountains, O, let us return!" in a way fit to break the heart of a Vermont boy near dead of homesickness already.

I watched her closely through the prelude to *Tristan and Isolde*, trying vainly to conjecture what that seething turmoil of strings and winds might mean to her, but she sat mutely staring at the violin bows that drove obliquely downward, like the pelting streaks of rain in a summer shower. Had this music any message for her? Had she enough left to at all comprehend this power which had kindled the world since she had left it? I was in a fever of curiosity, but Aunt Georgiana sat silent upon her peak in Darien.[25]

---

23. *The ancients* refers to those who lived in classical Greece and Rome.

24. Wolfgang Amadeus *Mozart* (woolf′ gang′   ä′ mə dā′ əs mōt′ särt), 1756–1791, was an Austrian composer. Giuseppe *Verdi* (jo͞o zep′ pe   ver′ dē), 1813–1901, was an Italian composer of opera.

25. The phrase *"peak in Darien"* (där′ ē en′) alludes to the poem "On First Looking into Chapman's Homer" by John Keats. The poem describes Spanish explorers on a mountain in Darien, now Panama, who stand silently and in awe, as the first Europeans to view the Pacific Ocean.

Vocabulary
turmoil (tur′ moil) *n.* a state of confused agitation; commotion
obliquely (ə blēk′ lē) *adv.* in a slanting or sloping direction

Rehearsal of the Pasdeloup Orchestra at the Cirque d'Hiver, 1879-1880. John Singer Sargent. Oil on canvas, 21¾ x 18¼ in. Museum of Fine Arts Boston. Charles Henry Hayden Fund.

Viewing the painting: How does this painting help you sense the "deluge of sound poured on and on"?

turned to my aunt. Her eyes were closed, but the tears were glistening on her cheeks, and I think, in a moment more, they were in my eyes as well. It never really died, then—the soul which can suffer so excruciatingly and so interminably; it withers to the outward eye only; like that strange moss which can lie on a dusty shelf half a century and yet, if placed in water, grows green again. She wept so throughout the development and elaboration of the melody.

During the intermission before the second half, I questioned my aunt and found that the "Prize Song" was not new to her. Some years before there had drifted to the farm in Red Willow County a young German, a tramp cowpuncher,[26] who had sung in the chorus at Bayreuth[27] when he was a boy, along with the other peasant boys and girls. Of a Sunday morning he used to sit on his gingham-sheeted bed in the hands' bedroom which opened off the kitchen, cleaning the leather of his boots and saddle, singing the "Prize

She preserved this utter immobility throughout the number from *The Flying Dutchman*, though her fingers worked mechanically upon her black dress, as if, of themselves, they were recalling the piano score they had once played. Poor hands! They had been stretched and twisted into mere tentacles to hold and lift and knead with; on one of them a thin, worn band that had once been a wedding ring. As I pressed and gently quieted one of those groping hands, I remembered with quivering eyelids their services for me in other days.

Soon after the tenor began the "Prize Song," I heard a quick drawn breath and

26. *Cowpuncher* means "cowboy."
27. *Bayreuth* (bī roit´) is a German city famous for its annual Wagnerian music festival.

Song," while my aunt went about her work in the kitchen. She had hovered over him until she had <u>prevailed</u> upon him to join the country church, though his sole fitness for this step, in so far as I could gather, lay in his boyish face and his possession of this divine melody. Shortly afterward, he had gone to town on the Fourth of July, been drunk for several days, lost his money at a faro[28] table, ridden a saddled Texas steer on a bet, and disappeared with a fractured collar-bone. All this my aunt told me huskily, wanderingly, as though she were talking in the weak lapses of illness.

"Well, we have come to better things than the old *Trovatore*[29] at any rate, Aunt Georgie?" I queried, with a well meant effort at jocularity.[30]

Her lip quivered and she hastily put her handkerchief up to her mouth. From behind it she murmured, "And you have been hearing this ever since you left me, Clark?" Her question was the gentlest and saddest of reproaches.

The second half of the program consisted of four numbers from the *Ring,* and closed with Siegfried's funeral march. My aunt wept quietly, but almost continuously, as a shallow vessel overflows in a rain-storm. From time to time her dim eyes looked up at the lights, burning softly under their dull glass globes.

The <u>deluge</u> of sound poured on and on; I never knew what she found in the shining current of it; I never knew how far it bore her, or past what happy islands. From the trembling of her face I could well believe that before the last number she had been carried out where the myriad[31] graves are, into the grey, nameless burying grounds of the sea; or into some world of death vaster yet, where, from the beginning of the world, hope has lain down with hope and dream with dream and, renouncing,[32] slept.

The concert was over; the people filed out of the hall chattering and laughing, glad to relax and find the living level again, but my kinswoman made no effort to rise. The harpist slipped the green felt cover over his instrument; the flute-players shook the water from their mouthpieces; the men of the orchestra went out one by one, leaving the stage to the chairs and music stands, empty as a winter cornfield.

I spoke to my aunt. She burst into tears and sobbed pleadingly. "I don't want to go, Clark, I don't want to go!"

I understood. For her, just outside the concert hall, lay the black pond with the cattle-tracked bluffs; the tall, unpainted house, with weather-curled boards, naked as a tower; the crook-backed ash seedlings where the dish-cloths hung to dry; the gaunt,[33] moulting turkeys picking up refuse about the kitchen door.

---

28. *Faro* (fār′ō) is a gambling game played with a deck of cards.
29. *Trovatore* (tro və tōr′e) refers to *Il Trovatore,* an opera by Giuseppe Verdi.
30. *Jocularity* means "joking" or "humor."

31. *Myriad* means "countless" or "innumerable."
32. *Renouncing* means "giving up."
33. *Gaunt* means "extremely thin."

Vocabulary
prevail (pri vāl′) *v.* to use persuasion successfully
deluge (del′ ūj) *n.* anything that overwhelms or rushes like a flood

Responding to Literature

Personal Response

What went through your mind as you read about Aunt Georgiana's reaction to the concert?

ANALYZING LITERATURE

RECALL

1. How does the narrator react to the letter from his uncle?
2. What changes occurred in Aunt Georgiana's life after she married?
3. The narrator says that he owed to his aunt "most of the good that ever came my way in my boyhood." What is he grateful for?
4. Why does the narrator grow doubtful that his aunt will enjoy the concert? How does she react to it?
5. How does Aunt Georgiana behave after the concert ends? How does the narrator explain this behavior?

INTERPRET

6. Why, do you think, does the narrator react so strongly to his uncle's letter?
7. What, in your opinion, did Aunt Georgiana give up in getting married and moving to Nebraska? Explain, using details from the story.
8. What do the narrator's thoughts and observations about his aunt reveal about his own character and personality?
9. Why do you think the concert affects Aunt Georgiana so deeply?
10. At the end of the story, what does the concert hall seem to symbolize for Aunt Georgiana?

EVALUATE AND CONNECT

11. How do Cather's descriptions of the Boston concert hall and the Nebraska prairie help you better understand the **theme,** or central message, of this story? Explain.
12. Look back at your response to the Focus Activity on page 531. How does your real or imagined experience with moving compare with Aunt Georgiana's experience?
13. How has this story affected your impressions of frontier life? Organize your response in a spider diagram like the one shown.
14. Describe a time when you experienced a deep, emotional response to a work of art, such as a painting, a poem, or a piece of music.
15. In what ways do the musical references contribute to or detract from your understanding of the story?

Literary ELEMENTS

Point of View

Point of view refers to the relationship of the narrator, or storyteller, to the story. The first-person pronouns *I, my,* and *me* in the opening paragraph of "A Wagner Matinée" reveal that this story is told from the **first-person point of view.** Everything that the reader learns is filtered through the eyes, ears, and thoughts of the narrator, a character named Clark.

1. How does the narrator help the reader understand Aunt Georgiana and her life? Use details from the story to support your answer.
2. How might the story be different if it had been told from Georgiana's point of view instead of Clark's? Give specific examples.

● See **Literary Terms Handbook,** p. R12.

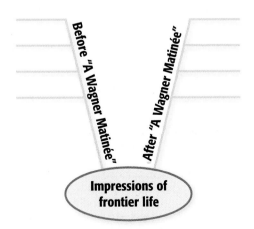

Before "A Wagner Matinée" After "A Wagner Matinée"

Impressions of frontier life

LITERATURE AND WRITING

Writing About Literature

Analyze Comparisons   Willa Cather compares Georgiana to an explorer, to a statue, and to moss; she compares aisles of corn to a treadmill, bowstrokes to the action of a conjurer's stick, and music to a water current. Choose a comparison and write a paragraph explaining how it contributes to the story's meaning.

Creative Writing

The Beat Goes On   Put yourself in Georgiana's place. Imagine that you have recently returned to your Nebraska home. Write a thank-you letter to Clark, updating him on your life since your return. Share with him your impressions of your visit to Boston and your trip home. Also include your thoughts about being back on the farm.

EXTENDING YOUR RESPONSE

Literature Groups

Time for a Rest?   In your group, discuss these questions: What might happen if Georgiana decided to stay in Boston for an extended vacation? Would she feel at home there? Why or why not? How might she spend her time? Who would do her work back home in Nebraska? Would she find it difficult to finally return home? Be sure to support your opinions with specific details from the story. Then summarize your group's opinions for the class.

Interdisciplinary Connection

Music: Appreciating Wagner   Locate a recording of one of Richard Wagner's operas and research the story behind it. Play some of the recording for the class, explaining the story.

Learning for Life

Mapping a Route   Aunt Georgiana traveled by train from Nebraska to Boston. Research and create a map that shows the route the train would have traveled (in about 1900), the terrain through which it would have passed, and major geographical landmarks along the way.

Reading Further

You might enjoy these novels by Willa Cather:

My Ántonia and *O Pioneers!* explore the life of the early pioneers in Nebraska.

📖 **Save your work for your portfolio.**

Skill Minilesson

VOCABULARY • Analogies

Analogies are comparisons based on relationships between words and ideas. The relationship in some analogies is that of an action and its significance.

    kiss : affection :: scowl : anger

A *kiss* is a sign of *affection;* a *scowl* is a sign of *anger.*

    To finish an analogy, decide what relationship is represented by the first pair of words. Then apply that relationship to the second pair.

● For more on analogies, see **Communications Skills Handbook**, p. R83.

PRACTICE   Choose the word that best completes each analogy.

1. reproaches : disapproval :: compliments :
   a. criticism   b. approval   c. affection
2. sweat : trepidation :: wink :
   a. anxiety   b. blink   c. mischief
3. riot : turmoil :: truce :
   a. peace   b. noise   c. conflict

Before You Read

Douglass and *We Wear the Mask*

Meet Paul Laurence Dunbar

"I know why the caged bird sings!"

—Dunbar

These words, perhaps better than any, describe the complex plight of Paul Laurence Dunbar. To get a hearing for his poetry he often felt he had to "sing" within the constraints of taste and prejudice that dominated his times.

One of the first African American writers to attain national recognition, Dunbar was the son of formerly enslaved people from Kentucky. Their stories of pre-Emancipation days would provide a sea of material for his work.

Dunbar was the only African American student at his Dayton, Ohio, high school. There he excelled at his studies, edited the school paper, and became class president. Despite his success in school, however, the adult world was reluctant to give Dunbar a chance to prove himself. When he could not find a job in a newspaper or a legal office because of his color, he took a four-dollar-a-week elevator operator job. Between calls for the elevator, he wrote.

Dunbar took out a loan to publish his first volume of poetry, *Oak and Ivy*. His second volume, *Majors and Minors*, came out in 1895. When the influential writer and critic William Dean Howells favorably reviewed it, Dunbar found himself famous. Much to Dunbar's growing despair, however, the poems that got a hearing were not those written with serious artistic intent, but those written in black dialect that he called "jingles in a broken tongue."

Paul Laurence Dunbar was born in 1872 and died in 1906.

FOCUS ACTIVITY

Do you sometimes feel that you have to "wear" more than one face? Are you one person at home, another at school, and yet another when you are out with friends?

SKETCH IT! Draw pictures showing different faces you might "wear" in different situations.

SETTING A PURPOSE Read "We Wear the Mask" to understand why some people show different faces at different times.

BACKGROUND

The Poet's Twin Masks

Who was Paul Laurence Dunbar? Was he a "city person" who in just one generation had lost touch with the reality of his parents' lives in slavery? Or was he a poet who understood his primarily white audience well enough to give them the poetry they wanted?

Dunbar wrote two kinds of poetry. Although he was known and loved for his sentimental verse, written in dialect, about an idyllic, pastoral, pre–Civil War plantation life, he has sometimes been criticized for this work and for failing to confront the issues of racial stereotypes and discrimination. However, Dunbar also produced poems in Standard English that meditate on love, nature, or death; express pride in African Americans; or lament thwarted efforts to live and create freely.

Douglass

Paul Laurence Dunbar

Ah, Douglass,° we have fall'n on evil days,
    Such days as thou, not even thou didst know,
    When thee, the eyes of that harsh long ago
Saw, salient,° at the cross of devious ways,
5   And all the country heard thee with amaze.
    Not ended then, the passionate ebb and flow,°
    The awful tide that battled to and fro;
We ride amid a tempest° of dispraise.°

Now, when the waves of swift dissension° swarm,
10   And Honor, the strong pilot, lieth stark,°
Oh, for thy voice high-sounding o'er the storm,
    For thy strong arm to guide the shivering bark,°
The blast-defying power of thy form,
    To give us comfort through the lonely dark.

---

1 Frederick *Douglass* escaped from slavery and became
  a great speaker and leader in the abolition movement.
4 *Salient* (sāl′ yənt) means "prominent" or "noticeable."
6 *Ebb and flow* means "fall and rise."
8 A *tempest* is a violent storm. *Dispraise* is disapproval.
9 *Dissension* means "disagreement" or "discord."
10 *Stark* means "stiffly" or "rigidly."
12 A *bark* is a type of boat.

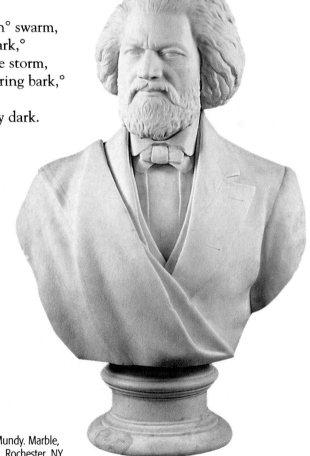

Frederick Douglass, 1873. Johnson Mundy. Marble,
height: 36 in. University of Rochester, Rochester, NY.

We Wear the Mask

Paul Laurence Dunbar ～

Lenox Avenue, c. 1938. Sargent Claude Johnson. Lithograph, 31.7 x 21.8 cm. National Museum of American Art, Washington, DC.

We wear the mask that grins and lies,
It hides our cheeks and shades our eyes,—
This debt we pay to human guile;°
With torn and bleeding hearts we smile,
5   And mouth with myriad° subtleties.°

Why should the world be overwise,
In counting all our tears and sighs?
Nay, let them only see us, while
     We wear the mask.

10   We smile, but, O great Christ, our cries
To thee from tortured souls arise.
We sing, but oh the clay is vile°
Beneath our feet, and long the mile;
But let the world dream otherwise,
15   We wear the mask!

---

3 *Guile* is deceit or slyness.
5 *Myriad* means "countless" or "innumerable." *Subtleties* are things so slight that they are barely perceptible.
12 *Vile* means "repulsive" or "disgusting."

Responding to Literature

Personal Response

Which lines in these poems had the greatest emotional impact on you? Explain your choices.

ANALYZING LITERATURE

Douglass

RECALL AND INTERPRET

1. Summarize what the speaker tells Douglass about the present time. How does the present compare with Douglass's time? Explain.
2. What does the speaker wish that Douglass could do? What does this wish seem to suggest about the problems of the present?

EVALUATE AND CONNECT

3. What **extended metaphor** does the speaker use (see page R6)? Evaluate how well this metaphor represents the struggle the speaker is describing.
4. Do you think the **theme**, or central message, of the poem is relevant today? Why or why not?

We Wear the Mask

RECALL AND INTERPRET

5. What words does the speaker use to describe the mask? Who wears the mask, and why must it be worn?
6. What reality is hidden behind the mask? What words and images describe that reality?

EVALUATE AND CONNECT

7. Look at the sketches you made for the Focus Activity on page 542. Do you "wear" different faces by choice, or are you forced to do so? Explain.
8. Why do you think Dunbar wrote this poem in Standard English rather than in dialect? How does this choice reinforce the speaker's **theme?**

Literary ELEMENTS

Sonnet

A **sonnet** is a fourteen-line poem typically written in **iambic pentameter**—a pattern of five stresses per line, each unstressed syllable followed by a stressed one. "Douglass" is a **Petrarchan**, or **Italian, sonnet**, which consists of two stanzas. The first stanza, an **octave**, contains eight lines and presents a situation, a question, or an idea; it is usually rhymed *abbaabba*. The second

stanza, a **sestet**, contains six lines and provides a resolution, an answer, or a comment; it is usually rhymed *cdecde* or *cdcdcd*.

1. What situation or problem is presented in the first stanza of "Douglass"?
2. What resolution is wished for in the second stanza?

● See **Literary Terms Handbook**, p. R15.

Before You Read

Lucinda Matlock and *Fiddler Jones*

Meet Edgar Lee Masters

"It is all very well, but for myself I know
I stirred certain vibrations in Spoon River
Which are my true epitaph, more lasting than stone."

—Masters

Edgar Lee Masters's poetry collection *Spoon River Anthology* did stir vibrations in early twentieth-century American literature. Its realism and irony contrasted sharply with the romantic and sentimental literature popular at the time.

Masters grew up in the small Illinois towns of Petersburg and Lewistown. As a boy, he spent a lot of time at his grandfather's farm where he fished, rode horses, and read. After graduating from high school, he worked as an apprentice for a local printer.

Although Masters wanted to study literature and be a writer, his father pushed him toward a career in law. So Masters took up both pursuits: he moved to Chicago and practiced law while also writing poetry, novels, essays, and biographies. Of all his works, *Spoon River Anthology* stands out for its originality and influence.

On Masters's tombstone in Petersburg appears this verse from his poem "Tomorrow is My Birthday":

"Good friends, let's to the fields . . .
After a little walk, and by your pardon
I think I'll sleep. There is no sweeter thing
Nor fate more blessed than to sleep."

Edgar Lee Masters was born in 1869 and died in 1950.

FOCUS ACTIVITY

Has an older person ever shared with you what he or she has learned from life? Have you done the same for someone younger than you?

LIST IDEAS If you were to sum up your life, what experiences would you share? What meaning would you find in those experiences? List your ideas.

SETTING A PURPOSE Read to learn how two speakers view their experiences.

BACKGROUND

Spoon River Anthology

When Edgar Lee Masters read the epigrams from the *Greek Anthology*—a collection of about 3,700 short poems—he was struck by their brevity, wit, and irony. He decided to write a similar collection comprising free-verse epitaphs in the form of monologues. The result was *Spoon River Anthology*. The dead inhabitants of a small midwestern town deliver the monologues with direct, sometimes frightening, honesty—after death there is nothing to hide. Because many of the monologues are related, a complex history of numerous families unfolds.

Who Am I?

The characters in *Spoon River Anthology* were inspired by people Masters knew in Petersburg and Lewistown. "Lucinda Matlock" is based on Lucinda Masters, the poet's grandmother. According to Masters, she was a simple, good-natured person who really did meet her future husband at a dance in Chandlerville, was married for seventy years, and died at the age of ninety-six.

Lucinda Matlock

Edgar Lee Masters

Woman at the Piano, c. 1917. Elie Nadelman. Wood, stained and painted, 35⅛ x 23¼ x 9 in., including base. The Museum of Modern Art, New York. Philip L. Goodwin Collection.

I went to the dances at Chandlerville,
And played snap-out° at Winchester.
One time we changed partners,
Driving home in the moonlight of middle June,
5   And then I found Davis.
We were married and lived together for seventy years,
Enjoying, working, raising the twelve children,
Eight of whom we lost
Ere I had reached the age of sixty.
10   I spun, I wove, I kept the house, I nursed the sick,
I made the garden, and for holiday
Rambled over the fields where sang the larks,
And by Spoon River gathering many a shell,
And many a flower and medicinal weed—
15   Shouting to the wooded hills, singing to the green valleys.
At ninety-six I had lived enough, that is all,
And passed to a sweet repose.°
What is this I hear of sorrow and weariness,
Anger, discontent and drooping hopes?
20   Degenerate° sons and daughters,
Life is too strong for you—
It takes life to love Life.

---

2 *Snap-out* (also known as crack-the-whip) is a game in which players link hands in a line and then run or skate so as to shake off those at the end of the line.

17 *Repose* means "rest"; here, it refers to death.

20 Here, *degenerate* (di jen′ ər it) means "having declined in condition or character."

Fiddler Jones

Edgar Lee Masters

Just in Tune, 1849. William Sidney Mount. Oil on canvas, 30 x 25 in. The Museums at Stony Brook, NY. Gift of Mr. and Mrs. Ward Melville.

The earth keeps some vibration going
There in your heart, and that is you.
And if the people find you can fiddle,
Why, fiddle you must, for all your life.
5   What do you see, a harvest of clover?
Or a meadow to walk through to the river?
The wind's in the corn; you rub your hands
For beeves° hereafter ready for market;
Or else you hear the rustle of skirts
10   Like the girls when dancing at Little Grove.
To Cooney Potter a pillar of dust
Or whirling leaves meant ruinous drouth;°
They looked to me like Red-Head Sammy
Stepping it off, to "Toor-a-Loor."°
15   How could I till my forty acres
Not to speak of getting more,
With a medley of horns, bassoons and piccolos
Stirred in my brain by crows and robins
And the creak of a wind-mill—only these?
20   And I never started to plow in my life
That some one did not stop in the road
And take me away to a dance or picnic.
I ended up with forty acres;
I ended up with a broken fiddle—
25   And a broken laugh, and a thousand memories,
And not a single regret.

---

8 *Beeves* is the plural form of *beef;* here, it refers to beef cattle.
12 A *drouth* (also *drought*) is a long period of dry weather.
14 *Toor-a-Loor* refers to a phrase in an Irish folk song.

Responding to Literature

Personal Response

Do you know anyone whose outlook resembles that of Lucinda Matlock or Fiddler Jones? Explain.

ANALYZING LITERATURE

Lucinda Matlock

RECALL AND INTERPRET

1. Describe how Lucinda Matlock spent her life. What were her joys? her sorrows?
2. What can you infer about Lucinda's character and outlook on life, based on the information she gives in lines 1–17? Support your answer, using details from the poem.
3. What is Lucinda talking about in lines 18–22? What do you think she means when she says, "It takes life to love Life"?
4. Describe Lucinda's **tone,** or attitude toward her subject, in lines 1–17. How does her tone change in lines 18–22? What might you infer from this change?

EVALUATE AND CONNECT

5. Find several examples of **alliteration** and describe the effect created by the repetition of initial consonant sounds.
6. Theme Connections   What advice might Lucinda give about facing the ups and downs of everyday life?
7. What simple pleasures in life do you most enjoy? Explain why.

Fiddler Jones

RECALL AND INTERPRET

8. What does Fiddler Jones say you must do if people find out that you can fiddle? What does this statement suggest about his outlook on life?
9. In lines 5–14, Fiddler describes different ways of perceiving the same things. Summarize these descriptions. What point do you think he is trying to make?
10. What reasons does Fiddler give for neglecting his farm? How does he seem to feel about his work habits?
11. What did Fiddler Jones have at the end of his life? Why might he have had no regrets?

EVALUATE AND CONNECT

12. What does Fiddler's philosophy of life seem to be? What do you think of his philosophy?
13. Theme Connections   Do you think Fiddler's life exemplifies "the energy of the everyday"? Give reasons for your answer.
14. Apply the statement in lines 1–2 to your own life. What "vibration" is at the center of your heart and your life? How does this force define who you are?

Literary ELEMENTS

Dramatic Monologue

A **dramatic monologue** is a form of dramatic poetry in which a single speaker addresses a silent audience. "Lucinda Matlock" and "Fiddler Jones" appear among a group of interrelated dramatic monologues in *Spoon River Anthology*. The speakers, who lived and died in Spoon River, all have something to say about their lives, and they want their audience–the living–to heed the lessons they have learned.

1. What did you learn about the meaning of life by reading "Lucinda Matlock" and "Fiddler Jones"?
2. Paraphrase one of the dramatic monologues you have just read. Do you think this work would be as effective in prose as it is in poetry? Explain your response.

◐ See **Literary Terms Handbook,** p. R5.

LITERATURE AND WRITING

Writing About Literature

Comparing Characters   Write several paragraphs in which you compare and contrast Lucinda Matlock and Fiddler Jones. What is similar about their outlooks and philosophies of life? What is different? How did they spend their lives? What was most important to each character? Do you think they would agree about what constitutes a good life? Why or why not?

Personal Writing

The Meaning of Life   Review the ideas you listed in response to the Focus Activity on page 546. What ideas would you add or change, now that you have read two poems about the meaning of life? After revising your list of ideas, write a statement that expresses your own philosophy of life.

EXTENDING YOUR RESPONSE

Literature Groups

What's the Scoop?   Lucinda Matlock and Fiddler Jones apparently led very active, full lives. Readers learn about the characters in a general way, but the details are missing. As a group, devise a list of questions that you would like to ask these characters. After you write the questions, discuss possible answers. Share your questions and answers with the class.

Performing

Dramatic Monologue   Prepare a dramatic reading of "Lucinda Matlock" or "Fiddler Jones." As you practice your monologue, try to vary the volume, pitch, and tone of your voice to communicate the speaker's message more effectively. You may want to use facial expressions and hand or body gestures to dramatize your presentation. Perform your monologue for your classmates.

Interdisciplinary Activity

Art: Character Sketch   After reading the two poems, can you imagine what each speaker might have looked like? Make a sketch of either Lucinda Matlock or Fiddler Jones. You might show the character engaged in an activity described in the poem. Share your sketch with the class.

Reading Further

You might enjoy another depiction of small-town America in the early twentieth century:

Our Town, by Thorton Wilder, is a play that affirms the simple values of life in a New Hampshire village.

📖 **Save your work for your portfolio.**

Grammar Link

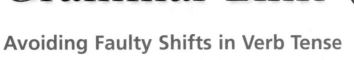

Avoiding Faulty Shifts in Verb Tense

Verb tenses indicate when an action occurs, so good writers pay close attention to the tenses they use. For example, "The author <u>reflected</u> on the books she <u>wrote</u>" means that the writing and the reflecting took place at the same time. But "The author <u>reflected</u> on the books she <u>had written</u>" means that she wrote the books and then reflected on them.

To make your writing clear, avoid the problems below.

Problem 1 An unnecessary shift in tense
In Edgar Lee Masters's poem "Fiddler Jones," the narrator is a farmer who plays the fiddle and ignored his plow.

Solution When two or more events occur at the same time, use the same verb tense to describe each event.
In Edgar Lee Masters's poem "Fiddler Jones," the narrator is a farmer who plays the fiddle and ignores his plow.

Problem 2 A failure to shift tenses to show that one event precedes or follows another
The narrator <u>didn't regret</u> that he <u>chose</u> music over farming.

Solution When the events being described have occurred at different times, shift tenses to show that one event precedes or follows another. Use the past perfect tense for the earlier action.
The narrator <u>didn't regret</u> that he <u>had chosen</u> music over farming.

● For more about verb tenses, see **Language Handbook,** pp. R26–R27.

EXERCISE

Rewrite the following paragraph, correcting any errors in shifting tenses.

> The poem "Lucinda Matlock" taught me an important lesson about life: that we should be grateful for all the experiences we have. As a young woman, Lucinda Matlock went to dances and stayed out late until she meets her husband, Davis. They got married and raised twelve children together. With her family, Lucinda finds out what life was about. She cleaned house, mended clothes, works in the garden, and helped the sick. By the time Lucinda turns sixty, eight of her children died. When she was ninety-six, she died. Her life was full of hard work, and she doesn't want it any other way.

Before You Read

Richard Cory and *Miniver Cheevy*

Meet Edwin Arlington Robinson

"You eyes, you large and all-
   inquiring Eyes,
That look so dubiously into me,
And are not satisfied with what
   you see,
Tell me the worst and let us have
   no lies"

—*Robinson*

Edwin Arlington Robinson himself had those inquiring eyes—eyes that searched, understood, and empathized with the people he knew.

Robinson grew up in Gardiner, Maine, the model for the fictional Tilbury Town where many of his most famous poems are set. From an early age, he felt "doomed, or elected, or sentenced for life, to the writing of poetry." As a high school student, he practiced writing in intricate verse forms under the guidance of a local poet. He continued to write during the two years he attended Harvard University.

There, he also read widely and published several poems. In 1893 financial problems forced Robinson to leave college and return home. He did, however, manage to publish two books of poems at his own expense.

At age twenty-eight, Robinson moved to New York City where he kept writing while living in poverty. President Theodore Roosevelt, who had read and admired some of his poems, came to Robinson's rescue by arranging a position for him at the U.S. Customs House in New York. Robinson dedicated his third collection, *The Town Down by the River*, to the president.

From the age of forty-one, Robinson devoted himself entirely to his writing. Eventually, he won three Pulitzer Prizes and became one of America's favorite poets.

Edwin Arlington Robinson was born in 1869 and died in 1935.

FOCUS ACTIVITY

Have you ever felt extreme sadness?

QUICKWRITE Spend five minutes writing about a time when you felt very sad. What was the cause? How did you deal with the situation?

SETTING A PURPOSE Read to learn about two unhappy characters.

BACKGROUND

The Time and Place

More than sixty of Robinson's best poems are set in Tilbury Town, a fictional setting modeled on the poet's hometown, Gardiner, Maine. The characters that Robinson portrayed tend to be loners and misfits as Robinson often felt himself to be. They live in places where people feel pressured to conform, and where the creative genius is ignored or misunderstood.

Gardiner, Maine, 1896.

John Lowell Gardner II, 1888. Dennis Miller Bunker. Oil on canvas, 50 x 36 in. Portland Museum of Art, ME.

Richard Cory

Edwin Arlington Robinson ∾

Whenever Richard Cory went down town,
We people on the pavement looked at him:
He was a gentleman from sole to crown,
Clean favored,° and imperially° slim.

5   And he was always quietly arrayed,°
And he was always human when he talked;
But still he fluttered pulses when he said,
"Good-morning," and he glittered when he walked.

And he was rich—yes, richer than a king—
10 And admirably schooled in every grace:
In fine,° we thought that he was everything
To make us wish that we were in his place.

So on we worked, and waited for the light,
And went without the meat, and cursed the bread;
15 And Richard Cory, one calm summer night,
Went home and put a bullet through his head.

4 Clean favored: having a tidy appearance. **imperially:** majestically; magnificently.
5 arrayed: dressed.

11 In fine: in short.

Miniver Cheevy

Edwin Arlington Robinson

Miniver Cheevy, child of scorn,
    Grew lean while he assailed the seasons;
He wept that he was ever born,
    And he had reasons.

5   Miniver loved the days of old
    When swords were bright and steeds were prancing;
The vision of a warrior bold
    Would set him dancing.

Miniver sighed for what was not,
10   And dreamed, and rested from his labors;
He dreamed of Thebes° and Camelot,°
    And Priam's° neighbors.

Miniver mourned the ripe renown
    That made so many a name so fragrant;
15   He mourned Romance, now on the town,°
    And Art, a vagrant.

Miniver loved the Medici,°
    Albeit he had never seen one;
He would have sinned incessantly
20   Could he have been one.

Miniver cursed the commonplace
    And eyed a khaki suit with loathing;
He missed the mediæval grace
    Of iron clothing.

25   Miniver scorned the gold he sought,
    But sore annoyed was he without it;
Miniver thought, and thought, and thought,
    And thought about it.

Miniver Cheevy, born too late,
30   Scratched his head and kept on thinking;
Miniver coughed, and called it fate,
    And kept on drinking.

11 Thebes (thēbz): a city-state in ancient Greece. **Camelot:** the legendary site of King Arthur's court.
12 Priam: in Homer's *Iliad,* King of Troy.

15 on the town: on welfare.

17 Medici (med′ i chē): a noble, rich, and powerful family in Florence, Italy (1300–1500).

Responding to Literature

Personal Response

What was your reaction to the last line in each poem? Give reasons for your answer.

ANALYZING LITERATURE

Richard Cory

RECALL AND INTERPRET

1. Summarize the speaker's description of Richard Cory. In what ways does Cory's life differ from the lives of the "people on the pavement"?
2. What does Richard Cory do "one calm summer night"? What does this action seem to suggest about the people's view of his life?

EVALUATE AND CONNECT

3. Evaluate how the poet's choice of speaker adds to your understanding of the poem's **theme,** or central message.
4. Explain why Richard Cory's fate is an example of **situational irony** (see page R8).
5. Have you ever envied someone, only to find out that his or her life was quite different from your perception of it? Explain.

Miniver Cheevy

RECALL AND INTERPRET

6. Describe how Miniver Cheevy spends his time. What does he seem to want from life? Do you think he can ever attain it? Why or why not?
7. What does Cheevy blame for his unhappiness? What do you think is the real reason he is unhappy? Explain.

EVALUATE AND CONNECT

8. How does the speaker's **tone** affect your attitude toward Cheevy (see page R16)?
9. Review your response to the Focus Activity on page 552. Compare your experience and the way you handled it with the way Cheevy copes with his own situation.
10. If you could live in a different time and place, what would you choose? Why?

EXTENDING YOUR RESPONSE

Listening and Speaking

Talk to Cheevy   With a partner, create a dialogue for a heart-to-heart talk with Miniver Cheevy in which you try to help him deal with his problems in a more constructive way. After creating and practicing the dialogue, present it to the class, with one partner playing the role of Cheevy and the other playing the role of a concerned friend.

Learning for Life

Crisis Intervention   What resources does your community offer for people such as Richard Cory or Miniver Cheevy—people who are depressed or suicidal, or those who abuse drugs or alcohol? Research available resources and create a brochure listing the services offered. Be sure to include names, addresses, and telephone numbers.

📖 **Save your work for your portfolio.**

Reading & Thinking Skills

Making Inferences

Your friend took a difficult test last period. Now she's walking toward you down the school hallway, smiling and brimming with energy. What conclusion could you draw, based on your friend's behavior and your knowledge of her previous activity? If you conclude that your friend felt she did well on the test, you are making an **inference,** an educated guess based on the available evidence and your own knowledge and experience.

Good readers constantly make inferences. They look for the following types of clues to help them understand what is happening in a selection:

- descriptive details
- events
- actions
- dialogue
- changes in the author's writing style
- their own knowledge and experience

The details in the first three stanzas of the poem "Richard Cory" might lead readers to infer that Cory led a full and rewarding life. However, the last stanza of the poem indicates that this inference is incorrect. Good readers revise their inferences when they come across new evidence.

You may have heard people confuse the words *imply* and *infer.* Remember that writers and speakers imply, or suggest. Readers and listeners infer, or draw conclusions. In his poems, Edwin Arlington Robinson makes implications; in response, his readers draw inferences.

Can different readers sometimes make different inferences concerning the same reading selection? Of course! Each of us applies his or her knowledge and experiences to the selection, so inferences can vary. In "Richard Cory," for example, some readers might infer that the towns-people were respectful, while others might infer that they were jealous. Discovering how differently others react to a reading selection can make class discussions unpredictable and fun.

● For more about making inferences, see **Reading Handbook,** pp. R86–R93.

EXERCISES

Reread "Richard Cory," then write your answers to these questions.

1. What inferences can you make about the main character?

2. What details from the poem support your inferences?

3. What personal knowledge or experience tells you that your inferences are correct?

Before You Read

The Open Boat

Meet Stephen Crane

"A man said to the universe:
'Sir, I exist!'
'However,' replied the
universe,
'The fact has not created
in me
A sense of obligation.'"

—*Crane*

Stephen Crane lived a life of rebellion—against his strict upbringing, his school and university, and what he considered a poorly regulated, unjust society.

As the fourteenth and youngest child of a Methodist minister, Crane first chafed against the constraints of his structured family life. The restrictions of university life, however, didn't agree with him any better. During his time at Syracuse University, Crane spent more time on the baseball diamond and on writing than he did in the classroom.

When he was twenty-two, Crane moved to New York City where he lived with medical students and magazine illustrators in a dilapidated boardinghouse in one of the city's slums. There he collected firsthand information for his first novel, *Maggie: a Girl of the Streets*. After several shocked publishers rejected the novel because of its frank, realistic depiction of life in the slums of New York City, Crane published it himself under a pseudonym. A few reviewers praised the book, but it did not sell well.

Crane continued to struggle as a journalist and began work on another novel. Befriended by the influential critic William Dean Howells, Crane's break came in 1895 with the publication of *The Red Badge of Courage: An Episode of the American Civil War*. This book, along with his first book of poems, *The Black Riders and Other Lines*, catapulted Crane into international literary fame.

Fascinated with danger and war, Crane went to Greece to cover the Greco-Turkish War for the *New York Journal*, and later, in 1898, to Cuba to cover the Spanish-American War for the *New York World* and then for the *Journal*.

In 1899 Crane settled in Sussex, England, but by this time, Crane was in a fierce battle against debts and illness. Years of exposure, poor food, and failure on his part to treat his tuberculosis and recurrent malarial fever finally proved fatal. Crane died while dictating notes for his final novel, *The O'Ruddy*. He was only twenty-eight years old.

"The good writers are Henry James, Stephen Crane, and Mark Twain. That's not the order they're good in. There is no order for good writers."

—*Ernest Hemingway*

Stephen Crane was born in 1871 and died in 1900.

FOCUS ACTIVITY

What might it be like to fight for your life after surviving a terrible accident?

DISCUSS Imagine that you have survived an airplane crash. You and your fellow survivors are in a remote, isolated area and have no way of calling for help. The nearest town is many miles away. Will you have enough courage, strength, and luck to survive? In a small group, discuss possible scenarios.

SETTING A PURPOSE Read about four men who struggle to survive after a terrible accident.

BACKGROUND

The Time and Place

On January 1, 1897, Stephen Crane was aboard the steamship *Commodore,* traveling from Jacksonville, Florida, to Cuba. The ship was on a mission to carry arms to Cuban rebels who were fighting for independence from Spain. On the morning of January 2, the ship sank. Crane and three others then faced a raging sea in a ten-foot dinghy. Crane wrote an account of the struggle for the *New York Press.* Five months later, he published his fictionalized account in *Scribner's Magazine.* The following year, the tale became the title story in Crane's book, *The Open Boat and Other Tales of Adventure.*

Literary Trends

Stephen Crane was one of the first writers to embrace a frank, often pessimistic realism in his work. He made no attempt to apologize for what he wrote. From his experience as a journalist he learned to be direct, precise, and accurate. He wrote about the way it was—not the way readers might wish it to be.

Crane was remarkable at creating and balancing contradiction. In "The Open Boat," the characters are pulled between self-pity and anger; illusion and reality; hope and despair.

The *New York Journal*'s depiction of the steamship *Commodore.*

VOCABULARY PREVIEW

profound (prə found′) *adj.* coming from the depth of one's being; intensely felt; p. 560

uncanny (un ka′ nē) *adj.* strangely unsettling; eerie; p. 562

emphatic (em fa′ tik) *adj.* forceful; p. 562

ingenuously (in jen′ ū əs lē) *adv.* honestly; frankly; candidly; p. 564

impudently (im′ pyə dənt lē) *adv.* in an offensively bold manner; arrogantly; p. 565

preposterous (pri pos′ tər əs) *adj.* absurd; ridiculous; p. 566

impious (im′ pē əs) *adj.* lacking in reverence; disrespectful; p. 568

coerce (kō urs′) *v.* to force; p. 573

Moonlit Shipwreck at Sea, 1901. Thomas Moran. Oil on canvas, 76.2 x 102.2 cm. Private collection.

The Open Boat

Stephen Crane ~

*A tale intended to be after the fact. Being the experience of
four men from the sunk steamer* Commodore . . .

The Open Boat

I

None of them knew the color of the sky. Their eyes glanced level, and were fastened upon the waves that swept toward them. These waves were of the hue of slate, save for the tops, which were of foaming white, and all of the men knew the colors of the sea. The horizon narrowed and widened, and dipped and rose, and at all times its edge was jagged with waves that seemed thrust up in points like rocks.

Many a man ought to have a bathtub larger than the boat which here rode upon the sea. These waves were most wrongfully and barbarously abrupt and tall, and each froth-top was a problem in small boat navigation.

The cook squatted in the bottom and looked with both eyes at the six inches of gunwale[1] which separated him from the ocean. His sleeves were rolled over his fat forearms, and the two flaps of his unbuttoned vest dangled as he bent to bail out the boat. Often he said: "Gawd! That was a narrow clip." As he remarked it he invariably gazed eastward over the broken sea.

The oiler,[2] steering with one of the two oars in the boat, sometimes raised himself suddenly to keep clear of water that swirled in over the stern.[3] It was a thin little oar and it seemed often ready to snap.

The correspondent, pulling at the other oar, watched the waves and wondered why he was there.

The injured captain, lying in the bow, was at this time buried in that profound dejection and indifference which comes, temporarily at least, to even the bravest and most enduring when, willy nilly,[4] the firm fails, the army loses, the ship goes down. The mind of the master of a vessel is rooted deep in the timbers of her, though he command for a day or a decade, and this captain had on him the stern impression of a scene in the grays of dawn of seven turned faces, and later a stump of a top-mast with a white ball on it that slashed to and fro at the waves, went low and lower, and down. Thereafter there was something strange in his voice. Although steady, it was deep with mourning, and of a quality beyond oration[5] or tears.

"Keep 'er a little more south, Billie," said he.

"'A little more south,' sir," said the oiler in the stern.

A seat in this boat was not unlike a seat upon a bucking bronco, and, by the same token, a bronco is not much smaller. The craft pranced and reared, and plunged like an animal. As each wave came, and she rose for it, she seemed like a horse making at a fence outrageously high. The manner of her scramble over these walls of water is a mystic thing, and, moreover, at the top of them were ordinarily these problems in white water, the foam racing down from the summit of each wave, requiring a new leap, and a leap from the air. Then, after scornfully bumping a crest, she would slide, and race, and splash down a long incline and arrive bobbing and nodding in front of the next menace.

A singular disadvantage of the sea lies in the fact that after successfully surmounting one wave you discover that there is another behind it just as important and just as nervously anxious to do something effective in the way of swamping boats. In a ten-foot dinghy one can get an idea of the resources of the sea in the line of waves that is not probable to the average experience, which is never

---

1. A *gunwale* is the upper edge of the side of a boat.
2. The *oiler* is the person responsible for oiling machinery in the engine room on a ship.
3. The *stern* is the rear part of a boat or ship.
4. *Willy nilly* means "whether one wishes it or not."

---

5. An *oration* is a formal speech.

Vocabulary

profound (prə found′) *adj.* coming from the depth of one's being; intensely felt

at sea in a dinghy. As each slaty[6] wall of water approached, it shut all else from the view of the men in the boat, and it was not difficult to imagine that this particular wave was the final outburst of the ocean, the last effort of the grim water. There was a terrible grace in the move of the waves, and they came in silence, save for the snarling of the crests.

In the wan[7] light, the faces of the men must have been gray. Their eyes must have glinted in strange ways as they gazed steadily astern. Viewed from a balcony, the whole thing would doubtlessly have been weirdly picturesque. But the men in the boat had no time to see it, and if they had had leisure there were other things to occupy their minds. The sun swung steadily up the sky, and they knew it was broad day because the color of the sea changed from slate to emerald green, streaked with amber lights, and the foam was like tumbling snow. The process of the breaking day was unknown to them. They were aware only of this effect upon the color of the waves that rolled toward them.

In disjointed sentences the cook and the correspondent argued as to the difference between a lifesaving station and a house of refuge. The cook had said: "There's a house of refuge just north of the Mosquito Inlet Light, and as soon as they see us, they'll come off in their boat and pick us up."

"As soon as who see us?" said the correspondent.

"The crew," said the cook.

"Houses of refuge don't have crews," said the correspondent. "As I understand them, they are only places where clothes and grub are stored for the benefit of shipwrecked people. They don't carry crews."

"Oh, yes, they do," said the cook.

"No, they don't," said the correspondent.

"Well, we're not there yet, anyhow," said the oiler, in the stern.

"Well," said the cook, "perhaps it's not a house of refuge that I'm thinking of as being near Mosquito Inlet Light. Perhaps it's a life-saving station."

"We're not there yet," said the oiler, in the stern.

II

As the boat bounced from the top of each wave, the wind tore through the hair of the hatless men, and as the craft plopped her stern down again the spray slashed past them. The crest of each of these waves was a hill, from the top of which the men surveyed, for a moment, a broad tumultuous[8] expanse, shining and wind-riven. It was probably splendid. It was probably glorious, this play of the free sea, wild with lights of emerald and white and amber.

"Bully good thing it's an onshore wind,"[9] said the cook. "If not, where would be we? Wouldn't have a show."

"That's right," said the correspondent.

The busy oiler nodded his assent.

Then the captain, in the bow, chuckled in a way that expressed humor, contempt, tragedy, all in one. "Do you think we've got much of a show, now, boys?" said he.

Whereupon the three were silent, save for a trifle of hemming and hawing. To express any particular optimism at this time they felt to be childish and stupid, but they all doubtless possessed this sense of the situation in their mind. A young man thinks doggedly[10] at such times. On the other hand, the ethics of their condition was decidedly against any open suggestion of hopelessness. So they were silent.

"Oh, well," said the captain, soothing his children, "we'll get ashore all right."

But there was that in his tone which made them think, so the oiler quoth: "Yes! If this wind holds!"

---

6. *Slaty* means "having the bluish-gray color of slate."
7. *Wan* means "pale."
8. *Tumultuous* means "agitated" or "turbulent."
9. An *onshore wind* is one that blows toward the shore.
10. *Doggedly* means "in a stubbornly persistent manner."

The Open Boat

The cook was bailing. "Yes! If we don't catch hell in the surf."

Canton flannel gulls[11] flew near and far. Sometimes they sat down on the sea, near patches of brown seaweed that rolled over the waves with a movement like carpets on a line in a gale. The birds sat comfortably in groups, and they were envied by some in the dinghy, for the wrath of the sea was no more to them than it was to a covey of prairie chickens a thousand miles inland. Often they came very close and stared at the men with black bead-like eyes. At these times they were <u>uncanny</u> and sinister[12] in their unblinking scrutiny, and the men hooted angrily at them, telling them to be gone. One came, and evidently decided to alight on the top of the captain's head. The bird flew parallel to the boat and did not circle, but made short sidelong jumps in the air in chicken-fashion. His black eyes were wistfully fixed upon the captain's head. "Ugly brute," said the oiler to the bird. "You look as if you were made with a jackknife." The cook and the correspondent swore darkly at the creature. The captain naturally wished to knock it away with the end of the heavy painter,[13] but he did not dare do it, because anything resembling an <u>emphatic</u> gesture would have capsized this freighted boat, and so with his open hand, the captain gently and carefully waved the gull away. After it had been discouraged from the pursuit the captain breathed easier on account of his hair, and others breathed easier because the bird struck their minds at this time as being somehow gruesome and ominous.

In the meantime the oiler and the correspondent rowed. And also they rowed.

They sat together in the same seat, and each rowed an oar. Then the oiler took both oars; then the correspondent took both oars; then the oiler; then the correspondent. They rowed and they rowed. The very ticklish part of the business was when the time came for the reclining one in the stern to take his turn at the oars. By the very last star of truth, it is easier to steal eggs from under a hen than it was to change seats in the dinghy. First the man in the stern slid his hand along the thwart[14] and moved with care, as if he were of Sèvres.[15] Then the man in the rowing seat slid his hand along the other thwart. It was all done with the most extraordinary care. As the two sidled past each other, the whole party kept watchful eyes on the coming wave, and the captain cried: "Look out now! Steady there!"

The brown mats of seaweed that appeared from time to time were like islands, bits of earth. They were traveling, apparently, neither one way nor the other. They were, to all intents, stationary. They informed the men in the boat that it was making progress slowly toward the land.

The captain, rearing cautiously in the bow, after the dinghy soared on a great swell, said that he had seen the lighthouse at Mosquito Inlet. Presently the cook remarked that he had seen it. The correspondent was at the oars, then, and for some reason he too wished to look at the lighthouse, but his back was toward the far shore and the waves were important, and for some time he could not seize an opportunity to turn his head. But at last there came

---

11. *Canton flannel gulls* are gulls whose feathers resemble Canton flannel, a strong cotton fabric that is soft on one side and ribbed on the other.
12. *Sinister* means "evil" or "ominous."
13. A *painter* is a rope attached to the front of a boat, used for tying up to a dock.

14. A *thwart* is a seat going across a boat, on which a rower or passenger sits.
15. *Sèvres* (sev′rə) refers to fine porcelain made in Sèvres, France.

Vocabulary

uncanny (un ka′nē) *adj.* strangely unsettling; eerie
emphatic (em fa′tik) *adj.* forceful

a wave more gentle than the others, and when at the crest of it he swiftly scoured the western horizon.

"See it?" said the captain.

"No," said the correspondent, slowly, "I didn't see anything."

"Look again," said the captain. He pointed. "It's exactly in that direction."

At the top of another wave, the correspondent did as he was bid, and this time his eyes chanced on a small still thing on the edge of the swaying horizon. It was precisely like the point of a pin. It took an anxious eye to find a lighthouse so tiny.

"Think we'll make it, Captain?"

"If this wind holds and the boat don't swamp, we can't do much else," said the captain.

The little boat, lifted by each towering sea, and splashed viciously by the crests, made progress that in the absence of seaweed was not apparent to those in her. She seemed just a wee thing wallowing, miraculously, top up, at the mercy of five oceans. Occasionally, a great spread of water, like white flames, swarmed into her.

"Bail her, cook," said the captain, serenely.

"All right, Captain," said the cheerful cook.

III

It would be difficult to describe the subtle brotherhood of men that was here established on the seas. No one said that it was so. No one mentioned it. But it dwelt in the boat, and each man felt it warm him. They were a captain, an oiler, a cook, and a correspondent, and

The Derelict, 1975. Donald McAdoo. Watercolor, 14 x 21 in. Collection Mr. & Mrs. Robert A. Kopp Jr.

Viewing the painting: What struggle might have occurred involving the boat in this painting? How does the struggle you imagine compare with the struggles faced by the men in "The Open Boat"?

they were friends, friends in a more curiously iron-bound degree than may be common. The hurt captain, lying against the water jar in the bow, spoke always in a low voice and calmly, but he could never command a more ready and swiftly obedient crew than the motley three of the dinghy. It was more than a mere recognition of what was best for the common safety. There was surely in it a quality that was personal and heartfelt. And after this devotion to the commander of the boat there was this comradeship that the correspondent, for instance, who had been taught to be cynical of men, knew even at the time was the best experience of his life. But no one said that it was so. No one mentioned it.

"I wish we had a sail," remarked the captain. "We might try my overcoat on the end of an oar and give you two boys a chance to rest." So the cook and the correspondent held the mast and spread wide the overcoat. The oiler steered, and the little boat made good way with her new rig. Sometimes the oiler had to scull[16] sharply to keep a sea from breaking into the boat, but otherwise sailing was a success.

Meanwhile the lighthouse had been growing slowly larger. It had now almost assumed color, and appeared like a little gray shadow on the sky. The man at the oars could not be prevented from turning his head rather often to try for a glimpse of this little gray shadow.

---

16. *Scull* means "to propel a boat forward by moving a single oar from side to side over the stern of a boat."

The **O**pen **B**oat

At last, from the top of each wave the men in the tossing boat could see land. Even as the lighthouse was an upright shadow on the sky, this land seemed but a long black shadow on the sea. It certainly was thinner than paper. "We must be about opposite New Smyrna,"[17] said the cook, who had coasted this shore often in schooners. "Captain, by the way, I believe they abandoned that lifesaving station there about a year ago."

"Did they?" said the captain.

The wind slowly died away. The cook and the correspondent were not now obliged to slave in order to hold high the oar. But the waves continued their old impetuous swooping at the dinghy, and the little craft, no longer under way, struggled woundily over them. The oiler or the correspondent took the oars again.

Shipwrecks are *apropos*[18] of nothing. If men could only train for them and have them occur when the men had reached pink condition, there would be less drowning at sea. Of the four in the dinghy none had slept any time worth mentioning for two days and two nights previous to embarking in the dinghy, and in the excitement of clambering about the deck of a foundering[19] ship they had also forgotten to eat heartily.

For these reasons, and for others, neither the oiler nor the correspondent was fond of rowing at this time. The correspondent wondered ingenuously how in the name of all that was sane could there be people who thought it amusing to row a boat. It was not an amusement; it was a diabolical punishment, and even a genius of mental aberrations could never conclude that it was anything but a horror to the muscles and a crime against the back. He mentioned to the boat in general how the amusement of rowing struck him, and the weary-faced oiler smiled in full sympathy. Previously to the foundering, by the way, the oiler had worked doublewatch in the engine-room of the ship.

"Take her easy, now, boys," said the captain. "Don't spend yourselves. If we have to run a surf you'll need all your strength, because we'll sure have to swim for it. Take your time."

Slowly the land arose from the sea. From a black line it became a line of black and a line of white—trees and sand. Finally, the captain said that he could make out a house on the shore. "That's the house of refuge, sure," said the cook. "They'll see us before long, and come out after us."

The distant lighthouse reared high. "The keeper ought to be able to make us out now, if he's looking through a glass," said the captain. "He'll notify the lifesaving people."

"None of those other boats could have got ashore to give word of the wreck," said the oiler, in a low voice. "Else the lifeboat would be out hunting us."

Slowly and beautifully the land loomed out of the sea. The wind came again. It had veered from the northeast to the southeast. Finally, a new sound struck the ears of the men in the boat. It was the low thunder of the surf on the shore. "We'll never be able to make the lighthouse now," said the captain. "Swing her head a little more north, Billie."

"'A little more north,' sir," said the oiler.

Whereupon the little boat turned her nose once more down the wind, and all but the oarsman watched the shore grow. Under the influence of this expansion doubt and direful apprehension was leaving the minds of the men. The management of the boat was still most absorbing, but it could not prevent a

---

17. *New Smyrna* refers to the town of New Smyrna Beach, on the east coast of Florida.
18. *Apropos* means "relevant" or "pertinent."
19. *Foundering* means "sinking."

Vocabulary
ingenuously (in jen′ ū əs lē) *adv.* honestly; frankly; candidly

quiet cheerfulness. In an hour, perhaps, they would be ashore.

Their backbones had become thoroughly used to balancing in the boat and they now rode this wild colt of a dinghy like circus men. The correspondent thought that he had been drenched to the skin, but happening to feel in the top pocket of his coat, he found therein eight cigars. Four of them were soaked with seawater; four were perfectly scatheless. After a search, somebody produced three dry matches, and thereupon the four waifs[20] rode impudently in their little boat, and with an assurance of an impending rescue shining in their eyes, puffed at the big cigars and judged well and ill of all men. Everybody took a drink of water.

IV

"Cook," remarked the captain, "there don't seem to be any signs of life about your house of refuge."

"No," replied the cook. "Funny they don't see us!"

A broad stretch of lowly coast lay before the eyes of the men. It was of dunes topped with dark vegetation. The roar of the surf was plain, and sometimes they could see the white lip of a wave as it spun up the beach. A tiny house was blocked out black upon the sky. Southward, the slim lighthouse lifted its little gray length.

Tide, wind, and waves were swinging the dinghy northward. "Funny they don't see us," said the men.

The surf's roar was here dulled, but its tone was, nevertheless, thunderous and mighty. As the boat swam over the great rollers, the men sat listening to this roar. "We'll swamp sure," said everybody.

It is fair to say here that there was not a lifesaving station within twenty miles in either direction, but the men did not know this fact and in consequence they made dark and opprobrious[21] remarks concerning the eyesight of the nation's lifesavers. Four scowling men sat in the dinghy and surpassed records in the invention of epithets.[22]

"Funny they don't see us."

The light-heartedness of a former time had completely faded. To their sharpened minds it was easy to conjure pictures of all kinds of incompetency and blindness and, indeed, cowardice. There was the shore of the populous land, and it was bitter and bitter to them that from it came no sign.

"Well," said the captain, ultimately, "I suppose we'll have to make a try for ourselves. If we stay out here too long, we'll none of us have strength left to swim after the boat swamps."

And so the oiler, who was at the oars, turned the boat straight for the shore. There was a sudden tightening of muscles. There was some thinking.

"If we don't all get ashore—" said the captain. "If we don't all get ashore, I suppose you fellows know where to send news of my finish?"

They then briefly exchanged some addresses and admonitions.[23] As for the reflections of the men, there was a great deal of rage in them. Perchance they might be formulated thus: "If I am going to be drowned—if I am going to be drowned—if I am going to be drowned, why, in the name of the seven mad gods who rule the sea,[24] was I allowed to come thus far and contemplate sand and trees? Was I brought here merely to have my nose dragged away as I was about to nibble the sacred cheese of life? It is

---

20. *Waifs* are persons having no apparent home.
21. *Opprobrious* (ə prō′ brē əs) means "derogatory."
22. *Epithets* are descriptive, sometimes abusive, words or phrases used with or in place of a name.
23. *Admonitions* are warnings or advice.
24. *[seven . . . the sea]* This description probably refers to the seven major seas, each at the mercy of a deity.

Vocabulary
impudently (im′ pyə dənt lē) *adv.* in an offensively bold manner; arrogantly

preposterous. If this old ninny-woman, Fate,[25] cannot do better than this, she should be deprived of the management of men's fortunes. She is an old hen who knows not her intention. If she has decided to drown me, why did she not do it in the beginning and save me all this trouble. The whole affair is absurd. . . . But, no, she cannot mean to drown me. She dare not drown me. She cannot drown me. Not after all this work." Afterward the man might have had an impulse to shake his fist at the clouds. "Just you drown me, now, and then hear what I call you!"

The billows that came at this time were more formidable. They seemed always just about to break and roll over the little boat in a turmoil of foam. There was a preparatory and long growl in the speech of them. No mind unused to the sea would have concluded that the dinghy could ascend these sheer heights in time. The shore was still afar. The oiler was a wily[26] surfman. "Boys," he said, swiftly, "she won't live three minutes more and we're too far out to swim. Shall I take her to sea again, Captain?"

"Yes! Go ahead!" said the captain.

This oiler, by a series of quick miracles, and fast and steady oarsmanship, turned the boat in the middle of the surf and took her safely to sea again.

There was a considerable silence as the boat bumped over the furrowed sea to deeper water. Then somebody in gloom spoke. "Well, anyhow, they must have seen us from the shore by now."

The gulls went in slanting flight up the wind toward the gray desolate east. A squall,[27] marked by dingy clouds, and clouds brick-red, like smoke from a burning building, appeared from the southeast.

"What do you think of those lifesaving people? Ain't they peaches?"

"Funny they haven't seen us."

"Maybe they think we're out here for sport? Maybe they think we're fishin'. Maybe they think we're damned fools."

It was a long afternoon. A changed tide tried to force them southward, but wind and wave said northward. Far ahead, where coastline, sea, and sky formed their mighty angle, there were little dots which seemed to indicate a city on the shore.

"St. Augustine?"

The captain shook his head. "Too near Mosquito Inlet."

And the oiler rowed, and then the correspondent rowed. Then the oiler rowed. It was a weary business. The human back can become the seat of more aches and pains than

Moonlight, c. 1885. Albert Pinkham Ryder. Oil on canvas, 16 x 17¾ in. National Museum of American Art, Smithsonian Institution, Washington, DC.

Viewing the painting: In your opinion, what is the mood of this painting? How does this mood help convey the experience of the men during their night at sea?

---

25. *Fate* implies a supernatural power guiding one to an inevitable end. In classical mythology, the three Fates were portrayed as old women.
26. *Wily* means "cunning" or "sly."

27. A *squall* is a short, sudden, strong windstorm, often accompanied by rain or snow.

Vocabulary
preposterous (pri pos′ tər əs) *adj.* absurd; ridiculous

are registered in books for the composite anatomy of a regiment. It is a limited area, but it can become the theater of innumerable muscular conflicts, tangles, wrenches, knots, and other comforts.

"Did you ever like to row, Billie?" asked the correspondent.

"No," said the oiler. "Hang it."

When one exchanged the rowing-seat for a place in the bottom of the boat, he suffered a bodily depression that caused him to be careless of everything save an obligation to wiggle one finger. There was cold seawater swashing to and fro in the boat, and he lay in it. His head, pillowed on a thwart, was within an inch of the swirl of a wave crest, and sometimes a particularly obstreperous[28] sea came inboard and drenched him once more. But these matters did not annoy him. It is almost certain that if the boat had capsized he would have tumbled comfortably out upon the ocean as if he felt sure that it was a great soft mattress.

"Look! There's a man on the shore!"

"Where?"

"There! See 'im? See 'im?"

"Yes, sure! He's walking along."

"Now he's stopped. Look! He's facing us!"

"He's waving at us!"

"So he is! By thunder!"

"Ah, now, we're all right! Now we're all right! There'll be a boat out here for us in half an hour."

"He's going on. He's running. He's going up to that house there."

The remote beach seemed lower than the sea, and it required a searching glance to discern the little black figure. The captain saw a floating stick and they rowed to it. A bath-towel was by some weird chance in the boat, and, tying this on the stick, the captain waved it. The oarsman did not dare turn his head, so he was obliged to ask questions.

"What's he doing now?"

"He's standing still again. He's looking, I think. . . . There he goes again. Toward the house. . . . Now he's stopped again."

"Is he waving at us?"

"No, not now! he was, though."

"Look! There comes another man!"

"He's running."

"Look at him go, would you."

"Why, he's on a bicycle. Now he's met the other man. They're both waving at us. Look!"

"There comes something up the beach."

"What the devil is that thing?"

"Why, it looks like a boat."

"Why, certainly it's a boat."

"No, it's on wheels."

"Yes, so it is. Well, that must be the lifeboat. They drag them along shore on a wagon."

"That's the lifeboat, sure."

"No, by——, it's—it's an omnibus."[29]

"I tell you it's a lifeboat."

"It is not! It's an omnibus. I can see it plain. See? One of those big hotel omnibuses."

"By thunder, you're right. It's an omnibus, sure as fate. What do you suppose they are doing with an omnibus? Maybe they are going around collecting the lifecrew, hey?"

"That's it, likely. Look! There's a fellow waving a little black flag. He's standing on the steps of the omnibus. There come those other two fellows. Now they're all talking together. Look at the fellow with the flag. Maybe he ain't waving it!"

"That ain't a flag, is it? That's his coat. Why, certainly, that's his coat."

"So it is. It's his coat. He's taken it off and is waving it around his head. But would you look at him swing it!"

"Oh, say, there isn't any lifesaving station there. That's just a winter resort hotel omnibus that has brought over some of the boarders to see us drown."

28. *Obstreperous* (əb strep′ ər əs) means "unruly."

29. An *omnibus*, or bus, would have been pulled by horses during this time period.

The Open Boat

"What's that idiot with the coat mean? What's he signaling, anyhow?"

"It looks as if he were trying to tell us to go north. There must be a lifesaving station up there."

"No! He thinks we're fishing. Just giving us a merry hand. See? Ah, there, Willie."

"Well, I wish I could make something out of those signals. What do you suppose he means?"

"He don't mean anything. He's just playing."

"Well, if he'd just signal us to try the surf again, or to go to sea and wait, or go north, or go south, or go to hell—there would be some reason in it. But look at him. He just stands there and keeps his coat revolving like a wheel. The ass!"

"There come more people."

"Now there's quite a mob. Look! Isn't that a boat?"

"Where? Oh, I see where you mean. No, that's no boat."

"That fellow is still waving his coat."

"He must think we like to see him do that. Why don't he quit it. It don't mean anything."

"I don't know. I think he is trying to make us go north. It must be that there's a lifesaving station there somewhere."

"Say, he ain't tired yet. Look at 'im wave."

"Wonder how long he can keep that up. He's been revolving his coat ever since he caught sight of us. He's an idiot. Why aren't they getting men to bring a boat out. A fishing boat—one of those big yawls[30]—could come out here all right. Why don't he do something?"

"Oh, it's all right, now."

"They'll have a boat out here for us in less than no time, now that they've seen us."

A faint yellow tone came into the sky over the low land. The shadows on the sea slowly deepened. The wind bore coldness with it, and the men began to shiver.

"Holy smoke!" said one, allowing his voice to express his impious mood, "if we keep on monkeying out here! If we've got to flounder out here all night!"

"Oh, we'll never have to stay here all night! Don't you worry. They've seen us now, and it won't be long before they'll come chasing out after us."

The shore grew dusky. The man waving a coat blended gradually into this gloom, and it swallowed in the same manner the omnibus and the group of people. The spray, when it dashed uproariously over the side, made the voyagers shrink and swear like men who were being branded.

"I'd like to catch the chump who waved the coat. I feel like soaking him one, just for luck."

"Why? What did he do?"

"Oh, nothing, but then he seemed so damned cheerful."

In the meantime the oiler rowed, and then the correspondent rowed, and then the oiler rowed. Gray-faced and bowed forward, they mechanically, turn by turn, plied the leaden oars. The form of the lighthouse had vanished from the southern horizon, but finally a pale star appeared, just lifting from the sea. The streaked saffron[31] in the west passed before the all-merging darkness, and the sea to the east was black. The land had vanished, and was expressed only by the low and drear thunder of the surf.

"If I am going to be drowned—if I am going to be drowned—if I am going to be drowned, why, in the name of the seven mad gods who rule the sea, was I allowed to come thus far and contemplate sand and trees? Was I brought here merely to have my nose dragged away as I was about to nibble the sacred cheese of life?"

---

30. A *yawl* is a sailboat with two masts, the large mast near the front of the boat and the smaller one near the back.

31. Here, *saffron* means "yellow-orange in color."

Vocabulary

impious (im′ pē əs) *adj.* lacking in reverence; disrespectful

The patient captain, drooped over the water jar, was sometimes obliged to speak to the oarsman.

"Keep her head up! Keep her head up!"

"'Keep her head up,' sir." The voices were weary and low.

This was surely a quiet evening. All save the oarsman lay heavily and listlessly in the boat's bottom. As for him, his eyes were just capable of noting the tall black waves that swept forward in a most sinister silence, save for an occasional subdued growl of a crest.

The cook's head was on a thwart, and he looked without interest at the water under his nose. He was deep in other scenes. Finally he spoke. "Billie," he murmured, dreamfully, "what kind of pie do you like best?"

V

"Pie," said the oiler and the correspondent, agitatedly. "Don't talk about those things, blast you!"

"Well," said the cook, "I was just thinking about ham sandwiches, and—"

A night on the sea in an open boat is a long night. As darkness settled finally, the shine of the light, lifting from the sea in the south, changed to full gold. On the northern horizon a new light appeared, a small bluish gleam on the edge of the waters. These two lights were the furniture of the world. Otherwise there was nothing but waves.

Two men huddled in the stern, and distances were so magnificent in the dinghy that the rower was enabled to keep his feet partly warmed by thrusting them under his companions. Their legs indeed extended far under the rowing seat until they touched the feet of the captain forward. Sometimes, despite the efforts of the tired oarsman, a wave came piling into the boat, an icy wave of the night, and the chilling water soaked them anew. They would twist their bodies for a moment and groan, and sleep the dead sleep once more, while the water in the boat gurgled about them as the craft rocked.

The plan of the oiler and the correspondent was for one to row until he lost the ability, and then arouse the other from his sea-water couch in the bottom of the boat.

The oiler plied the oars until his head drooped forward, and the overpowering sleep blinded him. And he rowed yet afterward. Then he touched a man in the bottom of the boat, and called his name. "Will you spell me for a little while?" he said, meekly.

"Sure, Billie," said the correspondent, awakening and dragging himself to a sitting position. They exchanged places carefully, and the oiler, cuddling down in the seawater at the cook's side, seemed to go to sleep instantly.

The particular violence of the sea had ceased. The waves came without snarling. The obligation of the man at the oars was to keep the boat headed so that the tilt of the rollers would not capsize her, and to preserve her from filling when the crests rushed past. The black waves were silent and hard to be seen in the darkness. Often one was almost upon the boat before the oarsman was aware.

In a low voice the correspondent addressed the captain. He was not sure that the captain was awake, although this iron man seemed to be always awake. "Captain, shall I keep her making for that light north, sir?"

The same steady voice answered him. "Yes. Keep it about two points off the port bow."[32]

The cook had tied a life belt around himself in order to get even the warmth which this clumsy cork contrivance could donate, and he seemed almost stove-like when a rower, whose teeth invariably chattered wildly as soon as he ceased his labor, dropped down to sleep.

The correspondent, as he rowed, looked down at the two men sleeping under foot. The cook's arm was around the oiler's shoulders, and, with their fragmentary clothing and haggard faces, they were the babes of the

---

32. The *bow* is the forward part of a boat or ship. The *port bow*, then, would be the left side of the forward part.

sea, a grotesque rendering of the old babes in the wood.

Later he must have grown stupid at his work, for suddenly there was a growling of water, and a crest came with a roar and a swash into the boat, and it was a wonder that it did not set the cook afloat in his life belt. The cook continued to sleep, but the oiler sat up, blinking his eyes and shaking with the new cold.

"Oh, I'm awful sorry, Billie," said the correspondent, contritely.

"That's all right, old boy," said the oiler, and lay down again and was asleep.

Presently it seemed that even the captain dozed, and the correspondent thought that he was the one man afloat on all the oceans. The wind had a voice as it came over the waves, and it was sadder than the end.

There was a long, loud swishing astern of the boat, and a gleaming trail of phosphorescence, like blue flame, was furrowed on the black waters. It might have been made by a monstrous knife.

Then there came a stillness, while the correspondent breathed with the open mouth and looked at the sea.

Suddenly there was another swish and another long flash of bluish light, and this time it was alongside the boat, and might almost have been reached with an oar. The correspondent saw an enormous fin speed like a shadow through the water, hurling the crystalline spray and leaving the long glowing trail.

The correspondent looked over his shoulder at the captain. His face was hidden, and he seemed to be asleep. He looked at the babes of the sea. They certainly were asleep. So, being bereft[33] of sympathy, he leaned a little way to one side and swore softly into the sea.

But the thing did not then leave the vicinity of the boat. Ahead or astern, on one side or the other, at intervals long or short, fled the long sparkling streak, and there was to be

heard the whiroo of the dark fin. The speed and power of the thing was greatly to be admired. It cut the water like a gigantic and keen projectile.

The presence of this biding thing did not affect the man with the same horror that it would if he had been a picnicker. He simply looked at the sea dully and swore in an undertone.

Nevertheless, it is true that he did not wish to be alone with the thing. He wished one of his companions to awaken by chance and keep him company with it. But the captain hung motionless over the water jar and the oiler and the cook in the bottom of the boat were plunged in slumber.

VI

"If I am going to be drowned—if I am going to be drowned—if I am going to be drowned, why, in the name of the seven mad gods who rule the sea, was I allowed to come thus far and contemplate sand and trees?"

During this dismal night, it may be remarked that a man would conclude that it was really the intention of the seven mad gods to drown him, despite the abominable injustice of it. For it was certainly an abominable injustice to drown a man who had worked so hard, so hard. The man felt it would be a crime most unnatural. Other people had drowned at sea since galleys[34] swarmed with painted sails, but still—

When it occurs to a man that nature does not regard him as important, and that she feels she would not maim the universe by disposing of him, he at first wishes to throw bricks at the temple, and he hates deeply the fact that there are no bricks and no temples. Any visible expression of nature would surely be pelleted with his jeers.

Then, if there be no tangible thing to hoot he feels, perhaps, the desire to confront a personification and indulge in pleas, bowed

---

33. *Bereft* means "lacking something needed."

34. A *galley* is a medieval ship propelled by sails and a row (or rows) of oars on either side.

to one knee, and with hands supplicant, saying: "Yes, but I love myself."

A high cold star on a winter's night is the word he feels that she says to him. Thereafter he knows the pathos[35] of his situation.

The men in the dinghy had not discussed these matters, but each had, no doubt, reflected upon them in silence and according to his mind. There was seldom any expression upon their faces save the general one of complete weariness. Speech was devoted to the business of the boat.

To chime the notes of his emotion, a verse mysteriously entered the correspondent's head. He had even forgotten that he had forgotten this verse, but it suddenly was in his mind.

> A soldier of the Legion[36] lay dying in
>   Algiers,[37]
> There was lack of woman's nursing,
>   there was dearth of woman's tears;
> But a comrade stood beside him, and he
>   took that comrade's hand,
> And he said: "I never more shall see my
>   own, my native land."[38]

In his childhood, the correspondent had been made acquainted with the fact that a soldier of the Legion lay dying in Algiers, but he had never regarded it as important. Myriads of his schoolfellows had informed him of the soldier's plight, but the dinning[39] had naturally ended by making him perfectly indifferent. He had never considered it his affair that a soldier of the Legion lay dying in Algiers, nor had it appeared to him as a matter for sorrow. It was less to him than the breaking of a pencil's point.

Now, however, it quaintly came to him as a human, living thing. It was no longer merely a picture of a few throes[40] in the breast of a poet, meanwhile drinking tea and warming his feet at the grate; it was an actuality—stern, mournful, and fine.

The correspondent plainly saw the soldier. He lay on the sand with his feet out straight and still. While his pale left hand was upon his chest in an attempt to thwart the going of his life, the blood came between his fingers. In the far Algerian distance, a city of low square forms was set against a sky that was faint with the last sunset hues. The correspondent, plying the oars and dreaming of the slow and slower movements of the lips of the soldier, was moved by a profound and perfectly impersonal comprehension. He was sorry for the soldier of the Legion who lay dying in Algiers.

The thing which had followed the boat and waited had evidently grown bored at the delay. There was no longer to be heard the slash of the cut water, and there was no longer the flame of the long trail. The light in the north still glimmered, but it was apparently no nearer to the boat. Sometimes the boom of the surf rang in the correspondent's ears, and he turned the craft seaward then and rowed harder. Southward, some one had evidently built a watch fire on the beach. It was too low and too far to be seen, but it made a shimmering, roseate reflection upon the bluff back of it, and this could be discerned from the boat. The wind came stronger, and sometimes a wave suddenly raged out like a mountain cat and there was to be seen the sheen and sparkle of a broken crest.

The captain, in the bow, moved on his water jar and sat erect. "Pretty long night," he observed to the correspondent. He looked at the shore. "Those lifesaving people take their time."

"Did you see that shark playing around?"

---

35. *Pathos* means "deep sadness."
36. *Legion* refers to the French Foreign Legion, an army composed mainly of foreign volunteers.
37. *Algiers* (al jērz′) is the capital of Algeria, a country in northern Africa that was once ruled by France.
38. This verse compresses the first stanza of "Bingen on the Rhine" by English poet Caroline E. S. Norton (1808–1877).
39. *Dinning* means "insistent repetition."

---

40. *Throes* are pains.

"Yes, I saw him. He was a big fellow, all right."

"Wish I had known you were awake."

Later the correspondent spoke into the bottom of the boat.

"Billie!" There was a slow and gradual disentanglement. "Billie, will you spell me?"

"Sure," said the oiler.

As soon as the correspondent touched the cold comfortable seawater in the bottom of the boat, and had huddled close to the cook's life belt he was deep in sleep, despite the fact that his teeth played all the popular airs. This sleep was so good to him that it was but a moment before he heard a voice call his name in a tone that demonstrated the last stages of exhaustion. "Will you spell me?"

"Sure, Billie."

The light in the north had mysteriously vanished, but the correspondent took his course from the wide-awake captain.

Later in the night they took the boat farther out to sea, and the captain directed the cook to take one oar at the stern and keep the boat facing the seas. He was to call out if he should hear the thunder of the surf. This plan enabled the oiler and the correspondent to get respite together. "We'll give those boys a chance to get into shape again," said the captain. They curled down and, after a few preliminary chatterings and trembles, slept once more the dead sleep. Neither knew they had bequeathed to the

Veiled Moon, 1995. Jane Wilson. Oil on linen, 18 x 18 in. Fischbach Gallery, New York.

Viewing the painting: Imagine the men on the boat viewing this scene. What might the scene make them think about? Explain.

cook the company of another shark, or perhaps the same shark.

As the boat caroused on the waves, spray occasionally bumped over the side and gave them a fresh soaking, but this had no power to break their repose. The ominous slash of the wind and the water affected them as it would have affected mummies.

"Boys," said the cook, with the notes of every reluctance in his voice, "she's drifted in pretty close. I guess one of you had better take her to sea again." The correspondent, aroused, heard the crash of the toppled crests.

As he was rowing, the captain gave him some whiskey and water, and this steadied the chills out of him. "If I ever get ashore and anybody shows me even a photograph of an oar—"

At last there was a short conversation.

"Billie . . . Billie, will you spell me?"

"Sure," said the oiler.

VII

When the correspondent again opened his eyes, the sea and the sky were each of the gray hue of the dawning. Later, carmine and gold was painted upon the waters. The morning appeared finally, in its splendor, with a sky of pure blue, and the sunlight flamed on the tips of the waves.

On the distant dunes were set many little black cottages, and a tall white windmill reared above them. No man, nor dog, nor bicycle appeared on the beach. The cottages might have formed a deserted village.

The voyagers scanned the shore. A conference was held in the boat. "Well," said the captain, "if no help is coming, we might better try a run through the surf right away. If we stay out here much longer we will be too weak to do anything for ourselves at all." The others silently acquiesced in this reasoning. The boat was headed for the beach. The correspondent wondered if none ever ascended the tall wind-tower, and if then they never looked seaward. This tower was a giant, standing with its back to the plight of the ants. It represented in a degree, to the correspondent, the serenity of nature amid the struggles of the individual—nature in the wind, and nature in the vision of men. She did not seem cruel to him then, nor beneficent, nor treacherous, nor wise. But she was indifferent, flatly indifferent. It is, perhaps, plausible that a man in this situation, impressed with the unconcern of the universe, should see the innumerable flaws of his life and have them taste wickedly in his mind and wish for another chance. A distinction between right and wrong seems absurdly clear to him, then, in this new ignorance of the grave-edge, and he understands that if he were given another opportunity he would mend his conduct and his words, and be better and brighter during an introduction, or at a tea.

"Now, boys," said the captain, "she is going to swamp sure. All we can do is to work her in as far as possible, and then when she swamps, pile out and scramble for the beach. Keep cool now, and don't jump until she swamps sure."

The oiler took the oars. Over his shoulders he scanned the surf. "Captain," he said, "I think I'd better bring her about, and keep her head-on to the seas and back her in."

"All right, Billie," said the captain. "Back her in." The oiler swung the boat then and, seated in the stern, the cook and the correspondent were obliged to look over their shoulders to contemplate the lonely and indifferent shore.

The monstrous inshore rollers heaved the boat high until the men were again enabled to see the white sheets of water scudding[41] up the slanted beach. "We won't get in very close," said the captain. Each time a man could wrest his attention from the rollers, he turned his glance toward the shore, and in the expression of the eyes during this contemplation there was a singular quality. The correspondent, observing the others, knew that they were not afraid, but the full meaning of their glances was shrouded.

As for himself, he was too tired to grapple fundamentally with the fact. He tried to coerce his mind into thinking of it, but the mind was dominated at this time by the muscles, and the muscles said they did not care. It merely occurred to him that if he should drown it would be a shame.

There were no hurried words, no pallor,[42] no plain agitation. The men simply looked at the shore. "Now, remember to get well clear of the boat when you jump," said the captain.

Seaward the crest of a roller suddenly fell with a thunderous crash, and the long white comber[43] came roaring down upon the boat.

"Steady now," said the captain. The men were silent. They turned their eyes from the shore to the comber and waited. The boat slid up the incline, leaped at the furious top, bounced over it, and swung down the long back of the wave. Some water had been shipped and the cook bailed it out.

---

41. *Scudding* means "moving swiftly."
42. *Pallor* is paleness or the lack of natural or healthy color.
43. A *comber* is a long, rolling wave that curls over and breaks.

Vocabulary
coerce (kō urs′) *v.* to force

The Open Boat

But the next crest crashed also. The tumbling boiling flood of white water caught the boat and whirled it almost perpendicular. Water swarmed in from all sides. The correspondent had his hands on the gunwale at this time, and when the water entered at that place he swiftly withdrew his fingers, as if he objected to wetting them.

The little boat, drunken with this weight of water, reeled and snuggled deeper into the sea.

"Bail her out, cook! Bail her out," said the captain.

"All right, Captain," said the cook.

"Now, boys, the next one will do for us, sure," said the oiler. "Mind to jump clear of the boat."

The third wave moved forward, huge, furious, implacable.[44] It fairly swallowed the dinghy, and almost simultaneously the men tumbled into the sea. A piece of lifebelt had lain in the bottom of the boat, and as the correspondent went overboard he held this to his chest with his left hand.

The January water was icy, and he reflected immediately that it was colder than he had expected to find it off the coast of Florida. This appeared to his dazed mind as a fact important enough to be noted at the time. The coldness of the water was sad; it was tragic. This fact was somehow so mixed and confused with his opinion of his own situation that it seemed almost a proper reason for tears. The water was cold.

When he came to the surface he was conscious of little but the noisy water. Afterward he saw his companions in the sea. The oiler was ahead in the race. He was swimming strongly and rapidly. Off to the correspondent's left, the cook's great white and corked back bulged out of the water, and in the rear the captain was hanging with his one good hand to the keel[45] of the overturned dinghy.

There is a certain immovable quality to a shore, and the correspondent wondered at it amid the confusion of the sea.

It seemed also very attractive, but the correspondent knew that it was a long journey, and he paddled leisurely. The piece of life preserver lay under him, and sometimes he whirled down the incline of a wave as if he were on a hand-sled.

But finally he arrived at a place in the sea where travel was beset with difficulty. He did not pause swimming to inquire what manner of current had caught him, but there his progress ceased. The shore was set before him like a bit of scenery on a stage, and he looked at it and understood with his eyes each detail of it.

As the cook passed, much farther to the left, the captain was calling to him, "Turn over on your back, cook! Turn over on your back and use the oar."

"All right, sir." The cook turned on his back, and, paddling with an oar, went ahead as if he were a canoe.

Presently the boat also passed to the left of the correspondent with the captain clinging with one hand to the keel. He would have appeared like a man raising himself to look over a board fence, if it were not for the extraordinary gymnastics of the boat. The correspondent marvelled that the captain could still hold to it.

They passed on, nearer to shore—the oiler, the cook, the captain—and following them went the water jar, bouncing gayly over the seas.

The correspondent remained in the grip of this strange new enemy—a current. The shore, with its white slope of sand and its green bluff, topped with little silent cottages, was spread like a picture before him. It was very near to him then, but he was impressed as one who in a gallery looks at a scene from Brittany[46] or Holland.

---

44. *Implacable* means "unrelenting" or "unyielding."
45. The *keel* runs along the center of the bottom of a boat. It supports the boat's frame and gives the boat stability.

46. *Brittany* is a region in northwestern France.

He thought: "I am going to drown? Can it be possible? Can it be possible? Can it be possible?" Perhaps an individual must consider his own death to be the final phenomenon of nature.

But later a wave perhaps whirled him out of this small deadly current, for he found suddenly that he could again make progress toward the shore. Later still, he was aware that the captain, clinging with one hand to the keel of the dinghy, had his face turned away from the shore and toward him, and was calling his name. "Come to the boat! Come to the boat!"

In his struggle to reach the captain and the boat, he reflected that when one gets properly wearied, drowning must really be a comfortable arrangement, a cessation of hostilities accompanied by a large degree of relief, and he was glad of it, for the main thing in his mind for some moments had been horror of the temporary agony. He did not wish to be hurt.

Presently he saw a man running along the shore. He was undressing with most remarkable speed. Coat, trousers, shirt, everything flew magically off him.

"Come to the boat," called the captain.

"All right, Captain." As the correspondent paddled, he saw the captain let himself down to bottom and leave the boat. Then the correspondent performed his one little marvel of the voyage. A large wave caught him and flung him with ease and supreme speed completely over the boat and far beyond it. It struck him even then as an event in gymnastics, and a true miracle of the sea. An overturned boat in the surf is not a plaything to a swimming man.

The correspondent arrived in water that reached only to his waist, but his condition did not enable him to stand for more than a moment. Each wave knocked him into a heap, and the undertow pulled at him.

Then he saw the man who had been running and undressing, and undressing and running, come bounding into the water. He dragged ashore the cook, and then waded toward the captain, but the captain waved him away, and sent him to the correspondent. He was naked, naked as a tree in winter, but a halo was about his head, and he shone like a saint. He gave a strong pull, and a long drag, and a bully heave at the correspondent's hand. The correspondent, schooled in the minor formulæ, said: "Thanks, old man." But suddenly the man cried: "What's that?" He pointed a swift finger. The correspondent said: "Go."

In the shallows, face downward, lay the oiler. His forehead touched sand that was periodically, between each wave, clear of the sea.

The correspondent did not know all that transpired afterward. When he achieved safe ground he fell, striking the sand with each particular part of his body. It was as if he had dropped from a roof, but the thud was grateful to him.

It seems that instantly the beach was populated with men with blankets, clothes, and flasks, and women with coffeepots and all the remedies sacred to their minds. The welcome of the land to the men from the sea was warm and generous, but a still and dripping shape was carried slowly up the beach, and the land's welcome for it could only be the different and sinister hospitality of the grave.

When it came night, the white waves paced to and fro in the moonlight, and the wind brought the sound of the great sea's voice to the men on shore, and they felt that they could then be interpreters.

Responding to Literature

Personal Response

How did you respond to each of the four main characters? Explain.

ANALYZING LITERATURE

RECALL

1. In part I, what is the situation in which the four men find themselves?
2. Summarize what happens in parts 2 and 3. What is the mood of the men at the end of part 3?
3. In part 4, why does the oiler take the boat out to sea again? What happens to give the men renewed hope?
4. How do the men spend the night (parts 5 and 6) at sea? What dangers and difficulties do they face? What discomforts do they endure?
5. What is the outcome of the story?

INTERPRET

6. Based on the discussion that three of the men have at the end of part 1, what might you infer about their situation and how each one will cope with it?
7. What is "the subtle brotherhood of men" at the beginning of part 3? How does this brotherhood help the men cope with their ordeal?
8. "Funny they don't see us." What does the repetition of this statement seem to suggest?
9. What can you infer about the character of each man, based on the way each behaves during the night on the sea?
10. What is **ironic** about the story's outcome (see page R8)? What lesson does this outcome seem to teach?

EVALUATE AND CONNECT

11. Explain how the use of **similes** and **metaphors** helps you better understand and appreciate the story. (See pages R14 and R9.)
12. How does Crane use **foreshadowing** (see page R7) to help prepare the reader for future events? Give specific examples.
13. Recall your discussion for the Focus Activity on page 558. Compare your imagined scenarios with the events that occur in this story. What role do courage, strength, and luck play in the story's outcome?
14. How does the statement "impressed with the unconcern of the universe" help you understand the story's **theme** (see page R16)?
15. Have you ever been part of a group in a difficult situation? How did you feel about the others in the group as a result?

Literary ELEMENTS

Naturalism

The literary movement called **Naturalism** is characterized by a certain pessimistic determinism—a belief that people have little or no control over their lives. Heredity and environment are seen as the main factors that affect the course of people's lives. In a broader sense, Naturalism also includes writing that depicts the effect of nature on human beings. In "The Open Boat," that effect is obvious—nature determines who will live and who will die. Nature is detached, unemotional, and seemingly random in its decisions.

1. Find three passages in the story that emphasize the power of nature over humans.
2. Although the men realize that ultimately they are at the mercy of nature, all of them struggle to survive. How does each one's struggle affect himself and the fate of the group?
3. Do you think the outcome of the story is fair? Why or why not? How might a follower of Naturalism respond to this question? Explain.

● See **Literary Terms Handbook**, p. R10.

LITERATURE AND WRITING

Writing About Literature

Analyzing Personification Write a paragraph or two in which you analyze Crane's **personification** of the sea (see page R11). Consider questions like these: How does the use of personification help to define the power of the sea? How does it intensify the conflict between the men and the sea? How does it help to personalize their struggle with an impersonal force?

Personal Writing

From Now On . . . Imagine that you have survived an ordeal similar to the one described in this story. How do you think you might have reacted? How do you think the experience might have changed your behavior and outlook on life? Record your ideas in your journal.

EXTENDING YOUR RESPONSE

Literature Groups

A Balancing Act Dramatic tension in the story is maintained with a careful balance between hope and despair. In a group, make a list of events or signs that give the men reason to hope. Make a second list of signs or occurrences that point to failure. Discuss which emotion you think is stronger in the story—hope or despair. Support your opinion with details from your lists. Then share your ideas with the class.

Learning for Life

Where in the World? Using a detailed map or atlas as a guide, outline the coasts of Florida, Cuba, and the surrounding waters on a large piece of posterboard. Label all important points of reference. Draw the probable course of the boat from the time the men first spot land until they reach the shore. Refer to the story for details.

Internet Connection

What Really Happened? "The Open Boat" is based on a true story (see the Background information on page 558). Research the incident using Internet and library resources. With a small group of classmates, present a multimedia account of the sinking of the *Commodore*.

📁 **Save your work for your portfolio.**

Skill Minilesson

VOCABULARY • Negative Prefixes

You know that a prefix at the beginning of a word affects the word's entire meaning. Negative prefixes, such as *dis-, im-, in-,* and *un-,* mean "not" or "the opposite of." Notice how negative prefixes contribute to the meanings of these words.

> *im*pious: not pious
> *in*competency: the opposite of competency

PRACTICE Use your knowledge of negative prefixes to write a definition for each of these words. Then use each word in an original sentence.

1. innumerable   4. unnatural
2. immovable   5. implacable
3. impersonal

~: Writing ✒ Workshop :~

Business Writing: Problem-Solution Proposal

Just by being human, you encounter problems—from basic ones, like keeping warm when it's cold, to more complicated problems, like repairing a strained friendship, finding time for homework and your favorite activity, or balancing your budget. Sometimes writing about a problem can help you work it out. Clearly stating the problem and recommending solutions can help lead others toward solving the problem. **In this workshop you will write a problem-solution proposal.**

● As you write your problem-solution proposal, refer to the **Writing Handbook,** pp. R62–R77.

The Writing Process

PREWRITING

PREWRITING TIP
Don't try to tackle a big problem like global warming. Instead, focus on a local problem that you have a chance of solving.

Explore ideas

Every day of your life, you face problems, some of which can pose serious challenges. Think back on the problems you read about in this theme. Which can you connect to your own experience?

● experiencing unfair treatment ("Let Us Examine the Facts")
● handling the obligations of daily life ("Lucinda Matlock," "Fiddler Jones")
● running away from one's problems ("Richard Cory," "Miniver Cheevy")
● finding oneself falsely accused of a wrongdoing ("Chief Sekoto Holds Court")

Start with a few of these ideas, and freewrite to see where they lead you. Then choose as your topic the problem you find most compelling or most serious.

Consider your audience

Who is touched by the problem? Who is in a position to help? Perhaps your audience is a teacher, an employer, or another adult who can help. Or your audience might be friends and other students whom you want to take action to solve the problem. In either case, your audience will determine the content, tone, and style of your proposal.

Consider your purpose

Your main purpose will be to present a problem and propose a solution. Along the way, you will consider a number of solutions and then select the one you think is best. You may want to use your proposal to encourage others to help you solve the problem.

Consider your strategy

Real-life problems don't often lend themselves to neat, easy solutions. To attack a problem effectively, try following this step-by-step process:

1. *Define the problem.* State it in words, as clearly and specifically as you can.
2. *Research the problem.* Gather information from several sources. Ask questions. Break the problem into parts.
3. *Consider various solutions.* Don't limit yourself to the obvious. Be creative. Try some unusual approaches.
4. *Explore each solution.* Can it be done? How? What effects might it have? What new problems might it create?
5. *Choose the solution you think is best.* Have good reasons to support your choice.

Decide on a solution

After checking your notes, write a statement that defines your problem. The clearer and more specific you are in stating the problem, the easier it will be to think about possible solutions. Review your ideas. Look for solutions that seem feasible and easy to explain, as well as effective. Mark your favorites. Then use a pro-con chart, like the one below, to help you evaluate each solution in detail and make your choice.

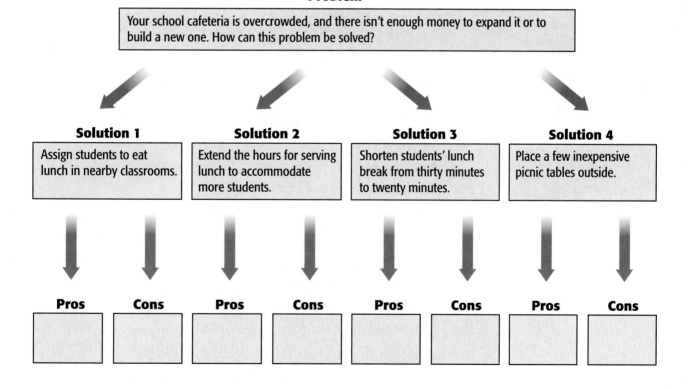

Problem

Your school cafeteria is overcrowded, and there isn't enough money to expand it or to build a new one. How can this problem be solved?

Solution 1
Assign students to eat lunch in nearby classrooms.

Solution 2
Extend the hours for serving lunch to accommodate more students.

Solution 3
Shorten students' lunch break from thirty minutes to twenty minutes.

Solution 4
Place a few inexpensive picnic tables outside.

Pros   **Cons**   **Pros**   **Cons**   **Pros**   **Cons**   **Pros**   **Cons**

DRAFTING

DRAFTING TIP

Include facts, statistics, examples, and personal anecdotes to persuade your readers to care about the problem.

TECHNOLOGY TIP

As you write, you may want to add facts or examples later. Most word processing programs allow you to leave special marks as reminders to fill in information.

Weigh your options

Is your problem particularly interesting? Is your solution a really creative one?

Write your draft

Start by describing the problem and explaining why it needs to be solved. Then describe your solution. Explain how it can be implemented and what its consequences might be, positive and negative. Draft a conclusion as well.

STUDENT MODEL

Our problem is overcrowding in the school cafeteria. Every day students have to eat while standing up because there isn't enough room. I propose having some of the students eat in nearby classrooms. The only additional cost would be the purchase of a few extra garbage cans, and every student could then eat comfortably.

REVISING

REVISING TIP

Try reading your work to two people—one who is involved in the problem and one who knows nothing about it. Ask for suggestions to make your proposal more convincing.

Review your work

Put your draft away for a while. Then, use a colored pencil or the highlight feature of a computer program to mark parts that may need more work. Be a tough critic.

Get another opinion

Ask for feedback from a friend, using the **Questions for Revising** as a guide.

QUESTIONS FOR REVISING

☑ Have I moved logically from the problem to the solution?

☑ Where can I add anecdotes or examples to stir the readers' interest?

☑ How might I make my conclusion stronger?

☑ How well does the content and style suit my purpose and audience?

STUDENT MODEL

More than 175 students spend their lunch period *crammed around tables* in a cafeteria for *designed to seat* 125. Students are tired of competing for a space to eat lunch. *and* The school doesn't have extra money to spend on *expanding* increasing the cafeteria. How can *this problem be solved* both these needs be met?

EDITING/PROOFREADING

When you think your proposal is as good as you can make it, proofread it for errors in spelling, grammar, and mechanics. Using the **Proofreading Checklist** on the inside back cover of this book as a guide, look for one kind of error at a time.

Grammar Hint

In an inverted sentence, the subject follows the verb. Take care to locate the simple subject and make sure the verb agrees with it.

There is *an important* issue *to consider here.*

Along with student needs come *budget* considerations.

● For more on subject-verb agreement, see **Language Handbook**, p. R21.

STUDENT MODEL

On one side is students tired of overcrowding and
                    ∂are
on the other side are a lack of money.
                    ∂is

PUBLISHING/PRESENTING

If you want to present your proposal outside your school, make a list of people you think would be interested in reading or hearing your proposal. Then send them a copy with a cover letter introducing yourself and explaining your purpose.

PRESENTING TIP

If you are using a computer, explore the design options in your word processing program and create a design that fits your proposal.

Reflecting

In your journal, reflect on your experience of writing about a problem and its solution. How might you use this experience to help you solve other problems? What did you learn about yourself as a problem solver? Finally, set goals for your next piece of writing. What will you do differently?

📖 **Save your work for your portfolio.**

Unit Wrap-Up

PERSONAL RESPONSE

1. Which selections in Unit 4 did you find most enjoyable? What was it about these selections that made them enjoyable?
2. Do you think great writing can come from recounting everyday events? Support your explanation using examples from the selections.
3. What have you learned from these selections about the geography and history of our country?
4. How did the poems in Unit 4 compare with other poems you have read in this book? Explain, using examples.

ANALYZING LITERATURE

Think About the Title Unit 4 is titled "Regionalism and Realism," and Theme 6 is called "Energy of the Everyday." Choose one of these titles and write an essay explaining what it means and how it ties together all the selections in the unit. Use at least five of the selections as support, including at least one story, one poem, and one nonfiction piece. You might quote passages from a selection or explain how a certain part of a selection supports your essay's main idea.

EVALUATE AND SET GOALS

Evaluate

1. List three contributions you made to the class as you studied this unit. Explain why each was important.
2. Which aspect of this unit did you find most difficult?
   ● What made it so difficult? How did you handle the difficulty?
   ● What lesson did you learn from handling the difficult parts of the unit?
3. Evaluate your work in this unit by using the following scale. Give at least two reasons for your assessment.
   4 = outstanding   **3** = good   **2** = fair   **1** = weak
4. If you had another week to work on this unit, which selections would you reread? Which ideas would you pursue further? Which skills would you hope to strengthen?

Set Goals

1. Set a goal for your work in the next unit. Focus on improving a skill, such as reading critically.
2. Discuss your goal with your teacher.
3. Plan specific steps to achieve your goal.
4. Plan checkpoints at which you can judge your work.
5. Think of a method to evaluate your finished work.

📁 BUILD YOUR PORTFOLIO

Select From the writing you have done for this unit, choose two pieces to put into your portfolio. Use the following questions as guides when choosing:
● Which pieces taught you the most?
● Which are you likely to share?
● Which taught you unexpected lessons?
● Which gave you the greatest sense of accomplishment?

Reflect Include some explanatory notes with each portfolio piece you have chosen. Use questions like these to guide you:
● What are the piece's strengths and weaknesses?
● How did you improve your writing by working on this piece?
● How would you revise the piece today to make it stronger?

Reading on Your Own

If you have enjoyed the literature in this unit, you might also be interested in the following books.

My Ántonia
by Willa Cather
Jim Burden recalls the Nebraska prairie and the people—most notably the Bohemian immigrant Ántonia—struggling to carve out a life there.

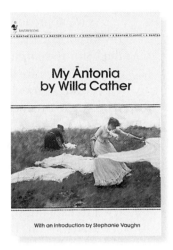

Edith Wharton Abroad: Selected Travel Writings, 1888–1920
edited by Sarah Bird Wright This collection of excerpts presents three decades of Wharton's travel writing. The book demonstrates Wharton's great skill at seeing the often overlooked treasures of everyday life.

Manners and Customs
by Jim Barmeier This book—from the series *Life in America 100 Years Ago*—chronicles details of everyday life at the beginning of the twentieth century. It shows how major forces such as immigration, technological advances, and the rise of the factory system brought great change to many spheres of life, including work, play, education, the family, and courtship.

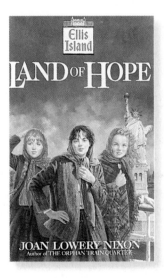

Ellis Island: Land of Hope
by Joan Lowery Nixon Rebekah Levinsky and her family, Russian Jews fleeing oppression, are the main characters in this story of the American immigrant experience of the early 1900s. The story tells of the Levinsky family's voyage to America and their struggle to survive on New York's Lower East Side.

Standardized Test Practice

The passage below is followed by seven questions based on its content. Select the best answer and write the corresponding letter on your paper.

This passage is taken from the memoir of a woman who emigrated as a young girl from Germany to America.

We all expected to see a long line of people waiting to be processed at Ellis Island. But what awaited us was not a
Line line, but rather a sea of people. It rippled
(5) like the ocean, with waves of felt hats, black and gray wool overcoats, and leather-strapped cases. As I caught my first glimpse of it, I felt my stomach rise into my throat. All those men, women,
(10) and children, from all over the world, waiting to get inside. What a wondrous place America must be!
My father's worried expression was now permanently engraved on his face. I was
(15) blissfully ignorant of the fact that we had spent everything we had to buy our passage. All that we had left was the telegram from my father's second cousin, stating his address and the promise that he would
(20) give my father a job and a room in which we could live. What if we couldn't find him? What if he were dead? How would we survive?
My mother, on the other hand, had no
(25) such cares. She never had designs on a great deal of money. Her concern was only for our health. She would wipe our hands and faces incessantly, and admonish us not to touch anything or anyone, lest we
(30) "catch our death." Hoping that her glances would escape our detection, she would furtively look over toward the side of the hall where she knew the medical examinations were administered, where
(35) those who were not healthy enough would have to wait in quarantine before being allowed into the country. She would

immediately re-examine our hands and faces, and rush to interpose herself
(40) between us and anyone whom she suspected of breathing on us.
As we approached the front of the line, my father tried to have all of our papers ready for the immigration officials.
(45) "Name?" the officer barked at my father. Uncertain as to whether he meant first name or last name, my father spoke hesitatingly, "Oskar . . . Oskar Schn—" and with that, the impatient officer cut him
(50) off, saying, "Good. Mr. and Mrs. Ossar." My father stared in disbelief as the hurried officer wrote "OSSAR" in his ledger. He tried to explain, in German, but the officer waved us off. I looked at my sister and
(55) we giggled to ourselves; how like a game it all seemed. Imagine that—an officer who didn't even understand German!
We had no conception of the enormity of what had just happened. Not only had
(60) we left behind our country and our acquaintances, but our name as well. A few minutes later we stood outside in the bright sun of our new home: re-born, re-baptized . . . like newborn infants, with
(65) nothing but possibilities in front of us.

1 The passage primarily serves to
(A) recount the author's experience of arriving in America
(B) describe the author's strength of character during a difficult time
(C) clarify the reasons for the emigration of the author's family
(D) describe in detail the process of becoming an American citizen
(E) explain why the author's name was changed upon arrival in America

2 In lines 3–11, the author's description of the crowd suggests that she feels

(A) overwhelmed by the experience of leaving her home country
(B) impressed by the widespread desire to immigrate
(C) depressed by the number of impoverished people in the world
(D) happy to have finished her long journey
(E) intimidated by the large number of people

3 According to the passage, the author differed from her parents in that she

(A) was more frightened by the crowd than they were
(B) disagreed with the decision to emigrate to America
(C) appreciated the freedom of the New World
(D) had no desire to remain in Germany
(E) was not as worried about the future as they were

4 In line 25, "had designs on" most nearly means

(A) created patterns for
(B) disliked
(C) had artwork of
(D) intended to have
(E) had a fear of

5 The author's statement that her mother "would furtively look over" suggests that her mother

(A) tried to protect her children from fatal diseases
(B) had no sympathy for the people in quarantine
(C) did not want her children to notice that she was worried
(D) was secretly thinking of going back to Germany
(E) had not wanted to leave Germany

6 The author's description in lines 55–57 of the customs officer at Ellis Island suggests that the author viewed him with

(A) anxiety
(B) disinterest
(C) respect
(D) amusement
(E) caution

7 The author claims to have been "re-born" and "re-baptized" (lines 63 and 64) in order to suggest that immigration

(A) is as painful and traumatic an experience as being born
(B) creates feelings of insecurity and helplessness
(C) is a fundamentally religious experience
(D) is like the beginning of a new life
(E) always involves receiving a new name

New York, 1911. George Bellows. Oil on canvas, 42 x 60 in. National Gallery of Art, Washington, DC. Collection of Mr. and Mrs. Paul Mellon.

Beginnings
of the
Modern Age
1910–1930

*"It was a long time ago.
I have almost forgotten my dream.
But it was there then,
In front of me,
Bright like a sun—
My dream."*

—Langston Hughes, from "As I Grew Older"

Theme 7
New Directions
pages 597–716

Theme 8
The Harlem Renaissance
pages 717–765

Setting the Scene

On March 3, 1913, a lanky, long-faced, scholarly man—Woodrow Wilson—arrived in Washington, D.C. Though he would be sworn in as President of the United States the following day, he arrived almost unnoticed. That same day, crowds flocked to a controversial march by women demanding the right to vote. As the women marched, supporters cheered and opponents yelled insults and jeered.

The next day, no competition drew attention from Wilson. A huge crowd of 50,000 people or more gathered to applaud his stirring inaugural address and his promise of a "New Freedom" for ordinary people. Women's right to vote, however, was not on his ambitious agenda, nor was the devastating world war that was to come. But these issues would come, and Wilson and the nation would face them.

U.S.A.

The National Urban League is formed to assist African Americans moving into cities

German submarines sink a British ship, the *Lusitania*, killing 1,198 people, including 128 Americans

1917
The United States declares war on Germany

1910

1911
Japan takes over Korea

Mexican President Porfirio Diaz is ousted; Manchu dynasty is overthrown in China

1914
The Panama Canal opens

1915

1915–16
Approximately one million Armenians die as Turkish troops force them from their land

1917
In Russia, a revolution overthrows the government of the Czar

World

History of the Time

The New Freedom

"There is one great basic fact which underlies all the questions that are discussed on political platforms at the present moment," declared Woodrow Wilson in 1913. "That singular fact is that nothing is done in this country as it was done twenty years ago." New technology—the automobile, the radio, the movies, the telephone, and the airplane—opened up the world and bound the expansive nation together.

Wilson's election reflected a number of popular demands. Many people wanted the government to limit the power of huge business interests. Congress passed laws to protect the rights of consumers and lowered tariffs, or taxes, on imports into the United States. Imported products could better compete with the products of large U.S. corporations, reducing the profits of these corporations. In addition, state governments ratified constitutional amendments that granted women the right to vote.

I WISH MA COULD VOTE

At the same time, more Americans left rural areas for cities. By 1920, for the first time in the nation's history, city inhabitants outnumbered rural dwellers. Many African Americans left the rural South with hopes of greater freedom in northern cities.

War!

In August 1914, Europe burst into war. Great Britain, France, Japan, Belgium, Serbia, Russia, and Italy formed an alliance against Germany, Austria-Hungary, Turkey, and Bulgaria. In the Atlantic Ocean, German submarines torpedoed ships carrying supplies to Great Britain. As American passengers died on these ships, anti-German sentiment grew in the United States. In 1917, with Wilson declaring that "the world must be made safe for democracy," the United States formally entered the war against Germany.

In this war, tanks, artillery, machine guns, planes, and poison gas caused death and destruction on a scale previously unmatched. Finally, on November 11, 1918, the exhausted, bloodied opponents stopped fighting after Germany and its allies surrendered. About 115,000 Americans died in the war, but Europe lost a generation—nearly 10 million people.

The Roaring Twenties

Repulsed by the senseless slaughter of the war, Americans attempted to withdraw from the rest of the world. Politicians rejected Wilson's pleas to join the new League of Nations and approved severe immigration restrictions.

Many Americans expressed a desperate yet creative hysteria in new jazz rhythms, outrageous fashions, and wacky fads, and in obsessions with money, motorcars, and youth. On October 29, 1929, however, the excitement ended. The stock market crashed and countless investors lost all their savings. An extraordinary era had come to an end.

The Nineteenth Amendment gives women the right to vote; prohibition on the sale of alcohol begins

1921
Congress passes the first law sharply limiting European immigration

1924
Congress declares all Native Americans to be citizens of the United States

1929
The stock market crashes, marking the beginning of the Great Depression

1920

The League of Nations meets for first time, in Geneva, Switzerland; Mohandas Gandhi starts a nonviolent movement against British rule in India

1925

1926
Economic turmoil leads to a general strike in Great Britain

1928
Fifteen countries sign the Kellogg-Briand Pact, renouncing war

1930

Life of the Time

People are talking about —

Three Tragedies In 1911 a fire at New York City's Triangle Shirtwaist Company kills 146 people—most of them female workers—trapped behind locked doors. The next year the *Titanic*, a luxury ship on its first voyage, hits an iceberg and sinks. About 1,500 of its 2,200 passengers die. In 1918 a deadly influenza epidemic kills 500,000 in the United States, and an estimated 30 million people worldwide—about three times the number killed in World War I. ▶

Triangle Shirtwaist Company, destroyed by fire, 1911.

Freedom for All? Congress continues to close the celebrated "open door" to America. Immigration restrictions in 1921 and 1924 target Asians and southern and eastern Europeans. Membership in the Ku Klux Klan surges past 4 million in 1924. The Klan directs hate and violence against African Americans, Jews, Roman Catholics, and union members.

Bessie Coleman

◀ **Wheels and Wings** By 1927 there are more than 20 million automobiles in the United States. In the air, stunt flyers become popular. In 1921 Bessie Coleman becomes the first licensed female African American pilot. In 1927 the country goes wild when Charles Lindbergh flies solo from New York to Paris in 33½ hours. Five years later, Amelia Earhart becomes the first woman to fly solo across the Atlantic Ocean.

Firsts

- Montana's Jeannette Rankin becomes the first woman elected to Congress. (1916)
- Gertrude Ederle becomes the first woman to swim the English Channel. (1926)
- Robert Goddard launches the first rocket powered by liquid fuel. (1926)
- Donald F. Duncan introduces the yo-yo, based on a traditional toy from East Asia. (1929)

U.S.A.			
1912 Native American Jim Thorpe stars at the Olympic Games in Sweden	**1914** African American sculptor Meta Vaux Warrick Fuller completes *Ethiopia Awakening*		**1918** The United States goes on daylight saving time for the first time

1910   **1915**

1911 Norwegian explorer Roald Amundsen reaches the South Pole; Marie Curie wins the Nobel Prize for Chemistry	**1916** German-born physicist Albert Einstein announces his general theory of relativity	**1918** A worldwide influenza epidemic kills an estimated 30 million people

World

Food & Fashion

New inventions and international events change the way people eat:

- Toast becomes easier to make with the development of the electric toaster in 1909—and easier still with the automatic toaster a few years later. ▶

- Anti-German sentiment is so powerful during World War I that sauerkraut is now called "liberty cabbage."

- In 1924 a typical family spends thirty-eight percent of its income on food, nearly three times what an American family spends today.

Fashions change dramatically in the 1920s:

- Fashionable young women wear shorter and shorter skirts, which finally skim the knee.

- Short "bobbed" hair shocks some people, who also watch in horror as women paint their lips and rouge their cheeks.

- ◀ Many of these fashion elements come together in the "flapper," a symbol of the new woman of the twenties. In reality, few women are "flappers."

- Men's clothes become more informal and more colorful.

Arts & Entertainment

- Many African Americans migrating from the South settle in New York's Harlem. By the mid-1920s, African American writers, artists, and musicians usher in the Harlem Renaissance.

- The rhythms of jazz come north from the African American clubs of New Orleans, spread by masters such as Louis Armstrong, Jelly Roll Morton, Duke Ellington, and Bessie Smith. The music gives the Jazz Age its name and influences composers such as George Gershwin and Aaron Copland.

Amusements

- "The Sultan of Swat," Babe Ruth, hits sixty home runs in 1927, setting a record that will last thirty-four years.

- Movies become the most popular form of entertainment. In 1930 weekly admissions totals reach ninety million.

1920

The population of the United States reaches 106 million

An earthquake in northwest China kills nearly 200,000 people

1924
Duke Ellington and the Washingtonians make their first recording

1924 **1925**
Chamonix, France, hosts the first Winter Olympics; anthropologists find the fossils of an ancient hominid, *Australopithecus,* in southern Africa

1927
The Jazz Singer is the first talking motion picture

1928
Walt Disney's Mickey Mouse makes his first appearance in *Steamboat Willie*

1930

The world population approaches 2 billion

Literature of the Time

PEOPLE ARE READING . . .

War Propaganda   When the United States goes to war in 1917, the government's Committee on Public Information blankets the country with 75 million leaflets, pamphlets, and posters aimed at recruiting soldiers and explaining President Wilson's war aims to the people. ▶

About Manners   The loosening of conventions after World War I leaves people confused about proper behavior. Their search for guidance makes Emily Post's 1922 book, *Etiquette*, a best-seller. Post remains America's chief arbiter of manners for more than three decades.

Magazines, Magazines, Magazines   New magazines reflect the changing times. In the *American Mercury*, H. L. Mencken expresses the critical, mocking spirit of the day. *Time* summarizes the news, and *Reader's Digest* condenses magazine articles. "Confession" magazines and gossipy movie magazines sell well.

People Are Writing

Parodies   Americans react to political and social events with clever slogans and humorous parodies in verse and song. Even the sacrifices of war (such as sending supplies to the armed forces through the Y.M.C.A.) are parodied in rhyme:

> **"My Tuesdays are meatless,**
> **My Wednesdays are wheatless,**
> **I'm getting more eatless each day.**
> **My coffee is sweetless,**
> **My bed it is sheetless.**
> **All sent to the Y.M.C.A."**

Petitions   Supporters of woman suffrage produce a petition 18,000 feet long with nearly 500,000 names. However, during World War I, the government jails petitioners demanding repeal of repressive laws designed to prevent antiwar protests. ▶

U.S.A.					
Jane Addams, *Twenty Years at Hull-House*	1912 Edna St. Vincent Millay, "Renascence"	1914 Gertrude Stein, *Tender Buttons*	Edgar Lee Masters, *Spoon River Anthology*	1917 William Carlos Williams, "All Que Quiere"	

1910	1912	1913	**1915**	1918
World	Switzerland: Carl Jung, *Psychology of the Unconscious*	England: George Bernard Shaw, *Pygmalion*	India: Muhammad Iqbāl, *The Secrets of the Self*; Japan: Akutagawa Ryūnosuke, *Rashōmon*	China: Lu Hsün, "A Madman's Diary"

Literary Trends: Modernism

"World War I . . . destroyed faith in progress, but it did more than that—it made clear to perceptive thinkers . . . that violence prowled underneath man's apparent harmony and rationality."

—William E. Leuchtenburg, *The Perils of Prosperity*

With their belief in human reason shaken by war, artists strive for new ways to portray the world. Painter Pablo Picasso, instead of reproducing what one sees from a single perspective, shows multiple perspectives in one painting. Composer Arnold Schoenberg abandons the traditional eight-note scale and creates music using a twelve-tone scale.

Writers also abandon conventions. Many create characters who, like real people, think in a continuous flow of ideas that seem to go in several directions at once. T. S. Eliot, William Faulkner, and Irish writer James Joyce make this stream-of-consciousness style famous. Another writer, E. E. Cummings, writes poetry without punctuation, capitalization, or even straight lines of text. These and other Modernists, with their emphasis on the new and untried, throw open the doors of possibility to all who follow.

Portrait of Gertrude Stein, 1906. Pablo Picasso. Oil on canvas, 100 x 81.3 cm. The Metropolitan Museum of Art, New York.

E. E. Cummings

FOCUS ON . . .

The Harlem Renaissance

African Americans who throng to New York's Harlem turn it into a vigorous, fertile cultural center. As W. E. B. Du Bois and others urge the expression of racial pride, writers focus on their own lives, culture, and identity. The fresh, new subjects and skillful writing attracts publishers and readers to the works of many writers, including Langston Hughes, Jean Toomer, Countee Cullen, and later, Zora Neale Hurston. However, with the economic depression of the 1930s, the Harlem Renaissance fades.

Harlem Renaissance novelist and literary editor Jessie Fauset

1923
Jean Toomer, "Song of the Son";
Claude McKay, *Harlem Shadows*

1922
T. S. Eliot,
The Waste Land

1924
Robert Frost wins the first of his
four Pulitzer Prizes for Poetry

1926
Langston Hughes,
The Weary Blues

1927
Carl Sandburg,
*The American
Songbag*

1928
Margaret Mead, *Coming
of Age in Samoa*

1920   **1922**
England: Katherine
Mansfield, *The
Garden Party*

1924
Chile: Pablo Neruda,
*Twenty Love Poems
and a Song of Despair*

1925

Germany: Adolf Hitler, *Mein Kampf*

1926
England: A. A. Milne,
Winnie-the-Pooh

1930

Novels of the Time

Like all of American culture, the novel is profoundly changed by World War I. Many writers and artists see the war as a tragic failure of the old ways and, more than ever, seek to cast off the traditions of the nineteenth century. "Make it new," is the cry of poet Ezra Pound, and novelists explore new subject matter, new styles and points of view, and new narrative techniques. In short, they create the modern novel.

The Great Gatsby
by F. Scott Fitzgerald (1925)

Both the glamor and the dark side of the twenties are reflected in Fitzgerald's story of Jay Gatsby, with his mysterious wealth, his lavish parties, and his idealistic but doomed pursuit of a woman and the American dream. Told from the point of view of Gatsby's neighbor, Nick Carraway, the story captures the spirit of the Jazz Age, a period that Fitzgerald called "an age of miracles, an age of art, and an age of excess."

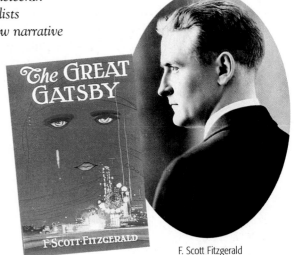

F. Scott Fitzgerald

Edith Wharton

The Age of Innocence
by Edith Wharton (1920)

Through the story of a doomed love, Edith Wharton presents an illuminating study of upper-class New York society in the late nineteenth century. In a perfect match, worldly and wealthy Newland Archer is engaged to May Welland, young, beautiful, and a member of the same elite social circle. Into this rosy picture steps the exotic Ellen Olenska, wellborn but bearing the burden of a mysterious past. Swept away by Olenska, Archer is torn between her and his bride-to-be.

U.S.A.

┌ **1911**
Edith Wharton, *Ethan Frome*

┌ **1912**
James Weldon Johnson, *Autobiography of an Ex-Colored Man*

┌ **1914**
Theodore Dreiser, *The Titan*

┌ **1918**
Willa Cather, *My Ántonia*

1910

1912 —
Germany: Thomas Mann, *Death in Venice*

1913 —
England: D. H. Lawrence, *Sons and Lovers*

└ **1914**
Japan: Natsume Sōseki, *Kokoro;*
Spain: Miguel de Unamuno, *Mist*

1915

Mexico: Mariano Azuela, *The Underdogs*

World

Scene from the movie, *The Sun Also Rises*.

Critics Corner

Too Much Sun

"There was a time, and it went on for weeks, when you could go nowhere without hearing of *The Sun Also Rises*. Some thought it was without excuse; and some, they of the cool, tall foreheads, called it the greatest American novel, tossing *Huckleberry Finn* and *The Scarlet Letter* lightly out the window. They hated it or they revered it. I may say, with due respect to Mr. Hemingway, that I was never so sick of a book in my life."

—Dorothy Parker in the *New Yorker*, October 29, 1927

The Sun Also Rises
by Ernest Hemingway (1926)

World War I, though long over, casts a heavy shadow over this story of members of Hemingway's own Lost Generation—young people psychologically and perhaps physically damaged by the war. Set in the cafes of Paris and the bullrings of Spain, Hemingway's novel paints in poignant detail the aimless lives of a group of cynical, disillusioned young people living in Paris, a life Hemingway himself had lived.

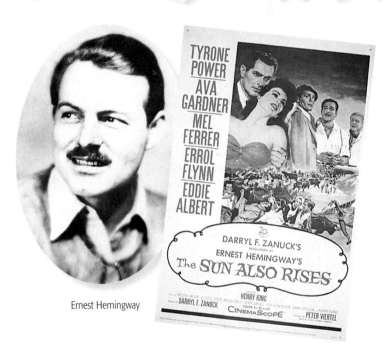

Ernest Hemingway

Sinclair Lewis, *Main Street*

1922 Sinclair Lewis, *Babbitt*

Theodore Dreiser, *An American Tragedy;* Ellen Glasgow, *Barren Ground*

1922 Germany: Hermann Hesse, *Siddhartha;* Ireland: James Joyce, *Ulysses,* published in Paris

1929 William Faulkner, *The Sound and the Fury;* Ernest Hemingway, *A Farewell to Arms*

1928 Claude McKay, *Home to Harlem*

1927 England: Virginia Woolf, *To the Lighthouse*

1928 India: Bibhuti Bushan Banerji, *The Song of the Road*

1920   **1925**   **1930**

Language of the Time

How People Speak

Radio Talk   Individuals and families spend hours in front of the radio, which delivers not only news and entertainment but a uniform English that begins to influence the way people talk.

Marvelous!   The Roaring Twenties generation goes to extremes in speech as in everything else. Things are not merely good, they are "divine," "keen," "super," or "marvelous!" People take delight in clever, slangy expressions, such as the following terms of approval:

- the cat's meow
- the bee's knees
- the tiger's spots

Wordplay

Jazz Horns, 1930s or early 1940s. Adolf Arthur Dehn. Watercolor on paper, 15⅛ x 22⅝ in. Private collection.

Jazz   What is the origin of *jazz,* the word that names a decade? Some believe it came from the name of an African American musician, Jasbo, or Jas, Brown. Others trace it to West Africa. The Tshilubia word *jaja* means "to cause one to dance," and the Temne word *yas* means "lively or energetic." No one knows for certain.

Crosswords   On December 21, 1913, the first crossword puzzle—called a word-cross—appears in the *New York World* newspaper. In the 1920s, a book of crosswords is published, setting off a national craze.

New Words and Expressions

"We could almost write the history of civilization merely from linguistic evidence." —*Albert C. Baugh* and *Thomas Cable*

From World War I

parachute	camouflage
bomber	shell shock
tank (weapon)	bail out
blimp	flame thrower
dog tag	slacker
gas mask	

From the Automobile

sedan	filling station, service
sports car	station, gas station
convertible	backseat driver
blowout	parking lot
retread	hitchhike
jalopy	

Theme 7 — New Directions

Do you ever feel like taking a new direction in your life, doing something quite different? What new directions might you take? The writers in this theme took new directions in their work and in their lives, creating new forms of writing to accompany the great social and economic changes of the "Modern Age."

Abstract Portrait of Marcel Duchamp, 1918. Katherine S. Dreier. Oil on canvas, 18 x 32 in. Museum of Modern Art, New York.

THEME PROJECTS

Learning for Life

Illustrate a Book   Imagine you are illustrating a book called *New Directions: Poetry and Stories from 1910 to 1930.*

1. Choose seven or more selections in this theme that you enjoy. For each, identify one image that has a strong effect on you.

2. On separate sheets of paper, sketch one image for each selection you have chosen.

3. In a small group, discuss your sketches and the reasons why you created each image. Then turn your sketches into color illustrations and put them in a book with copies of the selections. Share your book with the class.

Listening and Speaking

What Should Poetry Be?   With a small group, read ten poems in this theme to answer the question: "What should poetry be?"

1. As you read each poem, discuss how that poet might answer the question. Support your ideas with such details from the poem as subject, rhyme, rhythm, images, figurative language, and word choice.

2. After you have read and discussed all ten poems, decide whether the poets have similar or different ideas of what a poem should be. Then present your findings to the class in the form of a panel discussion.

Literature F O C U S

Imagist Poetry

The New Poets

At the beginning of the twentieth century, poetry was changing. A new group of poets known as the Imagists rebelled against traditional poetry forms. They wanted no part of predictable rhyme and rhythm or of conventionally "beautiful" subjects. Imagists found the tone of traditional poetry too sentimental and "high-minded."

Think, then, how a reader of the time, unfamiliar with the works of these new poets, might have responded to a poem describing the evening:

> "When the evening is spread out against the sky
> Like a patient etherised upon a table."

These lines, from "The Love Song of J. Alfred Prufrock," by T. S. Eliot, provide a classic example of imagist poetry.

Poetry Is . . .

The Imagists, including poets such as Eliot, Ezra Pound, Amy Lowell, Wallace Stevens, and Marianne Moore, held the following principles:

- The *image* is the essence, the raw material, of poetry.
- Poetry should be expressed economically—with brief, clear, concrete language to convey precise images.
- These images should instantly convey to the reader the poem's meaning and emotion.
- The language of these poetic images should be similar to the ways people speak—not made up of predictable rhythms and rhymes—but expressed in freer and more modern verse forms.
- Topics for poems do not have to be high-minded or "poetic." In fact, no topic is unsuitable for a poem.

The first poem in this theme is another classic imagist work. Titled "In a Station of the Metro," it tells of a vision in a subway station. The poet, Ezra Pound, had originally written a poem of thirty lines. He then cut words, making the poem more precise, until it contained only two lines, fourteen words, and two striking and powerful images.

Ezra Pound and other Imagists exerted a major influence on American poetry. Much of the poetry we read today stems from their poetic revolution.

Amy Lowell

ACTIVITY

In a small group, discuss some everyday scenes that might be good topics for imagist poetry. Choose one scene and decide what its central image is. Then list words and phrases that might clearly convey that image and its emotional tone. Try to appeal to senses other than just sight. Share your group's work with the class.

Before You Read

In a Station of the Metro and A Pact

Meet Ezra Pound

"Pound is a fine fellow, but not one person in a thousand likes him, and a great many people detest him."

—*William Carlos Williams*

Whatever their feelings about Ezra Pound may have been, many people agreed with the poet T. S. Eliot that Pound was "more responsible for the twentieth-century revolution in poetry than [was] any other individual."

Pound's achievements in poetry were no accident. As a young man, he determined that "at thirty [he] would know more about poetry than any man living," and he worked hard to achieve his goal. While attending Hamilton College and the University of Pennsylvania, he immersed himself in literature from around the world and remained a voracious reader throughout his life.

In 1908, at age twenty-three, Pound left for Europe, settling first in London and later in Paris and finally in Italy. There he wrote poetry and criticism and translated verse from nine different languages. He also served as an overseas editor for Chicago's *Poetry* magazine, a position he used to nurture the careers of Robert Frost, T. S. Eliot, and other writers. In 1912 Pound founded the literary movement known as Imagism, which called for "direct treatment of the 'thing'" and "the language of common speech, but always the exact word."

Though he urged other writers to "make it new," Pound himself often drew upon the literature of the past. In his best-known work, a collection of 117 poems called *The Cantos*, he combined his own ideas with material from different cultures and languages, historical texts, and newspaper articles.

During World War II, Pound supported the Fascist Italian dictator Benito Mussolini and made radio broadcasts openly criticizing the United States and its efforts in the war. Though arrested for treason after Italy fell to the Allies, Pound was declared mentally unfit to stand trial. He was then sent to a mental hospital, where he continued to write. Thirteen years later, the charges against him were dropped, and Pound returned to Italy.

Ezra Pound was born in 1885 and died in 1972.

FOCUS ACTIVITY

Think about a moment in time that captured your attention.

JOURNAL In your journal, describe the essence of that moment in two to three sentences.

SETTING A PURPOSE Read to find out how one poet captures a moment in time.

BACKGROUND

The Time and Place

These poems were written in 1913, a year after Pound joined *Poetry* magazine and a year before he edited the first anthology of imagist poetry, *Des Imagistes.*

Artistic Influences

Pound was influenced by the poems he read, as well as the paintings he saw and the music he heard. He was impressed with the brief but evocative Japanese **haiku** poetry (see page R7). One poet who particularly inspired Pound was Walt Whitman, whom Pound considered an original genius, but also "an exceedingly nauseating pill."

In a Station of the Metro

Ezra Pound ∾

The apparition° of these faces in the crowd;
Petals on a wet, black bough.°

The *Metro* refers to the Paris subway.

1 An *apparition* is a ghost or a phantom. It can also be a sight
that is unexpected or strange.
2 A *bough* is a branch of a tree, especially a main branch.

A Pact

Ezra Pound ∾

I make a pact with you, Walt Whitman—
I have detested you long enough.
I come to you as a grown child
Who has had a pig-headed father;
5   I am old enough now to make friends.
It was you that broke the new wood,
Now is a time for carving.
We have one sap and one root—
Let there be commerce° between us.

---

9 Here, *commerce* means "an exchange of views and attitudes."

Responding to Literature

Personal Response

Which poem do you think reveals more about the poet?

ANALYZING LITERATURE

In a Station of the Metro

RECALL AND INTERPRET

1. In the first line, what word does the speaker use to describe how the faces look to him? What might that word suggest about the faces?
2. To what image does the speaker compare the faces? Based on this image, how do you think the speaker feels about the faces? Explain.

EVALUATE AND CONNECT

3. Pound once wrote, "Painters realize that what matters is form and color. The image is the poet's pigment." In what ways is this poem like a painting?
4. In this poem, Pound focused on faces. What would you focus on if you were trying to capture the essence of the moment you described for the Focus Activity on page 599?

A Pact

RECALL AND INTERPRET

5. To whom is the poem addressed? How have the speaker's feelings changed?
6. What **extended metaphor** does the poet use in lines 6–9? In your opinion, what idea does the speaker express in these lines? (See Literary Terms Handbook, page R6.)

EVALUATE AND CONNECT

7. Theme Connections   How might this poem reflect the theme "New Directions"?
8. Name some people who have influenced your life. In what ways did they affect it?

Literary ELEMENTS

Juxtaposition

Juxtaposition is the placing of two or more distinct things side by side in order to compare or contrast them. Pound was inspired by Japanese verse forms, which often use juxtaposition to evoke an emotional response. In the following **haiku,** for example, the Japanese poet Matsuo Bashō expresses a melancholic view of spring by juxtaposing a line about spring with lines about the end of autumn:

First day of spring—
I keep thinking about
    the end of autumn.

1. What two images does Pound juxtapose in "In a Station of the Metro"?
2. In your opinion, what effect does this juxtaposition have? What emotion might it produce in the reader?

● See **Literary Terms Handbook,** p. R9.

Before You Read

The Love Song of J. Alfred Prufrock

Meet T. S. Eliot

Along with Ezra Pound, T. S. Eliot did more to revolutionize poetry in the twentieth century than any other writer. His experiments in language and form and his introduction into poetry of the scenes and concerns of everyday life forever changed literary tastes in this country and profoundly influenced the next generation of poets.

Eliot was born in St. Louis, Missouri, into a distinguished family that provided him with the best education available. In 1906 he entered Harvard University, where he steeped himself in literature and published his first poems. He then studied philosophy at the Sorbonne in Paris, at Harvard, and in England, where he would permanently settle. It was there, when he was twenty-six, that Eliot met the man who would champion his art and serve as an editor of his poems— Ezra Pound.

In 1915 Pound persuaded Harriet Monroe of *Poetry* magazine to publish "The Love Song of J. Alfred Prufrock." Often called the first modernist poem, "Prufrock" captures the emptiness and alienation many people feel living in modern, impersonal cities. The poem baffled, even angered, many readers. They found its subject matter "unpoetic," its fragmented structure off-putting, and its allusions, or references, difficult to understand.

The same month "Prufrock" was published, Eliot married Vivien Haigh-Wood. For six years he worked as a teacher and a bank clerk, and in his spare time he wrote numerous literary essays,

as well as his best-known work, *The Waste Land*. In this poem, Eliot expresses the disillusionment many people felt after the horrors of World War I, and their lack of and need for something to believe in. The work brought him international acclaim, but not happiness. Eliot was facing great strain in his marriage and in his job as a bank clerk.

Eventually, Eliot began a new, more satisfying career as a book editor and joined the Church of England, finding in Christianity a purpose in life. In poems such as "The Hollow Men" (1925), "Ash Wednesday" (1930), and his masterpiece, *Four Quartets* (1943), he described the importance and difficulty of belief in a spiritually impoverished world.

In his final years, Eliot wrote several plays. He also wrote essays of literary criticism that have had a permanent impact on poetry. In recognition of his achievements, he received in 1948 the Nobel Prize for Literature. At the time of his death, many considered Eliot to be the most important poet and critic writing in the English language.

"Genuine poetry can communicate before it is understood."

"Human kind cannot bear much reality."

—*Eliot*

T. S. Eliot was born in 1888 and died in 1965.

FOCUS ACTIVITY

The title of a poem often provides clues to its main idea. What do you think a "love song" should be like?

LIST IT! Create a list of words describing the nature of love songs.

SETTING A PURPOSE Read to find out one writer's version of a love song.

BACKGROUND

The Time and Place

When Eliot wrote "The Love Song of J. Alfred Prufrock," cities were growing at a rapid rate. In many countries, people in cities outnumbered those inhabiting rural areas. Factories were overrunning residential areas, people were crowding into huge apartment buildings, and skyscrapers were being built in great numbers. While factory owners were amassing great wealth, workers often toiled under miserable conditions.

In his poems, T. S. Eliot expressed the feelings of loneliness, alienation, and frustration that came with these changes. To help communicate these feelings, he sometimes made references to the work of fourteenth-century Italian poet Dante Alighieri (dän′ tā ä′ lē gyär′ ē). In "The Love Song of J. Alfred Prufrock," Eliot begins with a quote from Dante's epic poem *The Divine Comedy.* In this passage (*Inferno,* Canto XXVII, lines 61–66), presented in the original Italian, a condemned spirit in Hell confesses his sins to the speaker, wrongly believing that the speaker cannot return to Earth. "If I believed my answer were being given to someone who could ever return to the world, this flame [source of the spirit's voice] would shake no more; but since, if what I hear is true, no one ever did return alive from this depth, I answer you without fear of dishonor."

Stream of Consciousness

Stream of consciousness is a term first used by the American psychologist William James to describe the spontaneous flow of a person's thoughts, feelings, and emotions. Under the influence of James's ideas, writers in the early 1900s began trying to represent the random movements of a character's mind. To achieve their goal, they eliminated conjunctions and other connecting devices from their writing. They also linked thoughts and images that seemed dissimilar, but that could be associated in the mind.

Man viewing steel works, 1907.

The Love Song of J. Alfred Prufrock

T. S. Eliot

*S'io credessi che mia resposta fosse
a persona che mai tornasse al mondo,
questa fiamma staria senza più scosse.
Ma per ciò che giammai di questo fondo
non tornò vivo alcun, s'i'odo il vero,
senza tema d'infamia ti respondo.*

Let us go then, you and I,
When the evening is spread out against the sky
Like a patient etherised° upon a table;
Let us go, through certain half-deserted streets,
5   The muttering retreats
Of restless nights in one-night cheap hotels
And sawdust restaurants with oyster-shells:
Streets that follow like a tedious° argument
Of insidious° intent
10 To lead you to an overwhelming question . . .
Oh, do not ask, 'What is it?'
Let us go and make our visit.

In the room the women come and go
Talking of Michelangelo.°

15 The yellow fog that rubs its back upon the window-panes,
The yellow smoke that rubs its muzzle on the window-panes,

---

3 *Etherised (etherized)* (ē′ thə rīzd′) means "anesthetized with ether, as before
an operation"; in other words, "made insensitive to pain."
8 *Tedious* means "tiresome because of length" or "boring."
9 *Insidious* (in sid′ ē əs) means "slyly dangerous" or "deceitful."
14 *Michelangelo* Buonarroti (mī′ kəl an′ jə lō′   bwô nä rô′ tē) (1475–1564) was a gifted
Italian sculptor and painter.

Licked its tongue into the corners of the evening,
Lingered upon the pools that stand in drains,
Let fall upon its back the soot that falls from chimneys,
20   Slipped by the terrace, made a sudden leap,
And seeing that it was a soft October night,
Curled once about the house, and fell asleep.

And indeed there will be time
For the yellow smoke that slides along the street
25   Rubbing its back upon the window-panes;
There will be time, there will be time
To prepare a face to meet the faces that you meet;
There will be time to murder and create,
And time for all the works and days of hands
30   That lift and drop a question on your plate;
Time for you and time for me,
And time yet for a hundred indecisions,
And for a hundred visions and revisions,
Before the taking of a toast and tea.

35   In the room the women come and go
Talking of Michelangelo.

And indeed there will be time
To wonder, 'Do I dare?' and, 'Do I dare?'
Time to turn back and descend the stair,
40   With a bald spot in the middle of my hair—
(They will say: 'How his hair is growing thin!')

Rainy Night, 1930. Charles Burchfield. Watercolor, 30 x 42 in. San Diego Museum of Art.

Viewing the painting: Which images or lines from "The Love Song of J. Alfred Prufrock" would you use to describe this painting? Explain your choices.

My morning coat,° my collar mounting firmly to the chin,
My necktie rich and modest, but asserted° by a simple pin—
(They will say: 'But how his arms and legs are thin!')
45   Do I dare
Disturb the universe?
In a minute there is time
For decisions and revisions which a minute will reverse.

For I have known them all already, known them all—
50   Have known the evenings, mornings, afternoons,
I have measured out my life with coffee spoons;
I know the voices dying with a dying fall
Beneath the music from a farther room.
     So how should I presume?°

55   And I have known the eyes already, known them all—
The eyes that fix you in a formulated° phrase,
And when I am formulated, sprawling on a pin,
When I am pinned and wriggling on the wall,
Then how should I begin
60   To spit out all the butt-ends of my days and ways?
     And how should I presume?

And I have known the arms already, known them all—
Arms that are braceleted and white and bare
(But in the lamplight, downed with light brown hair!)?
65   Is it perfume from a dress
That makes me so digress?°
Arms that lie along a table, or wrap about a shawl.
     And should I then presume?
     And how should I begin?

70   Shall I say, I have gone at dusk through narrow streets
And watched the smoke that rises from the pipes
Of lonely men in shirt-sleeves, leaning out of windows? . . .

I should have been a pair of ragged claws
Scuttling across the floors of silent seas.

---

42 A *morning coat* is a man's jacket that slopes away from a front button at the waist to tails at the back. It was worn for formal daytime dress.

43 Here, *asserted* means "made more bold" or "enhanced."

54 *Presume* (pri zōōm′) means "to go beyond what is considered proper."

56 *Formulated* means "reduced to or expressed as a formula," thereby losing individuality.

66 *Digress* (dī gres′) means "to depart from the main subject" or "to ramble."

75 And the afternoon, the evening, sleeps so peacefully!
Smoothed by long fingers,
Asleep . . . tired . . . or it malingers,°
Stretched on the floor, here beside you and me.
Should I, after tea and cakes and ices,
80 Have the strength to force the moment to its crisis?
But though I have wept and fasted, wept and prayed,
Though I have seen my head (grown slightly bald) brought in upon a platter°
I am no prophet°—and here's no great matter;
I have seen the moment of my greatness flicker,
85 And I have seen the eternal Footman° hold my coat, and snicker,
And in short, I was afraid.

And would it have been worth it, after all,
After the cups, the marmalade, the tea,
Among the porcelain, among some talk of you and me,
90 Would it have been worth while,
To have bitten off the matter with a smile,
To have squeezed the universe into a ball
To roll it towards some overwhelming question,
To say: 'I am Lazarus, come from the dead,°
95 Come back to tell you all, I shall tell you all'—
If one, settling a pillow by her head,
    Should say: 'That is not what I meant at all.
    That is not it, at all.'

And would it have been worth it, after all,
100 Would it have been worth while,
After the sunsets and the dooryards and the sprinkled streets,
After the novels, after the teacups, after the skirts that trail along the floor—
And this, and so much more?—
It is impossible to say just what I mean!

---

77 Someone who *malingers* (mə ling′ gərz) pretends to be sick or injured in order to avoid working.
82 *[head . . . platter]* This biblical reference is to the beheading of the prophet John the Baptist (Matthew 14:1–11). King Herod was so pleased with the dancing of Salome, his stepdaughter, that he promised her anything she desired. Prompted by her mother, Salome asked for the head of John on a platter. Herod granted her request.
83 A *prophet* is a person who predicts the future or who speaks by divine inspiration.
85 The *eternal Footman* is Death.
94 *[I am Lazarus . . . dead]* This biblical reference is to (John 11:1–44) in which Jesus restored his friend Lazarus to life after he had been dead for four days.

105   But as if a magic lantern° threw the nerves in patterns on a screen:
Would it have been worth while
If one, settling a pillow or throwing off a shawl,
And turning toward the window, should say:
    'That is not it at all,
110   That is not what I meant, at all.'

No! I am not Prince Hamlet,° nor was meant to be;
Am an attendant lord, one that will do
To swell a progress,° start a scene or two,
Advise the prince; no doubt, an easy tool,
115   Deferential,° glad to be of use,
Politic,° cautious, and meticulous;
Full of high sentence,° but a bit obtuse;°
At times, indeed, almost ridiculous—
Almost, at times, the Fool.

120   I grow old . . . I grow old . . .
I shall wear the bottoms of my trousers rolled.

Shall I part my hair behind? Do I dare to eat a peach?
I shall wear white flannel trousers, and walk upon the beach.
I have heard the mermaids singing, each to each.

125   I do not think that they will sing to me.

I have seen them riding seaward on the waves
Combing the white hair of the waves blown back
When the wind blows the water white and black.

We have lingered in the chambers of the sea
130   By sea-girls wreathed with seaweed red and brown
Till human voices wake us, and we drown.

---

105 The *magic lantern,* a forerunner of the modern slide projector, was a device for projecting
enlarged images.

111 *Prince Hamlet* is the Prince of Denmark, the tragic hero of Shakespeare's play *Hamlet.*

113 *To swell a progress* is to participate in, and thereby increase (swell) the number of people in
a royal procession or a play.

115 *Deferential* (def′ ə ren′ shəl) means "yielding to someone else's opinions or wishes."

116 *Politic* (pol′ ə tik) means "characterized by prudence or shrewdness in managing, dealing, or
promoting a policy."

117 *High sentence* is fancy, pompous speech full of advice, like that of the old counselor Polonius
in *Hamlet. Obtuse* (əb tōōs′) means "slow in understanding" or "dull."

Responding to Literature

Personal Response

What are your impressions of J. Alfred Prufrock?

——— ANALYZING LITERATURE ———

RECALL

1. According to lines 1–10, with whom will Prufrock make his visit and through what places will they travel? To what will they be led?
2. What kinds of activities does Prufrock say he will have time for in lines 26–48?
3. How does Prufrock describe himself and his life in lines 49–74?
4. What does Prufrock debate with himself in lines 79–110?
5. In lines 111–121, how does Prufrock characterize himself?

INTERPRET

6. In your opinion, what do Prufrock's descriptions of the sky and of the places he will travel through suggest about his state of mind? What do these places have in common?
7. In your opinion, why does Prufrock emphasize having time for the activities mentioned in lines 26–48? Prufrock asks, "Do I dare / Disturb the universe?" What might he mean by that question?
8. What does Prufrock's description of his life and what he has known suggest about his self-image and the way he has conducted his life?
9. What, in your opinion, is Prufrock's "overwhelming question"? Why does he expect the woman to react in a certain way and what does this suggest about his relationship with women?
10. What do lines 111–131 suggest about how Prufrock sees himself and his future? In your opinion, what does the poem's final line mean?

EVALUATE AND CONNECT

11. In lines 15–22, Eliot compares the movements of the fog to those of a cat. In your opinion, how does this **extended metaphor** contribute to the meaning of the poem? (See Literary Terms Handbook, page R6.)
12. Prufrock says there will be time "To prepare a face to meet the faces that you meet." For what occasions do you prepare a "face" and why?
13. Compare the poem with the list you created for the Focus Activity on page 603. Do you think the title of the poem fits its content? Explain.
14. In what ways does the poem express Eliot's belief that society had become spiritually and morally empty?
15. Does Prufrock seem like a real person with real problems? Explain.

Literary ELEMENTS

Allusion

An **allusion** is a short reference to a person, a place, an event, or another work of literature. Writers use allusions to express an idea or to clarify its meaning. For example, in "The Love Song of J. Alfred Prufrock," Eliot includes an allusion to Michelangelo in order to indicate that the people discussing this great artist are well educated and from the middle or upper classes. The reader might even picture well-dressed women wandering about a room with a museum-like atmosphere.

1. To which biblical characters does Eliot refer in lines 82–83 and 94–95? Check the footnotes, if necessary.
2. In your opinion, why does he allude to these biblical characters?
3. Choose one of the allusions in lines 82–83, 94–95, or 111–119, and explain how it contributes to the poem's meaning.

● See **Literary Terms Handbook**, p. R1.

LITERATURE AND WRITING

Writing About Literature

Men and Women   A major theme in Eliot's poetry is the inability of a man and woman to communicate with each other. With a partner, look through "The Love Song of J. Alfred Prufrock" to find all the passages that explore this theme. Read over each passage carefully and discuss its meaning. Then, together, write two or three paragraphs explaining the theme of communication. Support your conclusions using details from the poem.

Creative Writing

Let Me Tell You   Eliot's poem is a **dramatic monologue,** or a long speech by a character in which the character discloses his or her thoughts and emotions. Invent a character who knows Prufrock intimately, and then create a dramatic monologue in which that character tells his or her impressions of Prufrock.

EXTENDING YOUR RESPONSE

Literature Groups

Tragedy or Comedy?   Is Prufrock a tragic character—is the reader supposed to feel real sorrow about his situation? Or is he a comic character—is the reader supposed to laugh at him or think he is foolish? Debate this question in your group, using examples from the poem to support your position. Then present your conclusions to the class.

Learning for Life

Interview   Imagine that you have the opportunity to interview J. Alfred Prufrock. Write a dialogue of the

interview as you think it might develop. Include in your dialogue references to the poem's central themes, such as Prufrock's inability to act and his feelings of alienation. Write at least ten questions and ten answers.

Performing

Put Yourself in Prufrock's Shoes   Choose a section of "The Love Song of J. Alfred Prufrock" to perform. In planning your performance, find or create a costume, select makeup, and decide what facial expressions, gestures, and movements you will use. Also practice speaking the lines to determine how loudly and quickly to deliver them. Finally, perform your piece for the class.

Reading Further

To read more by or about Eliot, try these works:

Poems: "The Hollow Men" and "The Waste Land" are included in Eliot's *Complete Poems and Plays: 1909–1950.*

Biography: *T. S. Eliot: A Life,* by Peter Ackroyd.

📖 **Save your work for your portfolio.**

Winter Night, 1928. Stefan Hirsch. Oil on panel, 22½ x 19¾ in. Collection of the Newark Museum, Newark, NJ.

Reading & Thinking Skills

Identifying the Author's Purpose

Have you ever laughed at the wrong time, thinking something was a joke when it was really serious? If so, then you know how important it is to recognize a speaker's purpose so you know how to respond. The same is true of recognizing an author's purpose: once you understand it, you can better evaluate what you are reading and respond appropriately.

An author typically writes to accomplish one or more of the following purposes: to persuade, to inform or explain, to entertain, to describe, or to tell a story. You can begin to figure out which of these is most likely the author's main purpose by thinking critically about the aspects you first encounter: the title and the first few paragraphs, lines, or stanzas.

Once you have formed an initial idea of the author's purpose, however, it's a good idea to double-check your notion against the information you gather from the rest of the piece. For example, the title of T. S. Eliot's "The Love Song of J. Alfred Prufrock" *might* lead you to believe that the purpose of the poem is to entertain or to tell a story. However, as you read on, the content, structure, and language of Eliot's poem reveal that the purpose of this poem is quite complex. At some points Eliot amuses the reader; at others he describes a sense of disillusionment with modern society.

To determine an author's main purpose, ask yourself questions like these:

Elements to Examine	Questions You Might Ask
Title	What might the title suggest about the nature of the topic and the author's attitude toward it?
Form	For what purposes is this form of writing most often used?
Tone	What is the nature of the tone: serious, formal, friendly, mocking? What might the tone suggest about the author's purpose?
Content	Is there a thesis statement? What kinds of details does the selection contain? For what purpose are such details most often used?
Structure/Organization	How is the content presented? For what purpose(s) might this type of organization be most appropriate?
Language	What kinds of transitional words are present? Are there many specialized terms? Are there a lot of descriptive words? For what purpose might an author use these kinds of words?

● For more about author's purpose, see **Reading Handbook,** p. R86–R93.

ACTIVITY

Choose a selection from this theme and use the questions above to try to identify the author's purpose. Explain to the class how you arrived at your conclusion.

Before You Read

The Red Wheelbarrow and *This Is Just to Say*

Meet William Carlos Williams

"Eyes stand first in the poet's equipment."

"Of mixed ancestry I felt from earliest childhood that America was the only home I could ever possibly call my own. I felt that it was expressly founded for me. . ."

—*Williams*

William Carlos Williams led a double life as a medical doctor and an award-winning poet. Often he would write between seeing patients, sometimes even jotting down poems on prescription pads. Despite his hectic schedule, Williams managed to compose groundbreaking poems that celebrate cultural diversity, colloquial speech, and everyday events.

Williams himself had a diverse background; his mother was born in Puerto Rico, and his father was British. He was raised in northern New Jersey, a part of the world he would mythologize in his five-volume epic, *Paterson*. At age twenty-three, he graduated from the University of Pennsylvania Medical School, where he wrote many of the poems that appear in his first book, *Poems*, published in 1909.

Williams believed that poetry should be grounded in everyday things and scenes, not abstract ideas, and was famous for saying, "No ideas but in things." He explored the world about him, writing of the gritty, industrial landscape of northern New Jersey and of his patients and neighbors, many of whom were impoverished immigrants struggling to fashion lives for themselves in the United States. Williams left an important legacy of work including poems, plays, essays, and stories. Somehow, while accomplishing all this, he also managed, as a doctor, to deliver more than two thousand babies.

William Carlos Williams was born in 1883 and died in 1963.

FOCUS ACTIVITY

What have you seen today that would make a good poem?

QUICKWRITE Look at the world as a poet might. What sights, smells, sounds, and situations could be used as subjects for poems? Jot down five possible subjects in your journal.

SETTING A PURPOSE Read to see how a poet turns everyday situations into vivid poems.

BACKGROUND

About the Poem
Williams saw the red wheelbarrow of this poem outside an old house. Rain was pouring down, and white chickens were walking nearby. Williams said, "The sight impressed me somehow as about the most important, the most integral [complete] that it had ever been my pleasure to gaze upon."

Literary Influences
While attending the University of Pennsylvania, Williams befriended poet Ezra Pound, who had a major influence on Williams's work. Pound originated the literary movement called Imagism, which emphasized the presentation of concrete images and the use of stripped-down language based on everyday speech. Williams himself recommended, "Cut and cut again whatever you write—while you leave by your art no trace of your cutting—and the final utterance will remain packed with what you have to say."

The Red Wheelbarrow

so much depends
upon

a red wheel
barrow

5   glazed° with rain
water

beside the white
chickens.

William Carlos Williams

The Red Wheelbarrow, 1992. Frank Jensen. Painted steel sculpture: approximately 27 x 73 x 34 in.; concrete base: approximately 2 x 73 x 42 in. Collection of the artist.

This Is Just to Say

William Carlos Williams

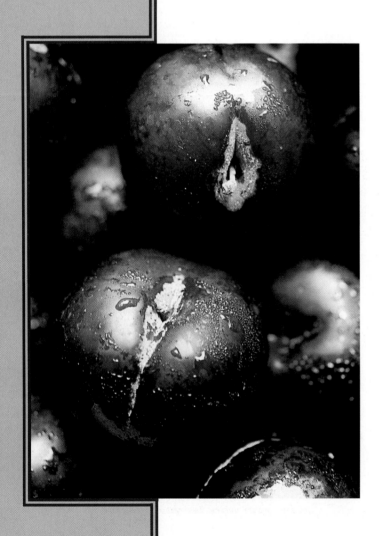

I have eaten
the plums
that were in
the icebox

5   and which
you were probably
saving
for breakfast

Forgive me
10   they were delicious
so sweet
and so cold

Responding to Literature

Personal Response

What thoughts came to your mind as you read these poems?

ANALYZING LITERATURE

The Red Wheelbarrow

RECALL AND INTERPRET

1. What do the first two lines suggest about the speaker's response to the scene?
2. What item is mentioned in stanza 2? What might be the significance of its color?
3. What two items does the poet describe in stanzas 3 and 4? What do you think Williams is saying in this poem?

EVALUATE AND CONNECT

4. Williams carefully arranges his words, including breaking up the words *rainwater* and *wheelbarrow*. How, in your opinion, does the arrangement of the words and stanzas affect the look, feel, sound, and pace of the poem?
5. Would you have picked this red wheelbarrow as a topic for a poem? How is it similar to or different from the subjects you listed for the Focus Activity on page 612?

This Is Just to Say

RECALL AND INTERPRET

6. How does the title connect to the poem?
7. What does the speaker admit in the first two stanzas? What does this suggest about the speaker's relationship to the person being addressed?
8. What does the speaker want from the other person? What does the speaker describe in the last three lines? In your opinion, why are these details included?

EVALUATE AND CONNECT

9. What **tone** does the speaker use? How would you react to this tone if you were the other person? Why? (See Literary Terms Handbook, page R16.)
10. Theme Connections   In what ways does this poem go in a new direction from earlier poems about abstract concepts such as *love* or *pleasure*?

EXTENDING YOUR RESPONSE

Literature Groups

The Perfect Poem?   Williams felt that the **meter** (see page R9) of "The Red Wheelbarrow" perfectly captured how pleased and impressed he was with the scene. Do you agree with Williams? Debate this issue in your group and share your results with the class.

Creative Writing

This Is Just to Respond   Write a brief reply to "This Is Just to Say" that is in keeping with the poem's **tone** and simplicity. Write your message as either a note or a poem.

📑 **Save your work for your portfolio.**

Before You Read

Anecdote of the Jar

Meet Wallace Stevens

"In the world of words, imagination is one of the forces of nature."

—*Stevens*

To those around him, Wallace Stevens probably didn't seem like a poet at all. He had a businesslike manner and worked as a lawyer in New York and later in the claims department of an insurance company in Connecticut. In fact, in his journal, Stevens expressed embarrassment about writing poetry: "Keep all this a great secret. There is something absurd about all this writing of verses; but the truth is, it elates and satisfies me to do it."

Stevens's poetry didn't stay a secret forever. He had published a few poems while attending Harvard University, but his more mature poems began to appear in magazines when he was thirty-five. Nine years later, in 1923, he published his first volume of poetry, *Harmonium*. The book received little attention until it was republished in 1931. With this revised edition and with other books that soon followed, Stevens gained a national reputation as an important and skilled poet. In 1955 he won a Pulitzer Prize for his *Collected Poems*.

Though Stevens never became a full-time writer, he believed very strongly in the importance and power of poetry. A poet, he once wrote, can "help people to live their lives." With their sensuous imagery, brilliant colors, and evocative language, Stevens's poems can indeed help people find joy and beauty in the world in which they live.

Wallace Stevens was born in 1879 and died in 1955.

FOCUS ACTIVITY

Think about a place in nature you like to visit, such as a park, a forest, or your own backyard. In what ways might the appearance of a jar or other manufactured object change the feel of that place?

FREEWRITE Spend three or four minutes freewriting to explore your response to this question. Let your imagination soar.

SETTING A PURPOSE Read to find out what happens to a wilderness in Tennessee when a jar is placed there.

BACKGROUND

Stevens and the Imagination

According to Stevens, the role of the poet is to use his or her imagination to "become the light in the minds of others." Stevens believed that only through the imagination could people understand the true nature of reality and experience a sense of order in a chaotic world. Through his poetry, Stevens explored the complex relationship between the physical world and the shaping power of the imagination.

Anecdote of the Jar

Wallace Stevens ~

I placed a jar in Tennessee,
And round it was, upon a hill.
It made the slovenly wilderness
Surround that hill.

5   The wilderness rose up to it,
And sprawled around, no longer wild.
The jar was round upon the ground
And tall and of a port° in air.°

It took dominion° everywhere.
10   The jar was gray and bare.
It did not give of bird or bush,
Like nothing else in Tennessee.

Rainy Day on a Farm, 1940. Jack Delano. Photograph. Library of Congress, Washington, DC.

---

8 Here, *port* means "the manner in which one carries oneself," and *air* means "the appearance or bearing of a person." The effect of the phrase *of a port in air* is that the jar has a certain dignified quality or manner in its appearance.
9 Here, *dominion* means "supreme authority."

Responding to Literature

Personal Response

What did the jar "upon a hill" look like in your imagination? Make a quick sketch to show what you pictured as you read the poem.

ANALYZING LITERATURE

RECALL AND INTERPRET

1. What action does the speaker in the poem take?
2. What word describes the wilderness in line 3? What might this word suggest about the speaker's attitude toward the wilderness?
3. What happens to the wilderness because of the jar? What seems to be the speaker's attitude toward this change?
4. How does the speaker describe the jar in lines 7–10? How powerful does the jar seem to be, based on the descriptions? What might it **symbolize?**
5. At the end of the poem, how is the jar different from the things around it? What, do you think, is the purpose of emphasizing this difference?

EVALUATE AND CONNECT

6. Examine the adjectives used to describe the jar and the wilderness. In your opinion, how does the contrast Stevens creates between the jar and its surroundings help clarify the meaning of the poem?
7. In what ways might this poem illustrate Stevens's belief in the power of the imagination?
8. Refer to your response to the Focus Activity on page 616. How do the changes you imagined occurring compare with the changes Stevens describes in the poem?

Literary ELEMENTS

Symbol

A **symbol** is a person, place, or thing that has meaning in itself and also stands for something other than itself. A symbol in a poem may have many meanings and feelings associated with it, or it may point to something that cannot be precisely defined.

In "Anecdote of the Jar," the symbolic meaning of the jar may be understood in more than one way, requiring readers to use their imaginations to come up with several possible meanings.

1. What do you think the wilderness is a symbol for?
2. Use your answer to question 1 to explain what you think the poem is saying.

● See **Literary Terms Handbook,** p. R16.

EXTENDING YOUR RESPONSE

Literature Groups

Sparking Your Imagination   In your group, debate whether or not "Anecdote of the Jar" helps readers understand the world. Does Stevens help you see the interaction between people and nature in a new light? Share your conclusions with the class.

Creative Writing

Anecdote Update   This poem tells the story of a jar on a hill in the wilderness. Rewrite the poem to fit the place where you live. What is the object (instead of the jar), what are the surroundings like, and what happens to the surroundings? What message do you want to convey?

📖 **Save your work for your portfolio.**

Newspaper Article

What does it feel like to be jilted or "dumped"? Read on to learn about one couple's experience of a canceled wedding and broken relationship—and what an expert had to say about their experience.

"Let's Call the Whole Thing Off"

Canceling a Wedding at the Last Minute Can Be Humiliating, Expensive . . . and Sensible

by Leila Cobo-Hanlon—*St. Louis Post-Dispatch,* August 16, 1995

Guests, flowers, champagne, band. One smiling clergyman and one nervous groom.

After months of preparation, the stage is set and the cast is ready. But instead of "Here Comes the Bride," the leading lady has opted for "Let's Call the Whole Thing Off."

Jilted at the altar. This is the stuff legends—and nightmares—are made of. Courtney Thorne-Smith fled before marrying Andrew Shue on "Melrose Place," and in a scene that made movie history, Dustin Hoffman stole his loved one from under her groom's nose in *The Graduate*.

The act is so devastating that, centuries ago, the Catholic Church was known to punish it with excommunication for the errant groom and exile to nunnery for the rejecting bride.

But no matter how embarrassing the circumstances, 'tis far better to be a scorned fiancee than an

unhappy spouse seeking a divorce.

"Thank God my wedding was canceled. I'd be divorced by now," said Robert, 44, of Los Angeles, whose fiancee called off their wedding a week before the Big Day.

"We planned this incredible wedding on the beach. The invitations were out for 200 people. We had met the rabbi and planned the honeymoon. I went for a jog on a Sunday morning, and when I came back, I found her crying in the living room. She said very coldly: 'Call your guests, the wedding is off.'"

Robert still doesn't know what made his bride-to-be

back out, and he admits he was devastated. But in hindsight he can see everything that was wrong about the relationship.

"The whole thing was my fault, because I should have seen it. She was more wrapped up in the wedding than in what the wedding meant."

Talking about expectations and goals in a marriage is a must for couples thinking about tying the knot, says Luz Patricia Bayer, a marriage, family, and child therapist in Woodland Hills, Calif.

"Sometimes I ask people what they expected from marriage, and they have no idea," she says. "They just know they liked each other. These are the marriages that end up having problems."

Respond

1. Do you agree or disagree with Luz Bayer's statement? Why?

2. In what ways might being jilted lead a person in a new direction? Explain.

Before You Read

The Jilting of Granny Weatherall

Meet
Katherine Anne Porter

"Ask what time it is in [Porter's] stories and you are certain to get the answer: the hour is fateful. It is not necessary to see the hands of the clock in her work. It is a time of racing urgency, and it is already too late."

—Eudora Welty

Over her long career, Katherine Anne Porter traveled far from the rural Texas landscape of her childhood. As a young woman she worked on newspapers in Chicago and Denver. She then spent most of her thirties living in Mexico and Europe, meeting other writers and gathering memories for some of her most famous stories.

Porter described herself as "a late starter," publishing her first collection of short stories, *Flowering Judas*, when she was forty. Several collections of short fiction and one novel, *Ship of Fools*, followed. At age seventy-six, Porter received a Pulitzer Prize and the National Book Award for *The Collected Stories of Katherine Anne Porter*.

Porter tried to tell each story "as clearly and purely and simply as I can." Many of her stories, like "The Jilting of Granny Weatherall," are set in the South and feature women who have profound self-realizations at crucial moments in their lives.

Katherine Anne Porter was born in 1890 and died in 1980.

FOCUS ACTIVITY

Life events occur in chronological order, but our conscious memories of them often unfold differently.

CHART IT! Chart five things you did yesterday in the order that you did them. Then chart five important events in your life in the order that they come to mind.

Yesterday's Events	Important Life Events

SETTING A PURPOSE Read to learn of one woman's memories and the order in which they unfold.

BACKGROUND

The Time and Place

Porter sets her story in the American South in the early twentieth century. This was an era in which many southerners, including Porter's family, lived in extreme poverty. In addition, women of the time were often confined to the traditional roles of wife, mother, and homemaker.

Roman Catholicism figures prominently in Porter's story. Granny Weatherall's religious beliefs and her ideas of guilt and forgiveness are important elements in the story.

VOCABULARY PREVIEW

tactful (takt′ fəl) *adj.* able to speak or act without offending others; p. 622

dutiful (do͞o′ ti fəl) *adj.* careful to fulfill obligations; p. 622

plague (plāg) *v.* to annoy; to pester; p. 623

vanity (van′ i tē) *n.* excessive pride, as in one's looks; p. 625

jilt (jilt) *v.* to drop or reject as a sweetheart; p. 625

piety (pī′ ə tē) *n.* religious devoutness; goodness; p. 627

dwindle (dwin′ dəl) *v.* to become gradually smaller; p. 628

The Jilting of Granny Weatherall

Katherine Anne Porter

She flicked her wrist neatly out of Doctor Harry's pudgy careful fingers and pulled the sheet up to her chin. The brat ought to be in knee-breeches. Doctoring around the country with spectacles on his nose. "Get along now, take your schoolbooks and go. There's nothing wrong with me."

Doctor Harry spread a warm paw like a cushion on her forehead where the forked green vein danced and made her eyelids twitch. "Now, now, be a good girl, and we'll have you up in no time."

"That's no way to speak to a woman nearly eighty years old just because she's down. I'd have you respect your elders, young man."

"Well, missy, excuse me." Doctor Harry patted her cheek. "But I've got to warn you, haven't I? You're a marvel,[1] but you must be careful or you're going to be good and sorry."

"Don't tell me what I'm going to be. I'm on my feet now, morally speaking. It's Cornelia. I had to go to bed to get rid of her."

Her bones felt loose, and floated around in her skin, and Doctor Harry floated like a balloon around the foot of the bed. He floated and pulled down his waistcoat[2] and swung his glasses on a cord. "Well, stay where you are, it certainly can't hurt you."

"Get along and doctor your sick," said Granny Weatherall. "Leave a well woman alone. I'll call for you when I want you . . . Where were you forty years ago when I pulled through milk-leg[3] and double pneumonia? You weren't even born. Don't let Cornelia lead you on," she shouted, because Doctor Harry appeared to float up to the ceiling and out. "I pay my own bills, and I don't throw my money away on nonsense!"

She meant to wave good-bye, but it was too much trouble. Her eyes closed of themselves, it was like a dark curtain drawn round the bed. The pillow rose and floated under her, pleasant as a hammock in a light wind. She listened to the leaves rustling outside the window. No, somebody was swishing newspapers: no, Cornelia and Doctor Harry were whispering together. She leaped broad awake, thinking they whispered in her ear.

"She was never like this, *never* like this!" "Well, what can we expect?" "Yes, eighty years old . . ."

Well, and what if she was? She still had ears. It was like Cornelia to whisper round doors. She always kept things secret in such a public way. She was always being tactful and kind. Cornelia was dutiful; that was the trouble with her. Dutiful and good: "So good and dutiful," said Granny, "that I'd like to spank her." She saw herself spanking Cornelia and making a fine job of it.

"What'd you say, Mother?"

Granny felt her face tying up in hard knots.

"Can't a body think, I'd like to know?"

"I thought you might want something."

"I do. I want a lot of things. First off, go away and don't whisper."

She lay and drowsed, hoping in her sleep that the children would keep out and let her rest a minute. It had been a long day. Not that she was tired. It was always pleasant to snatch a minute now and then. There was always so much to be done. Let me see: tomorrow.

Tomorrow was far away and there was nothing to trouble about. Things were finished somehow when the time came; thank God there was always a little margin over for peace: then a person could spread out the plan of life and tuck in the edges orderly. It was good to have everything clean and folded away, with the hairbrushes and tonic bottles sitting straight on the white embroidered linen; the day started without fuss and the pantry shelves laid out with rows of jelly glasses and brown jugs and white stone-china jars with blue whirligigs[4] and words painted on them: coffee, tea, sugar, ginger, cinnamon,

---

1. A *marvel* is a wonderful or astonishing thing.
2. A *waistcoat* is a vest.
3. *Milk-leg* is a painful swelling of the leg that may occur after childbirth.

---

4. *Whirligigs* (hwur′ li gigz′) are circular patterns, or swirls.

Vocabulary
tactful (takt′ fəl) *adj.* able to speak or act without offending others
dutiful (doo′ ti fəl) *adj.* careful to fulfill obligations

allspice; and the bronze clock with the lion on the top nicely dusted off. The dust that lion could collect in twenty-four hours! The box in the attic with all those letters tied up, well, she'd have to go through that tomorrow. All those letters—George's letters and John's letters and her letters to them both—lying around for the children to find afterwards made her uneasy. Yes, that would be tomorrow's business. No use to let them know how silly she had been once.

While she was rummaging round she found death in her mind and it felt clammy and unfamiliar. She had spent so much time preparing for death there was no need for bringing it up again. Let it take care of itself now. When she was sixty she had felt very old, finished, and went round making farewell trips to see her children and grandchildren, with a secret in her mind: This is the very last of your mother, children! Then she made her will and came down with a long fever. That was all just a notion like a lot of other things, but it was lucky too, for she had once for all got over the idea of dying for a long time. Now she couldn't be worried. She hoped she had better sense now. Her father had lived to be one hundred and two years old and had drunk a noggin[5] of strong hot toddy[6] on his last birthday. He told the reporters it was his daily habit, and he owed his long life to that. He had made quite a scandal and was very pleased

about it. She believed she'd just plague Cornelia a little.

"Cornelia! Cornelia!" No footsteps, but a sudden hand on her cheek. "Bless you, where have you been?"

"Here, mother."

"Well, Cornelia, I want a noggin of hot toddy."

"Are you cold, darling?"

"I'm chilly, Cornelia. Lying in bed stops the circulation. I must have told you that a thousand times."

Well, she could just hear Cornelia telling her husband that Mother was getting a little childish and they'd have to humor her. The thing that most annoyed her was that Cornelia thought she was deaf, dumb, and blind. Little hasty glances and tiny gestures tossed around her and over her head, saying, "Don't cross her, let her have her way, she's eighty years old," and she sitting there as if she lived in a thin glass cage. Sometimes Granny almost made up her mind to pack up and move back to her own house where nobody could remind her every minute that she was old. Wait, wait, Cornelia, till your own children whisper behind your back!

In her day she had kept a better house and had got more work done. She wasn't too old yet for Lydia to be driving eighty miles for advice when one of the children jumped the track, and Jimmy still dropped in and talked things over: "Now, Mammy, you've a good business head, I want to know what you think of this . . . ?" Old. Cornelia couldn't change the furniture round without asking. Little things, little things! They had been so sweet when they were little. Granny wished the old days were back again with the children young and everything to be done over. It had been a hard pull, but not too much for her. When she thought of all the food she had cooked, and all the clothes she had cut and sewed, and all the

---

5. A *noggin* is a small mug or cup.
6. A *hot toddy* is a drink made with liquor, hot water, sugar, and spices.

Vocabulary
plague (plāg) *v.* to annoy; to pester

gardens she had made—well, the children showed it. There they were, made out of her, and they couldn't get away from that. Sometimes she wanted to see John again and point to them and say, "Well, I didn't do so badly, did I?" But that would have to wait. That was for tomorrow. She used to think of him as a man, but now all the children were older than their father, and he would be a child beside her if she saw him now. It seemed strange and there was something wrong in the idea. Why, he couldn't possibly recognize her. She had fenced in a hundred acres once, digging the post holes herself and clamping the wires with just a Negro boy to help. That changed a woman. John would be looking for a young woman with the peaked Spanish comb in her hair and the painted fan. Digging post holes changed a woman. Riding country roads in the winter when women had their babies was another thing: sitting up nights with sick horses and sick Negroes and sick children and hardly ever losing one. John, I hardly ever lost one of them! John would see that in a minute; that would be something he could understand, she wouldn't have to explain anything!

It made her feel like rolling up her sleeves and putting the whole place to rights again. No matter if Cornelia was determined to be everywhere at once, there were a great many things left undone on this place. She would start tomorrow and do them. It was good to be strong enough for everything, even if all you made melted and changed and slipped under your hands, so that by the time you finished you almost forgot what you were working for. What was it I set out to do? she asked herself intently, but she could not remember. A fog rose over the valley, she saw it marching across the creek swallowing the trees and moving up the hill like an army of ghosts. Soon it would be at the near edge of the orchard, and then it was time to go in and light the lamps. Come in, children, don't stay out in the night air.

Lighting the lamps had been beautiful. The children huddled up to her and breathed like little calves waiting at the bars in the twilight. Their eyes followed the match and watched the flame rise and settle in a blue curve, then they moved away from her. The lamp was lit, they didn't have to be scared and hang on to mother any more. Never, never, never more. God, for all my life I thank Thee. Without Thee, my God, I could never have done it. Hail, Mary, full of grace.[7]

I want you to pick all the fruit this year and see that nothing is wasted. There's always someone who can use it. Don't let good things rot for want of using. You waste life when you waste good food. Don't let things get lost. It's bitter to lose things. Now, don't let me get to thinking, not when I am tired and taking a little nap before supper . . .

The pillow rose about her shoulders and pressed against her heart and the memory was being squeezed out of it: oh, push down the pillow, somebody; it would smother her if she tried to hold it. Such a fresh breeze blowing and such a green day with no threats in it. But he had not come, just the same. What does a woman do when she has put on the white veil and set out the white cake for a man and he doesn't come? She tried to remember. No, I swear he never harmed me but in that. He never harmed me but in that . . . and what if he did? There was the day, the day, but a whirl of dark smoke rose and covered it, crept up and over into the bright field where everything was planted so carefully in orderly rows. That was hell, she knew hell when she saw it. For sixty years she had prayed against remembering him and against losing her soul in the deep pit of hell, and now the two things were mingled in one, and the thought of him was a smoky cloud from hell that moved and crept in her head when she had just got rid of Doctor Harry and was trying to rest a minute.

---

7. *Hail, Mary, full of grace* is the beginning of a Roman Catholic prayer to the Virgin Mary.

Wounded vanity, Ellen, said a sharp voice in the top of her mind. Don't let your wounded vanity get the upper hand of you. Plenty of girls get jilted. You were jilted, weren't you? Then stand up to it. Her eyelids wavered and let in streamers of blue-gray light like tissue paper over her eyes. She must get up and pull the shades down or she'd never sleep. She was in bed again and the shades were not down. How could that happen? Better turn over, hide from the light; sleeping in the light gave you nightmares. "Mother, how do you feel now?" and a stinging wetness on her forehead. But I don't like having my face washed in cold water!

Hapsy? George? Lydia? Jimmy? No, Cornelia, and her features were swollen and full of little puddles. "They're coming, darling, they'll all be here soon." Go wash your face, child, you look funny.

Instead of obeying, Cornelia knelt down and put her head on the pillow. She seemed to be talking but there was no sound. "Well, are you tongue-tied? Whose birthday is it? Are you going to give a party?"

Cornelia's mouth moved urgently in strange shapes. "Don't do that, you bother me, daughter."

"Oh, no, Mother. Oh, no . . ."

Nonsense. It was strange about children. They disputed your every word. "No what, Cornelia?"

"Here's Doctor Harry."

"I won't see that boy again. He just left five minutes ago."

"That was this morning, Mother. It's night now. Here's the nurse."

"This is Doctor Harry, Mrs. Weatherall. I never saw you look so young and happy!"

"Ah, I'll never be young again—but I'd be happy if they'd let me lie in peace and get rested."

She thought she spoke up loudly, but no one answered. A warm weight on her forehead, a warm bracelet on her wrist and a breeze went on whispering, trying to tell her something. A shuffle of leaves in the everlasting hand of God, He blew on them and they danced and rattled. "Mother, don't mind, we're going to give you a little hypodermic." "Look here, daughter, how do ants get in this bed? I saw sugar ants yesterday." Did you send for Hapsy too?

It was Hapsy she really wanted. She had to go a long way back through a great many rooms to find Hapsy standing with a baby on her arm. She seemed to herself to be Hapsy also, and the baby on Hapsy's arm was Hapsy and himself and herself, all at once, and there was no surprise in the meeting. Then Hapsy melted from within and turned flimsy as gray gauze and the baby was a gauzy shadow, and Hapsy came up close and said, "I thought you'd never come," and looked at her very searchingly and said, "You haven't changed a bit!" They leaned forward to kiss, when Cornelia began whispering from a long way off, "Oh, is there anything you want to tell me? Is there anything I can do for you?"

Yes, she had changed her mind after sixty years and she would like to see George. I want you to find George. Find him and be sure to tell him I forgot him. I want him to know I had my husband just the same, and my children and my house, like any other woman. A good house too and a good husband that I loved and fine children out of him. Better than I hoped for, even. Tell him I was given back everything he took away, and more. Oh, no, O God, no, there was something else besides the house and the man and the children. Oh, surely they were not all? What was it? Something not given back . . . Her breath crowded down under her ribs and grew into a monstrous frightening shape with cutting

---

Vocabulary

vanity (van′ i tē) *n.* excessive pride, as in one's looks
jilt (jilt) *v.* to drop or reject as a sweetheart

The Seamstress, 1914.
Knud Larsen. Oil on canvas,
20 x 18½ in. Private collection.

Viewing the painting:
Why might the woman in
the painting be like Cornelia
at that age?

edges; it bored[8] up into her head, and the agony was unbelievable. Yes, John, get the doctor now, no more talk, my time has come.

When this one was born it should be the last. The last. It should have been born first, for it was the one she had truly wanted. Everything came in good time. Nothing left out, left over. She was strong, in three days she would be as well as ever. Better. A woman needed milk in her to have her full health.

"Mother, do you hear me?"

"I've been telling you—"

"Mother, Father Connolly's here."

"I went to Holy Communion only last week. Tell him I'm not so sinful as all that."

"Father just wants to speak to you."

He could speak as much as he pleased. It was like him to drop in and inquire about her soul as if it were a teething baby, and then stay on for a cup of tea and a round of cards and gossip. He always had a funny story of some sort, usually about an Irishman who made his little mistakes and confessed them, and the point lay in some absurd thing he would blurt out in the confessional[9] showing his struggles

---

8. Here, to *bore* means "to make a hole, as by drilling or pushing."

9. A *confessional* is a small booth in a Catholic church where a person confesses his or her sins to a priest and asks forgiveness from God through the priest.

between native <u>piety</u> and original sin. Granny felt easy about her soul. Cornelia, where are your manners? Give Father Connolly a chair. She had her secret comfortable understanding with a few favorite saints who cleared a straight road to God for her. All as surely signed and sealed as the papers for the new Forty Acres. For ever . . . heirs and assigns[10] for ever. Since the day the wedding cake was not cut, but thrown out and wasted. The whole bottom dropped out of the world, and there she was, blind and sweating, with nothing under her feet and the walls falling away. His hand had caught her under the breast, she had not fallen; there was the freshly polished floor with the green rug on it, just as before. He had cursed like a sailor's parrot and said, "I'll kill him for you." "Don't lay a hand on him, for my sake leave something to God." "Now, Ellen, you must believe what I tell you . . ."

So there was nothing, nothing to worry about any more, except sometimes in the night one of the children screamed in a nightmare, and they both hustled out shaking and hunting for the matches and calling, "There, wait a minute, here we are!" John, get the doctor now, Hapsy's time has come. But there was Hapsy standing by the bed in a white cap. "Cornelia, tell Hapsy to take off her cap. I can't see her plain."

Her eyes opened very wide and the room stood out like a picture she had seen somewhere. Dark colors with the shadows rising towards the ceiling in long angles. The tall black dresser gleamed with nothing on it but John's picture, enlarged from a little one, with John's eyes very black when they should have been blue. You never saw him, so how do you know how he looked? But the man insisted the copy was perfect, it was very rich and handsome. For a picture, yes, but it's not my husband. The table by the bed had a linen cover and a candle and a crucifix. The light was blue from Cornelia's silk lampshades. No sort of light at all, just frippery.[11] You had to live forty years with kerosene lamps to appreciate honest electricity. She felt very strong and she saw Doctor Harry with a rosy nimbus[12] around him.

"You look like a saint, Doctor Harry, and I vow that's as near as you'll ever come to it."

"She's saying something."

"I heard you, Cornelia. What's all this carrying-on?"

"Father Connolly's saying—"

Cornelia's voice staggered and bumped like a cart in a bad road. It rounded corners and turned back again and arrived nowhere. Granny stepped up in the cart very lightly and reached for the reins, but a man sat beside her, and she knew him by his hands, driving the cart. She did not look in his face, for she knew without seeing, but looked instead down the road where the trees leaned over and bowed to each other and a thousand birds were singing a Mass. She felt like singing too, but she put her hand in the bosom of her dress and pulled out a rosary, and Father Connolly murmured Latin in a very solemn voice and tickled her feet.[13] My God,

Did You Know?
A *rosary* is a string of beads used to help count specific prayers as they are recited.

---

10. *Assigns* are people to whom property is legally transferred.

11. *Frippery* is a showy, useless display.
12. A *nimbus* is a disk or ring of light; a halo.
13. The priest is administering the last rites, a Catholic ritual which includes saying prayers and applying oil to the dying person's feet.

will you stop that nonsense? I'm a married woman. What if he did run away and leave me to face the priest by myself? I found another a whole world better. I wouldn't have exchanged my husband for anybody except St. Michael[14] himself, and you may tell him that for me, with a thank you into the bargain.

Light flashed on her closed eyelids, and a deep roaring shook her. Cornelia, is that lightning? I hear thunder. There's going to be a storm. Close all the windows. Call the children in . . . "Mother, here we are, all of us." "Is that you, Hapsy?" "Oh, no, I'm Lydia. We drove as fast as we could." Their faces drifted above her, drifted away. The rosary fell out of her hands and Lydia put it back. Jimmy tried to help, their hands fumbled together, and Granny closed two fingers round Jimmy's thumb. Beads wouldn't do, it must be something alive. She was so amazed her thoughts ran round and round. So, my dear Lord, this is my death and I wasn't even thinking about it. My children have come to see me die. But I can't, it's not time. Oh, I always hated surprises. I wanted to give Cornelia the amethyst[15] set—Cornelia, you're to have the amethyst set, but Hapsy's to wear it when she wants, and, Doctor Harry, do shut up. Nobody sent for you. Oh, my dear Lord, do wait a minute. I meant to do something about the Forty Acres, Jimmy doesn't need it and

Lydia will later on, with that worthless husband of hers. I meant to finish the altar cloth and send six bottles of wine to Sister Borgia for her dyspepsia.[16] I want to send six bottles of wine to Sister Borgia, Father Connolly, now don't let me forget.

Cornelia's voice made short turns and tilted over and crashed. "Oh, Mother, oh, Mother, oh, Mother . . ."

"I'm not going, Cornelia. I'm taken by surprise. I can't go."

You'll see Hapsy again. What about her? "I thought you'd never come." Granny made a long journey outward, looking for Hapsy. What if I don't find her? What then? Her heart sank down and down, there was no bottom to death, she couldn't come to the end of it. The blue light from Cornelia's lampshade drew into a tiny point in the center of her brain, it flickered and winked like an eye, quietly it fluttered and dwindled. Granny lay curled down within herself, amazed and watchful, staring at the point of light that was herself; her body was now only a deeper mass of shadow in an endless darkness and this darkness would curl round the light and swallow it up. God, give a sign!

For the second time there was no sign. Again no bridegroom and the priest in the house. She could not remember any other sorrow because this grief wiped them all away. Oh, no, there's nothing more cruel than this—I'll never forgive it. She stretched herself with a deep breath and blew out the light.

---

14. *St. Michael* is an archangel, usually depicted as a handsome knight.
15. *Amethyst* (am′ ə thist) is purple or violet quartz, and is typically used in jewelry.

---

16. *Dyspepsia* is indigestion.

Vocabulary
dwindle (dwin′ dəl) *v.* to become gradually smaller

Responding to Literature

Personal Response

What was your reaction to Granny Weatherall's train of thought?

ANALYZING LITERATURE

RECALL

1. At the beginning of the story, what attitudes does Granny have toward the doctor, toward Cornelia, and toward her own illness?
2. How does Granny describe her life since her husband John died? What examples does she give?
3. Who is Hapsy, and where does Granny see her?
4. Which event does Granny recall with particular anger and sadness? What "message" does she have for the person involved?
5. What does Granny ask of God in the next-to-last paragraph? What happens "for the second time"?

INTERPRET

6. What do Granny's attitudes early in the story reveal about her state of mind?
7. How might Granny have changed due to her experiences since her husband died? How does the name *Weatherall* fit Granny?
8. How does Granny's vision of Hapsy **foreshadow** the end of the story? (See Literary Terms Handbook, page R7.)
9. Think about Granny's "message" to the person who has hurt and saddened her. What does this message tell you about her feelings toward him? Explain.
10. Why do you think the jilting incident comes back to Granny so frequently as she faces death?

EVALUATE AND CONNECT

11. In your opinion, does Porter bring this story to an effective **climax** (see page R3)? Explain your answer using details from the story. Use a plot graph like the one on this page to help organize your ideas.
12. Which of Granny's memories did you find most touching? Why?
13. In your opinion, did Granny live a full life? Support your answer with details from the story.
14. Look back at the chart you created for the Focus Activity on page 620. Did you list your five important life events in chronological order? How is the order of your list similar to or different from Granny Weatherall's death-bed memories?
15. Would you like to have had Granny as a grandmother? Explain.

Literary ELEMENTS

Stream of Consciousness

Stream of consciousness is a technique that a writer uses to imitate the flow of thoughts, feelings, images, and memories of a character in a literary work. Stream of consciousness replaces traditional chronological order with a seemingly jumbled collection of impressions, forcing the reader to piece together the plot or theme. In "The Jilting of Granny Weatherall," Porter uses stream of consciousness to represent Granny's thoughts and memories.

1. Is stream of consciousness a good choice for telling the story "The Jilting of Granny Weatherall"? Explain.
2. What kinds of clues help the reader follow Granny's thoughts?

● See **Literary Terms Handbook**, p. R15.

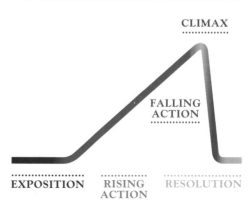

CLIMAX

FALLING ACTION

EXPOSITION   RISING ACTION   RESOLUTION

LITERATURE AND WRITING

Writing About Literature

Author's Use of Symbolism   The author uses several symbols for death in this story. Granny blowing out the light is one. Identify at least two more symbols that might represent death. Write a few paragraphs describing the effects of these symbols on the story's overall impression.

Creative Writing

Your Own Stream of Consciousness   Write your own stream-of-consciousness story. Make up a story or tell about an important person or event in your life. Do not plan the story, just write it as it comes to you. Then share and discuss your story with the class.

EXTENDING YOUR RESPONSE

Literature Groups

Discussing Women's Roles   Granny Weatherall grew up in the rural United States at a time when women's roles were very different from what they are today. With your group, discuss the kind of life Granny might have led if she had lived in the later years of the twentieth century.

Listening and Speaking

Dear George   What did Granny really want to say to George? Imagine that George arrives in Granny's room or calls on the phone. What would she really say to him? Write and present a monologue in which Granny talks to George. As you write and present your monologue, keep Granny's character in mind.

Performing

Granny on Stage   How would you turn a stream-of-consciousness narrative into a play? Discuss this question with a group of students. Think of a strategy for bringing "The Jilting of Granny Weatherall" to the stage. Have one group member take notes as you discuss ways to express Granny's thoughts, the jumbled time order, and other elements of the story. Then perform an improvised rendition of one part of the story for the class.

📖 **Save your work for your portfolio.**

Skill Minilesson

VOCABULARY • Analogies

Analogies are comparisons based on relationships between ideas. The relationship represented in some analogies is that of *antonym variants,* where the words are close to being, but are not exact opposites. For example:

   weak : strength :: cowardly : courage

Although *weak,* an adjective, and *strength,* a noun, are not exact opposites, you can still determine the relationship between the concepts they represent. Something *weak* lacks *strength.* Something *cowardly* lacks *courage.*

To finish an analogy, determine the relationship between the first two words. Then apply that relationship to the second set of words.

PRACTICE   Complete each analogy.

1. dwindle : increase :: stiffen :
   a. cringe   b. freeze   c. relax

2. humble : vanity :: kind :
   a. cruelty   b. humility   c. generosity

3. bad : piety :: polite :
   a. rudeness   b. sadness   c. courtesy

● For more about analogies, see **Communications Skills Handbook,** p. R83.

Before You Read

Richness

Meet Gabriela Mistral

"Speech is our second possession, after the soul, and perhaps we have no other possession in the world."

—*Mistral*

At age twenty-five, Gabriela Mistral (gä brē ā′ lä   mēs träl′) was so shy that she could not accept her first literary award. Instead, she sat unnoticed in the audience while another poet accepted it for her. Mistral eventually matured to become an internationally recognized poet and the first Latin American writer to receive the Nobel Prize for Literature.

She was born Lucila Godoy Alcayaga, in Vicuña, Chile, north of the capital city of Santiago. A solitary child, she found her classmates' teasing so unbearable that she left school in the sixth grade. Nevertheless, she read constantly, studied at home, and at age fifteen began her first job as a teacher, a vocation that she followed throughout her life.

The suicide of her fiancé prompted her to write "Sonetos de la muerte" ("Sonnets of Death"), which she entered in a national literary contest under the pen name Gabriela Mistral. Those poems, which later appeared in her first book, *Desolación (Desolation)*, brought her recognition that furthered both her teaching and her literary careers. "Material resources may be limited," Mistral once said, "but those of the spirit are more powerful than we could ever imagine." She proved the truth of that statement with many achievements—in teaching, in literature, and in diplomacy as Chilean consul to Italy and to the United States.

Gabriela Mistral was born in 1889 and died in 1957.

FOCUS ACTIVITY

How do you measure true richness in life? Is money the greatest measure? Do you find richness in family and good friends or perhaps in life experiences?

JOURNAL In your journal, note ways that you could measure true richness.

SETTING A PURPOSE Read to discover a speaker's idea of life's richness.

BACKGROUND

Did You Know?

Gabriela Mistral never forgot the sights and sounds of her birthplace, Vicuña, an agricultural community surrounded by the Andes Mountains. "I continue to speak Spanish with the sing-song of the Elqui Valley," she once said. "I have a sense of smell that comes from those vineyards and fig orchards, and even my sense of touch came from those hills covered with tender or hardy grasses."

Literary Influences

Besides the spoken language of her birthplace, Mistral also found inspiration in the language of the Bible and Spanish-language classics. Two of her favorite writers were the Italian poet Gabriele D'Annunzio and the (French) Provençal poet Frédéric Mistral. From these two names, the young poet developed her pen name, Gabriela Mistral.

Woman and the Cat, 1995. Maria Eugenia Terrazas. Watercolor, 60 x 70 cm. Private collection.

Richness

Gabriela Mistral
Translated by Doris Dana

I have a faithful joy
and a joy that is lost.
One is like a rose,
the other, a thorn.
5   The one that was stolen
I have not lost.
I have a faithful joy
and a joy that is lost.
I am as rich with purple
10   as with sorrow.

Ay! How loved is the rose,
how loving the thorn!
Paired as twin fruit,
I have a faithful joy
15   and a joy that is lost.

Responding to Literature

Personal Response

Which idea from the poem struck you as the most powerful or surprising? Why?

ANALYZING LITERATURE

RECALL AND INTERPRET

1. What joys does the speaker describe in the first two lines? What can you infer from these descriptions?
2. To what does the speaker compare her two joys in lines 3–4? What **connotations,** or associations, does each object have for you?
3. With what statement does the first stanza end? What does this statement suggest to you about the speaker's view of life?
4. What **simile,** or comparison using *like* or *as,* describes the relationship between the rose and the thorn? Why might the speaker describe the thorn as "loving"? What might the speaker be suggesting about the nature of joy?

EVALUATE AND CONNECT

5. What does the title of the poem lead you to expect? What might the title suggest about the different kinds of experiences people have?
6. What **repetition** does the speaker use? Where does it occur, and what effect does it have? (See Literary Terms Handbook, page R13.)
7. According to one critic, Mistral often wrote about "love and anguish, life and death, nature and man." Do you think this statement applies to "Richness"? Give details from the poem to support your answer.
8. How would you describe the speaker's emotional state? What life experiences might create similar emotions for you?

Literary ELEMENTS

Speaker

The **speaker** in a poem is the voice that communicates the ideas, actions, and emotions of a poem to the reader. In some poems, the speaker is the voice of the poet. In others, the speaker has his or her own identity and may be a real or a fictional person, an animal, or a thing such as a force of nature. In many cases, a poet invents a speaker with a particular identity to create a desired impression or impact. For example, the speaker in "Richness" is someone revealing very personal emotions.

1. How would you describe the speaker in "Richness"? Why?
2. What, in your opinion, is the speaker's tone in this poem? Explain.

● See **Literary Terms Handbook,** p. R15.

EXTENDING YOUR RESPONSE

Personal Writing

Personal Richness   Review your responses for the Focus Activity on page 631. Use one or more of these ideas in a brief poem that conveys your idea of personal richness. Before you write, select one or two powerful visual images to help express your idea.

Interdisciplinary Activity

Biology: Rose and Thorn   Do some research to discover why roses have thorns. Share your findings with the class and then discuss this question: How does knowing more about the relationship between roses and thorns affect your understanding of the poem?

📖 **Save your work for your portfolio.**

COMPARING selections

The Jilting of Granny Weatherall **and** *Richness*

COMPARE **CHARACTERS**

The speaker in "Richness" reveals herself through few words; Granny Weatherall provides many details as she sorts through a lifetime of memories. With a small group of students, discuss these questions:

1. In what ways are the characters' experiences similar? In what ways are they different?
2. How are their reactions to life alike? In what ways do they react differently?
3. How does love affect each speaker?

COMPARE **CULTURES**

Although the characters in both selections share certain kinds of experiences, they come from very different cultures. With a partner, investigate women's social roles in rural South America and in the rural southern United States in the early twentieth century. Consider these questions:

- What was expected of women in each culture?
- What customs and everyday activities reveal these expectations?
- Do Granny Weatherall and the speaker of "Richness" reveal much about the role of women in their respective cultures? Explain.

Then, create and perform a dialogue between Granny Weatherall and the speaker in "Richness." The dialogue should reflect the speakers' views of their lives and their possible attitudes toward the roles of women in each culture.

COMPARE **TECHNIQUES**

Both Porter and Mistral chose techniques they thought would best convey their ideas. In her story Porter uses stream of consciousness, presenting ideas, events, and images in the order in which a conscious mind might think of them. Mistral uses few words but powerful images. Write a paragraph comparing the two writers' techniques. Consider the other techniques each writer uses and which writer's techniques seem most effective.

Before You Read

Ars Poetica

Meet Archibald MacLeish

"But what, then, is the business of poetry? Precisely to make sense of the chaos of our lives. . . . To compose an order which the bewildered, angry heart can recognize."

—*MacLeish*

Archibald MacLeish was a poet with a purpose. He believed that through love and awareness, Americans could achieve the goals of freedom and equality set down in the Declaration of Independence. His ideals show in both his poetry and his public life.

MacLeish attended Yale University, where he played on the football team. Then, at the age of twenty-three, MacLeish entered Harvard Law School. Over the next two years he married singer Ada Hitchcock and enlisted in the army. After World War I he became a successful lawyer, then suddenly quit his job. He moved with his wife and two small children to Paris to become a writer. There, he published four poetry collections in five years. In 1928, at the age of thirty-six, he returned with his family to the United States. MacLeish continued writing poetry and in 1933 won his first Pulitzer Prize for *Conquistador*, an epic poem about the conquest of Mexico by the Spanish.

Concerned about the nation's social problems, MacLeish also wrote journalistic articles and supported President Franklin D. Roosevelt in his economic reforms and his arming against Hitler. In the 1940s, MacLeish served as director of a wartime office of propaganda, as assistant secretary of state, and as a librarian of Congress. Through all this, he continued to write. In the 1950s, MacLeish won two more Pulitzer Prizes—one for Poetry and one for Drama.

Critic Hayden Carruth said of the poet: "MacLeish wrote not as a personal crusader, never as a political crank or lonely visionary, but instead as the spokesman of the people. . . . His poems were outgoing . . . products of basic poetic and human loving kindness."

Archibald MacLeish was born in 1892 and died in 1982.

FOCUS ACTIVITY

Do you judge a poem by its sounds, its choice of words, the way you respond to it, or something else?

DISCUSS In small groups, complete the statement: "A good poem is . . ."

SETTING A PURPOSE Read to learn one writer's ideas about poetry.

BACKGROUND

The Time and Place

Ars Poetica is a Latin phrase meaning "the art of poetry." *Ars Poetica* was also the title of a work written around 13 B.C., in which the Roman poet Horace expressed his own rules for writing poetry. MacLeish published his "Ars Poetica" in 1926, in a collection titled *Streets in the Moon*. When he wrote the poem, MacLeish was living in Paris and was caught up in the study of poetry, working to perfect his own skills. He was part of a circle of innovative American writers who had settled in Paris. His friends included Ernest Hemingway, F. Scott Fitzgerald, and E. E. Cummings.

Ars Poetica

Archibald MacLeish

A POEM should be palpable° and mute°
As a globed fruit

Dumb°
As old medallions to the thumb

5   Silent as the sleeve-worn stone
Of casement° ledges where the moss has grown—

A poem should be wordless
As the flight of birds

A poem should be motionless in time
10   As the moon climbs

Leaving, as the moon releases
Twig by twig the night-entangled trees,

Leaving, as the moon behind the winter leaves,
Memory by memory the mind—

15   A poem should be motionless in time
As the moon climbs

A poem should be equal to:
Not true

For all the history of grief
20   An empty doorway and a maple leaf

For love
The leaning grasses and two lights above the sea—

A poem should not mean
But be

1 **palpable:** tangible; able to be touched or felt. **mute:** silent.

3 **Dumb:** here, unable to speak.

6 **casement:** a window that opens on hinges.

Responding to Literature

Personal Response

As you read the poem, which image could you see, feel, or hear most vividly in your imagination? Why?

——— ANALYZING LITERATURE ———

RECALL AND INTERPRET

1. What five adjectives in lines 1–8 describe what a poem should be? What is **ironic** about the use of these words to describe a poem? (See Literary Terms Handbook, page R8.)
2. To what does the speaker compare poetry in lines 9–16? What does this image suggest about the function of poetry?
3. How does the speaker suggest that grief and love be represented in poetry? What can you infer from this suggestion about the way poems should express emotions?
4. What does the speaker say poems should be in lines 17–18 and 23–24? What might the speaker be saying about poetry in these lines? Explain.

EVALUATE AND CONNECT

5. How would you rate the images in this poem based on their appeal to the senses? Explain your rating.
6. In your opinion, do lines 20 and 22 adequately capture the emotions of grief and love? Why or why not?
7. Do you agree with the statements made in lines 17–18 and lines 23–24? Explain.
8. How does the speaker's explanation of what a poem "should be" compare with the definition you created for the Focus Activity on page 635? Has your definition changed after reading this poem? Why or why not?

Literary ELEMENTS

Simile

A **simile** is a figure of speech that compares two things by using words such as *like* or *as*. The comparison to something familiar provides new insights about the thing being compared, and creates a more vivid experience for the reader. In "Ars Poetica," MacLeish uses several similes to clarify and expand his meaning. For example, he uses the simile "As old medallions to the thumb" to clarify what he means by saying that a poem should be "dumb."

1. To what does MacLeish compare the way a poem should be "motionless in time"?
2. What other similes can you find in the poem? Explain how each simile helps clarify and expand the term that comes before it.

● See **Literary Terms Handbook**, p. R14.

——— EXTENDING YOUR RESPONSE ———

Literature Groups

A Matter of Image   In your group, discuss each image MacLeish uses in "Ars Poetica." What exactly is the image describing? What pictures does it bring to mind? How effectively does it help readers understand what poetry should be? Then come up with additional images to convey MacLeish's view of what poetry should be and present them to the class.

Writing About Literature

Paraphrase the Poem   "Ars Poetica" is an argument about what a poem should be, but the argument is presented in the form of a poem. In your own words, rewrite the main ideas of the argument in paragraph form. Be sure your completed work has an effective introduction and conclusion.

📖 **Save your work for your portfolio.**

Before You Read

Dirge Without Music and *Recuerdo*

Meet Edna St. Vincent Millay

"O world, I cannot hold thee close enough!"

—*Millay*

"I am not a tentative person," wrote Edna St. Vincent Millay. "Whatever I do, I give my whole self up to it." Her passionate involvement with life made her a spokesperson for the generation that grew up in the Roaring Twenties. This was a carefree, exuberant period, and its spirit was captured in Millay's poem "The First Fig."

> My candle burns at both ends;
> It will not last the night;
> But ah, my foes, and oh, my friends—
> It gives a lovely light!

Millay began her writing career early and by the age of fourteen had won her first poetry award. By twenty, her poetry had landed her a patron who helped pay her tuition at Vassar College. After college, Millay moved to Greenwich Village, a section of New York City known for its writers, artists, and unconventional lifestyles. There she wrote, worked as an actress, fell in and out of love, and became one of the best-known poets of her day.

In 1923, when she was thirty-one, she won the Pulitzer Prize for Poetry. Eight years later, her book of fifty-two love sonnets, *Fatal Interview*, received enthusiastic reviews. As she grew older, Millay threw herself into politics and social issues with the same passion that she had put into her poetry. Critics complained, and many of Millay's fans deserted her. Though her popularity declined in her last years, she wrote constantly. Many of these later works have been published since her death, and her fame is once again on the rise.

Edna St. Vincent Millay was born in 1892 and died in 1950.

FOCUS ACTIVITY

What is your favorite memory?

LIST IT! Make a list of all the details you can recall from your favorite memory. What happened? What images do you associate with the memory?

SETTING A PURPOSE Read to learn about one speaker's memories.

BACKGROUND

The Time and Place

Recuerdo (rā kwer′ dō) is Spanish for "I remember," "remembrance," or "souvenir." The poem describes a ride on the Staten Island Ferry, a boat that travels back and forth between Manhattan and Staten Island in New York. The Spanish title suggests that the poem was inspired by a visit Millay made with the young Nicaraguan poet Salomón de la Selva (säl ō mōn′ dā lä sel′ vä) to Staten Island—a place many young couples went for picnics and walks.

Literary Influences

Millay was influenced by many arts, particularly music. In her early years, she studied to be a concert pianist but gave up because her hands were so small. Millay's love of music is reflected in her use of **repetition, rhyme,** and **alliteration** (see pages R13 and R1). For instance, Millay instills music in her poem "Recuerdo" by repeating the first line in each stanza and by using end rhyme throughout.

Dirge Without Music

Bramble, 1980. Louisa Chase. Oil on canvas, 182 x 243.8 cm. Private collection.

Edna St. Vincent Millay

I am not resigned° to the shutting away of loving hearts in the hard ground.
So it is, and so it will be, for so it has been, time out of mind:
Into the darkness they go, the wise and the lovely. Crowned
With lilies and with laurel° they go; but I am not resigned.

5   Lovers and thinkers, into the earth with you.
Be one with the dull, the indiscriminate° dust.
A fragment of what you felt, of what you knew,
A formula, a phrase remains,—but the best is lost.

The answers quick and keen, the honest look, the laughter, the love,—
10   They are gone. They are gone to feed the roses. Elegant and curled
Is the blossom. Fragrant is the blossom. I know. But I do not approve.
More precious was the light in your eyes than all the roses in the world.

Down, down, down into the darkness of the grave
Gently they go, the beautiful, the tender, the kind;
15   Quietly they go, the intelligent, the witty, the brave.
I know. But I do not approve. And I am not resigned.

A *dirge* is a funeral song or a song expressing grief.

1 To be *resigned* to something means "to have given in without complaint" or "to have adjusted to something undesirable."

4 The fragrant foliage from a *laurel* tree is often used to symbolize honor or victory. In ancient Greece and Rome, a person may have been crowned with a wreath of laurel to honor a particular achievement.

6 *Indiscriminate* means "not noting differences or making distinctions."

Staten Island Ferry, 1937. Minna Wright Citron. Oil on Masonite, 25¼ x 16⅜ in. ©Estate of Minna Citron/Licensed by VAGA, New York/Collection of The Newark Museum, Newark, NJ. Purchase, 1939. Felix Fuld Bequest Fund.

Recuerdo

Edna St. Vincent Millay

We were very tired, we were very merry—
We had gone back and forth all night on the ferry.
It was bare and bright, and smelled like a stable—
But we looked into a fire, we leaned across a table,
5   We lay on a hill-top underneath the moon;
And the whistles kept blowing, and the dawn came soon.

We were very tired, we were very merry—
We had gone back and forth all night on the ferry;
And you ate an apple, and I ate a pear,
10   From a dozen of each we had bought somewhere;
And the sky went wan,° and the wind came cold,
And the sun rose dripping, a bucketful of gold.

We were very tired, we were very merry,
We had gone back and forth all night on the ferry.
15   We hailed,° "Good-morrow, mother!" to a shawl-covered head,
And bought a morning paper, which neither of us read;
And she wept, "God bless you!" for the apples and pears,
And we gave her all our money but our subway fares.

---

11 *Wan* means "pale."
15 *Hailed* means "called out to greet."

Responding to Literature

Personal Response

With which of the two poems' speakers did you identify most? Why? Record your thoughts in your journal.

ANALYZING LITERATURE

Dirge Without Music

RECALL AND INTERPRET

1. Whom does the speaker mourn in the poem? What is her attitude toward losing these people? What does she say has been lost along with them?
2. What does the speaker say she does not approve of and is not resigned to? What does this suggest about her values and her view of humankind?

EVALUATE AND CONNECT

3. In your opinion, how effective is the **mood** of this poem in conveying the poem's message? Explain. (See Literary Terms Handbook, page R10.)
4. Based on this poem and on your own experiences, how well do you think the speaker understands losing someone? Support your answer with details from the poem.

Recuerdo

RECALL AND INTERPRET

5. What details in the first two stanzas tell you about the characters' actions? Why might they have felt the way they did?
6. What do the characters do in the last stanza? Why might they have done this?

EVALUATE AND CONNECT

7. What two lines are repeated in each stanza? What is the effect of this **repetition** (see page R13)?
8. In what ways might this poem reflect the poet's love of nineteenth-century poetry? For example, list words from the poem that seem old-fashioned.

EXTENDING YOUR RESPONSE

Personal Writing

Souvenirs of Experience   One critic wrote that Millay shared "souvenirs of experience" with readers. In "Recuerdo," she does this with images that focus on all five senses. Review your list for the Focus Activity on page 638. Using "Recuerdo" as a model, relate your own experience in a short poem or essay. Include strong sensory images as Millay does.

Interdisciplinary Activity

Music: Sorrow and Joy   Death and loss, as well as the joys of life, are common themes for Millay. Locate a piece of music that expresses grief comparable to "Dirge Without Music" and another that expresses the joy of "Recuerdo." Play them for the class and explain your choices.

📓 **Save your work for your portfolio.**

Before You Read

anyone lived in a pretty how town

Meet
E. E. Cummings

"to be nobody-but-myself—in a world which is doing its best, night and day, to make me everybody else—means to fight the hardest battle which any human being can fight, and never stop fighting."

—*Cummings*

To E. E. Cummings, being an individual—not giving in to pressures to be just like everyone else—was life's most important struggle. He challenged the forces that tend to suppress uniqueness and make people conform, a challenge that is reflected in his poetry.

Cummings grew up in Cambridge, Massachusetts, the son of a respected minister and a mother who loved poetry. Throughout his life, Cummings remained grateful to his mother for encouraging his poetic ambitions. He wrote, "if there are any heavens my mother will (all by herself) have / one."

A year after receiving a master's degree from Harvard University in 1916, Cummings volunteered to serve as an ambulance driver in World War I. Not long after, he was unjustly confined in a French detention camp on charges of espionage. Released a few months later, Cummings wrote an absorbing account of his imprisonment in *The Enormous Room.*

After the war, Cummings returned to New York City, settling in Greenwich Village. For much of the next two decades he divided his time between the Village and Paris and concentrated on writing poetry and painting. Though his writing, not his painting, brought him acclaim, the latter had a tremendous impact on his poetry.

The first things readers often notice about Cummings's poems are the unusual arrangement of the words, the lack of punctuation, and the use of lowercase letters. Cummings also experimented with words, breaking them apart or changing their parts of speech. Many times, he made a single word represent an entire idea. The experiments in language and grammar were Cummings's way of expressing his individuality and of encouraging readers to look at the world in a new way.

Edward Estlin Cummings was born in 1894 and died in 1962.

FOCUS ACTIVITY

What is the "average" or "typical" person of your age like?

QUICKWRITE Describe this person and his or her way of life. For example, what does he or she wear, do, think, and say?

SETTING A PURPOSE Read to learn how one speaker describes the "average" person's life.

BACKGROUND

The Poet's Themes

"Cummings was a lyric poet, ready to sing of love, the moon, the stars, and the beauties of nature," wrote one critic. Although Cummings's poems are innovative in style, they explore traditional poetic subjects such as love, the natural world, and death. Cummings was also, however, a master of satire. He coined the word "mostpeople" to describe people who follow the crowd. Cummings believed that individuals can only discover who they truly are if they don't worry what "mostpeople" think.

anyone lived in a pretty how town

E. E. Cummings

A Summer Evening on the Lake in Alexandra Park. Helen Bradley (1900–1979). Oil on canvas board, 24 x 30 in. Private collection.

anyone lived in a pretty how town
(with up so floating many bells down)
spring summer autumn winter
he sang his didn't he danced his did.

5 Women and men(both little and small)
cared for anyone not at all
they sowed their isn't they reaped their same
sun moon stars rain

children guessed(but only a few
10 and down they forgot as up they grew
autumn winter spring summer)
that noone loved him more by more

when by now and tree by leaf
she laughed his joy she cried his grief
15 bird by snow and stir by still
anyone's any was all to her

someones married their everyones
laughed their cryings and did their dance
(sleep wake hope and then)they
20 said their nevers they slept their dream

stars rain sun moon
(and only the snow can begin to explain
how children are apt to forget to remember
with up so floating many bells down)

25 one day anyone died i guess
(and noone stooped to kiss his face)
busy folk buried them side by side
little by little and was by was

all by all and deep by deep
30 and more by more they dream their sleep
noone and anyone earth by april
wish by spirit and if by yes.

Women and men(both dong and ding)
summer autumn winter spring
35 reaped their sowing and went their came
sun moon stars rain

Responding to Literature

Personal Response

What reactions did you have as you read this poem? Explain.

—— ANALYZING LITERATURE ——

RECALL AND INTERPRET

1. What is the name of the main character of the poem and what is the name of his wife? What do their names suggest to you?
2. According to the speaker, what do "women and men" do? What seems to be the speaker's attitude toward these people? How can you tell?
3. What does the speaker say about what children know? What happens to them? What might Cummings be trying to convey about the difference between children and adults?
4. What happens to the two main characters at the end of the poem? How do the townspeople seem to react to this event? What lesson about life do you think Cummings is trying to communicate with this poem?

EVALUATE AND CONNECT

5. What two series of words are repeated in the poem? What might the poet have meant to emphasize through the use of **repetition** (see page R13)?
6. The words in lines 2 and 24 don't seem to make much sense. How do these words contribute to your impression of the town?
7. How does the poem's depiction of the "average person" compare with your response to the Focus Activity on page 642? Based on your comparison, would you say the poem also describes people of today?
8. In this poem, Cummings uses unconventional word order and few capital letters and punctuation marks. In your opinion, how do these techniques contribute to the impact and meaning of the poem?

Literary ELEMENTS

Rhythm

In poetry, **rhythm** is the arrangement of stressed and unstressed syllables. Rhythm can convey meaning by emphasizing certain words and phrases. It can also add a musical quality to a poem and help set the tone. Regular rhythm has a predictable pattern, while irregular rhythm has no definite pattern. Although "anyone lived in a pretty how town" has irregular rhythm, the particular arrangement of stressed and unstressed syllables plays an important role in the poem.

> Wŏmĕn ánd mén (bŏth líttlĕ
>   ănd smáll)
> cáred fŏr ányŏne nót ăt áll

1. Which lines seem to have the same or nearly the same rhythm? Which have rhythm that is quite different?
2. What do you think the differences in rhythm emphasize?

● See **Literary Terms Handbook,** p. R13.

—— EXTENDING YOUR RESPONSE ——

Writing About Literature

What Does It Really Mean?   In choosing words, poets consider both the **denotation** (literal meaning) and **connotation** (suggested meaning). In a few paragraphs, describe how the difference between the denotation and the connotation of the words *little, small, same,* and *never* might affect the reading of the poem.

Internet Connection

E. E. Cummings on the Web   Look for Web sites devoted to Cummings. Print out or copy down two more of his poems. Compare your reactions to these poems with those you had to "anyone lived in a pretty how town." Share your thoughts with a partner.

📖 **Save your work for your portfolio.**

MEDIA Connection

Anecdote

Marianne Moore's fellow poet Alfred Kreymborg once decided to take her in a new direction—to a baseball game. Here's what happened, as Kreymborg described it in his autobiography.

from *The Oxford Book of American Literary Anecdotes*

edited by Donald Hall

Never having found her at a loss on any topic whatsoever, I wanted to give myself the pleasure of at least once hearing her stumped about something. Certain that only an experience completely strange to her would be the thing, I invited her to a game at the Polo Grounds [baseball stadium where the New York Giants played].

Well, I got her safely to her seat and sat down beside her. Without so much as a glance toward the players at practice grabbing grounders and chasing fungos [practice fly balls], she went on giving me her impression of the respective technical achievements of [poets] Mr. Pound and Mr. Aldington without missing a turn in the rhythm of her speech, until I, a little impatient, touched her arm and, indicating a man in the pitcher's box winding up with the movement Matty's [Hall of Fame pitcher Christy Mathewson] so famous for, interrupted: "But Marianne, wait a moment, the game's about to begin. Don't you want to watch the first ball?" "Yes indeed," she said, stopped, blushed and leaned forward. The old blond boy [Mathewson] delivered a tantalizing fadeaway [pitch] which hovered in the air and then, just as it reached the batter, Shorty Slagle, shot from his shoulders to his knees and across the plate. "Strike!" bawled Umpire Emslie. "Excellent," said Marianne.

Delighted, I quickly turned to her with: "Do you happen to know the gentleman who threw that strike?"

"I've never seen him before," she admitted, "but I take it it must be Mr. Mathewson."

I could only gasp, "Why?"

"I've read his instructive book on the art of pitching—"

"Strike two!" interrupted Bob Emslie.

"And it's a pleasure," she continued, "to note how unerringly his execution supports his theories."

Respond

1. Does Kreymborg really take Marianne Moore in a new direction? Explain.

2. If you were in Kreymborg's position, would you be so surprised? Why or why not?

Before You Read

Poetry

Meet
Marianne Moore

"We [writers] must not be too sensitive about not being liked or not being printed. . . . The thing is to see the vision and not deny it; to care and admit that we do."

—*Moore*

Marianne Moore followed her own advice: she cared more about writing poetry than about achieving fame. She wasn't discouraged when she was called a "poet's poet" (meaning that only other poets appreciated her "difficult" poetry) or when her *Selected Poems* sold only 864 copies in seven years.

This original and whimsical writer was born in Missouri, grew up in Pennsylvania, and attended Bryn Mawr College where she began writing poetry. At the age of thirty-one, Moore moved with her mother to New York City, a place that offered her "accessibility to experience." There she worked in a school and a library, edited an influential literary magazine called *The Dial*, and mingled with other avant-garde writers and painters. In her spare time, she wrote many books of poetry, one of which won a Pulitzer Prize.

Moore believed that poets should write with what she called "unbearable accuracy." She revised her own poems again and again, never really considering any to be truly finished. While her use of obscure words and complex stanza patterns gave Moore a reputation for being difficult, she was greatly admired by fellow poets, including T. S. Eliot and William Carlos Williams. The poet John Ashbery once said of her, "I am tempted to call her our greatest modern poet."

Marianne Moore was born in 1887 and died in 1972.

FOCUS ACTIVITY

Do you think you understand what poetry is?

THINK-PAIR-SHARE Spend three minutes jotting down a list of things you know about poetry. Then share your list with a partner.

SETTING A PURPOSE Read to learn one writer's ideas of what poetry is.

BACKGROUND

Scientific Influences

At Bryn Mawr College, Moore majored in biology and histology, the study of plant and animal tissue structure. She even considered pursuing a career in medicine. Moore's interest in science never left her, as is apparent in both the subject matter and the precision of her verse. Moore wrote extensively of the natural world, and in a 1961 interview she discussed the importance of her scientific training to her poetry: "Precision, economy of statement, logic employed to ends that are disinterested, drawing and identifying, liberate—at least have some bearing on—the imagination."

Poetry

Marianne Moore

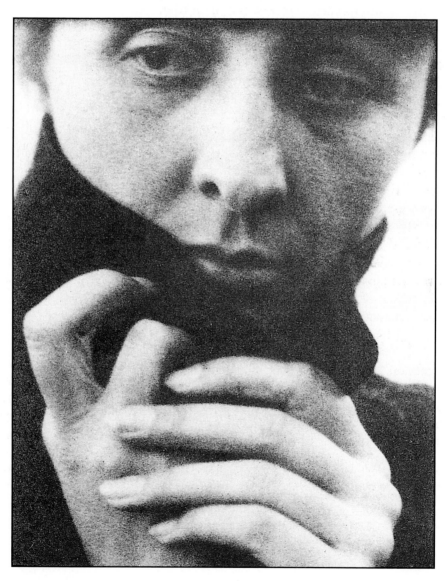

Georgia O'Keeffe, 1918. Alfred Stieglitz. Photograph. Metropolitan Museum of Art, New York.

Poetry

I, too, dislike it: there are things that are important beyond all this fiddle.°
  Reading it, however, with a perfect contempt for it, one discovers in
  it after all, a place for the genuine.
    Hands that can grasp, eyes
5   that can dilate,° hair that can rise
      if it must, these things are important not because a

high-sounding interpretation can be put upon them but because they are
  useful. When they become so derivative° as to become unintelligible,
  the same thing may be said for all of us, that we
10   do not admire what
    we cannot understand: the bat
      holding on upside down or in quest of something to

eat, elephants pushing, a wild horse taking a roll, a tireless wolf under
  a tree, the immovable critic twitching his skin like a horse that feels a flea, the base-
15 ball fan, the statistician—
    nor is it valid
      to discriminate against 'business documents and

school-books'; all these phenomena are important. One must make a distinction
  however: when dragged into prominence by half poets, the result is not poetry,
20 nor till the poets among us can be
    'literalists° of
    the imagination'—above
      insolence° and triviality and can present

for inspection, 'imaginary gardens with real toads in them', shall we have
25 it. In the meantime, if you demand on the one hand,
  the raw material of poetry in
    all its rawness and
    that which is on the other hand
      genuine, you are interested in poetry.

---

1 Here, *fiddle* means "nonsense" or "aimless, trifling, or experimental activity."
5 *Dilate* means "to become larger or wider."
8 Here, *derivative* (di riv′ ə tiv) may mean "unoriginal" or "based on someone else's experience."
21 Here, *literalists* are people who stick to observable facts.
23 *Insolence* is arrogance.

Responding to Literature

Personal Response
Were you convinced by the writer's argument? Why or why not?

ANALYZING LITERATURE

RECALL AND INTERPRET

1. What attitudes about poetry does the speaker express in lines 1–3?
2. What things does the speaker present in lines 4–5? Why are they important? What can you infer about the speaker's attitude toward poetry?
3. How does the speaker say people react to poems that "become so derivative as to become unintelligible"? According to the speaker, what kinds of "phenomena" make good subjects for poetry? What point do you think Moore is trying to make in lines 8–18?
4. According to lines 18–25, what accounts for the difference between the work of "half poets" and that of poets? How do you think presenting "'imaginary gardens with real toads in them'" results in poetry? Explain.
5. According to lines 25–29, what two demands indicate that a person is interested in poetry? In your opinion, what characteristics does the speaker believe a good poem should have?

EVALUATE AND CONNECT

6. Moore begins the poem by stating a provocative opinion. Do you think this is an effective way to begin the poem? Explain.
7. Look back at your response to the Focus Activity on page 646. How do the ideas presented in this poem help you understand what poetry is?
8. What subjects might the speaker suggest for poems written today?

Literary ELEMENTS

Enjambment
Enjambment is a verse technique in which the sense and grammatical structure of one line carries over to the next line without a punctuated pause. Enjambed lines contrast with end-stopped lines, in which both meaning and grammatical structure come to an end or a definitive pause. In "Poetry," enjambment serves to emphasize certain words or to expand their meanings by relating them to different contexts. This technique also serves to express the flow of the speaker's thought.

1. Identify three examples of enjambment in "Poetry."
2. In each example, what word or words might Moore be trying to emphasize or expand?

● See **Literary Terms Handbook**, p. R5.

EXTENDING YOUR RESPONSE

Writing About Literature
In Support of Poetry   Make poetry fans out of an audience of fourth or fifth graders. In your own words, rewrite Moore's ideas about poetry as stated in the poem. Be sure to write for your younger audience. Then make your presentation to a fourth- or fifth-grade class.

Listening and Speaking
Reading "Poetry"   Moore's **rhythm, rhyme,** and **enjambment** create challenges for reading aloud. (See Literary Terms Handbook, pages R13 and R5.) With a partner, prepare an oral reading of "Poetry." Present your reading to the class, alternating stanzas with your partner.

📖 **Save your work for your portfolio.**

Before You Read

The Bridal Party

Meet F. Scott Fitzgerald

F. Scott Fitzgerald once wrote that "all the stories that came into my head had a touch of disaster in them. . . . I was pretty sure living wasn't the reckless, careless business these people thought." Many of Fitzgerald's stories and novels describe the lifestyle of young, wealthy Americans in the 1920s. Fitzgerald shared this lifestyle, and the heroes in his fiction often have values and conflicts that are very similar to his own.

Fitzgerald was born in 1896 in St. Paul, Minnesota, into a family of little wealth but great social ambition. A failure at business, Fitzgerald's father was often criticized by his wife. She had high expectations for their children and sent them to the best schools so that they could mingle with the upper classes.

As a student, Fitzgerald had difficulty disciplining himself. He spent his time at Princeton University writing for the newspaper and participating in the drama club, trying to achieve social status through school clubs. After failing several courses, he left college in his junior year to enlist in the army. While stationed in the South, he fell in love with Zelda Sayre.

Following his stint in the army, Fitzgerald settled in New York City and struggled to earn a living. His financial worries ended with the publication of *This Side of Paradise* when he was twenty-four. This novel about his life at Princeton was an overnight success, making it possible for Fitzgerald to marry Zelda.

In the 1920s, Fitzgerald wrote short stories and novels and mingled with the rich in the United States and in Europe. While in France and Italy, he wrote and revised his most successful novel, *The Great Gatsby* (1925). However, he and Zelda also maintained a high style of living and spent money excessively. When the frantic decade ended with the 1929 stock market crash, Fitzgerald's private life and prosperous career also crashed. His wife suffered a series of nervous breakdowns from which she never recovered, and his high-paying magazine jobs dwindled with the onset of the Great Depression.

Though Fitzgerald struggled in the 1930s with alcoholism and with his marriage, he continued to write stories, novels, and essays; "The Bridal Party" was written during this period. He also spent some time in Hollywood as a screenwriter in an attempt to pay his debts. Fitzgerald then began work on a fifth novel, *The Last Tycoon*, but died of a heart attack at age forty-four before he completed it.

"Draw your chair up close to the edge of the precipice and I'll tell you a story."

"Show me a hero and I will write you a tragedy."

"Mostly, we authors repeat ourselves. . . . We have two or three great and moving experiences in our lives . . . and we tell our two or three stories—each time in a new disguise."

—*Fitzgerald*

F. Scott Fitzgerald was born in 1896 and died in 1940.

FOCUS ACTIVITY

Have you ever found yourself in a situation in which wanting to fit in with a group was an issue?

FREEWRITE Take a few minutes to freewrite about a time in your life when you especially wanted to fit in with a certain group. Why was it so important to fit in? How did you handle the situation?

SETTING A PURPOSE Read to see how the narrator hopes to "fit in."

BACKGROUND

The Time and Place

The Jazz Age   The 1920s have been called the Jazz Age for the relatively new musical form that was popular during the era. Jazz's vibrant and rebellious rhythms mirrored the spirit of a decade in which young people were rebelling against the social rules of the previous generation.

Economic prosperity fed the decade's party atmosphere. Business was booming, and some people made huge profits on their investments. Giddy from the sudden wealth, people partied and spent money recklessly.

The Stock Market Crash   In the 1920s, manufacturing experienced a great rise in productivity, but other sectors of the economy, most notably agriculture and energy, were sagging. Mergers between numerous small companies meant that by the end of the decade a relatively small number of corporations were earning nearly half of the nation's income. Stock prices rose sharply as many investors bought stocks, hoping to make quick profits before the boom ended. In August 1929, production dropped drastically, and two months later, panic began as many investors began selling off their stocks. Banks and

Paris, around 1930.

investment companies tried to intervene, but the situation proved irreversible; on October 29, 1929–"Black Tuesday"–the stock market collapsed completely. Stocks became worthless, and the Great Depression, the worst period of economic hardship in U.S. history, dragged on through most of the next decade.

VOCABULARY PREVIEW

imminent (im′ ə nənt) *adj.* about to take place; p. 652

reciprocate (ri sip′ rə kāt′) *v.* to give, feel, or show in return; p. 652

exhilarated (ig zil′ ə rā təd) *adj.* cheerful, lively, or excited; filled with vigor; p. 656

exploit (iks ploit′) *v.* to use or develop for profit, often in a selfish, unjust, or unfair way; p. 657

impetuously (im pech′ o͞o əs lē) *adv.* impulsively; suddenly; rashly; p. 658

tentative (ten′ tə tiv) *adj.* not fully worked out; somewhat undecided; p. 658

THE
BRIDAL PARTY

❧ I ❧

There was the usual insincere little note saying: "I wanted you to be the first to know." It was a double shock to Michael, announcing, as it did, both the engagement and the imminent marriage; which, moreover, was to be held, not in New York, decently and far away, but here in Paris under his very nose, if that could be said to extend over the Protestant Episcopal Church of the Holy Trinity, Avenue George-Cinq.[1] The date was two weeks off, early in June.

At first Michael was afraid and his stomach felt hollow. When he left the hotel that morning, the *femme de chambre*,[2] who was in love with his fine, sharp profile and his pleasant buoyancy, scented the hard abstraction that had settled over him. He walked in a daze to his bank, he bought a detective story at Smith's on the Rue de Rivoli,[3] he sympathetically stared for a while at a faded panorama of the battlefields in a tourist-office window and cursed a Greek tout who followed him with a half-displayed packet of innocuous[4] post cards warranted to be very dirty indeed.

But the fear stayed with him, and after a while he recognized it as the fear that now he would never be happy. He had met Caroline Dandy when she was seventeen, possessed her young heart all through her first season in New York, and then lost her, slowly, tragically, uselessly, because he had no money and could make no money; because, with all the energy and good will in the world, he could not find himself; because, loving him still, Caroline had lost faith and begun to see him as something pathetic, futile and shabby, outside the great, shining stream of life toward which she was inevitably drawn.

Since his only support was that she loved him, he leaned weakly on that; the support broke, but still he held on to it and was carried out to sea and washed up on the French coast with its broken pieces still in his hands. He carried them around with him in the form of photographs and packets of correspondence and a liking for a maudlin[5] popular song called "Among My Souvenirs." He kept clear of other girls, as if Caroline would somehow know it and reciprocate with a faithful heart. Her note informed him that he had lost her forever.

It was a fine morning. In front of the shops in the Rue de Castiglione,[6] proprietors and

---

1. *George-Cinq* (zhôrzh sănk)
2. The *femme de chambre* (fem də shäm′ br) is the hotel's housekeeper.
3. *Rue de Rivoli* (rōō də rē vo lē′); *Rue de* is French for "street of."
4. The *tout* (tōō), an aggressive peddler, offers pornographic pictures disguised as ordinary, innocent, or *innocuous*, post cards.
5. *Maudlin* means "overly sentimental."
6. *Castiglione* (käs′ tēl yō′ nä)

Vocabulary

imminent (im′ ə nənt) *adj.* about to take place
reciprocate (ri sip′ rə kāt′) *v.* to give, feel, or show in return

patrons were on the sidewalk gazing upward, for the Graf Zeppelin,[7] shining and glorious, symbol of escape and destruction—of escape, if necessary, through destruction—glided in the Paris sky. He heard a woman say in French that it would not her astonish if that commenced to let fall the bombs. Then he heard another voice, full of husky laughter, and the void in his stomach froze. Jerking about, he was face to face with Caroline Dandy and her fiancé.

"Why, Michael! Why, we were wondering where you were. I asked at the Guaranty Trust, and Morgan and Company, and finally sent a note to the National City——"

Why didn't they back away? Why didn't they back right up, walking backward down the Rue de Castiglione, across the Rue de Rivoli, through the Tuileries Gardens,[8] still walking backward as fast as they could till they grew vague and faded out across the river?

"This is Hamilton Rutherford, my fiancé."

"We've met before."

"At Pat's, wasn't it?"

"And last spring in the Ritz Bar."

"Michael, where have you been keeping yourself?"

"Around here." This agony. Previews of Hamilton Rutherford flashed before his eyes—a quick series of pictures, sentences. He remembered hearing that he had bought a seat in 1920 for a hundred and twenty-five thousand of borrowed money, and just before the break[9] sold it for more than half a million. Not handsome like Michael, but vitally attractive, confident, authoritative, just the right height over Caroline there—Michael had always been too short for Caroline when they danced.

Rutherford was saying: "No, I'd like it very much if you'd come to the bachelor dinner. I'm taking the Ritz Bar from nine o'clock on. Then right after the wedding there'll be a reception and breakfast at the Hotel George-Cinq."

"And, Michael, George Packman is giving a party day after tomorrow at Chez[10] Victor, and I want you to be sure and come. And also to tea Friday at Jebby West's; she'd want to have you if she knew where you were. What's your hotel, so we can send you an invitation? You see, the reason we decided to have it over here is because mother has been sick in a nursing home here and the whole clan is in Paris. Then Hamilton's mother's being here too——"

The entire clan; they had always hated him, except her mother; always discouraged his courtship. What a little counter he was in this game of families and money! Under his hat his brow sweated with the humiliation of the fact

---

7. The *Graf Zeppelin,* a German airship, carried passengers in the 1930s. During World War I, such airships served as bombers.
8. The *Tuileries* (twhēl′ rē) *Gardens* are located in Paris, France, and are noteworthy in that their design has changed little since they were created in 1664.

9. A *seat,* or membership, in a stock exchange is expensive because only a limited number of memberships exist. The *break* is the October 1929 stock market crash.
10. *Chez* (shā) is French for "at." It is often used in the names of restaurants, and here, means "at the house of."

Viewing the sketch: How do the people in the sketch seem similar to or different from the characters in "The Bridal Party"?

that for all his misery he was worth just exactly so many invitations. Frantically he began to mumble something about going away.

Then it happened—Caroline saw deep into him, and Michael knew that she saw. She saw through to his profound[11] woundedness, and something quivered inside her, died out along the curve of her mouth and in her eyes. He had moved her. All the unforgettable impulses of first love had surged up once more; their hearts had in some way touched across two feet of Paris sunlight. She took her fiancé's arm suddenly, as if to steady herself with the feel of it.

They parted. Michael walked quickly for a minute; then he stopped, pretending to look in a window, and saw them farther up the street, walking fast into the Place Vendôme,[12] people with much to do.

He had things to do also—he had to get his laundry.

"Nothing will ever be the same again," he said to himself. "She will never be happy in her marriage and I will never be happy at all any more."

The two vivid years of his love for Caroline moved back around him like years in Einstein's physics. Intolerable memories arose—of rides in the Long Island moonlight; of a happy time at Lake Placid with her cheeks so cold there, but warm just underneath the surface; of a despairing afternoon in a little café on Forty-eighth Street in the last sad months when their marriage had come to seem impossible.

"Come in," he said aloud.

The concierge with a telegram; brusque because Mr. Curly's clothes were a little shabby. Mr. Curly gave few tips; Mr. Curly was obviously a *petit client*.[13]

Michael read the telegram.

"An answer?" the concierge asked.

"No," said Michael, and then, on an impulse: "Look."

"Too bad—too bad," said the concierge. "Your grandfather is dead."

"Not too bad," said Michael. "It means that I come into a quarter of a million dollars."

Too late by a single month; after the first flush of the news his misery was deeper than ever. Lying awake in bed that night, he listened endlessly to the long caravan of a circus moving through the street from one Paris fair to another.

---

11. *Profound* means "deep" or "complete."
12. *Place Vendôme* (pläs vän dōm′)

13. A *concierge* (kōn syerzh′) assists hotel guests by taking messages, making reservations, and so on. A *brusque* person is blunt and rude. The French phrase *petit client* (pe′ tē klē′ ən) means "small (unimportant) customer."

When the last van had rumbled out of hearing and the corners of the furniture were pastel blue with the dawn, he was still thinking of the look in Caroline's eyes that morning—the look that seemed to say: "Oh, why couldn't you have done something about it? Why couldn't you have been stronger, made me marry you? Don't you see how sad I am?"

Michael's fists clenched.

"Well, I won't give up till the last moment," he whispered. "I've had all the bad luck so far, and maybe it's turned at last. One takes what one can get, up to the limit of one's strength, and if I can't have her, at least she'll go into this marriage with some of me in her heart."

⮑II⮐

Accordingly he went to the party at Chez Victor two days later, upstairs and into the little salon[14] off the bar where the party was to assemble for cocktails. He was early; the only other occupant was a tall lean man of fifty. They spoke.

"You waiting for George Packman's party?"

"Yes. My name's Michael Curly."

"My name's——"

Michael failed to catch the name. They ordered a drink, and Michael supposed that the bride and groom were having a gay time.

"Too much so," the other agreed, frowning. "I don't see how they stand it. We all crossed on the boat together; five days of that crazy life and then two weeks of Paris. You"—he hesitated, smiling faintly—"you'll excuse me for saying that your generation drinks too much."

"Not Caroline."

"No, not Caroline. She seems to take only a cocktail and a glass of champagne, and then she's had enough, thank God. But Hamilton drinks too much and all this crowd of young people drink too much. Do you live in Paris?"

"For the moment," said Michael.

"I don't like Paris. My wife—that is to say, my ex-wife, Hamilton's mother—lives in Paris."

"You're Hamilton Rutherford's father?"

"I have that honor. And I'm not denying that I'm proud of what he's done; it was just a general comment."

"Of course."

Michael glanced up nervously as four people came in. He felt suddenly that his dinner coat was old and shiny; he had ordered a new one that morning. The people who had come in were rich and at home in their richness with one another—a dark, lovely girl with a hysterical little laugh whom he had met before; two confident men whose jokes referred invariably to last night's scandal and tonight's potentialities, as if they had important rôles in a play that extended indefinitely into the past and the future. When Caroline arrived, Michael had scarcely a moment of her, but it was enough to note that, like all the others, she was strained and tired. She was pale beneath her rouge; there were shadows under her eyes. With a mixture of relief and wounded vanity,[15] he found himself placed far from her and at another table; he needed a moment to adjust himself to his surroundings. This was not like the immature set in which he and Caroline had moved; the men were more than thirty and had an air of sharing the best of this world's good. Next to him was Jebby West, whom he knew; and, on the other side, a jovial man who immediately began to talk to Michael about a stunt for the bachelor dinner: They were going to hire a French girl to appear with an actual baby in her arms, crying: "Hamilton, you can't desert me now!" The idea seemed stale and unamusing to Michael, but its originator shook with anticipatory laughter.

Farther up the table there was talk of the market—another drop today, the most appreciable[16] since the crash; people were kidding Rutherford about it: "Too bad, old man. You better not get married, after all."

---

14. The French word *salon* means "drawing room."

15. *Vanity* is excessive pride.
16. *Appreciable* means "enough to be noticed."

THE BRIDAL PARTY

Michael asked the man on his left, "Has he lost a lot?"

"Nobody knows. He's heavily involved, but he's one of the smartest young men in Wall Street. Anyhow, nobody ever tells you the truth."

It was a champagne dinner from the start, and toward the end it reached a pleasant level of conviviality,[17] but Michael saw that all these people were too weary to be exhilarated by any ordinary stimulant; for weeks they had drunk cocktails before meals like Americans, wines and brandies like Frenchmen, beer like Germans, whisky-and-soda like the English, and as they were no longer in the twenties, this preposterous *mélange*,[18] that was like some gigantic cocktail in a nightmare, served only to make them temporarily less conscious of the mistakes of the night before. Which is to say that it was not really a gay party; what gayety existed was displayed in the few who drank nothing at all.

But Michael was not tired, and the champagne stimulated him and made his misery less acute. He had been away from New York for more than eight months and most of the dance music was unfamiliar to him, but at the first bars of the "Painted Doll," to which he and Caroline had moved through so much happiness and despair the previous summer, he crossed to Caroline's table and asked her to dance.

She was lovely in a dress of thin ethereal[19] blue, and the proximity of her crackly yellow hair, of her cool and tender gray eyes, turned his body clumsy and rigid; he stumbled with their first step on the floor. For a moment it seemed that there was nothing to say; he wanted to tell her about his inheritance, but the idea seemed abrupt, unprepared for.

"Michael, it's so nice to be dancing with you again."

He smiled grimly.

"I'm so happy you came," she continued. "I was afraid maybe you'd be silly and stay away. Now we can be just good friends and natural together. Michael, I want you and Hamilton to like each other."

The engagement was making her stupid; he had never heard her make such a series of obvious remarks before.

"I could kill him without a qualm,"[20] he said pleasantly, "but he looks like a good man. He's fine. What I want to know is, what happens to people like me who aren't able to forget?"

As he said this he could not prevent his mouth from dropping suddenly, and glancing up, Caroline saw, and her heart quivered violently, as it had the other morning.

"Do you mind so much, Michael?"

"Yes."

For a second as he said this, in a voice that seemed to have come up from his shoes, they were not dancing; they were simply clinging together. Then she leaned away from him and twisted her mouth into a lovely smile.

"I didn't know what to do at first, Michael. I told Hamilton about you—that I'd cared for you an awful lot—but it didn't worry him, and he was right. Because I'm over you now—yes, I am. And you'll wake up some sunny morning and be over me just like that."

He shook his head stubbornly.

"Oh, yes. We weren't for each other. I'm pretty flighty, and I need somebody like Hamilton to decide things. It was that more than the question of—of——"

"Of money." Again he was on the point of telling her what had happened, but again something told him it was not the time.

---

17. *Conviviality* is merriment and the enjoyment of good company.
18. *Mélange* (mā´ länzh) means "mixture."
19. An *ethereal* (i thēr´ ē əl) blue would be very light and delicate.

---

20. *Qualm* means "doubt," "misgiving," or "twinge of conscience."

Vocabulary
exhilarated (ig zil´ ə rā təd) *adj.* cheerful, lively, or excited; filled with vigor

"Then how do you account for what happened when we met the other day," he demanded helplessly—"what happened just now? When we just pour toward each other like we used to—as if we were one person, as if the same blood was flowing through both of us?"

"Oh, don't," she begged him. "You mustn't talk like that; everything's decided now. I love Hamilton with all my heart. It's just that I remember certain things in the past and I feel sorry for you—for us—for the way we were."

Over her shoulder, Michael saw a man come toward them to cut in. In a panic he danced her away, but inevitably the man came on.

"I've got to see you alone, if only for a minute," Michael said quickly. "When can I?"

"I'll be at Jebby West's tea tomorrow," she whispered as a hand fell politely upon Michael's shoulder.

But he did not talk to her at Jebby West's tea. Rutherford stood next to her, and each brought the other into all conversations. They left early. The next morning the wedding cards arrived in the first mail.

Then Michael, grown desperate with pacing up and down his room, determined on a bold stroke; he wrote to Hamilton Rutherford, asking him for a rendezvous[21] the following afternoon. In a short telephone communication Rutherford agreed, but for a day later than Michael had asked. And the wedding was only six days away.

They were to meet in the bar of the Hotel Jena. Michael knew what he would say: "See here, Rutherford, do you realize the responsibility you're taking in going through with this marriage? Do you realize the harvest of trouble and regret you're sowing in persuading a girl into something contrary to the instincts of her heart?" He would explain that the barrier between Caroline and himself had been an artificial one and was now removed, and demand that the matter be put up to Caroline frankly before it was too late.

Rutherford would be angry, conceivably there would be a scene, but Michael felt that he was fighting for his life now.

He found Rutherford in conversation with an older man, whom Michael had met at several of the wedding parties.

"I saw what happened to most of my friends," Rutherford was saying, "and I decided it wasn't going to happen to me. It isn't so difficult; if you take a girl with common sense, and tell her what's what, and do your stuff damn well, and play decently square with her, it's a marriage. If you stand for any nonsense at the beginning, it's one of these arrangements—within five years the man gets out, or else the girl gobbles him up and you have the usual mess."

"Right!" agreed his companion enthusiastically. "Hamilton, boy, you're right."

Michael's blood boiled slowly.

"Doesn't it strike you," he inquired coldly, "that your attitude went out of fashion about a hundred years ago?"

"No, it didn't," said Rutherford pleasantly, but impatiently. "I'm as modern as anybody. I'd get married in an aeroplane next Saturday if it'd please my girl."

"I don't mean that way of being modern. You can't take a sensitive woman——"

"Sensitive? Women aren't so darn sensitive. It's fellows like you who are sensitive; it's fellows like you they exploit—all your devotion and kindness and all that. They read a couple of books and see a few pictures because they haven't got anything else to do, and then they say they're finer in grain than you are, and to prove it they take the bit in their teeth and

---

21. A *rendezvous* is an appointment to meet at a certain place or time.

Vocabulary
exploit (iks ploit´) *v.* to use or develop for profit, often in a selfish, unjust, or unfair way

THE BRIDAL PARTY

tear off for a fare-you-well—just about as sensitive as a fire horse."

"Caroline happens to be sensitive," said Michael in a clipped voice.

At this point the other man got up to go; when the dispute about the check had been settled and they were alone, Rutherford leaned back to Michael as if a question had been asked him.

"Caroline's more than sensitive," he said. "She's got sense."

His combative eyes, meeting Michael's, flickered with a gray light. "This all sounds pretty crude to you, Mr. Curly, but it seems to me that the average man nowadays just asks to be made a monkey of by some woman who doesn't even get any fun out of reducing him to that level. There are darn few men who possess their wives any more, but I am going to be one of them."

To Michael it seemed time to bring the talk back to the actual situation: "Do you realize the responsibility you're taking?"

"I certainly do," interrupted Rutherford. "I'm not afraid of responsibility. I'll make the decisions—fairly, I hope, but anyhow they'll be final."

"What if you didn't start right?" said Michael impetuously. "What if your marriage isn't founded on mutual love?"

"I think I see what you mean," Rutherford said, still pleasant. "And since you've brought it up, let me say that if you and Caroline had married, it wouldn't have lasted three years. Do you know what your affair was founded on? On sorrow. You got sorry for each other. Sorrow's a lot of fun for most women and for some men, but it seems to me that a marriage ought to be based on hope." He looked at his watch and stood up.

"I've got to meet Caroline. Remember, you're coming to the bachelor dinner day after tomorrow."

Michael felt the moment slipping away. "Then Caroline's personal feelings don't count with you?" he demanded fiercely.

"Caroline's tired and upset. But she has what she wants, and that's the main thing."

"Are you referring to yourself?" demanded Michael incredulously.[22]

"Yes."

"May I ask how long she's wanted you?"

"About two years." Before Michael could answer, he was gone.

During the next two days Michael floated in an abyss of helplessness. The idea haunted him that he had left something undone that would sever this knot drawn tighter under his eyes. He phoned Caroline, but she insisted that it was physically impossible for her to see him until the day before the wedding, for which day she granted him a tentative rendezvous. Then he went to the bachelor dinner, partly in fear of an evening alone at his hotel, partly from a feeling that by his presence at that function he was somehow nearer to Caroline, keeping her in sight.

The Ritz Bar had been prepared for the occasion by French and American banners and by a great canvas covering one wall, against which the guests were invited to concentrate their proclivities[23] in breaking glasses.

At the first cocktail, taken at the bar, there were many slight spillings from many trembling hands, but later, with the champagne, there was a rising tide of laughter and occasional bursts of song.

---

22. *Incredulously* means "with unwillingness or inability to believe."
23. At this bachelor party, the guests' tendencies, or *proclivities,* are to drink toasts repeatedly to the groom and then smash their drinking glasses.

Vocabulary
impetuously (im pech′ ōō əs lē) *adv.* impulsively; suddenly; rashly
tentative (ten′ tə tiv) *adj.* not fully worked out; somewhat undecided

Rooftop Café, 1925. Everett Shinn. Pastel on blue paper laid down on board, 11¼ x 15¼ in. Berry Hill Galleries Inc., New York.

Viewing the painting: In what ways does the mood of the painting reflect the mood of the parties described in "The Bridal Party"?

Michael was surprised to find what a difference his new dinner coat, his new silk hat, his new, proud linen made in his estimate of himself; he felt less resentment toward all these people for being so rich and assured. For the first time since he had left college he felt rich and assured himself; he felt that he was part of all this, and even entered into the scheme of Johnson, the practical joker, for the appearance of the woman betrayed, now waiting tranquilly in the room across the hall.

"We don't want to go too heavy," Johnson said, "because I imagine Ham's had a pretty anxious day already. Did you see Fullman Oil's sixteen points off this morning?"

"Will that matter to him?" Michael asked, trying to keep the interest out of his voice.

"Naturally. He's in heavily; he's always in everything heavily. So far he's had luck; anyhow, up to a month ago."

The glasses were filled and emptied faster now, and men were shouting at one another across the narrow table. Against the bar a group of ushers was being photographed, and the flash light surged through the room in a stifling cloud.

"Now's the time," Johnson said. "You're to stand by the door, remember, and we're both to try and keep her from coming in—just till we get everybody's attention."

He went on out into the corridor, and Michael waited obediently by the door. Several minutes passed. Then Johnson reappeared with a curious expression on his face.

"There's something funny about this."

"Isn't the girl there?"

"She's there all right, but there's another woman there, too; and it's nobody we engaged either. She wants to see Hamilton Rutherford, and she looks as if she had something on her mind."

THE BRIDAL PARTY

They went out into the hall. Planted firmly in a chair near the door sat an American girl a little the worse for liquor, but with a determined expression on her face. She looked up at them with a jerk of her head.

"Well, j'tell him?" she demanded. "The name is Marjorie Collins, and he'll know it. I've come a long way, and I want to see him now and quick, or there's going to be more trouble than you ever saw." She rose unsteadily to her feet.

"You go in and tell Ham," whispered Johnson to Michael. "Maybe he'd better get out. I'll keep her here."

Back at the table, Michael leaned close to Rutherford's ear and, with a certain grimness, whispered:

"A girl outside named Marjorie Collins says she wants to see you. She looks as if she wanted to make trouble."

Hamilton Rutherford blinked and his mouth fell ajar; then slowly the lips came together in a straight line and he said in a crisp voice:

"Please keep her there. And send the head barman to me right away."

Michael spoke to the barman, and then, without returning to the table, asked quietly for his coat and hat. Out in the hall again, he passed Johnson and the girl without speaking and went out into the Rue Cambon.[24] Calling a cab, he gave the address of Caroline's hotel.

His place was beside her now. Not to bring bad news, but simply to be with her when her house of cards came falling around her head.

Rutherford had implied that he was soft— well, he was hard enough not to give up the girl he loved without taking advantage of every chance within the pale[25] of honor. Should she turn away from Rutherford, she would find him there.

She was in; she was surprised when he called, but she was still dressed and would be down immediately. Presently she appeared in a dinner gown, holding two blue telegrams in her hand. They sat down in armchairs in the deserted lobby.

"But, Michael, is the dinner over?"

"I wanted to see you, so I came away."

"I'm glad." Her voice was friendly, but matter-of-fact. "Because I'd just phoned your hotel that I had fittings and rehearsals all day tomorrow. Now we can have our talk after all."

"You're tired," he guessed. "Perhaps I shouldn't have come."

"No. I was waiting up for Hamilton. Telegrams that may be important. He said he might go on somewhere, and that may mean any hour, so I'm glad I have someone to talk to."

Michael winced at the impersonality in the last phrase.

"Don't you care when he gets home?"

"Naturally," she said, laughing, "but I haven't got much say about it, have I?"

"Why not?"

"I couldn't start by telling him what he could and couldn't do."

"Why not?"

"He wouldn't stand for it."

"He seems to want merely a housekeeper," said Michael ironically.

"Tell me about your plans, Michael," she asked quickly.

"My plans? I can't see any future after the day after tomorrow. The only real plan I ever had was to love you."

Their eyes brushed past each other's, and the look he knew so well was staring out at him from hers. Words flowed quickly from his heart:

"Let me tell you just once more how well I've loved you, never wavering for a moment, never thinking of another girl. And now when I think of all the years ahead without you, without any hope, I don't want to live, Caroline darling. I used to dream about our home, our children, about holding you in my

---

24. *Cambon* (käm′ bon)
25. A *pale* is a boundary, an enclosure, or a limit.

arms and touching your face and hands and hair that used to belong to me, and now I just can't wake up."

Caroline was crying softly. "Poor Michael—poor Michael." Her hand reached out and her fingers brushed the lapel of his dinner coat. "I was so sorry for you the other night. You looked so thin, and as if you needed a new suit and somebody to take care of you." She sniffled and looked more closely at his coat. "Why, you've got a new suit! And a new silk hat! Why, Michael, how swell!" She laughed, suddenly cheerful through her tears. "You must have come into money, Michael; I never saw you so well turned out."

For a moment, at her reaction, he hated his new clothes.

"I have come into money," he said. "My grandfather left me about a quarter of a million dollars."

"Why, Michael," she cried, "how perfectly swell! I can't tell you how glad I am. I've always thought you were the sort of person who ought to have money."

"Yes, just too late to make a difference."

The revolving door from the street groaned around and Hamilton Rutherford came into the lobby. His face was flushed, his eyes were restless and impatient.

"Hello, darling; hello, Mr. Curly." He bent and kissed Caroline. "I broke away for a minute to find out if I had any telegrams. I see you've got them there." Taking them from her, he remarked to Curly, "That was an odd business there in the bar, wasn't it? Especially as I understand some of you had a joke fixed up in the same line." He opened one of the telegrams, closed it and turned to Caroline with the divided expression of a man carrying two things in his head at once.

"A girl I haven't seen for two years turned up," he said. "It seemed to be some clumsy form of blackmail, for I haven't and never have had any sort of obligation toward her whatever."

"What happened?"

"The head barman had a Sûreté Générale[26] man there in ten minutes and it was settled in the hall. The French blackmail laws make ours look like a sweet wish, and I gather they threw a scare into her that she'll remember. But it seems wiser to tell you."

"Are you implying that I mentioned the matter?" said Michael stiffly.

"No," Rutherford said slowly. "No, you were just going to be on hand. And since you're here, I'll tell you some news that will interest you even more."

He handed Michael one telegram and opened the other.

"This is in code," Michael said.

"So is this. But I've got to know all the words pretty well this last week. The two of them together mean that I'm due to start life all over."

Michael saw Caroline's face grow a shade paler, but she sat quiet as a mouse.

"It was a mistake and I stuck to it too long," continued Rutherford. "So you see I don't have all the luck, Mr. Curly. By the way, they tell me you've come into money."

"Yes," said Michael.

"There we are, then." Rutherford turned to Caroline. "You understand, darling, that I'm not joking or exaggerating. I've lost almost every cent I had and I'm starting life over."

Two pairs of eyes were regarding her—Rutherford's noncommittal[27] and unrequiring, Michael's hungry, tragic, pleading. In a minute she had raised herself from the chair and with a little cry thrown herself into Hamilton Rutherford's arms.

"Oh, darling," she cried, "what does it matter! It's better; I like it better, honestly I do! I want to start that way; I want to! Oh, please don't worry or be sad even for a minute!"

---

26. In Paris, *Sûreté Générale* (sœr′ tā zhen ä′ räl′) is the police department's criminal investigation unit.
27. *Noncommittal* means "unwilling to pledge oneself to a particular opinion, view, or course of action."

The Wedding. Walter Richard Sickert (1860–1942). Oil on canvas. Private collection.

Viewing the painting: What adjectives would you use to describe the bride in the painting? Could the adjectives you chose also apply to Caroline? Why or why not?

"All right, baby," said Rutherford. His hand stroked her hair gently for a moment; then he took his arm from around her.

"I promised to join the party for an hour," he said. "So I'll say good night, and I want you to go to bed soon and get a good sleep. Good night, Mr. Curly. I'm sorry to have let you in for all these financial matters."

But Michael had already picked up his hat and cane. "I'll go along with you," he said.

～III～

It was such a fine morning. Michael's cutaway[28] hadn't been delivered, so he felt rather uncomfortable passing before the cameras and moving-picture machines in front of the little church on the Avenue George-Cinq.

It was such a clean, new church that it seemed unforgivable not to be dressed properly, and Michael, white and shaky after a sleepless night, decided to stand in the rear. From there he looked at the back of Hamilton Rutherford, and the lacy, filmy back of Caroline, and the fat back of George Packman, which looked unsteady, as if it wanted to lean against the bride and groom.

The ceremony went on for a long time under the gay flags and pennons[29] overhead, under the thick beams of June sunlight slanting down through the tall windows upon the well-dressed people.

As the procession, headed by the bride and groom, started down the aisle, Michael realized with alarm he was just where everyone would dispense with their parade stiffness, become informal and speak to him.

So it turned out. Rutherford and Caroline spoke first to him; Rutherford grim with the strain of being married, and Caroline lovelier than he had ever seen her, floating all softly down through the friends and relatives of her youth, down through the past and forward to the future by the sunlit door.

Michael managed to murmur, "Beautiful, simply beautiful," and then other people passed and spoke to him—old Mrs. Dandy, straight from her sickbed and looking remarkably well, or carrying it off like the very fine old lady she was; and Rutherford's father and mother, ten years divorced, but walking side by side and looking made for each other and proud. Then all Caroline's sisters and their husbands and her little nephews in Eton suits,[30] and then a long parade, all speaking to Michael because he was still standing paralyzed just at that point where the procession broke.

He wondered what would happen now. Cards had been issued for a reception at the George-Cinq; an expensive enough place, heaven knew. Would Rutherford try to go through with that on top of those disastrous telegrams? Evidently, for the procession outside was streaming up there through the June morning, three by three and four by four. On the corner the long dresses of girls, five abreast, fluttered many-colored in the wind. Girls had become gossamer again, perambulatory flora;[31] such lovely fluttering dresses in the bright noon wind.

Michael needed a drink; he couldn't face that reception line without a drink. Diving into a side doorway of the hotel, he asked for the bar, whither a *chasseur*[32] led him through half a kilometer of new American-looking passages.

But—how did it happen?—the bar was full. There were ten—fifteen men and two—four girls, all from the wedding, all needing a drink. There were cocktails and champagne in the bar; Rutherford's cocktails and champagne, as

---

28. A *cutaway,* also called a morning coat, is a man's long, formal coat with tails sloping back from the waistline.
29. *Pennons* are long, triangular flags.
30. *Eton* is a prestigious boys' school near London; the *suits* are of the style—black, with short pants and waist-length jackets—worn by Eton students.
31. *Gossamer* is light, filmy, delicate, and cobweb-like. *Perambulatory flora* are walking plants or flowers.
32. A *chasseur* (shä sŏŏr´) runs errands and attends to guests' needs.

THE BRIDAL PARTY

it turned out, for he had engaged the whole bar and the ballroom and the two great reception rooms and all the stairways leading up and down, and windows looking out over the whole square block of Paris. By and by Michael went and joined the long, slow drift of the receiving line. Through a flowery mist of "Such a lovely wedding," "My dear, you were simply lovely," "You're a lucky man, Rutherford" he passed down the line. When Michael came to Caroline, she took a single step forward and kissed him on the lips, but he felt no contact in the kiss; it was unreal and he floated on away from it. Old Mrs. Dandy, who had always liked him, held his hand for a minute and thanked him for the flowers he had sent when he heard she was ill.

"I'm so sorry not to have written; you know, we old ladies are grateful for——" The flowers, the fact that she had not written, the wedding— Michael saw that they all had the same relative importance to her now; she had married off five other children and seen two of the marriages go to pieces, and this scene, so poignant,[33] so confusing to Michael, appeared to her simply a familiar charade in which she had played her part before.

A buffet luncheon with champagne was already being served at small tables and there was an orchestra playing in the empty ballroom. Michael sat down with Jebby West; he was still a little embarrassed at not wearing a morning coat, but he perceived now that he was not alone in the omission and felt better. "Wasn't Caroline divine?" Jebby West said. "So entirely self-possessed. I asked her this morning if she wasn't a little nervous at stepping off like this. And she said, 'Why should I be? I've been after him for two years, and now I'm just happy, that's all.'"

"It must be true," said Michael gloomily.

"What?"

"What you just said."

He had been stabbed, but, rather to his distress, he did not feel the wound.

He asked Jebby to dance. Out on the floor, Rutherford's father and mother were dancing together.

"It makes me a little sad, that," she said. "Those two hadn't met for years; both of them were married again and she divorced again. She went to the station to meet him when he came over for Caroline's wedding, and invited him to stay at her house in the Avenue du Bois[34] with a whole lot of other people, perfectly proper, but he was afraid his wife would hear about it and not like it, so he went to a hotel. Don't you think that's sort of sad?"

An hour or so later Michael realized suddenly that it was afternoon. In one corner of the ballroom an arrangement of screens like a moving-picture stage had been set up and photographers were taking official pictures of the bridal party. The bridal party, still as death and pale as wax under the bright lights, appeared, to the dancers circling the modulated semidarkness of the ballroom, like those jovial or sinister[35] groups that one comes upon in The Old Mill at an amusement park.

After the bridal party had been photographed, there was a group of the ushers; then the bridesmaids, the families, the children. Later, Caroline, active and excited, having long since abandoned the repose implicit[36] in her flowing dress and great bouquet, came and plucked Michael off the floor.

"Now we'll have them take one of just old friends." Her voice implied that this was best, most intimate of all. "Come here, Jebby, George—not you, Hamilton; this is just my friends—Sally——"

A little after that, what remained of formality disappeared and the hours flowed easily down

---

33. *Poignant* (poin′ yənt) means "calling up sad emotions."

34. *du Bois* (dōō bwä)

35. A *jovial* group is lively and full of fun; a *sinister* one threatens harm or evil.

36. *Repose* means "peacefulness." Something *implicit* is suggested but not directly expressed.

664 UNIT 5

the profuse stream of champagne. In the modern fashion, Hamilton Rutherford sat at the table with his arm about an old girl of his and assured his guests, which included not a few bewildered but enthusiastic Europeans, that the party was not nearly at an end; it was to reassemble at Zelli's after midnight. Michael saw Mrs. Dandy, not quite over her illness, rise to go and become caught in polite group after group, and he spoke of it to one of her daughters, who thereupon forcibly abducted her mother and called her car. Michael felt very considerate and proud of himself after having done this, and drank much more champagne.

"It's amazing," George Packman was telling him enthusiastically. "This show will cost Ham about five thousand dollars, and I understand they'll be just about his last. But did he countermand[37] a bottle of champagne or a flower? Not he! He happens to have it—that young man. Do you know that T. G. Vance offered him a salary of fifty thousand dollars a year ten minutes before the wedding this morning? In another year he'll be back with the millionaires."

The conversation was interrupted by a plan to carry Rutherford out on communal shoulders—a plan which six of them put into effect, and then stood in the four-o'clock sunshine waving good-bye to the bride and groom. But there must have been a mistake somewhere, for five minutes later Michael saw both bride and groom descending the stairway to the reception, each with a glass of champagne held defiantly on high.

"This is our way of doing things," he thought. "Generous and fresh and free; a sort of Virginia-plantation hospitality, but at a different pace now, nervous as a ticker tape."[38]

Standing unself-consciously in the middle of the room to see which was the American ambassador, he realized with a start that he hadn't really thought of Caroline for hours. He looked about him with a sort of alarm, and then he saw her across the room, very bright and young, and radiantly happy. He saw Rutherford near her, looking at her as if he could never look long enough, and as Michael watched them they seemed to recede as he had wished them to do that day in the Rue de Castiglione—recede and fade off into joys and griefs of their own, into the years that would take the toll of Rutherford's fine pride and Caroline's young, moving beauty; fade far away, so that now he could scarcely see them, as if they were shrouded[39] in something as misty as her white, billowing dress.

Michael was cured. The ceremonial function, with its pomp and its revelry,[40] had stood for a sort of initiation into a life where even his regret could not follow them. All the bitterness melted out of him suddenly and the world reconstituted[41] itself out of the youth and happiness that was all around him, profligate[42] as the spring sunshine. He was trying to remember which one of the bridesmaids he had made a date to dine with tonight as he walked forward to bid Hamilton and Caroline Rutherford good-bye.

---

37. To *countermand* is to revoke or reverse an order or command.

38. A ticker is a telegraphic instrument that prints stock market reports on a roll of narrow paper, or *ticker tape*.
39. *Shrouded* means "covered" or "concealed."
40. *Revelry* means "noisy festivity" or "merrymaking."
41. To be *reconstituted* is to be made over or renewed.
42. *Profligate* (prof′ lə git) means "over-abundant" or "recklessly extravagant."

Responding to Literature

Personal Response

What were your immediate responses to the main characters in the story?

ANALYZING LITERATURE

RECALL

1. How does Michael react to the news of Caroline's wedding? to his accidental meeting with Caroline and Hamilton? to his grandfather's death?
2. What comparisons does Michael make between himself and the other people at the parties before the wedding?
3. What are Michael's objections to Hamilton marrying Caroline? How does Hamilton defend himself?
4. Why does Michael leave the bachelor party? What news does Hamilton reveal to Caroline and Michael?
5. How does Michael's attitude toward Caroline change after the wedding? How do his views of the rich young people at the party change?

INTERPRET

6. What do Michael's reactions to the wedding invitation, the unexpected meeting with Caroline and Hamilton, and his grandfather's death tell you about his character?
7. What personal traits does Michael seem to equate with money and personal appearance? Explain.
8. What do Michael's objections to Hamilton and Hamilton's responses to Michael reveal about each character?
9. In your opinion, why does Caroline make the choice she does?
10. Do you think Michael has really changed by the end of the story? In your opinion, will this new attitude last? Explain.

EVALUATE AND CONNECT

11. Why do you think Fitzgerald describes the bridal party as both "jovial" and "sinister"?
12. Do you think Caroline made the better choice? Explain.
13. What do the references to actual places in Paris add to the story?
14. Does the **conflict,** or central struggle, faced by the characters in "The Bridal Party" seem realistic to you? Why or why not?
15. At the end of the story, Michael feels "cured" of his "bitterness" and "regret." How have you worked through personal disappointment or hurt? Compare a situation of your own with Michael's.

Literary ELEMENTS

Characterization

Characterization is the way an author reveals the personality of a character. In **direct characterization,** the writer makes direct statements about a character's personality. In **indirect characterization,** the writer reveals the personality of a character through physical description and the actions, thoughts, speech, or perceptions of that character or of other characters. The reader must then use these details to make inferences about the character's personality. For example, in "The Bridal Party," Fitzgerald shows Michael's impressions of Hamilton and Caroline through the use of indirect characterization.

1. What do Michael's thoughts and perceptions about those around him reveal about his own personality?
2. Explain two ways in which Fitzgerald indirectly reveals Hamilton's sense of confidence.

● See **Literary Terms Handbook,** p. R3.

LITERATURE AND WRITING

Writing About Literature

Point of View   A narrator who knows the thoughts and actions of all characters is a **third-person omniscient** (all-knowing) narrator. A narrator who tells the story from one character's point of view is a **third-person limited** narrator. Is the narrator of "The Bridal Party" omniscient or limited? Support your answer with at least three examples from the story. Then explain the effect of that point of view on this story.

Personal Writing

The Right Fit   Michael, obsessed about fitting in and with wearing the right clothing, believes that having money will bring him happiness. Look back at the writing you did for the Focus Activity on page 651. What did fitting in with a certain group represent for you? In your journal, compare your experience with Michael's.

EXTENDING YOUR RESPONSE

Literature Groups

Life Goals   Fitzgerald was both attracted to and repelled by wealth and social status. In "The Bridal Party," Michael voices these conflicting attitudes. Using Michael and other characters as examples, discuss the power of money. What can money buy? What can't it buy? Do you think that Michael's money will make him happy over time? Do you think Caroline and Hamilton will be happy?

Performing

Caroline's Story   Write and perform a monologue in which either Caroline or Hamilton discusses her or his thoughts about Michael. Review the story and try to determine what the character would say.

Interdisciplinary Activity

Music: Create a Sound Track   Jazz music came to define the spirit of the 1920s. At your local library, listen to the recordings of Jazz Age greats such as Louis Armstrong, Duke Ellington, and Count Basie. Then choose at least three pieces that could make up a sound track for the story. Decide at which point in the story you would play each piece. Play the pieces for the class and explain why you think each is appropriate for that part of the story.

📖 **Save your work for your portfolio.**

Skill Minilesson

VOCABULARY • Using Prior Knowledge to Understand New Words

Examining a new word can help you discover that the word is not as unfamiliar as it might seem. For example, Fitzgerald writes that Rutherford looked at Caroline in a *noncommittal* manner. You know what it means to *commit* yourself to a cause or a relationship. The negating prefix *non-* is familiar from such words as *nonsense* and *nonviolence*. By using what you know about other words, you can figure out that *noncommittal* means "not committed to a particular view or course of action."

PRACTICE   Use what you know about familiar words, word roots, prefixes, and suffixes to match each word to its meaning.

1. civility *(n.)*
2. inimitable *(adj.)*
3. malodorous *(adj.)*
4. antiquity *(n.)*
5. incertitude *(n.)*

a. bad smelling
b. politeness
c. doubtfulness
d. great age
e. too good to be copied

Vo·cab·u·lar·y Skills

Using a Semantic Features Chart

In "The Bridal Party," the narrator uses a number of words and phrases to describe Michael's character. Early in the story, Michael believes Caroline left him because she saw him as "pathetic, futile, and shabby." These words are similar in meaning, but they have subtle differences in both **denotation** (dictionary definition) and **connotation** (other meanings suggested by the word). You can use a **semantic features chart** like the one below to look more closely at these words—at their similarities, their differences, and their shades of meaning. The chart will help you understand Michael's character more fully, and you may find clues about how Fitzgerald built the character of Michael. In the process, you will also expand your own vocabulary.

Follow these instructions to create a semantic features chart.

- Place the words to be analyzed in the left-hand column of the chart.
- Check a dictionary and a thesaurus to gather denotations and connotations for each word.
- The different meanings become column heads at the top of the chart.
- Decide whether each word in the left column suggests the meanings at the top of the chart. If it does, mark a check in the corresponding box. If it doesn't, write a zero. If you are not sure, write a question mark.

A semantic features chart has been started below for the words describing Michael. It will help you understand the subtle differences between words that develop one part of Michael's character.

	Extremely pitiful, sad	Ineffective	Useless or hopeless	Worthless	Weak	Faded and dingy
Pathetic	✔	0	✔	0	✔	?
Futile						
Shabby						

EXERCISES

1. Draw this semantic features chart on a separate sheet of paper. Then complete the chart. Examine your finished chart. With your classmates, discuss the various meanings of the three words and why you think Fitzgerald uses them together to describe Caroline's view of Michael (as Michael sees it).

2. Find three or four similar words used to describe Caroline at various points in the story, and create a semantic features chart with these words. What does your analysis suggest about her character? Share your chart with classmates and compare findings.

Before You Read

Chicago

Meet Carl Sandburg

In his lifetime, Carl Sandburg had plenty of opportunities to collect material for his poetry. Besides being a poet and biographer, Sandburg worked as a milk truck driver, bricklayer, carpenter's assistant, housepainter, traveling salesman, and journalist.

Carl Sandburg grew up in Galesburg, Illinois, the son of Swedish immigrants. Feeling like an outsider, he changed his name for a time from Carl to Charles because he thought Charles sounded more American. Sandburg quit school after eighth grade and took odd jobs to help support his family. When he was nineteen, he set out to explore America, joining the many "hobos" of the period who hitched rides on freight trains. Returning from these journeys, he fought in the Spanish-American War, attended college, and then moved to Chicago. There he became a journalist, learning to write clearly and launching his lifelong involvement in protesting social and racial injustices.

When Sandburg was thirty-six, his first published poems appeared in *Poetry* magazine; two years later his first book, *Chicago Poems*, was published. With the publication of his second book, *Cornhuskers*, Sandburg's national reputation as a poet was established. Critics, however, were divided over Sandburg's poetic merits. Supporters praised his original subject matter and voice, while detractors criticized his free-verse technique and focus on social issues. In response, Sandburg wrote that his goal in writing poetry was simply "to sing, blab, chortle, yodel, like people."

In his lifetime, Sandburg published six original volumes of poetry. His poems are noted for their use of the rhythms of everyday language, for their democratic subjects and themes, and for their colorful use of sayings and anecdotes.

Sandburg was an extremely popular performer, lecturing, reading his poems aloud, and singing folk songs while playing the guitar. He won two Pulitzer Prizes: one for his four-volume biography, *Abraham Lincoln: The War Years*, and the other for his *Complete Poems*.

"I am the people—the mob—the crowd—the mass.
Do you know that all the great work of the world is done through me?"

"When [people] lose their poetic feeling for ordinary life, and cannot write poetry of ordinary things, their exalted poetry is likely to lose its strength of exaltation."

—*Sandburg*

Carl Sandburg was born in 1878 and died in 1967.

Reading Further

If you would like to read more by or about Carl Sandburg, you might enjoy these works:

Poems: "North Atlantic," "Prairie," and "The Windy City" are interesting poems that can be found in *The Complete Poems of Carl Sandburg.*

Biography: *Carl Sandburg: His Life and Works,* by North Callahan, is a complete and thorough story of the poet's life.

─────────── **FOCUS ACTIVITY** ───────────

Think of a significant time when you or someone else has been criticized and you argued against that criticism.

JOURNAL Write a journal entry describing the incident. Then describe how you felt about the criticism and how you responded to the person who made it.

SETTING A PURPOSE Read to discover how a speaker responds to criticisms of his city.

─────────── **BACKGROUND** ───────────

The Time and Place

During Sandburg's youth in the late nineteenth century, Chicago was an economic lifeline of the United States. Sandburg himself was excited and deeply impressed when, at age eighteen, he saw the bustling city for the first time. In 1896 Chicago's waterways and web of railroads united the nation, linking the wealth of the East with the agriculture of the West, Midwest, and South. From farms on the nearby prairies, wheat poured into the city's grain elevators, and cattle and hogs entered the city's slaughter-houses. From Chicago, meat and grain flowed out to feed the nation.

The city had grown amazingly fast, from a small trading post in 1830 to an expanding metropolis at the turn of the century. Beginning in the 1840s, waves of immigrants of many different nationalities settled in Chicago. By the 1880s, the city held more than half a million inhabitants; three-fourths of them immigrants from northern and eastern Europe or the sons and daughters of these immigrants. The city's rapid industrial growth brought many labor disputes, including riots and a strike of railroad workers. During his years as a Chicago newspaperman, Sandburg observed firsthand the struggles and triumphs of the growing city.

Literary Influences

Walt Whitman was one of Sandburg's greatest poetic inspirations. Sandburg's poetry shows the influence of Whitman's style, both in its free-verse form and its celebration of common American people. While one critic complained that Sandburg had "sat too long at the feet of Walt Whitman," most critics agree that Whitman's influence brought a lyrical energy to Sandburg's poetry.

Chicago skyline behind a railroad yard, 1909.

CHICAGO

Carl Sandburg

CHICAGO

          Hog Butcher for the World,
          Tool Maker, Stacker of Wheat,
          Player with Railroads and the Nation's Freight Handler;
          Stormy, husky, brawling,
5   City of the Big Shoulders:
They tell me you are wicked and I believe them, for I have seen your painted
     women under the gas lamps luring the farm boys.
And they tell me you are crooked and I answer: Yes, it is true I have seen the
     gunman kill and go free to kill again.
And they tell me you are brutal and my reply is: On the faces of women and
     children I have seen the marks of wanton° hunger.
And having answered so I turn once more to those who sneer at this my city,
     and I give them back the sneer and say to them:
10 Come and show me another city with lifted head singing so proud to be alive
     and coarse and strong and cunning.
Flinging magnetic curses amid the toil of piling job on job, here is a tall bold
     slugger set vivid against the little soft cities;
Fierce as a dog with tongue lapping for action, cunning as a savage pitted
     against the wilderness,
          Bareheaded,
          Shoveling,
15   Wrecking,
          Planning,
          Building, breaking, rebuilding,
Under the smoke, dust all over his mouth, laughing with white teeth,
Under the terrible burden of destiny laughing as a young man laughs,
20 Laughing even as an ignorant fighter laughs who has never lost a battle,
Bragging and laughing that under his wrist is the pulse, and under his ribs the
     heart of the people,
          Laughing!
Laughing the stormy, husky, brawling laughter of Youth, half-naked, sweat-
     ing, proud to be Hog Butcher, Tool Maker, Stacker of Wheat, Player
     with railroads and Freight Handler to the Nation.

---

8 *Wanton* means "resulting from extreme cruelty or neglect."

Responding to Literature

Personal Response

What are your impressions of the Chicago the speaker describes?

━━ ANALYZING LITERATURE ━━

RECALL AND INTERPRET

1. What names does the speaker give Chicago in lines 1–5? What do these names reveal about the city?
2. In lines 6–8, what three negative adjectives describe the city? What problems in the city do these adjectives indicate? What overall impressions do these problems give of Chicago? Explain.
3. Name some of the positive adjectives the speaker uses to describe Chicago. What do these words reveal about the city's inhabitants and the speaker's attitude toward them?
4. To what does Sandburg compare Chicago in lines 10–23? What final impression do these comparisons give of the city?

EVALUATE AND CONNECT

5. How does Sandburg's **diction**, or choice of words, help create a vivid image of the city? Provide examples from the poem.
6. Notice two **similes**, or comparisons using the word *like* or *as,* that Sandburg uses in lines 19–20. In your opinion, how effective are these similes in expressing the **theme** (see page R16) of the poem?
7. How does Sandburg's portrayal of early twentieth-century Chicago compare with a big city of today? Consider similarities as well as differences.
8. Review what you wrote for the Focus Activity on page 670. How does your defense compare with Sandburg's defense of Chicago? Would any of Sandburg's methods have helped you in your defense? Explain.

━━ EXTENDING YOUR RESPONSE ━━

Creative Writing

Defending Your Community   With a partner, write a poem or a brief essay defending your own city, town, or neighborhood. Use Sandburg's poem as a model. What special characteristics does your community have? What might some people say to criticize it? How will you defend it against those criticisms? Share your poem or essay with the class.

Literature Groups

Proud or Defensive?   Is the speaker in "Chicago" proud of the city or defensive about its poor public image? What do you think? Debate this question in your group, and provide examples from the poem to support your opinion. Share your group's ideas with the class.

📖 **Save your work for your portfolio.**

Before You Read

from *Songs of Gold Mountain*

"Right after we were wed, Husband,
    you set out on a journey.
How was I to tell you how I felt?
Wandering around a foreign country,
    when will you ever come home?"

—*Anonymous*

"Gold Mountain Poems" were written by numerous anonymous poets—Chinese immigrants to the United States who were detained at an immigration center in San Francisco.

In the mid-nineteenth century, Chinese people began immigrating to the United States in large numbers. Many left China to escape intense fighting between the British and the Chinese and between peasant farmers and the ruling class. Others left China hoping to improve their economic prospects by working in this country.

The first wave of Chinese immigrants consisted mostly of adventurous young men who dreamed of striking it rich in the mines of "Gold Mountain," as the United States was called. Circulars distributed by labor brokers fueled such dreams: "Americans are very rich people. They want the China man to come and make him very welcome. There you will have great pay, large houses, and food and clothing of the finest description."

Many of the young men who came to California were married and planned to remain just long enough to make their fortune. In reality, however, about half of this group never returned to China. When mining profits began to dwindle, many went to work on the Central Pacific Railroad and on farms in California.

FOCUS ACTIVITY

Think about a time when you experienced great disappointment. How did you feel? What did you do?

QUICKWRITE Spend three or four minutes exploring your response to these questions.

SETTING A PURPOSE Read to learn about the feelings of disappointment experienced by many Chinese immigrants as described by anonymous poets.

BACKGROUND

The Time and Place

In 1849, the first year of the great gold rush, 325 Chinese immigrants arrived in California to prospect for gold. In 1852 more than 20,000 arrived. Americans welcomed these newcomers at first, but they soon began crying "California for Americans," resulting in a special miner's tax for foreigners. In 1882 the Chinese Exclusion Act was passed, which prohibited the immigration of Chinese laborers and eventually of all Chinese. The law remained in effect until 1943. Because of it, Chinese arriving after 1882 were detained for anywhere from several weeks to more than a year in a place called the "Wooden Barracks" on San Francisco Bay. On the walls of this place, they wrote short, powerful poems expressing their reactions to being detained.

Chinese railroad workers, 1877.

from Songs of Gold Mountain

Anonymous

Writing carved on the wooden wall at Angel Island.

As soon as it is announced
    the ship has reached America:
I burst out cheering,
    I have found precious pearls.
5   How can I bear the detention upon arrival,
Doctors and immigration officials refusing
    to let me go?
All the abuse—
I can't describe it with a pen.
10   I'm held captive in a wooden barrack, like King Wen°
    in Youli:°
No end to the misery and sadness in my heart.

---

10 The popular and reportedly wise ruler Wen Wang became known as *King Wen* only after his death.

11 King Wen was imprisoned at *Youli* (yō lǐ′) by the ruling Shang-dynasty king, Zouxin (jō shin). King Wen's sons gained victory over the Shang and began the Zhou (jō) dynasty (c. 1122–221 B.C.).

The moment I hear
    we've entered the port,
I am all ready:
    my belongings wrapped in a bundle.
5 Who would have expected joy to become sorrow:
Detained in a dark, crude, filthy room?
What can I do?
Cruel treatment, not one restful breath of air.
Scarcity of food, severe restrictions—all
10   unbearable.
Here even a proud man bows his head low.

Fellow countrymen, four hundred million
    strong;
Many are great, with exceptional talents.
We want to come to the Flowery Flag Nation°
5   but are barred;
The Golden Gate° firmly locked, without even
    a crack to crawl through.
This moment—
Truly deplorable is the imprisonment.
10 Our hearts ache in pain and shame;
Though talented, how can we put on wings and
    fly past the barbarians?

4 The *Flowery Flag Nation* refers to the United States.
6 Literally, the *Golden Gate* is a narrow body of water in California that
  connects the Pacific Ocean with the San Francisco Bay.

I am a man of heroic deeds;
I am a man with pride and dignity.
My bosom encompasses the height of Heaven
    and the brilliance of Earth;
5 Everywhere they know me as a truly noble
    man.
In search of wealth—
Greed led me on the road to Golden Mountain.
Denied landing upon reaching the shore, I am
10   filled with rage.
With no means to pass the border, what can a
    person do?

Responding to Literature

Personal Response

Which lines from these poems do you find most memorable? Which do you find most surprising?

—— ANALYZING LITERATURE ——

RECALL AND INTERPRET

1. How do the speakers in the first two poems feel upon arriving in the United States? What behaviors suggest that they have these feelings?

2. Where are the speakers in the first two poems brought, and how are they treated? What thoughts and feelings do the speakers have regarding this treatment?

3. How do the speakers in the third and fourth poems describe themselves, their countrymen, and the events that follow their arrival in the United States?

4. How do the speakers in the third and fourth poems refer to the United States? What does this tell you about their hopes for immigration?

EVALUATE AND CONNECT

5. Do you think the people who wrote these poems regretted their decision to immigrate? Explain. How might they have evaluated their decision if they could see how Chinese Americans live today?

6. These poems were all translated from Chinese. In terms of **style, structure,** and **syntax** (ways of forming phrases and sentences), compare these poems with poems by native English speakers. How are they similar? How are they different? (See Literary Terms Handbook, page R15.)

7. Do you think it would have been helpful for later Chinese detainees to read poems like these on the walls of the barracks? Why or why not?

8. How do the thoughts and feelings you conveyed for the Focus Activity on page 674 compare with those expressed in these poems? Explain.

Literary ELEMENTS

Literal Language

Literal language is language that is simple, straightforward, and free of embellishment. It is the opposite of **figurative language**, or language that conveys meaning by comparing one thing to another. Examples of both types of language can be found in the poems from *Songs of Gold Mountain.* The line "Doctors and immigration officials refusing to let me go" is an example of literal language.

1. Find three more examples of literal language in this selection. How does the literal language affect your appreciation of the poems?

2. Find three examples of figurative language in this selection. Try rewriting them in literal language.

● See **Literary Terms Handbook,** p. R9.

—— EXTENDING YOUR RESPONSE ——

Creative Writing

Express Yourself   Write a short poem like the poems here, describing a time when you experienced great disappointment. Incorporate in your poem both figurative and literal language. As you write the poem, choose each word with care, avoiding any unnecessary words. Finally, read the poem aloud to decide on natural line breaks.

Literature Groups

Make a Case for a Poem   Debate the following question in your group: Which of these four poems conveys the difficulties faced by Chinese immigrants most powerfully? Have each person support his or her opinion with details from the poems. Then present your opinions to the class.

📖 **Save your work for your portfolio.**

Meet Ernest Hemingway

Born in Oak Park, Illinois, a suburb of Chicago, Ernest Hemingway began to write while in high school. By age eighteen, he was working as a reporter for the *Kansas City Star* and was determined to go to Europe to participate in World War I. Rejected by the U.S. military because of an eye defect, the adventure-seeking Hemingway became an ambulance driver for the American Red Cross. Less than one month before his nineteenth birthday, Hemingway was seriously wounded in Italy. The injury, according to American literary critic Alfred Kazin, "was a shock that went straight into Hemingway's early stories and fables of the war."

After recuperating at home in the United States, Hemingway accepted a position as a foreign correspondent for the *Toronto Star* and was sent to Paris. There, the young newsman met and sought the advice and encouragement of notable American writers of the time. In fact, Hemingway became part of a group of American artists and writers who formed a colony of expatriates, people who choose to live outside their homeland.

Hemingway's friend Gertrude Stein was a novelist and essayist who presided over this expatriate community. Stein, who acted as a mentor for the young Hemingway, summed up the alienation and disillusionment of these early Modernists when she told him, "You're all a lost generation." Stein applied the phrase to Hemingway and other young men who had experienced the horrors of World War I and had returned feeling demoralized and alienated from society. Her remark was later widely quoted as a concise expression of the aimlessness and despair felt by American expatriates in Paris in the 1920s.

In 1925, while in Paris, Hemingway published his first major work, *In Our Time*. This collection of short stories established Hemingway as an important new writer whose simple, unadorned style drew notice and praise.

Like Hemingway himself, the heroes of his fiction lead lives of great physical adventure. They are soldiers, big-game hunters, boxers, bullfighters, and deep-sea fishermen. Hemingway's major novels include *The Sun Also Rises* (1926) a novel of the "lost generation," set in Paris and Spain; *A Farewell to Arms* (1929), a love story set during World War I; *For Whom the Bell Tolls* (1940), a novel set in Spain during the Spanish Civil War of the 1930s where Hemingway had worked as a war correspondent; and *The Old Man and the Sea* (1952), a tale of a fisherman from Cuba. In 1954 Hemingway received the Nobel Prize for Literature.

"All good books are alike in that they are truer than if they had really happened. . . ."

"A man can be destroyed but not defeated."

—*Hemingway*

Ernest Hemingway was born in 1899 and died in 1961.

FOCUS ACTIVITY

How would you react if you suffered a serious injury to your leg or hand?

DISCUSS With a small group of classmates, briefly discuss how you would react to a life-changing injury. Explore how you might feel and how your outlook on the future might change.

SETTING A PURPOSE Read to discover how the narrator and other characters cope with their injuries and wounds.

BACKGROUND

Literary Influences

Hemingway recalled that when he was a young reporter on the *Kansas City Star,* the newspaper's style sheet instructed reporters to "avoid the use of adjectives, especially such extravagant ones as *splendid, gorgeous, grand, magnificent,* etc." Short sentences, brief opening paragraphs, and "vigorous English" were also required. Hemingway later called these "the best rules I ever learned for the business of writing." He learned much from Gertrude Stein's efforts to write with concise, spare prose that created repetitive sentence rhythms. Hemingway also noted that Stephen Crane, another American writer who had been trained as a journalist and served as a war correspondent, greatly influenced his prose style.

Kansas City Star newsroom, c. 1918.

VOCABULARY PREVIEW

lurch (lurch) *v.* to move suddenly and unevenly; p. 680
withered (with′ ərd) *adj.* shriveled; p. 680
detached (di tacht′) *adj.* not involved emotionally; indifferent; p. 681

jostle (jos′ əl) *v.* to bump, push, or shove while moving, as in a crowd; p. 681
resign (ri zīn′) *v.* to make oneself accept; p. 683

In Another Country

In the fall the war[1] was always there, but we did not go to it any more. It was cold in the fall in Milan[2] and the dark came very early. Then the electric lights came on, and it was pleasant along the streets looking in the windows. There was much game[3] hanging outside the shops, and the snow powdered in the fur of the foxes and the wind blew their tails. The deer hung stiff and heavy and empty, and small birds blew in the wind and the wind turned their feathers. It was a cold fall and the wind came down from the mountains.

We were all at the hospital every afternoon, and there were different ways of walking across the town through the dusk to the hospital. Two of the ways were alongside canals, but they were long. Always, though, you crossed a bridge across a canal to enter the hospital. There was a choice of three bridges. On one of them a woman sold roasted chestnuts. It was warm, standing in front of her charcoal fire, and the chestnuts were warm afterward in your pocket. The hospital was very old and very beautiful, and you entered through a gate and walked across a courtyard and out a gate on the other side. There were usually funerals starting from the courtyard. Beyond the old hospital were the new brick pavilions, and there we met every afternoon and were all very polite and interested in what was the matter, and sat in the machines that were to make so much difference.

The doctor came up to the machine where I was sitting and said: "What did you like best to do before the war? Did you practice a sport?"

I said: "Yes, football."

"Good," he said. "You will be able to play football again better than ever."

My knee did not bend and the leg dropped straight from the knee to the ankle without a calf, and the machine was to bend the knee and make it move as in riding a tricycle. But it did not bend yet, and instead the machine lurched when it came to the bending part. The doctor said: "That will all pass. You are a fortunate young man. You will play football again like a champion."

In the next machine was a major who had a little hand like a baby's. He winked at me when the doctor examined his hand, which was between two leather straps that bounced up and down and flapped the stiff fingers, and said: "And will I too play football, captain-doctor?" He had been a very great fencer, and before the war the greatest fencer in Italy.

The doctor went to his office in the back room and brought a photograph which showed a hand that had been withered almost as small as the major's, before it had taken a machine course, and after was a little larger. The major held the photograph with his good hand and looked at it very carefully. "A wound?" he asked.

"An industrial accident," the doctor said.

"Very interesting, very interesting," the major said, and handed it back to the doctor.

"You have confidence?"

"No," said the major.

There were three boys who came each day who were about the same age I was. They were all three from Milan, and one of them was to be a lawyer, and one was to be a painter, and

---

1. The *war* is World War I (1914–1918). The United States, Italy, and other countries fought Germany and its allies.
2. *Milan* is a city in northern Italy.
3. Here, *game* refers to wild animals and birds that have been hunted and killed for food.

Vocabulary

lurch (lurch) *v.* to move suddenly and unevenly
withered (with′ ərd) *adj.* shriveled

one had intended to be a soldier, and after we were finished with the machines, sometimes we walked back together to the Café Cova, which was next door to the Scala.[4] We walked the short way through the communist quarter because we were four together. The people hated us because we were officers, and from a wine-shop some one would call out, "A basso gli ufficiali!"[5] as we passed. Another boy who walked with us sometimes and made us five wore a black silk handkerchief across his face because he had no nose then and his face was to be rebuilt. He had gone out to the front[6] from the military academy and been wounded within an hour after he had gone into the front line for the first time. They rebuilt his face, but he came from a very old family and they could never get the nose exactly right. He went to South America and worked in a bank. But this was a long time ago, and then we did not any of us know how it was going to be afterward. We only knew then that there was always the war, but that we were not going to it any more.

We all had the same medals, except the boy with the black silk bandage across his face, and he had not been at the front long enough to get any medals. The tall boy with a very pale face who was to be a lawyer had been a lieutenant of Arditi[7] and had three medals of the

sort we each had only one of. He had lived a very long time with death and was a little detached. We were all a little detached, and there was nothing that held us together except that we met every afternoon at the hospital. Although, as we walked to the Cova through the tough part of town, walking in the dark, with light and singing coming out of the wine-shops, and sometimes having to walk into the street when the men and women would crowd together on the sidewalk so that we would have had to jostle them to get by, we felt held together by there being something that had happened that they, the people who disliked us, did not understand.

We ourselves all understood the Cova, where it was rich and warm and not too brightly lighted, and noisy and smoky at certain hours, and there were always girls at the tables and the illustrated papers on a rack on the wall. The girls at the Cova were very patriotic, and I found that the most patriotic people in Italy were the café girls—and I believe they are still patriotic.

The boys at first were very polite about my medals and asked me what I had done to get them. I showed them the papers, which were written in very beautiful language and full of *fratellanza* and *abnegazione*,[8] but which really said, with the adjectives removed, that I had been given the medals because I was an American. After that their manner changed a little toward me, although I was their friend against outsiders. I was a friend, but I was

---

4. *The Scala* (skä′ lə) is Milan's world-famous opera house.
5. In Italian, *A basso gli ufficiali!* (a̅ bä′ sō lyē o̅o̅ fē chä′ lē) means "Down with officers!"
6. The *front* is the line or area of conflict between opposing armies.
7. The *Arditi* (ar dē′ tē) was a corps of soldiers specially selected for dangerous operations.

8. *Fratellanza* (fra tāl än′ za) and *abnegazione* (ab nā ga tzyo′ nā) are Italian for "brotherhood" and "self-denial."

Vocabulary
detached (di tacht′) *adj.* not involved emotionally; indifferent
jostle (jos′ əl) *v.* to bump, push, or shove while moving, as in a crowd

never really one of them after they had read the citations,[9] because it had been different with them and they had done very different things to get their medals. I had been wounded, it was true; but we all knew that being wounded, after all, was really an accident. I was never ashamed of the ribbons, though, and sometimes, after the cocktail hour, I would imagine myself having done all the things they had done to get their medals; but walking home at night through the empty streets with the cold wind and all the shops closed, trying to keep near the street lights, I knew that I would never have done such things, and I was very much afraid to die, and often lay in bed at night by myself, afraid to die and wondering how I would be when I went back to the front again.

The three with the medals were like hunting-hawks; and I was not a hawk, although I might seem a hawk to those who had never hunted; they, the three, knew better and so we drifted apart. But I stayed good friends with the boy who had been wounded his first day at the front, because he would never know now how he would have turned out; so he could never be accepted either, and I liked him because I thought perhaps he would not have turned out to be a hawk either.

The major, who had been the great fencer, did not believe in bravery, and spent much time while we sat in the machines correcting my grammar. He had complimented me on how I spoke Italian, and we talked together very easily. One day I had said that Italian seemed such an easy language to me that I could not take a great interest in it; everything was so easy to say. "Ah, yes," the major said. "Why, then, do you not take up the use of grammar?" So we took up the use of grammar,

and soon Italian was such a difficult language that I was afraid to talk to him until I had the grammar straight in my mind.

The major came very regularly to the hospital. I do not think he ever missed a day, although I am sure he did not believe in the machines. There was a time when none of us believed in the machines, and one day the major said it was all nonsense. The machines were new then and it was we who were to prove them. It was an idiotic idea, he said, "a theory, like another." I had not learned my grammar, and he said I was a stupid impossible disgrace, and he was a fool to have bothered with me. He was a small man and he sat straight up in his chair with his right hand thrust into the machine and looked straight ahead at the wall while the straps thumped up and down with his fingers in them.

"What will you do when the war is over if it is over?" he asked me. "Speak grammatically!"

"I will go to the States."

"Are you married?"

"No, but I hope to be."

"The more of a fool you are," he said. He seemed very angry. "A man must not marry."

"Why, Signor Maggiore?"[10]

"Don't call me 'Signor Maggiore.'"

"Why must not a man marry?"

"He cannot marry. He cannot marry," he said angrily. "If he is to lose everything, he should not place himself in a position to lose that. He should not place himself in a position to lose. He should find things he cannot lose."

He spoke very angrily and bitterly, and looked straight ahead while he talked.

"But why should he necessarily lose it?"

"He'll lose it," the major said. He was looking at the wall. Then he looked down at the

9. *Citations* are specific references to military duties worthy of reward or praise.

10. *Signor Maggiore* (sē nyor′ ma jō′rā) means "Mr. Major." In Italy, one said *Signor* before an officer's rank as a sign of respect.

Piazza Corvetto in Genoa in 1918. Alessandro Milesi (1856–1945). Oil on canvas. Galleria d'Arte Moderna di Nervi, Genoa, Italy.

Viewing the painting: In what ways does this painting reflect the sense of detachment that the characters feel in "In Another Country"?

machine and jerked his little hand out from between the straps and slapped it hard against his thigh. "He'll lose it," he almost shouted. "Don't argue with me!" Then he called to the attendant who ran the machines. "Come and turn this thing off."

He went back into the other room for the light treatment and the massage. Then I heard him ask the doctor if he might use his telephone and he shut the door. When he came back into the room, I was sitting in another machine. He was wearing his cape and had his cap on, and he came directly toward my machine and put his arm on my shoulder.

"I am so sorry," he said, and patted me on the shoulder with his good hand. "I would not be rude. My wife has just died. You must forgive me."

"Oh—" I said, feeling sick for him. "I am *so* sorry."

He stood there biting his lower lip. "It is very difficult," he said. "I cannot <u>resign</u> myself."

He looked straight past me and out through the window. Then he began to cry. "I am utterly unable to resign myself," he said and choked. And then crying, his head up looking at nothing, carrying himself straight and soldierly, with tears on both his cheeks and biting his lips, he walked past the machines and out the door.

The doctor told me that the major's wife, who was very young and whom he had not married until he was definitely invalided[11] out of the war, had died of pneumonia. She had been sick only a few days. No one expected her to die. The major did not come to the hospital for three days. Then he came at the usual hour, wearing a black band on the sleeve of his uniform. When he came back, there were large framed photographs around the wall, of all sorts of wounds before and after they had been cured by the machines. In front of the machine the major used were three photographs of hands like his that were completely restored. I do not know where the doctor got them. I always understood we were the first to use the machines. The photographs did not make much difference to the major because he only looked out of the window.

11. *Invalided* means "removed from active duty because of sickness or disability."

Responding to Literature

Personal Response

How did you react to the end of the story? Which character or event left you with this reaction?

ANALYZING LITERATURE

RECALL AND INTERPRET

1. Why do the narrator and the major go to the hospital every afternoon? What are their attitudes toward the visits? Explain.
2. What does the narrator have in common with the other young men who go to the hospital? What happens to the narrator's relationship with three of the young men? What makes his relationship with the young man who wears the handkerchief on his face different?
3. What wounds besides physical ones might the narrator and the other soldiers have suffered? What might the machines represent for them?
4. What bad news does the major receive? Why do you think he feels "utterly unable to resign" himself to the news?
5. What strikes the narrator as odd about the photographs displayed by the doctor? How might the photographs affect the narrator's opinion of his treatments? What does this suggest about the character's future?

EVALUATE AND CONNECT

6. The author opens the story with a series of **sensory details** (see page R14). In your opinion, how effective are these details in setting the scene and in pulling the reader into the story? Explain.
7. The narrator compares the three young men with the medals to hunting-hawks. How does this comparison affect your view of the young men? of the narrator?
8. In your opinion, what does the narrator do to cope with his injury and rehabilitation? How do his methods compare with those suggested by your group for the Focus Activity on page 679?

Literary ELEMENTS

Style

Style is a writer's individual, characteristic way of writing. Elements such as diction, sentence structure, imagery, and tone make up a writer's style. Hemingway's simple language and sentence structure seem to reveal only the facts of an event or situation. Readers must draw their own conclusions about characters' motivations and Hemingway's purpose.

1. What repeated words, images, and sentence rhythms appear in the opening paragraph? What effect do these elements have on the story's mood or tone?
2. How does Hemingway's style bring out the story's theme?

● See **Literary Terms Handbook**, page R15.

EXTENDING YOUR RESPONSE

Literature Groups

Is There Any Hope?   Does this story show any signs of hope for its characters, or is it simply a sad story of isolation and loneliness? Debate this issue in your group. Consider each character's actions, words, and hope for the future. Share your conclusions with the class.

Personal Writing

Something to Lose   The major says, "A man must not marry." He goes on to explain that a man should not put himself in a position to lose something dear to him, but that "he should find things he cannot lose." Do you agree or disagree? Write a response to the major's comments.

🛍 **Save your work for your portfolio.**

Grammar Link

Using Commas in a Series

In Hemingway's writing, as in your own, you will often find a sentence with three or more elements in a series. These three elements might be words, phrases, or clauses. Use commas after each element in a series, including the element that precedes the conjunction.

Problem 1 Missing commas in a series of words
Hemingway writes of physical emotional and spiritual loss.

  Solution Use commas after the words in a series, including the word that comes before the conjunction.
Hemingway writes of physical, emotional, and spiritual loss.

Problem 2 Missing commas in a series of phrases
They were maimed in battle numbed by pain and defeated by loss.

  Solution Use commas after the phrases in a series, including the phrase that comes before the conjunction.
They were maimed in battle, numbed by pain, and defeated by loss.

Problem 3 Missing commas in a series of clauses
One boy wanted to be a lawyer one wanted to be a painter and the third had intended to be a soldier.

  Solution Use commas after the clauses in a series, including the clause that comes before the conjunction.
One boy wanted to be a lawyer, one wanted to be a painter, and the third had intended to be a soldier.

● For more about using commas in a series, see **Language Handbook,** p. R32.

EXERCISE

Rewrite each of the incorrect sentences, applying the solutions shown above. (One of the sentences is correct.)

1. In our band Larry plays guitar, Yolanda plays keyboards and Tom plays percussion.

2. He wants ice cream milk and cake.

3. They took a plane to Boston, a train to New York, and a bus to Baltimore.

4. Linda saw the balloon floating in the sky riding the air currents higher and higher, and disappearing into a cloud.

5. I cleaned my room swept the kitchen floor and took out the trash.

6. Hemingway has a concise, simple and unadorned style.

Technology Skills

Spreadsheet: Determining Productivity

Spreadsheet software can help you manage your time better by allowing you to see, in graphic form, how you actually spend your days. Start by listing everything you do on a typical school day. Group the activities into categories such as sleeping, school, homework, time spent with family, and so on. Then record how much time you spend on each group of activities during an average twenty-four-hour day. Round each figure to the nearest half hour, and record the times in decimals (for example, 3.5 hours). Make sure your hours add up to 24.

TECHNOLOGY TIP

Spreadsheet programs differ slightly, so if you have trouble at any time in this activity, browse through the program's Help menu or consult with your teacher or lab instructor.

Reviewing Spreadsheet Tools

Take a few minutes to review the major functions of spreadsheets.

TERM	FUNCTION
Worksheet	A worksheet is the "page" where you insert and manipulate data.
Cells	Each worksheet is divided into cells, the basic units for storing data.
Cell address	The intersection of a column and a row forms a cell. The cell at column D and row 4, for example, is called D4.
Chart	Various types of graphs (bar graph, line graph, and so on) are referred to as charts in spreadsheet programs. The data on a spreadsheet can be made into a chart.
Formulas	Formulas mathematically combine the data in cells to produce a new value. For example, a formula may tell the program to add up all the figures in a column or a row.

Estimating Your Productivity

Have your list of activities handy as you open your spreadsheet. Most spreadsheet software opens to a blank worksheet. You will see columns, rows, and empty cells. You will also see pull-down menus, one or more toolbars, a formula bar, and a cell-content space. When

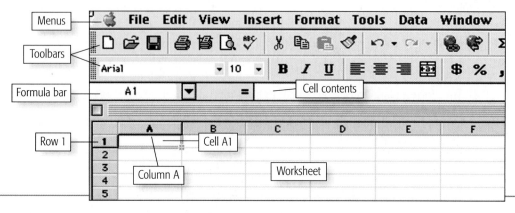

you select a cell, the cell-content space shows the data entered into that cell. If you wish to edit the data, do so in the cell-content space.

1. Activate Cell A1. To activate a cell, click on it. Type Weekday Activities. (Note: You can change the cell width to fit the long label by clicking and dragging on the line dividing columns A and B.)

2. Activate Cell B1, and type Time.

3. Activate Cell A2, and type the first of your activities. Then activate Cell B2, and type the average amount of time you spend on that activity. Continue in this way until all your activities and times are listed.

4. Skip a row and click in the A-column cell that follows your data. Type Total.

5. In the B column of that row, activate the cell that follows your data. You now want the computer to add the estimated times together. Click in the formula bar and type in the formula command =. Then type SUM. In parentheses, type in the first cell containing desired data, a colon, and the last cell containing desired data. The colon indicates that you want to add the first cell, the last cell, and all the cells in between. Your formula should look something like: =SUM(B2:B9).

6. Use your data to make a pie chart. Select the cells from A2 to the last entry above the total in column B. These contain your data for the chart.

7. Click on the icon for making a chart. (Or select **Chart** from the appropriate pull-down menu.) A series of dialogue boxes will then guide you through the process. Select a pie chart with labels and percentages, and include a title. When you finish, the chart will appear on your worksheet.

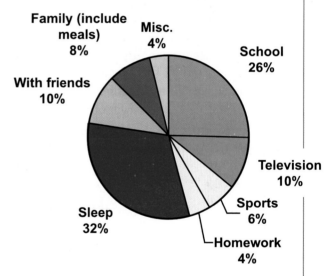

	A	B	C
		B11		=	=SUM(B2:B9)
1	Weekday Activities	Time	
2	School	6	
3	Television	2.5	
4	Sports	1.5	
5	Homework	1	
6	Sleep	7.5	
7	With friends	2.5	
8	Family (include meals)	2	
9	Misc.	1	
10			
11	Total	24	
12			
13			

Weekday Activities

Family (include meals) 8%
Misc. 4%
School 26%
With friends 10%
Television 10%
Sports 6%
Homework 4%
Sleep 32%

ACTIVITY

1. Repeat the process, using estimates of how you spend your time on weekends.

2. Think about ways you might change your data—for example, to spend more time studying or to get more time with your family. Experiment with the times. Note that your pie chart will adjust each time you make a change in the data on the worksheet.

3. Experiment with different types of charts. Which do you prefer? Why?

Before You Read

Soldiers of the Republic and *Penelope*

Meet Dorothy Parker

"I'd like to have money. And I'd like to be a good writer. These two can come together, and I hope they will, but if that's too adorable, I'd rather have money. I hate almost all rich people, but I think I'd be darling at it."

—*Parker*

As a writer, editor, and critic, Dorothy Parker was both famous and feared for her biting and clever wit. For example, she once described an actress's performance by saying, "She runs the gamut of emotion all the way from A to B."

Cofounder of a group of writers and humorists known collectively as the Algonquin Round Table, Parker wrote stories, poems, plays, screenplays, and reviews. Her celebrated wit and public pranks—she once displayed a sign reading "MEN" on her office door to attract company—often drew attention away from her involvement in social issues. Among her other causes, she chaired an anti-fascist committee during the Spanish Civil War, and she willed most of her money to Civil Rights leader, Martin Luther King Jr.

When Parker got older, she regretted some of her earlier snide remarks. "I wanted to be cute," she said. "That's the terrible thing. I should have had more sense." However, readers still recognize the quality of her writing and continue to enjoy her works.

Dorothy Parker was born in 1893 and died in 1967.

FOCUS ACTIVITY

What kind of people do you look up to and admire?

LIST IT! List some of the qualities you admire, and explain why you find each admirable.

SETTING A PURPOSE Read to notice the admirable qualities one writer gives her characters.

BACKGROUND

Did You Know?

- The Spanish Civil War began in 1936 as a military coup against Spain's Republican government. Soldiers from around the world came to help the Republicans fend off the Nationalists, who were supported by Fascist Italy and Nazi Germany. The war ended, with victory for the Nationalists, in March 1939.
- The poem "Penelope" refers to the wife of Odysseus, hero of the ancient Greek epic poem the *Odyssey,* by Homer. Penelope, traditionally associated with devotion and faithfulness, waits twenty years for her husband to return from war.

VOCABULARY PREVIEW

dissembling (di sem′ bling) *n.* the act of concealing one's true character, feelings, or intentions; p. 690

contrivance (kən trī′ vəns) *n.* a cleverly designed device; p. 690

vehemently (ve′ ə mənt lē) *adv.* in a strong or passionate manner; p. 690

whimsically (hwim′ zik lē) *adv.* in a quaintly humorous manner; p. 691

stoically (sto′ ik lē) *adv.* calmly and unemotionally, especially despite pain or suffering; p. 691

Soldiers of the Republic

Dorothy Parker ∾

That Sunday afternoon we sat with the Swedish girl in the big café in Valencia.[1] We had vermouth[2] in thick goblets, each with a cube of honeycombed gray ice in it. The waiter was so proud of that ice he could hardly bear to leave the glasses on the table, and thus part from it forever. He went to his duty—all over the room they were clapping their hands and hissing to draw his attention—but he looked back over his shoulder.

It was dark outside, the quick, new dark that leaps down without dusk on the day; but, because there were no lights in the streets, it seemed as set and as old as midnight. So you wondered that all the babies were still up. There were babies everywhere in the café, babies serious without solemnity[3] and interested in a tolerant way in their surroundings.

At the table next ours, there was a notably small one; maybe six months old. Its father, a little man in a big uniform that dragged his shoulders down, held it carefully on his knee. It was doing nothing whatever, yet he and his thin young wife, whose belly was already big again under her sleazy dress, sat watching it in a sort of ecstasy of admiration, while their coffee cooled in front of them. The baby was in Sunday white; its dress was patched so delicately that you would have thought the fabric whole had not the patches varied in their shades of whiteness. In its hair was a bow of new blue ribbon, tied with absolute balance of loops and ends. The ribbon was of no use; there was not enough hair to require restraint. The bow was sheerly an adornment, a calculated bit of dash.

"Oh, for God's sake, stop that!" I said to myself. "All right, so it's got a piece of blue ribbon on its hair. All right, so its mother went without eating so it could look pretty when its father came home on leave. All right, so it's her business, and none of yours. All right, so what have you got to cry about?"

The big, dim room was crowded and lively. That morning there had been a bombing from the air, the more horrible for broad daylight. But nobody in the café sat tense and strained, nobody desperately forced forgetfulness. They drank coffee or bottled lemonade, in the pleasant, earned ease of Sunday afternoon, chatting of small, gay matters, all talking at once, all hearing and answering.

There were many soldiers in the room, in what appeared to be the uniforms of twenty different armies until you saw that the variety lay in the differing ways the cloth had worn or faded. Only a few of them had been wounded; here and there you saw one stepping gingerly, leaning on a crutch or two canes, but so far on toward recovery that his face had color. There were many men, too, in civilian clothes—some of them soldiers home on leave, some of them governmental workers, some of them anybody's guess. There were plump, comfortable wives, active with paper fans, and old women as quiet as their grandchildren. There were many pretty girls and some beauties, of whom you did not remark, "There's a charming Spanish type," but

---

1. *Valencia* (vä len' sē' ä) is a port city and tourist resort on the Mediterranean coast of Spain.
2. *Vermouth* (vər mōōth') is a white wine used in cocktails.
3. *Solemnity* is deep seriousness.

said, "What a beautiful girl!" The women's clothes were not new, and their material was too humble ever to have warranted skillful cutting.

"It's funny," I said to the Swedish girl, "how when nobody in a place is best-dressed, you don't notice that everybody isn't."

"Please?" the Swedish girl said.

No one, save an occasional soldier, wore a hat. When we had first come to Valencia, I lived in a state of puzzled pain as to why everybody on the streets laughed at me. It was not because "West End Avenue" was writ across my face as if left there by a customs officer's chalked scrawl. They like Americans in Valencia, where they have seen good ones—the doctors who left their practices and came to help, the calm young nurses, the men of the International Brigade.[4] But when I walked forth, men and women courteously laid their hands across their splitting faces and little children, too innocent for dissembling, doubled with glee and pointed and cried, "Olé!"[5] Then, pretty late, I made my discovery, and left my hat off; and there was laughter no longer. It was not one of those comic hats, either; it was just a hat.

The café filled to overflow, and I left our table to speak to a friend across the room. When I came back to the table, six soldiers were sitting there. They were crowded in, and I scraped past them to my chair. They looked tired and dusty and little, the way that the newly dead look little, and the first things you saw about them were the tendons in their necks. I felt like a prize sow.

They were all in conversation with the Swedish girl. She has Spanish, French, German, anything in Scandinavian,[6] Italian, and English. When she has a moment for regret, she sighs that her Dutch is so rusty she can no longer speak it, only read it, and the same is true of her Rumanian.

They had told her, she told us, that they were at the end of forty-eight hours' leave from the trenches, and, for their holiday, they had all pooled their money for cigarettes, and something had gone wrong, and the cigarettes had never come through to them. I had a pack of American cigarettes—in Spain rubies are as nothing to them—and I brought it out, and by nods and smiles and a sort of breast stroke, made it understood that I was offering it to those six men yearning for tobacco. When they saw what I meant, each one of them rose and shook my hand. Darling of me to share my cigarettes with the men on their way back to the trenches. Little Lady Bountiful. The prize sow.

Each one lit his cigarette with a contrivance of yellow rope that stank when afire and was also used, the Swedish girl translated, for igniting grenades. Each one received what he had ordered, a glass of coffee, and each one murmured appreciatively over the tiny cornucopia[7] of coarse sugar that accompanied it. Then they talked.

They talked through the Swedish girl, but they did to us that thing we all do when we speak our own language to one who has no knowledge of it. They looked us square in the face, and spoke slowly, and pronounced their words with elaborate movements of their lips. Then, as their stories came, they poured them at us so vehemently, so emphatically that they were sure we must understand. They were so convinced we would understand that we were ashamed for not understanding.

But the Swedish girl told us. They were all farmers and farmers' sons, from a district so poor that you try not to remember there is that kind of poverty. Their village was next that

---

4. Allied with the Republicans, the *Brigade* was a military force composed of citizens from many nations.
5. *Olé!* (ō lā´) is similar to Hooray!
6. *Scandinavian* refers to Danish, Norwegian, and Swedish.

7. Here, *cornucopia* means "abundance." A cornucopia is a curved horn overflowing with fruit, grain, and vegetables.

Vocabulary

dissembling (di sem´ bling) *n.* the act of concealing one's true character, feelings, or intentions
contrivance (kən trī´ vəns) *n.* a cleverly designed device
vehemently (ve´ ə mənt lē) *adv.* in a strong or passionate manner

one where the old men and the sick men and the women and children had gone, on a holiday, to the bullring; and the planes had come over and dropped bombs on the bullring, and the old men and the sick men and the women and the children were more than two hundred.

They had all, the six of them, been in the war for over a year, and most of that time they had been in the trenches. Four of them were married. One had one child, two had three children, one had five. They had not had word from their families since they had left for the front. There had been no communication; two of them had learned to write from men fighting next them in the trench, but they had not dared to write home. They belonged to a union,[8] and union men, of course, are put to death if taken. The village where their families lived had been captured, and if your wife gets a letter from a union man, who knows but they'll shoot her for the connection?

They told about how they had not heard from their families for more than a year. They did not tell it gallantly or <u>whimsically</u> or <u>stoically</u>. They told it as if—Well, look. You have been in the trenches, fighting, for a year. You have heard nothing of your wife and your children. They do not know if you are dead or alive or blinded. You do not know where they are, or if they are. You must talk to somebody. That is the way they told about it.

One of them, some six months before, had heard of his wife and his three children—they had such beautiful eyes, he said—from a brother-in-law in France. They were all alive then, he was told, and had a

bowl of beans a day. But his wife had not complained of the food, he heard. What had troubled her was that she had no thread to mend the children's ragged clothes. So that troubled him, too.

"She has no thread," he kept telling us. "My wife has no thread to mend with. No thread."

We sat there, and listened to what the Swedish girl told us they were saying. Suddenly one of them looked at the clock, and then there was excitement. They jumped up, as a man, and there were calls for the waiter and rapid talk with him, and each of them shook the hand of each of us. We went through more swimming motions to explain to them that they were to take the rest of the cigarettes—fourteen cigarettes for six soldiers to take to war—and then they shook our hands again. Then all of us said *"Salud!"*[9] as many times as could be for six of them and three of us, and then they filed out of the café, the six of them, tired and dusty and little, as men of a mighty horde are little.

Only the Swedish girl talked, after they had gone. The Swedish girl has been in Spain since the start of the war. She has nursed splintered men, and she has carried stretchers into the trenches and, heavier laden, back to the hospital. She has seen and heard too much to be knocked into silence.

Presently it was time to go, and the Swedish girl raised her hands above her head and clapped them twice together to summon the waiter. He came, but he only shook his head and his hand, and moved away.

The soldiers had paid for our drinks.

---

8. The Republicans belonged to trade *unions.*

9. *Salud!* (sä lo͞od'), meaning "Health!" is a toast, like Cheers!

Vocabulary

whimsically (hwim' zik lē) *adv.* in a quaintly humorous manner
stoically (stō' ik lē) *adv.* calmly and unemotionally, especially despite pain or suffering

Return of Ulysses to Penelope: From 'The Odyssey,' c. 1509. Bernardino Pintoricchio. Fresco, 49½ x 59¾ in. National Gallery, London.

PENELOPE

Dorothy Parker

In the pathway of the sun,
  In the footsteps of the breeze,
Where the world and sky are one,
  He shall ride the silver seas,
5   He shall cut the glittering wave.
I shall sit at home, and rock;
Rise, to heed a neighbor's knock;
Brew my tea, and snip my thread;
Bleach the linen for my bed.
10   They will call him brave.

Responding to Literature

Personal Response

What surprised you most in the story and in the poem? Explain.

ANALYZING LITERATURE

Soldiers of The Republic

RECALL AND INTERPRET

1. What difficult circumstances do the people of Valencia and the soldiers in the café face? What kind of attitude do they seem to have toward these circumstances?
2. How do the soldiers react to the gift of cigarettes? How would you explain their reactions?

EVALUATE AND CONNECT

3. In your opinion, how does the author want readers to feel about the people of Valencia and about the soldiers? Do you think she was successful in making you feel a certain way? Explain, using examples from the story.
4. In your opinion, are the soldiers in this story like other people who face danger, or do they face danger differently than most people? Explain your answer.

Penelope

RECALL AND INTERPRET

5. What is the person called "he" doing? How does the speaker describe what "he" does? What is the speaker doing? How are her activities different from his?
6. Who are "they," and what will "they" say? What does the speaker's attitude seem to be about this outcome?

EVALUATE AND CONNECT

7. The poem's title is an **allusion,** or reference, to a well-known story—that of Odysseus. Does the allusion effectively help you understand the poem? Explain.
8. Who are some of the brave people you know whose strength, like that of the speaker, might not be recognized? Why do you consider them brave?

EXTENDING YOUR RESPONSE

Literature Groups

How to Tell a Hero   Keeping in mind the qualities you listed for the Focus Activity on page 688, discuss the admirable or heroic qualities of the characters in the story and in the poem. Then, as a group, choose five essential qualities a hero should have. Compare your group's list with those of other groups.

Writing About Literature

A Question of Attitude   From what you have read, what conclusions do you draw about Parker's attitude toward ordinary people during wartime? Using details from the story, the poem, or both, identify the writer's position, and write a few paragraphs to persuade your classmates to share your point of view.

📖 **Save your work for your portfolio.**

Before You Read

Robert Frost's Poetry

Meet Robert Frost

Robert Frost has been one of the most beloved as well as one of the most criticized poets of the twentieth century. During his lifetime, he received more awards than any other twentieth-century poet and had the honor of reciting one of his poems at the inauguration of President John F. Kennedy. Yet many critics felt he did not deserve such accolades. They faulted him for emphasizing the New England rural past over the urban, industrial present and for using "old-fashioned" verse forms instead of modernist innovations. To this day, many readers, while recognizing Frost's skill as a literary craftsman, consider his range of subjects narrow and his treatment of them often superficial. If, however, Frost's poems are read as he said poems must be written—"with the ear on the speaking voice"—they often reveal a startling freshness of perception.

Although widely equated with the New England farmer-sage he cultivated as a public persona, Frost actually spent his first eleven years in San Francisco. Following the death of his father, his family moved to the gritty industrial city of Lawrence, Massachusetts. Frost attended Dartmouth and Harvard colleges during the 1890s, but he left each school after a short period because of his frustration with academic life. Frost preferred real-life experiences to academic learning and worked as a mill hand, journalist, farmer, and schoolteacher.

At age twenty-six, Frost moved to a farm near Derry, New Hampshire, where he got to

know the rugged landscape and inhabitants of rural New England. There, between farm chores, Frost wrote poems describing the experiences of his fellow New Englanders and the feelings of awe and terror evoked in him by the New England countryside. In many of these poems, Frost deftly captured New England speech patterns in meter and rhyme.

Unable to find American publishers for his work, Frost, at age thirty-seven, uprooted his family and moved to England. There, his first two books, *A Boy's Will* and *North of Boston*, were published to critical acclaim, receiving positive reviews from literary notables, including Ezra Pound. Frost returned to New England in 1915 and found himself in great demand. Prominent publishers backed his work and the nation's most prestigious universities asked him to teach. He received the Pulitzer Prize for Poetry on four separate occasions and a congressional medal. By the time of Frost's death, his poetry had deeply embedded itself in the American imagination, and it continues to live there today.

"[Frost] reminds us that poems, like love, begin in surprise, delight, and tears, and end in wisdom."

—Robert Graves

"Poetry is a way of taking life by the throat."

—Frost

Robert Frost was born in 1874 and died in 1963.

FOCUS ACTIVITY

Think about the people who live near you. Do you see them often? Are you good friends, or do you barely speak? What activities, if any, bring you together? What things keep you apart?

FREEWRITE Spend three or four minutes freewriting to explore your responses to these questions.

SETTING A PURPOSE Read to find out how two neighbors relate to each other.

BACKGROUND

The Time and Place

From 1900 to 1909, Frost tried to earn a living on a small family farm he had bought in Derry, New Hampshire. In New England at this time, many farmers were moving west or to factory towns in search of regular wages. Farming there was difficult, owing to the rocky soil, short growing season, small yields, and harsh climate. After feeding their families, farmers had few surplus crops with which to support themselves.

Although Frost loved the outdoors enough to become an amateur botanist, he was basically unsuited for farm life. He found working around livestock awkward, disliked regular chores and early rising, feared darkness and storms, and had a somewhat frail build. Frost and his family were able to survive only because of the farming skills of Frost's friend Carl Burell and because of an annual sum of $500 Frost received from his grandfather's estate. Three years before Frost left for England, he abandoned farming and, with a sense of failure and frustration, resumed his teaching career. Despite his lack of success as a farmer, Frost drew inspiration for many poems from his memories of farm life.

Literary Influences

While living in England, Frost met the modernist writers W. B. Yeats, Ford Madox Ford, and Ezra Pound. He found their personalities pretentious and their writing style difficult to appreciate. Frost preferred the company and work of poets W. H. Davies, Wilfrid Gibson, Lascelles Ambercrombie, and Edward Thomas. Under the influence of William Wordsworth, these writers were composing lyrics about the natural world. They understood and appreciated Frost's poetry, bolstering his confidence in his decision to be a poet.

Mending Wall

Robert Frost

Something there is that doesn't love a wall,
That sends the frozen-ground-swell under it,
And spills the upper boulders in the sun;
And makes gaps even two can pass abreast.
5   The work of hunters is another thing:
I have come after them and made repair
Where they have left not one stone on a stone,
But they would have the rabbit out of hiding,
To please the yelping dogs. The gaps I mean,
10   No one has seen them made or heard them made,
But at spring mending-time we find them there.
I let my neighbour know beyond the hill;
And on a day we meet to walk the line
And set the wall between us once again.
15   We keep the wall between us as we go.
To each the boulders that have fallen to each.
And some are loaves and some so nearly balls
We have to use a spell to make them balance:
'Stay where you are until our backs are turned!'
20   We wear our fingers rough with handling them.
Oh, just another kind of out-door game,
One on a side. It comes to little more:
There where it is we do not need the wall:
He is all pine and I am apple orchard.
25   My apple trees will never get across
And eat the cones under his pines, I tell him.
He only says, 'Good fences make good neighbours.'
Spring is the mischief in me, and I wonder
If I could put a notion in his head:

30   '*Why* do they make good neighbours? Isn't it
        Where there are cows? But here there are no cows.
        Before I built a wall I'd ask to know
        What I was walling in or walling out,
        And to whom I was like to give offence.

35   Something there is that doesn't love a wall,
        That wants it down.' I could say 'Elves' to him,
        But it's not elves exactly, and I'd rather
        He said it for himself. I see him there
        Bringing a stone grasped firmly by the top

40   In each hand, like an old-stone savage armed.
        He moves in darkness as it seems to me,
        Not of woods only and the shade of trees.
        He will not go behind his father's saying,
        And he likes having thought of it so well

45   He says again, 'Good fences make good neighbours.'

The Last Stone Walls, Dogtown, 1936–1937. Marsden Hartley. Oil on canvas, 17½ x 23½ in. Yale University Art Gallery, New Haven, CT. Gift of Walter Bareiss, B.A. 1940.

Viewing the painting: In what ways might this wall be like the one in "Mending Wall"? In what ways might it be different?

Birches

Robert Frost

When I see birches bend to left and right
Across the lines of straighter darker trees,
I like to think some boy's been swinging them.
But swinging doesn't bend them down to stay
5   As ice-storms do. Often you must have seen them
Loaded with ice a sunny winter morning
After a rain. They click upon themselves
As the breeze rises, and turn many-colored
As the stir cracks and crazes their enamel.
10   Soon the sun's warmth makes them shed crystal shells
Shattering and avalanching on the snow-crust—
Such heaps of broken glass to sweep away
You'd think the inner dome of heaven had fallen.
They are dragged to the withered bracken° by the load,
15   And they seem not to break; though once they are bowed
So low for long, they never right themselves:
You may see their trunks arching in the woods

---

14 *Bracken* is a type of fern that grows in humid, temperate areas. It has large, triangular leaves.

Years afterwards, trailing their leaves on the ground
Like girls on hands and knees that throw their hair
20 Before them over their heads to dry in the sun.
But I was going to say when Truth broke in
With all her matter-of-fact about the ice-storm
I should prefer to have some boy bend them
As he went out and in to fetch the cows—
25 Some boy too far from town to learn baseball,
Whose only play was what he found himself,
Summer or winter, and could play alone.
One by one he subdued° his father's trees
By riding them down over and over again
30 Until he took the stiffness out of them,
And not one but hung limp, not one was left
For him to conquer. He learned all there was
To learn about not launching out too soon
And so not carrying the tree away
35 Clear to the ground. He always kept his poise°
To the top branches, climbing carefully
With the same pains you use to fill a cup
Up to the brim, and even above the brim.
Then he flung outward, feet first, with a swish,
40 Kicking his way down through the air to the ground.
So was I once myself a swinger of birches.
And so I dream of going back to be.
It's when I'm weary of considerations,
And life is too much like a pathless wood
45 Where your face burns and tickles with the cobwebs
Broken across it, and one eye is weeping
From a twig's having lashed across it open.
I'd like to get away from earth awhile
And then come back to it and begin over.
50 May no fate willfully misunderstand me
And half grant what I wish and snatch me away
Not to return. Earth's the right place for love:
I don't know where it's likely to go better.
I'd like to go by climbing a birch tree,
55 And climb black branches up a snow-white trunk
Toward heaven, till the tree could bear no more,
But dipped its top and set me down again.
That would be good both going and coming back.
One could do worse than be a swinger of birches.

---

28 *Subdued* means "brought under control" or "conquered."
35 Here, *poise* means "balance."

Responding to Literature

Personal Response

Which images from the poems did you find the most powerful?

ANALYZING LITERATURE

Mending Wall

RECALL AND INTERPRET

1. According to the speaker, what causes a wall to fall apart? To what might the "something" that "doesn't love a wall" refer?
2. Describe how the speaker and the neighbor fix the wall. How do the two differ on the issue of walls? What might walls and fences **symbolize** in this poem?

EVALUATE AND CONNECT

3. How does **dialogue** help emphasize the differences between the speaker and the neighbor? (See Literary Terms Handbook, page R4.)
4. Do you agree with the ideas suggested in this poem? Why or why not?

Birches

RECALL AND INTERPRET

5. What does the speaker want to think has caused the birches to bend? What really caused them to bend? Why might the speaker want to believe in the first cause?
6. To what does the speaker compare the ice that falls from the birches? To what does he compare their trunks and leaves? What can you infer about the speaker's feelings regarding the birches? What might the speaker mean when he says that "One could do worse than be a swinger of birches"?

EVALUATE AND CONNECT

7. In this poem, Frost compares life to a pathless wood. Do you think this is an appropriate **simile** (see page R14) for life? Why or why not? To what might you compare life?
8. This poem includes examples of **onomatopoeia**—words that imitate sounds. How, in your opinion, does onomatopoeia contribute to the impact of the poem?

EXTENDING YOUR RESPONSE

Performing

What They Might Have Said   With a partner, role-play the parts of the speaker and the neighbor in the poem "Mending Wall." Try to capture through words and gestures the rebellious and playful nature of the speaker. Elaborate on the single sentence spoken by the neighbor, without forgetting that he is a man of few words.

Writing About Literature

Analyzing Theme   Try to identify the **theme** of "Birches" (see page R16). First make a list of all the ideas expressed in the poem. Then determine which one is the most significant. Finally, write two or three paragraphs explaining how this idea is developed in the poem.

💾 **Save your work for your portfolio.**

Stopping by Woods on a Snowy Evening

Robert Frost

Whose woods these are I think I know.
His house is in the village though;
He will not see me stopping here
To watch his woods fill up with snow.

5   My little horse must think it queer
To stop without a farmhouse near
Between the woods and frozen lake
The darkest evening of the year.

He gives his harness bells a shake
10   To ask if there is some mistake.
The only other sound's the sweep
Of easy wind and downy flake.

The woods are lovely, dark and deep.
But I have promises to keep,
15   And miles to go before I sleep,
And miles to go before I sleep.

Country Doctor or *Night Call,* 1935. Horace Pippin. Oil on fabric, 28⅛ x 32⅛ in. Museum of Fine Arts, Boston. Abraham Shuman Fund.

Responding to Literature

Personal Response

Which lines from the poem did you find most powerful or meaningful?

ANALYZING LITERATURE

RECALL AND INTERPRET

1. Where does the owner of the woods live, and what will he not see? Why might the speaker care that the owner will not see this?
2. According to the speaker, what must the horse think, and why? What does the speaker describe the horse as doing? How might the horse's instincts differ from those of the speaker?
3. With what adjectives does the speaker describe the woods in line 13? What **mood** do these words create? What might the woods **symbolize?** (See Literary Terms Handbook, pages R10 and R16.)
4. What does the speaker do at the end of the poem? Why? What larger meaning might lines 14–16 convey?

EVALUATE AND CONNECT

5. Describe the **setting** (see page R14) of the poem. How does the setting contribute to the poem's meaning?
6. What specific sounds, sights, and tactile sensations does Frost include in this poem? Do you think these **sensory details** create a vivid portrait of the event described? Explain, using details from the poem. (See Literary Terms Handbook, page R14.)
7. The speaker finds comfort and peace in observing the snowy woods. Where do you go to find comfort and peace? Why?
8. In line 14, the speaker mentions that he has "promises to keep." What "promises" might prevent you from pausing and observing?

Rhyme Scheme

A **rhyme scheme** is the pattern of end rhymes in a poem. The rhyme scheme is identified by assigning a different letter of the alphabet to each new rhyming sound. For example, the rhyme scheme in the first stanza of this poem is *aaba.* Because the "b" sound is repeated in the second stanza, the rhyme scheme for that stanza is *bbcb.*

1. Determine the rhyme scheme for the final two stanzas.
2. What is the effect of repeating a sound from each stanza in the one that follows it?
3. How does the rhyme scheme in the last stanza reinforce the meaning of the poem?

● See **Literary Terms Handbook,** p. R13.

EXTENDING YOUR RESPONSE

Literature Groups

Discuss the Theme   Frost biographer Jeffrey Meyers wrote that the **theme** (see page R16) of this poem is "the temptation of death." In your group, discuss whether or not you agree with Meyers. Use details from the poem to support your opinions. Then summarize the results of your discussion for the class.

Interdisciplinary Activity

Geography: New England   Compare Robert Frost's New England with New England today. How have the following changed: flora (plants) and fauna (animals), climate, and land use? Choose two of the topics to investigate, then share your findings with the class.

📋 **Save your work for your portfolio.**

The Death of the Hired Man

Robert Frost

Breadloaf, 1982. Daniel Lang. Oil on canvas, 48 x 72 in. Collection of Harrison Young, Peking, China. Reproduced in *Spirit of Place* by John Arthur.

> Mary sat musing° on the lamp-flame at the table
> Waiting for Warren. When she heard his step,
> She ran on tip-toe down the darkened passage
> To meet him in the doorway with the news
> 5   And put him on his guard. 'Silas is back.'
> She pushed him outward with her through the door
> And shut it after her. 'Be kind,' she said.
> She took the market things from Warren's arms
> And set them on the porch, then drew him down
> 10   To sit beside her on the wooden steps.

---

1 *Musing* means "meditating" or "pondering."

'When was I ever anything but kind to him?
But I'll not have the fellow back,' he said.
'I told him so last haying, didn't I?
"If he left then," I said, "that ended it."

15   What good is he? Who else will harbour° him
At his age for the little he can do?
What help he is there's no depending on.
Off he goes always when I need him most.
"He thinks he ought to earn a little pay,

20   Enough at least to buy tobacco with,
So he won't have to beg and be beholden."°
"All right," I say, "I can't afford to pay
Any fixed wages, though I wish I could."
"Someone else can." "Then someone else will have to."

25   I shouldn't mind his bettering himself
If that was what it was. You can be certain,
When he begins like that, there's someone at him
Trying to coax° him off with pocket-money,—
In haying time, when any help is scarce.

30   In winter he comes back to us. I'm done.'

'Sh! not so loud: he'll hear you,' Mary said.

'I want him to: he'll have to soon or late.'

'He's worn out. He's asleep beside the stove.
When I came up from Rowe's I found him here,

35   Huddled against the barn-door fast asleep,
A miserable sight, and frightening, too—
You needn't smile—I didn't recognise him—
I wasn't looking for him—and he's changed.
Wait till you see.'

40   'Where did you say he'd been?'

'He didn't say. I dragged him to the house,
And gave him tea and tried to make him smoke.
I tried to make him talk about his travels.
Nothing would do: he just kept nodding off.'

---

15 *Harbour* means "to give shelter or protection to."
21 *Beholden* means "obligated" or "indebted."
28 *Coax* means "to persuade gently."

45 'What did he say? Did he say anything?'

'But little.'

                    'Anything? Mary, confess
He said he'd come to ditch° the meadow for me.'

'Warren!'

50   'But did he? I just want to know.'

'Of course he did. What would you have him say?
Surely you wouldn't grudge the poor old man
Some humble way to save his self-respect.
He added, if you really care to know,
55 He meant to clear the upper pasture, too.
That sounds like something you have heard before?
Warren, I wish you could have heard the way
He jumbled everything. I stopped to look
Two or three times—he made me feel so queer°—
60 To see if he was talking in his sleep.
He ran on° Harold Wilson—you remember—
The boy you had in haying four years since.
He's finished school, and teaching in his college.
Silas declares you'll have to get him back.
65 He says they two will make a team for work:
Between them they will lay this farm as smooth!
The way he mixed that in with other things.
He thinks young Wilson a likely lad, though daft°
On education—you know how they fought
70 All through July under the blazing sun,
Silas up on the cart to build the load,
Harold along beside to pitch it on.'

'Yes, I took care to keep well out of earshot.'

'Well, those days trouble Silas like a dream.
75 You wouldn't think they would. How some things linger!°

---

48 Here, *ditch* means "to dig long, narrow channels." These channels, or ditches,
are often used for drainage or irrigation.
59 *Queer* means "odd" or "strange."
61 *Ran on* means "talked continuously about."
68 *Daft* means "foolish."
75 *Linger* means "to continue to exist" or "to endure."

The Death of the Hired Man

Harold's young college boy's assurance piqued° him.
After so many years he still keeps finding
Good arguments he sees he might have used.
I sympathise.° I know just how it feels
80   To think of the right thing to say too late.
Harold's associated in his mind with Latin.
He asked me what I thought of Harold's saying
He studied Latin like the violin
Because he liked it—that an argument!
85   He said he couldn't make the boy believe
He could find water with a hazel prong°—
Which showed how much good school had ever done him.
He wanted to go over that. But most of all
He thinks if he could have another chance
90   To teach him how to build a load of hay—'

'I know, that's Silas' one accomplishment.
He bundles every forkful in its place,
And tags and numbers it for future reference,
So he can find and easily dislodge° it
95   In the unloading. Silas does that well.
He takes it out in bunches like big birds' nests.
You never see him standing on the hay
He's trying to lift, straining to lift himself.'

'He thinks if he could teach him that, he'd be
100   Some good perhaps to someone in the world.
He hates to see a boy the fool of books.
Poor Silas, so concerned for other folk,
And nothing to look backward to with pride,
And nothing to look forward to with hope,
105   So now and never any different.'

Part of a moon was falling down the west,
Dragging the whole sky with it to the hills.
Its light poured softly in her lap. She saw it
And spread her apron to it. She put out her hand
110   Among the harp-like morning-glory° strings,

---

76 *Piqued* means "aroused a feeling of anger or resentment in."
79 *Sympathise* means "to share in or to agree with the feelings or ideas of another."
86 A *hazel prong* is a stick believed to indicate the presence of underground water.
94 *Dislodge* means "to move or to force from a position."
110 A *morning glory* is a vine that produces trumpet-shaped flowers. Gardeners often position a lattice or strings for a vine to grow along.

Taut° with the dew from garden bed to eaves,
As if she played unheard some tenderness
That wrought° on him beside her in the night.
'Warren,' she said, 'he has come home to die:
115 You needn't be afraid he'll leave you this time.'

'Home,' he mocked gently.

                              'Yes, what else but home?
It all depends on what you mean by home.
Of course he's nothing to us, any more
120 Than was the hound that came a stranger to us
Out of the woods, worn out upon the trail.'

'Home is the place where, when you have to go there,
They have to take you in.'

                              'I should have called it
125 Something you somehow haven't to deserve.'

Warren leaned out and took a step or two,
Picked up a little stick, and brought it back
And broke it in his hand and tossed it by.
'Silas has better claim on us you think
130 Than on his brother? Thirteen little miles
As the road winds would bring him to his door.
Silas has walked that far no doubt to-day.
Why didn't he go there? His brother's rich,
A somebody—director in the bank.'

135 'He never told us that.'

                              'We know it though.'

'I think his brother ought to help, of course.
I'll see to that if there is need. He ought of right
To take him in, and might be willing to—
140 He may be better than appearances.
But have some pity on Silas. Do you think
If he had any pride in claiming kin
Or anything he looked for from his brother,
He'd keep so still about him all this time?'

---

111 *Taut* means "stretched tight."
113 *Wrought* means "worked."

145   'I wonder what's between them.'

                                              'I can tell you.
Silas is what he is—we wouldn't mind him—
But just the kind that kinsfolk can't abide.°
He never did a thing so very bad.
150   He don't know why he isn't quite as good
As anybody. Worthless though he is,
He won't be made ashamed to please his brother.'

'I can't think Si ever hurt anyone.'

'No, but he hurt my heart the way he lay
155   And rolled his old head on that sharp-edged chair-back.
He wouldn't let me put him on the lounge.
You must go in and see what you can do.
I made the bed up for him there to-night.
You'll be surprised at him—how much he's broken.
160   His working days are done; I'm sure of it.'

'I'd not be in a hurry to say that.'

'I haven't been. Go, look, see for yourself.
But, Warren, please remember how it is:
He's come to help you ditch the meadow.
165   He has a plan. You mustn't laugh at him.
He may not speak of it, and then he may.
I'll sit and see if that small sailing cloud
Will hit or miss the moon.'

                                         It hit the moon.
170   Then there were three there, making a dim row,
The moon, the little silver cloud, and she.

Warren returned—too soon, it seemed to her,
Slipped to her side, caught up her hand and waited.

'Warren?' she questioned.

175   'Dead,' was all he answered.

---

148 *Abide* means "to put up with" or "to tolerate."

Responding to Literature

Personal Response

How did you feel about the characters in the poem?

--- **ANALYZING LITERATURE** ---

RECALL

1. Describe what Mary does and says upon Warren's return in lines 1–10. What does Warren say in response to Mary's news?
2. How does Silas look when Mary first sees him? What labor does he promise her he will perform?
3. Who is Harold Wilson, and why does Silas want him to return to the farm? What about Harold bothers Silas, and what two skills does Silas want to teach him?
4. According to Mary, why has Silas come to the house? Why doesn't he go to his brother instead?
5. What news does Warren give Mary at the end of the poem?

INTERPRET

6. Based on lines 1–30, how would you characterize the differences between Mary and Warren?
7. In your opinion, why does Warren refuse to believe that Silas will tackle the chores he says he will?
8. What do Silas's thoughts and emotions regarding Harold reveal about Silas's personality?
9. In your opinion, why does Silas avoid asking his brother for help?
10. What does the end of the poem suggest about Warren's feelings toward Silas?

EVALUATE AND CONNECT

11. What can you infer about Frost's opinion of Silas? How do you feel about Silas? What details helped to shape your opinion?
12. In your opinion, how does Frost's use of **dialogue** affect the **tone** of the poem? (See Literary Terms Handbook, pages R4 and R16.)
13. What might you do if you found yourself in Mary and Warren's position?
14. In this poem, Frost presents two different definitions of home. Which definition do you prefer, and why?
15. In many of his poems, Frost described the difficult lives of New England farmers. What have you learned about their lives from reading "The Death of the Hired Man"?

Literary ELEMENTS

Dramatic Poetry

A **dramatic poem** is a poem that reveals the personalities of one or more characters by using dialogue and monologue as well as description. While a dramatic poem may include narrative, the focus is on the characters, not the events. In "The Death of the Hired Man," Frost used dialogue to reveal the personalities of Silas, Mary, and Warren. He also included purely descriptive passages.

1. In your opinion, how is this poem similar to a play?
2. Do you think this poem would have been as powerful if Frost had revealed Silas's personality through description instead of dialogue? Explain.
3. How does the language used in the dialogue between Mary and Warren differ from that used in the descriptive passages?

● See **Literary Terms Handbook**, p. R5.

LITERATURE AND WRITING

Writing About Literature

Analyzing Tone   The **tone** is the reflection of the writer's attitude toward the subject of a work. For example, the tone of "The Death of the Hired Man" could be described as quiet and somber. Choose two other Frost poems from this theme and write two to three paragraphs comparing their tones. Use specific examples from the selections to support your ideas.

Creative Writing

Home Is . . .   Write a dramatic poem expressing your concept of home. First choose an event and two or three characters through which to convey your ideas. Then write dialogue and monologue based on the speech patterns you hear at home and in school. To help enliven your poem, try also writing purely descriptive passages.

EXTENDING YOUR RESPONSE

Literature Groups

Debate the Question   In your group, debate the following question: Could Frost have chosen a better ending for "The Death of the Hired Man"? Have each side support its opinion with details from the poem. Then present the results of the debate to the class.

Learning for Life

Career Research   Use the Internet or library sources to research the kinds of jobs that are available on farms. Choose and describe one farm job, and list the formal education skills and experience necessary for that job. Based on your research, do you think there would still be work for a hired man such as Silas? Share the results of your research with the class.

Interdisciplinary Activity

Art: Visual Representation   Frost's poems are full of striking visual images. Choose one of the poems you have just read and create a painting, drawing, collage, or other visual representation of it. Portray the poem realistically or abstractly, depending on how you think you can best convey its meaning. Display your artwork in your classroom.

Reading Further

If you are interested in reading more by or about Robert Frost, look for the following:

Poetry Collections: *North of Boston* (1914) and *Mountain Interval* (1916) are collections of Frost's poems.

Biographies: *Frost: A Literary Life Reconsidered,* by William H. Pritchard, is a narrative exploring the interaction between Frost's life and work.

Into My Own: The English Years of Robert Frost, by John Evangelist Walsh, gives a detailed account of a major period in Frost's life.

📖 **Save your work for your portfolio.**

LISTENING, SPEAKING, and VIEWING

Oral Presentation of a Poem

Have you ever noticed that two people's reading of a poem can sound completely different? There is no "correct" way to read a particular poem. Anyone can give an oral presentation of a poem based on his or her own understanding and interpretation of that poem.

Preparing Your Oral Presentation

These suggestions can help you present your oral interpretation of a poem.

- Read the poem again. What is that speaker's tone? Think about ways to use your voice to convey that tone. For example, if the tone is angry, you might speak more slowly and at a lower pitch than you would if the tone were humorous.
- Read the poem to decide what the speaker is saying and why he or she is saying it. In other words, what is the meaning of the poem, and what is the poet's purpose?
- Read the poem once more, this time focusing on your own reactions to it. Think of ways to use your voice to communicate your reactions.
- Look for imagery and figurative language the poet has used. Think about ways to communicate these images and figures of speech. Should you read them more slowly or pause before or after important phrases?
- Examine how the poet has used sound devices, such as rhyme, rhythm, alliteration, assonance, and consonance. Decide how you will emphasize these elements in your oral presentation.
- Plan where you will pause for breath. Pause at the end of a line only if there is a punctuation mark or if it seems like a natural place to pause. Otherwise, read through the ends of lines, even those that end with a rhyme, until you reach an appropriate place to pause.
- Practice your oral presentation, experimenting with different uses of voice, volume, speed, and other vocal devices.

ACTIVITY

With a partner, choose a poem from this theme that you have enjoyed. Use the suggestions above to plan an oral interpretation of the poem. Discuss each point with your partner until you come up with a plan for presenting the poem. Determine how you will divide the poem for two readers. Then make your oral presentation to the class.

~: Writing ✦ Workshop :~

Persuasive Writing: Editorial

*N*ew. The word carries with it a sense of excitement, of unlimited possibilities, of better things. It's a word that enthralled writers in this theme, with their "New Art" and their urging to "Make it new." New doesn't always mean better, however. What do you think about the new things that are happening in the world around you? **In this workshop you will write an editorial persuading others to share your opinion about a timely issue.**

● As you write your editorial, refer to the **Writing Handbook,** pp. R62–R77.

The Writing Process

PREWRITING

PREWRITING TIP

Be sure you feel strongly about an issue before you try to persuade others to feel the same way. The most important person to have on your side is yourself.

Explore issues

An editorial is a short persuasive piece that appears in a periodical and focuses on a condition or an event of the moment. In an editorial you may use any of the following approaches:

● Suggest a new direction. *(A change I would like to see)*
● Criticize a new development or an existing situation. *(A situation that bothers me)*
● Express praise or support. *(A development I really like)*
● Promote an activity or a cause. *(Something I would like to do or to help happen)*

Idea webs can help you choose an issue to write about. In the center circle, write one of the parenthesized phrases above. In connecting circles, write any and all ideas that come to mind. Then go on to build webs around the three other phrases. Mark ideas that strike your interest.

You may get some ideas for your webs by going back to the selections in this theme. Although these writings spring from a time of emotional and cultural upheaval, new directions can be considered—and old ones reconsidered—at any time. Which of the authors' concerns are relevant today?

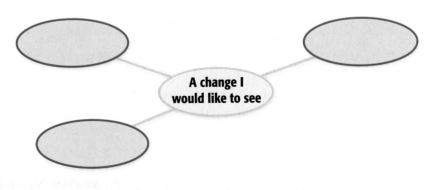

A change I would like to see

Consider your purpose

Your aim is to persuade readers to agree with you on a certain issue, but precisely how do you want them to react? Do you want them to take action? become enraged? become interested? Shape your editorial accordingly.

Consider your audience

To a large extent, your issue determines your audience. Who cares about the issue? Who is affected by it? Who can do something about it? Those are the people you want to address.

Make a plan

An editorial should pack a quick punch. In a relatively short space, you need to identify an issue, state your position on that issue, and provide evidence–facts and opinions–to support your position. One way to determine what kind of evidence to use is to list questions your audience may have and then provide the answers to them. You may also want to look into opposing arguments so that you can counter them.

When you're ready to make a plan, consider using a chart like the one below. Number your reasons in order of importance. This chart reflects one student's plan for an editorial on mandatory community service.

STUDENT MODEL

Issue	High school students' community service requirement
Position	Requiring high school students to perform community service is a plan with good intentions but bad results.
Evidence	Making community service compulsory turns it into a duty— another kind of homework. Half the students interviewed regarded it as a chore. Many said they'd do the easiest thing possible rather than the most useful or fulfilling.
Evidence	Students are wildly overscheduled already. Some admitted to doing homework or studying on the job.
Evidence	Is it the job of the school to fill volunteer slots in the community? Or is the job of the school to produce educated, concerned, compassionate citizens who will *want* to fill those slots?
Evidence	Who decides where students can volunteer to fulfill the service requirement? What if an organization is acceptable to some people but not to others?

DRAFTING

DRAFTING TIP

It's not enough just to present your evidence. You need to explain why it supports your position. Your reader reads your editorial, not your mind.

Write your draft

As you begin your draft, remind yourself of your purpose for writing and of your thesis. Because every element of your writing hinges on your thesis statement, write it down and refer to it often as you draft.

Think about your audience also. Be sure that your ideas and language are appropriate for your intended audience. You might want to share your draft with a group to discuss its appropriateness for your particular audience.

Once you are satisfied that your language and ideas are appropriate, ask yourself, "What will help my audience to understand why I feel the way I do?" It may be best to start out with your most convincing piece of evidence, or you may want to build up to it at the end. Either way, use appropriate transitions to lead the reader from one point to the next. At the end of your editorial, reaffirm your position. Don't worry about expressing your ideas perfectly—just get them down.

Watch your language

You want to make the reader feel as strongly as you do, but don't force the issue. Persuade rather than preach. Explain rather than attack. You can appeal to readers' emotions as well as their reason as long as you stay honest and avoid overdramatizing. Unless you are writing about a very serious topic, a little humor can also help to bring the reader over to your side.

STUDENT MODEL

Most importantly, people should perform community service because they want to, not because they have to. Otherwise, the volunteer spirit won't be very strong. If required to perform community service, many students will just go through the motions. Already, many choose the community service assignment that's easiest to complete rather than choosing something that will enrich themselves or someone else. If community service seems like homework, high school students are less likely to volunteer later in life. In the long run, everyone loses.

REVISING

TECHNOLOGY TIP
Search the Web sites of various periodicals to find some editorials. Identify which of these are the most persuasive, and use those techniques in your writing.

Evaluate your work

Put your editorial aside. After some time has passed, come back to it as if you were a first-time reader. What works? What doesn't? Mark sections that seem unclear, weak, or over-stated. Then use the **Questions for Revising** as a guide to improve your work.

Get some feedback

Read your editorial aloud to a member of your target audience. Is he or she persuaded to share your position? Why or why not? Ask questions about the piece and talk over the answers. Jot down suggestions that seem to make sense to you, and make use of them as you polish your editorial.

QUESTIONS FOR REVISING

☑ How might I state the issue and my position on it more clearly?

☑ Have I presented my evidence in the most effective order? Where might more transitions help?

☑ Is my evidence relevant? persuasive? Is there any-thing I should add or delete?

☑ Where can I add details to make my points clearer? Where can I add anecdotes to liven up the discussion?

☑ Where can I use more precise and powerful words?

☑ Where do I need to tone down my language?

☑ How can I make my conclusion stronger?

☑ Have I fit the content and style of my editorial to my purpose and audience?

STUDENT MODEL

I am not saying

~~Nobody denies~~ that community service is not a good thing, ~~in general.~~

I simply want to pose a number

~~However, there are a lot~~ of questions that have not been answered, such

as what counts as community service ~~and which organizations qualify~~

students

for student volunteers. ~~The plan does not say!~~ If ~~people~~ are left to make

some might choose activities that are not truly community service

these decisions on their own, ~~it will really be a ridiculous mess.~~ Does

taking a few neighborhood kids to the movies count as community

service, for example? ~~Think about that!~~

EDITING/PROOFREADING

Satisfy yourself that your editorial is as good as you can make it. Then proofread it for errors in grammar, usage, mechanics, and spelling. Using the **Proofreading Checklist** on the inside back cover of this book to guide you, check for one kind of error at a time.

Grammar Hint

If the subject is an indefinite pronoun, determine whether it is singular or plural and make the verb agree.

Each of the students **has** volunteered.

Few agree on what constitutes community service.

Some indefinite pronouns can be either singular or plural, depending on the nouns to which they refer.

Most organizations **seem** eager to have volunteers.

Most of the controversy **has** stemmed from a lack of free time.

STUDENT MODEL

Each of the students volunteer at one of our cities social service organizations.

PUBLISHING/PRESENTING

If you plan to submit your editorial to a newspaper or organization, you should include a cover letter explaining who you are and why you are sending your work. Try to find out the name of the person to whom the letter should be addressed, and submit a neat copy of your work. Send your editorial to as many places as you think might be interested. Submitting it to several venues increases your chance of getting heard.

Reflecting

With a classmate, discuss how the process of writing an editorial affected your views on the issue. What did you learn about yourself as a persuader? Consider what you might do differently if you write another editorial.

📖 **Save your work for your portfolio.**

Theme 8

When have you felt a creative spark to make or do something? In the 1920s, the Harlem neighborhood in New York City experienced a creative explosion of African American literature, art, and music. The selections in this theme celebrate this fertile era and reveal the unique vision of several of its writers.

Aspects of Negro Life: Song of the Towers, 1934. Aaron Douglas. Oil on canvas, 9 x 9 ft. Schomburg Center for Research in Black Culture, The New York Public Library.

THEME PROJECTS

Internet Project

Guide to the Harlem Renaissance
Essays, poetry, paintings, and sculpture from the Harlem Renaissance abound on the World Wide Web.

1. Use a search engine to find writings and artwork from the Harlem Renaissance. Be sure to look for some of the authors or works from this theme.

2. Evaluate each Web site you find. Is the information interesting? Does it seem to be accurate? Which artists and writings are represented?

3. Prepare an Internet guide to the Harlem Renaissance in which you recommend particular Web sites. For each site, include a written overview, sample pages, and reasons for your recommendation.

Listening and Speaking

A Writers' Debate   The writers of the Harlem Renaissance didn't always agree on the purpose of their work.

1. With a partner, research two Harlem Renaissance writers who held different beliefs about what their work should represent. Find examples of their writing that reflect these beliefs.

2. Take the role of one of these people while your partner takes the other, and stage a formal debate for your class on the purpose of African American literature during the Harlem Renaissance. Keep in mind the social and economic climate of the 1920s as you shape your arguments.

Before You Read

My City

Meet James Weldon Johnson

While many young writers were just starting out during the Harlem Renaissance, James Weldon Johnson was entering the most productive period of his highly successful life. At the beginning of the Harlem Renaissance, the forty-nine-year-old Johnson had already been a high school principal, a newspaper editor, a lawyer, a songwriter, a foreign consul, a novelist, an editorial writer, and the head of the National Association for the Advancement of Colored People (NAACP). For many, Johnson's vigorous artistic and intellectual activities represented the spirit of the age. For Johnson himself, the writing of poetry and the fight for African American equality served the same goal—winning a respected place in American society for people of African American heritage.

Johnson grew up in Jacksonville, Florida, in a middle-class family. As a student at Atlanta University, he responded to the school's philosophy that educated African Americans should devote their lives to public service, especially to helping less fortunate African Americans. When he finished college at age twenty-three, he took a job as the principal of the school he had attended in Jacksonville. He also worked for several summers as a teacher in poor, rural, African American schools.

At age thirty-one, Johnson resigned as school principal and began a varied and dazzling career. For a time, he was a successful composer, working in New York with his brother, Rosamond, also a composer. Among his many lyrics, Johnson wrote "Lift Every Voice and Sing," often referred to as the black national anthem. Later, he took up a post as U.S. consul, first in Venezuela and then in Nicaragua. When he returned to the United States, he became a journalist for an African American newspaper and later a Civil Rights activist and a lobbyist for the NAACP. His final career was as a professor of literature and writing at Fisk University in Nashville, Tennessee. The position was created specifically for him, due, in large part, to his literary accomplishments during the Harlem Renaissance. Throughout his life, Johnson wrote poetry. He also anthologized other African American poets in the popular and widely acclaimed collection, *Book of American Negro Poetry*.

❝The world does not know that a people is great until that people produces great literature and art.❞

—Johnson

James Weldon Johnson was born in 1871 and died in 1938.

Reading Further

If you would like to read more by or about James Weldon Johnson, try these books:

Poetry: *God's Trombones,* by James Weldon Johnson, presents seven sermons written in free verse and considered some of Johnson's most influential poems.

Autobiography: *Along This Way.*

Biography: *James Weldon Johnson,* by Robert E. Fleming, gives a clear chronology of his life.

FOCUS ACTIVITY

Visualize a place that you love. It might be a comfortable chair in your living room, a street you like to walk down, a lively beach, or some other place.

JOURNAL Describe the place in your journal and write about how you would feel if you could never visit that place again.

SETTING A PURPOSE Read "My City" to discover James Weldon Johnson's feelings about a particular place.

BACKGROUND

The Time and Place

During the 1920s and early 1930s, many African American writers and artists lived in the Harlem section of Manhattan (Manhattan is a borough of New York City). These writers and artists contributed to the Harlem Renaissance, a flowering of black culture that had its roots in the ideas of prominent African American leaders, such as W. E. B. DuBois. DuBois believed that to achieve social equality African Americans must not adopt the values of white America; instead they must work to express their own cultural heritage and, in doing so, renew their racial pride. James Weldon Johnson knew and respected DuBois. He agreed with many of DuBois's ideas and reflected them in his own writing.

W. E. B. DuBois
(1868–1963).

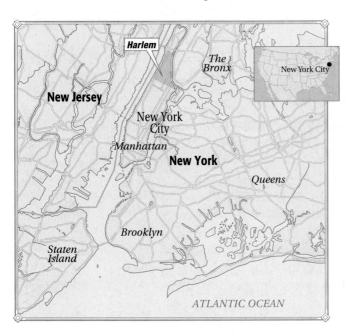

Literary Influences

Johnson was extremely well educated and well read. His mother, a schoolteacher, passed on to him a knowledge of, and love for, English literature. He earned both an undergraduate and a graduate degree from Atlanta University and studied for a time at Columbia University in New York City under the school's most distinguished professor of literature, Brander Matthews. At the beginning of his literary career, Johnson often modeled his writing after classic poets of the English language. He wrote poems in a formal style, using rhymed verse in conventional forms, such as the sonnet.

During the Harlem Renaissance of the 1920s, Johnson began experimenting with free verse. Inspired by the powerful speaking rhythms of African American preachers, he wrote a collection of poems styled after folk sermons, called *God's Trombones.*

Fulton and Nostrand, 1958. Jacob Lawrence. Tempera on Masonite, 24 x 30 in. Private collection. Courtesy Terry Dintenfass Gallery, New York.

My City

James Weldon Johnson〜

When I come down to sleep death's endless night,
The threshold of the unknown dark to cross,
What to me then will be the keenest loss,
When this bright world blurs on my fading sight?
5   Will it be that no more I shall see the trees
Or smell the flowers or hear the singing birds
Or watch the flashing streams or patient herds?
No. I am sure it will be none of these.

But, ah! Manhattan's sights and sounds, her smells,
10   Her crowds, her throbbing force, the thrill that comes
From being of her a part, her subtle° spells,
Her shining towers, her avenues, her slums—
O God! the stark,° unutterable° pity,
To be dead, and never again behold my city.

---

11 Things that are *subtle* are faint, barely noticeable, or not obvious.

13 Here, *stark* means "absolute" and *unutterable* means "too deep or great to be put into words."

Responding to Literature

Personal Response

What questions would you like to ask the speaker of "My City"? Jot them down. Next to each one, write a brief reason for your question.

——— **ANALYZING LITERATURE** ———

RECALL AND INTERPRET

1. What question does the speaker pose for himself at the beginning of the poem? What phase of life is implied in the question?
2. What possible answers does the speaker first explore? Why might he propose these answers?
3. What answer does the speaker finally provide? What reasons does he give? What does this answer tell you about the speaker's personality?
4. What, according to the speaker, is "the stark, unutterable pity"? Why might the speaker feel this way about the city?

EVALUATE AND CONNECT

5. How does the **rhyme scheme** contribute to the poem's impact? Explain. (See Literary Terms Handbook, page R13.)
6. A **caesura** is a pronounced pause in the middle of a line of poetry. Where does Johnson use caesuras in the poem? What do they help reveal about the speaker's emotions?
7. Overall, do you like this poem? Why or why not? Relate your answer to the poem's message, imagery, form, or all of these.
8. Refer back to your response to the Focus Activity on page 719. In this poem, the speaker expresses a preference for the city over the natural world. Which do you prefer? Why?

Octave and Sestet

Poets often divide their poems into **stanzas,** or groups of verse lines that form a unit. Stanzas organize a poem into thoughts, much as paragraphs help to organize prose. Two common types of stanzas are the **octave,** or stanza of eight lines, and the **sestet,** or stanza of six lines. Many sonnets, such as "My City," feature these two stanza forms. In such sonnets, the octave presents the main idea of the poem, and the sestet expands upon, contradicts, or develops this idea.

1. What idea is expressed in the octave of "My City"?
2. How is this idea developed in the sestet of the poem?
3. How does the division of this poem into an octave and sestet contribute to its effectiveness?

● See **Literary Terms Handbook,** p. R15.

——— **EXTENDING YOUR RESPONSE** ———

Interdisciplinary Activity

Art: Illustrate a Scene   In this poem, Johnson presents a rich and moving picture of Manhattan. Using crayons, pencils, or paints, create a work of art that captures Johnson's feelings about the city. Before you begin to work, reread the poem so that you remember which aspects of the city particularly appealed to Johnson. Share your work with the class.

Learning for Life

A Brochure of Poetic Places   What shining towers, avenues, and sights might Johnson be referring to in "My City"? Using a map and tourist information about Manhattan, locate places that match his descriptions. Then create an illustrated tourism guide for Johnson's "city."

🛍 **Save your work for your portfolio.**

Magazine Article

What's so special about the hometown of Harlem Renaissance writer Zora Neale Hurston's childhood? That's a controversial question for some people.

A Place to Be Free

by Constance Johnson—
U.S. News & World Report, March 2, 1992

PRINCEVILLE, N.C.—"We were first," says 84-year-old Susanna Thomas, thrusting her bony finger forward. "I don't know what those people are talking about." She means the residents of Eatonville, Florida, who claim that their 2-square-mile burg north of Orlando is the oldest all-black, self-governed town in the United States.

The origins of the dispute date back more than a century. In the decades after the Civil War, freed slaves moved across the United States creating hundreds of all-black towns. Some, like Princeville, were founded on unoccupied land in the shadows of nearby white towns. In others, like Eatonville, residents bought their land. Most of the towns offered the chance for blacks to govern themselves. Princeville was incorporated in 1885 and Eatonville in 1887. But Eatonville officials say their town, founded entirely by blacks, was the first incorporated all-black town because Princeville had about forty-five white residents until 1900, when it became nearly all black.

By 1920, many of these [all-black] towns had been wiped out by agricultural depressions and other calamities. Fewer than 30 all-black towns remain today. That's where the current dispute comes in. To save their town, Princeville's mayor and other leaders in the community of 1,700 people are trying to get it designated as the first all-black town in the National Register of Historic Places. Eatonville, with a population of 3,000, is pursuing the same designation. All the officials hope that the recognition will attract visitors who can help prop up their sagging economies.

In some ways, trying to win the battle over which was first . . . misses the real point of pride about these towns. Certain qualities already qualify Princeville as a national treasure.

Princeville Mayor Glennie Matthewson recalls that his desire to become a lawyer dawned as he sat on his uneducated father's lap while the elder Matthewson presided over misdemeanor cases in the black-run town. For 74-year-old Mable Dancy, Princeville may have failed to live up to its billing as "the center of the world." But it did fulfill another important role: "This was the only place we could be free," she says.

Respond

1. Why does each town want to be recognized as the nation's first all-African American town?

2. Which town do you think should get that designation? Explain.

Before You Read

from *Dust Tracks on a Road*

Meet Zora Neale Hurston

In 1973 the writer Alice Walker traveled to Fort Pierce, Florida, to visit Zora Neale Hurston's grave. What Walker found looked "more like an abandoned field" than a cemetery, she said. There among the waist-high weeds and yellow wildflowers was a large sunken rectangle—Hurston's grave. Walker ordered a headstone for the grave site.

"I wanted to mark Zora's grave so that one day all our daughters and sons would be able to locate the remains of a human mountain in Florida's and America's so frequently flat terrain," Walker explained.

Hurston grew up in Eatonville, Florida, one of the first incorporated black towns in the United States. There her father worked as a Baptist preacher and served as the town's mayor. Her mother, who taught her to read, was a great source of encouragement.

Only thirteen when her mother died, Hurston spent the next two decades working as a waitress, a manicurist, and a maid, while trying to get a high school education. Finally Hurston enrolled in Howard University, then later Barnard College, where she earned a degree in anthropology. Hurston used her training to collect the folklore of Eatonville and other southern African American communities. She later used this material as a source for much of her writing.

Although considered an important figure in the Harlem Renaissance, Hurston was a fierce individualist who resisted membership in any school of thought. Her ideas sometimes got her into trouble with fellow writers, and over the years, her popularity declined. Though she published widely, Hurston made little money from her books. By the time of her death, she was penniless.

Today, thanks to Walker and other admirers, Hurston's books are widely read, and she is remembered for her ability to capture the rich traditions and poetic speech of southern black culture. Her book *Mules and Men* is recognized as the first history of African American folklore written by an African American, and her most admired novel, *Their Eyes Were Watching God*, has sold more than a million copies since its republication in 1969.

❝All clumps of people turn out to be individuals on close inspection.❞

❝I am so put together that I do not have much of a herd instinct. Or if I must be connected with the flock, let *me* be the shepherd my ownself. That is just the way I am made.❞

❝There is no agony like bearing an untold story inside you.❞

—*Hurston*

Zora Neale Hurston was born in 1891 and died in 1960.

Before You Read

FOCUS ACTIVITY

Think about a time when a surprise event changed your life in some way.

CHART IT! Fill in a chart like the one below to show how a surprise event affected you. Add as many outcomes as you need.

SETTING A PURPOSE Read to learn about the outcomes of a surprise event in Zora Neale Hurston's life.

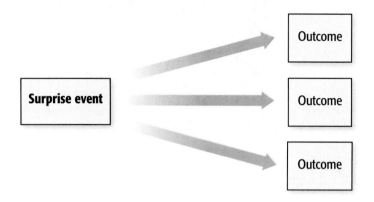

BACKGROUND

The Time and Place
This story takes place in Eatonville, Florida, around 1900, a time when white people controlled most communities in the United States. In Eatonville, however, African Americans were the leaders and decision makers. Zora Neale Hurston celebrated the customs and speech of her hometown in her writing.

Did You Know?
Although *Dust Tracks on a Road* is a fascinating autobiography, it hides as much as it reveals about the author's life. Hurston never tells when she was born, never mentions her second marriage, and contradicts details about her life that she wrote in private letters to friends.

VOCABULARY PREVIEW

brazenness (brā′ zən əs) *n.* defiant behavior; boldness; p. 725

exalt (ig zôlt′) *v.* to lift up; to put in high spirits; p. 726

snicker (sni′ kər) *n.* a snide, partly suppressed laugh, often expressing disrespect; p. 727

indifferent (in dif′ ər ənt) *adj.* lacking feeling or concern; p. 729

from Dust Tracks on a Road

Zora Neale Hurston ∾

Harlem Series, no. 28: The Libraries Are Appreciated, 1943. Jacob Lawrence. Gouache on paper, 14½ x 21¼ in. Philadelphia Museum of Art, PA.

I used to take a seat on top of the gate-post and watch the world go by. One way to Orlando ran past my house, so the carriages and cars would pass before me. The movement made me glad to see it. Often the white travelers would hail[1] me, but more often I hailed them, and asked, "Don't you want me to go a piece of the way with you?" They always did. I know now that I must have caused a great deal of amusement among them, but my self-assurance must have carried the point, for I was always invited to come along. I'd ride up the road for perhaps a half-mile, then walk back. I did not do this with the permission of my parents, nor with their foreknowledge. When they found out about it later, I usually got a whipping. My grandmother worried about my forward ways a great deal. She had known slavery and to her my brazenness was unthinkable.

"Git down offa dat gate-post! You li'l sow, you! Git down! Setting up dere looking dem white folks right in de face! They's gowine[2] to lynch you, yet. And don't stand in dat doorway gazing out at 'em neither. Youse too brazen to live long."

Nevertheless, I kept right on gazing at them, and "going a piece of the way" whenever I could make it. The village seemed dull to me most of the time. If the village was singing a chorus, I must have missed the tune.

Perhaps a year before the old man[3] died, I came to know two other white people for myself. They were women.

It came about this way. The whites who came down from the North were often brought by their friends to visit the village school. A Negro school was something strange to them, and while they were always sympathetic and kind, curiosity must have been present, also. They came and went, came and went. Always, the room was hurriedly put in order, and we were threatened with a prompt and bloody death if we cut one caper[4] while the visitors were present. We always sang a spiritual, led by Mr. Calhoun himself. Mrs. Calhoun always stood in the back, with a palmetto switch[5] in her hand as

---

1. *Hail* means "to greet."
2. *Gowine* is dialect for "going."

3. The *old man,* a white farmer who was a friend of Hurston's family, took Zora Neale fishing and gave her advice.
4. *Cut one caper* is slang for "play a trick or prank" or "behave extravagantly or noisily."
5. A *palmetto switch,* a whip used for discipline, was made from the flexible stem of a leaf from a palmetto palm.

Vocabulary

brazenness (brā′ zən əs) *n.* defiant behavior; boldness

from **Dust Tracks on a Road**

a squelcher. We were all little angels for the duration, because we'd better be. She would cut her eyes[6] and give us a glare that meant trouble, then turn her face towards the visitors and beam as much as to say it was a great privilege and pleasure to teach lovely children like us. They couldn't see that palmetto hickory in her hand behind all those benches, but we knew where our angelic behavior was coming from.

Usually, the visitors gave warning a day ahead and we would be cautioned to put on shoes, comb our heads, and see to ears and fingernails. There was a close inspection of every one of us before we marched in that morning. Knotty heads, dirty ears and fingernails got hauled out of line, strapped and sent home to lick the calf[7] over again.

This particular afternoon, the two young ladies just popped in. Mr. Calhoun was flustered,[8] but he put on the best show he could. He dismissed the class that he was teaching up at the front of the room, then called the fifth grade in reading. That was my class.

So we took our readers and went up front. We stood up in the usual line, and opened to the lesson. It was the story of Pluto and Persephone.[9] It was new and hard to the class in general, and Mr. Calhoun was very uncomfortable as the readers stumbled along, spelling out words with their lips, and in mumbling undertones before they exposed them experimentally to the teacher's ears.

Then it came to me. I was fifth or sixth down the line. The story was not new to me, because I had read my reader through from lid to lid, the first week that Papa had bought it for me.

That is how it was that my eyes were not in the book, working out the paragraph which I knew would be mine by counting the children ahead of me. I was observing our visitors, who held a book between them, following the lesson. They had shiny hair, mostly brownish. One had a looping gold chain around her neck. The other one was dressed all over in black and white with a pretty finger ring on her left hand. But the thing that held my eyes were their fingers. They were long and thin, and very white, except up near the tips. There they were baby pink. I had never seen such hands. It was a fascinating discovery for me. I wondered how they felt. I would have given those hands more attention, but the child before me was almost through. My turn next, so I got on my mark, bringing my eyes back to the book and made sure of my place. Some of the stories I had re-read several times, and this Greco-Roman myth was one of my favorites. I was <u>exalted</u> by it, and that is the way I read my paragraph.

"Yes, Jupiter[10] had seen her (Persephone). He had seen the maiden picking flowers in the field. He had seen the chariot of the dark monarch pause by the maiden's side. He had seen him when he seized Persephone. He had seen the black horses leap down Mount Aetna's[11] fiery throat. Persephone was now in Pluto's dark realm and he had made her his wife."

The two women looked at each other and then back to me. Mr. Calhoun broke out with a proud smile beneath his bristly moustache, and instead of the next child taking up where I had ended, he nodded to me to go on. So I read the story to the end, where flying Mercury, the messenger of the Gods, brought

---

6. *Cut her eyes* is slang for "look at with scorn or contempt."
7. *Lick the calf* is slang for "get cleaned up."
8. *Flustered* means "nervous" or "agitated."
9. The myth of *Pluto and Persephone* (pər sef′ ə nē) explains the origin of the seasons. Pluto is god of the underworld, and Persephone is his wife.

---

10. In Roman mythology, *Jupiter* is king of the gods and Pluto's brother.
11. *Mount Aetna* (et′ nə) (also spelled *Etna*) is a volcano in eastern Sicily, Italy.

Vocabulary
exalt (ig zôlt′) *v.* to lift up; to put in high spirits

Persephone back to the sunlit earth and restored her to the arms of Dame Ceres, her mother, that the world might have springtime and summer flowers, autumn and harvest. But because she had bitten the pomegranate while in Pluto's kingdom, she must return to him for three months of each year, and be his queen. Then the world had winter, until she returned to earth.

Did You Know?
A *pomegranate*
(pom′ ə gran′ it) is a round fruit containing many small seeds in a red pulp.

The class was dismissed and the visitors smiled us away and went into a low-voiced conversation with Mr. Calhoun for a few minutes. They glanced my way once or twice and I began to worry. Not only was I barefooted, but my feet and legs were dusty. My hair was more uncombed than usual, and my nails were not shiny clean. Oh, I'm going to catch it now. Those ladies saw me, too. Mr. Calhoun is promising to 'tend to me. So I thought.

Then Mr. Calhoun called me. I went up thinking how awful it was to get a whipping before company. Furthermore, I heard a <u>snicker</u> run over the room. Hennie Clark and Stell Brazzle did it out loud, so I would be sure to hear them. The smart-aleck was going to get it. I slipped one hand behind me and switched my dress tail at them, indicating scorn.

"Come here, Zora Neale," Mr. Calhoun cooed as I reached the desk. He put his hand on my shoulder and gave me little pats. The ladies smiled and held out those flower-looking fingers towards me. I seized the opportunity for a good look.

"Shake hands with the ladies, Zora Neale," Mr. Calhoun prompted and they took my hand one after the other and smiled. They asked me if I loved school, and I lied that I did. There was *some* truth in it, because I liked geography and reading, and I liked to play at recess time. Whoever it was invented writing and arithmetic got no thanks from me. Neither did I like the arrangement where the teacher could sit up there with a palmetto stem and lick me whenever he saw fit. I hated things I couldn't do anything about. But I knew better than to bring that up right there, so I said yes, I *loved* school.

"I can tell you do," Brown Taffeta gleamed. She patted my head, and was lucky enough not to get sandspurs[12] in her hand. Children who roll and tumble in the grass in Florida are apt to get sandspurs in their hair. They shook hands with me again and I went back to my seat.

When school let out at three o'clock, Mr. Calhoun told me to wait. When everybody had gone, he told me I was to go to the Park House, that was the hotel in Maitland, the next afternoon to call upon Mrs. Johnstone and Miss Hurd. I must tell Mama to see that I was clean and brushed from head to feet, and I must wear shoes and stockings. The ladies liked me, he said, and I must be on my best behavior.

The next day I was let out of school an hour early, and went home to be stood up in a tub of suds and be scrubbed and have my ears dug into. My sandy hair sported a red ribbon to match my red and white checked gingham dress, starched until it could stand alone. Mama saw to it that my shoes were on the right feet, since I was careless about left and right. Last thing, I was given a handkerchief to carry, warned again about my behavior, and sent off, with my big brother John to go as far as the hotel gate with me.

---

12. *Sandspurs* (also called *sandburs*) are spiny burs that grow on a grass of the same name.

Vocabulary
snicker (sni′ kər) *n.* a snide, partly suppressed laugh, often expressing disrespect

from **Dust Tracks on a Road**

First thing, the ladies gave me strange things, like stuffed dates and preserved ginger, and encouraged me to eat all that I wanted. Then they showed me their Japanese dolls and just talked. I was then handed a copy of *Scribner's Magazine*, and asked to read a place that was pointed out to me. After a paragraph or two, I was told with smiles, that that would do.

I was led out on the grounds and they took my picture under a palm tree. They handed me what was to me then a heavy cylinder done up in fancy paper, tied with a ribbon, and they told me goodbye, asking me not to open it until I got home.

My brother was waiting for me down by the lake, and we hurried home, eager to see what was in the thing. It was too heavy to be candy or anything like that. John insisted on toting it for me.

My mother made John give it back to me and let me open it. Perhaps, I shall never experience such joy again. The nearest thing to that moment was the telegram accepting my first book. One hundred goldy-new pennies rolled out of the cylinder. Their gleam lit up the world. It was not avarice[13] that moved me. It was the beauty of the thing. I stood on the mountain. Mama let me play with my pennies for a while, then put them away for me to keep.

That was only the beginning. The next day I received an Episcopal hymn-book bound in white leather with a golden cross stamped into the front cover, a copy of The Swiss Family Robinson, and a book of fairy tales.

I set about to commit the song words to memory. There was no music written there, just the words. But there was to my consciousness music in between them just the same. "When I survey the Wondrous Cross" seemed the most beautiful to me, so I committed that to memory first of all. Some of them seemed dull and without life, and I pretended they were not there. If white people liked trashy singing like that, there must be something funny about them that I had not noticed before. I stuck to the pretty ones where the words marched to a throb I could feel.

A month or so after the two young ladies returned to Minnesota, they sent me a huge box packed with clothes and books. The red coat with a wide circular collar and the red tam pleased me more than any of the other things. My chums pretended not to like anything that I had, but even then I knew that they were jealous. Old Smarty had gotten by them again. The clothes were not new, but they were very good. I shone like the morning sun.

Did You Know?
A *tam* (short for *tam-o'-shanter*) is a soft Scottish cap with a fitted headband. It often has a center pom-pom.

But the books gave me more pleasure than the clothes. I had never been too keen on dressing up. It called for hard scrubbings with Octagon soap suds getting in my eyes, and none too gentle fingers scrubbing my neck and gouging in my ears.

In that box were Gulliver's Travels, Grimm's Fairy Tales, Dick Whittington, Greek and Roman Myths, and best of all, Norse Tales. Why did the Norse tales strike so deeply into my soul? I do not know, but they did. I seemed to remember seeing Thor[14] swing his mighty short-handled hammer as he sped across the sky in rumbling thunder, lightning flashing from the tread of his steeds and the wheels of his chariot. The great and

---

13. *Avarice* is greed, or excessive desire for wealth.

14. In Norse mythology, *Thor* is the god of thunder. His magical hammer returns to him like a boomerang after being thrown.

good Odin,[15] who went down to the well of knowledge to drink, and was told that the price of a drink from that fountain was an eye. Odin drank deeply, then plucked out one eye without a murmur and handed it to the grizzly keeper, and walked away. That held majesty for me.

Of the Greeks, Hercules moved me most. I followed him eagerly on his tasks. The story of the choice of Hercules as a boy when he met Pleasure and Duty, and put his hand in that of Duty and followed her steep way to the blue hills of fame and glory, which she pointed out at the end, moved me profoundly. I resolved[16] to be like him. The tricks and turns of the other Gods and Goddesses left me cold. There were other thin books about this and that sweet and gentle little girl who gave up her heart to Christ and good works. Almost always they died from it, preaching as they passed.[17] I was utterly indifferent to their deaths. In the first place I could not conceive of death, and in the next place they never had any funerals that amounted to a hill of beans, so I didn't care how soon they rolled up their big, soulful, blue eyes and kicked the bucket. They had no meat on their bones.

But I also met Hans Andersen and Robert Louis Stevenson. They seemed to know what I wanted to hear and said it in a way that tingled me. Just a little below these friends was Rudyard Kipling in his Jungle Books. I loved his talking snakes as much as I did the hero.

I came to start reading the Bible through my mother. She gave me a licking one afternoon for repeating something I had overheard a neighbor telling her. She locked me in her room after the whipping, and the Bible was the only thing in there for me to read. I happened to open to the place where David[18] was doing some mighty smiting,[19] and I got interested. David went here and he went there, and no matter where he went, he smote 'em hip and thigh. Then he sung songs to his harp awhile, and went out and smote some more. Not one time did David stop and preach about sins and things. All David wanted to know from God was who to kill and when. He took care of the other details himself. Never a quiet moment. I liked him a lot. So I read a great deal more in the Bible, hunting for some more active people like David. Except for the beautiful language of Luke and Paul,[20] the New Testament still plays a poor second to the Old Testament for me. The Jews had a God who laid about[21] Him when they needed Him. I could see no use waiting till Judgment Day to see a man who was just crying for a good killing, to be told to go and roast.[22] My idea was to give him a good killing first, and then if he got roasted later on, so much the better.

---

15. *Odin* (ō′ din), the father of Thor, is the supreme god in Norse mythology and the creator of the first man and woman. Odin traded an eye for a drink from the well of wisdom, which was guarded by a giant.
16. *Resolved* means "decided."
17. *Passed* is short for "passed on" or "passed away" and means "died."
18. *David* was the second king of Judah and Israel. He killed the giant Goliath.
19. *Smiting* means "striking hard, as with a hand or a weapon, so as to cause serious injury or death."
20. *Luke* and *Paul* were authors of much of the New Testament of the Christian Bible.
21. *Laid about* means "hit out in all directions."
22. *Roast* is slang for "burn in hell."

Vocabulary
indifferent (in dif′ ər ənt) *adj.* lacking feeling or concern

Responding to Literature

Personal Response

How did you react to the narrator? Share your responses with the class.

—— ANALYZING LITERATURE ——

RECALL

1. What does Zora Neale do at the beginning of the selection? How do her parents and grandmother react?
2. How do the teachers and students react to the white visitors?
3. What draws the attention of the two white ladies to Zora Neale?
4. How do the ladies reward Zora Neale?
5. Which gifts does Zora Neale enjoy the most?

INTERPRET

6. How would you explain the difference between Zora Neale's attitude toward the white travelers passing through, and the attitudes of her parents and grandmother?
7. Why do you suppose the teachers and students react as they do to the white visitors?
8. When Zora Neale reads aloud from the story of Persephone, what does she reveal about her personality and abilities? Explain, using details from the selection.
9. Based on her reaction to the ladies and their gifts, how would you describe Zora Neale's attitude toward the ladies?
10. What do you think Zora Neale gains from the gifts she receives?

EVALUATE AND CONNECT

11. In your opinion, does Hurston do a good job of portraying the **setting** (the time and the place) in which she grew up? Explain.
12. Look back at the chart you made for the Focus Activity on page 724. How does the importance of your surprise event compare with Zora Neale's?
13. Think back to what you were like in the fifth grade. Does Hurston do a good job of recreating the thoughts of a fifth grader? Support your answer with examples.
14. How do you think you would have reacted if you were in Zora Neale's place in this story? Explain.
15. If you wanted to use books to describe your interests, opinions, and impressions—as Hurston does—which books would you choose, and why?

Literary ELEMENTS

Local Color

The use of details to show the unique character of a place and its inhabitants is called **local color.** When writers use local color, they look for details that appeal to the five senses. Some writers, including Zora Neale Hurston, specialize in bringing to life the customs, language, geography, and feeling of the places they write about.

1. What kinds of details does Hurston use to show the local color of Eatonville? List the categories of details, such as dress, dialect, and customs. Under each category, include a few examples from the selection.
2. What sense(s) does Hurston seem to appeal to most in the selection? Use examples in your answer.
3. Write a few sentences to show the local color of your school. Use details that appeal to each of the five senses.

● See **Literary Terms Handbook,** p. R9.

LITERATURE AND WRITING

Writing About Literature

Analyzing Characterization   You can learn about a character from his or her actions and words, from the reactions of others to the character, and from direct description. Write a few paragraphs explaining how the author shows young Zora Neale's self-confidence. Include examples from the selection.

Personal Writing

Meaningful Gift   Zora Neale is moved by the gifts she receives from the ladies who visit her school. Think of a time when you received a gift that was especially important to you. Write a letter to the person who gave it to you describing your reaction to the gift. You may or may not choose to send the letter.

EXTENDING YOUR RESPONSE

Literature Groups

True or False?   Critics have complained that Hurston's autobiography isn't always factual. In your group, discuss the following: Does it matter to you if Hurston's autobiography is absolutely true or not? What reasons might a writer have for distorting the facts in his or her autobiography? Do you think these are valid reasons? Why or why not? Share your conclusions with the class.

Performing

Storytelling   Choose one of the myths or stories mentioned in this selection. Read it several times, and practice telling it as a storyteller would. Use expressions, gestures, and different voices to capture the characters' personalities. Then tell the story to the class.

Listening and Speaking

Listening to the Locals   One of Hurston's trademarks as a writer is capturing the unique speech, or dialect, of the community in which she grew up. Write a few passages that capture the speech patterns of your own community. Share and discuss your writing with a partner. Did you notice similar speech patterns?

Save your work for your portfolio.

Skill Minilesson

VOCABULARY • Analogies

Analogies are comparisons based on relationships between words and ideas. The relationship between the words in some analogies is that of *worker* and *action*.

   tailor : sew :: chef : cook

   A *tailor sews*; a *chef cooks*.

To finish an analogy, decide on the relationship represented by the first two words. Then apply that relationship to the second set of words.

PRACTICE   Choose the word that best completes each analogy. Some of the analogies are based on the relationship of *worker* and *action*.

1. reporter : reveal :: critic :
   a. judge   b. discover   c. reprimand
2. snicker : laugh :: smirk :
   a. giggle   b. grin   c. frown
3. shyness : brazenness :: calmness :
   a. timidness   b. serenity   c. tension
4. police : regulate :: soldiers :
   a. complain   b. travel   c. fight

● For more about analogies, see **Communications Skills Handbook,** pp. R83–R84.

Writing Skills

Creating Unified Paragraphs

Clear, unified writing doesn't happen by accident. A writer must think carefully about the ideas he or she wants to present in a piece of writing and then plan how to develop those ideas in paragraphs. Each paragraph must support the main idea of the piece of writing, and each sentence in a paragraph must support the main idea of that paragraph. For example, look at this paragraph from *Dust Tracks on a Road.* Notice how the details provided in the body of the paragraph all support Hurston's claim that the Norse tales appealed to her very strongly.

> "In that box were Gulliver's Travels, Grimm's Fairy Tales, Dick Whittington, Greek and Roman Myths, and best of all, Norse Tales. Why did the Norse tales strike so deeply into my soul? I do not know, but they did. I seemed to remember seeing Thor swing his mighty short-handled hammer as he sped across the sky in rumbling thunder, lightning flashing from the tread of his steeds and the wheels of his chariot. The great and good Odin, who went down to the well of knowledge to drink, and was told that the price of a drink from that fountain was an eye. Odin drank deeply, then plucked out one eye without a murmur and handed it to the grizzly keeper, and walked away. That held majesty for me."

To write a unified paragraph, begin with a topic sentence that states the main idea of the paragraph, then add one or more pieces of supporting information such as

- descriptive details, which may be sensory—appealing to one or more of the five senses.
- reasons.
- facts and/or statistics.
- examples and/or incidents.

Be careful, however, to avoid supporting information that is not relevant. After you draft a paragraph, go back and cross out parts that do not support your main idea or that are weak.

EXERCISE

Write a paragraph explaining what you like or do not like about the selection from *Dust Tracks on a Road* or another selection from this theme. Be sure to include a topic sentence, and support it with details, reasons, facts, or examples.

Before You Read

If We Must Die and *The Tropics in New York*

Meet Claude McKay

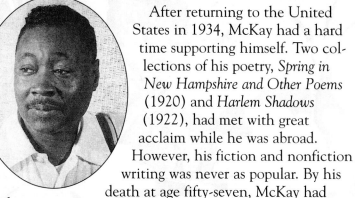

Some critics have identified the publication of "If We Must Die" in 1919 as the spark that ignited the Harlem Renaissance. This poem by Claude McKay inspired many African Americans and gave them a new sense of pride.

McKay was born and raised in rural Jamaica. When he first came to the United States at age twenty-two, he was shocked by the country's racial discrimination. "I had heard of prejudice in America but never dreamed of it being so intensely bitter," he later wrote. McKay spent much of his life looking for ways to counter the "ignoble cruelty" of racism. He grappled with different political beliefs and traveled and lived in Europe and Africa during the Harlem Renaissance.

After returning to the United States in 1934, McKay had a hard time supporting himself. Two collections of his poetry, *Spring in New Hampshire and Other Poems* (1920) and *Harlem Shadows* (1922), had met with great acclaim while he was abroad. However, his fiction and nonfiction writing was never as popular. By his death at age fifty-seven, McKay had become almost unknown.

❝There was among [the African American poets] a voice too powerful to be confined to the circle of race, a voice that carried further and made America in general aware; it was that of Claude McKay.❞

—*James Weldon Johnson*

Claude McKay was born in 1890 and died in 1948.

FOCUS ACTIVITY

What examples do you know of people who faced violence or death because of their race, religion, or ethnicity?

JOURNAL Write a journal entry about one of these examples. Describe how the person or people facing oppression responded to the situation.

SETTING A PURPOSE Read to find out how one poet responds to an unjust situation.

BACKGROUND

The Time and Place

Tensions between African Americans and whites erupted into race riots during the summer of 1919, when inflation was high and competition for jobs was fierce. The worst riot left thirty-eight people dead and more than three hundred injured in Chicago. A waiter in a railroad dining car, McKay and his fellow African American workers feared being attacked. It was during this summer that Claude McKay wrote "If We Must Die."

Literary Influences

Jamaica was a British colony when McKay was a child. English was the language of the schools, and McKay grew up reading the works of English writers, including William Shakespeare and Charles Dickens.

If We Must Die

Claude McKay ∾

If we must die, let it not be like hogs
Hunted and penned in an inglorious° spot,
While round us bark the mad and hungry dogs,
Making their mock at our accursed° lot.
5   If we must die, O let us nobly die,
So that our precious blood may not be shed
In vain; then even the monsters we defy
Shall be constrained° to honor us though dead!
O kinsmen! we must meet the common foe!
10   Though far outnumbered let us show us brave,
And for their thousand blows deal one deathblow!
What though before us lies the open grave?
Like men we'll face the murderous, cowardly pack,
Pressed to the wall, dying, but fighting back!

---

2 *Inglorious* means "shameful" or "disgraceful."
4 *Accursed* (ə kur′ sid) means "being under a curse" or "doomed."
8 *Constrained* means "forced."

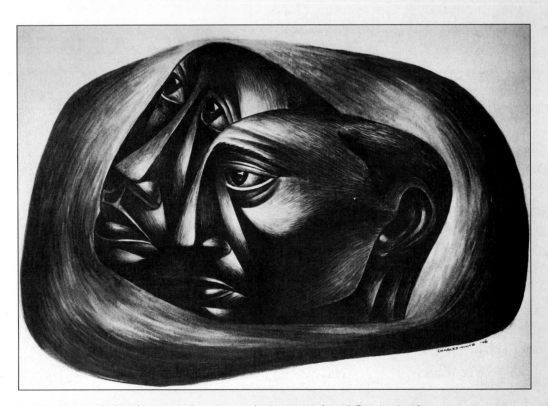

Two Heads, 1946. Charles White. Watercolor, 16¾ x 24¼ in. Courtesy Heritage Gallery, Los Angeles.

The Tropics in New York

Claude McKay

Fruit Stand Vendor, 1994. Hyacinth Manning. Acrylic on canvas, 28 x 22 in. Private collection. How does this painting help you visualize the tropics McKay describes?

Bananas ripe and green, and ginger-root,
    Cocoa in pods and alligator pears,
And tangerines and mangoes and grape fruit,
    Fit for the highest prize at parish fairs,

5   Set in the window, bringing memories
    Of fruit-trees laden by low-singing rills,
And dewy dawns, and mystical blue skies
    In benediction° over nun-like hills.

    My eyes grew dim, and I could no more gaze;
10   A wave of longing through my body swept,
And, hungry for the old, familiar ways,
    I turned aside and bowed my head and wept.

---

8 A *benediction* is a blessing.

Responding to Literature

Personal Response

Which image from the poems stands out in your mind? What effect does this image have on you?

ANALYZING LITERATURE

If We Must Die

RECALL AND INTERPRET

1. What two animals does the speaker name? Which is the hunter and which is the hunted? With whom does the speaker identify? Explain.
2. How does the speaker want his kinsmen to behave? Why is this important to him?

EVALUATE AND CONNECT

3. How do the reactions advocated by the speaker compare with those of the person or people you wrote about for the Focus Activity on page 733?
4. Theme Connections   Some critics believe "If We Must Die" marks the start of the Harlem Renaissance. Why might this poem have led to such a creative outpouring?

The Tropics in New York

RECALL AND INTERPRET

5. What does the speaker see in the window? What memories does the sight bring?
6. How does the speaker react physically when he recalls his memories? Why might he have this reaction?

EVALUATE AND CONNECT

7. Which **sensory details** (see page R14) in the poem help you picture the tropics best? Explain.
8. What feelings about times or places in your past does this poem express for you?

Literary ELEMENTS

Shakespearean Sonnet

A **Shakespearean**, or **English**, **sonnet** is a type of sonnet developed in England and made famous by William Shakespeare. It is organized into three **quatrains** (groups of four lines) followed by a rhymed **couplet** (a pair of lines). The lines have the rhyme scheme *abab cdcd efef gg*. A main thought is presented in the three quatrains, and the couplet contains the conclusion.

1. Which of the McKay poems is a Shakespearean sonnet? How do you know?
2. Explain the main idea presented in the three quatrains of the Shakespearean sonnet McKay wrote. Then describe the conclusion.

● See **Literary Terms Handbook,** p. R15.

Radio Transcript

People's lives are often influenced by
their communities and the events that
take place there. Artists, such as the
one featured below, help give expression to that influence.

Artist Jacob Lawrence

National Public Radio, from *Morning Edition*, June 9, 1998

BOB EDWARDS, host

As part of the Harlem Renaissance, Jacob
Lawrence was among those who helped
move the black experience into the mainstream of America's artistic consciousness
after World War I. Many of the writers and
musicians went on to gain worldwide recognition—Zora Neale Hurston, Langston
Hughes, Duke Ellington.

Behind those famous figures was a
vibrant community of visual artists whose
participation in the Harlem Renaissance
often is overlooked. Jacob Lawrence is the
last living member of the group and his
work is part of a touring exhibition dedicated to it.

WILLIAM DRUMMOND, reporter

One particular series of paintings stands
out. [Jacob Lawrence's] scenes from the life
of Toussaint l'Ouverture . . . consist of
forty-one panels depicting the life of the
Haitian general who came to be a symbol
of black pride in 1930s America because of
his successful rebellion against French rule
a century earlier.

The paintings were the subject of
Lawrence's first exhibition in 1938 at the
Harlem YMCA. By then, Jacob Lawrence
was just 20 years old and the Harlem
Renaissance was coming to an end.

When the movement began Lawrence
was just a toddler, but he grew up taking in
all that was going on around him.

LAWRENCE

I knew many of the older people. Some,
like Langston Hughes, I met. Claude
McKay I knew well. He befriended me. I'm
sure it had a great deal of influence on me
and my work.

DRUMMOND

Lawrence's paintings tell stories, says
Patricia Hills, who teaches art history at
Boston University and has written frequently about Lawrence. That's why she
calls him a pictorial Gryot.

PATRICIA HILLS

"Gryot," as you know, is a French word, it
comes from West Africa. It means "a storyteller." You know, the person in the community who knows the history and tells
the story. That's one of the reasons he's
[Lawrence] done a lot of works in series,
because the series allows him to tell the
kind of story that he wants to tell. He's
really interested in people. He's interested
in his own community.

Respond

1. Are storytellers important in
   today's society? Explain why or
   why not.

2. Based on this interview, what, in
   your opinion, is Jacob Lawrence's
   significance to the Harlem
   Renaissance?

Meet
Langston Hughes

When Langston Hughes was nineteen, his father offered to send him to college in Europe so Hughes could escape from the racism and segregation that affected every part of American life. Hughes refused, however, explaining, "More than Paris, or the Shakespeare country, or Berlin, or the Alps, I wanted to see Harlem, the greatest Negro city in the world." Hughes spent the rest of his life celebrating Harlem and African American life.

Despite having a wealthy father, Hughes knew what it meant to live in poverty. By the age of twelve he had already lived in six different cities because his divorced mother was always moving around looking for work. He also lived for a time with his grandmother, who told him stories about heroic ancestors who had fought slavery and racism. She helped instill in Hughes a lasting sense of pride in his heritage and culture.

Hughes began writing poetry in high school. He attended Columbia University for a year but found the school to be too large and impersonal. Instead he went to live in his beloved Harlem, where he had a hard time finding a job. Finally he took a job as a merchant sailor, traveling to Africa and Europe. When he returned to the United States he continued writing poetry and eventually earned a college degree from Lincoln University. In 1926 his first book, *The Weary Blues*, was published.

Throughout his life Hughes was a "poet of the people" who spent much time traveling across the country to read his poetry. He integrated the rhythms of blues and jazz music in his writings and used the language of the people he encountered. Hughes saw beauty in the wisdom, humor, and strength of the people he portrayed.

Although best known as a poet, Hughes also wrote fiction, drama, popular songs, and satirical sketches about an uneducated but perceptive character named Simple. In addition, he worked on anthologies and translations and helped the careers of many younger writers.

"It is the duty of the younger Negro artist . . . to change through the force of his art that old whispering 'I want to be white' to 'why should I want to be white? I am a Negro—and beautiful!'"

"I didn't know the upper-class Negroes well enough to write much about them. I knew only the people I had grown up with, and they weren't people whose shoes were always shined, who had been to Harvard, or who had heard of Bach. But they seemed to me good people, too."

—*Hughes*

"Hughes . . . was unashamedly black at a time when blackness was démodé [not fashionable], and he didn't go much beyond one of his earliest themes, black *is* beautiful."

—*Lindsay Patterson*

Langston Hughes was born in 1902 and died in 1967.

FOCUS ACTIVITY

What makes you who you are? Think about the forces that have shaped and influenced your life.

QUICKWRITE Jot down the names of some of the people and events that have helped shape your identity.

SETTING A PURPOSE Read to find out what the speakers of two poems reveal about themselves.

BACKGROUND

The Time and Place

When Hughes began writing in the 1920s, little progress had been made in securing basic rights for African Americans. In the South laws legalized segregation, and in the North black workers were generally hired only for low-wage jobs. Hughes's father had moved to Mexico because he was fed up with discrimination in the United States.

Hughes's college-educated mother moved from city to city looking for work, but found only menial jobs. In Harlem, many artists, writers, and intellectuals hoped their artistic movement would help bring about an end to such discrimination.

Harlem, New York City, 1920s or early 1930s.

I, Too

Langston Hughes 〜

I, too, sing America.

I am the darker brother.
They send me to eat in the kitchen
When company comes,
5   But I laugh,
And eat well,
And grow strong.

Tomorrow,
I'll be at the table
10   When company comes.
Nobody'll dare
Say to me,
"Eat in the kitchen,"
Then.

15   Besides,
They'll see how beautiful I am
And be ashamed—

I, too, am America.

Man or *Take My Mother Home #2*, 1959. Charles White. Pen and ink drawing. Collection of Harry Belafonte. Courtesy Heritage Gallery, Los Angeles. What qualities of the poem do you see reflected in this image? Explain.

The Negro Speaks of Rivers

Langston Hughes ~

I've known rivers:
I've known rivers ancient as the world and older than the
    flow of human blood in human veins.

My soul has grown deep like the rivers.

     I bathed in the Euphrates° when dawns were young.
5   I built my hut near the Congo° and it lulled me to sleep.
     I looked upon the Nile° and raised the pyramids above it.
     I heard the singing of the Mississippi when Abe Lincoln
        went down to New Orleans,° and I've seen its muddy
        bosom turn all golden in the sunset.

I've known rivers:
Ancient, dusky° rivers.

10   My soul has grown deep like the rivers.

---

4 The *Euphrates* (ū frā′ tēz) River flows from Turkey through Syria and Iraq. Many
  ancient civilizations flourished in the area between the Euphrates and Tigris rivers.
5 The *Congo,* also called the Zaire, is a river in central Africa.
6 The *Nile,* which runs through northeast Africa, is the longest river in the world.
7 According to legend, Abraham Lincoln decided that slavery should be abolished
  after witnessing his first slave auction in *New Orleans,* Louisiana, along the
  Mississippi River.
9 *Dusky* means "dark in color" or "murky."

Responding to Literature

Personal Response

Which lines from the poems did you find most memorable or powerful? Explain your choices to the class.

ANALYZING LITERATURE

I, Too

RECALL AND INTERPRET

1. How is the speaker of the poem treated? How does the speaker respond to this treatment? What is the identity of the speaker and of the other people in the poem?
2. How will things be different "tomorrow"? What do you think the change will represent? How do you think the speaker expects this change to come about?
3. What statement does the speaker make in the final line of the poem? Why might he feel the need to make this statement?

EVALUATE AND CONNECT

4. How would you describe the **mood** of this poem? What elements of the poem contribute to this mood? Explain. (See Literary Terms Handbook, page R10.)
5. What historical realities does this poem reflect?

The Negro Speaks of Rivers

RECALL AND INTERPRET

6. In line 2, how does the speaker describe the rivers he has known? For what reason might he emphasize their age?
7. To what rivers does the speaker refer in lines 4–7? What do the activities associated with these rivers communicate about the history of African Americans? In your opinion, what do the rivers **symbolize,** or stand for?
8. What is the final line of the poem? What does this line suggest about how the history of the speaker's people has affected the speaker?

EVALUATE AND CONNECT

9. Look carefully at the shape of this poem. In your opinion, does the poem's shape suit its content? Explain.
10. What do you know about the historical periods referred to in the poem? What more would you like to know after reading the poem?

Literary ELEMENTS

Repetition

Repetition occurs when a sound, word, phrase, or line is repeated within a piece of writing. In poetry, repetition can emphasize words or ideas and can add a musical quality. For example, the phrase "I've known rivers" appears three times in "The Negro Speaks of Rivers." This repetition sounds like a song refrain, and it ties together the beginning and ending of the poem.

1. Hughes repeats the title of "I, Too" in the first and final lines of the poem. What idea might he be trying to emphasize through this repetition?
2. What is the slight difference between these lines? What does the change emphasize?

● See **Literary Terms Handbook,** p. R13.

LITERATURE AND WRITING

Writing About Literature

Analyzing Theme   The **theme** of a literary work is the main idea that the writer is trying to communicate to the reader. Write a sentence for each of Hughes's poems that you think captures its theme. Then write a paragraph that compares the themes. Explore how the themes are similar and how they are different.

Creative Writing

A Bit About You   These poems emphasize the importance of history and nation in shaping one's identity. Look back at the items you listed for the Focus Activity on page 739. Write a poem, song lyrics, or a brief essay that conveys how these people and events have helped shape your identity.

EXTENDING YOUR RESPONSE

Literature Groups

Picture It   Work as a group to plan a sketch for each of the two poems. You may want to begin by discussing the feeling and meaning of each poem. Then discuss ways to convey your interpretations, and work together to create rough sketches. Share your sketches with other groups and discuss the similarities and differences between them.

Interdisciplinary Activity

Geography: River Country   In "The Negro Speaks of Rivers," the speaker refers to four rivers. Choose one of the rivers and research some of the cultures that grew up around it. Be sure to find out what contributions these cultures made to the rest of the world.

Performing

Choral Reading   Work with a small group to prepare a choral reading of one of the poems. Determine your audience and purpose—for example, to inspire pride among children. Decide how to divide up the reading of the poem. Practice your reading and perform it for the class.

Learning for Life

Evaluate Reviews   Use your library or the Internet to research reviews of and commentaries on Langston Hughes's poetry. Look for reviews of specific poems or of collections. Choose two or three of the reviews of poems you have read and write an evaluation of those reviews. Based on your reading of the poems, do the reviews you found seem accurate? Explain your answer in your evaluation.

📖 **Save your work for your portfolio.**

Before You Read

from *Songs for Signare*

Meet Léopold Sédar Senghor

Early in World War II, French soldier Léopold Sédar Senghor (sã′ där seng′ hor) was captured by the Nazis. He and fellow prisoners of African descent were made to line up against a wall. As the Nazis prepared to shoot them, Senghor shouted "Long live France! Long live Black Africa!" Before the shots were fired, a white French prisoner intervened, and Senghor and the others were allowed to live. The incident highlights Senghor's dual identity as an African and a Frenchman.

Senghor grew up in Senegal, which at that time was part of French West Africa. An exceptional student, he earned a scholarship to study in France. After graduating from the Sorbonne in Paris, he taught in French schools. After World War II, Senghor became involved in the African movement for independence. Under his leadership, Senegal gained nationhood in 1960. Senghor served as Senegal's president for twenty years, retiring in 1980.

Senghor began writing poetry as a student in Paris. Writing gave him an outlet for exploring his identity as an African immersed in French culture, and later for exploring the uniqueness of his own Senegalese culture. *Songs for Signare* was originally written in French, and it was published in 1961.

"**Tomorrow I will continue on my way to Europe, to the embassy, Already homesick for my black Land.**"

"**To assimilate, not to be assimilated**"
—Senghor

Léopold Sédar Senghor was born in 1906.

FOCUS ACTIVITY

Which objects in your home tell the most about your life and cultural heritage?

LIST IT! List the objects in your home that tell something about you and your heritage. Choose four objects that best represent you.

SETTING A PURPOSE Read to find out what objects tell about one poet's cultural heritage.

BACKGROUND

Senghor and African Culture

Although Senghor often wrote of his beloved homeland Senegal, in fact he was interested in all of Africa. In his poem he refers to masks, which play an important role in many different African cultures. He also mentions ritual stools, which were the seats of kings and other important people. The weaving of mats and cloth is a revered art form throughout Africa, as well.

Senghor wrote *Songs for Signare* to be read or sung to the accompaniment of the *khalam* (KHä′ läm), a four-stringed African lute.

Literary Influences

When Senghor was a student in Paris in the late 1920s, he was introduced to the works of Harlem Renaissance writers. He was so impressed by their works that, even though he knew very little English, he learned some of the Harlem Renaissance poems by heart.

from

SONGS FOR SIGNARE

Léopold S. Senghor 〜
Translated by John Reed and Clive Wake

(For khalam)

And we shall be steeped my dear in the presence of Africa.
Furniture from Guinea° and Congo,° heavy and polished,
    somber and serene.
On the walls, pure primordial° masks distant and yet present.
Stools of honor for hereditary guests, for the
    Princes of the High Lands.
5   Wild perfumes, thick mats of silence
Cushions of shade and leisure, the noise of a
    wellspring° of peace.
Classic words. In a distance, antiphonal singing
    like Sudanese° cloths
And then, friendly lamp, your kindness to soothe this
    obsessive presence
White black and red, oh red as the African soil.

Signare (si nä′ rē′)

2 *Guinea* is a region of West Africa that borders the Atlantic Ocean.
Congo is the name of a central African country.
3 *Primordial* means "primitive" or "existing at the beginning."
6 A *wellspring* is a source of continual supply.
7 Anything *Sudanese* is from Sudan, an African country located just
south of Egypt.

Antelope Headdress. Bamana people
of Upper Niger region of Mali, Africa.
Wood, height: 38½ in. Private collection.

Responding to Literature

Personal Response

What reactions did you have while reading this poem? What about the poem inspired you to react this way? Share your responses.

ANALYZING LITERATURE

RECALL AND INTERPRET

1. What is the speaker steeped in according to line 1? What do you think the speaker means by this?
2. List the objects that the speaker mentions in the poem. Based on the speaker's descriptions of these objects, how would you characterize the place that he imagines?
3. How does the speaker describe the "words" referred to in line 7? Why might the speaker describe these words in this way?
4. To what might the speaker be referring when he says "this obsessive presence"? How would you explain the speaker's strong feelings for Africa and African objects?

EVALUATE AND CONNECT

5. Is the writer successful in giving you an idea of what the "presence of Africa" looks, sounds, and feels like? Explain your answer.
6. What have you learned about the poem's **speaker?** (See Literary Terms Handbook, page R15.) What attitudes does the speaker communicate? Explain.
7. Think about the impressions you've gained about life on the continent of Africa from books, television, school, or firsthand experience. Does the poem match your impressions? Why or why not?
8. How do the objects mentioned in the poem compare with those you chose to represent yourself for the Focus Activity on page 744? Tell how they are alike and different.

Literary ELEMENTS

Lyric Poetry

Poems that tell a story are called **narrative poems.** In contrast, poems that focus on personal thoughts and feelings are called **lyric poems.** The word *lyric* refers to an ancient Greek musical instrument, the lyre. Long ago, the Greeks recited poetry to the music of the lyre.

Lyric poems can take many forms. They may follow a rhyme scheme, or they may be written in free verse. All the poems in this theme are examples of lyric poetry.

1. What are the main thoughts and emotions conveyed in the poem by Senghor?
2. What vivid words and phrases contribute to the effect these thoughts and emotions have?

● See **Literary Terms Handbook,** p. R9.

EXTENDING YOUR RESPONSE

Writing About Literature

Contrasting Images   Senghor uses opposites such as "somber and serene," "distant and yet present," and "noise of . . . peace." Choose one of these examples and write a paragraph explaining what you think it means in the poem.

Performing

The Song of the Poet   With a group, come up with music to accompany the poem, using either musical instruments or a recording. Consider the sounds, feelings, and ideas of the poem. Practice reading the poem with the music, then perform it for the class.

📖 **Save your work for your portfolio.**

COMPARING selections

I, Too **and** *The Negro Speaks of Rivers* **and** *from* SONGS FOR SIGNARE

COMPARE TONE

The **tone** of a piece of writing is the attitude the writer conveys toward the subject, characters, events, or audience. In a few paragraphs, answer the following questions about comparing the tones of these three poems:

1. What is the tone of each of the poems?
2. In what ways do details help bring out the tone of each poem?
3. Which of Hughes's poems has a tone more similar to Senghor's poem? Explain.

COMPARE CULTURES

Both Langston Hughes and Léopold Sédar Senghor were important poets who helped other Africans and African Americans appreciate their own cultures. With a group of classmates, list the images that Hughes and Senghor use to convey information about their cultures. Discuss what you learn about each culture from the poems. How are they similar? different? Share your conclusions with the class.

COMPARE POETIC DEVICES

Choose one of Hughes's poems to compare with Senghor's poem. Make a three-column chart like the one below. List poetic devices—alliteration, repetition, rhyme, and so on—in the first column and record examples of the devices that you find in each poem in the second and third columns. Then answer the questions.

Poetic Device	Hughes's poem	Senghor's poem

1. Which devices does each poet use most? What do they add to each poem?
2. Which poem do you like best? How did the use of poetic devices affect your choice?

Meet Helene Johnson

"[Johnson's] poetry is marked by an often lovely lyricism in which genteel sensuality and a usually muted expression of racial pride are blended."

—*The Norton Anthology of African American Literature*

When she was nineteen, Helene Johnson traveled from her hometown of Boston to New York City to accept her first poetry award. She had received an honorable mention in the annual poetry contest of the popular African American magazine *Opportunity*. Once Johnson saw and experienced New York City at the height of the Harlem Renaissance, she decided to stay.

When Johnson first moved to New York City, she lived in one of the few apartment buildings outside Harlem that rented to African Americans. She quickly became friends with the only other African American woman in the building, famed Harlem Renaissance writer Zora Neale Hurston. Before long, Johnson was socializing with Harlem's literary elite.

Today, Johnson is remembered as one of the youngest and most promising writers of the Harlem Renaissance, a woman who was very proud of her cultural heritage and exhibited strong concern for life in Harlem.

Helene Johnson was born in 1907 and died in 1995.

FOCUS ACTIVITY

Think about a person in your neighborhood who particularly stands out. What type of person is he or she?

CHART IT! In a chart like the one shown here, name one of this person's defining personality traits. Then list gestures, physical attributes, and behaviors that reveal this trait.

Personality Trait: Cheerful	
Gestures	
Physical attributes	
Behaviors	

SETTING A PURPOSE Read to understand one poet's impressions of someone who stands out.

BACKGROUND

The Time and Place

Harlem was known as a ghetto in the 1920s and 1930s. Despite its overcrowding and poverty, Harlem's African American residents found much better housing there than elsewhere in New York City. In her poetry, Johnson wanted to reflect the more modest and everyday realities of living in Harlem.

Literary Influences

Johnson's education and family strongly influenced her. She counted the British poets Alfred, Lord Tennyson and Percy Bysshe Shelley and American poets Walt Whitman and Carl Sandburg among her favorites. Johnson also received inspiration and support from her cousin, the writer Dorothy West, who moved with Johnson to New York and became an editor of *Challenge,* a publication that promoted young African American writers.

Sonnet to a Negro in Harlem

Helene Johnson

Negro Head, before 1930.
Nancy Elizabeth Prophet.
Wood, height: 20½ in.
Museum of Art, Rhode
Island School of Design.
Gift of Miss Eleanor B. Green.

You are disdainful° and magnificent—
Your perfect body and your pompous° gait,

Your dark eyes flashing solemnly with hate,
Small wonder that you are incompetent
5   To imitate those whom you so despise—
Your shoulders towering high above the throng,
Your head thrown back in rich, barbaric song,
Palm trees and mangoes stretched before your eyes.
Let others toil and sweat for labor's sake
10   And wring from grasping hands their meed° of gold.
Why urge ahead your supercilious° feet?
Scorn will efface° each footprint that you make.
I love your laughter arrogant and bold.
You are too splendid for this city street.

---

1 *Disdainful* means "full of scorn."
2 *Pompous* means "having an exaggerated sense of self-importance."
10 A *meed* is a well-deserved compensation or payment.
11 *Supercilious* (so͞o′ pər sil′ ē əs) means "haughty" or "arrogant."
12 *Efface* means "to rub out" or "to erase."

Responding to Literature

Personal Response

Which line or lines from the poem are most memorable to you? Why?

——— ANALYZING LITERATURE ———

RECALL AND INTERPRET

1. With what adjectives does the speaker first describe her subject? Why might she use both positive and negative adjectives?
2. In what way is the subject "incompetent"? Whom might the subject "despise"? Why?
3. What physical traits make the subject stand out? How would you characterize the subject based on the description in lines 6–8?
4. What does the speaker say is for others, not the subject, to do? Why?
5. What does the speaker love about her subject? Why might she describe the subject as "too splendid for this city street"?

EVALUATE AND CONNECT

6. What is the speaker's **tone** in this poem (see page R16)? Support your answer with details from the poem.
7. **Connotation** refers to the associations or suggestions that go beyond a word's literal meaning. What might Johnson be suggesting with the phrase "Palm trees and mangoes"?
8. In your opinion, is the subject of Johnson's poem a specific person or a representative for a group of people? Explain.
9. Johnson uses vivid language to convey her subject. What language would you use to describe the person you referred to for the Focus Activity on page 748?
10. Summarize the **theme,** or main idea, of this poem. Which words and phrases from the poem are most effective in supporting the theme?

Scansion

The analysis of a poem to determine its **meter,** or rhythmic pattern, is called **scansion.** When you scan a line of poetry, you notice its beats, or stressed and unstressed syllables, and determine whether or not the beats in a line form a particular pattern.

To scan a line of poetry, mark the stressed syllables with a (′) and unstressed syllables with a (˘). For example:

I love your laughter arrogant and bold
You are too splendid for this city
   street.

1. Copy the first two lines of Johnson's poem and mark the stressed and unstressed syllables.
2. Scan another poem in this theme. Does it have a regular rhythmic pattern or no pattern?

● See **Literary Terms Handbook,** p. R14.

——— EXTENDING YOUR RESPONSE ———

Writing About Literature

Analyze Diction   Write a two- or three-paragraph analysis of Johnson's **diction,** or word choice, in this poem. What does her diction suggest to you about the poem's setting, subject, and theme? How does her diction affect the way you read and understand the poem?

Interdisciplinary Activity

Music: Song of Myself   Johnson creates a vivid image of her subject's "rich, barbaric song." Compose a song that reveals a quality that defines you. Share your song with the class.

📖 **Save your work for your portfolio.**

Visions from Harlem

During the Harlem Renaissance, African American writers weren't the only people who flocked to a little-known district of Manhattan to explore their cultural identity. African American musicians, painters, and sculptors were as much a part of this artistic explosion of the 1920s and 1930s as were poets, novelists, and playwrights. Before long, the intense creative spirit spilled out of Harlem, which had become the heart and soul of African American culture. African American artists across the country began painting, sculpting, drawing, and taking photographs.

Artists of the Harlem Renaissance shared a single goal in their work: to express their identity as both Africans and Americans. However, their approaches varied. Some artists sought to capture details of everyday life, including the tensions of a segregated society. Others wanted to portray the dignity and independence of their people. Still other African American artists chose to focus on elements of folklore in their art.

The Harlem Renaissance marked the first time that many African American artists could work professionally at their craft. Foundations offered private funding to African American artists. Public art projects employed many artists during the Great Depression of the 1930s. As a result, African Americans were able to infuse America's cultural landscape with their vitality and their dreams.

Lift Every Voice and Sing or *The Harp*, 1939. Augusta Savage. Plaster with black paint finish, height: 9 ft. The Beinecke Rare Book and Manuscript Library, Yale University. Photograph by Carl van Vechten.

Self Portrait, 1934. Malvin Gray Johnson. Oil on canvas, mounted on canvas, 38½ x 30 in. National Museum of American Art, Smithsonian Institution, Washington, DC.

Activity

Work with a small group of classmates to research a Harlem Renaissance artist such as Jacob Lawrence, Aaron Douglas, Palmer Hayden, Malvin Gray Johnson, Hale Woodruff, or Augusta Savage. Plan a brief presentation that includes music from the time or a dramatic reading about the artist.

Before You Read

Storm Ending and November Cotton Flower

Meet Jean Toomer

Jean Toomer wrote only one major work, but it has been called "the most impressive product" of the Harlem Renaissance. Published in 1923, this book, *Cane,* is an experimental mixture of drama, prose, and poetry that includes the two poems you are about to read. In *Cane,* Toomer describes African American culture in both the rural South and the industrial North using rich, musical language.

Toomer was born in Washington, D.C., and attended college in several parts of the country. He taught school in Georgia, where he absorbed the sights and sounds that went into *Cane.* After settling in Harlem and contributing to a variety of literary journals, Toomer turned his interests to religion and philosophy, and he wrote a number of essays on these subjects. Ultimately, Toomer became a Quaker and lived his last years as a recluse.

Today, Toomer is recognized as one of the most talented figures of the Harlem Renaissance for his experimental style and his success in capturing both southern culture and the spiritual confusion experienced by many of his generation.

❝I was neither white nor black, but simply an American.❞

—Toomer

Jean Toomer was born in 1894 and died in 1967.

FOCUS ACTIVITY

What thoughts and images does the word *flower* bring to your mind?

FREEWRITE Write for two or three minutes about the word *flower.* Begin with the first image that forms in your mind and let your ideas flow.

SETTING A PURPOSE Read to discover how one poet uses images of flowers.

BACKGROUND

Did You Know?

For two months in the summer of 1921, Jean Toomer served as acting head of an agricultural school in Georgia. Traditionally, Georgia had depended heavily on cotton as a major crop, but during the 1920s, the state's cotton crop was devastated by boll weevils—destructive insects that attack cotton plants. Because so much of the cotton crop was destroyed, many farmers were ruined financially, and agricultural workers, many of them African American, were forced to migrate to the North in search of employment.

Boll weevil

Storm Ending

Jean Toomer

Thunder blossoms gorgeously above our heads,
Great, hollow, bell-like flowers,
Rumbling in the wind,
Stretching clappers to strike our ears . .
Full-lipped flowers
Bitten by the sun
Bleeding rain
Dripping rain like golden honey—
And the sweet earth flying from the thunder.

Landscape, 1914. Henry Ossawa Tanner. Oil on artist's board. Private collection.
Courtesy The Sheldon Ross Gallery, Birmingham, MI.

Sharecropper Boy, 1938. Hale Aspacio Woodruff. Oil on canvas, 20 x 15 in. The Harmon and Harriet Kelley Foundation for the Arts, San Antonio, TX. What characteristics do you find in this young man's face that help you understand the point of the poem? Explain.

November Cotton Flower

Jean Toomer ∾

Boll weevil's coming, and the winter's cold,
Made cotton stalks look rusty, seasons old,
And cotton, scarce as any southern snow,
Was vanishing; the branch,° so pinched and slow,
5 Failed in its function as the autumn rake;
Drought fighting soil had caused the soil to take
All water from the streams; dead birds were found
In wells a hundred feet below the ground—
Such was the season when the flower bloomed.
10 Old folks were startled, and it soon assumed
Significance. Superstition saw
Something it had never seen before:
Brown eyes that loved without a trace of fear,
Beauty so sudden for that time of year.

---

4 Here, *branch* means "creek" or "stream."

Responding to Literature

Personal Response

Which images from these poems do you find most surprising or unexpected? Why?

ANALYZING LITERATURE

Storm Ending

RECALL AND INTERPRET

1. To what does Toomer compare thunder in "Storm Ending"? What does this comparison suggest about his attitude toward the storm?
2. How does the earth respond to the thunder? Why might Toomer have chosen this response for the earth?

EVALUATE AND CONNECT

3. This poem is rich in **sensory details**—details that appeal to one or more of the five senses. How does the poem differ from a scientific description of a storm?
4. How does your attitude toward thunderstorms compare with those expressed in the poem? Explain.

November Cotton Flower

RECALL AND INTERPRET

5. What two things, according to lines 1–2, make the cotton look rusty? What happens to the cotton in lines 3–4?
6. What event startles "old folks"? Why might the event take on significance?
7. What two things has "Superstition" never seen before? What do these two things suggest about the effects of the sudden bloom on most people? What might the cotton flower symbolize? Explain.

EVALUATE AND CONNECT

8. The poem is a **Petrarchan sonnet,** a verse form consisting of an eight-line section followed by a six-line section. What change in thinking takes place from the first section to the second? Is the change significant? Explain.

EXTENDING YOUR RESPONSE

Interdisciplinary Activity

Art: Budding Responses   In these poems, Jean Toomer uses the images of flowers. Two visual artists who were captivated by flowers were Vincent van Gogh and Georgia O'Keeffe. Look for examples of their images of flowers and use them for inspiration to paint or draw a picture of a flower that could illustrate the poem "Storm Ending."

Creative Writing

Shall I Compare Thee?   Using your response to the Focus Activity on page 752, write a poem comparing a flower with something very different from a flower. Try to include details that appeal to at least two senses.

Save your work for your portfolio.

Before You Read

A black man talks of reaping and Any Human to Another

Meet Arna Bontemps

Proud of his heritage, Arna Bontemps (bän täm′) was disappointed by the lack of information on the history of African Americans available at his childhood school and his local library. As a writer, he spent much of his life filling the gaps in traditional accounts of African American history and literature.

Bontemps was born in Louisiana and grew up in California. In 1923, at the height of the Harlem Renaissance, Bontemps came to New York. He soon won recognition for his poetry and for his first novel, *God Sends Sunday*. He also began writing literature for children.

In 1943 Bontemps became the librarian at Fisk University in Nashville, Tennessee, where he devoted himself to recording the history of African Americans. He said that his book *The Story of the Negro* "consists mainly of things I learned after I left school that I wish I had known much earlier." Bontemps went on to write more than twenty-five books, including *The Harlem Renaissance Remembered* and *Golden Slippers*, the first children's anthology of African American poetry.

"How dare anyone, parent, schoolteacher, or merely literary critic, tell me not to act colored?"

—Bontemps

Arna Bontemps was born in 1902 and died in 1973.

Meet Countee Cullen

Countee Cullen's life was marked by contradictions. As a writer, he was known for speaking out against poetry that was "racial," yet he wrote forcefully about racial injustice. A twentieth-century American, he turned to highly structured and traditional verse forms from the European past. Although Cullen's early work won much praise, he received little recognition after he reached his thirties.

Cullen grew up and went to school in New York City. While a graduate student at Harvard University, he studied and admired traditional European poetic forms. He modeled his poetry after the work of John Keats, an English Romantic poet. Still, James Weldon Johnson noted that "the best of his poetry is motivated by race." Before Cullen had finished college, his first book of poems, *Color*, was published and received critical acclaim.

Cullen published several collections of poetry after *Color*, but his literary reputation declined gradually. In his thirties he began teaching junior high school in New York City, a job that he held until his death.

"I find that I am actuated by a strong sense of race consciousness."

—Cullen

Countee Cullen was born in 1903 and died in 1946.

FOCUS ACTIVITY

African American writer James Baldwin, who was once a student of Countee Cullen, wrote, "Color is not a human or a personal reality; it is a political reality."

DISCUSS With a group of students, discuss the meaning of this quotation. Do you agree or disagree with Baldwin?

SETTING A PURPOSE Read to discover how two poets view race and human relationships.

BACKGROUND

Literary Purposes

The Harlem Renaissance, like any literary movement, was not a club whose members all agreed. It was a collection of passionate artists who often disagreed on questions of style, content, and literary purpose. Many writers then and later criticized Countee Cullen for his use of conservative, "white" forms and themes. They felt that in his attempt to keep poetry colorblind, Cullen was betraying African Americans. Cullen answered these writers in a poem, "To Certain Critics," in which he wrote:

> For never shall the clan
> Confine my singing to its ways
> Beyond the ways of man.
> . . . . .
> How shall the shepherd heart then thrill
> To only the darker lamb?

Arna Bontemps, on the other hand, saw color-blind writing as neither possible nor desirable. He once wrote that "the shedding" of African American culture "is not only impossible but unthinkable."

A Collaboration

Bontemps and Cullen worked together in the mid-1940s to create a play based on *God Sends Sunday,* a novel by Bontemps. They called the play *St. Louis Woman.* Some African American critics objected to the play because it focused on African Americans living in poverty. Cullen was quite hurt by these criticisms. He never saw the play produced because he died suddenly, shortly before the play opened.

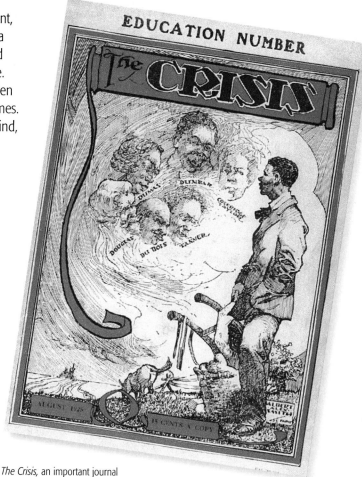

The Crisis, an important journal of the Harlem Renaissance.

Share Croppers, c. 1941. Robert Gwathmey. Watercolor, 45 x 32.4 cm. ©Estate of Robert Gwathmey/Licensed by VAGA, New York/San Diego Museum of Art. Museum purchase with funds provided by Mrs. Leon D. Bonnet.

A black man talks of reaping

Arna Bontemps ∿

I have sown beside all waters in my day.
I planted deep, within my heart the fear
that wind or fowl would take the grain away.
I planted safe against this stark, lean year.

5   I scattered seed enough to plant the land
in rows from Canada to Mexico
but for my reaping only what the hand
can hold at once is all that I can show.

Yet what I sowed and what the orchard yields
10   my brother's sons are gathering stalk and root;
small wonder then my children glean° in fields
they have not sown, and feed on bitter fruit.

---

11 *Glean* means "to gather grain left on a field after reaping."

Any Human to Another

Countee Cullen

Civilization is a method of living, an attitude of equal respect for all men. From the series *Great Ideas of Western Man,* 1955. George Giusti. India ink and gouache on paper sheet, 24⅞ x 18⁵⁄₁₆ in. National Museum of American Art, Smithsonian Institution, Washington, DC. In your opinion, which stanza from "Any Human to Another" does this painting best illustrate? Cite details from the painting and the poem to explain your response.

The ills I sorrow at
Not me alone
Like an arrow,
Pierce to the marrow,
5   Through the fat
And past the bone.

Your grief and mine
Must intertwine
Like sea and river,
10   Be fused and mingle,
Diverse yet single,
Forever and forever.

Let no man be so proud
And confident,
15   To think he is allowed
A little tent
Pitched in a meadow
Of sun and shadow
All his little own.

20   Joy may be shy, unique,
Friendly to a few,
Sorrow never scorned to speak
To any who
Were false or true.

25   Your every grief
Like a blade
Shining and unsheathed°
Must strike me down.
Of bitter aloes° wreathed,
30   My sorrow must be laid
On your head like a crown.

---

27 *Unsheathed* means "removed from a protective case."
29 *Aloes* refers to the spiny leaves of the aloe plant, whose juices are used to make a bitter medicine.

Responding to Literature

Personal Response

Which poem affected you more? Explain your choice.

——— ANALYZING LITERATURE ———

A black man talks of reaping

RECALL AND INTERPRET

1. What is the work done by the speaker in the poem? How would you explain the fears and concerns expressed in the first stanza?
2. Who are "my brother's sons," and what are they doing? Why, in your opinion, are they able to act in such a way?
3. What does the speaker mean by "my children glean in fields they have not sown"? What might be the "bitter fruit" the children feed on? Explain.

EVALUATE AND CONNECT

4. In this poem, Bontemps uses **end rhyme** (see page R13). What ideas might Bontemps be trying to emphasize through his use of rhyme?
5. How, in your opinion, might this poem illustrate the Baldwin quote you read in the Focus Activity on page 757?
6. In the poem, some people gain from the work of others. Is it fair to benefit from the labor of others? Explain.

Any Human to Another

RECALL AND INTERPRET

7. A **simile** is a comparison that uses words such as *like* or *as*. What similes does the writer use in the first and second stanzas? What ideas do they support?
8. What visual image does the poet use in the third stanza? What warning is implied here?
9. What qualities are contrasted in the two final stanzas? What images are attributed to each quality? Why, in your opinion, might Cullen have selected those particular images?
10. Whom does the speaker address? Why does the speaker say that his grief must be mixed with that of his audience?

EVALUATE AND CONNECT

11. In this poem, Cullen **personifies,** or gives human attributes to, the emotions of joy and sorrow. What might be the purpose of this personification?
12. Do you agree with the argument that the speaker makes? Why or why not? To which individuals or groups might you address this poem today?

Literary ELEMENTS

Stanza

A **stanza** is a group of lines that form a unit in a poem. The stanzas in a poem are separated by white space and are similar in structure, often having the same number of lines, **meter,** and **rhyme scheme** (see pages R9 and R13). A stanza usually focuses on a single idea, much like a paragraph does, and each new stanza typically has a new focus.

1. Look at "A black man talks of reaping." How many stanzas does it have? How many lines are in each stanza? What idea is presented in each stanza?

2. Cullen's "Any Human to Another" uses a freer type of stanza form than that used in Bontemps's "A black man talks of reaping." In what ways do the stanzas in Cullen's poem reflect the definition given above? How do they differ?

3. What effect does each poet create through his choice of stanza form?

● See **Literary Terms Handbook,** p. R15.

LITERATURE AND WRITING

Writing About Literature

Extended Metaphor   The poem "A black man talks of reaping" includes an **extended metaphor,** a metaphor that is developed over more than one line. The metaphor is implied instead of stated directly. What comparison is the poet making in this poem? Write two or three paragraphs stating what the metaphor is and how it is extended through the poem.

Creative Writing

Responding Through Poetry   Both poets wrote their poems in response to events and attitudes of the time. Think of an event or an issue that troubles you today. Write a poem responding to the topic. Include your personal thoughts and hopes, but also consider whether you plan to speak for just yourself or for a group of people. If you wish, share your finished poem with your class.

EXTENDING YOUR RESPONSE

Literature Groups

What's in a Name?   Bontemps has been called "the conscience of his era." Judging from "A black man talks of reaping," does the name fit Bontemps? Based on "Any Human to Another," do you think Cullen should share this title? Discuss these questions with your group. Then present the results of your discussion to the class.

Learning for Life

Interview Questions   Suppose that you are a reporter and you have the opportunity to interview Bontemps or Cullen about their poems. Choose the author you'd most like to interview, and prepare a list of questions. If possible, research the answers to your questions. Then share your findings with the class.

Interdisciplinary Activity

Music: Companion Piece   People have always used music to help tell their stories. Research one type of music, such as blues or folk music, and select a song that would be a good companion piece to one of the poems.

Reading Further

If you enjoyed these poems, you might try this collection:
The Lost Zoo, by Countee Cullen, a book for children that contains Cullen's poems with illustrations by Brian Pinkney.

📖 **Save your work for your portfolio.**

Creative Writing: Poem

Many of the poems you have read in this theme involve places or ideas that inspire deep affection or desire. Langston Hughes's expression of cultural hope and pride is evident in "The Negro Speaks of Rivers," as is Claude McKay's intense longing for the "dewy dawns, and mystical blue skies" of his native Jamaica in his poem "The Tropics in New York." What places or ideas inspire you? **In this workshop, you will write a poem about a place or idea that has influenced or affected you.**

● As you write your poem, refer to the **Writing Handbook,** pp. R62–R77.

The Writing Process

PREWRITING

PREWRITING TIP
You will be presenting your poem to others, so be sure to write about only those feelings, places, and ideas you are willing to share.

Explore ideas
Here are some suggestions for helping you find a subject for your poem.

● Skim the poems in Theme 8. Do any of the places or ideas in these poems remind you of something you want to write about?

● Think of a place or idea that intrigues you. Could you write about a childhood getaway place, an idea or feeling inspired by a trip, or a holiday with family or friends?

Explore your responses
Sometimes the ideas and feelings expressed in a poem are so similar to yours that you respond to the poem immediately. That poem might then inspire you to write on a similar topic or in a similar style. Choose a poem from this theme that especially appealed to you. In a chart like the one begun here, write the idea or place described in the poem and the poet's response to it. Then record connections the poem has to your life.

STUDENT MODEL

Poem	"My City"
Idea or Place	Manhattan
Poet's Response	Poet loves the sights, sounds, smells, and crowds
My Response	Reminds me of when I visit my uncle in Chicago. The bustling people downtown always interest me.

Choose your purpose and audience

Your purpose is to write a poem that expresses your feelings about a place or idea you choose. Think of friends or relatives who might enjoy your writing.

Freewrite about your place or idea

Most poems are concise—they are shorter than stories or essays. However, this doesn't mean that poets have little to say about their subject. To find the most precise, exciting words and phrases, poets usually draw from a large store of material. You can create a store of material for yourself by freewriting about your topic. The springboards below can help get you started.

- What specific images come to mind when you think about the place? What sights, sounds, and smells do you remember most?
- Do you associate certain feelings or ideas with the place? What are they?
- What actions can be associated with this place? What reactions do they evoke in you?

Exciting memories of visiting my uncle in Chicago—buildings are so big, sleek and shiny—boat trip on the river was amazing—shops and restaurants, inviting smells and cozy tables, majestic fountains with beautiful flowers nearby. Lake Michigan blue and turbulent, ominous, yet inviting—everything suggests movement and importance—boats and people—everyone is going somewhere—even the wind has important places to go and can't stay long.

After you finish your freewriting, underline main ideas, descriptions, or feelings you might want to include in your writing. Then plan your poem.

Make a plan

To plan your poem, ask yourself questions about possible themes, tone, and structure. Refer to the ideas you generated while prewriting, as the student did in the model below.

STUDENT MODEL

1. What ideas or feelings do I most want to express?

   Excitement, beauty, and fast pace of life in a big city.

2. What tone best expresses these feelings and ideas? Do I want my poem to sound wishful? anxious? overwhelmed?

   I'm excited and very much impressed, but also slightly overwhelmed at the size and speed of everything around me.

3. What form will I use for my poem? Do I prefer a strict or loose form? Do I want to use regular rhythm? How about rhyme?

   I think I can best express myself in a loose form, without regular rhythm or rhyme.

DRAFTING

DRAFTING TIP

Remember that a poem should have a distinctive sound as well as vivid words and images. As you write, think about how your poem sounds and if the sound supports the meaning.

Write your draft

To begin writing your draft, choose a word, an image, or a description from your prewriting that captures your impressions. Then start drafting your poem around it. For example, the student who decided to write about visiting the city of Chicago was impressed with the visual impact of the buildings, the lake, and the people.

STUDENT MODEL

Sleek and sophisticated,
City of strength and fortune.
Clad in stone and steel and glass,
Powerful sentries stand guard along the
    water's edge.
Antennas point like swords to the sky to
    bear witness and to
Secure a rightful place of honor.
Graceful and moving,
Boats persevere through calm or violently
    rocking waters,
Even the wind cannot stop for long.

REVISING

REVISING TIP

Take out phrases or images you thought were clever when you wrote them but that no longer appeal to you. Revise the poem so that it really says what *you* want it to say.

Get an audience reaction

Don't hand your poem to anyone yet. Read it aloud to a friend and ask for reactions based on the **Questions for Revising.** Then make any needed changes.

QUESTIONS FOR REVISING

☑ What message or feeling comes across?
☑ Have I used images, metaphors, and similes effectively?
☑ Where can I use more precise wording?
☑ Where might I add details?
☑ Are the rhythm and form appropriate?
☑ Is anything confusing or unclear?

STUDENT MODEL

Sleek and sophisticated,
overwhelming
City of strength and fortune.
With armament of
~~Clad in~~ stone and steel and glass,
~~Powerful~~ sentries stand guard along the water's edge.
aloft
Antennas point like swords ~~to the sky~~ to bear witness and to
Secure a rightful place of honor.

EDITING/PROOFREADING

Poets sometimes ignore traditional rules of grammar, usage, mechanics, and spelling to send a specific message or to create a desired tone in their work. If you choose to do so, you will still need to check over your work to make sure you haven't included unintentional errors that could confuse your readers. Use the **Proofreading Checklist** on the inside back cover of this book to check for unintentional errors.

Grammar Hint

You might choose to use parallel structure to state ideas that are equally important. Note, for example, the parallelism in lines from the student model. Both lines start with a plural noun followed by a plural verb:

Sentries stand guard along the water's edge,

With armament of stone and steel and glass.

Antennas point like swords aloft to bear witness and to

Secure a rightful place of honor.

STUDENT MODEL

Boats persevere ~~threw~~ through calm or ~~violently rocking~~ turbulent waters,

Always courageous, never tentative.

People, too, forge ahead, ~~determined,~~ around fountains and flowers. . . .

PUBLISHING/PRESENTING

If you are presenting your poem in written form, think about adding an illustration. You might also consider submitting your poem to a literary magazine.

PRESENTING TIP

Pay special attention to the appearance of your poem—its shape adds to its meaning. Where should the lines break? Which lines should be indented?

Reflecting

Use your journal to help you reflect on writing your poem. What did you find most difficult about writing this poem? What did you enjoy most? How has writing a poem changed your appreciation of the poems you have read? Then set some goals for your next piece of writing. How will you profit from what you've learned?

 Save your work for your portfolio.

Unit Wrap-Up

PERSONAL RESPONSE

1. Which selections would you like to discuss with someone a generation older than you are? Explain.
2. As a result of your work in this unit, how would you evaluate the following statements?
   - Literature is influenced by important events.
   - Literature opens new ways for people of each era to explore their own times.
   - Discussing poetry with a group is an aid to interpreting writers' ideas.

ANALYZING LITERATURE

What ideas do you think were most important in shaping the new directions that Americans took during the early decades of the twentieth century? Choose one concept, such as one of the following:
   - personal freedom
   - interaction among different peoples
   - increasing urbanization
   - attacking biases

Briefly define the concept you chose, and identify two or three selections that contain examples of the concept. Then explain how each selection increased your awareness and understanding of the concept.

EVALUATE AND SET GOALS

Evaluate

1. What did you contribute to your class's overall understanding of the issues in this unit?
2. What was most difficult for you in this unit? Why?
   - Explain why you found a particular selection or assignment to be difficult.
   - How did you handle the difficulty?
   - Do you expect to find the same difficulty with similar material? Why or why not?
3. How would you assess your work in this unit using the following scale? Give at least two reasons for your assessment.
   4 = outstanding   **3** = good   **2** = fair   **1** = weak
4. If you had another week to work on this unit, what would you hope to learn? Which skills would you hope to strengthen?

Set Goals

1. Set a goal for the next unit. Focus on improving a skill, such as listening or evaluating statements.
2. Discuss your goal with your teacher.
3. Plan steps to achieve your goal.
4. Plan checkpoints at which you can judge your work.
5. Think of ways to evaluate your finished work.

📂 BUILD YOUR PORTFOLIO_____

Select   Choose pieces of writing you completed for this unit and add them to your portfolio. Use these questions to help you make your selection:
   - Which was the most enjoyable for you?
   - Which represents your best work?
   - Which piece of writing contains ideas or information that you are most interested in researching further?

Reflect   Write a few notes to accompany the selections you have made for your portfolio. Use these questions to guide you:
   - What are the piece's strengths and weaknesses?
   - What did working on the piece teach you?
   - How would you revise the piece today?

Reading on Your Own

If you have enjoyed the literature in this unit, you might also be interested in the following books.

Their Eyes Were Watching God

by Zora Neale Hurston In Hurston's famous novel of the 1930s, Janie Crawford, a strong and self-reliant African American woman, makes a journey back to her roots in search of her own identity.

The Great Gatsby

by F. Scott Fitzgerald The "roaring 1920s" come to life in this famous story of Jay Gatsby, a self-made man, and the woman he has loved for years.

Having Our Say:
The Delaney Sisters' First 100 Years

by Sarah and A. Elizabeth Delaney Two feisty women who lived to be more than a century old tell their life stories. They describe the social history of the twentieth century as they witnessed and enjoyed it.

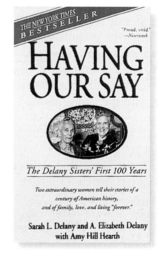

Collected Poems

by Edna St. Vincent Millay; Norma Millay, editor The definitive collection of Millay's poetry, this volume was compiled by Millay's sister after the poet's death. Published in 1957, the collection continues to appeal to today's readers. One reviewer of this book refers to the "grace and depth" and "stunning beauty" of Millay's poetry.

Standardized Test Practice

The passage below is followed by seven questions based on its content. Select the best answer and write the corresponding letter on your paper.

NATURAL SCIENCE: This passage is adapted from Stephen Hawking's *The Illustrated Brief History of Time* (©1988 and 1996 by Stephen Hawking).

Our present ideas about the motion of bodies date back to Galileo and Newton. Before them people believed Aristotle, who said that the natural state of a body was to be
5 at rest and that it moved only if driven by a force or impulse. It followed that a heavy body should fall faster than a light one, because it would have a greater pull toward the earth.

The Aristotelian tradition also held that
10 one could work out all the laws that govern the universe by pure thought: it was not necessary to check by observation. So no one until Galileo bothered to see whether bodies of different weight did in fact fall at different
15 speeds. It is said that Galileo demonstrated that Aristotle's belief was false by dropping weights from the leaning tower of Pisa. The story is almost certainly untrue, but Galileo did do something equivalent: he rolled balls
20 of different weights down a smooth slope. The situation is similar to that of heavy bodies falling vertically, but it is easier to observe because the speeds are lesser. Galileo's measurements indicated that each body
25 increased its speed at the same rate, no matter what its weight. For example, if a ball is released on a slope that drops by one meter for every ten meters of length, the ball will travel down the slope at a speed of about one
30 meter per second after one second, two meters per second after two seconds, and so on, however heavy the ball. Of course a lead weight would fall faster than a feather, but that is only because a feather is slowed by air
35 resistance. If one drops two bodies that don't have much air resistance, such as two different lead weights, they fall at the same rate. On the moon, where there is no air to slow things down, the astronaut David R. Scott
40 performed the feather and lead weight

experiment and found that indeed they did hit the ground at the same time.

Galileo's measurements were used by Newton as the basis of his laws of motion. In
45 Galileo's experiments, as a body rolled down the slope it was always acted on by the same force (its weight), and the effect was to make it constantly increase its speed. This showed that the real effect of a force is always to change the
50 speed of a body, rather than just to set it moving, as was previously thought. It also meant that whenever a body is not acted on by any force, it will keep on moving in a straight line at the same speed. This idea was first stated
55 explicitly in Newton's *Principia Mathematica*, published in 1687, and is known as Newton's first law. What happens to a body when a force does act on it is given by Newton's second law. This states that the body will accelerate, or
60 change its speed, at a rate that is proportional to the force. (For example, the acceleration is twice as great if the force is twice as great.) The acceleration is also smaller the greater the mass (or quantity of matter) of the body. (The
65 same force acting on a body of twice the mass will produce half the acceleration.) A familiar example is provided by a car: the more powerful the engine, the greater the acceleration, but the heavier the car, the smaller the accelera-
70 tion for the same engine. In addition to his laws of motion, Newton discovered a law to describe the force of gravity, which states that every body attracts every other body with a force that is proportional to the mass of each
75 body. Thus the force between two bodies would be twice as strong if one of the bodies (say, body A) had its mass doubled. This is what you might expect because one could think of the new body A as being made of two
80 bodies with the original mass. Each would attract body B with the original force. Thus the total force between A and B would be twice the original force. And if, say, one of the bodies had twice the mass, and the other had

85 three times the mass, then the force would be six times as strong. One can now see why all bodies fall at the same rate: a body of twice the weight will have twice the force of gravity pulling it down, but it will also have twice the
90 mass. According to Newton's second law, these two effects will exactly cancel each other, so the acceleration will be the same in all cases.

1. According to the passage, Galileo rolled balls of different weight down a smooth slope in order to:

   A. show that a body in motion will continue moving.
   B. measure the distance the balls traveled.
   C. compare the speed of the balls.
   D. demonstrate the force of gravity.

2. As it is used in line 55, the word *explicitly* most nearly means:

   F. definitively.
   G. scientifically.
   H. radically.
   J. vaguely.

3. According to the passage, Galileo determined that whenever a body is not acted on by another force, the body will:

   A. stop moving.
   B. decelerate and move at a slower speed.
   C. accelerate to move at a faster speed.
   D. continue to move at the current speed.

4. According to the passage, all of the following are involved in Newton's second law EXCEPT:

   F. proportional rate.
   G. force.
   H. air resistance.
   J. acceleration.

5. The passage suggests that one feature of the moon is that the moon:

   A. has no gravity.
   B. is a terrible place to perform experiments.
   C. has a large amount of air resistance.
   D. has no atmosphere to create air resistance.

6. One of the main observations made in the second paragraph (lines 9–42) is that:

   F. the natural state of a body is at rest.
   G. no one can tell if bodies of different weight fall at different times.
   H. Galileo dropped weights from the leaning tower of Pisa to prove Aristotle's theory.
   J. according to Aristotle, it was not necessary to prove the laws that govern the universe by observation.

7. How does the example of a car (lines 66–70) function in the passage?

   A. It distinguishes between heavy cars and lighter cars.
   B. It provides an example of Newton's second law in everyday terms.
   C. It makes the point that cars with bigger engines accelerate faster.
   D. It revises the theory that a heavy car will move more quickly.

STOP

Builders, 1980. Jacob Lawrence. Gouache on paper, 34¼ x 25⅝ in. SAFECO Insurance Company, Seattle, WA. Courtesy of the artist and the Francine Seders Gallery, Seattle, WA.

UNIT ❖ SIX

Midcentury Voices

1930–1960

"America is woven of many strands. I would recognize them and let it remain. . . . Our fate is to become one and yet many. This is not prophecy, but description."

—Ralph Ellison

Theme 9
Personal Discoveries

Theme 10
Acting on an Idea

Setting the Scene

"Everybody Ought to Be Rich," declared a Ladies' Home Journal *article in 1929. The soaring stock market of the time symbolized the nation's prosperity, a prosperity in which anyone with a little money to invest could share. Then, on October 29, came the Great Crash. According to the* New York Times: *"It came with a speed and ferocity that left men dazed. The bottom simply fell out of the [stock] market. From all over the country a torrent of selling orders poured onto the floor of the Stock Exchange and there were no buying orders to meet it. . . . Within a few moments the ticker service was hopelessly swamped and from then on no one knew what was really happening."*

The Great Crash was one of the most dramatic moments in an evolving global economic crisis—a crisis that would devastate the economy, the nation, and people's lives for longer than anyone could imagine.

Unemployment forced many families to become migrant workers. Photograph by Dorothea Lange.

U.S.A.

1932
Franklin Roosevelt is elected to the first of his four terms as president

The Social Security Act is passed
1936
Workers in Flint, Michigan, auto plants carry out a successful forty-four-day sit-down strike

1941
United States formally enters World War II

Roosevelt dies; Harry Truman becomes president

1930   **1935**   **1940**   **1945**

1931
Japanese seize Manchuria

1933
Hitler begins persecutions that result in the deaths of 6 million Jews and 2 million others

1936
Spanish Civil War breaks out

1939
Germany invades Poland, igniting World War II in Europe

Germany surrenders, May 8; Japan surrenders, September 2

World

History of the Time

Depression and New Deal

After the crash, the economic depression—a term chosen by President Herbert Hoover as less frightening than *panic* or *crisis*—steadily worsened. From 1929 to 1932, approximately 9,000 banks closed, 100,000 businesses failed, and 12 million people lost their jobs—and the numbers were still climbing. The unemployed filled city streets, breadlines, and soup kitchens.

Franklin Delano Roosevelt

With the economy crumbling, voters rejected Hoover's bid for a second term in 1932 and elected Franklin Delano Roosevelt, who promised "a new deal for the American people." Roosevelt's "alphabet agencies" poured out of the federal government, in hopes of pulling the nation out of its economic crisis. These included programs such as the Works Progress Administration (WPA) and the Civilian Conservation Corps (CCC), formed to provide emergency financial aid and temporary jobs. Besides easing the suffering caused by the depression, these agencies returned hope to people and established a larger role for the federal government in promoting prosperity.

World War II

As the depression of the 1930s worsened, some countries turned to menacing dictators for leadership: Benito Mussolini in Italy, Adolf Hitler in Germany, and a military government in Japan. Soon Japanese troops invaded China, and Hitler's army stormed through Europe. Then, on December 7, 1941, Japanese bombers attacked an American naval base at Pearl Harbor, Hawaii. America immediately went to war, joining the Allies, which included Great Britain and the Soviet Union.

Four years and some 45 to 50 million deaths later, peace returned to the world. Germany surrendered in May 1945. Japan surrendered four months later, after the United States dropped atomic bombs on the Japanese cities of Hiroshima and Nagasaki.

Progress and Anxiety

The years after World War II brought changes to the United States. Many Americans began to challenge racial discrimination at home. The devastation in Europe allowed American industries to dominate world markets and the wartime economic boom continued throughout the 1950s.

However, the United States and the Soviet Union became tense rivals in a worldwide struggle for power—a conflict that became known as the cold war. The two world powers never went to war against each other, but they continued developing and stockpiling nuclear weapons. An anxious world now lived under a new cloud—the mushroom cloud of the atomic age.

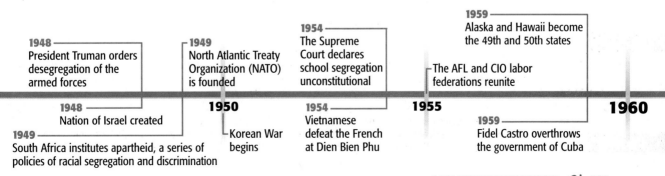

1948 — President Truman orders desegregation of the armed forces

1948 — Nation of Israel created

1949 — South Africa institutes apartheid, a series of policies of racial segregation and discrimination

1949 — North Atlantic Treaty Organization (NATO) is founded

1950

Korean War begins

1954 — The Supreme Court declares school segregation unconstitutional

1954 — Vietnamese defeat the French at Dien Bien Phu

1959 — Alaska and Hawaii become the 49th and 50th states

The AFL and CIO labor federations reunite

1955

1959 — Fidel Castro overthrows the government of Cuba

1960

Life of the Time

People are talking about

Broadcasts By 1940 about eighty percent of American households include radios. Listeners get to know President Roosevelt through his "fireside chats." In 1938 radio listeners fill the streets in panic, fearing that Martians are invading the earth, as Orson Welles broadcasts a very believable performance of H. G. Wells's *War of the Worlds*. After World War II, more and more families have a new form of entertainment in their living rooms—television. ▶

◀ The Road to Suburbia
America was the only nation "that ever went to the poorhouse in an automobile," notes humorist Will Rogers during the depression. The love of cars, combined with government subsidies for roads and new housing, leads to a postwar construction boom. Homes, malls, and motels engulf cities. Suddenly much of America becomes suburban.

Brown v. Board of Education Civil Rights activists, led by lawyer Thurgood Marshall, win a dramatic victory in 1954. The Supreme Court rules that "Separate educational facilities are inherently unequal," and, in a follow-up ruling, that schools should desegregate "with all deliberate speed." While more than 500 school districts obey quietly and quickly, more than seventy-five percent of southern schools are still segregated in 1965.

Thurgood Marshall (center), 1954.

Firsts

- Frances Perkins becomes Secretary of Labor—the first female cabinet member. (1933)
- Chuck Yeager flies the first airplane that breaks the sound barrier. (1947)
- Disneyland, the first theme park, opens. (1955)

U.S.A.

1931
The "Star Spangled Banner" becomes national anthem

1936
African American Jesse Owens wins four gold medals in Berlin Olympics

1937
Amelia Earhart disappears while attempting to fly across the Atlantic Ocean

1944
Aaron Copland's *Appalachian Spring* ballet opens, danced by Martha Graham and company

1930   **1935**   **1940**   **1945**

World

1931
The first trans-African railroad is completed

1934
In Germany, Wernher von Braun launches experimental rockets

1938
Geologists discover significant reserves of oil in Saudi Arabia; In Hungary, Ladislao and George Biró patent a ballpoint pen

Food & Fashion

Jean Harlow

- Some women dye their hair during the 1930s, attempting to copy the look of "platinum blonde bombshell" Jean Harlow and other movie stars. ▶

- Young "hepcats" show off their zoot suits in the 1940s, featuring thigh-length jackets with padded shoulders and baggy pants with narrow cuffs.

- With silk stockings unavailable and factory jobs common, wartime women turn to wearing slacks. ▶

- The drive for greater convenience continues to shape eating habits. Stores begin selling sliced bread in 1930 and TV dinners in 1953.

- Meat consumption increases to its highest level since 1909. Many more people can afford meat thanks to the wartime economic boom.

Women railroad mechanics, 1942.

Arts & Entertainment

Duke Ellington (at piano) and his orchestra.

- In the 1950s, television cuts into the appeal of movies, and theater attendance drops by half between 1948 and 1955.

◀ America's varied voices are heard through its music—swing tunes by Duke Ellington, bebop jazz by Charlie Parker, nightclub crooning by Frank Sinatra, country ballads by Hank Williams, and rock and roll by Chuck Berry and Elvis Presley.

- Artists stirred by the drama of real life and funded by a handful of New Deal programs use a documentary approach that influences every medium. Government-sponsored photographs, with their stark, vivid images of the depression, visually define the period for most Americans.

Amusements

- In 1947 Jackie Robinson becomes the major leagues' first African American player in the twentieth century.

- Critics condemn the acrobatic jitterbug of the 1930s as too wild for polite dancers. By 1943 it is so popular that *Life* magazine proclaims it "the true national folk dance."

1947
Levittown, the first mass-produced housing development, is started on Long Island, NY

Ralph Bunche becomes the first African American to win the Nobel Peace Prize

1951
The U.S. Census Bureau begins using UNIVAC, the first commercially available computer

1959
Frank Lloyd Wright's spiral building for the Guggenheim Museum opens in New York City

1946
In Italy, women gain the right to vote

1950

1953
Mountain climbers Edmund Hillary, New Zealand, and Tenzing Norgay, Nepal, conquer Mt. Everest in Nepal

1955

1959
Sirimavo Bandaranaike of Ceylon (Sri Lanka) becomes world's first woman prime minister

1960

Literature of the Time

PEOPLE ARE READING . . .

Paperbacks   Poverty in the 1930s and war shortages in the 1940s encourage publishers to shift toward smaller, less expensive soft-covered books. The public loves them, and the inexpensive paperback revolutionizes American reading habits. One paperpack, Dr. Benjamin Spock's *Baby and Child Care*, outsells every other book in American history—except the Bible.

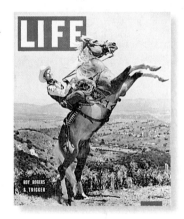

◄ **New Magazines**   New uses of technology stimulate new magazines. The powerful photographic images of the depression spur the founding of two magazines devoted to real-life photographs—*Life* (1936) and *Look* (1937). The advent of TV is followed in 1953 by the publication of *TV Guide*, which quickly becomes the most successful new periodical of the 1950s.

1940s paperback

The Lonely Crowd   This 1950 book by David Riesman and others helps define the era. Americans absorbed into large corporations, Riesman claims, find their independence and creativity squashed by their need for approval and hopes for advancement. Suffocating conformity and personal loneliness become themes in fictional works such as Sloan Wilson's *The Man in the Gray Flannel Suit*, Saul Bellow's *The Adventures of Augie March*, and J. D. Salinger's *Catcher in the Rye*.

People Are Writing

About America   Under the New Deal, the government hires writers to describe the sites and history of America in books, pamphlets, brochures, and other documentary literature. Among these writers are Conrad Aiken, Saul Bellow, and Ralph Ellison.

Letters   Even though wartime security censors check and edit personal letters, soldiers share their experiences with friends and family. Letters provide a vital link between the battlefront and the homefront.

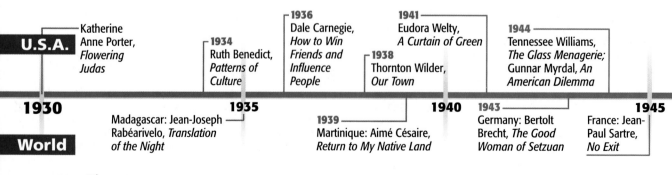

U.S.A.

Katherine Anne Porter, *Flowering Judas*

1934 Ruth Benedict, *Patterns of Culture*

1936 Dale Carnegie, *How to Win Friends and Influence People*

1938 Thornton Wilder, *Our Town*

1941 Eudora Welty, *A Curtain of Green*

1944 Tennessee Williams, *The Glass Menagerie;* Gunnar Myrdal, *An American Dilemma*

1930   **1935**   **1940**   **1945**

World

Madagascar: Jean-Joseph Rabéarivelo, *Translation of the Night*

1939 Martinique: Aimé Césaire, *Return to My Native Land*

1943 Germany: Bertolt Brecht, *The Good Woman of Setzuan*

France: Jean-Paul Sartre, *No Exit*

Literary Trends: Reflection and Protest

"In St. Louis, an Inquiring Reporter stopped a young mother and asked about her personal expectations for the postwar. 'Oh, things are going along just wonderfully,' she bubbled. 'Harry has a grand job, there's the new baby—'

Then she frowned. 'Do you think it's really all going to last?'

A zest in today, wondrous hopes for tomorrow—but always, in the America of V-J [Victory over Japan], there were shadows. A nation accustomed to the categorical yes and no, to war or peace and prosperity or depression, found itself in the nagging realm of maybe." —*Eric Goldman*

Some writers answer the "maybe" by setting off on personal journeys of discovery. For example, poet Robert Lowell revisits "My Father's Bedroom," and James Baldwin journeys back to his Harlem childhood in the short story "The Rockpile."

FOCUS ON . . .

Protest Writers

Many writers of the time respond to the uncertainty of their world by portraying human stories energized by social commitment. John Steinbeck and Arthur Miller demonstrate how writers can use their work as a weapon in the war for social justice. Steinbeck, stirred by the plight of migrant farm families, crafts one of the great novels of social protest, *The Grapes of Wrath*. In his play *The Crucible*, Arthur Miller uses the seventeenth-century Salem, Massachusetts, witch trials to protest the 1950s anticommunist hysteria. Both works arouse strong reactions, demonstrating how literature affects, as well as reflects, the world around it.

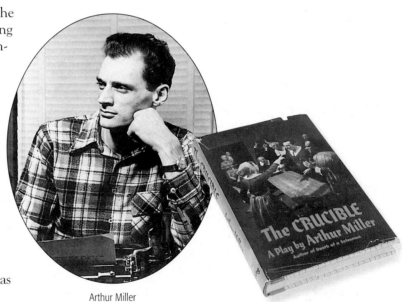

Arthur Miller

1947
W. H. Auden, *The Age of Anxiety*; James Michener, *Tales of the South Pacific*

1949
Arthur Miller, *Death of a Salesman*; Gwendolyn Brooks, *Annie Allen*

1951
Marianne Moore, *Collected Poems*; Langston Hughes, *Montage of a Dream Deferred*

1959
Lorraine Hansberry, *A Raisin in the Sun*

1947
1950
1955
1960

1947
Netherlands: Anne Frank, *The Diary of a Young Girl*

Chile: Pablo Neruda, *General Song*; Mexico: Octavio Paz, *The Labyrinth of Solitude*

1956
Soviet Union: Yevgeny Yevtushenko, *Zima Junction*

Novels of the Time

The literature of the period from 1930 through 1960 is as varied as the times that produce it. Some writers react directly to conditions in the world in which they find themselves, while others explore private experiences and feelings.

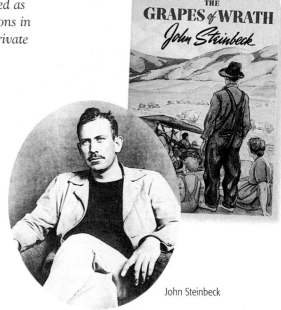

John Steinbeck

The Grapes of Wrath
by John Steinbeck (1939)

Set during the Great Depression, this gripping novel tells the story of the Joads, an Oklahoma farm family driven by poverty to seek out the natural paradise of California. Through the struggles of their journey and the disillusionment that awaits them, they learn how poor, exploited people can unite as a community to survive. The novel arouses widespread sympathy for the plight of migrant farm workers. In 1940 Steinbeck wins a Pulitzer Prize for *The Grapes of Wrath*, and the story is made into a memorable movie starring Henry Fonda.

Carson McCullers

The Member of the Wedding
by Carson McCullers (1946)

In this sensitive, beautifully written novel, as in much of her other work, Carson McCullers reveals the inner lives of isolated, lonely people. Frankie is a motherless twelve-year-old girl who, yearning for a connection, imagines that she will join her brother and his bride on their honeymoon trip. In the meantime, she finds refuge in her kitchen, talking with John Henry, her sickly six-year-old cousin, and Berenice, the wise and maternal cook. McCullers adapts the novel into a successful stage play in 1950 that is made into a film in 1952.

U.S.A.

1931
Pearl Buck, *The Good Earth*

1932
William Faulkner, *Light in August*

1934
F. Scott Fitzgerald, *Tender Is the Night*

1936
John Dos Passos, *The Big Money*

1937
Zora Neale Hurston, *Their Eyes Were Watching God*

Richard Wright, *Native Son;* Carson McCullers, *The Heart Is a Lonely Hunter;* Thomas Wolfe, *You Can't Go Home Again*

Jessamyn West, *Friendly Persuasion*

1930

1932
England: Aldous Huxley, *Brave New World*

1935

1937–40
Iceland: Halldór Laxness, *World Light*

1939
Ireland: James Joyce, *Finnegans Wake*

1940

1942
France: Albert Camus, *The Stranger*

China: Lao She, *Rickshaw Boy*

1945

World

Critics Corner

The Visible Ellison

"*Invisible Man* is not a great Negro novel; it is a work of art any contemporary writer could point to with pride."

—Harvey Curtis Wester, *Saturday Review*, April 12, 1952

"Ellison has an abundance of that primary talent without which neither craft nor intelligence can save a novelist; he is richly, wildly inventive; his scenes rise and dip with tension; his people bleed; his language stings. No other writer has captured so much of the confusion and agony, the hidden gloom and surface gaiety of Negro life."

—Irving Howe, *Nation*, May 10, 1952

Ralph Ellison

Invisible Man
by Ralph Ellison (1952)

Ralph Ellison spends seven years writing his only novel, which shocks and impresses readers when it first appears and goes on to win great acclaim and the 1953 National Book Award for fiction. Ellison looks at America through the eyes of a nameless young African American man. Full of idealism when he first leaves the South for the streets of Harlem, he journeys through a variety of strange and disillusioning experiences. Along the way, he realizes that he has been made invisible—that is, rejected and robbed of his identity—by racism and by an impersonal modern society.

1946
Robert Penn Warren, *All the King's Men*

1948
Japan: Kawabata Yasunari, *Snow Country*

1950

Uruguay: Juan Carlos Onetti, *A Brief Life*

1952
Ernest Hemingway, *The Old Man and the Sea*

1953
James Baldwin, *Go Tell It on the Mountain*

1955

1957
Soviet Union: Boris Pasternak, *Doctor Zhivago*

1957
Jack Kerouac, *On the Road*

1958

1960
Nigeria: Chinua Achebe, *Things Fall Apart*

Language of the Time

How People Speak

Cab Calloway

Jive Talk   Jive talk, the jargon of "cool" jazz musicians of the 1930s, works its way into American speech. Cab Calloway, a bandleader of the swing era, declares himself the heppest of hepcats and talks jive talk to his audiences, with the help of his "Hepster's Dictionary." During the decade, *hep* turns into *hip*. In the 1940s, jazz expressions move increasingly into general use, especially among the young, who take to describing good things as *cool, crazy, far out, real gone, out of sight, wild,* and *weird.*

American English Goes to War   Young Americans take their casual, slangy speech to war, creating expressions that enter the speech of the time. "Sighted sub. Sank same," radios a naval aviator. The most famous response of the war comes from General Anthony McAuliffe. When an opposing German general suggests that McAuliffe surrender, he replies simply, "Nuts!" The German general has no idea what McAuliffe means.

How People Write

Office Memos   Large corporations need a way to communicate with their employees, and the office memo is born. Memos are efficient, but they are also impersonal, reducing the human feeling in office life still further.

Braille   Louis Braille invented his raised-dot system of writing for the blind in 1824, when he was only sixteen years old. A universal braille code for English is adopted in 1932 and improved in 1957.

Office files in braille, 1955.

New Words and Expressions

Baseball, War, and Fashion   The years from 1930 to 1960 produce a multitude of new experiences that, in turn, produce a multitude of new words and expressions. Here are some examples:

Baseball	World War II	Korean War	Fashion
farm system	bazooka	brainwashing	bikini
send to the showers	GI	chopper	Bermuda shorts
All-Star Game	gung ho	germ warfare	button-down shirt
Little League	radar	honcho	Capri pants
have a strike against you	roger!		loafers
	walkie-talkie		

Theme 9 — *Personal Discoveries*

What are you like? What do you want out of life? Many of the characters and speakers in this theme make startling personal discoveries—about love, beauty, hope, family, and other crucial issues. Others teach lessons to help readers or listeners reach such personal discoveries.

THEME PROJECTS

Performing

Lessons to Be Learned   With a partner, role-play a five- to ten-minute dialogue between two characters or speakers from the selections in this theme.

1. Choose two characters or speakers who might have an interesting dialogue. Perhaps their discoveries are similar, opposite, or just seem interesting when compared.

2. Plan your dialogue. Make sure the two people explain their own discoveries or lessons; they should really listen and speak to each other—agreeing, disagreeing, comparing, and contrasting.

3. Present your dialogue to the class, allowing classmates to critique the content.

Interdisciplinary Project

Art: A Cast of Characters   With a small group, create a mural that includes characters or speakers from the selections and illustrates one discovery each has made.

1. Discuss the personal discoveries of the main character or speaker of each selection. How can you illustrate these discoveries?

2. Draw or paint your mural on a large sheet of paper. Divide the tasks among group members. Then, on the mural, write a small caption for each subject's personal discovery.

3. Display your mural on the classroom wall.

Study in Gray, 1933. Lucy Drake Marlow. Oil on Masonite, 28 x 23 in. The Lucy Drake Marlow Art Collection Trust.

Before You Read

The Second Tree from the Corner

Meet
E. B. White

"I arise in the morning torn between a desire to improve (or save) the world and a desire to enjoy (or savor) the world. This makes it hard to plan the day."

—White

Although the beloved children's classics *Charlotte's Web* and *Stuart Little* remain two of Elwyn Brooks (E. B.) White's best-known works, he is also highly acclaimed for his essays and short stories. In fact, it was while working for the *New Yorker* magazine in his late twenties that White first captivated the American public through his essays, sketches, and editing style. There he worked with other legendary writers such as James Thurber and Robert Benchley to create a sophisticated and clever "New York" voice for the newly established magazine.

White was born and raised in rural Mount Vernon, New York. In 1938, at age thirty-nine, after many years in New York City, he decided to leave the city and return to a simpler rural life, this time in Maine. There he continued writing essays and penned his famed children's stories, which were originally intended to entertain a visiting niece.

White was awarded the Presidential Medal of Freedom in 1963, the Laura Ingalls Wilder Award from the American Library Association in 1970, and, in 1973, he was elected to the American Academy of Arts and Letters.

E. B. White was born in 1899 and died in 1985.

FOCUS ACTIVITY

Imagine that someone asks you, "What do you want out of life?" How would you answer?

QUICKWRITE Jot down some answers to this question. Include tangible things, such as a college education or a car, as well as intangible things, such as wisdom or happiness.

SETTING A PURPOSE Read to see how two characters respond to the question "What do you want out of life?"

BACKGROUND

The Time and Place

This story takes place in Manhattan, a part of New York City, probably in the late 1940s. One clue to the story's time frame comes from a reference to Ethel Merman, a popular Broadway singer and actress of the time. Other references to famous New York institutions and places appear in the story as well. The narrator mentions the *Times,* which is the *New York Times* newspaper, the "Park," which is Central Park, and the "East Seventies," a section of Manhattan known for its wealthy residents.

VOCABULARY PREVIEW

amorphous (ə môr′ fəs) *adj.* without definite form; p. 784
retractable (ri trak′ tə bəl) *adj.* capable of being drawn back or in; p. 784
hemorrhage (hem′ ər ij) *n.* a severe discharge of blood; p. 785
inquisitor (in kwiz′ ə tər) *n.* one who asks questions; p. 786
intimation (in′ tə mā′ shən) *n.* a hint; a suggestion; p. 787
invigorated (in vig′ ə rā′ tid) *adj.* filled with strength and energy; p. 787

The Second Tree from the Corner

E. B. White

Washington Square Park. Anthony Springer (1928–1995). Oil on canvas. Private Collection. Permission courtesy of Mrs. Sylvia Springer.

"Ever have any bizarre thoughts?" asked the doctor.

Mr. Trexler failed to catch the word. "What kind?" he said.

"Bizarre," repeated the doctor, his voice steady. He watched his patient for any slight change of expression, any wince. It seemed to Trexler that the doctor was not only watching him closely but was creeping slowly toward him, like a lizard toward a bug. Trexler shoved his chair back an inch and gathered himself for a reply. He was about to say "Yes" when he realized that if he said yes the next question would be unanswerable. Bizarre thoughts, bizarre thoughts? Ever have any bizarre thoughts? What kind of thoughts *except* bizarre had he had since the age of two?

Trexler felt the time passing, the necessity for an answer. These psychiatrists were busy men, overloaded, not to be kept waiting. The next patient was probably already perched out there in the waiting room, lonely, worried, shifting around on the sofa, his mind stuffed with bizarre thoughts and <u>amorphous</u> fears. Poor fellow, thought Trexler. Out there all alone in that misshapen antechamber,[1] staring at the filing cabinet and wondering whether to tell the doctor about that day on the Madison Avenue bus.

Let's see, bizarre thoughts. Trexler dodged back along the dreadful corridor of the years to see what he could find. He felt the doctor's eyes upon him and knew that time was running out. Don't be so conscientious, he said to himself. If a bizarre thought is indicated here, just reach into the bag and pick anything at all. A man as well supplied with bizarre thoughts as you are should have no difficulty producing one for the record. Trexler darted into the bag, hung for a moment before one of his thoughts, as a hummingbird pauses in the delphinium. No, he said, not that one. He darted to another (the one about the rhesus monkey), paused, considered. No, he said, not that.

Trexler knew he must hurry. He had already used up pretty nearly four seconds since the question had been put. But it was an impossible situation—just one more lousy, impossible situation such as he was always getting himself into. When, he asked himself, are you going to quit maneuvering yourself into a pocket? He made one more effort. This time he stopped at the asylum, only the bars were lucite[2]— fluted, <u>retractable</u>. Not here, he said. Not this one.

He looked straight at the doctor. "No," he said quietly. "I never have any bizarre thoughts."

The doctor sucked in on his pipe, blew a plume of smoke toward the rows of medical books. Trexler's gaze followed the smoke. He managed to make out one of the titles, *The Genito-Urinary System*. A bright wave of fear swept cleanly over him and he winced under

Did You Know?
Delphinium (del fin′ ē əm), also called larkspur, is a tall, flowering plant. The flowers are usually blue or purple.

Did You Know?
Fluted means "having decorative, usually rounded grooves."

---

1. An *antechamber,* or waiting room, is a smaller room serving as an entrance to a larger or main room.

2. *Lucite* is the trademark name of a transparent plastic.

Vocabulary
amorphous (ə môr′ fəs) *adj.* without definite form
retractable (ri trak′ tə bəl) *adj.* capable of being drawn back or in

the first pain of kidney stones.[3] He remembered when he was a child, the first time he ever entered a doctor's office, sneaking a look at the titles of the books—and the flush of fear, the shirt wet under the arms, the book on t.b.,[4] the sudden knowledge that he was in the advanced stages of consumption,[5] the quick vision of the hemorrhage. Trexler sighed wearily. Forty years, he thought, and I still get thrown by the title of a medical book. Forty years and I still can't stay on life's little bucky horse. No wonder I'm sitting here in this dreary joint at the end of this woebegone[6] afternoon, lying about my bizarre thoughts to a doctor who looks, come to think of it, rather tired.

The session dragged on. After about twenty minutes, the doctor rose and knocked his pipe out. Trexler got up, knocked the ashes out of his brain, and waited. The doctor smiled warmly and stuck out his hand. "There's nothing the matter with you—you're just scared. Want to know how I know you're scared?"

"How?" asked Trexler.

"Look at the chair you've been sitting in! See how it has moved back away from my desk? You kept inching away from me while I asked you questions. That means you're scared."

"Does it?" said Trexler, faking a grin. "Yeah, I suppose it does."

They finished shaking hands. Trexler turned and walked out uncertainly along the passage, then into the waiting room and out past the next patient, a ruddy pin-striped man who was seated on the sofa twirling his hat nervously and staring straight ahead at the files. Poor, frightened guy, thought Trexler, he's probably read in the *Times* that one American male out of every two is going to die of heart disease by twelve o'clock next Thursday. It says that in the paper almost every morning. And he's also probably thinking about that day on the Madison Avenue bus.

A week later, Trexler was back in the patient's chair. And for several weeks thereafter he continued to visit the doctor, always toward the end of the afternoon, when the vapors hung thick above the pool of the mind and darkened the whole region of the East Seventies.[7] He felt no better as time went on, and he found it impossible to work. He discovered that the visits were becoming routine and that although the routine was one to which he certainly did not look forward, at least he could accept it with cool resignation, as once, years ago, he had accepted a long spell with a dentist who had settled down to a steady fooling with a couple of dead teeth. The visits, moreover, were now assuming a pattern recognizable to the patient.

Each session would begin with a resumé of symptoms—the dizziness in the streets, the constricting pain in the back of the neck, the apprehensions, the tightness of the scalp, the inability to concentrate, the despondency[8] and the melancholy times, the feeling of pressure and tension, the anger at not being able to work, the anxiety over work not done, the gas on the stomach. Dullest set of neurotic

---

3. *Kidney stones* are small, hard calcium deposits that sometimes form in the kidneys and cause pain.
4. Tuberculosis, a disease that often affects the lungs, is sometimes referred to as *t.b.*
5. *Consumption* is another name for tuberculosis.
6. *Woebegone* means "sorrowful" or "filled with grief"; it can also suggest "dreary and miserable."

7. Most of the streets that run east to west in Manhattan are identified by numbers rather than names. *East Seventies* refers to the section of streets from 70–79 that are on the east side of Manhattan.
8. *Despondency* means "hopelessness" or "depression."

Vocabulary
hemorrhage (hem′ ər ij) *n.* a severe discharge of blood

symptoms in the world, Trexler would think, as he obediently trudged back over them for the doctor's benefit.

As he became familiar with the pattern Trexler found that he increasingly tended to identify himself with the doctor, transferring himself into the doctor's seat—probably (he thought) some rather slick form of escapism. At any rate, it was nothing new for Trexler to identify himself with other people. Whenever he got into a cab, he instantly became the driver, saw everything from the hackman's angle (and the reaching over with the right hand, the nudging of the flag, the pushing it down, all the way down along the side of the meter), saw everything—traffic, fare, everything—through the eyes of Anthony Rocco, or Isidore Freedman, or Matthew Scott. In a barbershop, Trexler was the barber, his fingers curled around the comb, his hand on the tonic. Perfectly natural, then, that Trexler should soon be occupying the doctor's chair, asking the questions, waiting for the answers. He got quite interested in the doctor, in this way. He liked him, and he found him a not too difficult patient.

It was on the fifth visit, about halfway through, that the doctor turned to Trexler and said, suddenly, "What do you want?" He gave the word "want" special emphasis.

"I d'know," replied Trexler uneasily. "I guess nobody knows the answer to that one."

"Sure they do," replied the doctor.

"Do *you* know what *you* want?" asked Trexler narrowly.

"Certainly," said the doctor. Trexler noticed that at this point the doctor's chair slid slightly backward, away from him. Trexler stifled a small, internal smile. Scared as a rabbit, he said to himself. Look at him scoot!

"What *do* you want?" continued Trexler, pressing his advantage, pressing it hard.

The doctor glided back another inch away from his inquisitor. "I want a wing on the small house I own in Westport.[9] I want more money, and more leisure to do the things I want to do."

Trexler was just about to say, "And what are those things you want to do, Doctor?" when he caught himself. Better not go too far, he mused. Better not lose possession of the ball. And besides, he thought, what the hell goes on here, anyway—me paying fifteen bucks a throw for these séances[10] and then doing the work myself, asking the questions, weighing the answers. So he wants a new wing! There's a fine piece of theatrical gauze for you! A new wing.

Trexler settled down again and resumed the role of patient for the rest of the visit. It ended on a kindly, friendly note. The doctor reassured him that his fears were the cause of his sickness, and that his fears were unsubstantial. They shook hands, smiling.

Trexler walked dizzily through the empty waiting room and the doctor followed along to let him out. It was late; the secretary had shut up shop and gone home. Another day over the dam. "Goodbye," said Trexler. He stepped into the street, turned west toward Madison, and thought of the doctor all alone there, after hours, in that desolate hole—a man who worked longer hours than his secretary. Poor, scared, over-worked guy, thought Trexler. And that new wing!

It was an evening of clearing weather, the Park showing green and desirable in the distance, the last daylight applying a high

---

9. *Westport* is a residential community and summer resort on the coast of Connecticut.

10. A *séance* is a meeting in which people attempt to communicate with the spirits of the dead. Here, Trexler is questioning the scientific validity of his psychiatric sessions.

Vocabulary
inquisitor (in kwiz′ ə tər) *n.* one who asks questions

Did You Know?
Brownstone is the name of a reddish-brown sandstone as well as a type of house made with it.

lacquer to the brick and brownstone walls and giving the street scene a luminous and intoxicating splendor. Trexler meditated, as he walked, on what he wanted. "What do you want?" he heard again. Trexler knew what he wanted, and what, in general, all men wanted; and he was glad in a way, that it was both inexpressible and unattainable, and that it wasn't a wing. He was satisfied to remember that it was deep, formless, enduring, and impossible of fulfillment, and that it made men sick, and that when you sauntered along Third Avenue and looked through the doorways into the dim saloons, you could sometimes pick out from the unregenerate ranks the ones who had not forgotten, gazing steadily into the bottoms of the glasses on the long chance that they could get another little peek at it. Trexler found himself renewed by the remembrance that what he wanted was at once great and microscopic, and that although it borrowed from the nature of large deeds and of youthful love and of old songs and early intimations, it was not any one of these things, and that it had not been isolated or pinned down, and that a man who attempted to define it in the privacy of a doctor's office would fall flat on his face.

Trexler felt invigorated. Suddenly his sickness seemed health, his dizziness stability. A small tree, rising between him and the light, stood there saturated with the evening, each gilt-edged leaf perfectly drunk with excellence and delicacy. Trexler's spine registered an ever so slight tremor as it picked up this natural disturbance in the lovely scene. "I want the second tree from the corner, just as it stands," he said, answering an imaginary question from an imaginary physician. And he felt a slow pride in realizing that what he wanted none could bestow, and that what he had none could take away. He felt content to be sick, unembarrassed at being afraid; and in the jungle of his fear he glimpsed (as he had so often glimpsed them before) the flashy tail feathers of the bird courage.

Then he thought once again of the doctor, and of his being left there all alone, tired, frightened. (The poor, scared guy, thought Trexler.) Trexler began humming "Moonshine Lullaby," his spirit reacting instantly to the hypodermic of Merman's[11] healthy voice. He crossed Madison, boarded a downtown bus, and rode all the way to Fifty-second Street before he had a thought that could rightly have been called bizarre.

---

11. Ethel *Merman* (1909–1984) was an American actress and singer known for her powerful voice.

Vocabulary
intimation (in′ tə mā′ shən) *n.* a hint; a suggestion
invigorated (in vig′ ə rā′ tid) *adj.* filled with strength and energy

Responding to Literature

Personal Response

What questions would you like to ask Mr. Trexler? Explain.

ANALYZING LITERATURE

RECALL

1. What question does the doctor ask Mr. Trexler at the beginning of the story? What is Trexler's answer?
2. What, according to the doctor, is wrong with Trexler?
3. What two people does Trexler pity? What thoughts does he have about them?
4. Describe the ways that Trexler identifies with the cab driver, the barber, and the doctor.
5. How does Trexler respond to the question "What do you want?" What does the question make him think about after his visit to the doctor?

INTERPRET

6. In your opinion, what does Trexler's reaction to the doctor's first question reveal about his state of mind?
7. Do you agree with the doctor's early diagnosis of Trexler? Explain.
8. Why do you think Trexler pities others? Do you think his observations are accurate? Why or why not?
9. What does Trexler's tendency to identify with others suggest to you about his personality?
10. In your opinion, what does Trexler want?

EVALUATE AND CONNECT

11. Was Trexler's reaction to his discovery of what he wants in life realistic? Why or why not?
12. Do you think the "second tree from the corner" is an effective **symbol** for what Trexler wants from life? (See Literary Terms Handbook, page R16.)
13. Refer to your response to the Focus Activity on page 782. Are your answers more similar to Trexler's answer or to the doctor's? Explain.
14. In your opinion, is Trexler a sympathetic character or not? Use a chart like the one on this page to help organize your thoughts.
15. Theme Connections   What personal discovery does Trexler make? Describe a personal discovery you've made about yourself. What lesson did you learn? How did you learn that lesson?

Internal Conflict

At the center of each story there is usually a struggle, or **conflict,** between two opposing forces. The conflict might be **external**—between the main character and another person or an outside force—or it may be **internal**—between two opposing thoughts or desires within the mind of the main character.

1. Is the main struggle in this story an internal or external conflict? Describe that struggle, using details from the selection as evidence.
2. Does this story have a secondary conflict? If so, is it internal or external? Support your answer with details from the text.

● See **Literary Terms Handbook,** p. R3.

Trexler	
Positive traits	Negative traits
1.	1.

LITERATURE AND WRITING

Writing About Literature

"Like a Lizard Toward a Bug"   E. B. White uses many visual images to describe Trexler's feelings. For example, Trexler thinks the doctor "was creeping slowly toward him, like a lizard toward a bug." In a paragraph, explain how this image and two others fit Trexler's character.

Creative Writing

Trexler's Bizarre Thoughts   Select one of Trexler's incomplete references to a bizarre thought, such as "the Madison Avenue bus," "the rhesus monkey," or "the asylum." Write a journal entry for Trexler describing one of these thoughts more fully. Share your entry with the class.

EXTENDING YOUR RESPONSE

Literature Groups

What, Exactly, Does He Want?   With your group, look at the description on page 787 of Trexler's discovery and its effect on his outlook. Discuss what message the author intends to convey with this scene. Consider what events take place and the author's general attitude toward the characters. Share your group's views with the class.

Interdisciplinary Activity

Art: The Second Tree from the Corner   Visualize Trexler's view of the second tree from the corner. Why was it such a dramatic sight? Based on the details in the story, create a painting, a drawing, a collage, or other visual representation of what Trexler might have seen. Include a glimpse of a bird or other symbols you think might be appropriate.

Learning for Life

A Follow-Up Report   Following a session with a patient or client, psychiatrists and psychologists often write a report. Write a report that the psychiatrist might have written to summarize his observations and analysis of Trexler. The report should be based on details from the story.

Reading Further

If you would like to read more by E. B. White, you might enjoy these books:

Collections: *The Second Tree from the Corner* and *The Essays of E. B. White* showcase a variety of White's talents.

Children's Books: *Stuart Little, Charlotte's Web,* and *The Trumpet of the Swan,* are stories based on the ageless themes of friendship and love.

📖 **Save your work for your portfolio.**

Skill Minilesson

VOCABULARY • Parts of Speech

When a word is changed from one part of speech to another—such as from a noun to an adjective—the central part of the word's meaning remains the same. For example, if you know that the noun *despondency* means "hopelessness" or "depression," you can figure out that the adjective *despondent* means "hopeless" or "depressed."

PRACTICE   Use your knowledge of the vocabulary words in "The Second Tree from the Corner" to figure out the meanings of the words below. For each, write a definition of the word and use the word in a sentence.

1. inquisitive (adj.)
2. invigorate (v.)
3. intimate (v.)
4. retract (v.)

Television Transcript

What is happiness? What do you need in order to attain it? Is happiness something you can discover within yourself? See if your views change after reading the excerpt that follows.

The Mystery of Happiness

ABC Special Report, hosted by John Stossel, September 4, 1997

JOHN STOSSEL

If you had just one wish for your children, that they have wealth, high intelligence, a successful job or career, or an overall happy life, wouldn't you pick happiness? Actually, I know most of you would, because we just took an ABC News poll of 1,500 adults. A happy life outpolled all the other choices combined. . . .

What makes for a happy life—more possessions? And how would we know what makes for a happy life?

Psychologist David Myers, who spent six years examining hundreds of studies on happiness for [his] book, says once you get past poverty, money doesn't help, no matter how much stuff you buy.

DAVID MYERS

The stockpiles of CDs, the closets full of clothes, the big-screen stereo TV systems . . .

JOHN STOSSEL

Doesn't do it.

DAVID MYERS

Clearly it doesn't do it. People having achieved that level of wealth have now adapted to it, and it takes new increments— a faster computer, a bigger TV screen or whatever—to rejuice the joy that the initial purchase gained for them. . . . And that's why today, with double the incomes and double what money buys for us, we're no happier than we were 40 years ago. . . . Close, supportive, connected relationships

make for happiness, and we have fewer of those relationships today in the United States. Three times as many of us today live alone as lived alone a half century ago.

LEO WINGATE, guest

You don't have to search for happiness, you just have to know it, recognize it when you find it, when you see it. And it might be in the strangest places sometimes.

Respond

1. After reading this excerpt, do you agree with Myers's conclusion of what makes people happy? Why or why not?

2. Describe a time when you found happiness in an unexpected place.

Before You Read

Ode to My Socks

Meet Pablo Neruda

> "I have always wanted the hands of the people to be seen in poetry. I have always preferred a poetry where the fingerprints show. A poetry of loam where water can sing. A poetry of bread, where everyone may eat."
>
> —*Neruda*

Pablo Neruda (pä' blō   nä rōō' dä) was born in a small town in rural Chile. His father, a railway worker, and his mother, a teacher, named him Neftalí Ricardo Reyes Basoalto. His mother died of tuberculosis shortly after his birth, and two years later his father remarried.

Reyes began writing poetry at the age of ten. He published his first book of poems when he was just nineteen, under the pen name Pablo Neruda, a name most likely inspired by his appreciation of the works of Czech poet Jan Neruda. In 1924 his second book, *Twenty Love Poems and a Song of Despair*, became an instant success, and Neruda was well on his way to becoming a world-renowned poet. Not long after the publication of his first two books, Neruda went to Asia as Chile's honorary consul. It was the first position in a consular career that would take him to Spain, France, and Mexico.

Despite such high-ranking diplomatic positions and worldwide acclaim for his poetry, Neruda never lost the eloquent, yearning voice of his rural past. In 1945 Chile awarded him the National Literature Prize. In 1949, while living in France, he completed his major work, *Canto General*, a book of 340 poems, which took Neruda fourteen years to complete. In 1971 he received the Nobel Prize for Literature "for a poetry that with the action of an elemental force brings alive a continent's destiny and dreams."

Pablo Neruda was born in 1904 and died in 1973.

FOCUS ACTIVITY

What was the best gift that you ever received?

CHART IT! Use an idea tree like the one below to come up with reasons why the gift pleased you.

SETTING A PURPOSE Read to learn one speaker's reaction to a special gift.

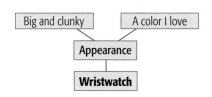

BACKGROUND

Literary Influences

Neruda felt that writers of the Americas, due to the relative youth of their countries, had great opportunities to explore creative possibilities and find fresh, new voices. As an example, he cited the often "unorthodox" poetic vision of Walt Whitman. Of Whitman he said, "He was not only intensely conscious, but he was open-eyed! He had tremendous eyes to see everything—he taught us to see things. He was our poet."

The Ode

Neruda calls this poem an **ode**—a type of lyric poem in which strong personal emotion is expressed directly and spontaneously. Traditionally odes have rhyming lines and are dignified in subject, feeling, and style. One famous ode glorifies a nightingale. Neruda's ode departs somewhat from the traditional style.

Ode to My Socks

Pablo Neruda ∾
Translated by Robert Bly

The Magician, 1992. Maria Angelica Ruiz-Tagle. Oil on canvas, 130 x 97 cm. Private collection.

Maru Mori brought me
a pair
of socks
which she knitted herself
5   with her sheepherder's hands,
two socks as soft
as rabbits.
I slipped my feet
into them
10 as though into
two
cases
knitted
with threads of
15 twilight
and sheepskin.

Violent socks,
my feet were
two fish made
20 of wool,
two long sharks
sea-blue, shot
through
by one golden thread,
25 two immense blackbirds,
two cannons:
my feet
were honored
in this way
30 by
these
heavenly
socks.
They were
35 so handsome
for the first time
my feet seemed to me
unacceptable
like two decrepit
40 firemen, firemen
unworthy
of that woven
fire,
of those glowing
45 socks.

Nevertheless
I resisted
the sharp temptation
to save them somewhere
50 as schoolboys
keep
fireflies,
as learned men
collect
55 sacred texts,
I resisted
the mad impulse
to put them
into a golden
60 cage
and each day give them
birdseed
and pieces of pink melon.
Like explorers
65 in the jungle who hand
over the very rare
green deer
to the spit°
and eat it
70 with remorse,
I stretched out
my feet
and pulled on
the magnificent
75 socks
and then my shoes.

The moral
of my ode is this:
beauty is twice
80 beauty
and what is good is doubly
good
when it is a matter of two socks
made of wool
85 in winter.

---

68 A *spit* is a rod on which meat is roasted.

Responding to Literature

Personal Response

What thoughts did you have while reading this poem? Describe your reactions in your journal.

ANALYZING LITERATURE

RECALL AND INTERPRET

1. What does the speaker say about the socks in lines 1–16? Why might the speaker have such strong emotions about wearing these socks?
2. How does the speaker describe his feet in the socks? How does this description emphasize his feelings for his socks?
3. What temptations and impulses does the speaker face? Why is he so tempted? Why, in your opinion, does he resist?
4. To whom does the speaker compare himself when he finally puts on the socks? Why do you think he makes this comparison?
5. A **moral** is a lesson taught by a written work or by a real event. What does the speaker say is the moral of the poem? What, in your opinion, is the meaning of this moral?

EVALUATE AND CONNECT

6. Review your response to the Focus Activity on page 791. How does your favorite gift compare with the speaker's? What moral might you write to sum up your reasons for valuing the gift you received?
7. A **simile** is a figure of speech that compares two things using the words *like* or *as,* as in "socks as soft as rabbits." Identify the other similes in the poem and suggest why Neruda may have made these comparisons.
8. Do the speaker's reactions seem realistic to you? Do you think it's possible to get so excited about a new pair of socks? Explain.

Literary ELEMENTS

Metaphor

A **metaphor** is a figure of speech that makes a comparison between two seemingly unlike things without using the words *like* or *as.* Poets use metaphors to suggest an underlying similarity between the two things and to show the first thing in a new light. For example, when Neruda says, "My feet were two fish made of wool," he's making a connection between the speaker's feet in the new socks and the shape and free movement of fish.

1. Identify three other metaphors in the poem. What is being compared?
2. Explain how each of these metaphors helps convey the poem's central idea.

⬤ See **Literary Terms Handbook,** p. R9.

EXTENDING YOUR RESPONSE

Creative Writing

Ode to a Different Kind of Gift   Think about a gift you or another person has received but did not really enjoy. Write a poem about that gift using Neruda's poem as a model. Include at least one metaphor and one simile, and end your poem with a moral as Neruda does.

Literature Groups

Pros and Cons   The speaker saw the socks as beautiful, and he considered saving the socks rather than wearing them. With a group, discuss what Neruda seems to think makes something beautiful. Do you agree with his ideas of beauty? Explain.

📖 **Save your work for your portfolio.**

COMPARING
selections

The Second Tree from the Corner **and** *Ode to My Socks*

COMPARE **IMAGES**

Mr. Trexler and the speaker in the poem both react to beauty in unusual ways. Using details from each selection, answer these questions:

1. How are the beautiful things they see alike, and how are they different?
2. How are their descriptions alike? How are they different?
3. In your opinion, who will gain more benefit and pleasure from the beauty he experiences, Trexler or the poem's speaker?

COMPARE **CHARACTERS**

With a partner, plan and role-play a conversation between Trexler and the speaker of the poem. Be sure there is a dialogue, or interchange, between the two. As these characters, discuss topics such as these:

- thoughts they try to resist
- their perceptions about other people
- their answers to the question "What do you want?"

COMPARE **CULTURES**

Each selection reflects a different cultural setting. In a small group, discuss how each setting affects the selection and the main characters.

- The cultural setting of "The Second Tree from the Corner" is New York City. In what kind of setting does "Ode to My Socks" seem to take place?
- Based on your own knowledge and experience, create a theory about how the cultural setting of each selection influences the main character's personality, challenges, perceptions of beauty, and quest for personal satisfaction and happiness.
- Test your theory by researching facts about each setting. Divide the research among group members. Discuss your findings, using these questions to guide you: Which facts support your theory? Which facts might cause you to revise or qualify your theory? Share your conclusions with the class.

Meet
John Steinbeck

"Very few people ever mature. . . . But sometimes . . . awareness takes place—not very often and always inexplainable. There are no words for it because there is no one ever to tell. This is a secret not kept a secret, but locked in wordlessness. The craft or art of writing is the clumsy attempt to find symbols for the wordlessness."

—*Steinbeck*

John Steinbeck was born and raised in Salinas, California, a small town nestled in a sprawling valley of lettuce farms. Bright and popular, Steinbeck was the president of his senior class in high school, wrote for the school newspaper, and played sports. He was accepted to Stanford University, but yearning for more life experiences, he drifted in and out of college, never earning a degree. Instead, he wrote and worked, taking jobs as a ranch hand, a factory worker, a sales clerk, a free-lance newspaper writer, a construction worker, and a farm laborer.

Steinbeck published four novels by the time he was thirty-three. His fourth book, the novel *Tortilla Flat*, was his first publicly acclaimed book. Set in his familiar Salinas Valley, it vividly and humorously describes the joys and sorrows of a group of unemployed men. The following year, Steinbeck used his experiences as a factory worker to produce and publish his next success, a novel entitled *In Dubious Battle*, which includes realistic and violent scenes based on labor strikes in California.

Perhaps Steinbeck's greatest work is the novel *The Grapes of Wrath*, written as the United States was getting back on its feet after the Great Depression of the 1930s. This 1940 Pulitzer Prize winner traces the difficult journey of poor farmers from the Dust Bowl poverty of Oklahoma to the rich farmland of California's Salinas Valley. There the farmers suffer tragically from injustice handed out by powerful landowners and corrupt officials. Today, the novel is universally respected for its depiction of the individual's quest for justice and dignity.

Steinbeck was awarded the Nobel Prize for Literature in 1962. He privately expressed fears about winning the prize, noting that authors whom he respected, including William Faulkner and Ernest Hemingway, had produced no further major works after receiving it. Six years after receiving the prize, Steinbeck died, without publishing another work.

"[T]he free, exploring mind of the individual human is the most valuable thing in the world. And this I would fight for: the freedom of the mind to take any direction it wishes, undirected. And this I must fight against: any idea, religion, or government which limits or destroys the individual. This is what I am and what I am about."

—*Steinbeck*

John Steinbeck was born in 1902 and died in 1968.

FOCUS ACTIVITY

What memories of people, places, or events are extremely vivid in your mind?

JOURNAL Write a journal entry describing one of these memories. Include a brief explanation of why you think the memory remains strong.

SETTING A PURPOSE Read to experience one person's vivid memory of an early morning.

BACKGROUND

The Time and Place

This story takes place in northern California in the 1930s. Steinbeck originally published this piece in a short-story collection called *The Long Valley* in 1938. He later adapted it and included it as part of a chapter in *The Grapes of Wrath*. The main character in "Breakfast" is not identified. In *The Grapes of Wrath*, however, the main character is Tom Joad, a young man who has traveled with his family from Oklahoma to California in search of work and opportunity.

Literary Influences

The odd jobs that Steinbeck held during the early 1920s gave him a firsthand look at the desperate working and living conditions forced upon most farm laborers. These observations helped Steinbeck develop the themes and plots of many of his major works. Steinbeck also was inspired by the terrain of his northern California background. He wrote about the working person's quest for dignity and deliverance, and the stark challenges presented by external forces, such as nature, society, and fate.

From the movie *The Grapes of Wrath*.

VOCABULARY PREVIEW

scuffle (skuf′ əl) *v.* to move with a quick, shuffling gait; p. 798
dissipate (dis′ ə pāt′) *v.* to cause to scatter and gradually vanish; to break up and drive off; p. 798
avert (ə vurt′) *v.* to turn away or aside; p. 800

Breakfast

John Steinbeck ∿

This thing fills me with pleasure. I don't know why, I can see it in the smallest detail. I find myself recalling it again and again, each time bringing more detail out of a sunken memory, remembering brings the curious warm pleasure.

It was very early in the morning. The eastern mountains were black-blue, but behind them the light stood up faintly colored at the mountain rims with a washed red, growing colder, grayer and darker as it went up and overhead until, at a place near the west, it merged with pure night.

And it was cold, not painfully so, but cold enough so that I rubbed my hands and shoved them deep into my pockets, and I hunched my shoulders up and scuffled my feet on the ground. Down in the valley where I was, the earth was that lavender gray of dawn. I walked along a country road and ahead of me I saw a tent that was only a little lighter gray than the ground. Beside the tent there was a flash of orange fire seeping out of the cracks of an old rusty iron stove. Gray smoke spurted up out of the stubby stovepipe, spurted up a long way before it spread out and dissipated.

I saw a young woman beside the stove, really a girl. She was dressed in a faded cotton skirt and waist.[1] As I came close I saw that she

_____

1. Here, a *waist* is a blouse.

Vocabulary
scuffle (skuf′ əl) *v.* to move with a quick, shuffling gait
dissipate (dis′ ə pāt′) *v.* to cause to scatter and gradually vanish; to break up and drive off

carried a baby in a crooked arm and the baby was nursing, its head under her waist out of the cold. The mother moved about, poking the fire, shifting the rusty lids of the stove to make a greater draft, opening the oven door; and all the time the baby was nursing, but that didn't interfere with the mother's work, nor with the light quick gracefulness of her movements. There was something very precise and practiced in her movements. The orange fire flicked out of the cracks in the stove and threw dancing reflections on the tent.

I was close now and I could smell frying bacon and baking bread, the warmest, pleasantest odors I know. From the east the light grew swiftly. I came near to the stove and stretched my hands out to it and shivered all over when the warmth struck me. Then the tent flap jerked up and a young man came out and an older man followed him. They were dressed in new blue dungarees[2] and in new dungaree coats with the brass buttons shining. They were sharp-faced men, and they looked much alike.

The younger had a dark stubble beard and the older had a gray stubble beard. Their heads and faces were wet, their hair dripped with water, and water stood out on their stiff beards and their cheeks shone with water. Together they stood looking quietly at the lightening east; they yawned together and looked at the light on the hill rims. They turned and saw me.

"Morning," said the older man. His face was neither friendly nor unfriendly.

"Morning, sir," I said.

2. *Dungarees* are blue denim pants.

Breakfast

"Morning," said the young man.

The water was slowly drying on their faces. They came to the stove and warmed their hands at it.

The girl kept to her work, her face averted and her eyes on what she was doing. Her hair was tied back out of her eyes with a string and it hung down her back and swayed as she worked. She set tin cups on a big packing box, set tin plates and knives and forks out too. Then she scooped fried bacon out of the deep grease and laid it on a big tin platter, and the bacon cricked[3] and rustled as it grew crisp. She opened the rusty oven door and took out a square pan full of high big biscuits.

When the smell of that hot bread came out, both of the men inhaled deeply.

The elder man turned to me, "Had your breakfast?"

"No."

"Well, sit down with us, then."

That was the signal. We went to the packing case and squatted on the ground about it. The young man asked, "Picking cotton?"

"No."

"We had twelve days' work so far," the young man said.

The girl spoke from the stove. "They even got new clothes."

The two men looked down at their new dungarees and they both smiled a little.

The girl set out the platter of bacon, the brown high biscuits, a bowl of bacon gravy and a pot of coffee, and then she squatted down by the box too. The baby was still nursing, its head

up under her waist out of the cold. I could hear the sucking noises it made.

We filled our plates, poured bacon gravy over our biscuits and sugared our coffee. The older man filled his mouth full and he chewed and chewed and swallowed. Then he said, "God Almighty, it's good," and he filled his mouth again.

The young man said, "We been eating good for twelve days."

We all ate quickly, frantically, and refilled our plates and ate quickly again until we were full and warm. The hot bitter coffee scalded our throats. We threw the last little bit with the grounds in it on the earth and refilled our cups.

There was color in the light now, a reddish gleam that made the air seem colder. The two men faced the east and their faces were lighted by the dawn, and I looked up for a moment and saw the image of the mountain and the light coming over it reflected in the older man's eyes.

Then the two men threw the grounds from their cups on the earth and they stood up together. "Got to get going," the older man said.

The younger turned to me. "'Fyou want to pick cotton, we could maybe get you on."

"No. I got to go along. Thanks for breakfast."

The older man waved his hand in a negative. "O.K. Glad to have you." They walked away together. The air was blazing with light at the eastern skyline. And I walked away down the country road.

That's all. I know, of course, some of the reasons why it was pleasant. But there was some element of great beauty there that makes the rush of warmth when I think of it.

---

3. Here, *cricked* means "turned or twisted."

Vocabulary

avert (ə vurt′) *v.* to turn away or aside

Responding to Literature

Personal Response

How did you react to this story? Jot down your reactions to the characters, their encounter, and the setting.

——————— **ANALYZING LITERATURE** ———————

RECALL AND INTERPRET

1. How does the narrator introduce this incident? What are the first things he describes? What do the introduction and the descriptions tell you about the narrator?
2. What observations does the narrator make about the family of migrant workers? What seems to be important to the family? Explain.
3. What do the narrator and the migrant workers talk about? What **tone** is conveyed by the family's words and actions? (See Literary Terms Handbook, page R16.) Support your answer with details from the story.
4. What does the narrator say about his memory at the end of the story? What might his attachment to this memory suggest about his life? What deeper understanding or awareness of life does he seem to gain?

EVALUATE AND CONNECT

5. Reread your response to the Focus Activity on page 797. What details would you add to your description after reading "Breakfast"?
6. Steinbeck wrote about migrant workers who lived in small, supportive communities. In what ways does Steinbeck portray the narrator as part of such a supportive community?
7. Steinbeck wrote to reach the heart of working people. Explain which aspects of this story might appeal to a farmer, a rancher, or a laborer.
8. What are some of your favorite **sensory details** (see page R14) in this story? How did these sensory details affect your reading of the story?

Literary
ELEMENTS

Implied Theme
The **theme** of a piece of literature is a dominant idea, often a universal message about life, that the writer communicates to the reader. Authors rarely state a theme outright. Instead, they use an **implied theme,** letting the main idea or message reveal itself through events, dialogue, or descriptions. In "Breakfast," the implied theme is built around the narrator's warm recollection of an encounter with a group of migrant workers.

1. What is the implied theme, or message about life, in this selection?
2. What details and descriptions support this theme?

● See **Literary Terms Handbook,** p. R16.

——————— **EXTENDING YOUR RESPONSE** ———————

Writing About Literature

Lively Description   Steinbeck creates vivid pictures of the setting by using specific, dramatic adjectives and verbs, such as "there was a flash of orange fire seeping out of the cracks of an old rusty iron stove." Select another example of vivid description from the selection. Describe the scene as you see it in your mind, adding details to your mental picture, if you wish.

Interdisciplinary Activity

History: California Farming   Research and prepare a brief report on the different groups of migrant workers in California during the 1900s. Begin with the 1930s and update your report with information about current migrant workers in the state. Include visuals, such as photographs, in your presentation to the class.

📑 **Save your work for your portfolio.**

Before You Read

A Rose for Emily and **Address upon Receiving the Nobel Prize for Literature**

Meet William Faulkner

As a young man, William Faulkner did not seem destined for literary renown. He was both a high school and college dropout and had difficulty holding a steady job. To his neighbors, who dubbed him "Count No'count," Faulkner seemed shiftless and peculiar. Few guessed that this seemingly lazy man was a literary genius who would one day write fiction that captured the struggles of the human heart.

Faulkner was born into a prominent southern family in Albany, Mississippi, and he was raised in nearby Oxford. During his youth, Faulkner read widely and began writing poetry. When World War I broke out, Faulkner tried to join the United States Army, but he was rejected because of his small size. Still eager for adventure and glory, he enlisted in the British Royal Air Force in Canada. The war ended, however, before he ever saw combat.

Following the war, Faulkner traveled abroad and to New Orleans where he befriended Sherwood Anderson and other writers and refined his writing style. When he was twenty-seven, his first book, a poetry collection entitled *The Marble Faun,* was published to little acclaim. At the advice of Anderson, he then attempted fiction, publishing his first novel, *Soldier's Pay,* in 1926, and his second novel, *Mosquitoes,* in 1927.

In his third novel, *Sartoris,* Faulkner invented the fictional world of Yoknapatawpha County, which was based on the region in northern Mississippi where he lived. Over the next thirty years, he continued to explore the "history" of this county and its tenant farmers, aristocrats, businesspeople, formerly enslaved people, and dispossessed Native Americans in novels now considered to be among the country's greatest. Yoknapatawpha County, wrote one critic, stands "as a parable or legend of all the Deep South."

Though Faulkner wrote of the conservative rural South, his writing methods were anything but conservative. He experimented with repetition, inconsistent punctuation, long and puzzling sentences, flashbacks, multiple points of view, and a stream-of-consciousness style. Often, the consciousness he presented was that of a child, a fool, or a person on the verge of madness. Because of the difficulty of his writing style, Faulkner was not widely read until *The Portable Faulkner* was published in 1946 and catapulted him to world fame. Three years later, he won the Nobel Prize for Literature.

“**[Faulkner showed] that the South . . . must bury the past; that it cannot remain true—without courting tragedy or absurdity—to the promises given to dead ancestors or to the illusions of former glory.**”
—*Robert Hemenway*

“**I felt a terrible torment in the man. He always kept his eyes down.**”
—*Tennessee Williams*

William Faulkner was born in 1897 and died in 1962.

FOCUS ACTIVITY

Miss Emily is described as "a tradition, a duty, and a care." Think about a person in your neighborhood who might fit this description. How does this person look and behave?

FREEWRITE Spend two or three minutes freewriting to explore your response to this question.

SETTING A PURPOSE Read to find out why Miss Emily is considered a tradition, a duty, and a care.

BACKGROUND

The Time and Place

- "A Rose for Emily" takes place in the Deep South in the early part of the twentieth century. During this period, women and African Americans were discriminated against both by law and by custom, an attitude that is reflected in this selection in the offensive language used to speak to and about African Americans and women. While today's readers might find this language disturbing, they should bear in mind that Faulkner used it to capture as accurately as possible the social conditions in the rural South at the turn of the century.

- By 1950, when Faulkner made his Nobel Prize acceptance speech, the Soviet Union had exploded its first nuclear bombs and the cold war with the United States had begun. Both sides were building and stockpiling nuclear weapons, and people worried about the threat of a nuclear war. Faulkner refers to these fears in his speech.

Literary Influences

As a young man, Faulkner was an avid reader who grew up surrounded by stories. His great-grandfather was, among other things, an accomplished novelist. In addition to his grandfather's works, Faulkner absorbed tales of the Civil War, regional folklore, French symbolist poetry, and stories from the Bible. Many of Faulkner's images and themes, such as the idea that a person will pay for the sins of his or her ancestors, are derived from the Old Testament.

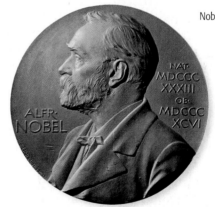

Nobel Prize medal

VOCABULARY PREVIEW

august (ô gust′) *adj.* well respected; distinguished; prominent; p. 804

sluggishly (slug′ ish lē) *adv.* slowly; without strength or energy; p. 805

obesity (ō bē′ sə tē) *n.* the condition of being extremely fat; p. 806

vindicate (vin′ də kāt′) *v.* to justify; to prove correct in light of later circumstances; p. 807

imperviousness (im pur′ vē əs nəs) *n.* the state of being unaffected or undisturbed; p. 808

haughty (hô′ tē) *adj.* conceited; arrogant; p. 808

circumvent (sur′ kəm vent′) *v.* to get around or to avoid by clever maneuvering; p. 810

virulent (vir′ yə lənt) *adj.* extremely poisonous or harmful; p. 810

A Rose for Emily

William Faulkner

When Miss Emily Grierson died, our whole town went to her funeral: the men through a sort of respectful affection for a fallen monument, the women mostly out of curiosity to see the inside of her house, which no one save an old man-servant—a combined gardener and cook—had seen in at least ten years. It was a big, squarish frame house that had once been white, decorated with cupolas[1] and spires and scrolled balconies in the heavily lightsome style of the seventies,[2] set on what had once been our most select street. But garages and cotton gins had encroached and obliterated even the august names of that neighborhood; only Miss Emily's house was left, lifting its stubborn and coquettish[3] decay above the cotton wagons and the gasoline pumps—an eyesore among eyesores. And now Miss Emily had gone to join the representatives of those august names where they lay in the cedar-bemused[4] cemetery among the ranked and anonymous graves of Union and Confederate soldiers who fell at the battle of Jefferson.

Alive, Miss Emily had been a tradition, a duty, and a care; a sort of hereditary obligation upon the town, dating from that day in 1894 when Colonel Sartoris, the mayor—he who fathered the edict that no Negro woman should appear on the streets without an apron—remitted her taxes, the dispensation dating from the death of her father on into perpetuity.[5] Not that Miss Emily would have accepted charity. Colonel Sartoris invented an involved tale to the effect that Miss Emily's father had loaned money to the town, which the town, as a matter of business, preferred this way of repaying. Only a man of Colonel Sartoris' generation and thought could have invented it, and only a woman could have believed it.

When the next generation, with its more modern ideas, became mayors and aldermen, this arrangement created some little dissatisfaction. On the first of the year they mailed her a tax notice. February came, and there was no reply. They wrote her a formal letter, asking her to call at the sheriff's office at her convenience. A week later the mayor wrote her himself, offering to call or to send his car for her, and received in reply a note on paper of an archaic[6] shape, in a thin, flowing calligraphy[7] in faded ink, to the effect that she no longer went out at all. The tax notice was also enclosed, without comment.

---

1. *Cupolas* are small, domed structures rising above a roof.
2. *Lightsome* means "light and graceful." *Seventies* refers to the 1870s.
3. *Coquettish* (kō ket′ ish) means "flirtatious."
4. *Cedar-bemused* means "lost among the cedar trees" (literally, "confused by cedars").

5. *[remitted . . . perpetuity]* This phrase means that Miss Emily was excused from paying taxes forever after her father's death.
6. Here, *archaic* means "old-fashioned."
7. *Calligraphy* is an elegant type of handwriting.

Vocabulary
august (ô gust′) *adj.* well respected; distinguished; prominent

They called a special meeting of the Board of Aldermen.[8] A deputation[9] waited upon her, knocked at the door through which no visitor had passed since she ceased giving china-painting lessons eight or ten years earlier. They were admitted by the old Negro into a dim hall from which a stairway mounted into still more shadow. It smelled of dust and disuse—a close, dank smell. The Negro led them into the parlor. It was furnished in heavy, leather-covered furniture. When the Negro opened the blinds of one window, they could see that the leather was cracked; and when they sat down, a faint dust rose <u>sluggishly</u> about their thighs, spinning with slow motes[10] in the single sun-ray. On a tarnished gilt[11] easel before the fireplace stood a crayon portrait of Miss Emily's father.

They rose when she entered—a small, fat woman in black, with a thin gold chain descending to her

My Mother, 1921. George Bellows. Oil on canvas, 83 x 49 in. The Art Institute of Chicago.

Viewing the painting: What similarities do you notice between this painting and Faulkner's description of Miss Emily and her parlor? Explain.

8. The *Board of Aldermen* is the group formed by members of a city or town council.

9. A *deputation* is a "a small group that represents a larger one."

10. *Motes* are particles or specks, as of dust.

11. *Gilt* means "covered with gold."

Vocabulary
sluggishly (slug′ ish lē) *adv.* slowly; without strength or energy

waist and vanishing into her belt, leaning on an ebony cane with a tarnished gold head. Her skeleton was small and spare; perhaps that was why what would have been merely plumpness in another was obesity in her. She looked bloated, like a body long submerged in motionless water, and of that pallid[12] hue. Her eyes, lost in the fatty ridges of her face, looked like two small pieces of coal pressed into a lump of dough as they moved from one face to another while the visitors stated their errand.

She did not ask them to sit. She just stood in the door and listened quietly until the spokesman came to a stumbling halt. Then they could hear the invisible watch ticking at the end of the gold chain.

Her voice was dry and cold. "I have no taxes in Jefferson. Colonel Sartoris explained it to me. Perhaps one of you can gain access to the city records and satisfy yourselves."

"But we have. We are the city authorities, Miss Emily. Didn't you get a notice from the sheriff, signed by him?"

"I received a paper, yes," Miss Emily said. "Perhaps he considers himself the sheriff . . . I have no taxes in Jefferson."

"But there is nothing on the books to show that, you see. We must go by the—"

"See Colonel Sartoris. I have no taxes in Jefferson."

"But, Miss Emily—"

"See Colonel Sartoris." (Colonel Sartoris had been dead almost ten years.) "I have no taxes in Jefferson. Tobe!" The Negro appeared. "Show these gentlemen out."

⮫ II ⮬

So she vanquished them, horse and foot, just as she had vanquished their fathers thirty years before about the smell. That was two years after her father's death and a short time after her sweetheart—the one we believed would marry her—had deserted her. After her father's death she went out very little; after her sweetheart went away, people hardly saw her at all. A few of the ladies had the temerity[13] to call, but were not received, and the only sign of life about the place was the Negro man—a young man then—going in and out with a market basket.

"Just as if a man—any man—could keep a kitchen properly," the ladies said; so they were not surprised when the smell developed. It was another link between the gross, teeming world and the high and mighty Griersons.

A neighbor, a woman, complained to the mayor, Judge Stevens, eighty years old.

"But what will you have me do about it, madam?" he said.

"Why, send her word to stop it," the woman said. "Isn't there a law?"

"I'm sure that won't be necessary," Judge Stevens said. "It's probably just a snake or a rat that nigger of hers killed in the yard. I'll speak to him about it."

The next day he received two more complaints, one from a man who came in diffident deprecation.[14] "We really must do something about it, Judge. I'd be the last one in the world to bother Miss Emily, but we've got to do something." That night the Board of Aldermen met—three graybeards and one younger man, a member of the rising generation.

"It's simple enough," he said. "Send her word to have her place cleaned up. Give her a certain time to do it in, and if she don't . . ."

"Dammit, sir," Judge Stevens said, "will you accuse a lady to her face of smelling bad?"

---

12. *Pallid* means "lacking healthy color" or "pale."

13. *Temerity* (tə mer′ ə tē) is excessive boldness.
14. *Diffident deprecation* means "timid disapproval."

Vocabulary
obesity (ō bē′ sə tē) *n.* the condition of being extremely fat

So the next night, after midnight, four men crossed Miss Emily's lawn and slunk about the house like burglars, sniffing along the base of the brickwork and at the cellar openings while one of them performed a regular sowing motion with his hand out of a sack slung from his shoulder. They broke open the cellar door and sprinkled lime there, and in all the outbuildings.[15] As they recrossed the lawn, a window that had been dark was lighted and Miss Emily sat in it, the light behind her, and her upright torso motionless as that of an idol. They crept quietly across the lawn and into the shadow of the locusts[16] that lined the street. After a week or two the smell went away.

That was when people had begun to feel really sorry for her. People in our town, remembering how old lady Wyatt, her great-aunt, had gone completely crazy at last, believed that the Griersons held themselves a little too high for what they really were. None of the young men were quite good enough for Miss Emily and such. We had long thought of them as a tableau,[17] Miss Emily a slender figure in white in the background, her father a spraddled[18] silhouette in the foreground, his back to her and clutching a horsewhip, the two of them framed by the backflung front door. So when she got to be thirty and was still single, we were not pleased exactly, but vindicated; even with insanity in the family she wouldn't have turned down all of her chances if they had really materialized.

When her father died, it got about that the house was all that was left to her; and in a way,

people were glad. At last they could pity Miss Emily. Being left alone, and a pauper,[19] she had become humanized. Now she too would know the old thrill and the old despair of a penny more or less.

The day after his death all the ladies prepared to call at the house and offer condolence and aid, as is our custom. Miss Emily met them at the door, dressed as usual and with no trace of grief on her face. She told them that her father was not dead. She did that for three days, with the ministers calling on her, and the doctors, trying to persuade her to let them dispose of the body. Just as they were about to resort to law and force, she broke down, and they buried her father quickly.

We did not say she was crazy then. We believed she had to do that. We remembered all the young men her father had driven away, and we knew that with nothing left, she would have to cling to that which had robbed her, as people will.

∾ III ∾

She was sick for a long time. When we saw her again her hair was cut short, making her look like a girl, with a vague resemblance to those angels in colored church windows—sort of tragic and serene.

The town had just let the contracts for paving the sidewalks, and in the summer after her father's death they began the work. The construction company came with niggers and mules and machinery, and a foreman named Homer Barron, a Yankee—a big, dark, ready man, with a big voice and eyes lighter than his face. The little boys would follow in groups to hear him cuss the niggers, and the niggers singing in time to the rise and fall of picks.

---

15. *Outbuildings* are separate buildings, such as a woodshed or barn, associated with a main building.
16. *Locusts* are deciduous trees. Several varieties have thorns and fragrant flowers that hang down in clusters.
17. A *tableau* (tab lō′) is a striking or artistic grouping of people or objects.
18. *Spraddled* means "sprawled" or "spread wide apart."

19. A *pauper* is a very poor person.

Vocabulary
vindicate (vin′ də kāt′) *v.* to justify; to prove correct in light of later circumstances

A Rose for Emily

Pretty soon he knew everybody in town. Whenever you heard a lot of laughing anywhere about the square, Homer Barron would be in the center of the group. Presently we began to see him and Miss Emily on Sunday afternoons driving in the yellow-wheeled buggy and the matched team of bays from the livery stable.

At first we were glad that Miss Emily would have an interest, because the ladies all said, "Of course a Grierson would not think seriously of a Northerner, a day laborer." But there were still others, older people, who said that even grief could not cause a real lady to forget *noblesse oblige*[20]—without calling it *noblesse oblige*. They just said, "Poor Emily. Her kinsfolk should come to her." She had some kin in Alabama; but years ago her father had fallen out with them over the estate of old lady Wyatt, the crazy woman, and there was no communication between the two families. They had not even been represented at the funeral.

And as soon as the old people said, "Poor Emily," the whispering began. "Do you suppose it's really so?" they said to one another. "Of course it is. What else could . . ." This behind their hands; rustling of craned[21] silk and satin behind jalousies closed upon the sun of Sunday afternoon as the thin, swift clop-clop-clop of the matched team passed: "Poor Emily."

She carried her head high enough—even when we believed that she was fallen. It was as if she demanded more than ever the recognition of her dignity as the last Grierson; as if it had wanted that touch of earthiness to reaffirm her imperviousness. Like when she bought the rat poison, the arsenic. That was over a year after they had begun to say "Poor Emily," and while the two female cousins were visiting her.

"I want some poison," she said to the druggist. She was over thirty then, still a slight woman, though thinner than usual, with cold, haughty black eyes in a face the flesh of which was strained across the temples and about the eye-sockets as you imagine a lighthouse-keeper's face ought to look. "I want some poison," she said.

"Yes, Miss Emily. What kind? For rats and such? I'd recom—"

"I want the best you have. I don't care what kind."

The druggist named several. "They'll kill anything up to an elephant. But what you want is—"

"Arsenic," Miss Emily said. "Is that a good one?"

"Is . . . arsenic? Yes, ma'am. But what you want—"

"I want arsenic."

The druggist looked down at her. She looked back at him, erect, her face like a strained flag. "Why, of course," the druggist said. "If that's what you want. But the law requires you to tell what you are going to use it for."

Miss Emily just stared at him, her head tilted back in order to look him eye for eye, until he looked away and went and got the arsenic and wrapped it up. The Negro delivery

Did You Know?
Jalousies (jal′ ə sēz) are overlapping, adjustable slats that cover a door or window.

---

20. The French expression *noblesse oblige* (nō bles′ ō blēzh′) suggests that those of high birth or rank have a responsibility to act kindly and honorably toward others.
21. *Craned* means "stretched."

Vocabulary
imperviousness (im pur′ vē əs nəs) *n.* the state of being unaffected or undisturbed
haughty (hô′ tē) *adj.* conceited; arrogant

Houses in Late Autumn, 1917. Charles Burchfield. Watercolor, 21½ x 17½ in. Private collection.

Viewing the painting: In your opinion, does the scene depicted in this painting resemble Miss Emily's neighborhood? Explain, using details to support your response.

boy brought her the package; the druggist didn't come back. When she opened the package at home there was written on the box, under the skull and bones: "For rats."

～ IV ～

So the next day we all said, "She will kill herself"; and we said it would be the best thing. When she had first begun to be seen with Homer Barron, we had said, "She will marry him." Then we said, "She will persuade him yet," because Homer himself had remarked— he liked men, and it was known that he drank with the younger men in the Elks' Club—that he was not a marrying man. Later we said, "Poor Emily" behind the jalousies as they passed on Sunday afternoon in the glittering buggy, Miss Emily with her head high and Homer Barron with his hat cocked and a cigar in his teeth, reins and whip in a yellow glove.

Then some of the ladies began to say that it was a disgrace to the town and a bad example to the young people. The men did not want to interfere, but at last the ladies forced the Baptist minister—Miss Emily's people were Episcopal— to call upon her. He would never divulge what happened during that interview, but he refused to go back again. The next Sunday they again drove about the streets, and the following day the minister's wife wrote to Miss Emily's relations in Alabama.

So she had blood-kin under her roof again and we sat back to watch developments. At first nothing happened. Then we were sure that they were to be married. We learned that Miss Emily had been to the jeweler's and ordered a man's toilet set[22] in silver, with the letters H. B. on each piece. Two days later we learned that she

___

22. A *toilet set* is a set of articles used for personal grooming (hairbrush, comb, etc.).

had bought a complete outfit of men's clothing, including a nightshirt, and we said, "They are married." We were really glad. We were glad because the two female cousins were even more Grierson than Miss Emily had ever been.

So we were not surprised when Homer Barron—the streets had been finished some time since—was gone. We were a little disappointed that there was not a public blowing-off,[23] but we believed that he had gone on to prepare for Miss Emily's coming, or to give her a chance to get rid of the cousins. (By that time it was a cabal,[24] and we were all Miss Emily's allies to help circumvent the cousins.) Sure enough, after another week they departed. And, as we had expected all along, within three days Homer Barron was back in town. A neighbor saw the Negro man admit him at the kitchen door at dusk one evening.

And that was the last we saw of Homer Barron. And of Miss Emily for some time. The Negro man went in and out with the market basket, but the front door remained closed. Now and then we would see her at a window for a moment, as the men did that night when they sprinkled the lime, but for almost six months she did not appear on the streets. Then we knew that this was to be expected too; as if that quality of her father which had thwarted her woman's life so many times had been too virulent and too furious to die.

When we next saw Miss Emily, she had grown fat and her hair was turning gray. During the next few years it grew grayer and grayer until it attained an even pepper-and-salt iron-gray, when it ceased turning. Up to the day of her death at seventy-four it was still that vigorous iron-gray, like the hair of an active man.

From that time on her front door remained closed, save for a period of six or seven years, when she was about forty, during which she gave lessons in china-painting. She fitted up a studio in one of the downstairs rooms, where the daughters and granddaughters of Colonel Sartoris' contemporaries were sent to her with the same regularity and in the same spirit that they were sent to church on Sundays with a twenty-five-cent piece for the collection plate. Meanwhile her taxes had been remitted.

Then the newer generation became the backbone and the spirit of the town, and the painting pupils grew up and fell away and did not send their children to her with boxes of color and tedious brushes and pictures cut from the ladies' magazines. The front door closed upon the last one and remained closed for good. When the town got free postal delivery, Miss Emily alone refused to let them fasten the metal numbers above her door and attach a mailbox to it. She would not listen to them.

Daily, monthly, yearly we watched the Negro grow grayer and more stooped, going in and out with the market basket. Each December we sent her a tax notice, which would be returned by the post office a week later, unclaimed. Now and then we would see her in one of the downstairs windows—she had evidently shut up the top floor of the house—like the carven torso of an idol in a niche,[25] looking or not looking at us, we could never tell which. Thus she passed from generation to generation—dear, inescapable, impervious, tranquil, and perverse.

And so she died. Fell ill in the house filled with dust and shadows, with only a doddering Negro man to wait on her. We did not even

---

23. A *blowing-off* is a celebration.
24. A *cabal* (kə bäl′) is a group united in a secret plot.

25. A *niche* (nich) is a recessed area in a wall, sometimes used for displaying a statue.

Vocabulary

circumvent (sur′ kəm vent′) *v.* to get around or to avoid by clever maneuvering
virulent (vir′ yə lənt) *adj.* extremely poisonous or harmful

know she was sick; we had long since given up trying to get any information from the Negro. He talked to no one, probably not even to her, for his voice had grown harsh and rusty, as if from disuse.

She died in one of the downstairs rooms, in a heavy walnut bed with a curtain, her gray head propped on a pillow yellow and moldy with age and lack of sunlight.

↝ V ↝

The Negro met the first of the ladies at the front door and let them in, with their hushed, sibilant[26] voices and their quick, curious glances, and then he disappeared. He walked right through the house and out the back and was not seen again.

The two female cousins came at once. They held the funeral on the second day, with the town coming to look at Miss Emily beneath a mass of bought flowers, with the crayon face of her father musing profoundly above the bier[27] and the ladies sibilant and macabre;[28] and the very old men—some in their brushed Confederate uniforms—on the porch and the lawn, talking of Miss Emily as if she had been a contemporary of theirs, believing that they had danced with her and courted her perhaps, confusing time with its mathematical progression, as the old do, to whom all the past is not a diminishing road but, instead, a huge meadow which no winter ever quite touches, divided from them now by the narrow bottle-neck of the most recent decade of years.

Already we knew that there was one room in that region above stairs which no one had

seen in forty years, and which would have to be forced. They waited until Miss Emily was decently in the ground before they opened it.

The violence of breaking down the door seemed to fill this room with pervading dust. A thin, acrid pall[29] as of the tomb seemed to lie everywhere upon this room decked and furnished as for a bridal:[30] upon the valance curtains of faded rose color, upon the rose-shaded lights, upon the dressing table, upon the delicate array of crystal and the man's toilet things backed with tarnished silver, silver so tarnished that the monogram was obscured. Among them lay a collar and tie, as if they had just been removed, which, lifted, left upon the surface a pale crescent in the dust. Upon a chair hung the suit, carefully folded; beneath it the two mute shoes and the discarded socks.

The man himself lay in the bed.

For a long while we just stood there, looking down at the profound and fleshless grin. The body had apparently once lain in the attitude of an embrace, but now the long sleep that outlasts love, that conquers even the grimace of love, had cuckolded[31] him. What was left of him, rotted beneath what was left of the nightshirt, had become inextricable from the bed in which he lay; and upon him and upon the pillow beside him lay that even coating of the patient and biding dust.

Then we noticed that in the second pillow was the indentation of a head. One of us lifted something from it, and leaning forward, that faint and invisible dust dry and acrid in the nostrils, we saw a long strand of iron-gray hair.

---

26. *Sibilant* (si′ bə lənt) means "making a hissing sound."
27. A *bier* is a stand for a coffin.
28. *Macabre* (mə kä′ brə) means "gruesome" or "suggesting the horror of death."

29. An *acrid pall* is a bitter-smelling covering.
30. Here, *bridal* means "wedding."
31. *Cuckolded* means "betrayed," in the sense of a husband deceived by an unfaithful wife.

Address upon Receiving
the Nobel Prize for Literature

Stockholm, December 10, 1950

William Faulkner

I feel that this award was not made to me as a man, but to my work—a life's work in the agony and sweat of the human spirit, not for glory and least of all for profit, but to create out of the materials of the human spirit something which did not exist before. So this award is only mine in trust. It will not be difficult to find a dedication for the money part of it commensurate[1] with the purpose and significance of its origin. But I would like to do the same with the acclaim too, by using this moment as a pinnacle[2] from which I might be listened to by the young men and women already dedicated to the same anguish and travail,[3] among whom is already that one who will some day stand here where I am standing.

Our tragedy today is a general and universal physical fear so long sustained by now that we can even bear it. There are no longer problems of the spirit. There is only the question: When will I be blown up? Because of this, the young man or woman writing today has forgotten the problems of the human heart in conflict with itself which alone can make good writing because only that is worth writing about, worth the agony and the sweat.

He must learn them again. He must teach himself that the basest of all things is to be afraid; and, teaching himself that, forget it forever, leaving no room in his workshop for anything but the old verities and truths of the heart, the old universal truths lacking which any story is ephemeral[4] and doomed—love and honor and pity and pride and compassion and sacrifice. Until he does so, he labors under a curse. He writes not of love but of lust, of defeats in which nobody loses anything of value, of victories without hope and, worst of all, without pity or compassion. His griefs grieve on no universal bones, leaving no scars. He writes not of the heart but of the glands.

Until he relearns these things, he will write as though he stood among and watched the end of man. I decline to accept the end of man. It is easy enough to say that man is immortal simply because he will endure: that when the last ding-dong of doom has clanged and faded from the last worthless rock hanging tideless in the last red and dying evening, that even then there will still be one more sound: that of his puny inexhaustible voice, still talking. I refuse to accept this. I believe that man will not merely endure: he will prevail. He is immortal, not because he alone among creatures has an inexhaustible voice, but because he has a soul, a spirit capable of compassion and sacrifice and endurance. The poet's, the writer's, duty is to write about these things. It is his privilege to help man endure by lifting his heart, by reminding him of the courage and honor and hope and pride and compassion and pity and sacrifice which have been the glory of his past. The poet's voice need not merely be the record of man, it can be one of the props, the pillars to help him endure and prevail.

---

1. *Commensurate* (kə men′ sər it) means "of equal measure."
2. *Pinnacle* (pin′ ə kəl) means "highest point" or "peak."
3. *Travail* (trə vāl′) is exhausting mental or physical work.

---

4. *Ephemeral* (i fem′ ər əl) means "lasting a very brief time" or "short-lived."

Responding to Literature

Personal Response

Were you surprised by the ending of "A Rose for Emily"? Explain.

ANALYZING LITERATURE

A Rose for Emily

RECALL AND INTERPRET

1. For what reason does a group of aldermen visit Miss Emily's house and with what result? Based on the first section, what can you infer about Miss Emily and her life?
2. Summarize what happens when Miss Emily's house begins to smell and when her father dies. How does the community interpret her response to these incidents?
3. Describe Homer Barron and his relationship to Miss Emily. Expain the community's involvement in their relationship and the results of that involvement.
4. What was Miss Emily's life like during her last years? What might have incited her to act as she apparently did? How much responsibility do you think the town bears?

EVALUATE AND CONNECT

5. How would you characterize the **narrator** (see page R10)? What can you infer about the narrator's attitude toward Miss Emily? Explain.
6. How is Miss Emily like the person you described in the Focus Activity on page 803? How is she different? Explain.

Address upon Receiving the Nobel Prize for Literature

RECALL AND INTERPRET

7. What are modern writers concerned with, according to Faulkner? Why is this a problem? What solution does Faulkner suggest?
8. What is Faulkner's view of humankind's future and of the writer's role in that future?

EVALUATE AND CONNECT

9. Do you agree with the ideas Faulkner presents in this speech? Why or why not?
10. If Faulkner were alive today, would he be someone you would like to meet? Explain.

Literary ELEMENTS

Flashback

A **flashback** is a portion of a story that interrupts the chronological sequence of events to describe what happened earlier. It provides background about a character, a setting, or an event. For example, Faulkner uses a flashback to illuminate the town's attitude toward Miss Emily and changes occurring in the South.

1. In the first paragraph of section 2, what events does the narrator describe? When did each occur? Why does the chronology turn out to be important?
2. What purpose do the flashbacks serve in this story?

● See **Literary Terms Handbook,** p. R6.

LITERATURE AND WRITING

Writing About Literature
Detective Work   In your opinion, exactly what happened to Homer Barron? Write a few paragraphs describing what you think happened and why. Use details from the story.

Creative Writing
Dear Diary   Imagine that Miss Emily kept a secret diary in which she recorded her thoughts and feelings. Write an entry that might be found in the diary, conveying Miss Emily's response to one of the events Faulkner describes.

EXTENDING YOUR RESPONSE

Literature Groups
The Human Struggle   Faulkner once described "A Rose for Emily" as "a manifestation of man's injustice to man, of the poor tragic human being struggling with its own heart, with others, with its environment, for the simple things which all human beings want." In your group, discuss what Faulkner might have meant by this statement and how this story illustrates it. Use evidence from the selection to support your conclusions, and share them with the class.

Internet Connection
Web Site Review   Conduct a search on the Internet to find Web sites devoted to Faulkner's life and work. Visit one site and present a short review of it to your classmates. Include the address, the options at the site, and aspects of the site that might make visiting it worthwhile.

Interdisciplinary Activity
Art: Research and Select   Faulkner's inspiration for this ghost story, as he called it, came from a "picture of a strand of hair on the pillow in [an] abandoned house." Create or find a picture that captures your feelings about the story, the setting, or one or more characters.

Reading Further
For more by Faulkner, look for the following books: *Collected Stories of William Faulkner,* edited by Erroll McDonald, contains more than forty stories, including many classics; *The Portable Faulkner,* the book that created his reputation.

Save your work for your portfolio.

Skill Minilesson

VOCABULARY • Denotation and Connotation

In describing Miss Emily, Faulkner writes ". . . perhaps that was why what would have been merely plumpness in another was obesity in her." The words *plumpness* and *obesity* have similar **denotations,** or literal meanings. Each word, however, has a different **connotation,** the feeling or impression it suggests. *Plumpness* has a positive connotation suggesting a pleasing roundness. *Obesity,* however, has a negative connotation implying an extreme fatness. Sometimes a word gives neither a positive nor a negative impression—its connotation is neutral.

PRACTICE   The words in each group have similar denotations. Tell whether each one has a positive, negative, or neutral connotation.

1. **haughty**   proud arrogant insolent
2. **archaic**   old antique venerable
3. **stubborn**   obstinate persistent determined
4. **sluggishly**   leisurely lethargically slowly

● For more on denotation and connotation, see **Literary Terms Handbook,** p. R4.

Vo·cab·u·lar·y Skills

Defining Compound Words

In his short story, "A Rose for Emily," William Faulkner uses compound words, such as *cotton gin, eyesore,* and *sun-ray.* A **compound word** consists of two words that together have a meaning different from either one. Compound words may be open *(cotton gin),* closed *(eyesore)*, or hyphenated *(sun-ray).* You can check a dictionary to find out whether a compound word is closed, open, or hyphenated.

The meanings of many compound words are obvious from the parts that make up the word. For example:

- What is a *passerby?* It is someone who passes by, or moves past.
- What is a *windowsill?* The word *window,* of course, is familiar. A *sill* is a horizontal strip that forms the lower part of a frame. So a *windowsill* is the strip at the bottom of a window opening.
- What do you do with a *viewfinder* on a camera? You look through it to find the view you will photograph.
- What is a *look-alike?* It's something that looks just like something else.

The meanings of other compound words, however, may be less obvious, and that's when you should consult a dictionary. For example, some greyhounds are not gray, and not all gray hounds are greyhounds.

EXERCISES

- Use your understanding of the following compounds to match each with its definition.

    1. swaybacked   a. a place-keeper
    2. bookmark   b. metal screen or grating
    3. grillwork   c. mistreated
    4. elbowroom   d. adequate space
    5. ill-used   e. having a sagging spine

- Define the following compound words based on their word parts. Discuss your definitions with a partner. Then look up the words in a dictionary to check your definitions.

    6. ivory tower
    7. dark horse
    8. wrongheaded
    9. monkey wrench
    10. green revolution

Before You Read

Father's Bedroom

Meet Robert Lowell

"So much of the effort of the poem is to arrive at something essentially human, to find the right voice for what we have to say. In life we speak with many false voices; occasionally, if we are lucky, we find a true one in our poems."

—*Lowell*

Robert Lowell was born into a family rich in New England tradition. He may even have had ancestors who arrived on the Mayflower. Numbering among Lowell's ancestors were the poets James Russell Lowell and Amy Lowell and the astronomer Percival Lowell. Lowell both embraced and rebelled against his aristocratic background.

At age eighteen, Lowell entered the family's alma mater, Harvard College, but dropped out after his first year. The next fall he enrolled in Kenyon College, where he studied under the poet John Crowe Ransom. A profound thinker and a gifted craftsman, Lowell achieved early success as a poet, winning a Pulitzer Prize before he was thirty.

In mid-life, Lowell began working on a new kind of poetry that has come to be called confessional poetry. In his new poems, he began to describe with great openness his personal experiences, including his struggles with manic-depressive disorder. Though this illness made it difficult for Lowell to function, it also, he believed, enabled him to perceive truths beyond the understanding of ordinary people.

In addition to being as one critic noted, "the most celebrated poet in English of his generation," Lowell was a political activist. He was imprisoned during World War II for refusing to join the Army, and in the 1960s he openly opposed United States involvement in Vietnam.

Robert Lowell was born in 1917 and died in 1977. What can you learn about people by their possessions

---

FOCUS ACTIVITY

or by how they arrange their possessions?

JOURNAL Think of someone close to you. Pick three or more objects that you associate with that person. Describe these objects in your journal and explain why you associate them with the person.

SETTING A PURPOSE Read to find out how one poet uses objects to characterize a person in his life.

Robert Lowell's

BACKGROUND

Father

Although he never used the title Jr., Robert Lowell was named after his father, Robert Traill Spence Lowell. The elder Lowell joined the United States Navy at age fourteen to help support his mother, who had been widowed before the birth of her only son. He sailed around the world, a tour referred to in the poem "Father's Bedroom."

Literary Influences

In interviews and in his own writing, Lowell named Allen Tate and William Carlos Williams as his greatest poetic influences. Tate schooled Lowell in traditional verse forms, which Lowell would use with great mastery in his early poetry. In describing Williams, Lowell once said, "For sheer language, Williams beats anybody. And who compares with him for aliveness and keenness of observation."

Father's Bedroom

Robert Lowell

In my Father's bedroom:
blue threads as thin
as pen-writing on the bedspread,
blue dots on the curtains,
5   a blue kimono,°
Chinese sandals with blue plush straps.
The broad-planked floor
had a sandpapered neatness.
The clear glass bed-lamp
10   with a white doily shade
was still raised a few
inches by resting on volume two
of Lafcadio Hearn's
Glimpses of Unfamiliar Japan.
15   Its warped olive cover
was punished like a rhinoceros hide.
In the flyleaf:
"Robbie from Mother."
Years later in the same hand:
20   "This book has had hard usage
on the Yangtze River, China.
It was left under an open
porthole in a storm."

Early Morning, 1966. Fairfield Porter. Oil on canvas, 32 x 28 in. Private collection. Courtesy Tibor de Nagy Gallery, New York.

---

5 A *kimono* (ki mō′ nə) is a loose robe or gown with wide sleeves and a broad sash traditionally worn by Japanese men and women.

Responding to Literature

Personal Response

List three adjectives that capture your perception of the father's life.

ANALYZING LITERATURE

RECALL AND INTERPRET

1. What kinds of objects does the speaker describe in lines 1–10? What do these objects tell you about the father?
2. What colors are mentioned in the poem? What association might Lowell want the reader to make with these colors?
3. How does Lowell describe the cover of *Glimpses of Unfamiliar Japan* in lines 15–16? What does this suggest about the personality of the father?
4. What do the inscriptions in *Glimpses of Unfamiliar Japan* tell you about the father's life and his relationship with his own mother?

EVALUATE AND CONNECT

5. Based on the poem's **tone** (see page R16), how would you describe Lowell's thoughts and feelings about his father? Explain.
6. What word does Lowell repeat in this poem? In what ways does this **repetition** contribute to the impact and meaning of the poem?
7. **Theme Connections**   What personal discoveries might Lowell have made by writing this poem? Explain with details from the selection.
8. In your opinion, does the reader learn more about Lowell or his father based on the objects described? Do the objects you listed for the Focus Activity on page 816 tell more about the person who owns them or more about you? Explain your answers.

Literary ELEMENTS

Confessional Poetry

Following the lead of Lowell, several poets in the 1950s, including Anne Sexton, Randall Jarrell, and Sylvia Plath, began writing poems that described their own personal experiences. Soon they were known as the **Confessional School** of poets. In their poetry, these writers used an open and direct style to describe their problems with mental illness, alcohol, and troubled relationships.

1. In what ways is "Father's Bedroom" an example of a confessional poem?
2. Would you characterize the style that Lowell uses in this poem as open and direct? Why or why not?

● See **Literary Terms Handbook,** p. R3.

EXTENDING YOUR RESPONSE

Literature Groups

Good Father/Good Son   In your group, discuss the following question: Does Lowell present his father as a good father and a good son in this poem, or does he suggest that his father had real shortcomings? Have each person support his or her opinions with details from the poem. Then present the results of your discussion to the class.

Creative Writing

Describe a Place   Through writing about a place, Lowell conveys an image of a person. What could you convey about someone you know by describing that person's room? Write a prose description of a place emphasizing details that help characterize the person who lives there.

📖 **Save your work for your portfolio.**

Writing Skills

Organizing Details

Strong writing often contains vivid images and colorful, exact details. When you write descriptions, essays, narratives, or reports, choose a strategy for ordering details that will help your readers understand your ideas. Here are four strategies for organizing details in your writing.

- **Chronological order** presents events in the order in which they occur. Words such as *now, then, later,* and *before* give readers clues to the sequence of events.
- **Spatial order** presents details according to their physical placement, allowing readers to visualize each scene or description. For example, details may be described from left to right, from front to back, from top to bottom, from near to far, clockwise, or counterclockwise.
- **Order of importance** presents details in order of their significance, either from the least important to the most important, or vice versa.
- **Categories** present details by feature, such as by color or by size.

It's important to consider your purpose for writing before choosing an organizational strategy. If you want to inform or persuade your readers, you might choose to organize your details in order of importance. If you need to narrate an account of a series of events, you may want to organize the details in chronological order, so readers can follow the sequence of events as they unfold. If you want to describe a real or fictional place or scene, you can organize your details in spatial order, so readers can "see" the scene exactly as you do.

Read the beginning of Robert Lowell's poem "Father's Bedroom," and think about the strategy or strategies he uses to organize the details.

> **In my Father's bedroom:**
> **blue threads as thin**
> **as pen-writing on the bedspread,**
> **blue dots on the curtains,**
> **a blue kimono,**
> **Chinese sandals with blue plush straps.**

Can you find a unifying pattern running through this description? Lowell uses the color blue to link the physical things in his father's bedroom as well as to create a mood of personal intimacy. He uses spatial order and color (a category) to organize details.

EXERCISE

Write a poem or a paragraph describing a memorable place, person, or event in your life. Choose a strategy for organizing your details that will allow your readers to clearly understand your thoughts and ideas.

Before You Read

from *Black Boy*

Meet Richard Wright

In April 1943, thirty-four-year-old Richard Wright, already a well-known writer, gave a speech at Fisk University in Nashville, Tennessee. Of that speech Wright later said:

"I gave a clumsy, conversational kind of speech to the folks, white and black, reciting what I felt and thought about the world, what I remembered about my life, about being a Negro. There was but little applause. Indeed, the audience was terribly still, and it was not until I was half way through my speech that it crashed upon me that I was saying things that Negroes were not supposed to say publicly."

After the speech, people inundated Wright with questions and comments. He realized that the truth he had shared about his life and about race relations had been a powerful stimulant to his audience. It was then that he decided to write his autobiography.

At the time he began his autobiography, Wright's novel *Native Son* had already sold tremendously well and had been adapted as a Broadway play. The play, in turn, was adapted into a movie made in Argentina and starred Wright as himself. Newspapers, magazines, and publishing companies flooded him with requests for book reviews, and he received loads of fan mail from readers around the world.

Wright's autobiography, *Black Boy*, which covers Wright's childhood in the South, was published in 1945. Like *Native Son*, Wright's autobiography sold very well. It depicts the deprivation, insecurity, and crushing lack of respect African Americans faced during the period in which Wright grew up.

Wright considered his childhood typical for African Americans of his time. Furthermore, he did not see social conditions changing quickly for the better in the United States. In fact, only two years after *Black Boy's* publication, Wright moved his family to Paris, France, to spare them the prejudices they might have faced in the United States. Although he continued writing and speaking, Wright never returned to live in the United States.

"I sweat over my work. I wish I could say it just flows out, but I can't. I usually write a rough draft, then go over it, page by page."

"I do not deal in happiness; I deal in meaning."

"It's strong, it's raw—but it's life as I see and lived it."

—*Wright*

Richard Wright was born in 1908 and died in 1960.

FOCUS ACTIVITY

What is the hungriest you have ever felt? What was the situation? How did it feel to be so hungry?

FREEWRITE In your journal, freewrite for three minutes about the experience. Write about how you might feel and act if you were always hungry. Jot down whatever words and images come to your mind.

SETTING A PURPOSE Read to learn of one writer's childhood experiences of hunger.

BACKGROUND

The Time and Place

Richard Wright was born on a farm near Natchez, Mississippi, in 1908. His father was a sharecropper—in return for planting, tending, and harvesting the fields, he and his family received a small cabin and some of the money from the cotton crop. Wright's mother gave up her career as a teacher to raise her family and help with the farm. Like many sharecropping families, the Wrights had a hard time making ends meet. They finally gave up share-cropping and moved to Natchez when Wright was three,

Sharecroppers, late 1800s.

and then to Memphis in 1912. Unfortunately, the Wrights were not successful in either place. By the time Richard Wright turned six, his father had abandoned the family. Wright, his mother, and his brother had little income and were facing starvation when the following selection from *Black Boy* begins.

Literary Influences

Richard Wright was always an avid reader, but he faced special handicaps during his youth. Public libraries in the South did not allow African Americans to take out books. However, he persuaded a white acquaintance to write a note giving Wright permission to take out books for him. The first library book he took out was by the fiery journalist H. L. Mencken. Realizing that he, too, could battle ignorance and prejudice with words, Wright set off on his path to be a writer.

Wright studied the lives and works of great Russian authors to learn how they wove their fictional tales from the material of their lives. He greatly admired many American authors as well, including William Faulkner and Ernest Hemingway. He also encouraged the next generation of African American writers, including Ralph Ellison and James Baldwin.

VOCABULARY PREVIEW

irk (urk) *v.* to annoy; to bother; p. 822
futile (fū′ til) *adj.* useless; worthless; pointless; p. 823
hostile (host′ əl) *adj.* feeling or showing hatred; antagonistic; p. 823
vindictive (vin dik′ tiv) *adj.* desiring revenge; p. 823
intrigue (in′ trēg) *n.* the use of devious schemes to achieve a goal; secret plotting; p. 823

vivid (viv′ id) *adj.* lifelike; realistic; distinct; p. 826
vital (vīt′ əl) *adj.* of critical importance; essential; p. 826
poised (poizd) *adj.* having a calm, controlled, and dignified manner; composed; p. 826
alien (ā′ lē ən) *adj.* strange; unfamiliar; foreign; p. 827

from Black Boy

Richard Wright ～

When I awakened one morning my mother told me that we were going to see a judge who would make my father support me and my brother. An hour later all three of us were sitting in a huge crowded room. I was overwhelmed by the many faces and the voices which I could not understand. High above me was a white face which my mother told me was the face of the judge. Across the huge room sat my father, smiling confidently, looking at us. My mother warned me not to be fooled by my father's friendly manner; she told me that the judge might ask me questions, and if he did I must tell him the truth. I agreed, yet I hoped that the judge would not ask me anything.

For some reason the entire thing struck me as being useless; I felt that if my father were going to feed me, then he would have done so regardless of what a judge said to him. And I did not want my father to feed me; I was hungry, but my thoughts of food did not now center about him. I waited, growing restless, hungry. My mother gave me a dry sandwich and I munched and stared, longing to go home. Finally I heard my mother's name called; she rose and began weeping so copiously[1] that she could not talk for a few moments; at last she managed to say that her husband had deserted her and her two children, that her children were hungry, that they stayed hungry, that she worked, that she was trying to raise them alone. Then my father was called; he came forward jauntily, smiling. He tried to kiss my mother, but she turned away from him. I only heard one sentence of what he said.

---

1. *Copiously* means "in great quantity."

"I'm doing all I can, Your Honor," he mumbled, grinning.

It had been painful to sit and watch my mother crying and my father laughing and I was glad when we were outside in the sunny streets. Back at home my mother wept again and talked complainingly about the unfairness of the judge who had accepted my father's word. After the court scene, I tried to forget my father; I did not hate him; I simply did not want to think of him. Often when we were hungry my mother would beg me to go to my father's job and ask him for a dollar, a dime, a nickel . . . But I would never consent to go. I did not want to see him.

My mother fell ill and the problem of food became an acute, daily agony. Hunger was with us always. Sometimes the neighbors would feed us or a dollar bill would come in the mail from my grandmother. It was winter and I would buy a dime's worth of coal each morning from the corner coalyard and lug it home in paper bags. For a time I remained out of school to wait upon my mother, then Granny came to visit us and I returned to school.

At night there were long, halting discussions about our going to live with Granny, but nothing came of it. Perhaps there was not enough money for railroad fare. Angered by having been hauled into court, my father now spurned us completely. I heard long, angrily whispered conversations between my mother and grandmother to the effect that "that woman ought to be killed for breaking up a home." What irked me was the ceaseless talk and no action. If someone had suggested that

---

Vocabulary

irk (urk) *v.* to annoy; to bother

my father be killed, I would perhaps have become interested; if someone had suggested that his name never be mentioned, I would no doubt have agreed; if someone had suggested that we move to another city, I would have been glad. But there was only endless talk that led nowhere and I began to keep away from home as much as possible, preferring the simplicity of the streets to the worried, <u>futile</u> talk at home.

Finally we could no longer pay the rent for our dingy flat;[2] the few dollars that Granny had left us before she went home were gone. Half sick and in despair, my mother made the rounds of the charitable institutions, seeking help. She found an orphan home that agreed to assume the guidance of me and my brother provided my mother worked and made small payments. My mother hated to be separated from us, but she had no choice.

The orphan home was a two-story frame building set amid trees in a wide, green field. My mother ushered me and my brother one morning into the building and into the presence of a tall, gaunt, mulatto[3] woman who called herself Miss Simon. At once she took a

Gamin, 1930. Augusta Savage. Plaster, height: 9¼ in. Schomberg Center for Research in Black Culture, The New York Public Library.

fancy to me and I was frightened speechless; I was afraid of her the moment I saw her and my fear lasted during my entire stay in the home.

The house was crowded with children and there was always a storm of noise. The daily routine was blurred to me and I never quite grasped it. The most abiding feeling I had each day was hunger and fear. The meals were skimpy and there were only two of them. Just before we went to bed each night we were given a slice of bread smeared with molasses. The children were silent, <u>hostile</u>, <u>vindictive</u>, continuously complaining of hunger. There was an overall atmosphere of nervousness and <u>intrigue</u>, of children telling tales upon others, of children being deprived of food to punish them.

The home did not have the money to check the growth of the wide stretches of grass by having it mown, so it had to be pulled by hand. Each morning after we had eaten a breakfast that seemed like no breakfast at all, an older child would lead a herd of us to the vast lawn and we would get to our knees and wrench the grass loose from the dirt with our fingers. At intervals Miss Simon would make a tour of inspection, examining the pile of pulled grass beside each child, scolding or praising according to the size of the pile. Many mornings I was too weak from

---

2. A *flat* is an apartment.
3. *Mulatto*, a word seldom used today, describes a biracial person, one of mixed African American and white ancestry.

Vocabulary
futile (fū′ til) *adj.* useless; worthless; pointless
hostile (host′ əl) *adj.* feeling or showing hatred; antagonistic
vindictive (vin dik′ tiv) *adj.* desiring revenge
intrigue (in′ trēg) *n.* the use of devious schemes to achieve a goal; secret plotting

from **Black Boy**

hunger to pull the grass; I would grow dizzy and my mind would become blank and I would find myself, after an interval of unconsciousness, upon my hands and knees, my head whirling, my eyes staring in bleak astonishment at the green grass, wondering where I was, feeling that I was emerging from a dream . . .

During the first days my mother came each night to visit me and my brother, then her visits stopped. I began to wonder if she, too, like my father, had disappeared into the unknown. I was rapidly learning to distrust everything and everybody. When my mother did come, I asked her why had she remained away so long and she told me that Miss Simon had forbidden her to visit us, that Miss Simon had said that she was spoiling us with too much attention. I begged my mother to take me away; she wept and told me to wait, that soon she would take us to Arkansas. She left and my heart sank.

Miss Simon tried to win my confidence; she asked me if I would like to be adopted by her if my mother consented and I said no. She would take me into her apartment and talk to me, but her words had no effect. Dread and distrust had already become a daily part of my being and my memory grew sharp, my senses more impressionable; I began to be aware of myself as a distinct personality striving against others. I held myself in, afraid to act or speak until I was sure of my surroundings, feeling most of the time that I was suspended over a void. My imagination soared; I dreamed of running away. Each morning I vowed that I would leave the next morning, but the next morning always found me afraid.

One day Miss Simon told me that thereafter I was to help her in the office. I ate lunch with her and, strangely, when I sat facing her at the table, my hunger vanished. The woman killed something in me. Next she called me to her desk where she sat addressing envelopes.

"Step up close to the desk," she said. "Don't be afraid."

I went and stood at her elbow. There was a wart on her chin and I stared at it.

"Now, take a blotter from over there and blot each envelope after I'm through writing on it," she instructed me, pointing to a blotter that stood about a foot from my hand.

I stared and did not move or answer.

"Take the blotter," she said.

I wanted to reach for the blotter and succeeded only in twitching my arm.

"Here," she said sharply, reaching for the blotter and shoving it into my fingers.

She wrote in ink on an envelope and pushed it toward me. Holding the blotter in my hand, I stared at the envelope and could not move.

"Blot it," she said.

I could not lift my hand. I knew what she had said; I knew what she wanted me to do; and I had heard her correctly. I wanted to look at her and say something, tell her why I could not move; but my eyes were fixed upon the floor. I could not summon enough courage while she sat there looking at me to reach over the yawning space of twelve inches and blot the wet ink on the envelope.

"Blot it!" she spoke sharply.

Still I could not move or answer.

"Look at me!"

I could not lift my eyes. She reached her hand to my face and I twisted away.

"What's wrong with you?" she demanded.

I began to cry and she drove me from the room. I decided that as soon as night came I would run away. The dinner bell rang and I did not go to the table, but hid in a corner of the hallway. When I heard the dishes rattling at the table, I opened the door and ran down the walk to the street. Dusk was falling. Doubt made me stop. Ought I go back? No; hunger was back there, and fear. I went on, coming to concrete sidewalks. People passed me. Where was I going? I did not know. The farther I walked the more frantic I became. In a confused and vague way I knew that I was doing more running *away* from than running *toward* something. I stopped. The streets seemed dangerous. The buildings were massive and dark. The moon shone and the trees loomed frighteningly. No, I could not go on. I would go back. But I had walked so far and had turned too many corners and had not kept track of the direction. Which way led back to the orphan home? I did not know. I was lost.

I stood in the middle of the sidewalk and cried. A "white" policeman came to me and I wondered if he was going to beat me. He asked me what was the matter and I told him that I was trying to find my mother. His "white" face created a new fear in me. I was remembering the tale of the "white" man who had beaten the "black" boy. A crowd gathered and I was urged to tell where I lived. Curiously, I was too full of fear to cry now. I wanted to tell the "white" face that I had run off from an orphan home and that Miss Simon ran it, but I was afraid. Finally I was taken to the police station where I was fed. I felt better. I sat in a big chair where I was surrounded by "white" policemen, but they seemed to ignore me. Through the window I could see that night had completely fallen and that lights now gleamed in the streets. I grew sleepy and dozed. My shoulder was shaken gently and I opened my eyes and looked into a "white" face of another policeman who was sitting beside me. He asked me questions in a quiet, confidential tone, and quite before I knew it he was not "white" any more. I told him that I had run away from an orphan home and that Miss Simon ran it.

It was but a matter of minutes before I was walking alongside a policeman, heading toward the home. The policeman led me to the front gate and I saw Miss Simon waiting for me on the steps. She identified me and I was left in her charge. I begged her not to beat me, but she yanked me upstairs into an empty room and lashed me thoroughly. Sobbing, I slunk off to

bed, resolved to run away again. But I was watched closely after that.

My mother was informed upon her next visit that I had tried to run away and she was terribly upset.

"Why did you do it?" she asked.

"I don't want to stay here," I told her.

"But you must," she said. "How can I work if I'm to worry about you? You must remember that you have no father. I'm doing all I can."

"I don't want to stay here," I repeated.

"Then, if I take you to your father . . ."

"I don't want to stay with him either," I said.

"But I want you to ask him for enough money for us to go to my sister's in Arkansas," she said.

Again I was faced with choices I did not like, but I finally agreed. After all, my hate for my father was not so great and urgent as my hate for the orphan home. My mother held to her idea and one night a week or so later I found myself standing in a room in a frame house. My father and a strange woman were sitting before a bright fire that blazed in a grate. My mother and I were standing about six feet away, as though we were afraid to approach them any closer.

"It's not for me," my mother was saying. "It's for your children that I'm asking you for money."

"I ain't got nothing," my father said, laughing.

"Come here, boy," the strange woman called to me.

I looked at her and did not move.

"Give him a nickel," the woman said. "He's cute."

"Come here, Richard," my father said, stretching out his hand.

I backed away, shaking my head, keeping my eyes on the fire.

"He is a cute child," the strange woman said.

"You ought to be ashamed," my mother said to the strange woman. "You're starving my children."

from **Black Boy**

"Now, don't you-all fight," my father said, laughing.

"I'll take that poker and hit you!" I blurted at my father.

He looked at my mother and laughed louder.

"You told him to say that," he said.

"Don't say such things, Richard," my mother said.

"You ought to be dead," I said to the strange woman.

The woman laughed and threw her arms about my father's neck. I grew ashamed and wanted to leave.

"How can you starve your children?" my mother asked.

"Let Richard stay with me," my father said.

"Do you want to stay with your father, Richard?" my mother asked.

"No," I said.

"You'll get plenty to eat," he said.

"I'm hungry now," I told him. "But I won't stay with you."

"Aw, give the boy a nickel," the woman said.

My father ran his hand into his pocket and pulled out a nickel.

"Here, Richard," he said.

"Don't take it," my mother said.

"Don't teach him to be a fool," my father said. "Here, Richard, take it."

I looked at my mother, at the strange woman, at my father, then into the fire. I wanted to take the nickel, but I did not want to take it from my father.

"You ought to be ashamed," my mother said, weeping. "Giving your son a nickel when he's hungry. If there's a God, He'll pay you back."

"That's all I got," my father said, laughing again and returning the nickel to his pocket.

We left. I had the feeling that I had had to do with something unclean. Many times in the years after that the image of my father and the strange woman, their faces lit by the dancing flames, would surge up in my imagination so vivid and strong that I felt I could reach out and touch it; I would stare at it, feeling that it possessed some vital meaning which always eluded me.

A quarter of a century was to elapse between the time when I saw my father sitting with the strange woman and the time when I was to see him again, standing alone upon the red clay of a Mississippi plantation, a sharecropper, clad in ragged overalls, holding a muddy hoe in his gnarled, veined hands—a quarter of a century during which my mind and consciousness had become so greatly and violently altered that when I tried to talk to him I realized that, though ties of blood made us kin, though I could see a shadow of my face in his face, though there was an echo of my voice in his voice, we were forever strangers, speaking a different language, living on vastly distant planes of reality. That day a quarter of a century later when I visited him on the plantation—he was standing against the sky, smiling toothlessly, his hair whitened, his body bent, his eyes glazed with dim recollection, his fearsome aspect of twenty-five years ago gone forever from him—I was overwhelmed to realize that he could never understand me or the scalding experiences that had swept me beyond his life and into an area of living that he could never know. I stood before him, poised, my mind aching as it embraced the simple nakedness of his life, feeling how completely his soul was imprisoned by the slow flow of the seasons, by wind and rain and sun, how fastened were his memories to a crude and raw past, how chained were his actions and emotions to the direct, animalistic impulses of his withering body . . .

From the white landowners above him there had not been handed to him a chance to learn

---

Vocabulary

vivid (viv′ id) *adj.* lifelike; realistic; distinct
vital (vīt′ əl) *adj.* of critical importance; essential
poised (poizd) *adj.* having a calm, controlled, and dignified manner; composed

Negro Cabin, Sedalia, North Carolina (No. 1), 1930. Loïs Mailou Jones. Watercolor on paper, 14⅛ x 19⅛ in. Collection of the artist.

Viewing the painting: In what ways does the scene depicted in the painting capture the difficult life of Wright's father and of sharecroppers in general?

the meaning of loyalty, of sentiment, of tradition. Joy was as unknown to him as was despair. As a creature of the earth, he endured, hearty, whole, seemingly indestructible, with no regrets and no hope. He asked easy, drawling questions about me, his other son, his wife, and he laughed, amused, when I informed him of their destinies. I forgave him and pitied him as my eyes looked past him to the unpainted wooden shack. From far beyond the horizons that bound this bleak plantation there had come to me through my living the knowledge that my father was a black peasant who had gone to the city seeking life, but who had failed in the city; a black peasant whose life had been hopelessly snarled in the city, and who had at last fled the city—that same city which had lifted me in its burning arms and borne me toward <u>alien</u> and undreamed-of shores of knowing.

Vocabulary
alien (ā′ lē ən) *adj.* strange; unfamiliar; foreign

Responding to Literature

Personal Response

What was your reaction to the events of Wright's life? Explain.

——— ANALYZING LITERATURE ———

RECALL

1. Why do Wright, his mother, and his brother go to court? What happens there?
2. Why do Wright and his brother go to the orphan home? What are the three main feelings Wright experiences while there?
3. Why does Wright run away? What happens during this incident?
4. What deal does Wright's mother make with him as she takes him out of the orphan home? How does Wright feel about the deal?
5. What ultimately happens to Wright's father?

INTERPRET

6. How do you think the events in court affect Wright's relationship with his father? Explain.
7. For Wright, how is the orphan home different from his old home? How is it similar? Why might his unhappiness increase there?
8. What do you learn about Wright's attitudes and perceptions about race from the runaway incident?
9. What do you learn about Wright's character from his interactions with his father just after he leaves the orphan home?
10. What does the visit with his elderly father reveal about Wright and what he values in life? Explain, using details from the selection.

EVALUATE AND CONNECT

11. Which **anecdote** from the selection did you find most moving? Why? (See Literary Terms Handbook, page R1.)
12. Theme Connections   What is the most important personal discovery you gained from reading this selection? Explain.
13. How did knowing that this selection is an **autobiography** (see page R2) affect your reaction to it? Would you have reacted differently if it were fiction? Explain.
14. How would you describe this selection's **tone**, or the author's attitude? How effective is this tone in expressing the author's main points?
15. Based on this selection, do you think you would like to read the rest of Richard Wright's autobiography? Why or why not?

Literary ELEMENTS

Flash-forward

Writers have different ways of ordering events in a story. Most often they describe events in chronological order, or the order in which events naturally occur. Sometimes, however, writers interrupt this flow of events. A skip back to the past is called a **flashback.** A leap forward into the future is called a **flash-forward.** A writer might signal a flash-forward with a new paragraph or with a description of a new setting, so readers know exactly how the time frame has shifted. In other instances, writers shift the setting back and forth in time without giving any signal.

1. Where is the flash-forward in this selection?
2. How does Wright signal that he is skipping ahead from the main narrative?
3. What effect does this flash-forward create in Wright's narrative? In your opinion, does it strengthen or weaken the narrative? Explain.

● See **Literary Terms Handbook,** p. R6.

LITERATURE AND WRITING

Writing About Literature

Author's Use of Dialogue   Find four examples of **dialogue** (see page R4) in the selection. Note the setting in which each occurs, the people who are talking, what they talk about, and any other details that you find significant. Then write several paragraphs explaining what each example reveals about the characters.

Creative Writing

Letters from the Heart   Imagine that you are Wright living in the orphan home. Write a letter to your mother describing the conditions, your feelings about being there, and your hopes for how things will change. Then imagine that you are Wright's mother, and write a reply. Use the selection as a guide for details and characterization.

EXTENDING YOUR RESPONSE

Literature Groups

What Is Hunger?   What does hunger feel like to you? Look back at your freewriting for the Focus Activity on page 821, and share your responses with your group. Then look in the selection for Wright's descriptions of hunger. How do his descriptions compare with those your group came up with? What "kills" his hunger? What else might he hunger for? Share your ideas with the class.

Interdisciplinary Activity

History: Life in the South   Find out what life was like for African Americans in the South around 1915. Look for interesting statistics as you research voting laws, Jim Crow laws, business ownership, farming, schools, or any other

topic of interest to you. Then, in an oral report, explain how what you have learned is related to Wright's story.

Listening and Speaking

Interview Richard Wright   What questions would you like to ask Richard Wright after reading this excerpt from his autobiography? With a partner, create a list of questions. Then discuss how Wright might answer each one. Finally, plan and perform your interview with Richard Wright for a group of classmates. After the interview, discuss its content with the class.

📕 **Save your work for your portfolio.**

Skill Minilesson

VOCABULARY • Latin Roots: *vit* and *viv*

Latin roots form the basis of many English words. The root is usually combined with a prefix, a suffix, or both. The meaning of the English word is usually related to the meaning of the root it contains. For example, the Latin roots *vit* and *viv* mean "life" or "to live." Notice how these roots affect the meanings of two vocabulary words:

vital—essential; necessary to continued existence or life

vivid—lifelike; realistic

PRACTICE   Write a definition that includes the meaning of the root *vit* or *viv* for each word below. Then write each word in an original sentence.

1. **vit**ality
2. re**viv**e
3. **viv**acious
4. **vit**a
5. con**viv**ial

Newspaper Article

Most professional athletes are relatively young, but amateurs of all ages can amaze people with their physical endurance. In California, the Angeles Crest 100-Mile Endurance Run attracts athletes who push their limits to the max.

100-Mile Run to Agony and Ecstasy

by Sonia Nazario, *Los Angeles Times*, September 30, 1996

Runner John Canby of La Canada Flintridge had been plodding on his feet most of the previous 29 hours when finally, at 11 A.M., he walked across the finish line, bowlegged, stepping as if walking on broken glass. His first request to friends: Could they pull the car closer to him, please, so he could escape without having to take another step? Some of the endurance runners [in this race] concede that this equivalent of four back-to-back marathons may seem a bit nutty to outsiders.

Frank Pitts, 65, began to ponder this point around midnight Saturday, as he ran up and down mountains in the wilderness darkness. Below, he could see the twinkling city lights.

"I thought: 'I could be in a nice soft bed,'" he said, quickly adding, "Then I thought: 'I'm out here having fun and all those people aren't.'" Pitts acknowledges some disadvantages to such a race, his eleventh:

Sometimes, in the dead of night, running, he hallucinates. During one race, he was convinced that he had to take a train between two first aid stops along the route. "Your legs feel like they've been beaten by baseball bats. You can't imagine taking another step. Yet you have to keep moving. And somehow you do," Pitts said. The retired Los Angeles County machinist, who began endurance running when he was 52, trained six to eight hours a day for the event.

Pitts, who had to drop out at the 74th mile but has finished the race six times before, plans to try again next year.

No matter one's age or fitness, the rocky trail is grueling, with eight major peaks, a total climb of 21,610 feet, and then 26,700 feet of quad-busting descent. Of the 140 who started the race Saturday, 18 finished in less than 24 hours. One Tarahumara Indian lost eight

pounds in the first 75 miles. [The Tarahumara of Mexico are noted for their ability to run long distances.]

And there are real dangers: rattlesnakes at night, and in the 1992 race, a mountain lion.

Respond

1. Does this endurance run sound appealing to you? Why or why not?

2. Why, in your opinion, do people push their physical limits? What might they discover about themselves by doing so?

A Worn Path

Meet
Eudora Welty

Eudora Welty admits to having lived a sheltered life. She grew up in Jackson, Mississippi, and has lived in her family's house there almost her entire life. Welty has maintained, though, that "a sheltered life can be a daring life as well. For all serious daring starts from within."

Welty's parents filled their house with books and loved to read on their own and to their children. Once she learned to read herself, Welty read everything she could get her hands on. Her mother, however, put one restriction on her reading. She told the town librarian that Eudora could read anything in the library except the then-popular novel *Elsie Dinsmore*. When Eudora asked why, her mother explained that the main character fainted and fell off her piano stool after being made to practice for a long time. Her mother told Eudora that she was too impressionable: "You'd read that and the very first thing you'd do, you'd fall off the piano stool." Thereafter, Welty could never hear the word *impressionable* without calling up the image of falling off a piano stool.

Welty's love of reading and her lively imagination inspired her decision to become a writer. Her first full-time job was as a publicity writer for the Works Progress Administration (WPA). This government agency, founded during the Great Depression, gave people work on public projects, such as constructing roads and buildings, clearing trails in parks, and painting murals. For her job, Welty traveled around Mississippi and wrote articles about WPA projects in the state. Welty later said that, through her travels, she gained her first glimpses of the very different ways that people live. Her musings and imaginings about the people she saw, talked to, and photographed inspired her writing throughout her life.

Welty had her first short story published when she was twenty-seven. Five years later, she published *A Curtain of Green*, a collection of short stories in which "A Worn Path" first appeared. In her thirties, she published her first novels, *The Robber Bridegroom* (1942) and *Delta Wedding*. Welty went on to write award-winning fiction for many years, until severe arthritis forced her to give up writing at age eighty-five.

"Through travel I first became aware of the outside world; it was through travel that I found my own introspective way into becoming part of it."

"Writing a story is one way of discovering *sequence* **in experience, of stumbling upon cause and effect in the happenings of a writer's own life. This has been the case with me. Connections slowly emerge."**

"Writing fiction has developed in me an abiding respect for the unknown in a human lifetime."

—*Welty*

Eudora Welty was born in 1909.

Before You Read

FOCUS ACTIVITY

Think about elderly people you respect and admire—people you know personally or people you know about.

LIST IDEAS Make a list of five to ten admirable elderly people, and write down what it is you admire about them.

SETTING A PURPOSE Read to discover the qualities of one elderly woman.

BACKGROUND

The Time and Place

"A Worn Path" is set near the city of Natchez (nach′ iz), Mississippi, probably sometime around 1930. The *Natchez Trace* mentioned in the story was an old trail that led from the Native American villages along the banks of the lower Mississippi River northeastward six hundred miles to settlements along the Cumberland River, in what is now Tennessee. Travelers who boated down the Mississippi had to walk or ride the Natchez Trace to return to locations upstream. In the 1700s, two towns grew up at the ends of the trail—Nashville and Natchez.

Around the turn of the nineteenth century, the Natchez Trace was one of the most well-traveled trails in the United States. However, it fell into disuse around 1820. New, powerful steamships that could travel against the Mississippi's strong current allowed river travelers to make their way upstream by boat, making the overland trail unnecessary. The Natchez Trace fell into disrepair. Some sections were farmed; others became parts of local roads.

Literary Influences

Eudora Welty has written that her story ideas come, in large part, from "what I see and hear and learn and feel and remember of my living world." In an interview, she explained an experience that inspired "A Worn Path":

"I was with a painter friend who was doing a landscape, and I just came along for company. I was reading under a tree, and just looking up saw this small, distant figure come out of the woods and move across the whole breadth of my vision and disappear into the woods on the other side. . . . I knew she was going somewhere. I knew that she was bent on an errand, even at that distance."

VOCABULARY PREVIEW

grave (grāv) *adj.* dignified and gloomy; somber; p. 833

quivering (kwiv′ ər ing) *n.* a shaking with a slight, rapid vibration; a trembling; p. 834

thicket (thik′ it) *n.* an area of dense growth, as of shrubs or bushes; p. 834

limber (lim′ bər) *adj.* able to bend or move easily; nimble; p. 834

vigorously (vig′ ər əs lē) *adv.* with power, energy, and strength; p. 835

ceremonial (ser′ ə mō′ nē əl) *adj.* formal; p. 838

solemn (sol′ əm) *adj.* serious; grave; p. 838

comprehension (kom pri hen′ shən) *n.* the act of grasping mentally; understanding; p. 839

A Worn Path

Eudora Welty ~

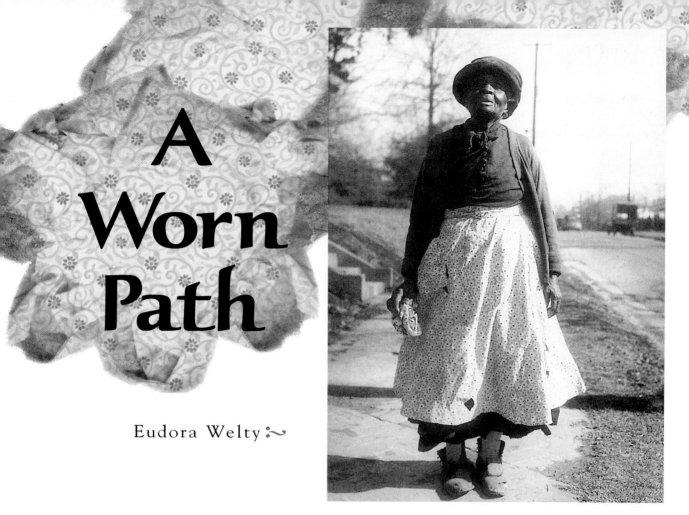

Day's End, Jackson, 1930s. Eudora Welty. Photograph. Mississippi Department of Archives and History, Jackson, MS. Eudora Welty Collection.

IT WAS DECEMBER—a bright frozen day in the early morning. Far out in the country there was an old Negro woman with her head tied in a red rag, coming along a path through the pinewoods. Her name was Phoenix Jackson. She was very old and small and she walked slowly in the dark pine shadows, moving a little from side to side in her steps, with the balanced heaviness and lightness of a pendulum in a grandfather clock. She carried a thin, small cane made from an umbrella, and with this she kept tapping the frozen earth in front of her. This made a <u>grave</u> and persistent noise in the still air, that seemed meditative like the chirping of a solitary little bird.

She wore a dark striped dress reaching down to her shoe tops, and an equally long apron of bleached sugar sacks, with a full pocket: all neat and tidy, but every time she took a step she might have fallen over her shoelaces, which dragged from her unlaced shoes. She looked straight ahead. Her eyes were blue with age. Her skin had a pattern all its own of numberless branching wrinkles and as though a whole little tree stood in the middle of her forehead, but a golden color ran underneath, and the two knobs of her cheeks were illumined by a yellow burning under the dark. Under the red rag her hair came down on her neck in the frailest of ringlets, still black, and with an odor like copper.

Vocabulary
grave (grāv) *adj.* dignified and gloomy; somber

Now and then there was a quivering in the thicket. Old Phoenix said, "Out of my way, all you foxes, owls, beetles, jack rabbits, coons and wild animals! . . . Keep out from under these feet, little bob-whites. . . .[1] Keep the big wild hogs out of my path. Don't let none of those come running my direction. I got a long way." Under her small black-freckled hand her cane, limber as a buggy whip, would switch at the brush as if to rouse up any hiding things.

On she went. The woods were deep and still. The sun made the pine needles almost too bright to look at, up where the wind rocked. The cones dropped as light as feathers. Down in the hollow[2] was the mourning dove—it was not too late for him.

The path ran up a hill. "Seem like there is chains about my feet, time I get this far," she said, in the voice of argument old people keep to use with themselves. "Something always take a hold of me on this hill—pleads I should stay."

After she got to the top she turned and gave a full, severe look behind her where she had come. "Up through pines," she said at length. "Now down through oaks."

Her eyes opened their widest, and she started down gently. But before she got to the bottom of the hill a bush caught her dress.

Her fingers were busy and intent, but her skirts were full and long, so that before she could pull them free in one place they were caught in another. It was not possible to allow the dress to tear. "I in the thorny bush," she said. "Thorns, you doing your appointed[3] work. Never want to let folks pass, no sir. Old eyes thought you was a pretty little *green* bush."

Finally, trembling all over, she stood free, and after a moment dared to stoop for her cane.

"Sun so high!" she cried, leaning back and looking, while the thick tears went over her eyes. "The time getting all gone here."

At the foot of this hill was a place where a log was laid across the creek.

"Now comes the trial," said Phoenix.

Putting her right foot out, she mounted the log and shut her eyes. Lifting her skirt, leveling her cane fiercely before her, like a festival figure

---

1. *Bob-whites,* also called quails or partridges, are birds with mottled brown plumage and white markings.

Road Between High Banks, Hinds County, 1940s. Eudora Welty. Photograph. Mississippi Department of Archives and History, Jackson, MS. Eudora Welty Collection.

Viewing the photograph: In what ways is the path in the photograph similar to or different from the path in the story?

---

2. A *hollow* is a small valley.
3. *Appointed* means "assigned" or "designated."

Vocabulary
quivering (kwiv′ ər ing) *n.* a shaking with a slight, rapid vibration; a trembling
thicket (thik′ it) *n.* an area of dense growth, as of shrubs or bushes
limber (lim′ bər) *adj.* able to bend or move easily; nimble

in some parade, she began to march across. Then she opened her eyes and she was safe on the other side.

"I wasn't as old as I thought," she said.

But she sat down to rest. She spread her skirts on the bank around her and folded her hands over her knees. Up above her was a tree in a pearly cloud of mistletoe. She did not dare to close her eyes, and when a little boy brought her a plate with a slice of marble-cake on it she spoke to him. "That would be acceptable," she said. But when she went to take it there was just her own hand in the air.

So she left that tree, and had to go through a barbed-wire fence. There she had to creep and crawl, spreading her knees and stretching her fingers like a baby trying to climb the steps. But she talked loudly to herself: she could not let her dress be torn now, so late in the day, and she could not pay for having her arm or her leg sawed off if she got caught fast where she was.

At last she was safe through the fence and risen up out in the clearing. Big dead trees, like black men with one arm, were standing in the purple stalks of the withered cotton field. There sat a buzzard.

"Who you watching?"

In the furrow[4] she made her way along.

"Glad this not the season for bulls," she said, looking sideways, "and the good Lord made his snakes to curl up and sleep in the winter. A pleasure I don't see no two-headed snake coming around that tree, where it come once. It took a while to get by him, back in the summer."

She passed through the old cotton and went into a field of dead corn. It whispered and shook and was taller than her head. "Through the maze now," she said, for there was no path.

Then there was something tall, black, and skinny there, moving before her.

At first she took it for a man. It could have been a man dancing in the field. But she stood still and listened, and it did not make a sound. It was as silent as a ghost.

"Ghost," she said sharply, "who be you the ghost of? For I have heard of nary[5] death close by."

But there was no answer—only the ragged dancing in the wind.

She shut her eyes, reached out her hand, and touched a sleeve. She found a coat and inside that an emptiness, cold as ice.

"You scarecrow," she said. Her face lighted. "I ought to be shut up for good," she said with laughter. "My senses is gone. I too old. I the oldest people I ever know. Dance, old scarecrow," she said, "while I dancing with you."

She kicked her foot over the furrow, and with mouth drawn down, shook her head once or twice in a little strutting way. Some husks blew down and whirled in streamers about her skirts.

Then she went on, parting her way from side to side with the cane, through the whispering field. At last she came to the end, to a wagon track where the silver grass blew between the red ruts. The quail were walking around like pullets,[6] seeming all dainty and unseen.

"Walk pretty," she said. "This the easy place. This the easy going."

She followed the track, swaying through the quiet bare fields, through the little strings of trees silver in their dead leaves, past cabins silver from weather, with the doors and windows boarded shut, all like old women under a spell sitting there. "I walking in their sleep," she said, nodding her head vigorously.

In a ravine[7] she went where a spring was silently flowing through a hollow log. Old

---

4. A *furrow* is a long, narrow channel in the ground made by a plow.

5. *Nary* means "not one."
6. *Pullets* are young hens.
7. A *ravine* is a deep, narrow valley, especially one eroded by running water.

Vocabulary
vigorously (vig′ ər əs lē) *adv.* with power, energy, and strength

Phoenix bent and drank. "Sweet-gum[8] makes the water sweet," she said, and drank more. "Nobody know who made this well, for it was here when I was born."

The track crossed a swampy part where the moss hung as white as lace from every limb. "Sleep on, alligators, and blow your bubbles." Then the track went into the road.

Deep, deep the road went down between the high green-colored banks. Overhead the live-oaks met, and it was as dark as a cave.

A black dog with a lolling tongue came up out of the weeds by the ditch. She was meditating, and not ready, and when he came at her she only hit him a little with her cane. Over she went in the ditch, like a little puff of milkweed.[9]

Down there, her senses drifted away. A dream visited her, and she reached her hand up, but nothing reached down and gave her a pull. So she lay there and presently went to talking. "Old woman," she said to herself, "that black dog come up out of the weeds to stall you off, and now there he sitting on his fine tail, smiling at you."

A white man finally came along and found her—a hunter, a young man, with his dog on a chain.

"Well, Granny!" he laughed. "What are you doing there?"

"Lying on my back like a June-bug waiting to be turned over, mister," she said, reaching up her hand.

He lifted her up, gave her a swing in the air, and set her down. "Anything broken, Granny?"

"No sir, them old dead weeds is springy enough," said Phoenix, when she had got her breath. "I thank you for your trouble."

"Where do you live, Granny?" he asked, while the two dogs were growling at each other.

"Away back yonder, sir, behind the ridge. You can't even see it from here."

"On your way home?"

"No sir, I going to town."

"Why, that's too far! That's as far as I walk when I come out myself, and I get something for my trouble." He patted the stuffed bag he carried, and there hung down a little closed claw. It was one of the bob-whites, with its beak hooked bitterly to show it was dead. "Now you go on home, Granny!"

"I bound to go to town, mister," said Phoenix. "The time come around."

He gave another laugh, filling the whole landscape. "I know you old colored people! Wouldn't miss going to town to see Santa Claus!"

But something held old Phoenix very still. The deep lines in her face went into a fierce and different radiation.[10] Without warning, she had seen with her own eyes a flashing nickel fall out of the man's pocket onto the ground.

"How old are you, Granny?" he was saying.

"There is no telling, mister," she said, "no telling."

Then she gave a little cry and clapped her hands and said, "Git on away from here, dog! Look! Look at that dog!" She laughed as if in admiration. "He ain't scared of nobody. He a big black dog." She whispered, "Sic him!"

"Watch me get rid of that cur," said the man. "Sic him, Pete! Sic him!"

Phoenix heard the dogs fighting, and heard the man running and throwing sticks. She even heard a gunshot. But she was slowly bending forward by that time, further and further forward, the lids stretched down over her eyes, as if she were doing this in her sleep. Her chin was lowered almost to her knees. The yellow palm of her hand came out from the fold of her apron. Her fingers slid down and along the ground under the piece of money with the grace and care they would have in lifting an egg from under a setting hen. Then she slowly straightened up, she stood erect, and the nickel was

---

8. The *sweet-gum* tree discharges a fragrant gum through cracks and crevices in its trunk.
9. The pods of a *milkweed* plant split open and release seeds with puffs of white, silky down.

10. Here, *radiation* means "a pattern of rays or waves."

School Children, Jackson, 1930s. Eudora Welty. Photograph. Mississippi Department of Archives and History, Jackson, MS. Eudora Welty Collection.

Viewing the photograph: Do you think Eudora Welty might have had her story "A Worn Path" in mind when she took this photograph? Why or why not?

in her apron pocket. A bird flew by. Her lips moved. "God watching me the whole time. I come to stealing."

The man came back, and his own dog panted about them. "Well, I scared him off that time," he said, and then he laughed and lifted his gun and pointed it at Phoenix.

She stood straight and faced him.

"Doesn't the gun scare you?" he said, still pointing it.

"No, sir, I seen plenty go off closer by, in my day, and for less than what I done," she said, holding utterly still.

He smiled, and shouldered the gun. "Well, Granny," he said, "you must be a hundred years old, and scared of nothing. I'd give you a dime if I had any money with me. But you take my advice and stay home, and nothing will happen to you."

"I bound to go on my way, mister," said Phoenix. She inclined her head in the red rag.

Then they went in different directions, but she could hear the gun shooting again and again over the hill.

She walked on. The shadows hung from the oak trees to the road like curtains. Then she smelled wood-smoke, and smelled the river, and she saw a steeple and the cabins on their steep steps. Dozens of little black children whirled around her. There ahead was Natchez shining. Bells were ringing. She walked on.

In the paved city it was Christmas time. There were red and green electric lights strung and crisscrossed everywhere, and all turned on in the daytime. Old Phoenix would have been lost if she had not distrusted her eyesight and depended on her feet to know where to take her.

She paused quietly on the sidewalk where people were passing by. A lady came along in the crowd, carrying an armful of red-, green- and silver-wrapped presents; she gave off perfume like the red roses in hot summer, and Phoenix stopped her.

"Please, missy, will you lace up my shoe?" She held up her foot.

"What do you want, Grandma?"

"See my shoe," said Phoenix. "Do all right for out in the country, but wouldn't look right to go in a big building."

"Stand still then, Grandma," said the lady. She put her packages down on the sidewalk beside her and laced and tied both shoes tightly.

"Can't lace 'em with a cane," said Phoenix. "Thank you, missy. I doesn't mind asking a nice lady to tie up my shoe, when I gets out on the street."

Moving slowly and from side to side, she went into the big building, and into a tower of steps, where she walked up and around and around until her feet knew to stop.

She entered a door, and there she saw nailed up on the wall the document that had been

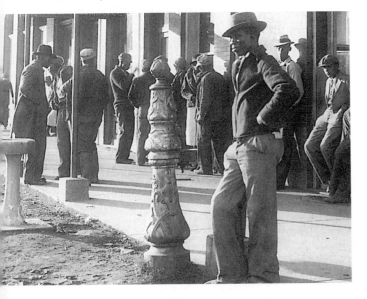

The Store, Madison County, 1930s. Eudora Welty. Photograph. Mississippi Department of Archives and History, Jackson, MS. Eudora Welty Collection.

stamped with the gold seal and framed in the gold frame, which matched the dream that was hung up in her head.

"Here I be," she said. There was a fixed and ceremonial stiffness over her body.

"A charity case, I suppose," said an attendant who sat at the desk before her.

But Phoenix only looked above her head. There was sweat on her face, the wrinkles in her skin shone like a bright net.

"Speak up, Grandma," the woman said. "What's your name? We must have your history, you know. Have you been here before? What seems to be the trouble with you?"

Old Phoenix only gave a twitch to her face as if a fly were bothering her.

"Are you deaf?" cried the attendant.

But then the nurse came in.

"Oh, that's just old Aunt Phoenix," she said. "She doesn't come for herself—she has a little grandson. She makes these trips just as regular as clockwork. She lives away back off the Old Natchez Trace." She bent down. "Well, Aunt Phoenix, why don't you just take a seat? We won't keep you standing after your long trip." She pointed.

The old woman sat down, bolt upright in the chair.

"Now, how is the boy?" asked the nurse.

Old Phoenix did not speak.

"I said, how is the boy?"

But Phoenix only waited and stared straight ahead, her face very solemn and withdrawn into rigidity.

"Is his throat any better?" asked the nurse. "Aunt Phoenix, don't you hear me? Is your grandson's throat any better since the last time you came for the medicine?"

With her hands on her knees, the old woman waited, silent, erect and motionless, just as if she were in armor.

Vocabulary
ceremonial (ser´ ə mō´ nē əl) *adj.* formal
solemn (sol´ əm) *adj.* serious; grave

"You mustn't take up our time this way, Aunt Phoenix," the nurse said. "Tell us quickly about your grandson, and get it over. He isn't dead, is he?"

At last there came a flicker and then a flame of <u>comprehension</u> across her face, and she spoke.

"My grandson. It was my memory had left me. There I sat and forgot why I made my long trip."

"Forgot?" The nurse frowned. "After you came so far?"

Then Phoenix was like an old woman begging a dignified forgiveness for waking up frightened in the night. "I never did go to school, I was too old at the Surrender,"[11] she said in a soft voice. "I'm an old woman without an education. It was my memory fail me. My little grandson, he is just the same, and I forgot it in the coming."

"Throat never heals, does it?" said the nurse, speaking in a loud, sure voice to old Phoenix. By now she had a card with something written on it, a little list. "Yes. Swallowed lye. When was it?—January—two-three years ago—"

Phoenix spoke unasked now. "No, missy, he not dead, he just the same. Every little while his throat begin to close up again, and he not able to swallow. He not get his breath. He not able to help himself. So the time come around, and I go on another trip for the soothing medicine."

"All right. The doctor said as long as you came to get it, you could have it," said the nurse. "But it's an obstinate case."

"My little grandson, he sit up there in the house all wrapped up, waiting by himself," Phoenix went on. "We is the only two left in the world. He suffer and it don't seem to put him back at all. He got a sweet look. He going to last. He wear a little patch quilt and peep out holding his mouth open like a little bird. I remembers so plain now. I not going to forget him again, no, the whole enduring time. I could tell him from all the others in creation."

"All right." The nurse was trying to hush her now. She brought her a bottle of medicine. "Charity," she said, making a check mark in a book.

Old Phoenix held the bottle close to her eyes, and then carefully put it into her pocket.

"I thank you," she said.

"It's Christmas time, Grandma," said the attendant. "Could I give you a few pennies out of my purse?"

"Five pennies is a nickel," said Phoenix stiffly.

"Here's a nickel," said the attendant.

Phoenix rose carefully and held out her hand. She received the nickel and then fished the other nickel out of her pocket and laid it beside the new one. She stared at her palm closely, with her head on one side.

Then she gave a tap with her cane on the floor.

"This is what come to me to do," she said. "I going to the store and buy my child a little windmill they sells, made out of paper. He going to find it hard to believe there such a thing in the world. I'll march myself back where he waiting, holding it straight up in this hand."

She lifted her free hand, gave a little nod, turned around, and walked out of the doctor's office. Then her slow step began on the stairs, going down.

---

11. The *Surrender* of Robert E. Lee to Ulysses S. Grant in 1865 ended the Civil War.

Vocabulary
comprehension (kom pri hen′ shən) *n.* the act of grasping mentally; understanding

Responding to Literature

Personal Response

What is your favorite incident or image from "A Worn Path"? What is it about the image or incident that especially appeals to you?

ANALYZING LITERATURE

RECALL

1. What does Phoenix Jackson look like?
2. Describe in detail the path Phoenix is taking.
3. Who is the first person Phoenix encounters? What happens?
4. What is Phoenix's destination and purpose? At what point in the story do you learn this?
5. How does Phoenix get her second nickel, and what does she decide to do with this money?

INTERPRET

6. What does Phoenix Jackson's appearance tell you about her?
7. From its description, what can you infer about the path Phoenix is on? What might the path be a **symbol** of? (See Literary Terms Handbook, page R16.) Support your answers with evidence from the selection.
8. What is the most important thing that Phoenix's first encounter reveals about her? Explain.
9. What does the purpose of Phoenix's trip tell you about her character?
10. What does Phoenix's decision about the way to spend her money tell you about her?

EVALUATE AND CONNECT

11. Do you feel empathy toward Phoenix? Why or why not? Relate your answer to events in the story as well as to your own experiences.
12. In Greek mythology, the *phoenix* is a bird that, at the end of its life, burns itself to death; from its ashes, a new phoenix rises. Why might Welty have named her main character Phoenix?
13. Refer to the list that you made for the Focus Activity on page 832. Would you put Phoenix Jackson on your list? Why or why not?
14. Theme Connections   Phoenix's approach to the physical challenges of the path reveals much about her. Think about a physical challenge you have faced. What did you discover about yourself as a result?
15. An author uses **descriptive writing** to create a picture of a person, place, or thing. In your opinion, how effective is Welty's descriptive writing in creating a picture of Phoenix Jackson? of the "worn path"?

Literary ELEMENTS

Characterization

Characterization is the way an author develops the personalities of characters. In **direct characterization,** the writer simply states a character's personality—for example, "The man was without imagination." In **indirect characterization,** the writer reveals a character's personality through the character's thoughts, words, and actions or through the way other characters react to him or her. The reader must then use these clues to infer the character's personality.

1. In developing Phoenix Jackson's personality, does Welty use mostly direct or indirect characterization? Explain briefly.
2. What do the things Phoenix says reveal about her personality?

● See **Literary Terms Handbook,** p. R3.

LITERATURE AND WRITING

Writing About Literature

Comparing Characters In "A Worn Path," Phoenix Jackson encounters several secondary characters on her journey. The character portrayed in most detail is the hunter. Make a chart comparing Phoenix with the hunter in terms of age, appearance, activities, attitudes, dialect, and any other elements you think important. Then write two to three paragraphs discussing what you have learned from comparing Phoenix with the hunter.

Creative Writing

On the Way Home What do you think Phoenix Jackson's trip home might be like? Whom and what might she encounter along the way? Will she make it home with the paper windmill intact? How might her grandson respond to her return? Write a short story two to four pages long about Phoenix's return trip. Try to keep your tone and characterization of Phoenix consistent with Welty's.

EXTENDING YOUR RESPONSE

Literature Groups

Analyzing Attitudes Over the course of the story, Phoenix Jackson interacts with a hunter, a hospital attendant, and a nurse. How do these characters treat Phoenix? In your group, discuss what factors might determine their attitudes—Phoenix's race, age, gender, financial situation, or something else. Use details from the story and your own observations about people as support. Share your group's conclusions with the rest of the class.

Listening and Speaking

Story Reading Pretend you are Eudora Welty, and read this story aloud for an interested audience. Before you read, look over the story, familiarize yourself with the pronunciation of any unfamiliar words, and decide how you will portray the different voices. Consider taping your reading as well.

Interdisciplinary Activity

Geography: Natchez and the Natchez Trace Use guidebooks, encyclopedias, and maps to help you learn about the geography of the city of Natchez and of the Natchez Trace today. Then write a brief report about these places.

📔 **Save your work for your portfolio.**

Skill Minilesson

VOCABULARY • **Analogies**

Analogies are comparisons based on relationships between words and ideas. Some analogies are based on *part-to-whole* relationships:

  student : class :: teacher : faculty

A *student* is part of a *class;* a *teacher* is part of a *faculty.*

  To finish an analogy, decide on the relationship represented by the first two words. Then apply that relationship to the second set of words.

● For more on analogies, see **Communications Skills Handbook,** p. R83.

PRACTICE Choose the word that best completes each analogy. One is a part-to-whole analogy.

1. acrobat : limber :: clown :
   a. solemn   b. humorous   c. flexible
2. study : comprehension :: practice :
   a. competence   b. ability   c. understanding
3. bush : thicket :: petal :
   a. stem   b. flower   c. bouquet
4. festive : party :: solemn :
   a. prayer   b. coffin   c. funeral

Before You Read

The Explorer

Meet Gwendolyn Brooks

"I want to write poems," said Gwendolyn Brooks, "that I could take . . . into the streets, into the halls of a housing project." In other words, she was interested in writing poems that would reach the people she wrote about—the African American urban poor. Perhaps more than any other poet, Brooks succeeded in capturing the hopes of this group, as well as their feelings of rage and despair in the face of racism and poverty.

The characters in Brooks's poems are based on people who lived in her neighborhood on Chicago's South Side. Brooks knew the South Side intimately, having spent most of her life there. She was born to parents who had little money but who did have a deep love of literature and high expectations for their children. When Brooks, at age seven, brought her mother her first poems, her mother said, "You are going to be the lady Paul Laurence Dunbar," referring to a prominent African American poet.

True to her mother's prediction, Brooks achieved literary stardom at an early age. She had her first poem published at seventeen, and her first book published at twenty-eight. With the publication of her second book, *Annie Allen*, she became the first African American writer to win the Pulitzer Prize for Poetry. Eventually Brooks was also named Poet Laureate of Illinois, poetry consultant to the Library of Congress, and a member of the National Women's Hall of Fame.

In her early books, Brooks chronicled the dreams and disappointments of the African American urban poor by using traditional verse forms such as the ballad and the sonnet. In the 1960s, Brooks's poetry underwent an immense change in tone and content. Inspired by black activism, Brooks began to write more overtly political poems that focused on issues important to African Americans, such as the need for racial unity. To reach an African American audience, she also began to incorporate black colloquial speech and free verse into her work. "It seems to me," she once said, "it's a wild, raw, ragged free verse time."

Although Brooks wrote primarily about urban African Americans, her poems, as Blyden Jackson notes, are brimming with "insights and revelations of universal application." They speak to the human condition and hence to all the citizens of the world.

"If you love songs and rap, you love poetry."

—Brooks

"From her poet's craft bursts a whole gallery of wholly alive persons, preening, squabbling, loving, weeping; many a novelist cannot do so well in ten times the space."

—Janet Overmeyer

"[In Brooks's work] each character, so neatly and precisely presented, is a racial protest in itself and a symbol of some sharply etched human dilemma."

—Richard K. Barksdale

Gwendolyn Brooks was born in 1917 and died in 2000.

What characteristics do you associate with explorers?

MAP IT! Use a word web like the one below to help you think of all the characteristics you associate wth explorers.

SETTING A PURPOSE Read to find out one speaker's conception of an explorer.

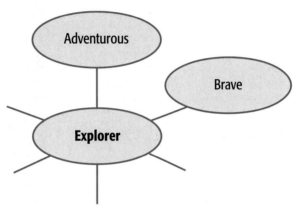

— BACKGROUND —

Literary Influences

When Gwendolyn Brooks was young, her mother arranged for her to meet the prominent Harlem Renaissance writers James Weldon Johnson and Langston Hughes. Both writers read and praised her poetry and encouraged her to continue writing. Johnson played the role of adviser, motivating Brooks to read, for instance, the modernist poets. Hughes became both mentor and friend. His poetry had a profound impact on Brooks, inspiring her to write about the world she knew and to incorporate African American idioms in her work. Brooks could have been describing herself, when she wrote of Hughes:

"Mightily did he use the street. He found its multiple heart, its tastes, smells, alarms, formulas, flowers, garbage and convulsions. He brought them all to his table-top. He crushed them to a writing paste. He himself became the pen."

Langston Hughes, 1939. Carl Van Vechten. 1983 photogravure from 1939 negative, 8¹³/₁₆ x 5⅞ in. National Portrait Gallery, Smithsonian Institution, Washington, DC. Photo copyright © Estate of Carl Van Vechten. Gravure and Compilation Copyright © Eakins Press Foundation.

Harlem Courtyard, 1954. Norman Lewis. Oil on canvas, 152.4 x 101.6 cm. Courtesy Raymond McGuire.

The Explorer

Gwendolyn Brooks ∾

Somehow to find a still spot in the noise
Was the frayed inner want, the winding, the frayed hope
Whose tatters he kept hunting through the din.°
A satin peace somewhere.
5   A room of wily° hush somewhere within.

So tipping down the scrambled halls he set
Vague hands on throbbing knobs. There were behind
Only spiraling, high human voices,
The scream of nervous affairs,
10 Wee griefs,
Grand griefs. And choices.

He feared most of all the choices, that cried to be taken.

There were no bourns.°
There were no quiet rooms.

---

3 *Din* means "a jumble of loud, usually discordant sounds."
5 *Wily* (wī′ lē) means "sly," "cunning," or "crafty."
13 *Bourns* (bôrnz) can refer to limits, boundaries, goals, or destinations.

Responding to Literature

Personal Response

How did this poem affect you? Write your response in your journal.

—— ANALYZING LITERATURE ——

RECALL AND INTERPRET

1. What does the subject of the poem want to find, according to line 1? Why might he want to find this thing?
2. What kinds of "noise" might the man be trying to escape from? What word does the speaker use to describe *peace?* What does this description tell you about the peace the man seeks?
3. Describe what the man does and hears in stanza 2. Where do you think he is? Explain.
4. What does the man fear most? What does this fear tell you about him?
5. What does the final stanza suggest about life?

EVALUATE AND CONNECT

6. What kinds of things do you think people fear most in life? Why?
7. In this poem, Brooks repeats several words, including *frayed, griefs,* and *choices.* Why might she have chosen to repeat these particular words? What ideas does this **repetition** emphasize?
8. Review the word web you made for the Focus Activity on page 843. Do you think "The Explorer" is a good title for this poem? Why or why not?
9. How would you describe the personality of the subject of this poem? What do you imagine his life is like? Use details from the poem to support your response.
10. Do you think this is a realistic and moving portrait of one individual's desires and fears? Explain using details from the poem.

Literary ELEMENTS

Alliteration

Poets work with words' sounds as well as their meanings. One device they use is **alliteration,** the repetition of sounds, usually at the beginnings of words. Alliteration can help create a musical effect, link words in the reader's ear, and reinforce the poem's meaning. For example, notice the repetition of the *s* sound in "A satin peace somewhere."

1. What effect does the repetition of the *s* sound convey in the above line?
2. Find another example of alliteration in the poem. How, in your opinion, does the alliteration contribute to the impact or meaning of the poem?

● See **Literary Terms Handbook,** p. R1.

—— EXTENDING YOUR RESPONSE ——

Personal Writing

Hushed Places   Write a short poem or two or three paragraphs describing a place where you experience a sense of peace. It could be a real place, or a place that exists only in your imagination. Like Brooks, use **repetition** and **sensory details** to capture the essence of the place and what it means to you.

Literature Groups

Unanswered Questions   In your group, review the poem sentence by sentence. Discuss each sentence and offer ways to interpret it. Based on everyone's combined input, build an interpretation of the poem. Share your interpretation with the class.

📖 **Save your work for your portfolio.**

Before You Read

February

Meet Ralph Ellison

"I am a novelist, not an activist, but I think that no one who reads what I write or who listens to my lectures can doubt that I am enlisted in the freedom movement."

—*Ellison*

Although Ralph Waldo Ellison was born in Oklahoma, he was named after the prominent New England author and philosopher Ralph Waldo Emerson. Ellison's father loved the works of Emerson and hoped that his own son would become a great writer. Just three years later Ellison's father died, but Ralph Ellison went on to fulfill his father's wish.

Ellison's first career interest, however, was to become a jazz musician and composer, and he went to Tuskegee Institute on a scholarship to study music. During his third year, Ellison began to read a lot. "I was much more under the spell of literature than I realized at the time," he later explained. In 1936 Ellison

went to New York City for the summer. There, he met Langston Hughes and Richard Wright, and he never returned to Tuskegee. After joining the Federal Writers' Project, a depression-era government program, Ellison began an extensive series of interviews in which he focused on capturing the speech patterns of African Americans. "I tried to use my ear for dialogue to give an impression of just how people sounded," he later wrote. Much of the dialogue he collected became the foundation of his novel *Invisible Man*.

At age thirty-eight, Ellison was awarded the National Book Award for *Invisible Man*. The novel was cited in a *Book Week* poll of American writers and critics as "the most significant work of fiction written between 1945 and 1965."

Ellison also taught at prestigious colleges and universities, such as Harvard, Yale, and the University of Chicago.

Ralph Ellison was born in 1914 and died in 1994.

FOCUS ACTIVITY

What comes to your mind when you think of February?

THINK-PAIR-SHARE Think about descriptive words and phrases that you associate with the month of February. Share your thoughts with a partner and list your combined words and phrases.

SETTING A PURPOSE Read to learn one writer's memories and descriptions of the month of February.

BACKGROUND

The Time and Place

This selection takes place on a February morning near Dayton, Ohio, in 1938. Saddened by his mother's death, Ellison has gone to live in the icy woods.

VOCABULARY PREVIEW

aura (ôr′ ə) *n.* a distinctive but intangible atmosphere surrounding a person or thing; p. 847

plumage (plo͞o′ mij) *n.* feathers of a bird; p. 847

exhilaration (ig zil′ ə rā′ shən) *n.* a feeling of strength and energy, joy, or excitement; p. 847

February

Ralph Ellison

February is a brook, birds, an apple tree—a day spent alone in the country. Unemployed, tired of reading, and weary of grieving the loss of my mother, I'd gone into the woods to forget. So that now all Februarys have the aura of that early morning coldness, the ghost of quail tracks on the snow-powdered brook which I brushed aside as I broke the brook to drink: and how the little quail tracks went up the ice, precise and delicate, into the darker places of the bank-ledge undisturbed. February is climbing up a hill into the full glare of the early sun, alone in all that immensity of snowscape with distant Dayton drowsing wavery to my eyes like the sound of distant horns. It's walking through a parklike grove, the tall trees stark, the knee-high snow windblown and pathless, to a decaying shed sheltering a fine old horsedrawn sleigh, carved and scrolled with traces of goldleaf clinging to its flaking wood.

And the birds: I descended into a little valley in the windless quiet and the smell of apples and saw the air erupt with red tracer-bullet[1] streaks of flight—across the snows, a carnival of cardinals. The red birds zoomed, the flickers flew, pheasants roared up like gaudy Chinese kimono rags. My heart beat hard and I saw the single tree, black-limbed against the sky, here and there the miracle of a dark red apple still hanging after months of ice and snow. I bent forward and knelt within the circle of the fruit-fall, searching out an apple missed by the birds. Sweet and mellow to the taste, it had been

Snow Bound Brook. Wilson Irvine (1869–1936). Oil on canvas, 29⅛ x 36 in. Private collection.

preserved by the leaves and grasses, protected by the snows. And I recalled the valley of two months before: *At the sound of my gun the birds came up along the hill in pairs and swooped with a circling down into the thicket on the other side, and I had gone down into the valley, soft, then, with the glow of sunset, and found the cock quail dead upon the snow, its plumage undisturbed, the vapor rising slowly from its sinking blood. . . .* And now in this place of hidden fruit and bird-tracked snow, I was seized with a kind of exhilaration. For I was in my early twenties then, and I had lived through my mother's death in that strange city, had survived three months off the fields and woods by my gun; through ice and snow and homelessness. And now in this windless February instant I had crossed over into a new phase of living. Shall I say it was in those February snows that I first became a man?

---

1. A *tracer-bullet* is a bullet treated with a chemical compound so that its path is visible during flight.

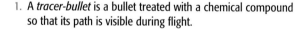

Vocabulary
aura (ôr′ ə) *n.* a distinctive but intangible atmosphere surrounding a person or thing
plumage (ploo′ mij) *n.* the feathers of a bird
exhilaration (ig zil′ ə rā′ shən) *n.* a feeling of strength and energy, joy, or excitement

Responding to Literature

Personal Response

What went through your mind at the end of this selection? Describe your reactions in your journal.

ANALYZING LITERATURE

RECALL AND INTERPRET

1. Why is Ellison in the woods? What does he seem to be seeking there?
2. What kinds of details does Ellison focus on in describing his time in the woods? What does his choice of details suggest to you about Ellison?
3. In your opinion, why did finding and tasting the apple remind Ellison of hunting the quail?
4. What does Ellison say caused his sense of exhilaration? Why, in your opinion, does he think he has become a man? What does this realization say about his view of life?

EVALUATE AND CONNECT

5. Ellison uses several **metaphors** (see page R9) to describe February. How well do they help you understand Ellison's view of February?
6. Refer to your response to the Focus Activity on page 846. How does your impression of the month compare with Ellison's? What do you think accounts for any differences?
7. At the beginning of the selection, Ellison states that he had "gone into the woods to forget." What advice might you have given him, based on your own methods of finding a place to think or "forget"?
8. Ellison reveals that he was living in a "strange city" at the time of this event. How might the event have been different, in actuality and in his memory, if it had occurred in his home city?

Literary ELEMENTS

Personal Essay

An **essay** is a brief nonfiction work that deals with one particular topic. A **formal essay** is carefully structured and has a serious tone. Its purpose is usually to inform or persuade. An **informal essay** has a looser structure, and commonly attempts to entertain. A **personal essay** is an informal essay that makes personal references and may reflect on a period in the writer's life.

1. What evidence can you give that "February" is a personal essay?
2. An essay is a brief work. What effects might the brevity of this selection have on the reader?

● See **Literary Terms Handbook, p. R5.**

EXTENDING YOUR RESPONSE

Literature Groups

Answer Ellison's Question   Ellison ends the selection by asking, "Shall I say it was in those February snows that I first became a man?" In your group, discuss the following: What does it mean to become a "man" or a "woman"? Do you think these experiences really made Ellison a mature person? Why or why not?

Creative Writing

A Calendar of Metaphors   With a group, create a "calendar" of descriptive paragraphs about the months of the year. Have each member write a paragraph listing details and images that describe his or her impressions of one or more months. Follow Ellison's model by using metaphors. Gather the paragraphs for all the months into a calendar.

💼 **Save your work for your portfolio.**

Grammar Link

Avoiding Run-on Sentences

> "It's walking through a parklike grove, the tall trees stark, the knee-high snow windblown and pathless, to a decaying shed sheltering a fine old horsedrawn sleigh, carved and scrolled with traces of goldleaf clinging to its flaking wood."

As Ralph Ellison does in the above excerpt from "February," you may want to create a rich description of something by presenting a series of images. However, this type of writing can lead to **run-on sentences,** two or more complete sentences written as though they were one sentence. Ellison has built a long sentence by using a series of phrases, but it is not a run-on sentence. His sentence has one subject, *it,* and one verb, *is,* contracted to form the single word, *it's.* Note the following run-on sentence problems.

Problem 1 Two main clauses with no punctuation between them
I will come next month I do want to see you.

   Solution A   Create two short sentences.
   I will come next month. I do want to see you.

   Solution B   Place a semicolon between the two clauses.
   I will come next month; I do want to see you.

   Solution C   Add a coordinating conjunction after the comma.
   I will come next month, and I do want to see you.

Problem 2 Two main clauses with no comma before the coordinating conjunction
The narrator is weary and he goes to the woods for solace.

   Solution   Add a comma before the coordinating conjunction to separate the main clauses.
   The narrator is weary, and he goes to the woods for solace.

● For more about run-on sentences, see **Language Handbook,** p. R19.

● EXERCISE ●

Rewrite each of the incorrect sentences, applying the solutions shown above. (One of the sentences is correct.)

1. February is very cold and the snow often piles high on the roads.

2. Birds come looking for sunflower seeds I keep the feeders filled.

3. I was worried last summer, but long walks soothed me.

4. The summer will come the snow will melt.

5. The blossoms promise fruit this summer, red and ripe cherries will lure me.

Before You Read

The Portrait

Meet Tomás Rivera

"He searched for stories about his people and finally gave their words sound, wrote the books he didn't have, we didn't have . . ."
—*Pat Mora*

The life of Tomás Rivera, the "Dean of Mexican American Literature," is a true rags-to-riches story. From modest beginnings he became a successful writer and educator—an inspiration to many. Rivera was born in Texas, the son of two agricultural workers. Until his early twenties, he, too, was a laborer, traveling with other migrant workers from Texas to the Midwest.

Despite all his traveling, he earned a formal education by attending different schools. After receiving degrees in education and Romance languages, he taught and published his only novel, *Y no se lo trago la tierra*, also known as *And the Earth Did Not Devour Him*. Written in Spanish, the book was published in both Spanish and English. It is an unconventional novel, made up of twenty-seven interrelated stories and sketches that describes, sometimes grimly, the indomitable spirit of migrant workers. The book was not meant to support any political point of view, but instead to reflect a world and experiences that Rivera knew well. The book's success inspired other Mexican Americans to add their voices to the literature of the United States.

Besides providing inspiration, Rivera also helped people in direct ways, serving on the boards of numerous Mexican American organizations. He also had a distinguished academic career, eventually becoming Chancellor of the University of California at Riverside. Known as a generous man, his goal, according to one source, was to develop "hospitable and fertile space for Hispanic Americans in America's institutions." He was working on a new book when he died.

Tomás Rivera was born in 1935 and died in 1984.

FOCUS ACTIVITY

What are the most precious items you and your family own—the things you would least want to lose?

QUICKWRITE Briefly describe one or two of these items, telling how you and your family feel about each.

SETTING A PURPOSE Read to learn how one family values a particular photograph.

BACKGROUND

The Time and Place

The story takes place in Texas during the 1950s, when the United States was involved in a war in Korea. Salespeople traveling from house to house were a familiar sight in America, selling everything from encyclopedias to vacuum cleaners. In this story, salespeople have timed their visit to coincide with the return of newly paid migrant workers—agricultural workers who follow the harvests around the United States.

The Portrait

Tomás Rivera

As soon as the people returned from up north the portrait salesmen began arriving from San Antonio. They would come to rake in. They knew that the workers had money and that was why, as Dad used to say, they would flock in. They carried suitcases packed with samples and always wore white shirts and ties; that way they looked more important and the people believed everything they would tell them and invite them into their homes without giving it much thought. I think that down deep they even longed for their children to one day be like them. In any event, they would arrive and make their way down the dusty streets, going house to house carrying suitcases full of samples.

I remember once I was at the house of one of my father's friends when one of these salesmen arrived. I also remember that that particular one seemed a little frightened and timid. Don Mateo asked him to come in because he wanted to do business.

"Good afternoon, traveler. I would like to tell you about something new that we're offering this year."

"Well, let's see, let's see . . ."

"Well, sir, see, you give us a picture, any picture you may have, and we will not only enlarge it for you but we'll also set it in a wooden frame like this one and we'll shape the image a little, like this—three dimensional, as they say."

"And what for?"

"So that it will look real. That way . . . look, let me show you . . . see? Doesn't he look real, like he's alive?"

"Man, he sure does. Look, vieja.[1] This looks great. Well, you know, we wanted to send some pictures to be enlarged . . . but now, this must cost a lot, right?"

"No, I'll tell you, it costs about the same. Of course, it takes more time."

"Well, tell me, how much?"

"For as little as thirty dollars we'll deliver it to you done with inlays just like this, one this size."

Did You Know?
Inlays are pieces of material, such as wood or ivory, set or embedded into the surface of something else to form a design.

"Boy, that's expensive! Didn't you say it didn't cost a lot more? Do you take installments?"

"Well, I'll tell you, we have a new manager and he wants everything in cash. It's very fine work. We'll make it look like real. Shaped like that, with inlays . . . take a look. What do you think? Some fine work, wouldn't you say? We can have it all finished for you in a month. You just tell us what color you want the clothes to

---

1. Here, the Spanish word *vieja* (vē ā′ hä′) is used as a term of endearment; literally, it means "old" or "old woman."

The Portrait

be and we'll come by with it all finished one day when you least expect, framed and all. Yes, sir, a month at the longest. But like I say, this man, who's the new manager, he wants the full payment in cash. He's very demanding, even with us."

"Yes, but it's much too expensive."

"Well, yes. But the thing is, this is very fine work. You can't say you've ever seen portraits done like this, with wood inlays."

"No, well, that's true. What do you think, vieja?"

"Well, I like it a lot. Why don't we order one? And if it turns out good . . . my Chuy . . . may he rest in peace. It's the only picture we have of him. We took it right before he left for Korea. Poor m'ijo,[2] we never saw him again. See . . . this is his picture. Do you think you can make it like that, make it look like he's alive?"

"Sure, we can. You know, we've done a lot of them in soldier's uniforms and shaped it, like you see in this sample, with inlays. Why, it's more than just a portrait. Sure. You just tell me what size you want and whether you want a round or square frame. What do you say? How should I write it down?"

"What do you say, vieja, should we have it done like this one?"

"Well, I've already told you what I think. I would like to have m'ijo's picture fixed up like that and in color."

"All right, go ahead and write it down. But you take good care of that picture for us because it's the only one we have of our son grown up. He was going to send us one all dressed up in uniform with the American and Mexican flags crossed over his head, but he no sooner got there when a letter arrived telling us that he was lost in action. So you take good care of it."

"Don't you worry. We're responsible people. And we understand the sacrifices that you people make. Don't worry. And you just wait and see, when we bring it, you'll see how pretty it's gonna look. What do you say, should we make the uniform navy blue?"

"But he's not wearing a uniform in that picture."

"No, but that's just a matter of fixing it up with some wood fiber overlays. Look at these. This one, he didn't have a uniform on but we put one on him. So what do you say? Should we make it navy blue?"

"All right."

"Don't you worry about the picture."

And that was how they spent the entire day, going house to house, street by street, their suitcases stuffed with pictures. As it turned out, a whole lot of people had ordered enlargements of that kind.

"They should be delivering those portraits soon, don't you think?"

"I think so, it's delicate work and takes more time. That's some fine work those people do. Did you see how real those pictures looked?"

"Yeah, sure. They do some fine work. You can't deny that. But it's already been over a month since they passed by here."

"Yes, but from here they went on through all the towns picking up pictures . . . all the way to San Antonio for sure. So it'll probably take a little longer."

"That's true, that's true."

And two more weeks had passed by the time they made the discovery. Some very heavy rains had come and some children, who were playing in one of the tunnels leading to the dump, found a sack full of pictures, all worm-eaten and soaking wet. The only reason that they could tell that these were pictures was because there were a lot of them and most of them the same size and with faces that could just barely be made out. Everybody caught on right away. Don Mateo was so angry that he took off to San Antonio to find the so and so who had swindled them.

---

2. In Spanish, *m'ijo* (mē' hō) is the colloquial form of mi hijo, meaning "my son."

"Well, you know, I stayed at Esteban's house. And every day I went with him to the market to sell produce. I helped him with everything. I had faith that I would run into that son of a gun some day soon. Then, after I'd been there for a few days, I started going out to the different barrios[3] and I found out a lot that way. It wasn't so much the money that upset me. It was my poor vieja, crying and all because we'd lost the only picture we had of Chuy. We found it in the sack with all the other pictures but it was already ruined, you know."

"I see, but tell me, how did you find him?"

"Well, you see, to make a long story short, he came by the stand at the market one day. He stood right in front of us and bought some vegetables. It was like he was trying to remember who I was. Of course, I recognized him right off. Because when you're angry enough, you don't forget a face. I just grabbed him right then and there. Poor guy couldn't even talk. He was all scared. And I told him that I wanted that portrait of my son and that I wanted it three dimensional and that he'd best get it for me or I'd let him have it. And I went with him to where he lived. And I put him to work right then and there. The poor guy didn't know where to begin. He had to do it all from memory."

"And how did he do it?"

"I don't know. I suppose if you're scared enough, you're capable of doing anything. Three days later he brought me the portrait all finished,

Adolfo, Zapote de Peralta, Guanajuato, Mexico, from the series *Family and Photography, A Portrait of a Family in Two Cultures,* 1979. Robert C. Buitron. Silver gelatin print, 20 x 16 in. Collection of the artist.

Viewing the photograph: How does the man in this photograph seem to feel about the portraits he's holding? What might he have in common with Don Mateo?

just like you see it there on that table by the Virgin. Now tell me, how do you like the way my boy looks?"

"Well, to be honest, I don't remember too well how Chuy looked. But he was beginning to look more and more like you, isn't that so?"

"Yes, I would say so. That's what everybody tells me now. That Chuy's a chip off the old block and that he was already looking like me. There's the portrait. Like they say, one and the same."

---

3. *Barrios* (bär′ ē ōs) are neighborhoods.

Responding to Literature

Personal Response

What would you say to Don Mateo about the portrait of his son? Why would you choose those words?

ANALYZING LITERATURE

RECALL AND INTERPRET

1. What does one salesman offer to Don Mateo? What is Don Mateo's first reaction? What do he and "vieja" finally decide to do? What deeper meaning might this offer have for them?
2. What has happened to the photographs the salesmen collected? As a result of this discovery, how does Don Mateo feel? How would you explain his strong feelings and his decisive action?
3. What happens when Don Mateo finds the salesman? Why do you think the salesman follows Don Mateo's orders?
4. How does Don Mateo feel about what he finally receives from the salesman? What does this reaction tell you about Don Mateo?

EVALUATE AND CONNECT

5. Review the items you wrote about for the Focus Activity on page 850. How does the importance of those items to your family compare with the importance of the photograph to Don Mateo and his wife?
6. How effective is the **dialogue** (see page R4) in conveying the message of this story? What does the dialogue reveal about the characters and their situations?
7. How would you describe the role and perspective of the **narrator** throughout this story? (See Literary Terms Handbook, page R10.)
8. Think of a time you had to stand up to someone who tricked you. How was your situation like Don Mateo's? How was it different?

Literary ELEMENTS

Idiom

An **idiom** is a saying, or group of words, that takes on special meaning. The narrator of "The Portrait" uses the term "rake in" to mean "make a lot of money." Idioms add realism to dialogue and expand characterization.

Often, idioms are difficult for non-native speakers of a language to understand because the meaning is not always clear. Thinking about the context of an idiom usually provides the best definition.

1. Don Mateo told the salesman that he would "let him have it" if he didn't get the portrait. What does this saying mean? Why might Don Mateo have said it that way?
2. At the end of the story, Don Mateo describes Chuy as "a chip off the old block." What does that mean? What does it suggest about the portrait?

● See **Literary Terms Handbook,** p. R8.

EXTENDING YOUR RESPONSE

Literature Groups

Winner or Loser? In your group, debate this question: Does Don Mateo really get what he wants or does he remain the victim of a swindler? Support your opinion with details from the story. Summarize the results of your debate for the class.

Creative Writing

Learn a Lesson Write a journal entry for one of the four characters–the narrator, Don Mateo, "vieja," or the salesman–explaining the personal discovery that character might have gained from the experience in the story.

📖 **Save your work for your portfolio.**

COMMUNICATIONS

Buyer Beware

In the story "The Portrait," migrant workers are tricked by the promise of a portrait service that doesn't exist. If you aren't careful, you too could be tricked by a slick sales pitch or by another type of communication that makes something sound better than it is.

Ten CDs for a Penny

Many music clubs run ads offering ten CDs for only a penny. It seems like a great deal—but is it? What the ads don't mention are the hidden commitments that go along with the initial purchase. For example, some clubs require that you buy a certain number of CDs at the regular price within a year. Also, while music club CDs seem inexpensive, their shipping costs can be outrageous. If you decide to join a club, read your contract carefully and don't forget to send in your reply cards.

Guaranteed Scholarships

Many teens fret about how to finance their college education. Some companies offer to spare you long hours in the library by finding college scholarships for you—for a fee. The companies may offer money-back guarantees or say that they are the exclusive source of the information. However, these companies are simply searching through computer databases of available scholarships—work you could do yourself for free.

Internet Scams

The Internet provides ample opportunities for scam artists. Whether you are signing up for a service agreement, accessing a database, or shopping on-line, it pays to be careful. Here are some guidelines:

- Ask for company references and get terms in writing.
- Watch out for ridiculously low prices or pressure selling.
- Be wary of ads. Companies that advertise on the Internet are not held accountable for the accuracy of their claims.
- If you do decide to buy something on the Internet, make sure it is a "secure" site, one that prevents others from viewing your personal information.

Activity

Look in magazines, newspapers, and on the Internet for offers that seem too good to be true. Study the advertisements. What claims do they make? Investigate whether the claims are true. Possible sources include the Better Business Bureau and your state attorney general's office.

Meet
Randall Jarrell

"His gifts . . . were wit, pathos, and brilliance of intelligence."

—*Robert Lowell*

"Jarrell tried to do the impossible: to observe and make poetry of a chaos."

—*Karl Shapiro*

No other critic could strike fear in the hearts of poets as Randall Jarrell could. In his literary reviews, he could be brutal, lambasting poetry he found mediocre. As many noted, however, the fierceness of Jarrell's reviews was a measure of his love for poetry. He was a passionate advocate of poetry that met his high standards.

Jarrell first became interested in poetry as a student at Vanderbilt University. There he studied under writers John Crowe Ransom and Robert Penn Warren, who nurtured Jarrell's skills as both a poet and a critic.

After earning a graduate degree at Vanderbilt, Jarrell began a satisfying career as a professor of English literature, which was interrupted only by the outbreak of World War II.

The war had a profound effect on Jarrell. As a member of the United States Air Force, he witnessed human carnage firsthand, which inspired him to write with great rancor, pity, and drama about the evils of war. Jarrell also displayed great compassion in the portraits he wrote of people trapped in meaningless lives, exhibiting particular sensitivity to the victimization of women and children. He had begun a new career as a children's book writer when a car struck and killed him on a dark road in October of 1965.

Randall Jarrell was born in 1914 and died in 1965.

FOCUS ACTIVITY

What comes to mind when you think of war?

MAP IT! Create a word web around the word *War*. Write the word in an oval at the center of a page, and in connecting ovals jot down words and images that you associate with the word.

SETTING A PURPOSE Read to learn one speaker's view of war.

BACKGROUND

The Time and Place

The aircraft that Jarrell mentions in his note were long-range bombers that the United States Army used in bombing raids over Europe and the Pacific during World War II. The B-17 was called the *Flying Fortress,* because it could withstand severe damage and still remain aloft. The B-24, also called the *Liberator,* was developed just a few years later. Its wingspan was slightly longer than that of the B-17, and it had a greater range. Although both the B-17 and B-24 were powerful aircraft, their plexiglass ball turrets made them vulnerable to attack.

A ball turret.

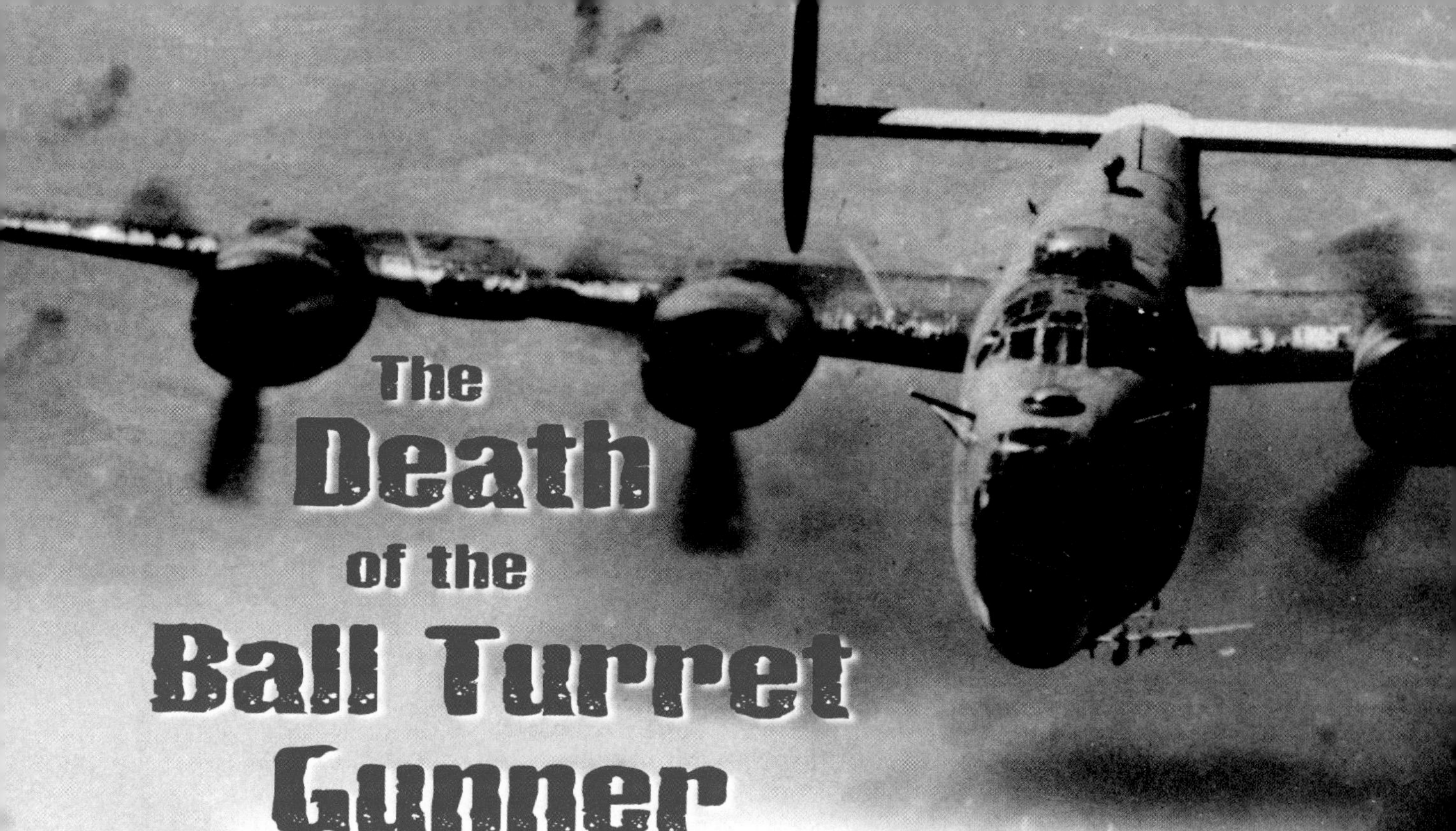

The Death of the Ball Turret Gunner

Randall Jarrell

From my mother's sleep I fell into the State,
And I hunched in its belly till my wet fur froze.
Six miles from earth, loosed from its dream of life,
I woke to black flak° and the nightmare fighters.
When I died they washed me out of the turret with a hose.

NOTE FROM THE AUTHOR:

A ball turret was a plexiglass sphere set into
the belly of a B-17 or B-24, and inhabited by
two .50 caliber machine guns and one man, a
short small man. When this gunner tracked
with his machine guns a fighter attacking his
bomber from below, he revolved with the
turret; hunched upside down in his little
sphere, he looked like the fetus in the womb.
The fighters which attacked him were armed
with cannon firing explosive shells. The hose
was a steam hose.

—*Randall Jarrell*

---

4 *Flak* is the fire of antiaircraft guns.

Responding to Literature

Personal Response

Which phrase or image struck you most forcefully? Why?

ANALYZING LITERATURE

RECALL AND INTERPRET

1. What is the speaker doing in lines 1–2? What do the images in these lines suggest about his attitude toward his situation? What do they suggest about the poet's view of the gunner?
2. According to line 3, where is the speaker? What do you think he means by "loosed from its dream of life"?
3. What happens to the speaker in line 4? What does the contrast of the nightmare in line 4 with the dream in line 3 suggest to you?
4. What happens to the speaker in the last line? What message about war does this line convey to you? Explain.

EVALUATE AND CONNECT

5. **Theme Connections** Review the word web that you created for the Focus Activity on page 856. What new insights about war has this poem given you? Add words to the web based on these insights.
6. How would you characterize Jarrell's attitude toward the "State"?
7. Jarrell compares the gunner in the ball turret to a fetus in the womb. What is **ironic** (see page R8) about this comparison? Explain.
8. Critics have characterized Jarrell as the "master of plain speech" and of clear, stark language. Do you think these statements apply to this poem? Explain.

Literary ELEMENTS

Author's Note

With some of his poems, Jarrell included an **author's note,** or a note containing explanatory information. "They are here for the reader only if he wants them," he wrote about these notes. Author's notes usually include helpful but nonessential information. In the note accompanying this poem, the reader learns that a gunner is often "a short small man"—a fact that doesn't necessarily alter the reader's basic understanding of the poem.

1. How does the author's note contribute to your understanding of specific details in the poem?
2. In what ways does the note contribute to or detract from the emotional impact of the poem? Explain.

● See **Literary Terms Handbook,** p. R2.

EXTENDING YOUR RESPONSE

Literature Groups

Analyzing Tone In your group, identify the **tone** (see page R16) of "The Death of the Ball Turret Gunner." Consider the specific words and images the poet uses, the sense of the speaker's personality that you get, even the sounds of the words in each line. Then compare the tone of lines 1-4 with that of line 5. What is the effect of the change in tone from line 4 to line 5? Share your ideas with the rest of the class.

Writing About Literature

First-Person Singular This poem was written from the **first-person point of view**—the ball turret gunner tells in his own voice what happened to him. In two or three paragraphs, explore how the use of the first-person point of view might affect how a reader responds to this poem. Also tell how it might affect the reader differently if written from the **third-person point of view** (see page R12).

📖 **Save your work for your portfolio.**

Reading & Thinking Skills

Summarizing

How often do you tell a friend about a movie you saw, a book you read, or a sports game you watched? When you do, you probably **summarize,** or state the main ideas or events in your own words. Summarizing is an important and useful skill, whether you are talking to your friends or completing a school assignment. In your reading, summarizing what you have just read can help you clarify difficult or confusing passages.

To summarize something you have just read, begin by identifying the main ideas, the key character, and the most important action in the passage. You might also include crucial details or reasons that support the main ideas. Then say to yourself, or jot down, the essential meaning of the passage without including extra information. By answering the questions *who, what, where, when, why,* and *how,* you can discover the main ideas and summarize most types of writing. The following example is a summary of the poem, "The Death of the Ball Turret Gunner."

> **"The Death of the Ball Turret Gunner"** is a personal account of a soldier's final moments. The soldier, locked inside the ball turret of a plane as it is attacked in the sky, is awakened by the shells that kill him.

In two sentences, the summary states the central event of the poem while leaving out its details and vivid imagery.

Summarizing is a useful tool that can help you understand and remember a wide range of information. The chart below suggests possible ways to summarize different kinds of information.

Information	Summary
Research report	Brief restatement of the important facts and ideas from various sources
Lecture or speech	Notes on the main ideas stated
Film	Notes on the theme, characters, and plot of the film
Textbook material	A restatement of the most important information
Historical documents	Notes on each paragraph as you read it

● For more about summarizing, see **Reading Handbook,** pp. R86–R93.

ACTIVITIES

1. Choose a favorite book to summarize in a paragraph. Trade summaries with a partner and discuss why you chose to include certain events or ideas.

2. Watch a television program or a film. Then write a brief summary to give to a friend who has not seen the program or film.

Before You Read

The Beautiful Changes

Meet Richard Wilbur

"Every poet is impelled to utter the whole of the world that is real to him, to respond to that world in some spirit, and to draw all its parts toward some coherence."

—*Wilbur*

"His intricately patterned poems reflect the discovery of patterns of natural beauty."

—*Robert B. Shaw*

In contrast to other major poets of the twentieth century, Richard Wilbur writes poems that are free of doubt and despair. These works celebrate the splendors of the natural world and the power of love, and reflect Wilbur's belief that "the universe is full of glorious energy." Whereas many critics have lauded Wilbur for the uplifting tone of his poems, others have faulted him for failing to address political themes in his work.

Wilbur's love of the visual aspects of nature may have derived in part from his background. His father was a commercial artist, and Wilbur himself considered pursuing a career in that field. Eventually, he settled on poetry, which he began to write in earnest after experiencing the horrors of World War II firsthand. Poetry, Wilbur claims, helped him to find a sense of order in a world in the throes of violence and chaos.

A prolific writer, Wilbur has published more than a dozen collections of verse, as well as books for children and translations of the works of French dramatist Molière. In recognition of his achievements in poetry he was named Poet Laureate of the United States and received two Pulitzer Prizes. Today he is considered among the best poets writing in the English language.

Richard Wilbur was born in 1921.

FOCUS ACTIVITY

Think about aspects of nature that strike you as being particularly beautiful.

FREEWRITE In a short freewriting session, describe why you find these aspects so beautiful.

SETTING A PURPOSE Read to find out what one speaker finds beautiful in nature.

BACKGROUND

The Poet's Craft

Wilbur is known for his skillful use of rhyme, meter, and different forms of stanzas. Because he uses these devices so well, readers may not notice them in his work. In "The Beautiful Changes," for example, he uses a rhyme scheme of *abacdc* that flows so smoothly it does not call attention to itself. He also invented a unique stanza form in which the middle lines of the stanza contract. Unlike the longer lines that enclose them, these middle lines consist of between four and seven syllables. The graceful and changing shape of the stanza reinforces the poem's central theme: that the beautiful changes and in "such kind ways."

The Beautiful Changes

Richard Wilbur

One wading a Fall meadow finds on all sides
The Queen Anne's Lace° lying like lilies
On water; it glides
So from the walker, it turns
5   Dry grass to a lake, as the slightest shade of you
Valleys my mind in fabulous blue Lucernes.°

The beautiful changes as a forest is changed
By a chameleon's tuning his skin to it;
As a mantis, arranged
10   On a green leaf, grows
Into it, makes the leaf leafier, and proves
Any greenness is deeper than anyone knows.

Your hands hold roses always in a way that says
They are not only yours; the beautiful changes
15   In such kind ways,
Wishing ever to sunder°
Things and things' selves for a second finding, to lose
For a moment all that it touches back to wonder.

---

2 *Queen Anne's Lace* is a meadow weed with delicate white flowers.
6 Here, *Lucernes* refers to the Lake of Lucerne, located in central Switzerland.
16 *Sunder* means "to separate" or "to tear apart."

Responding to Literature

Personal Response

Which lines from the poem did you find the most memorable or surprising? Take a few minutes to copy these lines into your journal.

--- **ANALYZING LITERATURE** ---

RECALL AND INTERPRET

1. What does the Queen Anne's lace turn the meadow into? What does the "you" in line 5 do to the speaker's mind?
2. How does a chameleon change a forest? How does a mantis change a leaf? In what ways are these beautiful changes?
3. How do the hands mentioned in stanza 3 hold roses, and why is this significant? To whom might the hands belong?
4. According to stanza 3, in what ways does the beautiful change? What opportunity do the changes offer to people?

EVALUATE AND CONNECT

5. Think about your response to the Focus Activity on page 860. How does your impression of what is beautiful in nature compare with what Wilbur describes in this poem?
6. The word *beautiful* can be a noun or an adjective, and the word *changes* can be a noun or a verb. How do you read the title of this poem: as an adjective and noun combination or as a noun and verb combination? Why? How would your reading of the poem change if you read the title differently?
7. Do you agree with the speaker that the beautiful is always changing and that it changes in "such kind ways"? Explain your response.
8. Why do you think Wilbur writes about changes in nature and a love relationship in the same poem?

Literary
ELEMENTS

Sensory Details
Sensory details are those images in a literary work that appeal to one or more of the five senses. Poets use sensory details to help the reader imagine or experience more deeply the content of their poems. "The Beautiful Changes" consists primarily of visual images, which help the reader to picture the splendors of the natural world. In the first stanza, for instance, the reader may visualize how lilies look floating on water.

1. Identify another image in the poem that appeals to your sense of sight. Tell what you see in your mind's eye.
2. What role do you think color plays in this poem? Use details to support your conclusions.

● See **Literary Terms Handbook,** p. R14.

--- **EXTENDING YOUR RESPONSE** ---

Writing About Literature

Identify the Sound Devices   In this poem, Wilbur enhances our appreciation of beautiful changes in nature by using such sound devices as **assonance,** the repetition of vowel sounds within words, and **alliteration,** the repetition of sounds at the beginnings of words. In a short paper, identify two or more examples of each device in the poem and explain how each example enriches the poem.

Performing

So from the Reader, It Turns   Create a dramatic reading of this poem. Begin by making a copy of the poem that you can write on. Make notes indicating where to speed up or slow down your reading, where to emphasize words, and where to add gestures or movements. Practice the reading several times; then perform it for the class.

📖 **Save your work for your portfolio.**

Before You Read

The Rockpile

Meet James Baldwin

"I am . . . listening to my own demons and no one else's, and I am going to keep working until they have all said what it is they are trying to tell me—and you. I am not going to stop until the last voice within me has been stilled."

—*Baldwin*

The world would agree that James Baldwin never did stop: he wrote, and wrote, and wrote, producing a body of work that is acclaimed in American literature. Baldwin overcame many handicaps to do so. His own grandparents had been enslaved, and Baldwin himself grew up in Harlem during the economic hard times of the depression.

During high school, Baldwin worked as a youth minister at the Fireside Pentecostal Assembly. After graduating from high school in 1942, Baldwin took a series of jobs to help support his brothers and sisters. He worked as a handyman, dish washer, office worker, and waiter.

The author of plays, short stories, and novels, Baldwin is perhaps most highly regarded as an essayist. Among his most famous essay collections are *Notes of a Native Son, Nobody Knows My Name,* and *The Fire Next Time.* In these essays, Baldwin explored, among other things, the forces that shaped American racial identity. In both fiction and nonfiction, Baldwin explored issues of African American identity in twentieth-century America.

Baldwin's first novel, *Go Tell It on the Mountain,* was published in 1953. This novel reflected Baldwin's search for his roots. More and more, however, Baldwin's eloquent voice became one of protest and social outrage against racial inequality. He urged whites to treat African Americans with fairness and justice. With uncompromising realism, he exposed his readers to some basic truths about the society in which they lived.

Besides achieving fame as a writer, Baldwin was in great demand as a speaker during the Civil Rights struggles of the 1950s and 1960s. His insights, his ear for the spoken language, and his early experience as a minister combined to make him a powerful force at the podium. As the years went by, however, Baldwin became disillusioned about the prospect of social change. In 1969 Baldwin moved to Europe, and he lived primarily in France for the rest of his life. In many respects, France proved friendlier to him than his own country. In the United States, Baldwin was for a time put under FBI surveillance, and, despite all his critical and popular success, he never won any major American literary prize during his lifetime. France, on the other hand, honored him with one of its most prestigious awards: Commander of the Legion of Honor.

In death, however, Baldwin returned to Harlem. His funeral was held only a few blocks from the house where he had been born. More than five thousand mourners gathered to pay respects to the man whom the writer E. L. Doctorow credited with the ability "not to make you question but to make you see."

"Trust life, and it will teach you, in joy and sorrow, all you need to know."

—*Baldwin*

James Baldwin was born in 1924 and died in 1987.

FOCUS ACTIVITY

Have you ever known someone who chose to side with a brother, a sister, or a friend even though it meant breaking the rules?

JOURNAL Explain what the person chose to do, and what happened as a result.

SETTING A PURPOSE Read to discover the choices two brothers make and the consequences of their choices.

BACKGROUND

The Time and Place

This story is set in the New York neighborhood of Harlem. Although no precise time is given, it appears to be the 1930s—the time of Baldwin's own youth. The story may well be set near the first home Baldwin remembered living in at Park Avenue and 131st Street. The author recalled playing at a garbage dump near the house.

Autobiographical References

Like John in "The Rockpile," Baldwin was the oldest child in a large family, and his stepfather was a minister. His mother married David Baldwin three years after James's birth. David Baldwin raised James, and James referred to him as Dad. Like the father in the story, David Baldwin was a stern man. He did not want his children playing in the streets. In fact, going outside, except to go to church or to the store, was certain, in his mind, to lead to sin. As John W. Roberts wrote, James Baldwin's "relationship with his stepfather served as a constant source of tension during his formative years." Yet Baldwin knew his father took care of him. He once said, "I would not be here had it not been for him."

Harlem, 1935.

VOCABULARY PREVIEW

intriguing (in trēg′ ing) *adj.* arousing curiosity or interest; fascinating; captivating; p. 865

grapple (grap′ əl) *v.* to struggle in hand-to-hand combat; to wrestle; p. 866

loiter (loi′ tər) *v.* to stand or linger idly or aimlessly about a place; p. 866

intimidated (in tim′ ə dāt′ əd) *adj.* made timid or fearful; frightened into submission or inaction; p. 866

engrossed (en grōst′) *adj.* fully attentive to; completely engaged in; absorbed; p. 867

clamber (klam′ bər) *v.* to climb hastily or awkwardly, using hands and feet; p. 867

jubilant (jōō′ bə lənt) *adj.* extremely happy; triumphantly joyful; p. 867

The Rockpile

James Baldwin ⁓

Across the street from their house, in an empty lot between two
houses, stood the rockpile. It was a strange place to find a mass of natural rock jutting out of the ground; and someone, probably Aunt
Florence, had once told them that the rock was there and could not be
taken away because without it the subway cars underground would fly
apart, killing all the people. This, touching on some natural mystery
concerning the surface and the center of the earth, was far too <u>intriguing</u>
an explanation to be challenged, and it invested the rockpile, moreover,
with such mysterious importance that Roy felt it to be his right, not to
say his duty, to play there.

Vocabulary
intriguing (in trēg′ ing) *adj.* arousing curiosity or interest; fascinating; captivating

The Rockpile

Other boys were to be seen there each afternoon after school and all day Saturday and Sunday. They fought on the rockpile. Sure-footed, dangerous, and reckless, they rushed each other and <u>grappled</u> on the heights, sometimes disappearing down the other side in a confusion of dust and screams and upended, flying feet. "It's a wonder they don't kill themselves," their mother said, watching sometimes from the fire escape. "You children stay away from there, you hear me?" Though she said "children," she was looking at Roy, where he sat beside John on the fire escape. "The good Lord knows," she continued, "I don't want you to come home bleeding like a hog every day the Lord sends." Roy shifted impatiently, and continued to stare at the street, as though in this gazing he might somehow acquire wings. John said nothing. He had not really been spoken to: he was afraid of the rockpile and of the boys who played there.

Did You Know?
A *fire escape* is a metal stairway attached to the outside of a building, used as an emergency exit in a fire.

Each Saturday morning John and Roy sat on the fire escape and watched the forbidden street below. Sometimes their mother sat in the room behind them, sewing, or dressing their younger sister, or nursing the baby, Paul. The sun fell across them and across the fire escape with a high, benevolent indifference; below them, men and women, and boys and girls, sinners all, <u>loitered</u>; sometimes one of the church-members passed and saw them and waved. Then, for the moment that they waved decorously back, they were <u>intimidated</u>. They watched the saint, man or woman, until he or she had disappeared from sight. The passage of one of the redeemed made them consider, however vacantly, the wickedness of the street, their own latent wickedness in sitting where they sat; and made them think of their father, who came home early on Saturdays and who would soon be turning this corner and entering the dark hall below them.

But until he came to end their freedom, they sat, watching and longing above the street. At the end of the street nearest their house was the bridge which spanned the Harlem River[1] and led to a city called the Bronx;[2] which was where Aunt Florence lived. Nevertheless, when they saw her coming, she did not come from the bridge, but from the opposite end of the street. This, weakly, to their minds, she explained by saying that she had taken the subway, not wishing to walk, and that, besides, she did not live in *that* section of the Bronx. Knowing that the Bronx was across the river, they did not believe this story ever, but, adopting toward her their father's attitude, assumed that she had just left some sinful place which she dared not name, as, for example, a movie palace.

In the summertime boys swam in the river, diving off the wooden dock, or wading in from the garbage-heavy bank. Once a boy, whose name was Richard, drowned in the river. His mother had not known where he was; she had even come to their house, to ask if he was

---

1. The *Harlem River* separates the Bronx and Manhattan, two boroughs of New York City.
2. The *Bronx* is actually one of five boroughs, or divisions, that make up New York City. It is not a separate city.

Vocabulary

grapple (grap′ əl) *v.* to struggle in hand-to-hand combat; to wrestle

loiter (loi′ tər) *v.* to stand or linger idly or aimlessly about a place

intimidated (in tim′ ə dāt′ əd) *adj.* made timid or fearful; frightened into submission or inaction

there. Then, in the evening, at six o'clock, they had heard from the street a woman screaming and wailing; and they ran to the windows and looked out. Down the street came the woman, Richard's mother, screaming, her face raised to the sky and tears running down her face. A woman walked beside her, trying to make her quiet and trying to hold her up. Behind them walked a man, Richard's father, with Richard's body in his arms. There were two white policemen walking in the gutter, who did not seem to know what should be done. Richard's father and Richard were wet, and Richard's body lay across his father's arms like a cotton baby. The woman's screaming filled all the street; cars slowed down and the people in the cars stared; people opened their windows and looked out and came rushing out of doors to stand in the gutter, watching. Then the small procession disappeared within the house which stood beside the rockpile. Then, *"Lord, Lord, Lord!"* cried Elizabeth, their mother, and slammed the window down.

One Saturday, an hour before his father would be coming home, Roy was wounded on the rockpile and brought screaming upstairs. He and John had been sitting on the fire escape and their mother had gone into the kitchen to sip tea with Sister McCandless. By and by Roy became bored and sat beside John in restless silence; and John began drawing into his schoolbook a newspaper advertisement which featured a new electric locomotive. Some friends of Roy passed beneath the fire escape and called him. Roy began to fidget, yelling down to them through the bars. Then a silence fell. John looked up. Roy stood looking at him.

"I'm going downstairs," he said.

"You better stay where you is, boy. You know Mama don't want you going downstairs."

"I be right *back*. She won't even know I'm gone, less you run and tell her."

"I ain't *got* to tell her. What's going to stop her from coming in here and looking out the window?"

"She's talking," Roy said. He started into the house.

"But Daddy's going to be home soon!"

"I be back before *that*. What you all the time got to be so *scared* for?" He was already in the house and he now turned, leaning on the windowsill, to swear impatiently, "I be back in *five* minutes."

John watched him sourly as he carefully unlocked the door and disappeared. In a moment he saw him on the sidewalk with his friends. He did not dare to go and tell his mother that Roy had left the fire escape because he had practically promised not to. He started to shout, *Remember, you said five minutes!* but one of Roy's friends was looking up at the fire escape. John looked down at his schoolbook: he became engrossed again in the problem of the locomotive.

When he looked up again he did not know how much time had passed, but now there was a gang fight on the rockpile. Dozens of boys fought each other in the harsh sun: clambering up the rocks and battling hand to hand, scuffed shoes sliding on the slippery rock; filling the bright air with curses and jubilant cries. They filled the air, too, with flying weapons: stones, sticks, tin cans, garbage, whatever could be picked up and thrown. John watched in a kind of absent amazement—until he remembered that Roy was still downstairs, and that he was one of the boys on the rockpile. Then he was afraid; he could not see his brother among the figures in the sun; and he stood up, leaning over the fire-escape railing. Then Roy appeared from the other side of the rocks; John

---

Vocabulary

engrossed (en grōst′) *adj.* fully attentive to; completely engaged in; absorbed

clamber (klam′ bər) *v.* to climb hastily or awkwardly, using hands and feet

jubilant (jōō′ bə lənt) *adj.* extremely happy; triumphantly joyful

The Rockpile

saw that his shirt was torn; he was laughing. He moved until he stood at the very top of the rockpile. Then, something, an empty tin can, flew out of the air and hit him on the forehead, just above the eye. Immediately, one side of Roy's face ran with blood, he fell and rolled on his face down the rocks. Then for a moment there was no movement at all, no sound, the sun, arrested, lay on the street and the side-walk and the arrested boys. Then someone screamed or shouted; boys began to run away, down the street, toward the bridge. The figure on the ground, having caught its breath and felt its own blood, began to shout. John cried, "Mama! Mama!" and ran inside.

"Don't fret, don't fret," panted Sister McCandless as they rushed down the dark, narrow, swaying stairs, "don't fret. Ain't a boy been born don't get his knocks every now and again. *Lord!*" they hurried into the sun. A man had picked Roy up and now walked slowly toward them. One or two boys sat silent on their stoops; at either end of the street there was a group of boys watching. "He ain't hurt bad," the man said, "Wouldn't be making this kind of noise if he was hurt real bad."

Elizabeth, trembling, reached out to take Roy, but Sister McCandless, bigger, calmer, took him from the man and threw him over her shoulder as she once might have handled a sack of cotton. "God bless you," she said to the man, "God bless you, son." Roy was still screaming. Elizabeth stood behind Sister McCandless to stare at his bloody face.

"It's just a flesh wound," the man kept saying, "just broke the skin, that's all." They were moving across the sidewalk, toward the house. John, not now afraid of the staring boys, looked toward the corner to see if his father was yet in sight.

Upstairs, they hushed Roy's crying. They bathed the blood away, to find, just above the left eyebrow, the jagged, superficial scar. "Lord, have mercy," murmured Elizabeth, "another inch and it would've been his eye." And she looked with apprehension toward the clock. "Ain't it the truth," said Sister McCandless, busy with bandages and iodine.

"When did he go downstairs?" his mother asked at last.

Sister McCandless now sat fanning herself in the easy chair, at the head of the sofa where Roy lay, bound and silent. She paused for a moment to look sharply at John. John stood near the window, holding the newspaper advertisement and the drawing he had done.

"We was sitting on the fire escape," he said. "Some boys he knew called him."

"When?"

"He said he'd be back in five minutes."

"Why didn't you tell me he was downstairs?"

He looked at his hands, clasping his note-book, and did not answer.

"Boy," said Sister McCandless, "you hear your mother a-talking to you?"

He looked at his mother. He repeated:

"He said he'd be back in five minutes."

"He said he'd be back in five minutes," said Sister McCandless with scorn, "don't look to me like that's no right answer. You's the man of the house, you supposed to look after your baby brothers and sisters—you ain't supposed to let them run off and get half-killed. But I expect," she added, rising from the chair, dropping the cardboard fan, "your Daddy'll make you tell the truth. Your Ma's way too soft with you."

He did not look at her, but at the fan where it lay in the dark red, depressed seat where she had been. The fan advertised a pomade[3] for the hair and showed a brown woman and her baby, both with glistening hair, smiling happily at each other.

"Honey," said Sister McCandless, "I got to be moving along. Maybe I drop in later tonight. I don't reckon you going to be at Tarry Service tonight?"

Tarry Service was the prayer meeting held every Saturday night at church to strengthen believers and prepare the church for the coming of the Holy Ghost on Sunday.

"I don't reckon," said Elizabeth. She stood up; she and Sister McCandless kissed each other on the cheek. "But you be sure to remember me in your prayers."

"I surely will do that." She paused, with her hand on the door knob, and looked down at Roy and laughed. "Poor little man," she said, "reckon he'll be content to sit on the fire escape *now*."

Elizabeth laughed with her. "It sure ought to be a lesson to him. You don't reckon," she asked nervously, still smiling, "he going to keep that scar, do you?"

"Lord, no," said Sister McCandless, "ain't nothing but a scratch. I declare, Sister Grimes, you worse than a child. Another couple of weeks and you won't be able to *see* no scar. No, you go on about your housework, honey, and thank the Lord it weren't no worse." She opened the door; they heard the sound of feet on the stairs. "I expect that's the Reverend," said Sister McCandless, placidly, "I *bet* he going to raise cain."[4]

A scene in Harlem, 1943.

"Maybe it's Florence," Elizabeth said. "Sometimes she get here about this time." They stood in the doorway, staring, while the steps reached the landing below and began again climbing to their floor. "No," said Elizabeth then, "that ain't her walk. That's Gabriel."

"Well, I'll just go on," said Sister McCandless, "and kind of prepare his mind." She pressed Elizabeth's hand as she spoke and started into the hall, leaving the door behind her slightly ajar. Elizabeth turned slowly back into the room. Roy did not open his eyes, or move; but she knew that he was not sleeping; he wished to delay until the last possible moment any contact with his father. John put

---

3. *Pomade* is a perfumed ointment, especially one used as a hair dressing.

4. *To raise cain* is an idiom meaning "to make a great disturbance" or "to lose one's temper."

The Rockpile

his newspaper and his notebook on the table and stood, leaning on the table, staring at her.

"It wasn't my fault," he said. "I couldn't stop him from going downstairs."

"No," she said, "you ain't got nothing to worry about. You just tell your Daddy the truth."

He looked directly at her, and she turned to the window, staring into the street. What was Sister McCandless saying? Then from her bedroom she heard Delilah's thin wail and she turned, frowning, looking toward the bedroom and toward the still open door. She knew that John was watching her. Delilah continued to wail, she thought, angrily, *Now that girl's getting too big for that*, but she feared that Delilah would awaken Paul and she hurried into the bedroom. She tried to soothe Delilah back to sleep. Then she heard the front door open and close—too loud, Delilah raised her voice, with an exasperated sigh Elizabeth picked the child up. Her child and Gabriel's, her children and Gabriel's: Roy, Delilah, Paul. Only John was nameless and a stranger, living, unalterable testimony to his mother's days in sin.

"What happened?" Gabriel demanded. He stood, enormous, in the center of the room, his black lunchbox dangling from his hand, staring at the sofa where Roy lay. John stood just before him, it seemed to her astonished vision just below him, beneath his fist, his heavy shoe. The child stared at the man in fascination and terror—when a girl down home she had seen rabbits stand so paralyzed before the barking dog. She hurried past Gabriel to the sofa, feeling the weight of Delilah in her arms like the weight of a shield, and stood over Roy, saying:

"Now, ain't a thing to get upset about, Gabriel. This boy sneaked downstairs while I had my back turned and got hisself hurt a little. He's alright now."

Roy, as though in confirmation, now opened his eyes and looked gravely at his father. Gabriel dropped his lunchbox with a clatter and knelt by the sofa.

"How you feel, son? Tell your Daddy what happened?"

Roy opened his mouth to speak and then, relapsing into panic, began to cry. His father held him by the shoulder

"You don't want to cry. You's Daddy's little man. Tell your Daddy what happened."

"He went downstairs," said Elizabeth, "where he didn't have no business to be, and got to fighting with them bad boys playing on that rockpile. That's what happened and it's a mercy it weren't nothing worse."

He looked up at her. "Can't you let this boy answer me for hisself?"

Ignoring this, she went on, more gently: "He got cut on the forehead, but it ain't nothing to worry about."

"You call a doctor? How you know it ain't nothing to worry about?"

"Is you got money to be throwing away on doctors? No, I ain't called no doctor. Ain't nothing wrong with my eyes that I can't tell whether he's hurt bad or not. He got a fright more'n anything else, and you ought to pray God it teaches him a lesson."

"You got a lot to say *now*," he said, "but I'll have *me* something to say in a minute. I'll be wanting to know when all this happened, what you was doing with your eyes *then*." He turned back to Roy, who had lain quietly sobbing eyes wide open and body held rigid: and who now, at his father's touch, remembered the height, the sharp, sliding rock beneath his feet, the sun, the explosion of the sun, his plunge into darkness and his salty blood; and recoiled, beginning to scream, as his father touched his forehead. "Hold still, hold still," crooned his father, shaking, "hold still. Don't cry. Daddy ain't going to hurt you, he just wants to see this bandage, see what they've done to his little man." But Roy continued to scream and would not be still and Gabriel dared not lift the bandage for fear of hurting him more. And he looked at Elizabeth in fury: "Can't you put that child down and help me with this boy? John, take your baby sister from your mother—don't look like neither of you got good sense."

John took Delilah and sat down with her in the easy chair. His mother bent over Roy, and held him still, while his father, carefully—but still Roy screamed—lifted the bandage and stared at the wound. Roy's sobs began to lessen. Gabriel readjusted the bandage. "You see," said Elizabeth, finally, "he ain't nowhere near dead."

"It sure ain't your fault that he ain't dead." He and Elizabeth considered each other for a moment in silence. "He came mightly close to losing an eye. Course, his eyes ain't as big as your'n, so I reckon you don't think it matters so much." At this her face hardened; he smiled. "Lord, have mercy," he said, "you think you ever going to learn to do right? Where was you when all this happened? Who let him go downstairs?"

"Ain't nobody let him go downstairs, he just went. He got a head just like his father, it got to be broken before it'll bow. I was in the kitchen."

"Where was Johnnie?"

"He was in here?"

"Where?"

"He was on the fire escape."

"Didn't he know Roy was downstairs?"

"I reckon."

"What you mean, you reckon? He ain't got your big eyes for nothing, does he?" He looked over at John. "Boy, you see your brother go downstairs?"

"Gabriel, ain't no sense in trying to blame Johnnie. You know right well if you have trouble making Roy behave, he ain't going to listen to his brother. He don't hardly listen to me."

"How come you didn't tell your mother Roy was downstairs?"

John said nothing, staring at the blanket which covered Delilah.

"Boy, you hear me? You want me to take a strap to you?"

"No, you ain't," she said. "You ain't going to take no strap to this boy, not today you ain't. Ain't a soul to blame for Roy's lying up there now but you—you because you done spoiled him so that he thinks he can do just anything and get away with it. I'm here to tell you that ain't no way to raise no child. You don't pray to the Lord to help you do better than you been doing, you going to live to shed bitter tears that the Lord didn't take his soul today." And she was trembling. She moved, unseeing, toward John and took Delilah from his arms. She looked back at Gabriel, who had risen, who stood near the sofa, staring at her. And she found in his face not fury alone, which would not have surprised her; but hatred so deep as to become insupportable in its lack of personality. His eyes were struck alive, unmoving, blind with malevolence—she felt, like the pull of the earth at her feet, his longing to witness her perdition.[5] Again, as though it might be propitiation,[6] she moved the child in her arms. And at this his eyes changed, he looked at Elizabeth, the mother of his children, the helpmeet given by the Lord. Then her eyes clouded; she moved to leave the room; her foot struck the lunchbox lying on the floor.

"John," she said, "pick up your father's lunchbox like a good boy."

She heard, behind her, his scrambling movement as he left the easy chair, the scrape and jangle of the lunchbox as he picked it up, bending his dark head near the toe of his father's heavy shoe.

---

5. *Perdition* (pər dish′ ən) means "the loss of one's soul and of heavenly salvation" or "eternal damnation."

6. *Propitiation* is a pleasing act intended to soothe, pacify, or win favor.

Responding to Literature

Personal Response

How did you react to the ending of this story?

ANALYZING LITERATURE

RECALL

1. What was the rockpile? What usually happened on the rockpile?
2. In what ways does the family in the story see themselves as different from others in the neighborhood?
3. What does Roy decide to do that he should not do? What is John's reaction? What happens to Roy?
4. What important fact is revealed about the father just before he arrives?
5. Describe the father's changing emotions toward his wife.

INTERPRET

6. Why might the rockpile seem to call out to Roy? Why might John not be tempted by the rockpile?
7. How, in your opinion, does the difference between John and Roy's family and others affect the brothers' attitudes toward the rockpile? toward the world outside their family?
8. Do you think John can be blamed for what has happened to Roy?
9. Why, do you think, do John's mother and father disagree over whether John can be blamed for what happens to his brother?
10. Do you think the **conflict** between the father and mother is resolved by the end of the story? Explain. (See Literary Terms Handbook, page R3.)

EVALUATE AND CONNECT

11. The author does not tell the reader an important fact about the father until well into the story. Why do you think the author uses this tactic and what effect did it have on you as a reader?
12. Using **foreshadowing,** a writer provides hints to something that will occur later in the story. In your opinion, what event or events are foreshadowed in this story? What effect does this foreshadowing have on the story? Explain, using details from the selection.
13. What do you think the rockpile symbolizes? Explain.
14. How important is the **setting** (see page R14) to the story? What picture of life does the author create with this setting?
15. Think about your response to the Focus Activity on page 864. How does John's experience compare with the one you described?

Literary ELEMENTS

Foil

In literature a **foil** is a character who is used as a contrast with a second character. The purpose of a foil is to highlight a particular quality of the second character. Although "The Rockpile" may appear to be about Roy, it actually tells just as much or more about John. The reader gets a clearer understanding of both John and Roy through the many contrasts presented between them, including the differences in their parents' reactions to them.

1. Explain how John and Roy differ in terms of their status within the family.
2. Name two more differences between John and Roy. Explain how these differences help the reader see both characters more clearly.
3. Who else might be a foil in this story? Support your response with evidence from the selection.

● See **Literary Terms Handbook,** p. R6.

LITERATURE AND WRITING

Writing About Literature

Identify Conflict   The plot of "The Rockpile" includes several **conflicts.** Remember that conflicts can be **external** or **internal.** Conflicts exist when a character struggles with another person, with himself or herself, with nature, with society, or with fate. Write a one-page analysis of the conflicts in this story, describing each conflict and telling how it affects the outcome of the story.

Personal Writing

Your Own "Rockpile"   Was there a "rockpile" in your childhood, or at least something like it? Is it the source of good memories, bad memories, or a mixture of both? In your journal, describe the "rockpile" in your own past. Tell how it helped make you the person you are today.

EXTENDING YOUR RESPONSE

Literature Groups

Defend Yourself   In your group, discuss how each character in the story might explain or defend his or her actions. For example, how might John explain why he did not tell his mother that Roy had gone to the rockpile? How might the father explain his reactions against Roy, John, and Elizabeth? Compile a list of your group's explanations and compare it with lists from other groups.

Internet Connection

Harlem on the Web   Use your research skills to locate four or more Web sites that present a picture of Harlem in the 1930s—what it looked like and what was going on there. Record each address, visit the site, and write a summary of the information that can be found there.

Performing

Later That Day   With a partner, write a conversation that might have occurred later on the same day between John and Roy. What might they have spoken about? What attitudes might they have had toward each other, toward the "rockpile" event, or toward their parents' reactions? Practice reading the conversation dramatically; then, when you are ready, perform it for the class.

📖 **Save your work for your portfolio.**

Skill Minilesson

VOCABULARY • Analogies

Analogies are comparisons based on relationships between words and ideas. Some analogies are based on a relationship of *manner,* for example:

> whisper : talk :: tap : hit

To *whisper* is to *talk* in a gentle manner; to *tap* is to *hit* in a gentle manner.

   To finish an analogy, decide on the relationship represented by the first two words. Then apply that relationship to the second set of words.

● For more on analogies, see **Communications Skills Handbook,** p. R83.

Choose the pair that best completes each analogy.

1. clamber : climb ::
   a. jump : leap
   b. run : jog
   c. creep : cringe
   d. strut : sway
   e. stroll : walk

2. loiter : stand ::
   a. dawdle : rush
   b. wander : travel
   c. wait : linger
   d. visit : depart
   e. search : ramble

Before You Read

The Magic Barrel

Meet Bernard Malamud

"People say I write so much about misery, but you write about what you know best."

—*Malamud*

Bernard Malamud was born to Russian Jewish immigrants who worked sixteen hours a day in their small grocery store on New York City's East Side. Reflecting on his childhood, he would recall that there were no books in his home, no records or musical instruments, and no pictures on the walls. He would, however, recall the generosity of his father, who bought him the twenty-volume *Book of Knowledge* when he was a nine-year-old recovering from pneumonia.

Malamud grew to become one of America's foremost writers. Most of the characters in his stories and novels are Jewish, but Malamud thought of Jewishness as a spiritual condition rather than his cultural heritage or a religious creed. To be Jewish, he felt, was to struggle with life's limitations and responsibilities. Malamud said that he wrote about Jews "because they set my imagination going. I know something about their history, the quality of experience and belief, and of their literature, though not as much as I would like."

Malamud's first novel, written when he was in his late thirties, was *The Natural*, the story of the rise and fall of a baseball player. The novel was later made into a popular movie starring Robert Redford. Malamud won highest acclaim, however, as a writer of short stories, and "The Magic Barrel" is considered one of his best.

Bernard Malamud was born in 1914 and died in 1986.

FOCUS ACTIVITY

How would you choose a spouse? Would you make a list of qualities you wanted, or would you simply rely on a gut feeling?

FREEWRITE Write about ways you think would be best to meet a spouse and about ways you've heard of.

SETTING A PURPOSE Read to learn of one young man's search for a wife.

BACKGROUND

The Time and Place

"The Magic Barrel" takes place in New York City, probably during the 1950s. Between 1880 and 1914, about two million Jews from eastern Europe immigrated to the United States. The largest concentration of Jewish immigrants settled on the Lower East Side of Manhattan. They brought with them their culture and traditions, which included the use of matchmakers, people paid to bring young men and women together for the purpose of marriage.

VOCABULARY PREVIEW

meager (mē′ gər) *adj.* deficient in quantity or completeness; p. 875
amiable (ā′ mē ə bəl) *adj.* friendly; p. 876
animated (an′ ə mā′ tid) *adj.* full of life; active; lively; p. 876
enamored (en am′ ərd) *adj.* inspired with love; charmed; captivated; p. 881
abjectly (ab jekt′ lē) *adv.* in a humiliating, mean, or degrading manner; p. 882
affirm (ə furm′) *v.* to declare firmly; to assert; p. 885

The Magic Barrel

Bernard Malamud ◞

Portrait of Abraham Wolkowitz, 1907. Max Weber. Oil on canvas, 25 x 30⅛ in. The Brooklyn Museum, New York.

NOT LONG AGO THERE LIVED IN UPTOWN New York in a small, almost <u>meager</u> room, though crowded with books, Leo Finkle, a rabbinical student in the Yeshivah University.[1] Finkle, after six years of study, was to be ordained in June and had been advised by an acquaintance that he might find it easier to win himself a congregation if he were married.

---

1. *Yeshivah* (yə shē′ və) *University* in New York City, originally a seminary for rabbis, today offers both theological and secular courses.

Vocabulary
meager (mē′ gər) *adj.* deficient in quantity or completeness

The Magic Barrel

Since he had no present prospects of marriage, after two tormented days of turning it over in his mind, he called in Pinye Salzman, a marriage broker whose two-line advertisement he had read in the *Forward*.[2]

The matchmaker appeared one night out of the dark fourth-floor hallway of the graystone rooming house where Finkle lived, grasping a black, strapped portfolio that had been worn thin with use. Salzman, who had been long in the business, was of slight but dignified build, wearing an old hat, and an overcoat too short and tight for him. He smelled frankly of fish, which he loved to eat, and although he was missing a few teeth, his presence was not displeasing, because of an <u>amiable</u> manner curiously contrasted with mournful eyes. His voice, his lips, his wisp of beard, his bony fingers were <u>animated</u>, but give him a moment of repose and his mild blue eyes revealed a depth of sadness, a characteristic that put Leo a little at ease although the situation, for him, was inherently tense.

He at once informed Salzman why he had asked him to come, explaining that his home was in Cleveland, and that but for his parents, who had married comparatively late in life, he was alone in the world. He had for six years devoted himself almost entirely to his studies, as a result of which, understandably, he had found himself without time for a social life and the company of young women. Therefore he thought it the better part of trial and error—of embarrassing fumbling—to call in an experienced person to advise him on these matters. He remarked in passing that the function of the marriage broker was ancient and honorable, highly approved in the Jewish community, because it made practical the necessary without hindering joy. Moreover, his own parents had been brought together by a matchmaker. They had made, if not a financially profitable marriage—since neither had possessed any worldly goods to speak of—at least a successful one in the sense of their everlasting devotion to each other. Salzman listened in embarrassed surprise, sensing a sort of apology. Later, however, he experienced a glow of pride in his work, an emotion that had left him years ago, and he heartily approved of Finkle.

The two went to their business. Leo had led Salzman to the only clear place in the room, a table near a window that overlooked the lamp-lit city. He seated himself at the matchmaker's side but facing him, attempting by an act of will to suppress the unpleasant tickle in his throat. Salzman eagerly unstrapped his portfolio and removed a loose rubber band from a thin packet of much-handled cards. As he flipped through them, a gesture and sound that physically hurt Leo, the student pretended not to see and gazed steadfastly out the window. Although it was still February, winter was on its last legs, signs of which he had for the first time in years begun to notice. He now observed the round white moon, moving high in the sky through a cloud menagerie,[3] and watched with half-open mouth as it penetrated a huge hen, and dropped out of her like an egg laying itself. Salzman, though pretending through eyeglasses he had just slipped on, to be engaged in scanning the writing on the cards, stole occasional glances at the young man's distinguished face, noting with pleasure the long, severe scholar's nose, brown eyes heavy with learning, sensitive yet ascetic[4] lips, and

---

2. The Yiddish-language newspaper the *Jewish Daily Forward* was published daily in New York.

3. A *menagerie* (mi naj′ ər ē) is a collection of wild or unusual animals.
4. Here, *ascetic* means "severe" or "stern."

Vocabulary
amiable (ā′ mē ə bəl) *adj.* friendly
animated (an′ ə mā′ tid) *adj.* full of life; active; lively

a certain, almost hollow quality of the dark cheeks. He gazed around at shelves upon shelves of books and let out a soft, contented sigh.

When Leo's eyes fell upon the cards, he counted six spread out in Salzman's hand.

"So few?" he asked in disappointment.

"You wouldn't believe me how much cards I got in my office," Salzman replied. "The drawers are already filled to the top, so I keep them now in a barrel, but is every girl good for a new rabbi?"

Leo blushed at this, regretting all he had revealed of himself in a curriculum vitae[5] he had sent to Salzman. He had thought it best to acquaint him with his strict standards and specifications, but in having done so, felt he had told the marriage broker more than was absolutely necessary.

He hesitantly inquired, "Do you keep photographs of your clients on file?"

"First comes family, amount of dowry,[6] also what kind promises," Salzman replied, unbuttoning his tight coat and settling himself in the chair. "After comes pictures, rabbi."

"Call me Mr. Finkle. I'm not yet a rabbi."

Salzman said he would, but instead called him doctor, which he changed to rabbi when Leo was not listening too attentively.

Salzman adjusted his horn-rimmed spectacles, gently cleared his throat and read in an eager voice the contents of the top card:

"Sophie P. Twenty-four years. Widow one year. No children. Educated high school and two years college. Father promises eight thousand dollars. Has wonderful wholesale business. Also real estate. On the mother's side comes teachers, also one actor. Well known on Second Avenue."

Leo gazed up in surprise. "Did you say a widow?"

"A widow don't mean spoiled, rabbi. She lived with her husband maybe four months. He was a sick boy she made a mistake to marry him."

"Marrying a widow has never entered my mind."

"This is because you have no experience. A widow, especially if she is young and healthy like this girl, is a wonderful person to marry. She will be thankful to you the rest of her life. Believe me, if I was looking now for a bride, I would marry a widow."

Leo reflected, then shook his head.

> **Salzman hunched his shoulders in an almost imperceptible gesture of disappointment.**

Salzman hunched his shoulders in an almost imperceptible gesture of disappointment. He placed the card down on the wooden table and began to read another:

"Lily H. High school teacher. Regular. Not a substitute. Has savings and new Dodge car. Lived in Paris one year. Father is successful dentist thirty-five years. Interested in professional man. Well Americanized family. Wonderful opportunity."

"I knew her personally," said Salzman. "I wish you could see this girl. She is a doll. Also very intelligent. All day you could talk to her about books and theyater[7] and what not. She also knows current events."

"I don't believe you mentioned her age?"

"Her age?" Salzman said, raising his brows. "Her age is thirty-two years."

Leo said after a while, "I'm afraid that seems a little too old."

---

5. A *curriculum vitae* (kə rik′ yə ləm   vē′ tī) is a summary of a person's education and work experience, usually given to a prospective employer. Finkle has provided Salzman with a summary of the "highlights" of his life.

6. A *dowry* is money or property a woman brings to her husband at the time of marriage.

7. *Theyater* is the way Salzman is pronouncing the word "theater."

The Magic Barrel

Salzman let out a laugh. "So how old are you, rabbi?"

"Twenty-seven."

"So what is the difference, tell me, between twenty-seven and thirty-two? My own wife is seven years older than me. So what did I suffer?—Nothing. If Rothschild's[8] a daughter wants to marry you, would you say on account her age, no?"

"Yes," Leo said dryly.

Salzman shook off the no in the yes. "Five years don't mean a thing. I give you my word that when you will live with her for one week you will forget her age. What does it mean five years—that she lived more and knows more than somebody who is younger? On this girl, God bless her, years are not wasted. Each one that it comes makes better the bargain."

---

8. The *Rothschilds* were a prominent, wealthy Jewish family.

Memoir, c. 1960. William Gropper. Watercolor. Marcus Gilden Collection.

Viewing the painting: What do you think the relationship might be between the two men in the painting? Do you think Finkle and Salzman have a similar relationship? Why or why not?

"What subject does she teach in high school?"

"Languages. If you heard the way she speaks French, you will think it is music. I am in the business twenty-five years, and I recommend her with my whole heart. Believe me, I know what I'm talking, rabbi."

"What's on the next card?" Leo said abruptly.

Salzman reluctantly turned up the third card:

"Ruth K. Nineteen years. Honor student. Father offers thirteen thousand cash to the right bridegroom. He is a medical doctor. Stomach specialist with marvelous practice. Brother-in-law owns own garment business. Particular people."

Salzman looked as if he had read his trump card.

"Did you say nineteen?" Leo asked with interest.

"On the dot."

"Is she attractive?" He blushed. "Pretty?"

Salzman kissed his finger tips. "A little doll. On this I give you my word. Let me call the father tonight and you will see what means pretty."

But Leo was troubled. "You're sure she's that young?"

"This I am positive. The father will show you the birth certificate."

"Are you positive there isn't something wrong with her?" Leo insisted.

"Who says there is wrong?"

"I don't understand why an American girl her age should go to a marriage broker."

A smile spread over Salzman's face.

"So for the same reason you went, she comes."

Leo flushed. "I am pressed for time."

Salzman, realizing he had been tactless, quickly explained. "The father came, not her. He wants she should have the best, so he looks around himself. When we will locate the right boy he will introduce him and encourage. This makes a better marriage than if a young girl without experience takes for herself. I don't have to tell you this."

"But don't you think this young girl believes in love?" Leo spoke uneasily.

Salzman was about to guffaw but caught himself and said soberly, "Love comes with the right person, not before."

Leo parted dry lips but did not speak. Noticing that Salzman had snatched a glance at the next card, he cleverly asked, "How is her health?"

"Perfect," Salzman said, breathing with difficulty. "Of course, she is a little lame on her right foot from an auto accident that it happened to her when she was twelve years, but nobody notices on account she is so brilliant and also beautiful."

Leo got up heavily and went to the window. He felt curiously bitter and upbraided himself for having called in the marriage broker. Finally, he shook his head.

"Why not?" Salzman persisted, the pitch of his voice rising.

"Because I detest stomach specialists."

"So what do you care what is his business? After you marry her do you need him? Who says he must come every Friday night in your house?"

Ashamed of the way the talk was going, Leo dismissed Salzman, who went home with heavy, melancholy eyes.

Though he had felt only relief at the marriage broker's departure, Leo was in low spirits the next day. He explained it as arising from Salzman's failure to produce a suitable bride for him. He did not care for his type of clientele. But when Leo found himself hesitating whether to seek out another matchmaker, one more polished than Pinye, he wondered if it

could be—his protestations to the contrary, and although he honored his father and mother—that he did not, in essence, care for the match making institution? This thought he quickly put out of mind yet found himself still upset. All day he ran around in the woods[9]—missed an important appointment, forgot to give out his laundry, walked out of a Broadway cafeteria without paying and had to run back with the ticket in his hand; had even not recognized his landlady in the street when she passed with a friend and courteously called out, "A good evening to you, Doctor Finkle." By nightfall, however, he had regained sufficient calm to sink his nose into a book and there found peace from his thoughts.

Almost at once there came a knock on the door. Before Leo could say enter, Salzman, commercial cupid, was standing in the room. His face was gray and meager, his expression hungry, and he looked as if he would expire on his feet. Yet the marriage broker managed, by some trick of the muscles, to display a broad smile.

"So good evening. I am invited?"

Leo nodded, disturbed to see him again, yet unwilling to ask the man to leave.

Beaming still, Salzman laid his portfolio on the table. "Rabbi, I got for you tonight good news."

"I've asked you not to call me rabbi. I'm still a student."

"Your worries are finished. I have for you a first-class bride."

"Leave me in peace concerning this subject." Leo pretended lack of interest.

"The world will dance at your wedding."

"Please, Mr. Salzman, no more."

"But first must come back my strength," Salzman said weakly. He fumbled with the portfolio straps and took out of the leather case an oily paper bag, from which he extracted a hard, seeded roll and a small, smoked white fish. With a quick motion of his hand he stripped the fish

---

9. *[ran . . . woods]* Here, this phrase means that Finkle "was nervous and distracted."

out of its skin and began ravenously to chew. "All day in a rush," he muttered.

Leo watched him eat.

"A sliced tomato you have maybe?" Salzman hesitantly inquired.

"No."

The marriage broker shut his eyes and ate. When he had finished he carefully cleaned up the crumbs and rolled up the remains of the fish, in the paper bag. His spectacled eyes roamed the room until he discovered, amid some piles of books, a one-burner gas stove. Lifting his hat he humbly asked, "A glass tea you got, rabbi?"

Conscience-stricken, Leo rose and brewed the tea. He served it with a chunk of lemon and two cubes of lump sugar, delighting Salzman.

After he had drunk his tea, Salzman's strength and good spirits were restored.

"So tell me, rabbi," he said amiably, "you considered some more the three clients I mentioned yesterday?"

"There was no need to consider."

"Why not?"

"None of them suits me."

"What then suits you?"

Leo let it pass because he could give only a confused answer.

Without waiting for a reply, Salzman asked, "You remember this girl I talked to you—the high school teacher?"

"Age thirty-two?"

But, surprisingly, Salzman's face lit in a smile. "Age twenty-nine."

Leo shot him a look. "Reduced from thirty-two?"

"A mistake," Salzman avowed. "I talked today with the dentist. He took me to his safety deposit box and showed me the birth certificate. She was twenty-nine years last August. They made her a party in the mountains where she went for her vacation. When her father spoke to me the first time I forgot to write the age and I told you thirty-two, but now I remember this was a different client, a widow."

"The same one you told me about? I thought she was twenty-four?"

"A different. Am I responsible that the world is filled with widows?"

"No, but I'm not interested in them, nor for that matter, in school teachers."

Salzman pulled his clasped hands to his breast. Looking at the ceiling he devoutly exclaimed, "Yiddishe kinder,[10] what can I say to somebody that he is not interested in high school teachers? So what then you are interested?"

Leo flushed but controlled himself.

"In what else will you be interested," Salzman went on, "if you not interested in this fine girl that she speaks four languages and has personally in the bank ten thousand dollars? Also her father guarantees further twelve thousand. Also she has new car, wonderful clothes, talks on all subjects, and she will give you a first-class home and children. How near do we come in our life to paradise?"

"If she's so wonderful, why wasn't she married ten years ago?"

"Why?" said Salzman with a heavy laugh. "—Why? Because she is *partikiler*.[11] This is why. She wants the *best*."

Leo went silent, amused at how he had entangled himself. But Salzman had aroused his interest in Lily H., and he began seriously to consider calling on her. When the marriage broker observed how intently Leo's mind was at work on the facts he had supplied, he felt certain they would soon come to an agreement.

Late Saturday afternoon, conscious of Salzman, Leo Finkle walked with Lily Hirschorn along Riverside Drive.[12] He walked briskly and erectly, wearing with

---

10. *Yiddishe kinder* (yid′ ish ə   kint′ ər) means "Jewish children" or "Jewish young people."

11. *Partikiler* is the way Salzman is pronouncing the word "particular."

12. *Riverside Drive,* a major road on the west side of Manhattan, runs beside the Hudson River.

distinction the black fedora[13] he had that morning taken with trepidation out of the dusty hat box on his closet shelf, and the heavy black Saturday coat he had thoroughly whisked clean. Leo also owned a walking stick, a present from a distant relative, but quickly put temptation aside and did not use it. Lily, petite and not unpretty, had on something signifying the approach of spring. She was au courant[14] animatedly, with all sorts of subjects, and he weighed her words and found her surprisingly sound—score another for Salzman, who he uneasily sensed to be somewhere around, hiding perhaps high in a tree along the street, flashing the lady signals with a pocket mirror; or perhaps a cloven-hoofed Pan, piping nuptial ditties as he danced his invisible way before them, strewing wild buds on the walk and purple grapes in their path, symbolizing fruit of a union, though there was of course still none.

Did You Know?
In Greek mythology, *Pan* was a god of pastures, flocks, and shepherds who was believed to foster reproduction and growth. He was traditionally depicted as a musician who was part man and part goat.

Lily startled Leo by remarking, "I was thinking of Mr. Salzman, a curious figure, wouldn't you say?"

Not certain what to answer, he nodded.

She bravely went on, blushing, "I for one am grateful for his introducing us. Aren't you?"

He courteously replied, "I am."

"I mean," she said with a little laugh—and it was all in good taste, or at least gave the effect of being not in bad—"do you mind that we came together so?"

He was not displeased with her honesty, recognizing that she meant to set the relationship aright, and understanding that it took a certain amount of experience in life, and courage, to want to do it quite that way. One had to have some sort of past to make that kind of beginning.

He said that he did not mind. Salzman's function was traditional and honorable—valuable for what it might achieve, which, he pointed out, was frequently nothing.

Lily agreed with a sigh. They walked on for a while and she said after a long silence, again with a nervous laugh, "Would you mind if I asked you something a little bit personal? Frankly, I find the subject fascinating." Although Leo shrugged, she went on half embarrassedly, "How was it that you came to your calling? I mean was it a sudden passionate inspiration?"

Leo, after a time, slowly replied, "I was always interested in the Law."

"You saw revealed in it the presence of the Highest?"

He nodded and changed the subject. "I understand that you spent a little time in Paris, Miss Hirschorn?"

"Oh, did Mr. Salzman tell you, Rabbi Finkle?" Leo winced but she went on, "It was ages ago and almost forgotten. I remember I had to return for my sister's wedding."

And Lily would not be put off. "When," she asked in a trembly voice, "did you become enamored of God?"

He stared at her. Then it came to him that she was talking not about Leo Finkle, but of a total stranger, some mystical figure, perhaps even passionate prophet that Salzman had dreamed up for her—no relation to the living

---

13. A *fedora* (fi dôr′ ə) is a soft felt hat with a curved brim and a lengthwise crease in the crown.
14. The French words *au courant* (ō′ kōō rän′) literally mean "in the current" but are most often used to mean "fully informed" or "up-to-date."

Vocabulary
enamored (en am′ ərd) *adj.* inspired with love; charmed; captivated

or dead. Leo trembled with rage and weakness. The trickster had obviously sold her a bill of goods, just as he had him, who'd expected to become acquainted with a young lady of twenty-nine, only to behold, the moment he laid eyes upon her strained and anxious face, a woman past thirty-five and aging rapidly. Only his self control had kept him this long in her presence.

"I am not," he said gravely, "a talented religious person," and in seeking words to go on, found himself possessed by shame and fear. "I think," he said in a strained manner, "that I came to God not because I loved Him, but because I did not."

This confession he spoke harshly because its unexpectedness shook him.

Lily wilted. Leo saw a profusion of loaves of bread go flying like ducks high over his head, not unlike the winged loaves by which he had counted himself to sleep last night. Mercifully, then, it snowed, which he would not put past Salzman's machinations.

H e was infuriated with the marriage broker and swore he would throw him out of the room the minute he reappeared. But Salzman did not come that night, and when Leo's anger had subsided,[15] an unaccountable despair grew in its place. At first he thought this was caused by his disappointment in Lily, but before long it became evident that he had involved himself with Salzman without a true knowledge of his own intent. He gradually realized—with an emptiness that seized him with six hands—that he had called in the broker to find him a bride because he was incapable of doing it himself. This terrifying insight he had derived as a result of his meeting and conversation with Lily Hirschorn. Her probing questions had somehow irritated him into

revealing—to himself more than her—the true nature of his relationship to God, and from that it had come upon him, with shocking force, that apart from his parents, he had never loved anyone. Or perhaps it went the other way, that he did not love God so well as he might, because he had not loved man. It seemed to Leo that his whole life stood starkly revealed and he saw himself for the first time as he truly was—unloved and loveless. This bitter but somehow not fully unexpected revelation brought him to a point of panic, controlled only by extraordinary effort. He covered his face with his hands and cried.

The week that followed was the worst of his life. He did not eat and lost weight. His beard darkened and grew ragged. He stopped attending seminars and almost never opened a book. He seriously considered leaving the Yeshivah, although he was deeply troubled at the thought of the loss of all his years of study—saw them like pages torn from a book, strewn over the city—and at the devastating effect of this decision upon his parents. But he had lived without knowledge of himself, and never in the Five Books and all the Commentaries[16]—mea culpa[17]—had the truth been revealed to him. He did not know where to turn, and in all this desolating loneliness there was no *to whom*, although he often thought of Lily but not once could bring himself to go downstairs and make the call. He became touchy and irritable, especially with his landlady, who asked him all manner of personal questions; on the other hand, sensing his own disagreeableness, he waylaid her on the stairs and apologized abjectly, until

---

15. *Subsided* means "decreased in intensity."

16. The Pentateuch (pen' tə took'), or first *Five Books* of the Hebrew Bible (Genesis, Exodus, Leviticus, Numbers, and Deuteronomy), are known collectively in Judaism as the Torah, or the Law. *Commentaries* provide explanatory and scholarly information about the biblical texts.

17. *Mea culpa* (mā' ə   kool' pə) means "my own fault" in Latin.

Vocabulary
abjectly (ab jekt' lē) *adv.* in a humiliating, mean, or degrading manner

The Bridge, 1926–1927. Raphael Soyer. Oil on canvas, 22¼ x 30⅛ in. Hirshhorn Museum and Sculpture Garden, Smithsonian Institution, Washington, DC.

Viewing the painting: In what ways might the attitudes of the couple walking in the painting reflect the way Lily and Leo walked together when they first met?

mortified, she ran from him. Out of this, however, he drew the consolation that he was a Jew and that a Jew suffered. But gradually, as the long and terrible week drew to a close, he regained his composure and some idea of purpose in life: to go on as planned. Although he was imperfect, the ideal was not. As for his quest of a bride, the thought of continuing afflicted him with anxiety and heartburn, yet perhaps with this new knowledge of himself he would be more successful than in the past. Perhaps love would now come to him and a bride to that love. And for this sanctified seeking who needed a Salzman?

The marriage broker, a skeleton with haunted eyes, returned that very night. He looked, withal, the picture of frustrated expectancy—as if he had steadfastly waited the week at Miss Lily Hirschorn's side for a telephone call that never came.

Casually coughing, Salzman came immediately to the point: "So how did you like her?"

Leo's anger rose and he could not refrain from chiding the matchmaker: "Why did you lie to me, Salzman?"

Salzman's pale face went dead white, the world had snowed on him.

"Did you not state that she was twenty-nine?" Leo insisted.

"I give you my word—"

"She was thirty-five, if a day. *At least* thirty-five."

"Of this don't be too sure. Her father told me—"

The Magic Barrel

"Never mind. The worst of it was that you lied to her."

"How did I lie to her, tell me?"

"You told her things about me that weren't true. You made me out to be more, consequently less than I am. She had in mind a totally different person, a sort of semi-mystical Wonder Rabbi."

"All I said, you was a religious man."

"I can imagine."

Salzman sighed. "This is my weakness that I have," he confessed. "My wife says to me I shouldn't be a salesman, but when I have two fine people that they would be wonderful to be married, I am so happy that I talk too much." He smiled wanly.[18] "This is why Salzman is a poor man."

Leo's anger left him. "Well, Salzman, I'm afraid that's all."

The marriage broker fastened hungry eyes on him.

"You don't want any more a bride?"

"I do," said Leo, "but I have decided to seek her in a different way. I am no longer interested in an arranged marriage. To be frank, I now admit the necessity of premarital love. That is, I want to be in love with the one I marry."

"Love?" said Salzman, astounded. After a moment he remarked, "For us, our love is our life, not for the ladies. In the ghetto they—"

"I know, I know," said Leo. "I've thought of it often. Love, I have said to myself, should be a by-product of living and worship rather than its own end. Yet for myself I find it necessary to establish the level of my need and fulfill it."

Salzman shrugged but answered, "Listen, rabbi, if you want love, this I can find for you also. I have such beautiful clients that you will love them the minute your eyes will see them."

Leo smiled unhappily. "I'm afraid you don't understand."

But Salzman hastily unstrapped his portfolio and withdrew a manila packet from it.

"Pictures," he said, quickly laying the envelope on the table.

Leo called after him to take the pictures away, but as if on the wings of the wind, Salzman had disappeared.

March came. Leo had returned to his regular routine. Although he felt not quite himself yet—lacked energy—he was making plans for a more active social life. Of course it would cost something, but he was an expert in cutting corners; and when there were no corners left he would make circles rounder. All the while Salzman's pictures had lain on the table, gathering dust. Occasionally as Leo sat studying, or enjoying a cup of tea, his eyes fell on the manila envelope, but he never opened it.

The days went by and no social life to speak of developed with a member of the opposite sex—it was difficult, given the circumstances of his situation. One morning Leo toiled up the stairs to his room and stared out the window at the city. Although the day was bright his view of it was dark. For some time he watched the people in the street below hurrying along and then turned with a heavy heart to his little room. On the table was the packet. With a sudden relentless gesture he tore it open. For a half-hour he stood by the table in a state of excitement, examining the photographs of the ladies Salzman had included. Finally, with a deep sigh he put them down. There were six, of varying degrees of attractiveness, but look at them long enough and they all became Lily Hirschorn: all past their prime, all starved behind bright smiles, not a true personality in the lot. Life, despite their frantic yoohooings, had passed them by; they were pictures in a brief case that stank of fish. After a while, however, as Leo attempted to return the photographs into the envelope, he found in it another, a snapshot of the type

---

18. Here, *wanly* means "sadly" or "in a dejected way."

taken by a machine for a quarter. He gazed at it a moment and let out a cry.

Her face deeply moved him. Why, he could at first not say. It gave him the impression of youth—spring flowers, yet age—a sense of having been used to the bone, wasted; this came from the eyes, which were hauntingly familiar, yet absolutely strange. He had a vivid impression that he had met her before, but try as he might he could not place her although he could almost recall her name, as if he had read it in her own handwriting. No, this couldn't be; he would have remembered her. It was not, he affirmed, that she had an extraordinary beauty—no, though her face was attractive; enough it was that *something* about her moved him. Feature for feature, even some of the ladies of the photographs could do better; but she leaped forth to his heart—had *lived,* or wanted to—more than just wanted, perhaps regretted how she had lived—had somehow deeply suffered: it could be seen in the depths of those reluctant eyes, and from the way the light enclosed and shone from her, and within her, opening realms of possibility: this was her own. Her he desired. His head ached and eyes narrowed with the intensity of his gazing, then as if an obscure fog had blown up in the mind, he experienced fear of her and was aware that he had received an impression, somehow, of evil. He shuddered, saying softly, it is thus with us all. Leo brewed some tea in a small pot and sat sipping it without sugar, to calm himself. But before he had finished drinking, again with excitement he examined the face and found it good: good for Leo Finkle. Only such a one could understand him and help him seek whatever he was seeking. She might, perhaps, love him. How she had happened to be among the discards in Salzman's barrel he could never guess, but he knew he must urgently go find her.

Leo rushed downstairs, grabbed up the Bronx[19] telephone book, and searched for Salzman's home address. He was not listed, nor was his office. Neither was he in the Manhattan book. But Leo remembered having written down the address on a slip of paper after he had read Salzman's advertisement in the "personals" column of the *Forward.* He ran up to his room and tore through his papers, without luck. It was exasperating. Just when he needed the matchmaker he was nowhere to be found. Fortunately Leo remembered to look in his wallet. There on a card he found his name written and a Bronx address. No phone number was listed, the reason— Leo now recalled— he had originally communicated with Salzman by letter. He got on his coat, put a hat on over his skullcap and hurried to the subway station. All the way to

Did You Know?
A *skullcap,* or yarmulke (yä′ məl kə), is a brimless cap worn by many Jewish men and boys, especially during religious services.

the far end of the Bronx he sat on the edge of his seat. He was more than once tempted to take out the picture and see if the girl's face was as he remembered it, but he refrained, allowing the snapshot to remain in his inside coat pocket, content to have her so close. When the train pulled into the station he was waiting at the door and bolted out. He quickly located the street Salzman had advertised.

The building he sought was less than a block from the subway, but it was not an office

---

19. The *Bronx* is one of five boroughs, or divisions, that make up New York City. Manhattan is another.

The Magic Barrel

building, nor even a loft, nor a store in which one could rent office space. It was a very old tenement[20] house. Leo found Salzman's name in pencil on a soiled tag under the bell and climbed three dark flights to his apartment. When he knocked, the door was opened by a thin, asthmatic, gray-haired woman in felt slippers.

"Yes?" she said, expecting nothing. She listened without listening. He could have sworn he had seen her, too, before but knew it was an illusion.

"Salzman—does he live here? Pinye Salzman," he said, "the matchmaker?"

She stared at him a long minute. "Of course."

He felt embarrassed. "Is he in?"

"No." Her mouth, though left open, offered nothing more.

"The matter is urgent. Can you tell me where his office is?"

"In the air." She pointed upward.

"You mean he has no office?" Leo asked.

"In his socks."

He peered into the apartment. It was sunless and dingy, one large room divided by a half-open curtain, beyond which he could see a sagging metal bed. The near side of a room was crowded with rickety chairs, old bureaus, a three-legged table, racks of cooking utensils, and all the apparatus of a kitchen. But there was no sign of Salzman or his magic barrel, probably also a figment of the imagination. An odor of frying fish made Leo weak to the knees.

"Where is he?" he insisted. "I've got to see your husband."

At length she answered, "So who knows where he is? Every time he thinks a new thought he runs to a different place. Go home, he will find you."

"Tell him Leo Finkle."

She gave no sign she had heard.

He walked downstairs, depressed.

But Salzman, breathless, stood waiting at his door.

Leo was astounded and overjoyed. "How did you get here before me?"

"I rushed."

"Come inside."

They entered. Leo fixed tea, and a sardine sandwich for Salzman. As they were drinking he reached behind him for the packet of pictures and handed them to the marriage broker.

Salzman put down his glass and said expectantly, "You found somebody you like?"

"Not among these."

The marriage broker turned away.

"Here is the one I want." Leo held forth the snapshot.

Salzman slipped on his glasses and took the picture into his trembling hand. He turned ghastly and let out a groan.

"What's the matter?" cried Leo.

"Excuse me. Was an accident this picture. She isn't for you."

Salzman frantically shoved the manila packet into his portfolio. He thrust the snapshot into his pocket and fled down the stairs.

Leo, after momentary paralysis, gave chase and cornered the marriage broker in the vestibule.[21] The landlady made hysterical outcries but neither of them listened.

"Give me back the picture, Salzman."

"No." The pain in his eyes was terrible.

"Tell me who she is then."

"This I can't tell you. Excuse me."

He made to depart, but Leo, forgetting himself, seized the matchmaker by his tight coat and shook him frenziedly.

"Please," sighed Salzman. *"Please."*

Leo ashamedly let him go. "Tell me who she is," he begged. "It's very important for me to know."

---

20. A *tenement* is an apartment building or rooming house that is built or maintained poorly and is often overcrowded.

21. A *vestibule* (ves′ tə būl′) is an entrance hall or lobby.

"She is not for you. She is a wild one—wild, without shame. This is not a bride for a rabbi."

"What do you mean wild?"

"Like an animal. Like a dog. For her to be poor was a sin. This is why to me she is dead now."

"In God's name, what do you mean?"

"Her I can't introduce to you," Salzman cried.

"Why are you so excited?"

"Why, he asks," Salzman said, bursting into tears. "This is my baby, my Stella, she should burn in hell."

Leo hurried up to bed and hid under the covers. Under the covers he thought his life through. Although he soon fell asleep he could not sleep her out of his mind. He woke, beating his breast. Though he prayed to be rid of her, his prayers went unanswered. Through days of torment he endlessly struggled not to love her; fearing success, he escaped it. He then concluded to convert her to goodness, himself to God. The idea alternately nauseated and exalted him.

He perhaps did not know that he had come to a final decision until he encountered Salzman in a Broadway cafeteria. He was sitting alone at a rear table, sucking the bony remains of a fish. The marriage broker appeared haggard, and transparent to the point of vanishing.

Salzman looked up at first without recognizing him. Leo had grown a pointed beard and his eyes were weighted with wisdom.

"Salzman," he said, "love has at last come to my heart."

"Who can love from a picture?" mocked the marriage broker.

"It is not impossible."

"If you can love her, then you can love anybody. Let me show you some new clients that they just sent me their photographs. One is a little doll."

"Just her I want," Leo murmured.

"Don't be a fool, doctor. Don't bother with her."

"Put me in touch with her, Salzman," Leo said humbly. "Perhaps I can be of service."

Salzman had stopped eating and Leo understood with emotion that it was now arranged.

Leaving the cafeteria, he was, however, afflicted by a tormenting suspicion that Salzman had planned it all to happen this way.

Leo was informed by letter that she would meet him on a certain corner, and she was there one spring night, waiting under a street lamp. He appeared, carrying a small bouquet of violets and rosebuds. Stella stood by the lamp post, smoking. She wore white with red shoes, which fitted his expectations, although in a troubled moment he had imagined the dress red, and only the shoes white. She waited uneasily and shyly. From afar he saw that her eyes—clearly her father's—were filled with desperate innocence. He pictured, in her, his own redemption. Violins and lit candles revolved in the sky. Leo ran forward with flowers outthrust.

Around the corner, Salzman, leaning against a wall, chanted prayers for the dead.

Responding to Literature

Personal Response

Were you surprised by the outcome of the story? Explain why or why not.

───── ANALYZING LITERATURE ─────

RECALL

1. Why does Leo Finkle decide to consult a marriage broker, or matchmaker?
2. Who are the first three women Salzman describes? How does Finkle react to the description of each?
3. What important personal discovery does Finkle make soon after the meeting with Lily Hirschorn?
4. How does Leo respond to the photo-machine snapshot that he finds in the envelope? What does Salzman reveal about the woman?
5. How does Finkle feel about Salzman at the end of the story?

INTERPRET

6. What do you think consulting a marriage broker represents for Finkle?
7. What does Finkle's attitude toward the women Salzman describes reveal about his personality?
8. Theme Connections   How do you think the personal discovery Finkle makes will change him? Do you think the change will last? Explain.
9. Why might Finkle have responded so strongly to the snapshot?
10. Do you think Finkle's suspicion about Salzman at the end of the story is correct? Support your answer with evidence from the story.

EVALUATE AND CONNECT

11. How does the **setting** (see page R14) of Salzman's apartment add to the author's characterization of the matchmaker? Explain with details from the selection.
12. What techniques does Malamud use to show the change in the relationship between Finkle and Salzman?
13. Imagine that you are buying something and the salesperson uses methods like Salzman's. How would you respond? Explain.
14. How does Malamud use **suspense** (see page R16) to draw the reader into the story? Support your response.
15. How does Finkle's method of finding a spouse compare with those you wrote about for the Focus Activity on page 874? Does this story cause you to reconsider your answers? Explain.

Literary ELEMENTS

Dialect

Dialect is a way of speaking and writing that is characteristic of a particular place and time. In "The Magic Barrel," Salzman speaks in a dialect of English influenced by Yiddish grammar and syntax. For example, he says, "She lived with her husband maybe four months. He was a sick boy she made a mistake to marry him." In Standard English, this passage might read, "She lived with her husband for perhaps four months. He was a sick boy; it was a mistake for her to marry him."

1. Find three more examples of dialect in Salzman's speech in the story.
2. Notice that Salzman speaks in dialect but Finkle does not. What do these differences in speech tell you about these characters?

● See **Literary Terms Handbook,** p. R4.

LITERATURE AND WRITING

Writing About Literature

Is It Love? Within the context of this story, would you say that Finkle truly loves Stella? Why or why not? Write a few paragraphs to answer this question, using evidence from the story to support your view. In particular, consider the different concepts of love presented by Finkle and by Salzman.

Creative Writing

Leo and Stella Write the story of Leo Finkle and Stella, beginning when they meet on the street. Write a two- or three-page story from the point of view of either Finkle, Stella, or Salzman. As you write, keep in mind the characterization Malamud has already developed for each one.

EXTENDING YOUR RESPONSE

Literature Groups

Salzman the Trickster? In your group, debate the following question: Does Salzman really trick Finkle into falling in love with Stella? Consider also whether Salzman really has everything all planned out, or if he truly included the photo by accident and hopes that Finkle stays away from Stella. Include in the debate your opinions on why the story ends with Salzman chanting "prayers for the dead." Come to a group conclusion, and compare it with the conclusions of other groups.

Listening and Speaking

Reading Dialogue Each of the scenes between Salzman and Finkle contains a great deal of dialogue. Have pairs of students take turns reading these dialogue segments aloud. As a class, discuss the different interpretations or presentations of Finkle and Salzman as presented by the different pairs.

Learning for Life

Dating Service Brochure For many people who are busy, shy, or have trouble meeting romantic partners for other reasons, dating services have taken the place of matchmakers. Imagine yourself as the owner of a dating service. Write the text for a brochure to persuade people like Leo Finkle and Lily Hirschorn to use your service.

📁 **Save your work for your portfolio.**

Skill Minilesson

You know that Latin roots form the basis of many English words and that the meaning of an English word is related to the meaning of its root. Study the meanings of these Latin roots:

ami–friend **anim**–mind; soul **ama** (also spelled **amo**)–to love

Now, notice how the roots affect the meanings of three vocabulary words from the selection:

***ami*able**–friendly ***anim*ated**–full of life, or soul **en*amo*red**–filled with love

Write each word below, and underline its Latin root. Then tell how the root contributes to the meaning of the word.

1. amateur
2. amicable
3. amity
4. magnanimous
5. amorous

Before You Read

from *Stride Toward Freedom*

Meet Martin Luther King Jr.

"Do your work so well that no one could do it better. Do it so well that all the hosts of heaven and earth will have to say: Here lived a man who did his job as if God Almighty called him at this particular time in history to do it."

—*King*

This was King's advice to others, but these words could be used to describe King himself and the role he played as one of the foremost leaders in the American Civil Rights movement.

Born the son of a minister in Atlanta, Georgia, King began his rise to leadership by distinguishing himself in school and entering college at the age of fifteen. After receiving his Ph.D. in theology, King accepted a position as a minister in a Montgomery, Alabama, church.

Shortly after King moved to Montgomery, the first major nonviolent protest of the Civil Rights movement took place: the Montgomery bus boycott. Led by the Montgomery Improvement Association, of which King was president, the boycott was an attempt to end the practice of segregation on public buses. For more than a year Montgomery's fifty thousand black citizens stayed off the buses. The boycott was successful, and King's outstanding public speaking and leadership skills drew national attention.

After the boycott, the Southern Christian Leadership Conference was founded to confront all forms of segregation, and King became its president. From then on, his role as a leader in the Civil Rights movement was assured.

When the center of the Civil Rights struggle shifted to Birmingham, Alabama, King was there. He was jailed, and violence exploded in the streets, but his stance on nonviolent resistance remained firm: "We will go on," he told his supporters, "because we have started a fire in Birmingham that water cannot put out. We are going on because we love Birmingham and we love democracy. And we are going to remain nonviolent."

One of the best-known triumphs of the Civil Rights movement was the March on Washington in 1963. There King delivered his famous "I Have a Dream" speech to an audience of approximately 250,000 people. One year later, he became the youngest person ever to win the Nobel Peace Prize.

Despite his commitment to nonviolence, King himself was the target of threats and violence. "I don't think I'm going to live until I reach 40," he once told his wife Coretta. In 1968, at the age of thirty-nine, he fell victim to an assassin's bullet.

"If a man has not discovered something that he is willing to die for, he is not fit to live."

"I'm happy tonight. I'm not worried about anything. I'm not fearing any man."

—*King*

Martin Luther King Jr. was born in 1929 and died in 1968.

FOCUS ACTIVITY

What do you already know about nonviolent resistance?

MAP IT! Make a cluster with the words *nonviolent resistance* in the center. Write down all the related words, ideas, and examples you can think of.

SETTING A PURPOSE Read to learn King's argument for nonviolent resistance against injustice.

BACKGROUND

The Time and Place

King's book *Stride Toward Freedom: The Montgomery Story* documents the bus boycott of 1955–56. In the 1950s, the South was entrenched in a system of legalized segregation. African Americans and whites used separate public facilities, such as schools and parks. The system was supposed to create "separate but equal" facilities, but in reality, those for African Americans were inferior.

Nonviolence

King based his theory of nonviolent resistance on the ideas of Henry David Thoreau, Mohandas Gandhi, and others. The movement got help from the Fellowship of Reconciliation, a group that promoted nonviolent direct action. James Lawson, a young African American pacifist, also helped by teaching workshops on nonviolence. As a missionary in India, Lawson had learned about Gandhi's nonviolent resistance strategies to help free that nation from British rule. In the end, nonviolence succeeded in the Civil Rights movement in the United States because of the courage of those who practiced it.

Demonstration in Hattiesburg, Mississippi, 1964.

VOCABULARY PREVIEW

oppressed (ə prest′) *adj.* controlled or governed by a cruel and unjust use of force or authority; p. 892

ordeal (ôr dēl′) *n.* a circumstance or experience that is painful or difficult; a trial; p. 892

corroding (kə rōd′ ing) *adj.* tending to eat or wear away gradually; slowly destructive; p. 893

succumb (sə kum′) *v.* to give in; to yield; p. 893

chaos (kā′ os) *n.* great confusion and disorder; p. 893

synthesis (sin′ thə sis) *n.* the combining of separate parts or elements to form a whole; p. 893

stature (stach′ ər) *n.* a level attained; standing; status; p. 894

imperative (im per′ ə tiv) *n.* something absolutely necessary; an essential; p. 894

repudiate (ri pū′ dē āt′) *v.* to refuse to accept as valid; to reject; to renounce; p. 894

advocate (ad′ və kit) *n.* one who supports or urges; a proponent; p. 894

from Stride Toward Freedom

Martin Luther King Jr. ∿

Freedom Now, 1965. Reginald Gammon. Acrylic on board, 40 x 30 in. Collection of the artist.

. . . Oppressed people deal with their oppression in three characteristic ways. One way is acquiescence:[1] the oppressed resign themselves to their doom. They tacitly[2] adjust themselves to oppression, and thereby become conditioned to it. In every movement toward freedom some of the oppressed prefer to remain oppressed. Almost 2,800 years ago Moses set out to lead the children of Israel from the slavery of Egypt[3] to the freedom of the promised land.[4] He soon discovered that slaves do not always welcome their deliverers. They become accustomed to being slaves. They would rather bear those ills they have, as Shakespeare pointed out, than flee to others that they know not of.[5] They prefer the "fleshpots of Egypt" to the ordeals of emancipation.

There is such a thing as the freedom of exhaustion. Some people are so worn down by the yoke of oppression that they give up. A few years ago in the slum areas of Atlanta, a Negro guitarist used to sing almost daily: "Ben down so long that down don't bother me." This is the type of negative freedom and resignation that often engulfs the life of the oppressed.

But this is not the way out. To accept passively an unjust system is to cooperate with that

1. *Acquiescence* means "the act of consenting or agreeing silently, without objections."
2. *Tacitly* means "silently."
3. *[Moses . . . of Egypt]* As Moses led the Israelites across the wilderness, supplies brought from Egypt ran out. The Bible (Exodus 16:2–3) tells how the people complained and began to regret having left Egypt where, although they were in bondage, they had sufficient food.
4. In the Bible, the *Promised Land* is the land of Canaan, promised by God to Abraham's descendants.
5. *[Shakespeare . . . know not of]* In Shakespeare's play *Hamlet,* the title character says (act 3, scene 1, lines 80–81): ". . . And makes us rather bear those ills we have, / Than fly to others that we know not of."

Vocabulary

oppressed (ə prest′) *adj.* controlled or governed by a cruel and unjust use of force or authority

ordeal (ôr dēl′) *n.* a circumstance or experience that is painful or difficult; a trial

system; thereby the oppressed become as evil as the oppressor. Noncooperation with evil is as much a moral obligation as is cooperation with good. The oppressed must never allow the conscience of the oppressor to slumber. Religion reminds every man that he is his brother's keeper. To accept injustice or segregation passively is to say to the oppressor that his actions are morally right. It is a way of allowing his conscience to fall asleep. At this moment the oppressed fails to be his brother's keeper. So acquiescence—while often the easier way—is not the moral way. It is the way of the coward. The Negro cannot win the respect of his oppressor by acquiescing; he merely increases the oppressor's arrogance and contempt. Acquiescence is interpreted as proof of the Negro's inferiority. The Negro cannot win the respect of the white people of the South or the peoples of the world if he is willing to sell the future of his children for his personal and immediate comfort and safety.

A second way that oppressed people sometimes deal with oppression is to resort to physical violence and corroding hatred. Violence often brings about momentary results. Nations have frequently won their independence in battle. But in spite of temporary victories, violence never brings permanent peace. It solves no social problem; it merely creates new and more complicated ones.

Violence as a way of achieving racial justice is both impractical and immoral. It is impractical because it is a descending spiral ending in destruction for all. The old law of an eye for an eye leaves everybody blind. It is immoral because it seeks to humiliate the opponent rather than win his understanding; it seeks to annihilate rather than to convert. Violence is immoral because it thrives on hatred rather than love. It destroys community and makes brotherhood impossible. It leaves society in monologue rather than dialogue. Violence ends by defeating itself. It creates bitterness in the survivors and brutality in the destroyers. A voice echoes through time saying to every potential Peter, "Put up your sword."[6] History is cluttered with the wreckage of nations that failed to follow this command.

If the American Negro and other victims of oppression succumb to the temptation of using violence in the struggle for freedom, future generations will be the recipients of a desolate night of bitterness, and our chief legacy to them will be an endless reign of meaningless chaos. Violence is not the way.

The third way open to oppressed people in their quest for freedom is the way of nonviolent resistance. Like the synthesis in Hegelian philosophy, the principle of nonviolent resistance seeks to reconcile the truths of two opposites—acquiescence and violence—while avoiding the extremes and immoralities of both. The nonviolent resister agrees with the person who acquiesces that one should not be physically aggressive toward his opponent;

Did You Know?
German philosopher Georg *Hegel* (hā′ gəl) (1770–1831) proposed the theory that for each idea or concept (thesis) there is an opposite (antithesis) and that these two eventually merge to form a new, unified idea or concept (synthesis).

---

6. *[Peter . . . sword]* In the Christian Bible (Matthew 26:52, John 18:11), when the soldiers and priests come to arrest Jesus, the disciple Peter cuts off the ear of the high priest's servant. Jesus condemns this use of violence.

Vocabulary

corroding (kə rōd′ ing) *adj.* tending to eat or wear away gradually; slowly destructive
succumb (sə kum′) *v.* to give in; to yield
chaos (kā′ os) *n.* great confusion and disorder
synthesis (sin′ thə sis) *n.* the combining of separate parts or elements to form a whole

but he balances the equation by agreeing with the person of violence that evil must be resisted. He avoids the nonresistance of the former and the violent resistance of the latter. With nonviolent resistance, no individual or group need submit to any wrong, nor need anyone resort to violence in order to right a wrong.

It seems to me that this is the method that must guide the actions of the Negro in the present crisis in race relations. Through nonviolent resistance the Negro will be able to rise to the noble height of opposing the unjust system while loving the perpetrators of the system. The Negro must work passionately and unrelentingly for full stature as a citizen, but he must not use inferior methods to gain it. He must never come to terms with falsehood, malice, hate, or destruction.

Nonviolent resistance makes it possible for the Negro to remain in the South and struggle for his rights. The Negro's problem will not be solved by running away. He cannot listen to the glib[7] suggestion of those who would urge him to migrate en masse[8] to other sections of the country. By grasping his great opportunity in the South he can make a lasting contribution to the moral strength of the nation and set a sublime example of courage for generations yet unborn.

---

7. *Glib* means "offhanded" or "showing little thought or concern."
8. The French expression *en masse* (än   mas′) means "in a group" or "all together."

By nonviolent resistance, the Negro can also enlist all men of good will in his struggle for equality. The problem is not a purely racial one, with Negroes set against whites. In the end, it is not a struggle between people at all, but a tension between justice and injustice. Nonviolent resistance is not aimed against oppressors but against oppression. Under its banner consciences, not racial groups, are enlisted.

If the Negro is to achieve the goal of integration, he must organize himself into a militant and nonviolent mass movement. All three elements are indispensable. The movement for equality and justice can only be a success if it has both a mass and militant character; the barriers to be overcome require both. Nonviolence is an imperative in order to bring about ultimate community.

A mass movement of a militant quality that is not at the same time committed to nonviolence tends to generate conflict, which in turn breeds anarchy. The support of the participants and the sympathy of the uncommitted are both inhibited by the threat that bloodshed will engulf the community. This reaction in turn encourages the opposition to threaten and resort to force. When, however, the mass movement repudiates violence while moving resolutely toward its goal, its opponents are revealed as the instigators and practitioners of violence if it occurs. Then public support is magnetically attracted to the advocates of nonviolence, while those who employ violence are literally disarmed by overwhelming sentiment against their stand.

Vocabulary
stature (stach′ ər) *n.* a level attained; standing; status
imperative (im per′ ə tiv) *n.* something absolutely necessary; an essential
repudiate (ri pū′ dē āt′) *v.* to refuse to accept as valid; to reject; to renounce
advocate (ad′ və kit) *n.* one who supports or urges; a proponent

Responding to Literature

Personal Response

What was your first reaction to King's argument? Explain.

ANALYZING LITERATURE

RECALL AND INTERPRET

1. According to King, what are people really doing when they passively accept an unjust system? Do you think this is a bold statement for King to make? Explain.
2. What does King think about violence as a means for bringing about social change? What does his opinion about violence tell you about King himself? Explain, using details from the selection.
3. What is nonviolent resistance? How is it similar to and different from both passive acceptance and violent resistance?
4. Against whom or what should nonviolence be aimed, according to King? Why do you suppose King took pains to make this target clear?

EVALUATE AND CONNECT

5. Identify three **allusions** (see page R1) in the selection. In your opinion, how effectively does King use these allusions to make his point? Support your response with evidence from the selection.
6. Booker T. Washington said, "Let no man pull you so low as to hate him." How might King respond to this quotation? Do you agree with it? Why or why not?
7. This selection was first published in 1958. Do you think King's ideas are still relevant? Explain.
8. After reading the selection, what would you add to the word cluster you made about nonviolent resistance for the Focus Activity on page 891? Explain.

Literary
ELEMENTS

Structure
Structure is the particular order or pattern a writer uses to best present ideas in a logical way. Narratives commonly follow a chronological order, while the structure of persuasive or expository writing may vary. Listing detailed information, using cause and effect, or describing a problem and then offering a solution are some ways of presenting a topic. In this selection, King uses a list to present his points.

1. What does King state in the first sentence? What does this opening suggest about the way his points might be organized?
2. Would switching the order of King's list affect the logic of his arguments? Why or why not?

● See **Literary Terms Handbook**, p. R15.

EXTENDING YOUR RESPONSE

Literature Groups
Evaluate Persuasive Techniques   Do you think King has written a successful persuasive piece? Discuss this question with your group. Consider the following questions: Does King's reputation make this argument more persuasive? Who is King's audience? What kinds of support does he use? Is his purpose clear? Share the results of your discussion with the class.

Learning For Life
Interview the Author   With a partner, write an interview with King based on this selection. Identify questions and issues the selection raises and how King might answer them. Perform your interview for the class.

📖 **Save your work for your portfolio.**

Before You Read

Choice: A Tribute to Dr. Martin Luther King Jr.

Meet Alice Walker

"Writing permits me to be more than I am," declares Alice Walker. Born into a poor, rural life in Eatonton, Georgia, Walker knew how it felt to be made to feel less than she was. She knew how it felt to bear the legacy of slavery, racism, and segregation. Her parents and grandparents worked on what had been a plantation, she recalled decades later, toiling "all their lives for barely enough food and shelter to sustain them. They were sharecroppers—landless peasants—the product of whose labor was routinely stolen from them."

Awarded a scholarship, Walker entered Spelman College in 1961, at the peak of the Civil Rights movement. There, she first met Martin Luther King Jr. She continued her education at Sarah Lawrence College in New York, and after graduation she worked in the New York City Welfare Department. Returning to the South in 1966, Walker became a Head Start worker in Mississippi and worked for voter registration in Georgia. Reflecting on the Civil Rights movement, she called it "a time of intense friendships, passions, and loves among the people who came south (or lived there), and who risked everything to change [the] system." She recalls the movement's many triumphs, but she also recalls that the cost "still bruises the heart." In 1967 Walker married another Civil Rights worker. She had to do so in the North, however, for she married a white man, and interracial marriage was still illegal in the South.

The Civil Rights leader Walker calls her "spiritual ancestor" is not however, King, nor anyone else from the Civil Rights movement, but Sojourner Truth. Walker says it gives her joy to realize she shares her name with Sojourner Truth: *walker* and *sojourner* can have roughly the same meaning, and *Alice* means "truth" in ancient Greek. Aside from their names, their common bond, Walker says, is a concern not only for the rights of African Americans but also for the rights of women. In fact, much of Walker's writing can be called *womanist*: to use a term Walker coined herself that describes work appreciating women's culture, their characters, and their feelings.

Since the publication of her novel *The Color Purple*, which won both a Pulitzer Prize and an American Book Award, and since the transformation of that book into a highly successful film, Walker has been a celebrity. Besides novels, she has written short stories, poems, essays, and children's books. She also has won acclaim for her nonfiction work, including *Anything We Love Can Be Saved: A Writer's Activism*.

❝We will be ourselves and free, or die in the attempt. Harriet Tubman was not our great-grandmother for nothing.❞

—*Walker*

Alice Walker was born in 1944.

Reading Further

For more about the Civil Rights movement, try these works:

The Civil Rights Movement: An Eyewitness History, by Sanford Wexler and Julian Bond, tells the story of the movement through numerous direct quotations from its participants.

The Civil Rights Movement: A Photographic History, by Steven Casher and Myrlie Evers-Williams, chronicles the movement with 150 gripping and dramatic photographs.

FOCUS ACTIVITY

If you were going to write a speech in honor of Martin Luther King Jr., what ideas would you want to include?

LIST IDEAS Make a list of topics you might explore and points you would like to make.

SETTING A PURPOSE Read to learn what Walker most wanted to express about King.

BACKGROUND

Walker's History and the History of African Americans

In some ways, Walker's speech reads like an abbreviated history of African Americans since the late nineteenth century. After mentioning an enslaved relative, Walker refers to the period after the Civil War called Reconstruction (1865–1877), a time when African Americans enjoyed new rights because of federal intervention in the South.

Following Reconstruction, southern whites regained control of state government and many used their power to keep African Americans down. This climate of oppression caused millions of African Americans to leave the South.

Walker then leaps to 1960, when a federal court, acting upon the landmark decision made in the case *Brown* v. *Board of Education* (1954), ordered the University of Georgia to admit African American students. Her final reference is to the desegregation of a Mississippi restaurant. Beginning in 1960, African Americans and many whites held sit-in demonstrations in restaurants in the South and even in some northern cities to force these restaurants to comply with desegregation laws.

Did You Know?

Dr. King's father, Martin Luther King Sr., was pastor of the Ebenezer Baptist Church in Atlanta, Georgia. The church was the site of the founding of the Southern Christian Leadership Conference, an important Civil Rights organization. Martin Luther King Jr. was the leader of this organization until his death in 1968.

VOCABULARY PREVIEW

ancestral (an ses′ trəl) *adj.* of or relating to those from whom one is descended; p. 899

colossal (kə los′ əl) *adj.* extraordinary in size or degree; enormous; p. 899

complex (kəm pleks′) *adj.* complicated; consisting of interrelated parts or elements; p. 900

embody (em bod′ ē) *v.* to give concrete or material form to; p. 900

continuity (kon′ tə nōō′ ə tē) *n.* the state or quality of going on without interruption; p. 900

ephemeral (i fem′ ər əl) *adj.* lasting for a very brief time; short-lived; p. 900

Choice:
A Tribute to
Dr. Martin Luther King Jr.

Alice Walker ❧

[This address was made in 1972 at a Jackson, Mississippi restaurant that refused to serve people of color until forced to do so by the Civil Rights movement a few years before.]

Stewart's Farm, 1995. Jonathan Green. Oil on canvas, 48 x 60 in. Collection of the artist.

MY GREAT-GREAT-GREAT-GRANDMOTHER walked as a slave from Virginia to Eatonton, Georgia—which passes for the Walker ancestral home—with two babies on her hips. She lived to be a hundred and twenty-five years old and my own father knew her as a boy. (It is in memory of this walk that I choose to keep and to embrace my "maiden" name, Walker.)

There is a cemetery near our family church where she is buried; but because her marker was made of wood and rotted years ago, it is impossible to tell exactly where her body lies. In the same cemetery are most of my mother's people, who have lived in Georgia for so long nobody even remembers when they came. And all of my great-aunts and uncles are there, and my grandfather and grandmother, and, very recently, my own father.

If it is true that land does not belong to anyone until they have buried a body in it, then the land of my birthplace belongs to me, dozens of times over. Yet the history of my family, like that of all black Southerners, is a history of dispossession. We loved the land and worked the land, but we never owned it; and even if we bought land, as my great-grandfather did after the Civil War, it was always in danger of being taken away, as his was, during the period following Reconstruction.

My father inherited nothing of material value from his father, and when I came of age in the early sixties I awoke to the bitter knowledge that in order just to continue to love the land of my birth, I was expected to leave it. For black people—including my parents—had learned a long time ago that to stay willingly in a beloved but brutal place is to risk losing the love and being forced to acknowledge only the brutality.

It is a part of the black Southern sensibility that we treasure memories; for such a long time, that is all of our homeland those of us who at one time or another were forced away from it have been allowed to have.

I watched my brothers, one by one, leave our home and leave the South. I watched my sisters do the same. This was not unusual; abandonment, except for memories, was the common thing, except for those who "could not do any better," or those whose strength or stubbornness was so colossal they took the risk that others could not bear.

In 1960, my mother bought a television set, and each day after school I watched Hamilton Holmes and Charlayne Hunter as they struggled to integrate—fair-skinned as they were—the University of Georgia. And then, one day, there appeared the face of Dr. Martin Luther King Jr. What a funny name, I thought. At the moment I first saw him, he was being handcuffed and shoved into a police truck. He had dared to claim his rights as a native son, and had been arrested. He displayed no fear, but seemed calm and serene, unaware of his own extraordinary courage. His whole body, like his conscience, was at peace.

At the moment I saw his resistance I knew I would never be able to live in this country without resisting everything that sought to disinherit me, and I would never be forced away from the land of my birth without a fight.

He was The One, The Hero, The One Fearless Person for whom we had waited. I hadn't even realized before that we *had* been waiting for

> *He displayed no fear, but seemed calm and serene, unaware of his own extraordinary courage.*

Vocabulary

ancestral (an ses′ trəl) *adj.* of or relating to those from whom one is descended
colossal (kə los′ əl) *adj.* extraordinary in size or degree; enormous

Martin Luther King Jr. but we had. And I knew it for sure when my mother added his name to the list of people she prayed for every night.

I sometimes think that it was literally the prayers of people like my mother and father, who had bowed down in the struggle for such a long time, that kept Dr. King alive until five years ago. For years we went to bed praying for his life, and awoke with the question "Is the 'Lord' still here?"

The public acts of Dr. King you know. They are visible all around you. His voice you would recognize sooner than any other voice you have heard in this century—this in spite of the fact that certain municipal libraries, like the one in downtown Jackson, do not carry recordings of his speeches, and the librarians chuckle cruelly when asked why they do not.

He gave us back our heritage. He gave us back our homeland . . .

You know, if you have read his books, that his is a <u>complex</u> and revolutionary philosophy that few people are capable of understanding fully or have the patience to <u>embody</u> in themselves. Which is our weakness, which is our loss.

And if you know anything about good Baptist preaching, you can imagine what you missed if you never had a chance to hear Martin Luther King Jr. preach at Ebenezer Baptist Church.

You know of the prizes and awards that he tended to think very little of. And you know of his concern for the disinherited: the American Indian, the Mexican American, and the poor American white—for whom he cared much.

You know that this very room, in this very restaurant, was closed to people of color not more than five years ago. And that we eat here together tonight largely through his efforts and his blood. We accept the common pleasures of life, assuredly, in his name.

But add to all of these things the one thing that seems to me second to none in importance: He gave us back our heritage. He gave us back our homeland; the bones and dust of our ancestors, who may now sleep within our caring *and* our hearing. He gave us the blueness of the Georgia sky in autumn as in summer; the colors of the Southern winter as well as glimpses of the green of vacation-time spring. Those of our relatives we used to invite for a visit we now can ask to stay. . . . He gave us full-time use of our own woods, and restored our memories to those of us who were forced to run away, as realities we might each day enjoy and leave for our children.

He gave us <u>continuity</u> of place, without which community is <u>ephemeral</u>. He gave us home.

Vocabulary
complex (kəm pleks′) *adj.* complicated; consisting of interrelated parts or elements
embody (em bod′ ē) *v.* to give concrete or material form to
continuity (kon′ tə nōō′ ə tē) *n.* the state or quality of going on without interruption
ephemeral (i fem′ ər əl) *adj.* lasting for a very brief time; short-lived

Responding to Literature

Personal Response
What ideas in this speech do you think you will remember?

——— ANALYZING LITERATURE ———

RECALL AND INTERPRET
1. Why did the author choose "to keep and to embrace" the name *Walker?* In what ways is this name more than just a name to her?
2. What circumstances kept Walker's family from owning land? How did the circumstances affect her family history? How does Walker seem to react to this course of events? Explain.
3. What was happening to Martin Luther King Jr. the first time Walker saw him? How did she know he was "The Hero"? In what ways did King's heroism affect Walker's life?
4. According to Walker, what was the most important thing King did for African Americans? Based on her description of this contribution, what can you infer about Walker and what she values?

EVALUATE AND CONNECT
5. If you had been in the audience the day Walker delivered this speech, how do you think it would have affected you? Explain your answer.
6. What examples of **repetition** do you find in this speech? In your opinion, how does the repetition affect the emotional impact of the speech?
7. Reread the first sentence of the final paragraph of this speech. Do you agree with what it says? Explain your answer.
8. What main point or points does Walker express about King? How does what she expresses compare with the points you listed for the Focus Activity on page 897? Explain.

——— EXTENDING YOUR RESPONSE ———

Literature Groups
Enough Said?   Is this tribute to Martin Luther King Jr. sufficient? In your group, examine Walker's speech. Decide how she best celebrates and honors King. Talk about what she might have said but didn't. Then present your group's opinion to another group.

Personal Writing
History Lesson   In your journal, explain how historical events have shaped the life of one of your ancestors or family members. Include in your discussion any historical figures who may have been involved.

📖 **Save your work for your portfolio.**

~: Writing \ Workshop :~

Narrative Writing: College Application

When authors write narratives about themselves, they allow readers to get to know them. In *Black Boy,* for example, readers learn about Richard Wright through his personal narratives. The same is true in Ralph Ellison's work, "February." One way for college admission officials or future employers to learn about you is through a personal narrative. Simply listing all your good qualities won't be as effective as telling a story that lets your character shine through. **In this workshop, you will write a personal narrative for a college application.**

● As you write your personal narrative, refer to the **Writing Handbook,** pp. R62–R67.

The Writing Process

PREWRITING

PREWRITING TIP
Ask three people in your life to describe an event or incident that stands out in their mind when they think about you. What do their answers tell you about yourself?

Consider your task
If you already have a college application, take a look at it. Chances are you'll be asked to write on a topic such as an experience or person important to you or a challenge that you faced and overcame. You may be asked to answer a question about yourself. As you plan your essay, keep the specific task in mind. Through this writing assignment, colleges are trying to find out what kind of person you are. Let your story reveal your character.

Consider your purpose
While the purpose of any narrative is to tell an interesting or entertaining story, the college application narrative has additional importance. It allows you to show that you have what it takes to face the challenges of higher education. By being able to think and write clearly, you have the chance to stand out from the crowd of students whose grades, scores, and activities are similar to yours.

Consider your audience
Try to forget that your audience consists of people who will be evaluating you. Write as if you know them. At the same time, remember that you are not addressing peers. Avoid expressions, jokes, or incidents that admissions officers might not appreciate or understand. Check with other adults if you are not sure whether something is appropriate.

Explore ideas

Which personal experiences reveal your most positive characteristics? Which are most interesting? Consider minor incidents as well as major ones. If nothing immediately comes to mind, flip through journals, photo albums, scrapbooks, and souvenirs to get ideas. Make a list of events you might be able to use. Next to each one, try to identify the personality trait that the incident reveals. Then focus on one experience.

STUDENT MODEL

I've fed the horses on our ranch every morning since I was ten. ➡ shows my discipline and commitment

I started a community newsletter. ➡ shows my motivation, creativity, and concern for community

I improved my grade from a C to an A in an advanced-level history class. ➡ shows my ability to learn and succeed in school

I won first place for barrel racing in the youth division. ➡ shows that I can achieve what I set out to do

Develop details

You want to recapture your experience for your reader. To do that, you first need to relive the experience in your own mind. Try running a mental movie of the experience, recalling each detail. Write down your actions and impressions in the order in which they occurred. For each step, note what you thought, felt, heard, saw, or smelled. Be specific. Even if you decide to relate events out of order when you draft, you can refer to these chronological notes to make sure you include all of the important aspects of your experience.

STUDENT MODEL

1. I DECIDED TO PUBLISH A COMMUNITY NEWSLETTER.

   My town gets the daily paper from the next town over; it never had anything about our town in it. I thought I could make a weekly newsletter full of local news and features.

2. I RODE MY BIKE AROUND AFTER DINNER, GATHERING NEWS AND INTERVIEWS.

   When I rode, the hot air turned cool around me. I was a little nervous, but people were friendly. Three different people offered me iced tea.

3. I TYPED THE STORIES INTO THE COMPUTER.

   The computer was in the sewing room on the third floor. The roof was low in there, and it was hot, but I was so involved I didn't notice.

DRAFTING

Write your draft

Gather your notes, keep your purpose in mind, and begin boldly. Write as yourself, using *I* and *me.* Don't try to sound impressive—just try to sound like you. If new thoughts about the experience occur to you as you write, include them as long as they reinforce the picture of yourself you want to convey. Later, you can decide which points will best capture the attention of the admissions officers.

Try different endings

The ending of your narrative will be particularly important. It determines whether or not your reader leaves with clear, focused memories of you. Try different endings—as many as you can think of, as long as you avoid a preachy statement or a simple summary. Here are some possibilities:

- End with a telling piece of dialogue.
- Connect the experience with the present.
- Tell how the issue was resolved.
- Consider what might occur in the future.
- End with a question or a speculation about the experience.
- Refer back to an important part of the event.
- Describe what you felt, how you reacted, or what you learned—but leave something for the reader's imagination.

STUDENT MODEL

FIRST CONCLUSION

As I mentioned, I got an idea to put out a newsletter because I knew people would like to see their names in print and read about their friends and neighbors. It didn't take me long to get some interesting news about the neighbors. I worked hard to get the first issue out, and I sold it by hand to almost every family in our town. By doing this, I believe I showed motivation, creativity, and concern for my community.

SECOND CONCLUSION

The newsletter ended up being profitable. People were happy to pay a dollar to receive it, and local businesses even took out some ads. However, I realize that the biggest reward was not monetary. By asking my neighbors questions about their farms and their lives, I learned a lot about the people I grew up around and also about myself. Although someone else will take over the newsletter when I go away, the lessons it taught me will stay with me wherever I am.

REVISING

Evaluate your work

Put your narrative aside for a few hours or, if possible, even a few days. Come back to it as a new reader. What impression does it give of you? Why? Are your word choices clear and specific? Use a thesaurus to help you choose more precisely the best words for the impression you want to convey.

Consult with others

Share your work with various people—someone who knows the event, someone who knows you, someone who does not know you well, someone older, someone your age. Ask each reader for comments and suggestions, based on the **Questions for Revising.** You don't need to address everyone's comments in your revisions, but if two or more people have similar remarks, pay special attention to those areas of your narrative.

REVISING TIP
Go back to the original question on the application form. Be sure your narrative answers that question. Does the application suggest a word limit? If so, adhere to it in your revision.

TECHNOLOGY TIP
If you have electronic mail on your computer, think about sending your draft to a few people who know you. Write first to ask their permission. Suggest that they respond by E-mail with comments and suggestions.

QUESTIONS FOR REVISING

☑ Does the beginning grab readers' attention?

☑ What unnecessary details can I eliminate? Which parts need more details?

☑ Which parts are confusing? boring?

☑ How can I use transitions to show the relationship of events in my narrative?

☑ Where do I sound pushy or preachy, pretentious or phony?

☑ Does the ending reinforce a true impression of me? Does it leave readers thinking favorably about me?

STUDENT MODEL

~~I was embarrassed. It seemed~~ like I was trying to pry into people's lives. I got up the courage to knock, though, ~~I knocked~~ and ~~on the door three times. Every knock made a clanking sound. I~~ before I knew it ~~was knocking on their screen door. Then it was OK. I had~~ my tape recorder was going and Mr. and Mrs. Klintock were telling me about what it had been like to go to school, down on Route 10, in the one-room schoolhouse that now sits empty.

> As I stood on the Klintocks's porch looking in through their screen door, butterflies rose in my stomach. What had seemed like a good idea at dinner now seemed like a bad idea,

EDITING/PROOFREADING

PROOFREADING TIP

Every time you see the word *its* or *it's,* double-check to make sure you're using it correctly. *Its* is a possessive pronoun. *It's* is a contraction for it is.

When you are satisfied with the picture you have created with your narrative, edit your writing carefully. Check the grammar, usage, mechanics, and spelling, looking for one kind of error at a time. Use the **Proofreading Checklist** on the inside back cover of this book.

Grammar Hint

Use an apostrophe and an *s* for the possessive form of a singular indefinite pronoun.

I noticed that everyone's stories were interesting to hear.

Never use an apostrophe with the possessive form of a personal pronoun.

Was the writing in the newsletter all yours?

● For more about possessive forms, see **Language Handbook,** p. R29.

STUDENT MODEL

After Mrs. Klintock told me about the time her famly was stranded for two weeks in a freak snow storm I thought no one's story could be more exciting than her's.

PUBLISHING/PRESENTING

PRESENTING TIP

As a final check, go back to the application one last time. Have you followed all the directions carefully?

Rarely will it be more important to present your writing in the best possible light. Whether you write by hand or on a word processor, be sure your narrative—and your application—are absolutely neat, clear, and legible. Use 8½-by-11-inch sheets of paper. Leave at least one-inch margins around all text, use a consistent style of heading, and remember to number your pages. Make copies of the entire application, in case it gets lost or in case you want to use it again. Check the date the application is due, and mail it in plenty of time. Be sure the package is addressed correctly and clearly, and have the post office weigh it to determine the correct postage. Then send it off—and good luck!

Reflecting

Think about your experience in writing this narrative. What advice about finding a topic, writing a draft, and revising would you give to someone else? What did you learn about yourself? What might you do differently for another application? Discuss these questions with a classmate.

📖 **Save your work for your portfolio.**

Theme 10 — Acting on an Idea

Think of a time when you acted on an idea—a time when you thought out something carefully and then took decisive action. Many characters in this theme have deeply held ideas, ideas that lead to bold and extreme deeds. Also, the playwright Arthur Miller uses a drama and "actors" to express his own powerful ideas about events of his time.

THEME PROJECTS

Learning for Life

Write a Preview   In movie theaters, you often see "coming attractions," or previews, of movies that will soon be out. With a small group, plan and perform a five- to ten-minute preview for *The Crucible*. Your preview should spark the viewer's interest without giving away too much of the plot.

1. After reading each act, discuss it with your group. What were the crucial moments? What moments would be best to portray in the preview? List these moments, and act out a few to see how they might work. Choose one or more moments to represent each act.

2. Then, develop a narration to make the play sound appealing and to connect the moments you will portray in your preview.

3. Perform your preview for the class. Then have a class discussion about your preview. Explain why you presented your preview the way you did.

Listening and Speaking

From Different Viewpoints   With a partner, role-play an interview with a different character from each act of *The Crucible*.

1. After reading each act, choose one character to interview. Develop a set of five questions to ask that character about the events that have just occurred, and plan answers.

2. Role-play all four interviews for the class after finishing the play.

"A POWERFUL AND EXCITING PLAY"
—BROOKS ATKINSON, N. Y. Times

THE CRUCIBLE

MARTIN BECK THEATRE
45th ST., WEST OF 8th AVE. EVES. 8:30 MATS. WED. & SAT. 2:30

Literature F O C U S

Drama

A **drama,** or play, is a story that has been written to be performed by actors for an audience. The story is told through the words and actions of the characters. When a playwright develops a script, he or she writes **dialogue** that the characters speak. The playwright also writes **stage directions** to help actors, directors, and readers visualize what is happening on-stage. These directions explain how characters should look, speak, act, and move on the stage.

The play's **protagonist** is the character around whom the action revolves. The protagonist usually has the audience's sympathy. In most plays, the protagonist has a **conflict** with one or more **antagonists.** Traditionally, a play in which the protagonist comes to an unhappy end is a **tragedy.** A light, humorous play with a happy ending is a **comedy.**

Understanding the major elements of drama can help you appreciate and discuss plays you see or read. The chart shown here provides examples of some of the important elements from Arthur Miller's play *The Crucible*, which appears on pages 913–995.

ELEMENTS OF DRAMA

Characters

The cast of characters is listed at the beginning of a play and might include a short description of each character. The playwright may further describe a character when he or she first appears in the play. Audiences learn about characters through their actions and through the dialogue.

Some of the characters in *The Crucible* are:
REVEREND PARRIS: clergyman in Salem, Massachusetts
ABIGAIL WILLIAMS: niece of Parris
JOHN PROCTOR: a farmer in his middle thirties
ELIZABETH PROCTOR: wife of John Proctor
GILES COREY: another farmer, eighty-three years old
REBECCA NURSE: farm wife, greatly respected by the people of Salem

Setting

The setting is the time and place in which the events of a play occur. Setting is often important in creating the **mood** of the play. Typically, the setting is described at the beginning. Additional details might appear throughout the play, such as at the beginning of acts and scenes, when the specific location or time changes.

PLACE: *Salem, Massachusetts*
TIME: *1692*

Plot

The plot of a drama, like the plots of other narratives, is the series of related events that revolve around a central conflict. The conflict may be a struggle involving people, ideas, or forces.

The Crucible dramatizes the story of a historical incident in Salem, Massachusetts, in which accusations made by a number of young women set off a witch hunt supported by local authorities. While some characters fiercely support the witch hunt, others resist, trying to stand up for the truth and save the lives of friends and loved ones, sometimes at the cost of their own lives.

Dialogue

Most plays consist largely of dialogue, or conversation between the characters. The dialogue helps reveal the plot and characters of the play.

PROCTOR. Mr. Hale, I never knew I must account to that man for I come to church or stay at home. My wife were sick this winter.
HALE. So I am told. But you, Mister, why could you not come alone?
PROCTOR. I surely did come when I could, and when I could not I prayed in this house.
HALE. Mr. Proctor, your house is not a church; your theology must tell you that.

Acts and Scenes

Many plays are divided into acts and scenes, which indicate a change in location or the passage of time. A one-act play, for example, takes place in one location over a brief, continuous span of time.

The Crucible is a play in four acts, each act taking place in a different location in Salem. Ordinarily the four acts are not divided into scenes, although Miller wrote one version in which act 2 has a second scene.

ACTIVITY

As you read *The Crucible,* answer these questions about the play:
1. Who is the protagonist? Is there more than one?
2. Who are the antagonists?
3. What is the central conflict?

Radio Transcript

Have you ever been accused unfairly? One woman's family, acting on the idea that she had been treated unjustly, took her case to court and won vindication for her.

Blacklisted Woman Vindicated by Federal Court Ruling

from *All Things Considered*, National Public Radio, March 16, 1996

Daniel Zwerdling, Host: Beatrice Braude died almost nine years ago, at the age of 75. But her relatives say it wasn't too late a few weeks ago for the U.S. court system to finally give her what they say she deserved, which [was] Washington justice. By all accounts, Braude was a lively, energetic and talented young woman when she went to work for the U.S. State Department after World War II. She spoke five languages, served for a time in Paris and got rave personnel reviews.

But in the early 1950s, Beatrice Braude got in trouble. This was the era when anti-communist hysteria swept the country. When the government and industry blacklisted thousands of people they believed might harbor unpopular political views. It was the era of Senator Joseph McCarthy.

Christopher Sipes, Braude Family Lawyer: . . . the McCarthy period was a period when many ordinary Americans were . . .

blacklisted . . . [and were] unable to have their rights vindicated.

Zwerdling: In 1951, the State Department's loyalty security board investigated Beatrice Braude, based on reports that she'd had some social contacts with two women who were suspected of being sympathetic to Communists. The board cleared her, but just two years later, mysteriously she was fired.

For the rest of her life, Braude tried to find out exactly what had happened to her, and after she died, her brother and niece convinced a leading law firm in Washington, D.C. to champion their case.

They sued the federal government, and won. A judge in the U.S. Claims Court ruled that the government unfairly blacklisted Beatrice Braude. He ordered the government to compensate her family. Justice Department officials disagree with the ruling. . . . But Sipes says their victory proves once and for

Senator Joseph McCarthy

all why Beatrice Braude lost her job one day in 1953.

Sipes: In the file there was evidence, both of the reason for her termination and additional documents suggesting that she had been black-listed . . . then talking to witnesses, we were able to find out, flesh out the full story.

This case . . . had a larger historical significance. . . . [An] ordinary American was able finally to vindicate her rights for the wrongs that were done to her in the McCarthy period.

Respond

1. Do you think this was a worthwhile case to pursue? Explain.

2. How might you react if you were in a similar situation?

Before You Read

The Crucible

Meet Arthur Miller

Arthur Miller saw a play for the first time when he was a boy. From that experience, he "learned that there were two kinds of reality, but that of the stage was far more real." Miller began writing plays of his own while in college, but it was not until 1947, when he was thirty-two, that he scored his first major critical success. That year, his play *All My Sons* was produced, received the New York Drama Critics Circle Award, and was sold for movie rights. Two years later, Miller's play *Death of a Salesman* began a highly successful run and received a Pulitzer Prize.

By his late thirties, Miller's work had won him fame. Fame, however, would involve him in a dark chapter of U.S. history. Fear of communism—the "Red Scare"—had taken hold of Americans. Congress established the House Un-American Activities Committee (HUAC) to investigate an alleged communist conspiracy. Among the main targets of the investigation were people in the entertainment business. These people were called before HUAC and asked not only to "confess" to earlier involvement in socialist or communist organizations but also to name others who had held similar views. People who refused to cooperate were often blacklisted, or denied employment.

The way HUAC questioned people and pressured them to testify against their colleagues reminded Miller of the witch trials in colonial America. In the spring of 1952, Miller visited Salem, Massachusetts. On his way, he stopped to visit his friend Elia Kazan. Kazan told Miller that he had been called to testify by HUAC, and that he had decided to save his career by confessing and naming names. Weighed down with his friend's news, Miller went on to Salem to bury himself in what he called "one of the strangest and most awful chapters in human history."

Miller's research inspired him to write *The Crucible*, which was first staged on Broadway in 1953. Its relevance to the political situation of the times was clear, even in other countries. When a Belgian group invited Miller to see its production of *The Crucible* late in 1953, the U.S. State Department refused to renew Miller's passport, so he could not travel abroad. This was Miller's first run-in with the government.

The second came in 1956 when Miller, too, was called to testify before HUAC. When he refused to name names, he was charged with contempt, fined, and sentenced to jail. His case, however, was reversed on appeal in 1958, and he never served a jail term.

In 1965 Miller became the president of P.E.N., an international literary organization. Through P.E.N. he helped free writers in many countries who had been imprisoned for their political views. Miller's most famous works have remained *Death of a Salesman* and *The Crucible*. In fact, on almost any given day, *The Crucible* is being produced somewhere in the world.

❝If only we could stop murdering one another we could be a wonderfully humorous species.❞

❝One of the strongest urges in the writer's heart . . . is to reveal what has been hidden and denied.❞

—*Miller*

Arthur Miller was born in 1915.

Before You Read

FOCUS ACTIVITY

Has your character ever been questioned? Or has someone you know or have heard about—perhaps even a character in a TV show or movie—undergone a test of character?

CHART IT! Create a flow chart like the one below to organize the details of that person's test of character.

| Event that led to test: | → | Response: | → | Reactions of others: | → | Outcome: |

SETTING A PURPOSE Read to learn how certain characters deal with their own tests of character.

BACKGROUND

The Time and Place

The Crucible takes place in 1692 in and near Salem, a small town in the Massachusetts Bay Colony that had been founded in the early 1600s by a group of Christians called Puritans. The Puritans had fled England for North America to establish a religious community. However, by the 1660s, English merchants had immigrated to the colony, attracted by business opportunities. Most did not share the religious beliefs of the Puritan founders. Against this backdrop, many Puritans felt they were losing hold of their ideals. Their sense of insecurity, frustration, and loss of control helped create a climate of guilt and blame. This climate pervaded the town of Salem and especially nearby Salem Village, where, in the winter of 1691–1692, several teenage girls began behaving strangely. Many people in the community suspected that the girls were victims of witchcraft. These events and the trials that followed form the basis for Miller's play *The Crucible*.

About the Title

A crucible is a pot or vessel commonly made from porcelain or other highly heat-resistant material. For centuries, people have used crucibles for melting metals, such as gold or silver, to test them for purity. In modern times, chemists use crucibles for heating materials in the process of chemical analysis and in conducting chemical reactions that require extremely high temperatures. Today the term *crucible* has also come to mean "a severe test," or "a place or situation in which concentrated forces interact to cause or influence change or development."

VOCABULARY PREVIEW

compromise (kom′ prə mīz′) *v.* to endanger the reputation or interests of; to expose to suspicion; p. 916

contention (kən ten′ shən) *n.* verbal argument or struggle; quarreling; p. 917

subservient (səb sur′ vē ənt) *adj.* useful, in an inferior capacity, to promote an end; submissive; p. 919

naive (nä ēv′) *adj.* lacking knowledge of the ways of the world; unsophisticated; innocent; p. 919

pretense (prē′ tens) *n.* a false show or appearance, especially for the purpose of deceiving; falseness; p. 922

evade (i vād′) *v.* to escape or avoid, as by cleverness; p. 931

The Crucible

Arthur Miller

CHARACTERS

(in order of appearance)

REVEREND PARRIS	MERCY LEWIS	FRANCIS NURSE
BETTY PARRIS	MARY WARREN	EZEKIEL CHEEVER
TITUBA	JOHN PROCTOR	MARSHAL HERRICK
ABIGAIL WILLIAMS	REBECCA NURSE	JUDGE HATHORNE
SUSANNA WALCOTT	GILES COREY	DEPUTY GOVERNOR DANFORTH
MRS. ANN PUTNAM	REVEREND JOHN HALE	SARAH GOOD
THOMAS PUTNAM	ELIZABETH PROCTOR	HOPKINS

Act One

(An Overture)

[*A small upper bedroom in the home of* REVEREND SAMUEL PARRIS, *Salem, Massachusetts, in the spring of the year 1692.*

There is a narrow window at the left. Through its leaded panes the morning sunlight streams. A candle still burns near the bed, which is at the right. A chest, a chair, and a small table are the other furnishings. At the back a door opens on the landing of the stairway to the ground floor. The room gives off an air of clean spareness. The roof rafters are exposed, and the wood colors are raw and unmellowed.

As the curtain rises, REVEREND PARRIS *is discovered kneeling beside the bed, evidently in prayer. His daughter,* BETTY PARRIS, *aged ten, is lying on the bed, inert.*

REVEREND PARRIS *is praying now, and, though we cannot hear his words, a sense of his confusion hangs about him. He mumbles, then seems about to weep; then he weeps, then prays again; but his daughter does not stir on the bed.*

The door opens, and his Negro slave enters. TITUBA[1] *is in her forties.* PARRIS *brought her with him from Barbados,*[2] *where he spent some years as a merchant before entering the ministry. She enters as one does who can no longer bear to be barred from the sight of her beloved, but she is also very frightened because her slave sense has warned her that, as always, trouble in this house eventually lands on her back.*]

TITUBA. [*Already taking a step backward.*] My Betty be hearty soon?

PARRIS. Out of here!

TITUBA. [*Backing to the door.*] My Betty not goin' die . . .

PARRIS. [*Scrambling to his feet in a fury.*] Out of my sight! [*She is gone.*] Out of my—[*He is overcome with sobs. He clamps his teeth against them and closes the door and leans against it, exhausted.*] Oh, my God! God help me! [*Quaking with fear, mumbling to himself through his sobs, he goes to the bed and gently takes* BETTY's *hand.*] Betty. Child. Dear child. Will you wake, will you open up your eyes! Betty, little one . . .

[*He is bending to kneel again when his niece,* ABIGAIL WILLIAMS, *seventeen, enters—a strikingly beautiful girl, an orphan, with an endless capacity for dissembling.*[3] *Now she is all worry and apprehension and propriety.*]

ABIGAIL. Uncle? [*He looks to her.*] Susanna Walcott's here from Doctor Griggs.

---

1. *Tituba* (ti tōō′ bə)
2. *Barbados* (bär bā′ dōz) is an island in the Caribbean that was, at the time of the play, an English colony.

3. *Dissembling* means "concealing one's true motives."

PARRIS. Oh? Let her come, let her come.

ABIGAIL. [*Leaning out the door to call to SUSANNA, who is down the hall a few steps.*] Come in, Susanna.

[*SUSANNA WALCOTT, a little younger than ABIGAIL, a nervous, hurried girl, enters.*]

PARRIS. [*Eagerly.*] What does the doctor say, child?

SUSANNA. [*Craning around PARRIS to get a look at BETTY.*] He bid me come and tell you, reverend sir, that he cannot discover no medicine for it in his books.

PARRIS. Then he must search on.

SUSANNA. Aye, sir, he have been searchin' his books since he left you, sir. But he bid me tell you, that you might look to unnatural things for the cause of it.

PARRIS. [*His eyes going wide.*] No—no. There be no unnatural cause here. Tell him I have sent for Reverend Hale of Beverly, and Mr. Hale will surely confirm that. Let him look to medicine and put out all thought of unnatural causes here. There be none.

SUSANNA. Aye, sir. He bid me tell you. [*She turns to go.*]

ABIGAIL. Speak nothin' of it in the village, Susanna.

PARRIS. Go directly home and speak nothing of unnatural causes.

SUSANNA. Aye, sir. I pray for her. [*She goes out.*]

ABIGAIL. Uncle, the rumor of witchcraft is all about; I think you'd best go down and deny it yourself. The parlor's packed with people, sir. I'll sit with her.

PARRIS. [*Pressed, turns on her.*] And what shall I say to them? That my daughter and my niece I discovered dancing like heathen in the forest?

ABIGAIL. Uncle, we did dance; let you tell them I confessed it—and I'll be whipped if I must be. But they're speakin' of witchcraft. Betty's not witched.

PARRIS. Abigail, I cannot go before the congregation when I know you have not opened[4] with me. What did you do with her in the forest?

ABIGAIL. We did dance, uncle, and when you leaped out of the bush so suddenly, Betty was frightened and then she fainted. And there's the whole of it.

PARRIS. Child. Sit you down.

ABIGAIL. [*Quavering, as she sits.*] I would never hurt Betty. I love her dearly.

PARRIS. Now look you, child, your punishment will come in its time. But if you trafficked[5] with spirits in the forest I must know it now, for surely my enemies will, and they will ruin me with it.

ABIGAIL. But we never conjured[6] spirits.

PARRIS. Then why can she not move herself since midnight? This child is desperate! [*ABIGAIL lowers her eyes.*] It must come out—my enemies will bring it out. Let me know what you done there. Abigail, do you understand that I have many enemies?

ABIGAIL. I have heard of it, uncle.

PARRIS. There is a faction[7] that is sworn to drive me from my pulpit. Do you understand that?

ABIGAIL. I think so, sir.

PARRIS. Now then, in the midst of such disruption, my own household is discovered to be the very center of some obscene practice. Abominations[8] are done in the forest—

ABIGAIL. It were sport,[9] uncle!

PARRIS. [*Pointing at BETTY.*] You call this sport? [*She lowers her eyes. He pleads.*] Abigail,

---

4. Here, *have not opened* means "have not been completely honest."
5. *Trafficked* means "dealt or did business."
6. Here, *conjured* means "summoned by using magic words or spells."
7. A *faction* is a small segment of people who disagree with the larger group on an issue or set of issues.
8. *Abominations* are vile or shameful acts.
9. Here, *sport* means "innocent recreation."

The Crucible

if you know something that may help the doctor, for God's sake tell it to me. [*She is silent.*] I saw Tituba waving her arms over the fire when I came on you. Why was she doing that? And I heard a screeching and gibberish coming from her mouth. She were swaying like a dumb beast over that fire!

ABIGAIL. She always sings her Barbados songs, and we dance.

PARRIS. I cannot blink[10] what I saw, Abigail, for my enemies will not blink it. I saw a dress lying on the grass.

ABIGAIL. [*Innocently.*] A dress?

PARRIS. [*It is very hard to say.*] Aye, a dress. And I thought I saw—someone naked running through the trees!

ABIGAIL. [*In terror.*] No one was naked! You mistake yourself, uncle!

PARRIS. [*With anger.*] I saw it! [*He moves from her. Then, resolved.*] Now tell me true, Abigail. And I pray you feel the weight of truth upon you, for now my ministry's at stake, my ministry and perhaps your cousin's life. Whatever abomination you have done, give me all of it now, for I dare not be taken unaware when I go before them down there.

ABIGAIL. There is nothin' more. I swear it, uncle.

PARRIS. [*Studies her, then nods, half convinced.*] Abigail, I have fought here three long years to bend these stiff-necked people to me, and now, just now when some good respect is rising for me in the parish, you compromise my very character. I have given you a home, child, I have put clothes upon your back—now give me upright answer. Your name in the town—it is entirely white, is it not?

ABIGAIL. [*With an edge of resentment.*] Why, I am sure it is, sir. There be no blush about my name.

PARRIS. [*To the point.*] Abigail, is there any other cause than you have told me, for your being discharged from Goody[11] Proctor's service? I have heard it said, and I tell you as I heard it, that she comes so rarely to the church this year for she will not sit so close to something soiled. What signified that remark?

ABIGAIL. She hates me, uncle, she must, for I would not be her slave. It's a bitter woman, a lying, cold, sniveling woman, and I will not work for such a woman!

PARRIS. She may be. And yet it has troubled me that you are now seven month out of their house, and in all this time no other family has ever called for your service.

ABIGAIL. They want slaves, not such as I. Let them send to Barbados for that. I will not black my face for any of them! [*With ill-concealed resentment at him.*] Do you begrudge my bed, uncle?

PARRIS. No—no.

ABIGAIL. [*In a temper.*] My name is good in the village! I will not have it said my name is soiled! Goody Proctor is a gossiping liar!

[*Enter* MRS. ANN PUTNAM. *She is a twisted soul of forty-five, a death-ridden woman, haunted by dreams.*]

PARRIS. [*As soon as the door begins to open.*] No—no, I cannot have anyone. [*He sees her, and a certain deference[12] springs into him, although his worry remains.*] Why, Goody Putnam, come in.

MRS. PUTNAM. [*Full of breath, shiny-eyed.*] It is a marvel. It is surely a stroke of hell upon you.

---

10. Here, *blink* means "to deliberately overlook or ignore."

11. *Goody* is short for *Goodwife,* a term of polite address for a married woman.

12. *Deference* is courteous respect or regard.

Vocabulary

compromise (kom' prə mīz') *v.* to endanger the reputation or interests of; to expose to suspicion

PARRIS. No, Goody Putnam, it is—

MRS. PUTNAM. [*Glancing at BETTY.*] How high did she fly, how high?

PARRIS. No, no, she never flew—

MRS. PUTNAM. [*Very pleased with it.*] Why, it's sure she did. Mr. Collins saw her goin' over Ingersoll's barn, and come down light as bird, he says!

PARRIS. Now, look you, Goody Putnam, she never—[*Enter THOMAS PUTNAM, a well-to-do, hard-handed landowner, near fifty.*] Oh, good morning, Mr. Putnam.

PUTNAM. It is a providence[13] the thing is out now! It is a providence. [*He goes directly to the bed.*]

PARRIS. What's out, sir, what's—?

[*MRS. PUTNAM goes to the bed.*]

PUTNAM. [*Looking down at BETTY.*] Why, her eyes is closed! Look you, Ann.

MRS. PUTNAM. Why, that's strange. [*To PARRIS.*] Ours is open.

PARRIS. [*Shocked.*] Your Ruth is sick?

MRS. PUTNAM. [*With vicious certainty.*] I'd not call it sick; the Devil's touch is heavier than sick. It's death, y'know, it's death drivin' into them, forked and hoofed.

PARRIS. Oh, pray not! Why, how does Ruth ail?

MRS. PUTNAM. She ails as she must—she never waked this morning, but her eyes open and she walks, and hears naught,[14] sees naught, and cannot eat. Her soul is taken, surely.

[*PARRIS is struck.*]

PUTNAM. [*As though for further details.*] They say you've sent for Reverend Hale of Beverly?

PARRIS. [*With dwindling conviction[15] now.*] A precaution only. He has much experience in all demonic arts, and I—

MRS. PUTNAM. He has indeed; and found a witch in Beverly last year, and let you remember that.

PARRIS. Now, Goody Ann, they only thought that were a witch, and I am certain there be no element of witchcraft here.

PUTNAM. No witchcraft! Now look you, Mr. Parris—

PARRIS. Thomas, Thomas, I pray you, leap not to witchcraft. I know that you—you least of all, Thomas, would ever wish so disastrous a charge laid upon me. We cannot leap to witchcraft. They will howl me out of Salem for such corruption in my house.

PUTNAM. [*At the moment, he is intent upon getting PARRIS, for whom he has only contempt, to move toward the abyss.*] Mr. Parris, I have taken your part in all contention here, and I would continue; but I cannot if you hold back in this. There are hurtful, vengeful spirits layin' hands on these children.

PARRIS. But, Thomas, you cannot—

PUTNAM. Ann! Tell Mr. Parris what you have done.

MRS. PUTNAM. Reverend Parris, I have laid seven babies unbaptized in the earth. Believe me, sir, you never saw more hearty babies born. And yet, each would wither in my arms the very night of their birth. I have spoke nothin', but my heart has clamored intimations.[16] And now, this year, my Ruth, my only—I see her turning strange. A secret child she has become this year, and shrivels like a sucking mouth

---

13. Here, *providence* means "a blessing" or "an act of divine care."
14. *Naught* means "nothing."
15. Here, *conviction* means "certainty."
16. A heart that has *clamored intimations* has nagged its owner with suggestions (of possible witchcraft).

Vocabulary
contention (kən ten′ shən) *n.* verbal argument or struggle; quarreling

were pullin' on her life too. And so I thought to send her to your Tituba—

PARRIS. To Tituba! What may Tituba—?

MRS. PUTNAM. Tituba knows how to speak to the dead, Mr. Parris.

PARRIS. Goody Ann, it is a formidable sin to conjure up the dead!

MRS. PUTNAM. I take it on my soul, but who else may surely tell us what person murdered my babies?

PARRIS. [*Horrified.*] Woman!

MRS. PUTNAM. They were murdered, Mr. Parris! And mark this proof! Mark it! Last night my Ruth were ever so close to their little spirits; I know it, sir. For how else is she struck dumb now except some power of darkness would stop her mouth? It is a marvelous sign, Mr. Parris!

PUTNAM. Don't you understand it, sir? There is a murdering witch among us, bound to keep herself in the dark. [*PARRIS turns to BETTY, a frantic terror rising in him.*] Let your enemies make of it what they will, you cannot blink it more.

PARRIS. [*To ABIGAIL.*] Then you were conjuring spirits last night.

ABIGAIL. [*Whispering.*] Not I, sir—Tituba and Ruth.

PARRIS. [*Turns now, with new fear, and goes to BETTY, looks down at her, and then, gazing off.*] Oh, Abigail, what proper payment for my charity! Now I am undone.

PUTNAM. You are not undone! Let you take hold here. Wait for no one to charge you—declare it yourself. You have discovered witchcraft—

PARRIS. In my house? In my house, Thomas? They will topple me with this! They will make of it a—

[*Enter MERCY LEWIS, the PUTNAMS' servant, a fat, sly, merciless girl of eighteen.*]

MERCY. Your pardons. I only thought to see how Betty is.

PUTNAM. Why aren't you home? Who's with Ruth?

MERCY. Her grandma come. She's improved a little, I think—she give a powerful sneeze before.

MRS. PUTNAM. Ah, there's a sign of life!

MERCY. I'd fear no more, Goody Putnam. It were a grand sneeze; another like it will shake her wits together, I'm sure. [*She goes to the bed to look.*]

PARRIS. Will you leave me now, Thomas? I would pray a while alone.

ABIGAIL. Uncle, you've prayed since midnight. Why do you not go down and—

PARRIS. No—no. [*To PUTNAM.*] I have no answer for that crowd. I'll wait till Mr. Hale arrives. [*To get MRS. PUTNAM to leave.*] If you will, Goody Ann . . .

PUTNAM. Now look you, sir. Let you strike out against the Devil, and the village will bless you for it! Come down, speak to them—pray with them. They're thirsting for your word, Mister! Surely you'll pray with them.

PARRIS. [*Swayed.*] I'll lead them in a psalm, but let you say nothing of witchcraft yet. I will not discuss it. The cause is yet unknown. I have had enough contention since I came; I want no more.

MRS. PUTNAM. Mercy, you go home to Ruth, d'y'hear?

MERCY. Aye, mum.

[*MRS. PUTNAM goes out.*]

PARRIS. [*To ABIGAIL.*] If she starts for the window, cry for me at once.

ABIGAIL. I will, uncle.

PARRIS. [*To PUTNAM.*] There is a terrible power in her arms today. [*He goes out with PUTNAM.*]

ABIGAIL. [*With hushed trepidation.*][17] How is Ruth sick?

MERCY. It's weirdish, I know not—she seems to walk like a dead one since last night.

ABIGAIL. [*Turns at once and goes to* BETTY, *and now, with fear in her voice.*] Betty? [BETTY *doesn't move. She shakes her.*] Now stop this! Betty! Sit up now!

[BETTY *doesn't stir.* MERCY *comes over.*]

MERCY. Have you tried beatin' her? I gave Ruth a good one and it waked her for a minute. Here, let me have her.

ABIGAIL. [*Holding* MERCY *back.*] No, he'll be comin' up. Listen, now; if they be questioning us, tell them we danced—I told him as much already.

MERCY. Aye. And what more?

ABIGAIL. He knows Tituba conjured Ruth's sisters to come out of the grave.

MERCY. And what more?

ABIGAIL. He saw you naked.

MERCY. [*Clapping her hands together with a frightened laugh.*] Oh, Jesus!

[*Enter* MARY WARREN, *breathless. She is seventeen, a* subservient, naive, *lonely girl.*]

MARY WARREN. What'll we do? The village is out! I just come from the farm; the whole country's talkin' witchcraft! They'll be callin' us witches, Abby!

MERCY. [*Pointing and looking at* MARY WARREN.] She means to tell, I know it.

MARY WARREN. Abby, we've got to tell. Witchery's a hangin' error, a hangin' like they done in Boston two year ago! We must tell the truth, Abby! You'll only be whipped for dancin', and the other things!

ABIGAIL. Oh, *we'll* be whipped!

MARY WARREN. I never done none of it, Abby. I only looked!

MERCY. [*Moving menacingly toward* MARY.] Oh, you're a great one for lookin', aren't you, Mary Warren? What a grand peeping courage you have!

[BETTY, *on the bed, whimpers.* ABIGAIL *turns to her at once.*]

ABIGAIL. Betty? [*She goes to* BETTY.] Now, Betty, dear, wake up now. It's Abigail. [*She sits* BETTY *up and furiously shakes her.*] I'll beat you, Betty! [BETTY *whimpers.*] My, you seem improving. I talked to your papa and I told him everything. So there's nothing to—

BETTY. [*Darts off the bed, frightened of* ABIGAIL, *and flattens herself against the wall.*] I want my mama!

ABIGAIL. [*With alarm, as she cautiously approaches* BETTY.] What ails you, Betty? Your mama's dead and buried.

BETTY. I'll fly to Mama. Let me fly! [*She raises her arms as though to fly, and streaks for the window, gets one leg out.*]

ABIGAIL. [*Pulling her away from the window.*] I told him everything; he knows now, he knows everything we—

BETTY. You drank blood, Abby! You didn't tell him that!

ABIGAIL. Betty, you never say that again! You will never—

BETTY. You did, you did! You drank a charm to kill John Proctor's wife! You drank a charm to kill Goody Proctor!

17. *Trepidation* means "fear" or "anxiety."

Vocabulary
subservient (səb sur′ vē ənt) *adj.* useful, in an inferior capacity, to promote an end; submissive
naive (nä ēv′) *adj.* lacking knowledge of the ways of the world; unsophisticated; innocent

The Crucible

ABIGAIL. [*Smashes her across the face.*] Shut it! Now shut it!

BETTY. [*Collapsing on the bed.*] Mama, Mama! [*She dissolves into sobs.*]

ABIGAIL. Now look you. All of you. We danced. And Tituba conjured Ruth Putnam's dead sisters. And that is all. And mark this. Let either of you breathe a word, or the edge of a word, about the other things, and I will come to you in the black of some terrible night and I will bring a pointy reckoning that will shudder you. And you know I can do it; I saw Indians smash my dear parents' heads on the pillow next to mine, and I have seen some reddish work[18] done at night, and I can make you wish you had never seen the sun go down! [*She goes to BETTY and roughly sits her up.*] Now, you—sit up and stop this!

[*But BETTY collapses in her hands and lies inert on the bed.*]

MARY WARREN. [*With hysterical fright.*] What's got her? [*ABIGAIL stares in fright at BETTY.*] Abby, she's going to die! It's a sin to conjure, and we—

ABIGAIL. [*Starting for MARY.*] I say shut it, Mary Warren!

[*Enter JOHN PROCTOR. On seeing him, MARY WARREN leaps in fright.*]

MARY WARREN. Oh! I'm just going home, Mr. Proctor.

PROCTOR. Be you foolish, Mary Warren? Be you deaf? I forbid you leave the house, did I not? Why shall I pay you? I am looking for you more often than my cows!

MARY WARREN. I only come to see the great doings in the world.

PROCTOR. I'll show you a great doin' on your arse one of these days. Now get you home; my wife is waitin' with your work! [*Trying to retain a shred of dignity, she goes slowly out.*]

MERCY LEWIS. [*Both afraid of him and strangely titillated.*][19] I'd best be off. I have my Ruth to watch. Good morning, Mr. Proctor.

[*MERCY sidles out. Since PROCTOR's entrance, ABIGAIL has stood as though on tiptoe, absorbing his presence, wide-eyed. He glances at her, then goes to BETTY on the bed.*]

ABIGAIL. Gah! I'd almost forgot how strong you are, John Proctor!

PROCTOR. [*Looking at ABIGAIL now, the faintest suggestion of a knowing smile on his face.*] What's this mischief here?

ABIGAIL. [*With a nervous laugh.*] Oh, she's only gone silly somehow.

PROCTOR. The road past my house is a pilgrimage to Salem all morning. The town's mumbling witchcraft.

ABIGAIL. Oh, posh! [*Winningly she comes a little closer, with a confidential, wicked air.*] We were dancin' in the woods last night, and my uncle leaped in on us. She took fright, is all.

PROCTOR. [*His smile widening.*] Ah, you're wicked yet, aren't y'! [*A trill of expectant laughter escapes her, and she dares come closer, feverishly looking into his eyes.*] You'll be clapped in the stocks[20] before you're twenty.

[*He takes a step to go, and she springs into his path.*]

ABIGAIL. Give me a word, John. A soft word. [*Her concentrated desire destroys his smile.*]

PROCTOR. No, no, Abby. That's done with.

ABIGAIL. [*Tauntingly.*][21] You come five mile to see a silly girl fly? I know you better.

PROCTOR. [*Setting her firmly out of his path.*] I come to see what mischief your uncle's brewin' now. [*With final emphasis.*] Put it out of mind, Abby.

---

18. *Reddish work* means "bloody deeds."

19. To be *titillated* is to be pleasantly excited or stimulated.
20. The word *stocks* refers to a heavy wooden frame with holes for confining the ankles and wrists of someone found guilty of a crime.
21. *Tauntingly* means "in a scornful or mocking way."

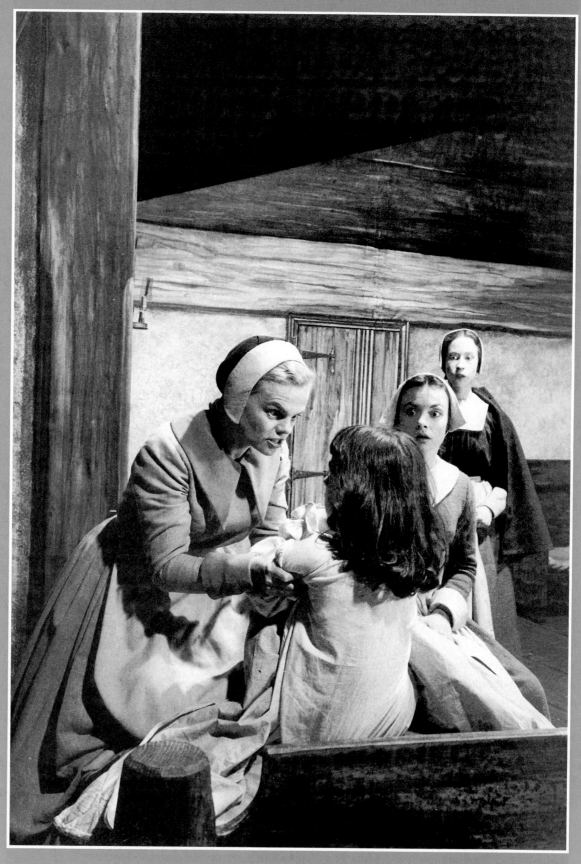

Photographs are from the original 1953 Broadway production of Arthur Miller's *The Crucible.*

The Crucible

ABIGAIL. [*Grasping his hand before he can release her.*] John—I am waitin' for you every night.

PROCTOR. Abby, I never give you hope to wait for me.

ABIGAIL. [*Now beginning to anger—she can't believe it.*] I have something better than hope, I think!

PROCTOR. Abby, you'll put it out of mind. I'll not be comin' for you more.

ABIGAIL. You're surely sportin' with me.

PROCTOR. You know me better.

ABIGAIL. I know how you clutched my back behind your house and sweated like a stallion whenever I come near! Or did I dream that? It's she put me out, you cannot pretend it were you. I saw your face when she put me out, and you loved me then and you do now!

PROCTOR. Abby, that's a wild thing to say—

ABIGAIL. A wild thing may say wild things. But not so wild, I think. I have seen you since she put me out; I have seen you nights.

PROCTOR. I have hardly stepped off my farm this sevenmonth.

ABIGAIL. I have a sense for heat, John, and yours has drawn me to my window, and I have seen you looking up, burning in your loneliness. Do you tell me you've never looked up at my window?

PROCTOR. I may have looked up.

ABIGAIL. [*Now softening.*] And you must. You are no wintry man. I know you, John. I *know* you. [*She is weeping.*] I cannot sleep for dreamin'; I cannot dream but I wake and walk about the house as though I'd find you comin' through some door. [*She clutches him desperately.*]

PROCTOR. [*Gently pressing her from him, with great sympathy but firmly.*] Child—

ABIGAIL. [*With a flash of anger.*] How do you call me child!

PROCTOR. Abby, I may think of you softly from time to time. But I will cut off my hand before I'll ever reach for you again. Wipe it out of mind. We never touched, Abby.

ABIGAIL. Aye, but we did.

PROCTOR. Aye, but we did not.

ABIGAIL. [*With a bitter anger.*] Oh, I marvel how such a strong man may let such a sickly wife be—

PROCTOR. [*Angered—at himself as well.*] You'll speak nothin' of Elizabeth!

ABIGAIL. She is blackening my name in the village! She is telling lies about me! She is a cold, sniveling woman, and you bend to her! Let her turn you like a—

PROCTOR. [*Shaking her.*] Do you look for whippin'?

[*A psalm is heard being sung below.*]

ABIGAIL. [*In tears.*] I look for John Proctor that took me from my sleep and put knowledge in my heart! I never knew what pretense Salem was, I never knew the lying lessons I was taught by all these Christian women and their covenanted[22] men! And now you bid me tear the light out of my eyes? I will not, I cannot! You loved me, John Proctor, and whatever sin it is, you love me yet! [*He turns abruptly to go out. She rushes to him.*] John, pity me, pity me!

[*The words "going up to Jesus" are heard in the psalm, and* BETTY *claps her ears suddenly and whines loudly.*]

---

22. A covenant is an agreement or promise. Among the Puritans, a *covenanted* person had made a commitment to the church and had signed an agreement testifying to his or her faith.

Vocabulary

pretense (prē′ tens) *n.* a false show or appearance, especially for the purpose of deceiving; falseness

ABIGAIL. Betty? [*She hurries to* BETTY, *who is now sitting up and screaming.* PROCTOR *goes to* BETTY *as* ABIGAIL *is trying to pull her hands down, calling "Betty!"*]

PROCTOR. [*Growing unnerved.*] What's she doing? Girl, what ails you? Stop that wailing!

[*The singing has stopped in the midst of this, and now* PARRIS *rushes in.*]

PARRIS. What happened? What are you doing to her? Betty! [*He rushes to the bed, crying, "Betty, Betty!"* MRS. PUTNAM *enters, feverish with curiosity, and with her* THOMAS PUTNAM *and* MERCY LEWIS. PARRIS, *at the bed, keeps lightly slapping* BETTY'S *face, while she moans and tries to get up.*]

ABIGAIL. She heard you singin' and suddenly she's up and screamin'.

MRS. PUTNAM. The psalm! The psalm! She cannot bear to hear the Lord's name!

PARRIS. No, God forbid. Mercy, run to the doctor! Tell him what's happened here! [MERCY LEWIS *rushes out.*]

MRS. PUTNAM. Mark it for a sign, mark it!

[REBECCA NURSE, *seventy-two, enters. She is white-haired, leaning upon her walking-stick.*]

PUTNAM. [*Pointing at the whimpering* BETTY.] That is a notorious sign of witchcraft afoot, Goody Nurse, a prodigious[23] sign!

MRS. PUTNAM. My mother told me that! When they cannot bear to hear the name of—

PARRIS. [*Trembling.*] Rebecca, Rebecca, go to her, we're lost. She suddenly cannot bear to hear the Lord's—

[GILES COREY, *eighty-three, enters. He is knotted with muscle, canny,[24] inquisitive, and still powerful.*]

REBECCA. There is hard sickness here, Giles Corey, so please to keep the quiet.

23. *Prodigious* means "amazing."
24. *Canny* means "sharp, clever, and careful in one's dealings with others."

GILES. I've not said a word. No one here can testify I've said a word. Is she going to fly again? I hear she flies.

PUTNAM. Man, be quiet now!

[*Everything is quiet.* REBECCA, *walks across the room to the bed. Gentleness exudes[25] from her.* BETTY *is quietly whimpering, eyes shut.* REBECCA *simply stands over the child, who gradually quiets.*]

MRS. PUTNAM. [*Astonished.*] What have you done?

[REBECCA, *in thought, now leaves the bedside and sits.*]

PARRIS. [*Wondrous and relieved.*] What do you make of it, Rebecca?

PUTNAM. [*Eagerly.*] Goody Nurse, will you go to my Ruth and see if you can wake her?

REBECCA. [*Sitting.*] I think she'll wake in time. Pray calm yourselves. I have eleven children, and I am twenty-six times a grandma, and I have seen them all through their silly seasons, and when it come on them they will run the Devil bowlegged keeping up with their mischief. I think she'll wake when she tires of it. A child's spirit is like a child, you can never catch it by running after it; you must stand still, and, for love, it will soon itself come back.

PROCTOR. Aye, that's the truth of it, Rebecca.

MRS. PUTNAM. This is no silly season, Rebecca. My Ruth is bewildered, Rebecca; she cannot eat.

REBECCA. Perhaps she is not hungered yet. [*To* PARRIS.] I hope you are not decided to go in search of loose spirits, Mr. Parris. I've heard promise of that outside.

PARRIS. A wide opinion's running in the parish that the Devil may be among us, and I would satisfy them that they are wrong.

25. *Exudes* means "gives forth."

PROCTOR. Then let you come out and call them wrong. Did you consult the wardens[26] before you called this minister to look for devils?

PARRIS. He is not coming to look for devils!

PROCTOR. Then what's he coming for?

PUTNAM. There be children dyin' in the village, Mister!

PROCTOR. I seen none dyin'. This society will not be a bag to swing around your head, Mr. Putnam. [*To PARRIS.*] Did you call a meeting before you—?

PUTNAM. I am sick of meetings; cannot the man turn his head without he have a meeting?

PROCTOR. He may turn his head, but not to Hell!

REBECCA. Pray, John, be calm. [*Pause. He defers to her.*] Mr. Parris, I think you'd best send

---

26. The church *wardens* were members who managed the congregation's business affairs.

Reverend Hale back as soon as he come. This will set us all to arguin' again in the society, and we thought to have peace this year. I think we ought rely on the doctor now, and good prayer.

MRS. PUTNAM. Rebecca, the doctor's baffled!

REBECCA. If so he is, then let us go to God for the cause of it. There is prodigious danger in the seeking of loose spirits. I fear it, I fear it. Let us rather blame ourselves and—

PUTNAM. How may we blame ourselves? I am one of nine sons; the Putnam seed have peopled this province. And yet I have but one child left of eight—and now she shrivels!

REBECCA. I cannot fathom that.

MRS. PUTNAM. [*With a growing edge of sarcasm.*] But I must! You think it God's work you should never lose a child, nor grandchild either, and I bury all but one? There are wheels within wheels in this village, and fires within fires![27]

PUTNAM. [*To PARRIS.*] When Reverend Hale comes, you will proceed to look for signs of witchcraft here.

PROCTOR. [*To PUTNAM.*] You cannot command Mr. Parris. We vote by name in this society, not by acreage.

PUTNAM. I never heard you worried so on this society, Mr. Proctor. I do not think I saw you at Sabbath meeting since snow flew.

PROCTOR. I have trouble enough without I come five mile to hear him preach only hellfire and bloody damnation. Take it to heart, Mr. Parris. There are many others who stay away from church these days because you hardly ever mention God any more.

PARRIS. [*Now aroused.*] Why, that's a drastic charge!

REBECCA. It's somewhat true; there are many that quail[28] to bring their children—

PARRIS. I do not preach for children, Rebecca. It is not the children who are unmindful of their obligations toward this ministry.

REBECCA. Are there really those unmindful?

PARRIS. I should say the better half of Salem village—

PUTNAM. And more than that!

PARRIS. Where is my wood? My contract provides I be supplied with all my firewood. I am waiting since November for a stick, and even in November I had to show my frostbitten hands like some London beggar!

GILES. You are allowed six pound a year to buy your wood, Mr. Parris.

PARRIS. I regard that six pound as part of my salary. I am paid little enough without I spend six pound on firewood.

PROCTOR. Sixty, plus six for firewood—

PARRIS. The salary is sixty-six pound, Mr. Proctor! I am not some preaching farmer with a book under my arm; I am a graduate of Harvard College.

GILES. Aye, and well instructed in arithmetic!

PARRIS. Mr. Corey, you will look far for a man of my kind at sixty pound a year! I am not used to this poverty; I left a thrifty business in the Barbados to serve the Lord. I do not fathom it, why am I persecuted here? I cannot offer one proposition but there be a howling riot of argument. I have often wondered if the Devil be in it somewhere; I cannot understand you people otherwise.

PROCTOR. Mr. Parris, you are the first minister ever did demand the deed to this house—

---

27. *[wheels within . . . fires!]* This expression means "things are not so simple or innocent as they seem."

28. To *quail* is to hesitate, to lose heart, or to retreat in fear.

The Crucible

PARRIS. Man! Don't a minister deserve a house to live in?

PROCTOR. To live in, yes. But to ask ownership is like you shall own the meeting house itself; the last meeting I were at you spoke so long on deeds and mortgages I thought it were an auction.

PARRIS. I want a mark of confidence, is all! I am your third preacher in seven years. I do not wish to be put out like the cat whenever some majority feels the whim. You people seem not to comprehend that a minister is the Lord's man in the parish; a minister is not to be so lightly crossed and contradicted—

PUTNAM. Aye!

PARRIS. There is either obedience or the church will burn like Hell is burning!

PROCTOR. Can you speak one minute without we land in Hell again? I am sick of Hell!

PARRIS. It is not for you to say what is good for you to hear!

PROCTOR. I may speak my heart, I think!

PARRIS. [*In a fury.*] What, are we Quakers? We are not Quakers here yet, Mr. Proctor. And you may tell that to your followers!

PROCTOR. My followers!

PARRIS. [*Now he's out with it.*] There is a party in this church. I am not blind; there is a faction and a party.

PROCTOR. Against you?

PUTNAM. Against him and all authority!

PROCTOR. Why, then I must find it and join it.

[*There is shock among the others.*]

REBECCA. He does not mean that.

PUTNAM. He confessed it now!

PROCTOR. I mean it solemnly, Rebecca; I like not the smell of this "authority."

REBECCA. No, you cannot break charity[29] with your minister. You are another kind, John. Clasp his hand, make your peace.

PROCTOR. I have a crop to sow and lumber to drag home. [*He goes angrily to the door and turns to* COREY *with a smile.*] What say you, Giles, let's find the party. He says there's a party.

GILES. I've changed my opinion of this man, John. Mr. Parris, I beg your pardon. I never thought you had so much iron in you.

PARRIS. [*Surprised.*] Why, thank you, Giles!

GILES. It suggests to the mind what the trouble be among us all these years. [*To all.*] Think on it. Wherefore is everybody suing everybody else? Think on it now, it's a deep thing, and dark as a pit. I have been six time in court this year—

PROCTOR. [*Familiarly, with warmth, although he knows he is approaching the edge of* GILES' *tolerance with this.*] Is it the Devil's fault that a man cannot say you good morning without you clap him for defamation?[30] You're old, Giles, and you're not hearin' so well as you did.

GILES. [*He cannot be crossed.*] John Proctor, I have only last month collected four pound damages for you publicly sayin' I burned the roof off your house, and I—

PROCTOR. [*Laughing.*] I never said no such thing, but I've paid you for it, so I hope I can call you deaf without charge. Now come along, Giles, and help me drag my lumber home.

PUTNAM. A moment, Mr. Proctor. What lumber is that you're draggin', if I may ask you?

PROCTOR. My lumber. From out my forest by the riverside.

PUTNAM. Why, we are surely gone wild this year. What anarchy[31] is this? That tract is in my bounds, it's in my bounds, Mr. Proctor.

PROCTOR. In your bounds! [*Indicating* REBECCA.] I bought that tract from Goody Nurse's husband five months ago.

---

29. For the Puritans, *charity* was Christian love, including mercy, forgiveness, kindness, and trust.

30. An attack on one's good name or reputation is an act of *defamation* (def′ ə mā′ shən).

31. *Anarchy* is lawless confusion and political disorder due to the absence of governmental authority. Here, Putnam uses the word to mean "lawlessness."

PUTNAM. He had no right to sell it. It stands clear in my grandfather's will that all the land between the river and—

PROCTOR. Your grandfather had a habit of willing land that never belonged to him, if I may say it plain.

GILES. That's God's truth; he nearly willed away my north pasture but he knew I'd break his fingers before he'd set his name to it. Let's get your lumber home, John. I feel a sudden will to work coming on.

PUTNAM. You load one oak of mine and you'll fight to drag it home!

GILES. Aye, and we'll win too, Putnam—this fool and I. Come on! [*He turns to* PROCTOR *and starts out.*]

PUTNAM. I'll have my men on you, Corey! I'll clap a writ³² on you!

[*Enter* REVEREND JOHN HALE *of Beverly. He appears loaded down with half a dozen heavy books.*]

HALE. Pray you, someone take these!

PARRIS. [*Delighted.*] Mr. Hale! Oh! it's good to see you again! [*Taking some books.*] My, they're heavy!

HALE. [*Setting down his books.*] They must be; they are weighted with authority.

PARRIS. [*A little scared.*] Well, you do come prepared!

---

32. A *writ* is a judge's order.

Ocean Greyness, 1953. Jackson Pollock. Oil on canvas, 4 ft 9¾ in x 7 ft 6⅛ in. Solomon R. Guggenheim Museum, New York.

Viewing the painting: Look at the interplay of colors in this painting. What characters or events in act 1 might these colors represent? Explain.

The Crucible

HALE. We shall need hard study if it comes to tracking down the Old Boy.[33] [*Noticing* REBECCA.] You cannot be Rebecca Nurse?

REBECCA. I am, sir. Do you know me?

HALE. It's strange how I knew you, but I suppose you look as such a good soul should. We have all heard of your great charities in Beverly.

PARRIS. Do you know this gentleman? Mr. Thomas Putnam. And his good wife Ann.

HALE. Putnam! I had not expected such distinguished company, sir.

PUTNAM. [*Pleased.*] It does not seem to help us today, Mr. Hale. We look to you to come to our house and save our child.

HALE. Your child ails too?

MRS. PUTNAM. Her soul, her soul seems flown away. She sleeps and yet she walks . . .

PUTNAM. She cannot eat.

HALE. Cannot eat! [*Thinks on it. Then, to* PROCTOR *and* GILES COREY.] Do you men have afflicted children?

PARRIS. No, no, these are farmers. John Proctor—

GILES COREY. He don't believe in witches.

PROCTOR. [*To* HALE.] I never spoke on witches one way or the other. Will you come, Giles?

GILES. No—no, John, I think not. I have some few queer questions of my own to ask this fellow.

PROCTOR. I've heard you to be a sensible man, Mr. Hale. I hope you'll leave some of it in Salem.

[PROCTOR *goes.* HALE *stands embarrassed for an instant.*]

PARRIS. [*Quickly.*] Will you look at my daughter, sir? [*Leads* HALE *to the bed.*] She has tried to leap out the window; we discovered her this

morning on the highroad, waving her arms as though she'd fly.

HALE. [*Narrowing his eyes.*] Tries to fly.

PUTNAM. She cannot bear to hear the Lord's name, Mr. Hale; that's a sure sign of witchcraft afloat.

HALE. [*Holding up his hands.*] No, no. Now let me instruct you. We cannot look to superstition in this. The Devil is precise; the marks of his presence are definite as stone, and I must tell you all that I shall not proceed unless you are prepared to believe me if I should find no bruise of hell upon her.

PARRIS. It is agreed, sir—it is agreed—we will abide by your judgment.

HALE. Good then. [*He goes to the bed, looks down at* BETTY. *To* PARRIS.] Now, sir, what were your first warning of this strangeness?

PARRIS. Why, sir—I discovered her—[*Indicating* ABIGAIL.]—and my niece and ten or twelve of the other girls, dancing in the forest last night.

HALE. [*Surprised.*] You permit dancing?

PARRIS. No, no, it were secret—

MRS. PUTNAM. [*Unable to wait.*] Mr. Parris's slave has knowledge of conjurin', sir.

PARRIS. [*To* MRS. PUTNAM.] We cannot be sure of that, Goody Ann—

MRS. PUTNAM. [*Frightened, very softly.*] I know it, sir. I sent my child—she should learn from Tituba who murdered her sisters.

REBECCA. [*Horrified.*] Goody Ann! You sent a child to conjure up the dead?

MRS. PUTNAM. Let God blame me, not you, not you, Rebecca! I'll not have you judging me any more! [*To* HALE.] Is it a natural work to lose seven children before they live a day?

PARRIS. Sssh!

[REBECCA, *with great pain, turns her face away. There is a pause.*]

HALE. Seven dead in childbirth.

---

33. *Old Boy* is another name for Satan.

MRS. PUTNAM. [*Softly.*] Aye. [*Her voice breaks; she looks up at him. Silence. HALE is impressed. PARRIS looks to him. He goes to his books, opens one, turns pages, then reads. All wait, avidly.*][34]

PARRIS. [*Hushed.*] What book is that?

MRS. PUTNAM. What's there, sir?

HALE. [*With a tasty love of intellectual pursuit.*] Here is all the invisible world, caught, defined, and calculated. In these books the Devil stands stripped of all his brute disguises. Here are all your familiar spirits—your incubi and succubi;[35] your witches that go by land, by air, and by sea; your wizards of the night and of the day. Have no fear now—we shall find him out if he has come among us, and I mean to crush him utterly if he has shown his face! [*He starts for the bed.*]

REBECCA. Will it hurt the child, sir?

HALE. I cannot tell. If she is truly in the Devil's grip we may have to rip and tear to get her free.

REBECCA. I think I'll go, then. I am too old for this. [*She rises.*]

PARRIS. [*Striving for conviction.*] Why, Rebecca, we may open up the boil of all our troubles today!

REBECCA. Let us hope for that. I go to God for you, sir.

PARRIS. [*With trepidation—and resentment.*] I hope you do not mean we go to Satan here! [*Slight pause.*]

REBECCA. I wish I knew. [*She goes out; they feel resentful of her note of moral superiority.*]

PUTNAM. [*Abruptly.*] Come, Mr. Hale, let's get on. Sit you here.

GILES. Mr. Hale, I have always wanted to ask a learned man—what signifies the readin' of strange books?

HALE. What books?

GILES. I cannot tell; she hides them.

HALE. Who does this?

GILES. Martha, my wife. I have waked at night many a time and found her in a corner, readin' of a book. Now what do you make of that?

HALE. Why, that's not necessarily—

GILES. It discomfits[36] me! Last night—mark this—I tried and tried and could not say my prayers. And then she close her book and walks out of the house, and suddenly—mark this—I could pray again!

HALE. Ah! The stoppage of prayer—that is strange. I'll speak further on that with you.

GILES. I'm not sayin' she's touched the Devil, now, but I'd admire to know what books she reads and why she hides them. She'll not answer me, y' see.

HALE. Aye, we'll discuss it. [*To all.*] Now mark me, if the Devil is in her you will witness some frightful wonders in this room, so please to keep your wits about you. Mr. Putnam, stand close in case she flies. Now, Betty, dear, will you sit up? [*PUTNAM comes in closer, ready-handed. HALE sits BETTY up, but she hangs limp in his hands.*] Hmmm. [*He observes her carefully. The others watch breathlessly.*] Can you hear me? I am John Hale, minister of Beverly. I have come to help you, dear. Do you remember my two little girls in Beverly? [*She does not stir in his hands.*]

PARRIS. [*In fright.*] How can it be the Devil? Why would he choose my house to strike? We have all manner of licentious[37] people in the village!

HALE. What victory would the Devil have to win a soul already bad? It is the best the Devil wants, and who is better than the minister?

GILES. That's deep, Mr. Parris, deep, deep!

---

34. *Avidly* means "with intense interest."
35. *Incubi* (ing′ kyə bī′) and *succubi* (suk′ yə bī′) are evil spirits or demons.
36. *Discomfits* means "confuses and frustrates."
37. *Licentious* people disregard commonly accepted standards of right and wrong or good and evil.

PARRIS. [*With resolution now.*] Betty! Answer Mr. Hale! Betty!

HALE. Does someone afflict you, child? It need not be a woman, mind you, or a man. Perhaps some bird invisible to others comes to you—perhaps a pig, a mouse, or any beast at all. Is there some figure bids you fly? [*The child remains limp in his hands. In silence he lays her back on the pillow. Now, holding out his hands toward her, he intones.*] In nomine Domini Sabaoth sui filiique ite ad infernos.[38] [*She does not stir. He turns to ABIGAIL, his eyes narrowing.*] Abigail, what sort of dancing were you doing with her in the forest?

ABIGAIL. Why—common dancing is all.

---

38. *[In nomine . . . infernos.]* "In the name of the God of the Heavenly Hosts and of His Son, go to hell." Hale is performing an exorcism, a ritual intended to drive out evil spirits.

PARRIS. I think I ought to say that I—I saw a kettle in the grass where they were dancing.

ABIGAIL. That were only soup.

HALE. What sort of soup were in this kettle, Abigail?

ABIGAIL. Why, it were beans—and lentils, I think, and—

HALE. Mr. Parris, you did not notice, did you, any living thing in the kettle? A mouse, perhaps, a spider, a frog—?

PARRIS. [*Fearfully.*] I—do believe there were some movement—in the soup.

ABIGAIL. That jumped in, we never put it in!

HALE. [*Quickly.*] What jumped in?

ABIGAIL. Why, a very little frog jumped—

PARRIS. A frog, Abby!

HALE. [*Grasping ABIGAIL.*] Abigail, it may be your cousin is dying. Did you call the Devil last night?

ABIGAIL. I never called him! Tituba, Tituba . . .

PARRIS. [*Blanched.*] She called the Devil?

HALE. I should like to speak with Tituba.

PARRIS. Goody Ann, will you bring her up? [*MRS. PUTNAM exits.*]

Omen, 1993. Katherine Bowling. Oil and spackle on wood, 24 x 24 in. The SBC Collection of Twentieth Century American Art. Courtesy SBC Communications.

Viewing the painting: What connections might you make between this painting and the description of the night the girls went to the forest?

HALE. How did she call him?

ABIGAIL. I know not—she spoke Barbados.

HALE. Did you feel any strangeness when she called him? A sudden cold wind, perhaps? A trembling below the ground?

ABIGAIL. I didn't see no Devil! [*Shaking BETTY.*] Betty, wake up. Betty! Betty!

HALE. You cannot evade me, Abigail. Did your cousin drink any of the brew in that kettle?

ABIGAIL. She never drank it!

HALE. Did you drink it?

ABIGAIL. No, sir!

HALE. Did Tituba ask you to drink it?

ABIGAIL. She tried, but I refused.

HALE. Why are you concealing? Have you sold yourself to Lucifer?

ABIGAIL. I never sold myself! I'm a good girl! I'm a proper girl!

[*MRS. PUTNAM enters with TITUBA, and instantly ABIGAIL points at TITUBA.*]

ABIGAIL. She made me do it! She made Betty do it!

TITUBA. [*Shocked and angry.*] Abby!

ABIGAIL. She makes me drink blood!

PARRIS. Blood!!

MRS. PUTNAM. My baby's blood?

TITUBA. No, no, chicken blood. I give she chicken blood!

HALE. Woman, have you enlisted these children for the Devil?

TITUBA. No, no, sir, I don't truck[39] with no Devil!

HALE. Why can she not wake? Are you silencing this child?

TITUBA. I love me Betty!

HALE. You have sent your spirit out upon this child, have you not? Are you gathering souls for the Devil?

ABIGAIL. She sends her spirit on me in church; she makes me laugh at prayer!

PARRIS. She have often laughed at prayer!

ABIGAIL. She comes to me every night to go and drink blood!

TITUBA. You beg *me* to conjure! She beg *me* make charm—

ABIGAIL. Don't lie! [*To HALE.*] She comes to me while I sleep; she's always making me dream corruptions!

TITUBA. Why you say that, Abby?

ABIGAIL. Sometimes I wake and find myself standing in the open doorway and not a stitch on my body! I always hear her laughing in my sleep. I hear her singing her Barbados songs and tempting me with—

TITUBA. Mister Reverend, I never—

HALE. [*Resolved now.*] Tituba, I want you to wake this child.

TITUBA. I have no power on this child, sir.

HALE. You most certainly do, and you will free her from it now! When did you compact with[40] the Devil?

TITUBA. I don't compact with no Devil!

PARRIS. You will confess yourself or I will take you out and whip you to your death, Tituba!

PUTNAM. This woman must be hanged! She must be taken and hanged!

TITUBA. [*Terrified, falls to her knees.*] No, no, don't hang Tituba! I tell him I don't desire to work for him, sir.

---

39. *Truck* is another way of saying "to have dealings."

40. To *compact with* is to make an agreement or contract with.

Vocabulary
evade (i vād′) *v.* to escape or avoid, as by cleverness

PARRIS. The Devil?

HALE. Then you saw him! [*TITUBA weeps.*] Now Tituba, I know that when we bind ourselves to Hell it is very hard to break with it. We are going to help you tear yourself free—

TITUBA. [*Frightened by the coming process.*] Mister Reverend, I do believe somebody else be witchin' these children.

HALE. Who?

TITUBA. I don't know, sir, but the Devil got him numerous witches.

HALE. Does he! [*It is a clue.*] Tituba, look into my eyes. Come, look into me. [*She raises her eyes to his fearfully.*] You would be a good Christian woman, would you not, Tituba?

TITUBA. Aye, sir, a good Christian woman.

HALE. And you love these little children?

TITUBA. Oh, yes, sir, I don't desire to hurt little children.

HALE. And you love God, Tituba?

TITUBA. I love God with all my bein'.

HALE. Now, in God's holy name—

TITUBA. Bless Him. Bless Him. [*She is rocking on her knees, sobbing in terror.*]

HALE. And to His glory—

TITUBA. Eternal glory. Bless Him—bless God . . .

HALE. Open yourself, Tituba—open yourself and let God's holy light shine on you.

TITUBA. Oh, bless the Lord.

HALE. When the Devil comes to you does he ever come—with another person? [*She stares up into his face.*] Perhaps another person in the village? Someone you know.

PARRIS. Who came with him?

PUTNAM. Sarah Good? Did you ever see Sarah Good with him? Or Osburn?

PARRIS. Was it man or woman came with him?

TITUBA. Man or woman. Was—was woman.

PARRIS. What woman? A woman, you said. What woman?

TITUBA. It was black dark, and I—

PARRIS. You could see him, why could you not see her?

TITUBA. Well, they was always talking; they was always runnin' round and carryin' on—

PARRIS. You mean out of Salem? Salem witches?

TITUBA. I believe so, yes, sir.

[*Now HALE takes her hand. She is surprised.*]

HALE. Tituba. You must have no fear to tell us who they are, do you understand? We will protect you. The Devil can never overcome a minister. You know that, do you not?

TITUBA. [*Kisses HALE's hand.*] Aye, sir, I do.

HALE. You have confessed yourself to witchcraft, and that speaks a wish to come to Heaven's side. And we will bless you, Tituba.

TITUBA. [*Deeply relieved.*] Oh, God bless you, Mr. Hale!

HALE. [*With rising exaltation.*][41] You are God's instrument put in our hands to discover the Devil's agents among us. You are selected, Tituba, you are chosen to help us cleanse our village. So speak utterly, Tituba, turn your back on him and face God—face God, Tituba, and God will protect you.

TITUBA. [*Joining with him.*] Oh, God, protect Tituba!

HALE. [*Kindly.*] Who came to you with the Devil? Two? Three? Four? How many?

[*TITUBA pants, and begins rocking back and forth again, staring ahead.*]

TITUBA. There was four. There was four.

PARRIS. [*Pressing in on her.*] Who? Who? Their names, their names!

---

41. Here, *exaltation* means "great enthusiasm" or "joyful ecstasy."

TITUBA. [*Suddenly bursting out.*] Oh, how many times he bid me kill you, Mr. Parris!

PARRIS. Kill me!

TITUBA. [*In a fury.*] He say Mr. Parris must be kill! Mr. Parris no goodly man, Mr. Parris mean man and no gentle man, and he bid me rise out of my bed and cut your throat! [*They gasp.*] But I tell him, "No! I don't hate that man. I don't want kill that man." But he say, "You work for me, Tituba, and I make you free! I give you pretty dress to wear, and put you way high up in the air, and you gone fly back to Barbados!" And I say, "You lie, Devil, you lie!" And then he come one stormy night to me, and he say, "Look! I have *white* people belong to me." And I look—and there was Goody Good.

PARRIS. Sarah Good!

TITUBA. [*Rocking and weeping.*] Aye, sir, and Goody Osburn.

MRS. PUTNAM. I knew it! Goody Osburn were midwife[42] to me three times. I begged you, Thomas, did I not? I begged him not to call Osburn because I feared her. My babies always shriveled in her hands!

HALE. Take courage, you must give us all their names. How can you bear to see this child suffering? Look at her, Tituba. [*He is indicating BETTY on the bed.*] Look at her God-given innocence; her soul is so tender; we must protect her, Tituba; the Devil is out and preying on her like a beast upon the flesh of the pure lamb. God will bless you for your help.

[*ABIGAIL rises, staring as though inspired, and cries out.*]

ABIGAIL. I want to open myself! [*They turn to her, startled. She is enraptured,[43] as though in a pearly light.*] I want the light of God, I want the sweet love of Jesus! I danced for the Devil; I saw him; I wrote in his book; I go back to Jesus; I kiss His hand. I saw Sarah Good with the Devil! I saw Goody Osburn with the Devil! I saw Bridget Bishop with the Devil!

[*As she is speaking, BETTY is rising from the bed, a fever in her eyes, and picks up the chant.*]

BETTY. [*Staring too.*] I saw George Jacobs with the Devil! I saw Goody Howe with the Devil!

PARRIS. She speaks! [*He rushes to embrace BETTY.*] She speaks!

HALE. Glory to God! It is broken, they are free!

BETTY. [*Calling out hysterically and with great relief.*] I saw Martha Bellows with the Devil!

ABIGAIL. I saw Goody Sibber with the Devil! [*It is rising to a great glee.*]

PUTNAM. The marshal, I'll call the marshal!

[*PARRIS is shouting a prayer of thanksgiving.*]

BETTY. I saw Alice Barrow with the Devil!

[*The curtain begins to fall.*]

HALE. [*As PUTNAM goes out.*] Let the marshal bring irons!

ABIGAIL. I saw Goody Hawkins with the Devil!

BETTY. I saw Goody Bibber with the Devil!

ABIGAIL. I saw Goody Booth with the Devil!

[*On their ecstatic cries.*]

THE CURTAIN FALLS

---

42. A *midwife* is a woman who assists other women in childbirth.

43. *Enraptured* means "filled with intense joy or delight."

Responding to Literature

Personal Response

What was your response to the end of act 1? Which events or details inspired your response?

ANALYZING ACT 1

RECALL AND INTERPRET

1. What is Reverend Parris praying about at the beginning of act 1? What else might explain why he is praying so desperately?
2. What reasons does Abigail give Parris for her discharge as the Proctors' servant? What might be another reason? What can you infer about Abigail's character from her words?
3. Describe the feelings the characters have toward each other: the Putnams toward John Proctor and Rebecca Nurse, Proctor toward the Putnams and Parris, and Parris toward the congregation. What effect might these feelings have on the future action of the play?
4. How does Tituba first respond to Hale's accusation of witchcraft? How does she change her response? Why might she, as well as Abigail and Betty, make accusations at the end of act 1?

EVALUATE AND CONNECT

5. Which character or characters arouse your sympathy most? Explain.
6. What is the overall **atmosphere,** or prevailing mood, of act 1? How does Miller create this atmosphere?
7. Is Miller's portrayal of the teenage girls and their behavior believable? Why or why not?
8. What similarities do you see between the interactions among the Salemites of 1692 and interactions among people today?

Literary ELEMENTS

Dialogue

Conversation between characters is called **dialogue.** Through dialogue, a playwright reveals the feelings, thoughts, and intentions of characters, sets out conflicts, and moves the plot forward. Much of the dialogue in *The Crucible* centers on series of questions and answers among the characters. In fact, the play opens with Tituba's question "My Betty be hearty soon?"

1. Which characters do the main questioning in act 1? Which characters are the subjects of the questioning?
2. What do the characters hope to determine by asking their questions?
3. Do you think the questions and methods of questioning are fair? Explain.

● See **Literary Terms Handbook,** p. R4.

EXTENDING YOUR RESPONSE

Writing About Literature

Setting the Stage   Miller called act 1 an overture—an introduction. In literary terms, it would be called an **exposition.** Write two or three paragraphs analyzing how Miller has "set the stage" for the rest of the play with the setting, characters, and plot of act 1. What, for you, is the **narrative hook,** or the story element that grabs your attention?

Literature Groups

Put Yourself in the Characters' Shoes   In your group, work together to create character webs that profile each character in act 1. Include the character's age, personality traits, standing in the community, and conflicts with others. Then, as a group, predict the role each character will play in this drama. Share your predictions with the class.

📖 **Save your work for your portfolio.**

Skill Minilesson

Often you must use clues outside a word to figure out its meaning. The dictionary and context clues are both useful. However, you will sometimes come across a new word that contains internal clues to its meaning—familiar parts that can provide significant help if you notice them. Every time you learn a new word, you learn something important about a number of other words, ones that share the same base or root or combining form. The more able you are to notice these similarities in words, the easier it is to use what you already know to figure out what you don't yet know.

PRACTICE   Use what you know about the vocabulary words in parentheses to complete the sentences.

1. (compromise) If you are in a compromising situation, you appear to be
   a. agreeable.   b. critical.   c. guilty.

2. (naive) An good antonym for naiveté is
   a. rudeness.   b. sophistication.   c. intelligence.

3. (contention) A contentious remark would be
   a. "Make me!"   b. "No, thanks!"   c. "I'm fine."

4. (evade) An evasive response to "When can we get together?" would be
   a. "Tonight."   b. "Soon."   c. "Never!"

Before You Read

The Crucible, Act 2

BACKGROUND

The Puritans and Their Beliefs

The Puritans believed that if one member of the community sinned, misfortune could befall the entire community. Blame, therefore, was a common way to deal with personal misfortune. The Puritans also believed that all aspects of life must be guided by the Christian Bible. In fact, communities built schools so that all could learn to read the Bible. These efforts were intended to counteract the work of Satan, who tried to "keep men from the knowledge of the scriptures."

For most Puritans, witchcraft and black magic were real. Books such as *The Discovery of Witches* (1647) and those used by Reverend Hale described how "bewitched" people behaved.

VOCABULARY PREVIEW

reprimand (rep′ rə mand′) *v.* to reprove or correct sharply; p. 937

base (bās) *adj.* morally low; dishonorable; p. 943

covet (kuv′ it) *v.* to desire, especially to an excessive degree, something belonging to another; p. 947

misgiving (mis giv′ ing) *n.* a feeling of doubt, distrust, or anxiety; p. 947

subtle (sut′ əl) *adj.* not open, direct, or obvious; crafty; sly; p. 949

ineptly (i nept′ lē) *adv.* incompetently; awkwardly; clumsily; p. 951

[_The common room of_ PROCTOR's _house, eight days later._

At the right is a door opening on the fields outside. A fireplace is at the left, and behind it a stairway leading upstairs. It is the low, dark, and rather long living room of the time. As the curtain rises, the room is empty. From above, ELIZABETH _is heard softly singing to the children. Presently the door opens and_ JOHN PROCTOR _enters, carrying his gun. He glances about the room as he comes toward the fireplace, then halts for an instant as he hears her singing. He continues on to the fireplace, leans the gun against the wall as he swings a pot out of the fire and smells it. Then he lifts out the ladle and tastes. He is not quite pleased. He reaches to a cupboard, takes a pinch of salt, and drops it into the pot. As he is tasting again, her footsteps are heard on the stair. He swings the pot into the fireplace and goes to a basin and washes his hands and face._ ELIZABETH _enters._]

ELIZABETH. What keeps you so late? It's almost dark.

PROCTOR. I were planting far out to the forest edge.

ELIZABETH. Oh, you're done then.

PROCTOR. Aye, the farm is seeded. The boys asleep?

ELIZABETH. They will be soon. [_And she goes to the fireplace, proceeds to ladle up stew in a dish._]

PROCTOR. Pray now for a fair summer.

ELIZABETH. Aye.

PROCTOR. Are you well today?

ELIZABETH. I am. [_She brings the plate to the table, and, indicating the food._] It is a rabbit.

PROCTOR. [_Going to the table._] Oh, is it! In Jonathan's trap?

ELIZABETH. No, she walked into the house this afternoon; I found her sittin' in the corner like she come to visit.

PROCTOR. Oh, that's a good sign walkin' in.

ELIZABETH. Pray God. It hurt my heart to strip her, poor rabbit. [_She sits and watches him taste it._]

PROCTOR. It's well seasoned.

ELIZABETH. [_Blushing with pleasure._] I took great care. She's tender?

PROCTOR. Aye. [_He eats. She watches him._] I think we'll see green fields soon. It's warm as blood beneath the clods.

ELIZABETH. That's well.

[PROCTOR _eats, then looks up._]

PROCTOR. If the crop is good I'll buy George Jacob's heifer. How would that please you?

ELIZABETH. Aye, it would.

PROCTOR. [_With a grin._] I mean to please you, Elizabeth.

ELIZABETH. [_It is hard to say._] I know it, John.

[_He gets up, goes to her, kisses her. She receives it. With a certain disappointment, he returns to the table._]

PROCTOR. [_As gently as he can._] Cider?

ELIZABETH. [_With a sense of reprimanding herself for having forgot._] Aye! [_She gets up and goes and pours a glass for him. He now arches his back._]

PROCTOR. This farm's a continent when you go foot by foot droppin' seeds in it.

ELIZABETH. [_Coming with the cider._] It must be.

PROCTOR. [_Drinks a long draught, then, putting the glass down._] You ought to bring some flowers in the house.

ELIZABETH. Oh! I forgot! I will tomorrow.

Vocabulary
reprimand (rep′ rə mand′) _v._ to reprove or correct sharply

The Crucible

PROCTOR. It's winter in here yet. On Sunday let you come with me, and we'll walk the farm together; I never see such a load of flowers on the earth. [*With good feeling he goes and looks up at the sky through the open doorway.*] Lilacs have a purple smell. Lilac is the smell of nightfall, I think. Massachusetts is a beauty in the spring!

ELIZABETH. Aye, it is.

[*There is a pause. She is watching him from the table as he stands there absorbing the night. It is as though she would speak but cannot. Instead, now, she takes up his plate and glass and fork and goes with them to the basin. Her back is turned to him. He turns to her and watches her. A sense of their separation rises.*]

PROCTOR. I think you're sad again. Are you?

ELIZABETH. [*She doesn't want friction, and yet she must.*] You come so late I thought you'd gone to Salem this afternoon.

PROCTOR. Why? I have no business in Salem.

ELIZABETH. You did speak of going, earlier this week.

PROCTOR. [*He knows what she means.*] I thought better of it since.

ELIZABETH. Mary Warren's there today.

PROCTOR. Why'd you let her? You heard me forbid her go to Salem any more!

ELIZABETH. I couldn't stop her.

PROCTOR. [*Holding back a full condemnation of her.*] It is a fault, it is a fault, Elizabeth—you're the mistress here, not Mary Warren.

ELIZABETH. She frightened all my strength away.

PROCTOR. How may that mouse frighten you, Elizabeth? You—

ELIZABETH. It is a mouse no more. I forbid her go, and she raises up her chin like the daughter of a prince and says to me, "I must go to Salem, Goody Proctor; I am an official of the court!"

PROCTOR. Court! What court?

ELIZABETH. Aye, it is a proper court they have now. They've sent four judges out of Boston, she says, weighty magistrates[1] of the General Court, and at the head sits the Deputy Governor of the Province.

PROCTOR. [*Astonished.*] Why, she's mad.

ELIZABETH. I would to God she were. There be fourteen people in the jail now, she says. [PROCTOR *simply looks at her, unable to grasp it.*] And they'll be tried, and the court have power to hang them too, she says.

PROCTOR. [*Scoffing, but without conviction.*] Ah, they'd never hang—

ELIZABETH. The Deputy Governor promise hangin' if they'll not confess, John. The town's gone wild, I think. She speak of Abigail, and I thought she were a saint, to hear her. Abigail brings the other girls into the court, and where she walks the crowd will part like the sea for Israel. And folks are brought before them, and if they scream and howl and fall to the floor—the person's clapped in the jail for bewitchin' them.

PROCTOR. [*Wide-eyed.*] Oh, it is a black mischief.

ELIZABETH. I think you must go to Salem, John. [*He turns to her.*] I think so. You must tell them it is a fraud.

PROCTOR. [*Thinking beyond this.*] Aye, it is, it is surely.

ELIZABETH. Let you go to Ezekiel Cheever—he knows you well. And tell him what she said to you last week in her uncle's house. She said it had naught to do with witchcraft, did she not?

PROCTOR. [*In thought.*] Aye, she did, she did. [*Now, a pause.*]

---

1. *Weighty* means "important." *Magistrates* are judges.

Painting, 1948. Willem de Kooning. Enamel and oil on canvas, 42⅝ x 56⅛ in. ©2000 Willem de Kooning Revocable Trust/Artists Rights Society (ARS), New York/ The Museum of Modern Art, New York.

Viewing the painting: What emotions does this painting evoke in you? How might it represent the emotions that John Proctor and Elizabeth are expressing at this point in the play?

ELIZABETH. [*Quietly, fearing to anger him by prodding.*] God forbid you keep that from the court, John. I think they must be told.

PROCTOR. [*Quietly, struggling with his thought.*] Aye, they must, they must. It is a wonder they do believe her.

ELIZABETH. I would go to Salem now, John—let you go tonight.

PROCTOR. I'll think on it.

ELIZABETH. [*With her courage now.*] You cannot keep it, John.

PROCTOR. [*Angering.*] I know I cannot keep it. I say I will think on it!

ELIZABETH. [*Hurt, and very coldly.*] Good, then, let you think on it. [*She stands and starts to walk out of the room.*]

PROCTOR. I am only wondering how I may prove what she told me, Elizabeth. If the girl's a saint now, I think it is not easy to prove she's fraud, and the town gone so silly. She told it to me in a room alone—I have no proof for it.

ELIZABETH. You were alone with her?

PROCTOR. [*Stubbornly.*] For a moment alone, aye.

ELIZABETH. Why, then, it is not as you told me.

PROCTOR. [*His anger rising.*] For a moment, I say. The others come in soon after.

ELIZABETH. [*Quietly—she has suddenly lost all faith in him.*] Do as you wish, then. [*She starts to turn.*]

PROCTOR. Woman. [*She turns to him.*] I'll not have your suspicion any more.

ELIZABETH. [*A little loftily.*] I have no—

PROCTOR. I'll not have it!

ELIZABETH. Then let you not earn it.

PROCTOR. [*With a violent undertone.*] You doubt me yet?

ELIZABETH. [*With a smile, to keep her dignity.*] John, if it were not Abigail that you must go to hurt, would you falter now? I think not.

PROCTOR. Now look you—

ELIZABETH. I see what I see, John.

PROCTOR. [*With solemn warning.*] You will not judge me more, Elizabeth. I have good reason to think before I charge fraud on Abigail, and I will think on it. Let you look to your own improvement before you go to judge your husband any more. I have forgot Abigail, and—

ELIZABETH. And I.

PROCTOR. Spare me! You forget nothin' and forgive nothin'. Learn charity, woman. I have gone tiptoe in this house all seven month since she is gone. I have not moved from there to there without I think to please you, and still an everlasting funeral marches round your heart. I cannot speak but I am doubted, every moment judged for lies, as though I come into a court when I come into this house!

ELIZABETH. John, you are not open with me. You saw her with a crowd, you said. Now you—

PROCTOR. I'll plead my honesty no more, Elizabeth.

ELIZABETH. [*Now she would justify herself.*] John, I am only—

PROCTOR. No more! I should have roared you down when first you told me your suspicion. But I wilted, and, like a Christian, I confessed. Confessed! Some dream I had must have mistaken you for God that day. But you're not, you're not, and let you remember it! Let you look sometimes for the goodness in me, and judge me not.

ELIZABETH. I do not judge you. The magistrate sits in your heart that judges you. I never thought you but a good man, John—[*With a smile.*]—only somewhat bewildered.

PROCTOR. [*Laughing bitterly.*] Oh, Elizabeth, your justice would freeze beer! [*He turns suddenly toward a sound outside. He starts for the door as* MARY WARREN *enters. As soon as he sees her, he goes directly to her and grabs her by her cloak, furious.*] How do you go to Salem when I forbid it? Do you mock me? [*Shaking her.*] I'll whip you if you dare leave this house again!

[*Strangely, she doesn't resist him, but hangs limply by his grip.*]

MARY WARREN. I am sick, I am sick, Mr. Proctor. Pray, pray, hurt me not. [*Her strangeness throws him off, and her evident pallor[2] and weakness. He frees her.*] My insides are all shuddery; I am in the proceedings all day, sir.

PROCTOR. [*With draining anger—his curiosity is draining it.*] And what of these proceedings here? When will you proceed to keep this house, as you are paid nine pound a year to do—and my wife not wholly well?

[*As though to compensate,* MARY WARREN *goes to* ELIZABETH *with a small rag doll.*]

MARY WARREN. I made a gift for you today, Goody Proctor. I had to sit long hours in a chair, and passed the time with sewing.

ELIZABETH. [*Perplexed, looking at the doll.*] Why, thank you, it's a fair poppet.

MARY WARREN. [*With a trembling, decayed voice.*] We must all love each other now, Goody Proctor.

ELIZABETH. [*Amazed at her strangeness.*] Aye, indeed we must.

MARY WARREN. [*Glancing at the room.*] I'll get up early in the morning and clean the house. I must sleep now. [*She turns and starts off.*]

---

2. *Pallor* refers to a pale complexion.

PROCTOR. Mary. [*She halts.*] Is it true? There be fourteen women arrested?

MARY WARREN. No, sir. There be thirty-nine now—[*She suddenly breaks off and sobs and sits down, exhausted.*]

ELIZABETH. Why, she's weepin'! What ails you, child?

MARY WARREN. Goody Osburn—will hang!

[*There is a shocked pause, while she sobs.*]

PROCTOR. Hang! [*He calls into her face.*] Hang, y'say?

MARY WARREN. [*Through her weeping.*] Aye.

PROCTOR. The Deputy Governor will permit it?

MARY WARREN. He sentenced her. He must. [*To ameliorate*[3] *it.*] But not Sarah Good. For Sarah Good confessed, y'see.

PROCTOR. Confessed! To what?

MARY WARREN. That she—[*In horror at the memory.*]—she sometimes made a compact with Lucifer, and wrote her name in his black book—with her blood—and bound herself to torment Christians till God's thrown down—and we all must worship Hell forevermore.

[*Pause.*]

PROCTOR. But—surely you know what a jabberer she is. Did you tell them that?

MARY WARREN. Mr. Proctor, in open court she near to choked us all to death.

PROCTOR. How, choked you?

MARY WARREN. She sent her spirit out.

ELIZABETH. Oh, Mary, Mary, surely you—

MARY WARREN. [*With an indignant*[4] *edge.*] She tried to kill me many times, Goody Proctor!

ELIZABETH. Why, I never heard you mention that before.

MARY WARREN. I never knew it before. I never knew anything before. When she come into the court I say to myself, I must not accuse this woman, for she sleep in ditches, and so very old and poor. But then—then she sit there, denying and denying, and I feel a misty coldness climbin' up my back, and the skin on my skull begin to creep, and I feel a clamp around my neck and I cannot breathe air; and then—[*Entranced.*]—I hear a voice, a screamin' voice, and it were my voice—and all at once I remembered everything she done to me!

PROCTOR. Why? What did she do to you?

MARY WARREN. [*Like one awakened to a marvelous secret insight.*] So many time, Mr. Proctor, she come to this very door, beggin' bread and a cup of cider—and mark this: whenever I turned her away empty, she *mumbled.*

ELIZABETH. Mumbled! She may mumble if she's hungry.

MARY WARREN. But *what* does she mumble? You must remember, Goody Proctor. Last month—a Monday, I think—she walked away, and I thought my guts would burst for two days after. Do you remember it?

ELIZABETH. Why—I do, I think, but—

MARY WARREN. And so I told that to Judge Hathorne, and he asks her so. "Sarah Good," says he, "what curse do you mumble that this girl must fall sick after turning you away?" And then she replies—[*Mimicking an old crone.*][5]—"Why, your excellence, no curse at all. I only say my commandments; I hope I may say my commandments," says she!

ELIZABETH. And that's an upright answer.

MARY WARREN. Aye, but then Judge Hathorne say, "Recite for us your commandments!"—[*Leaning avidly toward them.*]—and of all the ten she could not say a single one. She never knew no commandments, and they had her in a flat lie!

3. To *ameliorate* is to improve a situation that was unpleasant or unbearable before.
4. *Indignant* means "expressing righteous anger."
5. A *crone* is a withered old woman.

PROCTOR. And so condemned her?

MARY WARREN. [*Now a little strained, seeing his stubborn doubt.*] Why, they must when she condemned herself.

PROCTOR. But the proof, the proof!

MARY WARREN. [*With greater impatience with him.*] I told you the proof. It's hard proof, hard as rock, the judges said.

PROCTOR. [*Pauses an instant, then.*] You will not go to court again, Mary Warren.

MARY WARREN. I must tell you, sir, I will be gone every day now. I am amazed you do not see what weighty work we do.

PROCTOR. What work you do! It's strange work for a Christian girl to hang old women!

MARY WARREN. But, Mr. Proctor, they will not hang them if they confess. Sarah Good will only sit in jail some time—[*Recalling.*]—and here's a wonder for you; think on this. Goody Good is pregnant!

ELIZABETH. Pregnant! Are they mad? The woman's near to sixty!

MARY WARREN. They had Doctor Griggs examine her, and she's full to the brim. And smokin' a pipe all these years, and no husband either! But she's safe, thank God, for they'll not hurt the innocent child. But be that not a marvel? You must see it, sir, it's God's work we do. So I'll be gone every day for some time. I'm—I am an official of the court, they say, and I—[*She has been edging toward offstage.*]

PROCTOR. I'll official you! [*He strides to the mantel, takes down the whip hanging there.*]

MARY WARREN. [*Terrified, but coming erect, striving for her authority.*] I'll not stand whipping any more!

ELIZABETH. [*Hurriedly, as PROCTOR approaches.*] Mary, promise now you'll stay at home—

MARY WARREN. [*Backing from him, but keeping her erect posture, striving, striving for her way.*]

The Devil's loose in Salem, Mr. Proctor; we must discover where he's hiding!

PROCTOR. I'll whip the Devil out of you! [*With whip raised he reaches out for her, and she streaks away and yells.*]

MARY WARREN. [*Pointing at* ELIZABETH.] I saved her life today!

[*Silence. His whip comes down.*]

ELIZABETH. [*Softly.*] I am accused?

MARY WARREN. [*Quaking.*] Somewhat mentioned. But I said I never see no sign you ever sent your spirit out to hurt no one, and seeing I do live so closely with you, they dismissed it.

ELIZABETH. Who accused me?

MARY WARREN. I am bound by law, I cannot tell it. [*To* PROCTOR.] I only hope you'll not be so sarcastical no more. Four judges and the King's deputy sat to dinner with us but an hour ago. I—I would have you speak civilly to me, from this out.

PROCTOR. [*In horror, muttering in disgust at her.*] Go to bed.

MARY WARREN. [*With a stamp of her foot.*] I'll not be ordered to bed no more, Mr. Proctor! I am eighteen and a woman, however single!

PROCTOR. Do you wish to sit up? Then sit up.

MARY WARREN. I wish to go to bed!

PROCTOR. [*In anger.*] Good night, then!

MARY WARREN. Good night. [*Dissatisfied, uncertain of herself, she goes out. Wide-eyed, both,* PROCTOR *and* ELIZABETH *stand staring.*]

ELIZABETH. [*Quietly.*] Oh, the noose, the noose is up!

PROCTOR. There'll be no noose.

ELIZABETH. She wants me dead. I knew all week it would come to this!

PROCTOR. [*Without conviction.*] They dismissed it. You heard her say—

ELIZABETH. And what of tomorrow? She will cry me out until they take me!

PROCTOR. Sit you down.

ELIZABETH. She wants me dead, John, you know it!

PROCTOR. I say sit down! [*She sits, trembling. He speaks quietly, trying to keep his wits.*] Now we must be wise, Elizabeth.

ELIZABETH. [*With sarcasm, and a sense of being lost.*] Oh, indeed, indeed!

PROCTOR. Fear nothing. I'll find Ezekiel Cheever. I'll tell him she said it were all sport.

ELIZABETH. John, with so many in the jail, more than Cheever's help is needed now, I think. Would you favor me with this? Go to Abigail.

PROCTOR. [*His soul hardening as he senses . . .*] What have I to say to Abigail?

ELIZABETH. [*Delicately.*] John—grant me this. You have a faulty understanding of young girls. There is a promise made in any bed—

PROCTOR. [*Striving against his anger.*] What promise!

ELIZABETH. Spoke or silent, a promise is surely made. And she may dote on[6] it now—I am sure she does—and thinks to kill me, then to take my place.

[*PROCTOR's anger is rising; he cannot speak.*]

ELIZABETH. It is her dearest hope, John, I know it. There be a thousand names; why does she call mine? There be a certain danger in calling such a name—I am no Goody Good that sleeps in ditches, nor Osburn, drunk and half-witted. She'd dare not call out such a farmer's wife but there be monstrous profit in it. She thinks to take my place, John.

PROCTOR. She cannot think it! [*He knows it is true.*]

---

6. To *dote on* is to show extreme affection for or to pay excessive attention to.

ELIZABETH. [*"Reasonably."*] John, have you ever shown her somewhat of contempt? She cannot pass you in the church but you will blush—

PROCTOR. I may blush for my sin.

ELIZABETH. I think she sees another meaning in that blush.

PROCTOR. And what see you? What see you, Elizabeth?

ELIZABETH. [*"Conceding."*] I think you be somewhat ashamed, for I am there, and she so close.

PROCTOR. When will you know me, woman? Were I stone I would have cracked for shame this seven month!

ELIZABETH. Then go and tell her she's a whore. Whatever promise she may sense—break it, John, break it.

PROCTOR. [*Between his teeth.*] Good, then. I'll go. [*He starts for his rifle.*]

ELIZABETH. [*Trembling, fearfully.*] Oh, how unwillingly!

PROCTOR. [*Turning on her, rifle in hand.*] I will curse her hotter than the oldest cinder in hell. But pray, begrudge me not my anger!

ELIZABETH. Your anger! I only ask you—

PROCTOR. Woman, am I so <u>base</u>? Do you truly think me base?

ELIZABETH. I never called you base.

PROCTOR. Then how do you charge me with such a promise? The promise that a stallion gives a mare I gave that girl!

ELIZABETH. Then why do you anger with me when I bid you break it?

PROCTOR. Because it speaks deceit, and I am honest! But I'll plead no more! I see now your spirit twists around the single error of my life, and I will never tear it free!

Vocabulary
base (bās) *adj.* morally low; dishonorable

ELIZABETH. [*Crying out.*] You'll tear it free—when you come to know that I will be your only wife, or no wife at all! She has an arrow in you yet, John Proctor, and you know it well!

[*Quite suddenly, as though from the air, a figure appears in the doorway. They start slightly. It is* MR. HALE. *He is different now—drawn a little, and there is a quality of deference, even of guilt, about his manner now.*]

HALE. Good evening.

PROCTOR. [*Still in his shock.*] Why, Mr. Hale! Good evening to you, sir. Come in, come in.

HALE. [*To* ELIZABETH.] I hope I do not startle you.

ELIZABETH. No, no, it's only that I heard no horse—

HALE. You are Goodwife Proctor.

PROCTOR. Aye; Elizabeth.

HALE. [*Nods, then.*] I hope you're not off to bed yet.

PROCTOR. [*Setting down his gun.*] No, no. [HALE *comes further into the room. And* PROCTOR, *to explain his nervousness.*] We are not used to visitors after dark, but you're welcome here. Will you sit you down, sir?

HALE. I will. [*He sits.*] Let you sit, Goodwife Proctor.

[*She does, never letting him out of her sight. There is a pause as* HALE *looks about the room.*]

PROCTOR. [*To break the silence.*] Will you drink cider, Mr. Hale?

HALE. No, it rebels my stomach; I have some further traveling yet tonight. Sit you down, sir. [PROCTOR *sits.*] I will not keep you long, but I have some business with you.

PROCTOR. Business of the court?

HALE. No—no, I come of my own, without the court's authority. Hear me. [*He wets his lips.*] I know not if you are aware, but your wife's name is—mentioned in the court.

PROCTOR. We know it, sir. Our Mary Warren told us. We are entirely amazed.

HALE. I am a stranger here, as you know. And in my ignorance I find it hard to draw a clear opinion of them that come accused before the court. And so this afternoon, and now tonight, I go from house to house—I come now from Rebecca Nurse's house and—

ELIZABETH. [*Shocked.*] Rebecca's charged!

HALE. God forbid such a one be charged. She is, however—mentioned somewhat.

ELIZABETH. [*With an attempt at a laugh.*] You will never believe, I hope, that Rebecca trafficked with the Devil.

HALE. Woman, it is possible.

PROCTOR. [*Taken aback.*] Surely you cannot think so.

HALE. This is a strange time, Mister. No man may longer doubt the powers of the dark are gathered in monstrous attack upon this village. There is too much evidence now to deny it. You will agree, sir?

PROCTOR. [*Evading.*] I—have no knowledge in that line. But it's hard to think so pious[7] a woman be secretly a Devil's bitch after seventy year of such good prayer.

HALE. Aye. But the Devil is a wily[8] one, you cannot deny it. However, she is far from accused, and I know she will not be. [*Pause.*] I thought, sir, to put some questions as to the Christian character of this house, if you'll permit me.

PROCTOR. [*Coldly, resentful.*] Why, we—have no fear of questions, sir.

HALE. Good, then. [*He makes himself more comfortable.*] In the book of record that Mr. Parris keeps, I note that you are rarely in the church on Sabbath Day.

---

7. *Pious* means "having a sincere reverence for God."
8. *Wily* means "crafty" or "sly and full of tricks."

The Crucible

PROCTOR. No, sir, you are mistaken.

HALE. Twenty-six time in seventeen month, sir. I must call that rare. Will you tell me why you are so absent?

PROCTOR. Mr. Hale, I never knew I must account to that man for I come to church or stay at home. My wife were sick this winter.

HALE. So I am told. But you, Mister, why could you not come alone?

PROCTOR. I surely did come when I could, and when I could not I prayed in this house.

HALE. Mr. Proctor, your house is not a church; your theology[9] must tell you that.

PROCTOR. It does, sir, it does; and it tells me that a minister may pray to God without he have golden candlesticks upon the altar.

HALE. What golden candlesticks?

PROCTOR. Since we built the church there were pewter[10] candlesticks upon the altar; Francis Nurse made them, y'know, and a sweeter hand never touched the metal. But Parris came, and for twenty week he preach nothin' but golden candlesticks until he had them. I labor the earth from dawn of day to blink of night, and I tell you true, when I look to heaven and see my money glaring at his elbows—it hurt my prayer, sir, it hurt my prayer. I think, sometimes, the man dreams cathedrals, not clapboard meetin' houses.

HALE. [Thinks, then.] And yet, Mister, a Christian on Sabbath Day must be in church. [Pause.] Tell me—you have three children?

PROCTOR. Aye. Boys.

HALE. How comes it that only two are baptized?

PROCTOR. [Starts to speak, then stops, then, as though unable to restrain this.] I like it not that Mr. Parris should lay his hand upon my baby. I see no light of God in that man. I'll not conceal it.

HALE. I must say it, Mr. Proctor; that is not for you to decide. The man's ordained, therefore the light of God is in him.

PROCTOR. [Flushed with resentment but trying to smile.] What's your suspicion, Mr. Hale?

HALE. No, no, I have no—

PROCTOR. I nailed the roof upon the church, I hung the door—

HALE. Oh, did you! That's a good sign, then.

PROCTOR. It may be I have been too quick to bring the man to book, but you cannot think we ever desired the destruction of religion. I think that's in your mind, is it not?

HALE. [Not altogether giving way.] I—have—there is a softness in your record, sir, a softness.

ELIZABETH. I think, maybe, we have been too hard with Mr. Parris. I think so. But sure we never loved the Devil here.

HALE. [Nods, deliberating this. Then, with the voice of one administering a secret test.] Do you know your Commandments, Elizabeth?

ELIZABETH. [Without hesitation, even eagerly.] I surely do. There be no mark of blame upon my life, Mr. Hale. I am a covenanted Christian woman.

HALE. And you, Mister?

PROCTOR. [A trifle unsteadily.] I—am sure I do, sir.

HALE. [Glances at her open face, then at JOHN, then.] Let you repeat them, if you will.

PROCTOR. The Commandments.

HALE. Aye.

PROCTOR. [Looking off, beginning to sweat.] Thou shalt not kill.

HALE. Aye.

---

9. Here, Hale uses the term *theology* to refer to Proctor's own religious beliefs.

10. *Pewter* is an alloy, or a substance composed of two or more metals or of a metal and a nonmetal. Tin is the main metal in pewter, and it is often mixed with lead.

PROCTOR. [*Counting on his fingers.*] Thou shalt not steal. Thou shalt not <u>covet</u> thy neighbor's goods, nor make unto thee any graven image.[11] Thou shalt not take the name of the Lord in vain; thou shalt have no other gods before me. [*With some hesitation.*] Thou shalt remember the Sabbath Day and keep it holy. [*Pause. Then.*] Thou shalt honor thy father and mother. Thou shalt not bear false witness. [*He is stuck. He counts back on his fingers, knowing one is missing.*] Thou shalt not make unto thee any graven image.

HALE. You have said that twice, sir.

PROCTOR. [*Lost.*] Aye. [*He is flailing for it.*]

ELIZABETH. [*Delicately.*] Adultery, John.

PROCTOR. [*As though a secret arrow had pained his heart.*] Aye. [*Trying to grin it away—to* HALE.] You see, sir, between the two of us we do know them all. [HALE *only looks at* PROCTOR, *deep in his attempt to define this man.* PROCTOR *grows more uneasy.*] I think it be a small fault.

HALE. Theology, sir, is a fortress; no crack in a fortress may be accounted small. [*He rises; he seems worried now. He paces a little, in deep thought.*]

PROCTOR. There be no love for Satan in this house, Mister.

HALE. I pray it, I pray it dearly. [*He looks to both of them, an attempt at a smile on his face, but his* <u>misgivings</u> *are clear.*] Well, then—I'll bid you good night.

ELIZABETH. [*Unable to restrain herself.*] Mr. Hale. [*He turns.*] I do think you are suspecting me somewhat? Are you not?

HALE. [*Obviously disturbed—and evasive.*] Goody Proctor, I do not judge you. My duty is to add what I may to the godly wisdom of the court. I pray you both good health and good fortune. [*To* JOHN.] Good night, sir. [*He starts out.*]

ELIZABETH. [*With a note of desperation.*] I think you must tell him, John.

HALE. What's that?

ELIZABETH. [*Restraining a call.*] Will you tell him?

[*Slight pause.* HALE *looks questioningly at* JOHN.]

PROCTOR. [*With difficulty.*] I—I have no witness and cannot prove it, except my word be taken. But I know the children's sickness had naught to do with witchcraft.

HALE. [*Stopped, struck.*] Naught to do—?

PROCTOR. Mr. Parris discovered them sportin' in the woods. They were startled and took sick.

[*Pause.*]

HALE. Who told you this?

PROCTOR. [*Hesitates, then.*] Abigail Williams.

HALE. Abigail!

PROCTOR. Aye.

HALE. [*His eyes wide.*] Abigail Williams told you it had naught to do with witchcraft!

PROCTOR. She told me the day you came, sir.

HALE. [*Suspiciously.*] Why—why did you keep this?

PROCTOR. I never knew until tonight that the world is gone daft[12] with this nonsense.

HALE. Nonsense! Mister, I have myself examined Tituba, Sarah Good, and numerous others that have confessed to dealing with the Devil. They have *confessed* it.

PROCTOR. And why not, if they must hang for denyin' it? There are them that will swear to

---

11. Here, a *graven image* is an idol.

12. *Daft* means "without sense or reason," "crazy," or "silly."

Vocabulary

covet (kuv′ it) *v.* to desire, especially to an excessive degree, something belonging to another
misgiving (mis giv′ ing) *n.* a feeling of doubt, distrust, or anxiety

anything before they'll hang; have you never thought of that?

HALE. I have. I—I have indeed. [*It is his own suspicion, but he resists it. He glances at ELIZA-BETH, then at JOHN.*] And you—would you testify to this in court?

PROCTOR. I—had not reckoned with goin' into court. But if I must I will.

HALE. Do you falter here?

PROCTOR. I falter nothing, but I may wonder if my story will be credited in such a court. I do wonder on it, when such a steady-minded minister as you will suspicion such a woman that never lied, and cannot, and the world knows she cannot! I may falter somewhat, Mister; I am no fool.

HALE. [*Quietly—it has impressed him.*] Proctor, let you open with me now, for I have a rumor that troubles me. It's said you hold no belief that there may even be witches in the world. Is that true, sir?

PROCTOR. [*He knows this is critical, and is striving against his disgust with HALE and with himself for even answering.*] I know not what I have said, I may have said it. I have wondered if there be witches in the world—although I cannot believe they come among us now.

HALE. Then you do not believe—

Confrontation, 1964. Ben Shahn. Watercolor on rice paper, mounted on artist's board, 24 x 32 in. ©Estate of Ben Shahn/Licensed by VAGA, New York/The William H. Lane Collection. Courtesy Museum of Fine Arts, Boston.

Viewing the painting: How might this painting convey the confrontation between John Proctor and Mr. Hale?

PROCTOR. I have no knowledge of it; the Bible speaks of witches, and I will not deny them.

HALE. And you, woman?

ELIZABETH. I—I cannot believe it.

HALE. [*Shocked.*] You cannot!

PROCTOR. Elizabeth, you bewilder him!

ELIZABETH. [*To HALE.*] I cannot think the Devil may own a woman's soul, Mr. Hale, when she keeps an upright way, as I have. I am a good woman, I know it; and if you believe I may do only good work in the world, and yet be secretly bound to Satan, then I must tell you, sir, I do not believe it.

HALE. But, woman, you do believe there are witches in—

ELIZABETH. If you think that I am one, then I say there are none.

HALE. You surely do not fly against the Gospel, the Gospel—

PROCTOR. She believe in the Gospel, every word!

ELIZABETH. Question Abigail Williams about the Gospel, not myself!

[*HALE stares at her.*]

PROCTOR. She do not mean to doubt the Gospel, sir, you cannot think it. This be a Christian house, sir, a Christian house.

HALE. God keep you both; let the third child be quickly baptized, and go you without fail each Sunday in to Sabbath prayer; and keep a solemn, quiet way among you. I think—

[*GILES COREY appears in doorway.*]

GILES. John!

PROCTOR. Giles! What's the matter?

GILES. They take my wife.

[*FRANCIS NURSE enters.*]

GILES. And his Rebecca!

PROCTOR. [*To FRANCIS.*] Rebecca's in the *jail!*

FRANCIS. Aye, Cheever come and take her in his wagon. We've only now come from the jail, and they'll not even let us in to see them.

ELIZABETH. They've surely gone wild now, Mr. Hale!

FRANCIS. [*Going to HALE.*] Reverend Hale! Can you not speak to the Deputy Governor? I'm sure he mistakes these people—

HALE. Pray calm yourself, Mr. Nurse.

FRANCIS. My wife is the very brick and mortar of the church, Mr. Hale—[*Indicating GILES.*]— and Martha Corey, there cannot be a woman closer yet to God than Martha.

HALE. How is Rebecca charged, Mr. Nurse?

FRANCIS. [*With a mocking, half-hearted laugh.*] For murder, she's charged! [*Mockingly quoting the warrant.*] "For the marvelous and supernatural murder of Goody Putnam's babies." What am I to do, Mr. Hale?

HALE. [*Turns from FRANCIS, deeply troubled, then.*] Believe me, Mr. Nurse, if Rebecca Nurse be tainted,[13] then nothing's left to stop the whole green world from burning. Let you rest upon the justice of the court; the court will send her home, I know it.

FRANCIS. You cannot mean she will be tried in court!

HALE. [*Pleading.*] Nurse, though our hearts break, we cannot flinch; these are new times, sir. There is a misty plot afoot so <u>subtle</u> we should be criminal to cling to old respects and

---

13. Something *tainted* is spoiled, inferior, or corrupted.

Vocabulary
subtle (sut′ əl) *adj.* not open, direct, or obvious; crafty; sly

ancient friendships. I have seen too many frightful proofs in court—the Devil is alive in Salem, and we dare not quail to follow wherever the accusing finger points!

PROCTOR. [*Angered.*] How may such a woman murder children?

HALE. [*In great pain.*] Man, remember, until an hour before the Devil fell, God thought him beautiful in Heaven.[14]

GILES. I never said my wife were a witch, Mr. Hale; I only said she were reading books!

HALE. Mr. Corey, exactly what complaint were made on your wife?

GILES. That bloody mongrel Walcott charge her. Y'see, he buy a pig of my wife four or five year ago, and the pig died soon after. So he come dancin' in for his money back. So my Martha, she says to him, "Walcott, if you haven't the wit to feed a pig properly, you'll not live to own many," she says. Now he goes to court and claims that from that day to this he cannot keep a pig alive for more than four weeks because my Martha bewitch them with her books!

[*Enter EZEKIEL CHEEVER. A shocked silence.*]

CHEEVER. Good evening to you, Proctor.

PROCTOR. Why, Mr. Cheever. Good evening.

CHEEVER. Good evening, all. Good evening, Mr. Hale.

PROCTOR. I hope you come not on business of the court.

CHEEVER. I do, Proctor, aye. I am clerk of the court now, y'know.

[*Enter MARSHAL HERRICK, a man in his early thirties, who is somewhat shamefaced at the moment.*]

GILES. It's a pity, Ezekiel, that an honest tailor might have gone to Heaven must burn in Hell. You'll burn for this, do you know it?

CHEEVER. You know yourself I must do as I'm told. You surely know that, Giles. And I'd as lief[15] you'd not be sending me to Hell. I like not the sound of it, I tell you; I like not the sound of it. [*He fears PROCTOR, but starts to reach inside his coat.*] Now believe me, Proctor, how heavy be the law, all its tonnage I do carry on my back tonight. [*He takes out a warrant.*] I have a warrant for your wife.

PROCTOR. [*To HALE.*] You said she were not charged!

HALE. I know nothin' of it. [*To CHEEVER.*] When were she charged?

CHEEVER. I am given sixteen warrant tonight, sir, and she is one.

PROCTOR. Who charged her?

CHEEVER. Why, Abigail Williams charge her.

PROCTOR. On what proof, what proof?

CHEEVER. [*Looking about the room.*] Mr. Proctor, I have little time. The court bid me search your house, but I like not to search a house. So will you hand me any poppets that your wife may keep here?

PROCTOR. Poppets?

ELIZABETH. I never kept no poppets, not since I were a girl.

CHEEVER. [*Embarrassed, glancing toward the mantel where sits MARY WARREN's poppet.*] I spy a poppet, Goody Proctor.

ELIZABETH. Oh! [*Going for it.*] Why, this is Mary's.

CHEEVER. [*Shyly.*] Would you please to give it to me?

ELIZABETH. [*Handing it to him, asks HALE.*] Has the court discovered a text in poppets now?

CHEEVER. [*Carefully holding the poppet.*] Do you keep any others in this house?

PROCTOR. No, nor this one either till tonight. What signifies a poppet?

---

14. *[before the Devil fell . . . Heaven]* According to the Bible, the devil was heaven's highest angel before he was driven out because of his excessive pride.

15. *As lief* (lēv) means "prefer that."

CHEEVER. Why, a poppet—[*He gingerly turns the poppet over.*]—a poppet may signify—Now, woman, will you please to come with me?

PROCTOR. She will not! [*To* ELIZABETH.] Fetch Mary here.

CHEEVER. [*Ineptly reaching toward* ELIZABETH.] No, no, I am forbid to leave her from my sight.

PROCTOR. [*Pushing his arm away.*] You'll leave her out of sight and out of mind, Mister. Fetch Mary, Elizabeth. [ELIZABETH *goes upstairs.*]

HALE. What signifies a poppet, Mr. Cheever?

CHEEVER. [*Turning the poppet over in his hands.*] Why, they say it may signify that she—[*He has lifted the poppet's skirt, and his eyes widen in astonished fear.*] Why, this, this—

PROCTOR. [*Reaching for the poppet.*] What's there?

CHEEVER. Why—[*He draws out a long needle from the poppet.*]—it is a needle! Herrick, Herrick, it is a needle!

[HERRICK *comes toward him.*]

PROCTOR. [*Angrily, bewildered.*] And what signifies a needle!

CHEEVER. [*His hands shaking.*] Why, this go hard with her, Proctor, this—I had my doubts, Proctor, I had my doubts, but here's calamity. [*To* HALE, *showing the needle.*] You see it, sir, it is a needle!

HALE. Why? What meanin' has it?

CHEEVER. [*Wide-eyed, trembling.*] The girl, the Williams girl, Abigail Williams, sir. She sat to dinner in Reverend Parris's house tonight, and without word nor warnin' she falls to the floor. Like a struck beast, he says, and screamed a scream that a bull would weep to hear. And he goes to save her, and, stuck two inches in the flesh of her belly, he draw a needle out. And demandin' of her how she come to be so stabbed, she—[*To* PROCTOR *now.*]—testify it were your wife's familiar spirit pushed it in.

PROCTOR. Why, she done it herself! [*To* HALE.] I hope you're not takin' this for proof, Mister!

[HALE, *struck by the proof, is silent.*]

CHEEVER. 'Tis hard proof! [*To* HALE.] I find here a poppet Goody Proctor keeps. I have found it, sir. And in the belly of the poppet a needle's stuck. I tell you true, Proctor, I never warranted to see such proof of Hell, and I bid you obstruct me not, for I—

[*Enter* ELIZABETH *with* MARY WARREN. PROCTOR, *seeing* MARY WARREN, *draws her by the arm to* HALE.]

PROCTOR. Here now! Mary, how did this poppet come into my house?

MARY WARREN. [*Frightened for herself, her voice very small.*] What poppet's that, sir?

PROCTOR. [*Impatiently, pointing at the doll in* CHEEVER's *hand.*] This poppet, this poppet.

MARY WARREN. [*Evasively, looking at it.*] Why, I—I think it is mine.

PROCTOR. It is your poppet, is it not?

MARY WARREN. [*Not understanding the direction of this.*] It—is, sir.

PROCTOR. And how did it come into this house?

MARY WARREN. [*Glancing about at the avid faces.*] Why—I made it in the court, sir, and—give it to Goody Proctor tonight.

PROCTOR. [*To* HALE.] Now, sir—do you have it?

HALE. Mary Warren, a needle have been found inside this poppet.

MARY WARREN. [*Bewildered.*] Why, I meant no harm by it, sir.

PROCTOR. [*Quickly.*] You stuck that needle in yourself?

Vocabulary
ineptly (i nept′ lē) *adv.* incompetently; awkwardly; clumsily

The Crucible

MARY WARREN. I—I believe I did, sir, I—

PROCTOR. [*To* HALE.] What say you now?

HALE. [*Watching* MARY WARREN *closely*.] Child, you are certain this be your natural memory? May it be, perhaps, that someone conjures you even now to say this?

MARY WARREN. Conjures me? Why, no, sir, I am entirely myself, I think. Let you ask Susanna Walcott—she saw me sewin' it in court. [*Or better still*.] Ask Abby, Abby sat beside me when I made it.

PROCTOR. [*To* HALE, *of* CHEEVER.] Bid him begone. Your mind is surely settled now. Bid him out, Mr. Hale.

ELIZABETH. What signifies a needle?

HALE. Mary—you charge a cold and cruel murder on Abigail.

MARY WARREN. Murder! I charge no—

HALE. Abigail were stabbed tonight; a needle were found stuck into her belly—

ELIZABETH. And she charges me?

HALE. Aye.

ELIZABETH. [*Her breath knocked out*.] Why—! The girl is murder! She must be ripped out of the world!

CHEEVER. [*Pointing at* ELIZABETH.] You've heard that, sir! Ripped out of the world! Herrick, you heard it!

1954, 1954. Clyfford Still. Oil on canvas, 9 ft 5½ in x 13 ft. Albright-Knox Art Gallery, Buffalo, NY. Gift of Seymour H. Knox, 1957.

Viewing the painting: How, in your opinion, does this painting express the mood of Salem's community in act 2?

PROCTOR. [*Suddenly snatching the warrant out of* CHEEVER's *hands.*] Out with you.

CHEEVER. Proctor, you dare not touch the warrant.

PROCTOR. [*Ripping the warrant.*] Out with you!

CHEEVER. You've ripped the Deputy Governor's warrant, man!

PROCTOR. Damn the Deputy Governor! Out of my house!

HALE. Now, Proctor, Proctor!

PROCTOR. Get y'gone with them! You are a broken minister.

HALE. Proctor, if she is innocent, the court—

PROCTOR. If *she* is innocent! Why do you never wonder if Parris be innocent, or Abigail? Is the accuser always holy now? Were they born this morning as clean as God's fingers? I'll tell you what's walking Salem—vengeance is walking Salem. We are what we always were in Salem, but now the little crazy children are jangling the keys of the kingdom, and common vengeance writes the law! This warrant's vengeance! I'll not give my wife to vengeance!

ELIZABETH. I'll go, John—

PROCTOR. You will not go!

HERRICK. I have nine men outside. You cannot keep her. The law binds me, John, I cannot budge.

PROCTOR. [*To* HALE, *ready to break him.*] Will you see her taken?

HALE. Proctor, the court is just—

PROCTOR. Pontius Pilate! God will not let you wash your hands of this![16]

ELIZABETH. John—I think I must go with them. [*He cannot bear to look at her.*] Mary,

there is bread enough for the morning; you will bake, in the afternoon. Help Mr. Proctor as you were his daughter—you owe me that, and much more. [*She is fighting her weeping. To* PROCTOR.] When the children wake, speak nothing of witchcraft—it will frighten them. [*She cannot go on.*]

PROCTOR. I will bring you home. I will bring you soon.

ELIZABETH. Oh, John, bring me soon!

PROCTOR. I will fall like an ocean on that court! Fear nothing, Elizabeth.

ELIZABETH. [*With great fear.*] I will fear nothing. [*She looks about the room, as though to fix it in her mind.*] Tell the children I have gone to visit someone sick.

[*She walks out the door,* HERRICK *and* CHEEVER *behind her. For a moment,* PROCTOR *watches from the doorway. The clank of chain is heard.*]

PROCTOR. Herrick! Herrick, don't chain her! [*He rushes out the door. From outside.*] Damn you, man, you will not chain her! Off with them! I'll not have it! I will not have her chained!

[*There are other men's voices against his.* HALE, *in a fever of guilt and uncertainty, turns from the door to avoid the sight;* MARY WARREN *bursts into tears and sits weeping.* GILES COREY *calls to* HALE.]

GILES. And yet silent, minister? It is fraud, you know it is fraud! What keeps you, man?

[PROCTOR *is half braced, half pushed into the room by two deputies and* HERRICK.]

PROCTOR. I'll pay you, Herrick, I will surely pay you!

HERRICK. [*Panting.*] In God's name, John, I cannot help myself. I must chain them all. Now let you keep inside this house till I am gone! [*He goes out with his deputies.*]

[PROCTOR *stands there, gulping air. Horses and a wagon creaking are heard.*]

HALE. [*In great uncertainty.*] Mr. Proctor—

16. *[Pontius Pilate . . . this!]* According to the Christian Bible, the Roman official Pontius Pilate consented to the crucifixion of Jesus despite the lack of formal charges or evidence. Pilate then washed his hands and declared himself innocent of shedding Jesus' blood.

PROCTOR. Out of my sight!

HALE. Charity, Proctor, charity. What I have heard in her favor, I will not fear to testify in court. God help me, I cannot judge her guilty or innocent—I know not. Only this consider: the world goes mad, and it profit nothing you should lay the cause to the vengeance of a little girl.

PROCTOR. You are a coward! Though you be ordained in God's own tears, you are a coward now!

HALE. Proctor, I cannot think God be provoked so grandly by such a petty cause. The jails are packed—our greatest judges sit in Salem now—and hangin's promised. Man, we must look to cause proportionate. Were there murder done, perhaps, and never brought to light? Abomination? Some secret blasphemy[17] that stinks to Heaven? Think on cause, man, and let you help me to discover it. For there's your way, believe it, there is your only way, when such confusion strikes upon the world. [*He goes to* GILES *and* FRANCIS.] Let you counsel among yourselves; think on your village and what may have drawn from heaven such thundering wrath upon you all. I shall pray God open up our eyes.

[HALE *goes out.*]

FRANCIS. [*Struck by* HALE's *mood.*] I never heard no murder done in Salem.

PROCTOR. [*He has been reached by* HALE's *words.*] Leave me, Francis, leave me.

GILES. [*Shaken.*] John—tell me, are we lost?

PROCTOR. Go home now, Giles. We'll speak on it tomorrow.

GILES. Let you think on it. We'll come early, eh?

PROCTOR. Aye. Go now, Giles.

GILES. Good night, then.

[GILES COREY *goes out. After a moment.*]

MARY WARREN. [*In a fearful squeak of a voice.*] Mr. Proctor, very likely they'll let her come home once they're given proper evidence.

---

17. *Blasphemy* is an act or expression showing contempt for God or anything sacred.

Viewing the painting: In what ways might this painting echo John Proctor's words, "And the wind, God's icy wind, will blow!"?

PROCTOR. You're coming to the court with me, Mary. You will tell it in the court.

MARY WARREN. I cannot charge murder on Abigail.

PROCTOR. [*Moving menacingly toward her.*] You will tell the court how that poppet come here and who stuck the needle in.

MARY WARREN. She'll kill me for sayin' that! [PROCTOR *continues toward her.*] Abby'll charge lechery[18] on you, Mr. Proctor!

PROCTOR. [*Halting.*] She's told you!

MARY WARREN. I have known it, sir. She'll ruin you with it, I know she will.

PROCTOR. [*Hesitating, and with deep hatred of himself.*] Good. Then her saintliness is done with. [MARY *backs from him.*] We will slide together into our pit; you will tell the court what you know.

---

18. *Lechery* means "excessive indulgence of sexual desire." In Salem, this was sinful and, therefore, illegal.

MARY WARREN. [*In terror.*] I cannot, they'll turn on me—

[PROCTOR *strides and catches her, and she is repeating, "I cannot, I cannot!"*]

PROCTOR. My wife will never die for me! I will bring your guts into your mouth but that goodness will not die for me!

MARY WARREN. [*Struggling to escape him.*] I cannot do it, I cannot!

PROCTOR. [*Grasping her by the throat as though he would strangle her.*] Make your peace with it! Now Hell and Heaven grapple on our backs, and all our old pretense is ripped away—make your peace! [*He throws her to the floor, where she sobs, "I cannot, I cannot . . ."* And now, half to himself, staring, and turning to the open door.*] Peace. It is a providence, and no great change; we are only what we always were, but naked now. [*He walks as though toward a great horror, facing the open sky.*] Aye, naked! And the wind, God's icy wind, will blow!

[*And she is over and over again sobbing, "I cannot, I cannot, I cannot . . ."*]

THE CURTAIN FALLS

Responding to Literature

Personal Response

Which event in act 2 surprised you the most? the least?

ANALYZING ACT 2

RECALL AND INTERPRET

1. What has been going on between the close of act 1 and the opening of act 2? What role has Abigail Williams been playing in the proceedings?
2. Why might Proctor have previously hesitated to tell the court what Abigail told him about witchcraft? What does this hesitation suggest about his character?
3. What does the court accept as evidence that someone is a witch? Which characters seem to consider this evidence valid, and which do not? What, do you think, accounts for their differences of opinion?
4. Why does Hale come to the Proctors' house? How does Hale seem to feel about his own judgment and the court's? Explain.
5. How does Proctor react to Mary Warren's fears and her claim that Abigail will charge Proctor with lechery? What do you think Proctor means when he says, ". . . we are only what we always were, but naked now"?

EVALUATE AND CONNECT

6. Which character do you feel the most sympathy for now? Why? Does your answer differ from your response for act 1? Why or why not?
7. What is your opinion of Hale's questions to the Proctors? Do his methods of uncovering the devil's work seem valid to you? Explain.
8. How do the lies that are spoken and the truth that is revealed in act 2 compare with those of act 1? How might truth and lies relate to the development of the play's **theme**? (See Literary Terms Handbook, page R16.)

Literary ELEMENTS

Stage Directions
Stage directions are the instructions written by the playwright that describe the sets, costumes, and lighting as well as the appearance, actions, and tone of the characters. Stage directions are commonly written in italics and placed in brackets or parentheses to set them off in the script:

ELIZABETH. [*Unable to restrain herself.*] Mr. Hale. [*He turns.*] I do think you are suspecting me somewhat? Are you not?

1. What do you learn about the actions of the characters from the stage directions at the beginning of act 2?
2. How do the stage directions for Proctor's last speech of act 2 help you visualize the speech?

● See **Literary Terms Handbook**, p. R15.

EXTENDING YOUR RESPONSE

Literature Groups
The Dialect of Salem   In your group, discuss how the dialect Miller uses in *The Crucible* differs from the English spoken in your community today. Together, rewrite some of the lines in your own words and compare the impact each style has on the lines. Share your conclusions with the class.

Interdisciplinary Activity
Government: Guilty or Innocent?   Today, an accused person can be convicted only if proven "guilty beyond a reasonable doubt." Research the meaning of that phrase. Then write a paragraph or two responding to the following: Do you think any of the Salem defendants would have been convicted if that standard had been applied?

📖 **Save your work for your portfolio.**

Skill Minilesson

VOCABULARY • Dictionary Skills: Definitions

The best way to discover the meaning of an unfamiliar word is to use a dictionary. Remember, though, that most words have more than one meaning. A *pious* person may be sincerely religious, may pretend to have religious devotion, or may even pretend to be virtuous while not being virtuous at all. With this and other multiple-meaning words, you must rely on the context that a word appears in to know which meaning is the appropriate one.

The following is a sample dictionary entry containing only some of the meanings for *subtle.*

> **subtle** *adj.* **1.** sharp, quick, and keen; able to make fine distinctions: *a subtle thinker.* **2.** hard to see or understand: *The joke was too subtle for me.* **3.** not open, direct, or obvious; crafty or sly: *a subtle hint.* **4.** not sharp or strong; faint: *a subtle shade of purple.* **5.** delicately fine or skillful: *a subtle design.*

PRACTICE Write the number of the meaning of *subtle* that is used in each sentence.

1. I caught a *subtle* scent of lilacs.
2. The detective owed his success more to determination and thoroughness than to *subtle* reasoning.
3. Some people need a straightforward order; others respond to a *subtle* suggestion.
4. With this dress, a *subtle* necklace looks better than chunky jewelry.
5. Only an expert could detect the *subtle* differences between the original and the copy.

Before You Read

The Crucible, Act 3

BACKGROUND

Tyranny and *The Crucible*

Arthur Miller has expressed pride in *The Crucible,* which speaks about mass hysteria, social and political repression, and the tragic combination of the two. Deciding to present the play is often a response to similar circumstances. "I can almost tell what the political situation in a country is when the play is suddenly a hit there," Miller writes, "it is either a warning of tyranny on the way or a reminder of tyranny just past."

The Crucible played in Poland in the 1980s, a time of great resistance to the authoritarian government there. When it played in China, one Chinese writer told Miller that she was sure the play could have been written only by someone who had suffered persecution in China's Cultural Revolution. Miller adds, "It was chilling to realize what had never occurred to me until she mentioned it—that the tyranny of teenagers was almost identical in both instances."

VOCABULARY PREVIEW

vile (vīl) *adj.* evil; foul; repulsive; degrading; p. 960
immaculate (i mak′ yə lit) *adj.* unblemished; flawless; pure; p. 966
guile (gīl) *n.* cunning; deceit; slyness; p. 968

contemplation (kon′ təm plā′ shən) *n.* the act of thinking about something long and seriously; p. 970
unperturbed (un pər turbd′) *adj.* undisturbed; calm; p. 975

Act Three

[*The vestry room of the Salem meeting house, now serving as the anteroom[1] of the General Court.*

As the curtain rises, the room is empty, but for sunlight pouring through two high windows in the back wall. The room is solemn, even forbidding. Heavy beams jut out, boards of random widths make up the walls. At the right are two doors leading into the meeting house proper, where the court is being held. At the left another door leads outside.

There is a plain bench at the left, and another at the right. In the center a rather long meeting table, with stools and a considerable armchair snugged up to it.

Through the partitioning wall at the right we hear a prosecutor's voice, JUDGE HATHORNE's, asking a question; then a woman's voice, MARTHA COREY's, replying.]

HATHORNE'S VOICE. Now, Martha Corey, there is abundant evidence in our hands to show that you have given yourself to the reading of fortunes. Do you deny it?

MARTHA COREY'S VOICE. I am innocent to a witch. I know not what a witch is.

HATHORNE'S VOICE. How do you know, then, that you are not a witch?

MARTHA COREY'S VOICE. If I were, I would know it.

HATHORNE'S VOICE. Why do you hurt these children?

MARTHA COREY'S VOICE. I do not hurt them. I scorn it!

GILES' VOICE. [*Roaring.*] I have evidence for the court!

[*Voices of townspeople rise in excitement.*]

DANFORTH'S VOICE. You will keep your seat!

GILES' VOICE. Thomas Putnam is reaching out for land!

DANFORTH'S VOICE. Remove that man, Marshal!

GILES' VOICE. You're hearing lies, lies!

[*A roaring goes up from the people.*]

HATHORNE'S VOICE. Arrest him, excellency!

GILES' VOICE. I have evidence. Why will you not hear my evidence?

[*The door opens and GILES is half carried into the vestry room by HERRICK.*]

GILES. Hands off, damn you, let me go!

HERRICK. Giles, Giles!

GILES. Out of my way, Herrick! I bring evidence—

HERRICK. You cannot go in there, Giles; it's a court!

[*Enter HALE from the court.*]

HALE. Pray be calm a moment.

GILES. You, Mr. Hale, go in there and demand I speak.

HALE. A moment, sir, a moment.

GILES. They'll be hangin' my wife!

[*JUDGE HATHORNE enters. He is in his sixties, a bitter, remorseless Salem judge.*]

HATHORNE. How do you dare come roarin' into this court! Are you gone daft, Corey?

GILES. You're not a Boston judge yet, Hathorne. You'll not call me daft!

[*Enter DEPUTY GOVERNOR DANFORTH and, behind him, EZEKIEL CHEEVER and PARRIS. On his appearance, silence falls. DANFORTH is a grave man in his sixties, of some humor and sophistication that does not, however, interfere with an exact loyalty to his position and his cause. He comes down to GILES, who awaits his wrath.*]

---

1. The *meeting house* was both a community hall and the house of worship. Its *vestry* was an *anteroom,* or small outer room, that served as a waiting area and entrance to the main room.

DANFORTH. [*Looking directly at* GILES.] Who is this man?

PARRIS. Giles Corey, sir, and a more contentious—

GILES. [*To* PARRIS.] I am asked the question, and I am old enough to answer it! [*To* DAN-FORTH, *who impresses him and to whom he smiles through his strain.*] My name is Corey, sir, Giles Corey. I have six hundred acres, and timber in addition. It is my wife you be condemning now. [*He indicates the courtroom.*]

DANFORTH. And how do you imagine to help her cause with such contemptuous riot? Now be gone. Your old age alone keeps you out of jail for this.

GILES. [*Beginning to plead.*] They be tellin' lies about my wife, sir, I—

DANFORTH. Do you take it upon yourself to determine what this court shall believe and what it shall set aside?

GILES. Your Excellency, we mean no disrespect for—

DANFORTH. Disrespect indeed! It is disruption, Mister. This is the highest court of the supreme government of this province, do you know it?

GILES. [*Beginning to weep.*] Your Excellency, I only said she were readin' books, sir, and they come and take her out of my house for—

DANFORTH. [*Mystified.*] Books! What books?

GILES. [*Through helpless sobs.*] It is my third wife, sir; I never had no wife that be so taken with books, and I thought to find the cause of it, d'y'see, but it were no witch I blamed her for. [*He is openly weeping.*] I have broke charity with the woman, I have broke charity with her. [*He covers his face, ashamed.* DANFORTH *is respectfully silent.*]

HALE. Excellency, he claims hard evidence for his wife's defense. I think that in all justice you must—

DANFORTH. Then let him submit his evidence in proper affidavit.[2] You are certainly aware of our procedure here, Mr. Hale. [*To* HERRICK.] Clear this room.

HERRICK. Come now, Giles. [*He gently pushes* COREY *out.*]

FRANCIS. We are desperate, sir; we come here three days now and cannot be heard.

DANFORTH. Who is this man?

FRANCIS. Francis Nurse, Your Excellency.

HALE. His wife's Rebecca that were condemned this morning.

DANFORTH. Indeed! I am amazed to find you in such uproar. I have only good report of your character, Mr. Nurse.

HATHORNE. I think they must both be arrested in contempt, sir.

DANFORTH. [*To* FRANCIS.] Let you write your plea, and in due time I will—

FRANCIS. Excellency, we have proof for your eyes; God forbid you shut them to it. The girls, sir, the girls are frauds.

DANFORTH. What's that?

FRANCIS. We have proof of it, sir. They are all deceiving you.

[DANFORTH *is shocked, but studying* FRANCIS.]

HATHORNE. This is contempt, sir, contempt!

DANFORTH. Peace, Judge Hathorne. Do you know who I am, Mr. Nurse?

FRANCIS. I surely do, sir, and I think you must be a wise judge to be what you are.

DANFORTH. And do you know that near to four hundred are in the jails from Marblehead to Lynn, and upon my signature?

FRANCIS. I—

DANFORTH. And seventy-two condemned to hang by that signature?

---

2. An *affidavit* is a written declaration sworn to be true, usually before a judge.

FRANCIS. Excellency, I never thought to say it to such a weighty judge, but you are deceived.

[*Enter* GILES COREY *from left. All turn to see as he beckons in* MARY WARREN *with* PROCTOR. MARY *is keeping her eyes to the ground;* PROCTOR *has her elbow as though she were near collapse.*]

PARRIS. [*On seeing her, in shock.*] Mary Warren! [*He goes directly to bend close to her face.*] What are you about here?

PROCTOR. [*Pressing* PARRIS *away from her with a gentle but firm motion of protectiveness.*] She would speak with the Deputy Governor.

DANFORTH. [*Shocked by this, turns to* HERRICK.] Did you not tell me Mary Warren were sick in bed?

HERRICK. She were, Your Honor. When I go to fetch her to the court last week, she said she were sick.

GILES. She has been strivin' with her soul all week, Your Honor; she comes now to tell the truth of this to you.

DANFORTH. Who is this?

PROCTOR. John Proctor, sir. Elizabeth Proctor is my wife.

PARRIS. Beware this man, Your Excellency, this man is mischief.

HALE. [*Excitedly.*] I think you must hear the girl, sir, she—

DANFORTH. [*Who has become very interested in* MARY WARREN *and only raises a hand toward* HALE.] Peace. What would you tell us, Mary Warren?

[PROCTOR *looks at her, but she cannot speak.*]

PROCTOR. She never saw no spirits, sir.

DANFORTH. [*With great alarm and surprise, to* MARY.] Never saw no spirits!

GILES. [*Eagerly.*] Never.

PROCTOR. [*Reaching into his jacket.*] She has signed a deposition,[3] sir—

DANFORTH. [*Instantly.*] No, no, I accept no depositions. [*He is rapidly calculating this; he turns from her to* PROCTOR.] Tell me, Mr. Proctor, have you given out this story in the village?

PROCTOR. We have not.

PARRIS. They've come to overthrow the court, sir! This man is—

DANFORTH. I pray you, Mr. Parris. Do you know, Mr. Proctor, that the entire contention of the state in these trials is that the voice of Heaven is speaking through the children?

PROCTOR. I know that, sir.

DANFORTH. [*Thinks, staring at* PROCTOR, *then turns to* MARY WARREN.] And you, Mary Warren, how came you to cry out people for sending their spirits against you?

MARY WARREN. It were pretense, sir.

DANFORTH. I cannot hear you.

PROCTOR. It were pretense, she says.

DANFORTH. Ah? And the other girls? Susanna Walcott, and—the others? They are also pretending?

MARY WARREN. Aye, sir.

DANFORTH. [*Wide-eyed.*] Indeed. [*Pause. He is baffled by this. He turns to study* PROCTOR's *face.*]

PARRIS. [*In a sweat.*] Excellency, you surely cannot think to let so <u>vile</u> a lie be spread in open court!

DANFORTH. Indeed not, but it strike hard upon me that she will dare come here with

---

3. A *deposition* is a sworn, written statement given by a witness out of court and intended to be used as testimony in court.

Vocabulary
vile (vīl) *adj.* evil; foul; repulsive; degrading

such a tale. Now, Mr. Proctor, before I decide whether I shall hear you or not, it is my duty to tell you this. We burn a hot fire here; it melts down all concealment.

PROCTOR. I know that, sir.

DANFORTH. Let me continue. I understand well, a husband's tenderness may drive him to extravagance in defense of a wife. Are you certain in your conscience, Mister, that your evidence is the truth?

PROCTOR. It is. And you will surely know it.

DANFORTH. And you thought to declare this revelation in the open court before the public?

PROCTOR. I thought I would, aye—with your permission.

DANFORTH. [*His eyes narrowing.*] Now, sir, what is your purpose in so doing?

PROCTOR. Why, I—I would free my wife, sir.

DANFORTH. There lurks nowhere in your heart, nor hidden in your spirit, any desire to undermine this court?

PROCTOR. [*With the faintest faltering.*] Why, no, sir.

CHEEVER. [*Clears his throat, awakening.*] I— Your Excellency.

DANFORTH. Mr. Cheever.

CHEEVER. I think it be my duty, sir—[*Kindly, to PROCTOR.*] You'll not deny it, John. [*To DANFORTH.*] When we come to take his wife, he damned the court and ripped your warrant.

PARRIS. Now you have it!

DANFORTH. He did that, Mr. Hale?

HALE. [*Takes a breath.*] Aye, he did.

PROCTOR. It were a temper, sir. I knew not what I did.

DANFORTH. [*Studying him.*] Mr. Proctor.

PROCTOR. Aye, sir.

DANFORTH. [*Straight into his eyes.*] Have you ever seen the Devil?

PROCTOR. No, sir.

DANFORTH. You are in all respects a Gospel Christian?

PROCTOR. I am, sir.

PARRIS. Such a Christian that will not come to church but once in a month!

DANFORTH. [*Restrained—he is curious.*] Not come to church?

PROCTOR. I—I have no love for Mr. Parris. It is no secret. But God I surely love.

CHEEVER. He plow on Sunday, sir.

DANFORTH. Plow on Sunday!

CHEEVER. [*Apologetically.*] I think it be evidence, John. I am an official of the court, I cannot keep it.

PROCTOR. I—I have once or twice plowed on Sunday. I have three children, sir, and until last year my land give little.

GILES. You'll find other Christians that do plow on Sunday if the truth be known.

HALE. Your Honor, I cannot think you may judge the man on such evidence.

DANFORTH. I judge nothing. [*Pause. He keeps watching PROCTOR, who tries to meet his gaze.*] I tell you straight, Mister—I have seen marvels in this court. I have seen people choked before my eyes by spirits; I have seen them stuck by pins and slashed by daggers. I have until this moment not the slightest reason to suspect that the children may be deceiving me. Do you understand my meaning?

PROCTOR. Excellency, does it not strike upon you that so many of these women have lived so long with such upright reputation, and—

PARRIS. Do you read the Gospel, Mr. Proctor?

PROCTOR. I read the Gospel.

PARRIS. I think not, or you should surely know that Cain were an upright man, and yet he did kill Abel.[4]

PROCTOR. Aye, God tells us that. [*To* DANFORTH.] But who tells us Rebecca Nurse murdered seven babies by sending out her spirit on them? It is the children only, and this one will swear she lied to you.

[DANFORTH *considers, then beckons* HATHORNE *to him.* HATHORNE *leans in, and he speaks in his ear.* HATHORNE *nods.*]

HATHORNE. Aye, she's the one.

DANFORTH. Mr. Proctor, this morning, your wife send me a claim in which she states that she is pregnant now.

PROCTOR. My wife pregnant!

DANFORTH. There be no sign of it—we have examined her body.

PROCTOR. But if she say she is pregnant, then she must be! That woman will never lie, Mr. Danforth.

DANFORTH. She will not?

PROCTOR. Never, sir, never.

DANFORTH. We have thought it too convenient to be credited. However, if I should tell you now that I will let her be kept another month; and if she begin to show her natural signs, you shall have her living yet another year until she is delivered—what say you to that? [JOHN PROCTOR *is struck silent.*] Come now. You say your only purpose is to save your wife. Good, then, she is saved at least this year, and a year is long. What say you, sir? It is done now. [*In conflict,* PROCTOR *glances at* FRANCIS *and* GILES.] Will you drop this charge?

PROCTOR. I—I think I cannot.

DANFORTH. [*Now an almost imperceptible hardness in his voice.*] Then your purpose is somewhat larger.

PARRIS. He's come to overthrow this court, Your Honor!

PROCTOR. These are my friends. Their wives are also accused—

DANFORTH. [*With a sudden briskness of manner.*] I judge you not, sir. I am ready to hear your evidence.

PROCTOR. I come not to hurt the court; I only—

DANFORTH. [*Cutting him off.*] Marshal, go into the court and bid Judge Stoughton and Judge Sewall declare recess for one hour. And let them go to the tavern, if they will. All witnesses and prisoners are to be kept in the building.

HERRICK. Aye, sir. [*Very deferentially.*] If I may say it, sir, I know this man all my life. It is a good man, sir.

DANFORTH. [*It is the reflection on himself he resents.*] I am sure of it, Marshal. [HERRICK *nods, then goes out.*] Now, what deposition do you have for us, Mr. Proctor? And I beg you be clear, open as the sky, and honest.

PROCTOR. [*As he takes out several papers.*] I am no lawyer, so I'll—

DANFORTH. The pure in heart need no lawyers. Proceed as you will.

PROCTOR. [*Handing* DANFORTH *a paper.*] Will you read this first, sir? It's a sort of testament.[5] The people signing it declare their good opinion of Rebecca, and my wife, and Martha Corey. [DANFORTH *looks down at the paper.*]

PARRIS. [*To enlist* DANFORTH's *sarcasm.*] Their good opinion! [*But* DANFORTH *goes on reading, and* PROCTOR *is heartened.*]

PROCTOR. These are all landholding farmers, members of the church. [*Delicately, trying to point out a paragraph.*] If you'll notice, sir—they've known the women many years

---

4. According to the Bible, Adam and Eve's son Cain kills his brother Abel, becoming the first murderer.

5. Here, the *testament* is a statement of beliefs or opinions offered as evidence of the truth.

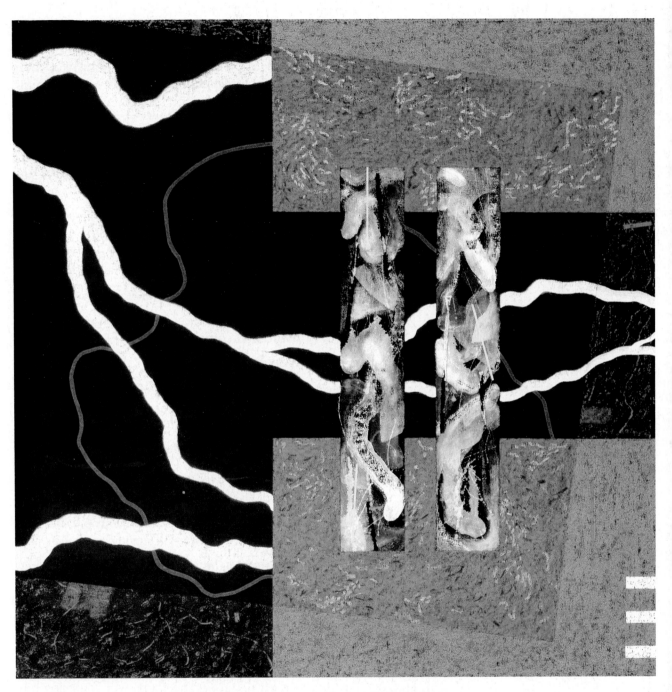

Window View-Scapeology #9, 1995. Nanette Carter. Oil on canvas, 41 x 40 in. Sande Webster Gallery, Philadelphia, PA.

Viewing the painting: Look closely at the painting. In what ways might it mirror the events and feelings evident so far in act 3?

and never saw no sign they had dealings with the Devil.

[PARRIS *nervously moves over and reads over* DANFORTH's *shoulder.*]

DANFORTH. [*Glancing down a long list.*] How many names are here?

FRANCIS. Ninety-one, Your Excellency.

PARRIS. [*Sweating.*] These people should be summoned. [DANFORTH *looks up at him questioningly.*] For questioning.

FRANCIS. [*Trembling with anger.*] Mr. Danforth, I gave them all my word no harm would come to them for signing this.

PARRIS. This is a clear attack upon the court!

HALE. [*To* PARRIS, *trying to contain himself.*] Is every defense an attack upon the court? Can no one—?

PARRIS. All innocent and Christian people are happy for the courts in Salem! These people are gloomy for it. [*To* DANFORTH *directly.*] And I think you will want to know, from each and every one of them, what discontents them with you!

HATHORNE. I think they ought to be examined, sir.

DANFORTH. It is not necessarily an attack, I think. Yet—

FRANCIS. These are all covenanted Christians, sir.

DANFORTH. Then I am sure they may have nothing to fear. [*Hands* CHEEVER *the paper.*] Mr. Cheever, have warrants drawn for all of these—arrest for examination. [*To* PROCTOR.] Now, Mister, what other information do you have for us? [FRANCIS *is still standing, horrified.*] You may sit, Mr. Nurse.

FRANCIS. I have brought trouble on these people; I have—

DANFORTH. No, old man, you have not hurt these people if they are of good conscience. But you must understand, sir, that a person is either with this court or he must be counted against it, there be no road between. This is a sharp time, now, a precise time—we live no longer in the dusky afternoon when evil mixed itself with good and befuddled the world. Now, by God's grace, the shining sun is up, and them that fear not light will surely praise it. I hope you will be one of those. [MARY WARREN *suddenly sobs.*] She's not hearty, I see.

PROCTOR. No, she's not, sir. [*To* MARY, *bending to her, holding her hand, quietly.*] Now remember what the angel Raphael said to the boy Tobias. Remember it.

MARY WARREN. [*Hardly audible.*] Aye.

PROCTOR. "Do that which is good, and no harm shall come to thee."

MARY WARREN. Aye.

DANFORTH. Come, man, we wait you.

[MARSHAL HERRICK *returns, and takes his post at the door.*]

GILES. John, my deposition, give him mine.

PROCTOR. Aye. [*He hands* DANFORTH *another paper.*] This is Mr. Corey's deposition.

DANFORTH. Oh? [*He looks down at it. Now* HATHORNE *comes behind him and reads with him.*]

HATHORNE. [*Suspiciously.*] What lawyer drew this, Corey?

GILES. You know I never hired a lawyer in my life, Hathorne.

DANFORTH. [*Finishing the reading.*] It is very well phrased. My compliments. Mr. Parris, if Mr. Putnam is in the court, will you bring him in? [HATHORNE *takes the deposition, and walks to the window with it.* PARRIS *goes into the court.*] You have no legal training, Mr. Corey?

GILES. [*Very pleased.*] I have the best, sir—I am thirty-three time in court in my life. And always plaintiff, too.

DANFORTH. Oh, then you're much put-upon.

GILES. I am never put-upon; I know my rights, sir, and I will have them. You know, your father tried a case of mine—might be thirty-five year ago, I think.

DANFORTH. Indeed.

GILES. He never spoke to you of it?

DANFORTH. No, I cannot recall it.

GILES. That's strange, he give me nine pound damages. He were a fair judge, your father. Y'see, I had a white mare that time, and this fellow come to borrow the mare—[Enter PARRIS with THOMAS PUTNAM. *When he sees* PUTNAM, GILES' *ease goes; he is hard.*] Aye, there he is.

DANFORTH. Mr. Putnam, I have here an accusation by Mr. Corey against you. He states that you coldly prompted your daughter to cry witchery upon George Jacobs that is now in jail.

PUTNAM. It is a lie.

DANFORTH. [*Turning to* GILES.] Mr. Putnam states your charge is a lie. What say you to that?

GILES. [*Furious, his fists clenched.*] A fart on Thomas Putnam, that is what I say to that!

DANFORTH. What proof do you submit for your charge, sir?

GILES. My proof is there! [*Pointing to the paper.*] If Jacobs hangs for a witch he forfeit up his property—that's law! And there is none but Putnam with the coin to buy so great a piece. This man is killing his neighbors for their land!

DANFORTH. But proof, sir, proof.

GILES. [*Pointing at his deposition.*] The proof is there! I have it from an honest man who heard Putnam say it! The day his daughter cried out on Jacobs, he said she'd given him a fair gift of land.

HATHORNE. And the name of this man?

GILES. [*Taken aback.*] What name?

HATHORNE. The man that give you this information.

GILES. [*Hesitates, then.*] Why, I—I cannot give you his name.

HATHORNE. And why not?

GILES. [*Hesitates, then bursts out.*] You know well why not! He'll lay in jail if I give his name!

HATHORNE. This is contempt of the court, Mr. Danforth!

DANFORTH. [*To avoid that.*] You will surely tell us the name.

GILES. I will not give you no name. I mentioned my wife's name once and I'll burn in hell long enough for that. I stand mute.

DANFORTH. In that case, I have no choice but to arrest you for contempt of this court, do you know that?

GILES. This is a hearing; you cannot clap me for contempt of a hearing.

DANFORTH. Oh, it is a proper lawyer! Do you wish me to declare the court in full session here? Or will you give me good reply?

GILES. [*Faltering.*] I cannot give you no name, sir, I cannot.

DANFORTH. You are a foolish old man. Mr. Cheever, begin the record. The court is now in session. I ask you, Mr. Corey—

PROCTOR. [*Breaking in.*] Your Honor—he has the story in confidence, sir, and he—

PARRIS. The Devil lives on such confidences! [*To* DANFORTH.] Without confidences there could be no conspiracy, Your Honor!

HATHORNE. I think it must be broken, sir.

DANFORTH. [*To* GILES.] Old man, if your informant tells the truth let him come here openly like a decent man. But if he hide in anonymity I must know why. Now sir, the government and central church demand of you the name of him who reported Mr. Thomas Putnam a common murderer.

HALE. Excellency—

DANFORTH. Mr. Hale.

HALE. We cannot blink it more. There is a prodigious fear of this court in the country—

DANFORTH. Then there is a prodigious guilt in the country. Are *you* afraid to be questioned here?

HALE. I may only fear the Lord, sir, but there is fear in the country nevertheless.

DANFORTH. [*Angered now.*] Reproach[6] me not with the fear in the country; there is fear in the country because there is a moving plot to topple Christ in the country!

HALE. But it does not follow that everyone accused is part of it.

DANFORTH. No uncorrupted man may fear this court, Mr. Hale! None! [*To* GILES.] You are under arrest in contempt of this court. Now sit you down and take counsel with yourself, or you will be set in the jail until you decide to answer all questions.

[GILES COREY *makes a rush for* PUTNAM. PROCTOR *lunges and holds him.*]

PROCTOR. No, Giles!

GILES. [*Over* PROCTOR's *shoulder at* PUTNAM.] I'll cut your throat, Putnam, I'll kill you yet!

PROCTOR. [*Forcing him into a chair.*] Peace, Giles, peace. [*Releasing him.*] We'll prove ourselves. Now we will. [*He starts to turn to* DANFORTH.]

GILES. Say nothin' more, John. [*Pointing at* DANFORTH.] He's only playin' you! He means to hang us all!

[MARY WARREN *bursts into sobs.*]

DANFORTH. This is a court of law, Mister. I'll have no effrontery[7] here!

PROCTOR. Forgive him, sir, for his old age. Peace, Giles, we'll prove it all now. [*He lifts up* MARY's *chin.*] You cannot weep, Mary. Remember the angel, what he say to the boy. Hold to it, now; there is your rock. [MARY *quiets. He takes out a paper, and turns to* DANFORTH.] This is Mary Warren's deposition. I—I would ask you remember, sir, while you read it, that until two week ago she were no different than the other children are today. [*He is speaking reasonably, restraining all his fears, his anger, his anxiety.*] You saw her scream, she howled, she swore familiar spirits choked her; she even testified that Satan, in the form of women now in jail, tried to win her soul away, and then when she refused—

DANFORTH. We know all this.

PROCTOR. Aye, sir. She swears now that she never saw Satan; nor any spirit, vague or clear, that Satan may have sent to hurt her. And she declares her friends are lying now.

[PROCTOR *starts to hand* DANFORTH *the deposition, and* HALE *comes up to* DANFORTH *in a trembling state.*]

HALE. Excellency, a moment. I think this goes to the heart of the matter.

DANFORTH. [*With deep misgivings.*] It surely does.

HALE. I cannot say he is an honest man; I know him little. But in all justice, sir, a claim so weighty cannot be argued by a farmer. In God's name, sir, stop here; send him home and let him come again with a lawyer—

DANFORTH. [*Patiently.*] Now look you, Mr. Hale—

HALE. Excellency, I have signed seventy-two death warrants; I am a minister of the Lord, and I dare not take a life without there be a proof so <u>immaculate</u> no slightest qualm[8] of conscience may doubt it.

---

6. To *reproach* is to blame or to express disapproval of.
7. *Effrontery* is boldness and disrespect.

---

8. *Qualm* (kwäm) means "doubt."

Vocabulary
immaculate (i mak′ yə lit) *adj.* unblemished; flawless; pure

DANFORTH. Mr. Hale, you surely do not doubt my justice.

HALE. I have this morning signed away the soul of Rebecca Nurse, Your Honor. I'll not conceal it, my hand shakes yet as with a wound! I pray you, sir, *this* argument let lawyers present to you.

DANFORTH. Mr. Hale, believe me; for a man of such terrible learning you are most bewildered—I hope you will forgive me. I have been thirty-two year at the bar, sir, and I should be confounded were I called upon to defend these people. Let you consider, now—[*To* PROCTOR *and the others.*] And I bid you all do likewise. In an ordinary crime, how does one defend the accused? One calls up witnesses to prove his innocence. But witchcraft is *ipso facto,*[9] on its face and by its nature, an invisible crime, is it not? Therefore, who may possibly be witness to it? The witch and the victim. None other. Now we cannot hope the witch will accuse herself; granted? Therefore, we must rely upon her victims—and they do testify, the children certainly do testify. As for the witches, none will deny that we are most eager for all their confessions. Therefore, what is left for a lawyer to bring out? I think I have made my point. Have I not?

HALE. But this child claims the girls are not truthful, and if they are not—

DANFORTH. That is precisely what I am about to consider, sir. What more may you ask of me? Unless you doubt my probity?[10]

HALE. [*Defeated.*] I surely do not, sir. Let you consider it, then.

DANFORTH. And let you put your heart to rest. Her deposition, Mr. Proctor.

[PROCTOR *hands it to him.* HATHORNE *rises, goes beside* DANFORTH, *and starts reading.* PARRIS *comes to his other side.* DANFORTH *looks at* JOHN PROCTOR, *then proceeds to read.* HALE *gets up, finds position near the judge, reads too.* PROCTOR *glances at* GILES. FRANCIS *prays silently, hands pressed together.* CHEEVER *waits placidly, the sublime official, dutiful.* MARY WARREN *sobs once.* JOHN PROCTOR *touches her head reassuringly. Presently* DANFORTH *lifts his eyes, stands up, takes out a kerchief and blows his nose. The others stand aside as he moves in thought toward the window.*]

PARRIS. [*Hardly able to contain his anger and fear.*] I should like to question—

DANFORTH. [*His first real outburst, in which his contempt for* PARRIS *is clear.*] Mr. Parris, I bid you be silent! [*He stands in silence, looking out the window. Now, having established that he will set the gait.*][11] Mr. Cheever, will you go into the court and bring the children here? [CHEEVER *gets up and goes out upstage.* DANFORTH *now turns to* MARY.] Mary Warren, how came you to this turnabout? Has Mr. Proctor threatened you for this deposition?

MARY WARREN. No, sir.

DANFORTH. Has he ever threatened you?

MARY WARREN. [*Weaker.*] No, sir.

DANFORTH. [*Sensing a weakening.*] Has he threatened you?

MARY WARREN. No, sir.

DANFORTH. Then you tell me that you sat in my court, callously lying, when you knew that people would hang by your evidence? [*She does not answer.*] Answer me!

MARY WARREN. [*Almost inaudibly.*] I did, sir.

DANFORTH. How were you instructed in your life? Do you not know that God damns all liars? [*She cannot speak.*] Or is it now that you lie?

MARY WARREN. No, sir—I am with God now.

DANFORTH. You are with God now.

---

9. The Latin legal term *ipso facto* means, literally, "by that very fact" or "by the fact itself."
10. *Probity* involves moral excellence, integrity, and honesty.
11. To *set the gait* is an expression that means "to determine how a matter will proceed."

The Crucible

MARY WARREN. Aye, sir.

DANFORTH. [Containing himself.] I will tell you this—you are either lying now, or you were lying in the court, and in either case you have committed perjury[12] and you will go to jail for it. You cannot lightly say you lied, Mary. Do you know that?

MARY WARREN. I cannot lie no more. I am with God, I am with God.

[But she breaks into sobs at the thought of it, and the right door opens, and enter SUSANNA WAL-COTT, MERCY LEWIS, BETTY PARRIS, and finally ABIGAIL. CHEEVER comes to DANFORTH.]

CHEEVER. Ruth Putnam's not in the court, sir, nor the other children.

DANFORTH. These will be sufficient. Sit you down, children. [Silently they sit.] Your friend, Mary Warren, has given us a deposition. In which she swears that she never saw familiar spirits, apparitions, nor any manifest of the Devil.[13] She claims as well that none of you have seen these things either. [Slight pause.] Now, children, this is a court of law. The law, based upon the Bible, and the Bible, writ by Almighty God, forbid the practice of witch-craft, and describe death as the penalty thereof. But likewise, children, the law and Bible damn all bearers of false witness. [Slight pause.] Now then. It does not escape me that this deposition may be devised to blind us; it may well be that Mary Warren has been con-quered by Satan, who sends her here to distract our sacred purpose. If so, her neck will break for it. But if she speak true, I bid you now drop your guile and confess your pretense, for a quick confession will go easier with you. [Pause.] Abigail Williams, rise. [ABIGAIL slowly rises.] Is there any truth in this?

ABIGAIL. No, sir.

DANFORTH. [Thinks, glances at MARY, then back to ABIGAIL.] Children, a very augur bit[14] will now be turned into your souls until your honesty is proved. Will either of you change your positions now, or do you force me to hard questioning?

ABIGAIL. I have naught to change, sir. She lies.

DANFORTH. [To MARY.] You would still go on with this?

MARY WARREN. [Faintly.] Aye, sir.

DANFORTH. [Turning to ABIGAIL.] A poppet were discovered in Mr. Proctor's house, stabbed by a needle. Mary Warren claims that you sat beside her in the court when she made it, and that you saw her make it and witnessed how she herself stuck her needle into it for safe-keeping. What say you to that?

ABIGAIL. [With a slight note of indignation.] It is a lie, sir.

DANFORTH. [After a slight pause.] While you worked for Mr. Proctor, did you see poppets in that house?

ABIGAIL. Goody Proctor always kept poppets.

PROCTOR. Your Honor, my wife never kept no poppets. Mary Warren confesses it was her poppet.

CHEEVER. Your Excellency.

DANFORTH. Mr. Cheever.

CHEEVER. When I spoke with Goody Proctor in that house, she said she never kept no pop-pets. But she said she did keep poppets when she were a girl.

---

12. *Perjury* is the act of swearing under oath to the truth of something that one knows to be untrue.

13. *Familiar spirits* are supernatural beings (not ghosts) believed to serve demons or humans; *apparitions* are ghosts of dead people; and a *manifest of the Devil* is a form in which the devil reveals himself.

14. Here, *augur bit* refers to an auger, a tool for boring holes.

Vocabulary
guile (gīl) *n.* cunning; deceit; slyness

PROCTOR. She has not been a girl these fifteen years, Your Honor.

HATHORNE. But a poppet will keep fifteen years, will it not?

PROCTOR. It will keep if it is kept, but Mary Warren swears she never saw no poppets in my house, nor anyone else.

PARRIS. Why could there not have been poppets hid where no one ever saw them?

PROCTOR. [*Furious.*] There might also be a dragon with five legs in my house, but no one has ever seen it.

PARRIS. We are here, Your Honor, precisely to discover what no one has ever seen.

PROCTOR. Mr. Danforth, what profit this girl to turn herself about? What may Mary Warren gain but hard questioning and worse?

DANFORTH. You are charging Abigail Williams with a marvelous cool plot to murder, do you understand that?

PROCTOR. I do, sir. I believe she means to murder.

DANFORTH. [*Pointing at* ABIGAIL, *incredulously.*][15] This child would murder your wife?

PROCTOR. It is not a child. Now hear me, sir. In the sight of the congregation she were twice this year put out of this meetin' house for laughter during prayer.

DANFORTH. [*Shocked, turning to* ABIGAIL.] What's this? Laughter during—!

PARRIS. Excellency, she were under Tituba's power at that time, but she is solemn now.

---

15. *Incredulously* means "in a disbelieving manner."

The Crucible

GILES. Aye, now she is solemn and goes to hang people!

DANFORTH. Quiet, man.

HATHORNE. Surely it have no bearing on the question, sir. He charges contemplation of murder.

DANFORTH. Aye. [*He studies* ABIGAIL *for a moment, then.*] Continue, Mr. Proctor.

PROCTOR. Mary. Now tell the Governor how you danced in the woods.

PARRIS. [*Instantly.*] Excellency, since I come to Salem this man is blackening my name. He—

DANFORTH. In a moment, sir. [*To* MARY WARREN, *sternly, and surprised.*] What is this dancing?

MARY WARREN. I—[*She glances at* ABIGAIL, *who is staring down at her remorselessly. Then, appealing to* PROCTOR.] Mr. Proctor—

PROCTOR. [*Taking it right up.*] Abigail leads the girls to the woods, Your Honor, and they have danced there naked—

PARRIS. Your Honor, this—

PROCTOR. [*At once.*] Mr. Parris discovered them himself in the dead of night! There's the "child" she is!

DANFORTH. [*It is growing into a nightmare, and he turns, astonished, to* PARRIS.] Mr. Parris—

PARRIS. I can only say, sir, that I never found any of them naked, and this man is—

DANFORTH. But you discovered them dancing in the woods? [*Eyes on* PARRIS, *he points at* ABIGAIL.] Abigail?

HALE. Excellency, when I first arrived from Beverly, Mr. Parris told me that.

DANFORTH. Do you deny it, Mr. Parris?

PARRIS. I do not, sir, but I never saw any of them naked.

DANFORTH. But she have *danced?*

PARRIS. [*Unwillingly.*] Aye, sir.

[DANFORTH, *as though with new eyes, looks at* ABIGAIL.]

HATHORNE. Excellency, will you permit me? [*He points at* MARY WARREN.]

DANFORTH. [*With great worry.*] Pray, proceed.

HATHORNE. You say you never saw no spirits, Mary, were never threatened or afflicted by any manifest of the Devil or the Devil's agents.

MARY WARREN. [*Very faintly.*] No, sir.

HATHORNE. [*With a gleam of victory.*] And yet, when people accused of witchery confronted you in court, you would faint, saying their spirits came out of their bodies and choked you—

MARY WARREN. That were pretense, sir.

DANFORTH. I cannot hear you.

MARY WARREN. Pretense, sir.

PARRIS. But you did turn cold, did you not? I myself picked you up many times, and your skin were icy. Mr. Danforth, you—

DANFORTH. I saw that many times.

PROCTOR. She only pretended to faint, Your Excellency. They're all marvelous pretenders.

HATHORNE. Then can she pretend to faint now?

PROCTOR. Now?

PARRIS. Why not? Now there are no spirits attacking her, for none in this room is accused of witchcraft. So let her turn herself cold now, let her pretend she is attacked now, let her faint. [*He turns to* MARY WARREN.] Faint!

MARY WARREN. Faint?

PARRIS. Aye, faint. Prove to us how you pretended in the court so many times.

MARY WARREN. [*Looking to* PROCTOR.] I—cannot faint now, sir.

Vocabulary

contemplation (kon′ təm plā′shən) *n.* the act of thinking about something long and seriously

PROCTOR. [*Alarmed, quietly.*] Can you not pretend it?

MARY WARREN. I—[*She looks about as though searching for the passion to faint.*] I—have no *sense* of it now, I—

DANFORTH. Why? What is lacking now?

MARY WARREN. I—cannot tell, sir, I—

DANFORTH. Might it be that here we have no afflicting spirit loose, but in the court there were some?

MARY WARREN. I never saw no spirits.

PARRIS. Then see no spirits now, and prove to us that you can faint by your own will, as you claim.

MARY WARREN. [*Stares, searching for the emotion of it, and then shakes her head.*] I—cannot do it.

PARRIS. Then you will confess, will you not? It were attacking spirits made you faint!

MARY WARREN. No, sir, I—

PARRIS. Your Excellency, this is a trick to blind the court!

MARY WARREN. It's not a trick! [*She stands.*] I—I used to faint because I—I thought I saw spirits.

DANFORTH. *Thought* you saw them!

MARY WARREN. But I did not, Your Honor.

HATHORNE. How could you think you saw them unless you saw them?

MARY WARREN. I—I cannot tell how, but I did. I—I heard the other girls screaming, and you, Your Honor, you seemed to believe them, and I—It were only sport in the beginning, sir, but then the whole world cried spirits, spirits, and I—I promise you, Mr. Danforth, I only thought I saw them but I did not.

[*DANFORTH peers at her.*]

PARRIS. [*Smiling, but nervous because DANFORTH seems to be struck by MARY WARREN's story.*] Surely Your Excellency is not taken by this simple lie.

DANFORTH. [*Turning worriedly to ABIGAIL.*] Abigail. I bid you now search your heart and tell me this—and beware of it, child, to God every soul is precious and His vengeance is terrible on them that take life without cause. Is it possible, child, that the spirits you have seen are illusion only, some deception that may cross your mind when—

ABIGAIL. Why, this—this—is a base question, sir.

DANFORTH. Child, I would have you consider it—

ABIGAIL. I have been hurt, Mr. Danforth; I have seen my blood runnin' out! I have been near to murdered every day because I done my duty pointing out the Devil's people—and this is my reward? To be mistrusted, denied, questioned like a—

DANFORTH. [*Weakening.*] Child, I do not mistrust you—

ABIGAIL. [*In an open threat.*] Let you beware, Mr. Danforth. Think you to be so mighty that the power of Hell may not turn *your* wits? Beware of it! There is—[*Suddenly, from an accusatory attitude, her face turns, looking into the air above—it is truly frightened.*]

DANFORTH. [*Apprehensively.*] What is it, child?

ABIGAIL. [*Looking about in the air, clasping her arms about her as though cold.*] I—I know not. A wind, a cold wind, has come. [*Her eyes fall on MARY WARREN.*]

MARY WARREN. [*Terrified, pleading.*] Abby!

MERCY LEWIS. [*Shivering.*] Your Honor, I freeze!

PROCTOR. They're pretending!

HATHORNE. [*Touching ABIGAIL's hand.*] She is cold, Your Honor, touch her!

MERCY LEWIS. [*Through chattering teeth.*] Mary, do you send this shadow on me?

MARY WARREN. Lord, save me!

SUSANNA WALCOTT. I freeze, I freeze!

ABIGAIL. [*Shivering visibly.*] It is a wind, a wind!

MARY WARREN. Abby, don't do that!

DANFORTH. [*Himself engaged and entered by ABIGAIL.*] Mary Warren, do you witch her? I say to you, do you send your spirit out?

[*With a hysterical cry MARY WARREN starts to run. PROCTOR catches her.*]

MARY WARREN. [*Almost collapsing.*] Let me go, Mr. Proctor, I cannot, I cannot—

ABIGAIL. [*Crying to Heaven.*] Oh, Heavenly Father, take away this shadow!

[*Without warning or hesitation, PROCTOR leaps at ABIGAIL and, grabbing her by the hair, pulls her to her feet. She screams in pain. DAN-FORTH, astonished, cries, "What are you about?" and HATHORNE and PARRIS call,* "Take your hands off her!" *and out of it all comes PROCTOR's roaring voice.*]

PROCTOR. How do you call Heaven! Whore![16] Whore!

[*HERRICK breaks PROCTOR from her.*]

HERRICK. John!

DANFORTH. Man! Man, what do you—

PROCTOR. [*Breathless and in agony.*] It is a whore!

DANFORTH. [*Dumfounded.*][17] You charge—?

ABIGAIL. Mr. Danforth, he is lying!

---

16. Here, *whore* refers to a "loose" woman, not that she has taken money for sexual services.

17. *Dumfounded* means "speechless."

PROCTOR. Mark her! Now she'll suck a scream to stab me with, but—

DANFORTH. You will prove this! This will not pass!

PROCTOR. [*Trembling, his life collapsing about him.*] I have known her, sir. I have known her.

DANFORTH. You—you are a lecher?

FRANCIS. [*Horrified.*] John, you cannot say such a—

PROCTOR. Oh, Francis, I wish you had some evil in you that you might know me! [*To DANFORTH.*] A man will not cast away his good name. You surely know that.

DANFORTH. [*Dumfounded.*] In—in what time? In what place?

PROCTOR. [*His voice about to break, and his shame great.*] In the proper place—where my beasts are bedded. On the last night of my joy, some eight months past. She used to serve me in my house, sir. [*He has to clamp his jaw to keep from weeping.*] A man may think God sleeps, but God sees everything, I know it now. I beg you, sir, I beg you—see her what she is. My wife, my dear good wife, took this girl soon after, sir, and put her out on the highroad. And being what she is, a lump of vanity, sir—[*He is being overcome.*] Excellency, forgive me, forgive me. [*Angrily against himself, he turns away from the Governor for a moment. Then, as though to cry out is his only means of speech left.*] She thinks to dance with me on my wife's grave! And well she might, for I thought of her softly. God help me, I lusted, and there *is* a promise in such sweat. But it is a whore's vengeance, and you must see it; I set myself entirely in your hands. I know you must see it now.

DANFORTH. [*Blanched,*[18] *in horror, turning to ABIGAIL.*] You deny every scrap and tittle of this?

ABIGAIL. If I must answer that, I will leave and I will not come back again!

---

18. Here, *blanched* means "drained of color."

[*DANFORTH seems unsteady.*]

PROCTOR. I have made a bell of my honor! I have rung the doom of my good name—you will believe me, Mr. Danforth! My wife is innocent, except she knew a whore when she saw one!

ABIGAIL. [*Stepping up to DANFORTH.*] What look do you give me? [*DANFORTH cannot speak.*] I'll not have such looks! [*She turns and starts for the door.*]

DANFORTH. You will remain where you are! [*HERRICK steps into her path. She comes up short, fire in her eyes.*] Mr. Parris, go into the court and bring Goodwife Proctor out.

PARRIS. [*Objecting.*] Your Honor, this is all a—

DANFORTH. [*Sharply to PARRIS.*] Bring her out! And tell her not one word of what's been spoken here. And let you knock before you enter. [*PARRIS goes out.*] Now we shall touch the bottom of this swamp. [*To PROCTOR.*] Your wife, you say, is an honest woman.

PROCTOR. In her life, sir, she have never lied. There are them that cannot sing, and them that cannot weep—my wife cannot lie. I have paid much to learn it, sir.

DANFORTH. And when she put this girl out of your house, she put her out for a harlot?

PROCTOR. Aye, sir.

DANFORTH. And knew her for a harlot?

PROCTOR. Aye, sir, she knew her for a harlot.

DANFORTH. Good then. [*To ABIGAIL.*] And if she tell me, child, it were for harlotry, may God spread His mercy on you! [*There is a knock. He calls to the door.*] Hold! [*To ABIGAIL.*] Turn your back. Turn your back. [*To PROCTOR.*] Do likewise. [*Both turn their backs—ABIGAIL with indignant slowness.*] Now let neither of you turn to face Goody Proctor. No one in this room is to speak one word, or raise a gesture aye or nay. [*He turns toward the door, calls.*] Enter! [*The door opens. ELIZABETH enters with PARRIS. PARRIS leaves her. She stands alone,*

The Crucible

her eyes looking for PROCTOR.] Mr. Cheever, report this testimony in all exactness. Are you ready?

CHEEVER. Ready, sir.

DANFORTH. Come here, woman. [ELIZABETH *comes to him, glancing at* PROCTOR'S *back.*] Look at me only, not at your husband. In my eyes only.

ELIZABETH. [*Faintly.*] Good, sir.

DANFORTH. We are given to understand that at one time you dismissed your servant, Abigail Williams.

ELIZABETH. That is true, sir.

DANFORTH. For what cause did you dismiss her? [*Slight pause. Then* ELIZABETH *tries to glance at* PROCTOR.] You will look in my eyes only and not at your husband. The answer is in your memory and you need no help to give it to me. Why did you dismiss Abigail Williams?

ELIZABETH. [*Not knowing what to say, sensing a situation, wetting her lips to stall for time.*] She—dissatisfied me. [*Pause.*] And my husband.

DANFORTH. In what way dissatisfied you?

ELIZABETH. She were—[*She glances at* PROCTOR *for a cue.*]

DANFORTH. Woman, look at me! [ELIZABETH *does.*] Were she slovenly?[19] Lazy? What disturbance did she cause?

ELIZABETH. Your Honor, I—in that time I were sick. And I—My husband is a good and righteous man. He is never drunk as some are, nor wastin' his time at the shovelboard,[20] but always at his work. But in my sickness—you see, sir, I were a long time sick after my last baby, and I thought I saw my husband somewhat turning from me. And this girl—[*She turns to* ABIGAIL.]

DANFORTH. Look at me.

ELIZABETH. Aye, sir. Abigail Williams—[*She breaks off.*]

DANFORTH. What of Abigail Williams?

ELIZABETH. I came to think he fancied her. And so one night I lost my wits, I think, and put her out on the highroad.

DANFORTH. Your husband—did he indeed turn from you?

ELIZABETH. [*In agony.*] My husband—is a goodly man, sir.

DANFORTH. Then he did not turn from you.

ELIZABETH. [*Starting to glance at* PROCTOR.] He—

DANFORTH. [*Reaches out and holds her face, then.*] Look at me! To your own knowledge, has John Proctor ever committed the crime of lechery? [*In a crisis of indecision she cannot speak.*] Answer my question! Is your husband a lecher!

ELIZABETH. [*Faintly.*] No, sir.

DANFORTH. Remove her, Marshal.

PROCTOR. Elizabeth, tell the truth!

DANFORTH. She has spoken. Remove her!

PROCTOR. [*Crying out.*] Elizabeth, I have confessed it!

ELIZABETH. Oh, God! [*The door closes behind her.*]

PROCTOR. She only thought to save my name!

HALE. Excellency, it is a natural lie to tell; I beg you, stop now before another is condemned! I may shut my conscience to it no more—private vengeance is working through this testimony! From the beginning this man has struck me true. By my oath to Heaven, I believe him now, and I pray you call back his wife before we—

DANFORTH. She spoke nothing of lechery, and this man has lied!

HALE. I believe him! [*Pointing at* ABIGAIL.] This girl has always struck me false! She has—

[ABIGAIL, *with a weird, wild, chilling cry, screams up to the ceiling.*]

---

19. To be *slovenly* is to be untidy or careless, especially in appearance.
20. *Shovelboard* is a tabletop version of shuffleboard.

ABIGAIL. You will not! Begone! Begone, I say!

DANFORTH. What is it, child? [*But* ABIGAIL, *pointing with fear, is now raising up her frightened eyes, her awed face, toward the ceiling—the girls are doing the same—and now* HATHORNE, HALE, PUTNAM, CHEEVER, HERRICK, *and* DANFORTH *do the same.*] What's there? [*He lowers his eyes from the ceiling, and now he is frightened; there is real tension in his voice.*] Child! [*She is transfixed—with all the girls, she is whimpering open-mouthed, agape at the ceiling.*] Girls! Why do you—?

MERCY LEWIS. [*Pointing.*] It's on the beam! Behind the rafter!

DANFORTH. [*Looking up.*] Where!

ABIGAIL. Why—? [*She gulps.*] Why do you come, yellow bird?

PROCTOR. Where's a bird? I see no bird!

ABIGAIL. [*To the ceiling.*] My face? My face?

PROCTOR. Mr. Hale—

DANFORTH. Be quiet!!

PROCTOR. [*To* HALE.] Do you see a bird?

DANFORTH. Be quiet!

ABIGAIL. [*To the ceiling, in a genuine conversation with the "bird," as though trying to talk it out of attacking her.*] But God made my face; you cannot want to tear my face. Envy is a deadly sin, Mary.

MARY WARREN. [*On her feet with a spring, and horrified, pleading.*] Abby!

ABIGAIL. [*Unperturbed, continuing to the "bird."*] Oh, Mary, this is a black art to change your shape. No, I cannot, I cannot stop my mouth; it's God's work I do.

MARY WARREN. Abby, I'm *here!*

PROCTOR. [*Frantically.*] They're pretending, Mr. Danforth!

ABIGAIL. [*Now she takes a backward step, as though in fear the bird will swoop down momentarily.*] Oh, please, Mary! Don't come down.

SUSANNA WALCOTT. Her claws, she's stretching her claws!

PROCTOR. Lies, lies.

ABIGAIL. [*Backing further, eyes still fixed above.*] Mary, please don't hurt me!

MARY WARREN. [*To* DANFORTH.] I'm not hurting her!

DANFORTH. [*To* MARY WARREN.] Why does she see this vision?

MARY WARREN. She sees nothin'!

ABIGAIL. [*Now staring full front as though hypnotized, and mimicking the exact tone of* MARY WARREN's *cry.*] She sees nothin'!

MARY WARREN. [*Pleading.*] Abby, you mustn't!

ABIGAIL AND ALL THE GIRLS. [*All transfixed.*] Abby, you mustn't!

MARY WARREN. [*To all the girls.*] I'm here, I'm here!

GIRLS. I'm here, I'm here!

DANFORTH. [*Horrified.*] Mary Warren! Draw back your spirit out of them!

MARY WARREN. Mr. Danforth!

GIRLS. [*Cutting her off.*] Mr. Danforth!

DANFORTH. Have you compacted with the Devil? Have you?

MARY WARREN. Never, never!

GIRLS. Never, never!

DANFORTH. [*Growing hysterical.*] Why can they only repeat you?

PROCTOR. Give me a whip—I'll stop it!

MARY WARREN. They're sporting. They—!

GIRLS. They're sporting!

Vocabulary
unperturbed (un pər turbd´) *adj.* undisturbed; calm

MARY WARREN. [*Turning on them all hysterically and stamping her feet.*] Abby, stop it!

GIRLS. [*Stamping their feet.*] Abby, stop it!

MARY WARREN. Stop it!

GIRLS. Stop it!

MARY WARREN. [*Screaming it out at the top of her lungs, and raising her fists.*] Stop it!!

GIRLS. [*Raising their fists.*] Stop it!!

[MARY WARREN, *utterly confounded, and becoming overwhelmed by* ABIGAIL's—*and the girls'*—*utter conviction, starts to whimper, hands half raised, powerless, and all the girls begin whimpering exactly as she does.*]

DANFORTH. A little while ago you were afflicted. Now it seems you afflict others; where did you find this power?

MARY WARREN. [*Staring at* ABIGAIL.] I—have no power.

GIRLS. I have no power.

PROCTOR. They're gulling[21] you, Mister!

DANFORTH. Why did you turn about this past two weeks? You have seen the Devil, have you not?

HALE. [*Indicating* ABIGAIL *and the girls.*] You cannot believe them!

MARY WARREN. I—

PROCTOR. [*Sensing her weakening.*] Mary, God damns all liars!

DANFORTH. [*Pounding it into her.*] You have seen the Devil, you have made compact with Lucifer, have you not?

PROCTOR. God damns liars, Mary!

[MARY *utters something unintelligible, staring at* ABIGAIL, *who keeps watching the "bird" above.*]

DANFORTH. I cannot hear you. What do you say? [MARY *utters again unintelligibly.*] You will confess yourself or you will hang! [*He turns her*

roughly *to face him.*] Do you know who I am? I say you will hang if you do not open with me!

PROCTOR. Mary, remember the angel Raphael—do that which is good and—

ABIGAIL. [*Pointing upward.*] The wings! Her wings are spreading! Mary, please, don't, don't—!

HALE. I see nothing, Your Honor!

DANFORTH. Do you confess this power! [*He is an inch from her face.*] Speak!

ABIGAIL. She's going to come down! She's walking the beam!

DANFORTH. Will you speak!

MARY WARREN. [*Staring in horror.*] I cannot!

GIRLS. I cannot!

PARRIS. Cast the Devil out! Look him in the face! Trample him! We'll save you, Mary, only stand fast against him and—

ABIGAIL. [*Looking up.*] Look out! She's coming down!

[*She and all the girls run to one wall, shielding their eyes. And now, as though cornered, they let out a gigantic scream, and* MARY, *as though infected, opens her mouth and screams with them. Gradually* ABIGAIL *and the girls leave off, until only* MARY *is left there, staring up at the "bird," screaming madly. All watch her, horrified by this evident fit.* PROCTOR *strides to her.*]

PROCTOR. Mary, tell the Governor what they—[*He has hardly got a word out, when, seeing him coming for her, she rushes out of his reach, screaming in horror.*]

MARY WARREN. Don't touch me—don't touch me! [*At which the girls halt at the door.*]

PROCTOR. [*Astonished.*] Mary!

MARY WARREN. [*Pointing at* PROCTOR.] You're the Devil's man!

[*He is stopped in his tracks.*]

PARRIS. Praise God!

GIRLS. Praise God!

---

21. *Gulling* means "deceiving."

Sympathizer, 1956. Elaine de Kooning. Oil on canvas, 40¼ x 31 in. Estate of Elaine de Kooning.

Viewing the painting: What are your reactions to this painting? Are they similar to or different from the reactions you have to Mary Warren in act 3? Explain.

PROCTOR. [*Numbed.*] Mary, how—?

MARY WARREN. I'll not hang with you! I love God, I love God.

DANFORTH. [*To* MARY.] He bid you do the Devil's work?

MARY WARREN. [*Hysterically, indicating* PROC-TOR.] He come at me by night and every day to sign, to sign, to—

DANFORTH. Sign what?

PARRIS. The Devil's book? He come with a book?

MARY WARREN. [*Hysterically, pointing at* PROC-TOR, *fearful of him.*] My name, he want my name. "I'll murder you," he says, "if my wife hangs! We must go and overthrow the court," he says!

[DANFORTH's *hand jerks toward* PROCTOR, *shock and horror in his face.*]

PROCTOR. [*Turning, appealing to* HALE.] Mr. Hale!

MARY WARREN. [*Her sobs beginning.*] He wake me every night, his eyes were like coals and his fingers claw my neck, and I sign, I sign . . .

HALE. Excellency, this child's gone wild!

PROCTOR. [*As* DANFORTH's *wide eyes pour on him.*] Mary, Mary!

MARY WARREN. [*Screaming at him.*] No, I love God; I go your way no more. I love God, I bless God. [*Sobbing, she rushes to* ABIGAIL.] Abby, Abby, I'll never hurt you more! [*They all watch, as* ABIGAIL, *out of her infinite charity, reaches out and draws the sobbing* MARY *to her, and then looks up to* DANFORTH.]

DANFORTH. [*To* PROCTOR.] What are you? [PROCTOR *is beyond speech in his anger.*] You are combined with anti-Christ, are you not? I have seen your power; you will not deny it! What say you, Mister?

HALE. Excellency—

DANFORTH. I will have nothing from you, Mr. Hale! [*To* PROCTOR.] Will you confess yourself befouled with Hell, or do you keep that black allegiance yet? What say you?

PROCTOR. [*His mind wild, breathless.*] I say—I say—God is dead!

PARRIS. Hear it, hear it!

PROCTOR. [*Laughs insanely, then.*] A fire, a fire is burning! I hear the boot of Lucifer, I see his filthy face! And it is my face, and yours, Danforth! For them that quail to bring men out of ignorance, as I have quailed, and as you quail now when you know in all your black hearts that this be fraud—God damns our kind especially, and we will burn, we will burn together!

DANFORTH. Marshal! Take him and Corey with him to the jail!

HALE. [*Starting across to the door.*] I denounce[22] these proceedings!

PROCTOR. You are pulling Heaven down and raising up a whore!

HALE. I denounce these proceedings, I quit this court! [*He slams the door to the outside behind him.*]

DANFORTH. [*Calling to him in a fury.*] Mr. Hale! Mr. Hale!

THE CURTAIN FALLS

---

22. Here, *denounce* means "to publicly pronounce something to be evil."

Responding to Literature

Personal Response

Which image from act 3 had the strongest impact on you? Explain.

RECALL AND INTERPRET

1. How and why does Giles Corey interrupt the court proceedings? What does the response of the judges to him and Francis Nurse suggest about the way the trials are being conducted?
2. Why does Proctor bring Mary Warren to court? How does Mary Warren's confession threaten Danforth, Parris, and Hathorne?
3. At what point does Abigail first begin feeling cold? What effect does this event have on Danforth? What does it suggest about her motives?
4. How does Danforth test Proctor's confession? Hale says that Elizabeth Proctor's response is a "natural" lie, but he condemns Abigail for her "falseness." What might account for the difference in his views?
5. What does Abigail do when Hale gives his opinion of her? What can you infer about the general emotional state surrounding these events?

EVALUATE AND CONNECT

6. What would you identify as the key **conflict** of act 3, and why? Do you consider this struggle the most important conflict of the play so far? Explain. (See Literary Terms Handbook, page R3.)
7. Which character or characters are undergoing a test at this point? How do their situations compare with the situation you described for the Focus Activity on page 912?
8. Theme Connections   Based on the information you read on page 911, do you think Miller successfully compared the HUAC hearings with the Salem witch trials? Why or why not? Use a Venn diagram like the one shown to help organize your ideas.

Literary ELEMENTS

Climax
When you read or see a play, the sequence of plot events builds to a point at which you feel the greatest emotional intensity, interest, or suspense. This point is called the **climax.** Usually the climax is a turning point after which the resolution of a conflict becomes clear.

1. Which event in act 3 do you see as the climax of *The Crucible*?
2. Which conflict or conflicts are now on the way to becoming resolved?

● See **Literary Terms Handbook,** p. R3.

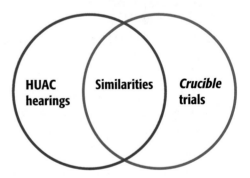

HUAC hearings   Similarities   *Crucible trials*

Literature Groups

Questioning the Questions   A question asked in a way that implies a particular answer is called a leading question. With your group, find examples of leading questions in act 3. Discuss how these questions affect the action of the play. Are these questions deceptive? Do they serve justice? Share your answers with other groups.

Creative Writing

A Revealing Diary   Imagine that you are Abigail Williams or Reverend Hale. Write a series of diary entries to explain your thoughts and motivations during the time period covered in act 3.

📖 **Save your work for your portfolio.**

Skill Minilesson

VOCABULARY • Synonyms—Shades of Meaning

Some words, such as *bad,* are general in their meaning. *Bad* can mean "poorly done," "naughty," or many other things. In many cases, the synonyms for such general words have much more specific meanings. For example, one synonym for *bad* is *vile.*

   Vile crimes are truly evil. *Vile* language is disgusting.

   You can speak and write more effectively if you pay attention to the small differences in the meanings of synonyms.

PRACTICE   Answer each question by thinking about the meanings of the underlined synonyms and selecting the one that is most fitting to the context.

1. Is rotten meat vile or corrupt?

2. If someone interrupts a joke to tell the punch line, is that rudeness or effrontery?

3. Is a fox who tricks the hounds by doubling back on its trail using fraud or guile?

4. When you check your roof for leaks, are you engaged in examination or contemplation?

Before You Read

The Crucible, Act 4

BACKGROUND

The People Behind the Characters
The characters in Miller's play are based on real people, though in some cases, Miller combined several people into one character, adjusted some of the characters' ages, and invented their possible motives. Even so, Miller states, "The fate of each character is exactly that of the historical model, and there is no one in the drama who did not play a similar—and in some cases exactly the same—role in history." For example, shortly after the girls started acting strangely, three women, including one named Tituba, were accused of being witches and were arrested. Before the witch hunt ended, nineteen people had been hanged as witches, and one had been pressed to death for refusing to testify.

VOCABULARY PREVIEW

conciliatory (kən sil′ ē ə tôr′ ē) *adj.* trying to gain the good will of another by friendly acts; p. 985
reprieve (ri prēv′) *n.* official postponement of the carrying out of a sentence; p. 985
retaliation (ri tal′ ē ā′ shən) *n.* the act of repaying an injury or wrong by committing the same, or a similar, act; p. 985

adamant (ad′ ə mənt) *adj.* completely firm and unyielding; p. 985
indictment (in dīt′ mənt) *n.* a formal legal accusation, charging the commission or omission of an act, which is punishable by law; p. 989

[*A cell in Salem jail, that fall.*

At the back is a high barred window; near it, a great, heavy door. Along the walls are two benches.

The place is in darkness but for the moonlight seeping through the bars. It appears empty. Presently footsteps are heard coming down a corridor beyond the wall, keys rattle, and the door swings open. MARSHAL HERRICK *enters with a lantern.*

He is nearly drunk, and heavy-footed. He goes to a bench and nudges a bundle of rags lying on it.]

HERRICK. Sarah, wake up! Sarah Good! [*He then crosses to the other bench.*]

SARAH GOOD. [*Rising in her rags.*] Oh, Majesty! Comin', comin'! Tituba, he's here, His Majesty's come!

HERRICK. Go to the north cell; this place is wanted now. [*He hangs his lantern on the wall.* TITUBA *sits up.*]

TITUBA. That don't look to me like His Majesty; look to me like the marshal.

HERRICK. [*Taking out a flask.*] Get along with you now, clear this place. [*He drinks, and* SARAH GOOD *comes and peers up into his face.*]

SARAH GOOD. Oh, is it you, Marshal! I thought sure you be the devil comin' for us. Could I have a sip of cider for me goin'-away?

HERRICK. [*Handing her the flask.*] And where are you off to, Sarah?

TITUBA. [*As* SARAH *drinks.*] We goin' to Barbados, soon the Devil gits here with the feathers and the wings.

HERRICK. Oh? A happy voyage to you.

SARAH GOOD. A pair of bluebirds wingin' southerly, the two of us! Oh, it be a grand transformation, Marshal! [*She raises the flask to drink again.*]

HERRICK. [*Taking the flask from her lips.*] You'd best give me that or you'll never rise off the ground. Come along now.

TITUBA. I'll speak to him for you, if you desire to come along, Marshal.

HERRICK. I'd not refuse it, Tituba; it's the proper morning to fly into Hell.

TITUBA. Oh, it be no Hell in Barbados. Devil, him be pleasureman in Barbados, him be singin' and dancin' in Barbados. It's you folks—you riles him up 'round here; it be too cold 'round here for that Old Boy. He freeze his soul in Massachusetts, but in Barbados he just as sweet and—[*A bellowing cow is heard, and* TITUBA *leaps up and calls to the window.*] Aye, sir! That's him, Sarah!

SARAH GOOD. I'm here, Majesty! [*They hurriedly pick up their rags as* HOPKINS, *a guard, enters.*]

HOPKINS. The Deputy Governor's arrived.

HERRICK. [*Grabbing* TITUBA.] Come along, come along.

TITUBA. [*Resisting him.*] No, he comin' for me. I goin' home!

HERRICK. [*Pulling her to the door.*] That's not Satan, just a poor old cow with a hatful of milk. Come along now, out with you!

TITUBA. [*Calling to the window.*] Take me home, Devil! Take me home!

SARAH GOOD. [*Following the shouting* TITUBA *out.*] Tell him I'm goin', Tituba! Now you tell him Sarah Good is goin' too!

[*In the corridor outside* TITUBA *calls on*—"*Take me home, Devil; Devil take me home!*" *and* HOPKINS' *voice orders her to move on.* HERRICK *returns and begins to push old rags and straw into a corner. Hearing footsteps, he turns, and enter* DANFORTH *and* JUDGE HATHORNE. *They are in greatcoats and wear hats against the bitter cold. They are followed in by* CHEEVER, *who carries a dispatch case and a flat wooden box containing his writing materials.*]

HERRICK. Good morning, Excellency.

The Crucible

DANFORTH. Where is Mr. Parris?

HERRICK. I'll fetch him. [*He starts for the door.*]

DANFORTH. Marshal. [*HERRICK stops.*] When did Reverend Hale arrive?

HERRICK. It were toward midnight, I think.

DANFORTH. [*Suspiciously.*] What is he about here?

HERRICK. He goes among them that will hang, sir. And he prays with them. He sits with Goody Nurse now. And Mr. Parris with him.

DANFORTH. Indeed. That man have no authority to enter here, Marshal. Why have you let him in?

HERRICK. Why, Mr. Parris command me, sir. I cannot deny him.

DANFORTH. Are you drunk, Marshal?

HERRICK. No, sir; it is a bitter night, and I have no fire here.

DANFORTH. [*Containing his anger.*] Fetch Mr. Parris.

HERRICK. Aye, sir.

DANFORTH. There is a prodigious stench in this place.

HERRICK. I have only now cleared the people out for you.

DANFORTH. Beware hard drink, Marshal.

Through the Fire, 1992. Gayle Ray. Acrylic on canvas. Private collection.
Viewing the painting: How might this painting illustrate the struggles of the characters in *The Crucible*?

HERRICK. Aye, sir. [*He waits an instant for further orders. But* DANFORTH, *in dissatisfaction, turns his back on him, and* HERRICK *goes out. There is a pause.* DANFORTH *stands in thought.*]

HATHORNE. Let you question Hale, Excellency; I should not be surprised he have been preaching in Andover lately.

DANFORTH. We'll come to that; speak nothing of Andover. Parris prays with him. That's strange. [*He blows on his hands, moves toward the window, and looks out.*]

HATHORNE. Excellency, I wonder if it be wise to let Mr. Parris so continuously with the prisoners. [DANFORTH *turns to him, interested.*] I think, sometimes, the man has a mad look these days.

DANFORTH. Mad?

HATHORNE. I met him yesterday coming out of his house, and I bid him good morning—and he wept and went his way. I think it is not well the village sees him so unsteady.

DANFORTH. Perhaps he have some sorrow.

CHEEVER. [*Stamping his feet against the cold.*] I think it be the cows, sir.

DANFORTH. Cows?

CHEEVER. There be so many cows wanderin' the highroads, now their masters are in the jails, and much disagreement who they will belong to now. I know Mr. Parris be arguin' with farmers all yesterday—there is great contention, sir, about the cows. Contention make him weep, sir; it were always a man that weep for contention. [*He turns, as do* HATHORNE *and* DANFORTH, *hearing someone coming up the corridor.* DANFORTH *raises his head as* PARRIS *enters. He is gaunt, frightened, and sweating in his greatcoat.*]

PARRIS. [*To* DANFORTH, *instantly.*] Oh, good morning, sir, thank you for coming, I beg your pardon wakin' you so early. Good morning, Judge Hathorne.

DANFORTH. Reverend Hale have no right to enter this—

PARRIS. Excellency, a moment. [*He hurries back and shuts the door.*]

HATHORNE. Do you leave him alone with the prisoners?

DANFORTH. What's his business here?

PARRIS. [*Prayerfully holding up his hands.*] Excellency, hear me. It is a providence. Reverend Hale has returned to bring Rebecca Nurse to God.

DANFORTH. [*Surprised.*] He bids her confess?

PARRIS. [*Sitting.*] Hear me. Rebecca have not given me a word this three month since she came. Now she sits with him, and her sister and Martha Corey and two or three others, and he pleads with them, confess their crimes and save their lives.

DANFORTH. Why—this is indeed a providence. And they soften, they soften?

PARRIS. Not yet, not yet. But I thought to summon you, sir, that we might think on whether it be not wise, to—[*He dares not say it.*] I had thought to put a question, sir, and I hope you will not—

DANFORTH. Mr. Parris, be plain, what troubles you?

PARRIS. There is news, sir, that the court—the court must reckon with. My niece, sir, my niece—I believe she has vanished.

DANFORTH. Vanished!

PARRIS. I had thought to advise you of it earlier in the week, but—

DANFORTH. Why? How long is she gone?

PARRIS. This be the third night. You see, sir, she told me she would stay a night with Mercy Lewis. And next day, when she does not return, I send to Mr. Lewis to inquire. Mercy told him she would sleep in *my* house for a night.

DANFORTH. They are both gone?!

PARRIS. [*In fear of him.*] They are, sir.

The Crucible

DANFORTH. [*Alarmed.*] I will send a party for them. Where may they be?

PARRIS. Excellency, I think they be aboard a ship. [DANFORTH *stands agape.*] My daughter tells me how she heard them speaking of ships last week, and tonight I discover my—my strongbox is broke into. [*He presses his fingers against his eyes to keep back tears.*]

HATHORNE. [*Astonished.*] She have robbed you?

PARRIS. Thirty-one pound is gone. I am penniless. [*He covers his face and sobs.*]

DANFORTH. Mr. Parris, you are a brainless man! [*He walks in thought, deeply worried.*]

PARRIS. Excellency, it profit nothing you should blame me. I cannot think they would run off except they fear to keep in Salem any more. [*He is pleading.*] Mark it, sir, Abigail had close knowledge of the town, and since the news of Andover has broken here—

DANFORTH. Andover is remedied. The court returns there on Friday, and will resume examinations.

PARRIS. I am sure of it, sir. But the rumor here speaks rebellion in Andover, and it—

DANFORTH. There is no rebellion in Andover!

PARRIS. I tell you what is said here, sir. Andover have thrown out the court, they say, and will have no part of witchcraft. There be a faction here, feeding on that news, and I tell you true, sir, I fear there will be riot here.

HATHORNE. Riot! Why at every execution I have seen naught but high satisfaction in the town.

PARRIS. Judge Hathorne—it were another sort that hanged till now. Rebecca Nurse is no Bridget that lived three year with Bishop before she married him. John Proctor is not Isaac Ward that drank his family to ruin. [*To* DANFORTH.] I would to God it were not so, Excellency, but these people have great weight yet in the town. Let Rebecca stand upon the gibbet[1] and send up some righteous prayer, and I fear she'll wake a vengeance on you.

HATHORNE. Excellency, she is condemned a witch. The court have—

DANFORTH. [*In deep concern, raising a hand to* HATHORNE.] Pray you. [*To* PARRIS.] How do you propose, then?

PARRIS. Excellency, I would postpone these hangin's for a time.

DANFORTH. There will be no postponement.

PARRIS. Now Mr. Hale's returned, there is hope, I think—for if he bring even one of these to God, that confession surely damns the others in the public eye, and none may doubt more that they are all linked to Hell. This way, unconfessed and claiming innocence, doubts are multiplied, many honest people will weep for them, and our good purpose is lost in their tears.

DANFORTH. [*After thinking a moment, then going to* CHEEVER.] Give me the list.

[CHEEVER *opens the dispatch case, searches.*]

PARRIS. It cannot be forgot, sir, that when I summoned the congregation for John Proctor's excommunication[2] there were hardly thirty people come to hear it. That speak a discontent, I think, and—

DANFORTH. [*Studying the list.*] There will be no postponement.

PARRIS. Excellency—

DANFORTH. Now, sir—which of these in your opinion may be brought to God? I will myself strive with him till dawn. [*He hands the list to* PARRIS, *who merely glances at it.*]

PARRIS. There is not sufficient time till dawn.

DANFORTH. I shall do my utmost. Which of them do you have hope for?

---

1. The *gibbet* (jib′ it) is the gallows.
2. *Excommunication* is the act, by church authorities, of expelling a person from membership in a church.

PARRIS. [*Not even glancing at the list now, and in a quavering voice, quietly.*] Excellency—a dagger—[*He chokes up.*]

DANFORTH. What do you say?

PARRIS. Tonight, when I open my door to leave my house—a dagger clattered to the ground. [*Silence. DANFORTH absorbs this. Now PARRIS cries out.*] You cannot hang this sort. There is danger for me. I dare not step outside at night!

[*REVEREND HALE enters. They look at him for an instant in silence. He is steeped in sorrow, exhausted, and more direct that he ever was.*]

DANFORTH. Accept my congratulations, Reverend Hale; we are gladdened to see you returned to your good work.

HALE. [*Coming to DANFORTH now.*] You must pardon them. They will not budge.

[*HERRICK enters, waits.*]

DANFORTH. [*Conciliatory.*] You misunderstand, sir; I cannot pardon these when twelve are already hanged for the same crime. It is not just.

PARRIS. [*With failing heart.*] Rebecca will not confess?

HALE. The sun will rise in a few minutes. Excellency, I must have more time.

DANFORTH. Now hear me, and beguile yourselves no more. I will not receive a single plea for pardon or postponement. Them that will not confess will hang. Twelve are already executed; the names of these seven are given out, and the village expects to see them die this morning. Postponement now speaks a floundering on my part; reprieve or pardon must cast doubt upon the guilt of them that died till now. While I speak God's law, I will not crack

its voice with whimpering. If retaliation is your fear, know this—I should hang ten thousand that dared to rise against the law, and an ocean of salt tears could not melt the resolution of the statutes. Now draw yourselves up like men and help me, as you are bound by Heaven to do. Have you spoken with them all, Mr. Hale?

HALE. All but Proctor. He is in the dungeon.

DANFORTH. [*To HERRICK.*] What's Proctor's way now?

HERRICK. He sits like some great bird; you'd not know he lived except he will take food from time to time.

DANFORTH. [*After thinking a moment.*] His wife—his wife must be well on with child now.

HERRICK. She is, sir.

DANFORTH. What think you, Mr. Parris? You have closer knowledge of this man; might her presence soften him?

PARRIS. It is possible, sir. He have not laid eyes on her these three months. I should summon her.

DANFORTH. [*To HERRICK.*] Is he yet adamant? Has he struck at you again?

HERRICK. He cannot, sir, he is chained to the wall now.

DANFORTH. [*After thinking on it.*] Fetch Goody Proctor to me. Then let you bring him up.

HERRICK. Aye, sir. [*HERRICK goes. There is silence.*]

HALE. Excellency, if you postpone a week and publish to the town that you are striving for their confessions, that speak mercy on your part, not faltering.

Vocabulary

conciliatory (kən sil′ ē ə tôr′ ē) *adj.* trying to gain the good will of another by friendly acts

reprieve (ri prēv′) *n.* official postponement of the carrying out of a sentence

retaliation (ri tal′ ē ā′ shən) *n.* the act of repaying an injury or wrong by committing the same, or a similar, act

adamant (ad′ ə mənt) *adj.* completely firm and unyielding

The Crucible

DANFORTH. Mr. Hale, as God have not empowered me like Joshua to stop this sun from rising, so I cannot withhold from them the perfection of their punishment.

HALE. [*Harder now.*] If you think God wills you to raise rebellion, Mr. Danforth, you are mistaken!

DANFORTH. [*Instantly.*] You have heard rebellion spoken in the town?

HALE. Excellency, there are orphans wandering from house to house; abandoned cattle bellow on the highroads, the stink of rotting crops hangs everywhere, and no man knows when the harlots' cry will end his life—and you wonder yet if rebellion's spoke? Better you should marvel how they do not burn your province!

DANFORTH. Mr. Hale, have you preached in Andover this month?

HALE. Thank God they have no need of me in Andover.

DANFORTH. You baffle me, sir. Why have you returned here?

HALE. Why, it is all simple. I come to do the Devil's work. I come to counsel Christians they should belie themselves. [*His sarcasm collapses.*] There is blood on my head! Can you not see the blood on my head!!

PARRIS. Hush! [*For he has heard footsteps. They all face the door. HERRICK enters with ELIZABETH. Her wrists are linked by heavy chain, which HERRICK now removes. Her clothes are dirty; her face is pale and gaunt. HERRICK goes out.*]

DANFORTH. [*Very politely.*] Goody Proctor. [*She is silent.*] I hope you are hearty?

ELIZABETH. [*As a warning reminder.*] I am yet six month before my time.

DANFORTH. Pray be at your ease, we come not for your life. We—[*Uncertain how to plead, for he is not accustomed to it.*] Mr. Hale, will you speak with the woman?

HALE. Goody Proctor, your husband is marked to hang this morning.

[*Pause.*]

ELIZABETH. [*Quietly.*] I have heard it.

HALE. You know, do you not, that I have no connection with the court? [*She seems to doubt it.*] I come of my own, Goody Proctor. I would save your husband's life, for if he is taken I count myself his murderer. Do you understand me?

ELIZABETH. What do you want of me?

HALE. Goody Proctor, I have gone this three month like our Lord into the wilderness. I have sought a Christian way, for damnation's doubled on a minister who counsels men to lie.

HATHORNE. It is no lie, you cannot speak of lies.

HALE. It is a lie! They are innocent!

DANFORTH. I'll hear no more of that!

HALE. [*Continuing to ELIZABETH.*] Let you not mistake your duty as I mistook my own. I came into this village like a bridegroom to his beloved, bearing gifts of high religion; the very crowns of holy law I brought, and what I touched with my bright confidence, it died; and where I turned the eye of my great faith, blood flowed up. Beware, Goody Proctor—cleave[3] to no faith when faith brings blood. It is mistaken law that leads you to sacrifice. Life, woman, life is God's most precious gift; no principle, however glorious, may justify the taking of it. I beg you, woman, prevail upon[4] your husband to confess. Let him give his lie. Quail not before God's judgment in this, for it may well be God damns a liar less than he that throws his life away for pride. Will you plead with him? I cannot think he will listen to another.

ELIZABETH. [*Quietly.*] I think that be the Devil's argument.

---

3. Here, *cleave* means "to stick tight," or "to remain attached."
4. To *prevail upon* means "to persuade."

HALE. [*With a climactic desperation.*] Woman, before the laws of God we are as swine! We cannot read His will!

ELIZABETH. I cannot dispute with you, sir; I lack learning for it.

DANFORTH. [*Going to her.*] Goody Proctor, you are not summoned here for disputation. Be there no wifely tenderness within you? He will die with the sunrise. Your husband. Do you understand it? [*She only looks at him.*] What say you? Will you contend with him? [*She is silent.*] Are you stone? I tell you true, woman, had I no other proof of your unnatural life, your dry eyes now would be sufficient evidence that you delivered up your soul to Hell! A very ape would weep at such calamity! Have the devil dried up any tear of pity in you? [*She is silent.*] Take her out. It profit nothing she should speak to him!

ELIZABETH. [*Quietly.*] Let me speak with him, Excellency.

PARRIS. [*With hope.*] You'll strive with him? [*She hesitates.*]

DANFORTH. Will you plead for his confession or will you not?

ELIZABETH. I promise nothing. Let me speak with him.

[*A sound—the sibilance[5] of dragging feet on stone. They turn. A pause. HERRICK enters with JOHN PROCTOR. His wrists are chained. He is another man, bearded, filthy, his eyes misty as though webs had overgrown them. He halts inside the doorway, his eye caught by the sight of ELIZABETH. The emotion flowing between them prevents anyone from speaking for an instant. Now HALE, visibly affected, goes to DANFORTH and speaks quietly.*]

HALE. Pray, leave them, Excellency.

DANFORTH. [*Pressing HALE impatiently aside.*] Mr. Proctor, you have been notified, have you

not? [*PROCTOR is silent, staring at ELIZABETH.*] I see light in the sky, Mister; let you counsel with your wife, and may God help you turn your back on Hell. [*PROCTOR is silent, staring at ELIZABETH.*]

HALE. [*Quietly.*] Excellency, let—

[*DANFORTH brushes past HALE and walks out. HALE follows. CHEEVER stands and follows, HATHORNE behind. HERRICK goes. PARRIS, from a safe distance, offers.*]

PARRIS. If you desire a cup of cider, Mr. Proctor, I am sure I—[*PROCTOR turns an icy stare at him, and he breaks off. PARRIS raises his palms toward PROCTOR.*] God lead you now. [*PARRIS goes out.*]

[*Alone. PROCTOR walks to her, halts. It is as though they stood in a spinning world. It is beyond sorrow, above it. He reaches out his hand as though toward an embodiment[6] not quite real, and as he touches her, a strange soft sound, half laughter, half amazement, comes from his throat. He pats her hand. She covers his hand with hers. And then, weak, he sits. Then she sits, facing him.*]

PROCTOR. The child?

ELIZABETH. It grows.

PROCTOR. There is no word of the boys?

ELIZABETH. They're well. Rebecca's Samuel keeps them.

PROCTOR. You have not seen them?

ELIZABETH. I have not. [*She catches a weakening in herself and downs it.*]

PROCTOR. You are a—marvel, Elizabeth.

ELIZABETH. You—have been tortured?

PROCTOR. Aye. [*Pause. She will not let herself be drowned in the sea that threatens her.*] They come for my life now.

ELIZABETH. I know it.

[*Pause.*]

---

5. A *sibilance* is a hissing sound.

6. *Embodiment,* here, suggests a vision or a spirit rather than a solid form.

The Last Judgment, 1955. Abraham Rattner. Watercolor on paper, 40 x 29½ in. The William H. Lane Collection, Boston.

Viewing the painting: In what ways might this painting and its title reflect the events in act 4?

PROCTOR. None—have yet confessed?

ELIZABETH. There be many confessed.

PROCTOR. Who are they?

ELIZABETH. There be a hundred or more, they say. Goody Ballard is one; Isaiah Goodkind is one. There be many.

PROCTOR. Rebecca?

ELIZABETH. Not Rebecca. She is one foot in Heaven now; naught may hurt her more.

PROCTOR. And Giles?

ELIZABETH. You have not heard of it?

PROCTOR. I hear nothin', where I am kept.

ELIZABETH. Giles is dead.

[He looks at her incredulously.]

PROCTOR. When were he hanged?

ELIZABETH. [Quietly, factually.] He were not hanged. He would not answer aye or nay to his indictment; for if he denied the charge they'd hang him surely, and auction out his property. So he stand mute, and died Christian under the law. And so his sons will have his farm. It is the law, for he could not be condemned a wizard without he answer the indictment, aye or nay.

PROCTOR. Then how does he die?

ELIZABETH. [Gently.] They press him, John.

PROCTOR. Press?

ELIZABETH. Great stones they lay upon his chest until he plead aye or nay. [With a tender smile for the old man.] They say he give them but two words. "More weight," he says. And died.

PROCTOR. [Numbed—a thread to weave into his agony.] "More weight."

ELIZABETH. Aye. It were a fearsome man, Giles Corey.

[Pause.]

PROCTOR. [With great force of will, but not quite looking at her.] I have been thinking I would confess to them, Elizabeth. [She shows nothing.] What say you? If I give them that?

ELIZABETH. I cannot judge you, John.

[Pause.]

PROCTOR. [Simply—a pure question.] What would you have me do?

ELIZABETH. As you will, I would have it. [Slight pause.] I want you living, John. That's sure.

PROCTOR. [Pauses, then with a flailing of hope.] Giles' wife? Have she confessed?

ELIZABETH. She will not.

[Pause.]

PROCTOR. It is a pretense, Elizabeth.

ELIZABETH. What is?

PROCTOR. I cannot mount the gibbet like a saint. It is a fraud. I am not that man. [She is silent.] My honesty is broke, Elizabeth; I am no good man. Nothing's spoiled by giving them this lie that were not rotten long before.

ELIZABETH. And yet you've not confessed till now. That speak goodness in you.

PROCTOR. Spite only keeps me silent. It is hard to give a lie to dogs. [Pause, for the first time he turns directly to her.] I would have your forgiveness, Elizabeth.

ELIZABETH. It is not for me to give, John, I am—

PROCTOR. I'd have you see some honesty in it. Let them that never lied die now to keep their souls. It is pretense for me, a vanity that will not blind God nor keep my children out of the wind. [Pause.] What say you?

ELIZABETH. [Upon a heaving sob that always threatens.] John, it come to naught that I should forgive you, if you'll not forgive yourself. [Now he turns away a little, in great agony.] It is not my

Vocabulary
indictment (in dīt′ mənt) n. a formal legal accusation, charging the commission or omission of an act, which is punishable by law

The Crucible

soul, John, it is yours. [*He stands, as though in physical pain, slowly rising to his feet with a great immortal longing to find his answer. It is difficult to say, and she is on the verge of tears.*] Only be sure of this, for I know it now: Whatever you will do, it is a good man does it. [*He turns his doubting, searching gaze upon her.*] I have read my heart this three month, John. [*Pause.*] I have sins of my own to count. It needs a cold wife to prompt lechery.

PROCTOR. [*In great pain.*] Enough, enough—

ELIZABETH. [*Now pouring out her heart.*] Better you should know me!

PROCTOR. I will not hear it! I know you!

ELIZABETH. You take my sins upon you, John—

PROCTOR. [*In agony.*] No, I take my own, my own!

ELIZABETH. John, I counted myself so plain, so poorly made, no honest love could come to me! Suspicion kissed you when I did; I never knew how I should say my love. It were a cold house I kept! [*In fright, she swerves, as HATHORNE enters.*]

HATHORNE. What say you, Proctor? The sun is soon up.

[*PROCTOR, his chest heaving, stares, turns to ELIZABETH. She comes to him as though to plead, her voice quaking.*]

ELIZABETH. Do what you will. But let none be your judge. There be no higher judge under Heaven than Proctor is! Forgive me, forgive me, John—I never knew such goodness in the world! [*She covers her face, weeping.*]

[*PROCTOR turns from her to HATHORNE; he is off the earth, his voice hollow.*]

PROCTOR. I want my life.

HATHORNE. [*Electrified, surprised.*] You'll confess yourself?

PROCTOR. I will have my life.

HATHORNE. [*With a mystical tone.*] God be praised! It is a providence! [*He rushes out the door, and his voice is heard calling down the corridor.*] He will confess! Proctor will confess!

PROCTOR. [*With a cry, as he strides to the door.*] Why do you cry it? [*In great pain he turns back to her.*] It is evil, is it not? It is evil.

ELIZABETH. [*In terror, weeping.*] I cannot judge you, John, I cannot!

PROCTOR. Then who will judge me? [*Suddenly clasping his hands.*] God in Heaven, what is John Proctor, what is John Proctor? [*He moves as an animal, and a fury is riding in him, a tantalized[7] search.*] I think it is honest, I think so; I am no saint. [*As though she had denied this he calls angrily at her.*] Let Rebecca go like a saint; for me it is fraud!

[*Voices are heard in the hall, speaking together in suppressed excitement.*]

ELIZABETH. I am not your judge, I cannot be. [*As though giving him release.*] Do as you will, do as you will!

PROCTOR. Would you give them such a lie? Say it. Would you ever give them this? [*She cannot answer.*] You would not; if tongs of fire were singeing you you would not! It is evil. Good, then—it is evil, and I do it!

[*HATHORNE enters with DANFORTH, and, with them, CHEEVER, PARRIS, and HALE. It is a businesslike, rapid entrance, as though the ice had been broken.*]

DANFORTH. [*With great relief and gratitude.*] Praise to God, man, praise to God; you shall be blessed in Heaven for this. [*CHEEVER has hurried to the bench with pen, ink, and paper. PROCTOR watches him.*] Now then, let us have it. Are you ready, Mr. Cheever?

PROCTOR. [*With a cold, cold horror at their efficiency.*] Why must it be written?

DANFORTH. Why, for the good instruction of the village, Mister; this we shall post upon the

---

7. Here, *tantalized* means "tormented."

church door! [*To PARRIS, urgently.*] Where is the marshal?

PARRIS. [*Runs to the door and calls down the corridor.*] Marshal! Hurry!

DANFORTH. Now, then, Mister, will you speak slowly, and directly to the point, for Mr. Cheever's sake. [*He is on record now, and is really dictating to CHEEVER, who writes.*] Mr. Proctor, have you seen the Devil in your life? [*PROCTOR's jaws lock.*] Come, man, there is light in the sky; the town waits at the scaffold; I would give out this news. Did you see the Devil?

PROCTOR. I did.

PARRIS. Praise God!

DANFORTH. And when he come to you, what were his demand? [*PROCTOR is silent. DANFORTH helps.*] Did he bid you to do his work upon the earth?

PROCTOR. He did.

DANFORTH. And you bound yourself to his service? [*DANFORTH turns, as REBECCA NURSE enters, with HERRICK helping to support her. She is barely able to walk.*] Come in, come in, woman!

REBECCA. [*Brightening as she sees PROCTOR.*] Ah, John! You are well, then, eh?

[*PROCTOR turns his face to the wall.*]

DANFORTH. Courage, man, courage—let her witness your good example that she may come to God herself. Now hear it, Goody Nurse! Say on, Mr. Proctor. Did you bind yourself to the Devil's service?

REBECCA. [*Astonished.*] Why, John!

PROCTOR. [*Through his teeth, his face turned from REBECCA.*] I did.

DANFORTH. Now, woman, you surely see it profit nothin' to keep this conspiracy any further. Will you confess yourself with him?

REBECCA. Oh, John—God send his mercy on you!

DANFORTH. I say, will you confess yourself, Goody Nurse?

REBECCA. Why, it is a lie, it is a lie; how may I damn myself? I cannot, I cannot.

DANFORTH. Mr. Proctor. When the Devil came to you did you see Rebecca Nurse in his company? [*PROCTOR is silent.*] Come, man, take courage—did you ever see her with the Devil?

PROCTOR. [*Almost inaudibly.*] No.

[*DANFORTH, now sensing trouble, glances at JOHN and goes to the table, and picks up a sheet—the list of condemned.*]

DANFORTH. Did you ever see her sister, Mary Easty, with the Devil?

PROCTOR. No, I did not.

DANFORTH. [*His eyes narrow on PROCTOR.*] Did you ever see Martha Corey with the Devil?

PROCTOR. I did not.

DANFORTH. [*Realizing, slowly putting the sheet down.*] Did you ever see anyone with the Devil?

PROCTOR. I did not.

DANFORTH. Proctor, you mistake me. I am not empowered to trade your life for a lie. You have most certainly seen some person with the Devil. [*PROCTOR is silent.*] Mr. Proctor, a score of people have already testified they saw this woman with the Devil.

PROCTOR. Then it is proved. Why must I say it?

DANFORTH. Why "must" you say it! Why, you should rejoice to say it if your soul is truly purged[8] of any love for Hell!

PROCTOR. They think to go like saints. I like not to spoil their names.

DANFORTH. [*Inquiring, incredulous.*] Mr. Proctor, do you think they go like saints?

PROCTOR. [*Evading.*] This woman never thought she done the Devil's work.

DANFORTH. Look you, sir. I think you mistake your duty here. It matters nothing what she

---

8. To be *purged* is to be cleansed of whatever is unclean or undesirable.

thought—she is convicted of the unnatural murder of children, and you for sending your spirit out upon Mary Warren. Your soul alone is the issue here, Mister, and you will prove its whiteness or you cannot live in a Christian country. Will you tell me now what persons conspired with you in the Devil's company? [PROCTOR *is silent*.] To your knowledge was Rebecca Nurse ever—

PROCTOR. I speak my own sins; I cannot judge another. [*Crying out, with hatred*.] I have no tongue for it.

HALE. [*Quickly to* DANFORTH.] Excellency, it is enough he confess himself. Let him sign it, let him sign it.

PARRIS. [*Feverishly*.] It is a great service, sir. It is a weighty name; it will strike the village that Proctor confess. I beg you, let him sign it. The sun is up, Excellency!

DANFORTH. [*Considers; then with dissatisfaction*.] Come, then, sign your testimony. [*To* CHEEVER.] Give it to him. [CHEEVER *goes to* PROCTOR, *the confession and a pen in hand.* PROCTOR *does not look at it*.] Come, man, sign it.

PROCTOR. [*After glancing at the confession*.] You have all witnessed it—it is enough.

DANFORTH. You will not sign it?

PROCTOR. You have all witnessed it; what more is needed?

DANFORTH. Do you sport with me? You will sign your name or it is no confession, Mister! [*His breast heaving with agonized breathing,* PROCTOR *now lays the paper down and signs his name.*]

PARRIS. Praise be to the Lord!

[PROCTOR *has just finished signing when* DANFORTH *reaches for the paper. But* PROCTOR *snatches it up, and now a wild terror is rising in him, and a boundless anger.*]

DANFORTH. [*Perplexed, but politely extending his hand.*] If you please, sir.

PROCTOR. No.

DANFORTH. [*As though* PROCTOR *did not understand.*] Mr. Proctor, I must have—

PROCTOR. No, no. I have signed it. You have seen me. It is done! You have no need for this.

PARRIS. Proctor, the village must have proof that—

PROCTOR. Damn the village! I confess to God, and God has seen my name on this! It is enough!

DANFORTH. No, sir, it is—

PROCTOR. You came to save my soul, did you not? Here! I have confessed myself; it is enough!

DANFORTH. You have not con—

PROCTOR. I have confessed myself! Is there no good penitence[9] but it be public? God does not need my name nailed upon the church! God sees my name; God knows how black my sins are! It is enough!

DANFORTH. Mr. Proctor—

PROCTOR. You will not use me! I am no Sarah Good or Tituba, I am John Proctor! You will not use me! It is no part of salvation that you should use me!

DANFORTH. I do not wish to—

PROCTOR. I have three children—how may I teach them to walk like men in the world, and I sold my friends?

DANFORTH. You have not sold your friends—

PROCTOR. Beguile me not! I blacken all of them when this is nailed to the church the very day they hang for silence!

DANFORTH. Mr. Proctor, I must have good and legal proof that you—

PROCTOR. You are the high court, your word is good enough! Tell them I confessed myself; say Proctor broke his knees and wept like a woman; say what you will, but my name cannot—

DANFORTH. [*With suspicion.*] It is the same, is it not? If I report it or you sign to it?

PROCTOR. [*He knows it is insane.*] No, it is not the same! What others say and what I sign to is not the same!

DANFORTH. Why? Do you mean to deny this confession when you are free?

PROCTOR. I mean to deny nothing!

DANFORTH. Then explain to me, Mr. Proctor, why you will not let—

PROCTOR. [*With a cry of his whole soul.*] Because it is my name! Because I cannot have another in my life! Because I lie and sign myself to lies! Because I am not worth the dust on the feet of them that hang! How may I live without my name? I have given you my soul; leave me my name!

DANFORTH. [*Pointing at the confession in* PROCTOR's *hand.*] Is that document a lie? If it is a lie I will not accept it! What say you? I will not deal in lies, Mister! [PROCTOR *is motionless.*] You will give me your honest confession in my hand, or I cannot keep you from the rope. [PROCTOR *does not reply.*] Which way do you go, Mister?

[*His breast heaving, his eyes staring,* PROCTOR *tears the paper and crumples it, and he is weeping in fury, but erect.*]

DANFORTH. Marshal!

PARRIS. [*Hysterically, as though the tearing paper were his life.*] Proctor, Proctor!

HALE. Man, you will hang! You cannot!

---

9. *Penitence* is humble sorrow for one's wrongdoing.

PROCTOR. [*His eyes full of tears.*] I can. And there's your first marvel, that I can. You have made your magic now, for now I do think I see some shred of goodness in John Proctor. Not enough to weave a banner with, but white enough to keep it from such dogs. [*ELIZABETH, in a burst of terror, rushes to him and weeps against his hand.*] Give them no tear! Tears pleasure them! Show honor now, show a stony heart and sink them with it! [*He has lifted her, and kisses her now with great passion.*]

REBECCA. Let you fear nothing! Another judgment waits us all!

DANFORTH. Hang them high over the town! Who weeps for these, weeps for corruption!

[*He sweeps out past them. HERRICK starts to lead REBECCA, who almost collapses, but PROCTOR catches her, and she glances up at him apologetically.*]

REBECCA. I've had no breakfast.

HERRICK. Come, man.

[*HERRICK escorts them out, HATHORNE and CHEEVER behind them. ELIZABETH stands staring at the empty doorway.*]

PARRIS. [*In deadly fear, to ELIZABETH.*] Go to him, Goody Proctor! There is yet time!

[*From outside a drumroll strikes the air. PARRIS is startled. ELIZABETH jerks about toward the window.*]

PARRIS. Go to him! [*He rushes out the door, as though to hold back his fate.*] Proctor! Proctor!

[*Again, a short burst of drums.*]

HALE. Woman, plead with him! [*He starts to rush out the door, and then goes back to her.*] Woman! It is pride, it is vanity. [*She avoids his eyes, and moves to the window. He drops to his knees.*] Be his helper!—What profit him to bleed? Shall the dust praise him? Shall the worms declare his truth? Go to him, take his shame away!

ELIZABETH. [*Supporting herself against collapse, grips the bars of the window, and with a cry.*] He have his goodness now. God forbid I take it from him!

[*The final drumroll crashes, then heightens violently. HALE weeps in frantic prayer, and the new sun is pouring in upon her face, and the drums rattle like bones in the morning air.*]

THE CURTAIN FALLS

Responding to Literature

Personal Response

What were your thoughts at the end of the play?

———— ANALYZING ACT 4 ————

RECALL

1. What has happened in Salem during the three months since the end of act 3?
2. What news does Parris give Danforth about Abigail?
3. What recommendation does Parris make about the condemned?
4. What has Hale been trying to do with the condemned?
5. Summarize the **conflict** (see page R3) that John Proctor is experiencing. How does Proctor finally meet the test before him?

INTERPRET

6. Describe the **mood** of Salem at the beginning of act 4. (See Literary Terms Handbook, page R10.) In what ways might this mood be responsible for what finally happens?
7. What is Danforth's reaction to Parris's news about Abigail? Why do you think he reacts this way?
8. What might Parris's motives be for his pleas with the judges and his attempts to get Proctor to confess? What is **ironic** about the officials' discussion of which of the condemned might be "brought to God"?
9. What do Hale's dealings with the condemned reveal about his values and his character?
10. What might Proctor's decision mean for him? for Salem? What might Elizabeth mean when she says that John has "his goodness now"?

EVALUATE AND CONNECT

11. What message do you think Miller was trying to give about the witch trials by his portrayal of Salem at the opening of act 4? How might this message also apply to the emotional environment of the HUAC hearings described on page 911?
12. Which characters in this play are **static,** or unchanging, and which ones are **dynamic characters,** capable of growth? How does Miller use these character types to stress his main points?
13. Besides the events of the 1950s, what other historical events might be similar to those covered in the play?
14. Theme Connections   In what ways are the characters in *The Crucible* acting on an idea? With which ideas do you identify most? Why?
15. What do you think makes this play universally popular?

LITERATURE AND WRITING

Writing About Literature

Community in Conflict Not only the characters, but the entire community of Salem went through a severe test during the witch trials. Using evidence from the play, first outline and then write an analysis of the impact the witch trials might have had on the community, the government, and the economy.

Creative Writing

The News from Salem Imagine that you are a news reporter covering the witch trials. Develop questions you would ask the judges, witnesses, and people on trial; then make up responses you think they would give. Finally, write up your news article. Try to present a balanced perspective and avoid **bias** (see page R2).

EXTENDING YOUR RESPONSE

Literature Groups

A Life-or-Death Question In your group, discuss the **internal conflicts** (see page R3) that torment John Proctor as he decides whether or not to confess to being a witch. Cite reasons given in the play for Proctor to confess and reasons not to confess. Construct a flow chart to follow his train of thought, showing not only the progression of his ideas, but also the emotional impact of each alternative as he weighs it. Then poll the members of your group to see who thinks Proctor's decision was right and who thinks it was wrong. Use evidence from the play, as well as predictions about what might happen after the end of the play, to support your opinion. Share your ideas with others in the class.

Internet Connection

The Red Scare Find all the information you can on the Internet about the HUAC hearings and the Red Scare of the 1950s. Use books or magazine articles to back up this information. Summarize what you learn in an oral report for the class.

Performing

Act It Out Work with a group to dramatize part of *The Crucible*. If you like, assign cooperative roles: actors, director, and set and costume designers. When your group is ready, perform your part of the play for the rest of the class.

▪ Save your work for your portfolio.

Skill Minilesson

VOCABULARY • Analogies

An analogy is a type of comparison that is based on the relationships between things or ideas. To complete an analogy, identify the relationship that exists between the first pair of words, then apply it to the other pair. The best way to identify the relationship is to come up with a sentence that describes it clearly and specifically.

● For more on analogies, see **Communications Skills Handbook**, p. R83.

PRACTICE Choose the word that best completes each analogy.

1. firm : adamant :: interested :
   a. curious   b. bored   c. fascinated
2. joined : connection :: purged :
   a. purity   b. clarity   c. union
3. apology : penitence :: hug :
   a. control   b. sorrow   c. affection
4. clear : puzzle :: conciliatory :
   a. gesture   b. threat   c. success

Before You Read

Nineteen Thirty-Seven

Meet Edwidge Danticat

Born in Haiti, Edwidge Danticat (ed wēj′ dän tē kä′) was only two when her father moved to New York City and four when her mother followed. Her parents planned to work hard, save money, and then send for their children. Meanwhile, Danticat was raised by her aunt in a poor neighborhood of the Haitian capital, Port-au-Prince. "While I was growing up, most of the writers I knew were either in hiding, missing or dead," Danticat says. "We were living under the brutal Duvalier dictatorship in Haiti, and silence was the law of the land." Yet Danticat wrote her first story when she was nine.

Danticat was reunited with her parents in New York when she was twelve. Teased by classmates because of her accent and dress, and torn between two languages—Haitian Creole (based on French) and English—Danticat found comfort in her writing.

Although her parents urged her to study medicine, Danticat studied writing instead. In 1993, when she was twenty-four, she received a master of fine arts degree from Brown University. Her first novel, *Breath, Eyes, Memory,* was published the following year. A short-story collection, *Krik? Krak!,* followed the year after. Danticat often writes of her native land. "I'm writing to save my life," she says, "to honor the sacrifices made by all those who came before me."

"I write to unearth all those things that scare me, to reach those places in my soul that may seem remote and dark to others."

—*Danticat*

Edwidge Danticat was born in 1969.

FOCUS ACTIVITY

Think of someone you know, or have heard about, who has survived a horrible ordeal.

JOURNAL Write about the ordeal in your journal. What do you know about it? To your knowledge, what have the people involved done to cope with the memory of it?

SETTING A PURPOSE Read to learn what some women do to deal with a horrible event in their past.

BACKGROUND

The Time and Place

"Nineteen Thirty-Seven" is set in Haiti in the 1950s or 1960s. Haiti is a Caribbean nation occupying the western third of the island of Hispaniola. The eastern two-thirds of the island make up the Spanish-speaking Dominican Republic. The title refers to the year in which a bloody incident occurred along the Haitian-Dominican border.

VOCABULARY PREVIEW

grimace (grim′ is) *v.* to contort the face, especially to express pain or displeasure; p. 1001

delirium (di lēr′ ē əm) *n.* a temporary state of mental disturbance characterized by confusion and disorientation; p. 1004

console (kən sōl′) *v.* to comfort; to cheer; p. 1004

rejuvenated (ri jōō′ və nā′ təd) *adj.* restored to youthful vigor or appearance; renewed; p. 1005

balmy (bä′ mē) *adj.* soothing; p. 1006

NINETEEN THIRTY-SEVEN

Edwidge Danticat ∾

1937: Grandmother Told Me That the Massacre River Was Bloody, c. 1975. Ernst Prophete. Oil on Masonite, 20 x 24 in. Collection of Jonathan Demme.

My Madonna[1] cried. A miniature teardrop traveled down her white porcelain face, like dew on the tip of early morning grass. When I saw the tear I thought, surely, that my mother had died. I sat motionless observing the Madonna the whole day. It did not shed another tear. I remained in the rocking chair until it was nightfall, my bones aching from the thought of another trip to the prison in Port-au-Prince.[2] But, of course, I had to go.

---

1. A *Madonna* is a representation of the Virgin Mary, the mother of Jesus Christ.
2. The capital city and main port in Haiti is *Port-au-Prince* (pōrt´ ō prins´).

The roads to the city were covered with sharp pebbles only half buried in the thick dust. I chose to go barefoot, as my mother had always done on her visits to the Massacre River, the river separating Haiti from the Spanish-speaking country that she had never allowed me to name because I had been born on the night that El Generalissimo, Dios Trujillo,[3] the honorable chief of state, had ordered the massacre of all Haitians living there.

The sun was just rising when I got to the capital. The first city person I saw was an old woman carrying a jar full of leeches.[4] Her gaze was glued to the Madonna tucked under my arm.

"May I see it?" she asked.

I held out the small statue that had been owned by my family ever since it was given to my great-great-great-grandmother Défilé by a French man who had kept her as a slave.

The old woman's index finger trembled as it moved toward the Madonna's head. She closed her eyes at the moment of contact, her wrists shaking.

"Where are you from?" she asked. She had layers of 'respectable' wrinkles on her face, the kind my mother might also have one day, if she has a chance to survive.

"I am from Ville Rose," I said, "the city of painters and poets, the coffee city, with beaches where the sand is either black or white, but never mixed together, where the fields are endless and sometimes the cows are yellow like cornmeal."

The woman put the jar of leeches under her arm to keep them out of the sun.

"You're here to see a prisoner?" she asked.

"Yes."

"I know where you can buy some very good food for this person."

She led me by the hand to a small alley where a girl was selling fried pork and plantains wrapped in brown paper. I bought some meat for my mother after asking the cook to fry it once more and then sprinkle it with spiced cabbage.

The yellow prison building was like a fort, as large and strong as in the days

Did You Know?
A *plantain* (plan′tən) is a starchy tropical fruit that resembles a banana.

when it was used by the American marines[5] who had built it. The Americans taught us how to build prisons. By the end of the 1915 occupation, the police in the city really knew how to hold human beings trapped in cages, even women like Manman[6] who was accused of having wings of flame.

The prison yard was quiet as a cave when a young Haitian guard escorted me there to wait. The smell of the fried pork mixed with that of urine and excrement was almost unbearable. I sat on a pile of bricks, trying to keep the Madonna from sliding through my fingers. I dug my buttocks farther into the bricks, hoping perhaps that my body might sink down to the ground and disappear before my mother emerged as a ghost to greet me.

The other prisoners had not yet woken up. All the better, for I did not want to see them, these bone-thin women with shorn[7] heads, carrying clumps of their hair in their bare hands, as they sought the few rays of sunshine that they were allowed each day.

My mother had grown even thinner since the last time I had seen her. Her face looked like

---

3. General Rafael Leónidas *Trujillo* Molina, (rä fä′ el   lā ō′ nē däs trōō hē′ yō   mō lē′ nä) the tyrannical dictator of the Dominican Republic from 1930 until his assassination in 1961, was responsible for the deaths of thousands of Haitians living in the Dominican Republic in 1937.

4. *Leeches* are bloodsucking worms once thought to cure the ill by sucking out "bad" blood.

---

5. Following years of political instability in Haiti, the United States *Marines* occupied the country from 1915 to 1934.

6. *Manman* (mä män′) is a Creole word meaning "mother."

7. *Shorn,* the past participle of *shear,* means "clipped" or "shaved."

the gray of a late evening sky. These days, her skin barely clung to her bones, falling in layers, flaps, on her face and neck. The prison guards watched her more closely because they thought that the wrinkles resulted from her taking off her skin at night and then putting it back on in a hurry, before sunrise. This was why Manman's sentence had been extended to life. And when she died, her remains were to be burnt in the prison yard, to prevent her spirit from wandering into any young innocent bodies.

I held out the fried pork and plantains to her. She uncovered the food and took a peek before <u>grimacing</u>, as though the sight of the meat nauseated her. Still she took it and put it in a deep pocket in a very loose fitting white dress that she had made herself from the cloth that I had brought her on my last visit.

I said nothing. Ever since the morning of her arrest, I had not been able to say anything to her. It was as though I became mute the moment I stepped into the prison yard. Sometimes I wanted to speak, yet I was not able to open my mouth or raise my tongue. I wondered if she saw my struggle in my eyes.

She pointed at the Madonna in my hands, opening her arms to receive it. I quickly handed her the statue. She smiled. Her teeth were a dark red, as though caked with blood from the initial beating during her arrest. At times, she seemed happier to see the Madonna than she was to see me.

She rubbed the space under the Madonna's eyes, then tasted her fingertips, the way a person tests for salt in salt water.

Head Against Flames, c. 1965. Wesner La Forest. Collection of Astrid and Halvor Jaeger, Neu-Ulm, Germany.

Viewing the painting: What characteristics do you see portrayed in the young woman in this painting that could be similar to those of the narrator of "Nineteen Thirty-Seven"? Support your answer with details from the selection.

"Has she cried?" Her voice was hoarse from lack of use. With every visit, it seemed to get worse and worse. I was afraid that one day, like me, she would not be able to say anything at all.

I nodded, raising my index finger to show that the Madonna had cried a single tear. She pressed the statue against her chest as if to reward the Madonna and then, suddenly, broke down and began sobbing herself.

I reached over and patted her back, the way one burps a baby. She continued to sob until a

---

Vocabulary

grimace (grim′ is) *v.* to contort the face, especially to express pain or displeasure

guard came and nudged her, poking the barrel of his rifle into her side. She raised her head, keeping the Madonna lodged against her chest as she forced a brave smile.

"They have not treated me badly," she said. She smoothed her hands over her bald head, from her forehead to the back of her neck. The guards shaved her head every week. And before the women went to sleep, the guards made them throw tin cups of cold water at one another so that their bodies would not be able to muster up enough heat to grow those wings made of flames, fly away in the middle of the night, slip into the slumber of innocent children and steal their breath.

Manman pulled the meat and plantains out of her pocket and started eating a piece to fill the silence. Her normal ration of food in the prison was bread and water, which is why she was losing weight so rapidly.

"Sometimes the food you bring me, it lasts for months at a time," she said. "I chew it and swallow my saliva, then I put it away and then chew it again. It lasts a very long time this way."

A few of the other women prisoners walked out into the yard, their chins nearly touching their chests, their shaved heads sunk low on bowed necks. Some had large boils on their heads. One, drawn by the fresh smell of fried pork, came to sit near us and began pulling the scabs from the bruises on her scalp, a line of blood dripping down her back.

All of these women were here for the same reason. They were said to have been seen at night rising from the ground like birds on fire. A loved one, a friend, or a neighbor had accused them of causing the death of a child. A few other people agreeing with these stories was all that was needed to have them arrested. And sometimes even killed.

I remembered so clearly the day Manman was arrested. We were new to the city and had been sleeping on a cot at a friend's house. The friend had a sick baby who was suffering with colic. Every once in a while, Manman would

wake up to look after the child when the mother was so tired that she no longer heard her son's cries.

One morning when I woke up, Manman was gone. There was the sound of a crowd outside. When I rushed out I saw a group of people taking my mother away. Her face was bleeding from the pounding blows of rocks and sticks and the fists of strangers. She was being pulled along by two policemen, each tugging at one of her arms as she dragged her feet. The woman we had been staying with carried her dead son by the legs. The policemen made no efforts to stop the mob that was beating my mother.

"*Lougarou*,[8] witch, criminal!" they shouted.

I dashed into the street, trying to free Manman from the crowd. I wasn't even able to get near her.

I followed her cries to the prison. Her face was swollen to three times the size that it had been. She had to drag herself across the clay floor on her belly when I saw her in the prison cell. She was like a snake, someone with no bones left in her body. I was there watching when they shaved her head for the first time. At first I thought they were doing it so that the open gashes on her scalp could heal. Later, when I saw all the other women in the yard, I realized that they wanted to make them look like crows, like men.

Now, Manman sat with the Madonna pressed against her chest, her eyes staring ahead, as though she was looking into the future. She had never talked very much about the future. She had always believed more in the past.

When I was five years old, we went on a pilgrimage to the Massacre River, which I had expected to be still crimson with blood, but which was as clear as any water that I had ever seen. Manman had taken my hand and pushed it into the river, no farther than my wrist. When we dipped our hands, I thought that the

---

8. The Creole word *lougarou* (lōō′ gä rōō′) means "witch" or "a follower of evil."

dead would reach out and haul us in, but only our own faces stared back at us, one indistinguishable from the other.

With our hands in the water, Manman spoke to the sun. "Here is my child, Josephine. We were saved from the tomb of this river when she was still in my womb. You spared us both, her and me, from this river where I lost my mother."

My mother had escaped El Generalissimo's soldiers, leaving her own mother behind. From the Haitian side of the river, she could still see the soldiers chopping up *her* mother's body and throwing it into the river along with many others.

We went to the river many times as I was growing up. Every year my mother would invite a few more women who had also lost their mothers there.

Until we moved to the city, we went to the river every year on the first of November.[9] The women would all dress in white. My mother would hold my hand tightly as we walked toward the water. We were all daughters of that river, which had taken our mothers from us. Our mothers were the ashes and we were the light. Our mothers were the embers and we were the sparks. Our mothers were the flames and we were the blaze. We came from the bottom of that river where the blood never stops flowing, where my mother's dive toward life—her swim among all those bodies slaughtered in flight—gave her those wings of flames. The river was the place where it had all begun.

"At least I gave birth to my daughter on the night that my mother was taken from me," she would say. "At least you came out at the right moment to take my mother's place."

—

Now in the prison yard, my mother was trying to avoid the eyes of the guard peering down at her.

9. On November 1, Haitians celebrate La Toussaint (lä too′ sän), or All Saints' Day, as a national holiday. The day is also a Roman Catholic holy day commemorating all Catholic saints.

"One day I will tell you the secret of how the Madonna cries," she said.

I reached over and touched the scabs on her fingers. She handed me back the Madonna.

I know how the Madonna cries. I have watched from hiding how my mother plans weeks in advance for it to happen. She would put a thin layer of wax and oil in the hollow space of the Madonna's eyes and when the wax melted, the oil would roll down the little face shedding a more perfect tear than either she and I could ever cry.

"You go. Let me watch you leave," she said, sitting stiffly.

I kissed her on the cheek and tried to embrace her, but she quickly pushed me away.

"You will please visit me again soon," she said.

I nodded my head yes.

"Let your flight be joyful," she said, "and mine too."

I nodded and then ran out of the yard, fleeing before I could flood the front of my dress with my tears. There had been too much crying already.

—

Manman had a cough the next time I visited her. She sat in a corner of the yard, and as she trembled in the sun, she clung to the Madonna.

"The sun can no longer warm God's creatures," she said. "What has this world come to when the sun can no longer warm God's creatures?"

I wanted to wrap my body around hers, but I knew she would not let me.

"God only knows what I have got under my skin from being here. I may die of tuberculosis, or perhaps there are worms right now eating me inside."

—

When I went again, I decided that I would talk. Even if the words made no sense, I would try to say something to her. But before I could even say hello, she was crying. When I handed her the Madonna, she did not want to take it. The guard was looking directly at us. Manman still had a fever that made her body tremble. Her eyes had the look of delirium.

"Keep the Madonna when I am gone," she said. "When I am completely gone, maybe you will have someone to take my place. Maybe you will have a person. Maybe you will have some *flesh* to console you. But if you don't, you will always have the Madonna."

"Manman, did you fly?" I asked her.

She did not even blink at my implied accusation.

"Oh, now you talk," she said, "when I am nearly gone. Perhaps you don't remember. All the women who came with us to the river, they could go to the moon and back if that is what they wanted."

A week later, almost to the same day, an old woman stopped by my house in Ville Rose on her way to Port-au-Prince. She came in the middle of the night, wearing the same white dress that the women usually wore on their trips to dip their hands in the river.

"Sister," the old woman said from the doorway. "I have come for you."

"I don't know you," I said.

"You *do* know me," she said. "My name is Jacqueline. I have been to the river with you."

I had been by the river with many people. I remembered a Jacqueline who went on the trips with us, but I was not sure this was the same woman. If she were really from the river, she would know. She would know all the things that my mother had said to the sun as we sat with our hands dipped in the water, questioning each other, making up codes and

disciplines by which we could always know who the other daughters of the river were.

"Who are you?" I asked her.

"I am a child of that place," she answered. "I come from that long trail of blood."

"Where are you going?"

"I am walking into the dawn."

"Who are you?"

"I am the first daughter of the first star."

"Where do you drink when you're thirsty?"

"I drink the tears from the Madonna's eyes."

"And if not there?"

"I drink the dew."

"And if you can't find dew?"

"I drink from the rain before it falls."

"If you can't drink there?"

"I drink from the turtle's hide."

"How did you find your way to me?"

"By the light of the mermaid's comb."

"Where does your mother come from?"

"Thunderbolts, lightning, and all things that soar."

"Who are you?"

"I am the flame, and the spark by which my mother lived."

"Where do you come from?"

"I come from the puddle of that river."

"Speak to me."

"You hear my mother who speaks through me. She is the shadow that follows my shadow. The flame at the tip of my candle. The ripple in the stream where I wash my face. Yes. I will eat my tongue if ever I whisper that name, the name of that place across the river that took my mother from me."

The Phoenix, 1985. Lafortune Félix. Yale University Art Gallery, New Haven, CT. Gift of Selden Rodman.

Viewing the painting: What connections can you make between the images in this painting and the images evoked by the river scenes in "Nineteen Thirty-Seven"?

Vocabulary
delirium (di lēr′ ē əm) *n.* a temporary state of mental disturbance characterized by confusion and disorientation
console (kən sōl′) *v.* to comfort or cheer

I knew then that she had been with us, for she knew all the answers to the questions I asked.

"I think you do know who I am," she said, staring deeply into the pupils of my eyes. "I know who *you* are. You are Josephine. And your mother knew how to make the Madonna cry."

I let Jacqueline into the house. I offered her a seat in the rocking chair, gave her a piece of hard bread and a cup of cold coffee.

"Sister, I do not want to be the one to tell you," she said, "but your mother is dead. If she is not dead now, then she will be when we get to Port-au-Prince. Her blood calls to me from the ground. Will you go with me to see her? Let us go to see her."

We took a mule for most of the trip. Jacqueline was not strong enough to make the whole journey on foot. I brought the Madonna with me, and Jacqueline took a small bundle with some black rags in it.

When we got to the city, we went directly to the prison gates. Jacqueline whispered Manman's name to a guard and waited for a response.

"She will be ready for burning this afternoon," the guard said.

My blood froze inside me. I lowered my head as the news sank in.

"Surely, it is not that much a surprise," Jacqueline said, stroking my shoulder. She had become <u>rejuvenated</u>, as though strengthened by the correctness of her prediction.

"We only want to visit her cell," Jacqueline said to the guard. "We hope to take her personal things away."

The guard seemed too tired to argue, or perhaps he saw in Jacqueline's face traces of some long-dead female relative whom he had not done enough to please while she was still alive.

He took us to the cell where my mother had spent the last year. Jacqueline entered first, and then I followed. The room felt damp, the clay breaking into small muddy chunks under our feet.

I inhaled deeply to keep my lungs from aching. Jacqueline said nothing as she carefully walked around the women who sat like statues in different corners of the cell. There were six of them. They kept their arms close to their bodies, like angels hiding their wings. In the middle of the cell was an arrangement of sand and pebbles in the shape of a cross for my mother. Each woman was either wearing or holding something that had belonged to her.

Vocabulary
rejuvenated (ri jōō′ və nā′ təd) *adj.* restored to youthful vigor or appearance; renewed

One of them clutched a pillow as she stared at the Madonna. The woman was wearing my mother's dress, the large white dress that had become like a tent on Manman.

I walked over to her and asked, "What happened?"

"Beaten down in the middle of the yard," she whispered.

"Like a dog," said another woman.

"Her skin, it was too loose," said the woman wearing my mother's dress. "They said prison could not cure her."

The woman reached inside my mother's dress pocket and pulled out a handful of chewed pork and handed it to me. I motioned her hand away.

"No no, I would rather not."

She then gave me the pillow, my mother's pillow. It was open, half filled with my mother's hair. Each time they shaved her head, my mother had kept the hair for her pillow. I hugged the pillow against my chest, feeling some of the hair rising in clouds of dark dust into my nostrils.

Jacqueline took a long piece of black cloth[10] out of her bundle and wrapped it around her belly.

"Sister," she said, "life is never lost, another one always comes up to replace the last. Will you come watch when they burn the body?"

---

10. The tying of a *black cloth* in this manner is a sign of mourning that precedes weeping for the deceased.

"What would be the use?" I said.

"They will make these women watch, and we can keep them company."

When Jacqueline took my hand, her fingers felt <u>balmy</u> and warm against the lifelines in my palm. For a brief second, I saw nothing but black. And then I *saw* the crystal glow of the river as we had seen it every year when my mother dipped my hand in it.

"I would go," I said, "if I knew the truth, whether a woman can fly."

"Why did you not ever ask your mother," Jacqueline said, "if she knew how to fly?"

Then the story came back to me as my mother had often told it. On that day so long ago, in the year nineteen hundred and thirty-seven, in the Massacre River, my mother did fly. Weighted down by my body inside hers, she leaped from Dominican soil into the water, and out again on the Haitian side of the river. She glowed red when she came out, blood clinging to her skin, which at that moment looked as though it were in flames.

In the prison yard, I held the Madonna tightly against my chest, so close that I could smell my mother's scent on the statue. When Jacqueline and I stepped out into the yard to wait for the burning, I raised my head toward the sun thinking, One day I may just see my mother there.

"Let her flight be joyful," I said to Jacqueline. "And mine and yours too."

Vocabulary
balmy (bä′ mē) *adj.* soothing

Responding to Literature

Personal Response

What were your thoughts at the end of the story?

——— ANALYZING LITERATURE ———

RECALL AND INTERPRET

1. At the beginning of the story, why does Josephine visit her mother in prison? How does Josephine seem to feel about the visit? Explain.
2. Why are Josephine's mother and the other women in prison? What do the charges against them and the treatment they receive tell you about the society in which they live?
3. What happened at the Massacre River the year Josephine was born? What meaning do you think the river holds for the women? Explain your answer by using details from the story.
4. Describe Josephine's last visit with her mother. What does the mother wish for her daughter? In your opinion, what does the mother mean when she says that the women who went to the river "could go to the moon and back if that is what they wanted"?
5. What do Josephine and Jacqueline find at the prison? What new insights do you think Josephine gains at the end of the story?

EVALUATE AND CONNECT

6. Does this story seem tragic or uplifting to you? Explain your answer.
7. Compare and contrast your answers to the questions in the Focus Activity on page 998 with the ways Josephine and her mother cope with the events at the Massacre River.
8. **Theme Connections**   In your opinion, what was the **author's purpose** (see page R2) in writing this story? What idea might she have been acting on?

Literary
ELEMENTS

Magical Realism
Magical realism is a literary style in which the writer combines realistic events, settings, characters, dialogue, and other details with elements that are magical, supernatural, fantastic, or bizarre. For example, in "Nineteen Thirty-Seven," the narrator's suggestion that certain women could fly with "wings of flames" implies a magical or supernatural quality about women whose lives have otherwise been filled with horrible realities.

1. What are other references to magical, supernatural, or bizarre events in "Nineteen Thirty-Seven"?
2. Which events does the narrator find ordinary explanations for? Which does she consider magical?

● See **Literary Terms Handbook**, p. R9.

——— EXTENDING YOUR RESPONSE ———

Literature Groups

I'll Fly Away   "Let her flight be joyful. . . . And mine and yours too." In this way, Danticat ended the story. In your group, discuss what this wish means. Do you think the author was implying physical flight? emotional flight? spiritual flight? metaphorical flight? How is the concept of flight important in the story? Find references to flight to support your ideas. Share your answers with the class.

Creative Writing

In Defense   Imagine that you are a lawyer defending Josephine's mother, trying to win her release from prison. Write a few paragraphs explaining what she is charged with and how you would argue in her defense. Will you ask for mercy or demand that she be released immediately? Support your argument with evidence from the story.

💼 **Save your work for your portfolio.**

COMPARING selections

The Crucible and Nineteen Thirty-Seven

COMPARE **RELATIONSHIPS BETWEEN THE GENERATIONS**

In both *The Crucible* and "Nineteen Thirty-Seven," interactions between young people and their elders form an important element of the plot. In a group, discuss the following questions:

1. How are the interactions between generations in the two works similar? How are they different?

2. Which of these interactions do you consider productive or healthy? Which do you consider unproductive or unhealthy?

3. How might the plot of each story change if the interactions between generations were different?

COMPARE **CULTURES**

While each selection is fiction, each is based on historical events. The two stories occur in widely different settings, however. Think about these distinct settings, and write a few paragraphs answering the following questions:

- What important things does each selection reveal about its cultural setting?
- In your opinion, why were such hysteria, accusations, and punishment able to arise in each setting? Are the reasons similar or different? Explain.

COMPARE **SITUATIONS**

How did you react to the characters' situations in each selection? What images come to mind that can represent your reaction? Create a visual piece, such as a painting, a drawing, or a collage, that shows your reaction to the characters' plights in each work, and attach a card with a sentence or two explaining your reaction. Then, with your classmates, assemble a display of the artwork. Come up with a title for your display that reflects your reactions to the selections. Invite other classes to view your display.

LISTENING, SPEAKING, and VIEWING

Critical Viewing of a Drama

Imagine yourself viewing a performance of *The Crucible*. How might viewing the play differ from reading it? Here are some guidelines that can help you analyze and evaluate a performance in depth as you watch and as you think back on the completed production.

First, look at the set.

- Does the set effectively transport you to the time and place of the story? What elements of the set are especially striking? What effects do they have on you?
- Do the lighting, sound effects, props, and costumes help set the mood and draw you into the play? What is most noteworthy about these elements?

Think about the acting.

- Do the performers make the characters come alive?
- What do the actors add to the written dialogue in terms of tone, facial expressions, gestures, and body language?
- How does the way the dialogue is spoken by these particular actors help reveal the characterization and the main events in the plot?
- Is the acting strong enough to make you care about what happens in the story? Which actor or actors gave the most effective performance?

Evaluate the completed production.

- Did the performance hold your attention? What might explain your answer—the acting, the plot, or something else about the play?
- What was your overall reaction to the play? What elements contributed most strongly to your reaction?
- Did you find the ending satisfying? Why or why not?
- What did you learn about the characters, about yourself, and about the human condition from viewing this play? Do you think that viewing the play instead of reading it had any effect on the lessons you learned?

ACTIVITY

As a class, watch a video of *The Crucible* or another play. Next, find and read reviews of the performance you watched. Then break into small groups. Beginning with the basic elements of **drama,** evaluate the reviews and conduct your own critical discussion of the play. Share your conclusions with the class.

~: Writing ✦ Workshop :~

Narrative Writing: Dramatic Scene

In the 1950s, Arthur Miller expressed his disapproval of the anticommunist hysteria sweeping the United States by writing a play about a similar historical incident. Because theater scenarios can grab an audience's attention, many other writers have also used drama to communicate a message about a particular issue.

In this workshop, you will write a dramatic scene focusing on an issue you feel strongly about. By doing so, you may move others to feel as you do.

● As you write your dramatic scene, refer to the **Writing Handbook,** pp. R62–R67.

The Writing Process

PREWRITING

PREWRITING TIP
Carry a small notebook. Jot down some of the persuasive arguments people make when they speak. These notes may help inspire you later.

Look for a story
A dramatic scene has the elements of any good story—such as characters, setting, conflict, and plot—but the telling is done through actions, dialogue, and stage directions. One way to find story ideas is to choose an issue that matters to you and imagine how that issue might affect specific people. To brainstorm for issues, ask yourself questions like these:

● What news story has stayed in my mind?
● What human condition makes me sad or angry?
● What traits do I admire most in people?
● What behaviors would I like to change?

To brainstorm for ideas about the people, or characters, who would be involved, ask:

● Who would be affected by this issue?
● What people or groups of people might conflict over this issue?
● How could someone overcome the problems or conflicts created by this issue?

Consider your audience
Who is most likely to see your scene performed? These people will be your audience. As you plan your scene, consider what kinds of material will grab their attention and keep them interested.

Consider your purpose
You want to entertain your audience, but your main purpose is to communicate a particular message. Consider which format has the best chance of getting your message across—a stage drama? a radio drama? a TV sitcom? a commercial?

Make a plan

After you've chosen an issue to dramatize, work out the story details, just as if you were writing a short story. What conflict will drive the plot? What characters will deal with the conflict? Where will the action take place? To begin, you might fill out a chart like the one shown.

STUDENT MODEL

Theme	We shouldn't discredit people who are different from us; we can learn from them.
Setting	Spaceship; year 2101
Conflict/Problem	The crew consists of people of different nationalities; they don't try to understand one another as individuals, which leads to conflicts.
Main Character(s)	Co-captains: one American woman, one Egyptian woman, and one Russian man.
Complications/Climax	Misunderstandings build around personal issues and leadership styles; then a technical crisis requires sudden and total cooperation.
Resolution	The ship is saved, but an officer is lost; survival depends on trust and the unique contribution each person makes.

A graphic like this can help you plan the plot of your scene.

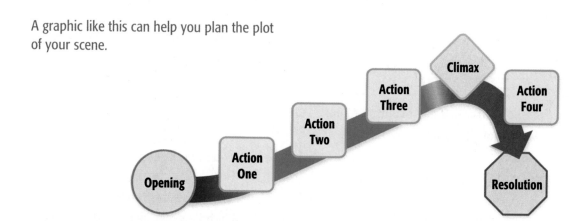

DRAFTING

DRAFTING TIP

Refer to published scripts to see what information playwrights generally include in their stage directions.

TECHNOLOGY TIP

If you're working on a word processor, choose a font that clearly distinguishes italic type from roman type. Use the italic for stage directions.

Write your draft
Get your ideas down in script format, but don't worry if everything doesn't flow smoothly yet. You'll have time later to perfect each character's dialogue.

Set the scene
Write stage directions that describe the set, the mood, the location, and the characters present in your opening scene.

STUDENT MODEL

[*The control cabin of spaceship Alyah in the year 2101. In the background, a large window shows stars and a few planets.* ~~The rest of the stage is black. As the curtain rises~~, *a woman, V. J., sits at a* one of two high-tech *console watching dials. A man, R. H., and another woman, L. C., move around busily.*]

V. J.: [*Jotting something on a clipboard, gets up, speaking animatedly.*]
We've got to get this ship moving. I'll have engineering check the fuel cells, again

R. H.: [*Annoyed, his back to V. J.*] Quite I've told you it's not ~~Don't bother with~~ the fuel cells!

REVISING

REVISING TIP

To give characters their own distinctive expressions, say the dialogue aloud, using a different voice for each character. Write down what you "hear."

Evaluate your script
Let your draft sit for at least a few hours, then read the scene and try to picture each detail as you read. Mark places that need improvement, using the **Questions for Revising**. Then ask classmates to read the scene aloud while you listen. Request feedback and make the changes that you think will improve your scene.

STUDENT MODEL

V. J.: [*Controlling her anger.*] It is absolutely clear to me that every calculation points to a problem in one of the fuel cells.

R. H.: If there *is* a problem, it is not in a fuel cell.

L. C.: I think—

R. H.: I am not interested. Just review the numbers.

QUESTIONS FOR REVISING

- ☑ How can I use dialogue and action to catch the audience's attention?
- ☑ Where do I need to speed up or slow down the action?
- ☑ What details can I add to further distinguish the characters?
- ☑ Which actions should I eliminate because they aren't relevant?
- ☑ Which stage directions need clarifying?

EDITING/PROOFREADING

When you feel satisfied with your scene, proofread for errors in grammar, usage, mechanics, and spelling. Use the **Proofreading Checklist** on the inside back cover of this book to check for one kind of error at a time.

PROOFREADING TIP

Decide how you are going to indicate stage directions, and then check to make sure that you do so consistently.

Grammar Hint

In contractions, use an apostrophe in place of letters that have been omitted.

This **shouldn't** be happening. **We've** got a real emergency here. **I've** checked the computer, but I **can't** find any problems there.

● For more on apostrophes, see **Language Handbook,** p. R56.

STUDENT MODEL

R. H.: Lets try it. We dont have any choice. As much as I hate to admitt it your calculashuns seems correct.

PUBLISHING/PRESENTING

Before you perform your scene, choose a cast, a director, and a stage manager. You may decide to direct, act, or do both. On a copy machine or computer printer, make a copy of your script for each person involved in the scene. Then start rehearsing, eventually adding the set and props. If you are presenting a radio production or readers theater, plan and rehearse sound effects. Consider audiotaping or videotaping your scene for presentation later.

PRESENTING TIP

To help your actors follow and read their dialogue, encourage each one to highlight his or her own lines on a copy of the script.

Reflecting

Reflect in your journal about whether your scene effectively communicated a message about a particular issue. If so, what made the scene effective? If not, did the scene succeed in other ways? Make a note of what you have learned by writing this dramatic scene. How might this knowledge help you in other kinds of writing?

👜 **Save your work for your portfolio.**

Unit Wrap-Up

PERSONAL RESPONSE

1. Which selections in Unit 6 did you find the most interesting? What made them interesting?
2. How did your work on *The Crucible* affect your ideas about drama? Explain.
3. What new ideas do you have about the power of literature to express important personal discoveries and deeply held convictions?
4. As a result of your work in this unit, what new ideas do you have about the ability of literature to portray a variety of cultural settings?

ANALYZING LITERATURE

A Dialogue of Characters Write a dialogue between characters, speakers, and/or authors in Unit 6. Choose five people from five selections—people who would have enough in common to hold a discussion. Develop a topic based on the themes of the selections, for example: "Why would people of a community falsely accuse and persecute their neighbors?" What would John Proctor say? How might Alice Walker respond? Draft the dialogue between the people you chose, and share it with the class. Use class comments to help you write your final dialogue.

EVALUATE AND SET GOALS

Evaluate

1. What was the most significant thing you contributed to the class as you studied this unit?
2. Which aspect of this unit was the most difficult for you?
   - What made it difficult?
   - How did you handle the difficulty? What did you learn from it?
3. How would you assess your work in this unit, using the following scale? Give at least two reasons for your assessment.
   4 = outstanding **3** = good **2** = fair **1** = weak
4. If you had another week to work on this unit, what would you hope to learn? What would you hope to create? What skills would you hope to strengthen?

Set Goals

1. Set a goal for your work in the next unit. Focus on improving a skill, such as expanding your vocabulary or reading more critically.
2. Explain to your teacher why you have decided to focus on this skill.
3. Develop a plan to achieve the goal.
4. Pause at regular intervals to judge your progress.
5. Think of a method to evaluate your finished work.

BUILD YOUR PORTFOLIO

Select From the writing you have done for this unit, choose two pieces to put into your portfolio. Use the following questions as guides when choosing:
- Which taught you the most?
- Which do you most want to share?
- Which was the most fun to do?
- Which might be most interesting for others to read?

Reflect Include explanatory notes with your portfolio pieces. Use these questions to guide you:
- What are the piece's strengths and weaknesses?
- What did working on the piece teach you about writing (or about other skills the piece displays)?
- How would you revise the piece today to make it stronger?

Reading on Your Own

If you have enjoyed the literature in this unit, you might also be interested in the following books.

A Separate Peace
by John Knowles A young man visits his old boarding school and remembers his life and friends there during the early days of World War II. This novel depicts a friendship between two extremely different people as well as life in a U.S. school during the war.

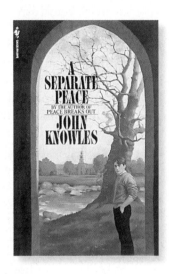

I Have a Dream: Writings and Speeches That Changed the World
by Martin Luther King Jr., edited by James Melvin Washington A collection of King's most memorable speeches and writings, as well as a biography of King and a historical review of the Civil Rights movement.

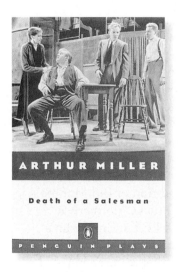

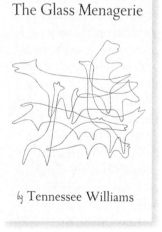

Death of a Salesman
by Arthur Miller In this classic Pulitzer Prize–winning drama, salesman Willy Loman faces his own empty, unhappy life as well as deep conflicts in his family.

The Glass Menagerie
by Tennessee Williams An emotion-charged play about a southern family shows how the dream world influences everyday life. The title comes from a collection of glass animals that belongs to the daughter in the family.

Standardized Test Practice

The passage below is followed by five questions based on its content. Select the
best answer and write the corresponding letter on your paper.

The following passage is taken from a collection of critical essays about Elvis Presley published on the twentieth anniversary of his death. It discusses Presley's contribution to American popular culture.

In the days following his death, Elvis Presley ascended to the level of lowbrow deity, a position he has maintained con-
Line tinually throughout the two decades that
(5) have followed. Kitschy Presleyana, includ-ing black velvet paintings, ceramic busts fashioned into lamps and decanters, and innumerable cynical repackagings of his music all attest to his preeminence.
(10) It is this canonization of Presley by common Americans—not his under-whelming cinematic career, not the bloated concert performances of his final years, and certainly not his recorded
(15) legacy—that leads so many critics to dis-miss Presley's greatness outright. How can anyone so enthusiastically embraced by the general public, these defenders of "culture" reason, be an artist of any real
(20) value?
And yet, to my mind, Presley's greatness is undeniable. It has nothing to do with the size of Presley's following nor with the magnitude of the devotion of his fans, even
(25) though it is impossible to separate Presley's artistic achievements from his phenomenal commercial appeal. Presley's desire—and ability—to please a dizzying variety of incompatible audiences drove his art, forc-
(30) ing him to try to reconcile his conflicting impulses in a single concert, on a single album, and often during a single song. It is Presley's struggle with these disparate strands of American culture (and his fre-
(35) quent victories in creating a temporary,

uneasy harmony among them in his music) that makes his art great.

Consider the young Presley, the teenage truck driver who cut his first
(40) records in a small Memphis studio in 1953. He was a church-going mama's boy, polite, shy, and respectful of his elders. He loved bluegrass great Bill Monroe, country superstar Hank Williams Sr., and crooner
(45) Dean Martin. Yet he was also the kid who grew his hair longer than any boy and most of the girls at his high school, who wore pink slacks with satin stripes and occasionally donned mascara. He was the
(50) rebel who would venture frequently into the black section of town—at a time when segregation in the South was virtu-ally unchallenged—to absorb the music of B. B. King, Arthur Crudup, and numerous
(55) other blues greats.

The young Presley transformed himself into a musical crucible, absorbing numer-ous strands of American popular music and fusing them into something singular,
(60) strange, and wonderful. His first single for the Memphis-based Sun Records label tells it all. On one side, Presley gave the blues song "Mystery Train" a revved-up country beat, then laid a pedal-to-the-
(65) metal vocal performance on top. The flip side was a new rendition of Bill Monroe's "Blue Moon of Kentucky," formerly a plaintive country waltz but, in Presley's hands, then and forever after a frantic
(70) two-step. Black, white, country, blues, gospel, jazz, and even crooning met on a single piece of vinyl and, if only for the duration of two three-minute bursts, man-aged to coexist.
(75) Of course, it helped that Presley was undeniably handsome and a remarkably

gifted singer. But it is also important to remember that his much-scorned legion of fans worship the image of an artist who
(80) was neither. The Elvis Presley commemorated on black velvet is the overweight, overblown Elvis of the 1970s, whose voice was but a shadow of what it had been before drug addiction sapped his strength.
(85) Even in the end—a period during which, tellingly, Presley performed numerous concerts and so was seen live by many of those who still carry the torch for him— Elvis Presley continued to embody numer-
(90) ous contradictions.

1 In lines 10–16 ("It is this canonization by . . . outright."), the author implies that she

(A) does not admire all of Presley's artistic efforts
(B) places great faith in the artistic tastes of the ordinary American
(C) owns a large collection of Presley memorabilia
(D) prefers gospel and blues music to country music
(E) believes that Elvis Presley should be canonized

2 In the second paragraph, the author suggests that many critics dismiss Elvis Presley's artistic achievements because they

(A) regard Presley as a major film star but only a minor musician
(B) have little respect for the majority of Presley's fans
(C) experience his music only through albums that have been artlessly repackaged
(D) are unaware of Presley's respect for such artists as Bill Monroe and B. B. King
(E) never had the chance to see Presley perform in concert

3 The passage implies that Elvis Presley's greatest contribution to American popular culture was that

(A) he introduced rock and roll fans to the music of Dean Martin and Arthur Craddup
(B) his movies realistically portrayed the struggles of working class Americans
(C) he made pop music respectable, because he was a polite and religious man
(D) his music blended many disparate strands of American culture
(E) he developed important new trends in men's fashion

4 The word "crucible" in line 57 most nearly means

(A) answer to a riddle
(B) defining characteristic
(C) vacuum cleaner
(D) cornerstone of a building
(E) melting pot

5 The author mentions Elvis Presley's good looks in order to

(A) dismiss Presley's fame as a result of his physical appeal
(B) explain how Presley was able to make movies despite the fact that his films are not very good
(C) criticize fans who admire Presley's appearance but not his artistic achievements
(D) assert that they play a minimal role in most fans' assessment of Presley
(E) justify the widespread use of Presley's image on velvet paintings and lamps.

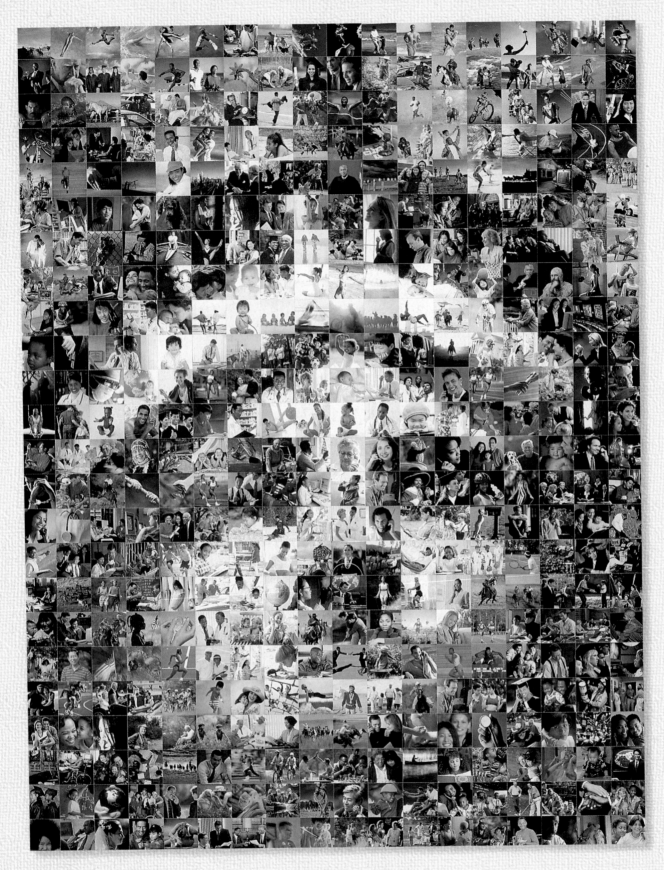

Liberty, 1996. Robert Silvers. Photomosaic™. Photos by The Stock Market.

1018

Toward the Twenty-First Century

1960 to the Present

> "Let the word go forth from this time and place, to friend and foe alike, that the torch has been passed to a new generation of Americans, born in this century, tempered by war, disciplined by a hard and bitter peace, proud of our ancient heritage, and unwilling to witness or permit the slow undoing of those human rights to which this nation has always been committed, and to which we are committed today, at home and around the world!"
>
> —John F. Kennedy, *Inaugural Address, 1961*

Theme 11
Generations
pages 1029–1116

Theme 12
Variety Is Richness
pages 1117–1203

Setting the Scene

"'Ten, nine, eight, seven, six . . .' At the count of five I put my right hand on the stopwatch button, which I had to push at liftoff to time the flight. I put my left hand on the abort handle, which I would move in a hurry only if something went seriously wrong and I had to activate the escape tower.

"Just after the count of zero, Deke said, 'Liftoff . . . you're on your way . . .'"

Astronaut Alan Shepard Jr. certainly was on his way— rocketing more than 115 miles above the earth. The flight, launched from Cape Canaveral, Florida, on May 5, 1961, traced a neat arc and landed Shepard about 300 miles from the launch site just fifteen minutes later. With this short flight, Shepard became the first American in space, less than a month after Soviet cosmonaut Yuri Gagarin had become the first person to circle the earth. The space age had arrived.

Alan Shepard, 1961, just before his successful flight into space.

U.S.A.

- 1963 Martin Luther King Jr. delivers his "I Have a Dream" speech in Washington, DC
- 1965 Voting Rights Act becomes law
- 1967 U.S. population passes 200 million
- 1972 President Nixon visits China
- 1976 U.S. celebrates its bicentennial birthday

1960

1970

World

- Mali, Senegal, Nigeria, and other African nations gain independence
- 1968 Soviets invade Czechoslovakia to stop liberal reforms
- 1979 In Iran, a revolution lead by Shiite Muslims overthrows the Shah; Soviet troops invade Afghanistan

History of the Time

Years of Turbulence

The stormy sixties were launched, appropriately, with a flight into space and an energetic young president—John F. Kennedy. The space program's great accomplishments included astronaut Neil Armstrong stepping onto the surface of the moon in 1969. President Kennedy's term ended in tragedy, however—he was assassinated on November 22, 1963, in Dallas, Texas.

Kennedy's successor, Texan Lyndon Baines Johnson, pushed landmark legislation through Congress, hoping to move the country toward becoming a Great Society without racial discrimination or poverty. Among Johnson's major achievements was the passage of the Civil Rights Act of 1964. With the help of Johnson's Great Society programs, the percentage of families living in poverty declined by one-third between 1964 and 1972.

However, in the words of Martin Luther King Jr., this Great Society was "shot down on the battlefields of Vietnam." The United States sent troops to the civil war in that nation hoping to halt a victory by communist forces. By the late 1960s, there were about 540,000 American troops in Vietnam.

At home, antiwar protests spread through the nation. In 1973 United States troops finally withdrew from Vietnam. The war ended two years later and Vietnam was united under communist rule.

A Change in Direction

In 1968 the assassinations of Martin Luther King Jr. and presidential candidate Robert Kennedy shocked Americans. In 1974 the nation witnessed the resignation of President Richard Nixon over the Watergate scandal. Disenchantment with government solutions to problems helped bring about the election in 1980 of Ronald Reagan, who promised cuts in taxes and social programs and increases in military spending.

In 1992 and again in 1996 Bill Clinton was elected president. Clinton focused on such issues as reducing the budget deficit and fostering free trade with Canada and Mexico.

Facing Challenges

With the breakup of the Soviet Union in 1991 into separate countries, the cold war ended. Other challenges and opportunities remained.

- Hispanics, Native Americans, and others struggled to seek their rightful place in American society.

- Women demanded equal access to good jobs, high salaries, and opportunities of all kinds.

- Immigration to the United States from Latin America, Asia, and the former Soviet Union created an even more diverse population.

- Computers and other technological innovations transformed the way people worked and lived.

1981
Henry Cisneros of San Antonio, Texas, is elected the first Mexican American mayor of a large U.S. city

1991
The United States attacks Iraq for invading Kuwait and defeats Iraqi forces

1996
Madeline Albright becomes the first female Secretary of State

1998
At age 77, John Glenn becomes the oldest astronaut in space

1980

1986
The overthrow of Jean-Claude Duvalier in Haiti ends a twenty-nine-year family dictatorship

1989
China crushes demonstrators in Tiananmen Square; Berlin Wall is torn down

1990

1991
Soviet Union dissolves into independent republics

1994
Nelson Mandela is elected president of South Africa

1998
India and Pakistan test nuclear weapons

2000

Life of the Time

People are talking about

Civil Rights   Inspired by Martin Luther King Jr., activists in the 1960s carry out nonviolent protests—sit-ins, marches, freedom rides—often confronted by tear gas, fire hoses, and dogs. In crowded urban ghettos of the North, frustration over the slow passage of Civil Rights programs erupts into riots each summer from 1964 through 1968. In addition to an impressive string of judicial and legislative victories, the Civil Rights movement creates a growing consciousness against racism. ▶

Martin Luther King Jr.

"High Tech"   Americans in the 1980s and 1990s use more and more amazing new devices. People begin to transmit documents by fax, chat on cell phones, and use personal computers for information, advice, and social interaction. By the late 1990s, the number of Internet users exceeds 30 million.

1960s computer

Laptop computer

The Changing American   As immigration soars in the 1980s and 1990s to levels not seen since the early 1900s, the American population becomes increasingly diverse. By 1995 almost nine percent of Americans are foreign born. Newcomers bring with them new ideas, new words, new foods, new literature, new music.

Firsts

- Dr. Michael DeBakey implants the first successful artificial heart. (1966)
- Margaret A. Brewer becomes the first female Marine Corps general. (1978)
- Chan Ho Park, first Korean major leaguer, pitches for Dodgers. (1994)

U.S.A.

1964 — The Beatles appear on television's *Ed Sullivan Show*

1967 — The Green Bay Packers win the first Super Bowl

1971 — Tennis player Billie Jean King becomes first female athlete to win more than $100,000 in a year

1972 — Educational Amendments Act prohibits sex discrimination in school programs

1977 — The movie *Star Wars* opens and becomes the largest-selling motion picture to date

1960

1962 — In Sweden, the Nobel Prize is awarded to three scientists who identified the structure and function of DNA

1967 1970 — In South Africa, Dr. Christiaan Barnard performs first successful human heart transplant

1974 — In China, archaeologists unearth statues of warriors more than 2,000 years old

World

Food & Fashion

- By the late 1960s, some young people wear "hippie" styles, such as scruffy blue jeans and brightly tie-dyed T-shirts. ▶

- Long hair becomes fashionable among men, and some African Americans demonstrate their pride in their heritage with full-shaped natural Afro hairstyles. ▶

- The growing concern with fitness and the environment begins to affect how Americans think about food. "Natural," "Pesticide-free," "No Preservatives," and "Organic" become increasingly sought-after terms on food labels in the 1970s, 1980s, and 1990s.

Arts & Entertainment

- Almost 90 percent of households own television sets by 1960. In 1981 MTV arrives, and its use of bright colors and quick cuts from scene to scene sets new trends in telecasting.

- Music lovers in the 1960s help the Supremes skyrocket to fame with the "Motown sound." In 1964 the Beatles explode on the U.S. scene. The 1971 musical *Godspell* draws huge crowds. In the 1990s, Garth Brooks wins numerous country music awards.

Amusements

- In the 1990s, the Latin dance style known as salsa grows in popularity, and the jitterbug, tango, and swing are revived.

The Supremes

Garth Brooks

1982
The Vietnam Veterans Memorial in Washington, DC, designed by Maya Lin, is dedicated

1993
The Family and Medical Leave Act requires that large companies allow unpaid leave for family emergencies

Americans with Disabilities Act protects rights of disabled people

1998
Singer Frank Sinatra dies

1980

1984
Toxic gas from a chemical plant kills thousands in Bhopal, India

1986
Polish composer Witold Lutoslawski's Third Symphony premiers in West Germany

1990
Total world population exceeds 5 billion

1996
Dolly, a cloned sheep, is born in Scotland

2000

Literature of the Time

PEOPLE ARE READING . . .

About Their Times In the "Me Decade" of the 1970s, self-help books such as Gail Sheehy's *Passages: Predictable Crises of Adult Life* are popular. In the 1980s and 1990s, racial and ethnic concerns, as well as poverty, continue to inspire thoughtful books. They include Richard Rodriguez's *Hunger of Memory* (1981) and *There Are No Children Here* (1991), by Alex Kotlowitz, which describes life in a housing project.

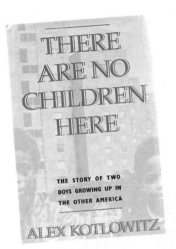

New-Style News In 1982 the new national newspaper *USA Today* zooms to success with its brief articles and bold use of color and graphics. Many Americans read news and feature articles in on-line magazines and news sources on the Internet.

Newcomer Publications The resurgence in immigration revives the foreign-language press. Among the 300 newspapers and magazines written in languages other than English are *La Voz de Houston* in Texas, *Nguoi Viet* in California, and *Korea Times* in New York City.

People Are Writing

Computer Programs As personal computers become more popular, a need arises for technical writers, software developers, and programmers. Some self-taught programmers distribute their creations without charge as "freeware," or for a minimal cost as "shareware."

U.S.A.				
Lillian Hellman, *Toys in the Attic*	**1965** Flannery O'Connor, *Everything That Rises Must Converge*	**1971** Dee Brown, *Bury My Heart at Wounded Knee*	**1974** Studs Terkel, *Working*	**1978** Adrienne Rich, *The Dream of a Common Language*; John Cheever, *The Stories of John Cheever*

1960		**1970**		
World				
Nigeria: Wole Soyinka, *A Dance of the Forests*	**1967** Japan: Ōe Kenzaburō, *The Silent Cry*	**1975** Argentina: Jorge Luis Borges, *The Book of Sand*; Ireland: Seamus Heaney, *North*		**1978** Czechoslovakia: Václav Havel, *Protest*

Literary Trends: Personalizing the Heritage

"The postwar world, the cultural drive toward what has become known as the Postmodern, can be viewed as . . . a root disagreement reducible to the distinction between the adjectives *the* and *a:* . . . can we hope for *the* meaning of a historical event or poem, or must we make do as best we can with *a* meaning?"

—*Richard Ruland* and *Malcolm Bradbury*

Greater diversity and amazing advances in communications greatly aid the proliferation of ideas, but many of these ideas do not quite fit together in a neat package. Writers of this period experiment with forms and topics, many insisting that no fixed standard exists for contemporary literature. This trend in writing—questioning an ordered view of the world— becomes known as Postmodernism.

In this period of uncertainty, topics such as personal change, generational change, and cultural identity concern such writers as Anne Sexton, John Updike, Simon J. Ortiz, Julia Alvarez, Maxine Hong Kingston, and many others. Writers search for the language and the form that help them make sense of and communicate their own experiences.

FOCUS ON . . .

Diversity

With immigration increasing and opportunities for women expanding, American literature draws upon a wider range of experience than ever before. Americans read stories, poems, and nonfiction by writers of African American heritage, such as Henry Louis Gates Jr. and Rita Dove; of Native American heritage, such as N. Scott Momaday and Louise Erdrich; of Latin American heritage, such as Sandra Cisneros and Victor Hernandez Cruz; and of Asian American heritage, such as Amy Tan and Garrett Hongo. Such writers show that their own cultural traditions have become part of the American cultural experience.

N. Scott Momaday

Rita Dove

1983
Sandra Cisneros, *The House on Mango Street;* Raymond Carver, *Cathedral*

1991
Diana Chang, *Earth, Water, Light: Landscape Poems Celebrating the East End of Long Island*

1988
Bharati Mukherjee, *The Middleman and Other Stories*

1992
Edward O. Wilson, *The Diversity of Life*

1993
Rita Dove is named the first African American poet laureate

1980

1983
Israel: Yehuda Amichai, *Great Tranquility*

1987
Mexico: Octavio Paz, *The Collected Poems of Octavio Paz, 1957–1987*

West Indies: Derek Walcott, *Omeros*

1990

1995
Poland: Wislawa Szymborska, *View with a Grain of Sand*

1997
India: Vikram Chandra, *Love and Longing in Bombay*

2000

Novels of the Time

The past and present, families, love, memory, heritage—the themes of late twentieth-century novels are as varied as the authors who write them. Still, many have a common element. They tell a good story, one that is the author's own, not strictly autobiographical, yet revealing and personal.

Breathing Lessons
by Anne Tyler (1988)

The events of Anne Tyler's Pulitzer-Prize novel take place in one day, as Maggie and Ira Moran—an ordinary middle-aged couple—drive to a friend's funeral. Flashbacks and the characters' own musings, however, take the reader deep into their lives. Maggie, a compulsive meddler, decides to reunite her son with his estranged wife and baby. In the process, she and Ira come to certain realizations about reality, hope, and their own relationship. With insight, compassion, and humor, Tyler portrays this family's private struggles.

Anne Tyler

The Joy Luck Club
by Amy Tan (1989)

Amy Tan

This novel by first-generation Chinese American Amy Tan draws upon her own family history. Four immigrant Chinese women meet regularly to play mahjong, eat, talk, raise money, and provide support for one another. Skillfully interweaving the voices of the immigrant mothers and their Chinese American daughters, Tan confronts issues of gender, generation, culture, and family through a powerful and touching narrative.

U.S.A.

Harper Lee, *To Kill a Mockingbird*

1961
Joseph Heller, *Catch-22*

1962
James Baldwin, *Another Country*

1967
William Styron, *The Confessions of Nat Turner*

1971
Wallace Stegner, *Angle of Repose*

1975
Anne Tyler, *Searching for Caleb*

1976
Ishmael Reed, *Flight to Canada*

1978
Isaac Bashevis Singer, *Shosha*

1960

1970

World

1961
Trinidad and Tobago: V. S. Naipaul, *A House for Mr. Biswas*

1964
Egypt: Naguib Mahfouz, *The Search*

1967
Colombia: Gabriel García Márquez, *One Hundred Years of Solitude*

1976
Canada: Margaret Atwood, *Lady Oracle*

1979
South Africa: Nadine Gordimer, *Burger's Daughter*

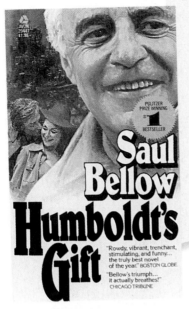

Critics Corner

Hurrahs for Humboldt

Humboldt's Gift is an exuberant comedy of success and failure, in which Bellow deals directly for the first time with the writer's life in America, including, implicitly, his own. It is his funniest book and his most openly affectionate, even in its satiric side glances. It speaks most movingly of aging and the felt loss of the sorely missed dead.

—Walter Clemons and Jack Kroll, *Newsweek*, September 1, 1975

Bellow's own great gifts as a storyteller and his talent for vital characterization save what could have been a morose and tedious novel.

—R. Z. Sheppard, *Time*, August 25, 1975

Humboldt's Gift
by Saul Bellow (1975)

Charles Citrine is an aging, award-winning writer, somewhat like Bellow himself. When his old friend and mentor, Von Humboldt Fleisher, dies, Citrine begins reviewing his life and thinking about death. Colorful characters, wild episodes, and Bellow's glorious writing create a thoughtful, at times comic, story. Bellow wins the 1976 Pulitzer Prize for Fiction for *Humbolt's Gift*; he also wins the 1976 Nobel Prize for Literature.

Saul Bellow

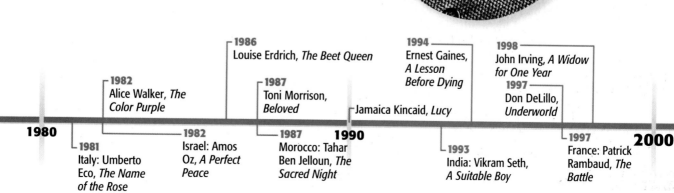

1986
Louise Erdrich, *The Beet Queen*

1982
Alice Walker, *The Color Purple*

1987
Toni Morrison, *Beloved*

1994
Ernest Gaines, *A Lesson Before Dying*

Jamaica Kincaid, *Lucy*

1998
John Irving, *A Widow for One Year*

1997
Don DeLillo, *Underworld*

1980

1981
Italy: Umberto Eco, *The Name of the Rose*

1982
Israel: Amos Oz, *A Perfect Peace*

1987
Morocco: Tahar Ben Jelloun, *The Sacred Night*

1990

1993
India: Vikram Seth, *A Suitable Boy*

1997
France: Patrick Rambaud, *The Battle*

2000

Language of the Time

How People Speak

Language Equality   The success of the feminist movement changes the way people talk, reflecting an effort to avoid gender stereotyping. For example, "fireman" becomes "firefighter," and "stewardess" becomes "flight attendant." ▶

CB Talk   Long before cellular phones become common, truckers talk to each other via citizens band (CB) radios. In the mid-1970s, automobile drivers discover CBs, and colorful code terms fill the airwaves. Each operator chooses a "handle," or nickname, such as "Lone Coyote," and uses terms such as "10-4 good buddy" for "good-bye."

Machine Messages   Talking to an answering machine makes many Americans feel silly and awkward at first, but they adjust. Some phone owners can't resist recording personal or funny messages, while others get right to the point with "Please leave your message after the beep."

How People Write

Out with the Old   The typewriter, the workhorse of the office for most of the century, gives way rapidly in the 1980s to the computer. The new machines help workers revise their memos with ease, allow companies to generate personalized form letters, and help everyone spell correctly.

In with the New   Speedy and convenient electronic mail, called E-mail, is rapidly replacing the personal letter—even the personal phone call. In 1995, more than one billion E-mail messages are sent. The new technology leads to new forms of expression, as writer John Seabrook noted of his E-mail correspondence with computer mogul Bill Gates:

"There was no beginning or end to Gates's messages—no time wasted on stuff like 'Dear' and 'Yours'. . . . Thoughts seemed to burst from his head *in medias res* [halfway formed] and to end in vapor trails of ellipses. He never signed his mail, but sometimes he put an '&' at the end, which, someone told me, means 'Write back' in E-mail language."

New Words and Expressions

From the Environmental Movement

alternative energy	biodiversity	ozone hole
biohazards	ecocatastrophe	PCBs
biodegradable	greenway	

From Politics

character issue	reinventing government
hot-button issue	shuttle diplomacy
new world order	silent majority

Theme 11 — Generations

Families pass down many things from generation to generation—stories, advice, and customs, for example. What has been passed down to you from previous generations? How does it affect who you are?

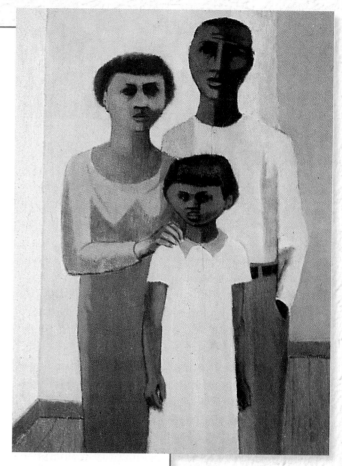

Family No. 9, 1968. Charles Alston. Oil on canvas.

THEME PROJECTS

Interdisciplinary Project

Psychology: Generation to Generation   A number of the selections in this theme illustrate problems or conflicts between generations. They also show valuable lessons that have been passed on. In a small group, do the following:

1. Choose five selections from this theme. On a large piece of paper, create a chart, recording for each selection: *Characters, Problems or conflicts, Lessons learned by a character.* As you read each selection, fill in the chart.

2. Once the chart is completed, discuss questions such as these: How are the problems and conflicts similar? How are they different? How are the lessons similar? How are they different?

3. Discuss general patterns that the group sees in comparing these problems and lessons. For example, does a certain kind of problem occur in more than one story? Present your group's findings to the class.

Learning for Life

Create a Video or a Magazine   With a group, create a video or a magazine on the topic of generations. Feature characters from three to five of the selections. As a group, decide how you will convey the idea of generations. For example, you might portray crucial scenes from each selection, or you might conduct interviews with the characters. When you have finished, present your work to the class.

Meet
Julia Alvarez

At the age of ten, Julia Alvarez found herself thrust into an entirely new culture. She had grown up in the Dominican Republic during the brutal regime of General Rafael Trujillo, a military dictator who terrorized the nation for thirty-one years. Fleeing their country in the last few months of Trujillo's rule, Alvarez and her family settled in New York City. "I consider this radical uprooting from my culture, my native language, my country, the reason I began writing," the award-winning poet and novelist has stated. "English, not the United States, was where I landed and sunk deep roots."

Although she learned her new language quickly and had an early interest in writing, Alvarez did not begin to consider a career in writing until she entered college. "I was raised in a very traditional, Old World family," she said, "so I never had thoughts about having a career. Moving to a new country, having to learn a new language, I got interested in words, and suddenly being in a world where there were books and encouragement of women to discover their talents contributed to my becoming a writer."

Alvarez graduated from Middlebury College and received a graduate degree from Syracuse University. She has taught writing in prisons and senior-citizen centers as well as in several schools and colleges, including Middlebury College, where she earned tenure as a member of the English Department. She has won several awards for her poetry and prose.

Her novels include *In the Time of the Butterflies*, *How the García Girls Lost Their Accents*, and its sequel, *¡Yo! (I!)* Her poetry collections include *Homecoming* and *The Other Side/El Otro Lado*.

❝Storytelling is a highly democratic practice. It's something we all do and most of us are pretty good at it.❞

❝I feel like one of the blessings in life is to be doing the work you think you were put here to do. You have to keep writing and achieving it day by day. The one thing I would want for myself is to keep writing and growing.❞

—*Alvarez*

❝Alvarez's style is blunt, but so light and eager it's absolutely captivating. Her eye for psychological detail can move the heart. And she's funny, too.❞

—*Sally Eckhoff*

Julia Alvarez was born in 1950.

FOCUS ACTIVITY

Imagine that you have never seen the sun setting over water, a flash of lightning, a rainstorm, or gently falling snow. How do you think you would react, experiencing one of these scenes for the first time?

FREEWRITE Jot down descriptive words and phrases to capture the reactions you might have.

SETTING A PURPOSE Read Alvarez's story to discover an immigrant girl's reaction to her first experience of snow.

BACKGROUND

The Time and Place

This selection takes place at the time of the 1962 Cuban Missile Crisis. Relations between Cuba and the United States began to disintegrate in 1959 after Fidel Castro took control of the Cuban government and asked the

Air-raid drill, 1960.

Soviet Union for economic and military aid. In 1962 Castro asked the Soviets to send nuclear missiles that could be aimed directly at the United States. The installation of these missiles later that year led to a tense period known as the Cuban Missile Crisis. President John F. Kennedy ordered a naval blockade to prevent further shipments of missiles to Cuba, and demanded that the Soviet Union remove all missiles and launch sites in Cuba. The world waited for the Soviets to respond, deeply fearful of a nuclear war.

All over the United States, schools established air-raid drills in an attempt to prepare and protect the nation's children against injury from nuclear attack. Like fire drills, air-raid drills began with a siren or other signal. Students then filed quickly to a hallway away from windows or doors. If there were no hallways away from windows, students crouched under their desks. They were to remain in this position until an all-clear signal sounded.

The Cuban Missile Crisis ended peacefully. The Soviet Union agreed to remove the missiles in return for a pledge from the United States that it would not attack Cuba.

VOCABULARY PREVIEW

enunciate (i nun′ sē āt′) v. to pronounce distinctly; p. 1032

holocaust (hol′ ə kôst′) n. great or complete destruction, especially by fire; p. 1032

ominous (om′ ə nəs) adj. like an evil omen; threatening; p. 1032

random (ran′ dəm) adj. lacking a definite pattern; haphazard; p. 1032

warily (wār′ ə lē) adv. in a watchful or alert manner; cautiously; p. 1032

Snow

Julia Alvarez

Our first year in New York we rented a small apartment with a Catholic school nearby, taught by the Sisters of Charity, hefty women in long black gowns and bonnets that made them look peculiar, like dolls in mourning. I liked them a lot, especially my grandmotherly fourth grade teacher, Sister Zoe. I had a lovely name, she said, and she had me teach the whole class how to pronounce it. *Yo-lan-da*. As the only immigrant in my class, I was put in a special seat in the first row by the window, apart from the other children so that Sister Zoe could tutor me without disturbing them. Slowly, she enunciated the new words I was to repeat: *laundromat, cornflakes, subway, snow*.

Soon I picked up enough English to understand holocaust was in the air. Sister Zoe explained to a wide-eyed classroom what was happening in Cuba. Russian missiles were being assembled, trained supposedly on New York City. President Kennedy, looking worried too, was on the television at home, explaining we might have to go to war against the Communists. At school, we had air-raid drills: an ominous bell would go off and we'd file into the hall, fall to the floor, cover our heads with our coats, and imagine our hair falling out, the bones in our arms going soft. At home, Mami and my sisters and I said a rosary[1] for world peace. I heard new vocabulary: *nuclear bomb, radioactive fallout,*[2] *bomb shelter*. Sister Zoe explained how it would happen. She drew a picture of a mushroom on the blackboard and dotted a flurry of chalkmarks for the dusty fallout that would kill us all.

The months grew cold, November, December. It was dark when I got up in the morning, frosty when I followed my breath to school. One morning as I sat at my desk daydreaming out the window, I saw dots in the air like the ones Sister Zoe had drawn—random at first, then lots and lots. I shrieked, "Bomb! Bomb!" Sister Zoe jerked around, her full black skirt ballooning as she hurried to my side. A few girls began to cry.

But then Sister Zoe's shocked look faded. "Why, Yolanda dear, that's snow!" She laughed. "Snow."

"Snow," I repeated. I looked out the window warily. All my life I had heard about the white crystals that fell out of American skies in the winter. From my desk I watched the fine powder dust the sidewalk and parked cars below. Each flake was different, Sister Zoe said, like a person, irreplaceable and beautiful.

---

1. For Roman Catholics, a *rosary* is a circle of beads and also the prayers said as one holds these beads.
2. *Fallout*, tiny radioactive particles, is released into the atmosphere after a nuclear explosion.

Vocabulary

enunciate (i nun′ sē āt′) *v.* to pronounce distinctly
holocaust (hol′ ə kôst′) *n.* great or complete destruction, especially by fire
ominous (om′ ə nəs) *adj.* like an evil omen; threatening
random (ran′ dəm) *adj.* lacking a definite pattern; haphazard
warily (wār′ ə lē) *adv.* in a watchful or alert manner; cautiously

Responding to Literature

Personal Response
What images or ideas from the selection do you find most memorable?

———— ANALYZING LITERATURE ————

RECALL AND INTERPRET
1. What words does Sister Zoe teach the narrator? Why might those words have been particularly useful for the narrator to understand?
2. What world event affects the children in the classroom? How do the children respond to the event? Do you think their response is justified? Explain.
3. What causes Yolanda to shriek suddenly? Why does she react in this way?
4. At the end of the selection, how does Sister Zoe describe snow? What deeper message might she be conveying to Yolanda?

EVALUATE AND CONNECT
5. Have you ever had to learn a second language quickly? If so, what or who helped? If not, imagine the concerns you might have if you were in such a position. To what or to whom would you look for help?
6. In your opinion, what words are among the first an immigrant should learn? List ten words that you would teach the narrator if she were a new student at your school.
7. The **setting** revolves around a particularly tense and fearful time in U.S. history. How does Alvarez convey the **mood,** or emotional atmosphere, of that time? (See Literary Terms Handbook, pages R14 and R10.)
8. Compare and contrast the reaction you described in the Focus Activity on page 1031 with the narrator's reactions to snow.

Literary ELEMENTS

Indirect Characterization

Alvarez uses **indirect characterization** to develop the character of Sister Zoe. That is, she reveals Sister Zoe's personality through her words and actions and through what the narrator, a character in the story, says about her.

1. Give two examples of Sister Zoe's actions or words that reveal a character trait, and name that trait.
2. Describe the age and physical appearance of Sister Zoe based on details the narrator supplies.
● See **Literary Terms Handbook,** p. R3.

———— EXTENDING YOUR RESPONSE ————

Literature Groups
Protecting the Children   Some experts criticized the air-raid drill policies of educators and government officials during the Cuban Missile Crisis, expressing their concerns that children were too young to understand what was happening and to cope with the stress of a possible attack. Discuss the issue with your group, using details from the story to support your opinions.

Personal Writing
A Tribute to Teachers   Like Yolanda, Alvarez learned English as a child in New York City. How might having a teacher like Sister Zoe have affected Alvarez's life? Write a tribute—a poem, an essay, or a letter of thanks—to Sister Zoe or to another teacher whose work changes lives. Use your imagination or the details of Alvarez's accomplishments to help you with your writing.

📖 **Save your work for your portfolio.**

Meet Maxine Hong Kingston

"I have no idea how people who don't write endure their lives . . . words and stories create order. And some of the things that happen to us in life seem to have no meaning, but when you write them down you find the meanings for them . . ."

—*Kingston*

Finding meaning was Maxine Hong Kingston's primary mission when she began to write *The Woman Warrior: Memoirs of a Girlhood among Ghosts.* She wanted to make sense out of her own life as the American daughter of Chinese immigrants, of her parents' lives and beliefs, and of the myths of powerful warrior women, which coexisted with the sexism she perceived in her culture. Kingston's mother would sing the *Ballad of Mu Lan,* about a young woman who took her father's place in battle. Kingston's mother would also tell the true story of the woman who invented white crane boxing only two hundred years ago. Despite these stories of strong women, though, Kingston's mother would often say, "It's better to raise geese than girls."

Kingston attended the University of California at Berkeley before marrying Earll Kingston, an actor. She taught English and creative writing for almost a decade before submitting her writing for publication.

The Woman Warrior won the National Book Critics Circle Award and was named one of the ten best nonfiction books of the 1970s by *Time* magazine. In the *New York Times,* John Leonard wrote, "As an account of growing up female and Chinese American in California . . . it is anti-nostalgic; it burns the fat right out of the mind. As a dream—of the 'female avenger'—it is dizzying, elemental, a poem turned into a sword."

While she was still writing the memoir, Kingston began another work, *China Men,* which was to win the American Book Award. She considers the two one big book. The first is the story of the women in her family; the second of the men.

Then came the novel *Tripmaster Monkey* and *The Fifth Book of Peace,* a combination of memoir and fiction. Kingston has also written many short stories and articles. In addition to her writing, she has taught English and math in Hawaii for years.

"I get a recurring dream in which my mother appears and she says to me: 'What have you done to educate America? Have you educated America yet? And what about the rest of the world? Have you gotten them educated yet?' . . . Those are my orders!"

—*Kingston*

Maxine Hong Kingston was born in 1940.

FOCUS ACTIVITY

Does someone you care about hold beliefs or attitudes or behave in ways that you just don't understand?

JOURNAL Think of a few examples of times when the attitudes or customs of a close friend or relative confused or embarrassed you. Describe one of these situations in your journal. Try to determine why you were confused or embarrassed and what the person's words or actions really meant.

SETTING A PURPOSE Read to discover the different attitudes of some close family members.

BACKGROUND

The Time and Place
This story about a family of Chinese immigrants takes place in 1969 in San Francisco, at the time United States forces were involved in the Vietnam War.

Did You Know?
Chinese immigrants first came to California during the gold rush of the late 1800s after hearing the region described as "Gold Mountain." Instead of finding gold and a land of plenty, many of these immigrants ended up with backbreaking jobs as laborers for the railroad that would connect the East and West Coasts.

Many more Chinese came to the United States in the 1930s and 1940s to escape warfare and poverty. After 1949, many left China to escape persecution by the communist government that had taken hold of China. The Communists persecuted many who owned land or were well educated.

Chinese railroad workers of the late 1800s.

VOCABULARY PREVIEW

downy (dou′ nē) *adj.* soft and fluffy, like the feathers of young birds; p. 1038

hover (huv′ ər) *v.* to remain nearby, as if suspended in the air over something; p. 1041

inaudibly (in ô′ də blē) *adv.* in a manner not able to be heard; p. 1041

gravity (grav′ ə tē) *n.* seriousness; importance; p. 1041

oblivious (ə bliv′ ē əs) *adj.* without conscious awareness; unmindful; p. 1041

dusk (dusk) *n.* the time of day just before nightfall; p. 1041

from The Woman Warrior

Maxine Hong Kingston ∿

When she was about sixty-eight years old, Brave Orchid took a day off to wait at San Francisco International Airport for the plane that was bringing her sister to the United States. She had not seen Moon Orchid for thirty years. She had begun this waiting at home, getting up a half-hour before Moon Orchid's plane took off in Hong Kong.

Brave Orchid would add her will power to the forces that keep an airplane up. Her head hurt with the concentration. The plane had to be light, so no matter how tired she felt, she dared not rest her spirit on a wing but continuously and gently pushed up on the plane's belly. She had already been waiting at the airport for nine hours. She was wakeful.

Next to Brave Orchid sat Moon Orchid's only daughter, who was helping her aunt wait. Brave Orchid had made two of her own children come too because they could drive, but they had been lured away by the magazine racks and the gift shops and coffee shops. Her American children could not sit for very long. They did not understand sitting; they had wandering feet. She hoped they would get back from the pay T.V.'s or the pay toilets or wherever they were spending their money before the plane arrived. If they did not come back soon, she would go look for them. If her son thought he could hide in the men's room, he was wrong.

"Are you all right, Aunt?" asked her niece.

"No, this chair hurts me. Help me pull some chairs together so I can put my feet up."

She unbundled a blanket and spread it out to make a bed for herself. On the floor she had two shopping bags full of canned peaches, real peaches, beans wrapped in taro[1] leaves, cookies, Thermos bottles, enough food for everybody, though only her niece would eat with her. Her bad boy and bad girl were probably sneaking hamburgers, wasting their money. She would scold them.

Many soldiers and sailors sat about, oddly calm, like little boys in cowboy uniforms. (She thought "cowboy" was what you would call a Boy Scout.) They should have been crying hysterically on their way to Vietnam. "If I see one that looks Chinese," she thought, "I'll go over and give him some advice." She sat up suddenly; she had forgotten about her own son, who was even now in Vietnam. Carefully she split her

---

1. *Taro* (tär′ ō) is a tropical Asian plant with broad leaves. It is customary in Chinese cooking to wrap rice, vegetables, or fish in the leaves for steaming.

A Sunny Day with Gentle Breeze, 1993. Zifen Qian. Oil on canvas, 56 x 42 in. Private collection.

Viewing the painting: In what way might this painting depict a scene from Brave Orchid's past? Explain.

attention, beaming half of it to the ocean, into the water to keep him afloat. He was on a ship. He was in Vietnamese waters. She was sure of it. He and the other children were lying to her. They had said he was in Japan, and then they said he was in the Philippines. But when she sent him her help, she could feel that he was on a ship in Da Nang.[2] Also she had seen the children hide the envelopes that his letters came in.

"Do you think my son is in Vietnam?" she asked her niece, who was dutifully eating.

"No. Didn't your children say he was in the Philippines?"

"Have you ever seen any of his letters with Philippine stamps on them?"

"Oh, yes. Your children showed me one."

"I wouldn't put it past them to send the letters to some Filipino they know. He puts Manila[3] postmarks on them to fool me."

"Yes, I can imagine them doing that. But don't worry. Your son can take care of himself. All your children can take care of themselves."

"Not him. He's not like other people. Not normal at all. He sticks erasers in his ears, and the erasers are still attached to the pencil stubs. The captain will say, 'Abandon ship,' or, 'Watch out for bombs,' and he won't hear. He doesn't listen to orders. I told him to flee to Canada, but he wouldn't go."

She closed her eyes. After a short while, plane and ship under control, she looked again at the children in uniforms. Some of the blond ones looked like baby chicks, their crew cuts like the downy yellow on baby chicks. You had to feel sorry for them even though they were Army and Navy Ghosts.[4]

Suddenly her son and daughter came running. "Come, Mother. The plane's landed early. She's here already." They hurried, folding up their mother's encampment. She was glad her children were not useless. They must have known what this trip to San Francisco was about then. "It's a good thing I made you come early," she said.

Brave Orchid pushed to the front of the crowd. She had to be in front. The passengers were separated from the people waiting for them by glass doors and walls. Immigration Ghosts were stamping papers. The travelers crowded along some conveyor belts to have their luggage searched. Brave Orchid did not see her sister anywhere. She stood watching for four hours. Her children left and came back. "Why don't you sit down?" they asked.

"The chairs are too far away," she said.

"Why don't you sit on the floor then?"

No, she would stand, as her sister was probably standing in a line she could not see from here. Her American children had no feelings and no memory.

To while away time, she and her niece talked about the Chinese passengers. These new immigrants had it easy. On Ellis Island[5] the people were thin after forty days at sea and had no fancy luggage.

"That one looks like her," Brave Orchid would say.

"No, that's not her."

Ellis Island had been made out of wood and iron. Here everything was new plastic, a ghost trick to lure immigrants into feeling safe and spilling their secrets. Then the Alien Office could send them right back. Otherwise, why did they lock her out, not letting her help her sister answer questions and spell

---

2. *Da Nang* (dä näng), a port city in South Vietnam, was the site of a major U.S. military base during the Vietnam War.
3. *Manila* (mə nil' ə) is the capital of the Philippines and its largest city.
4. Here, *ghosts* refers to white people.

---

5. From 1892 to 1943, *Ellis Island,* in upper New York Bay, was the chief U.S. immigration station.

Vocabulary
downy (dou' nē) *adj.* soft and fluffy, like the feathers of young birds

her name? At Ellis Island when the ghost asked Brave Orchid what year her husband had cut off his pigtail, a Chinese who was crouching on the floor motioned her not to talk. "I don't know," she had said. If it weren't for that Chinese man, she might not be here today, or her husband either. She hoped some Chinese, a janitor or a clerk, would look out for Moon Orchid. Luggage conveyors fooled immigrants into thinking the Gold Mountain was going to be easy.

Brave Orchid felt her heart jump—Moon Orchid. "There she is," she shouted. But her niece saw it was not her mother at all. And it shocked her to discover the woman her aunt was pointing out. This was a young woman, younger than herself, no older than Moon Orchid the day the sisters parted. "Moon Orchid will have changed a little, of course," Brave Orchid was saying. "She will have learned to wear western clothes." The woman wore a navy blue suit with a bunch of dark cherries at the shoulder.

"No, Aunt," said the niece. "That's not my mother."

"Perhaps not. It's been so many years. Yes, it is your mother. It must be. Let her come closer, and we can tell. Do you think she's too far away for me to tell, or is it my eyes getting bad?"

"It's too many years gone by," said the niece.

Brave Orchid turned suddenly—another Moon Orchid, this one a neat little woman with a bun. She was laughing at something the person ahead of her in line said. Moon Orchid was just like that, laughing at nothing. "I would be able to tell the difference if one of them would only come closer," Brave Orchid said with tears, which she did not wipe. Two children met the woman with the cherries, and she shook their hands. The other woman was met by a young man. They looked at each other gladly, then walked away side by side.

Up close neither one of those women looked like Moon Orchid at all. "Don't worry, Aunt," said the niece. "I'll know her."

"I'll know her too. I knew her before you did."

The niece said nothing, although she had seen her mother only five years ago. Her aunt liked having the last word.

Finally Brave Orchid's children quit wandering and drooped on a railing. Who knew what they were thinking? At last the niece called out, "I see her! I see her! Mother! Mother!" Whenever the doors parted, she shouted, probably embarrassing the American cousins, but she didn't care. She called out, "Mama! Mama!" until the crack in the sliding doors became too small to let in her voice. "Mama!" What a strange word in an adult voice. Many people turned to see what adult was calling, "Mama!" like a child. Brave Orchid saw an old, old woman jerk her head up, her little eyes blinking confusedly, a woman whose nerves leapt toward the sound anytime she heard "Mama!" Then she relaxed to her own business again. She was a tiny, tiny lady, very thin, with little fluttering hands, and her hair was in a gray knot. She was dressed in a gray wool suit; she wore pearls around her neck and in her earlobes. Moon Orchid *would* travel with her jewels showing. Brave Orchid momentarily saw, like a larger, younger outline around this old woman, the sister she had been waiting for. The familiar dim halo faded, leaving the woman so old, so gray. So old. Brave Orchid pressed against the glass. *That* old lady? Yes, that old lady facing the ghost who stamped her papers without questioning her was her sister. Then, without noticing her family, Moon Orchid walked smiling over to the Suitcase Inspector Ghost, who took her boxes apart, pulling out puffs of tissue. From where she was, Brave Orchid could not see what her sister had chosen to carry across the ocean. She wished her sister would look her way. Brave Orchid thought that if *she* were entering a new country, she would be at the windows. Instead

Moon Orchid <u>hovered</u> over the unwrapping, surprised at each reappearance as if she were opening presents after a birthday party.

"Mama!" Moon Orchid's daughter kept calling. Brave Orchid said to her children, "Why don't you call your aunt too? Maybe she'll hear us if all of you call out together." But her children slunk away. Maybe that shame-face they so often wore was American politeness.

"Mama!" Moon Orchid's daughter called again, and this time her mother looked right at her. She left her bundles in a heap and came running. "Hey!" the Customs Ghost yelled at her. She went back to clear up her mess, talking <u>inaudibly</u> to her daughter all the while. Her daughter pointed toward Brave Orchid. And at last Moon Orchid looked at her—two old women with faces like mirrors.

Their hands reached out as if to touch the other's face, then returned to their own, the fingers checking the grooves in the forehead and along the side of the mouth. Moon Orchid, who never understood the <u>gravity</u> of things, started smiling and laughing, pointing at Brave Orchid. Finally Moon Orchid gathered up her stuff, strings hanging and papers loose, and met her sister at the door, where they shook hands, <u>oblivious</u> to blocking the way.

"You're an old woman," said Brave Orchid.

"Aiaa. *You're* an old woman."

"But you are really old. Surely, you can't say that about me. I'm not old the way you're old."

"But *you* really are old. You're one year older than I am."

"Your hair is white and your face all wrinkled."

"You're so skinny."

"You're so fat."

"Fat women are more beautiful than skinny women."

The children pulled them out of the doorway. One of Brave Orchid's children brought the car from the parking lot, and the other heaved the luggage into the trunk. They put the two old ladies and the niece in the back seat. All the way home—across the Bay Bridge, over the Diablo hills,[6] across the San Joaquin River to the valley, the valley moon so white at <u>dusk</u>—all the way home, the two sisters exclaimed every time they turned to look at each other, "Aiaa! How old!"

Brave Orchid forgot that she got sick in cars, that all vehicles but palanquins made her dizzy. "You're so old," she kept saying. "How did you get so old?"

Brave Orchid had tears in her eyes. But Moon Orchid said, "You look older than

Did You Know?
A *palanquin* (pal′ ən kēn′) is a covered or enclosed couch, carried on the shoulders of two or more men by means of poles.

I. You *are* older than I," and again she'd laugh. "You're wearing an old mask to tease me." It surprised Brave Orchid that after thirty years she could still get annoyed at her sister's silliness.

---

6. The *Bay Bridge* crosses the San Francisco Bay, connecting the cities of San Francisco and Oakland. The *Diablo* (dē ä′ blō) *hills* are at the base of Mount Diablo, a peak located about twenty miles east of Oakland.

Vocabulary
hover (huv′ ər) *v.* to remain nearby, as if suspended in the air over something
inaudibly (in ô′ də blē) *adv.* in a manner not able to be heard
gravity (grav′ ə tē) *n.* seriousness; importance
oblivious (ə bliv′ ē əs) *adj.* without conscious awareness; unmindful
dusk (dusk) *n.* the time of day just before nightfall

Responding to Literature

Personal Response

Did you find this selection humorous, serious, or both? Describe your impressions.

ANALYZING LITERATURE

RECALL AND INTERPRET

1. In the opening paragraphs, what facts does the writer give about Brave Orchid? What character traits do you see in Brave Orchid?
2. Who has come to the airport with Brave Orchid? What does the presence of each person reveal about her?
3. What surprises Brave Orchid most when she sees her sister? Why, do you think, is she surprised?
4. How does Moon Orchid behave as her suitcases are inspected? How does Brave Orchid react? What do these actions reveal about each?

EVALUATE AND CONNECT

5. Since this narrative is from Kingston's memoir, a reader might expect a **first-person point of view.** Why might Kingston have chosen to use the third person here? (See Literary Terms Handbook, page R12.)
6. The author writes that the sisters have "faces like mirrors." How does she develop this **simile** (see page R14) throughout the selection?
7. This selection from Kingston's memoir uses different methods of **characterization** (see page R3). In what ways do these methods help you understand the selection? Support your responses with examples.
8. Brave Orchid finds her children a mystery. Why might she think this way? Compare your response to the Focus Activity on page 1035 with Brave Orchid's response to her children.

Literary ELEMENTS

Exposition in a Narrative

Exposition in a nonfiction narrative presents information that readers will need to understand the **characters,** the **setting,** and the situation. Like the exposition in a short story, this information usually comes at the beginning of the narrative. In this selection from *The Woman Warrior*, Kingston includes the exposition in the first two paragraphs.

1. What aspect of the story's setting is introduced in the exposition and developed further in the pages that follow?
2. Select one character and a trait of that character as introduced in the exposition. Explain briefly how that trait becomes important as the story unfolds.

● See **Literary Terms Handbook,** p. R6.

EXTENDING YOUR RESPONSE

Creative Writing

News Story   Imagine that you are a newspaper reporter who comes across Brave Orchid and her family at the airport. You sense a story and stop to interview Brave Orchid and Moon Orchid. Write a feature story about the reunion. Base the action and dialogue in your story on what you know about each character.

Literature Groups

Responding to Characters   The characters in this excerpt from *The Woman Warrior* display a variety of personalities. Why might each character act the way she or he does? What beliefs and ideas do you think each character values? In your group discuss these questions. Then share your answers with the class.

📖 **Save your work for your portfolio.**

Vo·cab·u·lar·y Skills

Using a Thesaurus

The selection from *The Woman Warrior* begins with a description of the main character, Brave Orchid, as she awaits her sister's flight from China. To ensure her sister's safety, Brave Orchid decides to "add her will power to the forces that keep an airplane up." *Power* and *forces* are **synonyms,** words with similar meanings. Many synonyms, like *force* and *power,* are interchangeable. However, some synonyms have small differences in meaning. Recognizing these differences can help a reader's understanding and improve a person's writing and speaking vocabularies. A **thesaurus** is a specialized dictionary of synonyms and antonyms, words with opposite meanings. There are two types of thesauruses.

Traditional Style

Probably the best-known thesaurus is the traditional *Roget's Thesaurus,* which organizes large categories of words related to a basic concept. To find a synonym for the verb *taste,* for example, browse the index of categories until you find the category *senses,* which includes the subentry *taste.* The index will refer you to the page for the subentry, where you will find a list of synonyms for *taste.*

Dictionary Style

This type of thesaurus presents words in alphabetical order, exactly as a dictionary does. Each word is followed by several synonyms, which are listed by parts of speech. The entry also refers the reader to cross-referenced entries. In this type of thesaurus, you must look for a specific word, such as "taste" or "sweet," to find its synonyms. When you find a synonym, look for it in the alphabetical listing to find additional synonyms.

EXERCISES

1. Using a thesaurus, find three synonyms for each word below. Then look up the definitions of these synonyms in a dictionary to identify the precise meanings for each one.

   a. wait   c. control   e. authorities

   b. scold   d. approval

2. For each word above, try to find one synonym whose meaning has a small but important difference from the original word. Then, for each pair of words, write two sentences—one using the original word and a second using the synonym. Be sure your sentences reflect the slight differences in meaning between the synonyms.

MEDIA
Connection

Comic Strip

Parents and children don't always see things the same way. How different can their perspectives be? *Calvin and Hobbes* cartoonist Bill Watterson finds humor in a misunderstanding between generations.

Calvin and Hobbes — by Bill Watterson

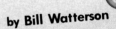

I CLEANED AND OILED YOUR BICYCLE, CALVIN. WHAT DO YOU SAY I TAKE SOME TIME AND HELP YOU LEARN HOW TO RIDE IT?

NO-O-O-O-O-O !!

YOU'RE WELCOME.

MOM! MOM! DAD *HATES* ME!

Calvin and Hobbes — by Bill Watterson

I'VE GOT THE BIKE, CALVIN. IT'S NOT GOING ANYWHERE.

I CAN FEEL IT'S GOING TO THROW ME! GET READY TO YANK ITS WHEELS OFF!

JUST RELAX. I'VE GOT YOU.

HOW CAN I RELAX?! I'M UNINSURED AND UNARMED! I'M AS GOOD AS DEAD!

PUSH BACK ON THE PEDALS. THAT'S YOUR BRAKE, OK?

YES, WELL, THAT WAS FUN! THANKS FOR THE LESSON!

GET BACK HERE.

NO, REALLY, I THINK I'VE GOT IT! YOU CAN SELL THE BIKE NOW.

Calvin and Hobbes — by Bill Watterson

THE TRICK TO BALANCING IS TO HAVE A LITTLE FORWARD MOMENTUM.

AAA! NO MOMENTUM! NO MOMENTUM!

JUST PEDAL SLOWLY. I'M HOLDING THE BIKE, SO YOU WON'T FALL.

YOU'LL LET GO AND THE BIKE WILL LAUNCH ME INTO THE IONOSPHERE!

TRUST ME, OK?

TRUST YOU? I HARDLY *KNOW* YOU!

I'M YOUR FATHER!!

WHAT, FOR SIX YEARS?! WHEN I'M 40, WE'LL SEE HOW THINGS ARE GOING!

Respond

1. Why would Calvin's father want to teach his son to ride a bike?
2. In what ways might Calvin represent all sons and daughters? How is he different?

Before You Read

Son

Meet John Updike

At an age when some people retire, John Updike stuck his head "into the mouth of the electronic lion"—cyberspace publishing. An on-line bookseller invited the sixty-five-year-old novelist to write the first and last installments of a serial mystery. On-line submissions from more than forty other writers completed the story that unfolded for thousands of readers in cyberspace. The project was a first for Updike, a prolific writer whose novels, short stories, and numerous other works had appeared only on paper. Despite his well-established literary reputation, Updike continues to take chances in his work and to meet new challenges. As he noted himself, "What's a writer for if not to venture out onto the thin ice."

An only child, Updike spent much of his childhood drawing and writing. As a teenager he dreamed of being a cartoonist. After graduating from Harvard University, he studied art at Oxford University in England.

Updike was in his early twenties when he returned to the United States and joined the staff of the *New Yorker*, where he wrote poetry, stories, reviews, and editorials.

When he was just twenty-six years old, Updike's first book, a collection of poetry titled *The Carpentered Hen and Other Tame Creatures*, was published. A year later, in 1959, his first novel, *Poorhouse Fair*, appeared in print. This book won an award, but it was Updike's second novel, *Rabbit, Run*, that brought him wider recognition the following year. It was the first of four novels about Harry "Rabbit" Angstrom, a suburban husband and father approximately Updike's age. Two books in this series won separate Pulitzer Prizes.

From the 1960s through the 1990s, Updike has continued to write novels and short stories. He has also written essays, poems, and a play. Many of these works focus on the small details of ordinary life: families, chores, and sports. Most are set either in the writer's native Pennsylvania or in New England, where Updike has lived since the 1960s. His fiction is precise and realistic, reflecting Updike's belief that "fiction is a tissue of lies that refreshes and informs our sense of actuality."

"Writing doesn't require drive. It's like saying a chicken has to have drive to lay an egg."

"I have from the start been wary of the fake, the automatic."

—Updike

"Those who admire [Updike's] work consider him one of the keepers of the language; those who don't say he writes beautifully about nothing very much."

—Joseph Kanon

John Updike was born in 1932.

FOCUS ACTIVITY

Do you think it is more difficult to be a parent or a child?

DISCUSS With a group, discuss this question. Consider all aspects of the roles of both parents and children. Think about the expectations and responsibilities that parents and children have for themselves and for each other.

SETTING A PURPOSE Read this short story to explore the different roles played by fathers and sons.

BACKGROUND

The Time and Place

Updike grew up in a small town in Pennsylvania and developed a keen eye and ear for its physical and emotional landscape. Like most Updike stories, "Son" is set mainly in suburban America; the time is somewhat different, though, in that events occur in 1973, 1949, 1913, and the 1880s.

Literary Influences

"I learned a lot from [J. D.] Salinger's short stories," wrote Updike. Salinger's first novel, *The Catcher in the Rye,* created a literary sensation while Updike was in college, and his shorter fiction appeared frequently in the *New Yorker.* Updike said, "Like most innovative artists, he made new room for shapelessness, for life as it is lived."

VOCABULARY PREVIEW

symmetrical (si met′ ri kəl) *adj.* having the same shape or structure on either side of a central line or plane; p. 1047

grotesque (grō tesk′) *adj.* bizarre; weird; p. 1047

heedless (hēd′ lis) *adj.* careless; thoughtless; reckless; p. 1047

charade (shə rād′) *n.* a false show or pretense; p. 1048

incessant (in ses′ ənt) *adj.* continuing or following without interruption; p. 1048

submissive (səb mis′ iv) *adj.* willing to yield to the power or authority of another; meek; p. 1048

radical (rad′ i kəl) *adj.* deviating greatly from the usual or customary; extreme; p. 1049

legible (lej′ ə bəl) *adj.* able to be read; p. 1049

valor (val′ ər) *n.* courage; bravery; p. 1049

lucid (lo͞o′ sid) *adj.* rational; sane; p. 1050

Son

John Updike ~

Portrait of a Young Man in a White Shirt. Bessie Lowenhaupt (1881–1968). Oil on canvas board, 23¾ x 18⅞ in. Collection of Mr. and Mrs. Charles A. Lowenhaupt.

[handwritten: narrator describes his son]

He is often upstairs, when he has to be home. He prefers to be elsewhere. He is almost sixteen, though beardless still, a man's mind indignantly captive in the frame of a child. I love touching him, but don't often dare. The other day, he had the flu, and a fever, and I gave him a back rub, marvelling at the symmetrical knit of muscle, the organic tension. He is high-strung. Yet his sleep is so solid he sweats like a stone in the wall of a well. He wishes for perfection. He would like to destroy us, for we are, variously, too fat, too jocular,[1] too sloppy, too affectionate, too grotesque and heedless in our ways. His mother smokes too much. His younger brother chews with his mouth open. His older sister leaves unbuttoned the top button of her blouses. His younger sister tussles with the dogs, getting them overexcited, avoiding doing her homework. Everyone in the house talks nonsense. He would be a better father than his father. But time has tricked him, has made him a son. After a quarrel, if he cannot go outside and kick a ball, he retreats to a corner of the house and reclines on the beanbag chair in an attitude of strange— infantile or leonine—torpor.[2] We exhaust him, without meaning to. He takes an interest in the newspaper now, the front page as well as the sports, in this tiring year of 1973.

---

1. *Jocular* (jok′ yə lər) means "tending to joke or jest" or "merry."
2. *Leonine* (lē′ ə nīn′) means "characteristic of, or resembling, a lion." *Torpor* is a state of inactivity.

Vocabulary

symmetrical (si met′ ri kəl) *adj.* having the same shape or structure on either side of a central line or plane
grotesque (grō tesk′) *adj.* bizarre; weird
heedless (hēd′ lis) *adj.* careless; thoughtless; reckless

Narrator describes himself as a teen

He is upstairs, writing a musical comedy. It is a Sunday in 1949. He has volunteered to prepare a high-school assembly program; people will sing. Songs of the time go through his head, as he scribbles new words. *Up in de mornin', down at de school, work like a debil for my grades.* Below him, irksome voices grind on, like machines working their way through tunnels. His parents each want something from the other. "Marion, you don't understand that man like I do; he has a heart of gold." His father's charade is very complex: the world, which he fears, is used as a flail[3] on his wife. But from his cringing attitude he would seem to an outsider the one being flailed. With burning red face, the woman accepts the role of aggressor as penance for the fact, the incessant shameful fact, that *he* has to wrestle with the world while she hides here, in solitude, at home. This is normal, but does not seem to them to be so. Only by convolution[4] have they arrived at the dominant/submissive relationship society has assigned them. For the man is maternally kind and with a smile hugs to himself his jewel, his certainty of being victimized; it is the mother whose tongue is sharp, who sometimes strikes. "Well, he gets you out of the house, and I guess that's gold to you." His answer is "Duty calls," pronounced mincingly.[5] "The social contract is a balance of compromises." This will infuriate her, the son knows; as his heart thickens, the downstairs overflows with her hot voice. "*Don't* wear that smile at me! And *take* your hands off your hips; you look silly!" Their son tries not to listen. When he does, visual details of the downstairs flood his mind: the two antagonists, circling with their coffee cups; the shabby mismatched

furniture; the hopeful books; the docile[6] framed photographs of the dead, docile and still like cowed[7] students. This matrix of pain that bore him—he feels he is floating above it, sprawled on the bed as on a cloud, stealing songs as they come into his head (*Across the hallway from the guidance room / Lives a French instructor called Mrs. Blum*), contemplating the view from the upstairs window (last summer's burdock[8] stalks like the beginnings of an alphabet, an apple tree holding three rotten apples as if pondering why they failed to fall), yearning for Monday, for the ride to school with his father, for the bell that calls him to homeroom, for the excitements of class, for Broadway, for fame, for the cloud that will carry him away, out of this, out.

Narrator describes his father as a teen

He returns from his paper-delivery route and finds a few Christmas presents for him on the kitchen table. I must guess at the year. 1913? Without opening them, he knocks them to the floor, puts his head on the table, and falls asleep. He must have been consciously dramatizing his plight: his father was sick, money was scarce, he had to work, to win food for the family when he was still a child. In his dismissal of Christmas, he touched a nerve: his love of anarchy,[9] his distrust of the social contract. He treasured this moment of revolt; else why remember it, hoard a memory so bitter, and confide it to his son many Christmases later? He had a teaching instinct, though he claimed that life miscast him as a schoolteacher. I suffered in his

---

3. A *flail* is a hand tool used to thresh grain by beating.
4. *Convolution* means "a twisting or turning."
5. *Mincingly* means "in an artificially dainty or refined manner."

6. *Docile* means "submissive" or "passive."
7. *Cowed* means "frightened" or "intimidated."
8. The weedy *burdock* plant produces purplish flowers and burs. Its stalks can grow from four to nine feet tall.
9. *Anarchy* (an′ ər kē) is confusion due to the absence of authority or law.

Vocabulary

charade (shə rād′) *n.* a false show or pretense
incessant (in ses′ ənt) *adj.* continuing or following without interruption
submissive (səb mis′ iv) *adj.* willing to yield to the power or authority of another; meek

classes, feeling the confusion as a persecution of him, but now wonder if his rebellious heart did not court confusion, not as Communists do, to intrude their own order, but, more radical still, as an end pleasurable in itself, as truth's very body. Yet his handwriting (an old pink permission slip recently fluttered from a book where it had been marking a page for twenty years) was always considerately legible, and he was sitting up doing arithmetic the morning of the day he died.

And letters survive from that yet prior son, written in brown ink, in a tidy tame hand, home to his mother from the Missouri seminary where he was preparing for his vocation. The dates are 1887, 1888, 1889. Nothing much happened: he missed New Jersey, and was teased at a church social for escorting a widow. He wanted to do the right thing, but the little sheets of faded penscript exhale a dispirited calm, as if his heart already knew he would not make a successful minister, or live to be old. His son, my father, when old, drove hundreds of miles out of his way to visit the Missouri town from which those letters had been sent. Strangely, the town had not changed; it looked just as he had imagined, from his father's descriptions: tall wooden houses, rain-soaked, stacked on a bluff. The town was a sepia[10] postcard mailed homesick home and preserved in an attic. My father cursed: his father's old sorrow bore him down into depression, into hatred of life. My mother claims his decline in health began at that moment.

He is wonderful to watch, playing soccer. Smaller than the others, my son leaps, heads, dribbles, feints, passes. When a big boy knocks him down, he tumbles on the mud, in his green-and-black school uniform, in an ecstasy of falling. I am envious. Never for me the jaunty pride of the school uniform, the solemn ritual of the coach's pep talk, the camaraderie of shook hands and slapped backsides, the shadow-striped hush of late afternoon and last quarter, the solemn vaulted universe of official combat, with its cheering mothers and referees exotic as zebras and the bespectacled timekeeper alert with his claxon.[11] When the boy scores a goal, he runs into the arms of his teammates with upraised arms and his face alight as if blinded by triumph. They lift him from the earth in a union of muddy hugs. What spirit! What valor! What skill! His father, watching him from the sidelines, inwardly registers only one complaint: he feels the boy, with his talent, should be more aggressive.

They drove across the Commonwealth of Pennsylvania to hear their son read in Pittsburgh. But when their presence was announced to the audience, they did not stand; the applause groped for them and died. My mother said afterwards she was afraid she might fall into the next row if she tried to stand in the dark. Next morning was sunny, and the three of us searched for the house where once they had lived. They had been happy there; I imagined, indeed, that I had been conceived there, just before the slope of the Depression steepened and fear gripped my family. We found the library where she used to read Turgenev,[12] and the little park where the bums slept close as paving stones in the summer night; but their street kept eluding us, though we circled in the car. On foot,

---

10. *Sepia* (sē′ pē ə) is a brown tone or pigment.

11. *Claxon* (more correctly, Klaxon) is an electronic warning signal or horn. It is also the trademark of such a device.

12. Ivan Sergeyevich *Turgenev* (toor gä′ nyev) (1818–1883) was a Russian novelist, short-story writer, and playwright.

Vocabulary
radical (rad′ i kəl) *adj.* deviating greatly from the usual or customary; extreme
legible (lej′ ə bəl) *adj.* able to be read
valor (val′ ər) *n.* courage; bravery

my mother found the tree. She claimed she recognized it, the sooty linden tree she would gaze into from their apartment windows. The branches, though thicker, had held their pattern. But the house itself, and the entire block, was gone. Stray bricks and rods of iron in the grass suggested that the demolition had been recent. We stood on the empty spot and laughed. They knew it was right, because the railroad tracks were the right distance away. In confirmation, a long freight train pulled itself east around the curve, its great weight gliding as if on a river current; then a silver passenger train came gliding as effortlessly in the other direction. The curve of the tracks tipped the cars slightly toward us. The Golden Triangle, gray and hazed, was off to our left, beyond a forest of bridges. We stood on the grassy rubble that morning, where something once had been, beside the tree still there, and were intensely happy. Why? We knew.

"'No,' Dad said to me, 'the Christian ministry isn't a job you choose, it's a vocation for which you got to receive a call.' I could tell he wanted me to ask him. We never talked much, but we understood each other, we were both scared devils, not like you and the kid. I asked him, Had he ever received the call? He said No. He said No, he never had. Received the call. That was a terrible thing, for him to admit. And I was the one he told. As far as I knew he never admitted it to anybody, but he admitted it to me. He felt like hell about it, I could tell. That was all we ever said about it. That was enough."

He has made his younger brother cry, and justice must be done. A father enforces justice. I corner the rat in our bedroom; he is holding a cardboard mailing tube like a sword. The challenge flares white-hot; I roll my weight toward him like a rock down a mountain, and knock the weapon from his hand. He smiles. Smiles! Because my facial expression is silly? Because he is glad that he can still be overpowered, and hence is still protected? Why? I do not hit him. We stand a second, father and son, and then as nimbly as on the soccer field he steps around me and out the door. He slams the door. He shouts obscenities in the hall, slams all the doors he can find on the way to his room. Our moment of smilingly shared silence was the moment of compression; now the explosion. The whole house rocks with it. Downstairs, his siblings and mother come to me and offer advice and psychological analysis. I was too aggressive. He is spoiled. What they can never know, my grief alone to treasure, was that lucid many-sided second of his smiling and my relenting, before the world's wrathful pantomime of power resumed.

As we huddle whispering about him, my son takes his revenge. In his room, he plays his guitar. He has greatly improved this winter; his hands getting bigger is the least of it. He has found in the guitar an escape. He plays the Romanza[13] wherein repeated notes, with a sliding like the heart's valves, let themselves fall along the scale:

The notes fall, so gently he bombs us, drops feathery notes down upon us, our visitor, our prisoner.

---

13. The *Romanza* (rō män′ zə) is a musical composition, written for the guitar, that has sentimental or romantic qualities.

Vocabulary
lucid (lōō′ sid) *adj.* rational; sane

Responding to Literature

Personal Response

Were you surprised by the final sentence of the story? Why or why not?

——— **ANALYZING LITERATURE** ———

RECALL AND INTERPRET

1. Who is the narrator at the beginning and the end of the story? How do you know?
2. Explain the different points of view from which this story is told.
3. Describe the characters in the passages from 1973, 1949, 1913, and the 1880s. What does each passage reveal about the attitudes of the time and the personalities of the characters?
4. How does the narrator of 1973 feel as he watches his son play soccer? Why might he feel this way?
5. What words does the narrator use to describe his son at the end of the story? What might he mean by these words?

EVALUATE AND CONNECT

6. Theme Connections   Find examples of father-son relationships from each time period in the story. What do these scenes suggest about the relationships between fathers and sons during the twentieth century?
7. Compare the relationships in this story with those in your own life. How are your relationships similar to any of those in the story? How are they different?
8. Think about your responses to the Focus Activity on page 1046. How do you think Updike might answer that same question? Explain.

Literary ELEMENTS

First-Person Point of View

In a story with **first-person point of view**, the story is told by a character who refers to himself or herself as "I." A first-person narrator can be a participant or an observer. In "Son," the narrator takes both roles. For example, he participates when he says that he gave his son a back rub. He observes in a later passage when he says, "I must guess at the year."

1. In what sections of the story is the narrator a participant? To whom does the pronoun *he* refer in each of those sections?
2. When the narrator is an observer, to whom does the pronoun *he* refer?
3. How might the effect be different if the story were written from third-person point of view?

● See **Literary Terms Handbook,** p. R12.

——— **EXTENDING YOUR RESPONSE** ———

Writing About Literature
Analyzing Title   Do you think the title "Son" is a good one for this story? Why or why not? Write your answer in a paragraph or two, and support it with information from your own experience and details from the story. If you disagree with the choice of title, suggest alternative titles.

Literature Groups
Identifying the Theme   A story's **theme** is its underlying message about life or human nature. What do you think is this story's theme? Discuss this question in your group, using details from the story as evidence. Then compare your answer with the answers of other groups.

📖 **Save your work for your portfolio.**

Before You Read

from *The Way To Rainy Mountain*

Meet
N. Scott Momaday

❝I believe that one can work miracles in language. Language itself is a kind of miracle.❞

—Momaday

The Man Made of Words, the title of one of his books, describes N. Scott Momaday (mə mä′ dā) well. He is a distinguished novelist, poet, and teacher who relishes words—their sounds, meanings, and power. "Words are instruments of infinite possibility," he observes, and he uses them to preserve the oral traditions and the culture of Native Americans.

Momaday, of Kiowa descent, was born in Oklahoma and grew up in the Southwest. His mother was a teacher and a writer; his father was an artist, a teacher, and a "great story-teller" who repeatedly told his son Kiowa tales and legends. When Momaday grew up, he realized how fragile these stories were: "They exist only by word of mouth, always just one generation away from extinction." He began retelling these stories on paper, thus starting down a lifelong path as a writer.

Momaday's first novel, *House Made of Dawn*, was groundbreaking for its realistic depiction of modern Native American life. The book won a Pulitzer Prize for Fiction, making Momaday the first Native American writer to win this award. In *The Way To Rainy Mountain*, Momaday blends Kiowa myths, legends, and history, as well as autobiographical details.

Through his writing, Momaday has helped to break down negative stereotypes of Native Americans as well as to share his Kiowa heritage with others.

"When I was growing up on the reservations of the Southwest, I saw people who were deeply involved in their traditional life, in the memories of their blood," he recalls. "They had, as far as I could see, a certain strength and beauty that I find missing in the modern world at large. I like to celebrate that involvement in my writing."

Momaday's talents extend beyond novels and stories, how-ever. He is also an artist and illustrator whose work has been displayed in Europe and appears in several of his books, including *The Gourd Dancer*. In addition, Momaday's trademark voice—described by many as rich, powerful, and booming—can be heard narrating many of the exhibits at the Smithsonian's Museum of the American Indian.

❝I believe that the Indian has an understanding of the physical world and of the earth as a spiritual entity that is his, very much his own. The non-Indian can benefit a good deal by having that perception revealed to him.❞

—Momaday

N. Scott Momaday was born in 1934.

Reading Further

If you would like to read more by or about N. Scott Momaday, you might enjoy the following:

Collections: *The Way To Rainy Mountain*, by N. Scott Momaday, is a collection of anecdotes and folktales about the Kiowas, with illustrations by Momaday's father.

Ancestral Voice: Conversations with N. Scott Momaday, by Charles L. Woodard, is a collection of discussions with Momaday about his writing and personal experiences.

Poetry: *The Gourd Dancer* contains poems and illustrations by Momaday.

FOCUS ACTIVITY

Where are you from? What places define who you are?

CHART IT! Chart the places that contribute to your identity. These might include your school, your place of birth, your native land, or your favorite place. Write words or phrases that explain how each place contributes to your identity.

Place	How It Defines Me

SETTING A PURPOSE Read to learn how a place influences a person, a family, and a culture.

BACKGROUND

The Time and Place

The story shifts in time between present-day Oklahoma, the childhood of the narrator's grandmother, and the more distant past.

Literary Influences

Two English-language writers who have influenced Momaday are writer Herman Melville and poet Emily Dickinson. In an interview, Momaday noted that Melville "had a wonderful ear, like the ear of a storyteller." He described Emily Dickinson as "a good teacher." Momaday believes that readers can learn a lot about language from Dickinson: "How it used to be used, how it ought to be used, what risks are involved in the use, and so on." For more about Melville and Dickinson, see pages 381–383 and 423–439.

VOCABULARY PREVIEW

writhe (rīth) v. to twist, as in great pain; p. 1054

preeminently (prē em′ ə nənt lē) adv. chiefly; primarily; p. 1054

pillage (pil′ ij) n. looting or plundering; p. 1054

luxuriant (lug zhoor′ ē ənt) adj. marked by rich or plentiful growth; abundant; p. 1056

profusion (prə fū′ zhen) n. a plentiful amount; abundance; p. 1056

engender (en jen′ dər) v. to give rise to; to cause; to produce; p. 1056

consummate (kon′ sə māt′) v. to bring to completion; to finish; p. 1057

opaque (ō pāk′) adj. not letting light through; p. 1058

domain (dō mān′) n. a territory over which control is exercised; a realm; p. 1058

enmity (en′ mə tē) n. deep-seated hatred; hostility; p. 1059

from The Way to

A single knoll rises out of the plain in Oklahoma, north and west of the Wichita Range. For my people, the Kiowas,[1] it is an old landmark, and they gave it the name Rainy Mountain. The hardest weather in the world is there. Winter brings blizzards, hot tornadic winds arise in the spring, and in summer the prairie is an anvil's edge. The grass turns brittle and brown, and it cracks beneath your feet. There are green belts along the rivers and creeks, linear groves of hickory and pecan, willow and witch hazel. At a distance in July or August the steaming foliage seems almost to <u>writhe</u> in fire. Great green and yellow grasshoppers are everywhere in the tall grass, popping up like corn to sting the flesh, and tortoises crawl about on the red earth, going nowhere in the plenty of time. Loneliness is an aspect of the land. All things in the plain are isolate;[2] there is no confusion of objects in the eye, but *one* hill or *one* tree or *one* man. To look upon that landscape in the early morning, with the sun at your back, is to lose the sense of proportion. Your imagination comes to life, and this, you think, is where Creation was begun.

I returned to Rainy Mountain in July. My grandmother had died in the spring, and I wanted to be at her grave. She had lived to be very old and at last infirm.[3] Her only living daughter was with her when she died, and I was told that in death her face was that of a child.

I like to think of her as a child. When she was born, the Kiowas were living the last great moment of their history. For more than a hundred years they had controlled the open range from the Smoky Hill River to the Red, from the headwaters of the Canadian to the fork of the Arkansas and Cimarron. In alliance with the Comanches, they had ruled the whole of the southern Plains. War was their sacred business, and they were among the finest horsemen the world has ever known. But warfare for the Kiowas was <u>preeminently</u> a matter of disposition rather than of survival, and they never understood the grim, unrelenting advance of the U.S. Cavalry. When at last, divided and ill-provisioned, they were driven onto the Staked Plains in the cold rains of autumn, they fell into panic. In Palo Duro Canyon they abandoned their crucial stores to <u>pillage</u> and had nothing then but their lives. In order to save themselves, they surrendered to the soldiers at

---

1. *Kiowas* (kī′ ə wäz)
2. *Isolate* (ī′ sə lāt) means "solitary."

3. *Infirm* means "physically weak" or "feeble."

Vocabulary
writhe (rīth) *v.* to twist, as in great pain
preeminently (prē em′ ə nənt lē) *adv.* chiefly; primarily
pillage (pil′ ij) *n.* looting or plundering

Rainy Mountain

N. Scott Momaday

Fort Sill and were imprisoned in the old stone corral that now stands as a military museum. My grandmother was spared the humiliation of those high gray walls by eight or ten years, but she must have known from birth the affliction of defeat, the dark brooding of old warriors.

Her name was Aho, and she belonged to the last culture to evolve in North America. Her forebears came down from the high country in western Montana nearly three centuries ago. They were a mountain people, a mysterious tribe of hunters whose language has never been positively classified in any major group. In the late seventeenth century they began a long migration to the south and east. It was a journey toward the dawn, and it led to a golden age. Along the way the Kiowas were befriended by the Crows, who gave them the culture and religion of the Plains. They acquired horses, and their ancient nomadic spirit was suddenly free of the ground. They acquired Tai-me,[4] the sacred Sun Dance doll, from that moment the object and symbol of their worship, and so shared in the divinity of the sun. Not least, they acquired the sense of destiny, therefore courage and pride. When they entered upon the southern Plains they had been transformed. No longer were they slaves to the simple necessity of survival; they were a lordly and dangerous society of fighters and thieves, hunters and priests of the sun. According to their origin myth, they entered the world through a hollow log. From one point of view, their migration was the fruit of an old prophecy, for indeed they emerged from a sunless world.

---

4. *Tai-me* (tī′ mā), the Sun Dance doll, wears a robe of white feathers.

Rock Tree, 1987. N. Scott Momaday. Graphite and wash, 14 x 11 in. Courtesy of the artist.

Although my grandmother lived out her long life in the shadow of Rainy Mountain, the immense landscape of the continental interior lay like memory in her blood. She could tell of the Crows, whom she had never seen, and of the Black Hills, where she had never been. I wanted to see in reality what she had seen more perfectly in the mind's eye, and traveled fifteen hundred miles to begin my pilgrimage.

Yellowstone, it seemed to me, was the top of the world, a region of deep lakes and dark timber, canyons and waterfalls. But, beautiful as it is, one might have the sense of confinement there. The skyline in all directions is close at hand, the high wall of the woods and deep cleavages of shade. There is a perfect freedom in the mountains, but it belongs to the eagle and the elk, the badger and the bear. The Kiowas reckoned their stature by the distance they could see, and they were bent and blind in the wilderness.

Descending eastward, the highland meadows are a stairway to the plain. In July the inland slope of the Rockies is luxuriant with flax and buckwheat, stonecrop and larkspur.[5] The earth unfolds and the limit of the land recedes. Clusters of trees, and animals grazing far in the distance, cause the vision to reach away and wonder to build upon the mind. The sun follows a longer course in the day, and the sky is immense beyond all comparison. The great billowing clouds that sail upon it are shadows that move upon the grain like water, dividing light. Farther down, in the land of the Crows and Blackfeet, the plain is yellow. Sweet clover takes hold of the hills and bends upon itself to cover and seal the soil. There the Kiowas paused on their way; they had come to the place where they must change their lives. The sun is at home on the plains. Precisely there does it have the certain character of a god. When the Kiowas came to the land of the Crows, they could see the dark lees[6] of the hills at dawn across the Bighorn River, the profusion of light on the grain shelves, the oldest deity ranging after the solstices.[7] Not yet would they veer southward to the caldron of the land that lay below; they must wean their blood[8] from the northern winter and hold the mountains a while longer in their view. They bore Tai-me in procession to the east.

A dark mist lay over the Black Hills, and the land was like iron. At the top of a ridge I caught sight of Devil's Tower[9] upthrust against the gray sky as if in the birth of time the core of the earth had broken through its crust and the motion of the world was begun. There are things in nature that engender an awful quiet in the heart of man; Devil's Tower is one of them. Two centuries ago, because they could not do otherwise, the Kiowas made a legend at the base of the rock. My grandmother said:

---

5. *Flax* is a flowering plant whose fibers are spun to make cloth. *Buckwheat* is a plant whose seeds are used as a cereal grain. *Stonecrop* is a flowering plant found on rocks and walls. *Larkspur* is known for its showy flower stalks.

6. *Lees* are sheltered places, as the sides of hills that are away from the wind.
7. The *solstices* (sol' sti sez) refers to the longest day of the year (about June 21) and the shortest day (about December 21) in the Northern Hemisphere.
8. *Wean their blood* means "to become acclimated by removing themselves gradually."
9. *Devil's Tower*, an 856-foot-high column of volcanic rock in Wyoming, was the first national monument in the United States.

Vocabulary
luxuriant (lug zhoor' ē ənt) *adj.* marked by rich or plentiful growth; abundant
profusion (prə fū' zhen) *n.* a plentiful amount; abundance
engender (en jen' dər) *v.* to give rise to; to cause; to produce

Eight children were there at play, seven sisters and their brother. Suddenly the boy was struck dumb; he trembled and began to run upon his hands and feet. His fingers became claws, and his body was covered with fur. Directly there was a bear where the boy had been. The sisters were terrified; they ran, and the bear after them. They came to the stump of a great tree, and the tree spoke to them. It bade them climb upon it, and as they did so it began to rise into the air. The bear came to kill them, but they were just beyond its reach. It reared against the tree and scored the bark all around with its claws. The seven sisters were borne into the sky, and they became the stars of the Big Dipper.[10]

From that moment, and so long as the legend lives, the Kiowas have kinsmen in the night sky. Whatever they were in the mountains, they could be no more. However tenuous their well-being, however much they had suffered and would suffer again, they had found a way out of the wilderness.

My grandmother had a reverence for the sun, a holy regard that now is all but gone out of mankind. There was a wariness in her, and an ancient awe. She was a Christian in her later years, but she had come a long way about, and she never forgot her birthright. As a child she had been to the Sun Dances; she had taken part in those annual rites, and by them she had learned the restoration of her people in the presence of Tai-me. She was about seven when the last Kiowa Sun Dance was held in 1887 on the Washita River above Rainy Mountain Creek. The buffalo were gone. In order to consummate the ancient sacrifice—to impale the head of a buffalo bull upon the medicine tree—a delegation of old men journeyed into Texas, there to beg and barter for an animal from the

Goodnight herd. She was ten when the Kiowas came together for the last time as a living Sun Dance culture. They could find no buffalo; they had to hang an old hide from the sacred tree. Before the dance could begin, a company of soldiers rode out from Fort Sill under orders to disperse the tribe. Forbidden without cause the essential act of their faith, having seen the wild herds slaughtered and left to rot upon the ground, the Kiowas backed away forever from the medicine tree. That was July 20, 1890, at the great bend of the Washita. My grandmother was there. Without bitterness, and for as long as she lived, she bore a vision of deicide.[11]

Now that I can have her only in memory, I see my grandmother in the several postures that were peculiar to her: standing at the wood stove on a winter morning and turning meat in a great iron skillet; sitting at the south window, bent above her beadwork, and afterwards, when her vision failed, looking down for a long time into the fold of her hands; going out upon a cane, very slowly as she did when the weight of age came upon her; praying. I remember her most often at prayer. She made long, rambling prayers out of suffering and hope, having seen many things. I was never sure that I had the right to hear, so exclusive were they of all mere custom and company. The last time I saw her she prayed standing by the side of her bed at night, naked to the waist, the light of a kerosene lamp moving upon her dark skin. Her long, black hair, always drawn and braided in the day, lay upon her shoulders and against her breasts like a shawl. I do not speak Kiowa, and I never understood her prayers, but there was something inherently sad in the sound, some merest hesitation upon the syllables of sorrow. She began in a high and

---

10. The *Big Dipper* is part of a larger constellation called Ursa Major, the Great Bear.

11. *Deicide* (dē′ ə sīd′) is the killing of a god.

Vocabulary
consummate (kon′ sə māt′) *v.* to bring to completion; to finish

Faces, 1987. N. Scott Momaday. Graphite and wash, 14 x 11 in. Courtesy of the artist.

Viewing the sketch: Which qualities of the Kiowas—according to Momaday— do you see portrayed in this sketch? Explain your reasoning.

little while, wood takes on the appearance of great age. All colors wear soon away in the wind and rain, and then the wood is burned gray and the grain appears and the nails turn red with rust. The windowpanes are black and opaque; you imagine there is nothing within, and indeed there are many ghosts, bones given up to the land. They stand here and there against the sky, and you approach them for a longer time than you expect. They belong in the distance; it is their domain.

Once there was a lot of sound in my grandmother's house, a lot of coming and going, feasting and talk. The summers there were full of excitement and reunion. The Kiowas are a summer people; they abide the cold and keep to themselves, but when the season turns and the land becomes warm and vital they cannot hold still; an old love of going returns upon them. The aged visitors who came to my grandmother's house when I was a child were made of lean and leather, and they bore themselves upright. They wore great black hats and bright ample shirts that shook in the wind. They rubbed fat upon their hair and wound

descending pitch, exhausting her breath to silence; then again and again—and always the same intensity of effort, of something that is, and is not, like urgency in the human voice. Transported so in the dancing light among the shadows of her room, she seemed beyond the reach of time. But that was illusion; I think I knew then that I should not see her again.

Houses are like sentinels in the plain, old keepers of the weather watch. There, in a very

---

Vocabulary

opaque (ō pāk′) *adj.* not letting light through
domain (dō mān′) *n.* a territory over which control is exercised; a realm

their braids with strips of colored cloth. Some of them painted their faces and carried the scars of old and cherished <u>enmities</u>. They were an old council of warlords, come to remind and be reminded of who they were. Their wives and daughters served them well. The women might indulge themselves; gossip was at once the mark and compensation of their servitude. They made loud and elaborate talk among themselves, full of jest and gesture, fright and false alarm. They went abroad[12] in fringed and flowered shawls, bright beadwork and German silver.[13] They were at home in the kitchen, and they prepared meals that were banquets.

There were frequent prayer meetings, and great nocturnal feasts. When I was a child I played with my cousins outside, where the lamplight fell upon the ground and the singing of the old people rose up around us and carried away into the darkness. There were a lot of good things to eat, a lot of laughter and surprise. And afterwards, when the quiet returned, I lay down with my grandmother and could hear the frogs away by the river and feel the motion of the air.

Now there is a funeral silence in the rooms, the endless wake of some final word. The walls have closed in upon my grandmother's house. When I returned to it in mourning, I saw for the first time in my life how small it was. It was late at night, and there was a white moon, nearly full. I sat for a long time on the stone steps by the kitchen door. From there I could see out across the land; I could see the long row of trees by the creek, the low light upon the rolling plains, and the stars of the Big Dipper. Once I looked at the moon and caught sight of a strange thing. A cricket had perched upon the handrail, only a few inches away from me. My line of vision was such that the creature filled the moon like a fossil. It had gone there, I thought, to live and die, for there, of all places, was its small definition made whole and eternal. A warm wind rose up and purled[14] like the longing within me.

The next morning I awoke at dawn and went out on the dirt road to Rainy Mountain. It was already hot, and the grasshoppers began to fill the air. Still, it was early in the morning, and the birds sang out of the shadows. The long yellow grass on the mountain shone in the bright light, and a scissortail hied[15] above the land. There, where it ought to be, at the end of a long and leg-

Did You Know?
A *scissortail,* a type of fly-catcher, is a small gray and pink bird with a forked tail.

endary way, was my grandmother's grave. Here and there on the dark stones were ancestral names. Looking back once, I saw the mountain and came away.

---

12. Here, *abroad* means "away from one's home."
13. *German silver* is an alloy that resembles real silver.

14. *Purled* means "rippled with a murmuring sound."
15. *Hied* means "went quickly."

Vocabulary
enmity (en′ mə tē) *n.* deep-seated hatred; hostility

Responding to Literature

Personal Response

What new insights did you gain from reading this selection? Share your thoughts with a classmate.

— ANALYZING LITERATURE —

RECALL

1. Where and what is Rainy Mountain? Why does Momaday return there?
2. What does Momaday call the era in which his grandmother was born? How did being born at that time affect her life?
3. Of what significance to the Kiowas is the **legend** the grandmother tells? (See Literary Terms Handbook, page R9.) What other elements of Kiowa traditional beliefs were part of the grandmother's life?
4. What memories does Momaday have of his grandmother and her "aged visitors"? What sparked their coming together?
5. What does Momaday notice during his last night and morning on Rainy Mountain? Where does he go, and what does he see?

INTERPRET

6. Why, do you think, does Momaday feel that Rainy Mountain "is where Creation was begun"?
7. What do you learn about the Kiowa people from the way that they respond to the end of their traditional lifestyle?
8. What do you think is the relationship between Momaday's "vision of deicide" and the changes in the environment of the Kiowa people?
9. What might the wealth of details Momaday recalls about his grandmother's life suggest about his childhood?
10. What, do you think, is symbolized in the description of the grandmother's grave?

EVALUATE AND CONNECT

11. In what ways, do you think, does the narrator capture the culture of the Kiowas? Give details from the selection to support your opinion.
12. How is this history like others you have read? How is it different?
13. Theme Connections   In your opinion, which generation witnessed more changes, that of the narrator or his grandmother? Explain your answer.
14. Compare and contrast Momaday's response to Rainy Mountain with the response a tourist today might have to the same place.
15. Momaday's grandmother was an important figure in his life. Who in your life has influenced you? In what ways?

Literary ELEMENTS

Narrative

A **narrative** tells a story. The story may be fiction, a legend, a memoir or an anecdote, a factual account, or even a poem or a song. Many writers use only one kind of story in a work. In *The Way To Rainy Mountain,* Momaday combines fiction, anecdotes, and historical facts. For example, the scene of the grandmother at prayer is an anecdote, and the account of the last Sun Dance and what followed is historical fact.

1. Momaday writes, "the Kiowas have kinsmen in the night sky." What type of narrative does Momaday use to support this idea?
2. What do anecdotes add to a narrative that historical facts cannot? What do historical facts provide that anecdotes or legends may not?

⬤ See **Literary Terms Handbook,** p. R10.

LITERATURE AND WRITING

Writing About Literature

Expanding a Narrative   What information about Momaday or his grandmother do you think could add to a reader's appreciation of this narrative? In a few paragraphs, describe the specific parts of the narrative that you would expand, what kinds of information you would include, and how the narrative would benefit from these additions.

Creative Writing

Time Travel   Reread the chart you made for the Focus Activity on page 1053. Select one place and think about how you would describe it. Consider Momaday's description of Rainy Mountain as you list details about your special place. Then create a travel brochure for your place. Include details about its landscape and its history.

EXTENDING YOUR RESPONSE

Literature Groups

Examine Ideas   Momaday once said, "I don't see any validity in the separation of man and landscape." He called human alienation from nature "one of the great afflictions of our time." In your group, discuss how Momaday's anecdote reflects the idea that people and places are linked and whether or not you agree with this idea. Share your conclusions with the class.

Listening and Speaking

Listen to Oral History   Momaday's grandmother witnessed many events in the history of the Kiowas. Whom do you know has been an eyewitness to important historical events? Interview a person about an event or period that the person is familiar with, asking questions to elicit detailed personal recollections about what the person saw and how she or he reacted to it. Share your notes in a brief discussion with the class.

Internet Connection

Other Native American Voices   There are many Internet sites that contain works by Native Americans, as well as reviews and discussions of those works. Search the Internet for sites about Native American writers and their writing. With your classmates, assemble a list of Native American authors and titles that you would like to read.

📖 **Save your work for your portfolio.**

Skill Minilesson

VOCABULARY • Etymology

A word's etymology is its history, the story of its origins. This information often gives clues to the meaning and spelling of a word.

   The word *wreit*, for example, is an Old English word meaning "to turn." Several modern words can be traced back to *wreit*; for example, *writhe, wreath, wriggle, wrench,* and *wring*. Notice how these words are similar to their ancestor in meaning and spelling.

PRACTICE   Use a dictionary and your understanding of word origins to trace the history of the words listed below from their original meanings and languages to their modern definitions.

1. knoll
2. range
3. panic
4. billow
5. canyon
6. cavalry

Before You Read

Ambush

Meet Tim O'Brien

"The object of storytelling, like the object of magic, is not to explain or to resolve, but rather to create and to perform miracles of the imagination," says Tim O'Brien. As a foot soldier in Vietnam, O'Brien had to perform miracles of the imagination just to get through each day. He was drafted into the army right after college in 1968. In Vietnam, he became a sergeant and earned a Purple Heart, an award given to U.S. soldiers wounded or killed in battle. His first book, *If I Die in a Combat Zone, Box Me Up and Ship Me Home*, was a memoir of his tour of duty.

O'Brien then wrote a novel called *Going After Cacciato* (kä chä′ tō), about a soldier who decides one day to simply walk away from the war. He won the National Book Award for it in 1979. O'Brien was nominated for a Pulitzer Prize in 1991 for his short-story collection *The Things They Carried*.

O'Brien's work has been compared to that of Ernest Hemingway and Joseph Heller. Like them, he builds a picture of soldiers' daily lives by compiling masses of sensory details. Unlike them, he intertwines fantasy with reality in his war stories.

Besides writing novels and short stories, O'Brien has worked as a national affairs reporter for the *Washington Post* and as a writing teacher.

"My passion[s] as a human being and as a writer intersect in Vietnam, not in the physical stuff but in the issues of Vietnam—of courage, rectitude, enlightenment, holiness, trying to do the right thing in the world."

—*O'Brien*

Tim O'Brien was born in 1946.

FOCUS ACTIVITY

When have you reacted quickly to a situation and then regretted your actions later?

JOURNAL In your journal, describe a situation in which you reacted without thinking, and what you later felt about your reaction.

SETTING A PURPOSE Read this short story to find out how a single action haunts a man for the rest of his life.

BACKGROUND

The Time and Place

The story takes place in Vietnam, near the village of My Khe (mē kā), around 1968. From 1965 to 1973, U.S. troops fought alongside the South Vietnamese in their struggle against a communist movement from the North.

The Vietcong, nicknamed *Charley* by U.S. soldiers, were guerrilla soldiers who supported communist North Vietnam. They sometimes disguised themselves as innocent civilians before ambushing South Vietnamese and U.S. troops.

VOCABULARY PREVIEW

grope (grōp) *v.* to feel about uncertainly with the hands; to search blindly; p. 1063

stooped (sto͞opt) *adj.* bent forward and downward; p. 1063

ponder (pon′ dər) *v.* to think about thoroughly and carefully; p. 1063

gape (gāp) *v.* to stare with the mouth open, as in wonder or surprise; p. 1064

dwell (dwel) *v.* to think about at length; p. 1064

AMBUSH

Tim O'Brien

When she was nine, my daughter Kathleen asked if I had ever killed anyone. She knew about the war; she knew I'd been a soldier. "You keep writing these war stories," she said, "so I guess you must've killed somebody." It was a difficult moment, but I did what seemed right, which was to say, "Of course not," and then to take her onto my lap and hold her for a while. Someday, I hope, she'll ask again. But here I want to pretend she's a grown-up. I want to tell her exactly what happened, or what I remember happening, and then I want to say to her that as a little girl she was absolutely right. This is why I keep writing war stories:

He was a short, slender young man of about twenty. I was afraid of him—afraid of something—and as he passed me on the trail I threw a grenade that exploded at his feet and killed him.

Or to go back:

Shortly after midnight we moved into the ambush site outside My Khe. The whole platoon[1] was there, spread out in the dense brush along the trail, and for five hours nothing at all happened. We were working in two-man teams—one man on guard while the other slept, switching off every two hours—and I remember it was still dark when Kiowa shook me awake for the final watch. The night was foggy and hot. For the first few moments I felt lost, not sure about directions, groping for my helmet and weapon. I reached out and found three grenades and lined them up in front of me; the pins had already been straightened for quick throwing. And then for maybe half an hour I kneeled there and waited. Very gradually, in tiny slivers, dawn began to break through the fog, and from my position in the brush I could see ten or fifteen meters up the trail. The mosquitoes were fierce. I remember slapping at them, wondering if I should wake up Kiowa and ask for some repellent, then thinking it was a bad idea, then looking up and seeing the young man come out of the fog. He wore black clothing and rubber sandals and a gray ammunition belt. His shoulders were slightly stooped, his head cocked to the side as if listening for something. He seemed at ease. He carried his weapon in one hand, muzzle down, moving without any hurry up the center of the trail. There was no sound at all—none that I can remember. In a way, it seemed, he was part of the morning fog, or my own imagination, but there was also the reality of what was happening in my stomach. I had already pulled the pin on a grenade. I had come up to a crouch. It was entirely automatic. I did not hate the young man; I did not see him as the enemy; I did not ponder issues of morality or politics or military duty. I crouched and kept my head low. I tried to swallow whatever was rising from my stomach, which tasted like lemonade, something fruity and sour. I was terrified. There were no thoughts about killing. The grenade was to make him go away—just evaporate—and I leaned back and felt my mind go empty and then felt it fill up again. I had already thrown the grenade before telling myself to throw it. The brush was thick and I had to lob it high, not aiming, and I remember the grenade seeming to freeze above

---

1. A *platoon* is a military unit, usually commanded by a lieutenant, that forms part of a company.

Vocabulary

grope (grōp) *v.* to feel about uncertainly with the hands; to search blindly
stooped (stoōpt) *adj.* bent forward and downward
ponder (pon′ dər) *v.* to think about thoroughly and carefully

Indiana Rangers: The Army Guard in Vietnam, 1984. Mort Künstler. Oil on canvas, 24 x 32 in. Collection National Guard Bureau, Pentagon, Washington, DC.

Viewing the painting: Look closely at the man in the foreground of the painting. In your opinion, which emotions expressed by the narrator of "Ambush" does his face convey?

me for an instant, as if a camera had clicked, and I remember ducking down and holding my breath and seeing little wisps of fog rise from the earth. The grenade bounced once and rolled across the trail. I did not hear it, but there must've been a sound, because the young man dropped his weapon and began to run, just two or three quick steps, then he hesitated, swiveling to his right, and he glanced down at the grenade and tried to cover his head but never did. It occurred to me then that he was about to die. I wanted to warn him. The grenade made a popping noise—not soft but not loud either—not what I'd expected—and there was a puff of dust and smoke—a small white puff—and the young man seemed to jerk upward as if pulled by invisible wires. He fell on his back. His rubber sandals had been blown off. There was no wind. He lay at the center of the trail, his right leg bent beneath him, his one eye shut, his other eye a huge star-shaped hole.

It was not a matter of live or die. There was no real peril. Almost certainly the young man would have passed by. And it will always be that way.

Later, I remember, Kiowa tried to tell me that the man would've died anyway. He told me that it was a good kill, that I was a soldier and this was a war, that I should shape up and stop staring and ask myself what the dead man would've done if things were reversed.

None of it mattered. The words seemed far too complicated. All I could do was <u>gape</u> at the fact of the young man's body.

Even now I haven't finished sorting it out. Sometimes I forgive myself, other times I don't. In the ordinary hours of life I try not to <u>dwell</u> on it, but now and then, when I'm reading a newspaper or just sitting alone in a room, I'll look up and see the young man coming out of the morning fog. I'll watch him walk toward me, his shoulders slightly stooped, his head cocked to the side, and he'll pass within a few yards of me and suddenly smile at some secret thought and then continue up the trail to where it bends back into the fog.

Vocabulary
gape (gāp) *v.* to stare with the mouth open, as in wonder or surprise
dwell (dwel) *v.* to think about at length

Responding to Literature

Personal Response

If you could speak with the narrator about his experience in Vietnam, what would you talk about?

Literary ELEMENTS

Mood

The **mood** of a story or a poem is the feeling or atmosphere that a writer creates for the reader. Writers develop a mood with carefully chosen words and details that vividly describe the **setting** and the events of the story. To determine the mood of a literary work, look closely at scene-setting descriptions and the reactions of characters to events.

1. How would you describe the mood of "Ambush"? Give examples of details that contribute to the mood.

2. How does the mood of the story affect its overall impact on you? Explain.

● See **Literary Terms Handbook,** p. R10.

--- ANALYZING LITERATURE ---

RECALL AND INTERPRET

1. How does the narrator respond to his daughter's question? In your opinion, why does he lie to her?

2. What does the narrator do when he sees the young man? What does he say he did not do? What does this episode suggest about the role of a soldier in wartime?

3. What does Kiowa tell the narrator, and how does the narrator feel about this advice? What does this exchange suggest to you about the narrator's values?

4. What do you think the story's title signifies? Who, besides the enemy soldier, might have been ambushed?

EVALUATE AND CONNECT

5. What would you have said to the daughter if you were in the narrator's position? Would you tell her the truth when she grows up? Why or why not?

6. Do the narrator's reactions to the killing of an enemy soldier seem believable to you? Explain.

7. A **frame** is a story that either surrounds or introduces a more important story. What effect does O'Brien achieve by using a frame?

8. The narrator of "Ambush" has a lot in common with O'Brien. What incidents in your own life would make good short stories? Why?

--- EXTENDING YOUR RESPONSE ---

Personal Writing

Regrets? I Have a Few   Years after the war, the narrator of "Ambush" continues to be haunted by his memory of killing the enemy soldier. Based on what you wrote for the Focus Activity on page 1062, choose one thing you have said or done that you'd like to change. In your journal, describe the event as you would have liked it to turn out.

Performing

Role-Play a Switch   In a group, role-play a scene that didn't take place in the story but could have happened years later. Assign roles and think about what the characters would say and do, using details from the story to support your ideas. Then perform the scene for the class.

📖 **Save your work for your portfolio.**

Before You Read

Rain Music

BACKGROUND

The Time and Place
Longhang Nguyen (long′ häng nōō yin′) was born in Vietnam. She came to the United States in 1979. This story takes place in present-day California.

Did You Know?
After the Vietnam War ended in 1975, hundreds of thousands of refugees came to the United States.

Today, more than 300,000 people of Vietnamese descent live in California. Other large Vietnamese communities are located in Texas, Florida, and Louisiana. Most Vietnamese Americans are foreign born, and many still maintain traditional Vietnamese customs and speak their native language at home. Their children, however, are influenced by U.S. culture as well as by Vietnamese ways.

FOCUS ACTIVITY

How do you make important decisions about your future?

MAP IT! Make a spider map like the one shown here to explore the factors that go into making a decision. On each diagonal line, name a decision you'll need to make in the future. On the horizontal lines, list the factors that might affect your decision.

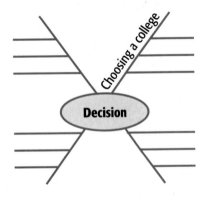

SETTING A PURPOSE Read to find out what one character considers when she makes an important life decision.

Vietnamese food court in Orange County, California.

VOCABULARY PREVIEW

sibling (sib′ ling) *adj.* relating to a brother or a sister; p. 1067

mimic (mim′ ik) *v.* to copy; to reproduce; to imitate; p. 1067

wistful (wist′ fəl) *adj.* full of wishful or sad longing; p. 1067

minutely (mī nōōt′ lē) *adv.* in a very small degree; p. 1068

resonant (rez′ ə nənt) *adj.* having a full, rich sound; p. 1068

ample (am′ pəl) *adj.* of great size or capacity; p. 1068

sumptuous (sump′ chōō əs) *adj.* involving great expense; extravagant; splendid; p. 1068

pigment (pig′ mənt) *n.* a substance that gives color; p. 1069

cascade (kas kād′) *v.* to fall or flow as if in a waterfall or series of waterfalls; p. 1069

Rain Music

Longhang Nguyen

Linh and I grew up penned in the same yard, so our <u>sibling</u> rivalry did not last very long. By third grade we had stopped physically assaulting one another and reached a permanent truce. At that time her hair was long and flowing, brushed daily by my mother as Linh closed her eyes and counted each stroke. It always felt like cool satin when I yanked it, her head jerking backward, <u>mimicking</u> the motion of my arm. In actuality, she was very kind and I was not too violent, so we became intimate friends. I have not had any trouble from her since.

She is the red rose of the family and I am the green thorn. We have both decided that we are beautiful, so she tells me, but I believe she is also very beautiful outside in face and gesture. I always pout when I accuse her of being a selfish firstborn, picking, stealing the best of our parents' genes and leaving me the rejected remainder. She has wide, almond-shaped eyes like black, pearl-black reflecting pools with brown-colored flecks swirling beneath the surface, light honey-color skin and even, velvet-smooth cheeks. Her nose is just slightly upturned, her lips rosebud shaped, her chin small and delicate.

Her hair still looks and feels the same now as in third grade. The vision, taken together as a whole, is breathtaking. There is something about it, a <u>wistful</u>, dandelion, orchid-like kind of beauty that feels like notes in a chord being played separately, finger by finger, harmonizing back and forth. I marvel even now.

My mother and father have polished her until she shines. She graduated summa cum laude[1] from the College of Chemistry at Cal[2] and double majored in Ethnic Studies. However, my parents don't count the latter. She is now a fourth-year student at UCSF[3] preparing to enter the surgical residency program next fall. My parents are bursting at the seams, gorged with devouring so much blessedness and good fortune.

"Will your daughter become a surgeon?" our relatives ask.

---

1. Someone who graduates *summa cum laude* (soom′ ə koom lou′ dē) graduates with highest honors. The Latin phrase means "with highest praise."
2. *Cal* is another name for the University of California at Berkeley.
3. *UCSF* is the University of California at San Francisco.

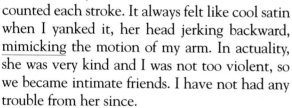

Vocabulary
sibling (sib′ ling) *adj.* relating to a brother or a sister
mimic (mim′ ik) *v.* to copy; to reproduce; to imitate
wistful (wist′ fəl) *adj.* full of wishful or sad longing

"It's possible," my father says, beaming.

"She is friends with this young man in her class. He's tall, distinguished-looking, loyal and respectful to his parents, hard-working but generous. He was even born in Vietnam! But he came over here with his family in 1975. He went to Harvard"—my mother pauses to let the relatives gasp in unison— "on a full scholarship!" She smiles modestly, then lowers her eyes.

"A possible son-in-law?" they ask.

She shrugs and sighs. "That is up to God."

Linh hasn't told my parents about David. She met him five years ago during her final year at Cal. That semester they were in three classes together: a choral class, an Afro-American literature class, and a creative writing class. They became good friends.

David is a writer. His subjects are ordinary preoccupations of other writers: his mother, the father he has never seen or known, the friends of his childhood. Some of them are dead now. The others are spread out across the country. One is a construction worker in St. Louis. Another is a teacher in Baton Rouge. The third is a journalist in Washington, D.C. They write to him once in a while or call him. Linh hasn't met any of them, but she knows them all.

After David feverishly completes a story, Linh cooks him dinner. Afterward, she tucks him into bed and sits nearby in the wicker chair, legs drawn up and hugged tightly to her chest, to watch him while he sleeps. His soft, black curls rest against the white of the pillow, his closed eyelids and long lashes flutter minutely while he dreams, his breath whistles through the evenness of his teeth as the cover grazes the dark honey of his skin.

They always have a good time together, and he makes her laugh in many different ways, wherever they happen to be. He always gets close to finishing her off during a tennis set, but then she cries out that he has cheated and treated her unfairly and he has to start over again. He never wins. Sometimes they sing together, his clear, resonant tenor melding with her flutelike, crystalline soprano. Then they have tea.

I know all about David. She won't stop talking about him, but I know less about Thanh, the Vietnamese friend at UCSF. I know he's nice but that's all. She woke me up this morning at ten thirty and said, "It's a bright, beautiful, Saturday morning. Let's go and have a picnic."

"No, no," I mumbled hazily in my sleep. "Take David. Leave me alone."

"I don't want to take David. I want to spend quality time with you, my darling sister. Get up, you piece of mutton. Toast on the table in five minutes and we're leaving in half an hour."

"Oh, lord," I groaned, "I'm being punished for sins from past lives."

We arrived at the park at twelve, lugged our ample picnic hamper heavily laden with cheese, fruits, sandwiches, ice, and bottles of juice from the car, and trudged into the heart of the lightly shaded, green forest. When I opened the basket and took out the butter, she started to talk.

"David kissed me last night . . ."

"He what?"

". . . or I kissed him. It just happened, I guess. He invited me to dinner, promised to cook a sumptuous Cajun[4] feast with Vietnamese desserts. Bánh flanc,[5] you know. My favorite."

---

4. *Cajun* refers to descendants of French colonists from the Acadia region of Canada who eventually settled in southern Louisiana. *Cajun* cuisine is spicy and commonly features seafood.
5. *Bánh flanc* (bän flänk) is a small cake made with coconut milk and a brown sugar topping.

Vocabulary

minutely (mī nōōt′ lē) *adv.* in a very small degree
resonant (rez′ ə nənt) *adj.* having a full, rich sound
ample (am′ pəl) *adj.* of great size or capacity
sumptuous (sump′ chōō əs) *adj.* involving great expense; extravagant; splendid

She plucked a blade of grass from its roots and twisted it back and forth, watching a streak of feeble, yellow sun play on its linear edges. "I expected it to be a celebration. He'd just finished his first novel, not quite a love story, he says, and he wanted me to read it." She spoke more softly. "When I arrived, he had set tiny blossoms in water dishes throughout the apartment. It smelled wonderful. The food was delicious, everything so lovely, so tranquil I didn't know where to begin. After dinner he led me into the living room.

" 'Rain music,' he said. 'It's for you.' After the last note on the piano had stopped to echo, he turned toward me and kissed me for a long, long time. I didn't know what I was doing. I just couldn't stop. I didn't breathe. When he let me go, I kept thinking of his hands and fingers, seeing them fly over the ivory keys like little Russian men dancing in their black fur hats and noticing how his brown was different from mine. I was raging inside, screaming in my head, 'Why can't his fingers be brown like mine, be my brown? Why is his hair curly, not straight, like mine?' I saw brown pigments run across my eyes, all different colored browns. Those pigments keep us apart. How do I stand there and tell this man who writes me music and whose hands burn my cheeks that I can't be who he wants me to be?"

"But he doesn't want to change you."

"No, I can't be who he thinks I am. He's a damned starving writer. He can't give me anything, just himself. And he doesn't even know that I'm using him. Damn it! He doesn't even know." She choked on her tears, swallowed, and cried quietly, hugging her knees, until exhausted. The leaves rustled softly while I waited.

After a while she grew calm, her eyes gazing steadily at the flashing water of the stream below. "I love Thanh. I would never hurt him for anything. Throughout the four years at UCSF, he has been so patient, so kind, so dedicated to medicine for its own good, not for just its technology, even though he's brilliant and understands these details completely. He's so perfect for me, just perfect. It's like he stepped out of my story and came to life. We speak the same language and share the same past. Everything. And Mom and Dad, they've done so much for us. Now they think they've won the lottery from God for being good all their life."

"But how do you feel about Thanh? How does he make you feel?"

"He will be my lifelong friend. He'll make a wonderful father. That's what a husband should be. Our children will know the culture and customs of our homeland. They'll speak Vietnamese and English, just like us."

"And how does David make you feel?" I tugged at her gently.

She bowed her head for a long while reflecting. Then she softly murmured, "It's just not possible."

"But why? I don't understand."

The picnic basket remained quite full. Neither of us was hungry. It threatened to rain as we packed up to go home. On the drive back, we were silent. I watched the windshield wipers swing back and forth, clearing rain cascading down the front window.

Vocabulary

pigment (pig′ mənt) *n.* a substance that gives color
cascade (kas kād′) *v.* to fall or flow as if in a waterfall or series of waterfalls

Responding to Literature

Personal Response
Do you think Linh made the right choice? Why or why not?

ANALYZING LITERATURE

RECALL AND INTERPRET

1. Describe Linh's personality, appearance, and achievements. What expectations do you think Linh's parents have for her?
2. What does the narrator learn on the picnic? How do you think the narrator feels about her sister's predicament? Explain.
3. What does Linh say about the pigment of her skin? What might pigment represent to her? Give reasons for your answer.
4. Describe Linh's relationship with David. How does she feel about him? How does she feel about Thanh? Support your answer with details from the story.
5. What problem does Linh struggle with in this story? What ideas or principles motivate her decision at the end of the story?

EVALUATE AND CONNECT

6. Is the conflict in this story an **internal conflict,** a struggle within a character, or an **external conflict,** a struggle between a character and an outside force? Use details from the story to support your answer.
7. In your opinion, how well does the writer capture the clash of cultures that some immigrants face when they settle in a new country? Explain.
8. What decisions in your life will be as important as the one Linh makes? Review the map you made for the Focus Activity on page 1066. Which factors will be most important to you when you make those decisions?

Literary ELEMENTS

Crisis

In many stories a character faces a **crisis,** a moment of high tension that requires a decision. In "Rain Music," the crisis occurs the evening that David and Linh kiss. Instead of just enjoying the moment or being repulsed by it, Linh experiences an emotional storm within herself.

In some stories, like this one, only one crisis occurs. In other stories and in novels, a character may face several crises.

1. What conflicting feelings does Linh have after the kiss?
2. What issues does this scene expose for Linh?
3. Why is this moment a crisis for Linh?

● See **Literary Terms Handbook,** p. R4.

EXTENDING YOUR RESPONSE

Literature Groups
Predict the Future   Do you think Linh will have a happy marriage with Thanh? Hold a debate in your group. Divide into two teams, one to argue in the affirmative and one in the negative. Use story details and personal knowledge to develop support for your team's position. Compare your conclusions with those of other groups.

Creative Writing
Dialogue with David   Imagine that Linh and David meet ten years after this story takes place. What kind of life might each have at that point, and what might they say to each other? Imagine both the situation and the conversation. Then write a dialogue that captures it.

📖 **Save your work for your portfolio.**

Reading & Thinking Skills

Identifying Cause and Effect

If you fail your driver's test, you immediately ask *why.* Did you forget to signal before pulling into traffic? Did you miss a stop sign? Whatever it was, your error **caused** you to fail a test. The **effect** of failing the test may be another few months without a license. These situations have a **cause-and-effect relationship.**

You will find cause-and-effect relationships in your reading as well as in your life. By identifying these relationships, you can better understand what you are reading and the author's purpose for writing. To determine a cause, ask *why.* Identify an effect by looking for a result. Note the following examples.

Heat causes water to evaporate. This is a clear, physical principal with an obvious cause and a predictable effect. The writer's purpose is to inform.

People are social beings. Every culture expects certain kinds of behavior. People of a culture often feel pressure to fulfill the group's expectations. This is a more complex relationship. More than one cause is named, and the effect is not automatic, as indicated by the word "often."

There are several kinds of cause-and-effect relationships:

- one cause, one effect
- several causes, one effect
- one cause, several effects
- a cause-and-effect chain

When reading about causal relationships, be alert for clues—words and phrases that signal the relationship. These clues can also indicate the degree of certainty that is present in the relationship.

As a result, because, if . . . then, and *therefore* are common indicators of cause-and-effect relationships. Words such as *may, perhaps, certainly,* and *possibly* are clues to the certainty of the relationship.

- For more about related comprehension skills, see **Reading Handbook,** pp. R86–R93.

ACTIVITIES

1. Find two examples of cause-and-effect relationships in "Rain Music" and explain each one. One example should be a cause-and-effect chain. In your explanations, point out any clue words that identify each cause and its effect, and the words that indicate the degree of certainty for each relationship.

2. From the reading you have done recently, identify examples of the four kinds of cause-and-effect relationships and explain each one briefly. You may use examples from nonfiction selections in any field you are studying, or from stories and articles.

Meet Aurora Levins Morales

"I have a commitment to myself not to take the easy route, to not say things that I don't believe in, to tackle things in a truthful way."

—*Morales*

Aurora Levins Morales (ə rōr′ ä le′ vinz mōr äl′ äs) was thirteen when her family came to the United States from Puerto Rico. It was 1967, and the feminist movement was spreading across the country. Morales read the works of many feminist writers and felt encouraged to write about her own experiences.

Morales joined women's writing groups and developed a love for the works of African American writers Alice Walker and Toni Morrison. She also began writing with her mother, Rosario Morales. Together, they have published their works in anthologies and in their own book, *Getting Home Alive*, a collection of prose and poetry about identity, family, and the experiences of immigrants.

Morales often writes about what it is like to be part Puerto Rican and part Jewish. "As a fiction writer, I feel a responsibility to write material that can be used by my communities in our struggle for survival and identity," she says.

Morales has a Ph.D. in women's studies and history. She teaches writing at the University of Minnesota. She also travels frequently, giving lectures on multicultural histories, especially those of women of Latin American or Jewish descent.

Aurora Levins Morales was born in 1954.

FOCUS ACTIVITY

Which of your senses is the first to respond when you think of the word *kitchen?* What sensory images come to mind?

LIST IT! Make a list of the sensory images the word *kitchen* evokes for you.

SETTING A PURPOSE Read to learn of an awakening that takes place amid the sensory images of a kitchen.

BACKGROUND

Puerto Rican Cuisine

The island of Puerto Rico is home to a number of Caribbean crops: rice, beans, pumpkins, guava, coconuts, and plantains. Puerto Rican meals commonly feature these foods served with fish or meat and seasoned delicately. Puerto Rican desserts include custards, puddings, and cakes, and many meals end with Puerto Rican coffee, served black or with hot milk and sugar.

VOCABULARY PREVIEW

deftly (deft′ lē) *adv.* skillfully; p. 1074
instinct (in′ stingkt) *n.* a natural ability or impulse; p. 1074

murky (mur′ kē) *adj.* characterized by dimness, as from fog or smoke; p. 1074

Vegetable Market (St. Kitts). Frane Lessac (b. 1954). Oil on board, 30 x 25 in. Private collection.

Kitchens

Aurora Levins Morales ⁓

Kitchens

I went into the kitchen just now to stir the black beans and rice, the shiny black beans floating over the smooth brown grains of rice and the zucchini turning black, too, in the ink of the beans. Mine is a California kitchen, full of fresh vegetables and whole grains, bottled spring water and yogurt in plastic pints, but when I lift the lid from that big black pot, my kitchen fills with the hands of women who came before me, washing rice, washing beans, picking through them so <u>deftly</u>, so swiftly, that I could never see what the defects were in the beans they threw quickly over one shoulder out the window. Some <u>instinct</u> of the fingertips after years of sorting to feel the rottenness of the bean with a worm in it or a chewed-out side. Standing here, I see the smooth red and brown and white and speckled beans sliding through their fingers into bowls of water, the gentle clicking rush of them being poured into the pot, hear the hiss of escaping steam, smell the bean scum floating on the surface under the lid. I see grains of rice settling in a basin on the counter, turning the water milky with rice polish and the talc they use to make the grains so smooth; fingers dipping, swimming through the <u>murky</u> white water, feeling for the grain with the blackened tip, the brown stain.

From the corner of my eye, I see the knife blade flashing, reducing mounds of onions, garlic, cilantro, and green peppers into *sofrito*[1] to be fried up and stored, and best of all is the pound and circular grind of the *pilón:*[2] pound, pound, thump, grind, pound, pound, thump, grind. Pound, *pound* (the garlic and oregano mashed together), THUMP! (the mortar lifted and slammed down to loosen the crushed herbs and spices from the wooden bowl), *grind* (the slow rotation of the pestle smashing the oozing mash around and around, blending the juices, the green stain of cilantro and oregano, the sticky yellowing garlic, the grit of black pepper).

Did You Know?
A *mortar* (môr′ tər) is a bowl in which grains, spices, or herbs are pounded into a powder or paste. A *pestle* (pes′ əl) is the instrument, usually club-shaped, used for pounding.

It's the dance of the *cocinera:*[3] to step outside
fetch the bucket of water, turn,
all muscular grace and striving,
pour the water, light dancing in the pot,
and set the pail down on the blackened wood.
The blue flame glitters in its dark corner,
and coffee steams in the small white pan.
Gnarled fingers, *mondando ajo,*
picando cebolla, cortando pan,
colando café,[4]
stirring the rice with a big long spoon
filling ten bellies
out of one soot-black pot.

It's a magic, a power, a ritual of love and work that rises up in my kitchen, thousands of miles from those women in cotton dresses who twenty years ago taught the rules of its observance to me, the apprentice, the novice, the girl child: "Don't go out without wrapping

---

1. *Cilantro* (sē län′ trō) is an herb that resembles parsley in shape but not in taste. *Sofrito* (sō frē′ tō) is a thick sauce used as a cooking base in many Puerto Rican dishes.
2. Here, *pilón* (pē lōn′) means "mortar."

3. A *cocinera* (cō sē när′ ä) is a female cook.
4. *Mondando ajo* (mōn dän′ dō ä′ hō) means "peeling garlic"; *picando cebolla* (pē cän′ dō sä boi′ yä) means "mincing onion"; *cortando pan* (côr tän′ dō pän) means "cutting bread"; and *colando café* (cō län′ dō kä fā′) means "preparing coffee by passing it through a strainer."

Vocabulary
deftly (deft′ lē) *adv.* skillfully
instinct (in′ stingkt) *n.* a natural ability or impulse
murky (mur′ kē) *adj.* characterized by dimness, as from fog or smoke

your head, child, you've been roasting coffee, *y te va' a pa'mar!*[5] "This much coffee in the *colador*,[6] girl, or you'll be serving brown water." "Dip the basin in the river, so, to leave the mud behind." "Always peel the green bananas under cold water, *mijita*,[7] or you'll cut your fingers and get *mancha*[8] on yourself and the stain never comes out: that black sap stain of *guineo verde* and *plátano*,[9] the stain that marks you forever."

So I peel my bananas under running water from the faucet, but the stain won't come out, and the subtle earthy green smell of that sap follows me, down from the mountains, into the cities, to places where banana groves are like a green dream, unimaginable by daylight: Chicago, New Hampshire, Oakland. So I travel miles on the bus to the immigrant markets of other people, coming home laden with bundles, and even, now and then, on the plastic frilled tables of the supermarket, I find a small curved green bunch to rush home, quick, before it ripens, to peel and boil, bathing in the

Produce market in Mayaguez, Puerto Rico.

scent of its cooking, bringing the river to flow through my own kitchen now, the river of my place on earth, the green and musty river of my grandmothers, dripping, trickling, tumbling down from the mountain kitchens of my people.

---

5. *Y te va' a pa'mar!* (ē tä vä ä pä mär) is an idiom meaning "you're going to die."

6. A *colador* (cō' lä dôr') is a strainer.

7. *Mijita* (mē hē' tä) means "my daughter" or "my child."

8. A *mancha* (män' chä) is a stain.

9. *Guineo verde* (gi nä' ō vär' dä) is a green banana. A *plátano* (plä' tä nō), or *plantain*, is a variety of banana that must be cooked. Plaintains are harvested as green vegetables and may be baked, fried, or boiled.

Responding to Literature

Personal Response

What kitchen sights and smells did you find most appealing?

— ANALYZING LITERATURE —

RECALL AND INTERPRET

1. Describe the narrator's kitchen. How does it compare with the kitchens of her childhood? Explain.
2. What is the narrator preparing in the kitchen, and what do these preparations remind her of? What seems to be her attitude toward these memories? Support your response with details from the selection.
3. Summarize the comparison the narrator makes between cooking and dance. What does this comparison suggest about her view of cooking?
4. What lessons has the narrator learned from her ancestors? What effect have those lessons had on her life as she has grown up and moved away from her childhood home? How do you know?

EVALUATE AND CONNECT

5. How do the sensory details the writer uses compare with those you listed for the Focus Activity on page 1072? In your opinion, does the writer effectively describe the sights and smells of a kitchen? Why or why not?
6. What bonds and traditions influence your behavior? Do they come from family, friends, or other groups? Explain.
7. Theme Connections   What do you think the narrator is saying about the connections between generations? What connections do you have to older generations in your family?
8. In your opinion, does Morales's use of Spanish terms contribute to the effectiveness of this piece? Why or why not?

Literary ELEMENTS

Onomatopoeia
The use of words that imitate the actual sounds associated with those words is known as **onomatopoeia** (on′ ə mat′ ə pē′ə). *Buzz, roar,* and *tap* are some examples of onomatopoetic words. This technique helps the reader not just to "see" the actions going on but to "hear" them as well. By combining onomatopoeia with repetition, ". . . circular grind of the pilón: *pound, pound, thump, grind, pound, pound, thump, grind,*" Morales brings to life the sound and motion of the mortar and pestle.

1. Find two more examples of onomatopoeia in the selection and explain how they add to the sensory description of the essay.
2. List five other onomatopoetic words that relate to kitchens or cooking. Explain your choices.
● See **Literary Terms Handbook**, p. R11.

— EXTENDING YOUR RESPONSE —

Literature Groups
Tales from the Refrigerator   In your group, discuss the following questions: In what ways do the contents of the narrator's refrigerator reflect her upbringing? her personality? the place where she lives? What can you learn about a person from the foods he or she eats? Outline your conclusions and present them to the class.

Learning for Life
Food for Thought   Create a dinner menu—a beverage, an appetizer, a main course with at least one side dish, and a dessert—that reflects your family's heritage. If you can, include recipes. Then share your menu with the class.

📖 **Save your work for your portfolio.**

Before You Read

Bread

Meet Margaret Atwood

"I became a poet at the age of sixteen. I did not intend to do it. It was not my fault."

—*Atwood*

Margaret Atwood has become one of Canada's most respected and most popular writers, producing award-winning poems, novels, children's books, short stories, and essays.

Atwood was born in Ottawa, Ontario, Canada, but her childhood was divided between a variety of Canadian cities and the forests of northwestern Quebec, where her father, a scientist, conducted research about insects. Both her parents were avid readers and encouraged her love of words.

Atwood earned a bachelor's degree from the University of Toronto in 1961 and a graduate degree from Radcliffe College a year later. For the next several years, she combined jobs waiting tables, working at a market research company, and teaching grammar, with off-and-on studies at Harvard University.

In 1966 Atwood won her first major literary prize, Canada's Governor General's Award, for her second book of poems, *The Circle Game*. The publication of her first novel in 1969 coincided with the growing feminist movement and helped put Atwood on the literary map. While much of her writing focuses on women, Atwood is also known for writing that ponders human behavior in general.

"I began as a profoundly apolitical writer, but then I began to do what all novelists and some poets do; I began to describe the world around me."

—*Atwood*

Margaret Atwood was born in 1939.

FOCUS ACTIVITY

What do you think of when you hear the word *bread*?

FREEWRITE Take three minutes to freewrite about bread and the things you associate with it.

SETTING A PURPOSE Read to discover some thoughts the idea of bread inspires in one writer.

BACKGROUND

Literary Influences

As a child, Margaret Atwood enjoyed reading E. Nesbit, Edgar Allan Poe, and Mark Twain, as well as *Grimm's Fairy Tales* and comic books. As a writer, she was influenced by a number of Canadian poets despite her claim that ". . . when I started, nobody took *Canadian writing* seriously." Today, Atwood is one of many internationally respected Canadian writers.

VOCABULARY PREVIEW

bloated (blō′ tid) *adj.* puffed up; swollen; p. 1078

scavenger (skav′ in jər) *n.* one who searches through discarded materials for something useful; p. 1078

subversive (səb vur′ siv) *adj.* intended to destroy or undermine; p. 1079

treacherous (trech′ ər əs) *adj.* likely to betray a trust; disloyal; p. 1079

hallucination (hə lōo′ sə nā′ shən) *n.* a false sensory perception of something that is not really there; p. 1079

dupe (dōop) *v.* to fool; to trick; p. 1079

Bread

Margaret Atwood ～

Imagine a piece of bread. You don't have to imagine it, it's right here in the kitchen, on the breadboard, in its plastic bag, lying beside the bread knife. The bread knife is an old one you picked up at an auction; it has the word BREAD carved into the wooden handle. You open the bag, pull back the wrapper, cut yourself a slice. You put butter on it, then peanut butter, then honey, and you fold it over. Some of the honey runs out onto your fingers and you lick it off. It takes you about a minute to eat the bread. This bread happens to be brown, but there is also white bread, in the refrigerator, and a heel of rye you got last week, round as a full stomach then, now going moldy. Occasionally you make bread. You think of it as something relaxing to do with your hands.

Imagine a famine. Now imagine a piece of bread. Both of these things are real but you happen to be in the same room with only one of them. Put yourself into a different room, that's what the mind is for. You are now lying on a thin mattress in a hot room. The walls are made of dried earth, and your sister, who is younger than you, is in the room with you. She is starving, her belly is bloated, flies land on her eyes; you brush them off with your hand. You have a cloth too, filthy but damp, and you press it to her lips and forehead. The piece of bread is the bread you've been saving, for days it seems. You are as hungry as she is, but not yet as weak. How long does this take? When will someone come with more bread? You think of going out to see if you might find something that could be eaten, but outside the streets are infested with scavengers and the stink of corpses is everywhere.

Should you share the bread or give the whole piece to your sister? Should you eat the piece of bread yourself? After all, you have a better chance of living, you're stronger. How long does it take to decide?

Imagine a prison. There is something you know that you have not yet told. Those in control of the prison know that you know. So do those not in control. If you tell, thirty or forty or a hundred of your friends, your comrades, will be caught and will die. If you refuse to tell, tonight will be like last night. They always choose the night. You don't think about the night however, but about the piece of bread they offered you. How long does it take? The piece of bread was brown and fresh and reminded you of sunlight falling across a wooden floor. It reminded you of a bowl, a yellow bowl that was once in your home. It held apples and pears; it stood on a table you can also remember. It's not the hunger or the pain that is killing you but the

---

Vocabulary

bloated (blō′ tid) *adj.* puffed up; swollen
scavenger (skav′ in jər) *n.* one who searches through discarded materials for something useful

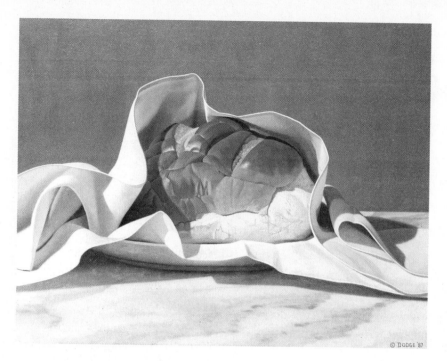

Bread in a Napkin, 1945. Joseph Jeffers Dodge. Oil on canvas. The Cummer Museum of Art and Gardens, Jacksonville, FL.

Viewing the painting: Compare and contrast this scene with one of the scenes in "Bread."

absence of the yellow bowl. If you could only hold the bowl in your hands, right here, you could withstand anything, you tell yourself. The bread they offered you is <u>subversive</u>, it's <u>treacherous</u>, it does not mean life.

There were once two sisters. One was rich and had no children, the other had five children and was a widow, so poor that she no longer had any food left. She went to her sister and asked her for a mouthful of bread. "My children are dying," she said. The rich sister said, "I do not have enough for myself," and drove her away from the door. Then the husband of the rich sister came home and wanted to cut himself a piece of bread; but when he made the first cut, out flowed red blood.

Everyone knew what that meant.

This is a traditional German fairy tale.

The loaf of bread I have conjured[1] for you floats about a foot above your kitchen table. The table is normal, there are no trap doors in it. A blue tea towel[2] floats beneath the bread, and there are no strings attaching the cloth to the bread or the bread to the ceiling or the table to the cloth, you've proved it by passing your hand above and below. You didn't touch the bread though. What stopped you? You don't want to know whether the bread is real or whether it's just a <u>hallucination</u> I've somehow <u>duped</u> you into seeing. There's no doubt that you can see the bread, you can even smell it, it smells like yeast, and it looks solid enough, solid as your own arm. But can you trust it? Can you eat it? You don't want to know, imagine that.

---

1. *Conjured* means "caused to appear, as by magic."
2. A *tea towel* is a towel for drying dishes.

Vocabulary

subversive (səb vur′ siv) *adj.* intended to destroy or undermine

treacherous (trech′ ər əs) *adj.* likely to betray a trust; disloyal

hallucination (hə loo′ sə nā′ shən) *n.* a false sensory perception of something that is not really there

dupe (doop) *v.* to fool; to trick

Responding to Literature

Personal Response

Which scene affected you most strongly? Why?

ANALYZING LITERATURE

RECALL AND INTERPRET

1. What does the narrator describe in the first paragraph? What attitude toward bread does the description convey?
2. Summarize the scenes related in the next two sections. What role does bread play in these scenes? What do you think is meant by the question, "How long does this take?"
3. How do you interpret the story about the two sisters?
4. What image does the narrator create in the last paragraph? What does she imply a reader should experience while envisioning this image? In your opinion, what is the author's message?

EVALUATE AND CONNECT

5. How does reading the first paragraph affect your perception of the next three scenes? Explain.
6. Compare the images in the first and last scenes. What is the effect of beginning the story with a concrete image and ending it with an image that may or may not be real?
7. How effectively does the author's use of **description** help you imagine each of the scenes? (See Literary Terms Handbook, page R4.) Explain your answer, using examples from the story.
8. Review your thoughts about bread from the Focus Activity on page 1077. What might you add after reading this selection?

> ## *Literary* ELEMENTS
>
> ### Voice
>
> **Voice** is the writer's or narrator's personality that comes across in a piece of writing. Voice is conveyed through sentence structure, word choice, and **tone**. For example, in the following sentence, Atwood's use of concrete words and the repetition of simple, direct clauses suggests a detached, quiet, almost hypnotic voice.
>
> > She is starving, her belly is bloated, flies land on her eyes; you brush them off with your hand.
>
> 1. How would you describe the voice of the narrator in "Bread"? Explain.
> 2. In your opinion, is this voice effective in helping to convey the author's message? Explain.
>
> ● See **Literary Terms Handbook**, p. R17.

EXTENDING YOUR RESPONSE

Writing About Literature

A Prisoner Without Hope   In a few paragraphs, analyze the scene of the prisoner. What do you think this prisoner has done? What might the yellow bowl be a **symbol** (see page R16) for? What does the narrator mean by calling the bread "subversive" and "treacherous"? What do you think will happen to this prisoner?

Interdisciplinary Activity

World Cultures: The Bread of Life   Research the role of bread in the diets of people around the world. Find out what kind of bread is common in various countries, how it is prepared and eaten, and what importance it has in relation to other foods. Then prepare a poster or other visual presentation to share your findings with your class

📖 **Save your work for your portfolio.**

COMPARING *selections*

Kitchens **and** Bread

COMPARE **NARRATORS**

Think about the narrator of each selection. Then, in a group, discuss the following:

- How do you think the narrator of "Bread" might respond to the kitchens described in "Kitchens"? Explain.
- Do you think the narrator of "Kitchens" would enjoy spending time in the first imagined kitchen of "Bread"? Why or why not?
- If you could have a conversation with one of the narrators, whom would you choose? What would you hope to learn from—or teach—this person?

COMPARE **KITCHENS**

Both writers use rich, specific details to help readers see, smell, taste, touch, and hear what is happening in the kitchens portrayed in the selections. Use these details to create a visual representation of one of the kitchen scenes described in each selection. Before you begin, consider the following questions:

- Which details help you to imagine the scenes in each selection?
- Which of the sensory details was most powerful or effective for you? Why?

COMPARE **CULTURES**

In both "Kitchens" and "Bread," the authors describe and compare more than one culture and the role of food in those cultures. Using these questions as a guide, write an analysis of how the authors use the subject of food to convey messages about the cultures they describe.

1. What cultures does Morales compare in "Kitchens"? What cultures does Atwood compare in "Bread"?
2. What similarities and differences do you find in the role of food in each of the cultures portrayed?
3. In your opinion, what is each author's purpose in presenting the comparisons she does?
4. Which author's comparison or comparisons had the strongest effect on you? Which do you think most readers would find strongest? Explain.

Before You Read

Picture Bride

Meet Cathy Song

"Song explores the nuances of intimacy with admirable clarity and passion."

—Pat Monaghan

Critics say that Cathy Song's poems are like "the muted tints of watercolor paintings." Her poetry is known for rich sensory imagery that celebrates the sights and sounds of Hawaii, from the smell of burning sugarcane to the thunder of the surf.

Song grew up in Hawaii, a place where many people place extreme importance on family and community. Her writing portrays the experiences of her Korean and Chinese ancestors and her own as an Asian American woman.

Her poems explore universal themes, such as the ties that bind family members to each other and people to community and tradition. Song's work also expresses her anger over the traditional roles of women and the history of unjust treatment of plantation workers in Hawaii.

Song spent her childhood in Wahiawa, a plantation town on the island of Oahu, and attended high school in Honolulu, where she discovered her love of writing. In pursuit of this passion, she enrolled in the graduate writing program at Boston University, receiving an M.A. in 1981.

Two years later, when she was twenty-eight, Song won the prestigious Yale Series of Younger Poets Award, for her first book of poetry, *Picture Bride*. This success has earned Song national recognition and has led to other awards and accolades.

Cathy Song was born in 1955.

FOCUS ACTIVITY

Think about a time when a friend or family member had to move from one city, town, or country to another.

JOURNAL In your journal, try to imagine how that person might have felt before and after the move. Write an entry describing those feelings.

SETTING A PURPOSE Read to find out how one poet imagines her grandmother may have felt when she immigrated to the United States.

BACKGROUND

The Time and Place

This poem is probably set in the late 1800s or early 1900s. During this time, Hawaiian plantations began importing laborers from Japan, China, Portugal, Korea, and other countries to perform backbreaking work in their sugarcane fields.

In Japan and Korea, arranged marriages were a tradition long before Japanese and Korean men

began immigrating to Hawaii. Thus, when these men sought Asian wives, people found it natural to arrange marriages by passing pictures among relatives and friends. Many young women agreed to become picture brides not because they wished to marry, but rather because they longed for adventure.

Picture Bride

Cathy Song

She was a year younger
than I,
twenty-three when she left Korea.
Did she simply close
5   the door of her father's house
and walk away? And
was it a long way
through the tailor shops of Pusan°
to the wharf where the boat
10   waited to take her to an island
whose name she had
only recently learned,
on whose shore
a man waited,
15   turning her photograph
to the light when the lanterns
in the camp outside
Waialua Sugar Mill° were lit
and the inside of his room
20   grew luminous
from the wings of moths
migrating out of the cane stalks?
What things did my grandmother
take with her? And when
25   she arrived to look
into the face of the stranger
who was her husband,
thirteen years older than she,

did she politely untie
30   the silk bow of her jacket,
her tent-shaped dress
filling with the dry wind
that blew from the surrounding fields
where the men were burning the cane?

Gisei/Kisaeng (A Korean Entertainer), c. 1936. Yasui
Sotaro. Oil on canvas, 24⅜ x 28¾ in. Private collection.

---

8 The city of *Pusan* (po͞o′ sän′) is a major port in South Korea.
18 The *Waialua* (wī′ ə lo͞o′ ə) *Sugar Mill* is a sugar refinery in
Hawaii.

Responding to Literature

Personal Response
What did this poem make you wonder about?

──── ANALYZING LITERATURE ────

RECALL AND INTERPRET

1. At what age does the young woman leave Korea, and how old is the speaker? What might be the purpose of comparing their respective ages?
2. What does the speaker wonder in the first ten lines of the poem? What attitude does the speaker seem to have toward her grandmother?
3. When does the man look at the photograph of his wife? What does his behavior suggest about his attitude toward her arrival?
4. What does the speaker wonder about in the last eleven lines of the poem? What does the **tone** of these lines suggest about the future of the grandparents' relationship? (See page R16.)

EVALUATE AND CONNECT

5. This poem is written as a series of questions. Why might Song have used this technique? What does it add to the overall effect of the poem?
6. Theme Connections   If the woman in this poem were to write a letter to her future granddaughter on the day she left Korea or the day she met her husband, what do you think she might say?
7. What have you learned about U.S. history from reading this poem? How does the type of information you learned differ from what you might find in a history book?
8. Review your response to the Focus Activity on page 1082. How do the thoughts and feelings experienced by your family member or friend compare with those described in this poem?

Literary
ELEMENTS

Verse Paragraph
A **verse paragraph** is a group of lines in a poem that form a unit. Unlike a **stanza**, a verse paragraph does not have a fixed number of lines. While poems written before the twentieth century usually contain stanzas, many contemporary poems are made up of verse paragraphs. Verse paragraphs help to organize a poem into thoughts, much as paragraphs help to organize prose. This poem includes two verse paragraphs, each of which chronicles a specific moment in time.

1. How do the two verse paragraphs compare in length? What might the difference in length contribute to the meaning of the poem?
2. Why might Song have begun the second verse paragraph in the middle of a sentence?

● See **Literary Terms Handbook,** p. R17.

──── EXTENDING YOUR RESPONSE ────

Interdisciplinary Activity
Sociology: Today's Picture Brides and Grooms   With a partner, research a culture where arranged marriages are still common. How are the arrangements made? How do the young people seem to feel about it? Are these unions typically successful? Prepare a brief oral report and present your findings to the class.

Creative Writing
First Words   Imagine the conversation the man and the woman in "Picture Bride" might have had when they first met. Drawing on the poem and your own imagination, write a page of dialogue between these two characters.

📖 **Save your work for your portfolio.**

Newspaper Article

Pictures still have their place in the world of matchmaking, but videos also have a place in today's dating market.

Love and Money
Singles Pay Services a Bundle for a Date—And Maybe a Mate

by Ellen Futterman, staff writer—*St. Louis Post-Dispatch*, June 12, 1994

In the wacky, unpredictable world of dating, mating, and relating, Jennifer Stephens knows exactly what she wants: a single man with whom she can fall in love, marry, and eventually raise a family.

Rather than leave the meeting to chance, Stephens shelled out big bucks to join Great Expectations, one of several pay-for-romance services in the St. Louis area that cater to singles. Between work and social obligations, Stephens says she doesn't have much time, or for that matter the inclination, to go searching for bright, attractive, available men. She'd rather let a dating service do the field work.

"I don't hang out at bars or attend church regularly," says Stephens, 33, who has bright blue eyes and a good-natured energy. "I've never met anyone at the grocery store. And I have my own washer and dryer, so I don't go to Laundromats."

Today, six months after joining, she hasn't fallen in love or, for that matter, in like. In fact, she hasn't even had what she would consider a good date with anyone she's met through Great Expectations' video-screening process.

The whole system felt awkward at first—especially the notion of paying to meet a man and talking into a camera about what she likes to do: watching *Seinfeld* on Thursday nights, going to movies, and reading (yes, she sheepishly admits) trashy Danielle Steel-type novels.

But Stephens, who works in accounting for a food distributor, says she has met nice people through the dating service. And she continues to visit the Great Expectations office in Maryland Heights each week to pore over books containing thumbnail descriptions and pictures of more than 1,500 eligible bachelors.

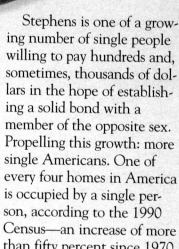

Stephens is one of a growing number of single people willing to pay hundreds and, sometimes, thousands of dollars in the hope of establishing a solid bond with a member of the opposite sex. Propelling this growth: more single Americans. One of every four homes in America is occupied by a single person, according to the 1990 Census—an increase of more than fifty percent since 1970.

Respond

1. In your opinion, what are the advantages and disadvantages of using a dating service?

2. Do you think your generation will rely on such a service? Explain.

Before You Read

Prime Time

Meet Henry Louis Gates Jr.

❝The society we have made simply won't survive without the values of tolerance. And cultural tolerance comes to nothing without cultural understanding.❞

—*Gates*

Bridging cultures is a habit for Henry Louis Gates Jr. He grew up in an Appalachian village and became a professor at Harvard. He faced segregation as a child, marched for black power, and spent a year in Tanzania at age twenty. "We were pioneers, people my age, in cross-race relations, able to get to know each other across cultures and classes in a way that was unthinkable in our parents' generation," he says.

After the Civil Rights movement of the 1960s, Gates studied at Yale University, where he was director of student affairs for John D. Rockefeller's campaign for governor. He later worked as a London correspondent for *Time*

magazine and earned a Ph.D. in English literature from Cambridge University in England. Gates went on to author several books and has won an American Book Award and a genius grant from the MacArthur Foundation. He also has written dozens of magazine articles, edited numerous anthologies, and created the Public Broadcasting System series, *The Image of the Black in the Western Imagination*.

❝I want to be black, to know black, to luxuriate in whatever I might be calling blackness at any particular time—but to do so in order to come out the other side, to experience a humanity that is neither colorless nor reducible to color. Bach *and* James Brown. Sushi *and* fried catfish.❞

—*Gates*

Henry Louis Gates Jr. was born in 1950.

FOCUS ACTIVITY

When you watch a movie or a television program, do you look for people you can identify with? Explain.

SHARE IDEAS With a partner list movies or TV shows with characters who remind you of yourself or people you know. Then list some movies and programs you don't relate to at all.

SETTING A PURPOSE Read to understand the influence of television on one writer's childhood.

BACKGROUND

The Time and Place

This selection takes place in the late 1950s and 1960s in a small town in West Virginia. During this time, many African Americans began to protest laws that denied them the same access to public places that white people enjoyed.

VOCABULARY PREVIEW

mundane (mun dān′) *adj.* ordinary or usual; commonplace; p. 1087
impediment (im ped′ ə mənt) *n.* an obstacle; p. 1087
allude (ə lood′) *v.* to refer to indirectly; p. 1088
facade (fə säd′) *n.* a false or artificial front; p. 1091
ritual (rich′ oo əl) *n.* a regularly followed routine; p. 1092
proverbial (prə vur′ bē əl) *adj.* commonly spoken of; well-known; p. 1094
tumult (too′ məlt) *n.* uproar; p. 1094

Prime Time

Henry Louis Gates Jr. ~

Family Group, 1955. Charles Alston. Oil on canvas, 48¼ x 35¾ in. Whitney Museum of American Art, New York.

I guess some chafed more than others against the <u>mundane</u> <u>impediments</u> of the color line. "It's no disgrace to be colored," the black entertainer Bert Williams famously observed early in this century, "but it is awfully inconvenient." For most of my childhood, we couldn't eat in restaurants or sleep in hotels, we couldn't use certain bathrooms or try on clothes in stores. Mama insisted that we dress up when we went to shop. She was a fashion plate when she went to clothing stores, and wore white pads called shields under her arms so her dress or blouse would show no sweat. We'd like to try this on, she'd say carefully, articulating[1] her words precisely and properly. We don't buy clothes we can't try on, she'd say when they declined, as we'd walk, in Mama's dignified manner, out of the store. She preferred to shop where we had an account and where everyone knew who she was.

---

1. *Articulating* (är tik′ yə lāt′ ing) means "pronouncing distinctly and carefully."

Vocabulary
mundane (mun dān′) *adj.* ordinary or usual; commonplace
impediment (im ped′ ə mənt) *n.* an obstacle

As for me, I hated the fact that we couldn't sit down in the Cut-Rate. No one colored was allowed to, with one exception: my father. It was as if there were a permanent TAKE-AWAY ONLY sign for colored people. You were supposed to stand at the counter, get your food to go, and leave. I don't know for certain why Carl Dadisman, the proprietor, wouldn't stop Daddy from sitting down. But I believe it was in part because Daddy was so light-complected, and in part because, during his shift at the phone company, he picked up orders for food and coffee for the operators, and Dadisman relied on that business. At the time, I never wondered if it occurred to Daddy not to sit down at the Cut-Rate when neither his wife nor his two children were allowed to, although now that I am a parent myself, the strangeness of it crosses my mind on occasion.

Even when we were with Daddy, you see, we had to stand at the counter and order take-out, then eat on white paper plates using plastic spoons, sipping our vanilla rickeys[2] from green-and-white paper cups through plastic flexible-end straws. Even after basketball games, when Young Doc Bess would set up the team with free Cokes after one of the team's many victories, the colored players had to stand around and drink out of paper cups while the white players and cheerleaders sat down in the red Naugahyde[3] booths and drank out of glasses. Integrate? I'll shut it down first, Carl Dadisman had vowed. He was an odd-looking man, with a Humpty-Dumpty sort of head and bottom, and weighing four or five hundred pounds. He ran the taxi service, too, and was just as nice as he could be, even to colored people. But he did not want us sitting in his booths, eating off his plates and silverware,

putting our thick greasy lips all over his glasses. He'd retire first, or die.

He had a heart attack one day while sitting in the tiny toilet at his place of business. Daddy and some other men tried to lift him up, while he was screaming and gasping and clutching his chest, but he was stuck in that cramped space. They called the rescue squad at the Fire Department. Lowell Taylor and Pat Amoroso came. Lowell was black and was the star of the soccer team at the high school across the river in Westernport. He looked like Pelé,[4] down to the shape of his head.

They sawed and sawed and sawed, while the ambulance and the rescue squad sat outside on Third Street, blocking the driveway to the town's parking lot. After a while, Carl Dadisman's cries and moans became quieter and quieter. Finally, they wedged in a couple of two-by-fours and dragged out his lifeless body. By then it made little difference to Carl that Lowell was black.

Maybe Carl never understood that the racial dispensation[5] he took for granted was coming to an end. As a child, I must once have assumed that this dispensation could no more be contested than the laws of gravity, or traffic lights. And I'm not sure when I realized otherwise.

I know that I had rich acquaintance early on with the inconveniences to which Bert Williams alluded. But segregation had some advantages, like the picnic lunch Mama would make for the five-hour train ride on the National Limited to Parkersburg,[6] where you had to catch the bus down to the state capital, Charleston, to visit her sister Loretta. So what if we didn't feel comfortable eating in the dining car? Our food was

---

2. *Rickeys* (ri′ kēz) are drinks often made with soda water, sugar, and flavoring.

3. *Naugahyde* (nô′ gə hīd) is a type of artificial leather.

4. *Pelé* (pā lā′) is a world-famous Brazilian soccer player.

5. A *dispensation* (dis′ pən sā′ shen) is a system of ordering things or of regulating human affairs.

6. *Parkersburg* is a city in northwestern West Virginia.

Vocabulary
allude (ə lōōd′) v. to refer to indirectly

Jackie Robinson, 1949.

Politics aside, though, we were starved for images of ourselves and searched TV to find them. Everybody, of course, watched sports, because Piedmont was a big sports town. Making the big leagues was like getting to Heaven, and everybody had hopes that they could, or a relative could. We'd watch the games day and night, and listen on radio to what we couldn't see. Everybody knew the latest scores, batting averages, rbi's, and stolen bases. Everybody knew the standings in the leagues, who could still win the pennant and how. Everybody liked the Dodgers because of Jackie Robinson,[8] the same way everybody still voted Republican because of Abraham Lincoln. Sports on the mind, sports in the mind. The only thing to rival the Valley in fascination was the big-league baseball diamond.

I once heard Mr. James Helms say, "You got to give the white man his due when it comes to technology. One on one, though, and it's even-steven. Joe Louis[9] showed 'em that." We were obsessed with sports in part because it was the only time we could compete with white people even-steven. And the white people, it often seemed, were just as obsessed with this primal confrontation between the races as we were. I think they integrated professional sports, after all those years of segregation, just to capitalize on this

better. Fried chicken, baked beans, and potato salad . . . a book and two decks of cards . . . and I didn't care if the train ever got there. We'd sing or read in our own section, munching that food and feeling sorry for the people who couldn't get any, and play 500 or Tonk or Fish with Mama and Daddy, until we fell asleep.

The simple truth is that the civil rights era came late to Piedmont, even though it came early to our television set. We could watch what was going on Elsewhere on television, but the marches and sit-ins were as remote to us as, in other ways, was the all-colored world of *Amos and Andy*[7]—a world full of black lawyers, black judges, black nurses, black doctors.

---

7. The television show *Amos and Andy* was a situation comedy based in Harlem. The show, which aired from 1951 to 1953, is now considered by many to be racist.

8. *Jackie Robinson* (1919–1972) was the first African American to play major league baseball in the twentieth century. He played for the Brooklyn *Dodgers* (1947–1956).

9. African American *Joe Louis* (1914–1981) was the world heavyweight boxing champion from 1937 to 1949.

voyeuristic thrill of the forbidden contact. What interracial sex was to the seventies, interracial sports were to the fifties. Except for sports, we rarely saw a colored person on TV.

Actually, I first got to know white people as "people" through their flickering images on television shows. It was the television set that brought us together at night, and the television set that brought in the world outside the Valley. We were close enough to Washington to receive its twelve channels on cable. Piedmont was transformed from a radio culture to one with the fullest range of television, literally overnight. During my first-grade year, we'd watch *Superman*, *Lassie*, Jack Benny, Danny Thomas, *Robin Hood*, *I Love Lucy*, *December Bride*, Nat King Cole (of course), *Wyatt Earp*, *Broken Arrow*, Phil Silvers, Red Skelton, *The $64,000 Question*, *Ozzie and Harriet*, *The Millionaire*, *Father Knows Best*, *The Lone Ranger*, Bob Cummings, *Dragnet*, *The People's Choice*, *Rin Tin Tin*, *Jim Bowie*, *Gunsmoke*, *My Friend Flicka*, *The Life of Riley*, *Topper*, *Dick Powell's Zane Grey Theater*, *Circus Boy*, and Loretta Young—all in prime time. My favorites were *The Life of Riley*, in part because he worked in a factory like Daddy did, and *Ozzie and Harriet*, in part because Ozzie never seemed to work at all. A year later, however, *Leave It to Beaver* swept most of the others away.

With a show like *Topper*, I felt as if I was getting a glimpse, at last, of the life that Mrs. Hudson, and Mrs. Thomas, and Mrs. Campbell, must be leading in their big mansions on East Hampshire Street. Smoking jackets and cravats, spats[10] and canes, elegant garden parties and martinis. People who wore suits to eat dinner! This was a world so elegantly distant from ours, it was like a voyage to another galaxy, light-years away.

Leave It to Beaver, on the other hand, was a world much closer, but just out of reach nonetheless. Beaver's street was where we wanted to live, Beaver's house where we wanted to eat and sleep, Beaver's father's firm where we'd have liked Daddy to work. These shows for us were about property, the property that white people could own and that we couldn't. About a level of comfort and ease at which we could only wonder. It was the world that the integrated school was going to prepare us to enter and that, for Mama, would be the prize.

If prime time consisted of images of middle-class white people who looked nothing at all like us, late night was about the radio, listening to *Randy's Record Shop* from Gallatin, Tennessee. My brother, Rocky, kept a transistor radio by his bed, and he'd listen to it all night, for all I knew, long after I'd fallen asleep. In 1956, black music hadn't yet broken down into its many subgenres, except for large divisions such as jazz, blues, gospel, rhythm and blues. On *Randy's*, you were as likely to hear The Platters doing "The Great Pretender" and Clyde McPhatter doing "Treasure of Love" as you were to hear Howlin' Wolf do "Smokestack Lightning" or Joe Turner do "Corrine, Corrine." My own favorite that year was the slow, deliberate sound of Jesse Belvin's "Goodnight, My Love." I used to fall asleep singing it in my mind to my Uncle Earkie's girlfriend, Ula, who was a sweet caffé latté[11] brown, with the blackest, shiniest straight hair and the fullest, most rounded red lips. Not even in your dreams, he had said to me one day, as I watched her red dress slink down our front stairs. It was my first brush with the sublime.

We used to laugh at the way the disc jockey sang "Black Strap Lax-a-teeves" during the commercials. I sometimes would wonder if the kids we'd seen on TV in Little Rock or

---

10. A *smoking jacket* is a man's loose-fitting jacket usually worn at home and made of a fine fabric. A *cravat* is a man's scarf. *Spats* are cloth or leather coverings worn over the upper shoe and ankle, usually fastened under the shoe with a strap.

11. *Caffé latté* (kä′ fā lä′ tā), a type of coffee with steamed milk, is a smooth tan color.

Birmingham earlier in the evening were singing themselves to sleep with *their* Ulas.

Lord knows, we weren't going to learn how to be colored by watching television. Seeing somebody colored on TV was an event.

"Colored, colored, on Channel Two," you'd hear someone shout. Somebody else would run to the phone, while yet another hit the front porch, telling all the neighbors where to see it. And *everybody* loved *Amos and Andy*—I don't care what people say today. For the colored people, the day they took *Amos and Andy* off the air was one of the saddest days in Piedmont, about as sad as the day of the last mill pic-a-nic.

What was special to us about *Amos and Andy* was that their world was *all* colored, just like ours. Of course, *they* had their colored judges and lawyers and doctors and nurses, which we could only dream about having, or becoming—and we *did* dream about those things. Kingfish ate his soft-boiled eggs delicately, out of an egg cup. He even owned an acre of land in Westchester County,[12] which he sold to Andy, using the <u>facade</u> of a movie set to fake a mansion. As far as we were concerned, the foibles of Kingfish or Calhoun the lawyer were the foibles of individuals who happened to be funny. Nobody was likely to confuse them with the colored people we knew, no more than we'd confuse ourselves with the entertainers and athletes we saw on TV or in *Ebony* or *Jet*, the magazines we devoured to keep up with what was happening with the race. And people took special relish in Kingfish's malapropisms.[13] "I denies the allegation, Your Honor, and I resents the alligator."

In one of my favorite episodes of *Amos and Andy*, "The Punjab[14] of Java-Pour,"[15] Andy Brown is hired to advertise a brand of coffee and is required to dress up as a turbaned Oriental potentate.[16] Kingfish gets the bright idea that if he dresses up as a potentate's servant, the two of them can enjoy a vacation at a luxury hotel for free. So attired, the two promenade around the lobby, running up an enormous tab and generously dispensing "rubies" and "diamonds" as tips. The plan goes awry when people try to redeem the gems and discover them to be colored glass. It was widely suspected that this episode was what promoted two Negroes in Baltimore to dress like African princes and demand service in a segregated four-star restaurant. Once it was clear to the management that these were not American Negroes, the two were treated royally. When the two left the restaurant, they took off their African headdresses and robes and enjoyed a hearty laugh at the restaurant's expense. "They weren't like our Negroes," the maître d' told the press in explaining why he had agreed to seat the two "African princes."

Whenever the movies *Imitation of Life* and *The Green Pastures* would be shown on TV, we watched with similar hunger—especially *Imitation of Life*. It was never on early; only the late *late* show, like the performances of Cab Calloway and Duke Ellington[17] at the Crystal Palace. And we'd stay up. Everybody colored. The men coming home on second shift from the paper mill would stay up. Those who had to go out on the day shift and who

---

12. *Westchester County* is an affluent suburban area just north of New York City.
13. *Malapropisms* are humorous misuses of words, especially those that are similar in sound (after the character Mrs. Malaprop in the play *The Rivals*).
14. The *Punjab* is a region divided between India and Pakistan. Here, the word refers to a person from this area.
15. *Java* is an island of Indonesia, where coffee is grown. The term is also used informally to mean "brewed coffee."
16. A *potentate* (pōt′ ən tāt′) is someone having great power or authority, such as a king.
17. *Cab Calloway* and *Duke Ellington* were celebrated African American jazz musicians.

Vocabulary
facade (fə säd′) *n.* a false or artificial front

normally would have been in bed hours earlier (because they had to be at work at 6:30) would stay up. As would we, the kids, wired for the ritual at hand. And we'd all sit in silence, fighting back the tears, watching as Delilah invents the world's greatest pancakes and a down-and-out Ned Sparks takes one taste and says, flatly, "We'll box it." Cut to a big white house, plenty of money, and Delilah saying that she doesn't want her share of the money (which should have been *all* of the money); she just wants to continue to cook, clean, wash, iron, and serve her good white lady and her daughter. (Nobody in our living room was going for *that*.) And then Delilah shows up at her light-complected daughter's school one day, unexpectedly, to pick her up, and there's the daughter, Peola, ducking down behind her books, and the white teacher saying, I'm sorry, ma'am, there must be some mistake. We have no little colored children here. And then Delilah, spying her baby, says, Oh, yes you do. Peola! Peola! Come here to your mammy, honey chile. And then Peola runs out of the room, breaking her poor, sweet mother's heart. And Peola continues to break her mother's heart, by passing, leaving the race, and marrying white. Yet her mama understands, always understands, and, dying, makes detailed plans for her own big, beautiful funeral, complete with six white horses and a carriage and a jazz band, New Orleans style. And she dies and is about to be buried, when, out of nowhere, comes grown-up Peola, saying, "Don't die, Mama, don't die, Mama, I'm sorry, Mama, I'm sorry," and throws her light-and-bright-and-damn-near-white self onto her mama's casket. By this time, we have stopped trying to fight back the tears and are boo-hooing all over the place. Then we turn to our *own* mama and tell her how much we love her and swear that we will

never, ever pass for white. I promise, Mama. I promise.

Peola had sold her soul to the Devil. This was the first popular Faust[18] in the black tradition, the bargain with the Devil over the cultural soul. Talk about a cautionary tale.

The Green Pastures was an altogether more uplifting view of things, our Afro Paradiso. Make way for the Lawd! Make way for the Lawd! And Rex Ingram, dressed in a long black frock coat[19] and a long white beard, comes walking down the Streets Paved with Gold, past the Pearly Gates, while Negroes with the whitest wings of fluffy cotton fly around Heaven, playing harps, singing spirituals, having fish fries, and eating watermelon. Hard as I try, I can't stop seeing God as that black man who played Him in *The Green Pastures* and seeing Noah as Rochester from the Jack Benny show, trying to bargain with God to let him take along an extra keg of wine or two.

Civil rights took us all by surprise. Every night we'd wait until the news to see what "Dr. King and dem" were doing. It was like watching the Olympics or the World Series when somebody colored was on. The murder of Emmett Till[20] was one of my first memories. He whistled at some white girl, they said; that's all he did. He was beat so bad they didn't even want to open the casket, but his mama made them. She wanted the world to see what they had done to her baby.

In 1957, when I was in second grade, black children integrated Central High School in

---

18. *Faust* (foust), a character in German legend, sells his soul to the devil in return for knowledge and power.
19. A *frock coat* is a man's dress coat reaching to the knees and fitted at the waist.
20. Teenager *Emmett Till* (1941–1955) was murdered in Mississippi after his friends dared him to ask out a white woman.

Vocabulary
ritual (rich′ o͞o əl) *n.* a regularly followed routine

Little Rock, Arkansas. We watched it on TV. All of us watched it. I don't mean Mama and Daddy and Rocky. I mean *all* the colored people in America watched it, together, with one set of eyes. We'd watch it in the morning, on the *Today* show on NBC, before we'd go to school; we'd watch it in the evening, on the news, with Edward R. Murrow on CBS. We'd watch the Special Bulletins at night, interrupting our TV shows.

The children were all well scrubbed and greased down, as we'd say. Hair short and closely cropped,

Elizabeth Ann Eckford, Little Rock High School, September 1957.

parted, and oiled (the boys); "done" in a "permanent" and straightened, with turned-up bangs and curls (the girls). Starched shirts, white, and creased pants, shoes shining like a buck private's spit shine. Those Negroes were *clean*. The fact was, those children trying to get the right to enter that school in Little Rock looked like black versions of models out of *Jack & Jill* magazine, to which my mama had subscribed for me so that I could see what children outside the Valley were up to. "They hand-picked those children," Daddy would say. "No dummies, no nappy hair, heads not too kinky, lips not too thick, no disses and no dats."[21] At seven, I was dismayed by his cynicism.[22] It bothered me somehow that those children would have been chosen, rather than just having shown up or volunteered or been nearby in the neighborhood.

Daddy was jaundiced[23] about the civil rights movement, and especially about the Reverend Dr. Martin Luther King, Jr. He'd say all of his names, to drag out his scorn. By the mid-sixties, we'd argue about King from sunup to sundown. Sometimes he'd just mention King to get a rise from me, to make a sagging evening more interesting, to see if I had *learned* anything real yet, to see how long I could think up counter arguments before getting so mad that my face would turn purple. I think he just liked the color purple on my face, liked producing it there. But he was not of two minds about those children in Little Rock.

The children would get off their school bus surrounded by soldiers from the National Guard and by a field of state police. They would stop at the steps of the bus and seem to take a very deep breath. Then the phalanx[24] would start to move slowly along this gulley of sidewalk and

---

21. *Disses* and *dats* are dialect for *thises* and *thats*.
22. *Cynicism* (sin′ ə siz′ əm) is an attitude of doubt about sincerity and goodness.

23. Here, *jaundiced* (jôn′ dist) means "bitter" or "hostile."
24. A *phalanx* (fā′ langks) is a compact body of people.

rednecks[25] that connected the steps of the school bus with the white wooden double doors of the school. All kinds of crackers[26] would be lining that gulley, separated from the phalanx of children by rows of state police, who formed a barrier arm in arm. Cheerleaders from the all-white high school that was desperately trying to stay that way were dressed in those funny little pleated skirts, with a big red C for "Central" on their chests, and they'd wave their pom-poms and start to cheer: "Two, four, six, eight—We don't want to integrate!" And all those crackers and all those rednecks would join in that chant as if their lives depended on it. Deafening, it was: even on our twelve-inch TV, a three-inch speaker buried along the back of its left side.

The TV was the ritual arena for the drama of race. In our family, it was located in the living room, where it functioned like a fireplace in the <u>proverbial</u> New England winter. I'd sit in the water in the galvanized tub in the middle of our kitchen, watching the TV in the next room while Mama did the laundry or some other chore as she waited for Daddy to come home from his second job. We watched people getting hosed and cracked over their heads, people being spat upon and arrested, rednecks siccing fierce dogs on women and children, our people responding by singing and marching and staying strong. Eyes on the prize. Eyes on the prize. George Wallace at the gate of the University of Alabama, blocking Autherine Lucy's way. Charlayne Hunter at the University of Georgia. President Kennedy interrupting our scheduled program with a special address, saying that James Meredith will *definitely* enter the University of Mississippi; and saying it like he believed it (unlike Ike),[27] saying it like the big kids said, "It's our turn to play" on the basketball court and walking all through us as if we weren't there.

Whatever <u>tumult</u> our small screen revealed, though, the dawn of the civil rights era could be no more than a spectator sport in Piedmont. It was almost like a war being fought overseas. And all things considered, white and colored Piedmont got along pretty well in those years, the fifties and early sixties. At least as long as colored people didn't try to sit down in the Cut-Rate or at the Rendezvous Bar, or eat pizza at Eddie's, or buy property, or move into the white neighborhoods, or dance with, date, or dilate upon white people. Not to mention try to get a job in the craft unions at the paper mill. Or have a drink at the white VFW, or join the white American Legion,[28] or get loans at the bank, or just generally get out of line. Other than that, colored and white got on pretty well.

---

25. The slang term *rednecks* usually refers to a white member of the southern rural laboring class.
26. *Crackers* is a derogatory term for poor white people, usually from the South.

---

27. President Dwight D. Eisenhower, known as *Ike,* held office (1953–1961) just prior to President John F. Kennedy.
28. The *VFW* (Veterans of Foreign Wars) is the second largest veterans' organization in the United States; the *American Legion* is the largest.

Vocabulary

proverbial (prə vur′ bē əl) *adj.* commonly spoken of; well-known
tumult (tōō′ məlt) *n.* uproar

Responding to Literature

Personal Response
What went through your mind when you finished this selection?

ANALYZING LITERATURE

RECALL AND INTERPRET

1. What were some of the barriers faced by African Americans in the 1950s? How did the author's mother respond to these obstacles, and what does this response reveal about her character?
2. What TV programs did the narrator watch? What new understandings about white people did the narrator gain from watching television?
3. Which TV programs featured African Americans? How did these programs affect the author? How did the community respond to them?
4. What does the author say about race relations in his town? Why might he say, "The TV was the ritual arena for the drama of race"?

EVALUATE AND CONNECT

5. In what ways might the author's description of the lunch counter's owner be considered **ironic** (see page R8)? What point do you think the author is trying to make in this part of the selection?
6. Gates says, "The simple truth is that the civil rights era came late to Piedmont, even though it came early to our television set." Use **anecdotes** (see page R1) from the selection and from your own experiences to describe how television reflects life and influences events. Use a chart like the one on the right to help organize your thoughts.
7. Review your notes from the Focus Activity on page 1086. Of the TV shows Gates describes, which might interest you? Why?
8. When the schools in Little Rock were integrated, the narrator's father was "jaundiced." Explain his response. In your opinion, was it an appropriate reaction? Why or why not?

Literary ELEMENTS

Sarcasm
Some writing is intended to be comical or amusing. However, writers also use humor in serious material, as Gates has done in his memoir. He uses **sarcasm**—satire or irony that often contains bitter and caustic language. An example is Gates's description of Carl Dadisman's death. He concludes, "By then it made little difference to Carl that Lowell was black."

1. Find two additional examples of sarcasm in the selection.
2. What does the use of sarcasm in this selection add to the story?

● See Literary Terms Handbook, p. R14.

Television	
reflects reality	influences reality
1.	1.

EXTENDING YOUR RESPONSE

Writing About Literature
Analyze Emotional Appeal   What types of emotional responses does this selection evoke? Identify techniques—such as anecdotes, quotations, or characterization—that the writer uses to achieve these responses. Find two or three examples of successful appeals to readers' emotions, and analyze them in a few paragraphs. Support your choices with details and quotations.

Literature Groups
Sports Fans   What reason does Gates give for the integration of sports? What message might this have sent to him and other children of the 1950s? Discuss these questions with your group. Share your thinking with the class.

📖 **Save your work for your portfolio.**

Before You Read

Se me enchina el cuerpo al oír tu cuento . . .

Meet Norma Elia Cantú

"Writing for me is like breathing," explains Norma Elia Cantú (nōr′mä el′yə kän tōō′). "I don't ask why, I just do it." She began writing in elementary school when she submitted a story to a kids' television program. In high school, she continued writing and began publishing her work in the school newspaper, the *Journal*.

"I am intimately inspired by the language and culture around me," she says, and this inspiration has resulted in dozens of books, poems, essays, stories, and articles. Her award-winning book, *Canicula: Snapshots of a Girlhood en la Frontera*, she categorizes as an "autobioethnography." It combines snapshots, autobiography, history, and fiction to create stories that are "truer than true." Rather than presenting factual details in chronological order, this book captures life as memory reflects it, "with our past and our present juxtaposed and bleeding, seeping back and forth."

Cantú, a professor of English at Texas A&M International University, not only writes and teaches, she also reads avidly. As a child, she enjoyed books, magazines, comics—even an encyclopedia that her father bought. Today, she reads a range of materials for different purposes: newspapers supply information and some entertainment; professional journals and essays aid her work; novels in Spanish maintain her fluency in that language; and other "fiction and poetry feed my soul."

"I write the kinds of things I like to read— stories, poems, essays that inspire me to do better, to change society for the better, to reflect on my own life."

—Cantú

Norma Elia Cantú was born in 1947.

FOCUS ACTIVITY

What have been some turning points in your life? Is a turning point always dramatic?

JOURNAL Describe a situation or event that changed the course of your life.

SETTING A PURPOSE Read to learn about a turning point in the life of one family.

BACKGROUND

Did You Know?

In the United States, about 500,000 people work as migrant laborers. They travel throughout the country harvesting crops. They often live and work in dangerous, unsanitary conditions. Some of these migrant workers are illegal immigrants. They are usually men under the age of thirty, and most have fewer than eight years of school.

VOCABULARY PREVIEW

valedictorian (val′ ə dik tôr′ ē ən) *n.* the student with the highest class rank; p. 1098

trek (trek) *n.* a journey, especially one that is slow or difficult; p. 1098

perplexed (pər plekst′) *adj.* puzzled; confused; p. 1098

demeaning (di mēn′ ing) *adj.* lowering in dignity or status; degrading; humiliating; p. 1098

cringe (krinj) *v.* to shrink back or flinch, as in fear or disgust; p. 1098

Self Portrait, 1927. Rufino Tamayo. Gouache over black chalk on paper, 9⁵⁄₁₆ x 7 in. Cleveland Museum of Art, Cleveland, OH.

Se me enchina el cuerpo al oír tu cuento . . .

Norma Elia Cantú ⁓

Se me enchina el cuerpo al oír tu cuento (sā mā en chē′ nä el kwār′ pō äl ō ēr′   tōō   kwen′ tō) means "I get goosebumps when I hear your story."

How the day after graduating as valedictorian from the high school in the Rio Grande Valley you helped your family board up the door and windows of the frame house and pack the old pick-up truck to make your annual trek north. After three days on the road arriving at the turkey farm and being led to your quarters. The family, tired, looks to you. "What's this?" you ask, for you, the favored son, speak English; you can communicate with the bosses.

"This is where you're gonna live."

Perplexed you say, "But it looks like a chicken coop."

"It is, but it's not good enough for the chickens," the Anglo responds with a sneer.

And you take it, and you suffer as your mother and your sisters make the best with the chicken coop. They hang curtains and sweep the floor and burn candles to the Virgen.[1]

Then the work, arduous[2] and demeaning, begins. Working night shifts after long days . . . plucking feathers, forcibly breeding the toms and the hens, and your Dad ages from day to day before your very eyes.

Until one day you've been working hard, and you look for your Dad, and barely see his head in one of the buried barrels full of feathers,

working away. Suddenly he's gone, and you think you're imagining things; how could he disappear? and you remove your gloves and risk the foreman's wrath. You run to your father; jump in; he is almost smothered by feathers, and you say, "Enough!"

You take control and pack the family off. "No pay for all your work if you leave."

And you say, "We're leaving." The favored son, who speaks to the bosses, has spoken. And driving the Midwest farm road almost crossing the state line you spy a sign "Labor Relations," and you stop. And, yes, you are owed your wages, and the bosses pay reluctantly. No one had ever done that before. But you read the language of the bosses. You move on with your family, and your father is pleased; your mother beams but is afraid in her heart for her son who speaks the language of the bosses.

Years later a lover will wonder why you refuse to sleep on feather-filled pillows, and you want to tell, to spill your guts, but you can't, you refuse. You hold your words like caged birds.

Memory's wound is too fresh.

And more years later when you tell the story, I cringe and get goosebumps; you tell your story and are healed, but there's still a scar and like an old war wound or surgical scar it hurts when the weather changes or the memory intersects with this time and place.

---

1. The *Virgen* (vēr′ hen) is Mary, the mother of Jesus Christ.
2. *Arduous* means "requiring great effort" or "difficult."

Vocabulary
valedictorian (val′ ə dik tôr′ ē ən) *n.* the student with the highest class rank
trek (trek) *n.* a journey, especially one that is slow or difficult
perplexed (pər plekst′) *adj.* puzzled; confused
demeaning (di mēn′ ing) *adj.* lowering in dignity or status; degrading; humiliating
cringe (krinj) *v.* to shrink back or flinch, as in fear or disgust

Responding to Literature

Personal Response

What is your response to the events in the story?

--------- **ANALYZING LITERATURE** ---------

RECALL AND INTERPRET

1. What honor does the young man receive? Where does the next day's trek lead him? What do these events tell you about the young man and his family's way of life?
2. Why is the son perplexed when his family sees their living quarters? What conclusions do you draw from his conversation with the farmer?
3. Briefly describe the living and working conditions at the farm. What does the family's response to them suggest about their situation?
4. What accident occurs in the story? What does the young man's reaction to the accident suggest about his values?
5. How does the young man carry the experience with him later in life? To whom does the man eventually tell the story, and how do you think telling it heals the man?

EVALUATE AND CONNECT

6. What effect do you think the writer achieves by using a Spanish title and leaving the characters unnamed?
7. Which situations or events in the story are catalysts for change? Compare and contrast these situations with the description you wrote for the Focus Activity on page 1096.
8. How would you describe the **point of view** in this story? In your opinion, what effect does this point of view have on the telling of the story?

Literary ELEMENTS

Protagonist and Antagonist

A story plot usually involves a conflict between a **protagonist,** the character who is the focus of readers' interest, and an **antagonist,** a person, a force, or even a feeling, such as excessive pride or fear. The antagonist may be a character who thwarts the hero. In some narratives, however, the antagonist is less obvious. The conflict between protagonist and antagonist develops until one overcomes the other. In Cantú's story the protagonist is the favored son.

1. Who, or what, is the antagonist in this story? Explain.
2. Is this a story in which the protagonist overcomes the antagonist? Explain.

● See **Literary Terms Handbook,** p. R12.

--------- **EXTENDING YOUR RESPONSE** ---------

Interdisciplinary Activity

History: U.S. Migrant Labor   What relevant, researchable questions can you develop about migrant work after reading this story? Research one of your questions, and prepare a brief report about some aspect of migrant work. For example, you might find out about any action to improve working and living conditions for these laborers. Then present your report to the class.

Personal Writing

Lessons Learned   According to Cantú, "Increased self-knowledge comes with the writing—both for me and, I hope, for my readers." How has this story increased your self-knowledge? Write a brief paragraph or two describing something you learned about yourself or about life.

📖 **Save your work for your portfolio.**

Before You Read

from *Kubota*

Meet
Garrett Hongo

Garrett Hongo felt like he was stepping back in time when, at the age of thirty-three, he returned to his birthplace: Volcano, Hawaii. It was the first time he had been there as an adult, and he was overwhelmed by Kilauea volcano, the mountain that looms over the town. "I suddenly wanted to be *better* than I had been," he remembers, "more a part of the earth I was born to, its rock and garland of ferns, more a part of the history which had been kept from me out of some mysterious shame, and more a part of my own poetic mind, an elusive and beleaguered thing, almost out of keeping with our own time."

Hongo, a poet who teaches English at the University of Oregon, didn't think he could find the words to describe what he saw. At the same time, he knew he had to write about the volcano, the rain forest, the mist, and the spew of hardened lava and rock.

Over the next several years, Hongo made seven visits to Volcano. Two of those visits were a year long. The journeys allowed him to explore his history and to discover a place that he says is like nowhere else on earth.

Hongo was born to Japanese American parents and grew up in southern California. There, he learned about the experiences of many groups of immigrants, including the forced internment of Japanese Americans during World War II. His writings frequently touch on the bitterness of prejudice and the trials immigrants face in American society.

"I find that the landscapes, folkways, and societies of Japan, Hawaii, and even Southern California continually charm and compel me to write about them."

—*Hongo*

Garrett Hongo was born in 1951.

FOCUS ACTIVITY

What lessons have your elders passed on to you through their stories?

SHARE IT! Tell a partner one of the stories you've heard.

SETTING A PURPOSE Read to find out how a grandfather's stories change the way one writer views the world.

BACKGROUND

The Time and Place
This story begins in Hawaii the day after the Japanese attacked Pearl Harbor on December 7, 1941, prompting the United States to enter World War II. It also takes place outside of Los Angeles during the 1950s and 1960s.

VOCABULARY PREVIEW

espionage (es′ pē ə näzh′) *n.* spying; p. 1102
access (ak′ ses) *n.* the right to approach, enter, or use; p. 1102
initially (i nish′ ə lē) *adv.* at the beginning; first; p. 1102
warranted (wôr′ ən tid′) *adj.* justified; p. 1102
idiom (id′ ē əm) *n.* an expression peculiar to a people or to a specific region; p. 1103
invoke (in vōk′) *v.* to call forth; p. 1105
concerted (kən sur′ tid) *adj.* planned or carried out by mutual agreement; p. 1106

from Kubota

Garrett Hongo

It was a Monday night, the day after Pearl Harbor, and there was a rattling knock at the front door. Two FBI agents presented themselves, showed identification, and took my grandfather in for questioning in Honolulu. He didn't return home for days. No one knew what had happened or what was wrong. But there was a roundup going on of all those in the Japanese-American community suspected of sympathizing with the enemy and worse.

Barracks, Tule Lake, California, 1945. Taneyuki Dan Harada. Oil on canvas, 27 x 31 in. Collection of Michael D. Brown.

from **Kubota**

My grandfather was suspected of espionage, of communicating with offshore Japanese submarines launched from the attack fleet days before the war began. Torpedo planes and escort fighters, decorated with the insignia of the Rising Sun, had taken an approach route from northwest of Oahu directly across Kahuku Point and on toward Pearl. They had strafed[1] an auxiliary air station near the fishing grounds my grandfather loved and destroyed a small gun battery there, killing three men. Kubota[2] was known to have sponsored and harbored Japanese nationals in his own home. He had a radio. He had wholesale access to firearms. Circumstances and an undertone of racial resentment had combined with wartime hysteria in the aftermath of the tragic naval battle to cast suspicion on the loyalties of my grandfather and all other Japanese Americans. The FBI reached out and pulled hundreds of them in for questioning in dragnets cast throughout the West Coast and Hawaii.

My grandfather was lucky; he'd somehow been let go after only a few days. Others were not as fortunate. Hundreds, from small communities in Washington, California, Oregon, and Hawaii, were rounded up and, after what appeared to be routine questioning, shipped off under Justice Department orders to holding centers in Leuppe on the Navaho reservation in Arizona, in Fort Missoula in Montana, and on Sand Island in Honolulu Harbor. There were other special camps on Maui in Ha'iku and on Hawaii—the Big Island—in my own home village of Volcano.

Many of these men—it was exclusively the Japanese-American men suspected of ties to Japan who were initially rounded up—did not see their families again for more than four years. Under a suspension of due process[3] that was only after the fact ruled as warranted by military necessity, they were, if only temporarily, "disappeared" in Justice Department prison camps scattered in particularly desolate areas of the United States designated as militarily "safe." These were grim forerunners of the assembly centers and concentration camps for the 120,000 Japanese-American evacuees that were to come later.

I am Kubota's eldest grandchild, and I remember him as a lonely, habitually silent old man who lived with us in our home near Los Angeles for most of my childhood and adolescence. It was the fifties, and my parents had emigrated from Hawaii to the mainland in the hope of a better life away from the old sugar plantation. After some success, they had sent back for my grandparents and taken them in. And it was my grandparents who did the work of the household while my mother and father worked their salaried city jobs. My grandmother cooked and sewed, washed our clothes, and knitted in the front room under the light of a huge lamp with a bright three-way bulb. Kubota raised a flower garden, read up on soils and grasses in gardening books, and planted a zoysia lawn in front and a dichondra[4] one in back. He planted a small patch near the rear block wall with green onions, eggplant, white Japanese radishes, and cucumber. While he hoed and spaded the loamless, clayey earth of Los Angeles, he sang

---

1. *Strafed* means "attacked with machine guns from low-flying aircraft."
2. *Kubota* (kōō bō′ tä)

3. *Due process* is the administration of the law according to prescribed procedures.
4. *Zoysia* (zoi′ zhə) is a type of grass. *Dichondra* (dī kän′ drə) is a type of herb used for lawns.

Vocabulary
espionage (es′ pē ə näzh′) *n.* spying
access (ak′ ses) *n.* the right to approach, enter, or use
initially (i nish′ ə lē) *adv.* at the beginning; first
warranted (wôr′ ən tid′) *adj.* justified

particularly plangent[5] songs in Japanese about plum blossoms and bamboo groves.

Once, in the mid-sixties, after a dinner during which, as always, he had been silent while he worked away at a meal of fish and rice spiced with dabs of Chinese mustard and catsup thinned with soy sauce, Kubota took his own dishes to the kitchen sink and washed them up. He took a clean jelly jar out of the cupboard—the glass was thick and its shape squatty like an old-fashioned. He reached around to the hutch below where he kept his bourbon. He made himself a drink and retired to the living room where I was expected to join him for "talk story," the Hawaiian idiom for chewing the fat.

I was a teenager and, though I was bored listening to stories I'd heard often enough before at holiday dinners, I was dutiful. I took my spot on the couch next to Kubota and heard him out.

Did You Know?
The Japanese word *soroban* (sō′ rō bän′) means "abacus."

Usually, he'd tell me about his schooling in Japan where he learned judo along with mathematics and literature. He'd learned the *soroban* there—the abacus, which was the original pocket calculator of the Far East—and that, along with his strong, judo-trained back, got him his first job in Hawaii. This was the moral. "Study *ha-ahd*," he'd say with pidgin[6] emphasis. "Learn read good. Learn speak da kine *good* English." The message is the familiar one taught to any children of immigrants: succeed through education. And imitation. But this time, Kubota reached down into

his past and told me a different story. I was thirteen by then, and I suppose he thought me ready for it. He told me about Pearl Harbor, how the planes flew in wing after wing of formations over his old house in La'ie in Hawaii, and how, the next day, after Roosevelt[7] had made his famous "Day of Infamy" speech about the treachery of the Japanese, the FBI agents had come to his door and taken him in, hauled him off to Honolulu for questioning, and held him without charge for several days. I thought he was lying. I thought he was making up a kind of horror story to shock me and give his moral that much more starch. But it was true. I asked around. I brought it up during history class in junior high school, and my teacher, after silencing me and stepping me off to the back of the room, told me that it was indeed so. I asked my mother and she said it was true. I asked my schoolmates, who laughed and ridiculed me for being so ignorant. We lived in a Japanese-American community, and the parents of most of my classmates were the *nisei*[8] who had been interned[9] as teenagers all through the war. But there was a strange silence around all of this. There was a hush, as if one were invoking the ill powers of the dead when one brought it up. No one cared to speak about the evacuation and relocation for very long. It wasn't in our history books, though we were studying World War II at the time. It wasn't in the family albums of the people I knew and whom I'd visit staying over

---

5. *Plangent* (plan′ jənt) can mean either "mournful" or "loud and echoing."
6. *Pidgin* (pij′ ən) is a hybrid language that is a mixture of two or more languages and that has a simplified vocabulary and grammatical structure.
7. President Franklin D. *Roosevelt* (1882–1945) addressed Congress the day after the bombing of Pearl Harbor on December 7, 1941, saying it was "a day which will live in infamy."
8. The Japanese word *nisei* (nē′ sā) refers to children of Japanese immigrants; that is, the first generation of Japanese Americans born in the United States.
9. *Interned* means "confined or restricted to a particular place, especially during war."

Vocabulary
idiom (id′ ē əm) *n.* an expression peculiar to a people or to a specific region

Portrait of Nishida, 1942. Sadayuki Uno. Oil on potato sack. Collection of Yo Kasai.

Viewing the painting: Look closely at this man's face. What kinds of memories might he have? Do you think his life might have been like Kubota's? Explain.

weekends with friends. And it wasn't anything that the family talked about or allowed me to keep bringing up either. I was given the facts, told sternly and pointedly that "it was war" and that "nothing could be done." "*Shikatta ga nai*"[10] is the phrase in Japanese, a kind of resolute and determinist pronouncement on how to deal with inexplicable tragedy. I was to know it but not to dwell on it. Japanese Americans were busy trying to forget it ever happened and were having a hard enough time building their new lives after "camp." It was as if we had no history for four years and the relocation was something unspeakable.

10. "*Shikatta ga nai*" (shē kä′ tä   gä   nī)

But Kubota would not let it go. In session after session, for months it seemed, he pounded away at his story. He wanted to tell me the names of the FBI agents. He went over their questions and his responses again and again. He'd tell me how one would try to act friendly toward him, offering him cigarettes while the other, who hounded him with accusations and threats, left the interrogation room. Good cop, bad cop, I thought to myself, already superficially streetwise from stories black classmates told of the Watts[11] riots and from my having watched too many episodes of *Dragnet* and *The Mod Squad*.[12] But Kubota was not interested in my experiences. I was not made yet, and he was determined that his stories be part of my making. He spoke quietly at first, mildly, but once into his narrative and after his drink was down, his voice would rise and quaver with resentment and he'd make his accusations. He gave his testimony to me and I held it at first cautiously in my conscience like it was an heirloom too delicate to expose to strangers and anyone outside of the world Kubota made with his words. "I give you story now," he once said, "and you learn speak good, eh?" It was my job, as the disciple of his preaching I had then become, Ananda to his Buddha,[13] to reassure him with a promise. "You learn speak good like the Dillingham," he'd say another time, referring to the wealthy scion of the grower family who had once run, unsuccessfully, for one of Hawaii's first senatorial seats. Or he'd then invoke a magical name, the name of one of his heroes, a man he thought particularly exemplary and righteous. "Learn speak dah good Ing-rish like *Mistah Inouye*," Kubota shouted. "He *lick* dah Dillingham even in debate. I saw on *terre-bision* myself." He was remembering the debates before the first senatorial election just before Hawaii was admitted to the Union as its fiftieth state. "You *tell* story," Kubota would end. And I had my injunction.[14]

Did You Know?
Daniel K. Inouye (in′ ō ye′) (born 1924), was the first Japanese American to serve in Congress as a U.S. Senator from Hawaii.

The town we settled in after the move from Hawaii is called Gardena, the independently incorporated city south of Los Angeles and north of San Pedro harbor. At its northern limit, it borders on Watts and Compton, black towns. To the southwest are Torrance and Redondo Beach, white towns. To the rest of L.A., Gardena is primarily famous for having legalized five-card draw poker after the war. On Vermont Boulevard, its eastern border, there is a dingy little Vegas-like strip of card clubs with huge parking lots and flickering neon signs that spell out "The Rainbow" and "The Horseshoe" in timed sequences of varicolored lights. The town is only secondarily famous as the largest community of Japanese Americans in the United States outside of Honolulu, Hawaii. When I was in high school there, it seemed to me that every *sansei*[15] kid I knew wanted to be a doctor, an engineer, or a pharmacist. Our fathers were gardeners or electricians or nurserymen or ran small businesses catering to other Japanese

---

11. *Watts,* a section of Los Angeles, was the site of severe racial violence in 1965.
12. *Dragnet* and *The Mod Squad* were popular television police shows.
13. *Buddha* (563?–483? B.C.) was the title given to Siddhartha Gautama (si där′ tə gou′ tə mə), the founder of Buddhism. *Ananda* (ä nän′ dä) was his cousin and "Beloved Disciple."

14. An *injunction* is a command or an order.
15. The *sansei* (sän′ sā′) are the children of the nisei.

Vocabulary
invoke (in vōk′) *v.* to call forth

from Kubota

Americans. Our mothers worked in civil service for the city or as cashiers for Thrifty Drug. What the kids wanted was a good job, good pay, a fine home, and no troubles. No one wanted to mess with the law—from either side—and no one wanted to mess with language or art. They all talked about getting into the right clubs so that they could go to the right schools. There was a certain kind of sameness, an intensely enforced system of conformity. Style was all. Boys wore moccasin-sewn shoes from Flagg Brothers, black A-1 slacks, and Kensington shirts with high collars. Girls wore their hair up in stiff bouffants solidified in hairspray and knew all the latest dances from the slauson to the funky chicken. We did well in chemistry and in math, no one who was Japanese but me spoke in English class or in history unless called upon, and no one talked about World War II. The day after Robert Kennedy was assassinated, after winning the California Democratic primary, we worked on calculus and elected class coordinators for

Did You Know?
A *bouffant* (bōō fänt′) is a hairstyle in which the hair is puffed out.

the prom, featuring the 5th Dimension.[16] We avoided grief. We avoided government. We avoided strong feelings and dangers of any kind. Once punished, we tried to maintain a concerted emotional and social discipline and would not willingly seek to fall out of the narrow margin of protective favor again.

But when I was thirteen, in junior high, I'd not understood why it was so difficult for my classmates, those who were themselves Japanese American, to talk about the relocation. They had cringed, too, when I tried to bring it up during our discussions of World War II. I was Hawaiian-born. They were mainland-born. Their parents had been in camp, had been the ones to suffer the complicated experience of having to distance themselves from their own history and all things Japanese in order to make their way back and into the American social and economic mainstream. It was out of this sense of shame and a fear of stigma I was only beginning to understand that the *nisei* had silenced themselves. And, for their children, among whom I grew up, they wanted no heritage, no culture, no contact with a defiled history. I recall the silence very well. The Japanese-American children around me were burdened in a way I was not. Their injunction was silence. Mine was to speak.

---

16. The *5th Dimension* was a popular music group in the late 1960s.

Vocabulary
concerted (kən sur′ tid) *adj.* planned or carried out by mutual agreement

Responding to Literature

Personal Response

What was your reaction to the events described in the memoir?

ANALYZING LITERATURE

RECALL AND INTERPRET

1. How does Hongo learn about his family's life at the outbreak of World War II? Why, do you think, does Hongo first disbelieve the stories?
2. What is the difference between the attitude of Kubota toward these events and the attitudes of his contemporaries? What might explain this difference? Use details from the selection to support your answer.
3. Where does Hongo live and go to school at the time he learns of Kubota's experience? How does the **setting** affect his acceptance of Kubota's story? (See Literary Terms Handbook, page R14.)
4. What does Kubota ask his grandson to do with the story he is telling? In your opinion, why does Kubota ask this?

EVALUATE AND CONNECT

5. Hongo begins with a vivid scene from the past and then moves to events that happened later. In your opinion, what does the opening scene contribute to the overall impact of the story?
6. What connection does Hongo make between his life as a writer and his family's past? Why, do you think, does he make this connection?
7. Suppose the author chose to delete the last paragraph from this selection. Would your view of his attitude toward his schoolmates be different? Explain.
8. How do your stories affect the way you view yourself and the world? Compare the impact of the stories you considered for the Focus Activity on page 1100 with the impact Kubota's story had on his grandson.

Literary ELEMENTS

Memoir

In a **memoir,** a writer narrates a portion of his or her past. Unlike an autobiography, a memoir focuses on a specific period or instance in history and deals peripherally with other parts of the writer's life. Many writers of memoirs, like Garrett Hongo, try to recreate an experience of discovery or growth. They may write about a new understanding of a time, a person, or an experience that is important to them. A memoir may include additional information about historical, scientific, or other developments of the time that are relevant to the writer.

1. What in-depth information must Hongo include in this portion of his memoir to make the story clear?
2. In what way does this memoir show a discovery or growth made by the narrator?

● See **Literary Terms Handbook,** p. R9.

EXTENDING YOUR RESPONSE

Literature Groups

To Speak, or Not to Speak   Is Kubota right to urge his grandson to tell about what happened to Japanese Americans during World War II? Debate this question in your group. Support your position with details from the selection and with historical information. Then share your group's opinions with the class.

Learning for Life

A Pilot Program   Imagine that you want to persuade a television station to air a documentary on *Kubota.* Create a storyboard for the program. Develop at least six scenes showing who is in the scene, where it takes place, and the major action of the scene.

📖 **Save your work for your portfolio.**

Before You Read

Speaking and *apprenticeship 1978*

Meet Simon J. Ortiz

Simon J. Ortiz (ôr tēz′) says that he has been a writer "forever," since his voice comes from the oral tradition of Native American storytelling. Ortiz, a Native American from Acoma Pueblo in New Mexico, has actually been writing for thirty years or more. He has published numerous books, including poetry and short-story collections and essay anthologies. Recently, Ortiz edited a book titled *Speaking for the Generations: Native Writers on Writing.*

Ortiz teaches creative writing and Native American literature at universities and writing workshops throughout the country.

Two of his recent works are *The Good Rainbow Road*, a children's book, and *Before the Lightning*, a poetry collection.

Simon J. Ortiz was born in 1941.

Meet Evangelina Vigil-Piñon

In her poetry, Evangelina Vigil-Piñon (vē hēl   pē nyōn′) explores a variety of themes and subjects ranging from the lively street life of Houston, Texas, to how Mexican American women experience motherhood. "In her attempt to capture . . . the many rhythms of ordinary life," writes critic Wendy Barker, "Vigil-Piñon seems partially descended from the earlier great American poet of the people, Walt Whitman."

Vigil-Piñon was born in San Antonio, Texas, and graduated from the University of Houston in 1974. Since then, she has taught literature at various universities. In 1983 Vigil-Piñon won the prestigious American Book Award for her poetry collection *Thirty an' Seen a Lot.*

Evangelina Vigil-Piñon was born in 1949.

FOCUS ACTIVITY

What family member or friend has taught you something that has influenced how you live your life? What exactly did you learn?

FREEWRITE Spend three or four minutes freewriting to explore your response to these questions.

SETTING A PURPOSE Read to find out what one speaker teaches a son and what another learns from a grandmother.

BACKGROUND

Oral tradition—the passing down of stories by word of mouth—is important to both Native American and Chicano cultures. Simon Ortiz believes that the oral tradition brings "a sense of cultural being, continuity, and identity" to Native Americans. Evangelina Vigil-Piñon, in her poem "apprenticeship 1978," celebrates the ways oral tradition keeps the past alive, and she works to reflect that tradition in her own writing. For example, the speaker of "apprenticeship 1978" describes how her grandmother's stories inspire and guide her. By remembering the oral tradition, Vigil-Piñon says, a writer can convey "values to her family members . . . and, as such, she represents a tie to the cultural past."

Speaking

Simon J. Ortiz

I take him outside
under the trees,
have him stand on the ground.
We listen to the crickets,
5   cicadas,° million years old sound.
Ants come by us.
I tell them,
"This is he, my son.
This boy is looking at you.
10   I am speaking for him."

The crickets, cicadas,
the ants, the millions of years
are watching us,
hearing us.
15   My son murmurs infant words,
speaking, small laughter
bubbles from him.
Tree leaves tremble.
They listen to this boy
20   speaking for me.

---

5 *Cicadas* (si kā′ däz) **are large, winged insects.**
The males produce a loud, shrill sound.

Yei's Collection of Mountains, Hills, and Plant Life. Emmi Whitehorse. Mixed media on paper and canvas,
38 x 48½ in. Telluride Gallery of Fine Art, Telluride, CO.

apprenticeship
1978

Evangelina Vigil-Piñon ∿

Retrato de Mujer, 1944. Maria Izquierdo. Watercolor on paper, 20 x 14 in.
Private collection.

I hunt for things
that will color my life
with brilliant memories
because I do believe
5   lo que nos dice
la mano del escritor:°
that life is remembering

when I join my grandmother
for a tasa de café°
10   and I listen to the stories
de su antepasado°
her words paint masterpieces
and these I hang
in the galleries of my mind:

15   I want to be an artist like her.

5–6 *lo que nos dice / la mano del escritor* (lō kā
nōs dē′sä / lä mä′nō del e skrē′tôr′)
means "what the writer's hand tells us."

9 *tasa de café* (tä′sä dä kä fā′) means "cup
of coffee."

11 *de su antepasado* (dä sōō än′tä pä sä′dō)
means "of her past."

Responding to Literature

Personal Response

What went through your mind when you finished each poem?

ANALYZING LITERATURE

Speaking

RECALL AND INTERPRET

1. Where does the speaker of this poem take his son and what does he have him do? Why might this place be important to the speaker?
2. What sounds does the son make? How would you describe the father's response to these sounds? What does this response suggest about the relationship between the father and son?

EVALUATE AND CONNECT

3. What two words does the poet **rhyme** in lines 3–5? What idea might he be trying to emphasize through this rhyme? (See Literary Terms Handbook, page R13.)
4. The speaker notices the ants, crickets, and cicadas all around him. What aspects of the natural world do you notice in your community? What can you learn from these natural elements? Explain.

apprenticeship
1978

RECALL AND INTERPRET

5. What does the speaker hunt for? How would you characterize the nature of her hunt?
6. What effect do the grandmother's words have on the speaker? What might the speaker mean when she says, "I want to be an artist like her"?

EVALUATE AND CONNECT

7. The poet incorporates Spanish words throughout "apprenticeship 1978." In your opinion, how do these words contribute to the meaning and impact of the poem?
8. In your opinion, is "apprenticeship 1978" a fitting title for this poem? What does it suggest about the speaker's relationship with her grandmother?

EXTENDING YOUR RESPONSE

Performing

Tell a Story   In Native American cultures, storytelling is an important activity. Storytellers pass on the myths and legends of the people. Imagine that you are a storyteller who feels that "Speaking" has an important message to preserve. Transform "Speaking" into an oral story and then perform it for a friend.

Creative Writing

Write a Poem   Using your response to the Focus Activity on page 1108 for inspiration, write a poem that conveys what you have learned from someone and how this knowledge has influenced you.

📖 **Save your work for your portfolio.**

~: Writing \ Workshop :~

Persuasive Writing: Speech

> "A living thing is distinguished from a dead thing by the multiplicity of the changes at any moment taking place in it."
>
> *—Herbert Spencer,* English philosopher

What were you like at thirteen? What songs were popular a year ago? What were schools like when your parents were young? The world is changing all the time.

Sometimes change happens by itself; sometimes people make it happen. Just as frequently, people try to resist change. **In this workshop you will write a speech to persuade others that something should or should not be changed.** What change would you like to promote? What change would you like to prevent?

● As you write your persuasive speech, refer to the **Writing Handbook,** pp. R62–R77.

The Writing Process

PREWRITING

PREWRITINGTIP

Keep your topic narrow and specific. You'll be able to target your audience more easily and cover your topic more effectively.

Explore ideas

Persuasive speeches are everyday events: an advertisement encourages you to buy a product, a candidate wants your vote, or a coach charges you up before the big game. When you try to persuade your parents to let you have a party, you become a persuasive speaker. Now you're going to focus your persuasive skills on change. In what ways would you like to go back to the past or move ahead? For ideas, just look around you—at your home, your school, your community, your world. Skim newspapers and magazines. Think about what is on television and radio. Talk to others. Consider the literature you read.

● Look back on the "good old days" an older person has described, as N. Scott Momaday does in *The Way to Rainy Mountain.* What do you think made those days better?

● As Longhang Nguyen does in "Rain Music," consider whether children of immigrant parents should follow traditional ways.

● Think about the lives of immigrants as described by Norma Elia Cantú and Julia Alvarez. How might their lives be made easier?

Focus on an issue that interests you—one about which you have an opinion and some information. Be sure you can justify your reasoning with good examples.

Choose an audience

Your topic will probably point you to your audience: a school audience for a school issue, a community audience for a community issue, and so on. Try to target listeners who are in a position to do something—such as pass a law, sign a petition, or write a letter. Talk to your audience in the kind of language they will understand, and give them the kind of information they will need to draw the conclusion you want.

Consider your purpose

Your purpose, as in any persuasive piece, is to persuade an audience to support your view on an issue and perhaps take some action. In this case, however, you will try to accomplish your goal with spoken words rather than written ones.

Build your argument

When you've found a compelling topic, map out your arguments. Include those that support your position and also those that oppose it. Do some research to back up your arguments, recording each fact and its source on one side of a note card. You can be profound and serious, or light and humorous, but in all cases, your arguments have to make sense. You might want to organize your thoughts on a diagram like this one:

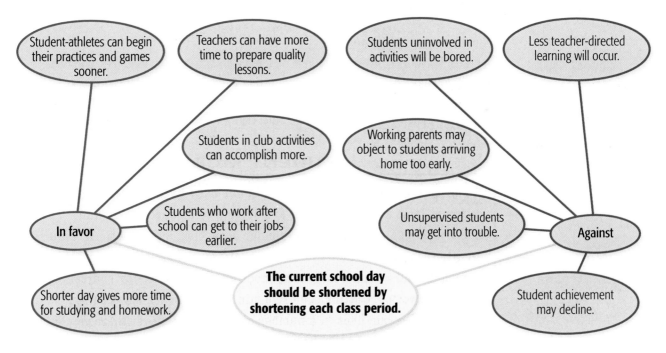

Make a plan

Check on whether you will be able to use visual aids, especially if any of your arguments involve data or diagrams that your audience will need to see. When you have all your information, spread out your note cards and make piles of those that speak to the same point. Then arrange your cards, with your arguments, in a logical order. You may want to prepare an outline from your cards to help you draft your speech.

DRAFTING

DRAFTING TIP

Find out if there is a time limit for your speech. If not, you may want to set a limit of about twelve minutes. A longer speech can lose its impact, as well as the attention of the audience.

Draft your speech

As you draft your speech, remember that you're writing to be *heard*. Read your draft aloud as you write, and determine if your word choices will *sound* good to an audience. Keep in mind that a persuasive speech is like a persuasive piece of writing. It demands strong arguments, and it is shaped by a good introduction, a cohesive body, and a logical conclusion.

Introduction

- Grab your audience's attention immediately. Try an anecdote, a startling fact, a challenging question, an interesting visual aid, a moving quotation, or a personal connection.
- Tell what the speech will be about.

Body

- Use your notes. Shift things around as you draft if you think of a better arrangement.
- Try building your arguments so that they peak with your most important point.

Conclusion

- Remind your audience of what your position is and why they should agree with it.
- Leave them with something to think about or something to do.

Develop your arguments

Don't just list your arguments, elaborate on them with facts, stories, examples, and visual aids. On the other hand, don't throw too much information at your listeners. They have to understand your argument from hearing it just once. Remember, listeners cannot turn back the pages for another look. Choose words that clarify, rather than confuse, your argument.

STUDENT MODEL

We never seem to have enough time in our busy lives. Students are no different from adults in this regard, having to balance school and homework with sports, extracurricular activities, and sometimes even an after-school job. Since there's not that much time in a day, one way to accomplish all we need to do is to modify the school day by shortening each class period. Cutting even five minutes from each class period would improve our lives in a number of significant ways. There would be more time to study and do homework. Those of us who participate in athletics or after-school clubs could begin practices and activities earlier, leaving more time later in the day for our studies. For those students who have after-school jobs, an earlier start might mean more money for college or more time for homework. Lastly, shortened class periods would mean more teacher preparation time and better lessons.

REVISING

Review your work

First read over your speech. Look for weak or incomplete arguments, words that need sharpening, or ideas that need linking. Then be your own audience. Practice your speech by yourself, thinking about how it sounds and how persuasive the arguments are. Mark places that strike you as awkward, unconvincing, unclear, or tedious.

Rehearse for others

Using your draft, your outline, or notes on cards, give your speech to family members, friends, classmates—anyone who is willing to listen and to make helpful comments. Ask your listeners to concentrate on how you look and sound as well as on what you say. The way a speech is delivered can significantly affect its message. Suggest that they use the **Questions for Revising** as a guide. Consider the comments you receive carefully, and incorporate those you find useful.

> **TECHNOLOGY TIP**
> With a computer, you can save and print out different versions of your speech. Test them all by reading them aloud—to yourself and to others. Use the one that seems most comfortable and convincing.

QUESTIONS FOR REVISING

☑ How might the opening be strengthened?

☑ Do the arguments flow smoothly? Where should the order be changed? Where do I need better transitions?

☑ Where can I eliminate weak arguments? Which points need more elaboration?

☑ Which parts are boring or hard to follow?

☑ Which parts have an inappropriately casual tone?

☑ How can I make the closing encourage action? Does it strongly support my opinion?

STUDENT MODEL

If your life is as hectic as mine, I think you'll agree that
~~To summarize, everybody's life is nuts.~~ Shortening the school day
is a good idea. Shortening each class period is one ~~good~~ solution. *by five minutes*
~~Five minutes isn't that much.~~ Athletes, ~~students in various clubs~~ *club members,*
~~and activities, kids~~ *students* with jobs ~~and stuff~~—all of us could benefit
from having extra time. ~~Then we'd be home for dinner early and~~ *Certainly our parents would be pleased*
~~our moms would be overjoyed.~~ *about that.* Finally, our teachers would have
extra planning time ~~and that would be good for us too.~~ *to prepare lessons*

EDITING/PROOFREADING

PROOFREADING TIP

Make sure that all changes from previous versions have been made correctly.

When you are satisfied with your speech, go over it for errors in grammar, usage, mechanics, and spelling, using the **Proofreading Checklist** on the inside back cover of this book. Even if no one but you will see the written version, you still want to be sure it is correct.

Grammar Hint

An irregular past participle cannot stand alone as a verb. Use the past participle with a form of *have*, or use the past tense form of the verb instead.

I have known many students who had after-school jobs.

● For information on related usage problems, see **Language Handbook,** pp. R27–R28.

STUDENT MODEL

Since september, I gone to work at the grocery store every day after school.

PUBLISHING/PRESENTING

PRESENTING TIP

The audience will be looking as well as listening. Don't wear or hold anything that will distract them from your speech.

Prepare any visual aids or props in advance. Also decide whether you prefer to read your speech, memorize it, or speak from brief notes. Reading guarantees you will say what you intend, but you may not connect as well with your audience. Memorizing carries the danger of forgetting things and may increase your nervousness. Speaking from notes also involves such dangers, but the notes do provide cues.

No matter how you deliver the speech, remember to speak slowly and loudly, make frequent eye contact with your audience, and vary your pace, volume, and tone to keep listeners awake. Stand straight, keep both feet on the floor, and avoid nervous movements.

Reflecting

What was most challenging about preparing a persuasive speech? What was most fun? Set goals for your next piece of writing. Will you do something differently? If so, what?

📕 **Save your work for your portfolio.**

Theme 12   Variety Is Richness

How do you respond to an unfamiliar place—a place where people act, speak, or dress differently than you? Variety can sometimes be confusing and disorienting, yet it can also help us learn. The writers in this theme come from diverse backgrounds and perspectives, and they write in a variety of forms—both traditional and experimental.

THEME PROJECTS

Learning for Life

Create a Brochure Suppose this theme were a book in itself, titled *Variety Is Richness.* With a small group, develop an advertising brochure to make the book appealing to high-school age readers.

1. Choose eight selections from the theme by authors from a variety of backgrounds and representing different kinds of writing. For each, consider what students might appreciate about it, and what it teaches about the theme "Variety Is Richness."

2. Create your brochure. Include pictures, captions, and promotional paragraphs. Use page-layout software or produce the brochure by hand on paper.

3. Present your brochure to the class, explaining how it conveys the appeal of this theme.

Performing

A Writers Conference With a small group, conduct a "writers conference" for the class. Have each member role-play one author from this theme. The authors should give brief talks about the influence of their cultural heritage on their writing and how their work contributes to the theme "Variety Is Richness." Then invite comments and questions from the class.

Crowd #16, 1990. Diana Ong. Watercolor, 11 x 14 in. Private collection.

Before You Read

Prayer to the Pacific

Meet Leslie Marmon Silko

"Storytelling always includes the audience and the listeners, and, in fact, a great deal of the story is believed to be inside the listener, and the storyteller's role is to draw the story out of the listeners."

—*Silko*

"Where I come from," said Leslie Marmon Silko, "the words that are most highly valued are those which are spoken from the heart." The place that Silko comes from is the Laguna Pueblo Reservation near Albuquerque, New Mexico. There she grew up hearing traditional Native American stories and myths. "Storytelling," she says, "lies at the heart of the Pueblo people." In her writing, Silko draws upon these stories, exploring traditional themes such as the importance of nature and ceremony in Pueblo life.

As a young woman, Silko commuted to a school fifty miles away because her father wanted her to receive the best education available. At sixteen, she entered the University of New Mexico, graduating with highest honors in 1969. She then began law school, but left after three semesters to devote her energies to writing. Silko's decision paid off. Her skillful interpretations of Pueblo stories and her complex portrayals of Native Americans in conflict with Anglo culture have earned her numerous awards and a grant from the MacArthur Foundation. Today, Silko is recognized as one of the finest writers of her generation.

Leslie Marmon Silko was born in 1948.

FOCUS ACTIVITY

What words, thoughts, and images do you associate with the ocean?

MAP IT! Create a word web with the word *ocean* in the center. Around it, write words that spring to mind when you think of the ocean.

SETTING A PURPOSE Read to discover one speaker's thoughts and feelings about a particular ocean.

BACKGROUND

Native American Origins
Sometime between 35,000 and 60,000 years ago, people first arrived in America from Asia. They most likely migrated across a land bridge where the Bering Strait now separates Asia and America.

Literary Influences
Creation myths are traditional, symbolic narratives that explain the origins of the world, of various gods, or of certain people. Different groups of people have different myths based on their particular experiences and concerns. While most creation myths share certain elements, they are also unique to the people who created them. According to Silko, a creation myth "functions basically as a maker of our identity—with the story we know who we are."

Our Life on His Back, 1993. Julie Lankford Olds. Oil on canvas, 12 x 16 in. Minnetrista Cultural Center & Oakhurst Gardens, Muncie, IN.

Prayer to the Pacific

Leslie Marmon Silko

Prayer to the Pacific

I traveled to the ocean
        distant
                from my southwest land of sandrock
              to the moving blue water
5   Big as the myth of origin.

Pale
pale water in the yellow-white light of
           sun   floating west
               to China
10   where ocean herself was born.
Clouds that blow across the sand are wet.

Squat in the wet sand and speak to the Ocean:
      I return to you   turquoise   the red coral you sent us,
        sister spirit of Earth.
15 Four round stones in my pocket   I carry back the ocean
        to suck and to taste.

Thirty thousand years ago
         Indians came riding across the ocean
        carried by giant sea turtles.
20 Waves were high that day
       great sea turtles waded   slowly out
            from the gray sundown sea.
Grandfather Turtle rolled in the sand   four times
       and disappeared
25   swimming into the sun.

And so   from that time
      immemorial,°
        as the old people say,
rain clouds drift from the west
30   gift from the ocean.

Green leaves in the wind
Wet earth on my feet
     swallowing raindrops
        clear from China.

---

27 Immemorial means "extending back beyond memory or record."

Responding to Literature

Personal Response

Which images appealed to you most? Note them in your journal.

—— ANALYZING LITERATURE ——

RECALL AND INTERPRET

1. Where did the speaker begin and end her journey? Why, in your opinion, did the speaker make this journey?
2. According to the speaker, where was the ocean born, and in what direction is it floating? Why might the speaker believe the ocean is floating in this direction?
3. What does the speaker say to the ocean? How would you characterize the speaker's relationship to the ocean? Why, in your opinion, is the ocean so important to her?
4. Summarize the story that the speaker tells. What natural phenomenon does the story explain? Why might this phenomenon be important to the Pueblo people?

EVALUATE AND CONNECT

5. Silko describes the Pacific Ocean as "Big as the myth of origin." Why is this comparison particularly fitting for this poem?
6. Review the word web that you created for the Focus Activity on page 1118. How is your view of the ocean different from or similar to the view expressed in this poem?
7. In what ways does the **form** of this poem connect to its subject?
8. Based on this poem, what can you infer about the Pueblos' relationship to nature? Do you think that other groups in American society have a similar relationship to nature? Explain.

Literary ELEMENTS

Poetic License

Poetic license is the freedom allowed poets to ignore the standard rules of grammar or proper diction in order to create a desired artistic effect. Although the term most frequently refers to liberties taken with language, it can also refer to liberties taken with facts. Silko uses poetic license throughout this poem. For example, in the line "Squat in the wet sand and speak to the Ocean," she does not include a subject in the clause.

1. What word in line 3 cannot be found in any dictionary? Why might Silko have coined this word?
2. What example of poetic license does line 25 include? How might this example contribute to the meaning of the poem?

● See **Literary Terms Handbook**, p. R12.

—— EXTENDING YOUR RESPONSE ——

Interdisciplinary Activity

History: Research Myths   According to this poem, "Indians came riding across the ocean / carried by giant sea turtles." Locate one or more collections of Pueblo myths in the library or on the Internet and look for myths that either describe the migration of the Pueblo people to North America or that include turtles. Then tell the class what you have learned about Pueblo origin myths and the significance of turtles in Pueblo culture.

Personal Writing

Picture Postcard   Create a postcard message about the Pacific Ocean to send to your family or a friend. If you have actually seen an ocean or another large body of water, describe your own response. If not, you might base your message on the impressions you get from the poem.

📖 **Save your work for your portfolio.**

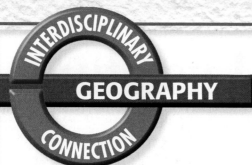

The Magnificent Pacific

Silko's "Prayer to the Pacific" describes the Pacific as an ocean of legend and myth, and indeed, the facts about the Pacific can be as fascinating as any legend or myth. The largest, deepest, and most life-sustaining ocean on Earth, this magnificent body of water stretches from Asia and Australia to the Americas.

Millions of Miles of Water The total surface area of the Pacific is about 63,800,000 square miles—an area greater than that of the entire land surface of the earth. In other words, the Pacific is so large that all of the continents could fit inside of it.

The widest part of the ocean from east to west lies between Colombia, South America, and the Malay Peninsula in Asia, a distance of about 12,000 miles. The longest part of the ocean from north to south stretches about 9,600 miles from the Bering Strait between Alaska and Asia to Antarctica.

Not Really So Pacific? Historians believe that the first people to sail the Pacific may have been seafaring Southeast Asians, about 3,000 years ago. It was Portuguese explorer Ferdinand Magellan (c. 1480–1521), however, who named the ocean *Pacífico*, which means "peaceful," after having sailed its calm waters for several weeks. The name is misleading, however. Underground volcanoes and earthquakes have caused powerful and deadly tidal waves called *tsunamis*, and typhoons have destroyed fleets of ships.

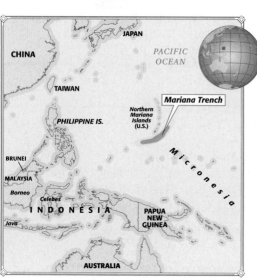

How Deep Is the Ocean? Although the Pacific Ocean bottom is extremely uneven, its average depth is about 14,000 feet. Its deepest spot—in fact, the deepest spot of any ocean—lies near Guam in the Mariana Trench. Here, the ocean bottom is about 36,200 feet below the surface.

Ocean Life The Pacific has the most varied mix of life forms of all the oceans. They range from tiny plankton, to species of seaweed that stretch 100 feet in length, to giant clams and whales. The western Pacific is also known for its spectacular coral reefs, ridges formed by the stacked skeletons of small sea creatures.

A Wealth of Resources　For centuries, traders have used the Pacific for transporting goods between continents. The ocean itself provides a wealth of products, including over half of the world's fish and shellfish catch. Northern Pacific fishers catch salmon, hake, and Alaska pollack. In addition, more than half of the world's tuna catch comes from the Pacific. Other products of the Pacific include pearls, seaweed, tropical fish for aquariums, and minerals, such as salt, sand, and magnesium. Major deposits of oil and natural gas from under the seafloor provide these important fuels for many countries.

Hot Vents　In the eastern Pacific, structures called hot vents occur where water, heated by underlying molten rock, rises to create mineral-rich hot water springs. Near these hot vents live large communities of unusual marine life, including giant clams, mussels, and tube worms.

Coral reef

Activity

Think of two or three questions you have about the Pacific Ocean and do research to find the answers. Then report your findings to the class.

Before You Read

Riding the Elevator into the Sky

Meet Anne Sexton

Anne Sexton once said that poetry "should almost hurt." In describing her personal nightmares with brutal honesty, Sexton's poems sometimes illuminate those of her readers as well and may, in fact, "hurt." After encountering many of her poems, readers may also find themselves feeling frustrated, as many critics have, by Sexton's exclusive focus on her own inner turmoil.

To outward appearances, Sexton led a fairly conventional life. She was born into a wealthy family in Newton, Massachusetts, and, like other young women of her background, attended a finishing school for girls.

At nineteen she dropped out of junior college to marry Alfred Muller Sexton, settling in a Boston suburb where she soon gave birth to the first of two daughters. For the next ten years, she focused on being a housewife and mother, roles that left her feeling restless and bored.

Sexton began writing poetry at the age of twenty-nine as a form of therapy for her ongoing struggles with depression. Through vivid imagery and bold metaphors, she explored motherhood, the breakdown of relationships, and the dramatic highs and tragic lows of mental illness. These poems catapulted Sexton into literary stardom and earned her a Guggenheim Fellowship and the Pulitzer Prize for Poetry in 1967. Despite her literary success, Sexton remained deeply troubled and ultimately took her own life.

Anne Sexton was born in 1928 and died in 1974.

FOCUS ACTIVITY

Think about a time in your life when you explored something unknown to you.

LIST IT! Make a list of images that describe the experience you had and the effects it had on your life.

SETTING A PURPOSE Read to learn about one speaker's experience exploring the unknown.

BACKGROUND

Literary Influences

In her poetry and in her emotionally charged life, Anne Sexton was greatly influenced by her fellow poets. Shortly after she began writing poetry, she attended the Antioch Writers' Conference, where she studied with the "confessional" poet W. D. Snodgrass. His very personal poems, she once said, "gave her permission" to explore her own emotional troubles. Later that year, Sexton participated in a writing seminar led by poet Robert Lowell at Boston University, where she forged lasting friendships with such poets as Sylvia Plath, Maxine Kumin, and Randall Jarrell.

Riding the Elevator into the Sky

Anne Sexton

City Night, 1926. Georgia O'Keeffe. Oil on canvas, 48 x 30 in.
©2000 The Georgia O'Keeffe Foundation/Artists Rights Society
(ARS), New York/Minneapolis Institute of Arts. Gift of the
Regis Corporation, W. John Driscoll, and the Beim Foundation;
the Larsen Fund; and by Public Subscription.

As the fireman said:
Don't book a room over the fifth floor
in any hotel in New York.
They have ladders that will reach further
5   but no one will climb them.
As the New York *Times* said:
The elevator always seeks out
the floor of the fire
and automatically opens
10   and won't shut.
These are the warnings
that you must forget
if you're climbing out of yourself.
If you're going to smash into the sky.

15   Many times I've gone past
the fifth floor,
cranking upward,
but only once
have I gone all the way up.
20   Sixtieth floor:
small plants and swans bending
into their grave.
Floor two hundred:
mountains with the patience of a cat,
25   silence wearing its sneakers.
Floor five hundred:
messages and letters centuries old,
birds to drink,
a kitchen of clouds.
30   Floor six thousand:
the stars,
skeletons on fire,
their arms singing.
And a key,
35   a very large key,
that opens something—
some useful door—
somewhere—
up there.

Responding to Literature

Personal Response

Which elements of this poem surprised or confused you? Explain.

ANALYZING LITERATURE

RECALL AND INTERPRET

1. What two warnings are stated in lines 1–10? Why might Sexton have begun her poem with two warnings?
2. Under what circumstances, according to the speaker, should such warnings be forgotten? What might lines 13–14 mean?
3. Describe what the speaker sees on floors sixty, two hundred, five hundred, and six thousand. How would you characterize the images that she encounters? What do they suggest about what it's like to "climb out of yourself"?
4. What is the final item that the speaker encounters? What possible uses might this item have? What might it represent?

EVALUATE AND CONNECT

5. Refer back to the list you made for the Focus Activity on page 1124. How did your experience compare with the one described in this poem?
6. What do you learn about Sexton from reading this poem?
7. This poem is composed of short lines, some containing as few as two syllables. How, in your opinion, might the structure of the poem connect to its subject?
8. The **mood** of a literary selection is its general emotional feeling. How would you describe the mood of this poem?

EXTENDING YOUR RESPONSE

Creative Writing

Riding into the Depths   Imagine that you are taking an elevator ride to the bottom of the sea. Write a poem describing the sights and sensations you might experience on your journey. Include as many evocative and daring images as you can. Also try experimenting with poetic devices that Sexton uses, such as short lines and **personification**—a figure of speech in which human characteristics are given to nonhuman subjects.

Literature Groups

The Mysterious Key   Many critics have noted that Sexton's poetry displays a preoccupation with the theme of death. In your group, discuss whether or not you think "Riding the Elevator into the Sky" explores this theme. Use details from the poem to support your conclusions. Then present your findings to the class.

📖 **Save your work for your portfolio.**

Magazine Article

What inspires people to create inventions that push the envelope of technology? Both in fantasy and reality, people have found a variety of ways to climb higher and reach for the sky.

Need a Lift?

by Randy Brown, *Buildings*, December 1996

No building system inspires flights of fancy more than the lowly elevator. In [the] cinema, elevators are used as a target for terrorism in *Speed* (1994); a tool for assassination in *Mission: Impossible* (1996); and a getaway vehicle in *In the Line of Fire* (1993).

Gene Roddenberry, creator of *Star Trek*, gave us the voice-activated, multidirectional "turbolift," and the beam-me-up immediacy of the "transporter."

Roald Dahl's "Willy Wonka" (*Charlie and the Chocolate Factory*) also had his Great Glass Elevator powered by candy and held to the sky with, well . . . a "skyhook." [It could] "go sideways and longways and slantways and any other way you can think of!"

In reality, even master builders can be carried away in their plans to achieve new heights. In his 1956 design for the Illinois-Sky City, Frank Lloyd Wright promised 56 quintuple-decked, atomic-powered elevators.

Why do we continue to collectively push the elevator envelope?

Is it the feeling of flight? Is it the fact that we may rise to new heights scraping the sky? Or is it, to revisit again the downside of our nature, the fleeting fear of freefall?

The latter would seem to explain the dropdead success of Walt Disney World's Twilight Zone Tower of Terror. The ride's set-up: a haunted 13-story, 13-star Hollywood hotel, site of a 1930s elevator accident. The pay-off, according to unofficial sources: 1.75 seconds of simulated freefall, zero-to-35 mph at the beat of a heart.

To solve the problems posed by ultra-high-rise structures, vertical thinkers and manufacturers are pursuing strategies similar to those used in the *Twilight Zone*. Otis Elevator Company unveiled Odyssey, a multidirectional system of "transitor" cabs, capable of commuting from parking lot to penthouse, even in structures more than 1,000 meters high.

While manufacturers aspire to break through the ceilings of height and speed, vertical speed demons will have to content themselves with a visit to Landmark Tower, in Yokohama, Japan. The world's fastest-moving passenger elevator is clocked at 750 meters (2,500 feet) per minute.

Respond

1. Which elevator system mentioned in the article is most appealing to you? Explain.

2. If you could develop a new elevator system, what would it do and why would it be beneficial?

Before You Read

Game

Meet Donald Barthelme

"**Donald Barthelme is [a] comedian who seems to have turned thinker.**"

—*Marvin Mudrick*

Donald Barthelme (bâr′ thəl mā′) was born in Philadelphia, Pennsylvania, and was raised outside of Houston, Texas. There, Barthelme's father, an architect, built the family a house that was noted for its modernity and that drew the attention of many in the community.

In 1953 Barthelme was drafted by the United States Army and served in Korea and Japan. Upon his return, he worked as a newspaper reporter, a museum director, a literary editor, and a teacher before establishing himself as a novelist and short-story writer. In the 1960s, Barthelme moved to New York City, where he became famous for the stories he contributed to the *New Yorker* magazine.

Throughout his literary career, Barthelme both puzzled and dazzled prominent reviewers and critics. Innovative and often eerie, his short stories usually contain bizarre characters forced to react to equally bizarre situations. As one critic put it, "Barthelme's writing verbalizes that semiconscious state we find ourselves in between sleep and wakefulness." Among his best-known works are the short-story collections *Come Back, Dr. Caligari* and *Sixty Stories* and the novel *Snow White*.

Donald Barthelme was born in 1931 and died in 1989.

FOCUS ACTIVITY

Have you ever been "stuck" in a situation with a person you did not know or did not like very well? How might you react, for example, if you were cooped up in a small room with such a person for a long period of time?

THINK-PAIR-SHARE Think about how you might react in such a situation. Would you make attempts to get along? Would you keep to yourself? Discuss your ideas with a partner.

SETTING A PURPOSE Read to find out how one character reacts to being cooped up with a coworker.

BACKGROUND

Literary Influences

Critics view Donald Barthelme as an *avant-garde* writer, one who experimented with new forms and new ideas. Barthelme has been compared to such experimental writers as Gertrude Stein and James Joyce. According to one critic, Barthelme's writing "depends on exaggeration, wit, elaborate hoax, playfulness." Barthelme is also noted for his use of **satire,** or writing that holds up its subject to ridicule or irony, usually with the intent of bringing about change.

VOCABULARY PREVIEW

simultaneously (sī′ məl tā′ nē əs lē) *adv.* at the same time; p. 1129

scrupulously (skrōō′ pyə ləs lē) *adv.* with extreme care and attention to detail; painstakingly; p. 1130

rigorously (rig′ ər əs lē) *adv.* precisely; strictly; p. 1130

exemplary (ig zem′ plə rē) *adj.* worthy of imitation; commendable; p. 1131

denounce (di nouns′) *v.* to condemn; to criticize; p. 1131

provoke (prə vōk′) *v.* to bring about; to incite; p. 1132

stolidly (stol′ id lē) *adv.* with little or no emotion; impassively; p. 1132

GAME

Donald Barthelme

Untitled, 1956. John Wilson. Painting.

Shotwell keeps the jacks and the rubber ball in his attaché case and will not allow me to play with them. He plays with them, alone, sitting on the floor near the console[1] hour after hour, chanting "onesies, twosies, threesies, foursies" in a precise, well-modulated voice, not so loud as to be annoying, not so soft as to allow me to forget. I point out to Shotwell that two can derive more enjoyment from playing jacks than one, but he is not interested. I have asked repeatedly to be allowed to play by myself, but he simply shakes his head. "Why?" I ask. "They're mine," he says. And when he has finished, when he has sated[2] himself, back they go into the attaché case.

It is unfair but there is nothing I can do about it. I am aching to get my hands on them.

Shotwell and I watch the console. Shotwell and I live under the ground and watch the console. If certain events take place upon the console, we are to insert our keys in the appropriate locks and turn our keys. Shotwell has a key and I have a key. If we turn our keys <u>simultaneously</u> the bird flies, certain switches are activated and the bird flies. But the bird never flies. In one hundred thirty-three days the bird has not flown. Meanwhile Shotwell and I watch each other. We each wear a .45 and if Shotwell behaves strangely I am supposed to shoot him. If I behave strangely Shotwell is supposed

---

1. A *console* (kon′ sōl) is a control panel for an electronic or mechanical system.
2. *Sated* (sā′ təd) means "completely satisfied."

GAME

to shoot me. We watch the console and think about shooting each other and think about the bird. Shotwell's behavior with the jacks is strange. Is it strange? I do not know. Perhaps he is merely selfish, perhaps his character is flawed, perhaps his childhood was twisted. I do not know.

Each of us wears a .45 and each of us is supposed to shoot the other if the other is behaving strangely. How strangely is strangely? I do not know. In addition to the .45 I have a .38 which Shotwell does not know about concealed in my attaché case, and Shotwell has a .25 caliber Beretta[3] which I do not know about strapped to his right calf. Sometimes instead of watching the console I pointedly watch Shotwell's .45, but this is simply a ruse,[4] simply a maneuver, in reality I am watching his hand when it dangles in the vicinity of his right calf. If he decides I am behaving strangely he will shoot me not with the .45 but with the Beretta. Similarly Shotwell pretends to watch my .45 but he is really watching my hand resting idly atop my attaché case, my hand resting idly atop my attaché case, my hand. My hand resting idly atop my attaché case.

In the beginning I took care to behave normally. So did Shotwell. Our behavior was painfully normal. Norms[5] of politeness, consideration, speech, and personal habits were scrupulously observed. But then it became apparent that an error had been made, that our

> ## Shotwell's behavior with the jacks is strange. Is it strange? I do not know.

relief was not going to arrive. Owing to an oversight. Owing to an oversight we have been here for one hundred thirty-three days. When it became clear that an error had been made, that we were not to be relieved, the norms were relaxed. Definitions of normality were redrawn in the agreement of January 1, called by us, The Agreement. Uniform regulations were relaxed, and mealtimes are no longer rigorously scheduled. We eat when we are hungry and sleep when we are tired. Considerations of rank and precedence were temporarily put aside, a handsome concession on the part of Shotwell, who is a captain, whereas I am only a first lieutenant. One of us watches the console at all times rather than two of us watching the console at all times, except when we are both on our feet. One of us watches the console at all times and if the bird flies then that one wakes the other and we turn our keys in the locks simultaneously and the bird flies. Our system involves a delay of perhaps twelve seconds but I do not care because I am not well, and Shotwell does not care because he is not himself. After the agreement was signed Shotwell produced the jacks and the rubber ball from his attaché case, and I began to write a series of descriptions of forms occurring in nature, such as a shell, a leaf, a stone, an animal. On the walls.

Shotwell plays jacks and I write descriptions of natural forms on the walls.

Shotwell is enrolled in a USAFI[6] course which leads to a master's degree in business

---

3. A *Beretta* (bə re′tə) is a type of semiautomatic pistol.
4. A *ruse* (rōōz) is an action or plan intended to deceive or trick.
5. *Norms* are accepted rules or standards.

6. The *USAFI* is the United States Armed Forces Institute.

Vocabulary

scrupulously (skrōō′ pyə ləs lē) *adv.* with extreme care and attention to detail; painstakingly
rigorously (rig′ ər əs lē) *adv.* precisely; strictly

administration from the University of Wisconsin (although we are not in Wisconsin, we are in Utah, Montana or Idaho). When we went down it was in either Utah, Montana or Idaho, I don't remember. We have been here for one hundred thirty-three days owing to an oversight. The pale green reinforced concrete walls sweat and the air conditioning zips on and off erratically[7] and Shotwell reads *Introduction to Marketing* by Lassiter and Munk, making notes with a blue ballpoint pen. Shotwell is not himself, but I do not know it, he presents a calm aspect and reads *Introduction to Marketing* and makes his exemplary notes with a blue ballpoint pen, meanwhile controlling the .38 in my attaché case with one-third of his attention. I am not well.

We have been here one hundred thirty-three days owing to an oversight. Although now we are not sure what is oversight, what is plan. Perhaps the plan is for us to stay here permanently, or if not permanently at least for a year, for three hundred sixty-five days. Or if not for a year for some number of days known to them and not known to us, such as two hundred days. Or perhaps they are observing our behavior in some way, sensors of some kind, perhaps our behavior determines the number of days. It may be that they are pleased with us, with our behavior, not in every detail but in sum. Perhaps the whole thing is very successful, perhaps the whole thing is an experiment and the experiment is very successful. I do not know. But I suspect that the only way they can persuade sun-loving creatures into their pale green sweating reinforced concrete rooms under the ground is to say that the system is twelve hours on, twelve hours off. And then lock us below for some number of days

known to them and not known to us. We eat well although the frozen enchiladas are damp when defrosted and the frozen devil's food cake is sour and untasty. We sleep uneasily and acrimoniously.[8] I hear Shotwell shouting in his sleep, objecting, denouncing, cursing sometimes, weeping sometimes, in his sleep. When Shotwell sleeps I try to pick the lock on his attaché case, so as to get at the jacks. Thus far I have been unsuccessful. Nor has Shotwell been successful in picking the locks on my attaché case so as to get at the .38. I have seen the marks on the shiny surface. I laughed, in the latrine, pale green walls sweating and the air conditioning whispering, in the latrine.

I write descriptions of natural forms on the walls, scratching them on the tile surface with a diamond. The diamond is a two and one-half carat solitaire I had in my attaché case when we went down. It was for Lucy. The south wall of the room containing the console is already covered. I have described a shell, a leaf, a stone, animals, a baseball bat. I am aware that the baseball bat is not a natural form. Yet I described it. "The baseball bat," I said, "is typically made of wood. It is typically one meter in length or a little longer, fat at one end, tapering to afford a comfortable grip at the other. The end with the handhold typically offers a slight rim, or lip, at the nether[9] extremity, to prevent slippage." My description of the baseball bat ran to 4500 words, all scratched with a diamond on the south wall. Does Shotwell read what I have written? I do not know. I am aware that Shotwell regards my writing-behavior as a little strange. Yet it is no stranger than his jacks-behavior, or the day he appeared in black bathing trunks

7. Here, *erratically* (ə rat′ ik lē′) means "irregularly," or "unpredictably."

8. *Acrimoniously* (ak′ rə mō′ nē əs lē) means "with bitterness and resentment."
9. *Nether* means "lower."

Vocabulary
exemplary (ig zem′ plə rē) *adj.* worthy of imitation; commendable
denounce (di nouns′) *v.* to condemn; to criticize

GAME

with the .25 caliber Beretta strapped to his right calf and stood over the console, trying to span with his two arms outstretched the distance between the locks. He could not do it, I had already tried, standing over the console with my two arms outstretched, the distance is too great. I was moved to comment but did not comment, comment would have provoked countercomment, comment would have led God knows where. They had in their infinite patience, in their infinite foresight, in their infinite wisdom already imagined a man standing over the console with his two arms outstretched, trying to span with his two arms outstretched the distance between the locks.

Shotwell is not himself. He has made certain overtures.[10] The burden of his message is not clear. It has something to do with the keys, with the locks. Shotwell is a strange person. He appears to be less affected by our situation than I. He goes about his business stolidly, watching the console, studying *Introduction to Marketing,* bouncing his rubber ball on the floor in a steady, rhythmical, conscientious manner. He appears to be less affected by our situation than I am. He is stolid. He says nothing. But he has made certain overtures, certain overtures have been made. I am not sure that I understand them. They have something to do with the keys, with the locks. Shotwell has something in mind. Stolidly he shucks the shiny silver paper from the frozen enchiladas, stolidly he stuffs them into the electric oven. But he has something in mind. But there must be a quid pro quo.[11] I insist on a quid pro quo. I have something in mind.

I am not well. I do not know our target. They do not tell us for which city the bird is targeted. I do not know. That is planning. That is not my responsibility. My responsibility is to watch the console and when certain events take place upon the console, turn my key in the lock. Shotwell bounces the rubber ball on the floor in a steady, stolid, rhythmical manner. I am aching to get my hands on the ball, on the jacks. We have been here one hundred thirty-three days owing to an oversight. I write on the walls. Shotwell chants "onesies, twosies, threesies, foursies" in a precise, well-modulated voice. Now he cups the jacks and the rubber ball in his hands and rattles them suggestively. I do not know for which city the bird is targeted. Shotwell is not himself.

Sometimes I cannot sleep. Sometimes Shotwell cannot sleep. Sometimes when Shotwell cradles me in his arms and rocks me to sleep, singing Brahms' "Guten abend, gute Nacht,"[12] or I cradle Shotwell in my arms and rock him to sleep, singing, I understand what it is Shotwell wishes me to do. At such moments we are very close. But only if he will give me the jacks. That is fair. There is something he wants me to do with my key, while he does something with his key. But only if he will give me my turn. That is fair. I am not well.

---

10. *Overtures* are actions or proposals that indicate a willingness to begin a new course of action or a new relationship.

11. The Latin expression *"quid pro quo"* (kwid′ prō kwō′) (literally, "what for what") means "an equal exchange."

12. The German words *"Guten abend, gute Nacht"* (gōō′ tən ä′ bənt, gōō′ tə näкнt) mean "good evening, good night." This is the opening phrase in the musical piece commonly known as "Brahms' Lullaby" by German composer Johannes Brahms (1833–1897).

Responding to Literature

Personal Response

If you could select only one word to describe this story, what would it be? Share your response with classmates, explaining your reasoning.

——— ANALYZING LITERATURE ———

RECALL AND INTERPRET

1. Where are the characters? According to the narrator, what are the details of their assignment? In your opinion, what is their actual assignment and how does it affect their behavior?
2. How long have the characters been in their current situation? Why, according to the narrator, have they been there for so long? Do you agree with the narrator? Why or why not?
3. What are the main tensions between the two men? What does each man's response to these tensions reveal about his character?
4. How does the narrator describe the "overtures" Shotwell makes? Are there any signs that the narrator may give in to these overtures? Explain, using details from the selection.

EVALUATE AND CONNECT

5. What methods does Barthelme use to reveal the character of the narrator? In your opinion, do these methods provide a clear picture of the narrator? Support your response with evidence from the story.
6. Based on your responses to the Focus Activity on page 1128, do you feel the narrator's reaction is realistic or unrealistic? Explain.
7. What words, phrases, and sentences does the narrator repeat in the story? What effect does this **repetition** (see page R13) have on your reading?
8. In your opinion, does the title "Game" simply refer to the game of jacks, or does it have deeper meanings? Explain.

Literary ELEMENTS

Irony

Irony is the contrast between what seems to be real and what actually is real. There are several types of irony. **Verbal irony** exists when a person says one thing and means another. **Dramatic irony** occurs when the reader has important information that characters in a literary work do not have. For example, readers of "Game" know that the narrator's actions are at times irrational. The narrator himself, though, does not seem to understand that his behavior is not always rational.

1. Find two examples of dramatic irony in the way the narrator and Shotwell interact. What do these examples contribute to the characterizations of the two men?
2. What, do you think, is most ironic in this story? What message might this irony convey?

● See **Literary Terms Handbook**, p. R8.

——— EXTENDING YOUR RESPONSE ———

Performing

I Am Not Well   One critic observed that Barthelme's tales "seem to plead for reading aloud. They're for feeling and effect, not narration." Select one long passage to read aloud as a monologue. Interpret the narrator's tone, mood, and frame of mind. Practice your dramatic reading and then present it to the class.

Learning for Life

Through Shotwell's Eyes   Imagine that you are Shotwell. Write an official report to your superiors detailing your observations and analyses of the situation and of your companion, the narrator.

💾 **Save your work for your portfolio.**

Before You Read

Waiting for the Barbarians

Meet Constantine P. Cavafy

"I could never write a novel or a play; but I hear inside me a hundred and twenty-five voices telling me that I could write history."

—*Cavafy*

Although he was born in Alexandria, Egypt, and lived most of his adult life there, Constantine P. Cavafy (kə vä′ fē) was fascinated by Greece, his parents' homeland. He became a Greek citizen as soon as he was old enough to vote, and today he is widely recognized as the most important modern poet of Greece. According to poet James Merrill, "Singlehanded in our century, Cavafy showed the Greek poets who followed him what could be done with their language."

From ages nine to sixteen, Cavafy lived and studied in England. He returned to Alexandria in his early twenties, and began to write poetry. He also worked as a journalist, a stockbroker, and a clerk for the Egyptian Ministry of Public Works. Although he wrote every day, he was highly self-conscious of his poetry and destroyed most of his writing. As a result, little of his work was published in his lifetime, and his international fame did not blossom until after his death.

Cavafy referred to himself as a "historical poet" because he wove into his work references to the history and literature of ancient Greece, as well as that of ancient Rome, Egypt, and Byzantium.

Although his poems often reflect historical cultures, Cavafy did not focus on famous events or individuals. Instead, he often focused, as he did in "Waiting for the Barbarians," on everyday individuals with whom the reader can identify. As one scholar noted, "[Cavafy] treated history not as an archaeological pageant but as a dramatic parable illustrating the facts of life and the ways of man."

Constantine P. Cavafy was born in 1863 and died in 1933.

FOCUS ACTIVITY

Have you ever thought of anyone as your "enemy"? Can you think of other people or groups who have publicly identified their enemies?

FREEWRITE Freewrite about what it means to have an enemy and what actions a person or a group might take against an enemy.

SETTING A PURPOSE Read to discover how one group thinks and acts as the enemy approaches.

BACKGROUND

Did You Know?

Barbarians The Romans considered the barbarians—groups of nomadic peoples—uncivilized because of differences in culture, language, and beliefs. In A.D. 476 a group of barbarians led by the Germanic chief Odoacer (ō′ də′ wā sər) overthrew the last Western Roman emperor.

The Roman Empire This empire was established in 27 B.C. and was distinguished for its cultural and political developments. "Waiting for the Barbarians" includes the following details of Roman government and city planning:

- **Consuls** were appointed officials who oversaw the administration of law.
- **Praetors** (prē′ tərz) were elected judicial officials.
- The **Forum** in a city was a public square or marketplace where legal and political activities took place and public assemblies were held.

Waiting for the
Barbarians

C. P. Cavafy

Translated by Edmund Keeley and Philip Sherrard

What are we waiting for, assembled in the forum?

    The barbarians are due here today.

Why isn't anything going on in the senate?
Why are the senators sitting there without legislating?

5   Because the barbarians are coming today.
    What's the point of senators making laws now?
    Once the barbarians are here, they'll do the legislating.

Waiting for the Barbarians

Why did our emperor get up so early,
and why is he sitting enthroned at the city's main gate,
10   in state, wearing the crown?

    Because the barbarians are coming today
    and the emperor's waiting to receive their leader.
    He's even got a scroll to give him,
    loaded with titles, with imposing names.

15   Why have our two consuls and praetors come out today
wearing their embroidered, their scarlet togas?°
Why have they put on bracelets with so many amethysts,°
rings sparkling with magnificent emeralds?
Why are they carrying elegant canes
20   beautifully worked in silver and gold?

    Because the barbarians are coming today
    and things like that dazzle the barbarians.

Why don't our distinguished orators turn up as usual
to make their speeches, say what they have to say?

25   Because the barbarians are coming today
    and they're bored by rhetoric° and public speaking.

Why this sudden bewilderment, this confusion?
(How serious people's faces have become.)
Why are the streets and squares emptying so rapidly,
30   everyone going home lost in thought?

    Because night has fallen and the barbarians haven't come.
    And some of our men just in from the border say
    there are no barbarians any longer.

Now what's going to happen to us without barbarians?
35   Those people were a kind of solution.

---

16 *Togas* (tō′ gəz), loose outer garments draped over the body, were worn by citizens of ancient Rome. The color and style of a toga reflected the wearer's social position.

17 *Amethysts* (am′ ə thists) are purple or violet gemstones.

26 *Rhetoric* (ret′ ər ik) is the art of using language effectively, especially for the purpose of persuasion.

Responding to Literature

Personal Response

How did you react to the speakers in this poem? Explain.

--- **ANALYZING LITERATURE** ---

RECALL AND INTERPRET

1. What anticipated event causes people to gather in the streets? How might the people assembled feel about the coming of the barbarians?
2. What leaders also assemble, and how do they prepare themselves for the upcoming event? In your opinion, why do they prepare themselves in such ways?
3. What happens in lines 27–33? In your opinion, how do the people in the poem feel about what has happened? Explain your response using details from the selection.
4. What does one of the speakers say in the last two lines? What do you think that speaker means? Explain.
5. What purpose do the barbarians serve in this society? How do you know? What does this function tell you about this particular society?

EVALUATE AND CONNECT

6. Refer back to your responses to the Focus Activity on page 1134. Compare and contrast your ideas about "enemies" with the ideas expressed by the speakers in the poem.
7. The **mood** of a poem is its overall emotional quality. How would you describe the mood of lines 1–26? How and why does the mood shift in lines 27–35?
8. Cavafy sets his poem in ancient Rome. In your opinion, what modern situation might be similar to the situation faced by the speakers in the poem? Explain.

Literary ELEMENTS

Motif

The **motif** of a literary work is any significant phrase, image, description, idea, or other element that is repeated throughout the work and is related to the theme. For example, the speaker of "Waiting for the Barbarians" repeats the phrase "Because the barbarians are coming today" in response to questions posed throughout the poem. This phrase becomes a motif, leading readers closer and closer to the poem's final response.

1. How does the use of this motif affect your understanding of the poem's theme?
2. What is the effect of having the last response differ from the other responses that create the motif?

● See **Literary Terms Handbook**, p. R10.

--- **EXTENDING YOUR RESPONSE** ---

Learning for Life

We Interrupt This Program . . .   How do you picture the barbarians and how do you imagine they would act if they arrived? What might their goals be? With a partner, create a three-minute television news report describing the arrival of the barbarians. Then, with one person acting as the news anchor and the other as the reporter on location, present a "live" or videotaped version to the class.

Writing About Literature

What's the Point?   In a few paragraphs, analyze the central message of this poem. Begin by considering the meaning of such questions as "What's the point?" and "Why this sudden bewilderment?" and the **denotation** and **connotation** (see page R4) of the word *solution*. What might Cavafy be saying about society in general?

📖 **Save your work for your portfolio.**

COMPARING selections

GAME and Waiting for the Barbarians

Untitled, 1956.

COMPARE **CONFLICTS**

The characters in each selection are coping with times packed with tension and emotion. With a group, discuss the following questions:

1. What **external conflict** does each set of characters face? How are these conflicts alike and how are they different?
2. What **internal conflict** does each set of characters face? How are these conflicts alike and how are they different?
3. How are the characters' reactions to these conflicts similar and how are they different?
4. Compare and contrast the ways that each selection expresses ideas about conflict and about relationships between people and groups.

COMPARE **CULTURES**

"Game" takes place in an unspecified setting, which might be the United States during the cold war. "Waiting for the Barbarians" is set during the end of the Western Roman Empire. With a partner, create a poster that depicts the physical signs of each culture—food, clothing, weapons, jewelry—as they appear in each selection and show how these objects are similar and different. Present your poster to the class and explain what these similarities and differences indicate about the two cultures.

COMPARE **SUSPENSE**

In both selections, **suspense** builds as the reader realizes that potential doom may await the characters. Write down answers to the following questions:

1. What event might bring doom to the characters in each selection?
2. What factors might contribute to doom in "Game"?
3. In each selection, the anticipated events never actually occur. How, in your opinion, does leaving questions unanswered affect the element of suspense?

Before You Read

Mirror

Meet Sylvia Plath

"In her poetry, . . . [Plath] had free and controlled access to depths formerly reserved to the primitive ecstatic priests, shamans and Holymen."

—*Ted Hughes*

To the world around her, Sylvia Plath's life seemed a model of brilliant success. She had her first poem published at the age of eight, earned straight A's in school, and as a teenager won many literary awards. At Smith College, Plath continued to win prizes and graduated with highest honors. Beneath her accomplished façade, however, was a person seething with rage and suffering from severe depression.

According to Plath, the death of her father when she was just eight may have triggered the emotional difficulties she experienced as an adult. While in college, she suffered a mental breakdown that led to the first of many suicide attempts—an experience that Plath chronicled with great candor in her novel *The Bell Jar.*

Despite her emotional troubles, Plath won a Fulbright Fellowship to the University of Cambridge in England, where she met and married the prominent English poet Ted Hughes. At first Plath and Hughes enjoyed a supportive relationship. In the early 1960s, however, their marriage began to crumble, and Plath plummeted into a state of deep despair.

In response, she began writing feverishly, completing the forty poems that would be published posthumously in *Ariel* less than two months after she began. It is these startlingly original and often violent poems about such topics as loneliness, human suffering, and death that brought Plath international acclaim. Sadly, she never enjoyed this fame; in February 1963 she killed herself in a cold London flat.

Sylvia Plath was born in 1932 and died in 1963.

FOCUS ACTIVITY

What are you searching for and what do you fear seeing when you look into a mirror?

JOURNAL Spend three or four minutes exploring your response to these questions in your journal.

SETTING A PURPOSE Read to find out what one person is searching for and fears seeing when she looks into a mirror.

BACKGROUND

Literary Influences

Plath attended a class taught by poet Robert Lowell, who was credited with originating the **Confessional school** of poetry and who inspired her to write about her own psychic anguish. Plath's husband, Ted Hughes, noted that she shared with Lowell and the poet Anne Sexton "the central experience of a shattering of the self, and the labor of fitting it together again or finding a new one."

Mirror

Sylvia Plath ∿

I am silver and exact. I have no preconceptions.°
Whatever I see I swallow immediately
Just as it is, unmisted by love or dislike.
I am not cruel, only truthful—
5   The eye of a little god, four-cornered.
Most of the time I meditate° on the opposite wall.
It is pink, with speckles. I have looked at it so long
I think it is a part of my heart. But it flickers.
Faces and darkness separate us over and over.

10   Now I am a lake. A woman bends over me,
Searching my reaches for what she really is.
Then she turns to those liars, the candles or the moon.
I see her back, and reflect it faithfully.
She rewards me with tears and an agitation of hands.
15   I am important to her. She comes and goes.
Each morning it is her face that replaces the darkness.
In me she has drowned a young girl, and in me an old
                    woman
Rises toward her day after day, like a terrible fish.

---

1 *Preconceptions* are ideas or opinions formed before acquiring actual knowledge or experience.
6 *Meditate* means "to think seriously and carefully" or "to contemplate."

Responding to Literature

Personal Response

Were you surprised by the way this poem ended? Explain.

——— ANALYZING LITERATURE ———

RECALL AND INTERPRET

1. What is the identity of the speaker in the first stanza? What qualities does the speaker possess? What does the **metaphor** (see page R9) in the first stanza suggest about the speaker?
2. How does the speaker view the wall in lines 7–8? How would you characterize the speaker's relationship to the wall?
3. How has the speaker changed in the second stanza? What does the woman want from the speaker? What might "those liars, the candle or the moon" offer the woman that the speaker can't?
4. In your opinion, why is the speaker important to the woman? What can you infer about the woman's attitude toward aging from lines 17–18?

EVALUATE AND CONNECT

5. Why might Plath have chosen the speaker of this poem to be an inanimate object instead of a human being? In what ways might the poem have been different if told from the perspective of the woman?
6. In this poem, the mirror claims that it is not cruel but truthful. Do you agree, or do you think this mirror distorts what it reflects? Explain.
7. Read over your response to the Focus Activity on page 1139. Are mirrors as important to you as they are to the woman in the poem? Explain.
8. The elderly are often valued because of their wisdom and experience. How might an elderly person react to this poem? Why?

Literary
ELEMENTS

Internal Rhyme

One of the sound devices that poets use is **rhyme,** or the repetition of sounds in the final accented syllables of words. When the rhyme occurs within a single line of poetry, it is called **internal rhyme.** Poets use internal rhyme, like **end rhyme,** to convey meaning, to evoke a mood, or simply to create a musical effect. In "Mirror," Plath incorporates internal rhyme as well as **alliteration** (looked, long) and **assonance** (reaches, really).

1. What two words rhyme in line 8? What is the effect of linking these two words?
2. What syllables rhyme in line 16? What image does this rhyme reinforce? What does this contribute to the meaning of the poem?

● See **Literary Terms Handbook,** p. R13.

——— EXTENDING YOUR RESPONSE ———

Performing

Mirror, Mirror on the Wall   Imagine that you are asked to read "Mirror" on the radio. How would you present it? Would you add sound effects, such as footsteps or a voice crying? How and where would you vary the volume and pitch of your voice? Plan a dramatic reading of the poem. As you plan, write down why you are making these choices about your performance. Then practice your reading and present it to the class.

Creative Writing

New View   Write a poem from the perspective of a mirror that describes what the mirror reflects in the course of an hour or a day. In your poem, try using the sound devices mentioned in the Literary Elements box above.

📖 **Save your work for your portfolio.**

Meet
William Stafford

"If I am to keep on writing, I cannot bother to insist on high standards. I must get into action and not let anything stop me, or even slow me much."

—*Stafford*

Writing, William Stafford once wrote, is like fishing. The writer must wait patiently for an idea or an impression to appear and then must seize upon it. "If I put something down," he adds, "that thing will help the next thing come, . . . a process that leads so wildly and originally into new territory." Stafford's method of writing certainly served him well. During his lifetime, he created an immense and compelling body of work that is recognized among the finest of the twentieth century.

Stafford was born in Kansas to parents who were avid readers. From his father he received a deep and abiding love of the natural world and from his mother, a particular view of events and people. "The voice I hear in my poems," he once said, "is my mother's voice." As a young man, Stafford worked on farms and oil refineries, and later he taught at various universities in the Midwest and West.

Stafford, wrote critic Stephen Stepanchev, is a "Western Robert Frost, forever amazed by the spaces of America, inner and outer." Like Frost, Stafford deftly captured American speech patterns in his poetry and discovered universal truths in the particulars of the natural world. Also like Frost, he was interested in exploring the ties that bind people to the earth and to each other.

William Stafford was born in 1914 and died in 1993.

FOCUS ACTIVITY

Think about a time in your life when you were forced to make a difficult decision.

SHARE IDEAS Share your experience with a partner. Describe the circumstances surrounding the decision and what happened as a result.

SETTING A PURPOSE Read to find out how one speaker responds when faced with a difficult decision.

BACKGROUND

The Time and Place

Many of Stafford's poem are set in rural areas of the Midwest and West in this century. The Kansas of his youth was primarily agricultural—what one critic called "rural, austere, inhabited by companionable neighbors and dominated by family." It was a beautiful, peaceful place that affected the poet deeply. "The earth was my home," he said. "I would never feel lost while it held me."

Kansas farmland, 1920s.

Moonlit, 1991. Benny Alba. Oil on paper, 25 x 18 in. Collection of the artist.

Traveling Through the Dark

William Stafford ⁓

Traveling through the dark I found a deer
dead on the edge of the Wilson River road.
It is usually best to roll them into the canyon:
that road is narrow; to swerve might make more dead.

5   By glow of the tail-light I stumbled back of the car
and stood by the heap, a doe, a recent killing;
she had stiffened already, almost cold.
I dragged her off; she was large in the belly.

My fingers touching her side brought me the reason—
10 her side was warm; her fawn lay there waiting,
alive, still, never to be born.
Beside that mountain road I hesitated.

The car aimed ahead its lowered parking lights;
under the hood purred the steady engine.
15 I stood in the glare of the warm exhaust turning red;
around our group I could hear the wilderness listen.

I thought hard for us all—my only swerving—
then pushed her over the edge into the river.

Responding to Literature

Personal Response

What did you think of the speaker in this poem? Explain.

───── ANALYZING LITERATURE ─────

RECALL AND INTERPRET

1. According to the speaker, what should one do with a dead deer? Why? Based on the first stanza, what can you infer about the personality of the speaker and his attitude toward deer?
2. What does the speaker notice about the deer? Why might he hesitate after touching the deer?
3. What is the speaker's car doing in the fourth stanza? In your opinion, what is the significance of the car in the poem?
4. What does the speaker hear in line 16? What does this line suggest about the relationship between human beings and the natural world?
5. What does the speaker finally decide to do with the deer? Why, in your opinion, does he make this decision?

EVALUATE AND CONNECT

6. In your opinion, did the speaker make the right decision about the deer? Explain your answer.
7. What connection can you make between the words *swerve* in the first stanza and *swerving* in the last stanza? What idea might Stafford have been trying to emphasize through this **repetition** (see page R13)?
8. Compare your response to the Focus Activity on page 1142 with the decision faced by the speaker. Who had the more difficult decision?

Literary
ELEMENTS

Caesura

Poets control the sound of a poem in many ways: they arrange stressed and unstressed syllables into patterns, and they place pauses in strategic locations. A pause that falls within a line of poetry is called a **caesura.** Generally, a caesura falls within the middle of a line and follows a punctuation mark. Sometimes, however, a pause occurs in the absence of punctuation. In the following line, the caesura is marked by double slanted lines: "I dragged her off;// she was large in the belly."

1. Find an example of a caesura in lines 1–2. What idea might it serve to emphasize?
2. What is the caesura in line 4? How does it affect how you read that line?

● See **Literary Terms Handbook,** p. R2.

───── EXTENDING YOUR RESPONSE ─────

Literature Groups

Where Do You Stand?   Stafford, writes critic Greg Orfalea, "is, at core, a moralist." In your group, debate whether or not "Traveling Through the Dark" includes a moral judgment. In other words, how might Stafford want the reader to view the speaker's decision? How do you know? Have each side give its opinion, using evidence from the poem as support. Then share your conclusions with the class.

Interdisciplinary Activity

Drivers Education: Heads Up   As deer populations in the United States increase, so does the likelihood of automobiles hitting deer on highways and back roads. Use the Internet or library resources to research this problem. Then write a guide for drivers showing how they might decrease the likelihood of hitting a deer on the road.

📖 Save your work for your portfolio.

Before You Read

Frederick Douglass

Meet Robert Hayden

"Hayden is ceaselessly trying to achieve . . . transcendence, which must not be an escape from the horror of history, . . . but an ascent that somehow transforms the horror and creates a blessed permanence."

—*Gary Zebrun*

Although Robert Hayden often wrote about African American heroes and history, he wanted to be known as a poet, not a black poet. Such labeling, Hayden believed, placed African American writers "in a kind of literary ghetto, where the standards of other writers" were not applied to them. It also, he felt, "restricted them to racial themes." During the Civil Rights movement, his beliefs provoked the ire of African American authors intent on writing political poetry. Hayden, however, continued to follow his own course.

Hayden's interest in African American history originated from research he did for the Federal Writers' Project in his native Detroit. He learned about the history of his people from the time of slavery to the present. Later, he used this material to write formal, graceful poems about the Underground Railroad, the Civil War, the experiences of enslaved people, and such historical figures as Frederick Douglass, Harriet Tubman, Nat Turner, and Malcolm X.

Although he taught for many years, Hayden saw himself as "a poet who teaches in order to earn a living." His first book of poetry, *Heart-Shape in the Dust,* was published in 1940. He received little critical attention, however, until the publication of *Selected Poems* in 1966. Ten years later, he became the first African American poet to become Poetry Consultant to the Library of Congress.

Robert Hayden was born in 1913 and died in 1980.

FOCUS ACTIVITY

Who has changed the world for you in ways that matter?

CHART IT! Use a simple chart like the one on this page to record the names of, and a few details about, people who have greatly influenced your life.

SETTING A PURPOSE Read to learn about one man and his influence on people's lives.

Person	Influence	Details

BACKGROUND

A Closer Look at Frederick Douglass

Frederick Douglass (c. 1818–1895) escaped from slavery and became an important figure in the Abolitionist movement. He was known both for his rousing speeches denouncing slavery and for his autobiography, *Life and Times of Frederick Douglass,* which poignantly described his experiences under slavery. Following the Civil War (1861–1865), Douglass fought for civil rights for newly emancipated African Americans and championed the women's rights movement. To learn more about Frederick Douglass, see pages 328–335.

FREDERICK DOUGLASS

Robert Hayden

When it is finally ours, this freedom, this liberty, this beautiful
and terrible thing, needful to man as air,
usable as earth; when it belongs at last to all,
when it is truly instinct, brain matter, diastole,° systole,°
5   reflex action; when it is finally won; when it is more
than the gaudy mumbo jumbo of politicians:
this man, this Douglass, this former slave, this Negro
beaten to his knees, exiled, visioning a world
where none is lonely, none hunted, alien,
10   this man, superb in love and logic, this man
shall be remembered. Oh, not with statues' rhetoric,
not with legends and poems and wreaths of bronze alone,
but with the lives grown out of his life, the lives
fleshing his dream of the beautiful, needful thing.

---

4 *Diastole* (dī as′ tə lē′) is the period of normal relaxation of the heart between beats.
The period of normal contraction between diastoles is called *systole* (sis′ tə lē).

The Contribution of the Negro to Democracy in America, 1943. Charles White. Egg tempera, 141 x 207 in.
Hampton University Museum, Hampton, VA. Choose two people in this painting whom you think exemplify what
Hayden describes as "fleshing [Douglass's] dream of the beautiful, needful thing." Explain your choices.

Responding to Literature

Personal Response

What is your impression of Frederick Douglass after reading this poem?

ANALYZING LITERATURE

RECALL AND INTERPRET

1. In what ways is freedom described in lines 1–5? What does the poet convey by using these particular details? Explain.
2. How does the speaker describe the talk of politicians? From this description, what can you infer about his attitude toward politicians?
3. In your own words, describe Frederick Douglass and the world he envisioned as portrayed in lines 7–10. What does this portrayal suggest to you about Hayden's opinion of Douglass? Explain.
4. According to lines 11–14, in what ways will Douglass be remembered? What does this tell you about the impact of Douglass's life?

EVALUATE AND CONNECT

5. Do you agree with the statement that freedom is both a "beautiful and terrible thing"? Why or why not?
6. In this poem, Hayden uses **parallelism**—the repeated use of phrases that are the same or similar in structure. In your opinion, how does the use of this device reinforce the message of the poem?
7. Do you think the tribute described in lines 13–14 is a fitting memorial to Douglass? Why or why not?
8. Many poets, including Langston Hughes and Paul Laurence Dunbar, have written about Frederick Douglass. Who from recent times might poets choose to honor? Explain.

Literary ELEMENTS

Diction

Poets choose words carefully, paying close attention to both their sounds and their meanings. Sometimes poets use specialized vocabulary, which can give a piece of writing more authority, enhance its sense of realism, create a certain musical effect, or provide contrast with other vocabulary. In this poem, Hayden's **diction,** or word choices, incorporates words commonly used by doctors and biologists, such as *diastole* and *systole.*

1. Why might Hayden have chosen to use specialized vocabulary in this poem?
2. How do the words *diastole* and *systole* contribute to the musical quality of the poem?

● See **Literary Terms Handbook,** p. R5.

EXTENDING YOUR RESPONSE

Literature Groups

Timely or Not?   In your group, discuss the following question: Is this poem still relevant to the lives of African Americans and other groups in this country, or is it interesting mainly as a historical piece? Use evidence from the poem to support your answer. Then summarize your opinions and share them with the class.

Personal Writing

Personal Tribute   Review your responses to the Focus Activity on page 1145. Then, using "Frederick Douglass" for inspiration, write a poem, song, or essay that celebrates the life of a person whom you admire. In your tribute, express the special qualities and accomplishments of this person and the impact he or she has had on the world.

📖 **Save your work for your portfolio.**

Writing Skills

Using Quotations

Hayden's poem "Frederick Douglass" is just one of many tributes to this American hero. If you were to write a research paper about Douglass, you would need quotations by and about Douglass to support and elaborate on your main points.

Citing Sources

When you use quotations in a research paper, you need to document the source of each quote by using a **citation**—the author's last name and the page number on which you found the material. *(McFeely 312)*

You will also need to include a **works-cited list,** which presents information about each source you refer to in your paper. The reader can then use the information in the citation to find the title of the book in the works-cited list.

Formatting Quotations

- When quoting an entire sentence, introduce it with your own words. Set off the quotation with quotation marks. Use a comma or colon before the quote:

    No historian can state Frederick Douglass's date of birth, because this important fact was unknown to Douglass himself: "I have no accurate knowledge of my age, never having seen any authentic record containing it." (Douglass 15).

- When quoting part of a sentence within your own sentence, set off the quotation with quotation marks:

    After the end of the Civil War, Douglass was not surprised that "all across the South black people were demonstrating a fierce interest in politics" (McFeely 240).

- When quoting only part of a sentence, use ellipses (three periods separated by spaces) to indicate omitted words:

    Douglass "did not wait . . . for a formal summons from the White House." *(McFeely 261).*

- When you use a quotation that runs more than four typed lines, create a **block quotation:**

    1. Set the quotation off from the rest of the text by beginning a new line.
    2. Indent the entire quotation one inch, or ten spaces, from the left margin.
    3. Type the quotation double-spaced, without quotation marks.

EXERCISE

Generate one or two questions about a topic that interests you. Then research the answers in more than one source. Write three paragraphs with four or five examples of quotations. Use at least one block quote. Be sure to document your sources and to include a works-cited list.

Before You Read

#2 Memory **and** *Poem*

Meet Victor Hernández Cruz

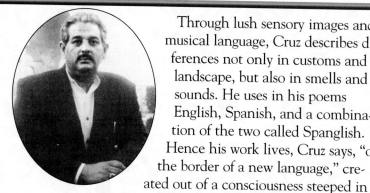

"My family life was full of music, guitars and conga drums, maracas and songs. . . . Even when it was five below zero in New York, [my mother] sang warm tropical ballads."

—*Cruz*

In both his poetry and his prose, Victor Hernández Cruz (ār nän′ dez krōōz) explores the contrasts between the traditional culture of Aguas Buenas, Puerto Rico, where he was born, and the multiracial and often harsh environment of New York City, where he grew up. "I write," Cruz explains, "from the center of a culture that is not on its native soil." In doing so, he has succeeded in capturing the experiences of many Puerto Ricans who try to bridge two cultural traditions.

Through lush sensory images and musical language, Cruz describes differences not only in customs and landscape, but also in smells and sounds. He uses in his poems English, Spanish, and a combination of the two called Spanglish. Hence his work lives, Cruz says, "on the border of a new language," created out of a consciousness steeped in two of the important world languages.

Cruz has produced many books of poetry and contributed poems to anthologies and magazines. In addition, he has contributed articles to the *New York Review of Books* and other publications. For his work, he has received a number of awards and honors, including a Guggenheim Fellowship.

In 1989 Cruz returned to Puerto Rico to live. There he continues to write what one critic has called Puerto Rican soul music.

Victor Hernández Cruz was born in 1949.

FOCUS ACTIVITY

Think about a time when you wished you could remember something you had said to a friend or family member.

JOURNAL In your journal, describe the gist of what you said and why you regret not remembering your exact words.

SETTING A PURPOSE Read to learn why one person thinks people should remember what they have said.

BACKGROUND

Free Verse

In these poems, Cruz uses **free verse**—a type of poetry that has no fixed pattern of **meter,** line length, and **rhyme** (if any). Although free verse lacks a regular pattern of stressed and unstressed syllables, it does not lack **rhythm.** Many poets use free verse to mimic the rising and falling cadences of normal speech. Cruz might have used it in "#2 Memory" for that very reason: specifically, to capture the rhythms of everyday speech in Don Arturo's words.

#2 Memory

Victor Hernández Cruz

Untitled. Sylvia Asturias. Pencil on paper. Collection of the artist.

Don Arturo° says:
You have to know
what you once said
Because it could
5   travel in the air
for years
And return in different
clothes
And then you have to
10   buy it.

---

1 Cruz also has written a short story
about the fictional character *Don
Arturo* (dôn   är tōōr′ ō). In Spanish,
the title *Don* is used before the first
name of a man to indicate respect.

Poem

Victor Hernández Cruz

Think with your body
And dance with your mind.

Responding to Literature

Personal Response

What new insights or ideas did these poems give you?

ANALYZING LITERATURE

#2 Memory

RECALL AND INTERPRET

1. According to Don Arturo, what do you need to know? In your own words, explain why you might need to know this.
2. What does Don Arturo's advice suggest to you about his character?

EVALUATE AND CONNECT

3. Do you agree with the opinion expressed in this poem? Why or why not?
4. Why might Cruz have chosen to quote a respected person in the poem? How might the impact of the poem be different if Cruz had called *Don Arturo* simply *Arturo?* Explain.

Poem

RECALL AND INTERPRET

5. With what does the speaker advise you to think in line 1? What do you think the speaker means by this?
6. How does the speaker advise you to dance? What, in your opinion, is the **theme**, or central message, of this poem? How might following this advice affect a person's life?

EVALUATE AND CONNECT

7. Do you agree with the point expressed in this poem? Explain.
8. Do you think this poem would have been more or less convincing if Cruz had provided examples of his ideas? Explain.

EXTENDING YOUR RESPONSE

Literature Groups

Find the Meaning   In your group, try to unravel the meaning of "#2 Memory." Discuss, for example, what Don Arturo means when he says that "what you once said" can "return in different clothes," and why you would then "have to buy it." Then share the results of your discussion with the class.

Creative Writing

Express Your Ideas   Cruz's poems express strong opinions about the importance of memory and of paying attention to the body. Using these works for inspiration, write a poem that communicates a truth about life that you hold dear. Express your ideas in as few words as possible.

📋 **Save your work for your portfolio.**

Before You Read

Weaver

Meet
Sandra María Esteves

"Esteves' poetry [is] an endless weave of incantation, made exceedingly powerful by her magical way of blending words and music."

—*Herb Boyd*

Sandra María Esteves (ā stā′ vās) works endlessly to bring her skills as a poet to her community and to the urban poor. As a literary consultant and writer-in-residence for the WritersCorps of New York City's Bronx Council on the Arts, Esteves teaches people of her community to appreciate poetry and to write poems about their own experiences.

Esteves calls upon her background in theater and as an artist to create and present poems rich in imagery and symbolism. Her poetry readings have been called "spectacular examples of poetry reading as performance art."

Born and raised in the Bronx, Esteves is of Puerto Rican and Dominican heritage. She published her first book, a collection of poetry and drawings, *Yerba Buena* (yār′ bä bwe′ nä), at age thirty-three. *Library Journal* named the collection the best small-press book of 1981. She has since published two more volumes of poetry, *Tropical Rains: A Bilingual Downpour* and *Bluestown Mockingbird Mambo*.

Esteves's poems have appeared in more than fifty literary journals, magazines, and anthologies, including *Aloud, Voices from the Nuyorican* (nōō yô rē′ kən) *Poets' Cafe* in 1994. (*Nuyorican* means "Puerto Rican from New York.") Esteves has been active for years in the New York City–based Nuyorican Cafe, where poets come to share their work and experiment with poetry, sometimes in Spanglish, a mix of Spanish and English.

The mother of four daughters and the grandmother of five, Esteves continues to support young Latino writers, particularly encouraging women writers.

Sandra María Esteves was born in 1948.

FOCUS ACTIVITY

How do you think our lives would be enriched if all peoples of the world were able to get along?

DISCUSS As a class, discuss your ideas about how peoples of the world can get along and how the world might be enriched if they did.

SETTING A PURPOSE Read to discover one speaker's thoughts on unity among peoples of the world.

BACKGROUND

A Dedication

Sandra María Esteves dedicated the poem "Weaver" to Phil George, a Native American writer and dancer. Esteves met George, who she says is a descendant of the famous Nez Percé leader Chief Joseph, at an ethnic writer's workshop held in Wisconsin in 1973. The workshop brought together minority writers both young and old and had a profound impact on Esteves. It was there that she decided to pursue a professional writing career. Esteves realized that, even though the writers came from a variety of backgrounds, as members of minority groups, "we all shared a common condition." Many of Esteves's writings bring out this theme.

Weaver

Sandra María Esteves

Awe Series, 1990.
Susan Stewart.
Monotype,
40⅛ x 28½ in.
Collection of the artist.

For Phil George

Weave us a song of many threads

Weave us a red of fire and blood
that tastes of sweet plum
fishing around the memories of the dead
5   following a scent wounded
our spines bleeding with pain

Weave us a red of passion
that beats wings against a smoky cloud
and forces motion into our lungs

10 Weave us a song
of yellow and gold and life itself
a wildgrowth
into the great magnetic center
topaz canyons
15 floral sweatseeds
in continuous universal suspension

Weave us a song of red and yellow and brown
that holds the sea and sky in its skin
the bird and mountain in its voice
20 that builds upon our graves a home
with fortifications
strength, unity and direction

And weave us a white song to hold us
when the wind blows so cold to make our children wail
25 submerged in furious ice
a song pure and raw
that burns paper
and attacks the colorless venom stalking hidden
in the petal softness of the black night

30 Weave us a rich round black that lives
in the eyes of our warrior child
and feeds our mouths with moon breezes
with rivers interflowing
through ALL spaces of existence

35 Weave us a song for our bodies to sing
a song of many threads
that will dance with the colors of our people
and cover us with the warmth of peace.

Responding to Literature

Personal Response

Which lines from the poem did you find most powerful? Why?

——— ANALYZING LITERATURE ———

RECALL AND INTERPRET

1. What does the speaker say in line 1? In your opinion, what does this mean and who is the speaker addressing? Explain.
2. In lines 2–22, what colors does the speaker note? What does the speaker associate with the colors and what might they add to the "song"?
3. What colors does the speaker ask for in lines 23–34? Why might she include these colors? Support your response with details from the poem.
4. What does the speaker think people could accomplish if they united? Review your response to the Focus Activity on page 1152. Do you agree with the speaker? Why or why not?

EVALUATE AND CONNECT

5. What contrasting images does Esteves use in lines 23–29? In your opinion, how does the contrast help get Esteves's main idea across? Support your response with evidence from the poem.
6. Which words and phrases are repeated throughout the poem? How does this **repetition** affect your reading of the poem? Explain.
7. What is the **tone** (see page R16) of this poem? Does the tone change at any point? How does the poem's tone help express the poet's main idea?
8. Theme Connections   Based on the ideas expressed in this poem, what do you think Esteves would say about the phrase, "variety is richness"? Explain, using details from the poem to support your response.

Assonance and Consonance

Poets commonly use sound devices to contribute to the tone or the musical quality of a poem. The repetition of similar vowel sounds is called **assonance**, and the repetition of consonant sounds within or at the ends of words is called **consonance**. For example, in the line "in continuous universal suspension," the repetition of the long *u* sound in "contin<u>uous</u>" and "<u>u</u>niversal" is assonance. The repetition of the *s* sound in "continuou<u>s</u> univer<u>s</u>al <u>s</u>u<u>s</u>pen<u>s</u>ion" is consonance.

1. What effect does the consonance in lines 11–12 have on your reading of the poem?
2. Find two more examples of consonance and assonance in the poem and explain the effects they have.

● See **Literary Terms Handbook,** pp. R2 and R4.

——— EXTENDING YOUR RESPONSE ———

Literature Groups

Lasting Peace?   In your group, discuss Esteves's message about breaking barriers. Does she seem to think people are capable of uniting? If they did unite, does she think peace would last? Support your ideas with details from the poem. Then sum up the poet's message in a sentence. Compare your statement with those of other groups.

Interdisciplinary Activity

Art: Weave a "Song of Many Threads"   Use the poem as inspiration to create your own weaving out of string, yarn, paper, or another material. Try to reflect the imagery and symbolism of the poem in your weaving. Then display your weaving in the classroom.

📕 **Save your work for your portfolio.**

Before You Read

For Georgia O'Keeffe and Most Satisfied by Snow

Meet Pat Mora

"The desert persists in me," writes Pat Mora, "both inspiring and compelling me to sing about her and her people."
Mora grew up in the Chihuahua desert in Texas and often writes about the Native Americans and Mexican Americans who live there, their rich cultural traditions, and their relationship to the land. "I write," she says, "because I believe Mexican Americans need to take their rightful place in U.S. literature. We need to be published . . . so that the stories and ideas of our people won't quietly disappear." Mora's books include a collection entitled *Borders and Chants* and *Nepantla: Essays from the Land in the Middle.*

Pat Mora was born in 1942.

Meet Diana Chang

"I guess it's in my temperament to seek variety and change." Diana Chang told an interviewer. "I not only write," she says, "but I also paint." Both Chang's life and work reflect her love of change. She was born in New York City, but spent her early years in China. After World War II, her family returned to New York, where Chang attended high school and Barnard College, graduating in 1955. Chang then worked as a book editor and creative writing instructor. In addition to writing poetry, Chang has produced six novels, which explore issues of identity through a vast array of characters.

Diana Chang was born in 1934.

FOCUS ACTIVITY

How might something in nature have an impact on one's life? Have you ever been changed by an experience related to nature? How?

FREEWRITE Spend a few minutes freewriting to explore your ideas about how nature can affect one's life.

SETTING A PURPOSE Read to discover how two speakers grow from their experiences related to nature.

BACKGROUND

Georgia O'Keeffe

The title of Pat Mora's poem refers to Georgia O'Keeffe, a painter who is linked with the southwestern United States. While in her thirties, O'Keeffe began painting magnified views of flowers. Then, following a visit to New Mexico in 1929, where she eventually settled, she turned her attention to the desert's spare beauty. She painted canvases that capture its colors and dramatic forms, including the bleached bones she found there. One series of studies from this period, the *Pelvis Series,* focuses exclusively on bones.

Georgia O'Keeffe, 1937.

For Georgia O'Keeffe

Pat Mora

I want

to walk
with you
on my Texas desert,
5   to stand near
you straight
as a Spanish Dagger,°
to see your fingers
pick a bone bouquet
10 touching life
where I touch death,
to hold a warm, white
pelvis up
to the glaring sun
15 and see
your red-blue world
to feel you touch
my eyes
as you touch canvas

20 to unfold
giant blooms.

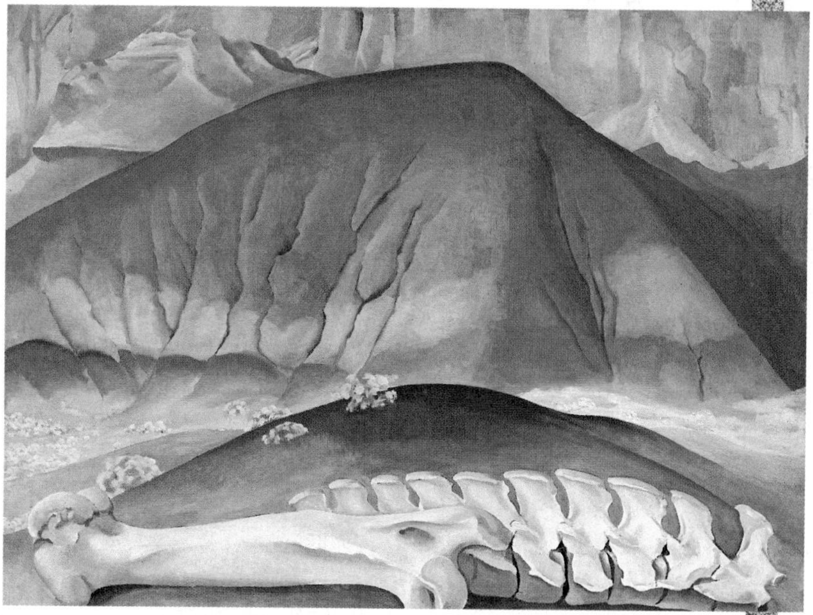

Red Hills and Bones, 1941. Georgia O'Keeffe. Oil on canvas, 30 x 40 in. ©2000 The Georgia O'Keeffe Foundation/Artists Rights Society (ARS), New York/Philadelphia Museum of Art, The Alfred Stieglitz Collection. What connections might you make between the poem and this painting by Georgia O'Keeffe?

---

7 A *Spanish dagger* is a type of yucca plant native to the Southwest and other areas of the United States. Its swordlike leaves end in a sharp point.

Passing Through, 1994. Karl J. Kuerner III. Acrylic on panel, 16 x 12 in.
David David Gallery, Philadelphia, PA.

Most Satisfied by Snow

Diana Chang

Against my windows,
fog knows
what to do, too

Spaces pervade°
5   us, as well

But occupied by snow,
I see

Matter
matters

10   I, too,
flowering

---

4 *Pervade* means "to spread through
every part of."

Responding to Literature

Personal Response
Which poem did you like better? Why?

ANALYZING LITERATURE

For Georgia O'Keeffe

RECALL AND INTERPRET
1. With whom does the speaker want to walk and where? Why might it be important to the speaker for this person to be in the place being described?
2. With what image does the poem end? To what might this image refer?
3. Based on the speaker's words to the other person, what do you think the speaker wants in life? Explain.

EVALUATE AND CONNECT
4. Did you find the visual **imagery** (see page R8) in this poem appealing? Why or why not? Why might Mora have selected the visual imagery that she did?
5. Theme Connections   In what ways does this poem expand your understanding of the idea "Variety Is Richness"?

Most Satisfied by Snow

RECALL AND INTERPRET
6. What do you think the speaker is saying about fog and spaces in lines 1–5? What makes you think that?
7. What does the speaker claim to learn from snow? What do you think this means?
8. According to lines 10–11, what does the speaker experience from observing the weather? What might this reveal about Chang's attitude toward nature? Explain.

EVALUATE AND CONNECT
9. What role does the simplicity of this poem play in conveying the poet's message?
10. How do you react to snow? How does it affect your mood?

EXTENDING YOUR RESPONSE

Interdisciplinary Activity
Ecology: Desert Life   Mora mentions a Spanish dagger, a plant of the Texas desert. Research another plant or animal that can be found in that region. Then write a brief report describing how desert conditions both challenge and support that plant or animal and what unique survival habits it has adopted. Present your findings to the class.

Writing About Literature
The Force of Nature   In a paragraph or two, discuss the ways these two poems describe nature's effect on people. Then review your responses to the Focus Activity on page 1156 and write another paragraph comparing your ideas with those expressed in the poems.

📖 **Save your work for your portfolio.**

Before You Read

Geometry

Meet Rita Dove

"A good poem is like a bouillon cube," says Rita Dove. "It's concentrated, you carry it around with you, and it nourishes you when you need it." Throughout her career, Dove has written poems that nourish her readers by appealing to both their imagination and their intellect. Her poems emphasize the significance of ordinary people and events and in doing so, encourage people to look at the world with fresh eyes.

Dove read in this way as a child, using books to make her imagination come alive. Although her parents were strict, even prohibiting Dove from watching much television, they allowed her freedom in choosing books to read. Her love for reading led to writing: "To me, writing was play. It was something you did to entertain yourself, like reading."

This early training paid off. Dove graduated with highest honors from Miami University in Oxford, Ohio in 1973. Next she studied in Germany on a Fulbright scholarship, and then she earned a master's degree from the University of Iowa in 1977, the same year her poetry was first published.

For Dove, poetry allows freedom of expression. "You don't have to be polite in poetry," she says. Dove wants students to value poetry the way she does, and not to regard it simply as a homework assignment. "I think that when a poem moves you, it moves you in a way that leaves you speechless."

The lives Dove describes in her poems are typically based on those of people she knows. In her narrative poem *Thomas and Beulah*, for example, she chronicles the experiences of her maternal grandparents, who migrated from the South to Akron, Ohio, in the early twentieth century. "It's not a dramatic story," she says. "But I think these are the people who often are ignored and lost." It is this "very absence of high drama," writes reviewer Peter Stitt, that "makes the poems so touching—these are ordinary people with ordinary struggles, successes, and failures."

In addition to several volumes of poetry, Dove has written a collection of short stories and a novel entitled *Through the Ivory Gate*. At the age of thirty-five, she became one of the youngest poets, and only the second African American woman, to win a Pulitzer Prize for Poetry. (The first was Gwendolyn Brooks.) At forty, Dove became the youngest poet ever named Poet Laureate of the United States.

"Literature gives one a chance to enter into another's world, to understand it intimately, and to not be afraid. Then we can relate to and empathize with other people's lives, whether it's Anna Karenina or James Baldwin growing up in Harlem."

—Dove

"[Dove's] images are indelible, the emotions always heartfelt and fresh."

—Barbara Hoffert

Rita Dove was born in 1952.

Think of a time when you have been baffled by homework, a difficult task, or a problem with a relationship and then suddenly understood what to do.

JOURNAL In your journal, describe how you felt when you understood something that had been a mystery.

SETTING A PURPOSE Read to find out how suddenly understanding the answer to a difficult problem makes one speaker feel.

BACKGROUND

Geometry: From Ancient Days to Modern Times

In mathematics, a theorem is a statement that can be proved based on certain other assumptions and definitions.

The word *geometry* literally means "earth measuring." The study of geometry began in ancient Egypt and Mesopotamia as people surveyed and farmed land. Knowledge about points, lines, planes, and solid objects was based on practical experience with landmarks, footpaths, farmers' fields, and blocks of granite. Around 300 B.C., the mathematician Euclid took hundreds of geometrical theorems that had accumulated over the centuries and developed ten postulates (fundamental rules or principles) that could explain them all. More than two thousand years later, in the 1820s, several mathematicians proved that Euclidian geometry is only one of many possible kinds of geometry.

Proving Theorems

Although geometry homework may be a chore for some students to hurry through, certain mathematicians devote much of their time—even years—to proving theorems. And some theorems go unproved for centuries. For example, a note left in a book by seventeenth-century mathematician Pierre Fermat stated that he had proved a proposition relating to an equation written in the sixth century. However, this proof—for Fermat's Last Theorem—was never found, and mathematicians tried unsuccessfully for years to prove the theorem.

Mathematician Andrew Wiles has been fascinated with the problem since he was just ten years old. Years of on-and-off work on the problem paid off when, in 1995, Wiles finally did prove Fermat's theorem. But is his proof the same as the one Fermat claimed to have developed? Impossible, according to Wiles, who says that his is a twentieth-century proof. In fact, he doubts that Fermat really had a proof but leaves the door open for future mathematical sleuths: ". . . What has made this problem special for amateurs is that there's a tiny possibility that there does exist an elegant seventeenth-century proof."

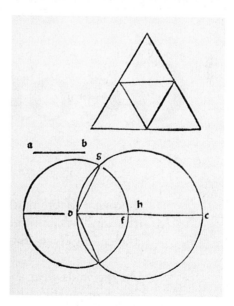

From Euclid's *Elementa geometria.*

Blue, 1994. Elizabeth B. Heuer. Collage. Collection of the artist. Look closely at the lines and shapes in this painting. How might they reflect the mood of "Geometry"?

Geometry

Rita Dove ∿

I prove a theorem and the house expands:
the windows jerk free to hover near the ceiling,
the ceiling floats away with a sigh.

As the walls clear themselves of everything
but transparency, the scent of carnations
leaves with them. I am out in the open

and above the windows have hinged into butterflies,
sunlight glinting where they've intersected.
They are going to some point true and unproven.

Responding to Literature

Personal Response

What questions would you like to ask the narrator of this poem?

ANALYZING LITERATURE

RECALL AND INTERPRET

1. In the first stanza, what happens to the house when the speaker proves a theorem? What might these events symbolize? What do they suggest about the speaker's sense of accomplishment?
2. At the end of the second stanza, where is the speaker? From what has the speaker freed herself? How do you know?
3. How does the event in lines 7–8 relate to the title of the poem?
4. What happens in line 9? What message might this line suggest?

EVALUATE AND CONNECT

5. Do you think Dove succeeds in conveying how the speaker feels when she proves a theorem? Why or why not?
6. A **metamorphosis** occurs when something changes drastically. What metamorphosis occurs in this poem? Is it presented convincingly? Support your answer with evidence from the poem.
7. Think about your response to the Focus Activity on page 1161. Compare the speaker's response with your own. How are they alike? How do they differ?
8. Theme Connections   Poet Adrienne Rich says that when she reads poetry, "I want voices speaking from lives and landscapes not necessarily known to me yet sharing boundaries with mine." In your opinion, does "Geometry" achieve this goal? Explain.

Literary ELEMENTS

Meter

Meter is the pattern of stressed and unstressed syllables in a line of poetry. Poets use meter to create special effects in their poems. For example, in "Geometry," Dove uses **iambic pentameter,** a meter in which each line has five pairs of syllables—one unstressed and one stressed. Iambic pentameter is associated with sonnets and other formal types of verse. Dove also uses **free verse,** which has no set meter and is often used to express freedom from stricter poetic forms.

1. Which part of "Geometry" is in iambic pentameter? in free verse?
2. How does Dove's use of meter help convey the meaning of the poem?

● See **Literary Terms Handbook,** p. R9.

EXTENDING YOUR RESPONSE

Creative Writing

Aha!   Write a poem that captures an **epiphany** for you, a moment of truth when you suddenly understood something. It can be something about a school subject, about yourself, or about life in general. Reread Dove's poem and use the journal entry you made for the Focus Activity on page 1161 to help you get started.

Interdisciplinary Connection

Mathematics: Geometry for Beginners   With a partner, create a "Geometry for Beginners" poster aimed at students who are about to study geometry. Design the poster to introduce students to basic geometry concepts and terms. Try to use a few words or phrases from Dove's poem in your poster. Present your poster to the class and, possibly, to a beginning geometry class.

📖 **Save your work for your portfolio.**

Before You Read

The Welder

Meet Cherríe Moraga

Cherríe Moraga (she rē′ môr ä′ gä) was a little girl when she fell in love with language and stories listening to the women in her family talk around the kitchen table at her home in southern California.

When Moraga went to college, she had the practical goal of becoming a teacher. She was one of the first in her family to earn a college degree, and after graduating she took a job at a high school. However, after two years of teaching, Moraga decided she wanted to write. Her writer's group inspired her, but they also told her she needed to improve her vocabulary. Moraga decided that for her, good writing did not mean a bigger vocabulary but "having your ear finely tuned to the many voices inside you."

When she was twenty-five, Moraga decided to devote a year to writing and reading as much as she could. A year later, in 1978, she read her poems in front of an audience at a coffeehouse. The response of the audience convinced Moraga that she had something important to say, and it encouraged her to continue her new career.

Since then, Moraga has written poems, essays, and plays that explore many facets of her identity. Moraga's relationship with her Mexican American mother, the Hispanic-Anglo culture of southern California, and the larger community of women of color are at the core of much of her writing.

"Frank and undaunted, Cherríe Moraga has managed to express feelings that many Hispanic women share."

—*Ronie-Richele Garcia-Johnson*

Cherríe Moraga was born in 1952.

FOCUS ACTIVITY

When might it be helpful to compare an activity, such as reading or writing, to another activity that is very different?

DISCUSS In a small group, discuss an activity you enjoy. Then think of ways in which it is similar to another activity you haven't tried before.

SETTING A PURPOSE Read to discover to what Moraga compares a welder's work.

BACKGROUND

Did You Know?
Among the earliest welders were Arab workers in Syria who made iron blades during the first millennium A.D. They heated soft and tough iron together until the substance was molten, then hammered the melted iron into shape to produce a strong, tough blade.

An *alchemist* was a person who practiced a combination of medieval chemistry and magic in an attempt to change one thing into another (cheap metal into gold, for instance).

The Welder

Cherríe Moraga

I am a welder.
Not an alchemist.
I am interested in the blend
of common elements to make
5   a common thing.

No magic here.
Only the heat of my desire to fuse°
what I already know
exists. Is possible.

10 We plead to each other,
we all come from the same rock
we all come from the same rock
ignoring the fact that we bend
at different temperatures
15 that each of us is malleable°
up to a point.

Yes, fusion *is* possible
but only if things get hot enough—
all else is temporary adhesion,°
20 patching up.

It is the intimacy of steel melting
into steel, the fire of our individual
passion to take hold of ourselves
that makes sculpture of our lives,
25 builds buildings.

And I am not talking about skyscrapers,
merely structures that can support us
without fear
of trembling.

30 For too long a time
the heat of my heavy hands
has been smoldering
in the pockets of other
people's business—
35 they need oxygen to make fire.

I am now
coming up for air.
Yes, I *am*
picking up the torch.

40 I am the welder.
I understand the capacity of heat
to change the shape of things.
I am suited to work
within the realm° of sparks
45 out of control.

I am the welder.
I am taking the power
into my own hands.

---

44 Here, a *realm* is a field of action or influence.

---

7 *Fuse* means "to join together or unite, as by melting."
15 Something that is *malleable* is flexible, and can be easily
    molded, shaped, or changed.
19 *Adhesion* means "the act or state of sticking fast."

Responding to Literature

Personal Response

Which lines from the poem did you find most surprising or intriguing?

———— ANALYZING LITERATURE ————

RECALL AND INTERPRET

1. What explanation does the speaker offer for calling herself a welder rather than an alchemist? What does this tell you about the kind of people the writer may hope to reach with her work? Explain.
2. According to the speaker, what are two things that heat can do? What do you think *heat* stands for, or represents, in this poem?
3. What does the speaker hope to build with her welding skills? What might this suggest to you about Moraga's purpose in writing this poem?
4. What is the speaker trying to weld? What, do you think, are her tools, and what does she want to change with her "welding"?

EVALUATE AND CONNECT

5. Theme Connections How are differences among people portrayed in this poem? Use evidence from the poem to support your answer.
6. Which lines or phrases in this poem convince you that the speaker in this poem is a welder? Why?
7. In "The Welder," how is your image of the speaker affected by the choice of occupation?
8. Write down some ideas you got from this poem for strengthening the comparison you made for the Focus Activity on page 1164 or, perhaps, for creating an entirely new comparison.

Literary ELEMENTS

Conceit

A **conceit** is a lengthy and elaborate **metaphor** or **simile** in a poem. Development of a conceit allows a writer to explore startling and witty ideas. In "The Welder," for example, Moraga develops her conceit by describing the actions, tools, materials, goals, and thoughts of a welder.

1. Identify several details and descriptions that develop the conceit in "The Welder."
2. List six words the speaker uses that relate to welding but that also have another meaning within the poem. For each word, write the literal definition that applies to welding as well as the deeper meaning.

● See **Literary Terms Handbook**, p. R3.

———— EXTENDING YOUR RESPONSE ————

Learning for Life

Job Interview With a partner, role-play an interview for a job as a welder or for any job you choose. First research the job and create a list of questions the employer might ask. Then role-play the interview for the class. The applicant should try to convince the employer of his or her unique qualifications. After the interview, have the employer explain to the class why the applicant did or did not get the job.

Writing About Literature

Paraphrase What do you think is the main point of this poem? Paraphrase, or state in your own words, the main point, mentioning passages or details from the poem that support your response. Compare your paraphrase with another student's and discuss each person's interpretation of the poem. Were your interpretations similar or different?

📖 **Save your work for your portfolio.**

Before You Read

The House/La Casa

Meet María Herrera-Sobek

"It's similar to when you hear a song and you can't get it out of your mind and you're humming it all day, that's the way a poem comes."

—Herrera-Sobek

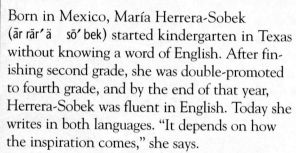

Born in Mexico, María Herrera-Sobek (ār rār' ä   sō' bek) started kindergarten in Texas without knowing a word of English. After finishing second grade, she was double-promoted to fourth grade, and by the end of that year, Herrera-Sobek was fluent in English. Today she writes in both languages. "It depends on how the inspiration comes," she says.

Herrera-Sobek has a degree in chemistry and sees an important parallel between the development of modern scientific knowledge and the literature of a culture. In the mid-twentieth century, Latin American literature was flowering, but most of the writers were male. Herrera-Sobek noted that these writers were building on the works of many nineteenth-century writers who were also men. "So I thought, I'm going to write to help create the tradition and maybe in 100 years there's going to be some really great Chicana writers. . . . In chemistry you depend on other scientists for progress. No one scientist can do it all alone. I see myself as creating bricks that will be used to build an edifice."

In fact, Herrera-Sobek worked briefly as a chemist before pursuing graduate degrees in Latin American studies and literature. As a professor of Chicano Studies, she hopes to inspire a new generation of Mexican American writers. She says, "I tell students when they read my poems, if you think they're not any good and you can do better, that's great! Go ahead and do it."

María Herrera-Sobek was born in 1942.

FOCUS ACTIVITY

Why might a person address an animal, a plant, or an inanimate object as if it were human?

JOURNAL Write a brief explanation of why you or someone else might "speak" to something other than a person.

SETTING A PURPOSE Read to find out what one speaker has to say to a house.

BACKGROUND

The Time and Place
Herrera-Sobek's poem was inspired by the view outside her home office, in a neighborhood of tract houses that were often empty when their occupants were at work or school.

Did You Know?
The average American family spends less time at home than it did thirty years ago. More parents work outside the home today than ever before, and many have longer commutes and work more hours than earlier generations did. Consequently, in typical families across the country, young children spend part of the day in day-care facilities. School age children, as well as teenagers, take advantage of opportunities for sports and other activities before and after school. In addition, many teenagers find after-school employment. As a result, neighborhoods may seem quiet and empty during much of the day.

THE HOUSE

María Herrera-Sobek ∽
Translated by Tey Diana Rebolledo

I see you standing
desolate
with the sun's rays
spattered
5   on your hair
of black roof-tiles.
Dark
alone
you remain like the cave
10   of a hermit
whose
fire has died down.
Your bowels°
send out only
15   silence.
The fire
that widened
your walls
that danced
20   on the windows
and opened your doors
has gone away.

Now
taciturn°
25   you dream alone
pensive°
you listen to
the slow steps
of the clouds
30   that murmur
at your shoulders
compassionate
of your enormous
emptiness.

13 bowels: intestines or deep and remote parts, as of a mountain or cave.

24 taciturn (tas′ ə turn′): silent.

26 pensive: engaged in deep and serious thought.

LA CASA

María Herrera-Sobek ~

Portals. Marsha Glaziere. Acrylic and collage on canvas, 66 x 52 in.
Gallery Contemporanea, Jacksonville, FL.

Te veo parada
desolada
con los rayos del sol
salpicados
5   en tu cabellera
de tejas negras.
Oscura
sola
quedas como la cueva
10   de un hermitaño
al cual se le ha
apagado su fuego.
Tus entrañas
sólo emiten
15   silencio.
El fuego
que ensanchaba
tus paredes
que bailaba
20   en las ventanas
y abría tus puertas
se ha alejado.

Ahora
taciturna
25   sólo sueñas
pensativa
escuchas
los pasos lentos
de las nubes
30   que a tus espaldas
murmuran
compadecidas
de tu enorme
vacío.

Responding to Literature

Personal Response

Does this poem make you look at inanimate objects differently? Why or why not?

━━━━ ANALYZING LITERATURE ━━━━

RECALL AND INTERPRET

1. Which word in the first sentence reflects the **mood** of the poem? What does this mood convey about the speaker's reaction to the situation she's describing? (See Literary Terms Handbook, page R10.)
2. What comparisons does the speaker make in lines 7–12 and 16–22? How do you interpret the word "fire" in each of these passages?
3. What **metaphor** (see page R9) does the speaker use at the beginning and the ending of the poem? What is the effect of this metaphor?
4. What two things besides the house are given human qualities? What is the relationship or connection between the house and each of these things? Use details from the poem to support your answers.

EVALUATE AND CONNECT

5. In what ways does the poet use images and metaphors effectively to create a picture in the reader's mind? Give examples to support your answer.
6. What other literature have you read that focuses on emptiness or loneliness? How was it like and unlike "The House"?
7. In which lines does the speaker address the house without comparing it to anything? In your opinion, is this technique needed in the poem?
8. Look again at your response to the Focus Activity on page 1167. What reason do you think Herrera-Sobek had for writing this poem? Do you agree with her reasoning? Explain.

Literary ELEMENTS

Form

Form is the structure of a poem. Many contemporary writers use loosely structured poetic forms instead of following traditional or formal patterns. These poets vary the lengths of lines and stanzas, relying on emphasis, rhythm, pattern, or the placement of words and phrases to convey meaning. This freedom of form may reflect the view that modern life is often unpredictable or it may show a poet's desire to experiment with line breaks and the juxtaposition of words.

1. Many words in the poem stand alone—one word to a line. How does this affect your response to the poem's mood?
2. What effect is created by dividing the poem into two stanzas?
- See **Literary Terms Handbook**, p. R7.

━━━━ EXTENDING YOUR RESPONSE ━━━━

Literature Groups

A New Mood   Suppose this poem had another speaker who saw the house in a different way. In a group, create a list of alternate words that would evoke a different mood. Then substitute your words for some of the words in the poem. Discuss whether or not your new poem creates the mood you intended. Share your results with the class.

Creative Writing

Dear Neighbor   In your journal, write a letter to the speaker of this poem from the house's point of view. Tell the speaker whether or not she's seeing you as you truly are. Explain what you think about your situation and anything else you want her to know.

📖 **Save your work for your portfolio.**

LISTENING, SPEAKING, and VIEWING

Discussing Literature

After reading a thought-provoking poem like "The House," readers often enjoy expressing their opinions. A group discussion is a useful way for people to exchange opinions and enhance their understanding of a piece of writing. People use discussions to solve problems, plan group actions, explore ideas, and exchange information. Here are some guidelines for planning and joining a group discussion about literature.

● Assign roles to people in your group, such as *group leader-facilitator, group participants,* and *note-taker.* This chart will help you understand these roles:

Role	Duties
Leader-facilitator	• introduces the discussion topic • invites each participant to speak • keeps the discussion focused and interactive • keeps track of the time • helps participants arrive at a consensus • summarizes major points at the end of the discussion
Group Participants	• form ideas and questions about the literature before the discussion • contribute throughout the discussion • support any opinions with facts • avoid repeating what has been said earlier • listen carefully to other group members • evaluate opinions of others • respect the opinions of others
Note-taker	• keeps track of the most important points • helps the group leader form conclusions based on the discussion • helps the group leader summarize the discussion

● If the topic for discussion has not been assigned, develop a topic and define a goal for the discussion. Choose a topic that interests the group. Try to state the topic as a question that will inspire an interesting discussion.
● After your discussion, take some time to evaluate how well you worked as a group.

ACTIVITY

Hold a twenty-minute discussion about "The House" or another piece of literature. Follow the guidelines above. Then together, write a brief evaluation of the discussion.

Before You Read

Salvador Late or Early

Meet Sandra Cisneros

When Sandra Cisneros (sis nā′ rōs) was a child, one of her favorite books was *The Little House,* by Virginia Lee Burton, the story of a stable family that lives permanently in one house even as the neighborhood around it changes. Perhaps she was drawn to the story because her own family moved constantly from one ghetto neighborhood to another. They also moved back and forth between Mexico and the United States, because her father was often homesick and was devoted to his mother in Mexico.

Cisneros was born in Chicago, Illinois, to a Mexican American mother and a Mexican father. As the only girl in a family of seven children, she often felt like she had "seven fathers," she says, because her six brothers, as well as her father, tried to control her. She felt shy and lost in the shuffle and retreated into books. Despite her love of reading, she did not do well in elementary school because her family moved so often and because she was too shy to participate.

In high school, with the encouragement of one particular teacher, Cisneros improved her grades and worked on the school literary magazine. Her father encouraged her to go to college because he thought it would be a good way for her to find a husband. Cisneros did attend college, but instead of searching for a husband, she found a teacher who helped her enroll in the prestigious graduate writing program at the University of Iowa. At the university's Writers' Workshop, however, she felt isolated—a Mexican American from a poor neighborhood among students from wealthy families and the best colleges. The feeling of being so different,

along with the friendship of Native American writer Joy Harjo, helped Cisneros find her "creative voice."

"It was not until this moment when I separated myself, when I considered myself truly distinct, that my writing acquired a voice. I knew I was a Mexican woman, but I didn't think it had anything to do with why I felt so much imbalance in my life, whereas it had everything to do with it! My race, my gender, my class! That's when I decided I would write about something my classmates couldn't write about."

Cisneros published her first prose work, *The House on Mango Street,* when she was twenty-nine. In a series of interlocking stories, the book tells about a young Chicana girl growing up in a Chicago barrio, much like the neighborhoods in which Cisneros lived as a child. The book was awarded the Before Columbus American Book Award in 1985 and has been used in classes from high school through graduate school level in many types of courses. Since then, Cisneros has published several books of poetry, a children's book, and a short-story collection. Many of her works, including "Salvador Late or Early," have appeared in literary journals.

"I'm trying to write the stories that haven't been written. I feel like a cartographer. I'm determined to fill a literary void."

"To me, the definition of a story is something that someone wants to listen to. If someone doesn't want to listen to you, then it's not a story."

—*Cisneros*

FOCUS ACTIVITY

What does it mean to be poor? In your opinion, how might poverty affect a person's personality and outlook on life?

MAP IT! Create a word web with the word *poverty* at the center. Around that word, write the words and images you associate with poverty. Then think about the reactions these words and images bring out in you.

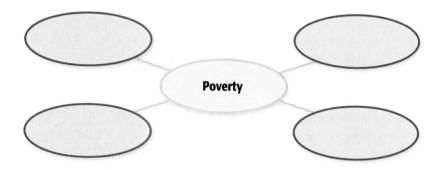

Poverty

SETTING A PURPOSE Read to discover one boy's experience of poverty.

BACKGROUND

Literary Influences

When Sandra Cisneros looks back on her years in high school and college, she admits she did not know that she was a Chicana, or Mexican American, writer. Although she had an identity that was Mexican, when it came to literature, she simply thought of herself as American because she read mainstream literature and wrote in English. Though she spoke Spanish at home, Cisneros did not know any Mexican American writers, so she did not think of them as belonging to a separate category. She admired the "big male voices" of poets such as James Wright, Richard Hugo, and Theodore Roethke. Those voices, however, "were all wrong for me," Cisneros now says. Not until graduate school in Iowa did she realize how different her experience was from that of most of her classmates.

Yet even as Cisneros was shaping her own Chicana identity, much of the inspiration for *The House on Mango Street* came from the memoirs of Russian American writer Vladimir Nabokov.

Cisneros admires Latin American writers such as Manuel Puig, for his compassion for the underdog, and Juan Rulfo, "for his rhythms and what he's doing with voices." She is also interested in the writing of American working-class women who publish with small presses, which Cisneros says can be "more fearless about things that they take" than large publishing companies. The writers who touch her "passion buttons" she says, are those who, like Rulfo and Puig, are "doing something new."

Salvador
Late or Early

Sandra Cisneros

Salvador with eyes the color of caterpillar, Salvador of the crooked hair and crooked teeth, Salvador whose name the teacher cannot remember, is a boy who is no one's friend, runs along somewhere in that vague direction where homes are the color of bad weather, lives behind a raw wood doorway, shakes the sleepy brothers awake, ties their shoes, combs their hair with water, feeds them milk and corn flakes from a tin cup in the dim dark of the morning.

Salvador, late or early, sooner or later arrives with the string of younger brothers ready. Helps his mama, who is busy with the business of the baby. Tugs the arms of Cecilio, Arturito, makes them hurry, because today, like yesterday, Arturito has dropped the cigar box of crayons, has let go the hundred little fingers of red, green, yellow, blue, and nub of black sticks that tumble and spill over and beyond the asphalt puddles until the crossing-guard lady holds back the blur of traffic for Salvador to collect them again.

Salvador inside that wrinkled shirt, inside the throat that must clear itself and apologize each time it speaks, inside that forty-pound body of boy with its geography of scars, its history of hurt, limbs stuffed with feathers and rags, in what part of the eyes, in what part of the heart, in that cage of the chest where something throbs with both fists and knows only what Salvador knows, inside that body too small to contain the hundred balloons of happiness, the single guitar of grief, is a boy like any other disappearing out the door, beside the schoolyard gate, where he has told his brothers they must wait. Collects the hands of Cecilio and Arturito, scuttles off dodging the many schoolyard colors, the elbows and wrists criss-crossing, the several shoes running. Grows small and smaller to the eye, dissolves into the bright horizon, flutters in the air before disappearing like a memory of kites.

El Patio de la Casa del Artista, 1884. Martin Tovar y Tovar. Oil on canvas, 18¼ x 21⅝ in. Private collection. Do you think Salvador might have liked to live in a house like this? Why or why not?

Responding to Literature

Personal Response

What would you want to say to Salvador if you were to meet him?

——— ANALYZING LITERATURE ———

RECALL AND INTERPRET

1. List the colors the narrator mentions in the first sentence of "Salvador Late or Early." What do these colors suggest about Salvador's life?
2. Describe Salvador's role in his household. What does his role reveal about how Salvador is viewed in his family?
3. What does the narrator reveal about Salvador's appearance in the third paragraph of the selection? about how Salvador speaks and feels? What do these details indicate about Salvador's history?
4. What images describe Salvador in the third paragraph? What do these images tell you about Salvador's character? about what he thinks of himself? about the narrator's attitude toward him?

EVALUATE AND CONNECT

5. **Theme Connections**   How might Cisneros's writing style reflect the idea that "variety is richness"? Support your answer with examples.
6. A major part of Cisneros's **style** (see page R15) in "Salvador Late or Early" is her use of unusually long sentences. In your opinion, do these long sentences add to or detract from the effectiveness of Cisneros's writing? Explain, using examples.
7. Think of someone you know who reminds you of Salvador. How is this person like Salvador? How is this person different?
8. Are the ideas about poverty you mapped out for the Focus Activity on page 1173 similar to those conveyed in "Salvador Late or Early"? Does Cisneros's story make you think differently about poverty? Explain.

Literary ELEMENTS

Imagery

Imagery is the word pictures a writer creates to evoke an emotional response. For example, Cisneros writes that Salvador "arrives with the string of younger brothers ready." These words create an image of a line of boys following behind Salvador. This image also conveys the idea that Salvador is always attached to his brothers.

1. What image do the words "Salvador inside that wrinkled shirt" create for you? How does this image make you feel about Salvador?
2. Which image in Cisneros's story do you find most striking? Why?

● See **Literary Terms Handbook**, p. R8.

——— EXTENDING YOUR RESPONSE ———

Writing About Literature

Poetic Prose   In "Salvador Late or Early," Cisneros uses many sound devices—**alliteration, assonance, rhyme,** and **rhythm**—that are more commonly associated with poetry than with prose. (See pages R1, R2, and R13.) Using specific examples from the story as evidence, write a paragraph explaining the effect these devices have on your reading of the story.

Internet Connection

Leading the Way   Sandra Cisneros is one of the leading figures in Hispanic American literature today. Search the Internet for information about other Hispanic Americans who are leaders in their fields. You may choose any area you like, such as art, science, sports, or politics. Present your findings to the class.

📖 **Save your work for your portfolio.**

Before You Read

Embroidering: A Response to "Somnad" by Carl Larrson and El Olvido (Según las Madres)

Meet Rita Magdaleno

The daughter of a Mexican American father and a German mother, Rita Magdaleno (mäg′ dä lā′ nō) writes to reconcile the two landscapes of her life. Born in Germany, she says that the sounds and landscapes of Germany shaped her, just as those of Phoenix, Arizona, did when she was growing up there.

Magdaleno remembers keeping a journal during her first visit to Germany, when she was ten years old. She traveled on a boat for seven days and kept a record of all that she observed.

She didn't consider writing professionally until her early thirties, when she entered a creative writing program. Since that time, she has published fiction and poetry in numerous anthologies. In addition, she has worked with high school students as a poet in the schools and has taught photo narrative writing, a type of writing that creates a story from a single photograph.

Rita Magdaleno was born in 1947.

Meet Judith Ortiz Cofer

Culture clash is a familiar theme in the work of Judith Ortiz Cofer (ôr tēz′ kō′ fer). Many of her poems, novels, and autobiographical essays touch on the conflicts between the old values of her Puerto Rican ancestors and those of the United States.

Cofer was born in Puerto Rico, but she moved with her family to New Jersey as a young girl. Her father worked for the U.S. Navy, and whenever he went to sea, the family visited relatives in Puerto Rico.

Cofer praises "Nuyoricans"—Americans of Puerto Rican descent—who use both Spanish and English in their writing. Although some criticize this practice, Cofer says, "My view is that these young people mixing English and Spanish are energizing the language. Writers do what teenagers do, taking on and changing the language."

A professor of literature and creative writing, Cofer continues to write.

Judith Ortiz Cofer was born in 1952.

FOCUS ACTIVITY

How does where you live affect the way you look at the world?

QUICKWRITE Jot down ways that the place, or places you've lived have affected your views.

SETTING A PURPOSE Read to discover how geography and culture affect two speakers.

BACKGROUND

Did You Know?
Rita Magdaleno wrote "Embroidering" after the death of her mother. A friend sent her a condolence card showing a sketch by artist Carl Larrson, of two women doing needlework. The sketch, "Somnad" (meaning "sewing"), inspired Magdaleno to reflect on her relationship with her mother.

Embroidering:
A Response to "Somnad" by Carl Larsson

Rita Magdaleno

A vase of hydrangeas on the table, this room
blue and clear, everything solid
and in its place. Here, two women
sit together, their knees
5   touching, stroking the beautiful
threads. One is pale green
like a single blade of weed
at the edge of a small pond. Another
strand is the color of deep wood
10   roses, wild and very sweet.
Also, threads like filaments°
of fish tails, gold
and a blue string curled
like a child's ball, color
15   of sky on early desert mornings.
This afternoon, pale
and warm, the daughter listens
to her mother's breath, soft

and steady like a small animal
20   full of milk, nearly asleep,
this rhythm of breathing and needles
sliding slowly through the cloth.
They have planned this thing,
a tablecloth to spread out
25   for guests who will come
to this room, who will sit
and bow their heads to the white
plates of food. And this will become
a cloth to be passed through
30   generations, needle of the mother,
needle of the daughter crossing
through the cloth over
and over. A choreography°
of hands and needles,
35   and the daughter wonders
how this cloth will sing.

---

11 Here, *filaments* probably refers to thin rods or rays that support the web of skin in fish fins.

33 *Choreography* (kôr′ ē og′ rə fē) is the composition and arrangement of dances.

Sömnad, 1916. Carl Larsson.
Watercolor. Private collection.

Ancestral Dream I, 1996. Maria Eugenia Terrazas.
Watercolor, 70 x 60 cm. Private collection.

El Olvido
(Según las Madres)

Judith Ortiz Cofer ∿

It is a dangerous thing
to forget the climate of
your birthplace; to choke out
the voices of the dead relatives when
5   in dreams they call you by
your secret name; dangerous
to spurn° the clothes you were
born to wear for the sake of fashion;
to use weapons and sharp instruments you
10   are not familiar with; dangerous
to disdain° the plaster saints before
which your mother kneels praying for you with
embarassing fervor that you survive in
the place you have chosen to live; a costly,
15   bare and elegant room with no pictures
on the walls: a forgetting place where
she fears you might die of exposure.
Jesús, María y José.
El olvido is a dangerous thing.

El Olvido (el ōl vē′ dō) is Spanish for "the forgotten." *Según las
Madres* (sə gōōn′ läs mä′drəs) means "according to mothers."

7 *Spurn* means "to reject with contempt" or "to scorn."
11 *Disdain* means "to look down on" or "to despise."

Responding to Literature

Personal Response

Which poem was more meaningful for you? Why?

ANALYZING LITERATURE

Embroidering:

A Response to "Somnad"
by Carl Larsson

RECALL AND INTERPRET

1. What are the mother and daughter in the poem doing? What feature of the threads does the speaker describe? What might the threads **symbolize,** or stand for, in the poem? Explain your response.
2. What do you think the tablecloth represents? Support your ideas with specific details from the poem.

EVALUATE AND CONNECT

3. How does the poet engage your senses in this poem? List several examples.
4. When have you made something with another person or for another person? How was it different from making something by yourself or for yourself?

El Olvido

(Según las Madres)

RECALL AND INTERPRET

5. According to lines 1–12, what kinds of things are dangerous? Why, do you think, does the speaker call them dangerous?
6. What fear does the mother have? Why might she have this fear? What seems to be the relationship between the speaker, the mother, and the person called "you"? What can you infer about their values?

EVALUATE AND CONNECT

7. Are you convinced that forgetting one's roots "is a dangerous thing"? Why or why not?
8. Consider one of the places you wrote about for the Focus Activity on page 1176. What aspects of this place or of a place your ancestors came from do you think are most important to remember? Why?

EXTENDING YOUR RESPONSE

Personal Writing

Your Point of View   "El Olvido" contains a Spanish subtitle that means "According to Mothers." Imagine that you are a young person living in a "costly, bare, and elegant room with no pictures on the walls." Compose an E-mail message that responds to the mother who has told you that forgetting is a dangerous thing.

Learning for Life

Letter of Request   Using Magdaleno's poem for inspiration, write a letter to a relative, asking him or her to help you create a visual-arts project celebrating an aspect of your family's culture or history. In your letter, describe what you want to make, the materials you will use, and how this person could help you carry out your project.

📖 **Save your work for your portfolio.**

Before You Read

The Names of Women

Meet Louise Erdrich

"People in [Native American] families make everything into a story. . . . People just sit and the stories start coming, one after another."

—*Erdrich*

The daughter of a German American father and an Ojibwa (ō jib′ wā′) mother, Louise Erdrich grew up in Wahpeton, North Dakota, the oldest of seven children. Erdrich's parents, who both worked in a Bureau of Indian Affairs boarding school, encouraged their daughter to write. "My father used to give me a nickel for every story I wrote, and my mother wove strips of construction paper together and stapled them into book covers. So at an early age I felt myself to be a

published author earning substantial royalties."

Erdrich entered Dartmouth College in 1972, the first year of the college's new Native American studies department. From Dartmouth, Erdrich went to the Johns Hopkins University, where she wrote poems and stories and earned a master's degree. She then returned to Dartmouth as a writer in residence.

Before she turned thirty, Erdrich published her first novel, *Love Medicine*. The book was well received by readers and critics, earning the National Book Award in 1984. Erdrich has continued her successful writing career, publishing novels, nonfiction, and children's books.

Louise Erdrich was born in 1954.

FOCUS ACTIVITY

What's in a name? Does your name tell people anything about you?

JOURNAL Write about your own name or the names of some of your relatives or ancestors. What can people learn about you and your family from your names?

SETTING A PURPOSE Read to learn what one writer thinks about the names in her family.

BACKGROUND

Erdrich's People

The *Anishinabe* (a nish′ i nä′ bä)—also known as the Ojibwa, Ojibway, or Chippewa—are one of the largest groups of Native Americans in North America. After the mid-1600s, they migrated west from the Great Lakes region to areas such as Wisconsin, North Dakota, and Montana.

VOCABULARY PREVIEW

decimated (des′ ə māt′ ed) *adj.* destroyed or killed in large numbers; p. 1182

presumptuous (pri zump′ chōō əs) *adj.* going beyond what is proper; excessively bold; p. 1182

ecclesiastical (i klē′ zē as′ ti kəl) *adj.* of or relating to the church; p. 1182

undeviating (un dē′ vē āt′ ing) *adj.* not turning away from; p. 1183

intricately (in′ tri kit lē) *adv.* in a complicated manner; elaborately; p. 1183

novel (nov′ əl) *adj.* new and unusual; p. 1183

wane (wān) *v.* to decrease gradually; to decline; p. 1184

The Names of Women

Louise Erdrich

Ikwe[1] is the word for woman in the language of the Anishinabe, my mother's people, whose descendants, mixed with and married to French trappers and farmers, are the Michifs[2] of the Turtle Mountain reservation in North Dakota. Every Anishinabe *Ikwe*, every mixed-blood descendant like me, who can trace her way back a generation or two, is the daughter of a mystery. The history of the woodland Anishinabe—decimated by disease, fighting Plains Indians tribes to the west and squeezed by European settlers to the east—is much like most other Native American stories, a confusion of loss, a tale of absences, of a culture that was blown apart and changed so radically in such a short time that only the names survive.

And yet, those names.

The names of the first women whose existence is recorded on the rolls of the Turtle Mountain Reservation, in 1892, reveal as much as we can ever recapture of their personalities, complex natures and relationships. These names tell stories, or half stories, if only we listen closely.

There once were women named *Standing Strong*, *Fish Bones*, *Different Thunder*. There once was a girl called *Yellow Straps*. Imagine what it was like to pick berries with *Sky Coming Down*, to walk through a storm with *Lightning Proof*. Surely, she was struck and lived, but what about the person next to her? People always avoided *Steps Over Truth*, when they wanted a straight answer, and *I Hear*, when they wanted to keep a secret. *Glittering* put coal on her face

and watched for enemies at night. The woman named *Standing Across* could see things moving far across the lake. The old ladies gossiped about *Playing Around*, but no one dared say anything to her face. *Ice* was good at gambling. *Shining One Side* loved to sit and talk to *Opposite the Sky*. They both knew *Sounding Feather*, *Exhausted Wind* and *Green Cloud*, daughter of *Seeing Iron*. *Center of the Sky* was a widow. *Rabbit*, *Prairie Chicken* and *Daylight* were all little girls. *She Tramp* could make great distance in a day of walking. *Cross Lightning* had a powerful smile. When *Setting Wind* and *Gentle Woman Standing* sang together the whole tribe listened. *Stop the Day* got her name when at her shout the afternoon went still. *Log* was strong, *Cloud Touching Bottom* weak and consumptive.[3] *Mirage* married *Wind*. Everyone loved *Musical Cloud*, but children hid from *Dressed in Stone*. *Lying Down Grass* had such a gentle voice and touch, but no one dared to cross *She Black of Heart*.

We can imagine something of these women from their names. Anishinabe historian Basil Johnston notes that 'such was the mystique and force of a name that it was considered presumptuous and unbecoming, even vain, for a person to utter his own name. It was the custom for a third person, if present, to utter the name of the person to be identified. Seldom, if ever, did either husband or wife speak the name of the other in public.'

Shortly after the first tribal roll, the practice of renaming became an ecclesiastical

> Imagine what it was like to pick berries with **Sky Coming Down**, to walk through a storm with **Lightning Proof**.

---

1. *Ikwe* (ik′ wā)
2. *Michifs* (mi′ chifz)

3. Someone who is *consumptive* suffers from a disease (especially tuberculosis) in which body tissue wastes away.

Vocabulary

decimated (des′ ə māt′ ed) *adj.* destroyed or killed in large numbers
presumptuous (pri zump′ chŏŏ əs) *adj.* going beyond what is proper; excessively bold
ecclesiastical (i klē′ zē as′ ti kəl) *adj.* of or relating to the church

exercise, and, as a result, most women in the next two generations bear the names of saints particularly beloved by the French. *She Knows the Bear* became Marie. *Sloping Cloud* was christened Jeanne. *Taking Care of the Day* and *Yellow Day Woman* turned into Catherines. Identities are altogether lost. The daughters of my own ancestors, *Kwayzancheewin*[4]—*Acts Like a Boy* and *Striped Earth Woman*—go unrecorded, and no hint or reflection of their individual natures comes to light through the scattershot records of those times, although they must have been genetically tough in order to survive: there were epidemics of typhoid, flu, measles and other diseases that winnowed the tribe each winter. They had to have grown up sensible, hard-working, undeviating in their attention to their tasks. They had to have been lucky. And if very lucky, they acquired carts.

It is no small thing that both of my great-grandmothers were known as women with carts.

The first was Elise Eliza McCloud, the great-granddaughter of *Striped Earth Woman*. The buggy she owned was somewhat grander than a cart. In her photograph, Elise Eliza gazes straight ahead, intent, elevated in her pride. Perhaps she and her daughter Justine, both wearing reshaped felt fedoras,[5] were on their way to the train that would take them from Rugby, North Dakota, to Grand Forks, and back again. Back and forth across the upper tier of the plains, they peddled their hand-worked tourist items—dangling moccasin brooches and little beaded hats, or, in the summer, the wild berries, plums and nuts that they had gathered from the wooded hills. Of Elise Eliza's industry there remains in the family only an intricately beaded pair of buffalo horns and a piece of real furniture, a 'highboy', an object once regarded with some awe, a prize she won for selling the most merchandise from a manufacturer's catalogue.

Did You Know?
A *highboy* is a tall chest of drawers having two sections and four legs.

The owner of the other cart, Virginia Grandbois, died when I was nine years old: she was a fearsome and fascinating presence, an old woman seated like an icon behind the door of my grandparents' house. Forty years before I was born, she was photographed on her way to fetch drinking water at the reservation well. In the picture she is seated high, the reins in her fingers connected to a couple of shaggy fetlocked draft ponies. The barrel she will fill stands behind her. She wears a man's sweater and an expression of vast self-pleasure. She might have been saying *Kaygoh*,[6] a warning, to calm the horses. She might have been speaking to whomever it was who held the camera, still a novel luxury.

Did You Know?
A *fetlocked* (fet' lokt) pony has a tuft of hair on the back of each leg, just above the hoof.

---

4. *Kwayzancheewin* (kwā′ zän chē′ win)

5. *Fedoras* (fi dôr′ əz) are soft felt hats with a curved brim and a lengthwise crease in the crown.

---

6. *Kaygoh* (kā gō′)

Vocabulary
undeviating (un dē′ vē āt′ ing) *adj.* not turning away from
intricately (in′ tri kit lē) *adv.* in a complicated manner; elaborately
novel (nov′ əl) *adj.* new and unusual

Virginia Grandbois was known to smell of flowers. In spite of the potato picking, water hauling, field and housework, she found the time and will to dust her face with pale powder, in order to look more French. She was the great-great-granddaughter of the daughter of the principal leader of the *A-waus-e*,[7] the Bullhead clan, a woman whose real name was never recorded but who, on marrying a Frenchman, was 'recreated' as Madame Cadotte. It was Madame Cadotte who acted as a liaison[8] between her Ojibway relatives and her husband so that, even when French influence waned in the region, Jean-Baptiste Cadotte stayed on as the only trader of importance, the last governor of the fort at Sault St. Marie.[9]

By the time I knew Virginia Grandbois, however, her mind had darkened, and her body deepened, shrunk, turned to bones and leather. She did not live in the present or in any known time at all. Periodically, she would awaken from dim and unknown dreams to find herself seated behind the door in her daughter's house. She then cried out for her cart and her horses. When they did not materialize, Virginia Grandbois rose with great energy and purpose. Then she walked towards her house, taking the straightest line.

That house, long sold and gone, lay over one hundred miles due east and still Virginia Grandbois charged ahead, no matter what lay in her path—fences, sloughs,[10] woods, the yards of other families. She wanted home, to get home, to be home. She wanted her own place back, the place she had made, not her daughter's, not anyone else's. Hers. There was no substitute, no kindness, no reality that would change her mind. She had to be tied to the chair, and the chair to the wall, and still there was no reasoning with Virginia Grandbois. Her entire life, her hard-won personality, boiled down in the end to one stubborn, fixed, desperate idea.

I started with the same idea—this urge to get home, even if I must walk straight across the world. Only, for me, the urge to walk is the urge to write. Like my great-grandmother's house, there is no home for me to get to. A mixed-blood, raised in the Sugarbeet Capital, educated on the Eastern seaboard, married in a tiny New England village, living now on a ridge directly across from the Swan Range in the Rocky Mountains, my home is a collection of homes, of wells in which the quiet of experience shales away into sweet bedrock.

Elise Eliza pieced the quilt my mother slept under, a patchwork of shirts, pants, other worn-out scraps, bordered with small rinsed and pressed Bull Durham[11] sacks. As if in another time and place, although it is only the dim barrel of a four-year-old's memory, I see myself lying wrapped under smoky quilts and dank green army blankets in the house in which my mother was born. In the fragrance of tobacco, some smoked in home-rolled cigarettes, some offered to the Manitous[12] whose presence still was honored, I dream myself home. Beneath the rafters, shadowed with bunches of plants

---

7. *A-waus-e* (ä′ wôs ē)
8. Here, a *liaison* (lē ä′ zon) is a person who maintains or improves communications between two parties.
9. *Sault St.* (or *Ste.*, meaning *Sainte*) Marie (sōō′ sänt mə rē′), Michigan, and its sister city, Sault Ste. Marie, Ontario, lie along the St. Mary's River between Lake Huron and Lake Superior.
10. *Sloughs* (slōōz) are marshes, swamps, or bogs.

11. *Bull Durham* was a brand of tobacco.
12. *Manitous* (man′ ə tōōs′) are spirits worshipped as governing forces of life and nature.

Vocabulary

wane (wān) *v.* to decrease gradually; to decline

and torn calendars, in the nest of a sagging bed, I listen to mice rustle and the scratch of an owl's claws as it paces the shingles.

Elise Eliza's daughter-in-law, my grandmother Mary LeFavor, kept that house of hand-hewed and stacked beams, mudded between. She managed to shore it up and keep it standing by stuffing every new crack with disposable diapers. Having used and reused cloth to diaper her own children, my grandmother washed and hung to dry the paper and plastic diapers that her granddaughters bought for her great-grandchildren. When their plastic-paper shredded, she gathered them carefully together and one day, on a summer visit, I woke early to find her tamping[13] the rolled stuff carefully into the cracked walls of that old house.

I t is autumn in the Plains, and in the little sloughs ducks land, and mudhens, whose flesh always tastes greasy and charred. Snow is coming soon, and after its first fall there will be a short, false warmth that brings out the sweet-sour odor of highbush cranberries. As a descendant of the women who skinned buffalo and tanned and smoked the hides, of women who pounded berries with the dried meat to make winter food, who made tea from willow bark and rosehips, who gathered snakeroot, I am affected by the change of seasons. Here is a time when plants consolidate[14] their tonic and drop seed, when animals store energy and grow thick fur. As for me, I start keeping longer hours, writing more, working harder, though I am obviously not a creature of a traditional Anishinabe culture. I was not raised speaking the old language, or adhering to the cycle of religious ceremonies that govern the Anishinabe spiritual relationship to the land and the moral order within human configurations. As the wedding of many backgrounds, I am free to do what simply feels right.

> As the wedding of many backgrounds, I am free to do what simply feels right.

My mother knits, sews, cans, dries food and preserves it. She knows how to gather tea, berries, snare rabbits, milk cows and churn butter. She can grow squash and melons from seeds she gathered the fall before. She is, as were the women who came before me, a repository[15] of all of the homely virtues, and I am the first in a long line who has not saved the autumn's harvest in birch bark *makuks*[16] and skin bags and in a cellar dry and cold with dust. I am the first who scratches the ground for pleasure, not survival, and grows flowers instead of potatoes. I record rather than practise the arts that filled the hands and days of my mother and her mother, and all the mothers going back into the shadows, when women wore names that told us who they were.

---

13. *Tamping* means "forcing or packing in with a series of light taps."

14. To *consolidate* (kən sol′ ə dāt′) means "to combine."
15. Here, a *repository* (ri poz′ ə tôr′ ē) is a person who stores something.
16. *makuks* (mä′ kuks)

Responding to Literature

Personal Response
Discuss your initial impression of this selection with a partner.

—————— ANALYZING LITERATURE ——————

RECALL
1. What does Erdrich reveal in the first paragraph about her ethnic heritage and about the history of her ancestors?
2. List five names that, according to Erdrich, appeared on the rolls of the Turtle Mountain Reservation in 1892.
3. What words does Erdrich use to describe her great-grandmothers?
4. What do Virginia Grandbois and Erdrich have in common?
5. Compare the things her mother does with the things Erdrich does.

INTERPRET
6. In your opinion, what is Erdrich's attitude about her ancestors' history?
7. What sense of the Anishinabe women do you get based on the listing of their names? Explain.
8. How do you think Erdrich feels about her great-grandmothers? Use specific details from the selection to explain your answer.
9. What do you think Erdrich is saying about herself when she explains what she has in common with her great-grandmother Virginia Grandbois? Use details from the selection to support your response.
10. What conclusions can you make about the kind of person Erdrich is, based on the last paragraph? How do you think she feels about being the kind of person she is? Explain.

EVALUATE AND CONNECT
11. In your opinion, what is the **theme,** or message, of this selection? Support your response with evidence from the selection.
12. Find three examples of **sensory details** (see page R14) in "The Names of Women," and describe how they affect your appreciation of the selection. Use a chart like the one on this page to help you.
13. Theme Connections   How does the fact that Erdrich's ancestors are both Anishinabe and French relate to the theme "Variety Is Richness"?
14. How do the names you wrote about for the Focus Activity on page 1180 compare with the ones in this selection for telling about the people they name? Which names do you prefer? Explain.
15. Do you think that writing about what people have done in the past is important? Why or why not?

Catalog
A **catalog** is a list of people, things, or attributes. Many forms of literature include catalogs. For example, ancient epic poems listed the names of heroes or ships. The poets Walt Whitman and Carl Sandburg often included catalogs in their poems as Erdrich does in "The Names of Women."
1. Describe two catalogs that appear in this selection.
2. Why might Erdrich present this information in the form of catalogs?
● See **Literary Terms Handbook,** p. R3.

Sensory detail	Effect
1.	
2.	
3.	

LITERATURE AND WRITING

Writing About Literature

Analyzing the Author's Use of Factual Information
Reread "The Names of Women" and find three facts that strike you as particularly interesting or surprising. Analyze each fact and explain how Erdrich uses it, what makes it so interesting, and how it adds to your understanding of the world she describes.

Creative Writing

Name Your Friends   Make a list of ten friends or relatives. What distinctive characteristics or events in their lives might best be used to illustrate their personalities? Make up names for these people, using the kind of descriptive names listed in the first part of "The Names of Women."

EXTENDING YOUR RESPONSE

Interdisciplinary Activity

History: Family Tree   Using the information in the selection, create a family tree for Louise Erdrich. Leave empty spaces where no information is provided, but show the relationships among the ancestors of Erdrich who are named in the selection.

Listening and Speaking

Readers Theater   Read parts of this selection aloud, dramatizing, through sound or pantomime, the names or activities described. You might use this technique for the opening paragraphs or for the final paragraphs.

Literature Groups

Will She Make It?   In this selection, Erdrich describes herself as someone with the "urge to get home, even if I must walk straight across the world." What does she mean? Will she make it? As a group, agree on a statement of Erdrich's goal and discuss why you think she will succeed or fail in reaching it. Use passages from the selection to support your view. Have one group member take notes on the explanations people offer. Outline your group's ideas and supporting details, and then share your conclusion with the class.

📕 **Save your work for your portfolio.**

Skill Minilesson

VOCABULARY • Antonyms

Antonyms are words that have opposite meanings from each other. Some antonyms are "true," with meanings that are exactly opposite; for example, *hot* and *cold* or *night* and *day*. Often, a word will have several antonyms, each with a slightly different meaning. For example, *courageous* and *valiant* are antonyms for *cowardly*.

While most words have at least one synonym, or word that has the same or nearly the same meaning, not all words have an antonym; for example, *run* and *dog* have no antonyms.

PRACTICE   Choose an antonym for each of the vocabulary words listed below.

1. decimate
   a. build   b. destroy   c. create
2. intricately
   a. simply   b. elaborately   c. curiously
3. novel
   a. innovative b. dated   c. literary
4. wane
   a. increase   b. slacken   c. subside

Newspaper Article

Names certainly come in a great variety. What is the origin of your name? In this article, you'll learn about recent trends in names for babies.

The Name Reign:
New Parents Balance the Trendy and Unique

by Janet Simons—*Rocky Mountain News*, January 18, 1998

Fashions in names seem as arbitrary as fashions in carpet. One day everyone wants orange shag, then suddenly it's green berber.

What else explains Mary, the top name for girls in 1930, 1940 and 1960? (It was temporarily displaced in 1950 by Linda.) At one point, one of every six females in the United States was named Mary. Now the name ranks 72nd. Or Heather, so popular in 1989 that the movie *Heathers* featured three popular girls all named Heather. At No. 100, Heather barely clings to the 1997 list.

On the flip side, countless parents thought Austin or Hannah sounded fresh when their children were born, then wound up inviting two kids with the same name to the third birthday party.

Duncan Drechsel is willing to predict which names will be popular in 1998. Drechsel is marketing director for the BabyCenter, a San Francisco–based Web site for expectant and new parents. The BabyCenter recently released

a list of the 100 most popular baby names based on a sample of new Social Security registrations from the first eight months of 1997. "Diana. I see a lot of Dianas in the future,"

he says. "And Mabel. I'd put money on Mabel moving up."

Diana, which ranked only 92 for the first eight months of 1997, before the princess died, seems obvious. But Mabel? It's not even on the current list of 100. Drechsel says Mabel meets several criteria for a name on the rise. It's an "antique" name, like Sarah and Emily, numbers 1 and 2 on the list. It has a long A sound, like Kaitlyn, Taylor and Megan, ranked 3,

7 and 8, respectively. Most important, it's the name of the baby in the television sitcom *Mad About You,* so it . . . is fresh in the minds of expectant parents.

"Parents today are looking for something different," Drechsel says. "That's why we're seeing so much more variation in the names on the list."

The nation's most popular names for 1997:

1. Michael	Sarah
2. Matthew	Emily
3. Nicholas	Kaitlyn
4. Jacob	Brianna
5. Christopher	Ashley
6. Austin	Jessica
7. Joshua	Taylor
8. Zachary	Megan
9. Andrew	Hannah
10. Brandon	Samantha

Respond

1. Which names in the article and on the list are your favorites? Which do you like least? Explain.

2. From this article, what do you learn about the theme "Variety Is Richness"? Explain.

Before You Read

Naming Myself

Meet Barbara Kingsolver

"I think what I need to do is respect my reader, begin from the premise that she or he is a reasonable person who doesn't need to be screamed at, would like to be entertained, would like to be moved, would like to read literature."

—*Kingsolver*

Barbara Kingsolver has been writing since she was a child. She first wrote stories, then essays. Since the age of eight, she has "continuously kept a journal in which I put personal revelations." Kingsolver didn't start writing poetry, however, until a college English teacher urged her to write sonnets. With this encouragement, she wrote hundreds of sonnets, which she now says were "pretty awful," but through them she learned a lot about "meter and economy and to pay attention to the sound of words." Today, Kingsolver is an accomplished and admired writer who has published poetry, short stories, novels, essays, and a nonfiction book. The poem "Naming Myself" is taken from her poetry collection *Another America/Otra America*.

Kingsolver is the daughter of a physician and a homemaker. She says she feels really blessed to have grown up in rural Kentucky, where she first heard and absorbed that area's poetic language. She acknowledges that people in other parts of the country make fun of rural speech and accents. "I lost my accent for exactly that reason: people made terrible fun of me for the way I used to talk." Later on, however, she realized that "this language was a precious and valuable thing." She tried to embody that language in the voice of Kentucky woman Taylor Greer, the protagonist of her first novel, *The Bean Trees*.

Barbara Kingsolver was born in 1955.

FOCUS ACTIVITY

Would you ever change your name?

LIST IT! Some people change their names when they marry, others when they take on a new identity or reach legal age, and many when they immigrate to another country. List reasons why you would or wouldn't change your name.

SETTING A PURPOSE Read to find out how the speaker of this poem feels about changing her name.

BACKGROUND

Women's Last Names

The famous social reformer Lucy Stone was one of the first American women to refuse to change her last name to her husband's after her marriage to Henry Blackwell in the mid-nineteenth century. Few women followed her in this practice until the 1970s. By that time, an increasing sense of the value of a woman's separate identity led more women, especially those with established careers, to keep their own names after they married.

Lucy Stone

Naming Myself

Barbara Kingsolver ∾

I have guarded my name as people
in other times kept their own clipped hair,
believing the soul could be scattered
if they were careless.

5   I knew my first ancestor.
His legend. I have touched
his boots and moustache, the grandfather
whose people owned slaves and cotton.
He was restless in Virginia
10   among the gentleman brothers, until
one peppered, flaming autumn he stole a horse,
rode over the mountains to marry
a leaf-eyed Cherokee.
The theft was forgiven but never
15   the Indian blood. He lost his family's name
and invented mine, gave it fruit and seeds.
I never knew the grandmother.
Her photograph has ink-thin braids
and buttoned clothes, and nothing that she was called.

20   I could shed my name in the middle of life,
the ordinary thing, and it would flee
along with childhood and dead grandmothers
to that Limbo° for discontinued maiden names.

But it would grow restless there.
25   I know this. It would ride over leaf smoke mountains
and steal horses.

Looking Within Myself I Am Many Parts,
1976. Helen Hardin. Acrylic on board,
approximately 20 x 16 in. © 1976 Helen
Hardin. Photo © Cradoc Bagshaw.

---

23 In Roman Catholic theology, *limbo* is the waiting place between heaven and hell.
The word is also used to refer to a place or condition of oblivion or neglect.

Poniéndome un Nombre

Barbara Kingsolver

He protegido mi nombre como la gente
de otras épocas guardaba mechones de su cabello,
creyendo que el alma podía fugarse
si no tenían cuidado.

5 Conocí a mi primer antepasado.
Su leyenda. He tocado
sus botas y el mostacho, el abuelo
cuya familia era dueña de esclavos y algodón.
Se sentía inquieto en Virginia
10 entre sus hermanos aristócratas, hasta que
un otoño llameante robó un caballo,
y galopó sobre las montañas para desposar
a una cheroki de ojos en forma de hojas.
El robo fue perdonado, pero nunca
15 la sangre indígena. Perdió el nombre de familia
e inventó el mío, le dió frutos y semillas.
Nunca conocí a la abuela.
Su fotografía tiene delgadas trenzas color tinta
y ropas abotonadas, y ningún nombre por el cual se le conociera.

20 Podría deshacerme de mi nombre en la mitad de la vida,
la cosa más común, y desaparecería
junto con la niñez y las abuelas muertas
hacia ese limbo creado para los nombres de soltera fuera de circulación.

Pero se inquietaría allí.
25 Lo sé. Cabalgaría sobre montañas con humo de hojas
para robar caballos.

Responding to Literature

Personal Response

What does this poem make you wonder about?

ANALYZING LITERATURE

RECALL AND INTERPRET

1. To what does the speaker compare her act of keeping her name in the first sentence of the poem? What does this comparison tell you about how the speaker regards her name?
2. What **legend** (see page R9) about her ancestor does the speaker recall? What does this legend reveal about the speaker's name? How do you think the speaker feels about her ancestor?
3. What does the speaker know about her grandmother's name? How do you think the speaker feels about it?
4. What is the "ordinary thing" to which the speaker refers in line 21? What does she say would happen if she did that "ordinary thing"? In your opinion, what is the meaning of the last sentence?

EVALUATE AND CONNECT

5. Theme Connections   How do you think the speaker of this poem would respond to the idea of immigrants changing their names? In your answer, consider the theme title, "Variety Is Richness."
6. Do you find the legend of the speaker's ancestor believable? Support your opinion with evidence from the poem.
7. Kingsolver wrote this poem in both English and Spanish. What reasons might she have had for doing this? Explain.
8. Look back at the list you made for the Focus Activity on page 1189. Has reading this poem changed your feelings about the possibility of changing your name? Explain.

(see page R9) ... Focus Activity on page 1189.

> ### Literary ELEMENTS
>
> **Personification**
>
> **Personification** is a figure of speech in which an animal, an object, a force of nature, or an idea is given human qualities or characteristics. In "Naming Myself," Barbara Kingsolver personifies the name of the speaker. For example, the speaker says that if she were to shed her name, "it would flee."
>
> 1. List three verbs, other than *flee*, that signal personification of the speaker's name.
> 2. Find another abstract idea that is personified in this poem.
> 3. In your opinion, what does the use of personification add to this poem?
>
> ● See **Literary Terms Handbook,** p. R11.

EXTENDING YOUR RESPONSE

Literature Groups

What's in a Name?   In your group, discuss the following questions: What can you tell about the personality of the speaker from this poem? What can you tell about the personalities of her grandfather and grandmother? Why do you think Kingsolver reveals what she does about each character? Why might she refer to her grandfather as her "first ancestor"? Share your conclusions with the class.

Creative Writing

Write a Legend   What stories have you heard about your ancestors? Which stories strike you as daring, humorous, frightening, or courageous? Turn a family story you've heard into a legend, using poetry or prose. Use Kingsolver's poem as a model.

📖 **Save your work for your portfolio.**

Grammar Link

Avoiding Misplaced and Dangling Modifiers

In a sentence, the position of a modifier determines what it modifies. For example, Barbara Kingsolver uses modifiers clearly and effectively when she says of her grandfather:

> one peppered, flaming autumn he stole a horse,
> rode over the mountains to marry
> a leaf-eyed Cherokee.

Some writers, however, are not so clear in their use of modifiers.

- A **misplaced modifier** seems to modify the wrong word or more than one word in a sentence.
- A **dangling modifier** does not seem to modify *any* word in the sentence. Such a modifier "dangles," attaching itself to nothing.

Correcting misplaced or dangling modifiers is easy if you think about what you are saying.

Problem 1 A misplaced modifier
Growing from memories of her heritage, the writer created her poems.

   Solution   Move the misplaced word or phrase as close as possible to the word it modifies. In some cases, this will require creating a subordinate clause, as in this example.
The writer created poems that grew from memories of her heritage.

Problem 2 A dangling modifier
After learning about my ancestors, the past began to seem valuable.

   Solution   Supply a word or phrase that the modifier can reasonably modify.
After learning about my ancestors, I began to value the past.

- For more on similar usage problems, see **Language Handbook,** pp. R28–R29.

EXERCISES

Rewrite these sentences, correcting any errors in modifiers. At least one sentence is correct.

1. After an English teacher encouraged her, writing became more important.

2. Finally written and edited, Kingsolver proudly reviewed her poem.

3. As a child, Kingsolver wrote stories and essays.

4. The poet discovered the works of Virginia Woolf when she was quite young.

5. Having gotten quite tired, the poem became difficult to complete.

Technology Skills

Word Processing: Publishing a Newsletter

Newsletters are publications that organizations use to inform and influence their target audiences. Schools and clubs publish newsletters to keep students and parents informed. Newsletters not only provide key facts and ideas in short, engaging articles and sidebars (the Technology Tip on this page is a sidebar), but also highlight them with such eye-catching visual elements as graphs, charts, or photographs.

Navigating the Keyboard and the Toolbar

Review these features on your keyboard and in the toolbar of your software. If you have trouble finding any of the keys or icons, click on the **Help** feature and find the topic in the index.

TERMS USED IN PRODUCING NEWSLETTERS AND BROCHURES	
Document builder	Some word processors include step-by-step guides to creating different kinds of documents.
Template	Some word processing programs include a style guide, or template, for newsletters and brochures.
Column	A document arranged in columns helps readers to move through articles quickly.
Heading	A heading is a line or two of text that appears above an article or section of an article. The type of a heading is usually larger and bolder than that of the body text.
Text box	A text box is an area of text that is smaller than the page and can be positioned anywhere upon it. Text boxes can be linked so that the text in one box flows into another.

Creating a Newsletter

Following the suggestions indicated on the sample newsletter on the next page, create a class newsletter to be distributed to your families that summarizes and promotes discussions and activities related specifically to your class. Make sure to list the names of people responsible for production, such as the editors, publishers, writers, artists, and photographers. This list is often found on page two. To organize your newsletter better, include a table of contents somewhere on page one.

TECHNOLOGY TIP

Text boxes must be empty before you link them. If you have selected **Create Text Box Link** but have not created another box to link to, press Esc to cancel.

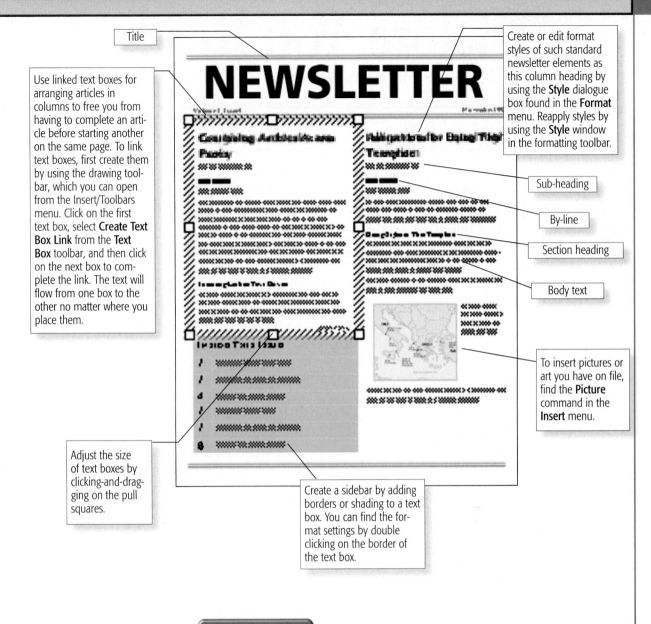

Title

Use linked text boxes for arranging articles in columns to free you from having to complete an article before starting another on the same page. To link text boxes, first create them by using the drawing toolbar, which you can open from the Insert/Toolbars menu. Click on the first text box, select **Create Text Box Link** from the **Text Box** toolbar, and then click on the next box to complete the link. The text will flow from one box to the other no matter where you place them.

Create or edit format styles of such standard newsletter elements as this column heading by using the **Style** dialogue box found in the **Format** menu. Reapply styles by using the **Style** window in the formatting toolbar.

Sub-heading

By-line

Section heading

Body text

NEWSLETTER

To insert pictures or art you have on file, find the **Picture** command in the **Insert** menu.

Adjust the size of text boxes by clicking-and-dragging on the pull squares.

Create a sidebar by adding borders or shading to a text box. You can find the format settings by double clicking on the border of the text box.

ACTIVITIES

1. Before opening a blank document on which to create a newsletter, check the **New** dialogue box under **File** to see if there is a newsletter template or builder (sometimes called a "wizard"). If your word processor includes one, access it to experiment with different formats for your class newsletter. Discuss with your classmates what formats work better for your purposes.

2. Write a one-page newsletter based on one of the short stories or nonfiction pieces in this book. For example, you could create a newsletter that the main character of Donald Barthelme's story "Game" might write.

3. Ask your history teacher if you can create a newsletter that covers a historical period you have studied.

Before You Read

A Poet's Job and *Emily Dickinson*

Meet Alma Luz Villanueva

❝Writing takes all your courage—to stand by your work and see it through to publication—courage and luck (and discipline, discipline, discipline).❞

—*Villanueva*

In her work as a poet and writer of fiction, Alma Luz Villanueva (vē′ yä nwä′ vä) expresses the personal and the public aspects of life with vivid images and sensory impressions. "[T]he paradox, the mystery of writing," she says, "[is] that when we touch the most personal, the most hidden within ourselves, we touch the other, the outer, the universal."

Villanueva won the American Book Award in 1989 for her novel *The Ultraviolet Sky*, and her work is found in many anthologies. In addition, the poet has read her own work for both audio and video performances.

Alma Luz Villanueva was born in 1944.

Meet Lucha Corpi

❝Lucha Corpi . . . is one of the most fully bilingual Hispanic writers in history.❞

—*Nicolás Kanellos*

Lucha Corpi writes about the places she knows: the sunny Mexican towns where she was born and spent her childhood, and California, where she has lived since the age of nineteen. She is a poet and author of essays, children's books, and an award-winning mystery. Corpi earned degrees from the University of California at Berkeley and San Francisco State University, and she teaches English for speakers of other languages. Like many Latina writers, Corpi is bilingual, writing both in English and in Spanish. "Emily Dickinson" was published in Corpi's collection *Palabras de mediodía (Noon Words)*.

Lucha Corpi was born in 1945.

FOCUS ACTIVITY

What does a poet really do as he or she writes a poem?

FREEWRITE Spend five minutes freewriting a response to this question.

SETTING A PURPOSE Read to learn how two poets describe what they do.

BACKGROUND

Poetry and Myth

In "A Poet's Job," Villanueva discusses **myth**—stories that try to explain the nature of the universe or the values of a society. Many cultures have used myths to explore unanswered questions about life. Myths help members of a culture ponder such age-old questions as, "Who am I?" and "How should I live my life?"

Emily Dickinson

The title of Corpi's poem refers to American poet Emily Dickinson (1830–1886). Dickinson was a poet far ahead of her time, a poet of great awareness and originality, who could describe an everyday occurrence in a way that made it seem miraculous. To learn more about Dickinson and her poetry, see pages 423–439.

A Poet's Job

Alma Luz Villanueva

A poet's job
is to see
the contours of the
world and make
5   a myth to share
for others to see
    to make a reality;
a point from where the
world spins—
10   and if stubborn and persistent enough,
   the point from where the
    universe whorls:°
right here.

---

12 *Whorls* means "spins," "spirals," or "whirls."

Emily Dickinson

Lucha Corpi ~
Translated by Catherine Rodríguez-Nieto

Like you, I belong to yesterday,
to the bays where
day is anchored to
wait for its hour.

5   Like me, you belong to today,
the progression of that hour
when what is unborn
begins to throb.

We are cultivators° of
10   the unsayable, weavers
of singulars,° migrant
workers in search of
floating gardens° as yet
unsown, as yet unharvested.

---

9 *Cultivator* means "grower" or "farmer."
11 Here, *singulars* are one-of-a-kind creations.
13 The speaker may be referring to the *floating gardens* of
Xochimilco (sō′ chi mēl′ kō) in Mexico City.

Responding to Literature

Personal Response

Which poem made the stronger impression on you? Why?

ANALYZING LITERATURE

A Poet's Job

RECALL AND INTERPRET

1. What does the speaker say a poet should see and do? What do you think this means?
2. In lines 7–9, what does the speaker suggest should become of the myth a poet creates? In your opinion, who or what must be "stubborn and persistent?" Why?
3. Where is the point from which the "world spins" and the "universe whorls"? What does this tell you about the speaker's ideas about the role of poetry and the job of the poet?

EVALUATE AND CONNECT

4. How do the ideas in this poem—and your own thinking in the Focus Activity on page 1196—contribute to your understanding of poets and their work?

Emily Dickinson

RECALL AND INTERPRET

5. What similarity to Emily Dickinson does the speaker mention in the first stanza? in the second?
6. In your opinion, what do the references to time convey in each of the first two stanzas? What do these references tell you about the speaker's view of what a poet does?
7. What **metaphors** does the speaker use to characterize herself and Dickinson in the last stanza? What more do these metaphors tell you about the speaker's ideas of what a poet does? (See Literary Terms Handbook, page R9.)

EVALUATE AND CONNECT

8. Why do you think the poet created a contrast between the first two stanzas? In what ways does this contrast help convey the poem's central message?

EXTENDING YOUR RESPONSE

Literature Groups

What Is a Poet?   With your group, complete this sentence: *A poet is* _____ . Use images and details from both poems to create a definition on which you all agree. Consider the work needed to create a poem, as well as the impact of a poem on its readers and on society. Then share your definition with the class.

Internet Connection

Star Search   Search the Internet for poems written by students. Print out or copy down one poem that you think is especially good. Then analyze how well you think the poet fulfills Villanueva's and Corpi's ideas of what a poet should do or what a poet is.

📖 **Save your work for your portfolio.**

Writing Workshop

Expository Writing: Research Report

By nature, human beings are curious, constantly asking "why?" and searching for answers. Long before there was a written language, folktales attempted to explain how the world works. Today, scientists, artists, writers, and other thinkers continue to raise questions, research ideas, and provide explanations about various aspects of life.

In this workshop, you will use information from several sources to write a research report about a topic that inspires your curiosity.

● As you write your research report, refer to the **Writing Handbook,** pp. R68–R75.

The Writing Process

PREWRITING

PREWRITING TIP

Don't eliminate possible topics just because they've been done before. Try looking at a familiar topic from a fresh new angle.

Explore ideas

A research report is a thoroughly investigated and documented response to a significant question. Since you'll be spending days or even weeks researching and writing about the question, it's important that you choose a topic that interests you. To find such a topic, think about books, documentaries, or articles that have inspired your curiosity. As you look for ideas, generate questions you might research. For example, after skimming the literature in this theme, you might ask questions like these.

● From reading "Game," you might ask, "What were the causes of the cold war?" "What are some of the psychological effects of the cold war?"
● After reading "For Georgia O'Keeffe," you might want to find out, "What kind of artwork did O'Keeffe create?" "How did she become an artist?"
● Based on "Salvador Late or Early," you might want to know how poverty is defined in the United States. "How extensive is poverty?" "What are the effects on young children of living in poverty?" "What measures have been taken by government and by private organizations to help people escape from poverty?"

Focus your topic

Once you've chosen a general topic, generate several research questions to guide your research. As you find answers to your questions you will get a feel for your subject's scope. Is there enough information available for you to consult a variety of sources? Is there so much information that you will be forced to make generalizations? Expand or narrow your topic until you feel you can write a specific, detailed report on it.

Consider your audience

You may write for your teacher and classmates, or you might look for a wider audience in your community. Just as with any other kind of writing, what you say and how you say it will be shaped by the interests and knowledge of your audience. What do they already know? What else do they need to know? What will capture their interest?

Consider your purpose

Your purpose is to inform others about your topic by supporting your main points with well-documented facts, statistics, and opinions.

Gather and evaluate sources

Using library catalogue systems, the Internet, and general reference books, look for sources relevant to your topic. Research the larger context of your topic—what historical events have influenced it, what other issues relate to it—as well as its specific aspects.

Keep track of all the sources you use on bibliography cards. Evaluate the credibility of your sources and make sure they are not outdated, biased, or ill informed.

Take notes

As they look through sources, many researchers note important ideas, facts, and quotes on index cards. No matter where you record your notes, you might find these techniques helpful:

- **Quote**   Record direct quotations exactly as they appear, including punctuation.
- **Paraphrase**   Restate someone else's original idea in your own words, giving credit to the author whose idea it is.
- **Summarize**   Condense information to its key points and most important details.

Make a plan

Write a *thesis statement*—a sentence that states the central idea guiding your report. Then use your notes to make an outline, including only the information that is relevant to your thesis.

STUDENT MODEL

THESIS STATEMENT

Although some people worry that Standard American English is threatened, it never really existed in the first place.

Bibliography Card

3

Franklin, Victoria and Robert Rodman.
An Introduction to Language.
Fort Worth: Harcourt Brace College Publishers, 1993.

Detroit Public Library   P 121.F75

Note Card

3

Standard American English—what is it?
Doesn't exist—just an ideal. No one's defined it, they don't know what it is. No agreement among linguists.

p. 284

DRAFTING

Begin your draft

Start to write, using your outline and note cards. Your completed report will need an introduction and a conclusion, as well as body paragraphs, but start with the section that will be easiest.

Think while you draft

Writing a report involves more than just reporting. As you cover each point on your outline or note cards, consider how it relates to other points and to your thesis statement. Explain those relationships to your reader. Think about ideas, think about connections, think about order, but do not think too much about exact words. You will revise for style later.

STUDENT MODEL

> People speak *about* Standard English, but no one really knows what it is. Even linguists who care about the notion have never managed to define it. (Fromkin and Rodman 284)

REVISING

Evaluate your report

Put your report aside for a while. When you read it over, use the **Questions for Revising** to help you identify places that need work. Then ask a classmate or family member to note any passages that seem unclear or irrelevant. Make the revisions that you think will improve your report. You may need to check facts or gather more information to support your points.

Cite your sources

A research report must include a works-cited page listing all sources used.

STUDENT MODEL

> Will the different kinds of English eventually turn into different languages? We should~~should~~ ^{be} not worry ^{~ing} that <s>about anything to do with the future of English, it should</s> ~the various strands of English will drift apart but <s>not be that the various strands</s> that they will grow indistinguishable. It seems to me that given that much of America watches the same TV programs, listens to the same songs, and reads the same magazines, we are probably closer to speaking one kind of English than ever before ⊙ ~as some fear? According to author Bill Bryson, "If" (Bryson, p. 245)

QUESTIONS FOR REVISING

☑ Does my introduction capture the reader's attention? Does it clearly state my thesis?

☑ Does each main point relate to my thesis? Does each detail elaborate on a main point?

☑ Where could I use transitions to help ideas flow more smoothly?

☑ Does my conclusion tie my main ideas together? Does it complement my introduction?

☑ Have I avoided *plagiarizing*—stating someone's words or ideas without giving credit?

EDITING/PROOFREADING

When your report is as effective as you can make it, review it for errors in grammar, usage, mechanics, and spelling, using the **Proofreading Checklist** on the inside back cover.

PROOFREADING TIP

Check your works-cited page against an appropriate model to make sure that you have formatted it properly.

Grammar Hint

Use the correct past or past-participle form of an irregular verb. Either memorize these forms or look them up.

INCORRECT: *Some children have* **growed** *up speaking English and Spanish.*

CORRECT: *Some children have* **grown** *up speaking English and Spanish.*

● For more on verb forms, see **Language Handbook,** pp. R27–R28.

STUDENT MODEL

> While one sister always ~~feeled~~ felt embarrassed by her father's English, the other had ~~choosed~~ chosen to write a story about it.

PUBLISHING/PRESENTING

Make a cover page that includes your name, the date, and the title of your report. Clip or bind the pages together and include your works-cited page at the end. If you decide to send your research report to a publication, an expert in the field, or a community group, be sure to include a neatly written letter explaining who you are, what the report is about, and how you came to write it.

TECHNOLOGY TIP

For the body of your paper, choose a font that is easy to read. Save decorative fonts for the title page, if you use them at all.

Reflecting

How did the process of writing a research report differ from the process you used for other kinds of writing? What different kinds of skills did you need to use? In your journal, jot down some instances when those skills might be useful. Then consider what you will do differently the next time you write a research report.

📔 **Save your work for your portfolio.**

Unit Wrap-Up

PERSONAL RESPONSE

1. Which selection in Unit 7 made the strongest impression on you? What created this impression— the events of a story, the language and imagery of a poem, or some other element?
2. Which selection or selections taught you the most about ways different generations relate to each other? about cultures other than your own?
3. What new ideas do you have about understanding our nation's diversity through different kinds of literature?
4. How did the poems in Unit 7 affect your ideas about poetry?

ANALYZING LITERATURE

A New Theme The selections in Unit 7 have been organized into two themes: "Generations" and "Variety Is Richness." Choose at least five of the selections from Unit 7 and organize them into a new theme of your own choosing. Write a few paragraphs explaining how the selections you have chosen relate to your new theme title.

EVALUATE AND SET GOALS

Evaluate

1. What was the most significant thing you contributed to the class as you studied this unit?
2. Which aspect of this unit was the most interesting to you?
   - What made it so interesting?
   - In what ways could you pursue this interest further?
3. How would you assess your work in this unit using the following scale? Give at least two reasons for your assessment.
   4 = outstanding   **3** = good   **2** = fair   **1** = weak
4. If you had another week to work on this unit, what would you hope to learn? What skills would you hope to strengthen?

Set Goals

1. What aspect of your work in this unit did you find the most difficult?
2. With your teacher, discuss ways to improve your performance in the future.
3. Write down several concrete goals that can help you improve. Then set checkpoints to monitor your future progress.

BUILD YOUR PORTFOLIO

Select From the writing you have done for this unit, choose two pieces to put into your portfolio. Use the following questions as guides when choosing:
- Which taught you the most?
- Which are you likely to share?
- Which was the most fun to do?
- Which was the most difficult to complete?

Reflect Include some explanatory notes with the portfolio pieces you have chosen. Use these questions to guide you:
- What are the piece's strengths and weaknesses?
- What skills did you practice and improve on by working on this piece?
- How would you revise the piece today to make it stronger?

Reading on Your Own

If you have enjoyed the literature in this unit, you might also be interested in the following books.

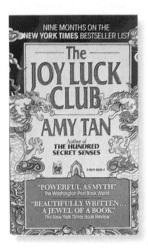

. . . And the Earth Did Not Devour Him

By Tomás Rivera This classic of Chicano literature tells the unique story of a young boy trying to recall the events of a "lost year," a year that has clearly been a difficult one for him.

The Joy Luck Club

by Amy Tan Spanning four decades, this novel traces the tragedies and joys of four Chinese women who immigrate to the United States and the complex lives of their American-born daughters.

The Piano Lesson

by August Wilson
Written by a Pulitzer Prize–winning author, this two-act play takes place in 1936, in the house of an African American family. Wilson tells the story of a brother and sister and their conflict over whether or not to sell a piano that has been in the family for three generations and is reminiscent of the family's painful history.

Eyes On the Prize: America's Civil Rights Years, 1954–1965

by Juan Williams This important and inspiring book about personal activism records eleven years that changed America's history. It includes the story of the Montgomery bus boycott and numerous other Civil Rights struggles.

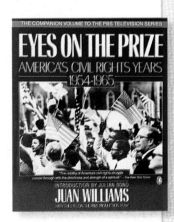

Standardized Test Practice

Directions: The following passage is an early draft of an essay. Some parts of the passage need to be rewritten.

Read the passage and answer the questions that follow. Some questions are about particular sentences or parts of sentences and ask you to improve sentence structure and word choice. Other questions refer to parts of the essay or the entire essay and ask you to consider organization and development. In making your decisions, follow the conventions of standard written English. Select the letter of the correct answer and write it on your paper.

(1) *In the last twenty years, automobiles in many forms have been increasingly necessary for modern life.* (2) *For example, today the compact car is regarded as indispensable for basic transportation for business people and homemakers.* (3) *The sedan, is something most executives, chauffeurs, and taxi drivers could not do without.* (4) *Moreover, many families use the mini-van to transport baseball teams to games, to travel on a vacation, and to help move their children to college.* (5) *Despite our obvious reliance on cars, some people do not want to buy new cars with advanced technology in them.* (6) *They fear that because the new automobiles have computers that they will take control over people and the road.* (7) *Because of this fear, cars that have computers that diagnose problems and control safety devices are not selling.* (8) *This is unfortunate.* (9) *The technology that is being developed for automobiles performs many important functions, and could do even more.* (10) *What would have happened if people had been afraid to buy the very first car, and it had been taken off the market?* (11) *Not only would the cost of transportation be greater, and many trips would require more time than before to make.* (12) *Further, major industries would never have been able to grow without trucks and other larger versions of the automobile.* (13) *Cars have become an essential part of almost everyone's lives.* (14) *To those of you who are afraid, we should remember that our new, high-tech cars are simply advanced model Ts!*

1. Which of the following would be the most suitable sentence to insert immediately after sentence 1?
   (A) The race is on to produce the "ultimate" car.
   (B) I have found the new automobiles somewhat difficult to learn to operate.
   (C) Many people are understandably intimidated by new technology.
   (D) They are now so common that they have a wide-ranging effect on daily life.
   (E) Motorcycles belong to the family of automobiles.

2. To best connect sentence 3 to the rest of the first paragraph, which is the best word or phrase to insert after "The sedan," in sentence 3 (shown below)?

   The sedan, is something most executives, chauffeurs, and taxi drivers could not do without.

   (A) surely,
   (B) however,
   (C) another form of automobile,
   (D) you see,
   (E) in contrast,

3. In context, sentence 8 could be made more precise by adding which of the following words after "*This*"?

   (A) technology
   (B) control
   (C) example
   (D) automobile
   (E) situation

4. The function of sentence 10 is to

   (A) set up a hypothetical condition
   (B) raise doubt in the reader's mind about the usefulness of automobiles
   (C) allow the writer to show modesty
   (D) contest a common claim about automobiles
   (E) show the writer's astonishment about the new automobiles

5. Which of the following is the best revision of the underlined portion of sentence 11 (reproduced below)?

   Not only would the cost of transportation be great, and many trips would require more time than before to make.

   (A) but so would the many trips require more time to make
   (B) and also many trips require more time to make
   (C) but they would require more time to make the trip
   (D) as well as to require more time for many trips to be made
   (E) but many trips would require more time to make, as well.

6. Which of the following versions of the underlined portion of sentence 14 (reproduced below) best suits the context?

   To those of you who are afraid, we should remember that our new, high-tech cars are simply advanced model Ts!

   (A) (As it is now)
   (B) You who are fearing it should remember that our new, high-tech cars
   (C) But remember, you may be afraid that our new, high-tech cars
   (D) Those who are fearful should remember that our new, high-tech cars
   (E) What we fear about the new, high-tech cars is that we see that they

Reference Section

Literary Terms Handbook

A

Abstract language   Language that expresses an idea or intangible reality, as opposed to a specific object or occurrence or a concrete reality. The Declaration of Independence uses such abstract language as *safety, happiness, prudence,* and *laws of nature.*

> See also CONCRETE LANGUAGE.

Act   A major unit of a **drama,** or play. Many modern dramas have two or three acts. A short drama may have only one act. Acts may comprise one or more scenes.

> See page 908.
> See also DRAMA, SCENE.

Allegory   A narrative work of fiction or drama in which the elements—characters, settings, and plot—work together to teach a moral lesson. Frequently, this involves using things, persons, and settings as symbols. Nathaniel Hawthorne sometimes used allegorical techniques—for example, in "The Minister's Black Veil."

> See also SYMBOL.

Alliteration   The repetition of similar sounds, most often consonant sounds, at the beginnings of words. For example, James Weldon Johnson uses alliteration in the following line from "My City":

But, ah! Manhattan's sights and sounds, her smells

> See pages 383, 399, and 845.
> See also SOUND DEVICES.

Allusion   A reference in a work of literature to a character, a place, or a situation from history or from music, art, or another work of literature. For example, in "A Narrative of the Captivity and Restoration of Mrs. Mary Rowlandson," Rowlandson makes a number of allusions to the Bible.

> See page 609.

Ambiguity   The expression in a single term or passage of more than one meaning. The richness of literary language lies in its ability to evoke multiple layers of meaning. The title of Richard Wilbur's poem "The Beautiful Changes" is intentionally ambiguous.

Analogy   A comparison to show similarities between two things that are otherwise dissimilar. Writers often use an analogy to explain something unfamiliar by comparing it to something familiar.

> See page 91.
> See also METAPHOR, SIMILE.

Anecdote   A brief account of an interesting event. An anecdote may be used to raise or illustrate a point, to explain an idea, or to describe a personality.

> See page 901.

Antagonist   A person or a force that opposes the protagonist, or central character, in a story or drama. The reader is generally meant not to sympathize with the antagonist. For example, in "The Open Boat," by Stephen Crane, the sea is the antagonist.

> See pages 472 and 1099.
> See also CONFLICT, PROTAGONIST.

Aphorism   A short, pointed statement that expresses a wise or clever observation about human experience. Américo Paredes's "Dichos" is composed largely of aphorisms.

> See page 136.
> See also EPIGRAM.

Apostrophe   A figure of speech in which a speaker addresses an inanimate object, an idea, or an absent person. Ezra Pound's poem "A Pact," in which he addresses the long-dead Walt Whitman, is an example of apostrophe.

> See pages 390 and 673.
> See also PERSONIFICATION.

Argument   Writing in which reason is used to influence ideas or actions. An argument is a form of persuasion. While some persuasive writing depends on emotion, an argument uses logic, reasons, and evidence.

See pages 262 and 521.
See also PERSUASION.

Aside   In a play, a comment made by a character that is heard by the audience or another character but is not heard by other characters on stage. The speaker turns to one side, or "aside," away from the main action on stage. Asides, which are rare in modern drama, reveal what a character is thinking or feeling.

Assonance   The repetition of similar vowel sounds, especially in a line of poetry. For example, the *o* sound is repeated in this line from an Emily Dickinson poem:

The Soul selects her own Society . . .

See pages 399 and 1155.
See also SOUND DEVICES.

Atmosphere   The dominant mood or feeling conveyed by a piece of writing.

See also MOOD.

Author's note   A note accompanying a piece of writing and containing explanatory information. Author's notes usually include helpful but nonessential information. Randall Jarrell provides an author's note along with his poem "The Death of the Ball Turret Gunner."

See page 858.

Author's purpose   An author's intent in writing a piece of literature. Authors typically write to accomplish one or more of the following purposes: to persuade, to inform, to explain, to entertain, or to describe.

See pages 150 and 611.
See also DICTION, STYLE, THEME.

Autobiography   The story of a person's life written by that person. An example of this genre is *The Autobiography of Benjamin Franklin*.

See page 335.
See also BIOGRAPHY, MEMOIR, NONFICTION.

B

Ballad   A narrative song or poem. **Folk ballads,** which usually recount an exciting or dramatic episode, were passed down by word of mouth for generations before being written down. **Literary ballads** are written in imitation of folk ballads.

See also FOLKLORE, NARRATIVE POETRY, ORAL TRADITION.

Bias   The author's personal inclination toward a certain opinion or position on a topic.

See page 67.
See also NONFICTION.

Biography   The account of a person's life written by someone other than the subject.

See pages 26–27.
See also AUTOBIOGRAPHY, MEMOIR, NONFICTION.

Blank verse   Poetry written in unrhymed **iambic pentameter.** Each line has five pairs of syllables, with each pair made up of an unstressed syllable followed by a stressed syllable. Because it may attempt to imitate spoken English, every line need not be perfectly regular. Robert Frost wrote "Birches" in blank verse:

When I see birches bend to left and right

See page 218.
See also IAMBIC PENTAMETER, SCANSION.

C

Caesura   A pause within a line of poetry. A caesura is used to produce variations in rhythm and to draw attention to certain words. The following lines from "The Tide Rises, the Tide Falls," by Henry Wadsworth Longfellow, have caesuras after the words *rises* and *darkens.*

The tide rises, the tide falls,

The twilight darkens, the curlew calls.

See page 1144.
See also RHYTHM.

Catalog The listing of images, details, people, or events in a piece of writing. In *Song of Myself,* for example, Walt Whitman catalogs different kinds of workers from all over the United States.

> See page 1186.

Character An individual in a literary work. A **main character** is central to the story and is typically characterized fully. A **minor character** displays few personality traits and is used to help develop the story. Characters who show varied and sometimes contradictory traits, such as Michael Curly in F. Scott Fitzgerald's "The Bridal Party," are called **round.** Characters who reveal only one personality trait are called **flat.** A **stereotype,** or stock character of a familiar type, is typically flat. A **dynamic character** grows and changes during the story, as does the captain in Stephen Crane's "The Open Boat." A **static character** remains basically the same throughout the story.

> See pages 472 and 485.
> See also CHARACTERIZATION, STEREOTYPE.

Characterization The methods a writer uses to reveal the personality of a character. In **direct characterization** the writer makes explicit statements about a character. In **indirect characterization** the writer reveals a character through the character's words and actions and through what other characters think and say about that character.

> See pages 666, 840, and 1033.
> See also CHARACTER.

Classicism A style that reflects the principles and concerns of the art and literature of ancient Greece and Rome. Typically, a classical style displays simple, harmonious purity of form.

Climax The point of greatest emotional intensity, interest, or suspense in a narrative. Usually the climax comes at the turning point in a story or drama, the point just before the resolution of the conflict, as in Ernest Hemingway's "In Another Country," when the bereft major loses his temper with the narrator.

> See pages 473, 492, and 979.
> See also CONFLICT, DÉNOUEMENT, PLOT, RESOLUTION.

Colloquial language Informal speech that people use in everyday conversation.

> See page 469.
> See also DIALECT, VERNACULAR.

Comedy A type of drama that often has a happy ending and is humorous. A **heroic comedy** focuses on the exploits of a larger-than-life hero.

> See also DRAMA, FARCE, HUMOR, PARODY, SATIRE, WIT.

Comic relief A humorous episode inserted into a serious drama, customarily used to break the tension yet highlight the seriousness of the story.

Conceit An elaborate extended metaphor that dominates a passage or an entire poem. The conceit makes an analogy between some object from nature or everyday life and the subject or theme of the poem.

> See page 1166.
> See also EXTENDED METAPHOR, IMAGERY.

Concrete language Clear language about actual things or occurrences. Words like *dog* and *sky* are concrete, while words like *truth* and *evil* are not concrete but abstract.

> See also ABSTRACT LANGUAGE.

Confessional poetry A movement in poetry begun in the 1950s in which the poet writes about his or her own personal experiences. These writers described their problems with mental illness, alcohol abuse, and troubled relationships in an open and direct style. Poets such as Robert Lowell, Anne Sexton, and Sylvia Plath became known as members of the **Confessional school** of poets.

> See page 818.

Conflict The central struggle between two opposing forces in a story or drama. An **external conflict** exists when a character struggles against some outside force, such as another person, nature, society, or fate. An **internal conflict** is a struggle between two opposing thoughts or desires within the mind of a character.

> See pages 473 and 788.
> See also ANTAGONIST, PLOT, PROTAGONIST.

Connotation   The suggested or implied meanings associated with a word beyond its dictionary definition, or **denotation.** A word can have a positive, negative, or neutral connotation.

> See pages 83 and 173.
> See also AMBIGUITY, DENOTATION, FIGURATIVE LANGUAGE.

Consonance   The repetition of similar consonant sounds typically within or at the ends of words, as in the succession of echoing *d* sounds in this line from "Naming Myself," by Barbara Kingsolver:

I could shed my name in the middle of life,

> See pages 399 and 1155.
> See also SOUND DEVICES.

Couplet   Two consecutive, paired lines of poetry, usually rhymed, and usually forming a stanza. For example, the following lines from "Recuerdo," by Edna St. Vincent Millay, make up a couplet:

We were very tired, we were very merry—
We had gone back and forth all night on the ferry.

> See page 180.
> See also HEROIC COUPLET, RHYME, SONNET, STANZA.

Crisis   In a narrative, a moment of high tension that requires a decision. In Bret Harte's "The Outcasts of Poker Flat," the crisis comes when the "outcasts" are stranded in a cabin during a blizzard and begin to run out of food.

> See page 1070.
> See also CLIMAX, RISING ACTION.

D

Denotation   The literal, or dictionary, meaning of a word. In his "Author's Note" to "The Death of the Ball Turret Gunner," Randall Jarrell uses many words that are intended simply to signify their literal, or exact, meanings.

"A ball turret was a plexiglass sphere set into the belly of a B-17 or B-24 . . ."

See also CONNOTATION, LITERAL LANGUAGE.

Dénouement   The outcome, or resolution, of the plot.

> See page 473.
> See also CLIMAX, CONFLICT, FALLING ACTION, PLOT, RESOLUTION.

Description   A detailed portrayal of a person, a place, an object, or an event. Description appeals to the senses, helping the reader see, hear, smell, taste, or feel what the writer is describing. The following passage from Eudora Welty's "A Worn Path" is an example of deft description:

Her eyes were blue with age. Her skin had a pattern all its own of numberless branching wrinkles and as though a whole little tree stood in the middle of her forehead. . . .

> See pages 18 and 186.
> See also FIGURATIVE LANGUAGE, SENSORY DETAILS.

Dialect   A variation of a language spoken by a particular group, often within a particular region and time. Dialects may differ from the standard form of a language in vocabulary, pronunciation, or grammatical form. Mark Twain's story "The Celebrated Jumping Frog of Calaveras County" contains the following example of dialect:

Well, thish-yer Smiley had a yaller one-eyed cow that didn't have no tail, only jest a short stump like a bannanner . . .

> See page 888.
> See also COLLOQUIAL LANGUAGE, LOCAL COLOR, REGIONALISM, VERNACULAR.

Dialogue   Conversation between characters in a literary work. These lines from "Rain Music," by Longhang Nguyen, provide an example of dialogue:

"Will your daughter become a surgeon?" our relatives ask.
"It's possible," my father says, beaming.

> See pages 909 and 935.
> See also MONOLOGUE.

Diary   An individual's personal, daily record of impressions, events, or thoughts, written for the individual's personal use rather than for publication.

> See also JOURNAL.

Diction A writer's choice of words; an important element in the writer's "voice" or style. Skilled writers choose their words carefully to convey a particular tone and meaning. Ernest Hemingway, for example, was known for his spare, simple, sturdy diction, as exemplified in these lines from "In Another Country":

In the fall the war was always there, but we did not go to it any more. It was cold in the fall in Milan and the dark came very early.

> See pages 73, 365, and 1147.
> See also AUTHOR'S PURPOSE, STYLE, VOICE.

Drama A story intended to be performed before an audience by actors on a stage. The script of a dramatic work may include **stage directions** that explain how characters should look, speak, move, and behave. The script might also specify details of the setting and scenery, such as lighting, **props,** and sound effects. A drama may be divided into **acts,** which may also be broken up into **scenes,** indicating changes in location or the passage of time.

> See pages 908–909.
> See also COMEDY, TRAGEDY.

Dramatic monologue A form of dramatic poetry in which one speaker addresses a silent listener. Edgar Allan Poe's poem "To Helen," in which the speaker passionately addresses his beloved, is an example of a dramatic monologue.

> See page 550.
> See also DRAMATIC POETRY, MONOLOGUE.

Dramatic poetry Poetry in which characters are revealed through dialogue and monologue, as well as through description. Robert Frost's "The Death of the Hired Man" is an example of dramatic poetry.

> See page 709.
> See also DIALOGUE, DRAMATIC MONOLOGUE.

E

Elegy A poem mourning a death or other great loss. Walt Whitman's "Sight in Camp in the Daybreak Gray and Dim" is an elegy to soldiers killed in the Civil War.

Enjambment In poetry, the continuation of a sentence across a line break without a punctuated pause between lines. For example, the following lines from Robert Frost's "Stopping by Woods on a Snowy Evening" are enjambed:

My little horse must think it queer
To stop without a farmhouse near

> See page 649.
> See also RHYTHM.

Epic A long narrative poem that traces the adventures of a hero. Epics intertwine myths, legends, and history, reflecting the values of the societies in which they originate. Homer's *Iliad* and *Odyssey* are two famous epics.

> See also LEGEND, MYTH, ORAL TRADITION.

Epigram A short, witty poem; a saying. For example, much of Benjamin Franklin's *Poor Richard's Almanack* is made up of epigrams.

> See also APHORISM.

Epiphany The sudden intuitive recognition of the meaning or essence of something. At the end of "The Second Tree from the Corner," by E. B. White, the main character has an epiphany when he finally realizes what he wants from life.

Epithet An apt phrase, nickname, or adjective; in oral or written epics, a formalized nickname or adjective phrase used to identify or describe a recurring character, place, event, or object. For example, in his poem "Fiddler Jones," Edgar Lee Masters uses an epithet when he refers to "Red-headed Sammy."

Essay A short piece of nonfiction writing on any topic. The purpose of the essay is to communicate an idea or opinion. The **formal essay** is serious and impersonal. The **informal essay** entertains while it informs, usually in light, conversational style. A **personal essay** is an informal essay that makes personal references. Ralph Waldo Emerson's "Nature" is an example of a formal essay. Ralph Ellison's "February" is a personal essay.

> See pages 34, 152–153, and 848.
> See also NONFICTION.

Exaggeration. See HYPERBOLE.

Exemplum A brief story that illustrates a moral point by serving as an example.

> See also ANECDOTE, FABLE, PARABLE.

Exposition At the beginning of a story, novel, or other narrative, the part of the plot line that sets the scene by introducing the characters, setting, and situation. Exposition also refers to expository writing, a type of prose that informs and explains.

> See pages 143, 473, and 1042.
> See also PLOT.

Extended metaphor A metaphor that compares two unlike things in various ways throughout a paragraph, a stanza, or an entire piece of writing. For example, in *Song of Myself,* Walt Whitman answers the question "What is the grass?" with this extended metaphor:

I guess it must be the flag of my disposition, out
of a hopeful green stuff woven.

Or I guess it is the handkerchief of the Lord,
A scented gift and remembrancer designedly dropt,
Bearing the owner's name someway in the
corners, that we may see and remark, and say
Whose?

> See page 81.
> See also METAPHOR.

F

Fable A short, usually simple tale that teaches a moral and sometimes uses animal characters. Themes are usually stated explicitly.

> See also LEGEND, PARABLE, THEME.

Falling action In a narrative, the action that follows the **climax.**

> See page 473.
> See also CLIMAX, DÉNOUEMENT, PLOT, RESOLUTION.

Farce A type of comedy with ridiculous situations, characters, or events.

> See COMEDY, HUMOR, PARODY, SATIRE.

Fiction A narrative in which situations and characters are invented by the writer. Some aspects of a fictional work may be based on fact or experience. Fictional works include short stories, novels, and dramas.

> See pages 4–5.
> See also DRAMA, NONFICTION, NOVEL, SHORT STORY.

Figurative language Language used for descriptive effect, in order to convey ideas or emotions. Figurative expressions are not literally true but express some truth beyond the literal level. Figurative language is especially prominent in poetry. A **figure of speech** is a specific device or kind of figurative language such as metaphor, personification, simile, or symbol.

> See pages 248 and 399.
> See also CONNOTATION, IMAGERY, METAPHOR, PERSONIFICATION, SIMILE, SYMBOL.

Flashback An interruption in the chronological order of a narrative to show an event that happened earlier. A flashback gives readers information that may help explain the main events of the story. For example, in "An Occurrence at Owl Creek Bridge," Ambrose Bierce presents a flashback in the middle of the story.

> See pages 380 and 813.
> See also FLASH-FORWARD.

Flash-forward An interruption in the chronological sequence of a narrative to leap forward in time. Richard Wright uses this device in his autobiography, *Black Boy,* when he describes a visit to his father that occurs many years after the time of the story.

> See page 828.
> See also FLASHBACK.

Foil A minor character whose contrast with a main character highlights particular traits of the main character. The dog in Jack London's "To Build a Fire," for example, exhibits a caution and respect for the cold of the Yukon that the man obviously lacks.

> See page 872.
> See also ANTAGONIST, CHARACTER, CHARACTERIZATION, PROTAGONIST.

Folklore The traditional beliefs, customs, stories, songs, and dances of a culture. Folklore is passed down through oral tradition and is based in the concerns of ordinary people.

> See also BALLAD, EPIC, FOLKTALE, LEGEND,
> MYTH, ORAL TRADITION, TALL TALE.

Folktale   An anonymous traditional story passed down orally long before being written down. Folktales include animal stories, trickster stories, fairy tales, myths, legends, and tall tales.

> See also EPIC, FOLKLORE, LEGEND, MYTH,
> ORAL TRADITION, TALL TALE.

Foot   The basic unit in the measurement of a line of metrical poetry. A foot usually contains one stressed syllable (´) and one or more unstressed syllables (˘). The basic metric feet are the **anapest** (˘˘´), the **dactyl** (´˘˘), the **iamb** (˘´), the **spondee** (´´), and the **trochee** (´˘).

> See also METER, RHYTHM, SCANSION, STANZA.

Foreshadowing   The use of clues by the author to prepare readers for events that will happen later in a story. In "The Portrait," by Thomas Rivera, the salesman's demand for full cash payment foreshadows the fact that the transaction is a swindle.

> See page 353.
> See also PLOT, RISING ACTION, SUSPENSE.

Form   The structure of a poem. Many contemporary writers use loosely structured poetic forms instead of following traditional or formal patterns. These poets vary the lengths of lines and stanzas, relying on emphasis, rhythm, pattern, or the placement of words and phrases to convey meaning.

> See page 1170.
> See also RHYTHM, STANZA, STRUCTURE.

Frame story   A plot structure that includes the telling of one story within another story. The frame is the **outer** story, which usually precedes and follows the **inner,** more important story. For example, Mark Twain uses a frame in "The Celebrated Jumping Frog of Calaveras County."

Free verse   Poetry that has no fixed pattern of meter, rhyme, line length, or stanza arrangement. "Prayer to the Pacific," by Leslie Marmon Silko, is an example of free verse.

> See pages 416 and 1149.
> See also RHYTHM.

G–H

Genre   A category or type of literature. Examples of genres are poetry, drama, fiction, and nonfiction.

Haiku   A traditional Japanese form of poetry that has three lines and seventeen syllables. The first and third lines have five syllables each; the middle line has seven syllables. Usually about nature, a haiku presents striking imagery to evoke in the reader a variety of feelings and associations.

Hero   The chief character in a literary work, typically one whose admirable qualities or noble deeds arouse the admiration of the reader. Although the word *hero* is applied only to males in traditional usage—*heroine* being the term used for females—contemporary usage applies the term to either gender.

> See also EPIC, LEGEND, MYTH, PROTAGONIST,
> TALL TALE, TRAGEDY.

Heroic couplet   A pair of rhymed lines in iambic pentameter. For example, Anne Bradstreet uses the heroic couplet in "To My Dear and Loving Husband":

Ĭ príze / thў lóve / mŏre thán / whŏle mínes / ŏf góld
Ŏr áll / the rích / ĕs thát / the Eást / dŏth hóld

> See page 180.
> See also IAMBIC PENTAMETER, METER,
> RHYTHM.

Historical fiction   A story that sets fictional characters against a backdrop of history and contains many details about the period in which it is set.

> See pages 110–113.
> See also FICTION.

Historical narrative   A work of nonfiction that tells the story of important historical events or developments. In *La Relación*, Cabeza de Vaca provides a historical narrative of the experiences of a group of Spanish explorers.

> See page 166.

Humor   The quality of a literary work that makes the characters and their situations seem funny, amusing, or ludicrous. Mark Twain's story "The Celebrated Jumping Frog of Calaveras County" is told with humor.

> See also COMEDY, FARCE, PARODY, SATIRE, WIT.

Hyperbole   A figure of speech that uses exaggeration to express strong emotion, to make a point, or to evoke humor. For example, the expression "I'm so hungry I could eat a horse" is hyperbole.

> See page 158.
> See also FIGURATIVE LANGUAGE, UNDERSTATEMENT.

I

Iambic pentameter   A specific poetic meter in which each line is composed of five feet (**pentameter**), most of which are iambs.

> See page 218.
> See also BLANK VERSE, FOOT, HEROIC COUPLET, METER, RHYTHM, SCANSION.

Idiom   A saying or group of words that takes on special meaning, different from the usual meaning of the words that make it up. For example, "I'm leading a hand-to-mouth existence" really means "I don't have much money." Idioms add realism to the dialogue in a story and can expand characterization.

> See page 854.
> See also DIALECT.

Imagery   The "word pictures" that writers create to evoke an emotional response. In creating effective images, writers use **sensory details,** or descriptions that appeal to one or more of the five senses: sight, hearing, touch, taste, and smell. For example, in the following lines from "Snow," Julia Alvarez uses visual imagery to make a scene vivid to the reader.

All my life I had heard about the white crystals that fell out of American skies in the winter. From my desk I watched the fine powder dust the sidewalk and parked cars below.

> See pages 105, 399, and 1175.
> See also FIGURATIVE LANGUAGE, SENSORY DETAILS.

Imagist poetry   The works of a group of early twentieth-century poets who believed that the image was the essence of poetry, conveying a poem's meaning and emotion. The language of poetry, they believed, should be brief, clear, and concrete, and it should also be similar to spoken language. A classic Imagist poem is "In a Station of the Metro," by Ezra Pound.

> See pages 598 and 612.
> See also MODERNISM.

Internal rhyme   Rhyme that occurs within a single line of poetry. Poets use internal rhyme to convey meaning, to evoke mood, or simply to create a musical effect. For example, Edgar Allan Poe uses internal rhyme in the poem "The Raven":

Once upon a midnight <u>dreary</u>, while I pondered, weak and <u>weary</u>

> See page 1141.
> See also RHYME.

Inversion   Reversal of the usual word order in a prose sentence or line of poetry, for emphasis or variety. Writers use inversion to maintain rhyme scheme or meter, or to emphasize certain words.

> See page 76.

Irony   A contrast or discrepancy between appearance and reality. **Situational irony** exists when the actual outcome of a situation is the opposite of someone's expectations, as at the end of Kate Chopin's "The Story of an Hour," when the narrator's husband, thought to be dead, arrives at the front door. In **verbal irony,** a person says one thing and means another, as when someone says of a mean person, "Nice guy!" **Dramatic irony** occurs when the audience has important information that the characters do not know.

> See pages 228 and 1133.

J–L

Journal. A daily record of events kept by a participant in those events or a witness to them.

> See page 361.

Juxtaposition The placing of two or more distinct things side by side in order to contrast or compare them. It is commonly used to evoke an emotional response in the reader. For example, in her poem "Richness," Gabriela Mistral juxtaposes the images of a rose and a thorn.

> I have a faithful joy
> And a joy that is lost.
> One is like a rose,
> The other, a thorn.

> See page 601.

Legend A traditional story handed down from the past, based on actual people and events, and tending to become more exaggerated and fantastical over time. For example, "The Sky Tree," as retold by Joseph Bruchac, is a legend about how the earth came to be.

> See also FABLE, FOLKLORE, FOLKTALE, HERO, MYTH, ORAL TRADITION, TALL TALE.

Literal language Language that is simple, straightforward, and free of embellishment. It is the opposite of figurative language, which conveys ideas indirectly.

> See page 677.
> See also DENOTATION.

Local color The evocative portrayal of a region's distinctive ways of talking and behaving. Bret Harte's story "The Outcasts of Poker Flats" is classic for its use of local color.

> See pages 455, 475, and 730.
> See also DIALECT, REGIONALISM, VERNACULAR.

Lyric poetry Poetry that expresses a speaker's personal thoughts and feelings. Lyric poems are usually short and musical. Emily Dickinson's "This is my letter to the World" is an example of a lyric poem.

> See page 746.
> See also POETRY.

M

Magical realism A literary style in which the writer combines realistic events, settings, characters, dialogue, and other details with elements that are magical, supernatural, fantastic, or bizarre. For example, in "Nineteen Thirty-Seven," the narrator's suggestion that certain women could fly with "wings of flames" implies a magical or supernatural quality about these women.

> See page 1007.

Memoir An account of an event or period emphasizing the narrator's own experience of it. "Prime Time," by Henry Louis Gates Jr., is an example of a memoir.

> See page 1107.
> See also AUTOBIOGRAPHY, BIOGRAPHY.

Metaphor A figure of speech that compares or equates two seemingly unlike things. In contrast to a simile, a metaphor implies the comparison instead of stating it directly; hence there is no use of connectives such as *like* or *as*. For example, in her story "Rain Music," Longhang Nguyen writes of her sister and herself:

> She is the rose of the family and I am the green thorn.

> See pages 399 and 794.
> See also EXTENDED METAPHOR, FIGURATIVE LANGUAGE.

Meter A regular pattern of stressed (ˊ) and unstressed (˘) syllables that gives a line of poetry a more or less predictable rhythm. The basic unit of meter is the **foot.** The length of a metrical line can be expressed in terms of the number of feet it contains: a **dimeter** has two feet, a **trimeter** three, a **tetrameter** four, a **pentameter** five, a **hexameter** six, and a **heptameter** seven. The following lines from "Old Ironsides," by Oliver Wendell Holmes, show one line of iambic tetrameter and one line of iambic trimeter:

> Aȳ, teár hȇr táttȇred énsiȋgn dówn!

> Lóng hăs ĭt wa̍ved ŏn hĭgh

> See page 1163.
> See also FOOT, IAMBIC PENTAMETER, METER, SCANSION.

Metonymy The use of one word to stand for a related term. When Emerson writes that the "sun shines into a child's heart," he uses *heart* to stand for soul, or deep emotions.

> See page 241.
> See also FIGURATIVE LANGUAGE.

Modernism A term applied to a variety of twentieth-century artistic movements that shared a desire to break with the past. The poetry of T. S. Eliot and Ezra Pound, with its novel subject matter, diction, and metrical patterns, came to define Modernism. One example is Eliot's "The Love Song of J. Alfred Prufrock."

> See page 593.
> See also IMAGIST POETRY, STREAM OF
>   CONSCIOUSNESS, SYMBOLIST POETRY.

Monologue A long speech by a character in a literary work.

> See also DRAMATIC MONOLOGUE, SOLILOQUY.

Mood The emotional quality or atmosphere of a literary work. A writer's choice of language, subject matter, setting, and tone, as well as such sound devices as rhyme and rhythm, contribute to creating mood.

> See page 1065.
> See also ATMOSPHERE, SETTING, TONE.

Moral A practical lesson about right and wrong conduct.

Motif A significant phrase, image, description, idea, or other element repeated throughout a literary work and related to the theme.

> See page 1137.

Motivation The stated or implied reason or cause for a character's actions.

> See also PSYCHOLOGICAL REALISM.

Myth A traditional story that deals with goddesses, gods, heroes, and supernatural forces. A myth may explain a belief, a custom, or a force of nature. "How the World Was Made" is an origin myth.

> See pages 46, 1118, and 1196.
> See also EPIC, FOLKLORE, FOLKTALE, LEGEND,
>   ORAL TRADITION.

N

Narrative Writing or speech that tells a story. Narrative writing is used in novels, short stories, and poetry, and it may also be an important element in biographies, autobiographies, memoirs, and essays.

> See page 1060.
> See also NARRATIVE POETRY.

Narrative poetry Verse that tells a story. Narrative poetry includes narrative ballads and epics as well as shorter forms that are usually more selective and concentrated than are prose stories. "The Raven," by Edgar Allan Poe, for example, is a narrative poem.

> See also BALLAD, EPIC, NARRATIVE.

Narrator The person who tells a story. The narrator may be a character in the story, as in Ali Deb's "The Three-Piece Suit." At other times the narrator stands outside the story, as in F. Scott Fitzgerald's "The Bridal Party."

> See page 66.
> See also NARRATIVE, POINT OF VIEW.

Naturalism The literary movement characterized by a belief that people have little control over their own lives. Naturalist writers such as Frank Norris and Stephen Crane focus on the powerful economic, social, and environmental forces that shape the lives of individuals. In Crane's "The Open Boat," for example, four men face the power of the relentless sea.

> See pages 455 and 576.
> See also PSYCHOLOGICAL REALISM.

Nonfiction Factual prose writing about real people, places, and events. Written from either the first- or third-person point of view, works of **narrative nonfiction** tell a story and commonly have characteristics of fiction, such as setting, characters, theme, and plot. Biographies, autobiographies, memoirs, and narrative essays are types of narrative nonfiction. Works of **informative nonfiction** include essays, speeches, and articles that explain a topic or promote an opinion.

> See pages 26–27.
> See also AUTOBIOGRAPHY, BIOGRAPHY, ESSAY,
>   FICTION.

Novel   A book-length fictional prose narrative. The novel has more scope than a short story in its presentation of plot, character, setting, and theme.

> See also FICTION, SHORT STORY.

O

Octave.   The first eight lines of a **Petrarchan,** or **Italian, sonnet.**

> See page 721.
> See also SONNET.

Ode   An elaborate **lyric poem** expressed in a dignified and sincere way. An ode may be imaginative as well as intellectual.

> See page 791.
> See also LYRIC POETRY.

Onomatopoeia   The use of a word or phrase that actually imitates or suggests the sound of what it describes. The word *murmur,* used in "Speaking," by Simon J. Ortiz, is an example of onomatopoeia.

> See pages 399 and 1076.
> See also SOUND DEVICES.

Oral tradition   Literature that passes by word of mouth from one generation to the next.

> See page 46.
> See also BALLAD, EPIC, FOLKLORE, FOLKTALE,
>   LEGEND, MYTH, TALL TALE.

Oxymoron   A figure of speech in which opposite ideas are combined. Examples are "bright darkness," "wise fool," and "hateful love."

> See also FIGURATIVE LANGUAGE, PARADOX.

P–Q

Parable   A simple story pointing to a moral or religious lesson. Nathaniel Hawthorne's short story "The Minister's Black Veil" is a parable.

> See page 265.
> See also FABLE.

Paradox   A situation or statement that seems to be impossible or contradictory but is nevertheless true, literally or figuratively. For example, in "The Useless," Chuang Tzu concludes with a paradox.

> This shows
> The absolute necessity
> Of what has "no use."

> See also OXYMORON.

Parallelism   The use of a series of words, phrases, or sentences that have similar grammatical form. Parallelism emphasizes the items that are arranged in similar structures. For example, Walt Whitman uses parallelism in *Song of Myself*:

> What do you think has become of the young and
>   old men?
> And what do you think has become of the
>   women and children?

> See page 386.
> See also REPETITION.

Parody   A humorous imitation of another literary work. A parody imitates another work's plot, characters, or style, usually through exaggeration. See the parodies of Emily Dickinson's poetry on page 439.

> See also COMEDY, FARCE, HUMOR, SATIRE.

Personification   A figure of speech in which an animal, an object, a force of nature, or an idea is given human characteristics. The following lines from Emily Dickinson's "Because I could not stop for Death" exemplify personification:

> Because I could not stop for Death—
> He kindly stopped for me—

> See pages 399 and 1192.
> See also APOSTROPHE, FIGURATIVE
>   LANGUAGE.

Persuasion   Writing, usually nonfiction, that attempts to influence the reader to think or act in a particular way. Writers of persuasive works use appeals to logic or emotion, entreaty, salesmanship, and other techniques to sway their readers. Thomas Paine's "The Crisis" is an excellent example of persuasive writing.

> See pages 347, 348, and 392–396.
> See also ARGUMENT.

Petrarchan sonnet. See SONNET.

Plain style   A style of writing common among the Puritan settlers that focused on communicating ideas as clearly as possible. This marked a change from ornate style, the complicated and decorative style used by writers in Europe at that time. Colonial writers such as William Bradford thought of writing as a practical tool for spiritual self-examination and religious instruction, not as an opportunity to demonstrate cleverness.

See page 43.

Plot   The sequence of events in a drama or a narrative work of fiction. The plot begins with **exposition,** which introduces the story's characters, setting, and situation. The plot catches the reader's attention with a **narrative hook.** The **rising action** adds complications to the **conflicts,** or problems, leading to the **climax,** or the point of highest emotional pitch. The **falling action** is the logical result of the climax, and the **resolution,** or **dénouement,** presents the final outcome.

See pages 276, 473, 528, and 909.
See also CLIMAX, CONFLICT, DÉNOUEMENT, EXPOSITION, FALLING ACTION, RESOLUTION, RISING ACTION.

Poetic license   The freedom given to poets to ignore standard rules of grammar or proper diction in order to create a desired artistic effect.

See page 1121.

Poetry   A form of literary expression that differs from prose in emphasizing the line, rather than the sentence, as the unit of composition. Many other traditional characteristics of poetry apply to some poems but not to others. Some of these characteristics are emotional, imaginative language; use of **metaphor, simile,** and other **figures of speech;** division into **stanzas;** and the use of **rhyme** and regular patterns of **meter.**

See pages 20–21, 398–399, 440–443, and 762–765.

Point of view   The relationship of the narrator, or storyteller, to the story. In a story with **first-person point of view,** the story is told by one of the characters, referred to as "I." The reader sees everything through that character's eyes. In a story with a **third-person limited point of view,** the narrator reveals the thoughts, feelings, and observations of only one character, but refers to that character as "he" or "she." In a story with an **omniscient,** or **all-knowing point of view,** the narrator knows everything about the characters and events and may reveal details that the characters themselves could not reveal.

See pages 377, 472, 540, and 1051.
See also NARRATOR, SPEAKER.

Props   Theater term (a shortened form of *properties*) for objects and elements of the scenery of a stage play or movie set. For example in act 1 of *The Crucible,* Arthur Miller writes:

[*There is a narrow window at the left. Through its leaded panes the morning sunlight streams. A candle still burns near the bed, which is at the right.*]

See also DRAMA.

Prose   Written language that is not versified. Novels, short stories, and essays are usually written in prose.

Protagonist   The central character in a literary work, around whom the main conflict revolves. Generally, the audience is meant to sympathize with the protagonist.

See pages 472 and 1099.
See also ANTAGONIST, CONFLICT, HERO.

Psychological realism   An attempt to portray characters in an objective, plausible manner. Above all else, psychological realism insists that characters be clearly motivated; they should not act without apparent reason.

See also MOTIVATION, NATURALISM, REALISM.

Quatrain   A four-line poem or stanza.

See also COUPLET, OCTAVE, SESTET, STANZA.

R

Rationalism   A philosophy that values reason over feeling or imagination.

See also ROMANTICISM.

Realism   A literary manner that seeks to portray life as it really is lived. More specifically, Realism was a nineteenth-century literary movement that usually focused on everyday middle- or working-class conditions and characters, often with reformist intent.

> See page 323.
> See also NATURALISM, PSYCHOLOGICAL REALISM.

Refrain   A line or lines repeated regularly, usually in a poem or song. For example, the line "If you follow the drinking gourd" is a refrain in the song "Follow the Drinking Gourd."

> See page 341.
> See also REPETITION.

Regionalism   An emphasis on themes, characters, and settings from a particular geographical region. For example, much of the work of Mark Twain deals with life in Missouri and along the Mississippi River, where he passed his boyhood and youth.

> See also DIALECT, LOCAL COLOR, VERNACULAR.

Repetition   The recurrence of sounds, words, phrases, lines, or stanzas in a speech or piece of writing. Repetition increases the sense of unity in a work and can call attention to particular ideas.

> See pages 58 and 743.
> See also PARALLELISM, REFRAIN.

Resolution   The part of a plot that concludes the falling action by revealing or suggesting the outcome of the central conflict.

> See pages 473 and 492.
> See also CLIMAX, CONFLICT, DÉNOUEMENT, FALLING ACTION, PLOT.

Rhetorical question   A question to which no answer is expected. A rhetorical question is used to emphasize the obvious answer to what is asked. In his biography, Olaudah Equiano uses rhetorical questions to argue against slavery:

Why are parents to lose their children, brothers their sisters, or husbands their wives?

> See page 97.

Rhyme   The repetition of the same stressed vowel sounds and any succeeding sounds in two or more words. For example, *notation* rhymes with *vacation*. **End rhyme** occurs at the ends of lines of poetry. **Internal rhyme** occurs within a single line. **Slant rhyme** occurs when words include sounds that are similar but not identical. Slant rhyme typically involves some variation of **consonance** (the repetition of similar consonant sounds) or **assonance** (the repetition of similar vowel sounds).

> See pages 398, 438, and 1141.
> See also ASSONANCE, CONSONANCE, INTERNAL RHYME, RHYME SCHEME, SOUND DEVICES.

Rhyme scheme   The pattern that end rhymes form in a stanza or a poem. The rhyme scheme is designated by the assignment of a different letter of the alphabet to each new rhyme. For example, the rhyme scheme in Edgar Allan Poe's "To Helen" is:

Helen, thy beauty is to me	*a*
Like those Nicéan barks of yore,	*b*
That gently, o'er a perfumed sea,	*a*
The weary, way-worn wanderer bore	*b*
To his own native shore.	*b*

> See pages 398 and 702.
> See also RHYME.

Rhythm   The pattern of beats created by the arrangement of stressed and unstressed syllables, especially in poetry. Rhythm gives poetry a musical quality, can add emphasis to certain words, and may help convey the poem's meaning. Rhythm can be regular, with a predictable pattern or meter, or irregular. Notice how the rhythm of the first two lines of E. E. Cummings's "anyone lived in a pretty how town" gives a lilting quality to the poem.

Anyone lived in a pretty how town

(with up so floating many bells down)

> See pages 237, 398, and 644.
> See also IAMBIC PENTAMETER, METER.

Rising action   The part of a plot in which actions, complications, and plot twists lead up to the **climax** of a story.

> See pages 282 and 473.
> See also CLIMAX, CONFLICT, PLOT.

Romanticism An artistic movement that valued imagination and feeling over intellect and reason. Ralph Waldo Emerson, Henry David Thoreau, and Walt Whitman were heavily influenced by Romanticism.

See pages 125, 218, and 323.
See also RATIONALISM, TRANSCENDENTALISM.

Round character. See CHARACTER.

S

Sarcasm Satire or irony that often uses bitter and caustic language to point out shortcomings or flaws.

See page 1095.
See also IRONY, SATIRE.

Satire Literature that exposes to ridicule the vices or follies of people or societies. Donald Barthelme's story "Game" is an example of satire.

See also COMEDY, FARCE, HUMOR, PARODY,
SARCASM, WIT.

Scansion The analysis of the meter of a line of verse. To scan a line of poetry means to note the stressed and unstressed syllables and to divide the line into its feet, or rhythmical units. Stressed syllables are marked (´) and unstressed syllables (˘). Note the scansion of these lines from Claude McKay's "The Tropics in New York":

Bă-nán / ăs rípe / ănd gréen, / ănd gín / gĕr-róot,

Có-cŏa / ĭn póds / ănd áll / ĭgát / ŏr peárs,

See page 750.
See also FOOT, METER, RHYTHM.

Scene A subdivision of an act in a play. Typically, each scene takes place in a specific setting and time. A scene is shorter than or as long as an act.

See page 909.
See also ACT, DRAMA.

Science fiction Fiction that deals with the impact of science and technology—real or imagined—on society and on individuals. Sometimes occurring in the future, science fiction commonly portrays space travel, exploration of other planets, and possible future societies.

Screenplay The script of a film, which, in addition to dialogue and stage directions, usually contains detailed instructions about camera shots and angles.

See also STAGE DIRECTIONS.

Sensory details Evocative words or phrases that appeal to one or more of the five senses. "The Beautiful Changes," by Richard Wilbur, uses sensory details that appeal to the sense of sight.

See page 862.
See also IMAGERY.

Sestet A six-line poem or stanza.

See page 721.
See also SONNET.

Setting The time and place in which the events of a literary work occur. Setting includes not only the physical surroundings, but also the ideas, customs, values, and beliefs of a particular time and place. The setting often helps create an atmosphere, or mood.

See pages 472, 510, and 908.
See also ATMOSPHERE, MOOD.

Shakespearean sonnet. See SONNET.

Short story A brief fictional narrative in prose that generally includes the following major elements: setting, characters, plot, point of view, and theme.

See pages 276 and 472–473.
See also CHARACTER, PLOT, POINT OF VIEW,
SETTING, THEME.

Simile A figure of speech using a word or phrase such as *like* or *as* to compare seemingly unlike things. For example, this famous simile appears at the opening of T. S. Eliot's "The Love Song of J. Alfred Prufrock":

Let us go then, you and I,
When the evening is spread out against the sky
Like a patient etherised upon a table. . . .

See pages 25, 399, and 637.
See also ANALOGY, FIGURATIVE LANGUAGE,
METAPHOR.

Slave narrative An autobiographical account of the life of a former enslaved person. These documents helped expose the cruelty and inhumanity of slavery.

See page 195.
See also AUTOBIOGRAPHY, MEMOIR.

Soliloquy   In a drama, a long speech by a character who is alone on stage. A soliloquy reveals the private thoughts and emotions of that character.

> See also DRAMATIC MONOLOGUE, MONOLOGUE.

Sonnet   A lyric poem of fourteen lines, typically written in iambic pentameter and usually following strict patterns of stanza divisions and rhymes.

The **Shakespearean,** or **English, sonnet** consists of three **quatrains,** or four-line stanzas, followed by a **couplet,** or pair of rhyming lines. The rhyme scheme is typically *abab, cdcd, efef, gg.* The rhyming couplet often presents a conclusion to the issues or questions presented in the three quatrains.

In the **Petrarchan,** or **Italian, sonnet,** fourteen lines are divided into two stanzas, the eight-line **octave** and the six-line **sestet.** The sestet usually responds to a question or situation posed by the octave. The rhyme scheme for the octave is typically *abbaabba;* for the sestet the rhyme scheme is typically *cdecde.*

> See page 545.
> See also COUPLET, RHYME SCHEME, STANZA.

Sound devices   Techniques used, especially in poetry, to appeal to the ear. Writers use sound devices to enhance the sense of rhythm, to emphasize particular sounds, or to add to the musical quality of their writing. Examples of sound devices include alliteration, assonance, consonance, onomatopoeia, and rhyme.

> See page 399.
> See also ALLITERATION, ASSONANCE, CONSONANCE, ONOMATOPOEIA, RHYME.

Speaker   The voice of a poem, similar to a narrator in a work of prose. Sometimes the speaker's voice is that of the poet, sometimes that of a fictional person or even a thing. The speaker's words communicate a particular **tone,** or attitude, toward the subject of the poem. For example, in Anne Bradstreet's "To My Dear and Loving Husband," the speaker addresses her husband in a tone of passionate devotion.

> See pages 398 and 633.
> See also TONE.

Stage directions   Instructions written by the dramatist to describe the appearance and actions of characters, as well as the sets, costumes, and lighting. Arthur Miller's play *The Crucible* contains numerous stage directions.

> See page 956.
> See also DRAMA, SCREENPLAY.

Stanza   A group of lines forming a unit in a poem. A stanza in a poem is similar to a paragraph in prose. Typically, stanzas in a poem are separated by a line of space.

> See page 761.
> See also COUPLET, OCTAVE, QUATRAIN, SESTET, SONNET, TRIPLET.

Stereotype   A character who is not developed as an individual, but instead represents a collection of traits and mannerisms supposedly shared by all members of a group.

> See also CHARACTER.

Stream of consciousness   The literary representation of a character's free-flowing thoughts, feelings, and memories. Much stream-of-consciousness writing does not employ conventional sentence structure or other rules of grammar and usage. Parts of T. S. Eliot's poem "The Love Song of J. Alfred Prufrock" exemplify stream of consciousness.

> See pages 603 and 629.
> See also SURREALIST POETRY.

Structure   The particular order or pattern a writer uses to present ideas. Narratives commonly follow a chronological order, while the structure of persuasive or expository writing may vary. Listing detailed information, using cause and effect, or describing a problem and then offering a solution are some other ways a writer can present a topic.

> See page 895.

Style   The expressive qualities that distinguish an author's work, including word choice and the length and arrangement of sentences, as well as the use of figurative language and imagery. Style can reveal an author's attitude and purpose in writing.

> See page 684.
> See also AUTHOR'S PURPOSE, FIGURATIVE LANGUAGE, IMAGERY, TONE.

Surrealist poetry   Poetry that expresses the workings of the unconscious mind and how these workings interact with outer reality. This poetry is characterized by the use of images from dreams and stream-of-consciousness associations. Anne Sexton's poem "Riding the Elevator into the Sky" has elements of surrealism.

> See page 1126.
> See also STREAM OF CONSCIOUSNESS.

Suspense   A feeling of curiosity, uncertainty, or even dread about what is going to happen next. Writers increase the level of suspense in a story by creating a threat to the central character, or **protagonist,** and giving readers clues to what might happen.

> See page 305.
> See also PROTAGONIST.

Symbol   Any object, person, place, or experience that exists on a literal level but also represents something else, usually something abstract. For example, in "The Bridal Party," F. Scott Fitzgerald writes:

> . . . the Graf Zeppelin, shining and glorious, symbol of escape and destruction—of escape, if necessary, through destruction—glided in the Paris sky.

> See pages 399 and 618.
> See also ALLEGORY, FIGURATIVE LANGUAGE.

Symbolist poetry   A kind of poetry that emphasizes suggestion and inward experience instead of explicit description. The symbolist poets influenced twentieth-century writers such as T. S. Eliot and Ezra Pound.

> See also IMAGIST POETRY, MODERNISM.

T

Tall tale   A type of folklore associated with the American frontier. Tall tales are humorous stories that contain wild exaggerations and invention. Typically, their heroes are bold but sometimes foolish characters who may have superhuman abilities or who may act as if they do. Tall tales are not intended to be believable;

their exaggerations are used for comic effect, as in Mark Twain's "The Celebrated Jumping Frog of Calaveras County," when Simon Wheeler describes the frog:

> "[Y]ou'd see that frog whirling in the air like a doughnut—see him turn one summerset, or maybe a couple, if he got a good start, and come down flat-footed and all right, like a cat."

> See page 214.
> See also FOLKLORE, FOLKTALE.

Technical vocabulary   Words that are unique to a particular art, science, profession, or trade. Technical vocabulary may provide authority or enhance the sense of realism. In her poem "Geometry," Rita Dove uses the terms *theorem* and *intersect* from the technical vocabulary of geometry.

> See also DICTION.

Theme   The central message of a work of literature that readers can apply to life. Some works have a **stated theme,** which is expressed directly. More works have an **implied theme,** which is revealed gradually through events, dialogue, or description. A literary work may have more than one theme.

> See pages 233, 276, 473, and 801.
> See also AUTHOR'S PURPOSE, FABLE, MORAL.

Thesis   The main idea of a work of nonfiction. The thesis may be stated directly or implied.

> See also NONFICTION.

Third-person point of view. See POINT OF VIEW.

Tone   A reflection of a writer's or a speaker's attitude toward the subject matter, as conveyed through elements such as word choice, punctuation, sentence structure, and figures of speech. A writer's tone might convey a variety of attitudes such as sympathy, objectivity, or humor.

> See pages 109 and 515.
> See also AUTHOR'S PURPOSE, DICTION, FIGURATIVE LANGUAGE, STYLE, VOICE.

Tragedy   A play in which a main character suffers a downfall. That character, the **tragic hero,** is typically a person of dignified or heroic stature. The downfall may result from outside forces or from a weakness within the character, which is known as a **tragic flaw.**

> See page 996.
> See also DRAMA, HERO.

Transcendentalism   A philosophical and literary movement whose followers believed that basic truths could be reached only by "going beyond," or transcending, reason and reflecting on the world of the spirit and on one's own deep and free intuition. Transcendentalists believed that the individual could transform the world—not only through writing, but also through utopian communities, antislavery activity, and other social action.

> See pages 125 and 239.
> See also RATIONALISM, ROMANTICISM.

Triplet   A stanza of three lines, sometimes rhymed *aaa*.

> See also RHYME, RHYME SCHEME, STANZA.

U–W

Understatement   Language that makes something seem less important than it really is.

> See also HYPERBOLE.

Vernacular   Ordinary speech of a particular country or region. Vernacular language is more casual than cultivated, formal speech. Slang and dialect are commonly described as vernacular language. Regional writers sometimes employ vernacular language for enhanced realism. Such use of vernacular is common in the works of Mark Twain, Zora Neale Hurston, and Alice Walker.

> See also COLLOQUIAL LANGUAGE, DIALECT,
> LOCAL COLOR, REGIONALISM.

Verse paragraph   A group of lines in a poem that form a unit. Unlike a stanza, a verse paragraph does not have a fixed number of lines. While poems written before the twentieth century usually contain stanzas, many contemporary poems are made up of verse paragraphs. Verse paragraphs help to organize a poem into thoughts, as paragraphs help to organize prose.

> See page 1084.
> See also STANZA.

Voice   The distinctive use of language that conveys the author's or narrator's personality to the reader. Voice is determined by elements of style such as word choice and tone.

> See page 1080.
> See also AUTHOR'S PURPOSE, DICTION,
> NARRATOR, STYLE, TONE.

Wit   An exhibition of cleverness and humor. For example, the works of Dorothy Parker, Mark Twain, and Donald Barthelme are all known for their wit.

> See also COMEDY, HUMOR, SARCASM, SATIRE.

Language Handbook

Troubleshooter

The Troubleshooter will help you recognize and correct errors that you might make in your writing.

Sentence Fragment

Problem: A fragment that lacks a subject

Ted put the dishes on the counter. (Should have put them in the dishwasher.) *frag*

Solution: Add a subject to the fragment to make it a complete sentence.

Ted put the dishes on the counter. He should have put them in the dishwasher.

Problem: A fragment that lacks a complete verb

He left without saying good-bye. (His anger apparent.) *frag*

Prospectors swarmed over the land. (Looking for gold.) *frag*

Solution A: Add a complete verb or a helping verb to make the sentence complete.

He left without saying good-bye. His anger was apparent.

Prospectors swarmed over the land. They were looking for gold.

Solution B: Combine the fragment with another sentence.

His anger apparent, he left without saying good-bye.

Prospectors swarmed over the land, looking for gold.

Problem: A fragment that is a subordinate clause

frag

Darnell didn't like the photograph. (Since he had closed his eyes at the flash.)

The recipe called for bananas and eggplant. (Which was a surprising combination.)

frag

Solution A: Combine the fragment with another sentence.

Darnell didn't like the photograph, since he had closed his eyes at the flash.

The recipe called for bananas and eggplant, which was a surprising combination.

Solution B: Rewrite the fragment as a complete sentence, eliminating the subordinating conjunction or the relative pronoun and adding a subject or other words necessary to make a complete thought.

Darnell didn't like the photograph. He had closed his eyes at the flash.

The recipe called for bananas and eggplant. This combination is surprising.

Problem: A fragment that lacks both a subject and a verb

(Not surprisingly.) The computer flashed the word "Error." *frag*

(For over a month.) No jobs were available at the employment center. *frag*

Solution: Combine the fragment with another sentence.

Not surprisingly, the computer flashed the word "Error."

For over a month, no jobs were available at the employment center.

> **Rule of Thumb:** Sentence fragments can make your writing hard to understand. Make sure every sentence has a subject and a verb.

Run-on Sentence

Problem: Comma splice—two main clauses separated by only a comma

run-on

(Scientists can now predict most earthquakes, the technology is still new.)

Solution A: Replace the comma with an end mark of punctuation, such as a period or a question mark, and begin the new sentence with a capital letter.

Scientists can now predict most earthquakes. The technology is still new.

Solution B: Place a semicolon between the two main clauses.

Scientists can now predict most earthquakes; the technology is still new.

Solution C: Add a coordinating conjunction after the comma.

Scientists can now predict most earthquakes, but the technology is still new.

Problem: Two main clauses with no punctuation between them

The ice skater glided on the ice she seemed to float on air. *run-on*

Solution A: Separate the main clauses with an end mark of punctuation, such as a period or a question mark, and begin the second sentence with a capital letter.

The ice skater glided on the ice. She seemed to float on air.

Solution B: Separate the main clauses with a semicolon.

The ice skater glided on the ice; she seemed to float on air.

Solution C: Add a comma and a coordinating conjunction between the main clauses.

The ice skater glided on the ice, and she seemed to float on air.

Problem: Two main clauses with no comma before the coordinating conjunction

run-on
Charlotte pivoted and passed to Rosa but the other team intercepted the ball.

The car was a silver color and it gleamed in the moonlight. *run-on*

Solution: Add a comma before the coordinating conjunction to separate the two main clauses.

Charlotte pivoted and passed to Rosa, but the other team intercepted the ball.

The car was a silver color, and it gleamed in the moonlight.

> **Rule of Thumb:** It often helps to have someone else read your longer sentences to see if they are clear. Since you know what the sentences are supposed to mean, you may sometimes miss the need for punctuation.

Lack of Subject-Verb Agreement

Problem: A subject that is separated from the verb by an intervening prepositional phrase

The first few sentences of the essay (was) very intriguing. *agr*

One group of tickets (were) lost. *agr*

Solution: Make the verb agree with the subject, which is never the object of a preposition.

The first few sentences of the essay were very intriguing.

One group of tickets was lost.

Problem: A predicate nominative that differs in number from the subject

The best part (are) the actors' performances. *agr*

Solution: Ignore the predicate nominative, and make the verb agree with the subject of the sentence.

The best part is the actors' performances.

Problem: A subject that follows the verb

There (goes) the two most admired people in the school. *agr*

In the attic (is) many boxes of clothes. *agr*

Solution: In an inverted sentence look for the subject *after* the verb. Then make sure the verb agrees with the subject.

There go the two most admired people in the school.

In the attic are many boxes of clothes.

> **Rule of Thumb:** Reversing the order of an inverted sentence may help you decide on the verb form to use: "Many boxes of clothes are in the attic."

Problem: A collective noun as the subject

The school council (are) holding a fund-raising dance. *agr*

The school council (is) voting for their new chairperson. *agr*

Solution A: If the collective noun refers to a group as a whole, use a singular verb.

The school council is holding a fund-raising dance.

Solution B: If the collective noun refers to each member of a group individually, use a plural verb.

The school council are voting for their new chairperson.

Problem: A noun of amount as the subject

Twenty miles (are) a long way to bicycle. *agr*

Two quarters (was) shining on the sidewalk. *agr*

Solution: Determine whether the noun of amount refers to one unit and is therefore singular or whether it refers to a number of individual units and is therefore plural.

Twenty miles is a long way to bicycle.

Two quarters were shining on the sidewalk.

Problem: A compound subject that is joined by *and*

Salt and pepper (seasons) most foods. *agr*

My friend and tutor (were) at the science fair to encourage me. *agr*

Solution A: If the parts of the compound subject do not belong to one unit or if they refer to different people or things, use a plural verb.

Salt and pepper season most foods.

Solution B: If the parts of the compound subject belong to one unit or if both parts refer to the same person or thing, use a singular verb.

My friend and tutor was at the science fair to encourage me.

Problem: A compound subject that is joined by *or* or *nor*

Neither Josh nor Ana get (up early.) *agr*

Either the defendant or his friends (is) guilty. *agr*

Solution: Make the verb agree with the subject that is closer to it.

Neither Josh nor Ana gets up early.

Either the defendant or his friends are guilty.

Problem: A compound subject that is preceded by *many a, every,* or *each*

Every candidate and voter (register) at this desk. *agr*

Solution: When *many a, every,* or *each* precedes a compound subject, the subject is considered singular. Use a singular verb.

Every candidate and voter registers at this desk.

Problem: A subject that is separated from the verb by an intervening expression

Lottie, together with Luis and Fatima, (plan) to be a camp counselor. *agr*

Solution: Certain expressions, such as those beginning with *as well as, in addition to,* and *together with,* do not change the number of the subject. Ignore these expressions between a subject and its verb. Make the verb agree with the subject.

Lottie, together with Luis and Fatima, plans to be a camp counselor.

Problem: An indefinite pronoun as the subject

Each of those cars (have) an electric motor. *agr*

Both of them (runs) well, too. *agr*

Solution: Determine whether the indefinite pronoun is singular or plural, and make the verb agree. Some indefinite pronouns are singular—*another, anyone, everyone, one, each, either, neither, anything, everything, something,* and *somebody.* Some are plural—*both, many, few, several,* and *others.* Some can be singular or plural—*some, all, any, more, most,* and *none.* Find the noun to which the pronoun refers to determine which verb form to use in these cases.

Each of those cars has an electric motor.

Both of them run well, too.

Lack of Pronoun-Antecedent Agreement

Problem: A singular antecedent that can be either male or female

A scientist announces (his) discoveries by publishing the results. *ant*

A famous person is often accompanied by (his) bodyguard. *ant*

Solution A: Traditionally, a masculine pronoun was used to refer to an antecedent that might be either male or female. This usage is not acceptable in contemporary writing because it ignores or excludes females. Reword the sentence to use *he or she, him or her,* and so on.

A scientist announces his or her discoveries by publishing the results.

A famous person is often accompanied by his or her bodyguard.

Solution B: Reword the sentence so that both the antecedent and the pronoun are plural.

Scientists announce their discoveries by publishing the results.

Famous people are often accompanied by their bodyguards.

Solution C: Reword the sentence to eliminate the pronoun.

A scientist announces a discovery by publishing the results.

A famous person is often accompanied by a bodyguard.

Problem: A second-person pronoun that refers to a third-person antecedent

The swimmers practice every day since (you) need to do that to win. *ant*

Solution A: Use the appropriate third-person pronoun.

The swimmers practice every day since they need to do that to win.

Solution B: Use an appropriate noun instead of a pronoun.

The swimmers practice every day since athletes need to do that to win.

Problem: A singular indefinite pronoun as an antecedent

Each of the lawyers believed (their) client was innocent. *ant*

Neither of the band members knew where (their) instruments were stored. *ant*

Solution: *Another, any, every, one, each, either, neither, anything, everything, something,* and *somebody* are singular; they therefore require singular personal pronouns even when followed by a prepositional phrase that contains a plural noun.

Each of the lawyers believed her client was innocent.

Neither of the band members knew where his instrument was stored.

> **Rule of Thumb:** To help you remember that pronouns such as *each, either, every,* and *neither* are singular, think *each one, either one, every one,* and *neither one.*

Lack of Clear Pronoun Reference

Problem: A pronoun reference that is weak or vague.

The cast performed well, (which) was the result of hard work. *ref*

There were no prices on the merchandise, and (that) bothered me. *ref*

The book says to sand (it) before painting it. *ref*

Solution A: Rewrite the sentence, adding a clear antecedent for the pronoun.

The cast gave a wonderful performance, which was the result of hard work.

Solution B: Rewrite the sentence, substituting a noun for the pronoun.

There were no prices on the merchandise, and the lack of information bothered me.

The book says to sand the wood before painting it.

Problem: A pronoun that could refer to more than one antecedent

When Marta and Helen picked up the magazines, (they) were dirty. *ref*

Midori told her mother that (she) should look for a new job. *ref*

Solution A: Rewrite the sentence, substituting a noun for the pronoun.

When Marta and Helen picked up the magazines, the covers were dirty.

Solution B: Rewrite the sentence, making the antecedent of the pronoun clear.

Midori told her mother to look for a new job.

Problem: The indefinite use of *you* or *they*

Is there still a law that (you) cannot drive faster than 55 miles per hour? *ref*

In Australia, (they) have winter when it is summer here. *ref*

Solution A: Rewrite the sentence, substituting a noun for the pronoun.

Is there still a law that motorists cannot drive faster than 55 miles per hour?

Solution B: Rewrite the sentence, eliminating the pronoun entirely.

In Australia, the winter season arrives when it is summer here.

Shift in Pronoun

Problem: An incorrect shift in person between two pronouns

I always study in the library because (you) can concentrate there. *pro*

One should feel lucky when (you) have good health. *pro*

They looked for a new television at the mall, where (you) can find bargains. *pro*

Solution A: Replace the incorrect pronoun with a pronoun that agrees with its antecedent.

I always study in the library because I can concentrate there.

One should feel lucky when one has good health.

They looked for a new television at the mall, where they can find bargains.

Solution B: Replace the pronoun with an appropriate noun.

I always study in the library because students can concentrate there.

They looked for a new television at the mall, where shoppers can find bargains.

Shift in Verb Tense

Problem: An unnecessary shift in tense

Since the clinic was so busy, the doctor (sees) ten patients in an hour. *shift t*

I rented a video while Maria (is making) popcorn for all of us. *shift t*

Solution: When two or more events occur at the same time, be sure to use the same verb tense to describe each event.

Since the clinic was so busy, the doctor saw ten patients in an hour.

I rented a video while Maria made popcorn for all of us.

Problem: A lack of correct shift in tenses to show that one event precedes or follows another

By the time I finished my homework, my sister (came) home from work. *shift t*

Solution: When two events have occurred at different times in the past, shift from the past tense to the past perfect tense to indicate that one action began and ended before another past action began.

By the time I finished my homework, my sister had come home from work.

> **Rule of Thumb:** When you need to use several verb tenses in your writing, it may help to first jot down the sequence of events you're writing about. Be clear in your mind what happened first, next, and last.

Incorrect Verb Tense or Form

Problem: An incorrect or missing verb ending

Krista (heat) the frying pan before she added the eggs. *tense*

The guard had (question) the visitor at the bank. *tense*

Solution: Add -*ed* to a regular verb to form the past tense and the past participle.

Krista heated the frying pan before she added the eggs.

The guard had questioned the visitor at the bank.

Problem: An improperly formed irregular verb

The pitcher (throwed) the ball to second base. *tense*

The runner on third had already (stealed) home. *tense*

Solution: Irregular verbs form their past and past participles in some way other than by adding -*ed.* Memorize irregular verb forms, or look them up.

The pitcher threw the ball to second base.

The runner on third had already stolen home.

Problem: Confusion between the past form and the past participle

Teka's new shoes (have tore) her pantyhose. *tense*

The poet (has wove) a theme of sorrow throughout her new poem. *tense*

Solution: Use the past participle form of an irregular verb, not the past form, when you use any form of the auxiliary verb *have.*

Teka's new shoes have torn her pantyhose.

The poet has woven a theme of sorrow throughout her new poem.

Problem: Improper use of the past participle

Jon (seen) the squirrel carry nuts from the tree. *tense*

The officers (given) medals to the war veterans. *tense*

Solution A: The past participle of an irregular verb cannot stand alone as a verb. Add a form of the auxiliary verb *have* to the past participle to form a complete verb.

Jon has seen the squirrel carry nuts from the tree.

The officers have given medals to the war veterans.

Solution B: Replace the past participle with the past form of the verb.

Jon saw the squirrel carry nuts from the tree.

The officers gave medals to the war veterans.

Misplaced or Dangling Modifier

Problem: A misplaced modifier

Emily borrowed a sweater from her cousin (that was too small.) *mod*

(With no horn or brakes,) the twins bought the old car. *mod*

Solution: Modifiers that modify the wrong word or that seem to modify more than one idea in a sentence are called misplaced modifiers. Move the misplaced phrase as close as possible to the word or words it modifies.

Emily borrowed a sweater that was too small from her cousin.

The twins bought the old car with no horn or brakes.

Problem: Incorrect placement of the adverb *only*

We (only) have study hall twice a week. *mod*

Solution: Place the adverb *only* immediately before the word or group of words it modifies.

Only we have study hall twice a week.

We have only study hall twice a week.

We have study hall only twice a week.

> **Rule of Thumb:** Note that each time *only* is moved, the meaning of the sentence changes. Check to be sure your sentence says what you mean.

Problem: A dangling modifier

(Knowing little Spanish,) the textbook was difficult to understand. *mod*

(Coming home late last night,) the front door was locked and bolted. *mod*

(Driving through the tunnel,) the tollbooth was blocked by traffic. *mod*

Solution: Dangling modifiers do not logically seem to modify any word in the sentence. Rewrite the sentence, adding a noun to which the dangling phrase clearly refers. Often you will have to add other words, too.

Knowing little Spanish, Jenny found that the textbook was difficult to understand.

Coming home late last night, I realized that the front door was locked and bolted.

Driving through the tunnel, my father reached the tollbooth, which was blocked by traffic.

Missing or Misplaced Possessive Apostrophe

Problem: Singular nouns

My (aunts) dog is a beagle. *poss*

(Jess) story was fascinating. *poss*

Solution: Use an apostrophe and *-s* to form the possessive of a singular noun or a proper name, even if the noun ends in *s*.

My aunt's dog is a beagle.

Jess's story was fascinating.

Problem: Plural nouns ending in -s

The (birds) songs sounded sweet, even so early in the morning. *poss*

Solution: Use an apostrophe alone to form the possessive of a plural noun that ends in -s.

The birds' songs sounded sweet, even so early in the morning.

Problem: Plural nouns not ending in -s

The (childrens) grandparents baked them chocolate chip cookies. *poss*

Solution: Use an apostrophe and -s to form the possessive of a plural noun that does not end in -s.

The children's grandparents baked them chocolate chip cookies.

Problem: Pronouns

(Someones) package is at the lost and found desk. *poss*

Is it (your's?) *poss*

Solution A: Use an apostrophe and -s to form the possessive of a singular indefinite pronoun.

Someone's package is at the lost and found desk.

Solution B: Do not use an apostrophe with any of the possessive personal pronouns.

Is it yours?

Problem: Confusion between *its* and *it's*

As the dragon roared, (it's) fiery breath consumed everything around it. *poss*

The detective said, ("Its) true that the butler committed the crime." *cont*

Solution A: Do not use an apostrophe to form the possessive of *it*.

As the dragon roared, its fiery breath consumed everything around it.

Solution B: Use an apostrophe to form the contraction of *it is*.

The detective said, "It's true that the butler committed the crime."

Missing Commas with Nonessential Elements

Problem: Missing commas with nonessential participles, infinitives, and their phrases

Lynda⌄delighted with the message⌄immediately called Rick with the news. *com*

The professor⌄browsing through some old books⌄found a rare first edition. *com*

To be honest⌄a gardener does not need a green thumb. *com*

Solution: Determine whether the participle, infinitive, or phrase is essential to the meaning of the sentence or not. If it is not essential, set off the phrase with commas.

Lynda, delighted with the message, immediately called Rick with the news.

The professor, browsing through some old books, found a rare first edition.

To be honest, a gardener does not need a green thumb.

Problem: Missing commas with nonessential adjective clauses

My running shoes⌄which have reflective patches⌄were falling apart. *com*

Solution: Determine whether the clause is essential to the meaning of the sentence or not. If it is not essential, set off the clause with commas.

My running shoes, which have reflective patches, were falling apart.

Problem: Missing commas with nonessential appositives

The librarian⌄a creative woman⌄held a story hour for beginning readers. *com*

Solution: Determine whether the appositive is essential to the meaning of the sentence or not. If it is not essential, set off the appositive with commas.

The librarian, a creative woman, held a story hour for beginning readers.

> **Rule of Thumb:** To determine whether a word, phrase, or clause is essential, try reading the sentence without it.

Problem: Missing commas with interjections and parenthetical expressions

OopsˌI dropped the glass on the floor! *con*

The junior class party, I think, will be held in the gym. *con*

Solution: Set off the interjection or parenthetical expression with commas.

Oops, I dropped the glass on the floor!

The junior class party, I think, will be held in the gym.

Missing Comma in a Series

Problem: Missing commas in a series of words, phrases, or clauses

Meg bought new pillows, sheets, and curtains. *ᴧ con*

I walked into the attic, through the closet, and behind the bed to find the trunk with the costumes. *ᴧ con*

Victor saved his money so he could fly to Chicago, stay in a hotel, and go sightseeing. *ᴧ con*

The clowns performed tricks, the lions roared, the elephants paraded, and the ringmaster cracked his whip. *ᴧ con*

Solution: When there are three or more elements in a series, use a comma after each element that precedes the conjunction.

Meg bought new pillows, sheets, and curtains.

I walked into the attic, through the closet, and behind the bed to find the trunk with the costumes.

Victor saved his money so he could fly to Chicago, stay in a hotel, and go sightseeing.

The clowns performed tricks, the lions roared, the elephants paraded, and the ringmaster cracked his whip.

> **Rule of Thumb:** When you're having difficulty with a rule of usage, try rewriting the rule in your own words. Then check with your teacher to be sure you have grasped the concept.

Troublesome Words

This section will help you choose between words that are often confused. It also alerts you to avoid certain words and expressions in school or business writing.

a, an

Use *a* when the word that follows begins with a consonant sound, including a sounded *h,* or with the "yew" sound. Use the article *an* when the word that follows begins with a vowel sound.

A little puppy might become **a** huge dog.

The ballplayer wore **a** uniform and carried **an** umbrella and **an** overcoat.

a lot, alot

The expression *a lot* means "a large amount" or "a great deal" (as in "I like him a lot") and should always be written as two words. Some authorities discourage its use in formal English.

Informal: There have been **a lot** of tourists in town this summer.

Formal: There have been **many** tourists in town this summer.

a while, awhile

An article and a noun form the expression *a while.* Often the preposition *in* or *for* precedes *a while,* forming a prepositional phrase. The single word *awhile* is an adverb.

Once in **a while,** I like to walk to the lake.

For **a while,** I walked to the lake each day.

I waited **awhile** before I walked to the lake.

ability, capacity

Ability and *capacity* both mean "the power to do something." *Ability* also means "skill or talent." *Capacity* also means "the maximum amount that can be contained."

Not all birds have the **ability** to fly. For example, the ostrich does not have the **capacity** to fly.

My guitar teacher says I have a great deal of musical **ability.**

The tank has a **capacity** of twenty gallons.

accept, except

Accept is a verb meaning "to receive" or "to agree to." *Except* may be a preposition or a verb. As a preposition, it means "but." As a verb, it means "to leave out."

I **accept** the nomination for president of the student council. **Except** for Ari, the other candidates are not good campaigners.

If we **except** him, I don't have any strong opponents.

adapt, adopt

Adapt means "to change something so that it can be used for another purpose" or "to adjust." *Adopt* means "to take something for one's own."

The writer will **adapt** his novel for a film.

Dogs often **adapt** to the cold weather by growing a thick undercoat of fur.

The city council agreed to **adopt** the new ordinance.

advice, advise

Advice (əd vīs′), a noun, means "helpful opinion." *Advise* (əd vīz′), a verb, means "to give advice or offer counsel."

To **advise** Ramona to exercise more and to eat less was good; unfortunately, she hasn't taken the **advice.**

affect, effect

Affect, a verb, means "to cause a change in" or "to influence." As a noun, *effect* means "result." *Effect* as a verb means "to bring about or accomplish."

Will the heavy traffic **affect** our travel time?

The **effect** of the heavy traffic was to make us late.

We should **effect** a right turn, away from the heavy traffic.

ain't

Ain't is never used in formal speaking or writing unless you are quoting the exact words of a character or real person. Instead of using *ain't,* say or write, *am not; is not;* and so on.

They **aren't** playing by the rules.

all ready, already

All ready means "completely ready." *Already,* an adverb, means "before" or "by this time."

By the time Danielle was **all ready** to go hiking, everyone else was **already** on the trail.

all right, alright

This expression should always be written as two words.

Everything seemed **all right** after the storm.

all together, altogether

All together means "in a group." *Altogether* is an adverb meaning "completely" or "on the whole."

Nana was **altogether** delighted when the family went **all together** to the reunion.

allusion, illusion

Allusion means "an indirect reference." *Illusion* refers to "a false idea or appearance."

Mr. Kim made an **allusion** to the designer's ability to create an **illusion** of elegance using commonplace objects.

anxious, eager

Anxious means "uneasy or worried about some event or situation." *Eager* means "having a keen interest, feeling impatient for something expected."

Anxious for the skiers' safety, the ski patrol closed the mountain. The skiers were **eager** to get back on the slopes.

anywheres, everywheres

Write these words and others like them without a final *s*: *anywhere, everywhere, somewhere.*

The family searched **everywhere** for their lost pet.

assure, ensure, insure

Assure means "to guarantee something to someone." *Ensure* means "to make a situation safe." *Insure* means "to assure the payment of a sum of money in certain circumstances."

At the garage sale, Cassie **assured** everyone that the stereo worked perfectly.

To **ensure** the financial security of the condominium, the board of directors voted to **insure** the building against fires.

bad, badly

Use *bad* as an adjective (to modify nouns and pronouns). *Bad* often follows a linking verb. Use *badly* as an adverb (to modify verbs, adjectives, or other adverbs). *Badly* almost always follows an action verb.

I felt **bad** after I snapped at my little sister.

The shortstop played so **badly** that the coach took him out of the game.

being as, being that

Although these expressions sometimes replace *because* or *since* in informal conversation, you should always avoid them in formal speaking and writing.

Because of my cold, I could not taste my food.

Since that galaxy is far away, the light we see in the telescope is thousands of years old.

beside, besides

Beside means "next to." *Besides* means "moreover" or "in addition to."

David insisted on sitting **beside** Sara at the restaurant. **Besides** eating three tacos, he finished the salad and the guacamole.

between, among

Between and *among* are prepositions that are used to state a relationship. Use *between* to refer to two persons or things or to compare one person or thing with another person or thing or with an entire group. Use *between* to refer to more than two persons or things considered equals in a close relationship or viewed individually in relation to one another.

Rosalia could not decide **between** the pink sweater and the beige blouse.

We had to choose **between** one large lilac bush and three small rose bushes.

The agreement was worked out **between** the president, the Senate, and the House of Representatives.

Use *among* to show a relationship in which more than two persons or things are considered as a group.

The teacher divided the toys **among** the children.

The eagles flew **among** the clouds.

bring, take

Bring means "to carry from a distant place to a closer one." *Take* means "to carry from a nearby place to a more distant one."

Tasha will **bring** her video camera when she comes.

"**Take** all of these groceries to Mrs. Hall's car," said the manager to the clerk.

can, may

Can implies the ability to do something. *May* implies permission to do something or the possibility of doing it.

I **can** run to the top of the hill without stopping.

May I have some fruit instead of ice cream?

> **Rule of Thumb:** Although *can* is sometimes used in place of *may* in informal speech, a distinction should be made when speaking and writing formally.

can't hardly, can't scarcely

Can't hardly and *can't scarcely* are considered double negatives, since *hardly* and *scarcely* by themselves have a negative meaning. Do not use *hardly* and *scarcely* with *not* or *-n't.*

I **can hardly** believe that the holiday is next week.

The cafeteria food is so bad I **can scarcely** eat it.

capital, capitol

Use *capital* to refer to the city that is the center of government of a state or nation, to money or other assets, or to an uppercase letter. Use *capitol* to refer to the building in which a state or national legislature meets.

She needed a loan, because she did not have enough **capital** to open a shop.

We saw members of Congress on our visit to the **Capitol,** in Washington D.C., the nation's **capital.**

complement, compliment

A *complement* is something that makes a thing complete. A *compliment* is an expression of praise or admiration.

The mathematics course is a **complement** to the physics course. The math teacher's **compliment** encouraged Reva to stay in physics.

compose, comprise

Compose means "to form by putting together." *Comprise* means "to contain, embrace."

Water is **composed** of hydrogen and oxygen.

David was sure he could **compose** a song for our band.

The ground floor **comprises** shops and a theater.

continual, continuous

Continual describes repetitive action with pauses between occurrences. *Continuous* describes an action that continues with no interruption in space or time.

The **continual** ringing of the phone was annoying, but not as disturbing as the **continuous** noise of the radio.

could of, might of, must of, should of, would of

The helping verb *have*, not the preposition *of*, should follow *could, might, must, should,* or *would.*

Doug **might have** won the swim meet if he hadn't caught the flu.

I **should have** asked Jenna to call.

different from, different than

The expression *different from* is generally preferred to *different than.*

An elk is **different from** a moose.

doesn't, don't

Doesn't is the contraction of *does not* and should be used with *he, she, it* and all singular nouns. *Don't* is the contraction of *do not* and should be used with *I, you, we, they,* and all plural nouns.

In spite of the clouds, it **doesn't** look like rain.

Don't you want to go to the baseball game with me?

emigrate, immigrate

Emigrate means "to leave one country to settle in another." Use *from* with *emigrate*. *Immigrate* means "to enter a country in order to live there permanently." Use *to* or *into* with *immigrate*.

Ellis Island was the first stop for people who **emigrated** from Europe in the early 1900s.

When my great-grandfather **immigrated** to the U.S., the customs official changed his name.

> **Rule of Thumb:** Remember that the *e-* in *emigrate* comes from *ex-* ("out of"); the *im-* in *immigrate* comes from *in-* ("into").

farther, further

Farther refers to physical distance. *Further* refers to time or degree.

The **farther** we walk, the more my feet hurt.

The more Devon talks, the **further** my patience is pushed to its limit.

fewer, less

Fewer is generally used to refer to things or qualities that can be counted. *Less* is generally used to refer to things or qualities that cannot be counted. In addition, *less* is sometimes used with figures that are regarded as single amounts of single quantities.

Fewer than ten students knew the answer.

Tim's cat has **less** energy now that she has kittens.

This jacket cost **less** than twenty dollars.

good, well

Good is always an adjective meaning "pleasing" or "able." *Well* may be used as an adverb of manner telling how ably something is done or as an adjective meaning "in good health."

Sachiko's perfume smelled **good.**

The band played especially **well** that evening.

I had the flu this winter, but now I'm **well** again.

had of

The word *of* should not be used between *had* and a past participle.

I wish I **had gone** to the dentist before my tooth started hurting.

hanged, hung

Use *hanged* to mean "put to death by hanging." In all other cases, use *hung*.

In what movie did the hero escape from being **hanged** by an angry mob?

Renoir's painting was **hung** in the main hall.

imply, infer

Imply means "to suggest without stating explicitly." *Infer* means "to come to a conclusion based on evidence or clues."

By his tone of voice, Jean-Luc meant to **imply** that he was efficient and professional, but the interviewer **inferred** that he was unfriendly.

in, into, in to

In means "inside" or "within." Use *into* to indicate movement or direction from outside to a point within. *In to* is made up of the adverb *in* followed by the preposition *to* and should be carefully distinguished from the preposition *into.*

The meeting took place **in** the community center. I walked **into** the meeting room with Maria.

The host took her **in to** dinner.

irregardless, regardless

Always use *regardless.* Both the prefix *ir-* and suffix *-less* have negative meanings. When used together, they produce a double negative, which is incorrect.

I am going ahead with my project **regardless** of their decision.

lay, lie

Lay means "to put" or "to place," and it takes a direct object. *Lie* means "to recline" or "to be positioned," and it never takes an object.

Lay the place mat on the table near the salt and pepper shakers.

Mom will be upset if you **lie** on the couch with your shoes on.

The past tense of *lay* is *laid.* The past tense of *lie* is *lay.*

Daisy **laid** the place mat on the table.

Was Mom upset when you **lay** on the couch with your shoes on?

learn, teach

Learn means "to gain knowledge." *Teach* means "to instruct" or "to give knowledge to."

People **learn** from experience.

People who **teach** often get a great deal of satisfaction from their work.

leave, let

Leave means "to go away; depart." *Let* means "to allow" or "to permit." With the word *alone* you may use either *let* or *leave.*

If you **leave** now, you will get to work on time.

"**Let** me see that cut," said the nurse.

Leave me alone. **Let** me alone.

lend, loan

Lend is a verb. *Loan* is a noun. Although *loan* is sometimes used informally as a verb, *lend* is preferred.

The bank agreed to **lend** Sharon the money for her college tuition.

The **loan** was immediately turned over to the school.

like, as

Use *like,* a preposition, to introduce a prepositional phrase. Use *as* and *as if,* subordinating conjunctions, to introduce subordinate clauses. Many authorities say that *like* should never be used before a clause.

Darren has red hair **like** his father and grandfather.

Mark arrived late for the concert, **as** he always does.

As if I didn't have enough homework, Mr. Phelps assigned another chapter.

> **Rule of Thumb:** *As* can be a preposition in some cases, as in *He posed as a secret agent.*

loose, lose

Use the adjective *loose* (lо̄о̅s) when you mean "free," "not firmly attached," or "not fitting tightly." Use the verb *lose* (lо̄о̅z) when you mean "to have no longer," "to misplace," or "to fail to win."

The news reported that a lion was **loose** at the zoo.

The gymnast felt sure she would **lose** the competition.

passed, past

Passed is the past and the past participle form of the verb *pass.*

He **passed** the bread but forgot the butter.

I have **passed** this corner many times.

Past is used as a noun, an adjective, a preposition, or an adverb.

The **past** comes to life in that novel.

Past mistakes can be forgiven.

To find the mall, go **past** the intersection and then turn left.

He lost the race as the other cars quickly moved **past.**

precede, proceed

Use *precede* when you mean "to go or come before." Use *proceed* when you mean "to continue" or "to move along."

A page **preceded** the queen as she **proceeded** to the throne.

principal, principle

Principal is an adjective meaning "the most important or first in rank." It is also used to refer to "the head of a school." A *principle* is a fundamental truth or a rule of conduct.

She was the **principal** financial officer for the company.

He remained true to his **principles,** even though it meant taking an unpopular stand.

raise, rise

The verb *raise* means "to cause to move upward" or "to lift up." It always takes an object. The verb *rise* means "to get up" or "to go up." It is an intransitive verb and never takes an object.

"**Raise** your right hand," said the judge.

"All **rise** as the judge enters the courtroom," said the bailiff.

reason . . . is that, because

Because means "for the reason that." Therefore, do not use *because* after *reason . . . is that*. Use either *reason . . . is that* or *because* alone.

The **reason** we are leaving early **is that** Doug is not feeling well.

We are leaving early **because** Doug is not feeling well.

respectfully, respectively

Use *respectfully* to mean "with respect." Use *respectively* to mean "in the order named."

Pierre **respectfully** waited for his grandfather to be served first.

Becky and Jenny were, **respectively,** the president and secretary of the junior class.

revenge, avenge

Revenge is used when the person who has been wronged or injured seeks retaliation. *Avenge* is a verb meaning "to punish someone for a wrong done to someone else"; it is followed by a direct object. *Revenge* can be a verb or a noun; *avenge* is always a verb.

Frank's father wanted to **revenge** the robbery of the family's store.

Frank also wanted to **avenge** the crime.

Finally they realized that **revenge** was not the answer.

says, said

Says is the present-tense, third-person singular form of the verb *say. Said* is the past tense of *say.* Do not use *says* when you are referring to the past.

Dr. Lee **says** that what he **said** yesterday is what he meant.

sit, set

Sit means "to be seated." It rarely takes an object. *Set* means "to put" or "to place," and it generally takes an object. When *set* is used to refer to the sun's going down, it does not take an object.

"**Sit** over here," said the waiter, as he **set** the glasses on the table.

The sun rises in the East and **sets** in the West.

stationary, stationery

Stationary is an adjective meaning "not moving." *Stationery* is writing paper.

She did not realize the bookcase was **stationary** until she tried to move it to another part of the room.

José created his own **stationery** on the computer.

than, then

Than is a conjunction that is used to introduce the second element in a comparison. *Than* also shows exception.

Although she is younger, Amy is taller **than** Jasmine.

Other **than** the goalie, does the soccer team have any outstanding players?

Then is an adverb that means "at that time," "soon afterward," "the time mentioned," "at another time," "for that reason," and "in that case."

It was **then** that the clock struck midnight.

Lea heard the footsteps and **then** a groan.

By **then** she was thoroughly frightened.

An old sea captain had lived in the house; **then** he had died.

Lea remembered there were no such things as ghosts, and **then** she felt better.

their, they're, there

Their is the possessive form of *they*. *They're* is the contraction of *they are*. *There* means "in that place." *There* is also sometimes used as an interjection, expressing a sense of completion.

Their house is down the street from our apartment building.

They're going to join us for lunch tomorrow.

My best friend lives **there.**

There! I finally finished my essay.

this here, that there

Avoid using *here* after *this* and *there* after *that.*

This is the pen and **that** is the paper, so write the thank-you note.

whereas, while

Both *whereas* and *while* can be used as conjunctions meaning "although." *Whereas* also means "it being the fact that." *While* can be used as a conjunction indicating a period of time.

Yoshi likes science fiction novels, **whereas** Jenny prefers biographies.

While Jake wanted to get a pizza, the rest of us wanted Thai food.

Whereas the majority of those present voted yes, the motion was carried.

Do you remember the song "Whistle **while** you work"?

who, whom

Use the nominative case pronoun *who* for subjects.

Who came to the party?

Please tell me **who** was there. [subject of the noun clause]

Who do you think was the guest of honor?

Rule of Thumb: When a question contains an interrupting expression such as *do you think,* it helps to omit the interrupting element to determine whether to use *who* or *whom.*

Use the objective pronoun *whom* for a direct object, an indirect object, or the object of a preposition.

Whom did the committee choose as chairperson? [direct object]

Ali gave **whom** the tape? [indirect object]

Michael Jordan is an athlete for **whom** I have a great deal of admiration. [object of the preposition *for*]

Rule of Thumb: When speaking informally, people often use *who* instead of *whom* in sentences like *Who did you see?* In writing and formal speech, distinguish between *who* and *whom.* Use the object pronoun *whom* for the direct or indirect object of a verb or verbal.

Grammar Glossary

This glossary will help you quickly locate information on parts of speech and sentence structure.

 A

Absolute phrase. *See* Phrase.

Abstract noun. *See* Noun chart.

Action verb. *See* Verb.

Active voice. *See* Voice.

Adjective A word that modifies a noun or pronoun by limiting its meaning. Adjectives appear in various positions in a sentence. (The *gray* cat purred. The cat is *gray.*)

Many adjectives have different forms to indicate degree of comparison. *(short, shorter, shortest)*

The **positive degree** is the simple form of the adjective. *(easy, interesting, good)*

The **comparative degree** compares two persons, places, things, or ideas. *(easier, more interesting, better)*

The **superlative degree** compares more than two persons, places, things, or ideas. *(easiest, most interesting, best)*

A **predicate adjective** follows a linking verb and further identifies or describes the subject. (The child is *happy.*)

A **proper adjective** is formed from a proper noun and begins with a capital letter. Many proper adjectives are created by adding these suffixes: *-an, -ian, -n, -ese,* and *-ish. (Chinese, African)*

Adjective clause. *See* Clause chart.

Adverb A word that modifies a verb, an adjective, or another adverb by making its meaning more specific. When modifying a verb, an adverb may appear in various positions in a sentence. (Cats *generally* eat less than dogs. *Generally,* cats eat less than dogs.) When modifying an adjective or another adverb, an adverb appears directly before the modified word. (I was *quite* pleased that they got along *so* well.) The word *not,* and the contraction *-n't* are adverbs. (Mike was*n't* ready for the test today.) Certain adverbs of time, place, and degree also have a negative meaning. (He's *never* ready.)

Some adverbs have different forms to indicate degree of comparison. *(soon, sooner, soonest)*

The **comparative** degree compares two actions. *(better, more quickly)*

The **superlative** degree compares three or more actions. *(fastest, most patiently, least rapidly)*

Adverb clause. *See* Clause chart.

Antecedent. *See* Pronoun.

Appositive A noun or a pronoun that further identifies another noun or pronoun. (My friend *Julie* lives next door.)

Appositive phrase. *See* Phrase.

Article The adjective *a, an,* or *the.*

Indefinite articles (*a* and *an*) refer to one of a general group of persons, places, or things. (I eat *an* apple *a* day.)

The **definite article** (*the*) indicates that the noun is a specific person, place, or thing. (*The* alarm woke me up.)

Auxiliary verb. *See* Verb.

 B

Base form. *See* Verb tense.

 C

Clause A group of words that has a subject and a predicate and that is used as part of a sentence. Clauses fall into two categories: *main clauses,* which are also called *independent clauses,* and *subordinate clauses,* which are also called *dependent clauses.*

A **main clause** can stand alone as a sentence. There must be at least one main clause in every sentence. (*The rooster crowed,* and *the dog barked.*)

A **subordinate clause** cannot stand alone as a sentence. A subordinate clause needs a main clause to complete its meaning. Many subordinate clauses begin with subordinating conjunctions or relative pronouns. (*When Geri sang her solo,* the audience became quiet.) The chart on this page shows the main types of subordinate clauses.

Collective noun. *See* Noun chart.

Common noun. *See* Noun chart.

Comparative degree. *See* Adjective; Adverb.

Complement A word or phrase that completes the meaning of a verb. The four basic kinds of complements are *direct objects, indirect objects, object complements,* and *subject complements.*

A **direct object** answers the question *What?* or *Whom?* after an action verb. (Kari found a *dollar.* Larry saw *Denise.*)

An **indirect object** answers the question *To whom? For whom? To what?* or *For what?* after an action verb. (Do *me* a favor. She gave the *child* a toy.)

An **object complement** answers the question *What?* after a direct object. An object complement is a noun, a pronoun, or an adjective that completes the meaning of a direct object by identifying or describing it. (The director made me the *understudy* for the role. The little girl called the puppy *hers.*)

A **subject complement** follows a subject and a linking verb. It identifies or describes a subject. The two kinds of subject complements are *predicate nominatives* and *predicate adjectives.*

A **predicate nominative** is a noun or pronoun that follows a linking verb and tells more about the subject. (The author of "The Raven" is *Poe.*)

A **predicate adjective** is an adjective that follows a linking verb and gives more information about the subject. (Ian became *angry* at the bully.)

Complex sentence. *See* Sentence.

Compound preposition. *See* Preposition.

Compound sentence. *See* Sentence.

Compound-complex sentence. *See* Sentence.

Conjunction A word that joins single words or groups of words.

A **coordinating conjunction** (*and, but, or, nor, for, yet, so*) joins words or groups of words that are equal in grammatical importance. (David *and* Ruth are twins. I was bored, *so* I left.)

Correlative conjunctions (*both . . . and, just as . . . so, not only . . . but also, either . . . or, neither . . . nor, whether . . . or*) work in pairs to join words and groups of words of equal importance. (Choose *either* the muffin *or* the bagel.)

A **subordinating conjunction** (*after, although, as if, because, before, if, since, so that, than, though, until, when, while*) joins a dependent idea or clause to a main clause. (Beth acted *as if* she felt ill.)

TYPES OF SUBORDINATE CLAUSES			
Clause	**Function**	**Example**	**Begins with . . .**
Adjective clause	Modifies a noun or pronoun	Songs *that have a strong beat* make me want to dance.	A relative pronoun such as *which, who, whom, whose,* or *that*
Adverb clause	Modifies a verb, an adjective, or an adverb	*Whenever Al calls me,* he asks to borrow my bike.	A subordinating conjunction such as *after, although, because, if, since, when,* or *where*
Noun clause	Serves as a subject, an object, or a predicate nominative	*What Philip did* surprised us.	Words such as *how, that, what, whatever, when, where, which, who, whom, whoever, whose,* or *why*

Conjunctive adverb An adverb used to clarify the relationship between clauses of equal weight in a sentence. Conjunctive adverbs are used to replace *and (also, besides, furthermore, moreover);* to replace *but (however, nevertheless, still);* to state a result *(consequently, therefore, so, thus);* to state equality *(equally, likewise, similarly).* (Ana was determined to get an A; *therefore,* she studied often.)

Coordinating conjunction. *See* Conjunction.

Correlative conjunction. *See* Conjunction.

Declarative sentence. *See* Sentence.

Definite article. *See* Article.

Demonstrative pronoun. *See* Pronoun.

Direct object. *See* Complement.

Emphatic form. *See* Verb tense.

Future tense. *See* Verb tense.

Gerund A verb form that ends in *–ing* and is used as a noun. A gerund may function as a subject, the object of a verb, or the object of a preposition. (*Smiling* uses fewer muscles than *frowning.* Marie enjoys *walking.*)

Gerund phrase. *See* Phrase.

Imperative mood. *See* Mood of verb.

Imperative sentence. *See* Sentence chart.

Indicative mood. *See* Mood of verb.

Indirect object. *See* Complement.

Infinitive A verb form that begins with the word *to* and functions as a noun, an adjective, or an adverb. (No one wanted *to answer.*) Note: When *to* precedes a verb, it is not a preposition but instead signals an infinitive.

Infinitive phrase. *See* Phrase.

Intensive pronoun. *See* Pronoun.

Interjection A word or phrase that expresses emotion or exclamation. An interjection has no grammatical connection to other words. Commas follow mild ones; exclamation points follow stronger ones. (*Well,* have a good day. *Wow!*)

Interrogative pronoun. *See* Pronoun.

Intransitive verb. *See* Verb.

Inverted order In a sentence written in *inverted order,* the predicate comes before the subject. Some sentences are written in inverted order for variety or special emphasis. (Up the beanstalk *scampered Jack.*) The subject also generally follows the predicate in a sentence that begins with here or there. (Here *was the solution* to his problem.) Questions, or interrogative sentences, are generally written in inverted order. In many questions, an auxiliary verb precedes the subject and the main verb follows it. (*Has* anyone *seen* Susan?) Questions that begin with *who* or *what* follow normal word order.

Irregular verb. *See* Verb tense.

Linking verb. *See* Verb.

Main clause. *See* Clause.

Mood of verb A verb expresses one of three moods: indicative, imperative, or subjunctive.

The indicative mood is the most common. It makes a statement or asks a question. (We *are* out of bread. *Will* you *buy* it?)

The imperative mood expresses a command or makes a request. (*Stop* acting like a child! Please *return* my sweater.)

The subjunctive mood is used to express, indirectly, a demand, suggestion, or statement of necessity (I demand that he *stop* acting like a child. It's necessary that she *buy* more bread.) The subjunctive is also used to state a condition or wish that is contrary to fact. This use of the subjunctive requires the past tense. (If you *were* a nice person, you *would return* my sweater.)

Nominative pronoun. *See* Pronoun.

Noun A word that names a person, a place, a thing, or an idea. The chart on this page shows the main types of nouns.

Noun clause. *See* Clause chart.

Noun of direct address. *See* Noun chart.

Number A noun, pronoun, or verb is *singular* in number if it refers to one; *plural* if it refers to more than one.

Object. *See* Complement.

Participle A verb form that can function as an adjective. Present participles always end in *–ing*. (The woman comforted the *crying* child.) Many past participles end in *–ed*. (We bought the beautifully *painted* chair.) However, irregular verbs form their past participles in some other way. (Cato was Caesar's *sworn* enemy.)

Passive voice. *See* Voice.

Past tense. *See* Verb tense.

Perfect tense. *See* Verb tense.

Personal pronoun. *See* Pronoun, Pronoun chart.

Phrase A group of words that acts in a sentence as a single part of speech.

An absolute phrase consists of a noun or pronoun that is modified by a participle or participial phrase but has no grammatical relation to the complete subject or predicate. (*The vegetables being done,* we finally sat down to eat dinner.)

An appositive phrase is an appositive along with any modifiers. If not essential to the meaning of the sentence, an appositive phrase is set off by commas. (Jack plans to go to the jazz concert, *an important musical event.*)

A gerund phrase includes a gerund plus its complements and modifiers. (*Playing the flute* is her hobby.)

An infinitive phrase contains the infinitive plus its complements and modifiers. (It is time *to leave for school.*)

A participial phrase contains a participle and any modifiers necessary to complete its meaning. (The woman *sitting over there* is my grandmother.)

A prepositional phrase consists of a preposition, its object, and any modifiers of the object. A prepositional phrase can function as an adjective, modifying a noun or a pronoun. (The dog *in the yard* is very gentle.) A prepositional phrase may also function as an adverb when it modifies a verb, an adverb, or

TYPES OF NOUNS		
Noun	**Function**	**Examples**
Abstract noun	Names an idea, a quality, or a characteristic	capitalism, terror
Collective noun	Names a group of things or people	herd, troop
Common noun	Names a general type of person, place, thing, or idea	city, building
Compound noun	Is made up of two or more words	checkerboard, globetrotter
Noun of direct address	Identifies the person or persons being spoken to	*Maria,* please stand.
Possessive noun	Shows possession, ownership, or the relationship between two nouns	my *sister's* room
Proper noun	Names a particular person, place, thing, or idea	Cleopatra, Italy, Christianity

an adjective. (The baby slept *on my lap.*)

A **verb phrase** consists of one or more auxiliary verbs followed by a main verb. (The job *will have been completed* by noon tomorrow.)

Positive degree. *See* Adjective.

Possessive noun. *See* Noun chart.

Predicate The verb or verb phrase and any objects, complements, or modifiers that express the essential thought about the subject of a sentence.

A **simple predicate** is a verb or verb phrase that tells something about the subject. (We *ran.*)

A **complete predicate** includes the simple predicate and any words that modify or complete it. (We *solved the problem in a short time.*)

A **compound predicate** has two or more verbs or verb phrases that are joined by a conjunction and share the same subject. (We *ran to the park* and *began to play baseball.*)

Predicate adjective. *See* Adjective; Complement.

Predicate nominative. *See* Complement.

Preposition A word that shows the relationship of a noun or pronoun to some other word in the sentence. Prepositions include *about, above, across, among, as, behind, below, beyond, but, by, down, during, except, for, from, into, like, near, of, on, outside, over, since, through, to, under, until, with.* (I usually eat breakfast *before* school.)

A **compound preposition** is made up of more than one word. *(according to, ahead of, as to, because of, by means of, in addition to, in spite of, on account of)* (We played the game *in spite of* the snow.)

Prepositional phrase. *See* Phrase.

Present tense. *See* Verb tense.

Progressive form. *See* Verb tense.

Pronoun A word that takes the place of a noun, a group of words acting as a noun, or another pronoun. The word or group of words that a pronoun refers to is called its **antecedent.** (In the following sentence, *Mari* is the antecedent of *she. Mari likes Mexican food, but she doesn't like Italian food.*)

A **demonstrative pronoun** points out specific persons, places, things, or ideas. *(this, that, these, those)*

An **indefinite pronoun** refers to persons, places, or things in a more general way than a noun does. *(all, another, any, both, each, either, enough, everything, few, many, most, much, neither, nobody, none, one, other, others, plenty, several, some)*

An **intensive pronoun** adds emphasis to another noun or pronoun. If an intensive pronoun is omitted, the meaning of the sentence will be the same. (Rebecca *herself* decided to look for a part-time job.)

An **interrogative pronoun** is used to form questions. *(who? whom? whose? what? which?)*

A **personal pronoun** refers to a specific person or thing. Personal pronouns have three cases: nominative, possessive, and objective. The case depends upon the function of the pronoun in a sentence. The chart on this page shows the case forms of personal pronouns.

A **reflexive pronoun** reflects back to a noun or pronoun used earlier in the sentence, indicating that the same person or thing is involved. (We told *ourselves* to be patient.)

PERSONAL PRONOUNS			
Case	**Singular Pronouns**	**Plural Pronouns**	**Function in Sentence**
Nominative	I, you, she, he, it	we, you, they	subject or predicate nominative
Objective	me, you, her, him, it	us, you, them	direct object, indirect object, or object of a preposition
Possessive	my, mine, your, yours, her, hers, his, its	our, ours, your, yours, their, theirs	replacement for the possessive form of a noun

A relative pronoun is used to begin a subordinate clause. *(who, whose, that, what, whom, whoever, whomever, whichever, whatever)*

Proper adjective. *See* Adjective.

Proper noun. *See* Noun chart.

Reflexive pronoun. *See* Pronoun.

Relative pronoun. *See* Pronoun.

Sentence A group of words expressing a complete thought. Every sentence has a subject and a predicate. Sentences can be classified by function or by structure. The chart on this page shows the categories by function; the following subentries describe the categories by structure. *See also* Subject; Predicate; Clauses.

A simple sentence has only one main clause and no subordinate clauses. *(Alan found an old violin.)* A simple sentence may contain a compound subject or a compound predicate or both. *(Alan and Teri found an old violin. Alan found an old violin and tried to play it. Alan and Teri found an old violin and tried to play it.)* The subject and the predicate can be expanded with adjectives, adverbs, prepositional phrases, appositives, and verbal phrases. As long as the sentence has only one main clause, however, it remains a simple sentence. *(Alan, rummaging in the attic, found an old violin.)*

A compound sentence has two or more main clauses. Each main clause has its own subject and predicate, and these main clauses are usually joined by a comma and a coordinating conjunction. *(Cats meow, and dogs bark, but ducks quack.)* Semicolons may also be used to join the main clauses in a compound sentence. *(The helicopter landed; the pilot had saved four passengers.)*

A complex sentence has one main clause and one or more subordinate clauses. *(Since the movie starts at eight, we should leave here by seven-thirty.)*

A compound-complex sentence has two or more main clauses and at least one subordinate clause. *(If we leave any later, we may miss the previews, and I want to see them.)*

Simple predicate. *See* Predicate.

Simple subject. *See* Subject.

Subject The part of a sentence that tells what the sentence is about.

A simple subject is the main noun or pronoun in the subject. *(Babies* crawl.)

A complete subject includes the simple subject and any words that modify it. *(The man from New Jersey* won the race.) In some sentences, the simple subject and the complete subject are the same. *(Birds* fly.)

A compound subject has two or more simple subjects joined by a conjunction. The subjects share the same verb. *(Firefighters* and *police officers* protect the community.)

Subjunctive mood. *See* Mood of verb.

Subordinate clause. *See* Clause.

Subordinating conjunction. *See* Conjunction.

Superlative degree. *See* Adjective; Adverb.

TYPES OF SENTENCES			
Sentence Type	**Function**	**Ends with . . .**	**Examples**
Declarative sentence	Makes a statement	A period	I did not enjoy the movie.
Exclamatory sentence	Expresses strong emotion	An exclamation point	What a good writer Consuela is!
Imperative sentence	Makes a request or gives a command	A period or an exclamation point	Please come to the party. Stop!
Interrogative sentence	Asks a question	A question mark	Is the composition due today?

Tense. *See* Verb tense.

Transitive verb. *See* Verb.

Verb A word that expresses action or a state of being. *(cooks, seem, laughed)*

An **action verb** tells what someone or something does. Action verbs can express either physical or mental action. (Crystal *decided* to *change* the tire herself.)

A **transitive verb** is an action verb that is followed by a word or words that answer the question *What?* or *Whom?* (I *held* the baby.)

An **intransitive verb** is an action verb that is *not* followed by a word that answers the question *What?* or *Whom?* (The baby *laughed.*)

A **linking verb** expresses a state of being by linking the subject of a sentence with a word or expression that identifies or describes the subject. (The lemonade *tastes* sweet. He *is* our new principal.) The most commonly used linking verb is *be* in all its forms *(am, is, are, was, were, will be, been, being).* Other linking verbs include *appear, become, feel, grow, look, remain, seem, sound, smell, stay, taste.*

An **auxiliary verb**, or helping verb, is a verb that accompanies the main verb to form a verb phrase. (I *have been* swimming.) The forms of *be* and *have* are the most common auxiliary verbs: *(am, is, are, was, were, being, been; has, have, had, having).* Other auxiliaries include *can, could, do, does, did, may, might, must, shall, should, will, would.*

Verb tense The tense of a verb indicates when the action or state of being occurs. All the verb tenses are formed from the four principal parts of a verb: a base form *(talk)*, a present participle *(talking)*, a simple past form *(talked)*, and a past participle *(talked)*. A **regular verb** forms its simple past and past participle by adding *-ed* to the base form. *(climb, climbed)* An **irregular verb** forms its past and past participle in some other way. *(get, got, gotten)*

In addition to present, past, and future tense, there are three perfect tenses.

The **present perfect tense** expresses an action or condition that occurred at some indefinite time in the past. This tense also shows an action or condition that began in the past and continues into the present. (She *has played* the piano for four years.)

The **past perfect tense** indicates that one past action or condition began *and* ended before another past action started. (Andy *had finished* his homework before I even began mine.)

The **future perfect tense** indicates that one future action or condition will begin *and* end before another future event starts. Use *will have* or *shall have* with the past participle of a verb. (By tomorrow, I *will have finished* my homework, too.)

The **progressive form** of a verb expresses a continuing action with any of the six tenses. To make the progressive forms, use the appropriate tense of the verb *be* with the present participle of the main verb. (She *is swimming.* She *has been swimming.*)

The **emphatic form** adds special force, or emphasis, to the present and past tense of a verb. For the emphatic form, use *do, does,* or *did* with the base form. (Toshi *did want* that camera.)

Verbal A verb form that functions in a sentence as a noun, an adjective, or an adverb. The three kinds of verbals are gerunds, infinitives, and participles. *See* Gerund; Infinitive; Participle.

Voice The **voice** of a verb shows whether the subject performs the action or receives the action of the verb.

A verb is in the **active voice** if the subject of the sentence performs the action. (The referee *blew* the whistle.)

A verb is in the **passive voice** if the subject of the sentence receives the action of the verb. (The whistle *was blown* by the referee.)

Mechanics

Capitalization

This section will help you recognize and use correct capitalization in sentences.

Rule	Example
Capitalize the first word in any sentence, including direct quotations and sentences in parentheses unless they are included in another sentence.	She said, "Come back soon." Emily Dickinson became famous only after her death. (She published only six poems during her lifetime.)
Rule of Thumb: Since people do not always speak in complete sentences, written dialogue may contain sentence fragments. In dialogue, capitalize the first word of each fragment, as well as of each complete sentence. For example: "Cute puppy," Ilse remarked.	
Always capitalize the pronoun *I* no matter where it appears in the sentence.	Some of my relatives think that I should become a doctor.
Capitalize proper nouns, including **a.** names of individuals and titles used in direct address preceding a name or describing a relationship.	George Washington; Dr. Morgan; Aunt Margaret
b. names of ethnic groups, national groups, political parties and their members, and languages.	Italian Americans; Aztec; the Republican party; a Democrat; Spanish
c. names of organizations, institutions, firms, monuments, bridges, buildings, and other structures.	Red Cross; Stanford University; General Electric; Lincoln Memorial; Tappan Zee Bridge; Chrysler Building; Museum of Natural History
d. trade names and names of documents, awards, and laws.	Microsoft; Declaration of Independence; Pulitzer Prize; Sixteenth Amendment
e. geographical terms and regions or localities.	Hudson River; Pennsylvania Avenue; Grand Canyon; Texas; the Midwest
f. names of planets and other heavenly bodies.	Venus; Earth; the Milky Way
g. names of ships, planes, trains, and spacecraft.	U.S.S. *Constitution*; *Spirit of St. Louis*; *Apollo 11*
h. names of most historical events, eras, calendar items, and religious names and items.	World War Two; Age of Enlightenment; June; Christianity; Buddhists; Bible; Easter; God

Rule	Example
i. titles of literary works, works of art, and musical compositions.	"Why I Live at the P.O."; *The Starry Night; Rhapsody in Blue*
j. names of specific school courses.	Advanced Physics; American History
Capitalize proper adjectives (adjectives formed from proper nouns).	Christmas tree; Hanukkah candles; Freudian psychology; American flag

Punctuation

This section will help you use these elements of punctuation correctly.

Rule	Example
Use a **period** at the end of a declarative sentence or a polite command.	I'm thirsty. Please bring me a glass of water.
Use an **exclamation point** to show strong feeling or after a forceful command.	I can't believe my eyes! Watch your step!
Use a **question mark** to indicate a direct question.	Who is in charge here?
Use a **colon** **a.** to introduce a list (especially after words such as *these*, *the following*, or *as follows*) and to introduce material that explains, restates, or illustrates previous material.	The following states voted for the amendment: Texas, California, Georgia, and Florida. The sunset was colorful: purple, orange, and red lit up the sky.

> **Rule of Thumb:** Do not use a colon between the verb and its complement. To be used correctly, a colon must follow a complete sentence.

Rule	Example
b. to introduce a long or formal quotation.	It was Mark Twain who stated the following proverb: "Man is the only animal that blushes. Or needs to."
c. in precise time measurements, biblical chapter and verse references, and business letter salutations.	3:35 P.M. 7:50 A.M. Gen. 1:10–11 Matt. 2:23 Dear Ms. Samuels: Dear Sir:

Rule	Example
Use a semicolon	
a. to separate main clauses that are not joined by a coordinating conjunction.	There were two speakers at Gettysburg that day; only Lincoln's speech is remembered.
b. to separate main clauses joined by a conjunctive adverb or by *for example* or *that is*.	Because of the ice storm, most students could not get to school; consequently, the principal canceled all classes for the day.
c. to separate the items in a series when these items contain commas.	The students at the rally came from Senn High School, in Chicago, Illinois; Niles Township High School, in Skokie, Illinois; and Evanston Township High School, in Evanston, Illinois.
d. to separate two main clauses joined by a coordinating conjunction when such clauses already contain several commas.	The designer combined the blue silk, brown linen, and beige cotton into a suit; but she decided to use the yellow chiffon, yellow silk, and white lace for an evening gown.
Use a comma	
a. between the main clauses of a compound sentence.	Ryan was late getting to study hall, and his footsteps echoed in the empty corridor.
b. to separate three or more words, phrases, or clauses in a series.	Mel bought carrots, beans, pears, and onions.
c. between coordinate modifiers.	That is a lyrical, moving poem.
d. to set off parenthetical expressions, interjections, and conjunctive adverbs.	Well, we missed the bus again.
	The weather is beautiful today; however, it is supposed to rain this weekend.
e. to set off nonessential words, clauses, and phrases, such as:	
—adverbial clauses	Since Ellen is so tall, the coach assumed she would be a good basketball player.
—adjective clauses	Scott, who had been sleeping, finally woke up.
—participles and participial phrases	Having found what he was looking for, he left.
—prepositional phrases	On Saturdays during the fall, I rake leaves.

> **Rule of Thumb:** Use a comma after a short introductory prepositional phrase only if the sentence would be misread without it.

Rule	Example
—infinitive phrases	To be honest, I'd like to stay awhile longer.
—appositives and appositive phrases	Ms. Kwan, a soft-spoken woman, ran into the street to hail a cab.
f. to set off direct quotations.	"My concert," Molly replied, "is tonight."
g. to set off an antithetical phrase.	Unlike Tom, Rob enjoys skiing.
h. to set a title after a person's name.	Margaret Thomas, Ph.D., was the guest speaker.
i. to separate the various parts of an address, a geographical term, or a date.	My new address is 324 Indian School Road, Albuquerque, New Mexico 85350. I moved on March 13, 1998.
j. after the salutation of an informal letter and after the closing of all letters.	Dear Helen, Sincerely,
k. to set off parts of a reference that direct the reader to the exact source.	You can find the article in the *Washington Post*, April 4, 1997, pages 33–34.
l. to set off words or names used in direct address and in tag questions.	Yuri, will you bring me my calculator? Lottie became a lawyer, didn't she?
Use a **dash** to signal a change in thought or to emphasize parenthetical material.	During the play, Maureen—and she'd be the first to admit it—forgot her lines. There are only two juniors attending—Mike Ramos and Ron Kim.

Rule of Thumb: A good test of the correct use of dashes is to delete the information that the dashes set off. If the remaining sentence retains its basic meaning, then the dashes were properly used. If the remaining sentence has lost crucial information, then the dashes were improperly used.

Use **parentheses** to set off supplemental material. Punctuate within the parentheses only if the punctuation is part of the parenthetical expression.	If you like jazz (and I assume you do), you will like this CD. (The soloist is Miles Davis.) The upper Midwest (which states does that include?) was hit by terrible floods last year.

Rule	Example
Use **brackets** to enclose information that you insert into a quotation for clarity or to enclose a parenthetical phrase that already appears within parentheses.	"He serves his [political] party best who serves the country best." —*Rutherford B. Hayes* The staircase (which was designed by a famous architect [Frank Lloyd Wright]) was inlaid with ceramic tile.
Use **ellipsis points** to indicate the omission of material from a quotation.	". . . Neither an individual nor a nation can commit the least act of injustice against the obscurest individual. . . ." —*Henry David Thoreau*

Use **quotation marks**

a. to enclose a direct quotation, as follows:

"Hurry up!" shouted Lisa.

When a quotation is interrupted, use two sets of quotation marks.

"A cynic," wrote Oscar Wilde, "is someone who knows the price of everything and the value of nothing."

Use single quotation marks for a quotation within a quotation.

"Did you say 'turn left' or 'turn right'?" asked Leon.

In writing dialogue, begin a new paragraph and use a new set of quotation marks every time the speaker changes.

"Do you really think the spaceship can take off?" asked the first officer.
"Our engineer assures me that we have enough power," the captain replied.

b. to enclose titles of short works, such as stories, poems, essays, articles, chapters, and songs.

"The Lottery" [short story]
"Provide, Provide" [poem]
"Civil Disobedience" [essay]

c. to enclose unfamiliar slang terms and unusual expressions.

The man called his grandson a "rapscallion."

d. to enclose a definition that is stated directly.

Gauche is a French word meaning "left."

Rule of Thumb: A good way to tell whether question marks and exclamation points go inside or outside quotation marks is to take the direct quotation out of the sentence and see how it would be punctuated if it stood alone. If it would end with a question mark or exclamation point, then that mark of punctuation should go within the quotation marks. If the new sentence would end with a period, then the question mark or exclamation point should go outside the quotation marks.

Rule	Example
Use italics **a.** for titles of books, lengthy poems, plays, films, television series, paintings and sculptures, long musical compositions, court cases, names of newspapers and magazines, ships, trains, airplanes, and spacecraft. Italicize and capitalize articles *(a, an, the)* at the beginning of a title only when they are part of the title.	*E.T.* [film]; *The Piano Lesson* [play]; *The Starry Night* [painting]; *The New Yorker* [magazine]; *Challenger* [spacecraft]; *Concorde* [airplane]; *The Great Gatsby* [book]; the *Chicago Tribune* [newspaper]
b. for foreign words and expressions that are not used frequently in English.	Luciano waved good-bye, saying, *"Arrivederci."*
c. for words, letters, and numerals used to represent themselves.	There is no *Q* on the telephone key pad. Number your paper from *1* through *10*.
Use an apostrophe **a.** for a possessive form, as follows: Add an apostrophe and *-s* to all singular nouns, plural nouns not ending in *-s*, singular indefinite pronouns, and compound nouns. Add only an apostrophe to a plural noun that ends in *-s*.	the tree's leaves the man's belt the bus's tires the children's pets everyone's favorite my mother-in-law's job the Attorney General's decision the baseball player's error the cats' bowls
If two or more persons possess something jointly, use the possessive form for the last person named. If they possess it individually, use the possessive form for each one's name.	Ted and Harriet's family Ted's and Harriet's bosses Lewis and Clark's expedition Lewis's and Clark's clothes
b. to express amounts of money or time that modify a noun.	two cents' worth three day's drive (You can use a hyphenated adjective instead: a three-day drive.)
c. in place of omitted letters or numerals.	haven't [have not] the winter of '95
d. to form the plural of letters, numerals, symbols, and words used to represent themselves. Use an apostrophe and *-s*.	You wrote two *5*'s instead of one. How many *s*'s are there in Mississippi? Why did he use three *l*'s at the end of the sentence?

Rule	Example
Use a **hyphen**	
a. after any prefix joined to a proper noun or proper adjective.	all-American pre-Columbian
b. after the prefixes *all-*, *ex-*, and *self-* joined to any noun or adjective, after the prefix *anti-* when it joins a word beginning with *i*, after the prefix *vice-* (except in *vice president*), and to avoid confusion between words that begin with *re-* and look like another word.	ex-president self-important anti-inflammatory vice-principal re-creation of the event recreation time re-pair the socks repair the computer

> **Rule of Thumb:** Remember that the prefix *anti-* requires a hyphen when followed by a word that begins with *i* in order to prevent spelling words with two successive *i*'s. Otherwise, *anti* does not require a hyphen except before a capitalized word.

Rule	Example
c. in a compound adjective that precedes a noun.	a bitter-tasting liquid
d. in any spelled-out cardinal or ordinal numbers up to *ninety-nine* or *ninety-ninth*, with a fraction used as an adjective, or to separate two numbers in a span.	twenty-three eighty-fifth one-half cup 1914-1918
e. to divide a word at the end of a line between syllables.	air-port scis-sors fill-ing fin-est

Abbreviations

Abbreviations are shortened forms of words.

Rule	Example
Use only one period if an abbreviation occurs at the end of a sentence. If the sentence ends with a question mark or exclamation point, use the period and the second mark of punctuation.	We didn't get home until 3:30 A.M. Did you get home before 4:00 A.M.? I can't believe you didn't get home until 3:30 A.M.!
Capitalize abbreviations of proper nouns and abbreviations related to historical dates.	John Kennedy Jr. P.O. Box 333 800 B.C. A.D. 456 C.E. 1066
Use all capital letters and no periods for most abbreviations of organizations and government agencies.	CBS CIA PIN CPA IBM NFL MADD GE FBI

Rule	Example
Use abbreviations for some personal titles.	Ms. Kasuga; Dr. Platt; Sandra Held, D.D.S.
Abbreviate units of measure used with numerals in technical or scientific writing, but not in ordinary prose.	ft. (foot) in. (inch) oz. (ounce) g (gram) l (liter) m (meter) km (kilometer)

Numbers and Numerals

This section will help you understand when to use numerals and when to spell out numbers.

Rule	Example
In general, spell out cardinal and ordinal numbers that can be written in one or two words.	We just celebrated my brother's twenty-third birthday.
Spell out any number that occurs at the beginning of a sentence.	One hundred forty people bought tickets for the concert.
In general, use numerals (numbers expressed in figures) to express numbers that would be written in more than two words. Extremely high numbers are often expressed as a numeral followed by the word *million* or *billion*.	There are 513 students in our school. The Suarez family donated $1.2 million to the new children's hospital.
If related numbers appear in the same sentence, use all numerals.	Our grammar school had 150 students, but my cousin's had more than 2,000.
Use numerals to express amounts of money, decimals, and percentages.	$45.99 4.59 20.5%
Use numerals to express the day and year in a date and to express the precise time with the abbreviations *A.M.* and *P.M.*	He was supposed to be at the airport on August 31, 1997, at 3:30 P.M.
To express a century when the word century is used, or a decade when the century is clear from the context, spell out the number. When a century and a decade are expressed as a single unit, use numerals followed by *-s*.	The nineteenth century was a time of turmoil in the United States, especially during the sixties. Do you remember the 1980s?
Use numerals for streets and avenues numbered above ten and for all house, apartment, and room numbers.	Ramona lived at the corner of Fourth and Elm streets. Todd worked in Suite 412, at 1723 West 18th Avenue.

Spelling

The following basic rules, examples, and exceptions will help you master the spellings of many words.

Forming plurals

English words form plurals in many ways. Most nouns simply add -s. The following chart shows other ways of forming plural nouns and some common exceptions to the pattern.

GENERAL RULES FOR FORMING PLURALS		
If a word ends in	**Rule**	**Example**
ch, s, sh, x, z	add -*es*	glass, glasses
a consonant + *y*	change *y* to *i* and add -*es*	caddy, caddies
a vowel + *y* or *o*	add only -*s*	cameo, cameos monkey, monkeys
a consonant + *o* common exceptions	generally add -*es* but sometimes add only -*s*	potato, potatoes cello, cellos
f or *ff* common exceptions	add -*s* change *f* to *v* and add -*es*	cliff, cliffs hoof, hooves
lf	change *f* to *v* and add -*es*	half, halves

A few plurals are exceptions to the rules in the previous chart, but they are easy to remember. The following chart lists these plurals and some examples.

SPECIAL RULES FOR FORMING PLURALS	
Rule	**Example**
To form the plural of proper names and one-word compound nouns, follow the general rules for plurals.	Cruz, Cruzes Mancuso, Mancusos crossroad, crossroads
To form the plural of hyphenated compound nouns or compound nouns of more than one word, make the most important word plural.	passer-by, passers-by ghost writer, ghost writers
Some nouns have unusual plural forms.	goose, geese child, children
Some nouns have the same singular and plural forms.	moose scissors pants

Adding prefixes

When adding a prefix to a word, keep the original spelling of the word. Use a hyphen only when the original word is capitalized or with the prefixes *all-, ex-,* and *self-* joined to a noun or adjective.

co + operative = cooperative   inter + change = interchange

pro + African = pro-African   ex + partner = ex-partner

Suffixes and the silent *e*

Many English words end in a silent letter *e.* Sometimes the *e* is dropped when a suffix is added. When adding a suffix that begins with a consonant to a word that ends in silent *e,* keep the *e.*

like + ness = likeness   sure + ly = surely

COMMON EXCEPTIONS awe + ful = awful; judge + ment = judgment

When adding a suffix that begins with a vowel to a word that ends in silent *e,* usually drop the *e.*

believe + able = believable   expense + ive = expensive

COMMON EXCEPTION mile + age = mileage

When adding a suffix that begins with *a* or *o* to a word that ends in *ce* or *ge,* keep the *e* so the word will retain the soft *c* or *g* sound.

notice + able = noticeable   courage + ous = courageous

When adding a suffix that begins with a vowel to a word that ends in *ee* or *oe,* keep the final *e.*

see + ing = seeing   toe + ing = toeing

Drop the final silent *e* after the letters *u* or *w.*

argue + ment = argument   owe + ing = owing

Keep the final silent *e* before the suffix *-ing* when necessary to avoid ambiguity.

singe + ing = singeing

Suffixes and the final *y*

When adding a suffix to a word that ends in a consonant + *y,* change the *y* to *i* unless the suffix begins with *i.* Keep the *y* in a word that ends in a vowel + *y.*

try + ed = tried   fry + ed = fried

stay + ing = staying   display + ed = displayed

copy + ing = copying   joy + ous = joyous

Adding *-ly* and *-ness*

When adding *-ly* to a word that ends in a single *l,* keep the *l,* but when the word ends in a double *l,* drop one *l.* When the word ends in a consonant + *le,* drop the *le.* When adding *-ness* to a word that ends in *n,* keep the *n.*

casual + ly = casually	practical + ly = practically
dull + ly = dully	probable + ly = probably
open + ness = openness	mean + ness = meanness

Doubling the final consonant

Double the final consonant in words that end in a consonant preceded by a single vowel if the word is one syllable, if it has an accent on the last syllable that remains there even after the suffix is added, or if it is a word made up of a prefix and a one-syllable word.

stop + ing = stopping	admit + ed = admitted
replan + ed = replanned	

Do not double the final consonant if the accent is not on the last syllable, or if the accent shifts when the suffix is added. Also do not double the final consonant if the final consonant is *x* or *w.* If the word ends in a consonant and the suffix begins with a consonant, do not double the final consonant.

benefit + ed = benefited	similar + ly = similarly
raw + er = rawer	box + like = boxlike
friend + less = friendless	rest + ful = restful

Forming compound words

When joining a word that ends in a consonant to a word that begins with a consonant, keep both consonants.

out + line = outline	after + noon = afternoon
post + card = postcard	pepper + mint = peppermint

ie and *ei*

Learning this rhyme can save you many misspellings: "Write *i* before *e* except after *c,* or when sounded like *a* as in *neighbor* and *weigh.*" There are many exceptions to this rule, including *seize, seizure, leisure, weird, height, either, neither, forfeit.*

-cede, -ceed, and *-sede*

Because of the relatively few words with *sēd* sounds, these words are worth memorizing.

These words use *-cede:* **accede, precede, secede.**
One word uses *-sede:* **supersede.**
Three words use *-ceed:* **exceed, proceed, succeed.**

The Writing Process

Writing is a process with five stages: *prewriting, drafting, revising, editing/proofreading,* and *publishing/presenting.* These stages often overlap, and their importance, weight, and even their order vary according to your needs and goals. Because writing is recursive, you almost always have to double back somewhere in this process, perhaps to gather more information or to re-evaluate your ideas.

The Writing Process

Prewriting

The prewriting stage includes coming up with ideas, making connections, gathering information, defining and refining the topic, and making a plan for a piece of writing.

Tips for prewriting

- Begin with an interesting idea (*what* you will write about).
- Decide the purpose of the writing (*why* you are writing).
- Identify the audience (for *whom* you are writing).
- Explore your idea through a technique such as freewriting, clustering, making diagrams, or brainstorming.

   Freewriting is writing nonstop for a set time, usually only five or ten minutes. The idea is to keep pace with your thoughts, getting them on paper before they vanish. Freewriting can start anywhere and go anywhere.

   Clustering begins with writing a word or phrase in the middle of a sheet of paper. Circle the word or phrase; then think of related words and ideas. Write them in bubbles connected to the central bubble. As you cluster, connect related ideas. The finished cluster will be a diagram of how your ideas can be organized.

Brainstorming is creating a free flow of ideas with a group of people—it's like freewriting with others. Start with a topic or question; encourage everyone to join in freely. Accept all ideas without judgment, and follow each idea as far as it goes. You can evaluate the ideas later.

- Search for information in print and nonprint sources.
- If you are writing a personal essay, all of the information may come from your own experiences and feelings. If you are writing a report or a persuasive essay, you will probably need to locate pertinent factual information and take notes on it. Besides library materials, such as books, magazines, and newspapers, you will want to use the Internet and other on-line resources. You may also want to interview people with experience or specialized knowledge related to your topic.
- As you gather ideas and information, jot them down on note cards to use as you draft.
- Evaluate all ideas and information to determine or fine-tune the topic.
- Organize information and ideas into a plan that serves as the basis of writing.
- Develop a rough outline reflecting the method of organization you have chosen. Include your main points and supporting details.
- Find and include missing information or ideas that might add interest or help accomplish the purpose of the writing.

Drafting

In this stage you translate into writing the ideas and information you gathered during prewriting. Drafting is an opportunity to explore and develop your ideas.

Tips for drafting

- Follow the plan made during prewriting, but be flexible. New and better ideas may come to you as you develop your ideas: be open to them.
- Transform notes and ideas into related sentences and paragraphs, but don't worry about grammar or mechanics. At this point it is usually better to concentrate on getting your ideas on paper. You might want to circle or annotate ideas or sections that need more work.
- Determine the tone or attitude of the writing.
- Try to formulate an introduction that will catch the interest of your intended audience.

Revising

In this stage, review and evaluate your draft to make sure it accomplishes its purpose and speaks to its intended audience. When revising, interacting with a peer reviewer can be especially helpful.

Using peer review

Ask one or more of your classmates to read your draft. Here are some specific ways in which you can direct their responses.

- Have readers tell you in their own words what they have read. If you do not hear your ideas restated, you will want to revise for clarity.
- Ask readers to tell you what parts of your writing they liked best and why. You may want to expand those elements when you revise.
- Discuss the ideas in your writing with your readers. Include any new insights you gain in your revision.
- Ask readers for their suggestions in specific areas, such as organization, word choice, or examples.

You may want to take notes on your readers' suggestions so you will have a handy reference as you revise.

Tips for the peer reviewer

When you are asked to act as a reviewer for a classmate's writing, the following tips will help you do the most effective job:

- Read the piece all the way through—without commenting—to judge its overall effect.
- Tell the writer how you responded to the piece. For example, did you find it informative? interesting? amusing?
- Jot down comments on a separate sheet of paper.
- Ask the writer about parts you don't understand.
- Think of questions to ask that will help the writer improve the piece.
- Be sure that your suggestions are constructive.
- Keep in mind that your job is not to criticize but to help the writer improve what he or she has written.
- Answer the writer's questions honestly. Think about how you would like someone to respond to you.

Tips for revising

- Be sure you have said everything you wanted to say. If not, *add.*
- If you find a section that does not relate to your topic, *cut it.*
- If your ideas are not in a logical order, *rearrange* sentences and paragraphs.
- *Rewrite* any unclear sentences.
- Evaluate your introduction to be sure it creates interest, leads the reader smoothly into your topic, and states your main idea. Also evaluate your conclusion to be sure it either summarizes your writing or effectively brings it to an end.
- Evaluate your word choices. Choose vivid verbs and precise nouns. Use a thesaurus to help you.
- Consider the comments of your peer reviewer. Evaluate them carefully and apply those that will help you create a more effective piece of writing.

Editing/Proofreading

In the editing stage, you polish your revised draft and proofread it for errors in grammar and spelling. Use this proofreading checklist to help you check for errors, and use the proofreading symbols in the chart below to mark places that need corrections.

☑ Have I avoided run-on sentences and sentence fragments and punctuated sentences correctly?

☑ Have I used every word correctly, including plurals, possessives, and frequently confused words?

☑ Do verbs and subjects agree? Are verb tenses correct?

☑ Do pronouns refer clearly to their antecedents and agree with them in person, number, and gender?

☑ Have I used adverb and adjective forms and modifying phrases correctly?

☑ Have I spelled every word correctly, and checked the unfamiliar ones in a dictionary?

Proofreading Symbols		
⊙	Lieut. Brown	Insert a period.
∧	No one came to the party.	Insert a letter or a word.
=	I enjoyed paris.	Capitalize a letter.
/	The Class ran a bake sale.	Make a capital letter lowercase.
⌒	The campers are home sick.	Close up a space.
🔘	They visited N.Y.	Spell out.
∧ ∧	Sue, please come, I need your help.	Insert a comma or a semicolon.
∩	He enjoyed feild day.	Transpose the position of letters or words.
#	alltogether	Insert a space.
ℐ	We went to to Boston.	Delete letters or words.
∨ ∨ ∨	She asked Who's coming?	Insert quotation marks or an apostrophe.
/ = /	mid January	Insert a hyphen.
¶	"Where?" asked Karl. "Over there," said Ray.	Begin a new paragraph.

Publishing/Presenting

There are a number of ways you can share your work. You could publish it in a magazine, a class anthology, or another publication, or read your writing aloud to a group. You could also join a writer's group and read one another's works.

Writing Modes

Writing may be classified as expository, descriptive, narrative, or persuasive. Each of these classifications, or modes, has its own purpose.

Expository Writing

Expository writing gives instructions, defines or explains new terms or ideas, explains relationships, compares one thing or opinion to another, or explains how to do something. Expository essays usually include a thesis statement in the introduction. The chart below shows types of expository writing. You might wish to combine several of them to achieve your purpose in an essay.

As you write an expository essay or report, use this checklist.

☑ Does the opening contain attention-grabbing details or intriguing questions to hook the reader?

☑ Have I provided sufficient information to my audience in a clear and interesting way?

☑ Have I presented information in a logical order?

☑ Have I used appropriate transitional words and phrases?

☑ Have I checked the accuracy of the information I have provided?

☑ Have I defined any unfamiliar terms and concepts?

☑ Are my comparisons and contrasts clear and logical?

☑ Have I supplied a satisfactory conclusion?

Type	Definition	Example
Process explanation	Explains how something happens, works, or is done, using step-by-step organization	The steps one young director took to make his first film
Cause and effect	Identifies the causes and/or effects of something and examines the relationship between causes and effects	The cause of the recent trend toward low-budget independent films
Comparison and contrast	Examines similarities and differences to find relationships and draw conclusions	How the features of a typical independent film compare with the features of a high-budget action film
Building a hypothesis	Uses patterns of facts to offer explanations or predictions and tests the hypothesis	More (or fewer) independent films to be made in the future
Problem and solution	Examines aspects of a complex problem and explores or proposes possible solutions	Ways in which young filmmakers can obtain funds to get their films made

Descriptive Writing

Description recreates an experience primarily through the use of sensory details. However, good descriptive writing is more than just a collection of sensory details. A writer should always strive to create a single impression that all the details support. To do so requires careful planning as well as choices about order of information, topic sentences, and figurative language.

Use the checklist at the right as you revise your descriptive writing.

☑ Did I create interest in my introduction?

☑ Are my perspective and my subject clearly stated in my topic sentence?

☑ Did I organize details carefully and consistently?

☑ Did I vary my sentences, including gerund, participial, and infinitive structures where appropriate?

☑ Did I order information effectively?

☑ Have I chosen precise, vivid words?

☑ Do transitions clearly and logically connect the ideas?

☑ Have I used fresh, lively figures of speech and sensory details?

☑ Have I created a strong, unified impression?

Narrative Writing

Narrative writing, whether factual or fictional, tells a story and has these elements: characters, plot, point of view, theme, and setting. The plot usually involves a conflict between a character and an opposing character or force.

Use this checklist as you revise your narrative writing.

☑ Did I introduce characters and a setting?

☑ Did I develop a plot that begins with an interesting problem or conflict?

☑ Did I build suspense, lead the reader to a climax, and end with a resolution?

☑ Did I use dialogue to move the story along?

☑ Did I present a clear and consistent point of view?

☑ Is my writing vivid and expressive?

Persuasive Writing

Persuasive writing expresses a writer's opinion. The goal of persuasion is to make an audience change its opinion and, perhaps, take action. Effective persuasive writing uses strong, relative evidence to support its claims. This kind of writing often requires careful research, organization, and attention to language.

Use this checklist for persuasive writing.

☑ Did I keep my audience's knowledge and attitudes in mind from start to finish?

☑ Did I state my position in a clear thesis statement?

☑ Have I included ample supporting evidence, and is it convincing?

☑ Have I addressed opposing viewpoints?

☑ Have I avoided errors in logic?

☑ Have I used strong, specific words to support my argument?

Research Paper Writing

More than any other type of paper, research papers are the product of a search—a search for data, for facts, for informed opinions, for insights, and for new information.

Kinds of Research Papers

Three common approaches to writing a research paper are listed below. Sometimes writers combine approaches. For example, they might evaluate the research of others and then conduct original research.

- A **summary paper** explores a topic by summing up the opinions of other writers. The author of the paper does not express an opinion about the subject.
- An **evaluative paper** states an opinion and backs it up with evidence found in primary and secondary sources.
- An **original paper** is based on the writer's own original research—for example, observation, experimentation, interviews. It leads to new insights or information about the topic.

Guidelines for Writing a Research Paper

A research paper is almost always a long-term assignment. Set a schedule. If you have six weeks to complete the assignment, your schedule might look like this.

Week 1	Week 2	Week 3	Week 4	Week 5	Week 6
Prewriting Researching and Outlining			Drafting	Revising	Editing and Presenting

Selecting a topic

- If a specific topic is not assigned, choose a topic. Begin with the assigned subject or a subject that interests you. Read general sources of information about that subject and narrow your focus to some aspect of it that interests you. Good places to start are encyclopedia articles and the tables of contents of books on the subject. A computerized library catalog will also display many subheads related to general topics. Find out if sufficient information about your topic is available.
- As you read about the topic, develop your paper's central idea, which is the purpose of your research. Even though this idea might change as you do more research, it can begin to guide your efforts. For example, if you were assigned the subject of the Civil War, you might find that you're interested

in women's roles during that war. As you read, you might narrow your topic down to women who went to war, women who served as nurses for the Union, or women who took over farms and plantations in the South.

Conducting a broad search for information

- Generate a series of researchable questions about your chosen topic. Then research to find answers to your questions.
- Among the many sources you might use are the card catalog, the computer catalog, the *Reader's Guide to Periodical Literature* (or a computerized equivalent, such as InfoTrac®), newspaper indexes, and specialized references such as biographical encyclopedias.
- If possible, use primary sources as well as secondary sources. A **primary source** is a firsthand account of an event—for example, the diary of a woman who served in the army in the Civil War is a primary source. **Secondary sources** are sources written by people who did not experience or influence the event. Locate specific information efficiently by using the table of contents, indexes, chapter headings, and graphic aids.

Developing a working bibliography

If a work seems useful, write a **bibliography card** for it. On an index card, write down the author, title, city of publication, publisher, and date of publication, and any other information you will need to identify the source. Number your cards in the upper right-hand corner so you can keep them in order.

Following are model bibliography, or source, cards.

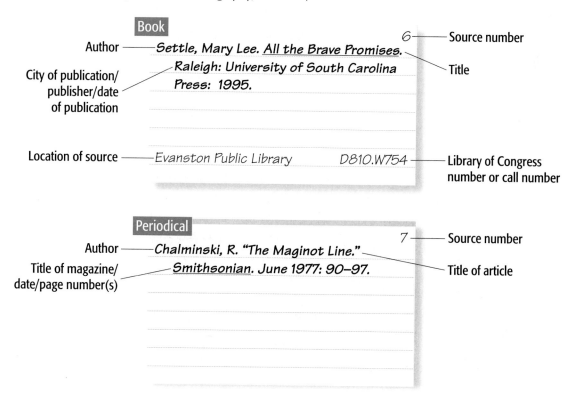

Book

Author —— Settle, Mary Lee. *All the Brave Promises*.

6 —— Source number

—— Title

City of publication/ publisher/date of publication —— Raleigh: University of South Carolina Press: 1995.

Location of source —— Evanston Public Library   D810.W754 —— Library of Congress number or call number

Periodical

Author —— Chalminski, R. "The Maginot Line."

7 —— Source number

Title of magazine/ date/page number(s) —— *Smithsonian*. June 1977: 90–97.

—— Title of article

Title ——— **"V for Victory: Women at War."**

Title of database ——— *cybersuperstores. On-line. Excite!*

Date of access ——— 12 Aug. 1998.

[On-line source]

17 ——— Source number

——— Publication medium/ name of computer service

Evaluating your sources

Your sources should be **a**uthoritative, **r**eliable, **t**imely, and **s**uitable. **(arts)**

- The source should be **authoritative.** The author should be well known in the field. An author who has written several books or articles about a subject or who is frequently quoted may be considered an authority. You might also consult *Book Review Index* and *Book Review Digest* to find out how other experts in the field have evaluated a book or an article.
- The source should be **reliable.** If possible, avoid material from popular magazines in favor of that from more scholarly journals. Be especially careful to evaluate material from on-line sources. For example, the Web site of a well-known university is more reliable than that of an individual. (You might also consult a librarian or your instructor for guidance in selecting reliable on-line sources.)
- The source should be **timely.** Use the most recent material available, particularly for subjects of current importance. Check the publication date of books as well as the month and year of periodicals.
- The source should be **suitable,** or **appropriate.** Consider only material that is relevant to the purpose of your paper. Do not waste time on books or articles that have little bearing on your topic. If you are writing on a controversial topic, you should include material that represents more than one point of view.

Compiling and organizing note cards

Careful notes will help you to organize the material for your paper.

- As you reread and study sources, write useful information on index cards. Be sure that each note card identifies the source (use the number of the bibliography card that corresponds to each source).
- Write the page number on which you found the information in the lower right-hand corner of the card. If one card contains several notes, write the page number in parentheses after the relevant material.

- Three helpful ways to take notes are paraphrasing, summarizing, and quoting directly.

   1. **Paraphrase** important details that you want to remember; that is, use your own words to restate specific information.

   2. **Summarize** main ideas that an author presents. When you summarize several pages, be sure to note the page on which the material begins and the page on which it ends—for example, 213–221.

   3. **Quote** the exact words of an author only when the actual wording is important. Be careful about placing the author's words in quotation marks.

- Identify the subject of each note card with a short phrase written in the upper left.

> Avoid **plagiarism**—presenting an author's words or ideas as if they were your own. Remember that you must credit the source not only for material directly quoted but also for any facts or ideas obtained from the source.

See the sample note card below, which includes information about careers and goals from three pages.

> 12
>
> *Careers and goals*
>
> *Many people "crave work that will spark . . . excitement and energy." (5) Sher recognizes that a career does not necessarily satisfy a person's aim in life. (24) She also offers advice on how to overcome obstacles that people experience in defining their goals. (101)*

- Organize your note cards to develop a **working outline.** Begin by sorting them into piles of related cards. Try putting the piles together in different ways that suggest an organizational pattern. (If, at this point, you discover that you do not have enough information, go back and do further research.) Many methods of organization are possible. You might also combine methods of organization. Three of the most common methods of organization are described on the next page.

Method	Description	Example
Chronological	Information arranged according to when it happened; often used in narratives and in papers describing historical change	A survey of early space-race events that led to the 1969 moon landing
Cause and effect	Items arranged showing how one development directly influenced another; often used in papers explaining why something happened	An analysis of how World War II changed the lives of African Americans and contributed to the rise of the Civil Rights movement
Cumulative	Items arranged according to how important or how familiar each one is; often used in persuasive papers and in those evaluating results	A discussion of the impact of the discovery of the laser on surgical techniques

Developing a thesis statement

A thesis statement tells what your topic is and what you intend to say about it—for example, "World War II changed the lives of African Americans and contributed to the rise of the Civil Rights movement."

- Start by examining your central idea.
- Refine it to reflect the information that you gathered in your research.
- Next, consider your approach to the topic. What is the purpose of your research? Are you proving or disproving something? illustrating a cause-and-effect relationship? offering a solution to a problem? examining one aspect of the topic thoroughly? predicting an outcome?
- Revise your central idea to reflect your approach.
- Be prepared to revise your thesis statement if necessary.

Drafting your paper

Consult your working outline and your notes as you start to draft your paper.

- Concentrate on getting your ideas down in a complete and logical order.
- Write an introduction and a conclusion. An effective introduction creates interest, perhaps by beginning with a question or a controversial quotation; it should also contain your thesis statement. An effective conclusion will summarize main points, restate your thesis, explain how the research points to important new questions to explore, and bring closure to the paper.

Documenting sources

Since a research paper, by its nature, is built on the work of others, you must carefully document all the sources you have used.

- Name the sources of words, ideas, and facts that you borrow.
- In addition to citing books and periodicals from which you take information, cite song lyrics, letters, and excerpts from literature.

- Also credit original ideas that are expressed graphically in tables, charts, and diagrams, as well as the sources of any visual aids you may include, such as photographs.
- You need not cite the source of any information that is common knowledge, such as "John F. Kennedy was assassinated in 1963 in Dallas, Texas."

In-text citations The Modern Language Association (MLA) recommends citations in the text that refer readers to a list of works cited. This style of documentation is parenthetical and consists of two main elements: the author's name and the page number or numbers on which the information is found. Put the documentation at the end of a clause or sentence. The parentheses that enclose it should come before commas and periods, but after quotation marks.

Type of Source	Style of Citation	Example
The author is named in text.	Put page number only in parentheses.	McDonald claims . . . (178)
The author is not named in the text.	Put author's last name and page number in parentheses.	(Goodrich 70–71)
The text has more than one author.	Put authors' last names in parentheses if all are not named in the text.	(McKnight and Williams 145)
No author is listed (usually in magazine articles).	Give title of article, or abbreviation of it, and page number in parentheses.	("Realism" 993)
More than one work by the same author is in the paper.	Include words from the title in the reference.	(Pratt, *Modern Art* 99–102)
You use a quotation that appears in a work written by another author.	Place the abbreviation "qtd. in" before author and page.	(qtd. in Dennis 47)
You refer to a novel, play, or poem.	Include: page and chapter in a novel; part (if there is more than one part) and line number in a poem; act and scene for a play, plus line number for a verse play	(Cather 72, ch. 3) (*Iliad* 9.19) (Jackson 2.2.15–18)
You cite more than one volume of a multivolume work.	Include the volume number and page number.	(Hawaii Volcano Observatory 2:140)
A work in an anthology.	Cite the name of the author not the anthology editor.	(Jeffers 16)

Compiling a list of works cited

At the end of your text, provide an alphabetized list of published works or other sources cited.

- Include complete publishing information for each source.
- For magazine and newspaper articles, include the page numbers. If an article is continued on a different page, use + after the first page number.
- For on-line sources, include the date accessed.
- Cite only those sources from which you actually use information.
- Arrange entries in alphabetical order according to the author's last name. Write the last name first. If no author is given, alphabetize by title.
- For long entries, indent five spaces every line after the first.

Some sample citations follow. Notice how each entry is punctuated and indented.

How to cite sources

Books	
One author	Settle, Mary Lee. <u>All the Brave Promises</u>. Charlotte: University of South Carolina Press, 1995.
Two or more authors	Haynesworth, Leslie, and David Toomey. <u>Amelia Earhart's Daughters</u>. New York: Morrow, 1998.
More than one work by an author	Levinson, Jay Conrad, and Seth Godin. <u>Get What You Deserve!</u> New York: Avon Books, 1997. ———. <u>The Guerilla Marketing Handbook</u>. New York: Houghton Mifflin, 1995.
One editor	Baker, Russell, ed. <u>The Norton Book of Light Verse</u>. New York: W.W. Norton, 1986.
Selections within books	
One selection from a book of one author's works	Bradstreet, Anne. "Of the Four Ages of Man." <u>The Works of Anne Bradstreet</u>. Ed. Jeannine Hensley. Cambridge: Harvard University Press, 1967. 51–64.
One selection from a book of several authors' works	Kingston, Maxine Hong. "The Grandfather of the Sierra Nevada Mountains." <u>American Mosaic</u>. Ed. Barbara Roche Rico and Sandra Mano. Boston: Houghton Mifflin, 1995. 122–141.
One selection from a collection of longer works	Shakespeare, William. <u>Cymbeline</u>. <u>The Riverside Shakespeare</u>. Ed. G. Blakemore Evans. Boston: Houghton Mifflin, 1974.

Articles from magazines, newspapers, and journals	
Weekly magazine article	Darr, A. "The Long Flight Home." <u>U. S. News and World Report</u> 17 Nov. 1997: 66–68.
Monthly magazine article	Chelminski, R. "The Maginot Line." <u>Smithsonian</u> June 1997: 90–96+.
Newspaper article with byline	Wells, Ken. "View from a Canoe." <u>The Wall Street Journal</u> 4 Aug. 1998: 1+.
Newspaper or magazine article, no byline	"Accounts of Blast at Odds." <u>Saint Paul Pioneer Press</u> 9 Aug. 1998: 1+.
Scholarly journal article	Rubinstein, William, and Richard Levy. "No Substitute for Victory." <u>The Wilson Quarterly</u> 21 (1997): 119–120.

Electronic sources: Sources accessed by computer, either on CD-ROM or on-line	
CD-ROM	"Time Warner, Inc.: Sales Summary, 1988–1992." <u>Disclosure/Worldscope. W/D Partners</u>. Oct. 1993.
Article in reference database	"Fresco." <u>Britannica Online</u>. Vers 97.1.1. Mar. 1997. Encyclopaedia Britannica. 18 Dec. 1998 <http://www.eb.com.180>.
Article in electronic journal	Machlis, Sharon. "Bookseller Beefs Up Products, Searches." <u>Computerworld</u> 2 Nov. 1998. 17 Dec. 1998 <http://www.elibrary.com/search.cgi?id=119940369x0y6229w3>.
Article at a professional site	<u>The Botany Libraries</u>. Harvard University. 17 Dec. 1998 <http://www.herbaria.harvard.edu/libraries/libraries.html>.

Other sources	
Radio/television interview	Berry, Wendell. Interview with Noah Adams. <u>All Things Considered</u>. Natl. Public Radio. WBEZ, Chicago. 24 Dec. 1998.
Television or radio program	"The cost of winning at all costs." <u>Dateline NBC</u>. NBC. WMAQ, Chicago. 31 July 1998.

Preparing a manuscript

Follow the guidelines of the Modern Language Association when you prepare the final copy of your research paper.

- **Heading** On separate lines in the upper left-hand corner of the first page, include your name, your teacher's name, the course name, and the date.
- **Title** Center the title on the line below the heading.
- **Numbering** Number the pages one-half inch from the top of the page in the right-hand corner. Write your last name before each page number after the first page.
- **Spacing** Use double spacing throughout.
- **Margins** Leave one-inch margins on all sides of every page.

Business and Technical Writing

Business writing and technical writing are specialized forms of expository writing.

Business Writing

Business writing might include documents such as letters, memorandums, reports, briefs, proposals, and articles for business publications. Business writing must be clear, concise, accurate, and correct in style and usage.

Business letters

Three common types of business letters are inquiry or order letters, complaint letters, and opinion letters. Whenever possible, address your letter to a specific person. Business letters are usually written in one of two forms: the modified block form (illustrated below) or the full block form.

> 66 Glenwood Drive
> Teller, NJ 07324
> June 8, 1999
>
> Ms. Barbara Neill
> Personnel Manager
> Riverside Press
> 35 Clinton Road
> Rutledge, NJ 07321
>
> Dear Ms. Neill:
>
> I am writing to express my interest in the summer word processing position, which you advertised in the *Rutledge Herald* of June 6.
>
> I have a great deal of word processing experience. This past semester, I typed and formatted every edition of our monthly school newspaper, *The Teller High News*. Mr. John Greene, faculty adviser to the newspaper, praised my neatness, attention to detail, and ability to work quickly under tight deadlines.
>
> I would be available to work full-time from the end of June until the beginning of September. I will be available for an interview at your convenience.
>
> Yours truly,
>
> Michael Costello

Memos

A memorandum (memo) conveys precise information to another person or a group of people. A memo begins with a heading block. It is followed by the text of the message. A memo does not have a formal closing.

TO: All interested students

FROM: Rebecca Riley

SUBJECT: New municipal basketball court hours

DATE: April 5, 1998

Municipal basketball courts will now be open until 9:00 P.M. seven days a week.

Proposals

A proposal describes a project the writer wishes to undertake. It is presented to the person or persons responsible for making a decision in that area. A proposal presents the advantages of the plan and provides an overview of the idea. The paragraphs below were written by a committee of high school seniors and submitted to the principal.

Proposal: Several members of the junior class would like to start a community volunteer program and are asking for the support of the Teller High School administration.

Four organizations are interested in participating in the program: the Learning Center preschool, St. Ann's Nursing Home, Little Ones Daycare, and Lakeside Hospital.

Schedule:

January 15   Administrative approval

February 1   Start recruitment drive for volunteers

February 15   Contact organizations and work out tentative schedules

March 1   Meet with volunteers and make assignments

Technical Writing

Technical writing is a type of expository writing that informs readers about specialized areas of science and technology. It is practical and objective. The following material is from a product information letter:

Antibody protocols include
- technical assistance in choosing appropriate peptide sequences
- purification of all peptides for antibody production to >90 percent
- synthesis of peptides up to 18 amino acids
- mass spec verification of all peptide sequences
        —from Quality Controlled Biochemicals, Inc., Product Information

Using Electronic Resources

Computers and computer networks are changing the ways in which people gather information. If you have access to a personal computer at home or in school, you can find information in two ways—through CD-ROMs or through the Internet.

CD-ROM

CD-ROMs (compact disc–read-only memory), which store a variety of information, can be purchased in stores or through a mail-order catalog. CD-ROMs may include sound, photographs, and video, as well as text. Types of information available in this form include the following:

- general reference books–encyclopedias, almanacs, histories
- literature collections
- biographies
- news reports from various sources
- back issues of magazines

The Internet

The Internet is, as its name implies, an extensive network that links computers. To access the Internet, you must purchase the services of an Internet service provider. Many Internet service providers are available.

The Internet gives you access to a wealth of information from universities, news organizations, researchers, government organizations, institutions, and individual experts in various fields. It also enables you to visit Web sites created by people who may or may not offer legitimate information and/or useful opinions.

Browsing the Web When you browse the Web, you search electronically for World Wide Web sites related to a particular subject.

Using a search engine Although you can browse the Web at large, you can narrow your search for selected information by using a search engine, such as Yahoo! or Webcrawler. When you select a specific search engine, it will identify a list of subject areas from which to choose.

Evaluating a Web site Consider the source of the material you locate when deciding whether the information on a Web site is reliable. Although many sites are maintained by educational institutions and other authorities, anyone can create a Web site and post information—or misinformation—on it. To evaluate a Web site, ask yourself these questions:

- Do I recognize the name of the author?
- Is the site associated with a well-known university or other reputable organization?
- Can the information be substantiated in another source?
- Is the writer citing a fact or offering an opinion?

Terms to know

On-line information services are commercial services that provide many resources: chat forums; bulletin boards; databases; publications; reference materials; news, weather, and sports; and E-mail and Internet access.

The **World Wide Web (WWW)** is a global system that uses the Internet. It allows a user to create and link fields of information, to retrieve related documents, and to access the data in any order.

Downloading is using a computer modem to transfer a copy of a file from a distant computer to your computer.

A **Web site** is a group of one or more related Web pages that are accessible on the Internet. A **Web page** is a file that contains the information you view when you access a Web site. When you search the World Wide Web, you use a **Web browser** to access Web sites that carry the information you are searching for.

Computerized Library Resources

Public libraries, as well as school and university libraries, offer a variety of ways to do research electronically.

Catalogs Most libraries have computerized catalogs. By typing in a title or an author's name, you can find out if the library has the book, how many copies are in the library's collection, if the book is currently available, and if not, when it will be returned. In large library systems, the computer also provides the name of other libraries from which the desired book is available.

Electronic databases Your library may provide access to electronic databases through on-line information services. These databases are being continually updated. One helpful database available in many libraries is InfoTrac® which provides an index and abstracts—short summaries—of articles from many periodicals. Other magazine indexes, some of which contain the full text of selected articles, may also be available.

Some libraries also have an extensive collection of CD-ROMs. Ask the librarian what is available at your library and how to access the information.

Study and Test-Taking Skills

Study Skills

Taking notes and budgeting your study time are skills essential for your success as a student.

Taking notes in class

Keeping notes based on classroom lectures and teachers' directions gives you a written record of important information. Try these tips for good note taking.

- Use loose-leaf paper if possible, so pages can be added and removed. Using a different notebook for each subject can help you organize your notes.
- Use a fresh page for every class. Write the name of the class and the date at the top of the page.
- Listen carefully. Do not try to write down every word. Instead, listen for the main ideas and express those in your own words.
- Be alert for signal terms such as *most importantly, remember this,* and *to summarize.*
- Spend at least twice as much time listening as writing. Don't risk missing an important point while writing.
- Leave enough space around your notes to add more information later. Some students find it useful to leave a wide left-hand margin in which they later write in key points to create an informal outline.
- As soon as possible after class, reread your notes and fill in any missing information. If possible, exchange notes with a peer and add to your notes any key points he or she has written down, but that you may have missed.
- Take notes not only on what your teacher presents in class, but also on your reading assignments. Your textbook can provide a framework for understanding the context of the material presented by your teacher. You might use the headings and subheadings in your textbook to create a basic outline.
- Try reviewing your notes in an active way. Recopying or typing them can help you commit key points to memory.

Using study time wisely

- Study in the same place each day. Choose a place that is quiet and free from distractions.
- If discussion helps you learn, find a study partner with whom you can work.
- Divide large assignments into smaller tasks. For example, reading four pages of a textbook each night is easier than trying to read twenty-eight pages in one sitting.

- Make a monthly assignment calendar. By writing down due dates, test dates, and notes about upcoming assignments, you can see at glance what work you need to do and when. It will also bring to your attention the times when you will be especially busy, allowing you to plan ahead.
- At the beginning of your study period, when your attention and energy are at their highest levels, work on the assignments you find hardest.
- Take a short break after completing each task. Stay alert by stretching, walking, or having a light snack.
- Review material before stopping. Even a short review will greatly increase the amount of material you are able to remember.

Preparing for Classroom Tests

This section will help you learn how to prepare for classroom tests.

Thinking ahead

- Write down information about an upcoming test–when it will be given, what it will cover, and so on–so you can plan your study time effectively.
- Review your textbook, quizzes, homework assignments, class notes, and handouts. End-of-chapter review questions often highlight key points from your textbook.
- Develop your own questions about main ideas and important details, and practice answering them. Writing your own practice tests is an excellent way to get ready for a real test.
- Make studying into an active process. Rather than simply rereading your notes or a chapter in your textbook, try to create a summary of the material. This can be an outline, a list of characters, or a time line. Try to include details from both your lecture notes and your textbook reading so you will be able to see connections between the two.
- Form study groups. Explaining information to a peer is one of the best ways to learn the material.
- Sleep well the night before a test. Spreading your study time over several days should have given you enough confidence to go to bed at your regular time the night before a test.
- Remember that eating well helps you remain alert. Students who eat a regular meal on the morning of a test generally score higher than those who do not.

Taking objective tests

Many of the tests you take in your high school classes will be objective tests, meaning that they ask questions that have specific, correct answers. Time is often limited for these tests, so be sure to use your time efficiently.

- First, read the directions carefully. If anything is unclear, ask questions.
- Try to respond to each item on the test, starting with the easier ones.
- Skip difficult questions rather than dwelling on them. You can always come back to them at the end of the test.
- Try to include some time to review your test before turning it in.

Below are tips for answering specific kinds of objective test items:

Kind of item	Tips
Multiple-choice	Read all the answer choices provided before choosing one; even if the first one seems nearly correct, a later choice may be a better answer. Be cautious when choosing responses that contain absolute words such as *always, never, all,* or *none.* Since most generalizations have exceptions, absolute statements are often incorrect.
True/False	If *any* part of the item is false, the correct answer must be "false."
Short-answer	Use complete sentences to help you write a clear response.
Fill-in	Restate fill-ins as regular questions if you are not sure what is being asked.
Matching	Note in the directions whether some responses can be used more than once, or not used at all.

Taking subjective (essay) tests

You will also take subjective tests during high school. Typically, these tests ask questions that require you to write an essay. Your grade is based more on how well you are able to make your point than on whether you choose a correct answer.

- When you receive the test, first read it through. If there are several questions, determine how much time to spend on each question.
- Begin your answer by jotting down ideas on scratch paper for several minutes. Read the test question again to make sure you are answering it. Then create a rough outline from which you can create your essay.
- Start your essay with a thesis statement in the first paragraph, and follow with paragraphs that provide supporting evidence. Give as much information as possible, including examples and illustrations where appropriate.
- Finish your essay with a conclusion, highlighting the evidence you have provided and restating your thesis.
- You will probably not have time to revise and recopy your essay. After you are finished writing, spend any remaining time proofreading your answer and neatly making any necessary corrections.

Preparing for Standardized Tests

Standardized tests are designed to be administered to very large groups of students, not just those in a particular class. Three of the most widely known standardized tests, all part of the college application process, are the ACT (American College Testing), the PSAT (Preliminary Scholastic Assessment Test), and the SAT (Scholastic Assessment Test). The strategies in this handbook refer specifically to the PSAT and SAT tests, but they also can apply to preparing for the ACT and other standardized tests.

The PSAT is generally administered to students in the 11th grade, though some schools offer it to students in the 10th grade as well. This test is designed to predict how well you will do on the SAT. For most students, the PSAT is simply a practice test. Those who perform exceptionally well on the 11th grade PSAT, however, will qualify for National Merit Scholarship competition.

The Scholastic Assessment Tests consist of the SAT-I: Reasoning Test and a variety of SAT-II: Subject Tests. The SAT-I is a three-hour test that evaluates your general verbal and mathematics skills. The SAT-II: Subject Tests are hour-long tests given in specific subjects and are designed to show specifically how much you have learned in a particular subject area.

Tips for taking standardized tests

Standardized tests are often administered outside of regular class time and require registration. Ask your teacher or guidance counselor how you can register early to ensure that you can take the test at a time and location most convenient for you. In addition, follow these tips:

- Skip difficult questions at first. Standardized tests are usually timed, so first answer items you know. You can return later to those you skipped.
- Mark only your answers on the answer sheet. Most standardized tests are scored by a computer, so stray marks can be read as incorrect answers.
- Frequently compare the question numbers on your test with those on your answer sheet to avoid putting answers in the wrong spaces.
- If time permits, check your answers. If you are not penalized for guessing, fill in answers for any items you might have skipped.

Preparing for the PSAT and the SAT-I

The verbal sections of the PSAT and SAT-I contain analogies, sentence completion items, and reading comprehension questions.

Analogies

Nearly half of the items on the verbal sections of the PSAT and SAT-I are designed to test your vocabulary. Therefore, the more words you know, the higher your score will be. Refer to pages R86–R87 of the **Reading Handbook** for information on how to build your vocabulary.

One type of vocabulary-based question is the analogy, which tests your ability to grasp the relationships between concepts. The best way to pinpoint the relationship is to connect the words in a simple sentence that defines one of the words. Some of the most common relationships seen on the PSAT and the SAT-I are shown below.

Relationship	Example
Cause and effect	heat : perspiration :: sadness : tears
A person to the normal action of that person	comedian : amuse :: journalist : write
An object to its normal function	telescope : magnify :: aircraft : fly
User to tool	teacher : book :: carpenter : hammer
Degree	terrified : frightened :: destitute : poor
Object to characteristic	water : wet :: brick : hard
Class to subclass (or subclass to class)	grain : rye :: music : rap

Answering analogy items will be easier if you know some facts about them.

- Each group of analogy items is roughly arranged from easiest to hardest.
- Many analogy items use only nouns. The rest involve a noun and an adjective, a noun and a verb, or a verb and an adjective.
- All the answer choices will have the same parts of speech, in the same order, as the words in the initial analogy.
- If you can eliminate even one answer choice, take a guess at the correct answer.

Sentence completion

Sentence completion items provide a sentence with one or two blanks and ask you to select the word or pair of words that best fits in the blank(s). Here is some general information to help you with these questions on the PSAT and SAT-I.

- Start by reading the sentence and filling in your own word to replace the blank. Look for words that show how the word in the blank is related to the rest of the sentence–*and, but, since, therefore, although.*
- Do not read the sentence with the words from each answer choice inserted. This may leave you with several choices that "sound good."
- Once you have chosen your own word to fill in the blank, pick the word from the answer choices that is closest in meaning to your word.
- If you have trouble coming up with a specific word to fill in the blank, try to determine whether the word should be positive or negative. Even this bit of information can help you eliminate some answer choices. If you can eliminate even one answer choice, take a guess at the correct answer.

Reading comprehension

Reading Comprehension questions on the PSAT and SAT-I measure your ability to understand and interpret what you read. Each reading passage is followed by a series of questions. Here are some points to keep in mind when working with these questions:

- You get points for answering questions correctly, not for reading passages thoroughly. Therefore, it is to your advantage to read the passages quickly and spend your time working on the questions.
- After quickly reading the passage, briefly summarize it. This will help you answer general questions, which are based on the passage as a whole.
- To answer specific questions based on details included in the passage, return to the passage to find the correct answers. Reading Comprehension is like an open-book test; you are expected to look at the passage while answering the questions.
- Reading Comprehension passages almost never include controversial opinions. Therefore, an answer choice like "advocated the overthrow of the government" is very likely to be incorrect.
- If you can eliminate even one answer choice, take a guess at the correct answer.

The Reading Process

Being an active reader is a crucial part of being a lifelong learner. It is also an ongoing task. Good reading skills are recursive; that is, they build on each other, providing the tools you'll need to understand text, to connect selections to your own life, to interpret ideas and themes, and to read critically.

Vocabulary Development

To develop a rich vocabulary, consider these four important steps:

- **Read** a wide variety of texts.
- **Enjoy** and engage in word play and word investigation.
- **Listen** carefully to how others use words.
- **Participate** regularly in good classroom discussions.

Using context to discover meaning

When you look at the words and sentences surrounding a new word, you are using context. **Look** before, at, and after a new word or phrase. **Connect** what you know with what an author has written. Then **guess** at a possible meaning. **Try again** if your guess does not make sense. Consider these strategies for using context:

- Look for a synonym or antonym nearby to provide a clue to the word.
- Notice if the text relates the word's meaning to another word.
- Check for a description of an action associated with the word.
- Try to find a general topic or idea related to the word.

Using word parts and word origins

Consider these basic elements when taking a word apart to determine meaning:

- Base words Locate the most basic part of a word to predict a core meaning.
- Prefixes Look at syllables attached before a base that add to or change a meaning.
- Suffixes Look at syllables added to the ends of base words that create new meanings.

Also consider **word origins**—Latin, Greek, and Anglo Saxon roots—that are the basis for much of English vocabulary. Knowing these roots can help you determine derivations and spellings, as well as meanings in English.

Using reference materials

When using context and analyzing word parts do not unlock the meaning of a word, go to a reference source like a dictionary, glossary, thesaurus, or even the Internet. Use these tips:

- **Locate a word** by using the guide words at the top of the pages.
- **Look at the parts of the reference entry,** like part of speech, definition, or synonym.
- **Choose between multiple meanings** by thinking about what makes sense.
- **Apply the meaning** to what you're reading.

Distinguishing between meanings

Determining subtle differences between word meanings also aids comprehension. **Denotation** refers to the dictionary meaning or meanings of a word. **Connotation** refers to an emotion or underlying value that accompanies a word's dictionary meaning. The word *fragrance* has a different connotation from the word *odor,* even though the denotation of both words is "smell."

Comprehension Strategies

Because understanding is the most critical reading task, lifelong learners use a variety of reading strategies before, during, and after reading to ensure their comprehension.

Establishing and adjusting purposes for reading

To establish a purpose for reading, preview or **skim** a selection by glancing quickly over the entire piece, reading headings and subheadings, and noticing the organizational pattern of the text.

If you are reading to learn, solve a problem, or perform a task involving complex directions, consider these tips:

- Read slowly and carefully.
- Reread difficult passages.
- Take careful notes or construct a graphic.

Adjust your strategies as your purpose changes. To locate specific information in a longer selection, or to enjoy an entertaining plot, you might allow yourself a faster pace. Know when to speed up or slow down to maintain your understanding.

Drawing on personal background

When you recall information and personal experiences that are uniquely your own, you **draw on your personal background.** By thus **activating prior knowledge,** and combining it with the words on a page, you create meaning in a selection. To expand and extend your prior knowledge, share it interactively in classroom discussions.

Monitoring and modifying reading strategies

Check or **monitor your understanding** as you read, using the following strategies:

- Summarize
- Clarify
- Question
- Predict what will come next

You can use these four important steps once or twice in an easy, entertaining passage, or after every paragraph in a conceptually dense nonfiction selection. As you read, think about asking interesting questions, rather than passively waiting to answer questions your teacher may ask later on.

All readers find that understanding sometimes breaks down when material is difficult. Consider these steps to modify or change your reading strategies when you don't understand what you've read:

- Reread the passage.
- Consult other sources, including text resources, teachers, and other students.
- Write comments or questions on another piece of paper for later review or discussion.

Constructing graphic organizers

Graphic organizers, like charts, maps, and diagrams, help you construct ideas in a visual way so you can remember them later on. Look at the following model. Like a Venn diagram, which compares and contrasts two ideas or characters, a **semantic features analysis** focuses on the discriminating features of ideas or words. The items or ideas you want to compare are listed down the side, and the discriminating features are listed across the top. In each box use a + if the feature or characteristic applies to the item, or use a − if the feature or characteristic does not apply.

People in Government	Elected	Appointed	Passes Laws	Vetoes Laws
President	+	−	−	+
State Governor	+	−	−	+
Supreme Court Justice	−	+	−	−
Secretary of Defense	−	+	−	−

A **flow chart** helps you keep track of the sequence of events. Arrange ideas or events in a logical, sequential order. Then draw arrows between your ideas to indicate how one idea or event flows into another. Look at the following flow chart to see how you might show the chronological sequence of a story. Use a flow chart to make a **change frame**, recording causes and effects in sequence to illustrate how something changed.

A **web** can be used for a variety of purposes as you read a selection.

- To **map out the main idea and details** of a selection, put the main idea in the middle circle, and, as you read, add supporting details around the main thought.
- To **analyze a character in a story,** put the character's name in the middle, and add that character's actions, thoughts, reputation, plot involvement, and personal development in the surrounding circles.
- To **define a concept,** put a word or idea in the middle circle, and then add a more general category, descriptions, examples, and non-examples in the surrounding circles.

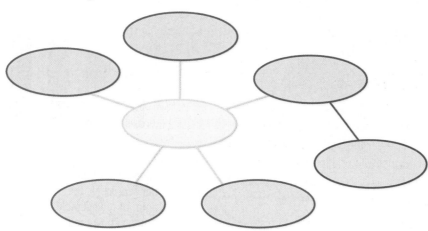

Analyzing text structures

To follow the logic and message of a selection and to remember it, analyze the **text structure,** or organization of ideas, within a writer's work. In narrative as well as in informational text, writers may embed one structure within another, but it is usually possible to identify one main pattern of organization. Recognizing the pattern of organization can help you discover the writer's purpose and will focus your attention on the important ideas in the selection. **Look for signal words** to point you to the structure.

- **Chronological order** often uses words like *first, then, after, later,* and *finally.*
- **Cause-and-effect order** can include words like *therefore, because, subsequently,* or *as a result of.*
- **Comparison-contrast order** may use words like *similarly, in contrast, likewise,* or *on the other hand.*

Interpreting graphic aids

Graphic aids provide an opportunity to see and analyze information at a glance. Charts, tables, maps, and diagrams allow you to analyze and compare information. Maps include a compass rose and legend to help you interpret direction, symbols, and scale. Charts and graphs compare information in categories running horizontally and vertically.

Tips for Reading Graphic Aids

- Examine the title, labels, and other explanatory features.
- Apply the labels to the graphic aid.
- Interpret the information.

Look carefully at the models below.

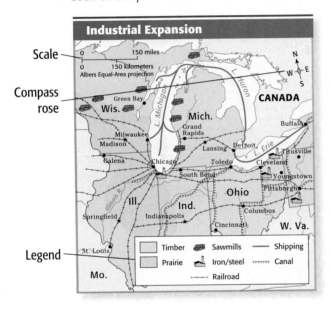

Scale

Compass rose

Legend

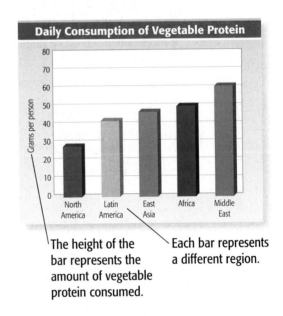

The height of the bar represents the amount of vegetable protein consumed.

Each bar represents a different region.

Sequencing

The order in which thoughts are arranged is called a **sequence**. A good sequence is one that is logical, given the ideas in a selection. **Chronological order, spatial order,** and **order of importance** are common forms of sequencing. Think about the order of a writer's thoughts as you read, and pay particular attention to sequence when **following complex written directions.**

Summarizing

A summary is a short restatement of the main ideas and important details of a selection. Summarizing what you have read is an excellent tool for understanding and remembering a passage.

Tips for Summarizing

- Identify the **main ideas** or most important thoughts within a selection.
- Determine the essential **supporting details.**
- Relate all the main ideas and the essential details in a **logical sequence.**
- **Paraphrase,** that is, use your own words.
- Answer **who, what, why, where,** and **when** questions when you summarize.

The best summaries can easily be understood by someone who has not read the selection. If you're not sure whether an idea is a main idea or a detail, try taking it out of your summary. Does your summary still sound complete?

Drawing inferences and supporting them

An **inference** involves using your reason and experience to come up with an idea based on what a writer implies or suggests, but does not directly state. The following strategic reading behaviors are examples of inference:

- **Making a prediction** is taking an educated guess about what a text will be about based on initial clues a writer provides.
- **Drawing a conclusion** is making a general statement you can explain with reason or with supporting details from a text.
- **Making a generalization** is generating a statement that can apply to more than one item or group.

What is most important when inferring is to be sure that you have accurately based your thoughts on supporting details from the text as well as on your own knowledge.

Reading silently for sustained periods

When you read for long periods of time, your task is to avoid distractions. Check your comprehension regularly by summarizing what you've read so far. Using study guides or graphic organizers can help get you through difficult passages. Take regular breaks when you need them, and vary your reading rate with the demands of the task.

Synthesizing information

You will often need to read across texts; that is, in different sources, combining or **synthesizing** what you've learned from varied sources to suit your purposes. Follow these suggestions:

- Understand the information you've read in each source.
- Interpret the information.
- Identify similarities and differences in ideas or logic.
- Combine like thoughts in a logical sequence.
- Add to the information or change the form to suit your purposes.

Literary Response

Whenever you share your thoughts and feelings about something you've read, you are responding to text. While the way you respond may vary with the type of text you read and with your individual learning style, as a strategic reader you will always need to adequately support your responses with proofs from the text.

Responding to informational and aesthetic elements

When you respond both intellectually *and* emotionally, you connect yourself with a writer and with other people. To respond in an intellectual way, ask yourself if the ideas you have read are logical and well supported. To respond emotionally, ask yourself how you feel about those ideas and events. Choose a way to respond that fits your learning style. Class discussions, journal entries, oral interpretations, enactments, and graphic displays are some of the many ways to share your thoughts and emotions about a writer's work.

Comparing responses with authoritative views

Critics' reviews may encourage you to read a book, see a movie, or attend an event. They may also warn you that whatever is reviewed is not acceptable entertainment or is not valued by the reviewer. Deciding whether or not to value a review depends on the credibility of the reviewer and also on your own personal views and feelings. Ask yourself the following questions:

- What is the reviewer's background?
- What qualifies the reviewer to write this evaluation?
- Is the review balanced? Does it include both positive and negative responses?
- Are arguments presented logically?
- Are opinions supported with facts?
- What bias does this reviewer show?
- Do I agree? Why or why not?

Analysis and Evaluation

Good readers want to do more than recall information or interpret thoughts and ideas. When you read, read critically, forming opinions about characters and ideas, and making judgments using your own prior knowledge and information from the text.

Analyzing characteristics of texts

To be a critical reader and thinker, start by analyzing the characteristics of the text. Think about what specific characteristics make a particular selection clear, concise, and complete. Ask yourself these questions:

- What **pattern of organization** has this writer used to present his or her thoughts? Cause/effect? Comparison/contrast? Problem/solution? Does this organization make the main ideas clear or vague? Why?

- What word order, or **syntax,** gives force and emphasis to this writer's ideas? Does the grammatical order of the words make ideas sound complete, or is the sentence structure confusing?
- What **word choices** reveal this writer's tone, or attitude about the topic? Is the language precise or too general? Is it economical and yet descriptive?

Evaluating the credibility of sources

Evaluating the credibility of a source involves making a judgment about whether a writer is knowledgeable and truthful. Consider the following steps:

- **Decide on the writer's purpose or motive.** What will the writer gain if you accept his or her ideas or if you act on his or her suggestions?
- **Investigate the writer's background.** How has the writer become an authority in his or her field? Do others value what he or she says?
- **Evaluate the writer's statements.** Is the writer's information factual? Can it be proved? Are opinions clearly stated as such? Are they adequately supported with details so that they are valid? Are any statements nonfactual? Check to be sure.

Analyzing logical arguments and modes of reasoning

When you analyze works you've read, ask yourself whether the reasoning behind a writer's works are logical. Two kinds of logical reasoning are

Inductive Reasoning By observing a limited number of particular cases, a reader arrives at a general or universal statement. This logic moves from the specific to the general.

Deductive Reasoning This logic moves from the general to the specific. The reader takes a general statement and, through reasoning, applies it to specific situations.

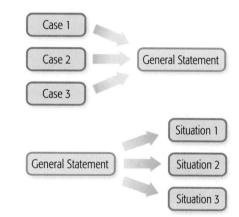

Faulty reasoning, on the other hand, is vague and illogical. Look for either/or reasoning or oversimplified statements when analyzing faulty reasoning. Failure to understand a writer's work may be the result of poorly presented, unsupported arguments, sequenced in a haphazard way.

A writer shows **bias** when he or she demonstrates a strong, personal, and sometimes unreasonable opinion. Look for bias when evaluating editorials, documentaries, and advertisements.

Writers use **persuasive techniques** when they try to get readers to believe a certain thing or act in a particular way. A writer may have a strong, personal bias and still compose a persuasive essay that is logical and well supported. On the other hand, deceptive arguments can be less than accurate in order to be persuasive. Read carefully to judge whether a writer's bias influences his or her writing in negative or positive ways.

Glossary

This glossary lists the vocabulary words found in the selections in this book. The definition given is for the word as it is used in the selection; you may wish to consult a dictionary for other meanings of these words. The key below is a guide to the pronunciation symbols used in each entry.

a	at	**ō**	hope	**ng**	sing
ā	ape	**ô**	fork, all	**th**	thin
ä	father	**oo**	wood, put	**th**	this
e	end	**oo**	fool	**zh**	treasure
ē	me	**oi**	oil	**ə**	ago, taken, pencil,
i	it	**ou**	out		lemon, circus
ī	ice	**u**	up	**′**	indicates primary stress
o	hot	**ū**	use	**′**	indicates secondary stress

A

abate (ə bāt′) v. to lessen or reduce in force or intensity; p. 102

abhor (ab hôr′) v. to regard with disgust; p. 103

abjectly (ab jekt′ lē) adv. in a humiliating, mean, or degrading manner; p. 882

abominable (ə bom′ ə nə bəl) adj. disgusting; detestable; p. 103

absolute (ab′ sə loot′) adj. complete; certain; final; p. 140

access (ak′ ses) n. the right to approach, enter, or use; p. 1102

accommodate (ə kom′ ə dāt′) v. to provide room or facilities for; p. 184

accost (ə kôst′) v. to approach and speak to, especially in an aggressive manner; p. 280

acquiesce (ak′ wē es′) v. to consent or agree silently, without objections; to comply passively; p. 172

acute (ə kūt′) adj. intense; severe; p. 506

adamant (ad′ ə mənt) adj. completely firm and unyielding; p. 985

admonition (ad′ mə nish′ ən) n. a warning; cautionary advice; p. 245

adorn (ə dôrn′) v. to make beautiful; to decorate; p. 369

advocate (ad′ və kit) n. one who supports or urges; a proponent; p. 894

affability (a fə′ bi′ lə tē) n. the quality of being easy to approach and talk to; friendliness; pleasantness; p. 280

affirm (ə furm′) v. to declare firmly; to assert; p. 885

agitated (aj′ ə tā′ təd) adj. disturbed; upset; p. 351

alacrity (ə lak′ rə tē) n. speed; swiftness; p. 258

alien (a′ lē ən) adj. strange; unfamiliar; foreign; p. 827

alight (ə līt′) v. to descend and come to rest; p. 48

allude (ə lood′) v. to refer to indirectly; p. 1088

allusion (ə loo′ zhən) n. an indirect or casual reference; an incidental mention; p. 358

ambulatory (am′ byə lə tôr′ē) adj. moving from place to place; p. 131

amiable (ā′ mē ə bəl) adj. friendly; p. 876

amorphous (ə môr′ fəs) adj. without definite form; p. 784

ample (am′ pəl) adj. of great size or capacity; p. 1068

anarchy (an′ ər kē) n. the absence of government; p. 363

ancestral (an ses′ trəl) *adj.* of or relating to those from whom one is descended; p. 899

animated (an′ ə mā′ tid) *adj.* full of life; active; lively; p. 876

apathetically (ap′ ə the′ ti klē) *adv.* in a manner showing little interest or concern; p. 507

appease (ə pēz′) *v.* to bring to a state of peace or quiet; to soothe; p. 102

apprehension (ap′ ri hen′ shən) *n.* a fear of what may happen in the future; anxiety; p. 191

ardently (ärd′ ent lē) *adv.* passionately; enthusiastically; p. 371

ardor (är′ dər) *n.* intensity of emotion; passion; enthusiasm; p. 157

arduous (ar′ jōō əs) *adj.* requiring great exertion or endurance; difficult; p. 148

aristocracy (ar′ is tok′ rə sē) *n.* people with high social status due to birth or title; p. 30

array (ə rā′) *v.* to place in proper or methodical order; p. 364

ashen (ash′ ən) *adj.* pale; p. 490

assent (ə sent′) *v.* to express agreement; p. 371

audaciously (ô dā′ shəs lē) *adv.* boldly; arrogantly; p. 358

august (ô gust′) *adj.* well respected; distinguished; prominent; p. 804

aura (ôr′ ə) *n.* a distinctive but intangible atmosphere surrounding a person or thing; p. 847

avarice (av′ ər is) *n.* excessive desire for wealth; greed; p. 333

avert (ə vurt′) *v.* to turn away or aside; p. 800

B

balmy (bä′ mē) *adj.* soothing; p. 1006

base (bās) *adj.* morally low; dishonorable; p. 943

benefactor (ben′ ə fak′ tər) *n.* one who gives help or financial aid; p. 246

benevolent (bə nev′ ə lent) *adj.* doing or desiring to do good; kind; p. 330

blithe (blīth) *adj.* lighthearted and carefree; cheerful; p. 243

bloated (blō′ tid) *adj.* puffed up; swollen; p. 1078

brazenness (brā′ zən əs) *n.* defiant behavior; boldness; p. 725

C

capitulate (kə pich′ ə lāt′) *v.* to surrender or yield; to give up; p. 358

cascade (kas kād′) *v.* to fall or flow as if in a waterfall or series of waterfalls; p. 1069

censure (sen′ shər) *v.* to express disapproval of; to find fault with; to blame; p. 334

ceremonial (ser′ ə mō′ nē əl) *adj.* formal; p. 838

chaos (kā′ os) *n.* great confusion and disorder; p. 893

charade (shə rād′) *n.* a false show or pretense; p. 1048

circumvent (sur′ kəm vent′) *v.* to get around or avoid by clever maneuvering; p. 810

clamber (klam′ bər) *v.* to climb hastily or awkwardly, using hands and feet; p. 867

clamor (klam′ ər) *n.* confused, insistent shouting; p. 194

coerce (kō urs′) *v.* to force; p. 573

cognizance (kog′ nə zəns) *n.* knowledge; awareness; p. 299

colossal (kə los′ əl) *adj.* extraordinary in size or degree; enormous; p. 899

commodity (kə mod′ ə tē) *n.* a product or economic good; an article of trade; p. 72

compassion (kəm pash′ ən) *n.* deep awareness of another's suffering combined with a desire to help; p. 86

compel (kəm pel′) *v.* to force; p. 501

complex (kəm pleks′) *adj.* complicated; consisting of interrelated parts or elements; p. 900

comprehension (kom pri hen′ shən) *n.* the act of grasping mentally; understanding; p. 839

compromise (kom′ prə mīz′) *v.* to endanger the reputation or interests of; to expose to suspicion; p. 916

concede (kən sēd′) *v.* to acknowledge as true; to admit; p. 489

conception (kən sep′ shən) *n.* a mental image or idea; a thought or notion; p. 108

concerted (kən sur′ tid) *adj.* planned or carried out by mutual agreement; p. 1106

conciliatory (kən sil′ ē ə tôr′ ē) *adj.* trying to gain the good will of another by friendly acts; p. 985

conflagration (kon′ flə grā′ shən) *n.* a large, destructive fire; p. 504

conjecture (kən jek′ chər) v. to form an opinion without definite evidence; to guess; p. 462

conjurer (kon′ jər ər) n. one who performs magic; a sorcerer; p. 49

consecrate (kon′ sə krāt′) v. to set apart as sacred; to make or declare holy; p. 385

console (kən sōl′) v. to comfort or cheer; p. 1004

conspire (kən spīr′) v. to join or act together, especially to carry out some secret or evil deed or for a hidden or illegal purpose; p. 141

consummate (kon′ sə māt′) v. to bring to completion; to finish; p. 1057

contemplation (kon′ təm plā′ shən) n. the act of thinking about something long and seriously; p. 970

contend (kən tend′) v. to argue; to dispute; p. 364

contention (kən ten′ shən) n. verbal argument or struggle; quarreling; p. 917

continuity (kon′ tə nōō′ ə tē) n. the state or quality of going on without interruption; p. 900

contrivance (kən trī′ vəns) n. a cleverly designed device; p. 690

convene (kən vēn′) v. to come together; to assemble; p. 56

copious (kō′ pē əs) adj. large in quantity; plentiful; p. 192

corroding (kə rōd′ ing) adj. tending to eat or wear away gradually; slowly destructive; p. 893

countenance (koun′ tə nens) n. a face; facial features; p. 190

covet (kuv′ it) v. to desire, especially to an excessive degree, something belonging to another; p. 947

cringe (krinj) v. to shrink back or flinch, as in fear or disgust; p. 1098

D

dally (dal′ ē) v. to linger; to delay; to waste time; p. 489

daunt (dônt) v. to overcome with fear; to intimidate; p. 86

decimated (des′ ə māt′ əd) adj. destroyed or killed in large numbers; p. 1182

decorum (di kôr′ əm) n. conformity to the approved standards of good taste; p. 243

deduce (di dōōs′) v. to draw a conclusion from something known or assumed; p. 294

deference (def′ ər əns) n. courteous respect or regard; p. 369

deftly (deft′ lē) adv. skillfully; p. 1074

deliberately (di lib′ ər it lē) adv. in a careful, thoughtful way; p. 253

deliberation (di lib′ ə rā′ shən) n. careful consideration; p. 57

delirium (di lēr′ ē əm) n. a temporary state of mental disturbance characterized by confusion and disorientation; p. 1004

deluge (del′ ūj) n. anything that overwhelms or rushes like a flood; p. 539

delusion (di lōō′ zhen) n. a false impression or belief; p. 359

demeaning (di mēn′ ing) adj. lowering in dignity or status; degrading; humiliating; p. 1098

denounce (di nouns′) v. to condemn; to criticize; p. 1131

depravity (di prav′ ə tē) n. the state of being morally bad or corrupt; p. 330

derangement (di rānj′ ment) n. disturbance of normal functioning; disorder; p. 491

desolation (des′ ə lā′ shən) n. devastation; misery; sadness; p. 85

detached (di tacht′) adj. not involved emotionally; indifferent; p. 681

didactic (dī dak′ tik) adj. intended to instruct, especially with regard to morals; p. 30

diffuse (di fūz′) v. to spread widely; to scatter in all directions; p. 303

dilapidated (di lap′ ə dā′ tid) adj. fallen into ruin or decay; shabby; p. 462

din (din) n. loud, continuous noise; p. 258

discern (di surn′) v. to recognize as different and distinct; to distinguish; p. 88

discord (dis′ kôrd) n. lack of agreement or harmony; conflict; p. 204

discreet (dis krēt′) adj. cautious; prudent; p. 280

disperse (dis purs′) v. to go off in different directions; to scatter; p. 163

disposition (dis′ pə zish′ ən) n. one's general way of thinking or feeling; p. 55

dissembling (di sem′ bling) *n.* the act of concealing one's true character, feelings, or intentions; p. 690

dissipate (dis′ ə pāt′) *v.* to cause to scatter and gradually vanish; to break up and drive off; p. 798

distinctive (dis ting′ tiv) *adj.* different in quality or kind; separate; p. 139

doctrine (dok′ trin) *n.* a principle that is taught and advocated; a tenet; p. 520

doggedly (dô′ gid lē) *adv.* in a stubbornly persistent manner; obstinately; p. 535

doleful (dōl′ fəl) *adj.* full of grief or sorrow; sad; p. 85

domain (dō mān′) *n.* a territory over which control is exercised; a realm; p. 1058

downy (dou′ nē) *adj.* soft and fluffy, like the feathers of young birds; p. 1038

dupe (do͞op) *v.* to fool; to trick; p. 1079

dusk (dusk) *n.* the time of day just before nightfall; p. 1041

dutiful (do͞o′ ti fəl) *adj.* careful to fulfill obligations; p. 622

dwell (dwel) *v.* to think about at length; p. 1064

dwindle (dwin′ dəl) *v.* to become gradually smaller; p. 628

E

ecclesiastical (i klē′ zē as′ ti kəl) *adj.* of or relating to the church; p. 1182

efface (i fās′) *v.* to destroy; to erase; p. 373

elusive (i lo͞o′ siv) *adj.* difficult to explain or grasp; p. 526

embark (em bärk′) *v.* to set out on a venture; p. 64

embody (em bod′ ē) *v.* to give concrete or material form to; p. 900

emphatic (em fa′ tik) *adj.* forceful; p. 562

enamored (en am′ ərd) *adj.* inspired with love; charmed; captivated; p. 881

endeavor (en dev′ ər) *v.* to make an effort to; to try; p. 171

engender (en jen′ dər) *v.* to give rise to; to cause; to produce; p. 1056

engrossed (en grōst′) *adj.* fully attentive to; completely engaged in; absorbed; p. 867

enlighten (en līt′ ən) *v.* to give knowledge or wisdom to; p. 31

enmity (en′ mə tē) *n.* deep-seated hatred; hostility; p. 1059

enormity (i nôr′ mə tē) *n.* outrageousness; the state of being monstrous; p. 93

ensure (en shoor′) *v.* to make certain; to guarantee; p. 96

enterprising (en′ tər prī′ zing) *adj.* showing energy and initiative, especially in beginning new projects; p. 468

enunciate (i nun′ sē āt′) *v.* to pronounce distinctly; p. 1032

ephemeral (i fem′ ər əl) *adj.* lasting for a very brief time; short-lived; p. 900

equanimity (ek′ wə nim′ ə tē) *n.* evenness of temper; calmness; p. 479

espionage (es′ pē ə näzh′) *n.* spying; p. 1102

esteem (es tēm′) *v.* to regard favorably; to value highly; p. 108

evade (i vād′) *v.* to escape or avoid, as by cleverness; p. 931

exalt (ig zôlt′) *v.* to lift up; to put in high spirits; p. 726

exalted (ig zôl′ təd) *adj.* elevated; p. 527

exclusively (iks′ klo͞o′ siv lē) *adv.* without the inclusion or involvement of others; p. 30

exemplary (ig zem′ plə rē) *adj.* worthy of imitation; commendable; p. 1131

exhilarated (ig zil′ ə rā təd) *adj.* cheerful, lively, or excited; filled with vigor; p. 656

exhilaration (ig zil′ ə rā′ shən) *n.* a feeling of strength and energy, joy, or excitement; p. 847

exorbitant (ig zôr′ bə tənt) *adj.* exceeding what is reasonable; excessive; p. 519

expatriated (eks pā′ trē āt′ əd) *adj.* banished; exiled; p. 477

expedient (iks pē′ dē ənt) *n.* something employed to bring about a desired result; a means to an end; p. 258

exploit (eks′ ploit) *n.* a notable, heroic deed; a feat; p. 156

exploit (iks ploit′) *v.* to use or develop for profit, often in a selfish, unjust, or unfair way; p. 657

extricate (eks′ trə kāt′) *v.* to set free from; to remove; p. 183

F

facade (fə säd´) *n.* a false or artificial front; p. 1091

feigned (fānd) *adj.* fictitious; not genuine; p. 72

feint (fānt) *n.* a deceptive movement intended to draw an opponent's attention from the real attack; a deception; p. 162

futile (fū´ til) *adj.* useless; worthless; pointless; p. 823

G

gape (gāp) *v.* to stare with the mouth open, as in wonder or surprise; p. 1064

garrulous (gar´ ə ləs) *adj.* talkative; p. 462

gaunt (gônt) *adj.* thin, bony, and hollow-eyed, as from hunger or illness; p. 8

grapple (grap´ əl) *v.* to struggle in hand-to-hand combat; to wrestle; p. 866

gratify (grat´ ə fī´) *v.* to satisfy or indulge; p. 193

grave (grāv) *adj.* dignified and gloomy; somber; p. 833

gravity (grav´ ə tē) *n.* seriousness; importance; p. 1041

grievously (grē´ vəs lē) *adv.* very seriously; gravely; p. 490

grimace (grim´ is) *v.* to contort the face, especially to express pain or displeasure; p. 1001

grope (grōp) *v.* to feel about uncertainly with the hands; to search blindly; p. 1063

grotesque (grō tesk´) *adj.* bizarre; weird; p. 1047

guile (gīl) *n.* cunning; deceit; slyness; p. 968

H

hallow (hal´ ō) *v.* to make or select as holy; to regard or honor as sacred; p. 385

hallucination (hə loo´ sə nā´ shən) *n.* a false sensory perception of something that is not really there; p. 1079

haughty (hô´ tē) *adj.* conceited; arrogant; p. 808

heedless (hēd´ lis) *adj.* careless; thoughtless; reckless; p. 1047

hemorrhage (hem´ ər ij) *n.* a severe discharge of blood; p. 785

holocaust (hol´ ə kôst´) *n.* great or complete destruction, especially by fire; p. 1032

hostile (host´ əl) *adj.* feeling or showing hatred; antagonistic; p. 823

hover (huv´ ər) *v.* to remain nearby, as if suspended in the air over something; p. 1041

hypocrisy (hi pok´ rə sē) *n.* an expression of feelings or beliefs not actually possessed or held; p. 156

hypothesis (hī poth´ ə sis) *n.* an unproved explanation or assumption; p. 480

I

idiom (id´ ē əm) *n.* an expression peculiar to a people or to a specific region; p. 1103

illumination (i loo´ mə nā´ shən) *n.* intellectual enlightenment; p. 527

immaculate (i mak´ yə lit) *adj.* unblemished; flawless; pure; p. 966

imminent (im´ ə nənt) *adj.* about to take place; p. 652

immortality (im´ ôr tal´ ə tē) *n.* the condition of having eternal life; p. 499

impede (im pēd´) *v.* to slow or block progress or action; to obstruct; p. 295

impediment (im ped´ ə mənt) *n.* an obstacle; p. 1087

imperative (im per´ ə tiv) *n.* something absolutely necessary; an essential; p. 894

imperious (im pēr´ ē əs) *adj.* imperative; urgent; p. 371

imperviousness (im pur´ vē əs nəs) *n.* the state of being unaffected or undisturbed; p. 808

impetuously (im pech´ oo əs lē) *adv.* impulsively; suddenly; rashly; p. 658

impious (im´ pē əs) *adj.* lacking in reverence; disrespectful; p. 568

impose (im pōz´) *v.* to inflict, as by authority; to dictate; p. 527

impregnable (im preg´ nə bəl) *adj.* incapable of being taken by force; able to resist attack; p. 205

impropriety (im´ prə prī´ ə tē) *n.* the quality of being improper; improper behavior; p. 477

impudently (im´ pyə dənt lē) *adv.* in an offensively bold manner; arrogantly; p. 565

inaudibly (in ô′ də blē) *adv.* in a manner not able to be heard; p. 1041

incensed (in senst′) *adj.* made very angry; p. 102

incessant (in ses′ ənt) *adj.* continuing or following without interruption; p. 1048

indentured (in den′ chərd) *adj.* bound by contract to serve another person for a period of time; p. 131

indictment (in dīt′ mənt) *n.* a formal legal accusation, charging the commission or omission of an act, which is punishable by law; p. 989

indifferent (in dif′ ər ənt) *adj.* lacking feeling or concern; p. 729

indignation (in′ dig nā′ shən) *n.* restrained, dignified anger in response to meanness, injustice, or ingratitude; p. 161

induce (in dōōs′) *v.* to lead by persuasion or influence; p. 330

ineptly (i nept′ lē) *adv.* incompetently; awkwardly; clumsily; p. 951

inert (i nurt′) *adj.* inactive; sluggish; p. 536

inevitable (i nev′ ə tə bəl) *adj.* incapable of being avoided or evaded; p. 96

infidel (in′ fə del′) *n.* an unbeliever; p. 131

ingenious (in jēn′ yəs) *adj.* exhibiting creative ability; inventive; p. 131

ingenuously (in jen′ ū əs lē) *adv.* honestly; frankly; candidly; p. 564

inherent (in hēr′ ənt) *adj.* existing as a basic quality; belonging to by nature; p. 258

iniquity (in ik′ wə tē) *n.* sin; wickedness; p. 268

initially (i nish′ ə lē) *adv.* at the beginning; first; p. 1102

inquisitor (in kwiz′ ə tər) *n.* one who asks questions; p. 786

insidious (in sid′ ē əs) *adj.* slyly treacherous and deceitful; deceptive; p. 148

instinct (in′ stingkt) *n.* a natural ability or impulse; p. 1074

intangible (in tan′ jə bəl) *adj.* not easily defined or evaluated by the mind; p. 498

integrate (in′ tə grāt) *v.* to bring all parts together into a whole; p. 242

integrity (in teg′ rə tē) *n.* moral uprightness; honesty; p. 247

interminable (in tur′ mi nə bəl) *adj.* seemingly endless; p. 463

intervene (in′ tər vēn′) *v.* to come or lie between; p. 502

intimation (in′ tə mā′ shən) *n.* a hint; a suggestion; p. 787

intimidated (in tim′ ə dāt′ əd) *adj.* made timid or fearful; frightened into submission or inaction; p. 866

intricately (in′ tri kit lē) *adv.* in a complex or complicated manner; elaborately; p. 1183

intrigue (in′ trēg) *n.* the use of devious schemes to achieve a goal; secret plotting; p. 823

intriguing (in trēg′ ing) *adj.* arousing curiosity or interest; fascinating; captivating; p. 865

invigorated (in vig′ ə rā′ tid) *adj.* filled with strength and energy; p. 787

invoke (in vōk′) *v.* to call forth; p. 1105

irk (urk) *v.* to annoy; to bother; p. 822

irreproachable (ir′ i prō′ chə bəl) *adj.* free from blame; faultless; p. 274

irrevocable (i rev′ ə kə bəl) *adj.* not possible to undo; p. 96

J

jilt (jilt) *v.* to drop or reject as a sweetheart; p. 625

jocular (jok′ yə lər) *adj.* humorous; p. 480

jostle (jos′ əl) *v.* to bump, push, or shove while moving, as in a crowd; p. 681

jubilant (jōō′ bə lənt) *adj.* extremely happy; triumphantly joyful; p. 867

K

kindle (kind′ əl) *v.* to stir up; to excite; p. 533

L

lament (lə ment′) *v.* to express deep sorrow or grief; p. 89

latent (lā′ tənt) *adj.* present but not evident; hidden; p. 245

legacy (leg′ ə sē) *n.* an inheritance; p. 533

legible (lej′ ə bəl) *adj.* able to be read; p. 1049

lethargy (leth′ ər jē) *n.* sluggish inactivity or drowsiness; p. 298

limber (lim′ bər) *adj.* able to bend or move easily; nimble; p. 834

list (list) *v.* to tilt or lean to one side; p. 8

loiter (loi′ tər) *v.* to stand or linger idly or aimlessly about a place; p. 866

lucid (loō′ sid) *adj.* rational; sane; p. 1050

lurch (lurch) *v.* to move suddenly and unevenly; p. 680

luxuriant (lug zhoor′ ē ənt) *adj.* marked by rich or plentiful growth; abundant; p. 1056

M

malevolence (mə lev′ ə ləns) *n.* a disposition to wish harm to others; ill will; p. 478

manifest (man′ ə fest′) *adj.* apparent to the eye or the mind; evident; obvious; p. 246

meager (mē′ gər) *adj.* deficient in quantity or completeness; p. 875

meandering (mē an′ dər ing) *adj.* following a winding course; p. 33

melancholy (mel′ ən kol′ ē) *adj.* depressing; dismal; gloomy; p. 205

mentor (men′ tər) *n.* a wise and trusted adviser; p. 57

mimic (mim′ ik) *v.* to copy; to reproduce; to imitate; p. 1067

minutely (mī noōt′ lē) *adv.* in a very small degree; p. 1068

misgiving (mis giv′ ing) *n.* a feeling of doubt, distrust, or anxiety; p. 947

mishap (mis′ hap′) *n.* an unfortunate accident or mistake; a misfortune; p. 520

morose (mə rōs′) *adj.* bad-tempered, gloomy, and withdrawn; p. 14

mortification (môr′ tə fi kā′ shən) *n.* a feeling of shame, humiliation, or embarrassment; p. 132

mundane (mun dān′) *adj.* ordinary; usual; commonplace; p. 1087

murky (mur′ kē) *adj.* characterized by dimness, as from fog or smoke; p. 1074

myriad (mir′ ē əd) *adj.* countless; innumerable; p. 255

N

naive (nä ēv′) *adj.* lacking knowledge of the ways of the world; unsophisticated; innocent; p. 919

novel (nov′ əl) *adj.* new and unusual; p. 1183

O

obesity (ō bē′ sə tē) *n.* the condition of being extremely fat; p. 806

obliquely (ə blēk′ lē) *adv.* in a slanting or sloping direction; p. 537

obliterate (ə blit′ ə rāt) *v.* to remove all traces of; to erase; p. 207

oblivious (ə bliv′ ē əs) *adj.* without conscious awareness; unmindful; p. 1041

occult (ə kult′) *adj.* beyond human understanding; mysterious; p. 243

ominous (om′ ə nəs) *adj.* like an evil omen; threatening; p. 1032

onslaught (on′ slôt′) *n.* a vigorous or destructive attack; p. 163

opaque (ō pāk′) *adj.* not letting light through; p. 1058

oppressed (ə prest′) *adj.* controlled or governed by a cruel and unjust use of force or authority; p. 892

ordeal (ôr dēl′) *n.* a circumstance or experience that is painful or difficult; a trial; p. 892

P

pall (pôl) *n.* that which covers with an atmosphere of darkness and gloom; p. 498

paradigm (par′ ə dīm′) *n.* an example that acts as a model; a pattern; p. 33

parsimony (pär′ sə mō nē) *n.* excessive frugality; stinginess; p. 211

perception (pər sep′ shən) *n.* an awareness; an insight; p. 527

perennial (pə ren′ ē əl) *adj.* continuing year after year; enduring; p. 243

perish (per′ish) *v.* to pass from existence; to disappear; p. 385

perpetual (pər pech′ oō əl) *adj.* lasting forever; eternal; p. 242

perplexed (pər plekst′) *adj.* puzzled; confused; p. 1098

persistence (pər sis′ təns) *n.* stubborn or determined continuance; p. 527

perturbation (pur′ tər bā′ shən) *n.* agitation; anxiety; uneasiness; p. 268

perusal (pə rōō′ zəl) *n.* the process of examining carefully; p. 363

pervade (pər vād′) *v.* to spread through every part; p. 360

petrified (pet′ rə fīd) *adj.* paralyzed with fear; stiff or like stone, p. 156

piety (pī′ ə tē) *n.* religious devoutness; goodness; p. 627

pigment (pig′ mənt) *n.* a substance that gives color; p. 1069

pillage (pil′ ij) *n.* looting or plundering; p. 1054

plague (plāg) *v.* to annoy; to pester; p. 623

plumage (plōō′ mij) *n.* the feathers of a bird; p. 847

poignant (poin′ yənt) *adj.* sharp; severe; causing emotional or physical anguish; p. 372

poised (poizd) *adj.* having a calm, controlled, and dignified manner; composed; p. 827

ponder (pon′ dər) *v.* to think about thoroughly and carefully; p. 1063

posterity (pos ter′ ə tē) *n.* generations of the future; all of one's descendants; p. 56

preeminently (prē em′ ə nənt lē) *adv.* chiefly; primarily; p. 1054

preposterous (pri pos′ tər əs) *adj.* absurd; ridiculous; p. 566

presumptuous (pri zump′ chōō əs) *adj.* going beyond what is proper; excessively bold; p. 1182

pretense (prē′ tens) *n.* a false show or appearance, especially for the purpose of deceiving; falseness; p. 922

pretension (pri ten′ shən) *n.* a claim; an assertion; p. 519

prevail (pri vāl′) *v.* to use persuasion successfully; p. 539

prevalent (prev′ ə lent) *adj.* widespread; p. 204

procure (prə kyōōr′) *v.* to obtain by care or effort; p. 72

profound (prə found′) *adj.* coming from the depth of one's being; intensely felt; p. 560

profusion (prə fū′ zhen) *n.* a plentiful amount; abundance; p. 1056

progenitor (prō jen′ ə tər) *n.* a direct ancestor; an originator of an ancestral line; p. 57

proposal (prə pō′ zəl) *n.* something put forward for consideration as a plan of action; p. 108

propriety (prə prī′ ə tē) *n.* the quality of being proper; appropriateness; p. 520

prosperity (pros per′ ə tē) *n.* success; wealth; good fortune; p. 364

prostrate (pros′ strāt) *adj.* bowing or kneeling down in humility, adoration, or submission; p. 359

protrude (prō trōōd′) *v.* to stick out; to project; p. 369

proverbial (prə vur′ bē əl) *adj.* commonly spoken of; well-known; p. 1094

providence (prov′ ə dəns) *n.* divine care or guidance; foresight; p. 70

provoke (prə vōk′) *v.* to bring about; to incite; p. 1132

proximity (prok sim′ ə tē) *n.* closeness in space, time, sequence, or degree; nearness; p. 302

prudence (prōōd′ əns) *n.* exercise of good and cautious judgment; p. 102

Q

querulous (kwer′ ə ləs) *adj.* complaining; whining; p. 483

quivering (kwiv′ ər ing) *n.* a shaking with a slight, rapid vibration; a trembling; p. 834

R

radical (rad′ i kəl) *adj.* deviating greatly from the usual or customary; extreme; p. 1049

random (ran′ dəm) *adj.* lacking a definite pattern; haphazard; p. 1032

ration (rash′ ən) *n.* a fixed portion or share; p. 62

ravage (rav′ ij) *n.* a destructive or ruinous action or its result; p. 156

ravenous (rav′ ə nəs) *adj.* extremely hungry; p. 11

reciprocate (ri sip′ rə kāt′) *v.* to give, feel, or show in return; p. 652

recourse (rē′ kôrs′) *n.* a resorting to a person or thing for help; p. 185

rectitude (rek′ tə to̅o̅d′) *n.* uprightness of moral character; honesty; p. 172

redress (rē′ dres′) *n.* compensation, as for wrong done; p. 364

refugee (ref′ū jē′) *n.* a person who flees to safety, especially one who leaves home or a homeland because of persecution, war, or danger; p. 352

rejuvenated (ri jo̅o̅′ və nā′ təd) *adj.* restored to youthful vigor or appearance; renewed; p. 1005

relinquish (ri ling′ kwish) *v.* to give up control of; to surrender; p. 156

reminiscence (rem′ ə nis′ əns) *n.* an account of a past experience or event; p. 462

remonstrate (ri mon′ strāt) *v.* to object; to protest; p. 148

remorselessly (ri môrs′ lis lē) *adv.* in a way that shows no pity or compassion; mercilessly; p. 165

render (ren′ dər) *v.* to cause to be; to make; p. 184

repertoire (rep′ ər twär′) *n.* the stock of skills that a person or group has and is prepared to demonstrate or perform; p. 280

repression (ri presh′ ən) *n.* the state of being held back or kept under control; p. 526

reprieve (ri prēv′) *n.* official postponement of the carrying out of a sentence; p. 985

reprimand (rep′ rə mand′) *v.* to reprove or correct sharply; p. 937

reproach (ri prōch′) *n.* an expression of disapproval; a reprimand; p. 533

repudiate (ri pū′ dē āt′) *v.* to refuse to accept as valid; to reject; to renounce; p. 894

resign (ri zīn′) *v.* to make oneself accept; p. 683

resignation (rez′ ig nā′ shən) *n.* unresisting acceptance; submission; p. 253

resolution (rez′ ə lo̅o̅′ shən) *n.* firmness of purpose; p. 156

resolve (ri zolv′) *v.* to decide; to determine; p. 70

resonant (rez′ ə nənt) *adj.* having a full, rich sound; p. 1068

retaliation (ri tal′ ē ā′ shən) *n.* the act of repaying an injury or wrong by committing the same, or a similar, act; p. 985

retractable (ri trak′ tə bəl) *adj.* capable of being drawn back or in; p. 784

revive (ri vīv′) *v.* to give new strength and vitality; to bring back to consciousness; p. 62

rigorously (rig′ ər əs lē) *adv.* precisely; strictly; p. 1130

ritual (rich′ o̅o̅ əl) *n.* a regularly followed routine; p. 1092

rouse (rouz) *v.* to awaken from sleep; p. 62

rudiment (ro̅o̅′ də mənt) *n.* an imperfect or undeveloped part; p. 254

rue (ro̅o̅) *v.* to regret; to be sorry for; p. 16

S

sagacious (sə gā′ shəs) *adj.* having or showing wisdom and keen perception; p. 269

sage (sāj) *n.* a person of profound wisdom and judgment; p. 245

sanction (sangk′ shən) *n.* approval or support; p. 261

savory (sā′ vər ē) *adj.* agreeable to the taste or smell; appetizing; p. 89

scavenger (skav′ in jər) *n.* one who searches through discarded materials for something useful; p. 1078

score (skôr) *n.* a group of twenty items; p. 385

scruple (skro̅o̅′ pəl) *n.* moral principle that restrains action; p. 194

scrupulously (skro̅o̅′ pyə ləs lē) *adv.* with extreme care and attention to detail; painstakingly; p. 1130

scuffle (skuf′ əl) *v.* to move with a quick, shuffling gait; p. 798

seclusion (si klo̅o̅′ zhən) *n.* separation from others; isolation; p. 481

sibling (sib′ ling) *adj.* relating to a brother or a sister; p. 1067

signal (sig′ nəl) *adj.* remarkable; striking; notable; p. 165

simultaneously (sī′ məl tā′ nē əs lē) *adv.* at the same time; p. 1129

sluggard (slug′ ərd) *n.* one who is usually or always lazy or idle; a loafer; p. 141

sluggishly (slug′ ish lē) *adv.* slowly; without strength or energy; p. 805

snicker (sni′ kər) *n.* a snide, partly suppressed laugh, often expressing disrespect; p. 727

solemn (sol′ əm) *adj.* serious; grave; p. 838

speculate (spek′ yə lāt′) *v.* to engage in risky business ventures, hoping to make quick profits; p. 210

spurn (spurn) *v.* to reject with disdain; p. 149

stately (stāt′ lē) *adj.* noble; dignified; majestic; p. 12

stature (stach′ ər) *n.* a level attained; standing; status; p. 894

stoically (stō′ ik lē) *adv.* calmly and unemotionally, especially despite pain or suffering; p. 691

stolidly (stol′ id lē) *adv.* with little or no emotion; impassively; p. 1132

stooped (sto͞opt) *adj.* bent forward and downward; p. 1063

subjugation (sub′ jə gā′ shən) *n.* the act of bringing under one's control; domination; p. 148

sublime (səb līm′) *adj.* of great spiritual or intellectual value; noble; p. 253

submissive (səb mis′ iv) *adj.* willing to yield to the power or authority of another; meek; p. 1048

subservient (səb sur′ vē ənt) *adj.* useful, in an inferior capacity, to promote an end; submissive; p. 919

subtle (sut′ əl) *adj.* not open, direct, or obvious; crafty; sly; p. 949

subversive (səb vur′ siv) *adj.* intended to destroy or undermine; p. 1079

succor (suk′ ər) *n.* assistance in time of need; relief; p. 71

succumb (sə kum′) *v.* to give in; to yield; p. 893

sumptuous (sump′ cho͞o əs) *adj.* involving great expense; extravagant; splendid; p. 1068

supplication (sup′ lə kā′ shən) *n.* an earnest and humble request; p. 280

surmise (sər mīz′) *v.* to infer from little or no evidence; to guess; p. 207

sustenance (sus′ tə nəns) *n.* that which sustains life, especially food; p. 520

symmetrical (si met′ ri kəl) *adj.* having the same shape or structure on either side of a central line or plane; p. 1047

synthesis (sin′ thə sis) *n.* the combining of separate parts or elements to form a whole; p. 893

T

tactful (takt′ fəl) *adj.* able to speak or act without offending others; p. 622

temper (tem′ pər) *v.* to modify or moderate; to soften; p. 57

tentative (ten′ tə tiv) *adj.* not fully worked out; somewhat undecided; p. 658

tenure (ten′ yər) *n.* the conditions or terms under which something is held; p. 171

thicket (thik′ it) *n.* an area of dense growth, as of shrubs or bushes; p. 834

torpor (tôr′ pər) *n.* a state of being unable to move or feel; p. 274

treacherous (trech′ ər əs) *adj.* likely to betray a trust; disloyal; p. 1079

trek (trek) *n.* a journey, especially one that is slow or difficult; p. 1098

trepidation (trep′ ə dā′ shən) *n.* nervous anticipation; anxiety; p. 536

tumult (to͞o′ məlt) *n.* uproar; p. 1094

tumultuously (to͞o mul′ cho͞o əs lē) *adv.* in an agitated manner; violently; p. 526

turmoil (tur′ moil) *n.* a state of confused agitation; commotion; p. 537

tyranny (tir′ ə nē) *n.* the cruel use of authority; oppressive power; p. 155

U

uncanny (un ka′ nē) *adj.* strangely unsettling; eerie; p. 562

undeviating (un dē′ vē āt′ ing) *adj.* not turning away from; not straying; p. 1183

unorthodox (un ôr′ thə doks′) *adj.* not customary or traditional; unusual; p. 33

unperturbed (un pər turbd′) *adj.* undisturbed; calm; p. 975

upbraiding (up brā′ding) *adj.* criticizing or harshly scolding; p. 333

usurpation (u′ sər pā′ shən) *n.* an act of seizing power without legal right or authority; p. 169

V

vagabond (vag′ ə bond′) *n.* someone who wanders from place to place, having no visible means of support; p. 468

valedictorian (val′ ə dik tôr′ ē ən) *n.* the student with the highest class rank; p. 1098

valor (val′ ər) *n.* courage; bravery; p. 1049

vanity (van′ i tē) *n.* excessive pride, as in one's looks; p. 625

vanquish (vang′ kwish) *v.* to defeat; p. 333

vault (vôlt) *n.* an arched structure forming a roof or ceiling; p. 48

vehemently (ve′ ə mənt lē) *adv.* in a strong, intense, or passionate manner; p. 690

venerable (ven′ ər ə bəl) *adj.* deserving respect because of age, character, or position; p. 268

venture (ven′chər) *n.* an undertaking, often involving risk or danger; p. 351

vigilance (vij′ ə ləns) *n.* the state of being alert or watchful; p. 520

vigorously (vig′ ər əs lē) *adv.* with power, energy, and strength; p. 835

vile (vīl) *adj.* evil; foul; repulsive; degrading; p. 960

vindicate (vin′ də kāt′) *v.* to justify; to prove correct in light of later circumstances; p. 807

vindictive (vin dik′ tiv) *adj.* desiring revenge; p. 823

virtuous (vur′choo əs) *adj.* righteous; good; p. 363

virulent (vir′ yə lənt) *adj.* extremely poisonous or harmful; p. 810

vital (vīt′ əl) *adj.* of critical importance; essential; p. 826

vivid (viv′ id) *adj.* lifelike; realistic; distinct; p. 826

W

wane (wān) *v.* to decrease gradually; to decline; p. 1184

warily (wār′ ə lē) *adv.* in a watchful or alert manner; cautiously; p. 1032

warranted (wôr′ ən tid′) *adj.* justified; p. 1102

whimsically (hwim′ zik lē) *adv.* in a quaintly humorous or fanciful manner; p. 691

wistful (wist′ fəl) *adj.* full of wishful or sad longing; p. 1067

withered (with′ ərd) *adj.* shriveled; p. 680

wrath (rath) *n.* extreme anger; vengeful punishment; p. 102

writhe (rīth) *v.* to twist, as in great pain; p. 1054

Z

zealous (zel′ əs) *adj.* filled with enthusiastic devotion; passionate; p. 274

Spanish Glossary

A

abate/aminorar *v.* disminuir o reducir en fuerza o intensidad; p. 102

abhor/aborrecer *v.* despreciar; odiar algo en particular; p. 103

abjectly/abyectamente *adv.* de modo humillante, infame o indecente; p. 882

abominable/abominable *adj.* espantoso; detestable; p. 103

absolute/absoluto *adj.* completo; total; categórico; p. 140

access/acceso *s.* derecho a acercarse, a entrar o a usar; p. 1102

accommodate/alojar *v.* proporcionar hospedaje o habitación; p. 184

accost/abordar *v.* acercarse o dirigirse a alguien de manera brusca; p. 280

acquiesce/acatar *v.* aceptar o consentir sin protestar; acceder pasivamente; p. 172

acute/agudo *adj.* intenso; severo; p. 506

adamant/obstinado *adj.* empeñado en un fin; terco; p. 985

admonition/amonestación *s.* advertencia; consejo severo; p. 245

adorn/adornar *v.* embellecer; decorar; p. 369

advocate/proponente *s.* que defiende o respalda una causa; p. 894

affability/afabilidad *s.* cualidad de ser amable y fácil de tratar; cordialidad; p. 280

affirm/afirmar *v.* declarar firmemente; asegurar; p. 885

agitated/agitado *adj.* alterado; intranquilo; p. 351

alacrity/alacridad *s.* prontitud; presteza; p. 258

alien/ajeno *adj.* extraño; foráneo; extranjero; p. 827

alight/apearse *v.* descender; bajar; p. 48

allude/aludir *v.* referirse a algo indirectamente; p. 1088

allusion/alusión *s.* referencia indirecta o casual; mención casual; p. 358

ambulatory/ambulatorio *adj.* que se mueve de un lugar a otro; p. 131

amiable/amigable *adj.* amistoso; p. 876

amorphous/amorfo *adj.* sin forma definida; p. 784

ample/amplio *adj.* de gran tamaño o capacidad; p. 1068

anarchy/anarquía *s.* ausencia de gobierno; p. 363

ancestral/ancestral *adj.* relativo o perteneciente a los antepasados; p. 899

animated/animado *adj.* lleno de vida; activo; vivaz; p. 876

apathetically/apáticamente *adv.* con una actitud que muestra poco interés o preocupación; p. 507

appease/apaciguar *v.* calmar o aquietar; tranquilizar; p. 102

apprehension/aprensión *s.* temor vago de lo que pueda pasar; ansiedad; p. 191

ardently/ardientemente *adv.* apasionadamente; con mucho entusiasmo; p. 371

ardor/ardor *s.* emoción intensa; pasión, entusiasmo; p. 157

arduous/arduo *adj.* que requiere gran esfuerzo o trabajo; difícil; p. 148

aristocracy/aristocracia *s.* personas de un nivel social alto por razón de nacimiento o título; p. 30

array/disponer *v.* colocar en el orden adecuado; arreglar; p. 364

ashen/ceniciento *adj.* pálido; p. 490

assent/asentir *v.* afirmar; expresar acuerdo; p. 371

audaciously/audazmente *adv.* atrevidamente; de manera osada; p. 358

august/augusto *adj.* que infunde respeto; distinguido; prominente; p. 804

aura/aura *s.* atmósfera distintiva pero intangible que rodea a una persona o cosa; p. 847

avarice/avaricia *s.* deseo excesivo de acumular riquezas; codicia; p. 333

avert/desviar *v.* apartar; evitar; p. 800

B

balmy/suave *adj.* balsámico; calmante; p. 1006

base/vil *adj.* de baja condición moral; deshonesto; p. 943

benefactor/benefactor *s.* que respalda una causa o ayuda con dinero; p. 246

benevolent/benevolente *adj.* que hace el bien; amable; p. 330

blithe/alegre *adj.* despreocupado; animado; p. 243

bloated/hinchado *adj.* inflamado; abotagado; p. 1078

brazenness/descaro *s.* actitud desafiante; atrevimiento; p. 725

C

capitulate/capitular *v.* rendirse o ceder; entregarse; p. 358

cascade/precipitarse *v.* caer o fluir como una cascada o torrente de agua; p. 1069

censure/censurar *v.* expresar desacuerdo; criticar algo; reprobar; p. 334

ceremonial/ceremonial *adj.* formal; relativo a las ceremonias; p. 838

chaos/caos *s.* gran confusión y desorden; p. 893

charade/charada *s.* acto falso o fingido; p. 1048

circumvent/circunvenir *v.* rodear o evitar mediante una acción astuta; p. 810

clamber/encaramarse *v.* trepar o subir apresuradamente con los pies y las manos; p. 867

clamor/algarabía *s.* griterío confuso e insistente; p. 194

coerce/constreñir *v.* forzar; p. 573

cognizance/conocimiento *s.* comprensión; p. 299

colossal/colosal *adj.* extraordinario en tamaño o intensidad; enorme; p. 899

commodity/mercancía *s.* producto o bien económico; artículo que se vende o compra; p. 72

compassion/compasión *s.* interés por el sufrimiento ajeno junto con el deseo de ayudar; p. 86

compel/compeler *v.* forzar; p. 501

complex/complejo *adj.* complicado; formado por partes o elementos diversos; p. 900

comprehension/comprensión *s.* acto de entender algo; p. 839

compromise/implicar *v.* comprometer la reputación o el interés; abrir a sospecha; p. 916

concede/admitir *v.* aceptar como cierto; consentir; p. 489

conception/concepción *s.* imagen o idea mental; pensamiento o noción; p. 108

concerted/concertado *adj.* planeado o llevado a cabo por mutuo acuerdo; p. 1106

conciliatory/conciliador *adj.* que trata de ganarse la buena voluntad con una actitud amistosa; p. 985

conflagration/conflagración *s.* incendio grande y destructivo; p. 504

conjecture/conjeturar *v.* formarse una opinión sin tener evidencia definitiva; suponer; p. 462

conjurer/mago *s.* que realiza magia; hechicero; p. 49

consecrate/consagrar *v.* declarar sagrado; santificar; p. 385

console/consolar *v.* alentar; tranquilizar; p. 1004

conspire/conspirar *v.* unirse o actuar en conjunto, especialmente para llevar a cabo un propósito secreto o maligno, o con fines ilegales; p. 141

consummate/consumar *v.* llevar a cabo; finalizar; p. 1057

contemplation/contemplación *s.* acto de pensar larga y seriamente; p. 970

contend/contender *v.* disputar; pelear; p. 364

contention/contienda *s.* lucha o disputa verbal; pelea; p. 917

continuity/continuidad *s.* estado o cualidad de seguir sin interrupción; p. 900

contrivance/artificio *s.* instrumento diseñado con astucia; p. 690

convene/congregarse *v.* reunirse; p. 56

copious/copioso *adj.* grande en cantidad; abundante; p. 192

corroding/corrosivo *adj.* que tiende a gastarse o consumirse gradualmente; que destruye lentamente; p. 893

countenance/semblante *s.* rostro; características faciales; p. 190

covet/codiciar *v.* desear de forma intensa algo ajeno; p. 947

cringe/contraerse *v.* encogerse, como cuando se tiene miedo o rabia; p. 1098

D

dally/demorarse *v.* perder el tiempo; holgazanear; flojear; p. 489

daunt/acobardar *v.* intimidar; atemorizar; p. 86

decimated/diezmado *adj.* destruido o liquidado en grandes cantidades; p. 1182

decorum/decoro *s.* conforme a las normas aprobadas de buen gusto; p. 243

deduce/deducir *v.* sacar una conclusión de algo que se sabe o se asume; p. 294

deference/deferencia *s.* tratamiento cortés o respetuoso; p. 369

deftly/diestramente *adv.* hábilmente; p. 1074

deliberately/deliberadamente *adv.* de modo cuidadoso y bien calculado; p. 253

deliberation/deliberación *s.* consideración cuidadosa; p. 57

delirium/delirio *s.* estado temporal de alteración mental que se caracteriza por confusión y desorientación; p. 1004

deluge/diluvio *s.* torrente; algo que abruma o cae como un diluvio; p. 539

delusion/ilusión *s.* impresión o creencia falsa; p. 359

demeaning/degradante *adj.* que rebaja dignidad o nivel social; humillante; p. 1098

denounce/denunciar *v.* condenar; criticar; p. 1131

depravity/depravación *s.* condición moral baja o corrupta; p. 330

derangement/trastorno *s.* alteración del funcionamiento normal; desorden p. 491

desolation/desolación *s.* devastación; miseria; p. 85

detached/indiferente *adj.* que no está involucrado emocionalmente; desinteresado; p. 681

didactic/didáctico *adj.* con fines instructivos, especialmente en lo relativo a la moral; p. 30

diffuse/difundir *v.* esparcir ampliamente; dispersar en todas las direcciones; p. 303

dilapidated/dilapidado *adj.* que ha sido gastado o arruinado; muy usado; p. 462

din/estrépito *s.* ruido fuerte y continuo; p. 258

discern/discenir *v.* reconocer como diferente; distinguir; p. 88

discord/discordia *s.* desacuerdo; conflicto; p. 204

discreet/discreto *adj.* cauteloso; prudente; p. 280

disperse/dispersar *v.* ir en diferentes direcciones; esparcir; p. 163

disposition/disposición *s.* modo de pensar o sentir; p. 55

dissembling/encubrimiento *s.* acto de ocultar el verdadero carácter, sentimientos o intenciones; p. 690

dissipate/disipar *v.* hacer que desaparezca gradualmente; disolver; p. 798

distinctive/distintivo *adj.* diferente en calidad o tipo; peculiar; p. 139

doctrine/doctrina *s.* principio que se enseña y promueve; dogma; p. 520

doggedly/obstinadamente *adv.* de manera persistente; firmemente; p. 535

doleful/afligido *adj.* lleno de pena o dolor; triste; p. 85

domain/dominio *s.* territorio sobre el que se ejerce control; reino; p. 1058

downy/aterciopelado *adj.* suave y velloso, como las plumas de un pájaro recién nacido; p. 1038

dupe/embaucar *v.* engañar o burlar; p. 1079

dusk/ocaso *s.* hora del día antes de que anochezca; p. 1041

dutiful/cumplidor *adj.* que cumple responsablemente sus obligaciones; p. 622

dwell/dilatarse *v.* pensar con calma; tomarse su tiempo p. 1064

dwindle/menguar *v.* reducir en tamaño gradualmente; p. 628

E

ecclesiastical/eclesiástico *adj.* relativo a la iglesia; p. 1182

efface/destruir *v.* arrasar; erradicar; p. 373

elusive/elusivo *adj.* difícil de explicar o entender; p. 526

embark/embarcar *v.* lanzarse a una empresa; partir en una aventura; p. 64

embody/encarnar *v.* tomar forma concreta o material; p. 900

emphatic/enfático *adj.* enérgico; categórico; p. 562

enamored/enamorado *adj.* prendado; encantado; cautivado; p. 881

endeavor/empeñarse *v.* esforzarse; tratar; p. 171

engender/engendrar *v.* dar lugar; causar; producir; p. 1056

engrossed/enfrascado *adj.* dedicado por completo a pensar en algo; ensimismado; absorto; p. 867

enlighten/ilustrar *v.* dar o revelar conocimientos o sabiduría; p. 31

enmity/enemistad *s.* odio profundo; hostilidad; p. 1059

enormity/enormidad *s.* monstruosidad; atrocidad; p. 93

ensure/garantizar *v.* asegurar; p. 96

enterprising/emprendedor *adj.* que muestra dinamismo e iniciativa, especialmente al iniciar nuevos proyectos; p. 468

enunciate/enunciar *v.* pronunciar claramente; p. 1032

ephemeral/efímero *adj.* que dura muy poco tiempo; fugaz; p. 900

equanimity/ecuanimidad *s.* igualdad y constancia de ánimo; calma; p. 479

espionage/espionaje *s.* acto de espiar o investigar; pesquisa; p. 1102

esteem/estimar *v.* apreciar; sentir simpatía; p. 108

evade/evadir *v.* evitar algo de modo astuto; p. 931

exalt/exaltar *v.* elevar; animar; p. 726

exalted/exaltado *adj.* elevado; p. 527

exclusively/exclusivamente *adv.* sin la participación de otros; p. 30

exemplary/ejemplar *adj.* digno de imitación; meritorio; p. 1131

exhilarated/alborozado *adj.* alegre, vivaz o muy entusiasmado; lleno de vigor; p. 656

exhilaration/alborozo *s.* sensación de vigor y energía, alegría o entusiasmo; p. 847

exorbitant/exorbitante *adj.* que excede a lo razonable; exagerado; p. 519

expatriated/expatriado *adj.* desterrado; exilado; p. 477

expedient/arbitrio *s.* algo que se usa para alcanzar un resultado deseado; recurso; p. 258

exploit/proeza *s.* acto heroico o notable; hazaña; p. 156

exploit/explotar *v.* usar o aprovechar para obtener ganancia, a menudo de manera egoísta o injusta; p. 657

extricate/redimir *v.* liberar; sacar; p. 183

F

facade/fachada *s.* apariencia falsa o artificial; p. 1091

feigned/fingido *adj.* falso; que no es genuino; p. 72

feint/finta *s.* movimiento o ademán con la intención de engañar al oponente; amago; p. 162

futile/fútil *adj.* inútil; insignificante; p. 823

G

gape/boquear *v.* quedar boquiabierto por sorpresa o asombro; p. 1064

garrulous/parlanchín *adj.* que habla mucho; locuaz p. 462

gaunt/enjuto *adj.* flaco y ojeroso por hambre o enfermedad; con aspecto enfermizo; p. 8

grapple/forcejear *v.* luchar cuerpo a cuerpo; bregar; p. 866

gratify/gratificar *v.* satisfacer o complacer; p. 193

grave/grave *adj.* solemne y severo; sombrío; p. 833

gravity/gravedad *s.* seriedad; importancia; p. 1041

grievously/penosamente *adv.* gravemente; seriamente; p. 490

grimace/gesticular *v.* hacer muecas con la cara, especialmente para expresar dolor o molestia; p. 1001

grope/tantear *v.* palpar algo sin certeza; buscar a ciegas; p. 1063

grotesque/grotesco *adj.* extravagante; raro; p. 1047

guile/ardid *s.* engaño; astucia; trampa; p. 968

H

hallow/consagrar *v.* santificar; honrar como sagrado; p. 385

hallucination/alucinación *s.* percepción sensorial falsa de algo que en realidad no está presente; p. 1079

haughty/altanero *adj.* presumido; arrogante; p. 808

heedless/incauto *adj.* descuidado; atolondrado; p. 1047

hemorrhage/hemorragia *s.* pérdida grave de sangre; p. 785

holocaust/holocausto *s.* destrucción grande o total, especialmente debida al fuego; p. 1032

hostile/hostil *adj.* que siente o demuestra odio; adverso; p. 823

hover/revolotear *v.* permanecer cerca; volar por los alrededores; p. 1041

hypocrisy/hipocresía *s.* expresión de sentimientos o creencias que en realidad no se tienen; falsedad; p. 156

hypothesis/hipótesis *s.* explicación no comprobada; p. 480

I

idiom/modismo *s.* expresión peculiar de un grupo de personas o de una región específica; p. 1103

illumination/iluminación *s.* claridad intelectual; p. 527

immaculate/inmaculado *adj.* sin mancha ni pecado; irreprochable; puro; p. 966

imminent/inminente *adj.* a punto de ocurrir; p. 652

immortality/inmortalidad *s.* vida eterna; p. 499

impede/impedir *v.* detener o aminorar; obstaculizar; p. 295

impediment/impedimento *s.* obstáculo; p. 1087

imperative/imperativo *s.* algo absolutamente necesario; algo esencial; p. 894

imperious/imperioso *adj.* imperativo; urgente; p. 371

imperviousness/insensibilidad *s.* condición de no experimentar sensación alguna o de no sentirse afectado; p. 808

impetuously/impetuosamente *adv.* de modo impulsivo y repentino; precipitado; p. 658

impious/impío *adj.* falto de piedad o reverencia; irrespetuoso; p. 568

impose/imponer *v.* obligar o exigir por medio de la autoridad; ordenar; p. 527

impregnable/inexpugnable *adj.* que no se deja vencer por la fuerza; que resiste cualquier ataque; p. 205

impropriety/impropiedad *s.* incorrección; indecencia; p. 477

impudently/descaradamente *adv.* de modo ofensivo y atrevido; sin decoro ni vergüenza; p. 565

inaudibly/inaudiblemente *adv.* de modo que no se puede escuchar; p. 1041

incensed/exasperado *adj.* muy molesto; colérico; irritado; p. 102

incessant/incesante *adj.* que continúa o persiste sin interrupción; p. 1048

indentured/ligado por contrato *adj.* obligado por un contrato a servir a una persona por un tiempo determinado; p. 131

indictment/acusación *s.* denuncia legal y formal por la comisión u omisión de un acto que castiga la ley; p. 989

indifferent/indiferente *adj.* que no demuestra sentimiento o preocupación; p. 729

indignation/indignación *s.* ira reprimida y digna en reacción a maldad, injusticia o ingratitud; p. 161

induce/inducir *v.* influir o persuadir; p. 330

ineptly/ineptamente *adv.* sin aptitud o destreza; torpemente; p. 951

inert/inerte *adj.* inactivo; inmóvil; p. 536

inevitable/inevitable *adj.* que no se puede evitar o eludir; irremediable; p. 96

infidel/infiel *s.* el que no cree; p. 131

ingenious/ingenioso *adj.* que tiene habilidad creativa; talentoso; p. 131

ingenuously/ingenuamente *adv.* de modo honesto; francamente; cándidamente; p. 564

inherent/inherente *adj.* que existe como cualidad básica; unido por naturaleza; p. 258

iniquity/iniquidad *s.* pecado; maldad; p. 268

initially/inicialmente *adv.* al comienzo; primeramente; p. 1102

inquisitor/inquisidor *s.* el que hace preguntas; p. 786

insidious/insidioso *adj.* engañoso; malicioso; p. 148

instinct/instinto *s.* habilidad o impulso natural; p. 1074

intangible/intangible *adj.* que no es fácil de definir o evaluar; p. 498

integrate/integrar *v.* unir todas las partes en un todo; p. 242

integrity/integridad *s.* rectitud moral; honestidad; p. 247

interminable/interminable *adj.* que parece no tener fin; p. 463

intervene/intervenir *v.* tomar parte en un asunto; p. 502

intimation/insinuación *s.* sugerencia; indirecta; p. 787

intimidated/intimidado *adj.* atemorizado o asustado; reprimido; p. 866

intricately/intrincadamente *adv.* de modo complejo o complicado; elaboradamente; p. 1183

intrigue/intriga *s.* manejos secretos para alcanzar una meta; complot; p. 823

intriguing/intrigante *adj.* que despierta curiosidad o interés; fascinante; cautivante; p. 865

invigorated/tonificado *adj.* lleno de fortaleza y energía; p. 787

invoke/invocar *v.* llamar en auxilio; p. 1105

irk/fastidiar *v.* molestar; disgustar; p. 822

irreproachable/irreprochable *adj.* libre de culpa; sin falta alguna; p. 274

irrevocable/irrevocable *adj.* que no se puede anular; p. 96

J

jilt/dejar plantado *v.* rechazar; incumplir una cita; p. 625

jocular/jocoso *adj.* chistoso; gracioso; p. 480

jostle/empujar *v.* empellar mientras se camina, como en una multitud; p. 681

jubilant/jubiloso *adj.* dichoso; muy feliz por un triunfo; p. 867

K

kindle/encender *v.* prender fuego; excitar o avivar; p. 533

L

lament/lamentar *v.* expresar gran pena o dolor; p. 89

latent/latente *adj.* presente pero no evidente; oculto; p. 245

legacy/legado *s.* herencia; p. 533

legible/legible *adj.* que puede leerse; p. 1049

lethargy/letargo *s.* estado de sopor o inactividad; p. 298

limber/flexible *adj.* que puede doblarse fácilmente; elástico; p. 834

list/ladear *v.* inclinar hacia un lado; p. 8

loiter/holgazanear *v.* permanecer en un lugar sin hacer nada; estar ocioso; p. 866

lucid/lúcido *adj.* racional; sensato; p. 1050

lurch/tambalearse *v.* caminar o moverse sin equilibrio; p. 680

luxuriant/frondoso *adj.* con una vegetación rica y abundante; abundante; p. 1056

M

malevolence/malevolencia *s.* deseo de lastimar a otros; mala voluntad; p. 478

manifest/manifiesto *adj.* evidente o claro a la vista; obvio; p. 246

meager/exiguo *adj.* muy escaso; limitado; p. 875

meandering/tortuoso *adj.* que sigue un camino con muchas curvas; p. 33

melancholy/melancólico *adj.* deprimente; funesto; desconsolador; p. 205

mentor/mentor *s.* persona que protege o guía a otra; tutor; consejero; p. 57

mimic/remedar *v.* copiar; imitar; p. 1067

minutely/minuciosamente *adv.* con gran detalle; p. 1068

misgiving/recelo *s.* sentimiento de duda, desconfianza o ansiedad; p. 947

mishap/percance *s.* accidente o error; contratiempo; desgracia; p. 520

morose/adusto *adj.* malhumorado; taciturno; p. 14

mortification/mortificación *s.* sentimiento de aflicción, humillación o vergüenza; p. 132

mundane/mundano *adj.* ordinario; usual; terrenal; p. 1087

murky/lóbrego *adj.* obscuro o sombrío; p. 1074

myriad/innumerable *adj.* que no se puede contar; incalculable; p. 255

N

naive/ingenuo *adj.* que no desconfía de nadie; inocente; p. 919

novel/novel *adj.* nuevo y original; p. 1183

O

obesity/obesidad *s.* gordura excesiva; p. 806

obliquely/oblicuamente *adv.* de manera inclinada o sesgada; p. 537

obliterate/arrasar *v.* borrar; destruir por completo; p. 207

oblivious/abstraído *adj.* distraído; ensimismado; p. 1041

occult/sobrenatural *adj.* más allá de la comprensión humana; misterioso; p. 243

ominous/ominoso *adj.* que da mal presagio; siniestro; p. 1032

onslaught/embestida *s.* ataque vigoroso o destructivo; p. 163

opaque/opaco *adj.* que no deja pasar la luz; p. 1058

oppressed/oprimido *adj.* controlado o gobernado mediante el uso cruel e injusto de la fuerza o autoridad; p. 892

ordeal/tribulación *s.* circunstancia o experiencia dolorosa o difícil; p. 892

P

pall/palio *s.* manto que obscurece o cubre y da una atmósfera sombría; p. 498

paradigm/paradigma *s.* ejemplo que sirve como modelo; p. 33

parsimony/parquedad *s.* excesiva moderación o economía; tacañería; p. 211

perception/percepción *s.* conocimiento; idea; p. 527

perennial/perenne *adj.* que continúa año tras año; duradero; p. 243

perish/perecer *v.* dejar de existir; desaparecer; p. 385

perpetual/perpetuo *adj.* que dura por siempre; eterno; p. 242

perplexed/perplejo *adj.* asombrado; confundido; p. 1098

persistence/persistencia *s.* perseverancia; continuación; p. 527

perturbation/perturbación *s.* agitación; ansiedad; inquietud; p. 268

perusal/escudriñamiento *s.* proceso de examinar cuidadosamente; p. 363

pervade/penetrar *v.* saturar; llenar por todos lados; p. 360

petrified/petrificado *adj.* paralizado de miedo; inmóvil como una piedra; p 156

piety/piedad *s.* devoción religiosa; bondad; p. 627

pigment/pigmento *s.* substancia que da color; p. 1069

pillage/pillaje *s.* robo o saqueo; p. 1054

plague/fastidiar *v.* molestar; importunar; p. 623

plumage/plumaje *s.* conjunto de plumas de un ave; p. 847

poignant/punzante *adj.* agudo; lacerante; que causa angustia emocional o física; p. 372

poised/sereno *adj.* que tiene un modo de ser calmado y equilibrado; p. 826

ponder/ponderar *v.* pensar algo detenida y cuidadosamente; p. 1063

posterity/posteridad *s.* generaciones del futuro; todos los descendientes; p. 56

preeminently/preeminentemente *adv.* de modo principal; predominantemente; p. 1054

preposterous/disparatado *adj.* absurdo; ridículo; p. 566

presumptuous/insolente *adj.* que va más allá de lo apropiado; atrevido; p. 1182

pretense/simulación *s.* falsa apariencia, especialmente con el propósito de engañar; falsedad; p. 922

pretension/pretensión *s.* reclamo; aspiración; p. 519

prevail/prevalecer *v.* persuadir; convencer; p. 539

prevalent/prevaleciente *adj.* frecuente; generalizado; p. 204

procure/procurarse *v.* obtener mediante esfuerzos; p. 72

profound/profundo *adj.* que viene del fondo; que se siente intensamente; p. 560

profusion/profusión *s.* gran cantidad; abundancia; p. 1056

progenitor/progenitor *s.* ancestro directo; ascendiente; padre o abuelo; p. 57

proposal/propuesta *s.* algo que se presenta a consideración como plan de acción; p. 108

propriety/corrección *s.* cualidad de ser correcto o apropiado; p. 520

prosperity/prosperidad *s.* éxito, riqueza o fortuna; p. 364

prostrate/postrado *adj.* agachado o arrodillado en señal de humillación, adoración o sumisión; p. 359

protrude/sobresalir *v.* resaltar; proyectarse; p. 369

proverbial/proverbial *adj.* conocido y notable; p. 1094

providence/providencia *s.* cuidado o guía divina; disposición; p. 70

provoke/provocar *v.* inducir; incitar; p. 1132

proximity/proximidad *s.* cercanía en espacio, tiempo, secuencia o grado; p. 302

prudence/prudencia *s.* ejercicio del buen juicio y la cordura; cautela; p. 102

Q

querulous/quejumbroso *adj.* que se queja mucho; lastimero; p. 483

quivering/estremecimiento *s.* temblor repentino; sacudida; sobresalto; p. 834

R

radical/radical *adj.* que se desvía de lo usual o común; extremo; p. 1049

random/causal *adj.* que no sigue un patrón definido; fortuito; p. 1032

ration/ración *s.* porción definida; p. 62

ravage/asolamiento *s.* acción destructiva o resultado de una acción destructiva; p. 156

ravenous/voraz *adj.* extremadamente hambriento; p. 11

reciprocate/corresponder *v.* dar, sentir o mostrar a cambio; p. 652

recourse/recurso *s.* ayuda; medio que, en caso de necesidad, sirve para conseguir lo que se pretende; p. 185

rectitude/rectitud *s.* buena condición moral; honestidad; p. 172

redress/desagravio *s.* compensación por un error o mala actitud; p. 364

refugee/refugiado *s.* persona que huye por razones de seguridad, especialmente quien abandona su hogar o país debido a persecución, guerra o peligro; p. 352

rejuvenated/rejuvenecido *adj.* que ha recuperado el vigor o la apariencia joven; renovado; p. 1005

relinquish/rendir *v.* ceder el control; doblegarse; p. 156

reminiscence/reminiscencia *s.* relato de una experiencia o suceso pasado; p. 462

remonstrate/rezongar *v.* objetar; protestar; p. 148

remorselessly/despiadadamente *adv.* de un modo que no muestra piedad ni compasión; sin misericordia; p. 165

render/producir *v.* causar; generar; p. 184

repertoire/repertorio *s.* conjunto de destrezas que una persona o grupo tiene y está preparado para demostrar en una actuación; p. 280

repression/represión *s.* situación en la que se frena o mantiene bajo control; p. 526

reprieve/aplazamiento *s.* demora oficial de una sentencia; p. 985

reprimand/reprender *v.* regañar o corregir severamente; p. 937

reproach/reproche *s.* expresión de desacuerdo; censura; p. 533

repudiate/repudiar *v.* negarse a aceptar como válido; rechazar; renunciar; p. 894

resign/resignarse *v.* obligarse a aceptar; conformarse; p. 683

resignation/resignación *s.* aceptación; conformismo; sumisión; p. 253

resolution/resolución *s.* acción de decidir con firmeza; p. 156

resolve/resolver *v.* decidir; determinar; p. 70

resonant/resonante *adj.* que tiene un sonido fuerte y vibrante; p. 1068

retaliation/represalia *s.* acto de vengarse o devolver un mal acto cometiendo un acto similar o igual; p. 985

retractable/retráctil *adj.* capaz de encogerse; p. 784

revive/revivir *v.* dar nueva fuerza y vitalidad; hacer que recupere el conocimiento; p. 62

rigorously/rigurosamente *adv.* precisamente; estrictamente; p. 1130

ritual/ritual *s.* rutina que se sigue regularmente; ceremonial; p. 1092

rouse/despertar *v.* dejar de dormir; p. 62

rudiment/rudimento *s.* parte imperfecta o sin desarrollar; p. 254

rue/deplorar *v.* lamentar; sentir; p. 16

S

sagacious/sagaz *adj.* que tiene o demuestra astucia y agudeza mental; p. 269

sage/sabio *s.* persona con profundo conocimiento y buen juicio; p. 245

sanction/ratificación *s.* aprobación o respaldo; p. 261

savory/apetitoso *adj.* agradable al paladar o al olfato; sabroso; p. 89

scavenger/trapero *s.* el que busca y recoge cosas útiles de la basura; p. 1078

score/veintena *s.* grupo de veinte objetos; p. 385

scruple/escrúpulo *s.* principio moral que limita una acción; p. 194

scrupulously/escrupulosamente *adv.* con extremo cuidado y atención; esmeradamente; p. 1130

scuffle/arrastrar los pies *v.* moverse con pasos rápidos y torpes; p. 798

seclusion/reclusión *s.* separación de otros; aislamiento; p. 481

sibling/fraterno *adj.* relativo a un hermano o hermana; p. 1067

signal/insigne *adj.* admirable; asombroso; notable; p. 165

simultaneously/simultáneamente *adv.* al mismo tiempo; p. 1129

sluggard/haragán *s.* alguien que por lo general es perezoso o vago; ocioso; p. 141

sluggishly/perezosamente *adv.* lentamente; sin energía ni entusiasmo; p. 805

snicker/risita burlona *s.* risa solapada que puede demostrar burla o falta de respeto; p. 727

solemn/solemne *adj.* serio; grave; p. 838

speculate/especular *v.* participar en negocios arriesgados con el deseo de obtener ganancias rápidas; p. 210

spurn/desdeñar *v.* rechazar con menosprecio o desdén; p. 149

stately/majestuoso *adj.* noble; imponente; espléndido; p. 12

stature/estatura *s.* nivel alcanzado; posición; p. 894

stoically/estoicamente *adv.* de modo calmado y sin emoción, especialmente en momentos de dolor o sufrimiento; p. 691

stolidly/impasiblemente *adv.* con poca o ninguna emoción; sin perturbarse; p. 1132

stooped/encorvado *adj.* doblado hacia adelante y hacia abajo; p. 1063

subjugation/subyugación *s.* acto de someter o poner bajo control; dominación; p. 148

sublime/sublime *adj.* de gran valor espiritual o intelectual; noble; p. 253

submissive/sumiso *adj.* dispuesto a ceder el poder o autoridad a otro; dócil; p. 1048

subservient/subordinado *adj.* útil, en una capacidad inferior, para conseguir un fin; sumiso; p. 919

subtle/sutil *adj.* que no es obvio ni directo; p. 949

subversive/subversivo *adj.* que busca destruir o debilitar; p. 1079

succor/socorro *s.* ayuda en momentos de necesidad; auxilio; p. 71

succumb/sucumbir *v.* rendirse; ceder; p. 893

sumptuous/suntuoso *adj.* que implica un gran gasto; extravagante; espléndido; p. 1068

supplication/súplica *s.* solicitud humilde de ayuda; ruego; p. 280

surmise/suponer *v.* conjeturar con poca o ninguna evidencia; presumir; p. 207

sustenance/sustento *s.* que conserva la vida, especialmente alimento; p. 520

symmetrical/simétrico *adj.* que tiene la misma forma o estructura a ambos lados de una línea o plano central; p. 1047

synthesis/síntesis *s.* combinación de partes o elementos separados para formar un todo; p. 893

T

tactful/discreto *adj.* capaz de hablar o actuar sin ofender a otros; p. 622

temper/atemperar *v.* modificar o moderar; suavizar; p. 57

tentative/tentativo *adj.* que no se ha definido por completo; p. 658

tenure/tenencia *s.* condiciones o términos bajo los cuales se posee algo; p. 171

thicket/espesura *s.* área de vegetación densa con muchos arbustos; p. 834

torpor/entumecimiento *s.* incapacidad de moverse o sentir; p. 274

treacherous/traicionero *adj.* que tiende a engañar; desleal; p. 1079

trek/travesía *s.* viaje, especialmente si es lento o difícil; p. 1098

trepidation/perturbación *s.* anticipación nerviosa; ansiedad; p. 536

tumult/tumulto *s.* alboroto; conmoción; p. 1094

tumultuously/tumultuosamente *adv.* de modo agitado; violentamente; p. 526

turmoil/disturbio *s.* estado de agitación; conmoción; p. 537

tyranny/tiranía *s.* uso cruel de la autoridad; poder opresivo; p. 155

U

uncanny/espectral *adj.* inquietante y extraño; misterioso; p. 562

undeviating/recto *adj.* que no se desvía o extravía; p. 1183

unorthodox/no ortodoxo *adj.* que no es usual ni tradicional; p. 33

unperturbed/inalterado *adj.* que no se molesta o altera; calmado; p. 975

upbraiding/reprochador *adj.* que da una crítica o recriminación severa; p. 333

usurpation/usurpación *s.* acto de tomar el poder sin derecho o autoridad legal; p. 169

V

vagabond/vagabundo *s.* alguien que vaga de un lugar a otro, sin tener medios aparentes de ganarse la vida; p. 468

valedictorian/orador *s.* estudiante de más alto rango que pronuncia el discurso de despedida; p. 1098

valor/valor *s.* coraje; valentía; p. 1049

vanity/vanidad *s.* orgullo excesivo, particularmente por la apariencia física; p. 625

vanquish/subyugar *v.* derrotar; conquistar p. 333

vault/bóveda *s.* estructura arqueada que forma un techo o cielo raso; p. 48

vehemently/vehementemente *adv.* de modo fuerte, intenso o apasionado; p. 690

venerable/venerable *adj.* que merece respeto debido a la edad, carácter o posición; p. 268

venture/empresa *s.* negocio o acto aventurado; p. 351

vigilance/vigilancia *s.* condición de estar alerta o vigilante; p. 520

vigorously/vigorosamente *adv.* con poder, energía y fuerza; p. 835

vile/vil *adj.* malvado; bajo; repulsivo; degradante; p. 960

vindicate/vindicar *v.* justificar; demostrar que es correcto ante nuevas circunstancias; p. 807

vindictive/vengativo *adj.* que desea venganza; p. 823

virtuous/virtuoso *adj.* recto; bueno; p. 363

virulent/virulento *adj.* extremadamente nocivo o dañino; p. 810

vital/vital *adj.* de enorme importancia; esencial; p. 826

vivid/vívido *adj.* auténtico; realista; distintivo; p. 826

W

wane/declinar *v.* menguar o disminuir gradualmente; p. 1184

warily/cautelosamente *adv.* de modo cuidadoso o alerta; p. 1032

warranted/justificado *adj.* que se explica en vista de las circunstancias; p. 1102

whimsically/caprichosamente *adv.* de modo extravagante; p. 691

wistful/nostálgico *adj.* lleno de melancolía o añoranza; p. 1067

withered/marchito *adj.* seco; arrugado; p. 680

wrath/ira *s.* furia extrema; castigo vengativo; p. 102

writhe/retorcerse *s.* flexionar, como cuando se siente gran dolor; p. 1054

Z

zealous/fervoroso *adj.* lleno de entusiasmo y devoción; apasionado; p. 274

Index of Skills

Reading & Thinking

Listening, Speaking, and Viewing

Research and Study Skills

Media and Technology

Life Skills

Interdisciplinary Studies

Index of Authors and Titles

INDEX OF AUTHORS AND TITLES

Index of Art and Artists

Acknowledgments

(Continued from page ii)

Literature
Active Reading Models

"The Life You Save May Be Your Own" from *A Good Man Is Hard to Find and Other Stories*, copyright © 1953 by Flannery O'Connor and renewed 1981 by Reginia O'Connor, reprinted by permission of Harcourt Brace & Company.

"The Fish" from *The Complete Poems 1927–1979* by Elizabeth Bishop. Copyright © 1979, 1983 by Alice Helen Methfessel. Reprinted by permission of Farrar, Straus & Giroux, Inc.

"Thoughts on the African-American Novel" by Toni Morrison, from *Black Women Writers (1950–1980)* by Mari Evans. Copyright © 1983 by Mari Evans. Used by permission of Doubleday, a division of Bantam Doubleday Dell Publishing Group, Inc.

Unit 1

"The Sky Tree" retold by Joseph Bruchac, from *Keepers of Life*, by Michael Caduto and Joseph Bruchac. Copyright © 1994, Fulcrum Publishing, 350 Indiana St., Suite 350, Golden, CO 80401. (800) 992–2908.

"Shipwreck Survivors Recall Ordeal" by Patrick McDonnell. Copyright © 1997, Los Angeles Times. Reprinted by permission.

Excerpt from *The Account: Alvar Nunez Cabeza de Vaca's Relacion*, edited and translated by José Fernandez and Martin Favata is reprinted with permission from the publisher (Houston: Arte Publico Press—University of Houston, 1993).

"In Your Eyes" by Peter Gabriel. Copyright © 1986 Real World Music, Ltd. Reprinted with permission of Lipservices.

From Lang, Amy Schrager, ed. "A True History of the Captivity and Restoration of Mary Rowlandson," in Andrews, William L., Sargent Bush Jr., Annette Kolodny, Amy Schrager Lang and Daniel B. Shea, eds. *Journeys in New Worlds: Early American Women's Narratives*. Copyright 1990. Reprinted by permission of The University of Wisconsin Press.

Reprinted with the permission of The Free Press, a Division of Simon & Schuster from *Stay Alive, My Son* by Pin Yathay. Copyright © 1987 by Pin Yathay. Excerpt from *Stay Alive, My Son*, copyright © 1987 by Pin Yathay. Reprinted by permission of the author.

Unit 2

"Dichos" by Americo Paredes from *Mexican-American Authors*. Copyright © 1976, 1972 by Houghton Mifflin Company. All rights reserved. Reprinted by permission of McDougal Littell Inc.

"Give Me Rhetoric!" by Wen Smith, from the *Saturday Evening Post*, September/October 1996. Reprinted by permission of the author.

"Thermopylae" from *The Histories* by Herodotus, translated by Aubrey de Selincourt, revised by A. R. Burn (Penguin Classics 1954, Revised edition 1972) copyright © the Estate of Aubrey de Selincourt, 1954 copyright © A. R. Burn, 1972. Reprinted by permission of Penguin Books Ltd.

"To His Excellency, George Washington" from *The Poems of Phillis Wheatley*, edited by Julian D. Mason. Copyright © 1989 by the University of North Carolina Press. Used by permission of the publisher.

"Amistad America" reprinted by permission of the Amistad Project, Mystic Seaport, Connecticut.

From "Bart Sells his Soul," *The Simpsons*™ and © 1996 Twentieth Century Fox Film Corporation. All rights reserved. Reprinted by permission.

"Dead Singer Buckley's Voice Haunts Poe Disc" by Steve James © Reuters Limited 1998. Used by permission.

Unit 3

"Swing Low, Sweet Chariot" and "Go Down, Moses" from *Religious Folk-Songs of the Negro*, edited by R. Nathaniel Dett. Reprinted courtesy of AMS Press, Inc.

"Follow the Drinking Gourd," adapted by John L. Haag, from *All American Folk, Vol. #1*. Copyright © 1982 and 1986 Creative Concepts Publishing Corp. Used by permission.

"Mars Robot 'Sojourner' Named by Black Girl to Honor Abolitionist Sojourner Truth," *Jet* magazine, July 29, 1997. Reprinted by permission.

From *His Promised Land: The Autobiography of John P. Parker* by Stuart Selly Sprague, editor. Copyright © 1996 by The John P. Parker Historical Society. Reprinted by permission of W. W. Norton & Company, Inc.

Excerpt from *Mary Chestnut's Civil War*, edited by C. Vann Woodward. Copyright © 1986 by C. Vann Woodward, Sally Bland Metts, Barbara G. Carpenter, Sally Bland Johnson, and Katherine W. Herbert. Reprinted by permission of Yale University Press.

"An Occurrence at Owl Creek Bridge" from *The Twilight Zone Companion* by Marc Scott Zicree. Copyright © 1982 by Marc Scott Zicree. Reprinted by permission of the author.

"The Gift in Wartime" by Tran Mong Tu. Reprinted by permission of the author.

"Stolen Whitman Papers Surface After 50 Years" by David Streitfeld and Elizabeth Kastor. Copyright © 1995, The Washington Post. Reprinted with permission.

"The Useless" by Thomas Merton from *The Way of Chuang Tzu*. Copyright © 1965 by The Abbey of Gethsemane. Reprinted by permission of New Directions Publishing Corp.

"Butterfly Dream" from *The Book of Chuang Tzu*, translated by Martin Palmer, with Elizabeth Breuilly, Chang Wai Ming, and Jay Ramsey (Arkana, 1996) copyright © ICOREC 1996. Reproduced by permission of Penguin Books Ltd.

Poems #511, #303, #67, #435, #1624, #1732, #465, #1078, #712, #258, #441 reprinted by permission of the publishers and the Trustees of Amherst College from *The Poems of Emily Dickinson*, Thomas H. Johnson, ed., Cambridge, Mass: The Belknap Press of Harvard University Press, copyright © 1951, 1955, 1979, 1983 by the President and Fellows of Harvard College.

Emily Dickinson parody ("The Apple falls—its own Society—") by Christopher C. Lund. Reprinted by permission of the author.

Emily Dickinson parody ("Punctuations * My forte"-") by Robert Hogge. Reprinted by permission of the author.

Unit 4

Excerpt from *Frogs,* text © David Badger, photo © John Netherton, reprinted with permission of the publisher, Voyageur Press, Inc., Stillwater, MN 55082. 1-800-888-9653.

"Chief Sekoto Holds Court" from *Tales of Tenderness and Power,* published by Heinemann International in their African Writers Series, 1990. Copyright © 1989 The Estate of Bessie Head.

Unit 5

"In a Station of the Metro" and "A Pact" by Ezra Pound, from *Personae.* Copyright © 1926 by Ezra Pound. Reprinted by permission of New Directions Publishing Corp.

"The Red Wheelbarrow," and "This Is Just to Say" by William Carlos Williams, from *Collected Poems: 1909–1939, Volume I.* Copyright © 1938 by New Directions Publishing Corp. Reprinted by permission of New Directions Publishing Corp.

"Anecdote of the Jar" from *Collected Poems* by Wallace Stevens. Copyright © 1923 and renewed 1951 by Wallace Stevens. Reprinted by permission of Alfred A. Knopf, Inc.

From "Let's Call the Whole Thing Off" by Leila Cobo-Hanlon. Reprinted with the permission of the *St. Louis Post-Dispatch,* copyright © 1995.

"The Jilting of Granny Weatherall" from *Flowering Judas and Other Stories,* copyright © 1930 and renewed 1958 by Katherine Anne Porter, reprinted by permission of Harcourt Brace & Company.

"Richness" by Gabriela Mistral, translated by Doris Dana. Reprinted by arrangement with Doris Dana, c/o Joan Daves Agency as agent for the proprietor. Copyright © 1971 by Doris Dana.

"Ars Poetica" from *Collected Poems 1917–1982* by Archibald MacLeish. Copyright © 1985 by The Estate of Archibald MacLeish. Reprinted by permission of Houghton Mifflin Company. All rights reserved.

"Dirge Without Music" by Edna St. Vincent Millay. From *Collected Poems,* HarperCollins. Copyright © 1928, 1955 by Edna St. Vincent Millay and Norma Millay Ellis. All rights reserved. Used by permission of Elizabeth Barnett, literary executor.

"Recuerdo" by Edna St. Vincent Millay. From *Collected Poems,* HarperCollins. Copyright © 1922, 1950 by Edna St. Vincent Millay. All rights reserved. Used by permission of Elizabeth Barnett, literary executor.

"anyone lived in a pretty how town," copyright 1940, © renewed 1968, 1991 by the Trustees for the E. E. Cummings Trust, from *Complete Poems: 1904–1962* by E. E. Cummings. Edited by George J. Firmage. Reprinted by permission of Liveright Publishing Corporation.

"Poetry," reprinted with the permission of Simon & Schuster from *Collected Poems* by Marianne Moore. Copyright © 1935 by Marianne Moore; copyright renewed © 1963 by Marianne Moore and T. S. Eliot.

"The Bridal Party," reprinted with the permission of Scribner, a division of Simon & Schuster, from *The Short Stories of F. Scott Fitzgerald,* edited by Matthew J. Bruccoli. Copyright © 1930 by Curtis Publishing. Copyright renewed © 1958 by Frances Scott Fitzgerald Lanahan.

Excerpts from *Songs of Gold Mountain: Rhymes from San Francisco Chinatown* by Marion K. Hom. Copyright © 1987 The Regents of the University of California. Reprinted by permission of the University of California Press.

"In Another Country," reprinted by permission of Scribner, a division of Simon & Schuster, from *Men Without Women* by Ernest Hemingway. Copyright © 1927 by Charles Scribner's Sons. Copyright renewed 1955 by Ernest Hemingway.

"Soldiers of the Republic" by Dorothy Parker, and "Penelope" by Dorothy Parker, from *The Portable Dorothy Parker* by Dorothy Parker, Introduction by Brendan Gill. Copyright 1928, renewed © 1956 by Dorothy Parker. Used by permission of Viking Penguin, a division of Penguin Books USA, Inc.

"Stopping by Woods on a Snowy Evening," "Mending Wall," "Birches," and "The Death of the Hired Man" from *The Poetry of Robert Frost,* edited by Edward Connery Lathem. Copyright 1944, 1951, © 1956, 1958 by Robert Frost, © 1967 by Lesley Frost Ballantine, copyright 1916, 1923, 1928, 1930, 1939 © 1969 by Henry Holt & Co., Inc. Reprinted by permission of Henry Holt & Co., Inc.

"My City," copyright 1935 by James Weldon Johnson, © renewed 1963 by Grace Nail Johnson, from *Saint Peter Relates an Incident* by James Weldon Johnson. Used by permission of Viking Penguin, a division of Penguin Books USA Inc.

"A Place to Be Free" by Constance Johnson. Copyright © March 2, 1992, *U.S. News & World Report.* Reprinted by permission.

Excerpt from *Dust Tracks on a Road* by Zora Neale Hurston. Copyright © 1942 by Zora Neale Hurston. Copyright renewed 1970 by John C. Hurston. Reprinted by permission of HarperCollins Publishers, Inc.

"Artist Jacob Lawrence" © Copyright NPR® 1998. The news report by NPR's William Drummond was originally broadcast on National Public Radio's "Morning Edition®" on June 9, 1998, and is used with the permission of National Public Radio, Inc. Any unauthorized duplication is strictly prohibited.

"I, Too" from *Collected Poems* by Langston Hughes. Copyright © 1996 by the Estate of Langston Hughes. Reprinted by permission of Alfred A. Knopf, Inc.

"The Negro Speaks of Rivers" from *Selected Poems* by Langston Hughes. Copyright © 1926 by Alfred A. Knopf and renewed 1954 by Langston Hughes. Reprinted by permission of the publisher.

"And We Shall Be Steeped" from *Nocturnes* by L. S. Senghor. Copyright © Editions du Seuil, 1964. Reprinted by permission of Editions du Seuil.

"Storm Ending" from *The Collected Poems of Jean Toomer,* edited by Robert B. Jones and Margery Toomer Latimer. Copyright © 1988 by the University of North Carolina Press. Used by permission of the publisher.

"November Cotton Flower" from *Cane* by Jean Toomer. Copyright 1923 by Boni & Liveright, renewed 1951 by Jean Toomer. Reprinted by permission of Liveright Publishing Corporation.

"A Black Man Talks of Reaping" from *Personals* by Arna Bontemps. Reprinted by permission of Harold Ober Associates Incorporated. Copyright © 1963 by Arna Bontemps.

"Any Human to Another" from *On These I Stand* by Countee Cullen. Copyrights held by the Amistad Research Center, administered by Thompson and Thompson, New York, NY.

"Love and Money" by Ellen Futterman. Reprinted with permission of the *St. Louis Post-Dispatch.* Copyright © 1994.

"Prime Time" from *Colored People* by Henry Louis Gates Jr. Copyright © 1994 by Henry Louis Gates Jr. Reprinted by permission of Alfred A. Knopf, Inc.

Excerpt from "Kubota" from *Volcano* by Garrett Hongo. Copyright © 1995 by Garrett Hongo. Reprinted by permission of Alfred A. Knopf, Inc.

"Speaking" from *Woven Stone* by Simon J. Ortiz. Copyright © 1992 by Simon J. Ortiz. Reprinted by permission of the author.

"apprenticeship" reprinted by permission of the author, Evangelina Vigil-Piñon.

"Prayer to the Pacific," copyright © 1981 by Leslie Marmon Silko. Reprinted from *Storyteller* by Leslie Marmon Silko, published by Seaver Books, New York, New York.

"Riding the Elevator Into the Sky" from *The Awful Rowing Toward God* by Anne Sexton. First published in the *New Yorker.* Copyright © 1975 by Loring Conant Jr., executor of the Estate of Anne Sexton. Reprinted by permission of Houghton Mifflin Company. All rights reserved.

Excerpt from "Need a Lift?" by Randy Brown, from *Buildings,* December 1996. Copyright © 1996 Stamats Communications. Reprinted by permission.

"Game" by Donald Barthelme. Copyright © 1982 by Donald Barthelme, as printed in *60 Stories.* Reprinted with the permission of The Wylie Agency.

"Waiting for the Barbarians" from Keeley, Edmund, and Sherrard, Philip (translators); *C. P. Cavafy: Selected Poems.* Copyright © 1972 by Edmund Keeley and Philip Sherrard. Reprinted by permission of Princeton University Press.

"Mirror" from *Crossing the Water* by Sylvia Plath. Copyright © 1963 by Ted Hughes. Originally appeared in the *New Yorker.* Reprinted by permission of HarperCollins Publishers, Inc.

"Traveling Through the Dark," copyright © 1962, 1998 by the Estate of William Stafford. Reprinted from *The Way It Is: New & Selected Poems* by William Stafford with the permission of Graywolf Press, Saint Paul, Minnesota.

"Frederick Douglass," copyright © 1966 by Robert Hayden, from *Collected Poems of Robert Hayden* by Frederick Glaysher, editor. Reprinted by permission of Liveright Publishing Corporation.

"#2 Memory" and "Poem" from *Mainland* by Victor Hernandez Cruz. Copyright © 1973 by Victor Hernandez Cruz. Reprinted by permission of Random House, Inc.

"Weaver" copyright © 1974 Sandra María Esteves, reprinted with permission from the author.

"For Georgia O'Keeffe," by Pat Mora, is reprinted with permission from the publisher of *Chants* (Houston: Arte Publico Press—University of Houston, 1985).

"Most Satisfied By Snow" first appeared in *The Virginia Quarterly Review,* Autumn, 1973. Copyrighted by Diana Chang and reprinted by permission of the author.

"Geometry" from *Rita Dove, Selected Poems,* © 1980, 1993 by Rita Dove. Used by permission of the author.

"The Welder" from *This Bridge Called My Back: Writings by Radical Women of Color.* Copyright © 1983 by Cherrie Moraga and Gloria Anzaldua. NY: Kitchen Table Press, 1983.

"The House" and "La Casa" by Maria Herrera-Sobek, from *Chasqui,* published in *Infinite Divisions,* by Tey Diana Rebolledo (University of Arizona Press, 1993).

"Salvador Late or Early" from *Woman Hollering Creek.* Copyright © 1991 by Sandra Cisneros. Published by Vintage Books, a division of Random House, Inc., and originally in hardcover by Random House, Inc. Reprinted by permission of Susan Bergholz Literary Services, New York. All rights reserved.

"Embroidering: A Response to 'Somnad' by Carl Larsson" by Rita Magdaleno, from *New Chicano/Chicana Writing 2,* University of Arizona Press, 1992. Reprinted by permission of the author.

"El Olvido" by Judith Ortiz Cofer is reprinted with permission from the publisher of *Terms of Survival* (Houston: Arte Publico Press - University of Houston, 1987).

"The Names of Women," copyright © 1992 by Louise Erdrich (from *Granta* 41, Autumn 1992). This story first appeared in Granta and was later adapted and made part of Ms. Erdrich's novel *Tales of Burning Love* (HarperCollins 1996). Reprinted by permission of the author.

"The name reign: new parents balance the trendy and the unique" by Janet Simons. Reprinted by permission from the Rocky Mountain News.

"Naming Myself" and "Poniendome un Nombre" by Barbara Kingsolver. Copyright © 1994 by Barbara Kingsolver. Reprinted from *Another America,* by Barbara Kingsolver, and published by Seal Press.

"A Poet's Job" by Alma Villanueva, from *Bloodroot,* Place of Herons Press, 1982. Reprinted by permission of the author.

Maps

Ortelius Design, Inc.

Photography

Abbreviation key: **AH** = Aaron Haupt Photography; **AP** = Archive Photos; **AR** = Art Resource, New York; **BAL** = Bridgeman Art Library, London/New York; **CB** = Corbis/Bettmann; **CI** = Christie's Images; **FMWPC** = Frank & Marie-Therese Wood Print Collections, Alexandria VA; **LPBC/AH** = book provided by Little Professor Book Company. Photo by Aaron Haupt; **LOC** = Library of Congress; **NWPA** = North Wind Picture Archives; **SIS** = Stock Illustration Source; **SS** = SuperStock; **TSI** = Tony Stone Images.

Cover (coin)Aaron Haupt, (painting)The Patrick Henry National Memorial, Brookneal VA; **vii** (t–b)NWPA, Chateau de Versailles, France/E.T. Archive, London/SS, Gene Ahren/Bruce Coleman Inc., Culver Pictures, private collection. Courtesy Terry Dintenfass Gallery, NY, CB, Wayne Miller/Magnum Photos; **viii** Ashmolean Museum, Oxford, UK/BAL; **ix** Robert Llewellyn/Uniphoto; **x** (t)Collection of the New York Public Library. Astor, Lenox and Tilden Foundations (b)Independence National Park; **xi** CI; **xii** (t)private collection, photo courtesy Robert M. Hicklin Jr., Inc., Spartanburg SC, (b)High Impact Photography/Time Life Books; **xiv** National Gallery of Art, Washington DC. Gift of the W.L. and May T. Mellon Foundation; **xv** The Museum of Modern Art, New York. Philip L. Goodwin Collection; **xvi** (t)National Gallery of Art, Washington DC. Collection of Mr. and Mrs. Paul Mellon, (b)CB; **xvii** Wide World Photos; **xviii** (t)CI, (b)Tom Till/DRK Photo; **xix** (l)First Image, (r)SAFECO Insurance Company, Seattle WA. Courtesy the artist and the

Francine Seders Gallery, Seattle WA; **xxi** The Stock Market; **xxii** Hampton University Museum, Hampton VA; **xxvii** Cambodian Artists Assistance Program; **xxviii** (t)Ron Watts/Corbis Los Angeles, (b)Art Wolfe/TSI; **xxix** LOC/CB; **4** AH; **6** Flannery O'Connor Collection, Ina Dillard Russell Library, GA College & State University; **7** Courtesy Hubert Shuptrine; **9** O.K. Harris Works of Art, New York; **10** Kactus Foto, Santiago, Chile/SS; **15** O.K. Harris Works of Art, New York; **17** Reprinted with permission of Mrs. Emil J. Kosa Jr.; **20, 21** AH; **22** UPI/CB; **24** BAL; **26, 27** AH; **28** Erin Elder/SABA; **29** Ackland Art Museum, University of NC at Chapel Hill. Ackland Fund; **31** Collection, High Museum at Georgia-Pacific Center, Atlanta GA; **32** Wadsworth Atheneum, Hartford CT. The Ella Galup Sumner and Mary Catlin Sumner Collection; **36** Ashmolean Museum, Oxford, UK/BAL; **38** SS; **39** Hand-colored engraving, NWPA; **40** (tl)AP, (tr)FMWPC, (b)CI; **41** (t)Robert Llewellyn/Uniphoto, (bl)from *Historic Samplers* by Patricia Ryan and Allen D. Bragdon, Bulfinch Press. Collection of The Bennington Museum, Bennington VT, (br)Peabody Essex Museum; **42** (l)American Bible Society, New York/SS, (r)CB; **43** Wadsworth Atheneum, Hartford CT; **44** (t)Culver Pictures/SS; (b)The Newberry Library/Stock Montage; **45** Philbrook Art Center, Tulsa OK; **46** Ron Watts/Corbis Los Angeles; **47** Jose Galvez/PhotoEdit; **50** Rochester Museum & Science Center, Rochester NY; **51** Stock Montage; **53** Arthur Rothstein/CI; **54** Drawing by Seth Eastman; **55** NY State Museum; **60** Flip Nicklin/Minden Pictures; **61** Amanita Pictures; **63** Frederic Remington Art Museum, Ogdensburg NY; **68** CB; **69** Museum of the City of New York/CB; **70** CB; **76** E.T. Archive; **77** Tom Stewart/The Stock Market; **79** The CT Historical Society, Hartford CT; **82** (t)John Henley/The Stock Market, (b)Peter Cade/TSI; **83** NWPA; **84** Trustees of the Boston Library; **85, 87** NWPA; **92** Sophie Bassouls/Sygma; **93** Gamma Liaison; **94** (t)Cambodian Artists Assistance Program, (b)Gamma Liaison; **95, 96** Gamma Liaison; **98** Cambodian Artists Assistance Program; **99** Larry Moore/SIS; **100** Yale University Art Gallery, New Haven CT; **101** Loaned by the Dept. of Parks and Recreation, City of Boston. Courtesy Museum of Fine Arts, Boston; **103** National Portrait Gallery, London; **108** Publishers Depot; **115** LPBC/AH; **118** Collection of the New York Public Library. Astor, Lenox and Tilden Foundations; **120** Private collection/BAL; **121** Bowdoin College of Art Museum; **122** (t)CB, (b)H. Armstrong Roberts; **123** (tl)The Newark Museum/AR, (tr)FMWPC, (b)Museum of Fine Arts, Boston. Gift of Joseph W. Revere, William B. Revere, and Edward H.R. Revere; **124** (l)Brown Brothers, hand coloring by Lorene Ward, (r)LOC/Corbis; **125** (tl)Peabody Essex Museum, Salem MA, (tr)H. Armstrong Roberts, (b)NWPA; **126** (t)Stock Montage/SS, (b)CB; **127** (c)CI, (others) NWPA; **128** (t)National Portrait Gallery, Washington DC/AR, (b)CB; **129** (t)file photo, (b)CB; **130, 132** Collection of The NY Historical Society; **135** AH; **138** Courtesy Arte Publico Press; **139** Reproducción autorizada por el Instituto Nacional De Belles Artes Y Literatura. © 2000 Reproducción autorizada por el Banco de México/Museu de Arte, Sao Paulo, Brazil; **144** Giraudon/AR; **145** Larry Moore/SIS; **146** National Portrait Gallery, Smithsonian Institution/AR; **147** VA Historical Society; **151** Photodisc; **154** AP; **155** Jim Barber; **156** Stock Montage; **160** Scala/AR; **161** Smithsonian Institution; **163** Ronald Sheridan/Ancient Art & Architecture; **164** The Trustees of the National Museums of Scotland; **168** H. Armstrong Roberts; **170** Yale University Art Gallery, New Haven CT; **176** Engraving published by Archibald Bell in 1773, LOC; **177** AH; **182** NY State Historical Association, (b)Smithsonian Institution; **183, 184** The White House Collection, ©White House Historical Association; **187** Courtesy Mystic Seaport; **188** The Royal Albert Memorial Musem, Exeter/BAL; **189** National Maritime Museum, London/BAL; **191** FMWPC; **192** Courtesy Tom Feelings. From *The Middle Passage, White Ships/Black Cargo*, ©1995 Dial Books;

193 The Newberry Library/Stock Montage; **201** Courtesy Robin Holder; **202** CB; **203** Cleveland Museum of Art. Mr. & Mrs. William H. Marlatt Fund, 1967.18; **204** Breck P. Kent/Earth Scenes; **205** (l) Photo Researchers, (r)John Gerlach/Animals Animals; **208** The Ogden Museum of Southern Art, University of New Orleans; **212** The Fine Arts Museums of San Francisco. Gift of Mr. & Mrs. John D. Rockefeller III. 1979.7.84; **216** The Simpsons™ and ©Twentieth Century Fox Film Corporation. All rights reserved; **218** National Academy, New York; **219** National Gallery of Art. Gift of Mrs. Walter B. James; **221** The Metropolitan Museum of Art, New York. Gift of J. Pierpont Morgan; **224** AP; **225** The PA Academy of the Fine Arts, Philadelphia. Gift of Caroline Gison Taitt; **226** Private collection/SS; **229** David M. Dennis; **230** FPG; **232** CI; **235** CB; **236** Dallas Museum of Art; **238** AP; **239** By permission of the Houghton Library, Harvard University. Shelf mark MS Am 1280H, vol. 918, pp. 68, 69; **240** SS; **246** National Portrait Gallery, London/SS; **247** Bruce Satterthwaite; **250** CB; **251** LOC; **254** CI; **257, 262** Charles Philip/Corbis Los Angeles; **264** H. Armstrong Roberts; **267** National Museum of American Art, Washington DC/AR; **268** NWPA; **273** The *Hartford Times*; **278** (t)Middle East News Agency, (b)CI; **279** Sotheby's; **281** Amanita Pictures; **283** NWPA; **285** CB; **286** David David Gallery, Philadelphia/SS; **287** CI; **293** Courtesy William Morrow & Company and R. Michelson Galleries; **295** Courtesy Christa Naher, photo by Lothar Schnepf; **299** Eric van den Brulle/Photonica; **300** Bowes Museum, Co. Durham, UK/BAL; **307** Steve Eichner/Retna Ltd; **313** LPBC/AH; **316, 317** Private collection, photo courtesy Robert M. Hicklin Jr., Inc., Spartanburg SC; **318** The Museum of the Confederacy, Richmond VA, photo by Katherine Wetzel; **320** (t)Mark Burnett; (inset)LOC/Corbis, (bl)National Portrait Gallery, Smithsonian Institution, Washington DC/AR, (br)CB; **321** (t)Mary Evans Picture Library, (bl)National Gallery of Art, Washington DC, (br)file photo; **322** (tl)from the collection of Edith Hariton/Antique Textile Resource, Bethesda, MD, (tr)file photo, (c)LOC, (b)National Portrait Gallery, Smithsonian Institution/AR; **323** CB; **324** (t)E.T. Archive, (b)NWPA; **325** (t)AP, (b)CB, hand coloring by Lorene Ward; **326** (t)Mark Twain Memorial, Hartford CT, (b)LOC/Corbis; **327** The Seventh Regiment Fund, Inc., photograph courtesy The Metropolitan Museum of Art, New York; **328** Corbis; **331** Hampton University Museum, Hampton VA; **336** Collection of the Blue Ridge Institute & Museums/Ferrum College; **337** National Museum of American Art, Washington DC/AR; **338, 339** Hampton University Museum, Hampton VA; **342** (t)Frank Driggs/AP, (b)David Redfern/Retna; **343** NASA; **344** AP; **345** Hampton University Museum, Hampton VA/©Elizabeth Catlett/Licensed by VAGA, New York, NY; **348** Larry Moore/SIS; **350** CB; **355** Doug Martin; **356** National Portrait Gallery, Smithsonian Institution/AR; **357** Corbis, hand coloring by Lorene Ward; **359** CB; **360** Museum of the Confederacy, Richmond VA; **362** West Point Museum Collections, U.S. Military Academy; **363** Cook Collection, Valentine Museum, Richmond VA; **364** High Impact Photography/Time Life Books; **367** CB; **368** The Metropolitan Museum of Art, New York. Gift of Mr. and Mrs. John A. Rutherford, 1914. (14.141). **369** (l)Time Life, (r)SS; **370** CB; **372** Courtesy Rodrigue Studios; **376** The Detroit Institute of Arts. Founders Society Purchase, Merrill Fund; **379** British Film Institute; **381** From a painting by Asa W. Twitchell/CB; **382** Gene Ahren/Bruce Colemman Inc.; **384** CB; **385** David Muench/Corbis; **388** Courtesy Tran Mong Tu; **389** Francis Bailly/Gamma Liaison; **391** David Muench/Corbis; **397** NWPA; **400** Assoc. Press Photo/Eric Miller; **401** Collection of Walt Whitman House, NJ State Historic Site, Camden NJ; **402** Museum of the Confederacy; Larry Sherer/Time Life Books, High Impact Photography; **403** The St. Louis Art Museum; **404** Peter Sickles/SS; **406** Archival Research International/

National Archives; **407** The Brooklyn Museum of Art, New York. Dick S. Ramsay Fund 59.9; **409** The Metropolitan Museum of Art, New York. Gift of Thomas Kensett; **411** The Columbus Museum of Art, Columbus OH. Museum Purchase, Howald Fund; **414** Brooklyn Museum, New York/SS; **419** Private collection/CI; **421** CI; **423** CB; **424** Trustees of Amherst College; **425** Private collection/CI; **426** Shiko Nakano/Photonica; **428** Fine Arts Museums of San Francisco. Gift of Mr. and Mrs. John D. Rockefeller III. 1993.35.20; **429** Collection of the Birmingham Museum of Art, Birmingham AL. Gift of John Meyer; **431** Jane Vollers/Photonica; **432** Tony Craddock/TSI; **435** Heath Robbins/Photonica; **436** CI; **445** LPBC/AH; **448–449** National Gallery of Art, Washington DC. Gift of the W.L. and May T. Mellon Foundation; **450** (l)CA State Railroad Museum, Sacramento/SS, (r)file photo; **451** Culver Pictures; **452** CB; **453** (l) Culver Pictures, (others)file photo; **454** (t)CB, (b)CI; **455** (t)NWPA, (b)The Metropolitan Museum of Art, New York/SS; **456** (tl)Culver Pictures, (tr)CI, (bl)CB, (br)Amanita Pictures; **457** (t)Culver Pictures, hand coloring by Lorene Ward, (b)painting by Isaac Radu, 1903. Photo: Archivio G.B.B./G. Neri/Woodfin Camp & Assoc.; **458** (l)CB, (r)LOC, hand coloring by Lorene Ward; **459** The Fine Arts Museums of San Francisco. Gift of the Charles E. Merrill Trust with matching funds from The de Young Museum Society; **460** AP; **461** North Wind Pictures; **462** Mark Burnett; **463** (t)Mark Burnett, (b)Hirshhorn Museum and Sculpture Garden, Smithsonian Institution. Gift of Joseph H. Hirshhorn; **464** LOC; **465** Museum of the City of New York/BAL; **466** SS; **471** John Netherton; **474** UPI/CB; **475** FMWPC; **476** SS; **478** Roy Bishop/Stock Boston; **481** file photo; **483** The Columbus Museum of Art, Columbus OH. Bequest of Frederick W. Schumacher; **487** J. Goldblatt/Globe Photos; **488** (l)courtesy Thames & Hudson Inc., (r)private collection/BAL; **490, 491** Courtesy Thames & Hudson Inc.; **494** Larry Moore/SIS; **496** AP; **497** CB; **498** Cavalry Club/E.T. Archive/SS; **500** Biophoto Assoc./Photo Researchers; **503** Tom Stock/TSI; **505** Photodisc; **507** Berhard Otto/FPG; **508** Giraudon/AR; **513** National Portrait Gallery, Washington DC/AR; **514** ©1979 Howard Terpning, courtesy The Greenwich Workshop Inc., Shelton CT. For information on limited edition fine art prints by Howard Terpning call 1-800-577-0666; **517** (t)MN Historical Society/Corbis, (b)LOC/Corbis; **519** The Philbrook Museum of Art, Tulsa OK; **523** MO Historical Society; **524** file photo; **525** The Butler Institute of American Art; **530** LOC/Corbis; **531** Ira Nowinski/Corbis; **532** The Hayden Collection, courtesy Museum of Fine Arts, Boston; **532–533** AH; **534** David David Gallery, Philadelphia/SS; **535** NWPA; **537** file photo; **538** Museum of Fine Arts, Boston. Charles Henry Hayden Fund; **542** AP; **543** University of Rochester, photo by Joe Gawlowicz; **544** National Museum of American Art, Washington DC/AR; **546** CB; **547** The Museum of Modern Art, New York. Philip L. Goodwin Collection; **548** The Museums at Stony Brook, NY; **552** (t)FPG, (b)ME Historic Preservation Commission; **553** Portland Museum of Art, Portland ME; **557** AP; **558** The *New York Journal;* **559** Private collection/CI; **563** Collection Mr. & Mrs. Robert A. Kopp Jr., courtesy Mrs. Carol McAdoo; **566** National Museum of American Art, Washington DC/AR; **572** Fischbach Gallery, NY; **583** LPBC/AH; **586–587** National Gallery of Art, Washington DC. Collection of Mr. and Mrs. Paul Mellon; **588** CB; **589** FPG; **590** (l)Underwood & Underwood/CB, (r)UPI/CB; **591** (l)courtesy AZ Historical Society, Tucson. AHS# 69493–Luisa Ronstadt Espinel, c. 1921, (r)PNI; **592** (t)James Westwater, (c)FMWPC, (b)UPI/CB; **593** (tl)by permission of the Houghton Library, Harvard University, (tr)The Metropolitan Museum of Art, New York. Bequest of Gertrude Stein, 1947, (b)Schomburg Center for Research in Black Culture; **594** (tl)CI, (tr)AP, (b)FPG; **595** (t)Wide World Photos, (bl)AP, (br)Photofest/Jagarts;

596 (l)FPG, (r)CI; **597** Museum of Modern Art, New York. Abby Aldrich Rockefeller Fund; **598, 599** CB; **602** Hulton Getty/TSI; **603** LOC; **605** San Diego Museum of Art. Gift of Anne R. and Amy Putnam; **610** Collection of the Newark Museum. Anonymous gift, 1929. (cat. No. 55); **612** UPI/CB; **613** Courtesy Frank Jensen, photo by Marlin Carter; **614** Kenneth Gabrielson Photography/Gamma Liaison; **616** (t)CB, (b)Carr Clifton/Minden Pictures; **617** LOC/Corbis; **619** Peter Gridley/FPG; **620** CB; **621** Collection, Hirschl & Adler Galleries; **623** E.T. Archive, London/SS; **626** CI; **627** Photodisc; **631** LOC/Corbis; **635** UPI/CB; **638** CB; **639** Private collection; **640** Collection of The Newark Museum. Purchase, 1939. Felix Fuld Bequest Fund. (cat. No. 22); **642** Culver/PNI; **643** CI; **645** Wide World Photos; **646** UPI/CB; **647** The Metropolitan Museum of Art, New York. Gift of Georgia O'Keeffe through the generosity of The Georgia O'Keeffe Foundation and Jennifer and Joseph Duke, 1997; **650** PhotoAssist/AP; **651** Hulton-Deutsch Collection/Corbis; **654** CB; **659** CI; **662** Private collection/BAL, London/SS; **669** Yousuf Karsh/Woodfin Camp & Assoc.; **670** LOC/Corbis; **671, 672** UPI/CB; **674** LOC/Corbis; **675, 676** Philip Gould/Corbis; **678** Karsh/Woodfin Camp & Assoc.; **679** file photo/The *Kansas City Star.* Reprinted by permission; **683** Scala/AR; **688** AP; **692** National Gallery, London/SS; **694** CB; **695** Walter Bibikow/FPG; **697** Yale University Art Gallery, New Haven CT. Gift of Walter Bareiss, B.A. 1940; **698** Geir Jordahl/Graphistock; **701** Museum of Fine Arts, Boston. Abraham Shuman Fund (1970.47); **703** Collection of Harrison Young, Beijing, China. Reproduced in *Spirit of Place* by John Arthur; **710** A. Corton/Visuals Unlimited; **711** Larry Moore/SIS; **717** The Schomburg Center for Research in Black Culture, The New York Public Library. Photo: Manu Sassoonian; **718** FPG; **719** LOC/Corbis; **720** Private collection. Courtesy Terry Dintenfass Gallery, New York; **723** National Portrait Gallery, Smithsonian Institution/AR; **724** Photograph owned by Louise Franklin. Courtesy The Association to Preserve the Eatonville; **725** Philadelphia Museum of Art: The Louis E. Stern Collection; **727** Anne Heimann/The Stock Market; **728** Geoff Butler; **733** National Portrait Gallery, Smithsonian Institution/AR; **734** Collection of Martin & Sondra Sperber, New York. Courtesy Heritage Gallery, Los Angeles; **735** Private collection/SS; **738** National Portrait Gallery, Smithsonian Institution/AR; **739** Penguin/CB; **740** Collection of Harry Belafonte. Courtesy Heritage Gallery, Los Angeles; **741** Tom Till/DRK Photo; **744** Peter Jordan/Network/SABA; **745** CI; **749** Museum of Art, Rhode Island School of Design. Gift of Miss Eleanor B. Green; **751** (t)The Beinecke Rare Book and Manuscript Library, Yale University, (b)National Museum of American Art, Smithsonian Institution, Washington DC/AR; **752** (t)UPI/CB, (b)George Lepp/Corbis; **753** Sheldon Ross Gallery, Birmingham MI; **754** The Harmon and Harriet Foundation for the Arts, San Antonio TX; **756** (l)Wide World Photos, (r)The Amistad Research Center, Tulane University, New Orleans; **757** Frank & Marie-Therese Wood Print Collections, Alexandria VA; **758** San Diego Museum of Art, San Diego CA. Museum purchase with funds provided by Mrs. Leon D. Bonnet; **759** National Museum of American Art, Washington DC/AR; **767** LPBC/AH; **770** SAFECO Insurance Company, Seattle WA. Courtesy the artist and the Francine Seders Gallery, Seattle WA; **772** (l)CB, (r)FPG; **773** Hulton Getty Collection/Liaison Agency; **774** (t)Camerique/AP, (c)FPG, (b)Wide World Photos; **775** (t)CB, (c)UPI/CB, (b)Everett Collection; **776** (tl)AH, (tr)Jon Hammer/AP, (b)Walter Sanders/Life Magazine ©Time, Inc.; **777** (t)Willinger/FPG, (bl)Wide World Photos, (br)Geoff Butler; **778** (tl)Hulton Getty Collection/Liaison Agency, (tr)CI, (bl)Geoff Butler, (br)UPI/CB; **779** (t)B. Gotfryd/Woodfin Camp & Assoc., (b)AH; **780** (t)AP, (b)Hulton Getty Collection/Liaison Agency; **781** The Lucy Drake

Marlow Collection Trust; **782** National Portrait Gallery, Smithsonian Institution. Gift of Irving Penn. Courtesy *Vogue*. ©1948 (renewed 1976) by The Conde Nast Publications Inc./AR; **783** David Findlay Jr. Fine Art, New York/BAL; **784** (t)Clay Perry/Corbis, (b)NWPA; **787** Jeff Greenberg/Photo Researchers; **790** The Stock Market; **791** Sovfoto/Eastfoto; **792** Kactus Foto, Santiago, Chile/SS; **796** CB; **797** Everett Collection; **798, 799** UPI/CB; **802** Cofield Collection, Center for the Study of Southern Culture, University of MS; **803** Ted Spiegel/Corbis; **804** First Image; **805** The Art Institute of Chicago. Frank Russell Wadsworth Memorial; **808** SS; **809** Columbus Museum of Art, Columbus OH; **811** First Image; **816** Hulton Getty/Gamma Liaison; **817** Private collection. Courtesy Tibor de Nagy Gallery, New York; **820, 821** AP; **823** Schomburg Center for Research in Black Culture, The New York Public Library; **827** Loïs Mailou Jones Pierre-Noel Trust; **830** Bob Gomel/The Stock Market; **831, 833, 834, 837, 838** Department of Archives and History; **842** The Contemporary Forum. Photo by Bill Tague; **843** National Portrait Gallery/AR; **844** Courtesy Raymond McGuire; **846** B. Gotfryd/Woodfin Camp & Assoc.; **847** Private collection/CI/SS; **850** Courtesy Arte Publico Press; **851** Scala/AR, (bkgd)courtesy Robert C Buitrón; **853** Courtesy Robert C. Buitrón; **855** Geoff Butler; **856** (t)Wide World Photos, (b)Hulton-Deutsch Collection/Corbis; **857** Baldwin H. Ward/CB; **860** Nancy Crampton; **863** Richard Kalvar/Magnum Photos; **864** UPI/CB; **865** Gwen Akin/Graphistock; **866** Jonathan Taylor Photography/Uniphoto; **868** E.C. Stangler/Uniphoto; **869** LOC/Corbis; **874** David Lee/Corbis; **875** The Brooklyn Museum, New York; **878** Marcus Gilden Collection; **881** NWPA; **883** Hirshhorn Museum and Sculpture Garden, Smithsonian Institution. Gift of Joseph H. Hirshhorn, May 14, 1981. Photo by Lee Stalsworth; **885** PNI; **890** Flip Schulke/Corbis; **891** Danny Lyon/Magnum Photos. From the book *Memories of the Southern Civil Rights Movement;* **892** Courtesy Reginald Gammon; **893** Culver Pictures; **896** F. Capri/Saga/AP; **897** Aristock, Inc.; **898** Collection of the artist; **907** Museum of the City of New York, Theatre Collection; **910** FPG; **911** UPI/CB; **912** Thomas Lindley/FPG; **913** Daniel Root/Photonica, (inset)Gjon Mili/Life Magazine ©Time, Inc.; **914** Daniel Root/Photonica; **921** Gjon Mili/Time Life Syndicate; **924** Sande Webster Gallery, Philadelphia, PA; **927** Solomon R. Guggenheim Museum, New York. 54.1408; **930** Courtesy SBC Communications; **933** Gjon Mili/Life Magazine ©Time, Inc.; **937** Daniel Root/Photonica; **939** The Museum of Modern Art, New York. Purchase/©2000 Willem de Kooning Revocable Trust/Artists Rights Society (ARS), New York; **944** Gjon Mili/Life Magazine ©Time, Inc.; **948** The Lane Collection, courtesy Museum of Fine Arts, Boston; **952** Albright-Knox Art Gallery, Buffalo, NY. Gift of Seymour H. Knox, 1957; **954** Courtesy The Robert Miller Gallery, NY/©2000 Pollock-Krasner Foundation/Artists Rights Society (ARS), New York; **958** Daniel Root/Photonica; **963** Sande Webster Gallery, Philadelphia PA; **969, 972** Gjon Mili/Life Magazine ©Time, Inc.; **977** Estate of Elaine DeKooning; **981** Daniel Root/Photonica; **982** Gayle Ray/SS; **989** The Lane Collection, courtesy Museum of Fine Arts, Boston; **992, 994** Gjon Mili/Life Magazine ©Time, Inc.; **998** Nancy Crampton; **999** Collection of Jonathan Demme; **1000** Amanita Pictures; **1001** Collection of Astrid and Halvor Jaeger, Neu-Ulm, West Germany; **1005** Yale University Art Gallery, New Haven CT. Gift of Seldon Rodman; **1008** Gjon Mili/Life Magazine ©Time, Inc.; **1009** Larry Moore/SIS; **1015** LPBC/AH; **1018** The Stock Market; **1020** NASA; **1021** Wayne Miller/Magnum Photos; **1022** (t)Hulton Getty/Gamma Liaison, (c)AP, (bl)H. Armstrong Roberts, (br)John Coletti/Stock Boston; **1023** (t)Gerald Israel/AP, (bl)UPI/CB, (br)Paul Natkin/Outline; **1024** (tl)AH, (tr)Amanita Pictures, (b)Dan Lamont/Corbis; **1025** (t)Cynthia Farah, (b)Tim Wright/Corbis; **1026** (tl)Diana Walker/Gamma Liaison, (tr bl)AH; (br)James D. Wilson/Gamma Liaison; **1027** (t)AH, (b)J. Lowenthal/Woodfin Camp & Assoc.; **1027** (tl)AH, (tr)Bob Peterson/FPG, (c)Geoff Butler, (b)Ian Lloyd/Corbis Los Angeles; **1030** Daniel Cima; **1031** UPI/CB; **1034** Miriam Berkley; **1035** CB; **1037** SS; **1039** Phil Schermeister/Corbis; **1041** NWPA; **1044** Calvin & Hobbes ©1995 Watterson. Reprinted with permission of UNIVERSAL PRESS SYNDICATE. All rights reserved; **1045** Levine/Gamma Liaison; **1046** Jerry Cooke/Corbis; **1047** The St. Louis Art Museum; **1052** Nancy Crampton. **1055, 1058** Courtesy N. Scott Momaday; **1059** Animals Animals/Bates Littlehales; **1062** Miriam Berkley; **1064** Collection National Guard Bureau, Pentagon, Washington DC. From the original painting by Mort Kunstler. ©1984 Mort Kunstler, Inc.; **1066** Jonathan Nourok/PhotoEdit; **1067** Color Box/FPG; **1072** Barry Kleider; **1074** Photodisc; **1075** Tony Arruza/Corbis; **1077** Sophie Bassouls/Sygma; **1079** The Cummer Museum of Art and Gardens, Jacksonville, FL/SS; **1082** (t)John Eddy, (b)Hawaiian Legacy Archive/Pacific Stock; **1083** CI; **1085** Photodisc; **1086** James M. Kelly/Globe Photos; **1087** Whitney Museum of American Art, New York; **1089** UPI/CB; **1093** Francis Miller/Life Magazine ©Time, Inc.; **1096** J. Michael Short; **1097** The Cleveland Museum of Art. Gift of Mrs. Malcolm L. McBride; **1100** Courtesy Alfred A. Knopf Inc. Photo by Shuzo Uemoto; **1101** Collection of Michael D. Brown; **1103** Richard Hutchings/PhotoEdit; **1104** Collection of Yo Kasai; **1105** Terry Ashe/Gamma Liaison; **1106** Corry/AP; **1108** (l)Nancy Crampton, (r)Arte Publico Press. Photo by George McInnis; **1109** Telluride Gallery of Fine Art; **1110** CI; **1117** SS; **1118** Nancy Crampton; **1119** Minnetrista Cultural Center & Oakhurst Gardens, Muncie IN; **1122** Vince Cavataio/Pacific Stock; **1122, 1123** Art Wolfe/TSI; **1123** Kelvin Aitken/Peter Arnold, Inc.; **1124** Wide World Photos; **1125** Minneapolis Institute of Arts. Gift of the Regis Corporation, W. John Driscoll, and the Beim Foundation; the Larsen Fund; and by Public Subscription. ©1999 The Georgia O'Keeffe Foundation; **1127** Walt Disney Company/Gamma Liaison; **1128** Nancy Crampton; **1129** Michael Barson Collection/Past Perfect; **1134** Margot Granitsas Archives/The Image Works; **1135** SS; **1138** Michael Barson Collection/Past Perfect; **1139** UPI/CB; **1140** Margo Weinstein/Swanstock; **1142** (t)Wide World Photos, (b)Culver Pictures; **1143** Courtesy Benny Alba; **1145** CB; **1146** Hampton University Museum, Hampton VA; **1149** Courtesy Coffee House Press, photo by William Lewis; **1150** Private collection of Sylvia Asturias; **1152** Courtesy Arte Publico Press; **1153** Courtesy Susan Stewart, photo by Pascale Productions; **1156** (tl)Cynthia Farah, (tr)Gordon Robotham, courtesy of Diana Chang, (b)Ansel Adams Publishing Rights Trust/Corbis; **1157** Philadelphia Museum of Art, The Alfred Stieglitz Collection; **1158** David David Gallery/SS; **1160** Robert Severi/Gamma Liaison; **1161** CB; **1162** Collection of the Artist/Elizabeth Heuer/SS; **1164** (t)Patrick "Pato" Hebert, (b)Kevin Laubacher/FPG; **1165** Steve Kahn/FPG; **1167** Courtesy Maria Herrera-Sobek; **1169** Gallery Contemporanea, Jacksonville, FL/SS; **1171** Larry Moore/SIS; **1172** Cynthia Farah; **1173** AH; **1174** CI; **1176** (l)courtesy Rita Magdaleno, (r)Miriam Berkley; **1177** Courtesy Nordén Auktioner AB, photo by Hans Winter; **1178** Kactus Foto/SS; **1180** Christopher Little/Outline; **1181** Courtesy Louise Erdrich, c/o Rembar and Curtis, (bkgd) William Self/Photonica; **1183** (t)Peter Harholdt/SS, (b)Richard B. Spencer/SS; **1188** Cydney Conger/Corbis Los Angeles; **1189** (t)Miriam Berkley, (b)LOC/Corbis; **1190** ©1976 Helen Hardin, photo ©2000 Cradoc Bagshaw; **1196** (l)courtesy Alma Luz Villanueva, (r)Bettina Larrude, courtesy Children's Press; **1197** Telegraph Colour Library/FPG; **1198** Danny Lehman/Corbis; **1205** LPBC/AH.